THE
ROYAL &
ANCIEN͏T
GOLFER'S
HANDBOOK
1991

88TH YEAR OF PUBLICATION

EDITOR
MARK WILSON

M
MACMILLAN

Copyright © Macmillan London Limited 1984, 1985, 1986, Macmillan Press Limited, 1987, 1988, 1989, 1990, 1991

This edition published 1991 by
MACMILLAN PRESS LIMITED
Stockton House, 1 Melbourne Place, London WC2B 4LF

British Library Cataloguing in Publication Data A CIP catalogue record for this book is available from the British Library

ISBN 0–333–54733–0
ISBN 0–333–54735–7 Pbk

Note
Whilst every care has been taken in compiling the information contained in this book, the Publishers, Editor and Sponsors accept no responsibility for any errors or omissions.

Correspondence
Letters on editorial matters should be addressed to:
The Editor, Royal & Ancient Golfer's Handbook
Macmillan Press Limited
Stockton House
1 Melbourne Place
London WC2B 4LF

Enquiries about despatch, invoicing and commercial matters should be addressed to:
Customer Services Department
Macmillan Press Limited
Houndmills
Basingstoke
Hampshire RG21 2XS

Advertising
Enquiries about advertising space in this book should be addressed to:
Communications Management International
Chiltern House
120 Eskdale Avenue
Chesham
Buckinghamshire HP5 3BD

Editorial co-ordination: Caroline Ball, Dot Robertson

Map by Chartwell

Cover photograph: Nick Faldo at St Andrews: © Matthew Harris

Typeset by Macmillan Production Limited, 4 Little Essex St, London WC2

Printed and bound in Great Britain by Richard Clay Ltd, Bungay, Suffolk.

Contents

John Jacobs
the first name in golf course design

Architects of the new and highly acclaimed Edinburgh Course at Wentworth, John Jacobs Golf Associates can offer a complete range of golf course design, project management and maintenance services.

The company is now at the very forefront of golf course design and development both at home and overseas with a number of major projects.

If you are considering a golf project, public or private, large or small, JJGA will be able to help. Send for a brochure or call David Pottage on 0438 861438.

John Jacobs
Golf Associates Limited

68a High Street Walkern Stevenage Herts SG2 7PG Tel: 0438 861438 Fax: 0438 861788

We're always interested in up and coming drivers.

Since the first Ford Amateur Golf Tournament teed off it has grown into Britain's premier amateur golf event. Last year well over 100,000 people competed for the opportunity to represent their country at the Belfry.

With our 26th Tournament about to start we'd like to congratulate all the Golf clubs, Ford dealers and competitors whose participation has made the tournament what it is today.

Ford's involvement in Golf, particularly this tournament, has now raised around £200,000 for The Golf Foundation; a scheme that coaches junior players to become tomorrow's top stars.

Combine this with our sponsorship of the 10th Ford Ladies' Classic and you'll see we're very interested in all types of drivers, whether on the road or the fairway.

FORD
in Golf

Ford

Ford in Golf
The chance to fulfil
a golfing dream

In 1991 The Ford Amateur Golf Tournament enters its 26th year and offers Club Golfers throughout the United Kingdom the unique opportunity to represent their country in the Home International Final at the Belfry in August. From fairly humble beginnings in 1966 the Ford Amateur Golf Tournament quickly grew into the largest participation amateur golf event in the world and since its inception a staggering 2.3 million rounds have been played in its preliminary stages alone!

The route to the Home International Final could not be more straightforward. Your own Golf Club should be sponsored by a local Ford Dealer as part of one of your Club's monthly medal competitions held between 16 March and 16 June. If you win the medal competition you will automatically qualify for an Area Final. Success in the Area Final will win you a place in your National 8 man Team representing either England, Scotland, Wales or Northern Ireland. Play at the Belfry will be in true Ryder-Cup style and you will be rubbing shoulders with some of the great personalities in golf including non-playing Team Coaches Tommy Horton for England, David Jones for Northern Ireland, George Will for Scotland and David Llewellyn for Wales. The Tournament is open to gentlemen aged 18 and over – and remember you play off full handicap allowance (max 28) so every Club Golfer in the land really does have the chance to fulfil a golfing dream.

Ford Motor Company is also proud to have been associated with the WPGET from the very beginning of the Ladies' Professional Tour and this year marks the 10th Anniversary of the Ford Ladies' Golf Classic. The event takes place between 2 and 5 May on the lovely Duchess Course of the Woburn Golf and Country Club. Recent winners of the Tournament have included Laura Davies, Muriel Thomson and Gillian Stewart and this year twice-champion Marie-Laure de Lorenzi will be defending her title in the chase for the £65,000 prize money on offer.

We are very pleased that our association with both the Ford Amateur Golf Tournament and the Ford Ladies Golf Classic has enabled us, through you, the Club Golfer, to raise nearly £200,000 for the Golf Foundation. This support, which goes towards the development of Junior Golf, will continue through 1991 and we sincerely hope that it might help this country produce the Sandy Lyles, Laura Davieses and Nick Faldos of the future.

Foreword: Encouragement Brings Rewards

The contribution made to golf history by each passing year needs to be judged on many different counts. Achievements at the highest level, even the ultimate of winning the Open Championship, have always to be measured against the progress made in safeguarding the future of the game by encouraging more people to play and, essentially, making room for them to do so. Happily, 1990 did well for the British Isles and the Continent of Europe in every way.

It was certainly a vintage season for international tournament golf. Nick Faldo's success in defending his US Masters title was remarkable enough, but to go on and win the Open Championship at St Andrews by the decisive margin of five shots left him without a serious challenger for the accolade of Golfer of the Year. And when the question is raised of how much professionals put back into the game, it should be remembered that Faldo is now helping fund his own 'Golf for All' programme to encourage much needed junior playing facilities.

The Continent has persevered with similar encouragement of young players in recent years and the deserved rewards are now to be seen. In 1990 Germany's professionals won the World Cup for the first time; Sweden's amateurs claimed the Eisenhower Trophy with a 13-stroke victory; a Dutchman, Rolf Muntz, became the Amateur Champion; a Frenchman, Olivier Edmond, shared victory at the English Open Amateur Stroke Play Championship; and two more triumphs for Sweden came with Helen Alfredsson's victory in the Ladies' British Open and Mathias Gronberg winning the British Youths title. It was all good for the game, as was the durability of Scotland's Charlie Green who won the Seniors Championship for a record third successive year, and the emergence of Boy champion Michael Welch as a British junior of enormous promise.

Inevitably, there were disappointments. In women's team golf, America inflicted defeats upon the Great Britain and Ireland amateurs to wrest back the Curtis Cup after losing the last two matches, and on Europe's professionals to hold the newly founded Solheim Cup. For consolation, however, there was the typical, exemplary grace and charm in victory of Angela Uzielli, who at 50 is now both the youngest British Seniors and oldest English Ladies champion. She is a great inspiration to all and this fact, it is to be hoped, will be recognised with her becoming captain of the Curtis Cup team before too long. Meantime, her contribution has been properly recognised with the 1990 Woman Golfer of the Year Award.

Off the course, the year provoked a number of lively, occasionally contentious, debates. The Amateur Championship at Muirfield produced a field in which there were no fewer than 123 players with plus handicaps, including one of plus four. Michael Bonallack, winner of the title five times

© Phil Sheldon

Golf history: from top hats to computers

before becoming Secretary of the Royal & Ancient Golf Club of St Andrews, was among the many to wonder how accurately such handicaps reflect true playing ability for championship purposes. The increasing need to ballot out entrants makes another review of this situation by the authority responsible for handicapping, the Council of National Golf Unions, a matter for serious consideration. Respectful attention is also owed to the concern expressed by Jack Nicklaus and Severiano Ballesteros, who share six Open Championship wins, over technical advances in the manufacturing of golf equipment.

Just how far equipment has advanced can be seen at the magnificent British Golf Museum, opened at St Andrews in 1990, and it is the subject of a special article by Museum Director Peter Lewis in this 88th edition of the *Royal & Ancient Golfer's Handbook*. The latest computerised programs are embraced to trace the history of the game in an extremely entertaining and informative manner – including exhibitions such as demonstrating the use of a top hat to measure the stuffing for the making of the feathery ball which stem from an age when others doubtless wondered if the game was courting technology too closely.

The 1989 publication of *The Demand for Golf*, a study commissioned by the Royal & Ancient which detailed the need for 691 more courses in Britain by the turn of the century, continued to concentrate the mind of many on a vital subject. Subsequent studies suggest that in Britain, where the number of new developments lags well behind some other European countries, as many as a third of all golfers are on waiting lists for club membership. The creation of luxurious and costly golf projects, of country club ambience and geared to fairway housing for financing, can do little to shorten this queue. Fortunately, there are signs of future emphasis being placed on more basic, pay-as-you-play courses which, properly administered, can also prove a rewarding investment for developers with initiative.

Finally, I express my sincere gratitude to so many administrators whose co-operation in providing information for the *Handbook* benefits all who enjoy and serve the game of golf throughout the world.

Mark Wilson
Editor
Sunningdale, January 1991

Introducing Dr David Marsh, Captain of the Royal & Ancient Golf Club of St Andrews

© John Cocks – Photographique

David Marsh began a distinguished international and championship golf career when he first played for England in the 1951 Boys' Team. After his student years at King George VI School, Southport, and Cambridge University (where he gained his golf Blue in 1953 and 1954, and again in 1955 as captain), Dr Marsh went on to win the English Amateur Championship in 1964 and 1970.

He was a member of the Walker Cup team in 1959 and again in 1971, when on the old course at St Andrews he played a memorable role in Great Britain and Ireland's first victory over the United States since 1938. Dr Marsh was subsequently Walker Cup team captain in 1973 and 1975. He also played for England between 1956 and 1972 (captain 1968–71). As an administrator his successes have been no less impressive in numerous capacities at national and international level. He was chairman of the R&A Selection Committee 1979–83 and chairman of the Rules of Golf Committee up to September 1990. He was also President of his county, Lancashire, in 1985, and President of the EGU in 1988. A member of the R&A since 1969, he is also an Honorary Member and Past Captain of Southport and Ainsdale Golf Club.

Part I
The Season

The Professional Golf Year

Michael Williams   Golf correspondent of *The Daily Telegraph*

As in 1987, Nick Faldo and Ian Woosnam were the dominant figures in European golf in 1990. Just as Faldo then won the Open championship at Muirfield, he was to do so again at St Andrews, while Woosnam repeated his performance of finishing top of the Volvo Order of Merit. This time, however, Faldo went one better in that he also took the Masters for the second successive year, the first man since Tom Watson (Open and US Open) to land two major championships in the same year. No one since Jack Nicklaus in 1965–66 had triumphed in consecutive years at Augusta National, the irony, or even tragedy, being that the 11th green on which Faldo had defeated Raymond Floyd in a play-off – as indeed he had also done against Scott Hoch 12 months earlier – was washed away by some unprecedented flooding in October.

Consequently, Faldo was comprehensively the Golfer of the Year, for it should not be forgotten either that he came to within a touch of a play-off for the United States Open Championship at

Nick Faldo, Golfer of the Year, in fine form at Wentworth.

© Phil Sheldon

Medinah, just missing a putt that would have tied him with Hale Irwin and Mike Donald. Irwin, at 45, went on to become the oldest champion.

Faldo's regard for the major championships is now as obsessive as it was for Nicklaus at the height of his power and the significance of his performance was that he won two of the four despite having renounced, along with Bernhard Langer, his American tournament player's card. Neither, with the responsibility of growing families, was prepared to commit himself to the minimum 15 tournaments in the States. It was a point not lost on the American policy board and some concession was made when it was announced that as from 1991, the Players Championship – which had attracted a meagre European entry in 1990 – was to be promoted alongside the Masters and US Open for 'special exemption'. This means that there are now 10 tournaments that a non-card holder like Faldo can still play in, five international events plus the Players Championship, the Masters, the US Open, the PGA and the World Series.

In the last 11 years there have been many painful reminders to the Americans that they are no longer the superpower they were. Not only have they lost two of the last three Ryder Cup matches – and tied the other – but they have seen Severiano Ballesteros win the Open Championship three times and the Masters twice, Faldo win the two of them twice, Sandy Lyle the two of them once and Langer the Masters once. It could nevertheless be argued that each of these four players might not have done so without considerable experience over the years of playing in America. Not so José Maria Olazabal, whose victory in the World Series was, from an American point of view, perhaps the most painful reminder of all. Olazabal, whose placings in the 1990 major championships was second only to that of Faldo, has never shown much interest in playing in America on a permanent basis. But on one of the most remorselessly long courses in the States, the Firestone Club in Ohio, he won by no less than 12 strokes from Lanny Wadkins with rounds of 61, 67, 67, 67. It left him 18 under par and the Americans wondering what had hit them. Never had it been made more clear how much is possi-

© Matthew Harris

José Maria Olazabal's Spanish salute to a record victory.

ble without an extensive American education. Olazabal had learned his craft almost exclusively in Europe and others will have taken notice.

Within a matter of weeks the PGA European Tour was to announce that it is to put its collective foot down over appearance money. This was first granted to Tony Jacklin after his victories in the Open Championship of 1969 and the US Open of 1970. He was at the time a European rarity but Ballesteros, Faldo, Lyle and Langer have since followed and each, together with Woosnam, Olazabal and even Ronan Rafferty, who won the Order of Merit in 1989, have also been in a position to bargain for their presence.

The longer it went on the more mutinous the rank and file of the European Tour became and it was at a committee meeting during the Portuguese Open in October that a decision was taken to stop appearance money being paid. To an extent it was the tail wagging the dog but once done Ken Schofield, Executive Director of the PGA European Tour, has no alternative but to make sure it is implemented. 'It is a moral issue', said Mr Schofield when he confronted the Press a week later. 'It is the payers who are the problem', and by that he meant the sponsors who have been prepared to meet the ransom to get the players they want to give their tournaments the standing they want.

However, such now is the strength of the European Tour that there is the possibility that all the cards are no longer in the hands of the sponsors. There is a long list of sponsors waiting in the wings and if any one of the existing ones steps out of line by paying appearance money, another is ready and waiting to fill the vacancy.

In 1991 there are to be 34 Volvo Order of Merit tournaments, stretching from February to the end of October, some of them opposite such special events as the World Match Play and Dunhill Cup, both of which have limited fields.

All of this will mean prize money of around £20,000,000 and it will not be lost on anyone that in 1990 Woosnam, the leading European money winner, did just as well financially and even marginally better than Greg Norman, who for the first time headed the American money list. Woosnam's official earnings were £574,166 which, in terms of the dollar, was within $52,000 of Norman's $1,165,477. However if one then adds the £100,000 Woosnam received for being match play champion, it could be said that the Welshman was the bigger earner. The same could also be said of Mark McNulty, second to Woosnam, against Wayne Levi, runner-up to Norman.

The PGA European Tour is therefore, at least at its top end, a very viable alternative to the American Tour and with European countries like Austria anxious to join the bandwagon, it was not surprising to hear Tom Kite predicting the day when the European Tour could become bigger than its counterpart.

For all the importance of money, the house of golf nevertheless remains an orderly one and it is to Faldo that one turns for the most lasting memories of 1990. His victories in the Masters and Open Championship came in very different circumstances. At Augusta he came from four behind Raymond Floyd with only six holes to play while at the Open he dominated the championship over the whole of the last two days.

At the end of the second day of the Open, the two supreme players in the game today, Faldo

Ian Woosnam discovers that, along with the money, the cups get bigger each year.

© Matthew Harris

and Norman, were locked together at the head of the field, both 10 under par for the 36 holes, Faldo with rounds of 67, 65; Norman with 66, 66. It had all the looks of a repeat of 1977 when at Turnberry Tom Watson and Jack Nicklaus were similarly joined at the halfway stage before Watson, with two concluding rounds of 65, won by a stroke. It was not, however, to be, for in the third round Norman could not stand the heat of Faldo's stove, taking 76 against a 67 and it was all over.

By then Irwin had already become US Open champion for a third time by resolving a tie with a play-off victory, his previous victories being in 1974 and 1979. He came from nowhere at Medinah with a last round of 67, holing a putt of some 50 feet on the last green and, in his excitement, doing a galloping lap of honour as the crowd rose to him.

It was at this stage of the season that Faldo revealed that he had a wrist injury caused, he first thought, by playing on hard ground earlier in the year in Britain. Subsequently he rather suspected that it might have had something to do with the new swing he had perfected under the guidance of David Leadbetter as he had neglected the exercises that would have strengthened his lower forearms. Consequently he dropped out of more than one tournament before taking a longer rest at the end of the season. Certainly he made no impact on the PGA where Wayne Grady, who had lost a play-off for the 1989 Open Championship, emerged triumphant on a highly controversial course at Shoal Creek, Alabama. A combination of severe rough and unpredictable greens frustrated everyone, Grady escaping the worst of it and with rounds of 72, 67, 72, 71, a total of 282, six under par, winning by three strokes from Fred Couples.

Having already in his time won the Australian and European orders of merit, Norman completed the set by now finishing top in America. The significance of this performance was that he accomplished it from 17 tournaments, six fewer than Wayne Levi's 23. Norman nevertheless won only twice, at Doral and the Memorial, whereas Levi was successful four times. It is just a little sad that a player as good as Levi holds little regard for the major championships, for which he has not picked up a single Sony world ranking point in three years.

In addition to the World Match Play, Woosnam won four tournaments in Europe – the Mediterranean, Monte Carlo and Scottish Opens and the Epson Grand Prix – playing, he felt, some of the best golf of his life though without quite the consistency of 1987. McNulty, with wins in the Cannes and German Opens, was also very consistent while Bernhard Langer, climbing back to fourth place, also with two victories, gave every indication that he is far from being a spent force. The two outstanding newcomers to the profes-

sional ranks were Russell Claydon and Steve Richardson, 28th and 29th in the money list, each with more than £100,000.

Of concern was the decline of Ballesteros, who won only once and dropped to 18th in the money list. Some of the fire seems to have gone out of him though it would be dangerous to predict that he will not be back. A talent like that does not disappear in 12 months, or not yet anyway.

There was a good deal of argument over Norman continuing to stay top of the Sony world rankings when most people regarded Faldo as the best player but less over those amassed behind them. The top 10 are now equally split, Faldo, Olazabal, Woosnam and Ballesteros from Europe, Payne Stewart, Paul Azinger, Mark Calcavecchia and Tom Kite from America. The other two at the top of the pile are Norman, an Australian, and Mark McNulty, of Zimbabwe, who is 10th.

European golf also enjoyed two other successes and these were the victory by Ireland in the Dunhill Cup at St Andrews and Germany's triumph at the World Cup in Florida. It was Ireland's second win in three years, the team of David Feherty, Ronan Rafferty and Philip Walton beating England in the final. It could not have been closer, the decisive point coming from Feherty, the captain, over extra holes against Mark James.

The most unsavoury note of the year came with the conflict between the European Tour and the British PGA over control of the Ryder Cup. It led to the resignation of Lord Derby as president of the Tour after his casting vote had gone to The Belfry as the venue for the 1993 match.

Nobody enjoys winning more than the Irish – Ronan Rafferty, David Feherty and Philip Walton after the Dunhill Cup.

© Phil Sheldon

The Amateurs

Raymond Jacobs   Golf correspondent of the *Glasgow Herald*

Contemplating the amateur side of golf, eclipsed as it is in the private mind and in the public prints by the infinitely more seductive professional game, to which it annually haemorrhages the best and the brightest of talent, the least impassioned observer is bound to ponder on the application to it of the definition of journalism by the novelist GK Chesterton. 'It consists', he wrote, 'of disclosing that Lord Jones is dead to an audience who did not even know that Lord Jones was alive.' But the amateur game is as alive and well as its role as graduate school for professionalism allows it to be.

Indeed, the theme of the 1990 season was the expanding role played by overseas golfers in the British Isles. Rolf Muntz won the Amateur Championship, the first Dutchman to do so; Olivier Edmond of France shared in the winning of the English stroke play title with Gary Evans; Mathias Gronberg of Sweden captured the British Youths' Championship; and two 72-hole tournaments of substance, the St Andrews Links Trophy and the Lagonda Trophy, were taken by Australians, Stuart Bouvier and Lucas Parsons. At opposing ends of the age scale, however, home players led by example: the indefatigable Charlie Green of Scotland at 58 won the Seniors' title for an unprecedented third successive year and England's Michael Welch at the age of 17 was almost unbeatable by his contemporaries.

In the midst of the alien achievements the relief was almost genuine that an Englishman (Ian Garbutt), a Scot (Craig Everett), an Irishman (Darren Clarke) and a Welshman (Andrew Barnett) were permitted the grace and favour of winning their own national championships. Yet the successes of the foreigners, in the act of broadening the field of potential winners, reflected, in a much less publicised and expansive way, the evolution of the Open Championship into the most international golfing event in the world. Whereas regret might properly be expressed at the exportation of so many of Britain's most important titles, their departure confirmed the growing strength of the game in countries until now given scarcely a passing consideration.

Nowhere was this development more vividly expressed than in the 13-stroke victory in New

Rolf Muntz, first Dutch winner of the Amateur Championship.

© Phil Sheldon

Zealand by Sweden in the Eisenhower Trophy, the World Team Championship and, therefore, golf's equivalent, if that were in any way possible, of the Olympic Games. It was surely not without significance that after the event in Christchurch the World Amateur Golf Council announced its intention to discuss with the International Olympic Committee the possibility of restoring golf to the Games, in which it has been a participant sport only twice, in Paris in 1900 and in St Louis four years later. The Swedish concept of amateur golf might well lend serious consideration to a sceptical ideal.

The thoroughness of Sweden's approach knew no limits. An hour-long video tape had been made of one of the team, Gabriel Hjerstedt, playing the course which incorporated a detailed sound analysis of each hole. Before the event the team spent a week in Australia warming up on courses with characteristics similar to those awaiting them in the championship – which

quickly developed into no sort of contest at all. Sweden led by 14 strokes at the halfway point and ultimately the host country and the United States tied a distant second. Great Britain and Ireland, who, ironically, had won in Sweden two years before, finished ninth, 31 strokes adrift.

In a population of 8,000,000 Sweden has some 240,000 golfers. Fewer than 30 clubs were formed before the Second World War while today there are over 200 courses and another 40 to 60 planned. The season lasts only six months, but the approach to the game is so intensively structured that coaching and competition start at club level at the age of 10. The Swedish Golf Federation has such a different attitude to golf that it has suggested that the European players with the 10 lowest aggregates in the Eisenhower should be given wild cards into the PGA European Tour's qualifying school – rejected, needless to say.

The Swedish philosophy, as it was applied to tennis 20 years ago, is for close co-operation between the amateur and professional sides of the game. There is even – a notoriously contentious element, this – a category of player defined as *non amateur*. There are not many of these golfers who will compete for prizes whose value is in excess of that provided for in the rules of amateur status, including paid holidays. Swedish successes in recent years seem to reflect their preference for stroke play over match and despite impressive progress as professionals, a place in Europe's Ryder Cup side has so far eluded them. That further step is probably only a matter of time.

Golf in the Netherlands – for that matter, everywhere on the continent except for Spain – has not reached the organised level of Sweden. There are only some 12000 Dutch players and Muntz, a 21-year-old psychology student from the Toxandria club near Breda, was only the third golfer from the Netherlands ever to compete in the Amateur Championship. He deservedly demolished Michael Macara by 7 and 6 in the 36-hole final at Muirfield with a well-drilled method and solid swing, although the Welsh internationalist's stamina clearly ran out after a more rigorous series of matches.

Muntz became the fourth continental golfer in 10 years to take the title, thwarting Macara's ambition to be the fifth player from Wales to take the championship in 11 years, a remarkable record for a country with so small a golfing population. In fact, in Macara's progress to the final he had to beat five opponents of international reputation, including the leading qualifier, Michael Brannan, a former American Walker Cup player and reinstated amateur, and his two matches before the final went to the 20th and 23rd holes respectively.

The finals of the four national championships took very different routes to reach their winning conclusions. At Woodhall Spa, 18-year-old Garbutt, who had been three down after nine holes, overwhelmed Evans by 8 and 7, to become, quite surprisingly, the first Yorkshireman for 62 years to win the English title. At Gullane, Everett, 22, who had won his semi-final match at the 20th after being four down at the turn to Andrew Coltart, beat Mike Thomson, aged 35 and an unranked competitor from the Border country, by 7 and 5 in the Scottish final, having been one down after the first round. At Prestatyn, Barnett became the Welsh champion with a 50 foot putt for an eagle 3 on the 36th green.

Given the Irish bent for the unorthodox, the result of their championship was peversely conventional. Darren Clarke, already with victories to his name in Ireland's North and South championships and in the Spanish Open, beat the immensely talented Padraig Harrington by 3 and 2 in the 18-hole final at Baltray. Ireland must obviously have expected Clarke to lead their side in the Home Internationals at Conwy, but by then he had turned professional. Instead, Harrington, aged 18, emerged as his team's most productive player. He gained the rare distinction of winning all his six games as Ireland, both for the second time in four years and since the series began in 1932, achieved the Triple Crown.

Separated by a gap of something like two generations, Charlie Green and Michael Welch nevertheless succeeded in setting new standards for their golfing age groups. Green, who was 37 when he won the first of three Scottish championships, took the British seniors' title by all of 10 strokes at The Berkshire, confirming that two decades later his competitive instincts had not deserted him. Welch, a protégé of Alex Lyle, the father of Sandy Lyle, carried almost all before him at boys' level. He won, among other events, the British match play and English stroke play titles, the Doug Sanders World Junior Championship, and his division of the Wilson PGA title.

In the broader field of the amateur game in 1990, however, there remained one other notably coincidental brace of performances. The common link between Phil Mickelson and Ben Collier was that each became the first left-handed player to win respectively the US Amateur and Scottish Boys titles. Mickelson had impressed everyone in the 1989 Walker Cup match and his victory made him the first player since Jack Nicklaus in 1961 to win the National title and the individual college championship in the same calendar year. It is 30 years since Bob Charles, of New Zealand, became the first left-hander to begin to impose himself on the awareness of world golf, as he still does as a senior. Perhaps one of these two will eventually fill a vacancy in the game which no other left-hander has lastingly been able to do.

The course that Jenti built

BODMIN GOLF & COUNTRY CLUB
BODMIN, CORNWALL, U.K.
Tel: 0208 73600 0208 74689

Proprietors: Jenti & Sue Madhvani

BODMIN GOLF AND COUNTRY CLUB

MY TRUST IS IN GOD

Limited number of Country
Memberships available

The World of Women's Golf

Lewine Mair

Angela Uzielli, a golfer fuelled by a love for the game and its gossip, became in May the oldest player, at 50, to win the English Women's Championship. The venue was Rye, where the dry and running fairways asked many of the same questions she had come up against at Hunstanton during her golfing childhood. Mrs Uzielli's performance – she defeated such as Helen Dobson, Julie Hall and Linzi Fletcher on her way to the title – was one which earned her a place in England's side for the Home Internationals, and which, to her great glee, were at Hunstanton.

That week, it was her proud and cheerful boast that she was as many as 27 years older than the next member of the team. Yet, one month later, she was revelling in being the youngest afield in the British Women's Senior

Championship she was to win at Harrogate. At the same time as she was finishing three shots ahead of Anne Thompson in the main event, her mother, Peggy Carrick, was winning the Over 70 section, and kicking herself for having missed out, by a shot, on the Over 60s. It was an impressive double for Mrs Uzielli and one which led to her winning the *Daily Telegraph's* Woman Golfer of the Year Award from Wales's Vicki Thomas.

Mrs Thomas, a little live-wire who is never less than outstanding in a team context, deserved her mention. She played in the Curtis Cup, went on to win the British Stroke Play Championship, and finished up playing alongside Claire Hourihane and Julie Hall in the three-strong side which came third in the Women's World Amateur Team Championship in New Zealand.

The Great Britain & Ireland and the US Curtis Cup teams.

The Welsh golfer's finest hour came on the first day of the Curtis Cup at a time when the Great Britain and Ireland side seemed in grave danger of bedding down at 2–7. Mrs Thomas, to her eternal credit, came from behind to win the sixth single on the home green and make the overnight scoreline 3–6. Sadly, the feat did not lead to any miracles on the following day, the Great Britain and Ireland side winning but one of the morning foursomes before losing all of the afternoon singles.

It had seemed at the outset, that this particular Curtis Cup would be the closest of contests. However, the Americans, who had lost in both 1986 and 1988, were this time properly prepared, with Lesley Shannon the first American captain in history to insist on her players practising the foursomes format prior to the week of the match. Her vision in pairing the veteran Anne Sander with Vicki Goetze was something of a master-stroke. Never, in the history of women's golf, can there have been a more disconcerting combination . . . . Mrs Sander was worrying about her hot flushes, while the youngster was complaining of toothache. Again, neither, as the saying goes, could hit the ball out of her shadow. Yet Mrs Sander's pride in the youngster and the youngster's great faith in Mrs Sander paved the way for two great wins.

The Americans had started the match playing the better golf, and the confidence they gathered early on no doubt had much to do with their spectacular play over the closing stages.

For the record, Vicki Thomas and Julie Hall won a singles apiece in an event in which Mrs Hall, with two points from four starts, did best among the Great Britain and Ireland contingent. It was entirely in keeping with the character she had shown, a few weeks earlier, in winning the British Women's Amateur Championship at Dunbar. The pressure on Mrs Hall, and others like her, had been considerable on those East Lothian links, for it was there that the international selectors had finalised their choices for the Curtis Cup team.

Scotland, who had contributed three players – Kathryn Imrie, Catriona Lambert and Elaine Farquharson – later in the season won what was a somewhat controversial Home International series. In the all-important Scotland–England clash, England claimed a hole from the Scots in the morning after Myra McKinlay had tapped her putter on what she saw as the correct path for her partner's putt. After lunch, Donna Jackson called a penalty on Katie Tebbet as the English player, having been asked to mark a second shot which had come to rest on the green's apron, made the mistake of cleaning her ball. The incidents sparked off a lively correspondence in *The Daily Telegraph*.

Though England failed to win at Hunstanton, their enviable strength in depth was amply

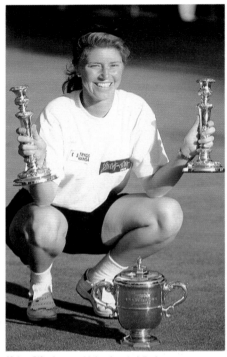

Helen Alfredsson, with her hands full of success on winning the Women's British Open.

© Phil Sheldon

demonstrated by the fact that Sarah Bennett won the amateur award at the Weetabix British Women's Open, only to fail to make England's Home International side. To no one's great surprise, this most impressive of competitors turned professional in time for the last WPGET event of the year, the Longines Classic in Nice.

Helen Alfredsson became the British champion after a never-to-be-forgotten four hole play-off with Jane Hill. This final act had these two most attractive of competitors playing under the evening sun and in front of an encouragingly large and enthusiastic crowd. Here, surely, was a dénouement to whet the appetite of TV people who have for long been so negative where the women's game is concerned. The Swede went on to finish the year in 3rd place on the Woolmark Order of Merit, topped by Trish Johnson with £83,043 winnings.

Miss Johnson, who had become just too technical for her own good in 1988 and 1989, threw most technical thoughts aside to win four titles over the year. True, she continued 'to think technique' when she was on the practice ground but, once out on the course, she decided to let rip.

As the leader on the Order of Merit, she was

© Matthew Harris

Trish Johnson, 1990's Order of Merit winner.

the first to make certain of her place on the European side which went down to America in the inaugural Solheim Cup match by a far from disgraceful 11½ to 4½.

Though she played good golf over the two November days at Lake Nona, Miss Johnson was not among the five Europeans to get in among the points. Laura Davies and Alison Nicholas, whose respective sizes had eveyone in those parts marvelling at just how 'cute' a pairing they made, defeated Pat Bradley and Nancy Lopez in the opening foursomes.

Pam Wright and Lotte Neumann, paired together because they play alongside each other on the American tour, combined magnificently to win a fourball on the second day. Then, in the final singles series, Laura Davies and Dale Reid both won points, while Pam Wright halved with the US Open champion, Betsy King.

Laura Davies, whose two points out of three added up to the best haul on the part of the Europeans, had struggled in the States over the first half of the year; and struggled, too, when she returned to Europe. Putting was a problem, while it did not help that she was trying over-hard to hang on to a record in which she had won on one side of the Atlantic, or the other, or both, since turning professional in 1985. Eventually she pinned down a title, albeit in less than ideal circumstances. In Biarritz, the penultimate tournament for the purposes of the Woolmark money list, Miss Davies opened with a scintillating 63, a score which gave her a three-shot lead. With Friday's play rained off, she returned on Saturday to hand in a second-round 73 which left her one stroke ahead of Alison Nicholas. The rain was back on the Sunday and no more golf was played. Laura was at once excited and exasperated, 'I wanted to

prove to myself that I still had what it takes to win, but to win in such a way proves nothing.' However, her sister professionals were quick to say that she deserved the title on the strength of an opening round which had been the talk of Biarritz.

The following week Laura teamed up with Brian Barnes for the Benson and Hedges Mixed Team Championship in Valencia which was won by Tania Abitbol and José Maria Canizares. Barnes marvelled at Laura's talent, but he left Valencia wondering just how much better she could be were she to stop holding the club so far down the shaft. His feeling was that if she were to stand up a little more and grip the club at a more orthodox point, she would add 30 yards to her shots and further benefit from being able 'to feel the clubhead.' For all this, he was adamant that the former US and British Open champion should not be talked into seeing a David Leadbetter or a Bob Torrance. 'There's nothing wrong with her swing . . . . She's a one off and should continue to be self-taught.'

If Laura's year was saved by that win in France, there were no redeeming features in Helen Dobson's season. Miss Dobson, who won the British Match and Stroke Play Championships of 1989, together with the English Women's Championship and English Girls', had seemed set to play amateur golf's leading role again in 1990. As it was she spent the summer nursing a bad case of tennis elbow. The injury had its origins in a swing adjustment in which she was working at hitting down on the ball rather than the reverse. The Lincolnshire girl had hoped that it would be right for the Curtis Cup but, though she was to share in a foursomes win, it was not. Far from it. Just as she had won Golfer of the Year honours in 1989, so one felt that she was worth another award for the way in which she accepted her misfortune. She was never less than sporting in defeat and always demonstrated an admirable knack of turning the conversation from her injury to the good golf played by her opponent.

After some initial hesitation Miss Dobson has now turned professional and she will undoubtedly prove a great asset to the Women's prize money tour.

Catherine Bailey's performance in the Senior's at Harrogate was in the same sporting mould. Mrs Bailey, the defending champion, was attending the pre-championship dinner in the clubhouse when her car, which was housing her clubs and the trophy, was stolen. Though many, in such circumstances, would have harped on about their misfortune, Mrs Bailey played uncomplainingly over the two days with borrowed clubs. The Ladies' Golf Union, for their part, had to find an alternative, if temporary, trophy to present to Mrs Uzielli. Harrogate Golf Club had just the thing. A men's monthly medal goblet!

The Ultimate Challenge with Unashamed Luxury

The Professionals

Unique and Prestigious
Residential Development

New Club House under Construction

BODMIN GOLF &COUNTRY CLUB

Outstanding Moments of 1990

Open Champion Nick Faldo and his caddie, Fanny Sunesson, dwell on a 'hair-raising' problem.

© Phil Sheldon

© Matthew Harris

© Matthew Harris

Delight – Hale Irwin

Despair – Curtis Strange
Disgust – Greg Norman

The US Open proved that golf is a game of emotions

© Matthew Harris

© Phil Sheldon

There's more than one way to celebrate winning the Open Championship – minutes after his victory at St Andrews, Nick Faldo was joined by the Red Arrows RAF Aerobatic team. And the morning after, when the crowds had gone, he still has the trophy and a place in golf history..

Golf's most exclusive club – 14 winners of the Open Championship and Michael Attenborough, the 1990 R&A Captain, hold a reunion on the Old Course at St Andrews.

© Phil Sheldon

Direct it – José Maria Olazabal

Lean on it – Howard Clark

Threaten it – Hale Irwin

How to influence a golf shot

Run after it – Mike Donald

Plead with it – Ian Woosnam

© Matthew Harris
© Matthew Harris
© Matthew Harris
© Matthew Harris
© Phil Sheldon

Tournament troubles come in many forms: Mark McNulty (above) with his back to the wall; Ian Woosnam (below left) digging in and Bobby Wadkins (below right) in deep water.

© Phil Sheldon

© Phil Sheldon

The settings for championship golf courses can be very different, as Nick Faldo discovered in action at the US Masters at Augusta National, Georgia (above left) and at the Spanish Open at Club de Campo, Madrid.

Goodbye, Arnie! After 30 years of priceless support, Arnold Palmer played his last Open Championship and waved farewell at St Andrews.

© Matthew Harris

EVERYTHING
JUST COMES TOGETHER.

Admittedly conditions were perfect (and the King's Course one of the world's finest) but the 13th, Braid's Brawest, is as hard a hole as they come.

I was playing it like a dream.

After a few days of complete relaxation in one of the world's greatest hotels something strange seems to happen to my game.

Distinctions between ball, club and action seem to blur. The swing is sweeter, the drives truer, the putting more assured.

There is a perfect balance between the demands of the fairways, the subtleties of the greens, the richness of the scenery and a wonderful stillness.

This is golf at its best. The least my game can do is rise to the occasion.

THE
GLENEAGLES
HOTEL

For full details of the Gleneagles Golfing Experience please write to the Leisure Manager,
THE GLENEAGLES HOTEL, AUCHTERARDER, PERTHSHIRE, SCOTLAND PH3 1NF
OR TELEPHONE 0764 62231. TELEX 76105.

one of The Leading Hotels of the World®

The Majors

Mitchell Platts   Golf correspondent of *The Times*

The Open

at St Andrews

Nick Faldo says that playing at St Andrews, the home of the Royal & Ancient Golf Club and of the game of golf, is like going to church. That the place has an air and beauty about it which induces an atmosphere second to none. In 1990, Faldo himself generated the atmosphere with a performance which enlivened Scotland's 'old grey toon' and overshadowed his rivals on the Old Course.

The Open is the most prestigious of championships. If any player questions that statement then there can at least be no doubt that for a European the primary objective each year as a golfer is to win the Open Championship. To win it at St Andrews is something special. Faldo has long since been aware of the traditions of St Andrews. He learned from experience. In 1978 – his first Open at St Andrews – he finished seventh. He returned in 1984 to be sixth behind Severiano Ballesteros. He learned, too, from Gerald Micklem, who at various times before his death had been the chairman of the Royal & Ancient Rules of Golf Committee, Selection Committee and Championship Committee. Micklem, who in 1969 received the Bobby Jones Award for his services to golf, furnished Faldo in 1978 with a blueprint on how to play the Old Course. 'He sat down at a desk, plotted the course and suggested how it should be played,' Faldo recalled. 'It has never ceased to amaze me how accurate those papers are.'

What is more, no player appeared more confident on the eve of the event than Faldo. 'Who will win? Me,' Faldo said. 'I'm sorry if that sounds arrogant but I have to be honest.' He was bristling with confidence, bursting with optimism. 'I know the course,' he added. 'I love it. Now what I'd love nothing more is to be at least two shots ahead coming into the 18th hole on Sunday because then I would really be able to enjoy the last walk home and drink in the atmosphere.'

It would eventually come down to such a scenario. Yet the first round belonged to an American and an Australian. Michael Allen, a Californian who some twelve months earlier had won the Bell's Scottish Open, had the audacity to sink a putt measured at some 150 feet during a first round of 66, a score equalled by Greg Norman. More than half the field shot below par on a warm day when there was hardly the hint of a breeze.

Faldo, however, refused to allow Allen and Norman to have it all their own way. He left himself at the 18th with a shot of some 40 yards through the Valley of Sin and he holed it, playing a bump and run with an eight iron, for an eagle 2.

'Who will win? Me,' asserts Nick Faldo.

© Phil Sheldon

That shot made the round for Faldo and it also gave him a 67. More importantly it endorsed the feeling for Faldo that this would be his week. He launched his second round with four birdies in the first seven holes. He finished with a 65 to tie with Norman, who shot a second successive 66, in the lead on 132.

Both Faldo and Norman had, with their record-equalling performances, matched the championship best for 36 holes established by Henry Cotton at Sandwich in 1934. What is more they held over their nearest rivals, Craig Parry of Australia and Payne Stewart of the United States, a lead of four strokes.

It seemed to all the world that Faldo and Norman were poised for a good, old-fashioned head to head over the last 36 holes. Yet just as Norman won the Open in 1986 with a second round of 63, so Faldo now virtually secured the 1990 edition with a 67 as his rival laboured to a 76.

Faldo went from strength to strength, so that by the end of the third day he not only held a five-stroke lead over Ian Baker-Finch and Stewart but with a 17 under par score of 199 he had established a championship record. His final round of 71 was a conservative affair although it was all that was necessary. He coasted home with an 18 under par aggregate of 270, five strokes from Mark McNulty, who finished with a 65, and Stewart, who also ended on 71. Even so it enabled him to enjoy the immense satisfaction of winning the Open at St Andrews.

The Results

Entries - 1,707.

Regional Qualifying Courses: Blackwell, Deer Park, Hankley Common, Langley Park, Ormskirk, Orsett, Sherwood Forest, South Herts.

Final Qualifying Courses: Ladybank, Leven Links, Lundin, Panmure, Scotscraig.

Qualified for final 36 holes: 72 (72 professionals, No Amateurs).

Non-qualifiers after 36 holes: 84 (80 Professionals and 4 Amateurs) with scores of 144 and above.

Pos	Name	Score	Prize£
1	N Faldo (Eng)	67-65-67-71—270	85000
2	M McNulty (Zim)	74-68-68-65—275	60000
	P Stewart (USA)	68-68-68-71—275	60000
4	I Woosnam (Wal)	68-69-70-69—276	40000
	J Mudd (USA)	72-66-72-66—276	40000
6	I Baker-Finch (Aus)	68-72-64-73—277	28500
	G Norman (Aus)	66-66-76-69—277	28500
8	S Pate (USA)	70-68-72-69—279	22000
	C Pavin (USA)	71-69-68-71—279	22000
	D Hammond (USA)	70-71-68-70—279	22000
	D Graham (Aus)	72-71-70-66—279	22000
12	V Singh (Fij)	70-69-72-69—280	16375
	T Simpson (USA)	70-69-69-72—280	16375
	R Gamez (USA)	70-72-67-71—280	16375
	P Broadhurst (Eng)	74-69-63-74—280	16375
16	M Roe (Eng)	71-70-72-68—281	11150
	S Jones (USA)	72-67-72-70—281	11150
	A Lyle (Sco)	72-70-67-72—281	11150
	JM Olazabal (Spa)	71-67-71-72—281	11150
	P Jacobsen (USA)	68-70-70-73—281	11150
	F Nobilo (NZ)	72-67-68-74—281	11150
22	E Darcy (Ire)	71-71-72-68—282	7933
	C Parry (Aus)	68-68-69-77—282	7933
	J Spence (Eng)	72-65-73-72—282	7933
25	N Price (Zim)	70-67-71-75—283	6383
	F Couples (USA)	71-70-70-72—283	6383
	C O'Connor Jr (Ire)	68-72-71-72—283	6383
	L Trevino (USA)	69-70-73-71—283	6383
	J Rivero (Spa)	70-70-70-73—283	6383
	J Sluman (USA)	72-70-70-71—283	6383
31	B Norton (USA)	71-72-68-73—284	5125
	L Mize (USA)	71-72-70-71—284	5125
	R Rafferty (N Ire)	70-71-73-70—284	5125
	B Crenshaw (USA)	74-69-68-73—284	5125
	M McCumber (USA)	69-74-69-72—284	5125
	M James (Eng)	73-69-70-72—284	5125

Pos	Name	Score	Prize£
	V Fernandez (Arg)	72-67-69-76—284	5125
	G Powers (USA)	74-69-69-72—284	5125
39	D Cooper (Eng)	72-71-69-73—285	4216
	N Ozaki (Jpn)	71-71-74-69—285	4216
	D Pooley (USA)	70-73-71-71—285	4216
	M Hulbert (USA)	70-70-70-75—285	4216
	M Reid (USA)	70-67-73-75—285	4216
	A North (USA)	71-71-72-71—285	4216
	S Simpson (USA)	73-70-69-73—285	4216
	R Floyd (USA)	72-71-71-71—285	4216
	S Torrance (Sco)	68-70-75-72—285	4216
48	M O'Meara (USA)	70-69-73-74—286	3720
	C Montgomerie (Sco)	72-69-74-71—286	3720
	B Langer (W.Ger)	74-69-75-78—286	3720
	P Fowler (Aus)	73-68-71-74—286	3720
	P Azinger (USA)	73-68-68-77—286	3720
53	H Irwin (USA)	72-68-75-72—287	3475
	E Romero (Arg)	69-71-74-73—287	3475
	J Bland (SA)	71-72-72-72—287	3475
	M Allen (USA)	66-75-73-73—287	3475
57	D Ray (Eng)	71-69-73-75—288	3225
	A Sorensen (Den)	70-68-71-79—288	3225
	B McCallister (USA)	71-68-75-74—288	3225
	J Rutledge (Can)	71-69-76-72—288	3225
	D Mijovic (USA)	69-74-71-74—288	3225
	M Clayton (Aus)	72-71-72-73—288	3225
63	M Poxon (Eng)	68-72-74-75—289	2950
	P Baker (Eng)	73-68-75-73—289	2950
	J Nicklaus (USA)	71-70-77-71—289	2950
	R Chapman (Eng)	72-70-74-73—289	2950
	D Canipe (USA)	72-70-69-78—289	2950
68	J Berendt (Arg)	75-66-72-77—290	2775
	D Feherty (N Ire)	74-69-71-76—290	2775
70	A Saavedra (Arg)	72-69-75-75—291	2700
71	M Mackenzie (Eng)	70-71-76-75—292	2700
72	JM Canizares (Spa)	72-70-78-76—296	2700

(The following players missed the cut)

Pos	Name	Score	Prize£	Pos	Name	Score	Prize£
73	J Woodland (Aus)	73-71—144	550		S Hoch (USA)	71-76—147	550
	T Kite (USA)	71-73—144	550		P Mitchell (Eng)	72-75—147	550
	G Turner (NZ)	69-75—144	550		I Gervas (Spa)	78-69—147	550
	R Hartman (USA)	73-71—144	550		D Smyth (Ire)	73-74—147	550
	J Quiros (Spa)	73-71—144	550		J Huston (USA)	77-70—147	550
	B Barnes (Sco)	73-71—144	550		P Senior (Aus)	72-75—147	550
	W Westner (SA)	72-72—144	550		M Ozaki (Jpn)	72-75—147	550
	M Harwood (Aus)	72-72—144	550		D Durnian (Eng)	73-74—147	550
	A Palmer (USA)	73-71—144	550	123	D Russell (Eng)	75-73—148	550
	J Morgan (Eng)	74-70—144	550		D Jones (N Ire)	74-74—148	550
83	A Oldcorn (Eng)	74-71—145	550		B Jones (Aus)	72-76—148	550
	L Wadkins (USA)	71-74—145	550		S Ginn (Aus)	73-75—148	550
	S Ballesteros (Spa)	71-74—145	550		P Archbold (Aus)	78-70—148	550
	T Watson (USA)	72-73—145	550		R Boxall (Eng)	78-70—148	550
	H Clark (Eng)	73-72—145	550		B Ogle (Aus)	78-70—148	550
	C Strange (USA)	74-71—145	550		J Hawkes (SA)	75-73—148	550
	A Hare (Eng)	73-72—145	550		K Green (USA)	73-75—148	550
	M Krantz (Swe)	72-73—145	550		D Love III (USA)	73-75—148	550
	D Williams (Eng)	74-71—145	550		K Trimble (Aus)	75-73—148	550
	C Moody (Eng)	71-74—145	550	134	P Walton (Ire)	74-75—149	550
	D Frost (SA)	72-73—145	550		M Mouland (Wal)	76-73—149	550
	S Elkington (Aus)	74-71—145	550		J Davila (Spa)	74-75—149	550
	G Player (SA)	72-73—145	550		Y Hagawa (Jpn)	78-71—149	550
	B Glasson (USA)	72-73—145	550		O Moore (Aus)	74-75—149	550
	S Bennett (Eng)	74-71—145	550		G Levenson (SA)	75-74—149	550
	P Hall (Eng)	74-71—145	550		C Patton (Am) (USA)	74-75—149	
	P Mayo (Wal)	73-72—145	550		Y Kuramoto (Am) (Jpn)	77-72—149	
	B Estes (USA)	73-72—145	550	142	A Murray (Eng)	74-76—150	550
	A Nash (Am) (Eng)	73-72—145			R Weir (Sco)	77-73—150	550
102	M Calcavecchia (USA)	71-75—146	550		K Waters (Eng)	76-74—150	550
	B Tway (USA)	73-73—146	550	145	B Charles (NZ)	76-75—151	550
	P Curry (Eng)	72-74—146	550		I Aoki (Jap)	73-78—151	550
	K Knox (USA)	74-72—146	550		J Higgins (Eng)	78-73—151	550
	P Hedblom (Swe)	75-71—146	550		C Beck (USA)	76-75—151	550
	MA Martin (Spa)	74-72—146	550		P Hoad (Eng)	75-76—151	550
	W Player (SA)	76-70—146	550	150	G Farr (Wal)	82-70—152	550
	R Drummond (Sco)	75-71—146	550		P Way (Eng)	75-77—152	550
110	P Harrison (Eng)	72-75—147	550		R Muntz (Am) (Neth)	78-74—152	
	T Weiskopf (USA)	73-74—147	550	153	P Lyons (Eng)	77-76—153	550
	G Brand Jr (Sco)	77-70—147	550		R Gonzalez (Arg)	75-78—153	550
	W Grady (Aus)	73-74—147	550		C Stadler (USA)	82-71—153	550
	T Armour III (USA)	74-73—147	550		R Davis (Aus)	82-71—153	550

We've developed some strong attachments for the Cushman Turf-Truckster.

No wonder some golf course Greenkeepers have grown attached to their Cushman Turf-Trucksters. Nothing even comes close to fulfilling as many functions with such beautiful results. It's state-of-the-art turf maintenance machinery in a class by itself.

A superior system.

More than a dozen attachments and implements can be interchanged with a minimum amount of effort, turning a Turf-Truckster into an entire fleet of turf maintenance vehicles. You can spray, aerate, pick up cores, haul, dump, fertilise, spread, seed and top dress. And you can do them all with

And so will you.

greater precision because of our unique ground speed governor control.

Pound for pound, function for function, nothing is as versatile or economical over more years of heavy use.

Now with Diesel engine option.

Now available with either petrol or economical diesel engine options, the Cushman Turf-Truckster is simply your best turf maintenance vehicle investment.

US Masters

at Augusta National GC, Augusta, Georgia

If the age of Nick Faldo had not already dawned, then it did so at Augusta National last April. There he thoroughly earned in the eyes of his peers, notably contemporaries such as Severiano Ballesteros and Greg Norman, the right to be regarded as the number one golfer in the world.

Faldo bloomed among the azaleas and the dogwood with a performance which smacked of character, courage and class. For he was obliged to emulate Jack Nicklaus, the only player in the past to accomplish a successful defence of the Masters, by clawing back four strokes in the last six holes on the redoubtable Raymond Floyd before closing out his opponent in a sudden-death finish reminiscent of 12 months earlier. Faldo had then overcome Scott Hoch at the 11th – the second extra hole – and Floyd, too, met his waterloo there when his approach to the green found a watery grave. Yet whereas Hoch had so unfairly, and unwisely, called Faldo the 'luckiest golfer in the world' in 1989, there were, following

Champion Nick Faldo at Augusta.

© Frank Christian Studios

his defeat of Floyd, only plaudits, rather than insults, for the 6ft 3in Englishman as he slipped once again into the ceremonial green jacket.

Faldo emerged as a true champion following a two–year hiatus when he remodelled his swing under the studious eye of the ubiquitous teacher, David Leadbetter. Throughout he was compelled to endure unnecessary intrusions into his private and professional life although he regarded the entire exercise of strengthening his game, and his mind, as a labour of love.

By the time the 1990 Masters began, Faldo felt under no pressure. After all, he had won the Open Championship in 1987 and the Masters in 1989. He had indelibly written his name into the record book. He was financially secure. He had never been happier. 'No one is leaning on me,' Faldo said before teeing–up at Augusta. 'I feel fine, my game is fine and I just want to play as well as I can.'

Faldo's 71 on the first day was overshadowed by Mike Donald, an American competing at Augusta for the first time, who shot 64, and his 72 on Friday left him trailing Floyd, the halfway leader, by five shots. Six of the leading 13 players following the second round were former Masters champions. Floyd had eagled the 8th and his hat–trick of birdies from the 13th gave him a total of 138, putting him one ahead of Hoch and three in front of Nicklaus.

Faldo was well aware when he arrived on Saturday that he would need to make a move if he was to retain the title and if Fanny Sunesson was to become the first woman to carry the bag of a major championship winner. He neither let himself nor his Swedish caddie down. Faldo launched his third round with an immaculate five iron approach to within one foot of the flag at the opening hole for the first of six birdies. Floyd, by virtue of storming home in 31 which included chipping in at the 14th, finished with a 68 for a ten under par score of 206. He led by two from John Huston, an improving American, and by three from Faldo.

After 12 holes of the final round, Floyd led by four shots. 'At that point, I didn't think I could lose,' he said. Faldo, however, eroded the deficit by one with a two–putt birdie at the long 13th. Then he pitched to six feet for another at the 15th and he extracted a two from the 16th with a six iron to eleven feet from where he holed.

Floyd came to the 17th, still one ahead, but he pulled his nine iron into three–putt range. Faldo playing alongside Nicklaus, had climbed the hill to the18th green. There were no cheers from down below, just an eerie hush. Floyd had taken three

putts. To Floyd's credit he saved his par at the 18th, despite visiting two bunkers. But his 72 meant that Faldo, with a 69, had tied with him on 278.

The impetus generated by Faldo carried him to victory. First, he salvaged his par at the 10th – the first extra hole – with a wonderful bunker shot and a four–foot putt. Then he hit an eight iron to 18 feet at the next. Floyd had put his seven iron in the lake. Faldo was walking on water and the Masters champion again.

Mitchell Platts

The Results

Pos	Name	Score	Prize $
1	N Faldo	71–72–66–69—278	225000
2	R Floyd	70–68–68–72—278	135000
(Faldo won play–off)			
3	J Huston	66–74–68–75—283	72500
	L Wadkins	72–73–70–68—283	72500
5	F Couples	74–69–72–69—284	50000
6	J Nicklaus	72–70–69–74—285	45000
7	S Ballesteros	74–73–68–71—286	35150
	B Britton	68–74–71–73—286	35150
	B Langer	70–73–69–74—286	35150
	S Simpson	74–71–68–73—286	35150
	C Strange	70–73–71–72—286	35150
	T Watson	77–71–67–71—286	35150
13	JM Olazabal	72–73–68–74—287	26300
14	B Crenshaw	72–74–73–69—288	20650
	S Hoch	71–68–73–76—288	20650
	T Kite	75–73–66–74—288	20650
	L Mize	70–76–71–71—288	20650
	R Rafferty	72–74–69–73—288	20650
	C Stadler	72–70–74–72—288	20650
20	M Calcavecchia	74–73–73–69—289	15100
	S Jones	77–69–72–71—289	15100
	F Zoeller	72–74–73–70—289	15100
23	M Ozaki	70–71–77–72—290	13000
24	L Trevino	78–69–72–72—291	11000

Pos	Name	Score	Prize $
	D Hammond	71–74–75–71—291	11000
	G Player	73–74–68–76—291	11000
27	W Grady	72–75–72–73—292	9267
	A North	71–73–77–71—292	9267
	J Sluman	78–68–75–71—292	9267
30	P Jacobsen	67–75–76–75—293	8133
	J Mudd	74–70–73–76—293	8133
	I Woosnam	72–75–70–76—293	8133
33	A Bean	76–72–74–72—294	7100
	B Glasson	70–75–76–73—294	7100
	N Ozaki	75–73–74–72—294	7100
36	M McCumber	74–74–76–71—295	6133
	P Stewart	71–73–77–74—295	6133
	B Tway	72–76–73–74—295	6133
39	C Beck	72–74–75–75—296	5500
	M Lye	75–73–73–75—296	5500
	C Patton (Am)	71–73–74–78—296	
42	J Mahaffey	72–74–75–76—297	4867
	D Pooley	73–73–72–79—297	4867
	P Senior	72–75–73–77—297	4867
45	M Hulbert	71–71–77–79—298	4250
	T Purtzer	71–77–76–74—298	4250
47	M Donald	64–82–77–76—299	3900
48	L Nelson	74–73–79–74—300	3600
49	G Archer	70–74–82–75—301	3400

(The following players missed the cut.)

Pos	Name	Score
50	B Casper	74–75—149
	D Frost	74–75—149
	R Gamez	73–76—149
	M O'Meara	75–74—149
	M Reid	76–73—149
55	H Green	73–77—150
	B McCallister	73–77—150
	G Norman	78–72—150
	T Pernice Jr	74–76—150
59	T Aaron	77–74—151
	I Baker–Finch	77–74—151
	D Forsman	79–72—151
	A Lyle	77–74—151
	D Rummells	77–74—151
	T Schulz	75–76—151
	T Sills	77–74—151
66	C Coody	75–77—152
	T Simpson	77–75—152

Pos	Name	Score
	H Sutton	81–71—152
69	T Armour III	75–78—153
	G Brewer	76–77—153
	C Byrum	76–77—153
	B Claar	74–79—153
	D Ishii	74–79—153
74	T Byrum	77–78—155
	S Dodd (Am)	77–78—155
	L Thompson	80–75—155
77	P Azinger	80–76—156
	A Palmer	76–80—156
	C Parry	80–76—156
80	K Green	78–80—158
	T Hobby (Am)	76–82—158
	W Levi	77–81—158
83	D Green (Am)	79–80—159
84	J Taylor (Am)	83–78—161
85	D Ford	78–85—163

US Open

at Medinah, Chicago, Illinois

Jack Nicklaus believes that of the four major championships, the US Open is the hardest to win. Hale Irwin would have reasonable grounds to disagree with his compatriot. Irwin has not won a Masters, Open Championship or USPGA Championship, but his success at Medinah in June was his third in the US Open following his previous wins in 1974 and 1979.

What is certain is that for Irwin it was the most unexpected triumph, right down to his inward 31 in the final round which culminated with a putt of 50 feet with which he earned a play–off against Mike Donald.

In the beginning Irwin teed–up only because the United States Golf Association, organisers of the US Open, gave him a special exemption. He teed–up, too, on a wing and a prayer, knowing that to succeed at the age of 45 would make him the oldest player to win the US Open. But he had dreamed a few weeks earlier that Medinah, on the outskirts of Chicago, would be his kind of course. 'I told my wife about it,' he said. 'I told her that I would win but that it would be an ordeal.'

Yet while Irwin proved that dreams do come true, so a dream died for Nick Faldo. He failed by only one shot to earn a place in the play–off alongside Irwin and Donald and that only after his putt for a birdie at the last kissed the hole. It would be a case of Hale the winner and farewell for Faldo to the Grand Slam.

Faldo is unquestionably suited by demanding conditions. They invariably encourage him because he is well aware that many players sabotage their own prospects by succumbing to the elements. Medinah has in the past been described as brutal. During the practice rounds it lived up to its reputation. Then came a thunderstorm on Wednesday evening which transformed the course. Scott Simpson, Tim Simpson and Jeff Sluman all shot first rounds of 66 as a US Open record was established with no fewer than 39 players returning sub–par scores, courtesy of the rain–softened greens. Moreover, the ink had hardly dried on that entry into the record book when in the second round, with the sun out but the wind still on holiday, 47 players broke the par of 72. Tim Simpson went on to lead on his own at the halfway stage following a second round of 69 for a score of 135, one shot ahead of Sluman.

The change in conditions had thrown the championship into confusion. Greg Norman survived the halfway cut only by virtue of holing a teasing putt at the 18th. Norman suggested that some of the players, as well as the officials, were disappointed and frustrated, because their expectations had been thwarted by the elements.

Then the pattern started to change. On Saturday the course which Simpson had dominated began

Hale Irwin – a man for whom dreams come true.

to dominate him. He took 75. Sluman, too, faltered with a 74. It was clear that Open pressure was now the keyword. Not that it made too much difference to Billy Ray Brown. He made his mark with a 69 to tie Donald (72) in the lead on 209 – seven under par, with Larry Nelson (69), Mark Brooks (72), Simpson and Sluman all one shot adrift.

Irwin stepped on to the first tee for the final round, four shots behind Donald and Brown. The wind was gusting up to 20mph. No fewer than 27 players were within four shots of the lead which accounted for the fact that Irwin would finish his round more than two hours before Donald. Irwin had birdied three holes in a row from the 11th before the television cameras finally swung towards him. Then he made another birdie at the 14th. He kept his act together moving through to the 18th where he stood motionless over his 50-foot putt. Irwin was not to remain motionless. The ball snaked towards its target and as it dropped into the sanctuary of the hole so Irwin set off on a lap of honour. He did one high–five after another with spectators and officials and he blew kiss after kiss into the air.

So with a final round of 67 and a total of 280, Irwin had set the target for the others. It proved to be out of reach for all but Donald who came through to tie Irwin with a 71, although he would regret dropping a shot at the 16th. For 24 hours later Irwin would win the 90th US Open at the 91st hole. There was no separating them after 18 holes of the play–off. Both scored 74. On they went. Irwin made no mistake from ten feet at that 91st hole for the sudden–death birdie that put him into the record book. 'It's a fabulous feeling,' he said. 'Because I'm so old, I feel blessed.'

Mitchell Platts

The Results

Pos	Name	Score	Prize $
1	H Irwin	69–70–74–67—280	180000
2	M Donald	67–70–72–71—280	108000

(Irwin won at first extra hole after tied 18–hole play–off)

Pos	Name	Score	Prize $
3	N Faldo	72–72–68–69—281	56878
	BR Brown	69–71–69–72—281	56878
5	G Norman	72–73–69–69—283	33271
	T Simpson	66–69–75–73—283	33271
	M Brooks	68–70–72–73—283	33271
8	S Jones	67–76–74–67—284	22236
	C Stadler	71–70–72–71—284	22236
	S Hoch	70–73–69–72—284	22236
	T Sieckmann	70–74–68–72—284	22236
	JM Olazabal	73–69–69–73—284	22236
	F Zoeller	73–70–68–73—284	22236
14	J Benepe	72–70–73–70—285	15712
	J Huston	68–72–73–72—285	15712
	J Inman	72–71–70–72—285	15712
	S Simpson	66–73–73–73—285	15712
	L Mize	72–70–69–74—285	15712
	J Sluman	66–70–74–75—285	15712
	L Nelson	74–67–69–75—285	15712
21	S Elkington	73–71–73–69—286	12843
	I Woosnam	70–70–74–72—286	12843
	C Strange	73–70–68–75—286	12843
24	M Ozaki	73–72–74–68—287	11308
	W Heintzelman	70–75–74–68—287	11308
	C Pavin	74–70–73–70—287	11308
	B Tuten	74–70–72–71—287	11308
	P Azinger	72–72–69–74—287	11308
29	P Mickelson (Am)	74–71–71–72—288	
	C Beck	71–71–73–73—288	10022
	M Hulbert	76–66–71–75—288	10022
	B Claar	70–71–71–76—288	10022
33	T Byrum	70–75–74–70—289	8221
	K Triplett	72–70–75–72—289	8221

Pos	Name	Score	Prize $
	B Lohr	71–74–72–72—289	8221
	I Aoki	73–69–74–73—289	8221
	D Frost	72–72–72–73—289	8221
	B Tway	69–72–74–74—289	8221
	S Pate	75–68–72–74—289	8221
	B Wadkins	71–73–71–74—289	8221
	S Ballesteros	73–69–71–76—289	8221
	J Nicklaus	71–74–68–76—289	8221
	J Gallagher Jr	71–69–72–77—289	8221
	T Schulz	73–70–69–77—289	8221
	M Reid	70–73–68–78—289	8221
46	C Parry	72–71–68–79—290	6687
47	D Barr	74–71–75–71—291	6140
	M McCumber	76–68–74–73—291	6140
	R Thompson	71–73–72–75—291	6140
	D Rummells	73–71–70–77—291	6140
51	R Stewart	70–74–75–73—292	5184
	B Glasson	71–73–73–76—292	5184
	A North	74–71–71–76—292	5184
	G Twiggs	72–70–73–77—292	5184
	L Wadkins	72–72–70–78—292	5184
56	T Kite	75–70–74–74—293	4694
	B McCallister	71–72–75–75—293	4694
	D Duval (Am)	72–72–72–77—293	
	B Gilder	71–70–74–78—293	4694
	G Morgan	70–72–73–78—293	4694
61	S Verplank	72–69–77–76—294	4529
	R Gamez	72–73–73–76—294	4529
63	R Rafferty	75–70–73–78—296	4507
64	D Graham	72–73–74–79—298	4507
65	H Twitty	73–72–77–77—299	4507
66	B Faxon	70–74–76–81—301	4507
67	ME Smith	72–72–82–80—308	4507
68	R Wylie	70–75–81–82—308	4507

(The following players missed the cut)

Pos	Name	Score
69	T Dodds	75–71—146
	P Blackmar	75–71—146
	T Moore	72–74—146
	D Hammond	71–75—146
	L Rinker	70–76—146
	T Lehman	75–71—146
	F Couples	74–72—146
	P Jacobsen	71–75—146
	C Patton (Am)	74–72—146
78	R McNamara	72–75—147
	J Wilson	80–67—147
	W Grady	74–73—147
	B Crenshaw	75–72—147
	W Levi	71–76—147
	JD Blake	72–75—147
	J Chaffee	76–71—147
	E Dougherty	74–73—147
	G Ladehoff	73–74—147
	J Estes	74–73—147
	B Jobe	73–74—147
	R Cochran	75–72—147
90	E Aubrey	69–79—148
	J Mudd	72–76—148

Pos	Name	Score
	P Stewart	73–75—148
	D Edwards	74–74—148
	M Wiebe	73–75—148
	M Lawrence	73–75—148
	I Smith	71–77—148
	J Gomez	71–77—148
	M James	74–74—148
	B Langer	78–70—148
	D Pooley	76–72—148
	B Mayfair	73–75—148
	B Sander	79–69—148
	H Green	71–77—148
104	R Eaks	74–75—149
	G Johnson	75–74—149
	B Fabel	77–72—149
	H Sutton	76–73—149
	T Watson	74–75—149
	P Senior	75–74—149
	M O'Meara	76–73—149
	M Schuchart	75–74—149
	G Hickman	75–74—149
	A Magee	79–70—149
114	K Gibson	72–78—150

Pos	Name	Score
	A Lyle	78–72—150
	B Buttner	76–74—150
	B Boyd	76–74—150
	B Vaughan	76–74—150
	J Snyder	78–72—150
	M Calcavecchia	73–77—150
121	L Rinker	79–75—154
122	J Flannery	75–80—155
	T Norby	78–77—155
	D Hepler	74–81—155
	C Peddicord	76–79—155
126	J Haas	78–78—156
	F Marrello	76–80—156
128	B Kelly	81–76—157
129	S Schroeder	87–71—158
	R Gaus	82–76—158
	J Julian	79–79—158
132	R Burgess	81–78—159
133	T Erwin	80–81—161
134	B Tuttle	78–84—162
	W Pitman (Am)	83–81—164
	B King	79–86—165

USPGA Championship

at Shoal Creek, Birmingham, Alabama

It mattered not a tee peg to Wayne Grady, as he cradled in his arms the USPGA Championship trophy, that many of the world's leading golfers were still incensed at being compelled to place their reputations on the line against rough which required a machete rather than a wedge. The Australian had won his first major championship and he had done so with the methodical care shown earlier by Nick Faldo at Augusta National and St Andrews and Hale Irwin at Medinah.

What is more, Grady succeeded on *terra firma* where not one but two controversies raged. Initially the prospect of demonstrations by civil rights groups was sparked following remarks made by Hall Thompson, Shoal Creek's founder. Thompson later apologised, but with the subject in the spotlight, once-exclusive private clubs found themselves seeking to satisfy new requirements for non-discriminatory membership policies.

In truth the competitors mostly distanced themselves from that controversy as one by one they arrived at the club. Payne Stewart, the defending champion, was more concerned over the way the grass had been allowed to grow. 'If you don't play from the fairways this week then you might as well pack your bags,' Stewart claimed. 'If the marshals can find your ball, then you can chop it back to the fairways. But that is where it ends. There's no way you can go for the greens out of it. They might as well paint red lines down either side of the fairway and make it all a lateral hazard.' Fuzzy Zoeller added, 'It's the hardest damn golf course I've played. Par will win.' In fact Grady won the title with six under par. Even so only three players managed to finish below par for the championship.

When the 36-hole qualifying guillotine fell on Saturday, it did so on some famous heads. Severiano Ballesteros was among the victims. He capitulated to his highest competitive score for more than a decade with a second round of 83. He had wondered almost aimlessly along the 7145 yards searching for a clue as to how to overcome Shoal Creek. He failed. So did Bernhard Langer, Mark James, Mark Calcavecchia, Jack Nicklaus (the course designer), Ronan Rafferty, Curtis Strange and Lee Trevino among others.

Grady, however, had set sail for home. He shot 67 for 139 – one ahead of Larry Mize and Fred Couples – and he cared not that there were still two punishing, pressurised rounds remaining. 'I don't mind being in the lead at all,' Grady said. 'I think its the best place to be.'

Gil Morgan, a doctor of optometry, found the prescription for success at Shoal Creek on Saturday when, by virtue of taking his driver on tees others feared to tread, he overpowered the course. He notched eight birdies and one bogey in a 65. Grady, however, stretched his lead by scoring a 72 for 211, two ahead of Couples and Stewart and three in front of Loren Roberts and Morgan.

Grady felt that if he compiled a sub-par round on the final day then the title would be his. He achieved his aim although it was not as easy as that. Couples followed a valiant outward 34 with successive birdies at the 11th and 12th to move one shot ahead. Grady, out in 35, had twice visited the rough at the 12th to drop a shot. Then Couples retreated, forfeiting his chance by missing three successive short putts, and as Morgan, too, failed to find the necessary inspiration, so Grady wriggled free of his rivals.

In the end his final round of 71 for a total of 282 gave him a winning margin of three over Couples (72), with Morgan (72) one stroke further adrift. Faldo, whose prospects of winning disintegrated with a third round of 80, produced the best last round with a 69. But there could be no question that Grady deserved to be champion.

Mitchell Platts

Wayne Grady kept his composure while others challenged.

© Frank Christian Studios

The Results

Pos	Name	Score	Prizes$		Pos	Name	Score	Prizes$
1	W Grady	72–67–72–71—282	225000			S Verplank	70–76–73–78—297	6500
2	F Couples	69–71–73–72—285	135000			I Woosnam	74–75–70–78—297	6500
3	G Morgan	77–72–65–72—286	90000		40	I Aoki	72–74–78–74—298	4750
4	B Britton	72–74–72–71—289	73500			T Kite	79–71–74–74—298	4750
5	C Beck	71–70–78–71—290	51666			D Love III	72–72–77–77—298	4750
	B Mayfair	70–71–75–74—290	51666			J Mahaffey	75–72–76–75—298	4750
	L Roberts	73–71–70–76—290	51666			C Parry	74–72–75–77—298	4750
8	M McNulty	74–72–75–71—292	34375		45	A Magee	75–74–73–77—299	3700
	D Pooley	75–74–71–72—292	34375			S Rachels	75–73–76–75—299	3700
	T Simpson	71–73–75–73—292	34375			M Reid	71–78–78–72—299	3700
	P Stewart	71–72–70–79—292	34375			B Tway	72–76–73–78—299	3700
12	H Irwin	77–72–70–74—283	27000		49	S Hoch	78–73–72–77—300	2865
	L Mize	72–68–76–77—293	27000			M McCumber	73–76–74–77—300	2865
14	B Andrade	75–72–73–74—294	20600			K Perry	73–76–78–73—300	2865
	M Hatalsky	73–78–71–72—294	20600			H Sutton	72–74–78–76—300	2865
	JM Olazabal	73–77–72–72—294	20600			R Floyd	72–77–74–77—300	2865
	C Pavin	73–75–72–74—294	20600			R Gamez	71–78–75–76—300	2865
	F Zoeller	72–71–76–75—294	20600			M Hulbert	71–75–79–75—300	2865
19	B Boyd	74–74–71–76—295	14000			S Utley	71–72–80–77—300	2865
	N Faldo	71–75–80–69—295	14000		57	I Baker–Finch	74–71–78–78—301	2525
	B McCallister	75–73–74–73—295	14000			B Gilder	73–78–73–77—301	2525
	G Norman	77–69–76–73—295	14000			J Huston	72–72–77–80—301	2525
	M O'Meara	69–76–79–71—295	14000			D Peoples	77–71–77–76—301	2525
	T Watson	74–71–77–73—295	14000			C Stadler	75–73–74–79—301	2525
	M Wiebe	74–73–75–73—295	14000		62	P Senior	74–75–72–81—302	2450
26	M Brooks	78–69–76–73—296	8650		63	J Delsing	75–73–73–82—303	2400
	P Jacobsen	74–75–71–76—296	8650			D Hammond	77–70–80–76—303	2400
	C Perry	75–74–72–75—296	8650			N Price	75–71–81–76—303	2400
	R Stewart	73–73–75–75—296	8650		66	D Graham	75–75–75–79—304	2325
	B Tennyson	71–77–71–77—296	8650			S Simpson	76–75–72–81—304	2325
31	P Azinger	76–70–74–77—297	6500			B Wadkins	68–75–80–81—304	2325
	B Crenshaw	74–70–78–75—297	6500		69	J Blair	73–76–76–80—305	2225
	D Frost	76–74–69–78—297	6500			E Fiori	75–76–77–77—305	2225
	S Pate	71–75–71–80—297	6500			C Hungate	72–77–79–77—305	2225
	T Purtzer	74–74–72–77—297	6500			R Mediate	75–72–77–81—305	2225
	D Rummells	73–73–77–74—297	6500			M Ozaki	75–74–79–77—305	2225
	J Sluman	74–74–73–76—297	6500		74	B Ford	75–75–79–77—306	2150

(The following players missed the cut)

Pos	Name	Score		Pos	Name	Score		Pos	Name	Score
75	BR Brown	75–77—152		100	M Donald	76–79—155		125	B Bryant	80–79—159
	S Elkington	75–77—152			B Faxon	80–75—155			G Cerulli	75–84—159
	R Fehr	77–75—152			B Sander	80–75—155			R Davis	81–78—159
	S Jones	74–78—152			K Schall	77–78—155			E Romero	84–75—159
	B Lietzke	78–74—152			C Strange	79–76—155			J Sobb	76–83—159
	B Lohr	78–74—152			L Wadkins	74–81—155		130	S Ballesteros	77–83—160
	L Nelson	77–75—152		106	L Emery	79–77—156			J Haas	82–78—160
	J Nicklaus	78–74—152			D Forsman	76–80—156			J Thorpe	77–83—160
	R Osberg	73–79—152			S Ingraham	75–81—156			E Whitman	84–76—160
	J Pate	73–79—152			J Overton	77–79—156		134	S Bowen	81–80—161
	T Schulz	78–74—152			B Passons	74–82—156		135	L Gilbert	83–72—162
	M Sullivan	75–77—152			R Rafferty	81–75—156			M Gove	86–76—162
	L Trevino	77–75—152			G Sauers	75–81—156			D Ishii	82–80—162
88	H Green	74–79—153			K Thompson	80–76—156			A Palmer	81–81—162
	K Hanefeld	76–77—153			K Triplett	74–82—156		139	J Gallagher Jr	82–81—163
	R Hoyt	74–79—153		115	T Armour III	78–79—157			D Johnson	79–84—163
	M James	77–76—153			P Fitzsimons	78–79—157		141	B Borowicz	81–84—165
	B Langer	75–78—153			P Hancock	82–75—157			C Dachisen	84–81—165
	L Nielsen	72–81—153			D Quigley	77–80—157			H Gilliland	82–83—165
	J Thomsen	77–76—153			D Stockton	80–77—157		144	C Schnell	82–84—166
95	M Calcavecchia	77–77—154		120	R Freeman	79–79—158		145	K Allard	81–86—167
	R Cochran	74–80—154			B Makoski	82–76—158			N Caruso	84–83—167
	B Estes	77–77—154			N Ozaki	77–81—158		147	D Fuller	82–87—169
	B Fleisher	78–76—154			M San Filippo	81–77—158		148	T Goin	87–83—170
	K Stauffer	78–76—154			C Tucker	76–82—158				

1990 Results

The 1990 Volvo Order of Merit (Official Money List)

Pos	Name	Official Prize Money £	Pos	Name	Official Prize Money £
1	I Woosnam (Wal)	574166.30	51	J Spence (Eng)	79929.03
2	M McNulty (Zim)	507540.95	52	M Roe (Eng)	77859.33
3	JM Olazabal (Spa)	434765.85	53	D Cooper (Eng)	77772.74
4	B Langer (Ger)	320449.65	54	MA Jimenez (Spa)	75932.73
5	R Rafferty (N Ire)	309851.08	55	J Rutledge (Can)	75273.61
6	M Harwood (Aus)	280084.43	56	C O'Connor Jr (Ire)	75254.82
7	S Torrance (Sco)	248203.32	57	M Persson (Swe)	72900.35
8	D Feherty (N Ire)	237830.16	58	J Rystrom (Swe)	67326.61
9	R Davis (Aus)	233841.87	59	A Lyle (Sco)	66551.50
10	M James (Eng)	229742.39	60	P Curry (Eng)	65740.73
11	E Romero (Arg)	200615.85	61	P McWhinney (Aus)	63708.34
12	N Faldo (Eng)	199937.33	62	C Mason (Eng)	63583.90
13	V Singh (Fij)	185677.68	63	B Malley (USA)	59934.40
14	C Montgomerie (Sco)	174852.26	64	GJ Brand (Eng)	59094.07
15	C Parry (Aus)	170867.85	65	R Drummond (Sco)	56772.31
16	J Bland (SA)	164891.06	66	J Van de Velde (Fra)	55893.25
17	R Boxall (Eng)	148798.67	67	T Charnley (Eng)	55862.22
18	S Ballesteros (Spa)	148033.34	68	B Lane (Eng)	55589.93
19	S McAllister (Sco)	147238.55	69	B Longmuir (Sco)	51390.88
20	P Walton (Ire)	142104.35	70	M Poxon (Eng)	51259.67
21	E Darcy (Ire)	138745.27	71	M Moreno (Spa)	49887.08
22	G Brand Jr (Sco)	135616.78	72	J Parnevik (Swe)	47795.85
23	MA Martin (Spa)	133977.50	73	B Marchbank (Sco)	47018.29
24	B Ogle (Aus)	133531.73	74	P Mitchell (Eng)	46956.85
25	M Mackenzie (Eng)	125307.25	75	S Bennett (Eng)	45955.43
26	T Johnstone (Zim)	124826.34	76	J Hawkes (SA)	44952.59
27	R Chapman (Eng)	114070.83	77	D Russell (Eng)	44897.56
28	R Claydon (Eng)	113968.09	78	P Smith (Sco)	44231.93
29	S Richardson (Eng)	109944.21	79	D Durnian (Eng)	43428.68
30	J Rivero (Spa)	109176.57	80	C Moody (Eng)	41624.99
31	P Fowler (Aus)	106452.05	81	H Baiocchi (SA)	41449.43
32	M Clayton (Aus)	104430.12	82	A Murray (Eng)	41259.07
33	D Smyth (Ire)	103331.86	83	J Quiros (Spa)	40637.86
34	D Williams (Eng)	103137.25	84	P Teravainen (USA)	40315.84
35	P Senior (Aus)	99539.55	85	K Waters (Eng)	40290.47
36	O Sellberg (Swe)	99508.00	86	E Dussart (Fra)	39896.93
37	V Fernandez (Arg)	97684.17	87	DA Russell (Eng)	38797.17
38	F Nobilo (NZ)	96740.94	88	S Bowman (USA)	38299.20
39	R Hartmann (USA)	93712.91	89	M Miller (Sco)	37905.71
40	A Sorensen (Den)	93285.36	90	J Heggarty (N Ire)	37369.00
41	H Clark (Eng)	93149.87	91	S Hamill (N Ire)	37168.62
42	M Mouland (Wal)	91328.26	92	M Farry (Fra)	36872.98
43	A Forsbrand (Swe)	90460.69	93	M Davis (Eng)	35389.60
44	M McLean (Eng)	89712.50	94	A Sherborne (Eng)	35169.78
45	M Lanner (Swe)	89085.66	95	D Gilford (Eng)	34620.29
46	JM Canizares (Spa)	86518.19	96	M Sunesson (Swe)	34448.79
47	P Broadhurst (Eng)	83812.33	97	P Parkin (Wal)	34206.83
48	C Rocca (Ita)	82612.15	98	K Brown (Sco)	33466.58
40	G Turner (Eng)	82323.00	99	B Norton (USA)	33237.88
50	P O'Malley (Aus)	81387.73	100	P Carrigill (Eng)	33109.61

PGA European Tour

(including Volvo Tour and Approved Special Events)

AGF Open
at La Grande Motte, Montpellier, France

Pos	Name	Score	Prize £
1	B Ogle	72-66-70-70–278	33330
2	P Curry	70-71-69-71–281	17360
	B Longmuir	71-72-69-69–281	17360
4	D Durnian	71-71-71-69–282	9235
	M McNulty	72-71-68-71–282	9235
6	M James	77-68-67-71–283	7000

American Express Mediterranean Open
at Las Brisas, Marbella, Spain

Pos	Name	Score	Prize £
1	I Woosnam	68-68-74–210	66660
2	E Romero	70-71-71–212	34720
	MA Martin	69-69-74–212	34720
4	C O'Connor Jr	71-71-71–213	20000
5	M James	67-71-76–214	16940
6	P Smith	72-72-72–216	13000
	A Murray	74-70-72–216	13000
(Reduced to three rounds because of poor weather)			

Austrian Open
at Gut Altentann, Salzburg

Pos	Name	Score	Prize £
1	B Langer*	65-66-72-68–271	41660
2	L Wadkins	67-68-68-68–271	27760
3	D Smyth	70-69-72-62–273	15650
4	M Moreno	74-67-67-67–275	11550
	MA Martin	68-69-70-68–275	11550
6	G Manson	72-67-72-65–276	8750

* Winner after play-off

Bell's Scottish Open

at King's Course, Gleneagles

Pos	Name	Score	Prize £
1	I Woosnam	72-62-67-68–269	66660
2	M McNulty	73-67-64-69–273	44400
3	G Brand Jr	65-67-72-71–275	22520
	M Mackenzie	71-72-65-67–275	22520
5	N Faldo	72-73-67-65–277	14313
	D Feherty	69-72-68-68–277	14313
	D Cooper	68-69-68-72–277	14313

Benson and Hedges International Open

at St Mellion G&CC, Cornwall

Pos	Name	Score	Prize £
1	JM Olazabal	69-68-69-73–279	58330
2	I Woosnam	69-69-69-73–280	38860
3	B Langer	72-72-68-70–282	21910
4	M McNulty	68-68-73-74–283	17500
5	J Bland	68-71-75-72–286	12526
	M Harwood	71-68-75-72–286	12526
	P Walton	70-71-75-70–286	12526

Benson and Hedges Trophy

at El Bosque G & CC, Valencia, Spain

Pos	Name	Score	Prize £
1	JM Canizares and T Abitbol	66-67-66-68–267	30500
2	M Mouland and A Nicholas	65-66-69-69–269	22500
3	B Barnes and L Davies	67-67-71-66–271	17250

BMW International Open

at Golfplatz München, Munich, Germany

Pos	Name	Score	Prize £
1	P Azinger*	63-73-73-68–277	66660
2	D Feherty	62-72-71-72–277	44400
3	P O'Malley	70-71-71-66–278	25040
4	R Claydon	66-76-67-70–279	20000
5	J Haas	73-70-68-69–280	16940
6	D Russell	66-79-69-67–281	13000
	JM Olazabal	70-73-69-69–281	13000

* Winner after play-off

El Bosque Open
at El Bosque G&CC, Valencia, Spain

Pos	Name	Score	Prize £
1	V Singh	66-69-74-69–276	33330
2	C Williams	68-71-70-71–280	17360
	R Boxall	70-69-70-71–280	17360
4	J Rystrom	72-72-69-68–281	9235
	B Marchbank	69-69-75-68–281	9235
6	P Parkin	68-72-71-71–282	5620
	T Charnley	72-72-67-71–282	5620
	MA Jimenez	74-70-66-72–282	5620
	J Hawksworth	73-72-68-69–282	5620

Carrolls Irish Open
at Portmarnock, Dublin

Pos	Name	Score	Prize £
1	JM Olazabal	67-72-71-72–282	57883
2	M Calcavecchia	66-75-72-72–285	30155
	F Nobilo	73-70-69-73–285	30155
4	R Hartmann	72-74-71-69–286	17369
5	J Bland	71-69-73-74–287	13441
	R Claydon	71-71-72-73–287	13441

Cepsa Madrid Open
at Real Club de la Puerta de Hierro, Madrid, Spain

Pos	Name	Score	Prize £
1	B Langer	70-67-66-67–270	45825
2	R Davies	67-70-68-66–271	30530
3	B Ogle	72-66-73-61–272	17215
4	M Sunesson	72-65-66-70–273	13750
5	R Stelten	73-68-67-68–276	11655
6	P Walton	70-69-71-67–277	8937
	J Rivero	67-71-70-69–277	8937

Crédit Lyonnais Cannes Open
at Cannes Mougins CC, France

Pos	Name	Score	Prize £
1	M McNulty	69-71-69-71–280	50000
2	R Rafferty	73-67-72-69–281	33300
3	M Roe	72-71-66-73–282	18780
4	V Singh	69-72-74-69–284	11800
	M O'Meara	70-70-75-69–284	11800
	J Parnevik	69-68-73-74–284	11800
	A Sorensen	68-68-75-73–284	11800

Dunhill British Masters
at Woburn G&CC

Pos	Name	Score	Prize £
1	M James	70-67-66-67–270	50000
2	D Feherty	65-70-68-69–272	33300
3	C Mason	69-70-68-67–274	18780
4	B Ogle	70-65-68-73–276	12733
	M McNulty	68-70-72-66–276	12733
	J Hawkes	69-69-72-66–276	12733

Ebel European Masters – Swiss Open
at Crans-Sur-Sierre

Pos	Name	Score	Prize £
1	R Rafferty	70-65-66-66–267	76636
2	J Bland	70-66-66-67–269	51060
3	J Spence	66-67-68-69–270	28796
4	C Parry	72-65-66-68–271	21252
	H Clark	64-66-72-69–271	21252
6	M McNulty	65-72-68-67–270	14950
	JM Canizares	69-67-65-71–272	14950

Emirates Airline Desert Classic
at Emirates GC, Dubai

Pos	Name	Score	Prize £
1	E Darcy	64-68-75-69–276	45825
2	D Feherty	73-69-70-68–280	30530
3	S Ballesteros	72-69-71-70–282	15482
	D Smyth	68-71-74-69–282	15482
5	D Gilford	70-73-69-72–284	11655
6	P Fowler	72-70-73-70–285	8250
	S Richardson	72-70-72-71–285	8250
	D Durnian	72-67-73-73–285	8250

Epson Grand Prix
at St Pierre G&CC, Chepstow

Pos	Name	Score	Prize £
1	I Woosnam	65-67-67-72–271	66660
2	JM Olazabal	71-67-67-69–274	34720
	M McNulty	67-67-68-72–274	34720
4	MA Martin	75-72-63-65–275	16780
	R Rafferty	72-71-65-67–275	16780
	B Ogle	66-70-71-68–275	16780

The Equity & Law Challenge
at Royal Mid-Surrey, Richmond

Pos	Name	Points*	Prize £
1	B Marchbank	22	20000
2	P Teravainen	21	9000
	D Cooper	21	9000
4	B Ogle	19	4750
5	P Broadhurst	18	3500

(*Modified Stableford format over 3 rounds)

KLM Dutch Open
at Kennemer GC, Zandvoort

Pos	Name	Score	Prize £
1	S McAllister	69-67-68-70–274	58330
2	R Chapman	73-68-66-71–278	38860
3	JM Olazabal	73-70-65-71–279	21910
4	C Montgomerie	71-68-73-68–280	16165
	D Mijovic	71-70-71-68–280	16165
6	P Baker	69-73-71-68–281	9268
	V Fernandez	72-69-69-71–281	9268
	P McWhinney	76-69-67-69–281	9268
	M Poxon	71-69-68-73–281	9268
	J Spence	71-72-69-69–281	9268

Lancia-Martini Italian Open
at Milano GC, Monza

Pos	Name	Score	Prize £
1	R Boxall	65-64-70-68–267	50000
2	JM Olazabal	67-69-68-68–272	33300
3	E Romero	72-69-66-68–275	18780
4	J Bland	67-74-68-68–277	15000
5	S Ballesteros	75-68-66-69–278	12700
6	G Cali	71-71-67-70–279	8430
	K Waters	70-70-71-68–279	8430
	A Sorensen	66-72-71-70–279	8430
	C Stadler	68-68-71-72–279	8430

Mercedes German Masters
at Stuttgarter GC, Stuttgart

Pos	Name	Score	Prize £
1	S Torrance	70-65-64-73–272	75000
2	B Langer	66-67-74-68–275	39065
	I Woosnam	75-69-69-62–275	39065
4	JM Olazabal	69-70-69-69–277	20780
	M Harwood	71-67-70-69–277	20780
6	D Feherty	69-68-74-67–278	15750

Motorola Classic
at East Sussex National

Pos	Name	Score	Prize £
1	P Broadhurst	68-73-67-69–277	10500
2	W Henry	73-75-66-66–280	7100
3	S Stephen	74-72-66-69–281	5100

Murphy's Cup
at Fulford, York

Pos	Name	Score					Prize £
1	T Johnstone	6	23	6	15	50	41660
2	M Mackenzie	8	13	16	11	48	27760
3	R Claydon	10	15	7	12	44	15650
4	A Lyle	9	10	8	13	40	12750
5	M Poxon	7	7	9	16	39	10800
6	B Lane	5	13	10	9	37	8900

NM English Open
at The Belfry, Sutton Coldfield

Pos	Name	Score	Prize £
1	M James*	76-68-65-75–284	66660
2	S Torrance	75-67-69-73–284	44400
3	D Feherty	73-75-69-68–285	25040
4	S Ballesteros	72-72-68-75–287	20000
5	D Cooper	77-73-71-67–288	13235
	S McAllister	74-74-72-68–288	13235
	H Clark	76-73-69-70–288	13235
	M Harwood	74-73-69-72–288	13235

Open Renault de Baleares
at Son Vida, Palma de Mallorca

Pos	Name	Score	Prize £
1	S Ballesteros*	66-65-70-68–269	45825
2	M Persson	65-65-66-73–269	30530
3	J Quiros	68-64-71-68–271	17215
4	M McNulty	67-70-69-66–272	13750
5	J Van de Velde	71-66-69-67–273	10640
	R Davis	70-64-70-69–273	10640

* Winner after play-off

Panasonic European Open
at Sunningdale

Pos	Name	Score	Prize £
1	P Senior	67-68-66-66–267	66660
2	I Woosnam	65-68-68-67–268	44400
3	JM Canizares	69-69-63-68–269	25040
4	T Simpson	67-72-64-67–270	15735
	JM Olazabal	65-69-70-66–270	15735
	N Faldo	68-70-64-68–270	15735
	GJ Brand	70-65-65-70–270	15735

Peugeot French Open
at Chantilly GC, Paris

Pos	Name	Score	Prize £
1	P Walton	73-66-67-69–275	58330
2	B Langer	71-65-72-67–275	38860
3	E Romero	68-69-69-70–276	21910
4	N Faldo	68-69-68-72–277	16165
	R Hartmann	68-65-73-71–277	16165
6	R Rafferty	70-70-66-72–278	9268
	M McNulty	71-65-69-73–278	9268
	R Boxall	70-69-66-73–278	9268
	B Gallacher	70-65-72-71–278	9268
	M Mackenzie	70-70-70-68–278	9268

Peugeot Spanish Open
at Club de Campo, Madrid

Pos	Name	Score	Prize £
1	R Davis	74-69-68-66–277	50000
2	N Faldo	70-71-72-65–278	22360
	B Langer	70-71-69-68–278	22360
	P Fowler	72-68-69-69–278	22360
5	S McAllister	74-71-65-70–280	12700
6	Y Beamonte	71-75-67-68–281	8430
	S Ballesteros	74-70-68-69–281	8430
	JM Olazabal	71-67-71-72–281	8430
	S Bowman	71-70-68-72–281	8430

Peugeot-Trends Belgian Open
at Royal Waterloo GC, Brussels

Pos	Name	Score	Prize £
1	O Sellberg	68-66-67-71–272	41660
2	I Woosnam	66-70-70-70–276	27760
3	E Romero	69-72-69-68–278	15650
4	G Turner	68-74-68-70–280	11550
	JM Olazabal	69-71-71-69–280	11550
6	R Rafferty	70-70-74-68–282	7500
	C Montgomerie	69-73-72-68–282	7500
	M Miller	68-72-74-68–282	7500

PLM Open
at Bokskogen GC, Malmo, Sweden

Pos	Name	Score	Prize £
1	R Rafferty	64-67-70-69–270	58330
2	V Singh	69-71-69-65–274	38860
3	B Langer	72-68-67-68–275	21910
4	O Sellberg	68-66-72-70–276	16165
	F Couples	70-72-69-65–276	16165
6	C Cookson	68-71-72-67–278	10500
	R Davis	70-70-73-65–278	10500
	J Pinsent	71-69-71-67–278	10500

Portuguese Open
at Quinta do Lago

Pos	Name	Score	Prize £
1	M McLean	69-69-65-71–274	45825
2	G Brand Jr	68-70-68-69–275	23872
	M Harwood	70-68-71-66–275	23872
4	M James	68-69-70-69–276	12702
	P Broadhurst	70-69-68-69–276	12702
6	R Hartmann	68-68-73-69–277	8937
	O Sellberg	67-68-70-72–277	8937

Scandinavian Enterprise Open
at Drottningholm GC, Stockholm

Pos	Name	Score	Prize £
1	C Stadler	68-72-67-61–268	66660
2	C Parry	66-70-69-67–272	44400
3	R Rafferty	70-71-65-67–273	25040
4	M Lanner	69-71-70-64–274	20000
5	MA Jimenez	67-69-72-67–275	15470
	M Harwood	68-69-69-69–275	15470

Suntory World Match Play Championship

at West Course, Wentworth

First Round:

C Beck beat R Kawagishi 4 and 3
R Rafferty beat S Ballesteros 8 and 6
W Grady beat B Langer 4 and 2
M McNulty beat BR Brown 4 and 2
(Each loser received £14000)

Second Round:

C Beck beat N Faldo 2 and 1
I Woosnam beat R Rafferty 5 and 4
G Norman beat W Grady at 38th hole
M McNulty beat G Norman 6 and 4
(Each loser received £18500)

Semi-Finals:

I Woosnam beat C Beck 5 and 3
M McNulty beat G Norman 3 and 2

Play-off for 3rd and 4th places:

C Beck halved with G Norman after 20 holes
(Each player received £30000)

Final:

I Woosnam beat M McNulty 4 and 2
(Woosnam won £100000 and McNulty £60000)

Tenerife Open

at Amarilla, Tenerife

Pos	Name	Score	Prize £
1	V Fernandez*	67-74-72-69–282	33330
2	M Mouland	70-73-71-68–282	22200
3	C O'Connor Jr	74-71-66-73–284	10330
	E Dussart	71-74-69-70–284	10330
	T Charnley	71-74-66-73–284	10330
6	MA Jimenez	68-72-75-70–285	7000

Torras Monte Carlo Open

at Mont Agel, Monte Carlo

Pos	Name	Score	Prize £
1	I Woosnam	66-67-65-60–258	59158
2	C Rocca	67-66-67-63–263	39411
3	M McNulty	67-66-66-65–264	19984
	M Mouland	63-67-65-69–264	19984
5	M Lanner	68-66-72-63–269	13732
	J Hawkes	70-66-67-66–269	13732

Trophée Lancôme
at St Nom-la-Breteche, Paris

Pos	Name	Score	Prize £
1	JM Olazabal	68-66-70-65–269	69970
2	C Montgomerie	69-63-71-67–270	46620
3	T Johnstone	68-69-70-64–271	26290
4	R Davis	69-66-71-69–275	17833
	M James	72-64-68-71–275	17833
	C Parry	69-70-66-70–275	17833

UAP Under 25's European Open
at Golf du Prieuré, Paris

Pos	Name	Score	Prize £
1	P Baker	74-69-74-65–282	14160
2	RN Roderick	73-71-70-71–285	9435
3	P Price	72-71-72-71–286	5320
4	M Piltz	72-68-76-73–289	4250
5	A Gillner	72-75-70-73–290	3290
	PU Johansson	72-74-70-74–290	3290

Vinho Verde Atlantic Open
at Campo Golfe, Estela, Oporto, Portugal

Pos	Name	Score	Prize £
1	S McAllister*	71-71-72-74–288	33330
2	R Rafferty	72-70-74-72–288	12038
	D Williams	70-71-73-74–288	12038
	S Hamill	71-67-74-76–288	12038
	R Boxall	71-73-73-71–288	12038
	A Sorensen	68-73-70-77–288	12038

Volvo German Open
at Hubbelrath GC, Dusseldorf

Pos	Name	Score	Prize £
1	M McNulty	67-68-70-65–270	77896
2	C Parry	66-65-72-70–273	51953
3	E Darcy	66-70-68-70–274	26310
	A Forsbrand	64-66-73-71–274	26310
5	J Rivero	70-71-70-64–275	16727
	P Walton	69-67-69-70–275	16727
	D Smyth	68-66-73-68–275	16727

* Winner after play-off

Volvo Masters
at Valderrama, Spain

Pos	Name	Score	Prize £
1	M Harwood	70-72-73-71–286	75000
2	S Torrance	69-73-72-73–287	39065
	S Richardson	71-73-70-73–287	39065
4	B Langer	72-71-72-73–288	17962
	A Forsbrand	75-69-71-73–288	17962
	JM Olazabal	72-69-74-73–288	17962
	M McNulty	73-73-71-71–288	17962
8	C Montgomerie	71-72-71-75–289	10955
6	D Feherty	70-77-67-75–289	10955
10	R Davis	74-71-74-72–291	9300

Volvo Open di Firenze
at Ugolino, Italy

Pos	Name	Score	Prize £
1	E Romero	68-66-64-67–265	33330
2	C Montgomerie	65-64-67-70–266	17360
	R Claydon	63-68-66-69–266	17360
4	R Davis	69-63-71-66–269	9235
	M Hallberg	71-63-67-68–269	9235
6	P O'Malley	67-64-68-71–270	7000

Volvo PGA Championship
at West Course, Wentworth

Pos	Name	Score	Prize £
1	M Harwood	69-68-67-67–271	66660
2	N Faldo	67-71-69-65–272	34720
	J Bland	67-67-71-67–272	34720
4	JM Olazabal	66-68-69-70–273	18470
	R Davis	68-68-71-66–273	18470
6	E Romero	66-71-69-68–274	14000
7	P Curry	66-70-72-68–276	11000
	T Johnstone	66-72-67-71–276	11000
9	C Montgomerie	70-70-68-69–277	8960
10	M Farry	68-71-71-68–278	7170
	J Hawkes	70-69-72-67–278	7170
	P Walton	70-67-71-70–278	7170
	D Williams	70-70-70-68–278	7170
14	J Rivero	72-67-67-73–279	5760
	M James	75-66-68-70–279	5760
	E Darcy	70-71-68-70–279	5760
	G Brand Jr	75-67-71-66–279	5760
18	W Grant	73-68-69-70–280	4900
	M McNulty	73-69-69-69–280	4900
	J Heggarty	68-70-73-69–280	4900
	C O'Connor Jr	76-68-70-66–280	4900

Volvo Seniors British Open
at Ailsa Course, Turnberry Hotel

Pos	Name	Score	Prize £
1	G Player	69-65-71-75–280	25000
2	D Beman	67-66-67-81–281	12775
	B Waites	66-70-69-76–281	12775
4	A Palmer	66-68-69-79–282	7350
5	S Hobday	67-70-67-79–283	6150
6	B Casper	70-70-70-74–284	4720
	B Charles	68-67-73-76–284	4720
8	D Simon	71-68-66-80–285	3422
	H Henning	72-75-62-76–285	3422
10	L Mowry	70-66-71-79–286	2795
	J Fourie	68-72-69-77–286	2795
12	N Coles	69-71-67-80–287	2560
13	C Mehok	70-68-72-80–290	2430
14	D Butler	70-77-68-76–291	2310
15	A Skerritt	71-71-70-80–292	2200
16	A Grubb	76-74-67-76–293	2040
	C O'Connor	72-71-74-76–293	2040
18	B Hunt	73-69-73-79–294	1870
	P Butler	73-72-73-76–294	1870
	C Green (Am)	71-69-72-83–295	

Wang Four Stars National Pro-Celebrity
at Moor Park GC, Rickmansworth

Pos	Name	Score	Prize £
1	R Davis*	67-72-65-67–271	36500
2	M McNulty	68-69-69-65–271	16716
	M Clayton	68-70-66-67–271	16716
	B Malley	68-66-67-70–271	16716
5	P Mitchell	66-66-69-71–272	9500
6	P Hoad	69-69-67-69–274	8000

* Winner after play-off

PGA European Tour Qualifying School

at La Grande Motte and Golf Massane, France

Pos	Name	Score
1	D Silva (Port)	69-74-72-74-65-70–424
2	JP Price (Wal)	75-71-70-67-78-69–430
3	J Anglada (Spa)	71-73-71-72-72-71–430
4	J Coceres (Arg)	72-72-71-73-75-68–431
5	F Lindgren (Swe)	71-75-72-70-73-70–431
6	S Luna (Spa)	70-69-73-73-71-75–431
7	J Townsend (USA)	71-68-71-73-72-76–431
8	J Bennett (Eng)	70-75-69-73-74-71–432
9	P Haugsrud (Nor)	72-69-73-70-70-78–432
10	R Huff (USA)	67-71-70-68-78-78–432
11	P Hall (Eng)	75-71-73-67-75-72–433
12	L Hederstrom (Swe)	75-65-79-75-66-73–433
13	S Bottomley (Eng)	69-69-75-73-72-75–433
14	G Day (USA)	75-74-71-68-75-71–434
15	T Dodds (Nam)	68-76-74-73-69-74–434
16	A Gillner (Swe)	71-70-76-74-69-74–434
17	M Thomas (Eng)	69-72-76-76-68-74–435
18	K Trimble (Aus)	73-72-72-73-70-75–435
19	PU Johansson (Swe)	72-70-70-68-77-78–435
20	D Stirling (Eng)	73-72-73-71-76-71–436
21	M Gates (Eng)	74-72-77-67-76-71–437
22	J Hobday (Eng)	73-73-75-71-71-74–437
23	P Hedblom (Swe)	75-71-71-71-74-75–437
24	C Van der Velde (Neth)	70-70-74-73-75-75–437
25	M Pendaries (Fra)	68-73-73-71-76-76–437
26	V Forsbrand (Swe)	71-74-75-73-71-74–438
27	P Lonard (Aus)	70-74-77-71-72-74–438
28	P Mayo (Wal)	77-68-73-71-75-74–438
29	R Karlsson (Swe)	74-73-74-73-68-76–438
30	H Green (Eng)	71-71-77-75-68-76–438
31	C Hardin (Swe)	73-73-74-69-73-76–438
32	L Vannet (Sco)	74-71-71-72-74-76–438
33	L Tinkler (Aus)	73-71-71-72-74-77–438
34	C Cookson (USA)	71-71-74-73-71-78–438
35	D Clarke (Ire)	69-75-73-74-75-73–439
36	R Lee (Eng)	75-71-78-69-70-76–439
37	M Fernandez (Arg)	75-69-73-72-72-78–439
38	A Hunter (Sco)	70-70-73-74-73-79–439
39	J Cantero (Arg)	71-72-75-74-74-74–440
40	I Mosey (Eng)	74-70-74-76-71-75–440
41	B Nelson (USA)	74-72-79-68-72-75–440
42	N Briggs (Eng)	69-73-77-73-73-75–440
43	T Stevens (Eng)	77-73-71-72-71-76–440
44	O Eskildsen (Den)	73-75-75-72-68-77–440
45	R Gregan (Sco)	71-72-76-73-76-73–441
46	P Carman (Eng)	68-76-72-72-78-75–441
47	T Levet (Fra)	76-73-73-70-72-77–441
48	B McColl (Sco)	73-75-72-75-68-78–441
49	K Jones (Wal)	73-71-72-71-75-79–441
50	R Winchester (Eng)	70-71-74-71-75-80–441

PGA European Tour Final Statistics, 1990

(provided by Philips Radio Communications Systems)

Driving Distance

		Yds
1	M Moreno	280.1
2	P McWhinney	279.8
3	M Lanner	279.7
4	S Richardson	279
5	M Farry	278
	A Lyle	278
	B Ogle	278
8	J Rutledge	277
	G Turner	277
10	M Davis	276
	B Marchbank	276
	I Woosnam	276

Fairways Hit

		%
1	A Murray	73.4
2	N Faldo	73.2
3	C Mason	72.8
4	G Levenson	70
	J Rivero	70
6	E Dussart	69
	M McNulty	69
	A Sorensen	69
9	MA Jimenez	67
10	S Bennett	66
	M Clayton	66
	M Harwood	66
	C O'Connor Jr	66

Greens in Regulation

		%
1	N Faldo	77
2	B Lane	75
	C Parry	75
4	A Lyle	73
	M Miller	73
	S Torrance	73
	I Woosnam	73
8	R Chapman	72
	R Davis	72
	J Heggarty	72
	J Rystrom	72

Putts Per Round

		Avg
1	B Langer	28.69
2	P Parkin	28.79
3	P Curry	28.88
4	G Turner	29.15
5	R Rafferty	29.18
6	M McNulty	29.36
7	D Feherty	29.50
8	JM Canizares	29.56
9	P Fowler	29.57
10	S Bennett	29.58

Sand Saves

		%
1	G Turner	73
2	P Curry	68
3	J Rystrom	67
4	A Lyle	64
	C Mason	64
6	C Montgomerie	62
7	D Feherty	61
	V Singh	61
9	JM Canizares	60
	B Langer	60
	D Smyth	60

Stroke Average

		Avg
1	C Parry	69.62
2	N Faldo	69.64
3	I Woosnam	69.66
4	M McNulty	69.76
5	JM Olazabal	69.89
5	B Langer	69.90
7	S Ballesteros	70.37
8	R Rafferty	70.40
9	E Romero	70.63
10	R Davis	70.76
11	J Bland	70.77
12	B Ogle	70.82
13	M Harwood	70.86
14	A Lyle	70.88
15	M James	70.94
16	D Feherty	70.96
17	J Rivero	71.01
18	T Johnstone	71.08
19	C Montgomerie	71.12
20	M Clayton	71.12

Professional Men's Internationals, 1990

Asahi Glass Four Tours World Championship
at Yomiuri, Tokyo

First Round:

PGA European Tour beat USPGA Tour 8–4
Australia/New Zealand PGA Tour halved with PGA of Japan 6–6

Second Round:

Australia/New Zealand PGA Tour beat PGA European Tour 8–4
USPGA Tour beat PGA of Japan 10–2

Third Round:

USPGA Tour halved with Australia/New Zealand PGA Tour 6–6
PGA European Tour halved with PGA of Japan 6–6

Overall totals after 54 holes round-robin:

USPGA Tour	20 points
Australia/New Zealand PGA Tour	20 points
PGA European Tour	18 points
PGA of Japan	14 points

Result:

Torrential rain made the course unplayable on the last day, so the tournament was decided on stroke average. Results as follows:

1	Australia/NZ PGA Tour	US$80,000 (£40,994.11) each	US$480,000 (£245,964.66)
2	USPGA Tour	US$45,000 (£23,059.18) each	US$270,000 (£138,355.08)
3	PGA European Tour	US$35,000 (£17,934.92) each	US$210,000 (£107,609.52)
4	PGA of Japan	US$30,000 (£15,372.79) each	US$180,000 (£92,236.74)

Kraft Foods World Cup
at Orlando, Florida

Pos	Country	Score	Prize £ (each)
1	GERMANY (556)		
	B Langer	278	
	T Giedeon	278	60960
2	ENGLAND (559)		
	M James	279	
	R Boxall	280	26416
	IRELAND (559)		
	R Rafferty	283	
	D Feherty	276	26416
4	WALES (561)		
	I Woosnam	276	
	M Mouland	285	16257
5	USA (562)		
	J Mudd	291	
	P Stewart	271	12700
6	ARGENTINA (566)		
	L Carbonetti	286	
	M Guzman	280	7958
	AUSTRALIA (566)		
	P Senior	280	
	B Jones	286	7958
	SPAIN (566)		
	J Rivero	282	
	MA Jimenez	284	7958
9	CANADA (570)		
	D Barr	282	
	R Gibson	288	4572
10	MEXICO (571)		
	C Pelaez	288	
	C Espinoza	283	3556
	SCOTLAND (571)		
	S Torrance	282	
	G Brand Jr	289	3556
	TAIPEI (571)		
	LH Chen	288	
	CC Yuan	283	3556

INDIVIDUAL TITLE (leading scores):

1	P Stewart (USA)	271	38100
2	A Sorensen (Den)	273	25400
3	D Feherty (Ire)	276	17780
	I Woosnam (Wal)	276	17780
5	B Langer (Ger)	278	8890
	T Giedeon (Ger)	278	8890

Dunhill Cup
at The Old Course, St Andrews

First Round:

Japan beat Argentina 2-1
France beat USA 2^{1}/$_{2}$-^{1}/$_{2}$
Spain beat Sweden 2-1
England beat Thailand 3-0
Scotland beat Mexico 2^{1}/$_{2}$-^{1}/$_{2}$
Ireland beat Korea 3-0
Wales beat Chinese Team Taipei 2-1
New Zealand beat Australia 2-1

Second Round:

Japan beat France 3-0
Ireland beat Spain 2-1
New Zealand beat Wales 2-1
England beat Scotland 2-1

Semi-Finals:

Ireland beat New Zealand 2^{1}/$_{2}$-^{1}/$_{2}$
England beat Japan 2-1

Play-off for 3rd and 4th places:

New Zealand beat Japan 2-1

Final:

Ireland beat England 3^{1}/$_{2}$-2^{1}/$_{2}$
P Walton halved with M James 72
R Rafferty beat R Boxall 71-73
D Feherty lost to H Clark 74-73

P Walton lost to M James 77-76
R Rafferty beat R Boxall 71-77
D Feherty beat H Clark 75-75 on 3rd play-off hole
(England received £25272 each and Ireland received £50505 each)

PGA Cup
at Kiawah Island, South Carolina, USA
(USA and European club professionals team event)

First Day - Foursomes

United States		Europe	
B Ford and B Boyd	^{1}/$_{2}$	A Webster and K Stables	^{1}/$_{2}$
B Fleisher and P Hancock (7 and 6)	1	B Waites and J Woof	0
S Rachels and K Thompson (3 and 2)	1	T Rastall and P Carman	0
R Freeman and S Ingraham (2 and 1)	1	R Weir and B Barnes	0
	3^{1}/$_{2}$		^{1}/$_{2}$

Fourball

United States		Europe	
D Fuller and J Thomsen (4 and 3)	1	A Webster and K Stables	0
B Fleisher and P Hancock (2 and 1)	1	P Carman and D Screeton	0
B Boyd and B Ford	0	R Weir and B Waites (3 and 2)	1
S Rachels and S Ingraham (8 and 7)	1	B Barnes and D Scott	0
	3		1

PGA Cup

continued

Second Day - Foursomes

United States		Europe	
R Freeman and S Ingraham	0	R Weir and B Waites (2 and 1)	1
J Thomsen and D Fuller (3 and 2)	1	P Carman and D Screeton	0
P Hancock and K Thompson (4 and 2)	1	T Rastall and J Woof	0
B Boyd and B Ford (2 and 1)	1	A Webster and K Stables	0
	3		1

Fourball

United States		Europe	
S Rachels and K Thompson (4 and 3)	1	B Barnes and P Carman	0
B Fleisher and P Hancock (3 and 2)	1	B Waites and R Weir	0
D Fuller and J Thomsen	1/2	T Rastall and D Scott	1/2
B Boyd and B Ford (1 hole)	1	A Webster and K Stables	0
	3 1/2		1/2

Third Day - Singles

United States		Europe	
R Freeman	0	A Webster (4 and 3)	1
D Fuller (1 hole)	1	B Barnes	0
B Fleisher (4 and 3)	1	B Waites	0
S Ingraham (7 and 6)	1	T Rastall	0
B Boyd	0	R Weir (1 hole)	1
S Rachels (1 hole)	1	K Stables	0
P Hancock	0	P Carman (3 and 2)	1
B Ford (5 and 4)	1	D Screeton	0
J Thomsen (4 and 3)	1	D Scott	0
K Thompson	0	J Woof (2 holes)	1
	6		4

Aggregate: USA 19, Europe 7

PGA European Challenge Tour

PGA European Challenge Tour Order of Merit

Pos	Name	Official Prize Money £	Pos	Name	Official Prize Money £
1	G Cali (Ita)	28382	26	P Mayo (Wal)	13396
2	E O'Connell (Ire)	24828	27	J Anglada (Spa)	13122
3	D James(Sco)	24619	28	J Bennett (Eng)	13113
4	M Hoegberg (Swe)	23900	29	A Gillner (Swe)	12979
5	Q Dabson (Fra)	21832	30	T Levet (Fra)	12752
6	E Bolognesi (Ita)	19339	31	J Rasmussen (Den)	12651
7	M Hallberg (Swe)	18774	32	J Lindberg (Swe)	12618
8	J Cantero (Arg)	18725	33	J Coceres (Arg)	12505
9	N Godin (Eng)	18560	34	D Westermark (Swe)	12264
10	W Henry (Eng)	18269	35	J Higgins (Eng)	11863
11	C Brooks (Sco)	18268	36	A Haglund (Swe)	11690
12	Y Beamonte (Spa)	17474	37	L Hederstrom (Swe)	11687
13	J McHenry (Ire)	17284	38	J Price(Wal)	11549
14	F Lindgren (Swe)	17257	39	J Saxton (USA)	11480
15	A Hare (Eng)	16796	40	K Trimble (Aus)	11352
16	C Cookson (USA)	16595	41	T Nilsson (Swe)	11244
17	V Forsbrand(Swe)	16015	42	O Nordberg (Swe)	10285
18	A Bossert(Swi)	15818	43	S Hurley (Eng)	10005
19	M Besanceney (Fra)	15279	44	T Planchin (Fra)	9995
20	P Affleck (Eng)	15261	45	O Eskildsen (Den)	9838
21	A Mednick (Swe)	15103	46	M Sterner (Swe)	9619
22	M Pendaries (Fra)	15039	47	J Rozadilla(Spa)	9562
23	P Haugsrud (Nor)	13823	48	J Lomas (Eng)	9434
24	CM Stromberg (Swe)	13689	40	R Gonzalez(Arg)	9430
25	M Mannelli (Ita)	13583	50	P Hedblom (Swe)	9361

1990 PGA European Challenge Tour

Tournament	Winner
Torras Hostench-Pals	S Hurley
Tessali Open	E Bolognesi
Open Renault de Vallromanas	W Henry
Boggi Open	J McHenry
Ercros Circuit 1	I Feliu
Ramlösa Open	CM Strömberg
Prince's Challenge	C Gillies
Jede Hot Cup Open	P Hedblom
Barnham Broom Challenge	C Brooks
Torras Hostench-Terramar	A Garrido
FLA Open	O Nordberg
Cerutti Open	G Cali
Open Vittel	M Besanceney
Bolton Old Links Challenge	K Trimble
Ercros Circuit 2	J Rosa
Martini Open	D James
Stiga Open	M Hallberg
Audi Open	B King
Open Ecco	Q Dabson
Memorial Barras	G Cali
Viking Open	P Carsbo
Wermland Open	J Haeggman
Neuchatel Open	A Bossert
Scand Tipo Trophy	F Lindgren
Leman Pro-Am	Q Dabson
Swedish Match Play	E O'Connell
Audi Quattro Trophy	N Godin
Gevalia Open	J Cantero
Rolex Pro-Am	J McHenry
Teleannons GP	M Hoegberg
Lansforsakringar Open	A Mednick
Vasteras Open	V Forsbrand
Brussels Pro-Am	P Golding
Ercros Circuit 3	J Pinero
SI/Compaq Open	J Parnevik
ESAB Open	R Gonzalez
Torras Hostench-El Prat	E O'Connell
Ercros Circuit 4	D Wood

Miscellaneous Professional Tournaments, 1990

Clydesdale Bank Northern Open

at Nairn GC, Dunbar

Name	Score	Prize £
C Brooks	67-68-69-70–274	3300
P Lyons	73-68-67-69–277	2050
B Barnes	72-68-68-69–277	2050
P Hinton	74-71-67-68–280	1050
P Lawrie	69-73-71-67–280	1050
F Mann	69-67-68-76–280	1050

Dunbar Professional Championship

at King's Links, Royal Aberdeen

Name	Score	Prize £
R Weir	68-69-68-73–278	2000
M McLaren	70-72-71-70–283	1360
K Walker	72-69-71-72–284	1000

Irish PGA Championship

at Woodbrook, Co Dublin

Name	Score	Prize £
D Smyth	70-69-65-67–271	8000
J Heggarty	71-69-71-69–280	5000
C O'Connor Jr	72-73-70-68–283	3800
E Darcy	72-69-75-68–284	2950
A O'Connor	72-69-71-74–286	2350

John Birnie Scottish Professional Championship
at Deer Park, Livingston

Name	Score	Prize £
R Drummond	73-67-69-69–278	5000
S Martin	67-71-69-72–279	3300
P Smith	71-70-70-69–280	1900
A Brooks	67-69-71-74–281	1500

Johnnie Walker International
at Hyatt Dorado Beach, Puerto Rico

Name	Score
D Gilford	66-67-72-69–274
N Briggs	69-70-68-71–278
R McFarlane	73-70-71-70–284
J Rodriguez	76-70-72-66–284
P Baker	73-71-70-71–285

Lord Derby Knowsley Safari Park Tournament
at Bury

Name	Score
E Wilson	64-71-69–204
J Murray	68-70-68–206
S Field	72-67-70–207

PGA Assistants' Championship
at Hillside, Southport

Name	Score
A Ashton (Huntercombe)	66-74-73–213
A Elliott (Ralston)	68-72-75–215
C Gillies (Glenbervie)	72-69-75–216
G Collinson (Windyhill)	72-73-73–218

Scottish Professional Match Play

at North Berwick

Quarter Finals:

A Hunter beat G Collinson 5 and 4
M Miller beat W Milne 2 and 1
S Stephen beat S Walker 2 holes
J Chillas beat A Oldcorn 1 hole

Semi-Finals:

A Hunter beat M Miller at 19th hole
J Chillas beat S Stephen 1 hole

Third place play-off:

S Stephen beat M Miller at 19th hole

Final:

J Chillas beat A Hunter 5 and 4

USPGA Tour Official Money List, 1990

Pos	Name	Official Prize Money $	Pos	Name	Official Prize Money $
1	G Norman (Aus)	1165477	51	B Britton	278977
2	W Levi	1024647	52	C Stadler	278482
3	P Stewart	976281	53	C Strange	277172
4	P Azinger	944731	54	K Green	267172
5	J Mudd	911746	55	R Floyd	264078
6	H Irwin	838249	56	J Sluman	264012
7	M Calcavecchia	834281	57	D Peoples	259367
8	T Simpson	809772	58	C Perry	259108
9	F Couples	757999	59	M Hatalsky	253639
10	M O'Meara	707175	60	M Reid	249148
11	G Morgan	702629	61	T Sills	243350
12	B Mayfair	693658	62	R Mediate	240625
13	L Wadkins	673433	63	S Simpson	235309
14	L Mize	668198	64	B Andrade	231362
15	T Kite	658202	65	R Cochran	230278
16	I Baker-Finch (Aus)	611492	66	P Persons	218505
17	C Beck	571816	67	M Hulbert	216002
18	S Elkington	548564	68	T Watson	213989
19	P Jacobsen	547279	69	B Estes	212090
20	D Love III	537172	70	J Thorpe	211297
21	W Grady (Aus)	527185	71	A Magee	210507
22	N Price (SA)	520777	72	M Wiebe	210435
23	B Tway	495862	73	K Knox	209679
24	L Roberts	478522	74	J Delsing	207740
25	J Gallagher Jr	476706	75	H Sutton	207084
26	C Pavin	468830	76	J Hallet	204059
27	R Gamez	461407	77	M Lye	201011
28	J Cook	448112	78	P Blackmar	200796
29	B Tennyson	443508	79	F Zoeller	199629
30	J Huston	435690	80	D Barr (Can)	197979
31	G Sauers	374485	81	B Faxon	197118
32	D Frost (SA)	372485	82	T Schulz	193127
33	B Crenshaw	351193	83	D Pooley	192570
34	S Jones	350982	84	R Zokol	191634
35	T Armour	348658	85	B Wadkins	190613
36	M Donald	348328	86	B Bryant	189795
37	N Faldo (GB)	345262	87	D Ishii	188000
38	JM Olazabal	337837	88	K Triplett	183464
39	S Pate	334505	89	J Haas	180023
40	S Hoch	333978	90	W Wood	179972
41	B Lietzke	329294	91	F Funk	179346
42	J Mahaffey	325115	92	R Wrenn	174308
43	D Forsman	319160	93	B Sander	172886
44	BR Brown	312466	94	M Smith	170034
45	M Brooks	307948	95	D Edwards	166028
46	J Sindelar	307207	96	B Fabel	165876
47	S Verplank	303589	97	M McCumber	163413
48	N Henke	294592	98	B Claar	161356
49	T Purtzer	285176	99	B Gardner	159737
50	K Perry	279881	100	B Glasson	156791

USPGA Tour, 1990

Anheuser-Busch Golf Classic
at Kingsmill GC, Williamsburg, Virginia

Pos	Name	Score	Prize $
1	L Wadkins	65-66-67-68–266	180000
2	L Mize	66-69-68-68–271	108000
3	S Verplank	69-64-69-70–272	58000
	B Wolcott	69-65-68-70–272	58000
5	I Baker-Finch	69-71-66-67–273	36500
	R Cochran	66-71-69-67–273	36500
	C Perry	67-67-68-71–273	36500

AT&T Pebble Beach National Pro-Am
at Pebble Beach, California

Pos	Name	Score	Prize $
1	M O'Meara	67-73-69-72–281	180000
2	K Perry	73-71-69-70–283	108000
3	T Kite	69-69-75-71–284	58000
	P Stewart	66-71-74-73–284	58000
5	D Frost	74-71-73-67–285	40000
6	M Calcavecchia	69-71-74-72–286	34750
	R Zokol	75-71-71-69–286	34750

Bank of Boston Classic
at Pleasant Valley, Sutton, Massachusetts

Pos	Name	Score	Prize $
1	M Hatalsky	70-68-69-68–275	162000
2	S Verplank	67-68-68-73–276	97200
3	R Fehr	68-71-68-70–277	46800
	M Smith	65-72-69-71–277	46800
	DA Weibring	68-69-72-68–277	46800
6	B Bryant	69-69-70-70–278	27225
	B Glasson	67-70-70-71–278	27225
	B Mayfair	70-68-72-68–278	27225
	S Pate	72-65-70-71–278	27225
	B Tennyson	71-68-65-74–278	27225
	W Wood	69-71-66-72–278	27225

BC Open
at En-Joie GC, Endicott, New York

Pos	Name	Score	Prize $
1	N Henke	66-64-70-68–268	126000
2	M Wiebe	70-69-68-64–271	75600
3	J Benepe	68-69-67-68–272	33600
	B Jaeckel	70-68-65-69–272	33600
	B Tennyson	70-70-66-66–272	33600
	D Tewell	71-64-70-67–272	33600

BellSouth Atlanta Golf Classic
at Atlanta GC, Georgia

Pos	Name	Score	Prize $
1	W Levi	72-66-68-69–275	180000
2	K Clearwater	70-68-66-72–276	74666
	L Mize	66-69-71-70–276	74666
	N Price	68-69-69-70–276	74666
5	M Donald	68-72-68-70–278	38000
	K Perry	69-70-70-69–278	38000

Bob Hope Chrysler Classic
at Palm Desert, California

Pos	Name	Score	Prize $
1	P Jacobsen	67-66-69-66-71–339	180000
2	S Simpson	68-69-67-68-68-340	88000
	B Tennyson	73-68-66-67-66-340	88000
4	T Simpson	70-70-67-68-66-341	41333
	T Kite	70-69-64-69-69-341	41333
	T Schulz	70-66-69-67-69-341	41333

Buick Classic
at Westchester CC, Rye, New York

Pos	Name	Score	Prize $
1	H Irwin	66-69-68-66–269	180000
2	P Azinger	67-70-69-65–271	108000
3	K Triplett	65-74-67-66–272	68000
4	K Green	70-67-69-67–273	48000
5	J Gallagher Jr	69-68-70-67–274	38000
	B McCallister	66-67-70-71–274	38000

Buick Open
at Warwick Hills, Grand Blanc, Michigan

Pos	Name	Score	Prize $
1	C Beck	66-70-71-65–272	180000
2	M Donald	65-69-69-70–273	74666
	F Zoeller	66-69-66-72–273	74666
	H Irwin	69-63-67-74–273	74666
5	F Funk	69-71-69-65–274	40000
6	K Green	71-63-71-70–275	36000

Canadian Open
at Glen Abbey GC, Ontario

Pos	Name	Score	Prize $
1	W Levi	68-68-72-70–278	180000
2	I Baker-Finch	68-70-73-68–279	88000
	J Woodward	68-71-74-66–279	88000
4	A North	71-71-70-69–281	48000
5	P Azinger	70-71-71-70–282	32750
	B Faxon	65-74-71-72–282	32750
	B Gardner	72-68-67-75–282	32750
	B Tennyson	70-67-73-72–282	32750
	B Wadkins	68-72-69-73–282	32750
	M Wiebe	69-73-68-72–282	32750

Canon Greater Hartford Open
at TPC Connecticut, Cromwell, Connecticut

Pos	Name	Score	Prize $
1	W Levi	67-66-67-67–267	180000
2	M Calcavecchia	67-67-68-67–269	66000
	B Fabel	67-65-67-70–269	66000
	R Mediate	65-69-70-65–269	66000
	C Perry	63-69-68-69–269	66000
6	N Henke	65-67-67-71–270	32375
	B Lohr	70-68-68-64–270	32375
	L Roberts	67-66-68-69–270	32375
	B Tennyson	69-69-65-67–270	32375

Centel Western Open
at Butler National, Oak Brook, Illinois

Pos	Name	Score	Prize $
1	W Levi	70-66-70-69–275	180000
2	P Stewart	68-67-72-72–279	108000
3	P Jacobsen	72-70-70-68–280	58000
	L Roberts	65-75-69-71–280	58000
5	M Brooks	71-65-73-72–281	38000
	G Norman	71-69-71-70–281	38000

Chattanooga Classic
at Valley Brook G&CC, Hixson, Tennessee

Pos	Name	Score	Prize $
1	P Persons	64-64-65-67–260	108000
2	R Zokol	65-66-65-66–262	64800
3	F Funk	65-67-66-66–264	34800
	K Knox	68-70-61-65–264	34800
5	R Pearce	70-66-64-66–266	21900
	D Peoples	67-66-67-66–266	21900
	H Taylor	66-66-67-67–266	21900

Deposit Guaranty Golf Classic
at Hattiesburg CC, Mississippi

Pos	Name	Score	Prize $
1	G Sauers	67-65-68-68–268	54000
2	J Ferenz	71-64-68-67–270	32400
3	M McCullough	68-67-70-66–271	17400
	D Ogrin	67-70-69-65–271	17400
5	L Janzen	69-64-71-68–272	12000

Doral Ryder Open
at Doral CC, Miami, Florida

Pos	Name	Score	Prize $
1	G Norman*	68-73-70-62–273	252000
2	M Calcavecchia	68-67-73-65–273	104533
	P Azinger	68-66-70-69–273	104533
	T Simpson	70-71-66-66–273	104533
5	T Purtzer	67-70-70-68–275	53200
	M Reid	67-72-66-70–275	53200

Federal Express St Jude Classic
at TPC Southwind, Germantown, Tennessee

Pos	Name	Score	Prize $
1	T Kite*	72-68-62-67–269	180000
2	J Cook	69-67-66-67–269	108000
3	D Canipe	66-73-64-69–272	68000
4	D Frost	69-70-68-67–274	41333
	B Estes	67-69-69-69–274	41333
	T Simpson	69-68-67-70–274	41333

* Winner after play-off

Greater Milwaukee Open
at Tuckaway CC, Franklin, Wisconsin

Pos	Name	Score	Prize $
1	J Gallagher Jr	69-70-66-66–271	162000
2	E Dougherty	69-69-67-66–271	79200
	B Mayfair	66-69-68-68–271	79200
4	S Hoch	70-66-69-67–272	37200
	S Lowery	69-67-71-65–272	37200
	R Stewart	63-70-67-72–272	37200

GTE Byron Nelson Golf Classic
at TPC Las Colinas, Irving, Texas

Pos	Name	Score	Prize $
1	P Stewart	67-68-67–202	180000
2	L Wadkins	72-67-65–204	108000
3	M Calcavecchia	69-69-69–207	58000
	B Lietzke	71-68-68–207	58000
5	A Magee	69-68-71–208	38000
	T Simpson	72-66-70–208	38000

Hardee's Golf Classic
at Oakwood CC, Coal Valley, Illinois

Pos	Name	Score	Prize $
1	J Sindelar*	70-65-67-66–268	180000
2	W Wood	68-63-68-69–268	108000
3	I Baker-Finch	67-69-69-64–269	45100
	D Barr	67-70-65-67–269	45100
	B Britton	69-67-68-65–269	45100
	J Delsing	66-65-70-68–269	45100
	J Gallagher Jr	68-66-67-68–269	45100

Hawaiian Open
at Waialae CC, Honolulu, Hawaii

Pos	Name	Score	Prize $
1	D Ishii	72-67-68-72–279	180000
2	P Azinger	68-71-71-70–280	108000
3	C Dennis	70-73-68-70–281	52000
	J Mudd	72-72-68-69–281	52000
	C Stadler	71-67-72-71–281	52000
6	BR Brown	72-71-69-70–282	30250
	J Hallet	69-73-70-70–282	30250
	B Mayfair	74-71-67-70–282	30250
	P Persons	72-68-73-69–282	30250
	T Simpson	72-69-71-70–282	30250
	G Waite	72-67-72-71–282	30250

* Winner after play-off

HEB Texas Open
at Oak Hills, San Antonio, Texas

Pos	Name	Score	Prize $
1	M O'Meara	64-68-66-63–261	144000
2	G Hallberg	63-69-64-66–262	86400
3	N Price	65-66-63-69–263	54400
4	L Roberts	70-65-64-65–264	38400
5	C Pavin	67-68-62-68–265	32000
	M Brooks	69-64-65-68–266	28800

Honda Classic
at TPC, Eagle Trace, Florida

Pos	Name	Score	Prize $
1	J Huston	68-73-70-71–282	180000
2	M Calcavecchia	70-76-69-69–284	108000
3	M Brooks	71-71-70-73–285	48000
	BR Brown	72-76-68-69–285	48000
	R Floyd	73-72-70-70–285	48000
	B Lietzke	75-69-73-68–285	48000

Independent Insurance Agent Open
at TPC Woodlands, Texas

Pos	Name	Score	Prize $
1	T Sills*	67-72-65–204	180000
2	G Morgan	67-70-67–204	108000
3	S Ballesteros	69-68-68–205	39062
	B Bryant	68-73-64–205	39062
	F Couples	67-69-69–205	39062
	B Lietzke	67-70-68–205	39062
	L Mize	68-69-68–205	39062
	D Peoples	67-66-72–205	39062
	S Simpson	68-68-69–205	39062
	I Woosnam	69-69-67–205	39062

* Winner after play-off

The International

at Castle Pines GC, Castle Rock, Colorado

FORMAT *Modified Stableford with points awarded as follows-double eagle +8; eagle +5; birdie +2; par 0; bogey –1; double bogey or worse –3*

Pos	Name	Points	Prize $
1	D Love III	+14	180000
2	S Pate	+11	74666
	P Senior	+11	74666
	E Romero	+11	74666
5	B Crenshaw	+9	40000
6	S Utley	+8	33500
	J Adams	+8	33500
	J Gallagher	+8	33500

Kemper Open

at TPC Avenel, Potomac, Maryland

Pos	Name	Score	Prize $
1	G Morgan	68-67-70-69–274	180000
2	I Baker-Finch	67-72-70-66–275	108000
3	S Hoch	68-68-69-71–276	58000
	H Irwin	69-73-65-69–276	58000
5	T Kite	70-70-67-70–277	38000
	D Watson	67-72-70-68–277	38000

K Mart Greater Greensboro Open

at Forest Oaks, North Carolina

Pos	Name	Score	Prize $
1	S Elkington	74-71-71-66–282	225000
2	M Reid	72-70-67-75–284	110000
	J Sluman	71-74-68-71–284	110000
3	P Azinger	72-73-73-67–285	51666
	M Hulbert	73-70-73-69–285	51666
	F Couples	71-70-71-73–285	51666

Las Vegas Invitational

at Las Vegas CC

Pos	Name	Score	Prize $
1	B Tway*	67-67-65-65-70–334	234000
2	J Cook	64-70-66-67-67–334	140400
3	P Blackmar	67-69-68-66-67–337	75400
	C Pavin	72-68-66-68-63–337	75400
5	N Henke	69-69-70-66-64–338	49400
	M O'Meara	67-64-67-69-71–338	49400

* Winner after play-off

MCI Heritage Classic
at Hilton Head, South Carolina

Pos	Name	Score	Prize $
1	P Stewart*	70-69-66-71–276	180000
2	S Jones	68-73-66-69–276	88000
	L Mize	71-69-70-66–276	88000
4	G Norman	70-70-67-70–277	44000
	S Pate	67-69-73-68–277	44000
6	A Bean	74-68-69-67–278	36000

Memorial Tournament
at Muirfield Village, Dublin, Ohio

Pos	Name	Score	Prize $
1	G Norman	73-74-69–216	180000
2	P Stewart	74-74-69–217	108000
3	M Brooks	76-70-72–218	48000
	F Couples	69-74-75–218	48000
	B Faxon	77-69-72–218	48000
	D Pooley	73-71-74–218	48000

Mony Tournament of Champions
at La Costa, California

Pos	Name	Score	Prize $
1	P Azinger	66-68-69-69–272	135000
2	I Baker-Finch	66-67-72-68–273	82000
3	M O'Meara	69-73-65-69–276	52000
4	W Grady	69-68-72-69–278	36800
5	S Hoch	69-68-71-71–279	29750
6	G Norman	66-72-71-70–279	29750

Nabisco Championship
at Champions GC, Houston, Texas

Pos	Name	Score	Prize $
1	J Mudd*	68-69-68-68–273	450000
2	B Mayfair	69-66-70-68–273	270000
3	I Baker-Finch	71-70-67-68–276	146250
	W Levi	75-71-67-63–276	146250
5	N Price	68-68-71-70–277	100000
6	C Beck	69-68-71-70–278	90000
7	G Norman	66-71-71-71–279	82500
	T Simpson	66-73-70-70–279	82500
9	W Grady	72-67-73-69–281	75000
10	S Elkington	72-72-66-72–282	71000

* Winner after play-off

NEC World Series of Golf
at Firestone CC, Ohio

Pos	Name	Score	Prize $
1	JM Olazabal	61-67-67-67–262	198000
2	L Wadkins	70-68-70-66–274	118000
3	H Irwin	70-67-66-74–277	74600
4	D Hammond	73-65-70-71–279	52600
5	L Mize	66-71-73-70–280	44000
	C Beck	71-69-69-72–281	38025
	G Norman	71-73-69-68–281	38025

The Nestlé Invitational
at Bay Hill, Orlando, Florida

Pos	Name	Score	Prize $
1	R Gamez	71-69-68-66–274	162000
2	G Norman	74-68-65-68–275	97200
3	L Mize	71-70-67-68–276	61200
4	F Allem	74-69-65-69–277	37200
	S Hoch	69-68-70-70–277	37200
	C Strange	69-70-68-70–277	37200

Nissan Los Angeles Open
at Riviera CC, Los Angeles, California

Pos	Name	Score	Prize $
1	F Couples	68-67-62-69–266	180000
2	G Morgan	67-67-65-70–269	108000
3	P Jacobsen	65-69-70-66–270	58000
	R Mediate	65-67-67-71–270	58000
5	T Kite	67-70-69-65–271	38000
	H Sutton	68-67-67-69–271	38000

Northern Telecom Tucson Open
at TPC Star Pass, Tucson, Arizona

Pos	Name	Score	Prize $
1	R Gamez	65-66-69-70–270	162000
2	M Calcavecchia	68-67-70-69–274	79200
	J Haas	66-64-72-72–274	79200
4	D Forsman	70-67-69-69–275	35437
	D Love III	68-65-73-69–275	35437
	C Pavin	67-70-69-69–275	35437
	B Sander	68-69-73-65–275	35437

Phoenix Open
at TPC Scottsdale, Arizona

Pos	Name	Score	Prize $
1	T Armour	65-67-67-68–267	162000
2	J Thorpe	69-69-66-68–272	97200
3	BR Brown	69-66-70-69–274	52200
	F Couples	75-66-66-67–274	52200
5	B Mayfair	73-66-70-66–275	32850
	B Tennyson	70-67-65-73–275	32850
	B Tway	71-67-71-66–275	32850

The Players Championship
at TPC Sawgrass, Florida

Pos	Name	Score	Prize $
1	J Mudd	67-72-70-69–278	270000
2	M Calcavecchia	67-75-68-69–279	162000
	S Jones	75-71-69-69–284	87000
	T Purtzer	71-73-69-71–284	87000
5	BR Brown	73-72-69-71–285	52687
	K Green	71-69-70-75–285	52687
	H Irwin	70-68-74-73–285	52687
	T Kite	72-70-70-73–285	52687

Shearson Lehman Hutton Open
at Torrey Pines, La Jolla, California

Pos	Name	Score	Prize $
1	D Forsman	68-63-72-72–275	162000
2	T Armour	66-66-73-72–277	97200
3	T Byrum	70-71-69-68–278	61200
4	F Couples	68-68-74-69–279	32625
	S Elkington	72-69-70-68–279	32625
	M O'Meara	66-74-67-72–279	32625
	T Sieckmann	69-64-76-70–279	32625
	C Stadler	67-70-70-72–279	32625
	K Triplett	71-66-72-70–279	32625

Southern Open
at Green Island, Columbus, Georgia

Pos	Name	Score	Prize $
1	K Knox*	69-62-68-66–265	108000
2	J Hallet	68-66-65-66–265	64800
3	J Booros	67-67-68-66–268	40000
4	T Moore	69-68-65-67–269	23625
	L Nelson	70-67-68-64–269	23625
	D Peoples	67-62-70-70–269	23625
	J Wilson	67-64-69-69–269	23625

* Winner after play-off

Southwestern Bell Colonial
at Colonial CC, Fort Worth, Texas

Pos	Name	Score	Prize $
1	B Crenshaw	69-65-72-66–272	180000
2	J Mahaffey	67-72-70-66–275	74666
	C Pavin	66-71-70-68–275	74666
	N Price	72-68-67-68–275	74666
5	M Hulbert	71-70-72-63–276	38000
	C Strange	68-69-69-70–276	38000

USF&G Classic
at English Turn G & CC, New Orleans, Louisiana

Pos	Name	Score	Prize $
1	D Frost	71-70-66-69–276	180000
2	G Norman	73-68-71-65–277	108000
3	R Cochran	72-69-71-67–279	68000
4	B Tennyson	69-70-69-75–283	48000
5	J Delsing	73-69-73-69–284	40000
6	T Simpson	73-69-71-72–285	36000

Walt Disney World/Oldsmobile Classic
at Lake Buena Vista, Florida

Pos	Name	Score	Prize $
1	T Simpson	64-64-65-71–264	180000
2	J Mahaffey	67-66-68-64–265	108000
3	D Love III	68-65-66-67–266	68000
4	G Sauers	68-65-67-67–267	48000
5	P Azinger	67-65-68-68–268	40000
6	D Peoples	68-69-65-67–269	36000

USPGA Tour Official Statistics

Scoring Leaders		Avg
1	G Norman	69.10
2	L Mize	69.49
3	T Simpson	69.73
4	H Irwin	69.76
5	P Azinger	69.88
	T Kite	69.88
7	P Jacobsen	69.91
8	F Couples	69.97
9	B Lietzke	70.06
10	B Mayfair	70.09

Driving Accuracy		%
1	C Peete	.837
2	L Mize	.792
3	D Tewell	.790
4	H Irwin	.778
5	D Edwards	.776
6	C Strange	.766
7	C Pavin	.757
	B Tennyson	.757
9	J Inman	.745
10	S Hoch	.742

Driving Distance		Yds
1	T Purtzer	279.6
2	J Adams	279.4
3	D Forsman	278.0
4	N Lancaster	277.6
	G Norman	277.6
6	L Hinkle	277.4
7	B Sander	276.7
8	D Love III	276.6
9	D Waldorf	275.8
10	T Armour	274.8

Putting Leaders		Avg
1	L Rinker	1.747
2	P Stewart	1.747
3	M Hatalsky	1.749
4	L Mize	1.752
5	I Baker-Finch	1.754
6	J Sluman	1.758
7	B Andrade	1.759
8	B Tway	1.760
9	3 tied with	1.762

Greens in Regulation		%
1	D Tewell	.709
2	R Mediate	.708
3	T Kite	.702
4	C Strange	.701
5	D Barr	.700
6	T Simpson	.699
7	M Lye	.696
8	B Wadkins	.696
9	L Roberts	.693
10	T Purtzer	.691

Sand Saves		%
1	P Azinger	.672
2	D Frost	.615
3	L Mize	.603
4	B Andrade	.600
5	B Mayfair	.599
6	E Fiori	.593
7	J Inman	.593
8	J Huston	.584
	B Jaeckel	.584
10	B Tennyson	.580

US Senior PGA Tour Money List, 1990

Pos	Name	Official Prize Money $	Pos	Name	Official Prize Money $
1	L Trevino	1190518	51	R Rawlins	95209
2	M Hill	895678	52	J Brodie	89386
3	C Coody	762901	53	C Evans	86446
4	G Archer	749691	54	B Devlin	83761
5	CC Rodriguez	729788	55	B Casper	78872
6	J Dent	693214	56	M Fetchick	78692
7	B Charles	584318	57	B Hiskey	76635
8	D Douglass	568198	58	D Dalziel	75681
9	G Player	507268	59	Q Gray	73844
10	R McBee	480329	60	JC Goosie	71724
11	B Crampton	464569	61	A Bardha	70958
12	H Henning	409879	62	C Owens	70314
13	A Geiberger	373624	63	J Fleck	69579
14	D Hill	354046	64	G Littler	66689
15	J Nicklaus	340000	65	A Palmer	66519
16	F Beard	327396	66	G Jones	63580
17	L Mowry	314657	67	C Sifford	63409
18	R Thompson	308915	68	L Elder	63164
19	T Dill	278372	69	P Moran	61419
20	W Zembriski	276292	70	B Wynn	59660
21	M Barber	274184	71	B Erickson	54706
22	O Moody	273224	72	R Gaona	53048
23	D Bies	265275	73	M Joyce	52050
24	A Kelley	263011	74	JC Snead	47494
25	J Jimenez	246067	75	L Mancour	46885
26	T Shaw	235683	76	R Boldt	38500
27	D Massengale	229184	77	D Simon	38337
28	D January	216243	78	B Maxwell	38162
29	JP Cain	208759	79	B Yancey	34850
30	J Powell	208183	80	D Sanders	31937
31	B Smith	201223	81	F Hawkins	31078
32	L Laoretti	165339	82	J Barber	29940
33	G Lanning	159768	83	H Johnson	28489
34	D Hendrickson	159070	84	C Lohren	26183
35	B Nichols	158144	85	R De Vincenzo	24101
36	H Blancas	157075	86	A Wall	23134
37	R Rhyan	156868	87	J Kiefer	21930
38	L Graham	154300	88	R Terry	20725
39	B Baird	150313	89	B Collins	19774
40	J Ferree	144680	90	B Rose	17650
41	G Brewer	128477	91	D Ford	17608
42	K Still	128110	92	A Sutton	17525
43	P Rodgers	127339	93	C Mehok	15483
44	J O'Hern	123625	94	T Naff	15121
45	D Weaver	118555	95	J Albus	14433
46	T Aaron	107651	96	J Schlee	14125
47	B Brue	106837	97	R Ginsberg	12745
48	D Morgan	104664	98	R Botts	12479
49	L Ziegler	102152	99	R Crawford	11044
50	B Betley	99503	100	A Balding	10900

US Senior PGA Tour, 1990

Aetna Challenge
at The Club at Pelican Bay, Naples, Florida

Pos	Name	Score	Prize $
1	L Trevino	66-67-67–200	60000
2	B Crampton	70-65-66–201	35000
3	C Coody	69-69-67–205	29000
4	M Hill	68-69-69–206	23000
5	B Baird	70-71-66–207	16150
	J Dent	69-68-70–207	16150

Ameritech Senior Open
at Grand Traverse Village, Michigan

Pos	Name	Score	Prize $
1	CC Rodriguez	67-70-66–203	75000
2	G Archer	69-70-71–210	40000
	A Kelley	69-71-70–210	40000
4	D Hill	68-71-72–211	23000
	M Hill	70-71-70–211	23000
	G Jones	68-71-72–211	23000
	P Rodgers	70-74-67–211	23000

Bell Atlantic Classic
at Chester Valley GC, Malvern, Pennsylvania

Pos	Name	Score	Prize $
1	D Douglass	70-66-70–206	75000
2	G Player	69-68-69–206	44000
3	B Charles	70-70-67–207	33000
	C Coody	69-68-70–207	33000
5	G Archer	68-72-68–208	24000
6	L Trevino	67-71-71–209	20000

Crestar Classic
at Hermitage CC, Manakin-Sabot, Virginia

Pos	Name	Score	Prize $
1	J Dent	73-64-65–202	52500
2	L Trevino	68-68-67–203	28000
3	G Player	67-64-73–204	23000
4	L Laoretti	69-69-68–206	20000
5	G Lanning	68-70-69–207	17000

Digital Seniors Classic
at Nashawtuc CC, Concord, Massachusetts

Pos	Name	Score	Prize $
1	B Charles	69-67-67–203	52500
2	L Trevino	67-72-66–205	28000
3	CC Rodriguez	64-71-71–206	23000
4	G Archer	67-70-70–207	18500
	H Henning	66-70-71–207	18500
6	T Shaw	71-72-66–209	12333
	F Beard	69-69-71–209	12333
	H Blancas	70-70-69–209	12333

Doug Sanders Kingwood Celebrity Classic
at Deerwood Park, Kingwood, Texas

Pos	Name	Score	Prize $
1	L Trevino	67-67-69–203	45000
2	G Player	70-74-65–209	27000
3	B Charles	70-68-72–210	22500
4	M Hill	73-69-71–213	15000
	G Lanning	69-71-73–213	15000
	O Moody	74-66-73–213	15000

Fairfield Barnett Space Coast Classic
at Suntree CC, Melbourne, Florida

Pos	Name	Score	Prize $
1	M Hill*	66-70-64–200	45000
2	D Douglass	66-67-67–200	25500
3	B Charles	65-66-70–201	20000
4	G Player	68-69-66–203	17000
5	D Hill	69-68-67–204	12800
	R Rawlins	66-71-67–204	12800

*Winner after play-off

Gatlin Brothers Southwest Classic

at Fairway Oaks, Abilene, Texas

Pos	Name	Score	Prize $
1	B Crampton	67-68-69–204	45000
2	L Trevino	71-70-67–208	25500
3	T Dill	68-72-70–210	18500
	CC Rodriguez	70-72-68–210	18500
5	R Rhyan	71-74-66–211	11866
	R Thompson	71-70-70–211	11866
	R Gaona	67-71-63–211	11866

Gold Rush at Rancho Murieta

at Rancho Murieta CC, California

Pos	Name	Score	Prize $
1	G Archer	70-68-66–204	60000
2	D Douglass	71-66-68–205	35000
3	C Coody	71-69-69–209	29000
4	B Charles	68-70-72–210	23000
5	B Betley	72-66-73–211	16150
	D Hendrickson	69-72-70–211	16150

Greater Grand Rapids Open

at Elks CC, Grand Rapids, Michigan

Pos	Name	Score	Prize $
1	D Massengale	69-65–134	45000
2	T Dill	69-66–135	20833
	D Hill	64-71–135	20833
	L Laoretti	68-67–135	20833
5	O Moody	67-69–136	14500
6	R Thompson	69-68–137	11100

GTE Kaanapali Classic

at Royal Kaanapali, Lahaina, Hawaii

Pos	Name	Score	Prize $
1	B Charles	65-71-70–206	67500
2	G Archer	67-70-73–210	36000
3	L Trevino	69-67-74–210	36000
4	H Henning	67-68-76–211	21750
	D January	68-70-73–211	21750
6	T Dill	74-66-73–213	16750
	J O'Hern	69-71-73–213	16750

GTE North Classic
at Broadmoor, Indianapolis

Pos	Name	Score	Prize $
1	M Hill	66-67-68–201	67500
2	B Crampton	68-67-66–201	40000
3	D Douglass	65-67-71–203	32000
4	H Henning	66-70-69–205	24500
5	G Archer	68-71-67–206	18250
	R Thompson	65-74-67–206	18250

GTE Northwest Classic
at Inglewood CC, Kenmore, Washington

Pos	Name	Score	Prize $
1	G Archer	69-66-70–205	52500
2	B Crampton	70-70-67–207	28000
3	D Bies	67-67-74–208	23000
4	A Geiberger	71-69-69–209	18500
	D January	71-68-70–209	18500
6	CC Rodriguez	68-70-72–210	14000

GTE Suncoast Classic
at Tampa Palms G&CC, Tampa, Florida

Pos	Name	Score	Prize $
1	M Hill	68-69-70–207	67500
2	L Trevino	69-71-69–209	40000
3	L Mowry	67-72-72–211	28250
	B Smith	69-73-69–211	28250
5	O Moody	68-77-67–212	19000

Kroger Senior Classic
at Jack Nicklaus Sports Centre, Kings Island, Ohio

Pos	Name	Score	Prize $
1	J Dent	67-66-133	90000
2	H Henning	70-64-134	53500
3	C Coody	67-68-135	42500
4	G Archer	67-69-136	24600
	H Blancas	67-69-136	24600
	D Hill	65-71-136	24600
	L Trevino	65-71-136	24600
	W Zembriski	66-70-136	24600

Las Vegas Senior Classic

at Desert Inn CC, Las Vegas, Nevada

Pos	Name	Score	Prize $
1	CC Rodriguez	68-67-69–204	67500
2	G Archer	69-66-70–205	36750
	C Coody	67-71-67–205	36750
4	B Charles	67-74-65–206	22433
	A Geiberger	69-69-68–206	22433
	L Trevino	67-72-67–206	22433

Mazda Senior TPC

at Dearborn CC, Dearborn, Michigan

Pos	Name	Score	Prize $
1	J Nicklaus	65-68-64-64–261	150000
2	L Trevino	66-68-66-67–267	88000
3	C Coody	68-70-68-66–272	66000
	J Dent	71-70-66-65–272	66000
5	D Hill	70-67-68-68–273	44000
	CC Rodriguez	70-67-68-68–273	44000

Mony Senior Tournament of Champions

at La Costa, California

Pos	Name	Score	Prize $
1	G Archer	73-69-67-74–283	37500
2	B Crampton	71-74-73-72–290	27500
	B Nichols	71-74-74-71–290	27500
4	A Geiberger	74-71-71-76–292	19500
	CC Rodriguez	73-71-75-73–292	19500
6	D Bies	73-73-75-73–294	13500
	D Hill	77-72-73-72–294	13500
	R McBee	74-74-74-72–294	13500

Mony Syracuse Senior Classic

at Lafayette CC, Jamesville, New York

Pos	Name	Score	Prize $
1	J Dent	66-67-66-199	60000
2	G Archer	70-65-65–200	35000
3	M Hill	66-67-69–202	26000
	L Mowry	66-68-68–202	26000
5	J Kiefer	68-71-64–203	16150
	R Rawlins	70-68-65–203	16150

Murata Reunion Pro-Am
at Stonebriar CC, Frisco, Texas

Pos	Name	Score	Prize $
1	F Beard	66-67-74–207	60000
2	W Zembriski	68-73-68–209	35000
3	D Douglass	69-70-71–210	29000
4	R Thompson	70-74-67–211	23000
5	P Rodgers	70-73-69–212	17600
6	B Wynn	69-71-73–213	14700

New York Life Champions
at Hyatt Dorado Beach, Puerto Rico

Pos	Name	Score	Prize $
1	M Hill*	69-64-68–201	150000
2	D Douglass	65-68-68–201	95000
	L Trevino	68-68-65–201	95000
4	CC Rodriguez	67-67-70–204	60000
5	A Geiberger	65-71-69–205	40500
	R Thompson	69-69-67–205	40500

Newport Cup
at Newport CC, Rhode Island

Pos	Name	Score	Prize $
1	A Kelley	66-68-134	45000
2	JP Cain	71-65-136	24750
	J Dent	69-67-136	24750
4	J Jimenez	68-69-137	15000
	R McBee	70-67-137	15000
	L Trevino	65-72-137	15000

Northville Long Island Classic
at Meadow Brook Club, Jericho, New York

Pos	Name	Score	Prize $
1	G Archer	69-67-72–208	67500
2	F Beard	69-69-71–209	36000
	C Coody	68-70-71–209	36000
4	D Hill	71-71-68–210	20333
	H Blancas	69-69-72–210	20333
	J Dent	68-71-71–210	20333

* Winner after play-off

Nynex Commemorative
at Sleepy Hollow CC, Scarborough, New York

Pos	Name	Score	Prize $
1	L Trevino*	66-66-67-199	52500
2	M Fetchick	67-68-64-199	23666
	J Powell	64-69-66-199	23666
	CC Rodriguez	69-64-66-199	23666
5	G Player	65-69-66–200	17000
6	G Archer	70-65-66–201	13000
	B Charles	67-64-70–201	13000

Painewebber Invitational
at TPC Piper Glen, Charlotte, North Carolina

Pos	Name	Score	Prize $
1	B Crampton	68-69-68–205	67500
2	T Shaw	72-65-69–206	40000
3	B Charles	66-70-71–207	28300
	L Mowry	71-71-65–207	28300
5	R McBee	69-71-68–208	18300
	R Rhyan	71-69-68–208	18300

PGA Seniors Championship
at PGA National GC, Palm Beach Gardens, Florida

Pos	Name	Score	Prize $
1	G Player	74-69-65-73–281	75000
2	CC Rodriguez	74-70-73-66–283	45000
3	J Nicklaus	68-78-67-72–285	25000
	L Trevino	77-67-70-71–285	25000
5	G Archer	72-72-73-72–289	16000
6	M Barber	75-73-68-76–292	15000
	D Douglass	71-73-74-75–293	14000
8	A Kelley	71-77-74-73–295	13000
9	D Bies	74-75-73-74–296	10500
	L Graham	76-76-72-72–296	10500
	H Henning	74-69-81-72–296	10500
	L Ziegler	73-75-75-73–296	10500
13	B Crampton	76-73-71-77–297	8000
	R McBee	75-75-72-75–297	8000
	A Palmer	80-73-73-71–297	8000

Royal Caribbean Classic
at Key Biscayne, Florida

Pos	Name	Score	Prize $
1	L Trevino	71-67-68–206	60000
2	B Baird	70-70-67–207	32000
	J Dent	66-68-73–207	32000
4	J Ferree	70-68-70–208	23000
	F Beard	69-68-72–209	16150
	B Crampton	70-68-71–209	16150

* Winner after play-off

Security Pacific Senior Classic
at Rancho Park, Los Angeles

Pos	Name	Score	Prize $
1	M Hill	70-68-63–201	75000
2	G Player	66-68-68–202	44000
3	CC Rodriguez	69-66-68–203	36000
4	D Douglass	68-70-67–205	24666
	J Jimenez	67-68-70–205	24666
	L Trevino	72-64-69–205	24666

Showdown Classic
at Jeremy Ranch GC, Park City, Utah

Pos	Name	Score	Prize $
1	R McBee	64-70-68–202	52500
2	D Bies	66-66-71–203	25500
	L Trevino	67-68-68–203	25500
4	G Archer	67-68-71–206	17000
	D Douglass	70-69-67–206	17000
	M Hill	66-68-72–206	17000

Southwestern Bell Classic
at Quail Creek, Oklahoma City, Oklahoma

Pos	Name	Score	Prize $
1	J Powell	72-71-65–208	67500
2	J Dent	75-68-68–211	28875
	T Dill	70-69-72–211	28875
	M Hill	72-69-70–211	28875
	R McBee	71-73-67–211	28875
6	D January	71-72-70–213	17500

Sunwest Bank/Charley Pride Classic
at Four Hills CC, Albuquerque, New Mexico

Pos	Name	Score	Prize $
1	CC Rodriguez	66-71-68–205	52500
2	J Dent	67-72-68–207	23666
	J Ferree	73-66-68–207	23666
	C Coody	70-66-71–207	23666
5	G Archer	74-67-68–209	14333
	B Betley	72-68-69–209	14333
	L Mowry	71-68-70–209	14333

The Tradition at Desert Mountain
at Golf Club at Desert Mountain (Cochise Course), Scottsdale, Arizona

Pos	Name	Score	Prize $
1	J Nicklaus	71-67-68–206	120000
2	G Player	71-69-71–210	65000
3	C Coody	73-71-68–212	48500
	B Crampton	69-71-72–212	48500
5	G Archer	70-72-71–213	35550
	F Beard	73-71-69–213	35550

Transamerica Seniors Golf Classic
at Silverado CC, Napa, California

Pos	Name	Score	Prize $
1	L Trevino	73-67-65–205	75000
2	M Hill	70-72-65–207	44000
3	M Barber	72-72-64–208	36000
4	R McBee	71-69-69–209	30000

USGA Senior Open
at Ridgewood, New Jersey

Pos	Name	Score	Prize $
1	L Trevino	67-68-73-67–275	90000
2	J Nicklaus	71-69-67-70–277	45000
3	CC Rodriguez	73-74-68-66–281	20881
	M Hill	72-67-73-69–281	20881
	G Player	75-65-68-73–281	20881
6	C Coody	68-73-72-69–282	12828
	H Henning	71-67-75-69–282	12828
8	M Barber	75-68-67-73–283	10550
	D Bies	75-69-67-72–283	10550
10	J Dent	68-68-72-76–284	9292
11	T Dill	71-73-73-68–285	8480
	O Moody	75-69-69-72–285	8480
13	G Archer	70-72-72-72–286	7623
	W Zembriski	68-73-73-72–286	7623
15	JP Cain	68-71-76-72–287	6614
	B Charles	73-71-69-74–287	6614
	D Hill	73-69-73-72–287	6614
	R Thompson	72-73-74-68–287	6614

Vantage at the Dominion
at The Dominion CC, San Antonio, Texas

Pos	Name	Score	Prize $
1	J Dent	69-70-66–205	45000
2	H Henning	69-69-70–208	25500
3	L Graham	73-68-69–210	18500
	M Hill	73-69-68–210	18500
5	D Douglass	66-72-73–211	12800
	D Hill	68-73-70–211	12800

Vantage Bank One Classic
at Kearney Hill Links, Lexington, Kentucky

Pos	Name	Score	Prize $
1	R McBee	66-67-68–201	45000
2	M Hill	70-71-64–205	25500
3	T Aaron	76-65-66–207	17166
	G Archer	73-66-68–207	17166
	H Henning	69-68-70–207	17166

Vantage Championship
at Tanglewood Park, Clemmons, North Carolina

Pos	Name	Score	Prize $
1	C Coody	67-65-70–202	202500
2	B Charles	72-69-64–205	126000
	A Geiberger	69-64-72–205	126000
4	L Mowry	68-70-68–206	81750
	L Trevino	68-68-70–206	81750
6	R McBee	66-73-68–207	56666
	CC Rodriguez	71-68-68–207	56666
	G Player	70-69-68–207	56666

Vintage Chrysler Invitational
at the Vintage Club (Mountain Course) Indian Wells, California

Pos	Name	Score	Prize $
1	L Trevino	66-67-72–205	60000
2	D Douglass	70-69-67–206	30050
	M Hill	67-73-66–206	30050
	D Massengale	67-69-70–206	30050
5	J Dent	68-70-70–208	20000
6	B Charles	72-69-68–209	13973
	R McBee	69-70-70–209	13973
	G Player	68-71-70–209	13973

US Senior Tour Official Statistics, 1990

Scoring Leaders

		Avg
1	L Trevino	68.89
2	G Player	69.96
3	G Archer	69.99
4	M Hill	70.06
5	CC Rodriguez	70.11
6	J Dent	70.34
7	B Charles	70.47
8	C Coody	70.77
9	B Crampton	70.86
10	D Hill	70.87

Driving Accuracy

		%
1	A Sutton	.766
2	C Sifford	.763
3	L Trevino	.740
4	J Barber	.738
	W Zembriski	.738
6	H Johnson	.722
7	J Fleck	.718
8	D Ford	.716
9	G Littler	.712
10	B Charles	.711

Driving Distance

		Yds
1	J Dent	276.8
2	T Dill	274.0
3	D Weaver	268.7
4	L Trevino	267.9
5	D January	265.8
6	D Hendrickson	265.7
7	J Ferree	264.1
8	G Archer	263.7
	R Boldt	263.7
10	R Gaona	263.3

Putting Leaders

		Avg
1	L Trevino	1.763
2	G Archer	1.755
	B Crampton	1.755
4	M Hill	1.757
5	G Player	1.760
6	H Henning	1.770
7	CC Rodriguez	1.772
9	F Beard	1.779
9	D Hill	1.784
10	3 tied with	1.788

Greens in Regulation

		%
1	L Trevino	.767
2	G Archer	.739
3	B Charles	.738
4	C Coody	.737
5	CC Rodriguez	.736
5	G Player	.735
7	D Douglass	.729
8	M Hill	.727
9	L Mowry	.725
10	J Dent	.723

Sand Saves

		%
1	CC Rodriguez	.582
2	O Moody	.544
3	D January	.536
	R Thompson	.536
5	L Trevino	.531
6	P Rodgers	.529
7	J Barber	.511
8	T Aaron	.504
	B Brue	.504
10	D Massengale	.500

Safari Tour, 1990

555 Kenya Open
at Muthaiga GC, Nairobi

Pos	Name	Score	Prize £
1	C O'Connor Jr	66-67-67-71–271	12500
2	C Platts	67-68-67-71–273	8329
3	P Eales	69-72-66-67–274	4697
4	S Richardson	68-73-68-66–275	3186
	P Affleck	69-70-69-67–275	3186
	M Litton	66-71-70-68–275	3186

Ivory Coast Open
at President GC, Yamoussoukro

Pos	Name	Score	Prize £
1	D Llewellyn	67-66-71-71–275	13643
2	J Pinsent	69-70-68-70–277	9095
3	A Hunter	72-67-71-69–279	4613
	GJ Brand	65-73-69-72–279	4613
5	G Ralph	71-71-67-71–280	3470
6	M Miller	72-74-68-67–281	2868

Nigerian Open
at Ikoyi GC, Lagos

Pos	Name	Score	Prize £
1	W˙ Stephens	68-64-66–198	12953
2	C Platts	66-70-68–204	8632
3	S Okpe	73-67-66–206	4015
	R Winchester	67-71-68–206	4015
	DR Jones	67-69-70–206	4015
6	G Krause	68-70-69–207	2720

Zambia Open
at Lusaka GC

Pos	Name	Score	Prize £
1	GJ Brand	70-74-68-72–284	12500
2	P Golding	71-73-70-74–288	6505
	C Maltman	71-74-75-68–288	6505
4	P Carrigill	75-72-72-70–289	3180
	S Richardson	75-67-75-72–289	3180
	P Carman	78-72-72-67–289	3180

Zimbabwe Open
at Chapman GC, Harare

Pos	Name	Score	Prize £
1	G Turner	68-71-71-71–281	7634
2	L Jones	69-72-71-70–282	5066
3	S Richardson	73-73-66-74–286	2871
4	S McAllister	74-73-68-72–287	2113
	GJ Brand	75-69-71-72–287	2113
6	B Barnes	74-73-68-73–288	1598

Australia/New Zealand Tour, 1990

Australian Masters
at Huntingdale GC, Melbourne

Pos	Name	Score	Prize Aus$
1	G Norman	68-67-70-68–273	90000
2	J Morse	71-69-68-67–275	37800
	M Clayton	64-74-69-68–275	37800
	N Faldo	68-67-68-72–275	37800
5	R Davis	69-71-68-69–277	19950
	D de Long	68-71-68-70–277	19950

Australian Match Play
at Kingston Heath, Melbourne

Quarter Finals:

D Smith beat B Shearer at 20th hole
M Clayton beat B Conran 2 and 1
P Fowler beat C Parry 1 hole
J Woodland beat B Ogle 4 and 3

Semi-Finals:

D Smith beat M Clayton 1 hole
P Fowler beat J Woodland 3 and 2

Final:

D Smith beat P Fowler 4 and 2

Australian Open
at The Australian, Sydney

Pos	Name	Score	Prize Aus$
1	J Morse*	72-70-73-68–283	108000
2	C Parry	72-70-69-72–283	64800
3	G Norman	70-68-76-72–286	35640
	W Riley	70-72-75-69–286	35640
5	I Baker-Finch	71-71-71-74–287	22800
	J Maggert	71-69-75-72–287	22800
	R Davis	70-71-75-71–287	22800

* Winner after play-off

Australian PGA Championship
at Riverside Oaks, Sydney

Pos	Name	Score	Prize Aus$
1	B Ogle	65-70-69-69–273	90000
2	D Davis	75-68-65-70–278	44250
	W Grady	65-71-75-67–278	44250
4	L Carter	69-74-64-72–279	24900
5	D Graham	70-71-70-69–280	19950
	L Stephen	69-73-69-69–280	19950
6	W Riley	71-73-68-69–281	16000

Johnnie Walker Australian Classic
at Royal Melbourne

Pos	Name	Score	Prize Aus$
1	G Turner	69-68-70-69–276	180000
2	R Davis	70-69-71-70–280	108000
3	I Baker-Finch	72-70-63-76–281	59400
	P McWhinney	70-70-70-71–281	59400
5	R Floyd	70-69-71-74–284	41600
6	M Harwood	70-72-72-71–285	36200
	D Mijovic	69-71-70-75–285	36200

Japan Tour, 1990

Casio World Open
at Ibusuki

Pos	Name	Score	Prize Yen
1	M Reid	69-70-65-70–274	21000000
2	Y Kaneko	70-71-70-65–276	12000000
3	S Ballesteros	71-67-68-71–277	5060000
	R Kawagishi	71-69-66-71–277	5060000
	D Ishii	71-71-72-63–277	5060000
	G Marsh	72-70-68-67–277	5060000
	M Kuramoto	74-68-66-69–277	5060000
	M Donald	70-68-69-70–277	5060000

Chunichi Crowns Open
at Nagoye

Pos	Name	Score	Prize Yen
1	N Sugai*	68-66-67-75–276	18000000
2	S Pate	66-67-69-74–276	10000000
3	H Makino	68-66-71-73–278	4480000
	T Chen	72-69-71-66–278	4480000
	M Ozaki	66-70-70-72–278	4480000
	D Love III	70-72-66-70–278	4480000
	J Sluman	71-75-67-65–278	4480000

Dunlop Phoenix Open
at Miyazaki

Pos	Name	Score	Prize Yen
1	L Mize	69-65-69-71–274	36000000
2	N Ozaki	67-72-67-71–277	20000000
3	T Nakajima	69-73-70-66–278	9600000
	D Ishii	65-74-71-68–278	9600000
	S Ballesteros	71-68-70-69–278	9600000
	L Nelson	71-63-73-71–278	9600000
7	G Marsh	69-71-69-70–279	6100000
	T Watson	69-71-69-70–279	6100000

* Winner after play-off

Japan PGA Championship
at Amanosan

Pos	Name	Score	Prize Yen
1	K Kase	71-66-67-70–274	13500000
2	S Fujiki	71-65-70-73–279	6300000
	M Kuramoto	73-67-65-74–279	6300000
4	Y Mizumaki	71-70-66-73–280	3600000

Japanese PGA Match Play Championship
at Green Academy

Quarter Finals:

N Ozaki beat M Kimura 1 hole
M Kuramoto beat T Sudo 4 and 3
B Jones beat A Ohmachi 3 and 2
Y Yamamoto beat Y Kaneko 2 and 1

Semi-Finals:

N Ozaki beat M Kuramoto 9 and 8
B Jones beat Y Yamamoto 4 and 3

Final:

N Ozaki beat B Jones 6 and 5

Asian Tour, 1990

Hong Kong Open
at Royal Hong Kong, Fanling

Pos	Name	Score
1	K Green	66-67-72–205
2	B Watts	71-71-67–209
	D Mijovic	70-72-67–209

Indian Open
at Royal Calcutta GC

Pos	Name	Score
1	A Debusk	71-74-73-70–288
2	C Espinosa	77-72-76-69–294
3	B Ali	72-72-78-73–295
	A Meeks	75-73-73-74–295

Indonesian Open
at Jakarta

Pos	Name	Score
1	F Minoza	69-69-66-71–275
2	D Mijovic	73-68-67-70–278
	R Gibson	72-71-67-68–278

Johnnie Walker Asian Classic
at Royal Hong Kong, Fanling

Pos	Name	Score
1	N Faldo	72-68-62-68–270
2	I Woosnam	69-68-70-67–274
3	M Clayton	72-70-66-67–275
4	L Porter	69-70-70-67–276
	C Montgomerie	68-70-68-70–276
	T Hamilton	69-69-69-69–276
7	R Rafferty	67-69-69-72–277

Malaysian Open
at Royal Perak GC, Ipoh

Pos	Name	Score
1	G Day	69-69-68-67–273
2	D Mijovic	70-72-72-63–277
	C Liang-Hsi	68-70-72-63–277

Philippine Open
at Wack Wack, Manila

Pos	Name	Score
1	R Pactolerin	68-75-72-72–287
2	L Porter	72-71-72-74–289
	L Chung Jen	73-70-71-75–289
	C Liang Hsi	74-69-72-74–289

Republic of China Open
at Taipei

Pos	Name	Score
1	F Minoza*	75-69-68-71–283
2	J Morse	71-72-69-71–283
3	L Tinkler	78-70-66-71–285

Singapore Open
at Singapore Island CC, Bukit

Pos	Name	Score
1	A Fernando*	66-71-67-69–273
2	F Minoza	70-65-72-66–273
3	C Sang-Ho	66-68-71-69–274

* Winner after play-off

South Korean Open

at Seoul

Pos	Name	Score
1	L Kang-sun	72-71-69–212
2	H Chin-sheng	73-69-73–215
3	T Power	72-70-74–216

Thailand Open

at Bangkok

Pos	Name	Score
1	L Wen-Ter	69-64-70-73–276
2	D Mijovic	66-69-71-71–277
	P Nam-Sin	68-67-72-70–277

South African Sunshine Circuit, 1990

Lexington PGA Championship

at Johannesburg

Pos	Name	Score	Prize Rand
1	F Allem	61-71-67-67–266	40000
2	C Davison	65-71-65-67–268	28750
3	R Kaplan	67-70-67-65-269	17500

Protea Assurance SA Open

at Royal Cape GC, Cape Town

Pos	Name	Score	Prize Rand
1	T Dodds	72-71-72-70–285	52000
2	H Royer	75-71-69-71–286	37375
3	M James	79-72-66-71–288	22750
4	R Stewart	75-71-73-70–289	12825
	S Hobday	74-73-69-73–289	12825
	D Terblanche	75-66-74-74–289	12825
	I Palmer	70-74-70-75–289	12825

TJ Masters

at Stellenbosch GC, Cape Winelands

Pos	Name	Score	Prize Rand
1	F Allem	69-69-69-70–276	55200
2	I Palmer	69-71-70-68–278	39675
3	J Bland	71-70-68-70–279	24150
4	R Wessels	69-70-70-71–280	17250
5	T Johnstone	71-70-68-72–281	14490
6	W Westner	71-72-71-70–284	12420

Trustbank Tournament of Champions
at Kensington, Johannesburg

Pos	Name	Score	Prize Rand
1	T Dodds	70-65-68-69–272	40000
2	F Quinn	66-70-70-67–273	28750
3	J Daly	67-71-67-69–274	17500

Million Dollar Challenge
at Sun City, Bophuthatswana

Pos	Name	Score	Prize $
1	D Frost	71-71-71-71–284	1000000
2	JM Olazabal	73-70-73-69–285	300000
3	B Langer	69-74-70-75-288	225000
	S Elkington	77-68-68-75–288	225000
5	F Allem	73-72-74-71–290	150000
6	R Gamez	79-76-69-69–293	135000
	K Green	75-72-70-76–293	135000
7	A Lyle	80-67-74-76–297	120000
8	T Armour	81-71-71-77–300	110000
9	T Simpson	75-74-73-81–303	100000

Sony Ranking 1990

The World Ranking System for Professional Golf

Introduction

In the spring of 1966 the Sony Corporation announced the launch of a world ranking system for professional golf. The Sony Ranking, which is sanctioned by The Championship is a specially developed computerised ranking which provides an authoritative reference source to the relative performance of the world's leading players.

The official events from all the geographical circuits are taken into account and points awarded according to the quality and strength of the players participating in each event. The number of points distributed to each player is dependent upon his finishing position and the scale of bonus points allocated on the basis of the number and ranking of the players in the field. The four Major Championships and the Players Championship have been weighted separately to reflect the higher quality of the events and the strong fields participating.

The Sony Ranking is based on a three year 'rolling' period weighted in favour of the more recent results, and a divisor is used to take account of the number of tournaments played by each ranked player

The Sony Ranking is issued every Monday at the completion of the week's tournaments from around the world.

Points

50 points are awarded to the winner of a Major Championship with 30 points for scond place, 20 for third, 15 for fourth, 12 for fifth down to a single point for a player completing the final round. The Players Championship is awarded 40 points for the winner down to a single point for 50th place.

All other events have a points system 'rated' on the strength of the field which is assessed upon the number and Ranking position of the top 100 Ranked players participating in each event.

Highest Points Earners in 1990

Name	1990 Sony Points	Sony Rank at end of 1990	Name	1990 Sony Points	Sony Rank at end of 1990
JM Olazabal	932	3	F Couples	496	11
N Faldo	848	2	B Langer	468	14
I Woosnam	816	4	T Simpson	468	18
G Norman	788	1	M Calcavecchia	456	10
M McNulty	624	9	W Levi	452	20
P Stewart	612	5	M Harwood	440	32
P Azinger	580	6	R Rafferty	428	19
H Irwin	512	16	I Baker-Finch	416	36
L Mize	504	13	M O'Meara	412	22
R Davis	500	23	J Mudd	404	25

Sony Ranking

at 31 December 1990

Pos	87–89	Player	Circuit		Points Average	Total Points
1	(1)	G Norman	ANZ	1	18.95	1402
2	(2)	N Faldo	Eur	1	18.54	1465
3	(7)	JM Olazabal	Eur	2	17.22	1343
4	(9)	I Woosnam	Eur	3	15.47	1207
5	(5)	P Stewart	USA	1	12.75	1109
6	(10)	P Azinger	USA	2	11.63	954
7	(3)	S Ballesteros	Eur	4	10.15	751
8	(6)	T Kite	USA	3	10.10	788
9	(31)	M McNulty	Afr	1	10.06	805
10	(8)	M Calcavecchia	USA	4	9.96	976
11	(15)	F Couples	USA	5	9.69	862
12	(4)	C Strange	USA	6	9.58	757
13	(19)	L Mize	USA	7	8.86	735
14	(16)	B Langer	Eur	5	8.78	746
15	(11)	C Beck	USA	8	8.58	695
16	(98)	H Irwin	USA	9	8.36	585
17	(12)	M Ozaki	Jpn	1	8.16	677
18	(35)	T Simpson	USA	10	7.78	708
19	(21)	R Rafferty	Eur	6	7.71	732
20	(67)	W Levi	USA	11	7.69	569
21	(25)	L Wadkins	USA	12	7.49	569
22	(27)	M O'Meara	USA	13	7.39	658
23	(43)	R Davis	ANZ	2	7.08	651
24	(13)	D Frost	Afr	2	7.01	631
25	(49)	J Mudd	USA	14	6.64	571
26	(61)	G Morgan	USA	15	6.35	457
27	(42)	W Grady	ANZ	3	6.32	588
28	(17)	B Crenshaw	USA	16	6.32	493
29	(46)	P Jacobsen	USA	17	6.27	483
30	(28)	S Jones	USA	18	6.18	507
31	(37)	M James	Eur	7	6.05	478
32	(68)	M Harwood	ANZ	4	5.88	594
33	(22)	M Reid	USA	19	5.81	447
34	(30)	C Stadler	USA	20	5.74	436
35	(53)	E Romero	SAm	1	5.68	420
36	(59)	I Baker-Finch	ANZ	5	5.65	588
37	(29)	C Parry	ANZ	6	5.30	535
38	(38)	N Price	Afr	3	5.28	459
39	(24)	S Hoch	USA	21	5.24	487
40	(18)	M McCumber	USA	22	5.18	383
41	(14)	A Lyle	Eur	8	5.12	456
42	(32)	B Lietzke	USA	23	5.05	333
43	(20)	T Watson	USA	24	5.03	307
44	(65)	D Love III	USA	25	4.91	437
45	(26)	P Senior	ANZ	7	4.67	495
46	(79)	D Feherty	Eur	9	4.62	448
47	(23)	L Nelson	USA	26	4.61	295
48	(74)	R Floyd	USA	27	4.56	292
49	(41)	S Pate	USA	28	4.53	453
50	(60)	S Torrance	Eur	10	4.41	357

Women's Professional International, 1990

Solheim Cup
at Lake Nona GC, Florida

Foursomes

USA	Matches	Europe	Matches
P Bradley and N Lopez	0	L Davies and A Nicholas (2 and 1)	1
C Gerring and D Mochrie (6 and 5)	1	P Wright and L Neumann	0
P Sheehan and R Jones (6 and 5)	1	D Reid and H Alfredsson	0
B Daniel and B King (5 and 4)	1	T Johnson and ML de Lorenzi	0
	3		1

Four-balls

USA	Matches	Europe	Matches
P Sheehan and R Jones (2 and 1)	1	T Johnson and ML de Lorenzi	0
P Bradley and N Lopez (2 and 1)	1	D Reid and H Alfredsson	0
B King and B Daniel (4 and 3)	1	L Davies and A Nicholas	0
C Gerring and D Mochrie	0	L Neumann and P Wright (4 and 2)	1
	3		1

Singles

USA	Matches	Europe	Matches
C Gerring (4 and 3)	1	H Alfredsson	0
R Jones	0	L Davies (3 and 2)	1
N Lopez (6 and 4)	1	A Nicholas	0
B King	1/2	P Wright	1/2
B Daniel (7 and 6)	1	L Neumann	0
P Sheehan	0	D Reid (2 and 1)	1
D Mochrie (4 and 2)	1	ML de Lorenzi	0
P Bradley (8 and 7)	1	T Johnson	0
	5 1/2		2 1/2

Result: USA 11 1/2; Europe 4 1/2

WPGET Woolmark Order of Merit, 1990

Pos	Name	Prize £	Pos	Name	Prize £
1	T Johnson	83043	51	A Shapcott	8379
2	A Nicholas	63199	52	P Grice-Whittaker	7894
3	H Alfredsson (Swe)	63079	53	A Munt (Aus)	7793
4	L Maritz-Atkins (SA)	56273	54	H Andersson (Swe)	7333
5	F Descampe (Bel)	51518	55	T Yarwood	7063
6	D Reid	49343	56	W-L Li (Tai)	7009
7	G Stewart	43531	57	S Moon	6893
8	ML de Lorenzi (Fra)	40351	58	E Quelhas (Aust)	6834
9	C Dibnah (Aus)	39665	59	M Lunn (Aus)	6824
10	D Barnard	39658	60	K Leadbetter (USA)	6624
11	K Douglas	38207	61	T Fernando (Sri Lanka)	6410
12	K Lunn (Aus)	36907	62	D Pavich (Aus)	6401
13	L Davies	36697	63	S Van Wyk (SA)	6374
14	S Gronberg (Swe)	34170	64	C Louw (SA)	6125
15	C Soules (Fra)	32936	65	D Petrizzi (USA)	5912
16	T Abitbol (Spa)	32600	66	S Prosser	5711
17	A Jones (Aus)	29387	67	S Moorcraft	5704
18	P Sinn (USA)	28407	68	K Lasken (USA)	5701
19	J Hill (Zim)	25485	69	B Huke	5683
20	D Dowling	22613	70	H Hopkins (Aus)	5401
21	F Dassu (Ita)	22573	71	B Helbig (Ger)	5165
22	X Wunsch-Ruiz (Spa)	21979	72	J Forbes	5058
22	M Garner (Ire)	21492	72	S Smith Cranmer (Can)	4843
24	J Connachan	20862	74	R Gawthrop (USA)	4775
25	S Strudwick	19439	75	S Etchevers (Fra)	4419
26	A Oxenstierna (Swe)	18008	76	K Dallas	4411
27	E Orley (Swi)	16482	77	K Imrie	4365
28	K Espinasse (Fra)	16107	78	M Burton	4249
29	D Hutton (Aus)	16035	79	C Griffiths	4035
30	A Dibos (Peru)	15926	80	R Comstock (USA)	4034
31	J Arnold (NZ)	15919	81	C Scholefield (USA)	4008
32	A Sheard (SA)	15632	82	L Mills (USA)	3920
33	M Estill (USA)	15498	83	S Nyhus (USA)	3685
34	C Panton	15380	84	L Neumann (Swe)	3612
35	T Craik	13702	85	T Hammond	3127
36	R Hast	13377	86	L Mullard (Aus)	3094
37	C Duffy	13196	87	C Mah-Lyford (USA)	3022
38	S Croce (Ita)	13062	88	J Brown	2875
39	C Nilsmark (Swe)	12436	89	N Way	2802
40	B New	11587	90	K Prechtl (USA)	2622
41	R Lautens (Swi)	11548	91	N McCormack	2365
42	J Soulsby	11247	92	D Clum (USA)	2279
43	M Navarro Corbachio (Spa)	10746	93	M Kelt (USA)	2135
44	N Hall (Aus)	10524	94	L Percival	2060
45	D Lofland (USA)	10261	95	E Glass	2051
46	P Gonzalez (Col)	9292	96	P Smillie	2001
47	S Shapcott	9095	97	J Hill	1955
48	P Conley (USA)	9032		M From (Swe)	1955
49	J Rumsey	8707	99	V Marvin	1949
50	J Furby	8498	100	R Bell (Aus)	1908

Women's Professional Golf European Tour, 1990

Weetabix Women's British Open
at Woburn G&CC

Pos	Name	Score	Prize £
1	H Alfredsson	70-71-74-73–288	20000
2	J Hill	77-74-69-68–288	13200
(H Alfredsson won play-off at 4th extra hole)			
3	L Davies	75-73-73-70–291	7353
	K Douglas	69-71-75-76–291	7353
	D Lofland	73-70-75-73–291	7353
6	ML de Lorenzi	72-70-72-79–293	4130
	T Johnson	71-74-73-75–293	4130
	M Blackwelder	73-70-78-72–293	4130
9	D Bernard	75-70-73-76–294	2750
	A Nicholas	75-75-68-76–294	2750
11	P Sinn	70-74-77-74–295	2390
12	A Shapcott	73-74-76-73–296	2230
13	C Duffy	76-74-74-73–297	2013
	L Len-Lin	73-69-76-79–297	2013
	M Estill	77-70-76-74–297	2013
16	T Fernando	74-73-74-77–298	1855
	A Dibos	76-73-72-77–298	1855
18	J Arnold	79-73-74-73–299	1712
	C Dibnah	71-81-74-73–299	1712
	B Huke	76-76-74-73–299	1712
	S Strudwick	79-71-71-78–299	1712
22	J Connachan	74-75-75-75–300	1570
	D Hutton	77-76-74-73–300	1570
	T Luckhurst	74-72-76-78–300	1570
25	T Abitbol	74-75-75-77–301	1430
	D Reid	76-70-77-78–301	1430
	M Sugimoto	76-74-79-72–301	1430
	T Craik	76-76-75-74–301	1430
29	A Sheard	72-80-77-73–302	1270
	G Stewart	74-73-77-78–302	1270
	X Wunsch-Ruiz	72-78-75-77–302	1270
	S Shapcott	72-75-76-79–302	1270
	S Bennett (Am)	75-77-78-72–302	
34	S Gronberg	74-78-77-74–303	1150
	L Maritz	71-76-76-80–303	1150
36	K Lasken	74-77-74-79–304	1070
	K Mills	74-75-74-81–304	1070
38	J Forbes	80-72-74-79–305	1010
	L Fairclough (Am)	73-78-79-75–305	
40	R Hast	76-77-77-76–306	910
	N Lowien	72-79-81-74–306	910
	H Andersson	78-71-78-79–306	910
	E Dahllof	79-73-77-77–306	910
44	P Grice-Whittaker	75-77-77-79–308	790
	C Panton	74-71-80-83–308	790
	M Spencer-Devlin	71-81-80-76–308	790
	S Morgan(Am)	75-75-76-82–308	

Pos	Name	Score	Prize £
49	C Mah-Lyford	79-74-76-80-309	700
	R Gawthrop	75-76-81-77-309	700
	C Scholefield	76-76-77-80-309	700
51	N Kessler	79-73-80-79-311	646
52	M Burton	72-75-85-81-313	598
	J Lawrence	73-77-82-81-313	598
	A Munt	73-80-81-79-313	598
55	J Morley(Am)	74-75-82-83-314	
	J Brown(Am)	74-78-80-82-314	
57	J Hill	77-74-79-85-315	550
58	R Lautens	76-77-84-81-318	526
59	S Moon	82-71-86-85-324	502
60	K Espinasse	70-81-75-DSQ	

Women's Professional European Golf Tour, 1990
continued

AGF Biarritz Ladies' Open
at Golf de Biarritz

Pos	Name	Score	Prize £
1	L Davies	63-73-136	12000
2	A Nicholas	71-66-137	8120
3	K Leadbetter	68-70-138	4960
	L Maritz-Atkins	69-69-138	4960
5	ML de Lorenzi	69-70-139	2648
	T Johnson	69-70-139	2648
	B New	69-70-139	2648
	H Alfredsson	66-73-139	2648

Bloor Homes Eastleigh Classic
at Flemming Park, Southampton

Pos	Name	Score	Prize £
1	T Johnson	61-66-58-64-249	9765
2	C Dibnah	61-69-64-60-254	6615
3	D Dowling	65-62-66-62-255	4565
4	K Douglas	62-62-65-67-256	3148
	D Reid	62-62-67-65-256	3148
	F Descampe	66-66-64-62-258	2127
	T Yarwood	61-67-65-65-258	2127

BMW European Masters
at Brussels, Belgium

Pos	Name	Score	Prize £
1	K Lunn	72-71-71-71-285	18000
2	C Soules	69-74-73-73-289	12180
3	C Stewart	70-76-73-72-291	8400
4	P Sinn	72-77-73-71-293	6480
5	C Dibnah	76-74-71-73-294	4644
	J Hill	74-75-72-73-294	4664

BMW Ladies' Classic
at Hubbelrath GC, Dusseldorf, Germany

Pos	Name	Score	Prize £
1	D Barnard	71-68-70-69–278	10500
2	C Dibnah	66-71-69-73–279	7105
3	A Nicholas	71-67-70-72–280	4900
4	K Lunn	67-69-73-72–281	3780
5	ML de Lorenzi	69-72-70-71–282	2958
6	P Conley	69-69-73-72–284	2450

Bonmont Ladies' Swiss Classic
at Club de Bonmont, Geneva

Pos	Name	Score	Prize $
1	E Orley*	71-72-71-75–289	10500
2	G Stewart	74-72-70-73–289	7105
3	T Abitbol	72-71-76-71–290	4340
	D Reid	70-74-75-71–290	4340
5	F Descampe	72-72-73-74–291	2968
6	F Dassu	77-69-71-75–292	2275
	S Gronberg	77-74-69-72–292	2275

Expedier Ladies' European Open
at Kingswood GC, Surrey

Pos	Name	Score	Prize £
1	T Johnson	71-67-69-69–276	11250
2	M Estill	67-70-68-73–278	6430
	P Sinn	70-68-72-68–278	6430
4	A Nicholas	69-72-66-74–281	4050
5	L Davies	69-70-73-70–282	2902
	S Croce	73-66-72-71–282	2902

Ford Ladies' Classic
at Woburn G&CC

Pos	Name	Score	Prize £
1	ML de Lorenzi	74-72-68-70–284	9750
2	L Maritz	70-73-71-73–287	6600
3	T Johnson	73-72-72-73–290	4550
4	R Hast	72-78-73-68–291	3133
	A Nicholas	71-75-70-75–291	3133
6	D Barnard	70-71-74-78–293	2112
	S Gronberg	73-73-74-73–293	2112

* Winner after play-off

Haninge Ladies' Open
at Haninge GC, Stockholm, Sweden

Pos	Name	Score	Prize £
1	D Reid	74-71-72-74–291	10500
2	M Garner	75-75-70-72–292	5261
	A Nicholas	72-73-71-76–292	5261
	S Strudwick	73-72-73-74–292	5261
5	G Stewart	71-74-74-74–293	2968
6	F Dassu	72-76-72-74–294	2450

Hennessy Ladies' Cup
at St Germain, France

Pos	Name	Score	Prize £
1	T Johnson	72-68-71-74–285	13500
2	ML de Lorenzi	75-71-69-73–288	7717
	T Green	72-75-66-75–288	7717
4	S Gronberg	72-69-73-75–289	4860
5	T Abitbol	77-69-72-72–290	3222
	D Barnard	71-74-71-74–290	3222
	C Panton	74-72-72-72–290	3222

Italian Ladies' Open
at Gardagolf

Pos	Name	Score	Prize £
1	F Descampe	72-74-66-70–282	13500
2	H Alfredsson	67-75-72-71–285	9135
3	K Espinasse	72-73-72-70–287	6300
4	D Reid	69-73-74-72–288	4860
5	ML de Lorenzi	72-73-71-73–289	3816
6	F Dassu	72-75-72-71–290	3150

Laing Ladies' Charity Classic
at Stoke Poges GC, Slough

Pos	Name	Score	Prize £
1	L Maritz	71-67-69-68–275	9750
2	A Nicholas	71-70-69-65–275	6800
3	M Garner	68-67-71-70–276	4550
4	C Soules	70-71-69-67–277	2510
5	P Gonzalez	71-69-70-73–283	2756
6	D Barnard	75-68-71-70–284	1950
	K Lunn	74-74-63-67–284	1950
	F Descampe	73-65-72-74–284	1950

Longines Classic
at Golf Esterel, Nice

Pos	Name	Score	Prize £
1	T Johnson	72-71-75-68–286	15000
2	G Stewart	71-79-69-73–292	10150
3	K Lunn	80-71-72-70–293	7000
4	H Hopkins	74-76-73-71–294	4820
	H Alfredsson	72-77-71-74–294	4820
6	K Douglas	77-72-75-71–295	3500

Lufthansa Ladies' German Open
at Worthsee GC, Munich

Pos	Name	Score	Prize £
1	A Okamoto*	68-70-69-67–274	13500
2	L Maritz	70-65-67-72–274	7717
	C Rarick	70-68-67-69–274	7717
4	T Johnson	67-67-72-70–276	4860
5	A Nicholas	71-70-71-66–278	3483
	H Alfredsson	71-65-71-71–278	3483

TEC Players' Championship
at Patshull Park Hotel, Wolverhampton

Pos	Name	Score	Prize £
1	A Jones	73-66-69-73–281	12000
2	L Maritz	72-70-70-71–283	8120
3	S Gronberg	74-69-72-70–285	4960
	H Alfredsson	75-70-68-72–285	4960
5	T Johnson	71-71-72-72–286	3392
6	T Abitbol	70-80-69-70–289	2118
	D Barnard	78-71-70-70–289	2118
	J Connachan	76-74-70-69–289	2118
	C Soules	68-75-72-74–289	2118
	C Nilsmark	72-74-71-72–289	2118

Trophée Internationale Coconut Skol
at Golf de Fourqueux, Paris

Pos	Name	Score	Prize £
1	C Dibnah	71-75-72-66–284	10500
2	T Johnson	71-73-70-71–285	6002
	H Alfredsson	70-73-71-71–285	6002
4	A Nicholas	72-73-69-74–288	3780
5	ML de Lorenzi	72-75-72-71–290	2709
	K Douglas	74-70-74-72–290	2709

* Winner after play-off

Trophée Urban-World Championship of Women's Golf
at Cely GC, Paris, France

Pos	Name	Score	Prize US$
1	C Gerring	69-69-69-71–278	100000
2	B Daniel	71-74-66-68–279	52000
3	B King	72-69-69-72–282	31000
4	P Sheehan	73-74-69-68–284	17167
	C Rarick	69-74-71-70–284	17167
	D Mochrie	70-72-72-70–284	17166
7	C Johnson	72-73-70-71–286	11000
8	C Johnston	72-76-67-76–291	10000
9	ML de Lorenzi	71-75-75-71–292	7167
	D Ammaccapane	71-70-74-77–292	7167
	P Bradley	74-71-73-74–292	7166

Valextra Classic
at Olgiata, Rome, Italy

Pos	Name	Score	Prize £
1	F Descampe	71-71-69-68–279	10500
2	D Reid	75-68-70-72–285	7105
3	L Davies	74-73-69-70–286	4900
4	D Hutton	73-74-69-72–288	3374
	P Sinn	73-68-73-74–288	3374
6	K Douglas	72-71-75-71–289	2450

Variety Club Celebrity Classic
at Calcot Park GC, Reading

Pos	Name	Score	Prize £
1	A Nicholas	68-68-68-71–275	7800
2	S Gronberg	72-70-65-69–276	5280
3	T Johnson	69-73-67-68–277	4080
4	K Douglas	67-66-70-75–278	3240
5	C Panton	72-70-67-71–280	2520
6	G Stewart	70-72-68-71–281	2040

Woolmark Ladies' Match Play Championship
at Club de Campo, Madrid

Semi-Finals:

F Descampe beat A Jones 5 and 4
D Reid beat X Wunsch 8 and 6
(Losers received £5200)

Final:

F Descampe beat D Reid
(F Descampe won £12000 and D Reid £8000)

WPG European Tour Classic
at Tytherington Club, Macclesfield

Pos	Name	Score	Prize £
1	T Abitbol	76-69-68–213	9000
2	A Oxenstierna	72-73-70–215	6090
3	S Shapcott	70-70-76–216	4200
4	D Barnard	73-72-72–217	2892
	S Gronberg	71-75-71–217	2892
6	D Dowling	72-74-72–218	1950
	C Soules	75-74-69–218	1950

USLPGA Money Winners, 1990

Pos	Name	Official Money $	Pos	Name	Official Money $
1	B Daniel	863578	51	L Neumann (Swe)	82323
2	P Sheehan	732618	52	J Dickinson	80784
3	B King	543844	53	M Edge	76797
4	C Gerring	487326	54	J Briles	73832
5	P Bradley	480018	55	R Walton	72519
6	R Jones	353832	56	M Blackwelder	72195
7	A Okamoto (Jpn)	302885	57	M Foyer	71196
8	N Lopez	301262	58	K Rogerson	69273
9	D Ammaccapane	300231	59	V Skinner	66577
10	C Rarick	259163	60	H Kobayashi (Jpn)	66325
11	D Coe	240478	61	K Monaghan	65725
12	D Mochrie	231410	62	T Purtzer (Can)	65293
13	C Walker	225518	63	M Figueras-Dotti (Spa)	64874
14	C Johnson	187486	64	L Davies (GB)	64863
15	D Richard	186464	65	H Stacy	64074
16	J Geddes	181874	66	C Hill	63348
17	C Keggi	180197	67	GL Hull	61088
18	E Crosby	169543	68	TJ Myers	61004
19	D Massey	166661	69	L Kean	59943
20	C Figg-Currier	157651	70	S Thomas	59316
21	CJ Johnston	156240	71	T Johnson (GB)	58729
22	T Green	155765	72	J Anderson	54879
22	B Mucha	149972	72	J Inkster	54251
24	D Eggeling	147990	74	C Marino	52992
25	P Rizzo	145377	75	D Andrews	52430
26	N Brown	140988	76	M Ward	50763
27	M Mallon	129381	77	L Baugh	50644
28	P Hammel	128753	78	N Rubin	50362
29	A Benz	128216	79	B Bunkowsky	48064
30	S Turner	122937	80	J Anschutz	47950
31	K Postlewait	121063	81	A Finney	47699
32	S Ertl	116422	82	L Merten	47263
33	A Ritzman	112840	83	K Cockerill	47125
34	J Crafter (Aus)	112225	84	K Ok-Hee (Kor)	47121
35	K Albers	111515	85	L Rinker	45605
36	M Will	110488	86	K Shipman	45376
37	S Steinhauer	109407	87	C Mackey	45017
38	M Berteotti	107030	88	J Portland Pitcock	44067
39	S Sanders	101446	89	J Lidback (Per)	42063
40	V Fergon	101049	90	A-M Palli (Fra)	40020
41	S Furlong	99215	91	K Tschetter	39469
42	A Alcott	99208	92	D Lasker	38268
43	D White	97084	93	H Drew	37615
44	P Wright (GB)	96817	94	L Walters	36047
45	M McGeorge	93721	95	M Bozarth	35568
46	L Connelly	90531	96	T Kerdyk	35199
47	C Morse	88661	97	B Pearson	35161
48	JA Carner	87218	98	M McGann	34846
49	L Rittenhouse	86478	99	NR Foust	32930
50	M Nause	83383	100	J Gibson	32404

US Ladies' PGA Tour, 1990

US Women's Open
at Atlanta Athletic Club, Duluth, Georgia

Pos	Name	Score	Prize $
1	B King	72-71-71-70–284	85000
2	P Sheehan	66-68-75-76–285	42500
3	D Mochrie	74-74-72-66–286	23956
	D Ammaccapane	72-73-70-71–286	23956
5	M Murphy	70-74-69-74–287	15904
6	E Crosby	71-74-73-70–288	12464
	T Green	70-74-73-71–288	12464
	B Daniel	71-71-74-72–288	12464
9	H Stacy	71-72-77-69–289	8533
	M Mallon	71-71-77-70–289	8533
	C Gerring	70-78-70-71–289	8533
	S Turner	74-72-71-72–289	8533
	C Walker	69-75-73-72–289	8533
	A Alcott	72-72-72-73–289	8533
	C Keggi	67-75-73-74–289	8533
16	M McGeorge	72-74-72-72–290	6727
	R Jones	72-70-74-74–290	6727
18	JA Carner	73-71-70-77–291	6287
19	A Ritzman	77-70-73-72–292	5424
	D Andrews	75-72-73-72–292	5424
	J Anschutz	72-73-74-73–292	5424
	P Bradley	74-70-75-73–292	5424
	N Lopez	68-76-75-73–292	5424
	J Geddes	66-74-79-73–292	5424
	C Rarick	73-74-70-75–292	5424
26	C Figg-Currier	76-72-73-72–293	4623
	B Mucha	74-72-75-72–293	4623
	L Davies	73-73-74-73–293	4623
29	K Postlewait	75-74-75-70–294	4221
	D Massey	70-73-75-76–294	4221
	A Finney	73-73-71-77–294	4221
32	C Morse	73-75-74-73–295	3694
	M Nause	75-71-76-73–295	3694
	A Okamoto	74-74-73-74–295	3694
	H Kobayashi	75-72-73-75–295	3694
	D Richard	74-72-74-75–295	3694
	P Wright	72-74-74-75–295	3694
	N Rubin	71-72-76-76–295	3694
	S Furlong	71-71-77-76–295	3694
40	J Anderson	70-72-80-74–296	3185
	N Brown	72-75-74-75–296	3185
	S Sanders	70-77-72-77–296	3185
43	C Marino	71-77-78-71–297	2817
	H Drew	75-74-74-74–297	2817
	G Hull	73-72-78-74–297	2817
	A Nicholas	75-73-74-75–297	2817
	J Gallagher	74-73-74-76–297	2817

Pos	Name	Score	Prize $
48	J Stephenson	75-72-73-78–298	2540
49	A Benz	74-75-76-74–299	2264
	M Blackwelder	75-71-78-75–299	2264
	K Tschetter	70-75-79-75–299	2264
	J Britz	69-74-78-78–299	2264
	J Delk	74-73-73-79–299	2264

LPGA Championship
at Bethesda CC, Bethesda, Maryland

Pos	Name	Score	Prize $
1	B Daniel	71-73-70-66–280	150000
2	R Jones	69-70-70-72–281	92500
3	D Coe	73-71-68-72–284	67500
4	S Ertl	70-67-79-69–285	52500
5	B King	72-73-72-69–286	33250
	P Sheehan	75-71-70-70–286	33250
	T Green	72-72-70-72–286	33250
	C Figg-Currier	72-68-73-73–286	33250
9	A-M Palli	75-72-70-70–287	19500
	P Bradley	73-71-71-72–287	19500
	A Okamoto	75-69-70-73–287	19500
	D Richard	71-72-70-74–287	19500
	C Johnston	70-70-71-76–287	19500
14	M Nause	73-73-75-67–288	13500
	A Benz	69-75-76-68–288	13500
	N Lopez	78-70-70-70–288	13500
	C Rarick	74-71-72-71–288	13500
	D Ammaccapane	73-71-68-74–288	13500
	S Sanders	73-73-68-74–288	13500
20	L Hurlbut	73-75-72-69–289	10179
	M Ward	76-73-71-69–289	10179
	M Mallon	72-71-75-71–289	10179
	J Dickinson	71-75-71-72–289	10179
	J Briles	72-72-71-74–289	10178
	P Hammel	71-74-70-74–289	10178
	C Johnson	67-77-68-77–289	10178
27	P Wright	71-76-73-70–290	8200
	N Brown	70-74-73-73–290	8200
	G Hull	70-76-71-73–290	8200
	L Neumann	75-71-71-73–290	8200
	T Johnson	73-71-71-75–290	8200
32	C Gerring	75-73-72-71–291	6975
	J Crafter	77-68-74-72–291	6975
	L Baugh	75-70-73-73–291	6975
	T Kerdyk	72-75-69-75–291	6975
36	J Geddes	75-75-72-70–292	5608
	S Furlong	71-74-76-71–292	5607
	SA McGetrick	73-73-75-71–292	5607
	T-J Myers	74-74-73-71–292	5607
	B Mucha	74-72-73-73–292	5607
	S Steinhauer	75-75-68-74–292	5607
	J Wyatt	72-74-72-74–292	5607
43	B Pearson	73-75-74-71–293	4500
	L Merten	72-75-73-73–293	4500
	D White	73-77-70-73–293	4500
46	M Berteotti	75-73-73-73–294	3900
	A Alcott	76-70-74-74–294	3900
	J Stephenson	71-74-72-77–294	3900
49	K Postlewait	76-74-77-68–295	3238
	V Fergon	76-73-75-71–295	3238
	E Crosby	72-73-74-76–295	3237
	M Figueras-Dotti	72-69-78-76–295	3237

Atlantic City Classic
at Sands CC, Somers Point, New Jersey

Pos	Name	Score	Prize $
1	C Johnson	69-67-69-70–275	45000
2	P Wright	72-69-64-72–277	27750
3	N Lopez	67-72-68-71–278	20250
4	D Eggeling	67-71-67-74–279	15750
5	L Rittenhouse	70-68-71-71–280	12750
6	M Edge	68-72-72-70–282	10500

Boston Five Classic
at Tara Ferncroft CC, Danvers, Massachusetts

Pos	Name	Score	Prize $
1	B Mucha*	71-70-67-69–277	52500
2	L Rittenhouse	72-69-71-65–277	32375
3	C Rarick	69-74-69-66–278	23625
4	A Alcott	73-72-66-69–280	16625
	O-H Ku	64-77-69-70–280	16625
6	N Brown	72-69-70-70–281	11288
	L Baugh	71-70-68-72–281	11287

Centel Classic
at Killearn CC, Tallahassee, Florida

Pos	Name	Score	Prize $
1	B Daniel	71-63-68-69–271	150000
2	N Lopez	70-67-69-66–272	92500
3	P Sheehan	67-65-74-72–278	67500
4	C Gerring	63-78-67-71–279	52500
5	D Coe	69-73-70-68–280	42500
6	D Ammaccapane	71-71-69-70–281	32250
	S Thomas	70-72-69-70–281	32250

Circle K LPGA Tucson Open
at Randolph North GC, Tucson, Arizona

Pos	Name	Score	Prize $
1	C Walker	71-68-65-72–276	45000
2	P Bradley	70-74-71-66–281	19125
	K Rogerson	69-71-74-67–281	19125
	H Drew	73-68-69-71–281	19125
	B King	71-70-69-71–281	19125
6	J Geddes	76-70-68-69–283	10500

* Winner after play-off

LPGA Corning Classic
at Corning CC, Corning, New York

Pos	Name	Score	Prize $
1	P Bradley	69-70-66-69–274	52500
2	P Sheehan	71-69-69-68–277	32375
3	A Ritzman	68-68-74-68–278	23625
4	R Jones	72-68-73-66–279	16625
	D Coe	72-68-70-69–279	16625
6	A Okamoto	70-72-68-70–280	12250
7	T Johnson	68-70-72-71–281	10325

Crestar Classic
at Greenbrier CC, Chesapeake, Virginia

Pos	Name	Score	Prize $
1	D Mochrie	67-65-68–200	52500
2	C Johnson	73-67-69–209	32375
3	M Mallon	70-72-68–210	23625
4	J Dickinson	71-71-69–211	16625
	P Sheehan	70-71-70–211	16625
6	C Hill	70-72-70–212	12250

Desert Inn LPGA International
at Desert Inn CC, Las Vegas, Nevada

Pos	Name	Score	Prize $
1	M Will	73-66-75–214	60000
2	A Okamoto	73-69-73–215	28334
	V Skinner	71-70-74–215	28333
	P Rizzo	66-70-79–215	28333
5	S Steinhauer	74-69-73–216	14267
	C Morse	73-70-73–216	14267
	C Gerring	71-70-75–216	14266

du Maurier Classic
at Westmount G&CC, Kitchener, Ontario

Pos	Name	Score	Prize $
1	C Johnston	65-70-70-71–276	90000
2	P Sheehan	69-70-70-69–278	55500
3	B Daniel	74-66-71-70–281	40500
4	L Neumann	68-72-70-72–282	31500
5	M Berteotti	74-68-69-72–283	25500
6	G Hull	70-68-76-70–284	19350
	J Anschutz	70-72-70-72–284	19350

JAL Big Apple Classic
at Wykagyl CC, New Rochelle, New York

Pos	Name	Score	Prize $
1	B King	75-67-63-68–273	60000
2	B Daniel	70-70-68-68–276	37000
3	R Jones	69-69-71-70–279	27000
4	T Green	68-69-74-70–281	21000
5	D Coe	70-70-72-70–282	17000
6	K Albers	72-70-73-69–284	12067
	P Bradley	73-71-69-71–284	12067
	P Sheehan	70-73-70-71–284	12066

The Jamaica Classic
at The Tryall Club, Montego Bay

Pos	Name	Score	Prize $
1	P Sheehan	69-68-75–212	75000
2	P Bradley	74-74-67–215	35417
	J Geddes	73-73-69–215	35417
	L Connelly	74-68-73–215	35416
5	M Spencer-Devlin	76-72-68–216	19375
	P Rizzo	72-75-69–216	19375

Jamie Farr Toledo Classic
at Highland Meadows GC, Sylvania, Ohio

Pos	Name	Score	Prize $
1	T Purtzer	67-72-66–205	48750
2	JA Carner	67-73-69–209	26000
	C Johnson	68-71-70–209	25999
4	C Gerring	72-72-67–211	12058
	S Ertl	73-69-69–211	12057
	R Walton	74-67-70–211	12057
	P Rizzo	70-70-71–211	12057
	B King	68-70-73–211	12057

Women's Kemper Open
at Wailea Resort, Maui, Hawaii

Pos	Name	Score	Prize $
1	B Daniel	73-75-66-69–283	75000
2	R Jones	71-73-69-71–284	40000
	L Davies	70-71-72-71–284	40000
4	C Gerring	71-71-73-70–285	23750
	M Edge	68-71-73-73–285	23750
6	D Richard	73-74-70-69–286	17500

Lady Keystone Open
at Hershey CC, Hershey, Pennsylvania

Pos	Name	Score	Prize $
1	C Gerring	70-67-71–208	45000
2	P Bradley	72-69-68–209	24000
	E Crosby	70-69-70–209	24000
4	K Postlewait	70-71-69–210	14250
	B Mucha	71-69-70–210	14250
6	J Briles	70-73-68–211	9675
	K Rogerson	67-76-68–211	9675

Mazda Japan Classic
at Musashigaoka GC, Tokyo

Pos	Name	Score	Prize $
1	D Massey	69-64–133	82500
2	D Ammaccapane	66-67–136	44000
3	C Keggi	68-68–136	44000
4	B King	72-65–137	23834
	E Crosby	69-68–137	23833
	C Gerring	69-68–137	23833

MBS LPGA Classic
at Los Coyotes CC, Buena Park, California

Pos	Name	Score	Prize $
1	N Lopez*	69-70-74-68–281	48750
2	C Gerring	71-70-68-72–281	30062
3	C Keggi	70-69-68-75–282	21937
4	K Shipman	70-71-74-69–284	15437
	N Brown	69-72-71-72–284	15437
6	D Ammaccapane	74-71-68-72–285	11375

McDonald's Championship
at Du Pont CC, Wilmington, Delaware

Pos	Name	Score	Prize $
1	P Sheehan	70-67-68-70–275	97500
2	K Albers	69-73-69-68–279	41438
	B King	70-70-70-69–279	41438
	C Gerring	69-72-67-71–279	41437
	A Okamoto	70-69-69-71–279	41437
6	C Walker	69-71-71-69–280	19609
	J Geddes	68-68-74-70–280	19608
	B Mucha	68-72-67-73–280	19608
9	P Bradley	70-73-71-67–281	14463
	D Richard	68-71-73-69–281	14462

* Winner after play-off

Nabisco Dinah Shore
at Mission Hills CC, Rancho Mirage, California

Pos	Name	Score	Prize $
1	B King	69-70-69-75–283	90000
2	S Furlong	74-73-70-68–285	42000
	K Postlewait	73-72-68-72–285	42000
4	C Rarick	72-72-72-70–286	28000
5	C Walker	74-72-67-74–287	24000
6	A Okamoto	73-72-72-71–288	17217
	B Daniel	71-73-72-72–288	17217
	R Jones	72-71-71-74–288	17216
9	P Bradley	74-73-69-73–289	12699
	M Mallon	74-72-70-73–289	12698

Northgate LPGA Classic
at Edinburgh USA GC, Brooklyn Park, Minnesota

Pos	Name	Score	Prize $
1	B Daniel	66-69-68–203	56250
2	C Johnson	66-75-68–209	30000
	P Hammel	69-71-69–209	29999
4	B Bunkowsky	65-75-71–211	16250
	C Keggi	71-68-72–211	16250
	C Rarick	66-71-74–211	16249
7	P Wright	72-71-69–212	10406
	E Crosby	72-69-71–212	10406

Oldsmobile LPGA Classic
at Wycliffe G&CC, Lake Worth, Florida

Pos	Name	Score	Prize $
1	P Bradley*	66-65-74-76–281	45000
2	D Eggeling	72-73-67-69–281	27750
3	D Mochrie	72-71-67-72–282	20250
4	M Blackwelder	73-73-70-68–284	10450
	B Daniel	72-71-72-69–284	10450
	D McHaffie	71-69-74-70–284	10450
	E Crosby	70-69-73-72–284	10450
	S Thomas	71-70-70-73–284	10450
	L Kean	71-68-72-73–284	10450

* Winner after play-off

Orix Hawaiian Ladies' Open
at Ko Olina GC, Ewa Beach, Hawaii

Pos	Name	Score	Prize $
1	B Daniel	71-67-72–210	52500
2	P Sheehan	69-73-71–213	28000
	A Benz	70-70-73–213	28000
4	M Blackwelder	71-74-70–215	12985
	M Berteotti	73-70-72–215	12985
	P Rizzo	73-70-72–215	12985
	L Poling	70-72-73–215	12985
	S Turner	70-71-74–215	12985

Phar-Mor Inverrary Classic
at Inverrary CC&R, Fort Lauderdale, Florida

Pos	Name	Score	Prize $
1	J Crafter	70-67-72–209	60000
2	N Lopez	73-67-70–210	37000
3	M Mallon	72-68-71–211	21667
	D Ammaccapane	72-68-71–211	21667
	D Eggeling	69-68-74–211	21666
6	P Sheehan	72-70-70–212	12900
	E Crosby	68-71-73–212	12900

The Phar-Mor in Youngstown
at Squaw Creek CC, Vienna, Ohio

Pos	Name	Score	Prize $
1	B Daniel*	65-69-73–207	60000
2	P Sheehan	70-68-69–207	37000
3	D Ammaccapane	69-67-72–208	27000
4	A Okamoto	70-68-71–209	19000
	D Massey	71-65-73–209	19000
6	R Jones	72-68-70–210	12900
	D Mochrie	67-71-72–210	12900

Ping Cellular One LPGA Golf Championship
at Columbia Edgewater CC, Portland, Oregon

Pos	Name	Score	Prize $
1	P Sheehan	70-71-67–208	52500
2	D Ammaccapane	72-73-64–209	32375
3	P Bradley	70-68-72–210	23625
4	S Turner	69-70-74–213	16625
	D Mochrie	68-71-74–213	16625
6	D White	71-72-71–214	12250

* Winner after play-off

Planters Pat Bradley International
at Willow Creek GC, High Point, North Carolina

Pos	Name	Points					Prize $
1	C Rarick	3	4	12	6 – 25		60000
2	B Daniel	8	1	5	10 – 24		37000
3	H Stacy	5	3	5	10 – 23		27000
4	S Steinhauer	4	7	5	6 – 22		21000
5	J Inkster	9	4	7	9 – 21		17000
6	D Richard	10	5	0	5 – 20		12900
	D Ammaccapane	1	5	3	11 – 20		12900

Rail Charity Golf Classic
at Rail GC, Springfield, Illinois

Pos	Name	Score	Prize $
1	B Daniel	67-69-67–203	45000
2	S Sanders	71-69-66–206	27750
3	N Brown	69-71-67–207	18000
	A Ritzman	69-70-68–207	18000
5	D Andrews	70-68-70–208	12750
	K Rogerson	72-68-69–209	10500

Red Robin Kyocera Inamori Classic
at Stoneridge CC, Poway, California

Pos	Name	Score	Prize $
1	K Monaghan	72-67-70-67–276	45000
2	C Gerring	70-72-67-69–278	27750
3	R Jones	70-74-67-68–279	18000
	A Okamoto	71-70-69-69–279	18000
5	K Tschetter	69-72-72-67–280	11625
	P Rizzo	72-68-70-70–280	11625

Rochester International
at Locust Hill CC, Pittsford, New York

Pos	Name	Score	Prize $
1	P Sheehan	72-64-68-67–271	60000
2	A Alcott	69-65-68-73–275	37000
3	N Lopez	68-70-70-68–276	27000
4	T Green	76-67-68-69–280	21000
5	K Postlewait	68-68-68-77–281	17000
6	J Geddes	72-72-67-71–282	14000

Safeco Classic
at Meridian Valley CC, Kent, Washington

Pos	Name	Score	Prize $
1	P Sheehan	69-65-66-70–270	45000
2	D Richard	75-67-71-66–279	27750
3	M Foyer	74-70-68-68–280	20250
4	V Fergon	71-74-68-69–282	13000
	T Green	76-67-68-71–282	13000
	D Coe	74-68-68-72–282	13000

Sara Lee Classic
at Hermitage GC, Old Hickory, Tennessee

Pos	Name	Score	Prize $
1	A Okamoto	71-71-68–210	63750
2	B King	72-71-68–211	24650
	C Walker	71-70-70–211	24650
	JA Carner	73-67-71–211	24650
	D Coe	70-69-72–211	24649
	P Bradley	70-68-73–211	24649

Standard Register Turquoise Classic
at Moon Valley CC, Phoenix, Arizona

Pos	Name	Score	Prize $
1	P Bradley	70-71-68-71–280	75000
2	A Okamoto	72-69-69-71–281	46250
3	B King	69-72-70-71–282	33750
4	B Daniel	72-71-71-71–285	21667
	C Figg-Currier	68-74-72-71–285	21667
	K Albers	70-70-71-74–285	21666

Stratton Mountain LPGA Classic
at Stratton Mountain CC, Stratton Mountain, Vermont

Pos	Name	Score	Prize $
1	C Gerring*	71-70-72-68–281	67500
2	C Keggi	71-72-70-68–281	41625
3	L Connelly	70-71-71-71–283	27000
	C Figg-Currier	68-72-72-71–283	27000
5	A Benz	69-72-70-73–284	19125
6	M Will	74-70-73-68–285	14513
	N Harvey	68-78-67-72–285	14512

Winner after play-off

Men's Amateur

The Amateur Championship
at Muirfield and Luffness New

Starting field: 288. There were 75 qualifiers (64 plus ties with scores of 148 or better) for the match-play stage at Muirfield after a 36-hole stroke-play competition held at Muirfield and Luffness New (one round on each course).

First Round (Preliminary Round):

A Rogers beat E Valimaa 4 and 2
R Eggo beat B Burns at 21st hole
K Weeks beat G Shaw 3 and 2
G Homewood beat D Beech 4 and 2
A Hill beat M Moore 1 hole
D Brookreson beat G Patterson 4 and 3
D Gammon beat R Oliveira 3 and 2
G Wolstenholme beat N Graves 1 hole
J Kiley beat P MacLeod 2 and 1
L Parsons beat A Harrhy 2 holes
M Macara beat F Stewart 4 and 3

Second Round:

G Kennedy beat A Hart 3 and 2
A Sandywell beat G Zahringer 7 and 5
R Muntz beat M Wiggett 2 and 1
A Nicholson beat D Kirkpatrick 3 and 2
G Millar beat P Blaikie at 19th hole
E Nistri beat S Henderson 4 and 3
J Carvill beat V Phillips 5 and 4
W Bryson beat M Stanford 1 hole
J Payne beat J Noon 3 and 2
G Lawrie beat R Russell 2 and 1
C Cassells beat S Knight 6 and 4
L White beat B Barnes 3 and 2
N Walton beat K Hird 8 and 6
W Hewlett beat T Nielson 3 and 1
M McGuire beat M Hastie 4 and 2
G Winter beat A Butler 2 holes

C Cuthbert beat B Shields 2 and 1
R Johnson beat L Peterson at 23rd hole
G Pooley beat I Garbutt 2 and 1
J Bickerton beat J Metcalfe 5 and 3
C Pottier beat S Green 1 hole
J Fanagan beat A Jones 2 and 1
G Evans beat M Goodin 6 and 5
D Clarke beat D McToldridge 3 and 2
T Spence beat M Dove 1 hole
O Edmond beat P Sefton 4 and 3
R Eggo beat A Rogers 1 hole
K Weeks beat G Homewood 3 and 2
A Hill beat D Brookreson 2 and 1
G Wolstenholme beat D Gammon 3 and 2
L Parsons beat J Kiley 6 and 4
M Macara beat M Brannan 1 hole

Third Round:

A Sandywell beat G Kennedy 8 and 7
R Muntz beat A Nicholson 4 and 3
E Nistri beat G Millar 8 and 7
J Carvill beat W Bryson 6 and 4
G Lawrie beat J Payne 1 hole
C Cassells beat L White 4 and 3
N Walton beat W Hewlett 3 and 1
G Winter beat M McGuire 2 holes

R Johnson beat C Cuthbert 1 hole
G Pooley beat J Bickerton at 19th hole
C Pottier beat J Fanagan 5 and 4
G Evans beat D Clarke 7 and 6
O Edmond beat T Spence 2 and 1
K Weeks beat R Eggo 2 and 1
G Wolstenholme beat A Hill 5 and 3
M Macara beat L Parsons 3 and 2

Fourth Round:

R Muntz beat A Sandywell 5 and 4
J Carvill beat E Nistri 1 hole
C Cassells beat G Lawrie 2 holes
G Winter beat N Walton 1 hole

R Johnson beat G Pooley 1 hole
G Evans beat C Pottier 2 and 1
O Edmond beat K Weeks 2 and 1
M Macara beat G Wolstenholme at 23rd

Quarter Finals:

R Muntz beat J Carvill at 19th hole
C Cassells beat G Winter 5 and 4
R Johnson beat G Evans 2 and 1
M Macara beat O Edmond at 20th hole

Semi-Finals:

R Muntz beat C Cassells 2 and 1
M Macara beat R Johnson 1 hole

The Amateur Championship
continued

Final:

R Muntz beat M Macara 7 and 6

World Amateur Team Championship for the Eisenhower Trophy
at Christchurch, New Zealand

Leading Team Scores

SWEDEN	215 -212 -229 -223 –879			
M Gronberg	70 - 67 - 77 - 72 –286			
G Hjertstedt	73 - 71 - 74 - 74 –292			
K Eriksson	72 - 74 - 78 - 74 –301			
P Nyman	(77) -(78) -(82) -(80) –317			

NEW ZEALAND	222 -222 -223 -220 –892
M Long	71 - 71 - 79 - 73 –294
B Paterson	76 - 76 - 74 -(77) –301
S Alker	75 -(77) - 77 - 73 –302
G Moorhead	(76) - 75 -(82) - 72 –305

USA	227 -222 -223 -220 –892
P Mickelson	(78) - 78 - 72 - 71 –299
D Duval	77 - 69 -(77) -(76) –299
D Eger	74 -(80) - 75 - 73 –302
A Doyle	76 - 75 - 76 - 76 –303

In ninth position	
GB&I	228 -226 -226 -230 –910
J Milligan	77 - 75 - 79 - 74 –305
R Willison	77 - 74 -(79) - 79 –309
A Coltart	(77) -(87) - 73 - 77 –314
G Evans	74 - 77 - 74 -(93) –318

Leading Individual Scores

M Gronberg (Swe)	70-67-77-72–286
G Hjerstedt (Swe)	73-71-74-74–292
M Long (NZ)	71-71-79-73–294
S Maruyama (Jpn)	72-75-75-72–294
O Edmond (Fra)	75-72-74-75–296

(Discarded scores in brackets)

St Andrews Trophy
at El Saler, Valencia, Spain

First Day–Foursomes

Continent of Europe		Great Britain and Ireland	
K Eriksson and G Hjertstedt	0	C Cassells and J Metcalfe (1 hole)	1
B Queipo de Llano and E Nistri (2 and 1)	1	G McGimpsey and J Carvill	0
O Edmond and E de la Riva	½	J Milligan and A Coltart	½
R Muntz and T Bjorn	0	R Willison and J Payne (1 hole)	1
	1½		2½

Singles

Continent of Europe		Great Britain and Ireland	
K Eriksson (6 and 5)	1	C Cassells	0
B Queipo de Llano	1/2	J Milligan	1/2
U Jonsson	1/2	G McGimpsey	1/2
E Nistri	0	R Willison (5 and 3)	1
E de la Riva (1 hole)	1	J Payne	0
G Hjertstedt	1/2	D Clarke	1/2
O Edmond (5 and 3)	1	J Metcalfe	0
R Muntz (5 and 4)	1	J Carvill	0
	5 1/2		2 1/2

Second Day–Foursomes

Continent of Europe		Great Britain and Ireland	
K Eriksson and G Hjertstedt	1/2	R Willison and J Payne	1/2
B Queipo de Llano and E Nistri	0	C Cassells and J Metcalfe (6 and 5)	1
E de la Riva and O Edmond (1 hole)	1	D Clarke and J Carvill	0
T Bjorn and R Muntz	0	J Milligan and A Coltart (5 and 4)	1
	1 1/2		2 1/2

Singles

Continent of Europe		Great Britain and Ireland	
K Eriksson	0	R Willison (2 and 1)	1
B Queipo de Llano (1 hole)	1	D Clarke	0
T Bjorn	0	C Cassells (3 and 2)	1
O Edmond	1/2	G McGimpsey	1/2
U Jonsson (1 hole)	1	J Milligan	0
R Muntz	0	J Payne (3 and 2)	1
E de la Riva	0	A Coltart (5 and 4)	1
G Hjertstedt	0	J Metcalfe (1 hole)	1
	2 1/2		5 1/2

Result: Continent of Europe 11, Great Britain and Ireland 13

English Amateur Championship
at Woodhall Spa

Fifth Round:

L Yearn beat K Fairbairn 4 and 3
D Thomson beat R Tuddenham 3 and 2
P Sefton beat R Walton at 19th hole
G Evans beat D McToldridge 3 and 1
L White beat M Caswell 3 and 2
A Duffin beat P Little 5 and 3
M Dove beat D Lee 5 and 3
I Garbutt beat N Willis 5 and 3

Semi–Finals:

G Evans beat L Yearn 3 and 1
I Garbutt beat L White 4 and 3

Final:

I Garbutt beat G Evans 8 and 7

Quarter Finals:

L Yearn beat D Thomson 1 hole
G Evans beat P Sefton 3 and 2
L White beat A Duffin 1 hole
I Garbutt beat M Dove 5 and 3

The Senior Open Amateur Golf Championship
at The Berkshire GC,

Name	Club/Country	Score
CW Green	Dumbarton	68-71-68–207
D Frame	Worplesdon	68-74-75–217
R Remsen	USA	74-71-73–218
P McIlvenny	Dyke	76-71-74–221
J McMurtrey	USA	72-76-74–222
C Ribelin	USA	72-76-74–222
R Coogan	South Bedfordshire	72-73-78–223
CC Moore	USA	78-74-71–223
D Goerlich	USA	77-75-72–224
I Hughes	Abergele & Pensarn	78-75-71–224

English Open Amateur Championship
at Burnham and Berrow

Name	Score
O Edmond	75-73-66-73–287
G Evans	74-71-71-71–287
R Eggo	74-73-73-68–288
D Gammon	66-76-68-78–288
J Metcalfe	74-70-72-72–288
J Lee	72-71-69-77–289

English Open Seniors Championship
at Enville and Bridgnorth

Name	Score
NA Paul	74-75-68–217
I Caldwell	75-73-76–224
R Coogan	75-76-73–224
D Frame	72-77-76–225
R Hiatt	82-73-73–228
H Dooley	74-78-78–230
J Flanders	77-78-76–231
G Edwards	80-78-74–232

Men's Home Internationals
at Conwy

England beat Wales 10-5
Ireland beat Scotland 9-6
Scotland beat England 9½-5½
Ireland beat Wales 11-4
Wales beat Scotland 8-7
Ireland beat England 8-7

Result: Ireland 3, England 1, Scotland 1, Wales 1

Berkhamsted Trophy
at Berkhamsted

Name	Score
J Barnes	71-73–144
J Metcalfe	75-71–146
R Willison	71-75–146
J Scott Hodgson	73-75–148

The Berkshire Trophy
at The Berkshire GC

Name	Score
J O'Shea	67-68-68-68–271
D Gammon	70-71-71-64–276
L White	68-69-70-70–277
M Stanford	72-69-69-68–278
N Walton	68-71-70-69–278
N Leconte	72-69-69-68–278
M Dove	68-70-70-70–278

British Universities Men's Championship
at Musselburgh

Quarter Finals:

M Church (Leeds) beat S Docherty (Aberdeen) 4 and 3
N Deans (Liverpool) beat R Payne (Nottingham) 3 and 1
I Main (Aberdeen) beat R Krefting (Southampton) 5 and 3
I Fraser (Heriot Watt) beat D Hawsell (Dundee) 1 hole

Semi-Finals:

M Church beat N Deans at 19th hole
I Fraser beat I Main 5 and 4

Final:

M Church beat I Fraser 4 and 2

County Champion of Champions
at Olton, Solihull

Name	Score
P Streeter	68-68–136
R Sloman	68-68–136
J Good	68-69–137
J Cook	69-69–138
L White	71-68–139
D Charlton	70-70–140

Daily Mail/ Golf Illustrated Gold Vase
at Walton Heath

Name	Score
A Rogers	78-68–138
D Lee	71-69–140
R Hodgkinson	69-72–141
M Pinner	71-71–142
T Greenwood	76-67–143
B Ingleby	75-69–144
G Carter	76-68–144
S Barwick	77-67–144

Duncan Putter
at Southerndown

Name	Score
R Willison	71-81-77-82–311
M Macara	74-76-83-82–315
J Peters	78-73-84-81–316
A Jones	74-79-83-82–318
A Rogers	73-82-82-81–318
S Wilkinson	80-77-81-80–318

East of Ireland Championship
at Baltray

Name	Score
D O'Sullivan	74-74-74-69–291
G McNeill	76-73-72-72–293
G McGimpsey	71-75-72-76–294
L McNamara	71-71-75-79–296

East of Scotland Stroke Play Championship
at Lundin Links

Name	Score
G Lawrie	69-70-71-75–285
S Bannerman	73-69-72-71–285
G Lowson	70-69-71-76–286

European Amateur Championship
at Aalborg, Denmark

Name	Score
K Eriksson	67-70-71-71–279
P Moloney	69-70-74-71–284
C Cassells	71-66-74-76–287
M Florioli	68-73-72-75–288
V Pagel	75-75-67-72–289
T Bjorn	73-69-69-78–289
E Nistri	71-69-73-76–289
J Payne	70-69-74-76–289

France *v* England
at Morfontaine, France

First Day:

France 4$\frac{1}{2}$, England 7$\frac{1}{2}$

Second Day:

France 3, England 9

Result:

France 7$\frac{1}{2}$, England 16$\frac{1}{2}$

Halford Hewitt Public Schools Society Cup
at Royal Cinque Ports, Deal

Quarter Finals:

Malvern 3, Edinburgh Academy 2
Watsons 4$\frac{1}{2}$, Eton $\frac{1}{2}$
Tonbridge 3, Repton 2
Liverpool 3, Whitgift 2

Semi-Finals:

Malvern 3$\frac{1}{2}$, Watsons 1$\frac{1}{2}$
Tonbridge 4, Liverpool 1

Final:

Tonbridge 3, Malvern 2

Hampshire Hog
at North Hants

Name	Score
J Metcalfe	69-67–136
N Williamson	69-69–138
G Evans	73-66–139
A Mew	67-72–139

Irish Amateur Close Championship
at Baltray

Semi-Finals:

D Clarke beat G McGimpsey 2 and 1
P Harrington beat M Gannon 2 and 1

Final:

D Clarke beat P Harrington 3 and 2

Italy *v* Scotland
at Venice

First Day:	Second Day:
Italy 4½, Scotland 4½	Italy 3½, Scotland 5½

Result:

Italy 8, Scotland 10

J&B Scottish Amateur Championship
at Gullane

Semi-Finals:

C Everett beat A Coltart at 20th hole
M Thomson beat P Blaikie 2 and 1

Final:

C Everett beat M Thomson 7 and 5

John Cross Bowl
at Worplesdon

Name	Score
D Lee*	71-71–142
N Williamson	73-69–142
A Mew	71-71–142

---

* Winner after play-off

King George V Challenge Cup
at Porters Park

Name	Score
C Boal	69-72–141
P Page	72-72–144
M Deal	75-70–145
J Bickerton	72-74–146

Lagonda Trophy
at Gog Magog

Name	Score
L Parsons	66-71-69-67–273
M Dove	69-68-73-65–275
L White	70-69-67-70–276
S Amor	69-69-68-72–278
N Graves	72-70-66-70–278

Lytham Trophy
at Royal Lytham & St Annes

Name	Score
G Evans	68-76-74-73–291
D Bathgate	69-71-72-80–292
J Dockar	69-71-76-77–293
C Poxon	71-71-78-75–295
P Wharton	70-79-72-76–297
I Garbutt	74-73-73-77–297
N Graves	74-71-76-76–297

Nixdorf Cup
at Oporto, Portugal

Pos	Name	Team	Score
1	(G Evans, I Garbutt, J Cook, B Eggo)	England	629
1		Sweden	637
3		Spain	640
4		Scotland	641
5		Denmark	653
6		Portugal	673

Oxford *v* Cambridge University Match
at Muirfield

Oxford		Cambridge	
Foursomes		**Foursomes**	
	Matches		**Matches**
S Jenkins and P Gerrans	1/2	B Ingleby and S Scott	1/2
J Hampel and N Burke	0	J Packham and J Shinton	
J Higgo and K Froggatt	0	(1 hole)	1
P Eayres and I Henderson	0	M Williams and N Peplow	
S Ritchie and A Woolnough		(4 and 3)	1
(6 and 5)	1	J Turner and R Sherwin	
	—	(13 and 12)	1
	1 1/2	R Hall and C Dale	0
			—
Singles		**Singles**	
N Burke	0	R Sherwin (4 and 3)	1
S Jenkins	0	B Ingleby (6 and 5)	1
A Woolnough	1/2	S Scott	1/2
J Higgo (3 and 2)	1	J Packham	0
J Hampel	0	N Peplow (7 and 6)	1
K Froggatt (3 and 2)	1	J Shinton	0
P Eayres	0	J Turner (4 and 3)	1
I Henderson	0	M Williams (2 and 1)	1
P Gerrans	0	C Dale (12 and 10)	1
S Ritchie	0	R Hall (5 and 4)	1
	—		—
	2 1/2		7 1/2

Result: Oxford 4; Cambridge 11

St Andrews Links Trophy
at St Andrews

Name	Score
S Bouvier	69-69-71-71–280
M Brannan	69-74-71-73–287
G Hickman	67-76-72-73–288
S Knowles	73-75-69-72–289
J Milligan	73-78-68-70–289

Scotland v Sweden
at Carnoustie

First Day:

Scotland 3 1/2, Sweden 5 1/2

Second Day:

Scotland 6, Sweden 3

Result:

Scotland 9 1/2, Sweden 8 1/2

Scottish Equitable Scottish Stroke Play Championship
at Royal Aberdeen

Name	Score
G Hay	65-68–133
S MacKenzie	69-67–136
K Yonemoto	69-69–138
M Hastie	70-69–139
A Tait	69-70–139

Scottish Seniors Championship
at Royal Burgess

Name	Score
C Hartland	72-74–146
CW Green	73-74–147
G Donaldson	74-73–147
J Haynes	76-74–150
D Galbraith	74-79–153

Selborne Salver
at Blackmoor

Name	Score
J Metcalfe	70-66–136
R Willison	71-70–141
G Wolstenholme	76-66–142
G Homewood	69-73–142
J Barnes	74-68–142

Tillman Trophy
at Royal Porthcawl

Name	Score
M Wiggett	75-74-76-75–300
B Austin	80-76-71-74–301
J Cook	80-74-78-70–302
J Peters	75-81-74-73–303

Ulster Seniors' Championship
at Shandon Park

Name	Score
J Daly	153

US Amateur Championship
at Cherry Hills, Englewood, Colorado

Quarter Finals:

P Mickelson beat B May 1 hole
D Eger beat M Brannan 2 and 1
T Scherrer beat H Albertsson 3 and 2
M Zerman beat M Sposa 3 and 2

Semi-Finals:

P Mickelson beat D Eger 5 and 3
M Zerman beat T Scherrer 4 and 2

Final:

P Mickelson beat M Zerman 5 and 4

Welsh Amateur Championship
at Prestatyn

Semi-Finals:

A Barnett beat J McLaughlin 3 and 2
A Jones beat M Calvert 2 and 1

Final:

A Barnett beat A Jones 1 hole

Welsh Amateur Open Stroke Play Championship
at Pyle and Kenfig

Name	Score
G Houston	76-69-71-72–288
C Evans	74-72-73-71–290
A Jones	72-73-71-74–290
N Clarke	74-72-70-76–292
N Williamson	79-71-69-76–295
H Roberts	73-75-72-75–295
C Rivett	71-74-75-75–295
R Goosen	75-69-76-75–295

Women's Amateur

Curtis Cup
at Somerset Hills, New Jersey

First Day – Foursomes

United States		Great Britain & Ireland	
V Goetze and A Sander (4 and 3)	1	H Dobson and C Lambert	0
K Noble and M Platt	0	J Hall and K Imrie (2 and 1)	1
C Semple-Thompson and R Weiss (3 and 1)	1	E Farquharson and H Wadsworth	0
	2		1

Singles

United States		Great Britain & Ireland	
V Goetze	0	J Hall (2 and 1)	1
K Peterson (3 and 2)	1	K Imrie	0
B Burton (3 and 1)	1	E Farquharson	0
R Weiss (4 and 3)	1	L Fletcher	0
K Noble (1 hole)	1	C Lambert	0
C Semple-Thompson	0	V Thomas (1 hole)	1
	4		2

Second Day – Foursomes

United States		Great Britain & Ireland	
V Goetze and A Sander (3 and 1)	1	J Hall and K Imrie	0
K Noble and M Platt	0	C Lambert and H Dobson (1 hole)	1
K Peterson and B Burton (5 and 4)	1	E Farquharson and H Wadsworth	0
	2		1

Singles

United States		Great Britain & Ireland	
V Goetze (4 and 3)	1	H Dobson	0
B Burton (4 and 3)	1	C Lambert	0
K Peterson (1 hole)	1	K Imrie	0
K Noble (2 holes)	1	J Hall	0
R Weiss (2 and 1)	1	E Farquharson	0
C Semple-Thompson (3 and 1)	1	V Thomas	0
	6		0

Aggregate: United States 14, Great Britain and Ireland 4

Women's World Amateur Team Championship for the Espirito Santo Trophy
at Christchurch, New Zealand

Leading Team Scores

US	148 - 143 - 153 - 141 –585	NEW ZEALAND	152 - 149 - 150 - 146 –597
V Goetze	74 -(76)- 74 - 67 –291	J Higgins	74 - 72 - 74 -(75)–295
P Hurst	74 - 71 -(81)- 74 –300	A Stott	78 - 77 -(82)- 74 –311
K Noble	(77)- 72 - 79 -(77)–305	L Aldridge	(88)-(80)- 76 - 72 –316
GB&I	153 - 146 - 155 - 151 –605	JAPAN	156 - 156 - 154 - 141 –607
C Hourihane	79 - 72 - 79 - 74 –304	M Hattori	79 - 78 - 78 - 71 –306
J Hall	74 -(77)- 76 -(79)–306	A Takamura	77 - 78 -(82)- 70 –307
V Thomas	(79)- 74 - (79)- 77 –309	M Saito	(80)-(80)- 76 -(80)–316

Leading Individual Scores

V Goetze (US)	74-76-74-67–291
J Higgins (NZ)	74-72-74-75–295
J Won (Kor)	77-77-72-69–295
P Hurst (US)	74-71-81-74–300
A Sorenstam (Swe)	78-71-77-74–300
M Hageman (Neth)	75-76-78-73–302
E Valera (Spa)	78-74-76-75–303
C Hourihane (GB&I)	79-72-79-74–304
D Bourson (Fra)	75-78-79-73–305
L Briers (Aus)	78-76-73-78–305
K Noble (US)	77-72-79-77–305
M Olivero (Arg)	78-76-74-77–305

(Discarded scores in brackets)

Women's Home Internationals
at Hunstanton

Scotland beat Wales 5-4
Scotland beat Ireland 5-4
Scotland beat England 6-3
England beat Wales 6-3
England halved with Ireland 4$\frac{1}{2}$-4$\frac{1}{2}$.
Wales halved with Ireland 4$\frac{1}{2}$.-4$\frac{1}{2}$.

Result: Scotland 3, England 1$\frac{1}{2}$., Ireland 1, Wales $\frac{1}{2}$.

British Women's Stroke Play Championship
at Strathaven

Name	Score
V Thomas	72-72-70-73–287
C Hourihane	72-73-70-73–288
E Valera	76-72-71-71–290
P Carlson	72-73-73-72–290
H Wadsworth	74-73-68-77–292
D Bourson	77-72-70-74–293
S Gautrey	74-74-76-71–295

Name	Score
L Hackney	76-77-72-72–297
M Bergman	73-76-75-73–297
L Fairclough	73-80-69-76–298
W Doolan	74-78-71-75–298
W Dicks	76-75-73-74–298
C Lambert	78-74-78-69–299
T Samuel	75-74-75-75–299
L Dermott	76-76-72-76–300

British Women's Stroke Play Championship

continued

Astor Salver

at The Berkshire

Name	Score
J Hall	72-72–144
J Morley	73-71–144
J Thornhill	76-70–146

British Universities Women's Championship

at Musselburgh

Name	Score
C Lambert	73-73–146
A MacDonald	73-76–149
F McKay	77-73–150
K Speak	79-75–154
K Baird	78-78–156

Critchley Salver

at Sunningdale

Name	Score
C Hourihane	68-71–139
J Hall	72-74–146
K Tebbet	76-72–148
V Thomas	75-74–149

English Women's Championship
at Rye

Semi-Finals:

L Fletcher beat S Bennett 1 hole
A Uzielli beat H Dobson 6 and 4

Final:

A Uzielli beat L Fletcher 2 and 1

English Women's County Finals
at East Devon

Hampshire beat Glamorgan 6½-2½
Cheshire beat Nottinghamshire 6-3
Nottinghamshire beat Glamorgan 7½-1½
Cheshire beat Hampshire 5½-3½
Hampshire beat Nottinghamshire 8½-½
Cheshire beat Glamorgan 5-4

Result: Cheshire 3; Hampshire 2; Nottinghamshire 1; Glamorgan 0

English Intermediate Championship
at Whitley Bay

Semi-Finals:

L Fletcher beat A Johns at 19th hole
K Speak beat K Tebbet 4 and 3

Finals:

L Fletcher beat K Speak 7 and 6

English Ladies' Seniors Championship
at Fairhaven

Name	Score
A Thomson	81-81–162
C Atack	86-79–165
R Watters	84-83–167
C Balley	87-80–167
A Howard	87-80–167
A Uzielli	85-83–168

Helen Holm Trophy
at Troon Portland and Royal Troon

Name	Score
C Lambert	74-74-77–225
L Fletcher	75-76-76–227
V Thomas	72-76-80–228
L Bayman	77-79-74–230
J Hall	73-80-77–230

Team	Scores
Scotland	457
Wales	459
England	460
Ireland	474
Sweden	481

Irish Women's Championship
at The Island

Semi-Finals:

L Callen beat M McKenna 4 and 3
E McDaid beat A Ferguson 5 and 4

Final:

E McDaid beat L Callen 2 and 1

North of Scotland Women's Championship
at Forfar

Semi-Finals:

K Imrie beat L Urquhart 3 and 2
C Middleton beat A Laing 3 and 1

Final:

K Imrie beat C Middleton 5 and 4

Roehampton Gold Cup

at Roehampton Club

Name	Score
K Imrie	75-75–150
C Caldwell	74-78–152
C Duffy(Pro)	80-72–152
S Moon(Pro)	77-77–154
H Wadsworth	78-76–154
K Hurley(Pro)	80-75–155

St Rule Trophy

at St Andrews

Name	Score
A Sorenstam	81-76-71–228
J Allmark	79-72-77–228
A Rose	77-79-74–230
J Forbes	76-77-78–231
E Kruuse	77-77-78–232

Scottish Women's Championship

at Machrihanish

Semi-Finals:

E Farquharson beat K Imrie 2 and 1
S Huggan beat M McKinlay 3 and 2

Final:

E Farquharson beat S Huggan 3 and 2

Welsh Women's Championship

at Ashburnham

Semi-Finals:

S Roberts beat V Thomas at 19th hole
H Wadsworth beat S Thomas at 21st hole

Final:

S Roberts beat H Wadsworth 3 and 2

Team Championship

Semi-Finals:

Maesdu beat Pennard 3 and 2
Whitchurch beat Royal Porthcawl 3 and 2

Final:

Whitchurch beat Maesdu 3 and 2

Welsh Open Stroke Play
at Newport

Name	Score
L Hackney	71-73-74–218
H Dobson	77-73-73–223
H Wadsworth	70-78-76–224
K Nicholls	78-73-76–227

Wentworth Scratch Trophy
at Wentworth

Name	Score
L Fletcher	74-67–141
C Hall	74-69–143
H Wadsworth	75-69–144
V Thomas	77-71–148

Juniors and Youths

British Boys' Championship
at Hunstanton

Quarter Finals:

G Campbell beat R Coles 3 and 2
M Welch beat D De Vooght 2 holes
M Ellis beat A Kellock 5 and 3
G Jack beat G Sproule 3 and 2

Semi-Finals:

M Welch beat G Campbell 5 and 3
M Ellis beat G Jack 4 and 3

Final:

M Welch beat M Ellis 3 and 1

Boys' Internationals
at Hunstanton

Result:

Scotland 10½, England 4½
Ireland 8½, Wales 6½

R&A Trophy
at Hunstanton

This trophy is played between the winners of the England v Scotland and Wales v Ireland
Boys' International Matches and was introduced in 1985.

Result:

Scotland 12½, Ireland 2½

International Match for Jacques Leglise Trophy

(Great Britain and Ireland Boys v Continent of Europe Boys)
at Hunstanton

Foursomes

Great Britain & Ireland		Continent of Europe	
M Welch and G Jack (5 and 3)	1	M Persson and J Stalberg	0
R Burns and R Coughlan (2 and 1)	1	K Ekjord and A Townhill	0
N Archibald and N Macrae (1 hole)	1	F Duger and R Bleze-Pascau	0
M Ellis and L Westwood (6 and 4)	1	F De Pablo and P Beautell	0
	—		—
	4		0

Singles

Great Britain & Ireland		Continent of Europe	
M Welch (4 and 3)	1	M Persson	0
G Jack (5 and 4)	1	K Ekjord	0
R Burns (1 hole)	1	J Stalberg	0
M Ellis	0	F Duger (2 holes)	1
N Archibald (1 hole)	1	F De Pablo	0
R Coughlan	0	A Townhill (2 holes)	1
N Macrae (5 and 4)	1	R Bleze-Pascau	0
L Westwood (1 hole)	1	P Beautell	0
	—		—
	6		2

Result: Great Britain and Ireland 10, Continent of Europe 2

British Youth's Open Amateur Championship

at Southerness

Pos	Name	Score
1	M Gronberg	70-69-65-71–275
2	A Coltart	71-69-68-68–276
3	J Payne	70-69-69-70–278
4	D Bathgate	67-68-75-70–280
5	T Munoz	70-67-71-72–280
6	M Watson	73-69-66-73–281
7	J Webber	70-70-69-73–282
8	D Robertson	72-68-70-73–283
9	O Edmond	72-70-67-74–283
10	C Ciesielski	73-71-70-70–284
	R Johnson	71-71-71-71–284
	C O'Carroll	73-71-69-71–284
	P Sefton	71-66-73-74–284
	J Wilshire	70-72-75-67–284

Youths' International

at Southerness

Foursomes: Scotland 5, England 0

Singles: Scotland 4, England 6

Result: Scotland 9, England 6

Great Britain and Ireland *v* Continent of Europe (Youths)

for the EGA Trophy
at Oporto, Portugal

First Day – Foursomes

Continent of Europe		Great Britain and Ireland	
O Edmond and M Florioli	½	I Garbutt and D Bathgate	½
J Greisen and J-E Schapmann	0	A Coltart and J Payne (4 and 3)	1
C Beautell and D Borrego	0	R Johnson and P Harrington (4 and 3)	1
C Cevaer and C Pottier (6 and 4)	1	A Jones and S Mackenzie	0
	1½		2½

Singles

Continent of Europe		Great Britain and Ireland	
O Edmond	½	I Garbutt	½
E Canonica	0	A Coltart (3 and 2)	1
J Greisen (2 holes)	1	D Bathgate	0
M Florioli (1 hole)	1	R Johnson	0
J-E Schapmann (2 and 1)	1	P Harrington	0
C Beautell	½	G McNeill	½
D Borrego (4 and 3)	1	J Payne	0
C Cevaer	0	S Mackenzie (4 and 3)	1
	5		3

Second Day – Foursomes

Continent of Europe		Great Britain and Ireland	
O Edmond and M Florioli	0	A Coltart and J Payne (4 and 3)	1
C Beautell and D Borrego	0	I Garbutt and D Bathgate (4 and 3)	1
J Greisen and J-E Schapmann	0	G McNeill and P Harrington (3 and 1)	1
C Cevaer and C Pottier	0	R Johnson and A Jones (3 and 1)	1
	0		4

Singles

Continent of Europe		Great Britain and Ireland	
M Florioli	0	A Coltart (3 and 2)	1
O Edmond	0	J Payne (1 hole)	1
E Canonica	1/2	R Johnson	1/2
J Greisen	0	I Garbutt (4 and 3)	1
D Borrego (5 and 4)	1	A Jones	0
C Pottier	0	D Bathgate (3 and 2)	1
J-E Schapmann (5 and 4)	1	S Mackenzie	0
C Cevaer	1/2	P Harrington	1/2
	—		—
	3		5

Result: Continent of Europe 9 1/2, Great Britain and Ireland 14 1/2

Great Britain and Ireland *v* Continent of Europe (Youths)

continued

European Boys' Team Championship
at Reykjavik, Iceland

Semi-Finals:

Scotland beat Ireland 4-3
Spain beat England 4-3

Final:

Spain beat Scotland 3-2

European Youths' Team Championship
at I Roveri, Turin

Pos	Country
1	Italy
2	Sweden
3	England
4	Scotland

Scottish Boys' Championship (Stroke Play)
at Monifieth

Name	Score
N Archibald	72-77-71-72–292
G Jack	75-77-75-68–295
G McGlinchey	72-78-75-73–293
G Russell	78-72-72-76–298
C MacDougall	76-78-78-67–299

Scottish Boys' Championship (Match Play)
at West Kilbride

Semi-Finals:

D Keeney beat G Jack 2 holes
B Collier beat R Russell 5 and 3

Final:

B Collier beat D Keeney 2 and 1

Scottish Boys' Under-16 Championship
at West Linton

Name	Score
G Davidson	78-70–148
D Patrick	76-72–148
S Gallacher	79-73–152
R Hall	78-74–152
G Vogwell	76-76–152

English Boys' Stroke Play Championship
at Luffenham Heath, Stamford

Name	Score
M Welch	64-69-74-69–276
S Williams	69-68-74-71–282
L Westwood	70-66-74-73–283
G Harris	70-70-75-71–286
D Harding	71-69-74-72–286
K Saunders	71-70-74-71–286
G Lord	67-76-72-71–286
P Easto	75-71-69-71–286

Irish Boys' Championship
at Kilkenny

Name	Score
R Burns	213

Ulster Boys' Championship
at Cairndhu

Final:

G Sproule beat A Adair at 20th hole

English Boys' County Finals
at Burford, Oxfordshire

Pos	County
1	Lancashire
2	Wiltshire
3	Shropshire and Hereford

Welsh Boys' Championship
at Maesdu, Llandudno

Semi-Finals:

M Ellis beat L Cox 4 and 3
C Sheppard beat A Cooper 2 holes

Final:

M Ellis beat C Sheppard 3 and 2

Welsh Boys' Under-15 Championship
at Llandrindod Wells

Name	Score
R Morgan	71
S Raybould	72
S Austerberry	74

Scottish Youths' Championship
at Portpatrick and Stranraer

Name	Score
S Bannerman	74-65-74–213
P Harrington	73-70-71–214
S Mackenzie	69-66-82–217
C Ronald	73-71-75–219
D Kirkpatrick	76-65-79–220
A Coltart	69-69-82–220

Ulster Youths' Championship
at Royal County Down

Final:

N Crawford beat C Feenan 3 and 2

Scotland Youths *v* Ireland Youths
at Stranraer

Foursomes

Scotland		Ireland	
A Coltart and C Ronald (2 and 1)	1	G McNeil and S Paul	0
S Bannerman and S Henderson (3 and 2)	1	F Howley and P Harrington	0
S Mackenzie and R Russell	1/2	I Walker and K O'Flaherty	1/2
	2 1/2		1/2

Singles

Scotland		Ireland	
A Coltart	1/2	I Walker	1/2
S Mackenzie (2 and 1)	1	S Paul	0
S Henderson	0	G McNeil (5 and 4)	1
R Russell	0	P Harrington (5 and 4)	1
C Ronald	0	F Howley (2 holes)	1
S Bannerman	0	K O'Flaherty (1 hole)	1
	1 1/2		4 1/2

Result: Scotland 4, Ireland 5

Peter McEvoy Trophy
at Copt Heath

Name	Score
P Sherman	76-69-74-71—290
D Cottrell	76-73-71-78—298
N Osmond	75-74-72-78—299
M Ellis	74-72-76-78—300
R Hussey	69-80-79-73—301

Doug Sanders European Junior Championship
at King's Links, Aberdeen

Name	Country	Score
M Welch	England	70-65-67-68–270
A Castelo	Portugal	66-67-71-70–274
D de Vooght	Belgium	72-72-68-68–280
M Ellis	Wales	69-77-66-71–283
N Boyson	Netherlands	72-71-70-70–283
A Berg	Norway	70-69-76-69–284
K Nolan	Ireland	73-74-70-68–285
A Archibald	Scotland	74-71-70-72–287
M Persson	Sweden	75-73-70-70–288
J Dahlstrom	France	71-72-76-70–289

Doug Sanders World Junior Championship
at King's Links, Aberdeen

Name	Country	Score
M Welch	England	66-69-69-72–276
B Ellam	Australia	71-68-72-75–286
C Thompson	Canada	70-72-70-78–290
W Chang	Taiwan	82-72-68-74–296
C Taylor	Australia	76-72-71-77–296
A Castelo	Portugal	78-76-68-75–297
J Chang	USA	75-72-73-78–298

British Girls' Open Amateur Championship
at Penrith

Quarter Finals:

S Cavalleri beat E Knuth at 19th hole
E Valera beat M McKinley 2 holes
L Navarro beat C Hall 5 and 4
B Chretien beat F Fehlaver at 19th hole

Semi-Finals:

S Cavalleri beat L Navarro 6 and 5
E Valera beat B Chretien 4 and 3

Final:

S Cavalleri beat E Valera 5 and 4

English Girls' Championship
at Bolton Old Links, Manchester

Semi-Finals:

C Hall beat J Berry 7 and 5
J Hockley beat K Stupples 3 and 2

Final:

C Hall beat J Hockley at 20th hole

Scottish Girls' Stroke Play Championship
at Portland Course, Royal Troon

Name	Score
J Moodie	73-68-76–217
M McKinlay	77-75-78–230
F McKay	72-79-79–230
V Melvin	71-79-80–230
R MacRae	81-74-77–232

Scottish Girls' Championship (Match Play)
at Duff House Royal, Banff

Quarter Finals:

J Moodie beat C Wilson 3 and 2
V Melvin beat C MacDonald 5 and 3
M McKay beat J Anderson 4 and 3
M McKinlay beat L Brabender 9 and 7

Semi-Finals:

J Moodie beat V Melvin 4 and 3
M McKay beat M McKinlay 3 and 2

Final:

M McKay beat J Moodie 3 and 2

Welsh Girls' Amateur Championship
at Padeswood & Buckley

Semi-Finals:

L Dermott beat R Morgan at 21st hole
N Stroud beat B Jones at 19th hole

Final:

L Dermott beat N Stroud 6 and 4

England v Scotland Schoolgirls
at Hillside

Foursomes: England 3, Scotland 0

Singles: England 4, Scotland 2

Result: England 7, Scotland 2

European Girls' Team Championship
at Shannon

Pos	Country	Pos	Country
1	Sweden	8	Italy
2	England	9	Denmark
3	West Germany	10	Ireland
4	France	11	Netherlands
5	Spain	12	Wales
6	Scotland	13	Norway
7	Belgium	14	Switzerland

Wilson PGA Junior Championship
at Selsdon Park Hotel

Boys Name	Score	Girls Name	Score
M Welch	73-68–141	J Moodie	74-73–147
J Brien	70-74–144	N Buxton	76-77–153
I Pyman	75-71–146	K Rostron	83-75–158
G Bretherton	76-73–149	J Williamson	80-78–158
M Butler	76-73–149	G Doran	78-80–158
I Porthouse	74-75–149	A Rogers	78-80–158
P Easto	73-76–149	J Berry	76-83–159

Winner of Selsdon Park Salvers (*Best gross score of the Championship*)

Boys: 68 M Welch

Girls: 73 J Moodie

Nick Faldo Trophies (*Best gross score in the first round*)

Boys: 70 J Brien

Girls: 74 J Moodie

The Golf Foundation

Chris Plumridge   Press consultant to the Golf Foundation

The first year of the new decade saw the Golf Foundation expanding its activities to cope with the enormous interest in the game from youngsters all over Great Britain and Ireland. The number of schools and junior groups in the Golf Foundation Coaching Scheme increased, as did entries for the Golf Foundation/NatWest Age Group Championships and other sponsored junior events. Indeed the Golf Foundation Calendar of Junior Events listed over 600 opportunities for youngsters to hone their competitive skills at club, county and national levels.

The flagship of the Golf Foundation events, the Team Championship for Schools, attracted entries from over 2000 schools around the world and after the qualifying rounds were completed, 11 teams gathered at St Andrews for the International Final in May. The Old Course was unavailable due to the Open being held on it in July so the 36 holes of the Final were contested over the New Course. Sweden, which had won the R & A Trophy for three consecutive years, were

installed as favourites but it was the team from France which took the honours. Led by Jean-Yan Dusson, whose rounds of 69 and 72 earned him the PGA European Tour Trophy for the best individual score, the French ran away with the title by 14 strokes from Wales. It was yet another significant event in the development of European golf and was emphasised later in the year when another French team defeated America in the Dunhill Cup.

It was during that Dunhill week in October that the world of golf came to St Andrews to pay its last respects to one of the game's great administrators. Since his retirement as Secretary of the R & A in 1983, Keith Mackenzie had been President of the Golf Foundation. He brought to that office the same enthusiasm and commercial acumen he had applied to the promotion of the Open Championship. Travelling the length and breadth of the country, Keith persuaded and cajoled everybody to support the Foundation's work. His battle-cry, delivered in his distinctive

Michael Attenborough, 1990 Captain of the R&A, presents the R&A Trophy to the victorious French team.

© Golf Foundation

Champions all. From left to right: Katy Wrigglesworth (Hornsea), Vicki Hanks (Broome Manor), Tina Poulton (Boyce Hill), Christopher Lane (Kingsthorpe), Gary Harris (Broome Manor), Patrick Collier (Limerick), Sam Walker (Bold-mere).

gravelly voice, was that every golfer should donate the price of half a bottle of tonic water. If they were in Keith's company they would find themselves donating a couple of large gins as well! There is no doubt that his influence was responsible for the increased financial support from the R & A, both for the Foundation's general activities and for the Team Championship for Schools. His death at the age of 69 was a sad loss to the game.

The fourth year of the Golf Foundation/ NatWest Age Group Championships attracted a record entry of over 3000 youngsters. Following regional qualifying rounds, 55 boys and 30 girls won through to the final at Patshull Park. Christopher Lane from Kingsthorpe, who won the Under-15 category in 1989, won the Under-16s this time with two rounds of 75. Tina Poulton of Boyce Hill took the girls' Under-16 title after a play-off with Denbigh's Bethan Jones. The Broome Manor pair of Gary Harris and Vicki Hanks also repeated their victories of the previous year – Gary in the boys Under-15s and Vicki in the girls'. Patrick Collier from Limerick took the boys' Under-14 title with an excellent round

of 74 which was tied by Christopher Leach of Gillingham who lost the play-off. A remarkable 77 from Sam Walker of Boldmere secured the boys' Under-13 section. In the girls' Under-14s, Katy Wrigglesworth from Hornsea, a club which really encourages its juniors, led the way with an 84. All scores were off scratch with no account taken of handicap. Our two Golf Foundation Award winners, Lee Westwood and Lynn McCool continued to distinguish themselves in the game while another previous Award winner, Ian Garbutt, proved his potential by winning the English Amateur Championship.

The present economic conditions mean that the Foundation will have to promote its message even harder but we believe that commerce, industry and golfers everywhere will continue to respond. In the words of Keith Mackenzie, all it takes is the price of half a bottle of tonic from every golfer in the country.

The Golf Foundation, 57 London Road, Enfield, Middlesex EN2 6DU. *Tel*: 081-367 4404 *Fax*: 081-366 5758

Golf Foundation Tournament Winners

Team Championship for Schools

International Final at St Andrews (New Course)

1st France

Lycée Bellevue, Toulouse

Jean-Yan Dusson	144
Nicolas Kalouguine	163
Jean-Jacques Roditti	153
	460

2nd Wales

Neath College, West Glamorgan

Matthew Peet	149
Chris Hanford	161
Andrew Thomas	164
	474

3rd Australia

Ballina High School, New South Wales

Dean Larsson	161
Scott Hayter	152
Justin Saxby	166
	479

4th England

Haslingden High School, Lancashire

Mark Parsons	164
Gary Morton	157
Mathew Andrew	159
	480

5th Sweden

Osterangsskolan, Kristianstad

Ola Cederblad	164
Henrik Johansson	156
Johan Annerfelt	161
	481

6th Scotland

Millburn Academy, Inverness

Murray Urquhart	154
Paul Johnston	172
Gordon McIntosh	157
	483

7th Ireland

Abbey Grammar School, Newry

Raymond Burns	149
Brian Powell	166
Francis O'Connor	175
	490

8th Iceland

Akranes College, Akranes

Hjalti Nielsen	167
Kristinn G Bjarnason	160
Ingi R Gislason	168
	495

9th New Zealand

Hamilton High School, Hamilton

Kent Lyall	165
Terry King	166
Adam Hays	166
	497

10th Netherlands

Rijksscholen Gemeenschap, Brielle

Laura Thijssen	170
Geert Jan Engelsman	168
Ramon v Wingerden	171
	509

11th India

The Modern School, New Delhi

Pawan Pratap	166
Aman Behl	160
Amit Sood	187
	513

Golf Foundation/NatWest Age Group Championships

Grand Final at Patshull Park, Shropshire

Under 16

Boys

Christopher Lane (Kingsthorpe)	75–75—150
Glen Evans (Normanton)	80–75—155
Russell Binney (Newquay)	78–77—155
Andrew McAllister (King's Lynn)	76–79—155
Mark Foster (Kilton Forest)	80–76—156
Jonathan Palmer (Enmore Park)	77–79—156

Girls

Tina Poulton (Boyce Hill)	80–84—164
Bethan Jones (Denbigh)	83–81—164
(Tina Poulton won at 1st hole of sudden death play-off)	
Stacia Scrimshire (Nottingham City)	87–80—167
Sarah Potts (Ely City)	88–83—171

Under 15

Boys

Gary Harris (Broome Manor)	72–79—151
Christopher Rodgers (Royal Mid-Surrey)	77–76—153
Ben Sandry (Exeter)	79–76—155

Girls

Vicki Hanks (Broome Manor)	83–76—159
Georgina Simpson (Cleckheaton)	81–82—163
Lisa McGowan (Coombs Wood)	90–78—168

Under 14

Boys

Patrick Collier (Limerick)	74
Christopher Leach (Gillingham)	74
(Collier won at 1st hole of sudden death play-off)	
Denny Lucas (Worksop)	77
James Davidson (Thornhill)	79

Girls

Katy Wrigglesworth (Hornsea)	84
Kerry Robinson (Ingestre Park)	87
Laura McLardy (Duff House Royal)	87
Anne-Marie Power (Tramore)	93
Emma Sharpe (St Augustines)	93

Under 13

Sam Walker (Boldmere)	77
Paul Dunton (Nevill)	78
Justin Smith (West Essex)	81
Mark Gordon (Pyle & Kenfig)	81

Golf Foundation Team Championship for Schools

for the R & A Trophy

Year	Winner	Country	Venue
1986	Tonbridge School	England	Sunningdale
1987	Klippans Gymnasieskola	Sweden	Foxhills
1988	Klippans Gymnasieskola	Sweden	Sunningdale
1989	Marks Gymnasium	Sweden	St Andrews
1990	Lycée Bellevue	France	St Andrews

Golf Foundation Award Winners

Year	Winner	Club	Year	Winner	Club
1982	Lindsey Anderson	Tain	1988	*Boys* Ian Garbutt	Wheatley
1983	Nigel Osborne Clarke	Shirehampton		*Girls* Lisa Dermott	St Melyd
1984	Wayne Henry	Redbourn	1989	*Boys* Lee Westwood	Worksop
1985	David Grantham	Hull		*Girls* Lynn McCool	Strabane
1986	Matthew Stanford	Saltford	1990	*Boys* Keith Law	Forfar
1987	Jane Marchant	Whittington Barracks		*Girls* Mhairi McKay	Turnberry

Awards

Golf Writers' Association Trophy

Awarded to the man or woman who, in the opinion of Golf Writers, has done most for golf during the year

1951 Max Faulkner
1952 Miss Elizabeth Price
1953 JB Carr
1954 Mrs Roy Smith (Miss Frances Stephens)
1955 Ladies' Golf Union's Touring Team
1956 JC Beharrell
1957 DJ Rees
1958 Harry Bradshaw
1959 Eric Brown
1960 Sir Stuart Goodwin (sponsor of international golf)
1961 Commdr RCT Roe (ex-hon secretary, PGA)
1962 Mrs Marley Spearman, British Ladies' Champion 1961–1962
1963 MSR Lunt, Amateur Champion, 1963
1964 Great Britain and Ireland Team, winners of Eisenhower Trophy – JB Carr (non-playing Captain), MF Bonallack, MSR Lunt, RDBM Shade, R Foster
1965 Gerald Micklem, golf administrator, President, English Golf Union
1966 RDBM Shade, Scottish Amateur Champion for fourth successive year; Eisenhower Trophy Best individual score, 1966; runner-up Amateur Championship, 1966
1967 John Panton
1968 Michael Bonallack
1969 Tony Jacklin
1970 Tony Jacklin
1971 British Walker Cup Team – MF Bonallack, R Carr, R Foster, CW Green, W Humphreys, JS Macdonald, G McGregor, GC Marks, DM Marsh, HB Stuart
1972 Miss Michelle Walker
1973 PA Oosterhuis
1974 PA Oosterhuis
1975 Golf Foundation
1976 Great Britain and Ireland Team, winners of Eisenhower Trophy – Sandy Saddler (non-playing Captain), John Davies, Ian Hutcheon, Mike Kelly, Steve Martin
1977 C O'Connor
1978 Peter McEvoy
1979 S Ballesteros
1980 AWB Lyle
1981 B Langer
1982 G Brand Jr
1983 N Faldo
1984 S Ballesteros
1985 European Ryder Cup Team
1986 Great Britain and Ireland Curtis Cup Team
1987 European Ryder Cup Team
1988 AWB Lyle
1989 British Walker Cup Team – Peter McEvoy, Darren Prosser, Garth McGimpsey, Andrew Hare, Russell Claydon, Craig Cassells, Jim Milligan, Neil Roderick, Stephen Dodd, Eoghan O'Connell
1990 N Faldo

Harry Vardon Trophy

Currently awarded to the PGA member heading the Order of Merit at the end of the season

1937	CA Whitcombe	1967	ME Gregson
1938	TH Cotton	1968	BGC Huggett
1939	RA Whitcombe	1969	B Gallacher
1940–45	*In abeyance*	1970	NC Coles
1946	AD Locke	1971	PA Oosterhuis
1947	NG Von Nida	1972	PA Oosterhuis
1948	CH Ward	1973	PA Oosterhuis
1949	CH Ward	1974	PA Oosterhuis
1950	AD Locke	1975	Dale Hayes
1951	J Panton	1976	S Ballesteros
1952	H Weetman	1977	S Ballesteros
1953	F van Donck	1978	S Ballesteros
1954	AD Locke	1979	AWB Lyle
1955	DJ Rees	1980	AWB Lyle
1956	H Weetman	1981	B Langer
1957	EC Brown	1982	G Norman
1958	BJ Hunt	1983	N Faldo
1959	DJ Rees	1984	B Langer
1960	BJ Hunt	1985	AWB Lyle
1961	C O'Connor	1986	S Ballesteros
1962	C O'Connor	1987	I Woosnam
1963	NC Coles	1988	S Ballesteros
1964	P Alliss	1989	R Rafferty
1965	BJ Hunt	1990	I Woosnam
1966	P Alliss		

Rookie of the Year

1960	T Goodwin	1969	PA Oosterhuis
1961	A Caygill	1970	S Brown
1962	*No Award*	1971	D Llewellyn
1963	A Jacklin	1972	S Torrance
1964	*No Award*	1973	P Elson
1966	R Liddle	1974	C Mason
1967	*No Award*	1975	*No Award*
1968	B Gallacher	1976	M James

1977	N Faldo	1984	AP Parkin
1978	AWB Lyle	1985	P Thomas
1979	MJ Miller	1986	JM Olazabal
1980	P Hoad	1987	P Baker
1981	J Bennett	1988	C Montgomerie
1982	G Brand Jr	1989	P Broadhurst
1983	G Turner	1990	R Claydon

Daily Telegraph Woman Golfer of the Year

(Formerly The Avia Award)

1982	Jane Connachan
1983	Jill Thornhill
1984	Gillian Stewart
	Claire Waite
1985	Belle Robertson
1986	Great Britain and Ireland Curtis Cup Team
1987	Linda Bayman
1988	Great Britain and Ireland Curtis Cup Team
1989	Helen Dobson
1990	Angela Uzielli

Ritz Club-PGA European Tour Golfer of the Year

1987	Ian Woosnam
1988	Severiano Ballesteros
1989	Nick Faldo
1990	Nick Faldo

The US Vardon Trophy

The award is made to the member of the USPGA who completes 80 rounds or more, with the lowest scoring average over the calendar year.

1948	Ben Hogan	1970	Lee Trevino
1949	Sam Snead	1971	Lee Trevino
1950	Sam Snead	1972	Lee Trevino
1951	Lloyd Mangrum	1973	Bruce Crampton
1952	Jack Burke	1974	Lee Trevino
1953	Lloyd Mangrum	1975	Bruce Crampton
1954	Ed Harrison	1976	Don January
1955	Sam Snead	1977	Tom Watson
1956	Cary Middlecoff	1978	Tom Watson
1957	Dow Finsterwald	1979	Tom Watson
1958	Bob Rosburg	1980	Lee Trevino
1959	Art Wall	1981	Tom Kite
1960	Billy Casper	1982	Tom Kite
1961	Arnold Palmer	1983	Ray Floyd
1962	Arnold Palmer	1984	Calvin Peete
1963	Billy Casper	1985	Don Pooley
1964	Arnold Palmer	1986	Scott Hoch
1965	Billy Casper	1987	Dan Pohl
1966	Billy Casper	1988	Chip Beck
1967	Arnold Palmer	1989	Greg Norman
1968	Billy Casper	1990	Greg Norman
1969	Dave Hill		

Bobby Jones Award

Awarded by USGA for distinguished sportsmanship in golf

1955	Francis Ouimet	1974	Byron Nelson
1956	Bill Campbell	1975	Jack Nicklaus
1957	Babe Zaharias	1976	Ben Hogan
1958	Margaret Curtis	1977	Joseph C Dey
1959	Findlay Douglas	1978	Bob Hope and
1960	Charles Evans Jr		Bing Crosby
1961	Joe Carr	1979	Tom Kite
1962	Horton-Smith	1980	Charles Yates
1963	Patty Berg	1981	Mrs JoAnne Carner
1964	Charles Coe	1982	WJ Patton
1965	Mrs Edwin Vare	1983	Mrs Maureen Garrett
1966	Gary Player	1984	J Sigel
1967	Richard Tufts	1985	Fuzzy Zoeller
1968	Robert Dickson	1986	Jess W Sweetser
1969	Gerald Micklem	1987	Tom Watson
1970	Roberto De Vicenzo	1988	Isaac B Grainger
1971	Arnold Palmer	1989	Chi-Chi Rodriquez
1972	Michael Bonallack	1990	Peggy Kirk Bell
1973	Gene Littler	1991	Ben Crenshaw

USPGA Player of the Year Award

1948	Ben Hogan	1970	Billy Casper
1949	Sam Snead	1971	Lee Trevino
1950	Ben Hogan	1972	Jack Nicklaus
1951	Ben Hogan	1973	Jack Nicklaus
1952	Julius Boros	1974	Johnny Miller
1953	Ben Hogan	1975	Jack Nicklaus
1954	Ed Furgol	1976	Jack Nicklaus
1955	Doug Ford	1977	Tom Watson
1956	Jack Burke	1978	Tom Watson
1957	Dick Mayer	1979	Tom Watson
1958	Dow Finsterwald	1980	Tom Watson
1959	Art Wall	1981	Bill Rogers
1960	Arnold Palmer	1982	Tom Watson
1961	Jerry Barner	1983	Hal Sutton
1962	Arnold Palmer	1984	Tom Watson
1963	Julius Boros	1985	Lanny Wadkins
1964	Ken Venturi	1986	Bob Tway
1965	Dave Marr	1987	Paul Azinger
1966	Billy Casper	1988	Curtis Strange
1967	Jack Nicklaus	1989	Tom Kite
1968	*not awarded*	1990	Nick Faldo
1969	Orville Moody		

Arnold Palmer

Awarded to the USPGA leading money-winner

1981	Tom Kite	1986	Greg Norman
1982	Craig Stadler	1987	Paul Azinger
1983	Hal Sutton	1988	Curtis Strange
1984	Tom Watson	1989	Tom Kite
1985	Curtis Strange	1990	Greg Norman

USPGA Player of the Year

1990   Wayne Levi

US Rolex Player of the Year

1980	Beth Daniel
1981	JoAnne Carner
1982	JoAnne Carner
1983	Patty Sheehan
1984	Betsy King
1985	Nancy Lopez
1986	Pat Bradley
1987	Ayako Okamoto
1988	Nancy Lopez
1989	Betsy King
1990	Beth Daniel

US Vare Trophy

		Scoring average
1980	Amy Alcott	71.51
1981	JoAnne Carner	71.75
1982	JoAnne Carner	71.49
1983	JoAnne Carner	71.41
1984	Patty Sheehan	71.40
1985	Nancy Lopez	70.73
1986	Pat Bradley	71.10
1987	Betsy King	71.14
1988	Colleen Walker	71.26
1989	Beth Daniel	70.38
1990	Beth Daniel	70.54

US Gatorade Rookie of the Year

1980	Myra Van Hoose
1981	Patty Sheehan
1982	Patti Rizzo
1983	Stephanie Farwig
1984	Juli Inster
1985	Penny Hammel
1986	Jody Rosenthal
1987	Tammie Green
1988	Liselotte Neumann
1989	Pamela Wright
1990	Hiromi Kobayashi

1991 Schedule of Events

PGA European Tour	WPGA European Tour	GB & Ireland Men's Amateur	GB & Ireland Women's Amateur	USPGA Tour	USLPGA Tour	Others		
							January	
				•			3-6	Tournament of Champions, Carlsbad, California
				•			10-13	Northern Telecom Tucson Open, Tucson, Arizona
				•			17-20	Hawaiian Open, Honolulu
				•			24-27	Phoenix Open, Scottsdale, Arizona
						•	30-2	South African Open, Durban
				•			31-3	AT&T National Pro-Am, Pebble Beach, California
							February	
				•			6-10	Bob Hope Chrysler Classic, Palm Springs, California
						•	7-10	Hong Kong Open, Fanling
						•	7-10	Australian Match Play Championship, Melbourne
				•			14-17	Shearson Lehman Hutton Open, La Jolla, California
						•	14-17	Australian Masters, Melbourne
						•	14-17	Philippine Open, Manila
•							21-24	Barcelona Open, El Prat
				•			21-24	Nissan Los Angeles Open, California
						•	21-24	Singapore Open, Tanah Merah
						•	21-24	Australian PGA Tournament Players Championship, Canberra
•							28-3	Mediterranean Open, Nice, France
				•			28-3	Doral Ryder Open, Miami, Florida
						•	28-3	Malaysia Open, Kuala Lumpur
							March	
•							7-10	Open de Baleares, Son Vida, Majorca
				•			7-10	Honda Classic, Coral Springs, Florida
						•	7-10	New Zealand Open, Wellington
						•	7-10	Indonesia Open, Jakarta
•							14-17	Catalan Open, Bonmont, Tarragona
				•			14-17	Nestlé Invitational, Orlando, Florida
•							21-24	Atlantic Open, Estela, Oporto
				•			21-24	USF & G Classic, New Orleans, Louisiana

PGA European Tour	WPGA European Tour	GB & Ireland Men's Amateur	GB & Ireland Women's Amateur	USPGA Tour	USLPGA Tour	Others	Date	Event
								March cont'd
						•	21-24	Wills India Open, Delhi
•							28-31	Volvo Firenze, Ugolino, Florence
				•			28-31	The Players Championship Ponte Vedra, Florida
					•		28-31	Nabisco Dinah Shore, Rancho Mirage, California
						•	28-31	Thai Open, Bangkok
								April
•							4-7	AGF Open
				•			4-7	Independent Insurance Agent Open, Houston, Texas
		•					6-7	Scottish Champion of Champions, Leven
•							11-14	Jersey Open, La Moye
				•			11-14	**The US Masters, Augusta, Georgia**
				•			11-14	Deposit Guaranty Golf Classic, Hattiesburg, Mississippi
						•	11-14	Republic of China Open, Taipei
		•					17-18	Peter McEvoy Trophy, Copt Heath
•							18-21	Benson and Hedges International Open, St Mellion
	•						18-21	Valextra Classic
				•			18-21	MCI Heritage Classic, Hilton Head Island, South Carolina
						•	18-21	PGA Seniors Championship, Palm Beach Gardens, Florida
						•	18-21	Korean Maekyung Open, Seoul
•							25-28	Madrid Open, Puerta de Hierro
	•						25-28	Ford Ladies' Classic
				•			25-28	K Mart Greater Greensboro Open, Greensboro, North Carolina
						•	25-28	Dunlop Open, Ibaraki, Japan
								May
•							2-5	Crédit Lyonnais Cannes Open, Cannes Mougins
				•			2-5	GTE Byron Nelson Classic, Irving, Texas
		•					4-5	Lytham Trophy, R Lytham & St Annes
		•					4-5	Berkshire Trophy, The Berkshire
•							9-12	Spanish Open, Club de Campo, Madrid
				•			9-12	BellSouth Atlanta Classic, Marietta, Georgia
	•						10-12	Welsh Open Stroke Play Championship, R Porthcawl
	•						11-12	England v Spain, Lindrick
			•				12-14	Welsh Ladies' Close Championship
						•	13-14	Golf Foundation International Schools Final, Sunningdale
			•				14-18	Scottish Ladies' Close Championship, Carnoustie

PGA European Tour	WPGA European Tour	GB & Ireland Men's Amateur	GB & Ireland Women's Amateur	USPGA Tour	USLPGA Tour	Others	Date	Event
							May cont'd	
			•				15-18	Welsh Ladies' Team Championship
•							16-19	Lancia Martini Italian Open, Castelconturbia, Milan
	•						16-19	French Ladies' Open
				•			16-19	Memorial Tournament, Dublin, Ohio
						•	16-19	JPGA Match Play Championship, Shinyo, Gufi
		•					17-19	Brabazon Trophy, Hunstanton
			•				21-25	Irish Ladies' Close Championship, Ballybunion
•							23-26	BMW European Masters
				•			23-26	Southwestern Bell Colonial, Fort Worth, Texas
•							24-27	Volvo PGA Championship, Wentworth
		•					29-30	Lagonda Trophy, Gog Magog
						•	29-31	English Open Seniors Championship, Gerrards Cross/ Denham
•							30-2	Dunhill British Masters, Woburn
				•			30-2	Kemper Open, Potomac, Maryland
						•	30-2	Northern Open
							June	
		•					1-2	St Andrews Links Trophy
						•	5	Youths England v Scotland, Woodhall Spa
	•						5-8	Swiss Ladies' Classic
		•					6-8	Commonwealth Tournament, Northumberland
						•	6-8	Youths' Championship, Woodhall Spa
•							6-9	Murphy's Cup, Fulford, York
				•			6-9	Buick Classic, Rye, New York
			•				11-15	Ladies' British Open Amateur Championship, Pannal
•							13-16	Belgian Open, Royal Waterloo, Brussels
	•						13-16	Hennessy Ladies' Cup
				•			13-16	**US Open, Chaska, Minnesota**
						•	13-16	THF PGA Seniors, Wollaton Park
		•					13-16	Scottish Amateur Stroke Play Championship
•							20-23	Carrolls Irish Open, Killarney, Co Kerry
	•						20-23	Trophée Coconut Skol
				•			20-23	Anhauser-Busch Classic, Kingsmill, Virginia
		•					26-30	European Men's Team Championship, Puerta de Hierro
•							27-30	Peugeot French Open, National Golf Course, Paris
				•			27-30	Federal Express St Jude Classic, Germantown, Tennessee

PGA European Tour	WPGA European Tour	GB & Ireland Men's Amateur	GB & Ireland Women's Amateur	USPGA Tour	USLPGA Tour	Others	Date	Event
							June cont'd	
					•		27-30	Mazda LPGA Championship, Bethesda, Maryland
		•					28-29	Midland Open Amateur Championship, Little Aston/Sutton Coldfield
			•				29-30	Welsh Ladies' Open Stroke Play Championship
							July	
						•	**2-5**	Wilson Club Professional Championship, Kings Lynn
•							3-6	Torras Monte Carlo Open, Mont Agel
				•			4-7	Centel Western Open, Oak Brook, Illinois
•		•					8	Open Championship Regional Qualifying
•							10-13	Bell's Scottish Open, Gleneagles
	•						10-14	European Ladies' Championship, Wentworth
		•					**10-14**	European Boys' Team Championship, Oslo
•							11-14	Seniors British Open, R Lytham & St Annes
	•						11-14	Bloor Homes Eastleigh Classic, Fleming Park
				•			11-14	Bank of Boston Classic, Sutton, Massachusetts
					•		**11-14**	**US Women's Open Championship, Colonial CC, Fort Worth, Texas**
•		•					14-15	Open Championship Final Qualifying
•				•			**18-21**	**120th Open Championship, R Birkdale, Southport**
				•			18-21	Chattanooga Classic, Hixson, Tennessee
		•					**23-25**	Carris Trophy, Long Ashton
•							25-28	KLM Dutch Open, Noordwijk, Leiden
•							25-28	Lufthansa German Open
				•			25-28	Canon Greater Hartford Open, Cromwell, Connecticut
						•	**25-28**	US PGA Seniors Open Championship, Detroit, Michigan
		•					29-3	English Amateur Championship, Formby
		•					29-3	Scottish Amateur Championship, Downfield
							August	
•							1-4	Scandinavian Masters, Stockholm
	•						**1-4**	**Weetabix British Open, Woburn**
				•			1-4	Buick Open, Grand Blanc, Michigan
		•					7-9	Seniors Championship, Prestwick/Prestwick St Nicholas
			•				**7-9**	Girls' Internationals, Whitchurch
		•					**8-9**	Boys' Internationals, Montrose Links
•							8-11	European Pro-Celebrity

PGA European Tour	WPGA European Tour	GB & Ireland Men's Amateur	GB & Ireland Women's Amateur	USPGA Tour	USLPGA Tour	Others	Date	Event
							August cont'd	
				•			8-11	**PGA Championship, Indianapolis, Indiana**
		•					10	Boys' International: GB&I v Continent of Europe, Montrose Links
	•						10-14	Irish Amateur Close Championship, Ballybunion
		•					12-16	Boys' Championship, Montrose Links
		•					13-16	Girls' British Open Amateur Championship, Whitchurch
•							15-18	NM English Open, The Belfry
•							15-18	Swedish Open
				•			15-18	The International, Castle Rock, Colorado
						•	15-18	JPGA Championship, Osaka
		•					16-17	Youths' International: GB & Ireland v Continent of Europe, Dalmahoy
		•					19-20	Golf Foundation/NatWest Championships, Patshull Park
		•					19-22	Peugeot PGA Assistants' Championship, Wentworth
			•				21-23	Ladies' British Open Amateur Stroke Play Championship, Long Ashton
•							22-25	Volvo German Open, Hubbelrath, Dusseldorf
	•						22-25	European Open
		•					22-25	International European Amateur Championship, Hillside
				•			22-25	NEC World Series of Golf, Akron, Ohio
		•					29-30	PGA Junior Championship, Selsdon Park
•							29-1	Variety Club Classic
				•			29-1	Greater Milwaukee Open, Franklin, Wisconsin
•							29-1	GA European Open, Walton Heath
							September	
			•				4-6	Women's Home Internationals, Aberdovey
		•					5-6	**Walker Cup, Portmarnock**
•							5-8	European Masters – Swiss Open, Crans-sur-Sierre
	•						5-8	TEC Players Championship
				•			5-8	Canadian Open, Oakville, Ontario
		•					6-7	English Champion Club Tournament, Porters Park
		•					10-15	**Amateur Championship, Ganton/Scarborough North Cliff**
•							12-15	Lancôme Trophy, St Nom la Breteche, Paris
•							12-15	Irish Open
				•			12-15	Hardee's Golf Classic, Coal Valley, Illinois
•							16-17	Equity & Law Challenge, Royal Mid-Surrey
•							19-22	Epson Grand Prix, St Pierre, Chepstow
•							19-22	Italian Open

PGA European Tour	WPGA European Tour	GB & Ireland Men's Amateur	GB & Ireland Women's Amateur	USPGA Tour	USLPGA Tour	Others		
							September cont'd	
				•			19-22	BC Open, Endicott, New York
			•				20-21	Vagliano Trophy, Nairn
		•					22	English County Champions Tournament, Clitheroe
		•					25-27	Home Internationals, Co Sligo
•							26-29	Austrian Open, Gut Altentann, Salzburg
				•			26-29	Buick Southern Open, Columbus, Ohio
•							27-29	**Johnnie Walker Ryder Cup, Kiawah Island, South Carolina**
							October	
			•				1-2	Senior Ladies British Open Amateur Championship, Ladybank
•							3-6	Mercedes German Masters, Stuttgart
				•			3-6	Texas Open, San Antonio
					•		3-6	Centel Classic, Tallahassee, Florida
		•					4-6	English County Finals, R Liverpool
				•			9-13	Las Vegas Invitational, Las Vegas
•							10-13	Dunhill Cup, St Andrews
•			•				10-13	Trophée Urban – World Championship, Cely, Paris
						•	10-13	Japan Open
						•	16-18	PGA European Team Championship, La Manga
				•			16-19	Walt Disney World/Oldsmobile Classic, Orlando, Florida
•							17-20	World Match Play, Wentworth
	•						17-20	Woolmark Ladies Match Play Championship
•							24-27	Volvo Masters, Valderrama, Spain
•							24-27	Biarritz Open
				•			24-27	US Tour Championship
•							31-3	World Cup, Rome
							November	
•							7-10	Asahi Glass Four Tours World Championship of Golf
•	•						7-10	Benson and Hedges Trophy (Mixed Team)
•							9-14	PGA European Tour Qualifying School
•							31-3	Longines Classic
							December	
					•		12-15	Itoman LPGA Match Play Championship, Kauai, Hawaii
						•	13-15	US Seniors New York Life Championship, Puerto Rico
						•	19-22	Johnnie Walker World Championship of Golf, Jamaica

Royal & Ancient Venues and Dates for Championships in 1991–3

	1991	1992	1993

The Youths' Championship

Internationals	5 June Woodhall Spa	3 June Northumberland	2 June Glasgow Gailes
Championship	6–8 June Woodhall Spa	4–6 June Northumberland	3–5 June Glasgow Gailes

St Andrews Trophy

	–	26–7 June R Cinque Ports	–

The Open Championship

Regional qualifying competitions	8 July Blackwell Deer Park Hankley Common Langley Park Ormskirk Orsett Sherwood Forest	TBA	TBA
Final qualifying competitions	14–15 July Hesketh Hillside Southport & Ainsdale West Lancashire	12–13 July Dunbar Gullane Luffness New North Berwick	11–12 July R Cinque Ports Prince's Littlestone North Foreland
Championship	18–21 July R Birkdale	16–19 July Hon Company of Edinburgh Golfers (Muirfield)	15–18 July R St George's

The Seniors' Championship

	7–9 Aug Preswick/Prestwick St Nicholas	5–7 Aug Ipswich (Purdis Heath)/Woodbridge	4–6 Aug R Aberdeen/Murcar

	1991	**1992**	**1993**

The Boys' Championship

	1991	1992	1993
Internationals	8–10 Aug Montrose Links	6–8 Aug R Mid-Surrey	5–7 Aug Glenbervie
Championship	12–16 Aug Montrose Links	10–14 Aug R Mid-Surrey	9–13 Aug Glenbervie

The Walker Cup

5–6 Sept Portmarnock	–	18–19 Aug Chicago, Illinois

The Amateur Championship

10–15 Sept Ganton/Scarborough North Cliff	31 Aug–5 Sept Carnoustie (Championship)/ Panmure	6–11 Sept R Portush/Dunluce & Valley

Espirito Santo Trophy

–	1–4 Oct Marine Drive, Vancouver	–

Eisenhower Trophy

–	8–11 Oct Capiland, Vancouver	–

Part II
Past Tournament Results

The Major Championships

The Open Golf Championship

The Belt

Year	Winner	Score	Venue	Entrants
1860	W Park, Musselburgh	174	Prestwick	8
1861	T Morris, Sr, Prestwick	163	Prestwick	12
1862	T Morris, Sr, Prestwick	163	Prestwick	6
1863	W Park, Musselburgh	168	Prestwick	14
1864	T Morris, Sr, Prestwick	167	Prestwick	6
1865	A Strath, St Andrews	162	Prestwick	10
1866	W Park, Musselburgh	169	Prestwick	12
1867	T Morris, Sr, St Andrews	170	Prestwick	10
1868	T Morris, Jr, St Andrews	157	Prestwick	10
1869	T Morris, Jr, St Andrews	154	Prestwick	8
1870	T Morris, Jr, St Andrews	149	Prestwick	17

The Belt having been won thrice in succession by young Tom Morris, it became his property, and the Championship remained in abeyance for one year, when the present cup was offered for yearly competition.

The Cup

Year	Winner	Score	Venue	Entrants
1872	T Morris, Jr, St Andrews	166	Prestwick	8
1873	T Kidd, St Andrews	179	St Andrews	26
1874	M Park, Musselburgh	159	Musselburgh	32
1875	W Park, Musselburgh	166	Prestwick	18
1876	B Martin, St Andrews	176	St Andrews	34
(D Strath tied but refused to play off)				
1877	J Anderson, St Andrews	160	Musselburgh	24
1878	J Anderson, St Andrews	157	Prestwick	26
1879	J Anderson, St Andrews	169	St Andrews	46
1880	B Ferguson, Musselburgh	162	Musselburgh	30
1881	B Ferguson, Musselburgh	170	Prestwick	22
1882	B Ferguson, Musselburgh	171	St Andrews	40
1883	W Fernie, Dumfries	159	Musselburgh	41
After a tie with B Ferguson, Musselburgh				
1884	J Simpson, Carnoustie	160	Prestwick	30
1885	B Martin, St Andrews	171	St Andrews	51
1886	D Brown, Musselburgh	157	Musselburgh	46
1887	W Park, Jr, Musselburgh	161	Prestwick	36
1888	J Burns, Warwick	171	St Andrews	53
1889	W Park, Jr, Musselburgh	155	Musselburgh	42
After a tie with A Kirkaldy				
1890	J Ball, Royal Liverpool (Am)	164	Prestwick	40
1891	H Kirkaldy, St Andrews	166	St Andrews	82
After 1891 the competition was extended to 72 holes and for the first time entry money was imposed				
1892	H Hilton, Royal Liverpool (Am)	305	Muirfield	66
1893	W Auchterlonie, St Andrews	322	Prestwick	72
1894	J Taylor, Winchester	326	Sandwich, R St George's	94
1895	J Taylor, Winchester	322	St Andrews	73
1896	H Vardon, Ganton	316	Muirfield	64

After a tie with J Taylor. Play-off scores for 36 holes: H Vardon 157; Taylor 161

Year	Winner	Score	Venue	Entrants
1897	H Hilton, Royal Liverpool (Am)	314	Hoylake, R Liverpool	86
1898	H Vardon, Ganton	307	Prestwick	78
1899	H Vardon, Ganton	310	Sandwich, R St George's	98
1900	J Taylor, Mid-Surrey	309	St Andrews	81
1901	J Braid, Romford	309	Muirfield	101
1902	A Herd, Huddersfield	307	Hoylake, R Liverpool	112
1903	H Vardon, Totteridge	300	Prestwick	127
1904	J White, Sunningdale	296	Sandwich, R St George's	144
1905	J Braid, Walton Heath	318	St Andrews	152
1906	J Braid, Walton Heath	300	Muirfield	183
1907	A Massy, La Boulie	312	Hoylake, R Liverpool	193

The Open Golf Championship

continued

Year	Winner	Score	Venue	Qual	Ents
1908	J Braid, Walton Heath	291	Prestwick	180	
1909	J Taylor, Mid-Surrey	295	Deal, R Cinque Ports	204	
1910	J Braid, Walton Heath	299	St Andrews	210	
1911	H Vardon, Totteridge	303	Sandwich, R St George's	226	

After a tie with A Massy. The tie was over 36 holes, but Massy picked up at the 35th hole before holing out. He had taken 148 for 34 holes, and when Vardon holed out at the 35th hole his score was 143.

Year	Winner	Score	Venue	Qual	Ents
1912	E Ray, Oxhey	295	Muirfield	215	
1913	J Taylor, Mid-Surrey	304	Hoylake, R Liverpool	269	
1914	H Vardon, Totteridge	306	Prestwick	194	
1915-19	*No Championship owing to the Great War*				
1920	G Duncan, Hanger Hill	303	Deal, R Cinque Ports	81	190
1921	J Hutchison, Glenview, Chicago	296	St Andrews	85	158

After a tie with R Wethered (Am). Royal and Ancient-Play-off scores: Hutchison 150; Wethered 159.

Year	Winner	Score	Venue	Qual	Ents
1922	W Hagen, Detroit, USA	300	Sandwich, R St George's	80	225
1923	A Havers, Coombe Hill	295	Troon	88	222
1924	W Hagen, Detroit, USA	301	Hoylake, R Liverpool	86	277
1925	J Barnes, USA	300	Prestwick	83	200
1926	R Jones, USA (Am)	291	R Lytham and St Annes	117	293
1927	R Jones, USA (Am)	285	St Andrews	108	207
1928	W Hagen, USA	292	Sandwich, R St George's	113	271
1929	W Hagen, USA	292	Muirfield	109	242
1930	R Jones, USA (Am)	291	Hoylake, R Liverpool	112	296
1931	T Armour, USA	296	Carnoustie	109	215
1932	G Sarazen, USA	283	Sandwich, Prince's	110	224
1933	D Shute, USA	292	St Andrews	117	287

After a tie with C Wood, USA-Play-off scores: Shute 149; Wood 154.

Year	Winner	Score	Venue	Qual	Ents
1934	T Cotton, Waterloo, Belgium	283	Sandwich, R St George's	101	312
1935	A Perry, Leatherhead	283	Muirfield	109	264
1936	A Padgham, Sundridge Park	287	Hoylake, R Liverpool	107	286
1937	T Cotton, Ashridge	290	Carnoustie	141	258
1938	R Whitcombe, Parkstone	295	Sandwich, R St George's	120	268
1939	R Burton, Sale	290	St Andrews	129	254
1940-45	*No Championship owing to Second World War*				
1946	S Snead, USA	290	St Andrews	100	225
1947	F Daly, Balmoral	293	Hoylake, R Liverpool	100	263
1948	T Cotton, Royal Mid-Surrey	284	Muirfield	97	272
1949	A Locke, South Africa	283	Sandwich, R St George's	96	224

After a tie with H Bradshaw, Kilcroney-Play-off scores: Locke 135; Bradshaw 147.

Year	Winner	Score	Venue	Qual	Ents
1950	A Locke, South Africa	279	Troon	93	262
1951	M Faulkner, GB	285	R Portrush	98	180
1952	A Locke, South Africa	287	R Lytham and St Annes	96	275
1953	B Hogan, USA	282	Carnoustie	91	196

The Open Golf
Championship
continued

Year	Winner	Score	Venue	Qual	Ents
1954	P Thomson, Australia	283	Birkdale	97	349
1955	P Thomson, Australia	281	St Andrews	94	301
1956	P Thomson, Australia	286	Hoylake,		
			R Liverpool	96	360
1957	A Locke, South Africa	279	St Andrews	96	282
1958	P Thomson, Australia	278	R Lytham and		
			St Annes	96	362

After a tie with D Thomas, Sudbury-Play-off scores: Thomson 139; Thomas 143.

1959	G Player, South Africa	284	Muirfield	90	285
1960	K Nagle, Australia	278	St Andrews	74	410
1961	A Palmer, USA	284	Birkdale	101	364
1962	A Palmer, USA	276	Troon	119	379
1963	R Charles, New Zealand	277	R Lytham and		
			St Annes	119	261

After a tie with P Rodgers, USA-Play-off scores: Charles 140; Rodgers 148

1964	T Lema, USA	279	St Andrews	119	327
1965	P Thomson, Australia	285	R Birkdale	130	372
1966	J Nicklaus, USA	282	Muirfield	130	310
1967	R De Vicenzo, Argentina	278	Hoylake,		
			R Liverpool	130	326
1968	G Player, South Africa	289	Carnoustie	130	309
1969	A Jacklin, GB	280	R Lytham and		
			St Annes	129	424
1970	J Nicklaus USA	283	St Andrews	134	468

After a tie with Doug Sanders, USA-Play-off scores: Nicklaus 72; Sanders 73.

1971	L Trevino, USA	278	R Birkdale	150	528
1972	L Trevino, USA	278	Muirfield	150	570
1973	T Weiskopf, USA	276	Troon	150	569
1974	G Player, South Africa	282	R Lytham and		
			St Annes	150	679
1975	T Watson, USA	279	Carnoustie	150	629

After a tie with J Newton. Australia-Play-off scores: Watson 71; Newton 72.

1976	J Miller, USA	279	R Birkdale	150	719
1977	T Watson, USA	268	Turnberry	150	730
1978	J Nicklaus, USA	281	St Andrews	150	788
1979	S Ballesteros, Spain	283	R Lytham and		
			St Annes	150	885
1980	T Watson, USA	271	Muirfield	151	994
1981	B Rogers, USA	276	Sandwich, R		
			St George's	153	971
1982	T Watson, USA	284	R Troon	176	1,121
1983	T Watson, USA	275	R Birkdale	151	1,107
1984	S Ballesteros, Spain	276	St Andrews		1,413
1985	A Lyle, GB	282	Sandwich, R		
			St George's	149	1,361
1986	G Norman, Australia	280	Turnberry	152	1,347
1987	N Faldo, GB	279	Muirfield	153	1,407
1988	S Ballesteros, Spain	273	R Lytham and		
			St Annes	153	1,393
1989	M Calcavecchia, USA	275	R Troon	156	1,481

After a tie with W Grady,. Australia, and G Norman, Australia-Calcavecchia won a 4-hole play-off.

1990	N Faldo, GB	270	St Andrews	152	1,707

1981 at Sandwich, R St George's

Entries 972. Qualifying aggregates: 146 Littlestone. 146 North Foreland. 148 Princes. 144 Deal. Qualified for final 36 holes: 82 competitors (75 Professionals, 7 Amateurs) with scores of 150 and below. Qualified for final 18 holes: 61 competitors (59 Professionals, 2 Amateurs) with scores of 222 and below.

Name	Score	Prize Money £
B Rogers (USA)	72, 66, 67, 71-276	25,000
B Langer (WG)	73, 67, 70, 70-280	17,500
R Floyd (USA)	74, 70, 69, 70-283	11,750
M James (GB)	72, 70, 68, 73-283	11,750
S Torrance (GB)	72, 69, 73, 70-284	8,500
B Lietzke (USA)	76, 69, 71, 69-285	7,750
M Pinero (Spa)	73, 74, 68, 70-285	7,750
H Clark (GB)	72, 76, 70, 68-286	6,500
B Crenshaw (USA)	72, 67, 76, 71-286	6,500
B Jones (GB)	73, 76, 66, 71-286	6,500
L Trevino (USA)	77, 67, 70, 73-287	5,000
N Faldo (GB)	77, 68, 69, 73-287	5,000
I Aoki (Jpn)	71, 73, 69, 74-287	5,000
E Darcy (Ire)	79, 69, 70, 70-288	3,240
A Lyle (GB)	73, 73, 71, 71-288	3,240

The Open Golf Championship
continued

Name	Score	Prize Money £
D Graham (Aus)	71, 71, 74, 72-288	3,240
B Barnes (GB)	76, 70, 70, 72-288	3,240
N Job (GB)	70, 69, 75, 74-288	3,240
G Marsh (Aus)	75, 71, 72, 71-289	2,013
G Brand (GB)	78, 65, 74, 72-289	2,013
P Townsend (GB)	73, 70, 73, 73-289	2,013
J Pate (USA)	73, 73, 69, 74-289	2,013
M McNulty (SA)	74, 74, 74, 68-290	1,218
N Price (Zim)	77, 68, 76, 69-290	1,218
H Green (USA)	75, 72, 74, 69-290	1,218
J Nicklaus (USA)	83, 66, 71, 70-290	1,218
A Palmer (USA)	72, 74, 73, 71-290	1,218
T Watson (USA)	73, 69, 75, 73-290	1,218
A Jacklin (GB)	71, 71, 73, 75-290	1,218
S Owen (NZ)	71, 74, 70, 75-290	1,218
J Morgan (GB)	77, 72, 73, 69-291	875
G Norman (Aus)	72, 75, 72, 72-291	875
D Smyth (Ire)	77, 67, 73, 74-291	875
T Powell (GB)	75, 68, 73, 75-291	875

Other Totals

T Horton (GB), E Dunk (Aus), B Charles (NZ), M Ozaki (Jpn) 292; S Ballesteros (Spa), F Molina (Arg), N Coles (GB), R Davis (Aus), J Miller (USA) 293; K Brown (GB), R Streck (USA), T Gale (Aus) 294; J Gonzales (Bra), M O'Meara (USA), H Sutton (USA) (Am) 295; D Jones (GB), D Thorpe (GB), B Waites (GB) 296; E Polland (Ire), G Cullen (GB), M Ferguson (GB) 297; N Hunt (GB), W Humphreys (GB) 298; J O'Leary (Ire), D Stewart (GB), G Godwin (GB) (Am) 299; D McLean (USA) 300.

1982 at R Troon

Entries 1,121. Qualifying aggregates: 144 Glasgow Gailes. 143 Kilmarnock (Barassie). 140 Prestwick St Nicholas. 145 Western Gailes. Qualified for final 36 holes: 90 competitors (89 Professionals, 1 Amateur) with scores of 152 and below. Qualified for final 18 holes: 60 competitors (59 Professionals, 1 Amateur) with scores of 226 and below.

Name	Score	Prize Money £
T Watson (USA)	69, 71, 74, 70-284	32,000
P Oosterhuis (GB)	74, 67, 74, 70-285	19,300
N Price (SA)	69, 69, 74, 73-285	19,300
T Purtzer (USA)	76, 66, 75, 69-286	11,000
N Faldo (GB)	73, 73, 71, 69-286	11,000
M Kuramoto (Jpn)	71, 73, 71, 71-286	11,000
D Smyth (Ire)	70, 69, 74, 73-286	11,000
F Zoeller (USA)	73, 71, 73, 70-287	8,750
A Lyle (GB)	74, 66, 73, 74-287	8,750
J Nicklaus (USA)	77, 70, 72, 69-288	7,350
B Clampett (USA)	67, 66, 78, 77-288	7,350
S Torrance (GB)	73, 72, 73, 71-289	6,300
S Ballesteros (Spa)	71, 75, 73, 71-290	5,400
B Langer (WG)	70, 69, 78, 73-290	5,400
R Floyd (USA)	74, 73, 77, 67-291	3,900
C Strange (USA)	72, 73, 76, 70-291	3,900
B Crenshaw (USA)	74, 75, 72, 70-291	3,900
D Watson (GB)	75, 69, 73, 74-291	3,900
K Brown (GB)	70, 71, 79, 72-292	2,900
T Nakamura (Jpn)	77, 68, 77, 71-293	2,500
I Aoki (Jpn)	75, 69, 75, 74-293	2,500
JM Canizares (Spa)	71, 72, 79, 72-294	2,200
J Miller (USA)	71, 76, 75, 72-294	2,200
B Rogers (USA)	73, 70, 76, 75-294	2,200
G Marsh (Aus)	76, 76, 72, 71-295	1,950
B Gallacher (GB)	75, 71, 74, 75-295	1,950
J Haas (USA)	78, 72, 75, 71-296	1,600
G Norman (Aus)	73, 75, 76, 72-296	1,600
A Palmer (USA)	71, 73, 78, 74-296	1,600
L Trevino (USA)	78, 72, 71, 75-296	1,600
D Graham (Aus)	73, 70, 76, 77-296	1,600
L Nelson (USA)	77, 69, 77, 74-297	1,200
M Thomas (GB)	72, 74, 75, 76-297	1,200
M Miller (Sco)	74, 72, 78, 73-297	1,200

Other Totals

E Darcy (Ire), J Ferenz (USA), P Way (GB), C Stadler (USA), B Barnes (GB), D Russell (GB) 298;
H Henning (SA) 299; B Shearer (NZ), M Lewis (GB) (Am), G Player (SA), T Gale (Aus), N Coles
(GB) 300; B Longmuir (GB), T Britz (USA), R Chapman (GB), B Waites (GB) 301; M James (GB),
H Sheng-San (Tai), M Pinero (Spa) 302; M McNulty (Zim), P Townsend (GB), M Poxton (GB),
K Waters (GB) 303; P Harrison (GB) 304; M King (GB) 305; M Cahill (Aus) 306.

The Open Golf Championship

continued

1983 at R Birkdale

Entries 1,107. Qualifying aggregates: 143 Hesketh. 145 Southport and Ainsdale. 147 Hillside. 148
West Lancs. Qualified for final 36 holes: 83 competitors (all Professionals) with scores of 146 and
below. Qualified for final 18 holes: 63 competitors with scores of 217 and below.

Name	Score	Prize Money £
T Watson (USA)	67, 68, 70, 70-275	40,000
H Irwin (USA)	69, 68, 72, 67-276	23,000
A Bean (USA)	70, 69, 70, 67-276	23,000
G Marsh (Aus)	69, 70, 74, 64-277	15,000
L Trevino (USA)	69, 66, 73, 70-278	13,600
S Ballesteros (Spa)	71, 71, 69, 68-279	12,500
H Henning (SA)	71, 69, 70, 69-279	12,250
D Durnian (GB)	73, 66, 74, 67-280	9,625
C O'Connor, Jr (Ire)	72, 69, 71, 68-280	9,625
B Rogers (USA)	67, 71, 73, 69-280	9,625
N Faldo (GB)	68, 68, 71, 73-280	9,625
P Jacobsen (USA)	72, 69, 70, 70-281	7,250
C Stadler (USA)	64, 70, 72, 75-281	7,250
M Sullivan (USA)	72, 68, 74, 68-282	5,040
G Koch (USA)	75, 71, 66, 70-282	5,040
F Zoeller (USA)	71, 71, 67, 73-282	5,040
R Floyd (USA)	72, 66, 69, 75-282	5,040
D Graham (Aus)	71, 69, 67, 75-282	5,040
G Norman (Aus)	75, 71, 70, 67-283	2,957
H Green (USA)	69, 74, 72, 68-283	2,957
T Britz (SA)	71, 74, 69, 69-283	2,957
B Waites (GB)	70, 70, 73, 70-283	2,957
B Gallacher (GB)	72, 71, 70, 70-283	2,957
S Hobday (SA)	70, 73, 70, 70-283	2,957
J Haas (USA)	73, 72, 68, 70-283	2,957
E Darcy (Ire)	69, 72, 74, 69-284	2,150
H Clark (GB)	71, 72, 69, 72-284	2,150
R Davis (Aus)	70, 71, 70, 73-284	2,150

Other Totals

C-S Lu (Tai), L Wadkins (USA), J Nicklaus (USA), T Kite (USA), M McCullough (USA), H Sutton
(USA), M James (GB), T Nakamura (Jpn), C Strange (USA), T Gale (Aus) 285; A Jacklin (GB),
K Arai (Jpn), B Gilder (USA), V Fernandez (Arg), C Moody (GB), I Collins (GB) 286; C Tucker
(GB), M Muramoto (Jpn), M Pinero (Spa), G Burroughs (GB), T Weiskopf (USA), V Somers (Aus),
T Simpson (USA), M McNulty (Zim) 287; B Clampett (USA), L Nelson (USA), S Torrance (GB) 288;
B Langer (WG), A Palmer (USA), M Johnson (GB) 289; M Calero (Spa), J O'Leary (Ire) 290;
R Rafferty (Ire) 291; M Ingham (GB) 292; Y-S Hseih (Tai) 295.

1984 at St Andrews

Entries 1,413. Regional qualifying courses: Glenbervie, Pleasington, Lindrick, Little Aston,
Porters Park, Camberley Heath. Final qualifying courses: Ladybank, Leven, Lundin, Scotscraig.
Qualified for final 36 holes: 94 competitors (92 Professionals, 2 Amateurs) with scores of 148 and
below. Qualified for final 18 holes: 63 competitors with scores of 219 and below.

Name	Score	Prize Money £
S Ballesteros (Spa)	69, 68, 70, 69-276	55,000
B Langer (W Ger)	71, 68, 68, 71-278	31,900
T Watson (USA)	71, 68, 66, 73-278	31,900
F Couples (USA)	70, 69, 74, 68-281	19,800
L Wadkins (USA)	70, 69, 73, 69-281	19,800
N Faldo (GB)	69, 68, 76, 69-282	16,390
G Norman (Aus)	67, 74, 74, 67-282	16,390
M McCumber (USA)	74, 67, 72, 70-283	14,300
G Marsh (Aus)	70, 74, 73, 67-284	11,264
S Torrance (GB)	74, 74, 66, 70-284	11,264
R Rafferty (Ire)	74, 72, 67, 71-284	11,264
H Baiocchi (SA)	72, 70, 70, 72-284	11,264
I Baker-Finch (Aus)	68, 66, 71, 79-284	11,264

The Open Golf Championship
continued

Name	Score	Prize Money £
A Lyle (GB)	75, 71, 72, 67-285	6,751
K Brown (GB)	74, 71, 72, 68-285	6,751
A Bean (USA)	72, 69, 75, 69-285	6,751
F Zoeller (USA)	71, 72, 71, 71-285	6,751
P Senior (Aus)	74, 70, 70, 71-285	6,751
W Bergin (USA)	75, 73, 66, 71-285	6,751
H Irwin (USA)	75, 68, 70, 72-285	6,751
L Trevino (USA)	70, 67, 75, 73-285	6,751
C Pavin (USA)	71, 74, 72, 69-286	3,850
B Crenshaw (USA)	72, 75, 70, 69-286	3,850
T Kite (USA)	69, 71, 74, 72-286	3,850
P Way (GB)	73, 72, 69, 72-286	3,850
P Jacobsen (USA)	67, 73, 73, 73-286	3,850
G Morgan (USA)	71, 71, 71, 73-286	3,850
T Gale (Aus)	71, 74, 72, 70-287	2,970
J Gonzales (Bra)	69, 71, 76, 71-287	2,970
C Stadler (USA)	75, 70, 70, 72-287	2,970

Other Totals

P Parkin (GB), R Drummond (GB), B Gallacher (GB), J Miller (USA), J Nicklaus (USA) 288;
M Pinero (Spa), J Haas (USA), G Levenson (SA), J Heggarty (GB), E Murray (GB), D Dunk (GB),
T Nakajima (Jpn), JM Canizares (Spa) 289; N Price (SA), M Poxon (GB), M James (GB) 290; M
Calero (Spain), I Aoki (Jpn), D Frost (SA), R Charles (NZ), R Chapman (GB), H Clark (GB),
J Chillas (GB), R Boxall (GB) 292; M Mackenzie (GB), D Russell (GB), W Longmuir (GB),
E Rodriguez (Spa) 293; S Fujiki (Jpn) 294; J Garner (GB), G Koch (USA), R Hartman (USA),
N Ozaki (Jpn) 295.

1985 at Sandwich, R St George's

Entries 1,361. Regional qualifying courses: Camberley Heath, Glenbervie, Lindrick, Little Aston,
Pleasington, Porters Park, Wildernesse. Final qualifying courses: Royal Cinque Ports Deal,
Littlestone, North Foreland. Qualified for final 36 holes: 85 (83 Professionals, 2 Amateurs) with
scores of 149 and below. Qualified for final 18 holes: 60 (59 Professionals, 1 Amateur) with scores
of 221 and below.

Name	Score	Prize Money £
A Lyle (GB)	68, 71, 73, 70-282	65,000
P Stewart (USA)	70, 75, 70, 68-283	40,000
J Rivero (Spa)	74, 72, 70, 68-284	23,600
C O'Connor Jr (Ire)	64, 76, 72, 72-284	23,600
M O'Meara (USA)	70, 72, 70, 72-284	23,600
D Graham (Aus)	68, 71, 70, 75-284	23,600
B Langer (W Ger)	72, 69, 68, 75-284	23,600
A Forsbrand (Swe)	70, 70, 69, 70-285	15,566
DA Weibring (USA)	69, 71, 74, 71-285	15,566
T Kite (USA)	73, 73, 67, 72-285	15,566
E Darcy (Ire)	76, 68, 74, 68-286	11,400
G Koch (USA)	75, 72, 70, 69-286	11,400
JM Canizares (Spa)	72, 75, 70, 69-286	11,400
F Zoeller (USA)	69, 76, 70, 71-286	11,400
P Jacobsen (USA)	71, 74, 68, 73-286	11,400
S Bishop (GB)	71, 75, 72, 69-287	7,900
S Torrance (GB)	74, 74, 69, 70-287	7,900
G Norman (Aus)	71, 72, 71, 73-287	7,900
I Woosnam (GB)	70, 71, 71, 75-287	7,900
I Baker-Finch (Aus)	71, 73, 74, 70-288	5,260
J Gonzales (Bra)	72, 72, 73, 71-288	5,260
L Trevino (USA)	73, 76, 68, 71-288	5,260
G Marsh (Aus)	71, 75, 69, 73-288	5,260
M James (GB)	71, 78, 66, 73-288	5,260
P Parkin (GB)	68, 76, 77, 68-289	3,742
K Moe (USA)	70, 76, 73, 70-289	3,742
JM Olazabal (Spa) (Am)	72, 76, 71, 70-289	3,742
M Cahill (Aus)	72, 74, 71, 72-289	3,742
D Frost (SA	70, 74, 73, 72-289	3,742
GJ Brand (GB)	73, 72, 72, 72-289	3,742
M Pinero (Spa)	71, 73, 72, 73-289	3,742
R Lee (GB)	68, 73, 74, 74-289	3,742

Other Totals

O Sellberg (Swe), W Riley (Aus) 290; H Baiocchi (SA), B Crenshaw (USA), A Bean (USA),
R Shearer (Aus) 291; A Johnstone (Zim), M Parsson (Swe), J Pinsent (GB), S Ballesteros (Spa),
C Pavin (USA) 292; P Senior (Aus), R Rafferty (N Ire), D Russell (GB) 293; D Watson (SA),
M Mouland (GB), G Brand, Jr (GB), H Clark (GB), T Watson (USA) 294;
N Faldo (GB), E Rodriguez (Spa) 295; L Nelson (USA), P Fowler (Aus) 296; D Whelan (GB) 298; D
Williams (GB) 300; V Somers (Aus) 301; R Charles (NZ) retired.

The Open Golf Championship
continued

1986 at Turnberry

Entries 1,347. Regional qualifying courses: Glenbervie, Haggs Castle, Hankley Common,
Langley Park, Lindrick, Little Aston, Ormskirk, Porters Park. Final qualifying courses: Glasgow
Gailes, Kilmarnock (Barassie), Prestwick St Nicholas, Western Gailes. Qualified for final 36 holes:
77 Professionals. Non-qualifiers after 36 holes: 74 (71 Professionals, 3 Amateurs) with scores of
152 and above.

Name	Score	Prize Money £
G Norman (Aus)	74, 63, 74, 69-280	70,000
GJ Brand (GB)	71, 68, 75, 71-285	50,000
B Langer (W Ger)	72, 70, 76, 68-286	35,000
I Woosnam (GB)	70, 74, 70, 72-286	35,000
N Faldo (GB)	71, 70, 76, 70-287	25,000
S Ballesteros (Spa)	76, 75, 73, 64-288	25,000
G Koch (USA)	73, 72, 72, 71-288	25,000
F Zoeller (USA)	75, 73, 72, 69-289	17,333
B Marchbank (GB)	78, 70, 72, 69-289	17,333
T Nakajima (Jpn)	74, 67, 71, 77-289	17,333
C O'Connor Jr (Ire)	75, 71, 75, 69-290	14,000
D Graham (Aus)	75, 73, 70, 72-290	14,000
JM Canizares (Spa)	76, 68, 73, 73-290	14,000
C Strange (USA)	79, 69, 74, 69-291	11,500
A Bean (USA)	74, 73, 73, 71-291	11,500
A Forsbrand (Swe)	71, 73, 77, 71-292	9,000
JM Olazabal (Spa)	78, 69, 72, 73-292	9,000
R Floyd (USA)	78, 67, 73, 74-292	9,000
R Charles (NZ)	76, 72, 73, 72-293	7,250
M Pinero (Spa)	78, 71, 70, 74-293	7,250
R Rafferty (N Ire)	75, 74, 75, 70-294	5,022
D Cooper (GB)	72, 79, 72, 71-294	5,022
V Somers (Aus)	73, 77, 72, 72-294	5,022
B Crenshaw (USA)	77, 69, 75, 73-294	5,022
R Lee (GB)	71, 75, 75, 73-294	5,022
P Parkin (GB)	78, 70, 72, 74-294	5,022
D Edwards (USA)	77, 73, 70, 74-294	5,022
V Fernandez (Arg)	78, 70, 71, 75-294	5,022
S Torrance (GB)	78, 69, 71, 76-294	5,022

Other Totals

I Stanley (Aus), J Mahaffey (USA), M Karamoto (Jpn), DA Weibring (USA), A Lyle (Sco) 295;
T Watson (USA), R Chapman (Eng), A Brooks (Sco), R Commans (USA), M James (Eng),
P Stewart (USA), G Player (SA), G Turner (NZ) 296; R Maltbie (USA), M O'Meara (USA),
HM Chung (Tai) 297; J Nicklaus (USA), M O'Grady (USA), T Charnley (Eng), F Couples (USA),
M Clayton (Aus), L Mize (USA), J Hawkes (SA), LS Chuen (Tai), R Tway (USA), T Armour III (USA)
298; S Randolph (USA), G Marsh (Aus), C Mason (Eng) 300; M McNulty (Zim),
M Mackenzie (Eng), L Trevino (USA), E Darcy (Ire), T Lamore (USA), F Nobilo (NZ) 301;
A Chandler (Eng), J Heggarty (N Ire), M Gray (Sco), D Hammond (USA), S Simpson (USA) 302;
O Moore (Aus), P Fowler (Aus) 303; D Jones (N Ire), R Drummond (Sco) 305; T Horton (Sco) 306;
G Weir (Sco) 307; K Moe (USA) 314; H Green (USA) retired

1987 at Muirfield

The Open Golf
Championship
continued

Entries 1,407. Regional qualifying courses: Glenbervie, Haggs Castle, Hankley Common, Langley Park, Lindrick, Little Aston, Ormskirk, Porters Park. Final qualifying courses: Gullane No 1, Longniddry, Luffness New, North Berwick. Qualified for final 36 holes: 78 (76 Professionals, 2 Amateurs). Non-qualifiers after 36 holes: 75 (65 Professionals, 10 Amateurs) with scores of 147 and above.

Name	Score	Prize Money £
N Faldo (GB)	68, 69, 71, 71-279	75,000
R Davis (Aus)	64, 73, 74, 69-280	49,500
P Azinger (USA)	68, 68, 71, 73-280	49,500
B Crenshaw (USA)	73, 68, 72, 68-281	31,000
P Stewart (USA)	71, 66, 72, 72-281	31,000
D Frost (SA)	70, 68, 70, 74-282	26,000
T Watson (USA)	69, 69, 71, 74-283	23,000
I Woosnam (GB)	71, 69, 72, 72-284	18,666
N Price (Zim)	68, 71, 72, 73-284	18,666
C Stadler (USA)	69, 69, 71, 75-284	18,666
M McNulty (Zim)	71, 69, 75, 70-285	13,500
H Sutton (USA)	71, 70, 73, 71-285	13,500
JM Olazabal (Spa)	70, 73, 70, 72-285	13,500
M Ozaki (Jpn)	69, 72, 71, 73-285	13,500
M Calcavecchia (USA)	69, 70, 72, 74-285	13,500
G Marsh (Aus)	69, 70, 72, 74-285	13,500
W Grady (Aus)	70, 71, 76, 69-286	7,450
A Lyle (GB)	76, 69, 71, 70-286	7,450
E Darcy (Ire)	74, 69, 72, 71-286	7,450
B Langer (W Ger)	69, 69, 76, 72-286	7,450
L Trevino (USA)	67, 74, 73, 72-286	7,450
M Roe (GB)	74, 68, 72, 72-286	7,450
K Brown (GB)	69, 73, 70, 74-286	7,450
R Floyd (USA)	72, 68, 70, 76-286	7,450
G Taylor (Aus)	69, 68, 75, 75-287	5,300
D Feherty (Ire)	74, 70, 77, 67-288	4,933
G Brand Jr (GB)	73, 70, 75, 70-288	4,933
L Mize (USA)	68, 71, 76, 73-288	4,933

Other Totals

L Wadkins (USA), F Zoeller (USA), K Green (USA), D Edwards (USA), A Forsbrand (Swe) 289; D Graham (Aus) 290; R Drummond (GB), M Calero (Spa), J Haas (USA), G Norman (Aus), R Tway (USA) 291; D Cooper (GB), F Couples (USA), A Bean (USA), GJ Brand (GB) 292; F Allem (SA), B Marshbank (GB), O Moore (Aus), C Mason (GB), L Nelson (USA), J Slaughter (USA) 294; M Lanner (Swe), S Torrance (GB), S Ballesteros (Spa), P Walton (Ire) 295; J O'Leary (Ire), R Chapman (GB), W Andrade (USA) 296; O Sellberg (Swe), P Mayo (GB) 297; B Jones (Aus), W McColl (GB), T Nakajima (Jpn) 298; S Simpson (USA), N Hansen (GB), H Clark (GB), M Martin (Spa) 299; M O'Meara (USA), G Player (SA), T Ozaki (Jpn), H Baiocchi (SA), B Chamblee (USA) 300; W Westner (SA) 301; J Nicklaus (USA), T Kite (USA) 302; J Hawkes (SA) 303; R Willison (GB) 305; C Moody (GB) 306; D Jones (Ire) 307; A Stevens (GB) 312.

1988 at R Lytham & St Annes

Entries 1,393. Regional qualifying courses: Beau Desert, Camberley Heath, Glenbervie, Hankley Common, Langley Park, Lindrick, Little Aston, Ormskirk, Porters Park. Final qualifying courses: Blackpool North Shore, Fairhaven, Lytham Green Drive, St Annes Old Links. Qualified for final 36 holes: 71 (70 Professionals, 1 Amateur). Non-qualifiers after 36 holes: 83 (76 Professionals, 7 Amateurs) with scores of 149 and above.

Name	Score	Prize Money £
S Ballesteros (Spa)	67, 71, 70, 65-273	80,000
N Price (Zim)	70, 67, 69, 69-275	60,000
N Faldo (Eng)	71, 69, 68, 71-279	47,000
F Couples (USA)	73, 69, 71, 68-281	33,500
G Koch (USA)	71, 72, 70, 68-281	33,500
P Senior (Aus)	70, 73, 70, 69-282	27,000
I Aoki (Jpn)	72, 71, 73, 67-283	21,000
P Stewart (USA)	73, 75, 68, 67-283	21,000
D Frost (SA)	71, 75, 69, 68-283	21,000
A Lyle (Sco)	73, 69, 67, 74-283	21,000
D Russell (Eng)	71, 74, 69, 70-284	16,500
B Faxon (USA)	69, 74, 70, 71-284	16,500
C Strange (USA)	79, 69, 69, 68-285	14,000
E Romero (Arg)	72, 71, 69, 73-285	14,000
L Nelson (USA)	73, 71, 68, 73-285	14,000
J Rivero (Spa)	75, 69, 70, 72-286	10,500

Name	Score	Prize Money £
B Crenshaw (USA)	73, 73, 68, 72-286	10,500
A Bean (USA)	71, 70, 71, 74-286	10,500
D Pooley (USA)	70, 73, 69, 74-286	10,500
T Kite (USA)	75, 71, 73, 68-287	7,000
R Davis (Aus)	76, 71, 72, 68-287	7,000
G Brand Jr (Sco)	72, 76, 68, 71-287	7,000
B Tway (USA)	71, 71, 72, 73-287	7,000
R Charles (NZ)	71, 74, 69, 73-287	7,000
J Nicklaus (USA)	75, 70, 75, 68-288	5,500
I Woosnam (Wal)	76, 71, 72, 69-288	5,500
M O'Meara (USA)	75, 69, 75, 70-289	5,200
H Clark (Eng)	71, 72, 75, 72-290	4,600
M McNulty (Zim)	73, 73, 72, 72-290	4,600
T Watson (USA)	74, 72, 72, 72-290	4,600
C Beck (USA)	72, 71, 74, 73-290	4,600
T Armour III (USA)	73, 72, 72, 73-290	4,600
J Benepe III (USA)	75, 72, 70, 73-290	4,600
W Riley (Aus)	72, 71, 72, 76-291	4,150
L Wadkins (USA)	73, 71, 71, 76-291	4,150
G Brand (Eng)	73, 74, 72, 73-292	3,950
JM Olazabal (Spa)	73, 71, 73, 75-292	3,950

Other Totals

J Haas (USA), N Ratcliffe (Eng), B Marchbank (Eng), R Rafferty (Ire), G March (Aus), C Pavin (USA), D Russell (Eng), W Grady (Aus), K Brown (Eng) 293; P Kent (Eng), S Torrance (Sco), P Azinger (USA), A North (USA), M McCumber (USA) 294; P Fowler (Aus), F Zoeller (USA), P Walton (Eng), H Green (USA), J Miller (USA) 295; M Smith (Eng), C Mason (Eng), P Broadhurst (Am.) (Eng) 296; C Stadler (USA), G Player (SA) 297; M James (Eng), S Bishop (Eng), A Sherborne (Eng) 298; M Pinero (Spa) 299; P Carman 301; G Bruckner, C-H Hsieh 302; B Langer (W Ger) 303; G Stafford 305; P Mitchell 308.

1989 at R Troon

Entries 1,481. Regional qualifying courses: Glenbervie, Hankley Common, Langley Park, Lindrick, Little Aston, Ormskirk, Porters Park, South Herts. Final qualifying courses: Glasgow Gailes, Irvine (Bogside), Kilmarnock (Barassie), Western Gailes. Qualified for final 36 holes: 80 (78 Professionals, 2 Amateurs). Non-qualifiers after 36 holes: 76 (68 Professionals, 8 Amateurs) with scores of 147 and above.

Name	Score	Prize Money £
M Calcavecchia (USA)	71, 68, 68, 68-275	80,000
W Grady (Aus)	68, 67, 69, 71-275	55,000
G Norman (Aus)	69, 70, 72, 64-275	55,000
(Calcavecchia won 4-hole play-off)		
T Watson (USA)	69, 68, 68, 72-277	40,000
J Mudd (USA)	73, 67, 68, 70-278	30,000
F Couples (USA)	68, 71, 68, 72-279	26,000
D Feherty (Ire)	71, 67, 69, 72-279	26,000
E Romero (Arg)	68, 70, 75, 67-280	21,000
P Azinger (USA)	68, 73, 67, 72-280	21,000
P Stewart (USA)	72, 65, 69, 74-280	21,000
N Faldo (GB)	71, 71, 70, 69-281	17,000
M McNulty (Zim)	75, 70, 70, 66-281	17,000
P Walton (Ire)	69, 74, 69, 70-282	13,000
H Clark (GB)	72, 68, 72, 70-282	13,000
S Pate(USA)	69, 70, 70, 73-282	13,000
R Chapman (GB)	76, 68, 67, 71-282	13,000
M James (GB)	69, 70, 71, 72-282	13,000
C Stadler (USA)	73, 69, 69, 71-282	13,000
L Mize (USA)	71, 74, 66, 72-283	8,575
D Cooper (GB)	69, 70, 76, 68-283	8,575
T Kite (USA)	70, 74, 67, 72-283	8,575
D Pooley (USA)	73, 70, 69, 71-283	8,575
V Singh (Fiji)	71, 73, 69, 71-284	6,733
D Love III (USA)	72, 70, 73, 69-284	6,733
JM Olazabal (Spa)	68, 72, 69, 75-284	6,733
S Bennett (GB)	75, 69, 68, 73-285	5,800
L Wadkins (USA)	72, 70, 69, 74-285	5,800
C Beck (USA)	75, 69, 68, 73-285	5,800
S Simpson (USA)	73, 66, 72, 74-285	5,800
J Hawkes (SA)	75, 67, 69, 75-286	4,711
G Koch (USA)	72, 71, 74, 69-286	4,711
J Nicklaus (USA)	74, 71, 71, 70-286	4,711
P Jacobsen (USA)	71, 74, 71, 70-286	4,711
B Marchbank (GB)	69, 74, 73, 70-286	4,711

The Open Golf Championship
continued

Name	Score	Prize Money £
M Martin (Spa)	68, 73, 73, 72-286	4,711
I Baker-Finch (Aus)	72, 69, 70, 75-286	4,711
M Ozaki (Jpn)	71, 73, 70, 72-286	4,711
M Davis (GB)	77, 68, 67, 74-286	4,711

The Open Golf Championship
continued

Other Totals

M Harwood (Aus), T Armour III (USA), J Woodland (Aus) 287; M O'Meara (USA), L Trevino (USA), R Floyd (USA), J Rivero (Spa) 288; M McCumber (USA), A Lyle (GB), N Ozaki (Jpn) 289; J Miller (USA), I Woosnam (GB), C O'Connor Jr (Ire) 290; B Ogle (Aus), M Roe (GB), T Ozaki (Jpn), M Allen (USA), T Johnstone (Zim), E Dussart (Fra), R Boxall (GB), G Sauers (USA), B Crenshaw (USA) 291; C Strange (USA), D Graham (Aus), K Green (USA), P Hoad (GB), B Tway (USA), R Rafferty (Ire), M Reid (USA), W`Stephens (GB) 292; L Carbonetti (Arg), A`Stephen (GB), R Claydon (Am) (GB) 293; C Gillies (GB) 294; B Faxon (USA), P Teravainen (USA) 295; E Aubrey (USA) 296; M Sludds (Ire) 297; S Ballesteros (Spa), R Karlsson (Am) (Swe) 299; G Levenson (SA) 301; B Langer (W Ger) 309.

For 1990 results see page 30

United States Open Championship

Year	Winner	Runner-up	Venue	By
1894	W Dunn	W Campbell	St Andrews, NY	2 holes

After 1894 decided by medal play

Year	Winner	Venue	Score
1895	HJ Rawlins	Newport	173
1896	J Foulis	Southampton	152
1897	J Lloyd	Wheaton, Ill	162
1898	F Herd	Shinnecock Hills	328
72 holes played from 1898			
1899	W Smith	Baltimore	315
1900	H Vardon (Eng)	Wheaton, Ill	313
1901	W Anderson	Myopia, Mass	315
1902	L Auchterlonie	Garden City	305
1903	W Anderson	Baltusrol	307
1904	W Anderson	Glenview	304
1905	W Anderson	Myopia, Mass	335
1906	A Smith	Onwentsia	291
1907	A Ross	Chestnut Hill, Pa	302
1908	F McLeod	Myopia, Mass	322
1909	G Sargent	Englewood, NJ	290
1910	A Smith	Philadelphia	289
(After a tie with J McDermott and M Smith)			
1911	J McDermott	Wheaton, Ill	307
1912	J McDermott	Buffalo, NY	294
1913	F Ouimet (Am)	Brookline, Mass	304
(After a tie with H Vardon and E Ray)			
1914	W Hagen	Midlothian	297
1915	J Travers (Am)	Baltusrol	290
1916	C Evans (Am)	Minneapolis	286
1917-18	*No Championship*		
1919	W Hagen	Braeburn	301
1920	E Ray (Eng)	Inverness	295
1921	J Barnes	Washington	289
1922	G Sarazen	Glencoe	288
1923	R Jones, Jr (Am)	Inwood, LI	295
(After a tie with R Cruikshank. Play-off: 76; Cruikshank 78)			
1924	C Walker	Oakland Hills	297
1925	W MacFarlane	Worcester	291
1926	R Jones, Jr (Am)	Scioto	293
1927	T Armour	Oakmont	301
(After a tie with H Cooper. Play-off: Armour 76; Cooper 79)			
1928	J Farrell	Olympia Fields	294
(After a tie with R Jones, Jr. Play-off: Farrell 143; Jones 144)			
1929	R Jones, Jr (Am)	Winged Foot, NY	294
(After a tie with A Espinosa. Play-off: Jones 141; Espinosa 164)			
1930	R Jones, Jr (Am)	Interlachen	287
1931	B Burke	Inverness	292
(After a tie with G von Elm. Play-off: Burke 149, 148; von Elm 149, 149)			
1932	G Sarazen	Fresh Meadow	286

Year	Winner	Venue	Score
1933	J Goodman (Am)	North Shore	287
1934	O Dutra	Merion	293
1935	S Parks	Oakmont	299
1936	T Manero	Springfield	282
1937	R Guldahl	Oakland Hills	281
1938	R Guldahl	Cherry Hills	284
1939	B Nelson	Philadelphia	284

(After a tie with C Wood and D Shute)

| 1940 | W Lawson Little | Canterbury, Ohio | 287 |

(After a tie with G Sarazen. Tie scores: Little 70; Sarazen 73)

1941	Craig Wood	Fort Worth, Texas	284
1942-45	*No Championship*		
1946	L Mangrum	Canterbury	284

(After a tie with B Nelson and V Ghezzie)

| 1947 | L Worsham | St Louis | 282 |

(After a tie with S Snead. Replay scores: Worsham 69; Snead 70)

1948*	B Hogan	Los Angeles	276
1949	Dr C Middlecoff	Medinah, Ill	286
1950	B Hogan	Merion, Pa	287

(After a tie with L Mangrum and G Fazio. Replay scores: Hogan 69; Mangrum 73; Fazio 75)

1951	B Hogan	Oakland Hills, Mich	287
1952	J Boros	Dallas, Texas	281
1953	B Hogan	Oakmont	283
1954	E Furgol	Baltusrol	284
1955	J Fleck	San Francisco	287

(After a tie with B Hogan. Replay scores: Fleck 69; Hogan 72)

| 1956 | Dr C Middlecoff | Rochester | 281 |
| 1957 | D Mayer | Inverness | 282 |

(After a tie with Dr C Middlecoff. Tie scores: Mayer 72; Middlecoff 79)

1958	T Bolt	Tulsa, Okla	283
1959	W Casper	Winged Foot, NY	282
1960	A Palmer	Denver, Col	280
1961	G Littler	Birmingham, Mich	281
1962	J Nicklaus	Oakmont	283

(After a tie with A Palmer: Nicklaus 71; Palmer 74)

| 1963 | J Boros | Brookline, Mass | 293 |

(After a tie. Play-off: J Boros 70; J Cupit 73, A Palmer 76)

| 1964 | K Venturi | Washington | 278 |
| 1965 | G Player (SA) | St Louis, Mo | 282 |

(After a tie with K Nagle (Aus). Replay scores: Player 71; Nagle 74)

| 1966 | W Casper | San Francisco | 278 |

(After a tie with A Palmer. Replay scores: Casper 69; Palmer 73)

1967	J Nicklaus	Baltusrol	275
1968	L Trevino	Rochester	275
1969	O Moody	Houston, Texas	281
1970	A Jacklin (Eng)	Chaska, Minn	281
1971	L Trevino	Merion, Pa	280

(After a tie with J Nicklaus. Play-off: Trevino 68; Nicklaus 71)

1972	J Nicklaus	Pebble Beach	290
1973	J Miller	Oakmont, Pa	279
1974	H Irwin	Winged Foot, NY	287
1975	L Graham	Medinah, Ill	287

(After a tie with Mahaffey. Play-off: Graham 71; Mahaffey 73)

1976	J Pate	Atlanta, Georgia	277
1977	H Green	Southern Hills, Tulsa	278
1978	A North	Cherry Hills	285
1979	H Irwin	Inverness, Ohio	284
1980	J Nicklaus	Baltusrol	272
1981	D Graham (Aus)	Merion, Pa	273
1982	T Watson	Pebble Beach	282
1983	L Nelson	Oakmont, Pa	280
1984	F Zoeller	Winged Foot	276

(After tie with G Norman (Aus). Play-off: Zoeller 67; Norman 75)

1985	A North	Oakland Hills, Mich	279
1986	R Floyd	Shinnecock Hills, NY	279
1987	S Simpson	Olympic, San Francisco, Cal	277
1988	C Strange	Brookline, Mass.	278

(After a tie with N Faldo (GB). Play-off Strange 71, Faldo 75)

| 1989 | C Strange | Rochester, NY | 278 |
| 1990 | H Irwin | Medinah | 280 |

(After a tie with M Donald, at 1st extra hole after 18-hole play-off tie)

United States Masters' Championship

Venue – Augusta National Golf Course, Augusta, Georgia

Year	Winner	Score	Year	Winner	Score
1934	H Smith	284	1964	A Palmer	276
1935	G Sarazen	282	1965	J Nicklaus	271
1936	H Smith	285	1966	J Nicklaus	288
1937	B Nelson	283	1967	G Brewer	280
1938	H Picard	285	1968	R Goalby	277
1939	R Guldahl	279	1969	G Archer	281
1940	J Demaret	280	1970	W Casper*	279
1941	C Wood	280	1971	C Coody	279
1942	B Nelson*	280	1972	J Nicklaus	286
1946	H Keiser	282	1973	T Aaron	283
1947	J Demaret	281	1974	G Player (SA)	278
1948	C Harmon	279	1975	J Nicklaus	276
1949	S Snead	283	1976	R Floyd	271
1950	J Demaret	282	1977	T Watson	276
1951	B Hogan	280	1978	G Player (SA)	277
1952	S Snead*	286	1979	F Zoeller*	280
1953	B Hogan	274	1980	S Ballesteros (Spa)	275
1954	S Snead	289	1981	T Watson	280
1955	C Middlecoff	279	1982	C Stadler*	284
1956	J Burke	289	1983	S Ballesteros (Spa)	280
1957	D Ford	283	1984	B Crenshaw	277
1958	A Palmer	284	1985	B Langer (WGer)	282
1959	A Wall	284	1986	J Nicklaus	279
1960	A Palmer	282	1987	L Mize*	285
1961	G Player (SA)	280	1988	A Lyle (GB)	281
1962	A Palmer*	280	1989	N Faldo (GB)*	283
1963	J Nicklaus	286	1990	N Faldo (GB)*	278

* Winner in play-off

United States PGA Championship

Year	Winner	Runner-up	Venue	By
1916	J Barnes	J Hutchison	Siwanoy	1 hole
1919	J Barnes	F McLeod	Engineers' Club	6 and 5
1920	J Hutchison	D Edgar	Flossmoor	1 hole
1921	W Hagen	J Barnes	Inwood Club	3 and 2
1922	G Sarazen	E French	Oakmont	4 and 3
1923	G Sarazen	W Hagen	Pelham	38th hole
1924	W Hagen	J Barnes	French Lick	2 holes
1925	W Hagen	W Mehlhorn	Olympic Fields	6 and 4
1926	W Hagen	L Diegel	Salisbury	4 and 3
1927	W Hagen	J Turnesa	Dallas, Texas	1 hole
1928	L Diegel	A Espinosa	Five Farms	6 and 5
1929	L Diegel	J Farrell	Hill Crest	6 and 4
1930	T Armour	G Sarazen	Fresh Meadow	1 hole
1931	T Creavy	D Shute	Wannamoisett	2 and 1
1932	O Dutra	F Walsh	St Paul, Minnesota	4 and 3
1933	G Sarazen	W Goggin	Milwaukee	5 and 4
1934	P Runyan	C Wood	Buffalo	38th hole
1935	J Revolta	T Armour	Oklahoma	5 and 4
1936	D Shute	J Thomson	Pinehurst	3 and 2
1937	D Shute	H McSpaden	Pittsburgh	37th hole
1938	P Runyan	S Snead	Shawnee	8 and 7
1939	H Picard	B Nelson	Pomonok	37th hole
1940	B Nelson	S Snead	Hershey, Pa	1 hole
1941	V Ghezzie	B Nelson	Denver, Colo	38th hole
1942	S Snead	J Turnesa	Atlantic City	2 and 1
1943	*No Championship*			
1944	B Hamilton	B Nelson	Spokane, Wash	1 hole
1945	B Nelson	S Byrd	Dayton, Ohio	4 and 3
1946	B Hogan	E Oliver	Portland	6 and 4
1947	J Ferrier	C Harbert	Detroit	2 and 1
1948	B Hogan	M Turnesa	Norwood Hills	7 and 6
1949	S Snead	J Palmer	Richmond, Va	3 and 2
1950	C Harper	H Williams	Scioto, Ohio	4 and 3
1951	S Snead	W Burkemo	Oakmont, Pa	7 and 6
1952	J Turnesa	C Harbert	Big Spring, Louisville	1 hole
1953	W Burkemo	F Lorza	Birmingham, Michigan	2 and 1
1954	C Harbert	W Burkemo	St Paul, Minnesota	4 and 3
1955	D Ford	C Middlecoff	Detroit	4 and 3
1956	J Burke	T Kroll	Boston	3 and 2
1957	L Hebert	D Finsterwald	Miami Valley, Dayton	3 and 1

Changed to Stroke Play

Year	Winner	Venue	Score
1958	D Finsterwald	Llanerch, PA	276
1959	B Rosburg	Minneapolis, MN	277
1960	J Hebert	Firestone, Akron, OH	281
1961	J Barber*	Olympia Fields, IL	277
1962	G Player	Aronimink, PA	278
1963	J Nicklaus	Dallas, TX	279
1964	B Nichols	Columbus, OH	271
1965	D Marr	Laurel Valley, PA	280
1966	A Geiberger	Firestone, Akron, OH	280
1967	D January*	Columbine, CO	281
1968	J Boros	Pecan Valley, TX	281
1969	R Floyd	Dayton, OH	276
1970	D Stockton	Southern Hills, OK	279
1971	J Nicklaus	PGA National, FL	281
1972	G Player	Oakland Hills, MI	281
1973	J Nicklaus	Canterbury, OH	277
1974	L Trevino	Tanglewood, NC	276
1975	J Nicklaus	Firestone, Akron, OH	276
1976	D Stockton	Congressional, MD	281
1977	L Wadkins*	Pebble Beach, CA	287
1978	J Mahaffey*	Oakmont, PA	276
1979	D Graham*	Oakland Hills, MI	272
1980	J Nicklaus	Oak Hill, NY	274
1981	L Nelson	Atlanta, GA	273
1982	R Floyd	Southern Hills, OK	272
1983	H Sutton	Pacific Palisades, CA	274
1984	L Trevino	Shoal Creek, AL	273
1985	H Green	Cherry Hills, Denver, CO	278
1986	R Tway	Inverness, Toledo, OH	276
1987	L Nelson*	PGA National, FL	287
1988	J Sluman	Oaktree, OK	272
1989	P Stewart	Kemper Lakes, IL	276
1990	W Grady	Shoal Creek, AL	282

*Winner in play-off

Ladies' Major Championships

Weetabix Ladies' British Open Championship

Year	Winner	Club/Country	Venue	Score
1976	J Lee Smith	Gosforth Park	Fulford	299
1977	V Saunders	Tyrrells Wood	Lindrick	306
1978	J Melville	Furness	Foxhills	310
1979	A Sheard	South Africa	Southport and Ainsdale	301
1980	D Massey	USA	Wentworth (East)	294
1981	D Massey	USA	Northumberland	295
1982	Figueras-Dotti	Spain	R Birkdale	296
1983	Not played			
1984	A Okamoto	Japan	Woburn	289
1985	B King	USA	Moor Park	300
1986	L Davies	GB	R Birkdale	283
1987	A Nicholas	GB	St Mellion	296
1988	C Dibnah / S Little	Australia / South Africa } tie	Lindrick	296
(Dibnah won at second play-off hole)				
1989	J Geddes	USA	Ferndown	274
1990	H Alfredsson	Sweden	Woburn	288

United States Ladies' Open Championship
(American unless stated)

Year	Winner	Venue	By
1946	P Berg	Spokane	5 and 4
Changed to stroke play			

Year	Winner	Venue	Score
1947	B Jamieson	Greensboro	300
1948	B Zaharias	Atlantic City	300
1949	L Suggs	Maryland	291
1950	B Zaharias	Wichita	291
1951	B Rawls	Atlanta	294
1952	L Suggs	Bala, Philadelphia	284
1953	B Rawls	Rochester, NY	302
(After a tie with J Pung)			
1954	B Zaharias	Peabody, Mass	291
1955	F Crocker	Wichita	299
1956	K Cornelius	Duluth	302
(After a tie with B McIntire)			
1957	B Rawls	Mamaroneck	299
1958	M Wright	Bloomfield Hills, Mich	290
1959	M Wright	Pittsburgh, Pa	287
1960	B Rawls	Worchester, Mass	292
1961	M Wright	Springfield, NJ	293
1962	M Lindstrom	Myrtle Beach	301

Year	Winner	Venue	Score
1963	M Mills	Kenwood	289
1964	M Wright	San Diego	290
(After a tie with R Jessen, Seattle)			
1965	C Mann	Northfield, NJ	290
1966	S Spuzich	Hazeltine National GC, Minn	297
1967	C Lacoste (Fra)	Hot Springs, Virginia	294
1968	S Berning	Moselem Springs, Pa	289
1969	D Caponi	Scenic-Hills	294
1970	D Caponi	Muskogee, Okla	287
1971	J Gunderson-Carner	Erie, Pa	288
1972	S Berning	Mamaroneck, NY	299
1973	S Berning	Rochester, NY	290
1974	S Haynie	La Grange, Ill	295
1975	S Palmer	Northfield, NJ	295
1976	J Carner	Springfield, Pa	292
(After a tie with S Palmer)			
1977	H Stacy	Hazeltine, Minn	292
1978	H Stacy	Indianapolis	299
1979	J Britz	Brooklawn, Conn	284
1980	A Alcott	Richland, Tenn	280
1981	P Bradley	La Grange, Illinois	279
1982	J Alex	Del Paso, Sacramento	283
1983	J Stephenson (Aus)	Broken Arrow, Oklahoma	290
1984	H Stacy	Salem, Mass	290
1985	K Baker	Baltusrol, NJ	280
1986	J Geddes	NCR	287
1987	L Davies (GB)	Plainfield	285
(After a tie with J Carner and A Akamoto (Jpn))			
1988	L Neumann (Swe)	Baltimore	277
1989	B King	Indianwood, MI	278
1990	B King	Atlanta Athletic Club, GA	284

United States Ladies' Open Championship

continued

British and Irish National Championships

Amateur Championship

Year	Winner	Runner-up	Venue	By	Ent
1885	A MacFie	H Hutchinson	Hoylake, R Liverpool	7 and 6	44
1886	H Hutchinson	H Lamb	St Andrews	7 and 6	42
1887	H Hutchinson	J Ball	Hoylake, R Liverpool	1 hole	33
1888	J Ball	J Laidlay	Prestwick	5 and 4	38
1889	J Laidlay	L Melville	St Andrews	2 and 1	40
1890	J Ball	J Laidlay	Hoylake, R Liverpool	4 and 3	44
1891	J Laidlay	H Hilton	St Andrews	20th hole	50
1892	J Ball	H Hilton	Sandwich, R St George's	3 and 1	45
1893	P Anderson	J Laidlay	Prestwick	1 hole	44
1894	J Ball	S Fergusson	Hoylake, R Liverpool	1 hole	64
1895	L Melville	J Ball	St Andrews	19th hole	68
1896*	F Tait	H Hilton	Sandwich, R St George's	8 and 7	64

36 holes played on and after this date

Year	Winner	Runner-up	Venue	By	Ent
1897	A Allan	J Robb	Muirfield	4 and 2	74
1898	F Tait	S Fergusson	Hoylake, R Liverpool	7 and 5	77
1899	J Ball	F Tait	Prestwick	37th hole	101
1900	H Hilton	J Robb	Sandwich, R St George's	8 and 7	68
1901	H Hilton	J Low	St Andrews	1 hole	116
1902	C Hutchings	S Fry	Hoylake, R Liverpool	1 hole	114
1903	R Maxwell	H Hutchinson	Muirfield	7 and 5	142
1904	W Travis (USA)	E Blackwell	Sandwich, R St George's	4 and 3	104
1905	A Barry	Hon O Scott	Prestwick	3 and 2	148
1906	J Robb	C Lingen	Hoylake, R Liverpool	4 and 3	166
1907	J Ball	C Palmer	St Andrews	6 and 4	200
1908	E Lassen	H Taylor	Sandwich, R St George's	7 and 6	197
1909	R Maxwell	Capt C Hutchison	Muirfield	1 hole	170
1910	J Ball	C Aylmer	Hoylake, R Liverpool	10 and 9	160
1911	H Hilton	E Lassen	Prestwick	4 and 3	146
1912	J Ball	A Mitchell	Westward Ho!, R North Devon	38th hole	134
1913	H Hilton	R Harris	St Andrews	6 and 5	198
1914	J Jenkins	C Hezlet	Sandwich, R St George's	3 and 2	232
1915-19	No Championship owing to the Great War				
1920	C Tolley	R Gardner (USA)	Muirfield	37th hole	165
1921	W Hunter	A Graham	Hoylake, R Liverpool	12 and 11	223
1922	E Holderness	J Caven	Prestwick	1 hole	252
1923	R Wethered	R Harris	Deal, R Cinque Ports	7 and 6	209
1924	E Holderness	E Storey	St Andrews	3 and 2	201
1925	R Harris	K Fradgley	Westward Ho!, R North Devon	13 and 12	151
1926	J Sweetser (USA)	A Simpson	Muirfield	6 and 5	216

Amateur Championship
continued

Year	Winner	Runner-up	Venue	By	Ent
1927	Dr W Tweddell	D Landale	Hoylake, R Liverpool	7 and 6	197
1928	T Perkins	R Wethered	Prestwick	6 and 4	220
1929	C Tolley	J Smith	Sandwich, R St George's	4 and 3	253
1930	R Jones (USA)	R Wethered	St Andrews	7 and 6	271
1931	E Smith	J De Forest	Westward Ho!, R North Devon	1 hole	171
1932	J De Forest	E Fiddian	Muirfield	3 and 1	235
1933	Hon M Scott	T Bourn	Hoylake, R Liverpool	4 and 3	269
1934	W Lawson Little (USA)	J Wallace	Prestwick	14 and 13	225
1935	W Lawson Little (USA)	Dr W Tweddell	R Lytham and St Annes	1 hole	232
1936	H Thomson	J Ferrier (Aus)	St Andrews	2 holes	283
1937	R Sweeney, Jr (USA)	L Munn	Sandwich, R St George's	3 and 2	223
1938	C Yates (USA)	R Ewing	Troon	3 and 2	241
1939	A Kyle	A Duncan	Hoylake, R Liverpool	2 and 1	167
1940-45	*Suspended during Second World War*				
1946	J Bruen	R Sweeny (USA)	Birkdale	4 and 3	263
1947	W Turnesa (USA)	R Chapman (USA)	Carnoustie	3 and 2	200
1948	F Stranahan (USA)	C Stowe	Sandwich, R St George's	5 and 4	168
1949	S McCready	W Turnesa (USA)	Portmarnock	2 and 1	204
1950	F Stranahan (USA)	R Chapman (USA)	St Andrews	8 and 6	324
1951	R Chapman (USA)	C Coe (USA)	R Porthcawl	5 and 4	192
1952	E Ward (USA)	F Stranahan (USA)	Prestwick	6 and 5	286
1953	J Carr	E Harvie Ward (USA)	Hoylake, R Liverpool	2 holes	279
1954	D Bachli (Aus)	W Campbell (USA)	Muirfield	2 and 1	286
1955	J Conrad (USA)	A Slater	R Lytham and St Annes	3 and 2	240
1956*	J Beharrell	L Taylor	Troon	5 and 4	200
1957*	R Reid Jack	H Ridgley (USA)	Formby	2 and 1	200

In 1956 and 1957 the Quarter Finals, Semi-Finals and Final were played over 36 holes

Year	Winner	Runner-up	Venue	By	Ent
1958*	J Carr	A Thirlwell	St Andrews	3 and 2	488

In 1958, Semi-Finals and Final only were played over 36 holes

Year	Winner	Runner-up	Venue	By	Ent
1959	D Beman (USA)	W Hyndman (USA)	Sandwich, R St George's	3 and 2	362
1960	J Carr	R Cochran (USA)	R Portrush	8 and 7	183
1961	M Bonallack	J Walker	Turnberry	6 and 4	250
1962	R Davies (USA)	J Povall	Hoylake, R Liverpool	1 hole	256
1963	M Lunt	J Blackwell	St Andrews	2 and 1	256
1964	G Clark	M Lunt	Ganton	39th hole	220
1965	M Bonallack	C Clark	R Porthcawl	2 and 1	176
1966	R Cole (SA)	R Shade	Carnoustie (18 holes)	3 and 2	206
1967	R Dickson (USA)	R Cerrudo (USA)	Formby	2 and 1	
1968	M Bonallack	J Carr	Troon	7 and 6	249
1969	M Bonallack	W Hyndman (USA)	Hoylake, R Liverpool	3 and 2	245
1970	M Bonallack	W Hyndman (USA)	Newcastle, R Co Down	8 and 7	256
1971	S Melnyk (USA)	J Simons (USA)	Carnoustie	3 and 2	256
1972	T Homer	A Thirlwell	Sandwich, R St George's	4 and 3	253
1973	R Siderowf (USA)	P Moody	R Porthcawl	5 and 3	222
1974	T Homer	J Gabrielsen (USA)	Muirfield	2 holes	330
1975	M Giles (USA)	M James	Hoylake, R Liverpool	8 and 7	206
1976	R Siderowf (USA)	J Davies	St Andrews	37th hole	289
1977	P McEvoy	H Campbell	Ganton	5 and 4	235
1978	P McEvoy	P McKellar	R Troon	4 and 3	353
1979	J Sigel (USA)	S Hoch (USA)	Hillside	3 and 2	285
1980	D Evans	D Suddards (SA)	R Porthcawl	4 and 3	265
1981	P Ploujoux (Fra)	J Hirsch (USA)	St Andrews	4 and 2	256
1982	M Thompson	A Stubbs	Deal, R Cinque Ports	4 and 3	245
1983	A Parkin	J Holtgrieve (USA)	Turnberry	5 and 4	288
1984	JM Olazabal (Spa)	C Montgomerie	Formby	5 and 4	291
1985	G McGimpsey	G Homewood	R Dornoch	8 and 7	457
1986	D Curry	G Birtwell	R Lytham and St Annes	11 and 9	427
1987	P Mayo	P McEvoy	Prestwick	3 and 1	373
1988	C Hardin (Swe)	B Fouchee (SA)	R Porthcawl	1 hole	391
1989	S Dodd	C Cassells	R. Birkdale	5 and 3	378
1990	R Muntz (Neth)	A Macara	Muirfield	7 and 6	510

Senior Open Amateur Championship

Year	Winner	Venue	Score
1969	R Pattinson	Formby	154
1970	K Bamber	Prestwick	150
1971	GH Pickard	Deal, R Cinque Ports; Sandwich, R St George's	150
1972	TC Hartley	St Andrews	147
1973	JT Jones	Longniddry	142
1974	MA Ivor-Jones	Moortown	149
1975	HJ Roberts	Turnberry	138
1976	WM Crichton	Berkshire	149
1977	Dr TE Donaldson	Panmure	228
1978	RJ White	Formby	225
1979	RJ White	Harlech, R St David's	226
1980	JM Cannon	Prestwick St Nicholas	218
1981	T Branton	Hoylake, R Liverpool	227
1982	RL Glading	Blairgowrie	218
1983	AJ Swann (USA)	Walton Heath	222
1984	JC Owens (USA)	Western Gailes	222
1985	D Morey (USA)	Hesketh	223
1986	AN Sturrock	Panmure	229
1987	B Soyars (USA)	Deal, R Cinque Ports	226
1988	CW Green	Barnton, Edinburgh	221
1989	CW Green	Moortown and Alwoodley	226
1990	CW Green	The Berkshire	207

Ladies' British Open Amateur Championship

Year	Winner	Runner-up	Venue	By
1893	Lady Margaret Scott	Miss I Pearson	St Annes	7 and 5
1894	Lady Margaret Scott	Miss I Pearson	Littlestone	3 and 2
1895	Lady Margaret Scott	Miss E Lythgoe	Portrush	5 and 4
1896	Miss Pascoe	Miss L Thomson	Hoylake, R Liverpool	3 and 2
1897	Miss EC Orr	Miss Orr	Gullane	4 and 2
1898	Miss L Thomson	Miss EC Neville	Yarmouth	7 and 5
1899	Miss M Hezlet	Miss Magill	Newcastle Co Down	2 and 1
1900	Miss Adair	Miss Neville	Westward Ho!, R North Devon	6 and 5
1901	Miss Graham	Miss Adair	Aberdovey	3 and 1
1902	Miss M Hezlet	Miss E Neville	Deal	19th hole
1903	Miss Adair	Miss F Walker-Leigh	Portrush	4 and 3
1904	Miss L Dod	Miss M Hezlet	Troon	1 hole
1905	Miss B Thompson	Miss ME Stuart	Cromer	3 and 2
1906	Mrs Kennon	Miss B Thompson	Burnham	4 and 3
1907	Miss M Hezlet	Miss F Hezlet	Newcastle Co Down	2 and 1
1908	Miss M Titterton	Miss D Campbell	St Andrews	19th hole
1909	Miss D Campbell	Miss F Hezlet	Birkdale	4 and 3
1910	Miss Grant Suttie	Miss L Moore	Westward Ho!, R North Devon	6 and 4
1911	Miss D Campbell	Miss V Hezlet	Portrush	3 and 2
1912	Miss G Ravenscroft	Miss S Temple	Turnberry	3 and 2
(Final played over 36 holes after 1912)				
1913	Miss M Dodd	Miss Chubb	St Annes	8 and 6
1914	Miss C Leitch	Miss G Ravenscroft	Hunstanton	2 and 1
1915-18	*No Championship owing to the Great War*			
1919	*Should have been played at Burnham in October, but abandoned owing to Railway Strike*			
1920	Miss C Leitch	Miss M Griffiths	Newcastle Co Down	7 and 6
1921	Miss C Leitch	Miss J Wethered	Turnberry	4 and 3
1922	Miss J Wethered	Miss C Leitch	Prince's, Sandwich, R St George's	9 and 7
1923	Miss D Chambers	Miss A Macbeth	Burnham, Somerset	2 holes
1924	Miss J Wethered	Mrs Cautley	Portrush	7 and 6
1925	Miss J Wethered	Miss C Leitch	Troon	37th hole
1926	Miss C Leitch	Mrs Garon	Harlech	8 and 7
1927	Miss Thion de la Chaume (Fra)	Miss Pearson	Newcastle Co Down	5 and 4
1928	Miss N Le Blan (Fra)	Miss S Marshall	Hunstanton	3 and 2
1929	Miss J Wethered	Miss G Collett (USA)	St Andrews	3 and 1
1930	Miss D Fishwick	Miss G Collett (USA)	Formby	4 and 3

Ladies' British
Open Amateur
Championship
continued

Year	Winner	Runner-up	Venue	By
1931	Miss E Wilson	Miss W Morgan	Portmarnock	7 and 6
1932	Miss E Wilson	Miss CPR Montgomery	Saunton	7 and 6
1933	Miss E Wilson	Miss D Plumpton	Gleneagles	5 and 4
1934	Mrs AM Holm	Miss P Barton	Porthcawl	6 and 5
1935	Miss W Morgan	Miss P Barton	Newcastle Co Down	3 and 2
1936	Miss P Barton	Miss B Newell	Southport and Ainsdale	5 and 3
1937	Miss J Anderson	Miss D Park	Turnberry	6 and 4
1938	Mrs AM Holm	Miss E Corlett	Burnham	4 and 3
1939	Miss P Barton	Mrs T Marks	Portrush	2 and 1
1940-45	No Championship owing to Second World War			
1946	GW Hetherington	P Garvey	Hunstanton	1 hole
1947	B Zaharias (USA)	J Gordon	Gullane	5 and 4
1948	L Suggs (USA)	J Donald	Lytham St Annes	1 hole
1949	F Stephens	V Reddan	Harlech	5 and 4
1950	Vicomtesse de Saint Sauveur (Fra)	J Valentine	Newcastle Co Down	3 and 2
1951	PJ MacCann	F Stephens	Broadstone	4 and 3
1952	M Paterson	F Stephens	Troon	39th hole
1953	M Stewart (Can)	P Garvey	Porthcawl	7 and 6
1954	F Stephens	E Price	Ganton	4 and 3
1955	J Valentine	B Romack (USA)	Portrush	7 and 6
1956	M Smith (USA)	M Janssen (USA)	Sunningdale	8 and 7
1957	P Garvey	J Valentine	Gleneagles	4 and 3
1958	J Valentine	E Price	Hunstanton	1 hole
1959	E Price	B McCorkindale	Ascot	37th hole
1960	B McIntyre (USA)	P Garvey	Harlech	4 and 2
1961	M Spearman	DJ Robb	Carnoustie	7 and 6
1962	M Spearman	A Bonallack	Birkdale	1 hole
1963	B Varangot (Fra)	P Garvey	Newcastle Co Down	3 and 1
1964	C Sorenson (USA)	BAB Jackson	Sandwich, Prince's, R St George's	37th hole
1965	B Varangot (Fra)	IC Robertson	St Andrews	4 and 3
1966	E Chadwick	V Saunders	Ganton	3 and 2
1967	E Chadwick	M Everard	Harlech	1 hole
1968	B Varangot (Fra)	C Rubin (Fra)	Walton Heath	20th hole
1969	C Lacoste (Fra)	A Irvin	Portrush	1 hole
1970	D Oxley	IC Robertson	Gullane	1 hole
1971	M Walker	B Huke	Alwoodley	3 and 1
1972	M Walker	C Rubin (Fra)	Hunstanton	2 holes
1973	A Irvin	M Walker	Carnoustie	3 and 2
1974	C Semple (USA)	A Bonallack	Porthcawl	2 and 1
1975	N Syms (USA)	S Cadden	St Andrews	3 and 2
1976	C Panton	A Sheard	Silloth	1 hole
1977	A Uzielli	V Marvin	Hillside	6 and 5
1978	E Kennedy (Aus)	J Greenhalgh	Notts	1 hole
1979	M Madill	J Lock (Aus)	Nairn	2 and 1
1980	A Quast (USA)	L Wollin (Swe)	Woodhall Spa	3 and 1
1981	IC Robertson	W Aitken	Conway	20th hole
1982	K Douglas	G Stewart	Walton Heath	4 and 2
1983	J Thornhill	R Lautens (Switz)	Silloth	4 and 2
1984	J Rosenthal (USA)	J Brown	Royal Troon	4 and 3
1985	L Beman (Ire)	C Waite	Ganton	1 hole
1986	McGuire (NZ)	L Briars (Aus)	West Sussex	2 and 1
1987	J Collingham	S Shapcott	Harlech	19th hole
1988	J Furby	J Wade	Deal	4 and 3
1989	H Dobson	E Farquharson	Hoylake, R Liverpool	6 and 5
1990	J Hall	H Wadsworth	Dunbar	3 and 2

Ladies' British Open Amateur Stroke Play Championship

Year	Winner	Club	Venue	Score
1969	A Irvin	R Lytham and St Annes	Gosforth Park	295
1970	M Everard	Hallamshire	Birkdale	313
1971	IC Robertson	Dunaverty	Ayr Belleisle	302
1972	IC Robertson	Dunaverty	Silloth	296
1973	A Stant	Beau Desert	Purdis Heath	298
1974	J Greenhalgh	Pleasington	Seaton Carew	302
1975	J Greenhalgh	Pleasington	Gosforth Park	298

Year	Winner	Club	Venue	Score
1976*	J Lee Smith	Gosforth Park	Fulford	299
1977*	M Everard	Hallamshire	Lindrick	306
1978*	J Melville	Furness	Foxhills	310
1979	M McKenna	Donabate	Moseley	305
1980	M Mahill	Portstewart	Brancepeth Castle	304
(After a tie with P Wright)				
1981	J Soulsby	Prudhoe	Norwich	300
1982	J Connachan	Musselburgh	Downfield	294
1983	A Nicholas		Moortown	292
1984	C Waite	Swindon	Caernarvonshire	295
1985	IC Robertson	Dunaverty	Formby	300
1986	C Hourihane		Blairgowrie	291
(After a tie with P Johnson)				
1987	L Bayman	Princes	Ipswich	297
1988	K Mitchell	Worthing	Porthcawl	317
1989	H Dobson	Seacroft	Southerness	298
1990	V Thomas	Pennard	Strathaven	287

Played concurrently with Ladies' British Open Championship

Ladies' British Open Amateur Stroke Play Championship

continued

Senior Ladies' British Open Amateur Stroke Play Championship

Year	Winner	Club	Venue	Score
1981	BM King	Pleasington	Formby	159
1982	P Riddiford	Royal Ashdown Forest	Ilkley	161
1983	M Birtwistle		Troon Portland	167
1984	O Semelaigne	France	Woodbridge	152
1985	Dr G Costello	Formby Ladies	Prestatyn	158
1986	P Riddiford	Royal Ashdown Forest	Longniddry	154
1987	O Semelaigne	France	Copt Heath	152
1988	C Bailey	Tandridge	Littlestone	156
1989	C Bailey	Tandridge	Wrexham	149
1990	A Uzielli	The Berkshire	Harrogate	153

English Amateur Championship

Year	Winner	Runner-up	Venue	By
1925	TF Ellison	S Robinson	Hoylake, R Liverpool	1 hole
1926	TF Ellison	Sq Ldr CH Hayward	Walton Heath	6 and 4
1927	TP Perkins	JB Beddard	Little Aston	2 and 1
1928	JA Stout	TP Perkins	R Lytham and St Annes	3 and 2
1929	W Sutton	EB Tipping	Northumberland	3 and 2
1930	TA Bourn	CE Hardman	Burnham	3 and 2
1931	LG Crawley	W Sutton	Hunstanton	1 hole
1932	EW Fiddian	AS Bradshaw	Sandwich, R St George's	1 hole
1933	J Woollam	TA Bourn	Ganton	4 and 3
1934	S Lunt	LG Crawley	Formby	37th hole
1935	J Woollam	EW Fiddian	Hollinwell	2 and 1
1936	HG Bentley	JDA Langley	Deal	5 and 4
1937	JJ Pennink	LG Crawley	Saunton	6 and 5
1938	JJ Pennink	SE Banks	Moortown	2 and 1
1939	AL Bentley	W Sutton	R Birkdale	5 and 4
1946	IR Patey	K Thom	Mid-Surrey	5 and 4
1947	GH Micklem	C Stow	Ganton	1 hole
1948	AGB Helm	HJR Roberts	Little Aston	2 and 1
1949	RJ White	C Stowe	Formby	5 and 4
1950	JDA Langley	IR Patey	Deal	1 hole
1951	GP Roberts	H Bennett	Hunstanton	39th hole
1952	E Millward	TJ Shorrock	Burnham and Berrow	2 holes
1953	GH Micklem	RJ White	R Birkdale	2 and 1
1954	A Thirlwell	HG Bentley	Sandwich, R St George's	2 and 1
1955	A Thirlwell	M Burgess	Ganton	7 and 6

Year	Winner	Runner-up	Venue	By
1956	GB Wolstenholme	H Bennett	R Lytham and St Annes	1 hole
1957	A Walker	G Whitehead	Hoylake, R Liverpool	4 and 3
1958	DN Sewell	DA Procter	Walton Heath	8 and 7
1959	GB Wolstenholme	MF Bonallack	Formby	1 hole
1960	DN Sewell	MJ Christmas	Hunstanton	41st hole
1961	I Caldwell	GJ Clark	Wentworth	37th hole
1962	MF Bonallack	MSR Lunt	Moortown	2 and 1
1963	MF Bonallack	A Thirlwell	Burnham and Berrow	4 and 3
1964	Dr D Marsh	R Foster	Hollinwell	1 hole
1965	MF Bonallack	CA Clark	Berkshire	3 and 2
1966	MSR Lunt	DJ Millensted	R Lytham and St Annes	3 and 2
1967	MF Bonallack	GE Hyde	Woodhall Spa	4 and 2
1968	MF Bonallack	PD Kelley	Ganton	12 and 11
1969	JH Cook	P Dawson	Sandwich, R St George's	6 and 4
1970	Dr D Marsh	SG Birtwell	R Birkdale	6 and 4
1971	W Humphreys	JC Davies	Burnham and Berrow	9 and 8
1972	H Ashby	R Revell	Northumberland	5 and 4
1973	H Ashby	SC Mason	Formby	5 and 4
1974	M James	JA Watts	Woodhall Spa	6 and 5
1975	N Faldo	D Eccleston	R Lytham and St Annes	6 and 4
1976	P Deeble	JC Davies	Ganton	3 and 1
1977	TR Shingler	J Mayell	Walton Heath	4 and 3
1978	P Downes	P Hoad	R Birkdale	1 hole
1979	R Chapman	A Carman	Sandwich, R St George's	6 and 5
1980	P Deeble	P McEvoy	Moortown	4 and 3
1981	D Blakeman	A Stubbs	Burnham and Berrow	3 and 1
1982	A Oldcorn	I Bradshaw	Hoylake, R Liverpool	4 and 3
1983	G Laurence	A Brewer	Wentworth	7 and 6
1984	D Gilford	M Gerrard	Woodhall Spa	4 and 3
1985	R Winchester	P Robinson	Little Aston	1 hole
1986	J Langmead	B White	Hillside	2 and 1
1987	K Weeks	R Eggo	Frilford Heath	37th hole
1988	R Claydon	D Curry	R Birkdale	38th hole
1989	S Richardson	R Eggo	Sandwich, R St George's	2 and 1
1990	I Garbutt	G Evans	Woodhall Spa	8 and 7

English Open Amateur Stroke Play Championship

(Formerly Brabazon Trophy)

Year	Winner	Club	Venue	Score
1957	D Sewell	Hook Heath	Moortown	287
1958	AH Perowne	Norwich	Birkdale	289
1959	D Sewell	Hook Heath	Hollinwell	300
1960	GB Wolstenholme	Sunningdale	Ganton	286
1961	RDBM Shade	Duddingston	Hoylake, R Liverpool	284
1962	A Slater	Wakefield	Woodhall Spa	209
1963	RDBM Shade	Duddingston	R Birkdale	306
1964	MF Bonallack	Thorpe Hall	Deal, R Cinque Ports	290
1965	CA Clark / DJ Millensted / MJ Burgess } tie	Ganton / Wentworth / West Sussex	Formby	289
1966	PM Townsend	Porters Park	Hunstanton	282
1967	RDBM Shade	Duddingston	Saunton	299
1968	MF Bonallack	Thorpe Hall	Walton Heath	210
1969	R Foster / MF Bonallack } tie	Bradford / Thorpe Hall	Moortown	290
1970	R Foster	Bradford	Little Aston	287
1971	MF Bonallack	Thorpe Hall	Hillside	294
1972	PH Moody	Notts	Hoylake, R Liverpool	296
1973	R Revell	Farnham	Hunstanton	294
1974	N Sundelson	South Africa	Moortown	291
1975	A Lyle	Hawkstone Park	Hollinwell	298
1976	P Hedges	Langley Park	Saunton	294

**English Open
Amateur
Stroke Play
Championship**

continued

Year	Winner	Club	Venue	Score
1977	A Lyle	Hawkstone Park	Hoylake, R Liverpool	293
1978	G Brand, Jr	Knowle	Woodhall Spa	289
1979	D Long	Shandon Park	Little Aston	291
1980	R Rafferty / P McEvoy } tie	Warrenpoint / Copt Heath }	Hunstanton	293
1981	P Way	Neville	Hillside	292
1982	P Downes	Coventry	Woburn	299
1983	C Banks	Stanton-on-the-Wolds	Hollinwell	294
1984	M Davis	Thorndon Park	Deal, R Cinque Ports	286
1985	R Roper / P Baker } tie	Catterick Garrison / Lillieshall Park }	Seaton Carew	296
1986	R Kaplan	South Africa	Sunningdale	286
1987	JG Robinson	Woodhall Spa	Ganton	287
1988	R Eggo	L'Ancresse	Saunton	289
1989	C Rivett / RN Roderick } tie	}	Hoylake, R Liverpool	293
1990	O Edmond / G Evans } tie	Fontainbleau / Worthing }	Burnham and Berrow	287

English Seniors Championship

Year	Winner	Venue	Score
1981	CR Spalding	Copt Heath	152
1982	JL Whitworth	Lindrick	152
1983	B Cawthray	Ross-on-Wye	154
1984	RL Glading	Thetford	150
1985	JR Marriott	Bristol and Clifton	153
1986	R Hiatt	Northants County	153
1987	I Caldwell	North Hants, Fleet (curtailed due to storm)	72
1988	G Edwards	Bromborough	222
1989	G Clark	West Sussex	212
1990	N Paul	Enville and Bridgnorth	217

English Open Over 35s Championship

(Formerly English Mid-Amateur)

Year	Winner	Club	Venue	Score
1988	P McEvoy	Copt Heath	Little Aston	284
1989	A Mew	Stoneham	Moortown	290
1990	A Mew	Stoneham	Wentworth	214

English Club Champions

Year	Winner	Club	Venue	Score
1989	Ealing	Southport and Ainsdale	Southport and Ainsdale	289
1990	Ealing	Porters Park	Goring and Streatley	277

English County Championship (Men)

Year	Winner	Year	Winner
1928	Warwickshire	1964	Northumberland
1929	Lancashire	1965	Northumberland
1930	Lancashire	1966	Surrey
1931	Yorkshire	1967	Lancashire
1932	Surrey	1968	Surrey
1933	Yorkshire	1969	Berks, Bucks, Oxon
1934	Worcestershire	1970	Gloucestershire
1935	Worcestershire	1971	Staffordshire
1936	Surrey	1972	Berks, Bucks, Oxon
1937	Lancashire	1973	Yorkshire
1938	Staffordshire	1974	Lincolnshire
1939	Worcestershire	1975	Staffordshire
1947	Staffordshire	1976	Warwickshire
1848	Staffordshire	1977	Warwickshire
1949	Lancashire	1978	Kent
1950	*Not Played*	1979	Gloucestershire
1951	Lancashire	1980	Surrey
1952	Yorkshire	1981	Surrey
1953	Yorkshire	1982	Yorkshire
1954	Cheshire	1983	Berks, Bucks, Oxon
1955	Yorkshire	1984	Yorkshire
1956	Staffordshire	1985 }	Devon Hertfordshire
1957	Surrey	1986	Hertfordshire
1958	Surrey	1987	Yorkshire
1959	Northumberland	1988	Warwickshire
1961	Lancashire	1989	Middlesex
1962	Northumberland	1990	Warwickshire
1963	Yorkshire		

English Ladies' Amateur Championship

Year	Winner	Runner-up	Venue	By
1960	M Nichol	A Bonallack	Burnham	3 and 1
1961	R Porter	P Reece	Littlestone	2 holes
1962	J Roberts	A Bonallack	Woodhall Spa	3 and 1
1963	A Bonallack	E Chadwick	Liphook	7 and 6
1964	M Spearman	M Everard	R Lytham and St Annes	6 and 5
1965	R Porter	C Cheetham	Whittington Barracks	6 and 5
1966	J Greenhalgh	JC Holmes	Hayling Island	3 and 1
1967	A Irwin	A Pickard	Alwoodley	3 and 2
1968	S Barber	D Oxley	Hunstanton	5 and 4
1969	B Dixon	M Wenyon	Burnham and Berrow	6 and 4
1970	D Oxley	S Barber	Rye	3 and 2
1971	D Oxley	S Barber	Hoylake	5 and 4
1972	M Everard	A Bonallack	Woodhall Spa	2 and 1
1973	M Walker	C Le Feuvre	Broadstone	6 and 5
1974	A Irvin	J Thornhill	Sunningdale	1 hole
1975	B Huke	L Harrold	R Birkdale	2 and 1
1976	L Harrold	A Uzielli	Hollinwell	3 and 2
1977	V Marvin	M Everard	Burnham and Berrow	1 hole
1978	V Marvin	R Porter	West Sussex	2 and 1
1979	J Greenhalgh	S Hedges	Hoylake	2 and 1
1980	B New	J Walker	Aldeburgh	3 and 2
1981	D Christison	S Cohen	Cotswold Hills	2 holes
1982	J Walter	C Nelson	Brancepeth Castle	4 and 3
1983	L Bayman	C Mackintosh	Hayling Island	4 and 3
1984	C Waite	L Bayman	Hunstanton	3 and 2
1985	P Johnson	L Bayman	Ferndown	1 hole
1986	J Thornhill	S Shapcott	Sandwich, Princes	3 and 1
1987	J Furby	M King	Alwoodley	4 and 3
1988	J Wade	S Shapcott	Little Aston	19th hole
1989	H Dobson	S Morgan	Burnham and Berrow	4 and 3
1990	A Uzielli	L Fletcher	Rye	2 and 1

English Ladies' Under-23 Championship

Year	Winner	Venue	Score
1978	S Bamford	Caldy	228
1979	B Cooper	Coxmoor	223
1980	B Cooper	Porters Park	226
1981	J Soulsby	Willesley Park	220
1982	M Gallagher	High Post	221
1983	P Grice	Hallamshire	219
1984	P Johnson	Moor Park	300
1985	P Johnson	Northants County	301
1986	S Shapcott	Broadstone	301
1987	J Wade	Northumberland	296
1988	J Wade	Wentworth	299
1989	A Shapcott	Notts Ladies	302
1990	K Tebbet	Saunton	299

English Ladies' Seniors Championship

Year	Winner	Venue	Score
1988	A Thompson	Wentworth	158
1989	C Bailey	Notts Ladies	163
1990	A Thompson	Fairhaven	162

English Ladies' Stroke-Play Championship

Year	Winner	Venue	Score
1984	P Grice	Moor Park	300
1985	P Johnson	Northants County	301
1986	S Shapcott	Broadstone	301
1987	J Wade	Northumberland	296
1988	S Prosser	Wentworth	297
1989	S Robinson	Notts	302
1990	K Tebbet	Saunton	299

English Ladies' Intermediate Championship

Year	Winner	Venue	Score
1982	J Rhodes	Headingley	19th hole
1983	L Davies	Worksop	2 and 1
1984	P Grice	Whittington Barracks	3 and 2
1985	S Lowe	Caldy	2 and 1
1986	S Moorcroft	Hexham	6 and 5
1987	J Wade	Sheringham	2 and 1
1988	S Morgan	Enville, Staffs	20th hole
1989	L Fairclough	Warrington	4 and 3
1990	L Fletcher	Whitley Bay	7 and 6

England and Wales (Ladies') County Championship

Year	Winner	Year	Winner	Year	Winner
1908	Lancashire	1937	Surrey	1968	Surrey
1909	Surrey	1938	Lancashire	1969	Lancashire
1910	Cheshire	1947	Surrey	1970	Yorkshire
1911	Cheshire	1948	Yorkshire	1971	Kent
1912	Cheshire	1949	Surrey	1972	Kent
1913	Surrey	1950	Yorkshire	1973	Northumberland
1920	Middlesex	1951	Lancashire	1974	Surrey
1921	Surrey	1952	Lancashire	1975	Glamorgan
1922	Surrey	1953	Surrey	1976	Staffordshire
1923	Surrey	1954	Warwickshire	1977	Essex
1924	Surrey	1955	Surrey	1978	Glamorgan
1925	Surrey	1956	Kent	1979	Essex
1926	Surrey	1957	Middlesex	1980	Lancashire
1927	Yorkshire	1958	Lancashire	1981	Glamorgan
1928	Cheshire	1959	Middlesex	1982	Surrey
1929	Yorkshire	1960	Lancashire	1983	Surrey
1930	Surrey	1961	Middlesex	1984	Surrey/Yorkshire
1931	Middlesex	1962	Staffordshire	1985	Surrey
1932	Cheshire	1963	Warwickshire	1986	Glamorgan
1933	Yorkshire	1964	Lancashire	1987	Lancashire
1934	Surrey	1965	Staffordshire	1988	Surrey
1935	Essex	1966	Lancashire	1989	Cheshire
1936	Surrey	1967	Lancashire	1990	Cheshire

Irish National Professional Championship

Year	Winner	Club	Venue	Score
1960	C O'Connor	Royal Dublin	Warrenpoint	271
1961	C O'Connor	Royal Dublin	Lahinch	280
1962	C O'Connor	Royal Dublin	Bangor	264
1963	C O'Connor	Royal Dublin	Little Island	271
1964	E Jones	Bangor	Knock	279
1965	C O'Connor	Royal Dublin	Mullingar	283
1966	C O'Connor	Royal Dublin	Warrenpoint	269
1967	H Boyle	Jacobs Golf Centre	Tullamore (3 rounds)	214
1968	C Greene	Mill Town	Knock	282
1969	J Martin	Unattached	Dundalk	268
1970	H Jackson	Knockbracken	Massareene	283
1971	C O'Connor	Royal Dublin	Galway	278
1972	J Kinsella	Castle	Bundoran	289
1973	J Kinsella	Castle	Limerick	284
1974	E Polland	Balmoral	Portstewart	277
1975	C O'Connor	Royal Dublin	Carlow	275
1976	P McGuirk	Co Louth	Waterville	291
1977	P Skerritt	St Annes	Woodbrook	281
1978	C O'Connor	Royal Dublin	Dollymount	286
1979	D Smyth	Bettystown	Dollymount (54 holes)	215
1980	D Feherty	Balmoral	Dollymount	283
1981	D Jones	Bangor	Woodbrook	283
1982	D Feherty	Balmoral	Woodbrook	287
1983	L Higgins	Waterville	Woodbrook	275
1984	M Sludds	—	Skerries	277
1985	D Smyth	—	Co Louth	204
(Played over 54 holes due to bad weather)				
1986	D Smyth	—	Waterville	282
1987	P Walton	Malahide	Co Louth	144
(Played over 36 holes due to bad weather. Walton won play-off)				
1988	E Darcy	Delgany	Castle, Dublin	269
1989	P Walton	Malahide	Castle, Dublin	266
1990	D Smyth	—	Woodbrook	271

Irish Amateur Championship

Year	Winner	Runner-up	Venue	By
1960	M Edwards	N Fogarty	Portstewart	6 and 5
1961	D Sheahan	J Brown	Rosses Point	5 and 4
1962	M Edwards	J Harrington	Baltray	42nd hole
1963	JB Carr	EC O'Brien	Killarney	2 and 1
1964	JB Carr	A McDade	Co Down	6 and 5
1965	JB Carr	T Craddock	Rosses Point	3 and 2
1966	D Sheahan	J Faith	Dollymount	3 and 2
1967	JB Carr	PD Flaherty	Lahinch	1 hole
1968	M O'Brien	F McCarroll	Portrush	2 and 1
1969	V Nevin	J O'Leary	Co Sligo	1 hole
1970	D Sheahan	M Bloom	Grange	2 holes
1971	P Kane	M O'Brien	Ballybunion	3 and 2
1972	K Stevenson	B Hoey	Co Down	2 and 1
1973	RKM Pollin	RM Staunton	Rosses Point	1 hole
1974	R Kane	M Gannon	Portmarnock	5 and 4
1975	MD O'Brien	JA Bryan	Cork	5 and 4
1976	D Brannigan	D O'Sullivan	Portrush	2 holes
1977	M Gannon	A Hayes	Westport	19th hole
1978	M Morris	T Cleary	Carlow	1 hole
1979	J Harrington	MA Gannon	Ballybunion	2 and 1
1980	R Rafferty	MJ Bannon	Co Down	8 and 7
1981	D Brannigan	E McMenamin	Co Sligo	19th hole
1982	P Walton	B Smyth	Woodbrook	7 and 6
1983	T Corridan	E Power	Killarney	2 holes
1984	CB Hoey	L McNamara	Malone	20th hole
1985	D O'Sullivan	D Branigan	Westport	1 hole
1986	J McHenry	P Rayfus	Dublin	4 and 3
1987	E Power	JP Fitzgerald	Tranmore	2 holes
1988	G McGimpsey	D Mulholland	Portrush	2 and 1
1989	P McGinley	N Goulding	Rosses Point	3 and 2
1990	D Clarke	P Harrington	Baltray	3 and 2

Irish Seniors' Open Amateur Championship

Year	Winner	Venue	Score
1980	GN Fogarty	Galway	144
1981	GN Fogarty	Bundoran	149
1982	J Murray	Douglas	141
1983	F Sharpe	Courtown	153
1984	J Boston	Connemara	147
1985	J Boston	Newcastle	155
1986	J Coey	Waterford	141
1987	J Murray	Castleroy	150
1988	WB Buckley	Westport	154
1989	B McCrea	Royal Belfast	150
1990	C Hartland	Cork	149

Irish Ladies' Amateur Championship

Year	Winner	Runner-up	Venue	By
1960	P Garvey	PG McGann	Cork	5 and 3
1961	K McCann	A Sweeney	Newcastle	5 and 3
1962	P Garvey	M Earner	Baltray	7 and 6
1963	P Garvey	E Barnett	Killarney	9 and 7
1964	Z Fallon	P O'Sullivan	Portrush	37th hole
1965	E Purcell	P O'Sullivan	Mullingar	3 and 2
1966	E Bradshaw	P O'Sullivan	Rosslare	3 and 2
1967	G Brandom	P O'Sullivan	Castlerock	3 and 2
1968	E Bradshaw	M McKenna	Lahinch	3 and 2
1969	M McKenna	C Hickey	Ballybunion	3 and 2
1970	P Garvey	M Earner	Portrush	2 and 1

Year	Winner	Runner-up	Venue	By
1971	E Bradshaw	M Mooney	Baltray	3 and 1
1972	M McKenna	I Butler	Killarney	5 and 4
1973	M Mooney	M McKenna	Bundoran	2 and 1
1974	M McKenna	V Singleton	Lahinch	3 and 2
1975	M Gorry	E Bradshaw	Tramore	1 hole
1976	C Nesbitt	M McKenna	Rosses Point	20th hole
1977	M McKenna	R Hegarty	Ballybunion	2 holes
1978	M Gorry	I Butler	Grange	4 and 3
1979	M McKenna	C Nesbitt	Donegal	6 and 5
1980	C Nesbitt	C Hourihane	Lahinch	1 hole
1981	M McKenna	M Kenny	Laytown & Bettystown	1 hole
1982	M McKenna	M Madill	Portrush	2 and 1
1983	C Hourihane	V Hassett	Cork	6 and 4
1984	C Hourihane	M Madill	Rosses Point	19th hole
1985	C Hourihane	M McKenna	Waterville	4 and 3
1986	T O'Reilly	E Higgins	Castlerock	4 and 3
1987	C Hourihane	C Hickey	Lahinch	5 and 4
1988	L Bolton	E Higgins	Tramore	2 and 1
1989	M McKenna	C Wickham	West Port	19th hole
1990	ER McDaid	L Callan	The Island	2 and 1

Scottish Professional Championship

Year	Winner	Club	Venue	Score
1960	EC Brown	Buchanan Castle	West Kilbride	278
1961	RT Walker	Downfield, Dundee	Forres	271
1962	EC Brown	Unattached	Dunbar	283
1963	WM Miller	Cardross	Crieff	284
1964	RT Walker	Downfield, Dundee	Machrihanish	277
1965	EC Brown	Cruden Bay	Forfar	271
1966	EC Brown / J Panton } tie	Cruden Bay / Glenbervie }	Cruden Bay (36 holes)	137
1967	H Bannerman	Aberdeen	Montrose	279
1968	EC Brown	Cruden Bay	Monktonhall	286
1969	G Cunningham	Troon Municipal	Machrihanish	284
1970	RDBM Shade	Duddingston	Montrose	276
1971	NJ Gallacher	Wentworth	Lundin Links	282
1972	H Bannerman	Banchory	Strathaven	268
1973	BJ Gallacher	Wentworth	Kings Links, Aberdeen	276
1974	BJ Gallacher	Wentworth	Drumpellier	276
1975	D Huish	North Berwick	Duddingston	279
1976	J Chillas	Crow Wood	Haggs Castle	286
1977	BJ Gallacher	Wentworth	Barnton	282
1978	S Torrance	Caledonian Hotel	Strathaven	269
1979	AWB Lyle	Hawkstone Park	Glasgow Gailes	274
1980	S Torrance	Caledonian Hotel	East Kilbride	273
1981	B Barnes	Caledonian Hotel	Dalmahoy	275
1982	B Barnes	Caledonian Hotel	Dalmahoy	286
1983	B Gallacher	Wentworth	Dalmahoy	276
(After play-off)				
1984	I Young	Dalmahoy	Dalmahoy	276
1985	S Torrance	Unattached	Dalmahoy	277
1986	R Drummond	Strathclyde Hardware	Glenbervie	270
1987	R Drummond	Strathclyde Hardware	Glenbervie	268
1988	S Stephen	Stephen Architects	Haggs Castle	283
1989	R Drummond	Continental Airlines	Monktonhall	274
1990	R Drummond	Continental Airlines	Deer Park	278

Scottish Amateur Championship

Year	Winner	Runner-up	Venue	By
1922	J Wilson	E Blackwell	St Andrews	19th hole
1923	TM Burrell	Dr A McCallum	Troon	1 hole
1924	WW Mackenzie	W Tulloch	Aberdeen	3 and 2
1925	JT Dobson	W Mackenzie	Muirfield	3 and 2
1926	WJ Guild	SO Shepherd	Leven	2 and 1
1927	A Jamieson, Jr	Rev D Rutherford	Gailes	22nd hole
1928	WW Mackenzie	W Dodds	Muirfield	5 and 3

Scottish Amateur Championship
continued

Year	Winner	Runner-up	Venue	By
1929	JT Bookless	J Dawson	Aberdeen	5 and 4
1930	K Greig	T Wallace	Carnoustie	9 and 8
1931	J Wilson	A Jamieson, Jr	Prestwick	2 and 1
1932	J McLean	K Greig	Dunbar	5 and 4
1933	J McLean	KC Forbes	Aberdeen	6 and 4
1934	J McLean	W Campbell	Western Gailes	3 and 1
1935	H Thomson	J McLean	St Andrews	2 and 1
1936	ED Hamilton	R Neill	Carnoustie	1 hole
1937	H McInally	K Patrick	Barassie	6 and 5
1938	ED Hamilton	R Rutherford	Muirfield	4 and 2
1939	H McInally	H Thomson	Prestwick	6 and 5
1946	EC Brown	R Rutherford	Carnoustie	3 and 2
1947	H McInally	J Pressley	Glasgow Gailes	10 and 8
1948	AS Flockhart	G Taylor	Balgownie, Aberdeen	7 and 6
1949	R Wright	H McInally	Muirfield	1 hole
1950	WC Gibson	D Blair	Prestwick	2 and 1
1951	JM Dykes	J Wilson	St Andrews	4 and 2
1952	FG Dewar	J Wilson	Carnoustie	4 and 3
1953	DA Blair	J McKay	Western Gailes	3 and 1
1954	JW Draper	W Gray	Nairn	4 and 3
1955	RR Jack	AC Miller	Muirfield	2 and 1
1956	Dr FWG Deighton	A MacGregor	Troon	8 and 7
1957	JS Montgomerie	J Burnside	Balgownie	2 and 1
1958	WD Smith	I Harris	Prestwick	6 and 5
1959	Dr FWG Deighton	R Murray	St Andrews	6 and 5
1960	JR Young	S Saddler	Carnoustie	5 and 3
1961	J Walker	ST Murray	Western Gailes	4 and 3
1962	SWT Murray	R Shade	Muirfield	2 and 1
1963	RDBM Shade	N Henderson	Troon	4 and 3
1964	RDBM Shade	J McBeath	Nairn	8 and 7
1965	RDBM Shade	G Cosh	St Andrews	4 and 2
1966	RDBM Shade	C Strachan	Western Gailes	9 and 8
1967	RDBM Shade	A Murphy	Carnoustie	5 and 4
1968	GB Cosh	R Renfrew	Muirfield	4 and 3
1969	JM Cannon	A Hall	Troon	6 and 4
1970	CW Green	H Stewart	Balgownie, Aberdeen	1 hole
1971	S Stephen	C Green	St Andrews	3 and 2
1972	HB Stuart	A Pirie	Prestwick	3 and 1
1973	IC Hutcheon	A Brodie	Carnoustie	3 and 2
1974	GH Murray	A Pirie	Western Gailes	2 and 1
1975	D Greig	G Murray	Montrose	7 and 6
1976	GH Murray	H Stuart	St Andrews	6 and 5
1977	A Brodie	P McKellar	Troon	1 hole
1978	IA Carslaw	J Cuddihy	Downfield	7 and 6
1979	K Macintosh	P McKellar	Prestwick	5 and 4
1980	D Jamieson	C Green	Balgownie, Aberdeen (18 holes)	2 and 1
1981	C Dalgleish	A Thomson	Western Gailes	7 and 6
1982	CW Green	G McGregor	Carnoustie	1 hole
1983	CW Green	J Huggan	Gullane	1 hole
1984	A Moir	K Buchan	Renfrew	3 and 3
1985	D Carrick	D James	Southerness	4 and 2
1986	C Brooks	A Thomson	Monifieth	3 and 2
1987	C Montgomerie	A Watt	Nairn	9 and 8
1988	J Milligan	A Colthart	Barassie	1 hole
1989	A Thomson	A Tait	Moray	1 hole
1990	C Everett	M Thomson	Gullane	7 and 5

Scottish Open Amateur Stroke Play Championship

Year	Winner	Club	Venue	Score
1967	BJ Gallacher	Bathgate	Muirfield and Gullane	291
1968	RDBM Shade	Duddingston	Prestwick and Prestwick St Nicholas	282
1969	JS Macdonald	Dalmahoy	Carnoustie and Monifieth	288
1970	D Hayes	South Africa	Glasgow Gailes and Barassie	275
1971	IC Hutcheon	Monifieth	Leven and Lundin Links	277
1972	BN Nicholas	Nairn	Dalmahoy and Ratho Park	290
1973	{ DM Robertson	Dunbar } tie	Dunbar and North Berwick	284
	{ GJ Clark	Whitley Bay }		

Scottish Open Amateur Stroke Play Championship

continued

Year	Winner	Club	Venue	Score
1974	IC Hutcheon	Monifieth	Blairgowrie and Alyth	283
1975	CW Green	Dumbarton	Nairn and Nairn Dunbar	295
1976	S Martin	Downfield	Monifieth and Carnoustie	299
1977	PJ McKellar	East Renfrewshire	Muirfield and Gullane	299
1978	AR Taylor	East Kilbride	Keir and Cawder	281
1979	IC Hutcheon	Monifieth	Lansdowne and Rosemount	286
1980	G Brand Jr	Knowle	Musselburgh and R Musselburgh (54 holes)	207
1981	F Walton	Malahide	Erskine and Renfrew	287
1982	C Macgregor	Glencourse	Downfield and Camperdown	287
1983	C Murray	Fereneze	Irvine	291
1984	CW Green	Dumbarton	Blairgowrie	287
1985	C Montgomerie	Royal Troon	Dunbar	274
1986	KH Walker	Royal Burgess	Carnoustie	289
1987	D Carrick	Douglas Park	Lundin Links	282
1988	S Easingwood	Dunbar	Cathkin Braes	277
1989	F Illouz	France	Blairgowrie	281
1990	G Hay	Hilton Park	R Aberdeen	133 (36 holes)

Scottish Open Amateur Seniors' Championship

Year	Winner	Club	Venue	Score
1978	JM Cannon / GR Carmichael } tie	Irvine / Ladybank	Glasgow Killermont	149
1979	A Sinclair	Drumpellier	Glasgow Killermont	143
1980	JM Cannon	Irvine	Royal Burgess	149
1981	IR Harris / Dr J Hastings } tie / AN Sturrock	Royal Troon / Royal Troon / Royal Troon	Glasgow Killermont	146
1982	JM Cannon / J Niven } tie	Irvine / Newbury & Crookham	Royal Burgess	143
1983	WD Smith	Prestwick	Glasgow Killermont	145
1984	A Sinclair	Drumpellier	Royal Burgess	148
1985	AN Sturrock	Prestwick	Glasgow Killermont	143
1986	RL Glading	Mitcham	Royal Burgess	153
1987	I Hornsby	Ponteland	Glasgow Killermont	145
1988	J Hayes	Gosforth	Royal Burgess	143
1989	AS Mayer	Torwoodlee	Glasgow Killermont	
1990	G Hartland	Huddersfield	Royal Burgess	146

Scottish Ladies' Amateur Championship

Year	Winner	Runner-up	Venue	By
1960	JS Robertson	DT Sommerville	Turnberry	2 and 1
1961	JS Wright (née Robertson)	AM Lurie	St Andrews	1 hole
1962	JB Lawrence	C Draper	R Dornoch	5 and 4
1963	JB Lawrence	IC Robertson	Troon	2 and 1
1964	JB Lawrence	SM Reid	Gullane	5 and 3
1965	IC Robertson	JB Lawrence	Nairn	5 and 4
1966	IC Robertson	M Fowler	Machrihanish	2 and 1
1967	J Hastings	A Laing	North Berwick	5 and 3
1968	J Smith	J Rennie	Carnoustie	10 and 9
1969	JH Anderson	K Lackie	West Kilbride	5 and 4
1970	A Laing	IC Robertson	Dunbar	1 hole
1971	IC Robertson	A Ferguson	R Dornoch	3 and 2
1972	IC Robertson	CJ Lugton	Machrihanish	5 and 3
1973	I Wright	Dr AJ Wilson	St Andrews	2 holes
1974	Dr AJ Wilson	K Lackie	Nairn	22nd hole
1975	LA Hope	JW Smith	Elie	1 hole
1976	S Needham	T Walker	Machrihanish	3 and 2
1977	CJ Lugton	M Thomson	R Dornoch	1 hole
1978	IC Robertson	JW Smith	Prestwick	2 holes
1979	G Stewart	LA Hope	Gullane	2 and 1
1980	IC Robertson	F Anderson	Carnoustie	1 hole
1981	A Gemmill	W Aitken	Stranraer	2 and 1
1982	J Connachan	P Wright	R Troon	19th hole

Year	Winner	Runner-up	Venue	By
1983	G Stewart	F Anderson	North Berwick	3 and 1
1984	G Stewart	A Gemmill	R Dornoch	3 and 2
1985	A Gemmill	D Thomson	Barassie	2 and 1
1986	IC Robertson	L Hope	St Andrews	3 and 2
1987	F Anderson	C Middleton	Nairn	4 and 3
1988	S Lawson	F Anderson	Southerness	3 and 1
1989	J Huggon	L Anderson	Lossiemouth	5 and 4
1990	E Farquharson	S Huggan	Machrihanish	3 and 2

Scottish Ladies' Amateur Championship
continued

Welsh Professional Championship

Year	Winner	Club	Venue	Score
1960	RH Kemp, Jr	Unattached	Llandudno	288
1961	S Mouland	Glamorganshire	Southerndown	286
1962	S Mouland	Glamorganshire	Porthcawl	302
1963	H Gould	Southerndown	Wrexham	291
1964	B Bielby	Portmadoc	Tenby	297
1965	S Mouland	Glamorganshire	Penarth	281
1966	S Mouland	Glamorganshire	Conway	281
1967	S Mouland	Glamorganshire	Pyle and Kenfig	
			(54 holes, fog)	219
1968	RJ Davies	South Herts	Southerndown	292
1969	S Mouland	Glamorganshire	Llandudno	277
1970	W Evans	Pennard	Tredegar Park	289
1971	J Buckley	North Wales	St Pierre	291
1972	J Buckley	Rhos-on-Sea	Porthcawl	298
1973	A Griffiths	Wrexham	Newport	289
1974	M Hughes	Aberystwyth	Cardiff	284
1975	C DeFoy	Bryn Meadows	Whitchurch	285
1976	S Cox	Wenvoe Castle	Radyr	284
1977	C DeFoy	Calcot Park	Glamorganshire	135
1978	BCC Huggett	Cambridgeshire Hotel	Whitchurch	145
1979	Cancelled			
1980	A Griffiths	Llanymynech	Cardiff	139
1981	C DeFoy	Coombe Hill	Cardiff	139
1982	C DeFoy	Coombe Hill	Cardiff	137
1983	S Cox	Wenvoe Castle	Cardiff	136
1984	K Jones	Caldy	Cardiff	135
1985	D Llewellyn	Thirsk	Whitchurch	132
1986	P Parkin	Blue Arrow	Whitchurch	142
1987	A Dodman	St Pierre	Cardiff	132
1988	I Woosnam	Wang	Cardiff	137
1989	K Jones	Caldy	Royal Porthcawl	140
1990	P Mayo	Powell Duffryn	Fairwood Park	136

Welsh Amateur Championship

Year	Winner	Runner-up	Venue	By
1934	SB Roberts	GS Noon	Prestatyn	4 and 3
1935	R Chapman	GS Noon	Tenby	1 hole
1936	RM de Lloyd	G Wallis	Aberdovey	1 hole
1937	DH Lewis	R Glossop	Porthcawl	2 holes
1938	AA Duncan	SB Roberts	Rhyl	2 and 1
1946	JV Moody	A Marshman	Porthcawl	9 and 8
1947	SB Roberts	G Breen Turner	Harlech	8 and 7
1948	AA Duncan	SB Roberts	Porthcawl	2 and 1
1949	AD Evans	MA Jones	Aberdovey	2 and 1
1950	JL Morgan	DJ Bonnell	Southerndown	9 and 7
1951	JL Morgan	WI Tucker	Harlech	3 and 2
1952	AA Duncan	JL Morgan	Ashburnham	4 and 3
1953	SB Roberts	D Pearson	Prestatyn	5 and 3
1954	AA Duncan	K Thomas	Tenby	6 and 5
1955	TJ Davies	P Dunn	Harlech	38th hole
1956	A Lockley	WI Tucker	Southerndown	2 and 1
1957	ES Mills	H Griffiths	Harlech	2 and 1
1958	HC Squirrell	AD Lake	Conway	4 and 3
1959	HC Squirrell	N Rees	Porthcawl	8 and 7
1960	HC Squirrell	P Richards	Aberdovey	2 and 1
1961	AD Evans	J Toye	Ashburnham	3 and 2
1962	J Povall	HC Squirrell	Harlech	3 and 2

Year	Winner	Runner-up	Venue	By
1963	WI Tucker	J Povall	Southerndown	4 and 3
1964	HC Squirrell	WI Tucker	Harlech	1 hole
1965	HC Squirrell	G Clay	Porthcawl	6 and 4
1966	WI Tucker	EN Davies	Aberdovey	6 and 5
1967	JK Povall	WI Tucker	Asburnham	3 and 2
1968	J Buckley	J Povall	Conway	8 and 7
1969	JL Toye	EN Davies	Porthcawl	1 hole
1970	EN Davies	J Povall	Harlech	1 hole
1971	CT Brown	HC Squirrell	Southerndown	6 and 5
1972	EN Davies	JL Toye	Prestatyn	40th hole
1973	D McLean	T Holder	Ashburnham	6 and 4
1974	S Cox	EN Davies	Caernarvonshire	3 and 2
1975	JL Toye	WI Tucker	Porthcawl	5 and 4
1976	MPD Adams	WI Tucker	Harlech	6 and 5
1977	D Stevens	JKD Povall	Southerndown	3 and 2
1978	D McLean	A Ingram	Caernarvonshire	11 and 10
1979	TJ Melia	MS Roper	Ashburnham	5 and 4
1980	DL Stevens	G Clement	Prestatyn	10 and 9
1981	S Jones	C Davies	Porthcawl	5 and 3
1982	D Wood	C Davies	Harlech	8 and 7
1983	JR Jones	AP Parkin	Southerndown	2 holes
1984	JR Jones	A Llyr	Prestatyn	1 hole
1985	ED Jones	MA Macara	Ashburnham	2 and 1
1986	C Rees	B Knight	Conwy	1 hole
1987	PM Mayo	DK Wood	Porthcawl	2 holes
1988	K Jones	RN Roderick	Harlech	40th hole
1989	S Dodd	K Jones	Tenby	2 and 1
1990	A Barnett	A Jones	Prestatyn	1 hole

Welsh Amateur Championship

continued

Welsh Amateur Stroke Play Championship

(Became open event 1990)

Year	Winner	Club	Venue	Score
1967	EN Davies	Llantrisant	Harlech	295
1968	JA Buckley	Rhos-on-Sea	Harlech	294
1969	DL Stevens	Llantrisant	Tenby	288
1970	JK Povall	Whitchurch	Newport	292
1971	EN Davies / JL Toye } tie	Llantrisant / Radyr	Harlech	296
1972	JR Jones	Wrexham	Pyle and Kenfig	299
1973	JR Jones	Caernarvonshire	Llandudno (Maesdu)	300
1974	JL Toye	Radyr	Tenby	307
1975	D McLean	Holyhead	Wrexham	288
1976	WI Tucker	Monmouthshire	Newport	282
1977	JA Buckley	Abergele and Pensarn	Prestatyn	302
1978	HJ Evans	Llangland Bay	Pyle and Kenfig	300
1979	D McLean	Holyhead	Holyhead	289
1980	TJ Melia	Cardiff	Tenby	291
1981	D Evans	Leek	Wrexham	270
1982	JR Jones	Langland Bay	Cradoc	287
1983	G Davies	Pontypool	Aberdovey	287
1984	RN Roderick	Portardawe	Newport	292
1985	MA Macara	Llandudno	Harlech	291
1986	M Calvert	Aberystwyth	Pyle and Kenfig	299
1987	MA Macara	Llandudno	Llandudno (Maesdu)	290
1988	RN Roderick	Portardawe	Tenby	283
1989	SC Dodd	Brynhill	Conwy (Carnarfonshire)	304
1990	G Houston	Flint	Pyle and Kenfig	288

Welsh Seniors' Amateur Championship

Year	Winner	Club	Venue	Score
1975	A Marshman	Brecon	Aberdovey	77 (18 holes)
1976	AD Evans	Ross on Wye	Aberdovey	156
1977	AE Lockley	Swansea Bay	Aberdovey	154
1978	AE Lockley	Swansea Bay	Aberdovey	75 (18 holes)
1979	CR Morgan	Monmouthshire	Aberdovey	158
1980	ES Mills	Llandudno (Maesdu)	Aberdovey	152
1981	T Branton	Newport	Aberdovey	153
1982	WI Tucker	Monmouthshire	Aberdovey	147
1983	WS Gronow	East Berks	Aberdovey	153
1984	WI Tucker	Monmouthshire	Aberdovey	150
1985	NA Lycett	Aberdovey	Aberdovey	149
1986	E Mills	Aberdovey	Aberdovey	154
1987	WS Gronow	East Berks	Aberdovey	146
1988	NA Lycett	Aberdovey	Aberdovey	150
1989	WI Tucker	Monmouthshire	Aberdovey	160
1990	I Hughes	Abergele and Pensarn	Aberdovey	159

Welsh Ladies' Amateur Championship

Year	Winner	Runner-up	Venue	By
1960	M Barron	E Brown	Tenby	8 and 6
1961	M Oliver	N Sneddon	Aberdovey	5 and 4
1962	M Oliver	P Roberts	Radyr	4 and 2
1963	P Roberts	N Sneddon	Harlech	7 and 5
1964	M Oliver	M Wright	Southerndown	1 hole
1965	M Wright	E Brown	Prestatyn	3 and 2
1966	A Hughes	P Roberts	Ashburnham	5 and 4
1967	M Wright	C Phipps	Harlech	21st hole
1968	S Hales	M Wright	Porthcawl	3 and 2
1969	P Roberts	A Hughes	Caernarvonshire	3 and 2
1970	A Briggs	J Morris	Newport	19th hole
1971	A Briggs	EN Davies	Harlech	2 and 1
1972	A Hughes	J Rogers	Tenby	3 and 2
1973	A Briggs	J John	Holyhead	3 and 2
1974	A Briggs	Dr H Lyall	Ashburnham	3 and 2
1975	A Johnson (née Hughes)	K Rawlings	Prestatyn	1 hole
1976	T Perkins	A Johnson	Porthcawl	4 and 2
1977	T Perkins	P Whitley	Aberdovey	5 and 4
1978	P Light	A Briggs	Newport	2 and 1
1979	V Rawlings	A Briggs	Caernarvonshire	2 holes
1980	M Rawlings	A Briggs	Tenby	2 and 1
1981	M Rawlings	A Briggs	Harlech	5 and 3
1982	V Thomas (née Rawlings)	M Rawlings	Ashburnham	7 and 6
1983	V Thomas	T Thomas (née Perkins)	Llandudno	1 hole
1984	S Roberts	K Davies	Newport	5 and 4
1985	V Thomas	S Jump	Prestatyn	1 hole
1986	V Thomas	L Isherwood	Porthcawl	7 and 6
1987	V Thomas	S Roberts	Aberdovey	3 and 1
1988	S Roberts	F Connor	Tenby	4 and 2
1989	H Lawson	V Thomas	Conwy	2 and 1
1990	S Roberts	H Wadsworth	Ashburnham	3 and 2

Welsh Ladies' Open Amateur Stroke Play Championship

Year	Winner	Club	Venue	Score
1981	V Thomas	Pennard	Aberdovey	224
1982	V Thomas	Pennard	Aberdovey	225
1983	J Thornhill	Walton Heath	Aberdovey	239
1984	L Davies	West Byfleet	Aberdovey	230
1985	C Swallow		Aberdovey	219
1986	H Wadsworth	Princes	Aberdovey	223
1987	S Shapcott	Knowle	Newport	225
1988	S Shapcott	Knowle	Newport	218
1989	V Thomas	Pennard	Newport	220
1990	L Hackney	Trentham	Newport	218

Welsh Ladies' Senior Championship

Year	Winner	Club	Venue	Score
1990	E Higgs	Wrexham	Vale of Llangollen	171

Overseas National Championships

except PGA European Tour Events

Argentine Open Championship

Year	Winner	Year	Winner
1981	V Fernandez	1986	V Fernandez
1982	J Soto	1987	M Fernandez
1983	A Sowa	1988	M Fernandez
1984	V Fernandez	1989	E Romero
1985	V Fernandez	1990	V Fernandez

Argentine Amateur Championship

Year	Winner	Year	Winner
1981	J Devoto	1986	D Ventureira
1982	D Vizzolini	1987	J Rivas
1983	D Vizzolini	1988	J Nougues, Jr
1984	M Prado	1989	F Alemán
1985	F Curutchet	1990	R Damm

Argentine Ladies' Amateur Championship

Year	Winner	Year	Winner
1981	S Garmendia	1986	M Abramoff
1982	S Garmendia	1987	V Podrug
1983	M Noguerol	1988	M Noguerol
1984	A Lagrutta	1989	M Noguerol
1985	M Noguerol	1990	M Olivero

Australian Open Championship

Year	Winner	Score	Year	Winner	Score
1975	J Nicklaus	279	1984	T Watson	281
1976	J Nicklaus	286	1985	G Norman	212
1977	D Graham	284	*(54 holes only–rain)*		
1978	J Nicklaus	284	1986	R Davies	
1979	J Newton	288	1987	G Norman	273
1980	G Norman	284	1988	M Calcavecchia	269
1981	B Rogers	282	1989	P Senior	271
1982	R Shearer	287	1990	J Morse	283
1983	P Fowler	285			

Australian Professional Championship

Year	Winner	Year	Winner
1981	S Ballesteros	1986	G Norman
1982	G Marsh	1987	R Mackay
1983	B Shearer	1988	W Grady
1984	G Norman	1989	P Senior
1985	G Norman	1990	B Ogle

Australian Amateur Championship

Year	Winner	Year	Winner
1981	O Moore	1986	D Ecob
1982	E Couper	1987	B Johns
1983	W Smith	1988	S Bouvier
1984	B King	1989	S Conran
1985	S Ruangit	1990	C Gray

Australian Ladies' Amateur Championship

Year	Winner	Year	Winner
1981	C Dibnah	1986	E Kennedy
1982	R Lautens	1987	E Cavill
1983	S McCaw	1988	C Bourtayre
1984	S McCaw	1989	J Higgins
1985	H Greenwood	1990	J Shearwood

Austrian Amateur Open Championship

Year	Winner	Year	Winner
1981	C Kilian	1986	D Carrick
1982	C-C Yuan	1987	Y-S Chen
1983	C-C Yuan	1988	L Peterson
1984	C-H Yu	1989	U Zilg
1985	C-S Hsieh	1990	A Peterskovsky

Austrian Ladies' Open Championship

Year	Winner	Year	Winner
1981	N Le Roux	1986	W-L Li
1982	J Orley	1987	Y-S Chen
1983	Y-Y Chen	1988	H-F Tseng
1984	M-C Cheng	1989	K Poppmeier
1985	P Peter	1990	A Rast

BMW European Ladies' Masters
(formerly Belgian Ladies' Open Championship)

Year	Winner
1985	L Davies
1986	P Grice-Whittaker
1987	ML de Lorenzi
1988	K Lunn
1989	K Douglas
1990	K Lunn

Canadian Open Championship

Year	Winner	Year	Winner
1975	T Weiskopf	1983	J Cook
1976	J Pate	1984	G Norman
1977	L Trevino	1985	C Strange
1978	B Lietzke	1986	B Murphy
1979	L Trevino	1987	C Strange
1980	B Gilder	1988	K Green
1981	P Oosterhuis	1989	S Jones
1982	B Lietzke	1990	W Levi

Canadian Amateur Championship

Year	Winner	Year	Winner
1981	R Zokol	1986	B Franklin
1982	D Roxburgh	1987	B Franklin
1983	D Mijovic	1988	D Roxburgh
1984	W Swartz	1989	P Major
1985	B Franklin	1990	W Sye

Canadian Ladies' Open Amateur Championship

Year	Winner	Year	Winner
1981	J Lock	1986	M O'Connor
1982	C Pleger	1987	T Kerdyk
1983	D Coe	1988	M Hattori
1984	K Williams	1989	C Damphouse
1985	K Williams	1990	S Lebrun

Czechoslovak Open Amateur Championship

Year	Winner	Year	Winner
1981	P Fulín	1986	D Kraljic
1982	M Brtek	1987	G Nikitaidis
1983	J Kunsta	1988	M Brtek
1984	Ch Czerny	1989	A Krag
1985	J Juhaniak	1990	J Janda

Czechoslovak Ladies' Open Amateur Championship

Year	Winner	Year	Winner
1981	L Krenková	1986	L Krenková
1982	G Hobbs	1987	A Hudcová
1983	L Krenková	1988	A Hudcová
1984	A Robetínová	1989	A Kugelmüller
1985	L Krenková	1990	A Kugelmüller

Danish Amateur Stroke Play Championship

Year	Winner	Year	Winner
1981	I Andersen	1986	P Digebjerg
1982	A Sørensen	1987	M Brodersen
1983	T Morsbol	1988	B Tinning
1984	J Rasmussen	1989	R Budde
1985	A Sørensen	1990	T Bjørn

Danish Ladies' Open Championship

Year	Winner
1988	F Descampe
1989	T Abitbol
1990	*Not played*

Danish Ladies' Stroke Play Championship

Year	Winner	Year	Winner
1981	A Peitersen	1986	M Meiland
1982	L Eliasen	1987	A Peitersen
1983	M Meiland	1988	J Kragh
1984	M Meiland	1989	M Brandt Anderson
1985	M Meiland	1990	P Carlson

French Open Amateur Championship

Year	Winner	Year	Winner
1981	F Illouz	1986	*Not played*
1982	F Illouz	1987	F Lindgren
1983	A Godillot	1988	*Not played*
1984	A Godillot	1989	G Shemano
1985	R Taher	1990	*Not played*

French Men's Close Amateur Championship

Year	Winner	Year	Winner
1981	T Planchin	1986	J van der Velde
1982	A Godillot	1987	G Brizay
1983		1988	P Barquez
1984	Y Houssin	1989	C Cevaer
1985	J-F Remesy	1990	O Edmond

French Ladies' Open Championship

Year	Winner	Score
1987	L Neumann	293
1988	ML de Lorenzi	285
1989	S Strudwick	285
1990	Not played	

French Ladies' Open Amateur Championship

Year	Winner
1984	LA Chen
1985	M Campomanes
1986	Not played
1987	S Louapre
1988	Not played
1989	E Orley
1990	Not played

French Ladies' Close Championship

Year	Winner	Year	Winner
1981	C Soules	1986	ML de Lorenzi
1982	E Berthet	1987	S Louapre
1983	ML de Lorenzi	1988	C Marty
1984	C Soules	1989	C Bourtayre
1985	V Pammard	1990	C Bourson

International PGA Championship of Germany

(formerly German Close Professional Championship)

Year	Winner	Year	Winner
1981	M Kessler	1986	S Vollrath
1982	H-P Thül	1987	H-P Thül
1983	T Gideon	1988	T Gideon
1984	H-J Kupitz	1989	T Gideon
1985	H-P Thül	1990	S Strüver

German Open Amateur Championship

Year	Winner	Year	Winner
1981	K Flint	1986	*Not played*
1982	F Schlig	1987	N Sallmann
1983	C Stadler	1988	*Not played*
1984	T Hübner	1989	J Steenkamer
1985	R Thielemann	1990	*Not played*

German Close Amateur Championship

Year	Winner	Year	Winner
1981	U Schulte	1986	S Strüver
1982	F Schlig	1987	HG Reiter
1983	C Domin	1988	U Zilg
1984	A Stamm	1989	H Reiter
1985	F Schlig	1990	M Von Hagen

German Ladies' Open Championship

Year	Winner
1984	B Huke
1985	J Brown
1986	L Neumann
1987	ML de Lorenzi
1988	L Neumann
1989	A Nicholas
1990	A Okamoto

International PGA Championship of Germany (Ladies)
(formerly German Ladies' Close Professional Championship)

Year	Winner
1986	S Eckrodt
1987	S Eckrodt
1988	D Franz
1989	D Franz
1990	D Franz

German Ladies' Open Amateur Championship

Year	Winner	Year	Winner
1981	S Blecher	1986	*Not played*
1982	S Knodler	1987	S Lambert
1983	I Bockelmann	1988	*Not played*
1984	S Lampert	1989	M Fischer
1985	M Koch	1990	*Not played*

German Ladies' Close Championship

Year	Winner	Year	Winner
1981	Dr B Bohm	1986	I Bockelmann
1982	E Peter	1987	P Peter
1983	S Knodler	1988	C Grundherr
1984	M Koch	1989	M Fischer
1985	R Ruland	1990	L Gehlen

Hong Kong Open Championship

Year	Winner	Year	Winner
1981	CT Ming	1986	S Kanai
1982	K Cox	1987	I Woosnam
1983	G Norman	1988	H Chin-sheng
1984	B Brask	1989	B Claar
1985	M Aebli	1990	K Green

Iceland Amateur Championship

Year	Winner	Year	Winner
1981	R Olafsson	1986	U Jónsson
1982	P Sigurdur	1987	U Jónsson
1983	G Kristinnsson	1988	S Sigurdsson
1984	S Pétursson	1989	U Jónsson
1985	S Pétursson	1990	U Jónsson

Iceland Ladies' Championship

Year	Winner	Year	Winner
1981	S Thorsteinsdóttir	1986	S Saemundsdóttir
1982	S Thorsteinsdóttir	1987	Th Geirsdóttir
1983	A Sverrisdóttir	1988	S Saemundsdóttir
1984	A Sverrisdóttir	1989	K Saevarsdóttir
1985	R Sigurdardótir	1990	K Saevarsdóttir

India Open Championship

Year	Winner	Year	Winner
1981	P Stewart	1986	L Hsi-Chuen
1982	HS San	1987	B Tennyson
1983	J Takahashi	1988	L Chien-Soon
1984	R Alarcon	1989	R Bouchard
1985	A Grimes	1990	A Debusk

India Men's Amateur Championship

Year	Winner
1984	R Narain
1985	A Sharma
1986	R Mehta
1987	L Singh
1988	KN Perera
1989	A Johl
1990	V Bhandari

India Ladies' Championship

Year	Winner	Year	Winner
1981	M Wallis	1986	R Grewal
1982	R Grewal	1987	E Cavill
1983	K Kanwar	1988	N Lal
1984	S Saheed	1989	S Sobti
1985	N Lal	1990	J Higgins

Italian Professional Championship

Year	Winner	Year	Winner
1981	M Mannelli	1986	M Mannelli
1982	D Lovato	1987	G Cali
1983	S Locatelli	1988	A Canessa
1984	C Rocca	1989	C Rocca
1985	G Cali	1990	M Mannelli

Italian Open Amateur Championship

Year	Winner	Year	Winner
1981	M Durante	1986	A Binaghi
1982	C Francis	1987	P Quirici
1983	JM Olazabal	1988	E Giraud
1984	M Luzzi	1989	R Victor
1985	JM Olazabal	1990	M Tadini

Italian Close Amateur Championship

Year	Winner	Year	Winner
1981	A Canessa	1986	A Binaghi
1982	L Silva	1987	M Grabau
1983	S Grappasonni	1988	M de Rossi
1984	S Prati	1989	G Ferrero
1985	E Nistri	1990	M Aragnetti

Italian Ladies' Open Championship

Year	Winner	Year	Winner
1981	E Berthet	1986	S Moorcroft
1982	M Figueras-Dotti	1987	R Lautens
1983	C Maestre	1988	L Davies
1984	R Lautens	1989	X Wunsch-Ruiz
1985	R Lautens	1990	F Descampe

Japan Open Championship

Year	Winner	Year	Winner
1981	Y Hagawa	1986	T Nakajima
1982	A Yabe	1987	I Aoki
1983	I Aoki	1988	M Ozaki
1984	K Uehara	1989	M Ozaki
1985	T Nakajima	1990	T Nakajima

Japan Professional Championship

Year	Winner
1984	T Nakajima
1985	T Ozaki
1986	I Aoki
1987	D Ishii
1988	T Ozaki
1989	M Ozaki
1990	H Kase

Japan Amateur Championship

Year	Winner	Year	Winner
1981	M Naito	1986	Y Ito
1982	L Karamoto	1987	T Suzuki
1983	K Kato	1988	R Kawagishi
1984	K Nagarta	1989	K Oie
1985	T Nakagawa	1990	Y Kuramoto

Kenya Open Championship

Year	Winner	Year	Winner
1981	B Barnes	1986	I Woosnam
1982	E Darcy	1987	C Mason
1983	K Brown	1988	C Platts
1984	JM Canizares	1989	D Jones
1985	G Harvey	1990	C O'Connor Jr

Korea Open Championship

Year	Winner	Year	Winner
1981	Chen Tze Ming	1986	Choi Yoon Soo
1982	Choi Yoon Soo	1987	K Lang-Sun
1983	Choi Sang Ho	1988	Kwak Yu Hyun
1984	Yeom Se Woon	1989	Chul Sang Cho
1985	Cho Ho Sang	1990	L Kang-Sun

Malaysian Open Championship

Year	Winner	Year	Winner
1981	H-C Lu	1986	S Ginn
1982	D Hepler	1987	T Gale
1983	T Gale	1988	T Tyner
1984	L Chien-Soon	1989	J Maggert
1985	T Gale	1990	G Day

Malaysian Women's Open Championship

Year	Winner
1987	I Shiotani
1988	B New
1989	N Terazawa
1990	C Nishida

New Zealand Open Championship

Year	Winner	Year	Winner
1981	R Shearer	1986	C Pavin
1982	T Gale	1987	R Rafferty
1983	I Baker-Finch	1988	R Rafferty
1984	B Devlin	1989	G Turner
1985	DA Weibring	1990	*Not played*

New Zealand Amateur Championship

Year	Winner	Year	Winner
1981	T Cochrane	1986	P O'Malley
1982	I Peters	1987	O Kendall
1983	C Taylor	1988	B Hughes
1984	J Wagner	1989	L Peterson
1985	G Power	1990	M Long

New Zealand Ladies' Open Championship

Year	Winner
1984	D Smith
1985	E Kennedy
1986	A Kita
1987	J Wyatt
1988	E Cavill
1989	W Sook
1990	L Brooky

Nigerian Open Championship

Year	Winner	Year	Winner
1981	P Tupling	1986	GJ Brand
1982	D Jagger	1987	not played
1983	GJ Brand	1988	V Singh
1984	E Murray	1989	V Singh
1985	B Longmuir	1990	W Stephens

Nordic Amateur Championship

(Previously Scandinavian Men's Amateur Open)

Year	Winner
1984	S Tinning
1985	C Härdin
1986	J Ryström
1987	P Hedblom
1988	H Simonsen
1989	P-U Johansson
1990	P Magnebrandt

Nordic Ladies' Amateur Championship

(Previously Scandinavian Ladies' Amateur Open)

Year	Winner
1984	T Pors
1985	M Meiland
1986	A. Öquist
1987	H Anderssen
1988	M Binau
1989	K Orum
1990	A Dönnestad

Pakistan Open Championship

Year	Winner	Year	Winner
1981		1986	M Ali
1982	G Nabi	1987	T Hassan
1983	G Nabi	1988	G Nabi
1984	G Nabi	1989	F Minosa
1985	G Muhammad	1990	F Qureshi

Pakistan Men's Amateur Championship

Year	Winner	Year	Winner
1981	T Hassan	1986	T Hassan
1982	I Ahmed	1987	T Hassan
1983	T Hassan	1988	F Qureshi
1984	F Qureshi	1989	M Sajid
1985	T Hassan	1990	K Perera

Pakistan Ladies' Amateur Championship

Year	Winner	Year	Winner
1981	T Butt	1986	N Shahban
1982	*Not played*	1987	N Shahban
1983	*Not played*	1988	Y Mubarik
1984	Y Mubarik	1989	C Amluwalia
1985	N Shahban	1990	V Aggarwal

Portuguese Open Amateur Championship

Year	Winner	Year	Winner
1981	G Brand Jr	1986	R Nissen
1982	M Higgins	1987	S Struven
1983	U Schulte	1988	C Waesberg
1984	A Dantas	1989	S Bjorn
1985	M Grabbau	1990	R Oliveira

Portuguese Close Amateur Championship

Year	Winner	Year	Winner
1981	A Dantas	1986	JS Melo
1982	J Silva Bento	1987	D Silva
1983	A Guerreiro	1988	R Uliveira
1984	J Santos	1989	A Castelo
1985	C Marta	1990	J Grahja

Portuguese Ladies' Open Amateur Championship

Year	Winner	Year	Winner
1981	V Dulout	1986	MC Navarizo
1982	S Blecher	1987	MC Navarizo
1983	K Douglas	1988	H Andersson
1984	M Campohanes	1989	S Clauset
1985	T Abitbol	1990	S Navarro

Singapore Open Championship

Year	Winner	Year	Winner
1981	M Aye	1986	G Turner
1982	HC San	1987	P Fowler
1983	C-S Lu	1988	G Bruckner
1984	T Sieckmann	1989	C-S Lu
1985	CT Ming	1990	A Fernando

Singapore Open Amateur Championship

Year	Winner	Year	Winner
1981	J Steward	1986	M Sukamdi
1982	Sudjiono	1987	T Wiratchant
1983	P Sachdev	1988	KN Perera
1984	D Ooi	1989	S Gimson
1985	D Lim	1990	K Nandasena

South African Open Championship

Year	Winner	Year	Winner
1981	G Player	1986	D Frost
1982	*Not played*	1987	M McNulty
1983	C Bolling	1988	W Westner
1984	A Johnstone	1989	F Wadsworth
1985	G Levenson	1990	T Dodds

South African Masters

Year	Winner	Year	Winner
1981	M McNulty	1986	M McNulty
1982	M McNulty	1987	D Frost
1983	*Not played*	1988	J Bland
1984	A Johnstone	1989	H Baiocchi
1985	M McNulty	1990	H Baiocchi

South African PGA Championship

Year	Winner	Year	Winner
1981	*Not played*	1986	B Cole
1982	G Player	1987	F Allem
1983	C Pavin	1988	D Feherty
1984	G Levenson	1989	A Johnstone
1985	C Williams	1990	F Allem

South African Amateur Championship

Year	Winner	Year	Winner
1981	D Suddards	1986	E Els
1982	N James	1987	B Fouchee
1983	G-C Yuan	1988	N Clarke
1984	M Wiltshire	1989	C Rivett
1985	N Clarke	1990	R Goosen

South African Amateur Stroke Play Championship

Year	Winner	Year	Winner
1981	CC Yuan	1986	C-S Hsieh
1982	WS Li	1987	B Fouchee
1983	P van der Riet	1988	N Clarke
1984	D James	1989	E Els
1985	D van Staden	1990	P Pascoe

South African Ladies' Championship

Year	Winner
1984	G Whitfield
1985	W Warrington
1986	W Warrington
1987	C Louw
1988	G Tebbutt
1989	L Rose
1990	G Tebbutt

Spanish Open Amateur Championship

Year	Winner	Year	Winner
1981	P Walton	1986	A Haglund
1982	D Williams	1987	M Quirke
1983	JM Olazabal	1988	S Atako
1984	JM Olazabal	1989	E Giraud
1985	B Quippe de Llano	1990	D Clarke

Spanish Amateur Close Championship

Year	Winner
1984	L Garbarda
1985	L Garbarda
1986	BQ de Llano
1987	JM Arruti
1988	T Muñoz
1989	T Muñoz
1990	G de la Riva

Qualitair Ladies' Classic
(formerly Spanish Ladies' Open)

Year	Winner
1986	L Davies
1987	C Dibnah
1988	ML de Lorenzi
1989	A Nicholas
1990	*Not played*

Spanish Ladies' Open Amateur Championship

Year	Winner	Year	Winner
1981	Marquesa de Artasona	1986	R Lautens
		1987	C Hourihane
1982	C Mourgue D'Algue	1988	I Calogero
1983	ML de Lorenzi	1989	I Calogero
1984	C Navarro	1990	D Bourson
1985	C Espinasse		

Spanish Ladies' Amateur Close Championship

Year	Winner
1984	C Maestre
1985	C Navarro
1986	C Navarro
1987	C Navarro
1988	S Navarro
1989	S Navarro
1990	E Valera

Swedish Professional Championship

Year	Winner	Year	Winner
1981	G Mueller	1986	M Persson
1982	A Forsbrand	1987	C-M Strömberg
1983	M Lanner	1988	V Singh
1984	P Brostedt	1989	L Hederström
1985	P Brostedt	1990	A Mednick

Swedish Open International Stroke Play Championship

(Before 1984: Amateur)

Year	Winner	Year	Winner
1981	D Carrick	1986	M Lanner
1982	D Carrick	1987	M Pendaries
1983	M Hogberg	1988	P Haugsrud
1984	A Forsbrand	1989	A Gillner
1985	Y Nilson	1990	J Parnevik

Swedish Open Championship

(Before 1984: Amateur; 1984-9: Close)

Year	Winner	Year	Winner
1981	G Knutsson	1986	M Grankvist
1982	B Svedin	1987	C-M Strömberg
1983	K-G Drotz	1988	M Krantz
1984	M Lanner	1989	M Grankvist
1985	Nillso	1990	E O'Connell

Swedish Ladies' International Open Stroke Play Championship

(Before 1984: Amateur)

Year	Winner	Year	Winner
1981	L Neumann	1986	P Neilsson
1982	L Neumann	1987	M Hattori
1983	A Oxenstierna	1988	H Alfredsson
1984	C Montgomery	1989	S Norberg
1985	K Espinasse	1990	M Bjurö

Swedish Ladies' Open Championship

(Before 1989: Close)

Year	Winner	Year	Winner
1981	M Wennersten	1986	H Alfredsson
1982	M Wennersten	1987	H Alfredsson
1983	G Linner	1988	H Alfredsson
1984	L Neumann	1989	P Nilsson
1985	S Gronberg	1990	J Allmark

Swiss Open Amateur Championship

Year	Winner	Year	Winner
1981	C Staedler	1986	A Binaghi
1982	F Illouz	1987	M Durante
1983	J Lamberg	1988	A Bossert
1984	F Illouz	1989	M Frank
1985	T Hubner	1990	M Santi

Swiss Close Amateur Championship

Year	Winner	Year	Winner
1981	J Storjohann	1986	M Frank
1982	C Rampone	1987	M Frank
1983	P Jaquet	1988	A Bossert
1984	M Buchter	1989	M Frank
1985	M Gottstein	1990	T Gottstein

Swiss Ladies' Open Amateur Championship

Year	Winner	Year	Winner
1981	R Lautens	1986	M Koch
1982	MC de Werra	1987	R Lautens
1983	E Berthet	1988	M Koch
1984	E Girardi	1989	V Pamard
1985	M Koch	1990	M Hageman

Swiss Ladies' Close Amateur Championship

Year	Winner	Year	Winner
1981	A Hadorn	1986	E Orley
1982	R Lautens	1987	E Orley
1983	R Lautens	1988	E Orley
1984	R Lautens	1989	C Vannini
1985	E Orley	1990	C Vannini

United States Amateur Championship

Year	Winner	Runner-up	Venue	By
1946	SE Bishop	S Quick	Baltusrol	37th hole
1947	RH Riegel	J Dawson	Pebble Beach	2 and 1
1948	WP Turnesa	R Billows	Memphis	2 and 1
1949	C Coe	R King	Rochester	11 and 10
1950	S Urzetta	FR Stranahan	Minneapolis	39th hole
1951	WJ Maxwell	J Cagliardi	Saucon Valley, Pa	4 and 3
1952	J Westland	A Mengert	Seattle	3 and 2
1953	G Littler	D Morey	Oklahoma City	1 hole
1954	A Palmer	R Sweeney	Detroit	1 hole
1955	E Harvie Ward	W Hyndman	Richmond, Va	9 and 8
1956	E Harvie Ward	C Kocsis	Lake Forest, Ill	5 and 4
1957	H Robbins	Dr F Taylor	Brookline	5 and 4
1958	C Coe	T Aaron	San Francisco	5 and 4
1959	J Nicklaus	C Coe	Broadmoor	1 hole
1960	DR Beman	R Gardner	St Louis, Mo	6 and 4
1961	J Nicklaus	D Wysong	Pebble Beach	8 and 6
1962	LE Harris, Jr	D Gray	Pinehurst	1 hole
1963	DR Beman	D Sikes	Des Moines	2 and 1
1964	W Campbell	E Tutweiler	Canterbury, Ohio	1 hole
Changed to stroke play				
1965	R Murphy		Tulsa, Okla	291
1966	G Cowan		Ardmore, Penn	285
1967	R Dickson		Colorado	285
1968	B Fleisher		Columbus	284
1969	S Melnyk		Oakmont	286
1970	L Wadkins		Portland	280
1971	G Cowan		Wilmington	280
1972	M Giles		Charlotte, NC	285
Reverted to match play				
1973	C Stadler	D Strawn	Inverness, Ohio	6 and 5
1974	J Pate	J Grace	Ridgewood, NJ	2 and 1
1975	F Ridley	K Fergus	Richmond, Va	2 holes
1976	B Sander	P Moore	Bel-Air	8 and 6
1977	J Fought	D Fischesser	Aronimonk, Pa	9 and 8
1978	J Cook	S Hoch	Plainfield, NJ	5 and 4
1979	M O'Meara	J Cook	Canterbury, Ohio	8 and 7
1980	H Sutton	B Lewis	North Carolina	9 and 8
1981	N Crosby	B Lyndley	San Francisco	37th hole
1982	J Sigel	D Tolley	The Country Club, Brookline	8 and 7
1983	J Sigel	C Perry	North Shore, Chicago	8 and 7
1984	S Verplank	S Randolph	Oak Tree, Okla	4 and 3
1985	S Randolph	P Persons	Montclair, NJ	1 hole
1986	S Alexander	C Kite	Shoal Creek	5 and 3
1987	W Mayfair	E Rebmann	Jupiter Hills, Fl	4 and 3
1988	E Meeks	D Yates	Hot Springs, VA	7 and 6
1989	C Patton	D Green	Merion, PA	3 and 1
1990	P Mickelson	M Zerman	Cherry Hills, CO	5 and 4

United States Ladies' Amateur Championship

Year	Winner	Runner-up	Venue	By
1960	J Gunderson	J Ashley	Tulsa, Okla	6 and 5
1961	A Quast	P Preuss	Tacoma	14 and 13
1962	J Gunderson	A Baker	Rochester, NY	9 and 8
1963	A Quast	P Conley	Williamstown	2 and 1
1964	B McIntyre	J Gunderson	Prairie Dunes, Kansas	3 and 2
1965	J Ashley	A Quast	Denver	5 and 4
1966	J Carner (*née* Gunderson)	JD Streit	Pittsburgh	41st hole
1967	L Dill	J Ashley	Annandale, Pasadena	5 and 4
1968	J Carner	A Quast	Birmingham, Mich	5 and 4
1969	C Lacoste (Fra)	S Hamlin	Las Colinas, Texas	3 and 2
1970	M Wilkinson	C Hill	Darien, Conn	3 and 2
1971	L Baugh	B Barry	Atlanta	1 hole
1972	M Budke	C Hill	St Louis, Mo	5 and 4
1973	C Semple	A Quast	Montclair, NJ	1 hole
1974	C Hill	C Semple	Broadmoor, Seattle	5 and 4

Year	Winner	Runner-up	Venue	By
1975	B Daniel	D Horton	Brae Burn, Mass	3 and 2
1976	D Horton	M Bretton	Del Paso, California	2 and 1
1977	B Daniel	C Sherk	Cincinnati	3 and 1
1978	C Sherk	J Oliver	Sunnybrook, Pa	4 and 3
1979	C Hill	P Sheehan	Memphis	7 and 6
1980	J Inkster	P Rizzo	Prairie Dunes, Kansas	2 holes
1981	J Inkster	L Coggan (Aus)	Portland, Oregon	1 hole
1982	J Inkster	C Hanton	Colorado Springs	4 and 3
1983	J Pacillo	S Quinlan	Canoe Brook, NJ	2 and 1
1984	D Richard	K Williams	Broadmoor, Seattle	37th hole
1985	M Hattori (Jpn.)	C Stacy	Pittsburgh, PA	5 and 4
1986	K Cockerill	K McCarthy	Pasatiempo, California	9 and 7
1987	K Cockerill	T Kerdyk	Barrington, RI	3 and 2
1988	P Sinn	K Noble	Minikahde, MN	6 and 5
1989	V Goetze	B Burton	Pinehurst, NC	4 and 3
1990	P Hurst	S Davis	Canoe Brook, NJ	37th hole

United States Ladies' Amateur Championship

continued

Zambian Open Championship

Year	Winner	Year	Winner
1981	B Barnes	1986	G Cullen
1982	B Waites	1987	P Carrigill
1983	B Calfee	1988	D Llewellyn
1984	C Mason	1989	C Maltman
1985	I Woosnam	1990	GJ Brand

PGA European Tour

and other Men's Professional Tournaments

AGF Open Championship

Year	Winner	Venue	Score
1988	D Llewellyn	Biarritz	258
1989	M James	Montpellier	277
1990	B Ogle	Montpellier	278

Peugeot-Trends Belgian Open

Year	Winner	Venue	Score
1987	E Darcy	Royal Waterloo	200
(three rounds only—rain)			
1988	JM Olazabal	Bercuit	269
1989	GJ Brand	Royal Waterloo	273
1990	O Sellberg	Royal Waterloo	272

Bells' Scottish Open

Formerly Glasgow Classic, 1983-85

Year	Winner	Venue	Score
1983	B Langer	Haggs Castle	274
1984	K Brown	Haggs Castle	266
1985	H Clark	Haggs Castle	274
1986	D Feherty	Haggs Castle	270
1987	I Woosnam	Gleneagles	264
1988	B Lane	Gleneagles	271
1989	M Allen	Gleneagles	272
1990	I Woosnam	Gleneagles	269

Benson and Hedges International Open

Year	Winner	Score	Year	Winner	Score
1981	T Weiskopf	272	1986	M James	274
1982	G Norman	283	1987	N Ratcliffe	275
1983	J Bland	273	1988	P Baker	271
1984	S Torrance	270	1989	G Brand, Jr	272
1985	A Lyle	274	1990	JM Olazabal	279

Benson and Hedges Trophy

Year	Winner	Venue	Score
1988	M McNulty/ML de Lorenzi	La Moraleja	276
1989	MA Jimenez/X Wunsch-Ruiz	Aloha	281
1990	JM Canizares/T Abitbol	El Bosque	267

Crédit Lyonnais Cannes Open
at Cannes Mougins

Year	Winner	Score
1984	D Frost	280
1985	R Lee	280
1986	J Bland	276
1987	S Ballesteros	275
1988	M McNulty	279
1989	P Broadhurst	207*
1990	M McNulty	280

*(*54 holes only)*

Carrolls Irish Open
Formerly Carrolls International

Year	Winner	Club/Country	Venue	Score
1981	S Torrance	GB	Portmarnock	276
1982	J O'Leary	Unattached	Portmarnock	287
1983	S Ballesteros	Spain	R Dublin	271
1984	B Langer	Germany	R Dublin	267
1985	S Ballesteros	Spain	R Dublin	278
1986	S Ballesteros	Spain	Portmarnock	285
1987	B Langer	Germany	Portmarnock	269
1988	I Woosnam	Wales	Portmarnock	278
1989	I Woosnam	Wales	Portmarnock	278
1990	JM Olazabal	Spain	Portmarnock	282

Dunhill British Masters'
Formerly sponsored by Dunlop, 1946-62 (1963-83: Silk Cut)

Year	Winner	Club/Country	Venue	Score
1981	G Norman	Australia	Woburn	273
1982	G Norman	Australia	St Pierre	267
1983	I Woosnam	Wales	St Pierre	269
1984	*Not played*			
1985	L Trevino	USA	Woburn	278
1986	S Ballesteros	Spain	Woburn	275
1987	M McNulty	Zimbabwe	Woburn	274
1988	A Lyle	Scotland	Woburn	273
1989	N Faldo	England	Woburn	267
1990	M James	England	Woburn	270

KLM Dutch Open

Year	Winner	Score	Year	Winner	Score
1981	H Henning	280	1986	S Ballesteros	271 (70 holes)
1982	P Way	276	1987	G Brand, Jr	272
1983	K Brown	274	1988	M Mouland	274
1984	B Langer	275	1989	JM Olazabal	277
1985	G Marsh	282	1990	S McAllister	274

NM English Open

Year	Winner	Venue	Score
1988	H Clark	R Birkdale	279
1989	M James	The Belfry	279
1990	M James	The Belfry	284

Epson Grand Prix

Match play 1986-89, then stroke play

Year	Winner	Venue
1986	O Sellberg beat H Clark 3 and 2	St Pierre
1987	M Lanner beat J Hawkes 1 hole	St Pierre
1988	B Langer beat M McNulty 4 and 3	St Pierre
1989	S Ballesteros beat D Durnian 4 and 3	St Pierre
1990	I Woosnam (271)	St Pierre

Equity & Law Challenge

Year	Winner	Country	Score
1987	B Lane	England	22 points
1988	R Rafferty	England	21 points
1989	B Ogle	Australia	25 points
1990	B Marchbank	Scotland	22 points

Peugeot French Open

Year	Winner	Score	Year	Winner	Score
1981	A Lyle	270	1986	S Ballesteros	269
1982	S Ballesteros	278	1987	J Rivero	269
1983	N Faldo	277	1988	N Faldo	274
1984	B Langer	270	1989	N Faldo	273
1985	S Ballesteros	263	1990	P Walton	275

Mercedes German Masters

Year	Winner	Score
1987	A Lyle	278
1988	JM Olazabal	279
1989	B Langer	276
1990	S Torrance	272

Volvo German Open

Year	Winner	Score	Year	Winner	Score
1981	B Langer	272	1986	B Langer	273
1982	B Langer	279	1987	M McNulty	259
1983	C Pavin	275	1988	S Ballesteros	263
1984	W Grady	268	1989	C Parry	266
1985	B Langer	183	1990	M McNulty	270
(54 holes only—rain)					

Lancia-Martini Italian Open

Year	Winner	Score	Year	Winner	Score
1981	JM Canizares	280	1986	D Feherty	270
1982	M James	280	1987	S Torrance	271
1983	B Langer	271	1988	G Norman	270
1984	A Lyle	277	1989	R Rafferty	273
1985	M Pinero	267	1990	R Boxall	267

Jersey Open
Formerly British Airways-Avis Tournament and Billy Butlin Open

Year	Winner	Score	Year	Winner	Score
1981	A Jacklin	279	1986	J Morgan	275
1982	B Gallacher	273	1987	I Woosnam	279
1983	J Hall	278	1988	D Smyth	273
1984	B Gallacher	274	1989	C O'Connor Jr	281
1985	H Clark	279	1990	*Not played*	

Lancôme Trophy

Year	Winner	Score	Year	Winner	Score
1981	D Graham	280	1986	S Ballesteros	274
1982	D Graham	276	1987	I Woosnam	264
1983	S Ballesteros	269	1988	S Ballesteros	269
1984	A Lyle	278	1989	E Romero	266
1985	N Price	275	1990	JM Olazabal	269

Cepsa Madrid Open

Year	Winner	Score	Year	Winner	Score
1981	M Pinero	279	1986	H Clark	274
1982	S Ballesteros	273	1987	I Woosnam	269
1983	A Lyle	285	1988	D Cooper	275
1984	H Clark	274	1989	S Ballesteros	272
1985	M Pinero	278	1990	B Langer	270

Monte Carlo Open

at Mont Agel

Year	Winner	Score
1984	I Mosey	131
(36 holes only)		
1985	S Torrance	264
1986	S Ballesteros	265
1987	P Senior	260
1988	J Rivero	261
1989	M McNulty	261
1990	I Woosnam	258

Open Renault de Baleares

Year	Winner	Score
1988	S Ballesteros	272
1989	O Sellberg	279
1990	S Ballesteros	269

Panasonic European Open

Year	Winner	Venue	Score
1978	R Wadkins	Walton Heath	283
1979	A Lyle	Turnberry	275
1980	T Kite	Walton Heath	284
1981	G Marsh	Liverpool	275
1982	M Pinero	Sunningdale	266
1983	I Aoki	Sunningdale	274
1984	G Brand, Jr	Sunningdale	270
1985	B Langer	Sunningdale	269
1986	G Norman	Sunningdale	269
1987	P Way	Walton Heath	279
1988	I Woosnam	Sunningdale	260
1989	A Murray	Walton Heath	277
1990	P Senior	Sunningdale	267

Volvo PGA Championship

Year	Winner	Venue	Score
1955	K Bousfield	Pannal	277
1956	C Ward	Maesdu	282
1957	P Alliss	Maesdu	286
1958	H Bradshaw	Llandudno	287

Volvo PGA
Championship
continued

Year	Winner	Venue	Score
1959	D Rees	Ashburnham	283
1960	A Stickley	Coventry (63	
		holes)	247
1961	B Bamford	R Mid-Surrey	266
1962	P Alliss	Little Aston	287
1963	P Butler	R Birkdale	306
1964	A Grubb (Asst)	Western Gailes	287
1965	P Alliss	Sandwich, Prince's	286
1966	G Wostenholme	Saunton	278
1967	M Gregson*	Hunstanton	275
1968	D Talbot*	Dunbar	276
1969	B Gallacher	Ashburnham	291
1970-71	Not played		
1972	A Jacklin	Wentworth	279
1973	P Oosterhuis	Wentworth	280
1974	M Bembridge	Wentworth	278
1975	A Palmer	Sandwich, R St George's	285
1976	NC Coles	Sandwich, R St George's	280
1977	M Pinero	Sandwich, R St George's	283
1978	N Faldo	R Birkdale	278
1979	V Fernandez	St Andrews	288
1980	N Faldo	Sandwich, R St George's	283
1981	N Faldo	Ganton	274
1982	A Jacklin	Hillside	284
1983	S Ballesteros	Sandwich, R St George's	278
1984	H Clark	Wentworth	204
(3 rounds only due to weather)			
1985	P Way	Wentworth	282
1986	R Davis	Wentworth	281
1987	B Langer	Wentworth	270
1988	I Woosnam	Wentworth	274
1989	N Faldo	Wentworth	272
1990	M Harwood	Wentworth	271

* Until 1966 restricted to UK and Irish Pros. In 1967 and 1968 PGA 'open' and
'closed' were contested. From 1969 Championship has been open.

PLM Open Championship

Year	Winner	Venue	Score
1986	P Senior	Falsterbo	273
1987	H Clark	Ljunghusen	271
1988	F Nobilo	Flommen	270
1989	M Harwood	Bokskogen	271
1990	R Rafferty	Bokskogen	270

Portuguese Open TPC Championship

Year	Winner	Score	Year	Winner	Score
1981	Not played		1986	M McNulty	270
1982	S Torrance	207	1987	R Lee	195
(3 rounds only)			(3 rounds only)		
1983	S Torrance	286	1988	M Harwood	280
1984	A Johnstone	274	1989	C Montgomerie	264
1985	W Humphreys	279	1990	M McLean	274

Scandinavian Enterprise Open

Year	Winner	Score	Year	Winner	Score
1981	S Ballesteros	273	1986	G Turner	270
1982	B Byman	275	1987	G Brand, Jr	277
1983	S Torrance	280	1988	S Ballesteros	270
1984	I Woosnam	280	1989	R Rafferty	268
1985	I Baker-Finch	274	1990	C Stadler	268

Peugeot Spanish Open

Year	Winner	Score	Year	Winner	Score
1981	S Ballesteros	273	1986	H Clark	272
1982	S Torrance	273	1987	N Faldo	286
1983	E Darcy	277	1988	M James	262
1984	B Langer	275	1989	B Langer	281
1985	S Ballesteros	266	1990	R Davis	277

Suntory World Match Play
at Wentworth

Sponsored by Piccadilly until 1976 and by Colgate 1977 and 1978

Year	Winner	Runner-up	By
1964	A Palmer	N Coles	2 and 1
1965	G Player	P Thomson	3 and 2
1966	G Player	J Nicklaus	6 and 4
1967	A Palmer	P Thomson	1 hole
1968	G Player	R Charles	1 hole
1969	R Charles	G Littler	37th hole
1970	J Nicklaus	L Trevino	2 and 1
1971	G Player	J Nicklaus	5 and 4
1972	T Weiskopf	L Trevino	4 and 3
1973	G Player	G Marsh	40th hole
1974	H Irwin	G Player	3 and 1
1975	H Irwin	A Geiberger	4 and 2
1976	D Graham	H Irwin	38th hole
1977	G Marsh	R Floyd	5 and 3
1978	I Aoki	S Owen	3 and 2
1979	W Rogers	I Aoki	1 hole
1980	G Norman	A Lyle	1 hole
1981	S Ballesteros	B Crenshaw	1 hole
1982	S Ballesteros	A Lyle	37th hole
1983	G Norman	N Faldo	3 and 2
1984	S Ballesteros	B Langer	2 and 1
1985	S Ballesteros	B Langer	6 and 5
1986	G Norman	A Lyle	2 and 1
1987	I Woosnam	A Lyle	1 hole
1988	A Lyle	N Faldo	2 and 1
1989	N Faldo	I Woosnam	1 hole
1990	I Woosnam	M McNulty	4 and 2

Ebel European Masters – Swiss Open

Year	Winner	Score	Year	Winner	Score
1981	M Pinero	277	1986	JM Olazabal	262
1982	I Woosnam	272	1987	A Forsbrand	263
1983	N Faldo	268	1988	C Moody	268
1984	J Anderson	261	1989	S Ballesteros	266
1985	C Stadler	267	1990	R Rafferty	267

Volvo Masters

Year	Winner	Score
1988	N Faldo	284
1989	R Rafferty	282
1990	M Harwood	286

Volvo Seniors British Open

Year	Winner	Score
1987	N Coles	279
1988	G Player	272
1989	R Charles	269
1990	G Player	280

Wang Four Stars National Pro-Celebrity Tournament

Year	Winner	Score
1985	K Brown	277
1986	A Garrido	275
1987	M McNulty	273
1988	R Davies	275
1989	C Parry	273
1990	R Davis	271

Other Men's Professional Tournaments

PGA Seniors Championship

From 1957 to 1968 sponsored by Teachers; from 1969 to 1974 sponsored by Pringle; from 1975 sponsored by Ben Sayers and Allied Hotels; from 1977 by Cambridgeshire Hotel; from 1983 by Trust House Forte

Year	Winner	Club/Country	Venue	Score
1970	M Faulkner	Ifield	Longniddry	288
1971	K Nagle	Australia	Elie	269
1972	K Bousfield	Coombe Hill	Longniddry	291
1973	K Nagle	Australia	Elie	270
1974	E Lester	Astbury	Lundin	282
1975	K Nagle	Australia	Longniddry	268
1976	C O'Connor	Royal Dublin	Cambridgeshire Hotel	284
1977	C O'Connor	Royal Dublin	Cambridgeshire Hotel	288
1978	P Skerritt	St Annes, Dublin	Cambridgeshire Hotel	288
1979	C O'Connor	Royal Dublin	Cambridgeshire Hotel	280
1980	P Skerritt	St Annes, Dublin	Gleneagles Hotel	286
1981	C O'Connor	Royal Dublin	North Berwick	287
1982	C O'Connor	Royal Dublin	Longniddry	285
1983	C O'Connor	Royal Dublin	Burnham and Berrow	277
1984	E Jones	Royal Co Down	Stratford-upon-Avon	280
1985	N Coles	Expotel	Pannal, Harrogate	284
1986	N Coles	Expotel	Mere, Cheshire	276
1987	N Coles	Expotel	Turnberry	279
1988	P Thomson	Australia	North Berwick	287
1989	N Coles	Expotel	West Hill	277
1990	B Waites	Notts	.Brough	269

Club Professionals' Championship

Year	Winner	Club	Venue	Score
1973	DN Sewell	Ferndown	Calcot Park	276
1974	WB Murray	Coombe Wood	Calcot Park	275
1975	DN Sewell	Ferndown	Calcot Park	276
1976	WJ Ferguson	Ilkley	Moortown	283
1977	D Huish	North Berwick	Notts	284
1978	D Jones	Bangor	Pannal	281
1979	D Jones	Bangor	Pannal	278
1980	D Jagger	Selby	Turnberry	286
1981	M Steadman	Cleeve Hill Mun	Woburn	289
1982	D Durnian	Northenden	Hill Valley	285
1983	J Farmer		Heaton Park	270
1984	D Durnian		Bolton Old Links	278
1985	R Mann	Thorpeness	The Belfry	291
1986	D Huish	North Berwick	R Birkdale	278
1987	R Weir		Sandiway	273
1988	R Weir		Harlech	269
1989	B Barnes	W Chiltington	Sandwich, Prince's	280
1990	A Webster	Edzell	Carnoustie	292

Krystal Klear Assistants' Scottish Championship

Year	Winner	Club	Venue	Score
1980	F Mann	Banchory	Dunbar	294
1981	M Brown	Strathclyde	West Kilbride	290
1982	R Collinson	Windyhill	West Kilbride	294
1983	A Webster	Edzell	Stirling	285
1984	C Elliott	Falkirk Tryst	Stirling	285
1985	C Elliott	Falkirk Tryst	Falkirk Tryst	284
1986	P Helsby	Hilton Park	Erskine	295
1987	C Innes	Turnberry	Hilton Park	284
1988	G Collinson	Windyhill	Turnberry	289
1989	C Brooks	Grangemouth	Windyhill	282
1990	P Lawrie	Banchory	Cruden Bay	279

PGA Assistants' Championship

Year	Winner	Venue	By
1984	G Weir	Coombe Hill	286
1985	G Coles	Coombe Hill	284
1986	J Brennand	Sand Moor	280
1987	J Hawksworth	Coombe Hill	282
1988	J Oates	Coventry	284
1989	C Brooks	Hillside	291
1990	A Ashton	Hillside	213 (54 holes)

Men's Professional Internationals

Great Britain & Ireland (Europe from 1979) *v* USA

Year	Great Britain & Ireland			USA			Venue
1921	Foursomes	4		Foursomes	1		
(June 6)	Singles	6½	10½	Singles	3½	4½	Gleneagles
1926	Foursomes	5		Foursomes	0		
(June 4-5)	Singles	8½	13½	Singles	1½	1½	Wentworth

The Ryder Cup
Instituted 1927

Year	Great Britain & Ireland			USA			Venue
1927	Foursomes	1		Foursomes	3		
(June 3-4)	Singles	1½	2½	Singles	6½	9½	Worcester, Mass
1929	Foursomes	1½		Foursomes	2½		
(May 26-27)	Singles	5½	7	Singles	2½	5	Moortown
1931	Foursomes	1		Foursomes	3		
(June 26-27)	Singles	2	3	Singles	6	9	Columbus, Ohio
1933	Foursomes	2½		Foursomes	1½		
(June 26-27)	Singles	4	6½	Singles	4	5½	Southport and Ainsdale
1935	Foursomes	1		Foursomes	3		
(Sept 28-29)	Singles	2	3	Singles	6	9	Ridgewood, NJ
1937	Foursomes	1½		Foursomes	2½		
(June 29-30)	Singles	2½	4	Singles	5½	8	Southport and Ainsdale
1947	Foursomes	0		Foursomes	4		
(Nov 1-2)	Singles	1	1	Singles	7	11	Portland, Oregon
1949	Foursomes	3		Foursomes	1		
(Sept 16-17)	Singles	2	5	Singles	6	7	Ganton
1951	Foursomes	1		Foursomes	3		
(Nov 2 and 4)	Singles	1½	2½	Singles	6½	9½	Pinehurst, N Carolina
1953	Foursomes	1		Foursomes	3		
(Oct 2-3)	Singles	4½	5½	Singles	3½	6½	Wentworth
1955	Foursomes	1		Foursomes	3		
(Nov 5-6)	Singles	3	4	Singles	5	8	Palm Springs, California
1957	Foursomes	1		Foursomes	3		
(Oct 4-5)	Singles	6½	7½	Singles	1½	4½	Lindrick
1959	Foursomes	1½		Foursomes	2½		
(Nov 6-7)	Singles	2	3½	Singles	6	8½	Eldorado, California
1961	Foursomes	2		Foursomes	6		
(Oct 13-14)	Singles	7½	9½	Singles	8½	14½	R Lytham and St Annes
1963	Foursomes	2		Foursomes	6		
(Oct 11-13)	Four-ball	2		Four-ball	6		
	Singles	5	9	Singles	11	23	Atlanta, Ga.
1965	Foursomes	4		Foursomes	4		
(Oct 7-9)	Four-ball	3		Four-ball	5		
	Singles	5½	12½	Singles	10½	19½	R Birkdale
1967	Foursomes	2½		Foursomes	5½		
(Oct 20-22)	Four-ball	½		Four-ball	7½		
	Singles	5½	8½	Singles	10½	23½	Houston, Tex.

Ryder Cup
continued

Year	Great Britain & Ireland			USA			Venue
1969	Foursomes	4½		Foursomes	3½		
(Oct 18-20)	Four-ball	3½	16	Four-ball	4½	16	R Birkdale
	Singles	8		Singles	8		
1971	Foursomes	4½		Foursomes	3½		
(Sept 16-18)	Four-ball	1½	13½	Four-ball	6½	18½	St Louis, Missouri
	Singles	7½		Singles	8½		
1973	Foursomes	4½		Foursomes	3½		
(Sept 20-22)	Four-ball	3½	13	Four-ball	4½	19	Muirfield
	Singles	5		Singles	11		
1975	Foursomes	1		Foursomes	7		
(Sept 19-21)	Four-ball	2½	11	Four-ball	5½	21	Laurel Valley, Pa.
	Singles	7½		Singles	8½		
1977	Foursomes	1½		Foursomes	3½		
(Sept 15-17)	Four-ball	1	7½	Four-ball	4	12½	R Lytham and St Annes
	Singles	5		Singles	5		
1979	Foursomes	4½		Foursomes	3½		
(Sept 14-16)	Four-ball	3	11	Four-ball	5	17	Greenbrier, WVa
	Singles	3½		Singles	8½		

From 1979 players from the Continent of Europe became available for selection in addition to those from Great Britain and Ireland

At Walton Heath, 18th, 19th and 20th September, 1981

First Day—Foursomes

Europe	Matches	USA	Matches
B Langer and M Pinero	0	L Trevino and L Nelson (1 hole)	1
A Lyle and M James (2 and 1)	1	W Rogers and B Lietzke	0
B Gallacher and D Smyth (3 and 2)	1	H Irwin and R Floyd	0
P Oosterhuis and N Faldo	0	T Watson and J Nicklaus (4 and 3)	1
	2		2

Four-ball

S Torrance and H Clark (halved)	½	T Kite and J Miller (halved)	½
A Lyle and M James (3 and 2)	1	B Crenshaw and J Pate	0
D Smyth and JM Canizares (6 and 5)	1	W Rogers and B Leitzke	0
B Gallacher and E Darcy	0	H Irwin and R Floyd (2 and 1)	1
	2½		1½

Second Day—Four-ball

N Faldo and S Torrance	0	L Trevino and J Pate (7 and 5)	1
A Lyle and M James	0	L Nelson and T Kite (1 hole)	1
B Langer and M Pinero (2 and 1)	1	R Floyd and H Irwin	0
JM Canizares and D Smyth	0	J Nicklaus and T Watson (3 and 2)	1
	1		3

Foursomes

P Oosterhuis and S Torrance	0	L Trevino and J Pate (2 and 1)	1
B Langer and M Pinero	0	J Nicklaus and T Watson (3 and 2)	1
A Lyle and M James	0	W Rogers and R Floyd (3 and 2)	1
D Smyth and B Gallacher	0	T Kite and L Nelson (3 and 2)	1
	0		4

Third Day—Singles

S Torrance	0	L Trevino (5 and 3)	1
A Lyle	0	T Kite (3 and 2)	1
B Gallacher (halved)	½	W Rogers (halved)	½
M James	0	L Nelson (2 holes)	1
D Smyth	0	B Crenshaw (6 and 4)	1
B Langer (halved)	½	B Leitzke (halved)	½
M Pinero (4 and 2)	1	J Pate	0
JM Canizares	0	H Irwin (1 hole)	1
N Faldo (2 and 1)	1	J Miller	0
H Clark (4 and 3)	1	T Watson	0
P Oosterhuis	0	R Floyd (2 holes)	1
E Darcy	0	J Nicklaus (5 and 3)	1
	4		8

Match Aggregate: Great Britain and Europe 9½; USA 18½.
Non-playing Captains: J Jacobs (Europe); D Marr (USA).

At PGA National, Florida, 14th, 15th and 16th October, 1983

Ryder Cup
continued

First Day—Foursomes

USA		Europe	
Matches	Matches		
T Watson and B Crenshaw (5 and 4)	1	B Gallacher and A Lyle	0
L Wadkins and C Stadler	0	N Faldo and B Langer (4 and 2)	1
R Floyd and B Gilder	0	JM Canizares and S Torrance (4 and 3)	1
T Kite and C Peete (2 and 1)	1	S Ballesteros and P Way	0
	2		2

Four-ball

G Morgan and F Zoeller	0	B Waites and K Brown (2 and 1)	1
T Watson and J Haas (2 and 1)	1	N Faldo and B Langer	0
R Floyd and C Strange	0	S Ballesteros and P Way (1 hole)	1
B Crenshaw and C Peete (halved)	1/2	S Torrance and I Woosnam (halved)	1/2
	11/2		21/2

Second Day—Four-ball

C Stadler and L Wadkins (1 hole)	1	K Brown and B Waites	0
C Peete and B Crenshaw	0	N Faldo and B Langer (4 and 2)	1
G Morgan and J Haas (halved)	1/2	S Ballesteros and P Way (halved)	1/2
T Watson and B Gilder (5 and 4)	1	S Torrance and I Woosnam	0
	21/2		11/2

Foursomes

R Floyd and T Kite	0	N Faldo and B Langer (3 and 2)	1
L Wadkins and G Morgan (7 and 5)	1	S Torrance and JM Canizares	0
B Gilder and T Watson	0	S Ballesteros and P Way (2 and 1)	1
J Haas and C Strange (3 and 2)	1	K Brown and B Waites	0
	2		2

Third Day—Singles

F Zoeller (halved)	1/2	S Ballesteros (halved)	1/2
J Haas	0	N Faldo (2 and 1)	1
G Morgan	0	B Langer (2 holes)	1
B Gilder (2 holes)	1	GJ Brand	0
B Crenshaw (3 and 1)	1	A Lyle	0
C Peete (1 hole)	1	B Waites	0
C Strange	0	P Way (2 and 1)	1
T Kite (halved)	1/2	S Torrance (halved)	1/2
C Stadler (3 and 2)	1	I Woosnam	0
L Wadkins (halved)	1/2	JM Canizares (halved)	1/2
R Floyd	0	K Brown (4 and 3)	1
T Watson (2 and 1)	1	B Gallacher	0
	61/2		51/2

Match Aggregate USA 141/2; Europe 131/2.
Non-playing Captains: J Nicklaus, USA; A Jacklin, Europe.

At The Belfry, Sutton Coldfield, 13th, 14th and 15th September, 1985

First Day—Foursomes

Europe	Matches	USA	Matches
S Ballesteros and M Pinero (2 and 1)	1	C Strange and M O'Meara	0
B Langer and N Faldo	0	C Peete and T Kite (3 and 2)	1
A Lyle and K Brown	0	L Wadkins and R Floyd (4 and 3)	1
H Clark and S Torrance	0	C Stadler and H Sutton (3 and 2)	1
	1		3

Four-ball

P Way and I Woosnam (1 hole)	1	F Zoeller and H Green	0
S Ballesteros and M Pinero (2 and 1)	1	A North and P Jacobsen	0
B Langer and JM Canizares (halved)	1/2	C Stadler and H Sutton (halved)	1/2
S Torrance and H Clark	0	R Floyd and L Wadkins (1 hole)	1
	2 1/2		1 1/2

Second Day—Four-ball

S Torrance and H Clark (2 and 1)	1	T Kite and A North	0
P Way and I Woosnam (4 and 3)	1	H Green and F Zoeller	0
S Ballesteros and M Pinero	0	M O'Meara and L Wadkins (3 and 2)	1
B Langer and A Lyle (halved)	1/2	C Stadler and C Strange (halved)	1/2
	2 1/2		1 1/2

Foursomes

JM Canizares and J Rivero (7 and 5)	1	T Kite and C Peete	0
S Ballesteros and M Pinero (5 and 4)	1	C Stadler and H Sutton	0
P Way and I Woosnam	0	C Strange and P Jacobsen (4 and 2)	1
B Langer and K Brown (3 and 2)	1	R Floyd and L Wadkins	0
	3		1

Third Day—Singles

M Pinero (3 and 1)	1	L Wadkins	0
I Woosnam	0	C Stadler (2 and 1)	1
P Way (2 holes)	1	R Floyd	0
S Ballesteros (halved)	1/2	T Kite (halved)	1/2
A Lyle (3 and 2)	1	P Jacobsen	0
B Langer (5 and 4)	1	H Sutton	0
S Torrance (1 hole)	1	A North	0
H Clark (1 hole)	1	M O'Meara	0
N Faldo	0	H Green (3 and 1)	1
J Rivero	0	C Peete (1 hole)	1
JM Canizares (2 holes)	1	F Zoeller	0
K Brown	0	C Strange (4 and 2)	1
	7 1/2		4 1/2

Match Aggregate: Europe 16 1/2; USA 11 1/2.
Non-playing Captains: A Jacklin, Europe; L Trevino, USA.

At Muirfield Village, Ohio, 25th, 26th and 27th September, 1987

First Day—Foursomes

USA	Matches	Europe	Matches
C Strange and T Kite (4 and 2)	1	S Torrance and H Clark	0
H Sutton and D Pohl (2 and 1)	1	K Brown and B Langer	0
L Wadkins and L Mize	0	N Faldo and I Woosnam (2 holes)	1
L Nelson and P Stewart	0	S Ballesteros and JM Olazabal (1 hole)	1
	2		2

Four-ball

B Crenshaw and S Simpson	0	G Brand Jr and J Rivero (3 and 2)	1
A Bean and M Calcavecchia	0	A Lyle and B Langer (1 hole)	1
H Sutton and D Pohl	0	N Faldo and I Woosnam (2 and 1)	1
C Strange and T Kite	0	S Ballesteros and JM Olazabal (2 and 1)	1
	0		4

Second Day—Foursomes

C Strange and T Kite (3 and 1)	1	J Rivero and G Brand Jr	0
H Sutton and L Mize (halved)	1/2	N Faldo and I Woosnam (halved)	1/2
B Crenshaw and P Stewart	0	S Ballesteros and JM Olazabal	1
L Wadkins and L Nelson	0	A Lyle and B Langer (2 and 1)	1
	1 1/2		2 1/2

Second Day—Foursomes

T Kite and C Strange	0	I Woosnam and N Faldo (5 and 4)	1
A Bean and P Stewart (3 and 2)	1	E Darcy and G Brand Jr	0
H Sutton and L Mize (2 and 1)	1	S Ballesteros and JM Olazabal	0
L Wadkins and L Nelson	0	A Lyle and B Langer (1 hole)	1
	2		2

Four-ball

A Bean (1 hole)	1	I Woosnam	0
D Pohl	0	H Clark (1 hole)	1
L Mize (halved)	1/2	S Torrance (halved)	1/2
M Calcavecchia (1 hole)	1	N Faldo	0
P Stewart (2 holes)	1	JM Olazabal	0
B Crenshaw	0	E Darcy (1 hole)	1
S Simpson (2 and 1)	1	J Rivero	0
L Nelson (halved)	1/2	B Langer (halved)	1/2
T Kite (3 and 2)	1	A Lyle	0
C Strange	0	S Ballesteros (2 and 1)	1
H Sutton (halved)	1/2	G Brand Jr (halved)	1/2
L Wadkins (3 and 2)	1	K Brown	0
	7 1/2		4 1/2

Match Aggregate: USA 13; Europe 15.
Non-playing Captains: J Nicklaus, USA; A Jacklin, Europe.

At The Belfry, Sutton Coldfield, 22nd, 23rd and 24th September, 1989

First Day—Foursomes

Europe		USA	
Matches		**Matches**	
N Faldo and I Woosnam (halved)	1/2	T Kite and C Strange (halved)	1/2
H Clark and M James	0	L Wadkins and P Stewart (1 hole)	1
S Ballesteros and JM Olazabal (halved)	1/2	T Watson and C Beck (halved)	1/2
B Langer and R Rafferty	0	M Calcavecchia and K Green (2 and 1)	1
	1		3

Four-ball

S Torrance and G Brand Jr (1 hole)	1	C Strange and P Azinger	0
H Clark and M James (3 and 2)	1	F Couples and L Wadkins	0
N Faldo and I Woosnam (2 holes)	1	M Calcavecchia and M McCumber	0
S Ballesteros and JM Olazabal (6 and 5)	1	T Watson and M O'Meara	0
	4		0

Second Day—Foursomes

I Woosnam and N Faldo (3 and 2)	1	L Wadkins and P Stewart	0
G Brand Jr and S Torrance	0	C Beck and P Azinger (4 and 3)	1
C O'Connor Jr and R Rafferty	0	M Calcavecchia and K Green (3 and 2)	1
S Ballesteros and JM Olazabal (1 hole)	1	T Kite and C Strange	0
	2		2

Four-ball

N Faldo and I Woosnam	0	C Beck and P Azinger (2 and 1)	1
B Langer and JM Canizares	0	T Kite and M McCumber (2 and 1)	1
H Clark and M James (1 hole)	1	P Stewart and C Strange	0
S Ballesteros and JM Olazabal (4 and 2)	1	M Calcavecchia and K Green	0
	2		2

Third Day—Singles

S Ballesteros	0	P Azinger (1 hole)	1
B Langer	0	C Beck (3 and 2)	1
JM Olazabal (1 hole)	1	P Stewart	0
R Rafferty (1 hole)	1	M Calcavecchia	0
H Clark	0	T Kite (8 and 7)	1
M James (3 and 2)	1	M O'Meara	0
C O'Connor Jr (1 hole)	1	F Couples	0
JM Canizares (1 hole)	1	K Green	0
G Brand Jr	0	M McCumber (1 hole)	1
S Torrance	0	T Watson (3 and 2)	1
N Faldo	0	L Wadkins (1 hole)	1
I Woosnam	0	C Strange (2 holes)	1
	5		7

Match Aggregate: Europe 14; USA 14.
Non-playing Captains: A Jacklin, Europe; R Floyd, USA.

Individual Records

(Matches were contested as Great Britain v USA from 1927-71; as Great Britain and Ireland from 1973-7; and as Europe v USA from 1979.)

Bold type indicates captain; in brackets did not play.

Europe

Name	Year	Played	Won	Lost	Halved
Jimmy Adams	*1939-47-49-51-53	7	2	5	0
Percy Alliss	1929-33-35-37	6	3	2	1
Peter Alliss	1953-57-59-61-63-65-67-69	30	10	15	5
Laurie Ayton	1949	0	0	0	0
Severiano Ballesteros	1979-83-85-87-89	25	13	8	4
Harry Bannerman	1971	5	2	2	1
Brian Barnes	1969-71-73-75-77-79	25	10	14	1
Maurice Bembridge	1969-71-73-75	16	5	8	3
Aubrey Boomer	1927-29	4	2	2	0
Ken Bousfield	1949-51-55-57-59-61	10	5	5	0
Hugh Boyle	1967	3	0	3	0
Harry Bradshaw	1953-55-57	5	2	2	1
Gordon J Brand	1983	1	0	1	0
Gordon Brand Jr	1987-89	7	2	4	1
Eric Brown	1953-55-57-59-**(69)**-**(71)**	8	4	4	0
Ken Brown	1977-79-83-85-87	13	4	9	0
Stewart Burns	1929	0	0	0	0
Dick Burton	1935-37-*39-49	5	2	3	0
Jack Busson	1935	2	0	2	0
Peter Butler	1965-69-71-73	14	3	9	2
Jose Maria Canizares	1981-83-85-89	11	5	4	2
Alex Caygill	1969	1	0	0	1
Clive Clark	1973	1	0	1	0
Howard Clark	1977-81-85-87-89	13	6	6	1
Neil Coles	1961-63-65-67-69-71-73-77	40	12	21	7
Archie Compston	1927-29-31	6	1	4	1
Henry Cotton	1929-37-*39-**47**-**(53)**	6	2	4	0
Bill Cox	1935-37	3	0	2	1
Allan Dailey	1933	0	0	0	0
Fred Daly	1947-49-51-53	8	3	4	1
Eamonn Darcy	1975-77-81-87	11	1	8	2
William Davies	1931-33	4	2	2	0
Peter Dawson	1977	3	1	2	0
Norman Drew	1959	1	0	0	1
George Duncan	1927-**29**-31	5	2	3	0
Syd Easterbrook	1931-33	3	2	1	0
Nick Faldo	1977-79-81-83-85-87-89	27	16	9	2
John Fallon	1955-**(63)**	1	1	0	0
Max Faulkner	1947-49-51-53-57	8	1	7	0
George Gadd	1927	0	0	0	0
Bernard Gallacher	1969-71-73-75-77-79-81-83-**(91)**	31	13	13	5
John Garner	1971-73	1	0	1	0
Antonio Garrido	1979	5	1	4	0
Eric Green	1947	0	0	0	0
Malcolm Gregson	1967	4	0	4	0
Tom Haliburton	1961-63	6	0	6	0
Jack Hargreaves	1951	0	0	0	0
Arthur Havers	1927-31-33	6	3	3	0
Jimmy Hitchcock	1965	3	0	3	0
Bert Hodson	1931	1	0	1	0
Reg Horne	1947	0	0	0	0
Tommy Horton	1975-77	8	1	6	1
Brian Huggett	1963-67-69-71-73-75-**(77)**	25	9	10	6
Bernard Hunt	1953-57-59-61-63-65-67-69-**(73)**-**(75)**	28	6	16	6
Geoffrey Hunt	1963	3	0	3	0
Guy Hunt	1975	3	0	2	1
Tony Jacklin	1967-69-71-73-75-77-79-**(83)**-**(85)**-**(87)**-**(89)**	35	13	14	8
John Jacobs	1955-**(79)**-**(81)**	2	2	0	0
Mark James	1977-79-81-89	14	5	8	1
Edward Jarman	1935	1	0	1	0
Herbert Jolly	1927	2	0	2	0
Michael King	1979	1	0	1	0
Sam King	1937-*39-47-49	5	1	3	1
Arthur Lacey	1933-37-**(51)**	3	0	3	0
Bernhard Langer	1981-83-85-87-89	22	10	8	4
Arthur Lees	1947-49-51-55	8	4	4	0

Ryder Cup

continued

Name	Year	Played	Won	Lost	Halved
Sandy Lyle	1979-81-83-85-87	18	7	9	2
Jimmy Martin	1965	1	0	1	0
Peter Mills	1957-59	1	1	0	0
Abe Mitchell	1929-31-33	6	4	2	0
Ralph Moffitt	1961	1	0	1	0
Christy O'Connor, Jr	1975-89	4	1	3	0
Christy O'Connor, Sr	1955-57-59-61-63-65-67-69-71-73	36	11	21	4
Jose Maria Olazabal	1987-89	10	7	2	1
John O'Leary	1975	4	0	4	0
Peter Oosterhuis	1971-73-75-77-79-81	28	14	11	3
Alf Padgham	1933-35-37-*39	6	0	6	0
John Panton	1951-53-61	5	0	5	0
Alf Perry	1933-35-37	4	0	3	1
Manuel Pinero	1981-85	9	6	3	0
Lionel Platts	1965	5	1	2	2
Eddie Polland	1973	2	0	2	0
Ronan Rafferty	1989	3	1	2	0
Ted Ray	1927	2	0	2	0
Dai Rees	1937-*39-47-49-51-53-**55**-**57**-**59**-**61**-**(67)**	18	7	10	1
Jose Rivero	1985-87	5	2	3	0
Fred Robson	1927-29-31	6	2	4	0
Syd Scott	1955	2	0	2	0
Des Smyth	1979-81	7	2	5	0
Dave Thomas	1959-63-65-67	18	3	10	5
Sam Torrance	1981-83-85-87-89	18	4	10	4
Peter Townsend	1969-71	11	3	8	0
Brian Waites	1983	4	1	3	0
Charlie Ward	1947-49-51	6	1	5	0
Paul Way	1983-85	9	6	2	1
Harry Weetman	1951-53-55-57-59-61-63-**(65)**	15	2	11	2
Charles Whitcombe	1927-29-**31**-33-**35**-**37**-*39-**(49)**	9	3	2	4
Ernest Whitcombe	1929-31-35	6	1	4	1
Reg Whitcombe	1935-*39	1	0	1	0
George Will	1963-65-67	15	2	11	2
Norman Wood	1975	3	1	2	0
Ian Woosnam	1983-85-87-89	17	7	7	3

(Great Britain named eight members of their 1939 side, but the match was not played because of the Second World War.)

United States of America

Name	Year	Played	Won	Lost	Halved
Tommy Aaron	1969-73	6	1	4	1
Skip Alexander	1949-51	2	1	1	0
Paul Azinger	1989	4	3	1	0
Jerry Barber	1955-**61**	5	1	4	0
Miller Barber	1969-71	7	1	4	2
Herman Barron	1947	1	1	0	0
Andy Bean	1979-87	6	4	2	0
Frank Beard	1969-71	8	2	3	3
Chip Beck	1989	4	3	0	1
Homero Blancas	1973	4	2	1	1
Tommy Bolt	1955-57	4	3	1	0
Julius Boros	1959-63-65-67	16	9	3	4
Gay Brewer	1967-73	9	5	3	1
Billy Burke	1931-33	3	3	0	0
Jack Burke	1951-53-55-**57**-59-**(73)**	8	7	1	0
Walter Burkemo	1953	1	0	1	0
Mark Calcavecchia	1987-89	7	3	4	0
Billy Casper	1961-63-65-67-69-71-73-75-**(79)**	37	20	10	7
Bill Collins	1961	3	1	2	0
Charles Coody	1971	3	0	2	1
Fred Couples	1989	2	0	2	0
Wilfred Cox	1931	2	2	0	0
Ben Crenshaw	1981-83-87	9	3	5	1
Jimmy Demaret	**1941-47-49-51	6	6	0	0
Gardner Dickinson	1967-71	10	9	1	0
Leo Diegel	1927-29-31-33	6	3	3	0
Dale Douglass	1969	2	0	2	0
Dave Douglas	1953	2	1	0	1
Ed Dudley	1929-33-37	4	3	1	0
Olin Dutra	1933-35	4	1	3	0
Lee Elder	1979	4	1	3	0
Al Espinosa	1927-29-31	4	2	1	1
Johnny Farrell	1927-29-31	6	3	2	1
Dow Finsterwald	1957-59-61-63-**(77)**	13	9	3	1
Ray Floyd	1969-75-77-81-83-85-**(89)**	23	7	13	3
Doug Ford	1955-57-59-61	9	4	4	1
Ed Furgol	1957	1	0	1	0

Ryder Cup

continued

Name	Year	Played	Won	Lost	Halved
Marty Furgol	1955	1	0	1	0
Al Geiberger	1967-75	9	5	1	3
Vic Ghezzi	*1939-**41	0	0	0	0
Bob Gilder	1983	4	2	2	0
Bob Goalby	1963	5	3	1	1
Johnny Golden	1927-29	3	3	0	0
Lou Graham	1973-75-77	9	5	3	1
Hubert Green	1977-79-85	7	4	3	0
Ken Green	1989	4	2	2	0
Ralph Guldahl	1937-*39	2	2	0	0
Fred Haas, Jr	1953	1	0	1	0
Jay Haas	1983	4	2	1	1
Walter Hagen	**1927-29-31-33-35-(37)**	9	7	1	1
Bob Hamilton	1949	2	0	2	0
Chick Harbert	1949-**55**	2	2	0	0
Chandler Harper	1955	1	0	1	0
Dutch (EJ) Harrison	1947-49-51	3	2	1	0
Fred Hawkins	1957	2	1	1	0
Mark Hayes	1979	3	1	2	0
Clayton Heafner	1949-51	4	3	0	1
Jay Hebert	1959-61-**(71)**	4	2	1	1
Lionel Hebert	1957	1	0	1	0
Dave Hill	1969-73-77	9	6	3	0
Jimmy Hines	*1939	0	0	0	0
Ben Hogan	**1941-**47**-**(49)**-51-**(67)**	3	3	0	0
Hale Irwin	1975-77-79-81	16	11	4	1
Tommy Jacobs	1965	4	3	1	0
Peter Jacobsen	1985	3	1	2	0
Don January	1965-77	7	2	3	2
Herman Keiser	1947	1	0	1	0
Tom Kite	1979-81-83-85-87-89	24	13	7	4
Ted Kroll	1953-55-57	4	3	1	0
Ky Laffoon	1935	1	0	1	0
Tony Lema	1963-65	11	8	1	2
Bruce Lietzke	1981	3	0	2	1
Gene Littler	1961-63-65-67-69-71-75	27	14	5	8
John Mahaffey	1979	3	1	2	0
Mark McCumber	1989	3	2	1	0
Jerry McGee	1977	2	1	1	0
Harold McSpaden	*1939-**41	0	0	0	0
Tony Manero	1937	2	1	0	1
Lloyd Mangrum	**1941-47-49-51-**53**	8	6	2	0
Dave Marr	1965-**(81)**	6	4	2	0
Billy Maxwell	1963	4	4	0	0
Dick Mayer	1957	2	1	0	1
Bill Mehlhorn	1927	2	1	1	0
Dick Metz	*1939	0	0	0	0
Cary Middlecoff	1953-55-59	6	2	3	1
Johnny Miller	1975-81	6	2	2	2
Larry Mize	1987	4	1	1	2
Gil Morgan	1979-83	6	1	2	3
Bob Murphy	1975	4	2	1	1
Byron Nelson	1937-*39-**41-47-**(65)**	4	3	1	0
Larry Nelson	1979-81-87	13	9	3	1
Bobby Nichols	1967	5	4	0	1
Jack Nicklaus	1969-71-73-75-77-81-**(83)-(87)**	28	17	8	3
Andy North	1985	3	0	3	0
Ed Oliver	1947-51-53	5	3	2	0
Mark O'Meara	1985-89	5	1	4	0
Arnold Palmer	1961-**63**-65-67-71-73-**(75)**	32	22	8	2
Johnny Palmer	1949	2	0	2	0
Sam Parks	1935	1	0	0	1
Jerry Pate	1981	4	2	2	0
Calvin Peete	1983-85	7	4	2	1
Henry Picard	1935-37-*39	4	3	1	0
Dan Pohl	1987	3	1	2	0
Johnny Pott	1963-65-67	7	5	2	0
Dave Ragan	1963	4	2	1	1
Henry Ransom	1951	1	0	1	0
Johnny Revolta	1935-37	3	2	1	0
Chi Chi Rodriguez	1973	2	0	1	1
Bill Rogers	1981	4	1	2	1
Bob Rosburg	1959	2	2	0	0
Mason Rudolph	1971	3	1	1	1
Paul Runyan	1933-35-*39	4	2	2	0
Doug Sanders	1967	5	2	3	0
Gene Sarazen	1927-29-31-33-35-37-**41	12	7	2	3
Densmore Shute	1931-33-37	6	2	2	2
Dan Sikes	1969	3	2	1	0
Scott Simpson	1987	2	1	1	0
Horton Smith	1929-31-33-35-37-*39-**41	4	3	0	1
JC Snead	1971-73-75	11	9	2	0

Ryder Cup
continued

Name	Year	Played	Won	Lost	Halved
Sam Snead	1937-*39-**41-47-49-**51**-53-55-**59**-**(69)**	13	10	2	1
Ed Sneed	1977	2	1	0	1
Mike Souchak	1959-61	6	5	1	0
Craig Stadler	1983-85	8	4	2	2
Payne Stewart	1987-89	8	3	5	0
Ken Still	1969	3	1	2	0
Dave Stockton	1971-77-**(91)**	5	3	1	1
Curtis Strange	1983-85-87-89	17	6	9	2
Hal Sutton	1985-87	9	3	3	3
Lee Trevino	1969-71-73-75-79-81-**(85)**	30	17	7	6
Jim Turnesa	1953	1	1	0	0
Joe Turnesa	1927-29	4	1	2	1
Ken Venturi	1965	4	1	3	0
Lanny Wadkins	1977-79-83-85-87-89	25	15	9	1
Art Wall, Jnr	1957-59-61	6	4	2	0
Al Watrous	1927-29	3	2	1	0
Tom Watson	1977-81-83-89	15	10	4	1
Tom Weiskopf	1973-75	10	7	2	1
Craig Wood	1931-33-35-**41	4	1	3	0
Lew Worsham	1947	2	2	0	0
Fuzzy Zoeller	1979-83-85	10	1	8	1

(US teams were selected in 1939 (*) and 1941 (**), but the matches were not played because of the Second World War.)

Asahi Glass Four Tours Championship
Formerly Nissan Cup and Kirin Cup

Year	Pos		Year	Pos	
1985	1	US PGA Tour	1988	1	US PGA Tour
	2	PGA European Tour		2	PGA European Tour
	3	PGA Japan Tour		3	Australia/New Zealand Tour
	4	Australia/New Zealand Tour		4	PGA Japan Tour
1986	1	PGA Japan Tour	1989	1	US PGA Tour
	2	PGA European Tour		2	PGA European Tour
	3	Australia/New Zealand Tour		3	PGA Japan Tour
	4	US PGA Tour		4	Australia/New Zealand Tour
1987	1	US PGA Tour	1990	1	Australia/New Zealand Tour
	2	PGA European Tour		2	US PGA Tour
	3	Australia/New Zealand Tour		3	PGA European Tour
	4	PGA Japan Tour		4	PGA Japan Tour

Dunhill Cup
Venue: St Andrews
Instituted 1985

Year	Winner	Runner-up
1985	Australia	USA
1986	Australia	Japan
1987	England	Scotland
1988	Ireland	Australia
1989	USA	Japan
1990	Ireland	England

PGA Cup
Instituted 1973

Year	Winner	Venue	Result
1973	USA	Pinehurst, USA	13-3
1974	USA	Pinehurst, USA	11½-4½
1975	USA	Hillside	9½-6½
1976	USA	Moortown	9½-6½
1977	Halved	Miss Hills, USA	8½-8½
1978	GB & I	St Mellion	10½-6½

Year	Winner	Venue	Result
1979	GB&I	Castletown	12^1/2-4^1/2
1980	USA	Oak Tree	15-6
1981	Halved	Turnberry, Isle	10^1/2-10^1/2
1982	USA	Knoxville, Tennessee	13-7
1983	GB & I	Muirfield	14^1/2-6^1/2
1984	GB & I	Turnberry	12^1/2-8^1/2
To be played alternate years			
1986	USA	Knollwood	16-9
1988	USA	The Belfry	15^1/2-10^1/2
1990	USA	Kiawah Island, S Carolina	19-7

PGA Cup
continued

World Cup of Golf
Until 1966, called Canada Cup

Year	Winner	Runners-up	Venue	Score
1953	Argentina (A Cerda and R De Vincenzo)	Canada (S Leonard and B Kerr)	Montreal	287
	(Individual: A Cerda, Argentina, 140)			
1954	Australia (P Thomson and K Nagle)	Argentina (A Cerda and R De Vincenzo)	Laval-Sur-Lac	556
1955	United States (C Harbert and E Furgol)	Australia (P Thomson and K Nagle)	Washington	560
	(Individual: E Furgol, USA, after a play-off with P Thomson and F van Donck, 279)			
1956	United States (B Hogan and S Snead)	South Africa (A Locke and G Player)	Wentworth	567
	(Individual: B Hogan, USA, 277)			
1957	Japan (T Nakamura and K Ono)	United States (S Snead and J Demaret)	Tokyo	557
	(Individual: T Nakamura, Japan, 274)			
1958	Ireland (H Bradshaw and C O'Connor)	Spain (A Miguel and S Miguel)	Mexico City	579
	(Individual: A Miguel, Spain, after a play-off with H Bradshaw, 286)			
1959	Australia (P Thomson and K Nagle)	United States (S Snead and C Middlecoff)	Melbourne	563
	(Individual: S Leonard, Canada, 275, after a tie with P Thomson, Australia)			
1960	United States (S Snead and A Palmer)	England (H Weetman and B Hunt)	Portmarnock	565
	(Individual: F van Donck, Belgium, 279)			
1961	United States (S Snead and J Demaret)	Australia (P Thomson and K Nagle)	Puerto Rico	560
	(Individual: S Snead, USA, 272)			
1962	United States (S Snead and A Palmer)	Argentina (F de Luca and R De Vicenzo)	Buenos Aires	557
	(Individual: R De Vincenzo, Argentina, 276)			
1963	United States (A Palmer and J Nicklaus)	Spain (S Miguel and R Sota)	St Nom-La-Breteche	482
	(Individual: J Nicklaus, USA, 237 [63 holes])			
1964	United States (A Palmer and J Nicklaus)	Argentina (R De Vicenzo and L Ruiz)	Maui, Hawaii	554
	(Individual: J Nicklaus, USA, 276)			
1965	South Africa (G Player and H Henning)	Spain (A Miguel and R Sota)	Madrid	571
	(Individual: G Player, South Africa, 281)			
1966	United States (J Nicklaus and A Palmer)	South Africa (G Player and H Henning)	Tokyo	548
	(Individual: G Knudson, Canada, and H Sugimoto, Japan, each 272; Knudson won play-off)			
1967	United States (J Nicklaus and A Palmer)	New Zealand (R Charles and W Godfrey)	Mexico City	557
	(Individual: A Palmer, USA, 276)			
1968	Canada (A Balding and G Knudson)	United States (J Boros and L Trevino)	Olgiata, Rome	569
	(Individual: A Balding, Canada, 274)			
1969	United States (O Moody and L Trevino)	Japan (T Kono and H Yasuda)	Singapore	552
	(Individual: L Trevino, USA, 275)			
1970	Australia (B Devlin and D Graham)	Argentina (R De Vicenzo and V Fernandez)	Buenos Aires	545
	(Individual: R De Vicenzo, Argentina, 269)			
1971	United States (J Nicklaus and L Trevino)	South Africa (H Henning and G Player)	Palm Beach, Florida	555
	(Individual: J Nicklaus, USA, 271)			

Year	Winner	Runners-up	Venue	Score
1972	Taiwan (H Min-Nan and LL Huan)	Japan (T Kono and T Murakami)	Melbourne	438
	(Individual: H Min-Nan, Taiwan, 217 [3 rounds only])			
1973	United States (J Nicklaus and J Miller)	South Africa (G Player and H Baiocchi)	Marbella, Spain	558
	(Individual: J Miller, USA, 277)			
1974	South Africa (R Cole and D Hayes)	Japan (I Aoki and M Ozaki)	Caracas	554
	(Individual: R Cole, South Africa, 271)			
1975	United States (J Miller and L Graham)	Taiwan (H Min-Nan and KC Hsiung)	Bangkok	554
	(Individual: J Miller, USA, 275)			
1976	Spain (S Ballesteros and M Pinero)	United States (J Pate and D Stockton)	Palm Springs, USA	574
	(Individual: EP Acosta, Mexico, 282)			
1977	Spain (S Ballesteros and A Garrido)	Philippines (R Lavares and B Arda)	Manilla, Philippines	591
	(Individual: G Player, South Africa, 289)			
1978	United States (J Mahaffey and A North)	Australia (G Norman and W Grady)	Hawaii	564
	(Individual: J Mahaffey, USA, 281)			
1979	United States (J Mahaffey and H Irwin)	Scotland (A Lyle and K Brown)	Glyfada, Greece	575
	(Individual: H Irwin, USA, 285)			
1980	Canada (D Halldorson and J Nelford)	Scotland (A Lyle and S Martin)	Bogota	572
	(Individual: A Lyle, Scotland, 282)			
1981	Not played			
1982	Spain (M Pinero and JM Canizares)	United States (B Gilder and B Clampett)	Acapulco	563
	(Individual: M Pinero, Spain, 281)			
1983	United States (R Caldwell and J Cook)	Canada (D Barr and J Anderson)	Pondok Inah, Jakarta	565
	(Individual: D Barr, Canada, 276)			
1984	Spain (JM Canizares and J Rivero)	Scotland (S Torrance and G Brand, Jr)	Olgiata, Rome	414
	(Individual: JM Canizares, Spain, 205. Played over 54 holes due to storm)			
1985	Canada (D Halidorson and D Barr)	England (H Clark and P Way)	La Quinta, Calif.	559
	(Individual: H Clark, England, 272)			
1986	Not played			
1987	Wales (I Woosnam and D Llewelyn)	Scotland (S Torrance and A Lyle)	Kapalua, Hawaii	574
	(Wales won play-off)			
	(Individual: I Woosnam, Wales, 274)			
1988	United States (B Crenshaw and M McCumber)	Japan (T Ozaki and M Ozaki)	Royal Melbourne, Australia	560
1989	Australia (P Fowler and W Grady)	Spain (JM Olazabal and JM Canizares)	Las Brisas, Spain	
	(Individual: P Fowler. Played over 36 holes due to storms.)			
1990	Germany (B Langer and Giedeon)	England (M James and R Boxall) Ireland (R Rafferty and D Feherty) } tie	Grand Cypress Resort, Orlando, Florida	556

World Cup

continued

Men's Amateur

Berkhamsted Trophy

Year	Winner	Score	Year	Winner	Score
1970	R Hunter	145	1980	R Knott	143
1971	A Millar	144	1981	P Dennett	146
1972	C Cieslewicz	148	1982	DG Lane	148
1973	SC Mason	141	1983	J Hawksworth	146
1974	P Fisher	144	1984	R Willison	139
1975	P Deeble	147	1985	F George	144
1976	J Davies	144	1986	P McEvoy	144
1977	A Lyle	144	1987	F George	141
1978	JC Davies	146	1988	J Cowgill	146
1979	JC Davies	147	1989	J Payne	142
			1990	J Barnes	144

Berkshire Trophy

Year	Winner	Score	Year	Winner	Score
1970	MF Bonallack	274	1980	P Downes	280
1971	MF Bonallack	277	1981	D Blakeman	280
	J Davies		1982	S Keppler	278
1972	DP Davidson	280	1983	S Hamer	288
1973	P Hedges	278	1984	JL Plaxton	276
1974	J Downie	280	1985	P McEvoy	279
1975	N Faldo	281	1986	R Muscroft	280
1976	P Hedges	284	1987	J Robinson	275
1977	A Lyle	279	1988	R Claydon	276
1978	P Hedges	281	1989	J Metcalfe	
1979	D Williams	274	1990	J O'Shea	271

Boyd Quaich Tournament

Year	Winner	Year	Winner
1981	P Gallagher	1986	A Roberts
1982	ME Lewis	1987	M Pask
1983	R Risan	1988	A Mathers
1984	J Huggan	1989	A Mathers
1985	S Elgie	1990	A Mathers

Duncan Putter

Year	Winner	Score
1981	{ R Chapman P Way	294
1982	D McLean	283
1983	JG Jermine	297
1984	JP Price	297
1985	P McEvoy	299
1986	D Wood	300
1987	P McEvoy	278
1988	S Dodd	290
1989	RN Roderick	280
1990	R Willison	311

Edward Trophy

Year	Winner	Year	Winner
1981	A Liddle	1986	J Noon
1982	F Dunsmore	1987	S Easingwood
1983	S Morrison	1988	R Blair
1984	K Walker	1989	A Elliott
1985	GK MacDonald	1990	A Gourlay

Frame Trophy

Venue: Worplesdon

Year	Winner	Score
1986	DW Frame	220
1987	JRW Walkinshaw	225
1988	DW Frame	229
1989	JRW Walkinshaw	219
1990	WJ Williams	224

Golf Illustrated Gold Vase

Year	Winner	Year	Winner
1948	RD Chapman	1970	D Harrison
1949	RJ White	1971	MF Bonallack
1950	AW Whyte		{ H Ashby
1951	JB Carr	1972	DP Davidson
1952	JDA Langley		R Hunter
1953	JDA Langley	1973	J Davies
1954	H Ridgeley	1974	P Hedges
1955	Major DA Blair	1975	MF Bonallack
1956	Major DA Blair	1976	A Brodie
1957	G Wolstenholme	1977	J Davies
1958	M Lunt	1978	P Thomas
1959	A Bussell	1979	KJ Miller
1960	D Sewell	1980	G Brand, Jr
1961	{ DJ Harrison MF Bonallack	1981	P Garner
		1982	I Carslaw
1962	BHG Chapman	1983	S Keppler
1963	RH Mummery	1984	JV Marks
1964	D Moffat	1985	M Davis
1965	C Clark	1986	R Eggo
1966	PM Townsend	1987	D Lane
1967	{ RA Durrant MF Bonallack	1988	M Turner
		1989	G Wolstenholme
1968	MF Bonallack	1990	A Rogers
1969	{ MF Bonallack J Hayes		

Grafton Morrish Trophy
Public Schools Old Boys' Golf Association

Year	Winner	Year	Winner
1963	Tonbridge	1977	Haileybury
1964	Tonbridge	1978	Charterhouse
1965	Charterhouse	1979	Harrow
1966	Charterhouse	1980	Charterhouse
1967	Charterhouse	1981	Charterhouse
1968	Wellington	1982	Marlborough
1969	Sedbergh	1983	Wellington
1970	Sedbergh	1984	Sedbergh
1971	Dulwich	1985	Warwick
1972	Sedbergh	1986	Tonbridge
1973	Pangbourne	1987	Harrow
1974	Millfield	1988	Robert Gordon's
1975	Oundle	1989	Tonbridge
1976	Charterhouse	1990	Clifton

Halford-Hewitt Challenge Cup
Public Schools Old Boys' Tournament

Year	Winner	Year	Winner
1947	Harrow	1969	Eton
1948	Winchester	1970	Merchiston
1949	Charterhouse	1971	Charterhouse
1950	Rugby	1972	Marlborough
1951	Rugby	1973	Rossall
1952	Harrow	1974	Charterhouse
1953	Harrow	1975	Harrow
1954	Rugby	1976	Merchiston
1955	Eton	1977	Watsons
1956	Eton	1978	Harrow
1957	Watsons	1979	Stowe
1958	Harrow	1980	Shrewsbury
1959	Wellington	1981	Watsons
1960	Rossall	1982	Charterhouse
1961	Rossall	1983	Charterhouse
1962	Oundle	1984	Charterhouse
1963	Repton	1985	Harrow
1964	Fettes	1986	Repton
1965	Rugby	1987	Merchiston
1966	Charterhouse	1988	Stowe
1967	Eton	1989	Stowe
1968	Eton	1990	Tonbridge

Hampshire Hog
Played annually at North Hants GC

Year	Winner	Year	Winner
1981	G Brand Jr	1986	R Eggo
1982	A Sherborne	1987	A Rogers
1983	I Gray	1988	S Richardson
1984	J Hawkesworth	1989	P McEvoy
1985	A Clapp	1990	J Metcalfe

The Lagonda Trophy

Year	Winner	Year	Winner
1981	N Mitchell	1986	D Gilford
1982	A Sherborne	1987	DG Lane
1983	I Sparkes	1988	R Claydon
1984	M Davis	1989	T Spence
1985	J Robinson	1990	L Parsons

Leven Amateur Championship Gold Medal

Year	Winner	Year	Winner
1981	IC Hutcheon	1986	P-U Johansson
1982	IC Hutcheon	1987	G Macgregor
1983	J Huggan	1988	CE Everett
1984	S Stephen	1989	AJ Coltart
1985	A Turnball	1990	C Everett

The Lytham Trophy

Venue: R Lytham and St Annes

Year	Winner	Score	Year	Winner	Score
1965	{ MF Bonallack / CA Clark	295	1976	MJ Kelley	292
			1977	P Deeble	296
1966	PM Townsend	290	1978	B Marchbank	288
1967	R Foster	296	1979	P McEvoy	279
1968	R Foster	286	1980	IC Hutcheon	293
1969	T Craddock	290	1981	R Chapman	221
			1982	MF Sludds	306
1970	{ SG Birtwell / JC Farmer / CW Green / GC Marks	296	1983	S McAllister	299
			1984	J Hawksworth	289
			1985	L Macnamara	144
1971	W Humphreys	292	1986	S McKenna	297
1972	MF Bonallack	281	1987	D Wood	293
1973	{ MG King / SG Birtwell	292	1988	P Broadhurst	296
			1989	N Williamson	286
1974	CW Green	291	1990	G Evans	291
1975	G Macgregor	299			

Oxford *v* Cambridge

Year	Winner	Venue
1946	Cambridge	R Lytham and St Annes
1947	Oxford	Rye
1948	Oxford	Sandwich, R St George's
1949	Cambridge	Hoylake
1950	Oxford	R Lytham and St Annes
1951	Cambridge	Rye
1952	Cambridge	Rye
1953	Cambridge	Rye
1954	Cambridge	Rye
1955	Cambridge	Rye
1956	Oxford	Formby
1957	Oxford	Sandwich, R St George's

Oxford *v*
Cambridge
continued

Year	Winner	Venue
1958	Cambridge	Rye
1959	Cambridge	Burnham & Berrow
1960	Cambridge	R Lytham and St Annes
1961	Oxford	Sandwich, R St George's
1962	Halved	Hunstanton
1963	Cambridge	R Birkdale
1964	Oxford	Rye
1965	Cambridge	Sandwich, R St George's
1966	Cambridge	Hunstanton
1967	Cambridge	Rye
1968	Cambridge	Porthcawl
1969	Cambridge	Formby
1970	Halved	Sandwich, R St George's
1971	Oxford	Rye
1972	Cambridge	Formby
1973	Oxford	Saunton
1974	Cambridge	Ganton
1975	Cambridge	Hoylake
1976	Cambridge	Woodhall Spa
1977	Cambridge	Porthcawl
1978	Oxford	Rye
1979	Oxford	Harlech
1980	Oxford	Hoylake
1981	Cambridge	Formby
1982	Cambridge	Hunstanton
1983	Cambridge	Sandwich, R St George's
1984	Cambridge	Sunningdale
1985	Oxford	Rye
1986	Oxford	Ganton
1987	Cambridge	Formby
1988	Cambridge	Royal Porthcawl
1989	Cambridge	Rye
1990	Cambridge	Muirfield

Oxford and Cambridge Golfing Society's "President's" Putter

Year	Winner	Year	Winner
1947	LG Crawley	1969	P Moody
1948	Major AA Duncan	1970	DMA Steel
1949	PB Lucas	1971	GT Duncan
1950	DHR Martin	1972	P Moody
1951	LG Crawley	1973	AD Swanston
1952	LG Crawley	1974	R Biggs
1953	GH Micklem	1975	CJ Weight
1954	G Huddy	1976	MJ Reece
1955	G Huddy	1977	AWJ Holmes
1956	GT Duncan	1978	MJ Reece
1957	AE Shepperson	1979	*Cancelled due to snow*
1958	Lt-Col AA Duncan	1980	S Melville
1959	ID Wheater	1981	AWJ Holmes
1960	JME Anderson	1982	DMA Steel
1961	ID Wheater	1983	ER Dexter
1962	MF Attenborough	1984	A Edmond
1963	JG Blackwell	1985	ER Dexter
1964	DMA Steel	1986	J Caplan
1965	WI Uzielli	1987	CD Meacher
1966	MF Attenborough	1988	G Woollett
1967	JR Midgley	1989	M Froggatt
1968	AWJ Holmes	1990	G Woollett

Parliamentary Handicap

Year	Winner	Year	Winner
1981	R Foster	1986	Sir Anthony Grant MP
1982	S Clinton Davis MP	1987	Sir Anthony Grant MP
1983	S Clinton Davis MP	1988	Sir Peter Hordern
1984	S Clinton Davis	1989	Lord Vaux
1985	M Morris MP	1990	Rt Hon T Raison MP

HRH Prince of Wales Challenge Cup
Venue: Deal

Year	Winner	Score	Year	Winner	Score
1981	JM Baldwin	146	1986	JM Baldwin	149
1982	G Homewood	145	1987	S Finch	148
1983	M Davis	141	1988	MP Palmer	144
1984	{ DH Niven / F Wood } tie	146	1989	{ T Lloyd / NA Farrell } tie	146
1985	RJ Tickner	141	1990	{ BS Ingleby / G Homewood } tie	145

Rosebery Challenge Cup
Venue: Ashridge

Year	Winner	Year	Winner
1981	{ RY Mitchell / JB Berney (RY Mitchell won play-off) }	1985	P Wharton
		1986	JE Ambridge
		1987	HA Wilkerson
1982	DG Lane	1988	N Leconte
1983	N Briggs	1989	C Slattery
1984	DG Lane	1990	C Tingey

St David's Gold Cross
Venue: Royal St David's, Harlech

Year	Winner	Year	Winner
1981	G Broadbent	1986	RN Roderick
1982	MW Calvert	1987	SR Andrew
1983	RD James	1988	MW Calvert
1984	RJ Green	1989	AJ Barnett
1985	KH Williams	1990	M Macara

St George's Challenge Cup

Venue: Royal St George's, Sandwich

Year	Winner	Year	Winner
1981	MF Bonallack	1985	SJ Wood
1982	{ SJ Wood, G	1986	R Claydon
	{ Broadbent, N Taylor	1987	MR Goodin
	(Wood won play-off)	1988	T Ryan
1983	R Willison	1989	S Green
1984	SJ Wood	1990	P Sullivan

Selborne Salver

Venue: Blackmoor GC, Hampshire

Year	Winner	Year	Winner
1981	A Sherborne	1986	TE Clarke
1982	I Gray	1987	AJ Clapp
1983	D Lane	1988	N Holman
1984	D Curry	1989	M Stanford
1985	SM Bottomley	1990	J Metcalfe

Sunningdale Open Foursomes

Year	Winners
1970	R Barrell and Miss A Willard beat R Hunter and Miss M Everard, 2 and 1
1971	A Bird and H Flatman beat J Putt and Miss K Phillips, 3 and 2
1972	JC Davies and MG King beat JK Tullis and AJ Howard, 6 and 5
1973	JA Putt and Miss M Everard beat H Clark and SC Mason, 6 and 5
1974	PJ Butler and C Clark beat HK Clark and DN Brunyard, 1 hole
1975	*Cancelled due to snow*
1976	C Clark and M Hughesdon beat BJ Hunt and IM Stungo, 2 and 1
1977	GN Hunt and D Matthew beat D Huish and G Logan, 3 and 2
1978	GA Caygill and Miss J Greenhalgh beat A Stickley and Mrs C Caldwell, 5 and 4
1979	G Will and R Chapman beat NC Coles and D McClelland, 3 and 2
1980	NC Coles and D McClelland beat SC Mason and J O'Leary, 2 and 1
1981	A Lyddon and G Brand beat MG King and MH Dixon, 1 hole
1982	Miss MA McKenna and Miss M Madill beat Miss C Langford and Miss M Walker, 1 hole
1983	J Davies and M Devetta beat M Hughesdon and Mrs L Bayman, 4 and 3
1984	Miss M McKenna and Miss M Madill beat Miss M Walker and Miss C Langford
1985	J O'Leary and S Torrance beat B Gallacher and P Garner at 25th
1986	R Rafferty and R Chapman beat Mrs M Garner and Miss M McKenna, 1 hole
1987	I Mosey and W Humphries beat Miss G Stewart and D Huish, 3 and 2
1988	C Mason and A Chandler beat Miss M McKenna and Mrs J Garner, 5 and 3
1989	A Hare and R Claydon beat Miss V Thomas and Miss J Wade, 4 and 3
1990	Miss D Reid and Miss C Dibnah beat Miss T Craik and P Hughes, 7 and 6

Tennant Cup

This trophy was presented by Sir Charles Tennant to the Glasgow Club in 1880.
It is the oldest open amateur stroke play competition in the world

Year	Winner	Year	Winner
1970	CW Green	1980	Allan Brodie
1971	Andrew Brodie	1981	G MacDonald
1972	Allan Brodie	1982	LS Mann
1973	PJ Smith	1983	C Dalgleish
1974	D McCart	1984	E Wilson
1975	CW Green	1985	CJ Brooks
From 1976, 72 holes		1986	PG Irvan
1976	IC Hutcheon	1987	J Rasmussen
1977	S Martin	1988	C Dalgleish
1978	IA Carslaw	1989	DG Carrick
1979	G Hay	1990	C Everett

West of England Open Amateur Championship

Venue: Burnham-on-Sea

Year	Winner	Year	Winner
1981	M Mouland	1986	J Bennett
1982	M Higgins	1987	D Rosier
1983	C Peacock	1988	N Holman
1984	GB Hickman	1989	N Holman
1985	AC Nash	1990	J Payne

West of England Open Amateur Stroke Play Championship

Year	Winner	Year	Winner
1981	N Taee	1986	P Baker
1982	MP Higgins	1987	G Wolstenholme
1983	P McEvoy	1988	M Evans
1984	A Sherborne	1989	AD Hare
1985	P McEvoy	1990	J Payne

West of Scotland Open Amateur Championship

Year	Winner	Year	Winner
1981	H McMorran	1986	C Brooks
1982	G MacDonald	1987	R Jenkins
1983	C Barrie	1988	S Savage
1984	G Shaw	1989	AJ Elliott
1985	JA Thomson	1990	ST Knowles

Worplesdon Mixed Foursomes

Year	Winners
1980	Mrs L Bayman and I Boyd beat Mrs L Davies and R Hurst, 1 hole
1981	Mrs J Nicholsen and MN Stern beat Mrs S Birley and RL Glading, 2 and 1
1982	Miss B New and K Dobson beat Miss S Cohen and J Tarbuck, 2 and 1
1983	Miss B New and K Dobson beat Miss N McCormack and N Briggs at 19th
1984	Miss L Bayman and MC Hughesdon beat Miss N McCormack and N Briggs, 5 and 4
1985	Mrs H Kaye and D Longmuir beat Mrs J Collingham and GS Melville, 5 and 3
1986	Miss P Johnson and RN Roderick beat Miss C Duffy and L Hawkins, 2 and 1
1987	Mrs J Nicholsen and B White beat Miss T Craik and P Hughes, 4 and 3
1988	Mme A Larrezac and JJ Caplan beat Miss S Bennett and BK Turner, 4 and 3
1989	Miss J Kershaw and M Kershaw beat Mrs H Kaye and D Longmuir, 2 and 1
1990	Miss S Keogh and A Rogers beat Miss J Rhodes and C Banks, 3 and 1

Amateur International Tournaments and Matches

United States *v* Great Britain & Ireland
Unofficial

Year	Great Britain		USA		Venue
1921	Foursomes	0	3	Foursomes	4	9	Hoylake
(May 21)	Singles	3		Singles	5		

Year	Great Britain		USA		Venue
1921 (May 21)	Foursomes 0 / Singles 3 = 3	Foursomes 4 / Singles 5 = 9	Hoylake

The Walker Cup
Instituted 1922

Year	Great Britain & Ireland			USA			Venue
1922	Foursomes	1	4	Foursomes	3	8	Long Island, NY
(August 29)	Singles	3		Singles	5		
1923	Foursomes	3	5½	Foursomes	1	6½	St Andrews
(May 18-19)	Singles	2½		Singles	5½		
1924	Foursomes	1	3	Foursomes	3	9	Garden City, NY
(Sept 12-13)	Singles	2		Singles	6		
1926	Foursomes	1	5½	Foursomes	3	6½	St Andrews
(June 2-3)	Singles	4½		Singles	3½		
1928	Foursomes	0	1	Foursomes	4	11	Chicago
(Aug 30-31)	Singles	1		Singles	7		
1930	Foursomes	1	2	Foursomes	3	10	Sandwich
(May 15-16)	Singles	1		Singles	7		
1932	Foursomes	0	2½	Foursomes	4	9½	Brookline, Mass
(Sept 1-2)	Singles	2½		Singles	5½		
1934	Foursomes	1	2½	Foursomes	3	9½	St Andrews
(May 11-12)	Singles	1½		Singles	6½		
1936	Foursomes	1	1½	Foursomes	3	10½	Pine Valley, NJ
(Sept 2-3)	Singles	0½		Singles	7½		
1938	Foursomes	2½	7½	Foursomes	1½	4½	St Andrews
(June 3-4)	Singles	5		Singles	3		
1947	Foursomes	2	4	Foursomes	2	8	St Andrews
(May 16-17)	Singles	2		Singles	6		
1949	Foursomes	1	2	Foursomes	3	10	Winged Foot, NY
(Aug 19-20)	Singles	1		Singles	7		
1951	Foursomes	1	4½	Foursomes	3	7½	Royal Birkdale
(May 11-12)	Singles	3½		Singles	4½		
1953	Foursomes	1	3	Foursomes	3	9	Kittansett, Mass
(Sept 4-5)	Singles	2		Singles	6		
1955	Foursomes	0	2	Foursomes	4	10	St Andrews
(May 20-21)	Singles	2		Singles	6		
1957	Foursomes	1½	3½	Foursomes	2½	8½	Minikahda
(Sept 1-2)	Singles	2		Singles	6		
1959	Foursomes	0	3	Foursomes	4	9	Muirfield
(May 15-16)	Singles	3		Singles	5		
1961	Foursomes	0	1	Foursomes	4	11	Seattle, Wash
(Sept 1-2)	Singles	1		Singles	7		

From 1963 Foursomes and Singles matches were played on both days, each match over 18 holes.

Year	Great Britain & Ireland			USA			Venue
1963	Foursomes	1	8	Foursomes	6	12	Turnberry
(May 24-25)	Singles	7		Singles	6		

Year	Great Britain & Ireland				USA				Venue
1965	Foursomes	4			Foursomes	3			
(Sept 3-4)	Singles	7	11		Singles	8	11		Baltimore, M'land
1967	Foursomes	3			Foursomes	4			
(May 15-20)	Singles	4	7		Singles	9	13		Sandwich
1969	Foursomes	3			Foursomes	3			
(Aug 22-23)	Singles	5	8		Singles	7	10		Milwaukee, Wisc.
1971	Foursomes	5½			Foursomes	2½			
(May 26-27)	Singles	7½	13		Singles	8½	11		St Andrews
1973	Foursomes	1			Foursomes	7			
(Aug 24-25)	Singles	9	10		Singles	7	14		Brookline, Mass.
1975	Foursomes	3			Foursomes	5			
(May 28-29)	Singles	5½	8½		Singles	10½	15½		St Andrews
1977	Foursomes	3			Foursomes	5			
(Aug 26-27)	Singles	5	8		Singles	11	16		Shinnecock Hills, NY
1979	Foursomes	4			Foursomes	4			
(May 30-31)	Singles	4½	8½		Singles	11½	15½		Muirfield

At Cypress Point, 28th and 29th August, 1981

First Day—Foursomes

USA	Matches	Great Britain and Ireland	Matches
H Sutton and J Sigel	0	P Walton and R Rafferty (4 and 2)	1
J Holtgrieve and F Fuhrer (1 hole)	1	R Chapman and P McEvoy	0
B Lewis and D von Tacky (2 and 1)	1	P Deeble and T Hutcheon	0
R Commans and C Pavin (5 and 4)	1	D Evans and P Way	0
	3		1

Singles

USA	Matches	Great Britain and Ireland	Matches
H Sutton (3 and 1)	1	R Rafferty	0
J Rassett (1 hole)	1	C Dalgleish	0
R Commans	0	P Walton (1 hole)	1
B Lewis	0	R Chapman (2 and 1)	1
C Pavin (4 and 3)	1	T Hutcheon	0
J Mudd (1 hole)	1	J Godwin	0
D von Tacky	0	P Way (3 and 1)	1
J Sigel (4 and 2)	1	P McEvoy	0
	5		3

First-days' aggregate: USA, 8; Great Britain and Ireland, 4.

Second Day—Foursomes

USA	Matches	Great Britain and Ireland	Matches
H Sutton and J Sigel	0	R Chapman and P Way (1 hole)	1
J Holtgrieve and F Fuhrer	0	P Walton and R Rafferty (6 and 4)	1
B Lewis and D von Tacky	0	D Evans and C Dalgleish (3 and 2)	1
J Rassett and J Mudd (5 and 4)	1	T Hutcheon and J Godwin	0
	1		3

Singles

USA	Matches	Great Britain and Ireland	Matches
H Sutton	0	R Chapman (1 hole)	1
J Holtgrieve (2 and 1)	1	R Rafferty	0
F Fuhrer (4 and 2)	1	P Walton	0
J Sigel (6 and 5)	1	P Way	0
J Mudd (7 and 5)	1	C Dalgleish	0
R Commans (halved)	½	J Godwin (halved)	½
J Rassett (4 and 3)	1	P Deeble	0
C Pavin (halved)	½	D Evans (halved)	½
	6		2

Second-days' aggregate: USA, 7; Great Britain and Ireland, 5.
Grand Match aggregate: USA, 15; Great Britain and Ireland, 9.

At Hoylake, 25th and 26th May, 1983

Walker Cup
continued

First Day—Foursomes

Great Britain and Ireland	Matches	USA	Matches
M Lewis and M Thompson	0	B Lewis and J Holtgrieve (7 and 6)	1
G Macgregor and P Walton (3 and 1)	1	J Sigel and R Fehr	0
L Mann and A Oldcorn (5 and 4)	1	W Hoffer and D Tentis	0
S Keppler and A Pierse	0	W Wood and B Faxon (3 and 1)	1
	2		2

Singles

Great Britain and Ireland	Matches	USA	Matches
P Parkin (6 and 4)	1	N Crosby	0
L Mann	0	J Holtgrieve (6 and 5)	1
A Oldcorn (4 and 3)	1	B Tuten	0
P Walton (1 hole)	1	J Sigel	0
S Keppler	0	R Fehr (1 hole)	1
D Carrick	0	B Faxon (3 and 1)	1
G Macgregor (halved)	1/2	W Wood (halved)	1/2
A Pierse	0	B Lewis (3 and 1)	1
	3 1/2		4 1/2

First day's aggregate: Great Britain and Ireland, 5 1/2; USA, 6 1/2.

Second Day—Foursomes

Great Britain and Ireland	Matches	USA	Matches
G Macgregor and P Walton	0	N Crosby and W Hoffer (2 holes)	1
P Parkin and M Thompson (1 hole)	1	B Faxon and W Wood	0
L Mann and A Oldcorn (1 hole)	1	B Lewis and J Holtgrieve	0
S Keppler and A Pierse (halved)	1/2	J Sigel and R Fehr	1/2
	2 1/2		1 1/2

Singles

Great Britain and Ireland	Matches	USA	Matches
P Walton (2 and 1)	1	W Wood	0
P Parkin	0	B Faxon (3 and 2)	1
G Macgregor	0	R Fehr (2 and 1)	1
M Thompson	0	B Tuten (3 and 2)	1
L Mann (halved)	1/2	D Tentis (halved)	1/2
S Keppler	0	B Lewis (6 and 5)	1
A Oldcorn (3 and 2)	1	J Holtgrieve	0
D Carrick	0	J Sigel (3 and 1)	1
	2 1/2		5 1/2

Second day's aggregate: Great Britain and Ireland, 5; USA, 7.
Grand Match aggregate: Great Britain and Ireland, 10 1/2; USA 13 1/2.

At Pine Valley, New Jersey, 21st and 22nd August, 1985

Walker Cup
continued

First Day—Foursomes

USA	Matches	Great Britain and Ireland	Matches
S Verplank and J Sigel (1 hole)	1	C Montgomerie and G Macgregor	0
D Waldorf and S Randolph	0	J Hawksworth and G McGimpsey	
R Sonnier and J Haas	0	(4 and 3)	1
M Podolak and D Love	1/2	P Baker and P McEvoy (6 and 5)	1
		C Bloice and S Stephen	1/2
	1 1/2		2 1/2

Singles

USA	Matches	Great Britain and Ireland	Matches
S Verplank (2 and 1)	1	G McGimpsey	0
S Randolph (5 and 4)	1	P Mayo	0
R Sonnier	1/2	J Hawksworth	1/2
J Sigel (5 and 4)	1	C Montgomerie	0
B Lewis	0	P McEvoy (2 and 1)	1
C Burroughs	0	G Macgregor (2 holes)	1
D Waldorf (4 and 2)	1	D Gilford	0
J Haas	0	S Stephen (2 and 1)	1
	4 1/2		3 1/2

First-days' aggregate: Great Britain and Ireland, 6; USA, 6.

Second Day—Foursomes

USA	Matches	Great Britain and Ireland	Matches
S Verplank and J Sigel	1/2	P Mayo and C Montgomerie	1/2
S Randolph and J Hass (3 and 2)	1	J Hawksworth and G McGimpsey	0
B Lewis and C Burroughs (2 and 1)	1	P Baker and P McEvoy	0
M Podolak and D Love (3 and 2)	1	C Bloice and S Stephen	0
	3 1/2		1/2

Singles

USA	Matches	Great Britain and Ireland	Matches
S Randolph	1/2	G McGimpsey	1/2
S Verplank (1 hole)	1	C Montgomerie	0
J Sigel	0	J Hawksworth (4 and 3)	1
D Love (5 and 3)	1	P McEvoy	0
R Sonnier	0	P Baker (5 and 4)	1
C Burroughs	0	G Macgregor (3 and 2)	1
B Lewis (4 and 3)	1	C Bloice	0
D Waldorf	0	S Stephen (2 and 1)	1
	3 1/2		4 1/2

Second-days' aggregate: Great Britain and Ireland, 5; USA, 7.
Grand Match aggregate: Great Britain and Ireland, 11; USA, 13.

At Sunningdale, Berkshire, 27th and 28th May, 1987

Walker Cup

continued

First Day—Foursomes

USA	Matches	Great Britain and Ireland	Matches
B Alexander and B Mayfair (5 and 4)	1	C Montgomerie and G Shaw	0
C Kite and L Mattice (2 and 1)	1	D Curry and P Mayo	0
B Lewis and B Loeffler (2 and 1)	1	G Macgregor and J Robinson	0
J Sigel and B. Andrade (3 and 2)	1	J McHenry and P Girvan	0
	4		0

Singles

USA	Matches	Great Britain and Ireland	Matches
B Alexander	0	D Curry (2 holes)	1
B Andrade (7 and 5)	1	J Robinson	0
J Sorenson	0	C Montgomerie (3 and 2)	1
J Sigel (3 and 2)	1	R Eggo	0
B Montgomery (1 hole)	1	J McHenry	0
B Lewis (3 and 2)	1	P Girvan	0
B Mayfair (2 holes)	1	D Carrick	0
C Kite	0	G Shaw (1 hole)	1
	5		3

First day's aggregate: Great Britain and Ireland, 3; USA, 9.

Second Day—Foursomes

USA	Matches	Great Britain and Ireland	Matches
B Lewis and B Loeffler (4 and 3)	1	D Curry and D Carrick	0
C Kite and L Mattice (5 and 3)	1	C Montgomerie and G Shaw	0
J Sorenson and B Montgomery (4 and 3)	1	P Mayo and G Macgregor	0
J Sigel and B Andrade	0	J McHenry and J Robinson (4 and 2)	1
	3		1

Singles

USA	Matches	Great Britain and Ireland	Matches
B Alexander (5 and 4)	1	D Curry	0
B Andrade	0	C Montgomerie (4 and 2)	1
B Loeffler	0	J McHenry (3 and 2)	1
J Sorenson (half)	1/2	G Shaw (half)	1/2
L Mattice	0	J Robinson (1 hole)	1
B Lewis (3 and 2)	1	D Carrick	0
B Mayfair (1 hole)	1	R Eggo	0
J Sigel (6 and 5)	1	P Girvan	0
	4 1/2		3 1/2

Second day's aggregate: Great Britain and Ireland, 4 1/2; USA, 7 1/2.
Grand Match aggregate: Great Britain and Ireland, 7 1/2 USA 16 1/2.

At Peachtree, Atlanta, 16th and 17th August, 1989

Walker Cup
continued

First Day—Foursomes

USA	Matches	Great Britain and Ireland	Matches
R Gamez and D Martin (3 and 2)	1	R Claydon and D Prosser	0
D Yates and P Mickelson	1/2	S Dodd and G McGimpsey	1/2
G Lesher and J Sigel	0	P McEvoy and E O'Connell (6 and 5)	1
D Eger and K Johnson	0	J Milligan and A Hare (2 and 1)	1
	1 1/2		2 1/2

Singles

USA	Matches	Great Britain and Ireland	Matches
R Gamez (7 and 6)	1	J Milligan	0
D Martin	0	R Claydon (5 and 4)	1
E Meeks	1/2	S Dodd	1/2
R Howe	0	E O'Connell (5 and 4)	1
D Yates	0	P McEvoy (2 and 1)	1
P Mickelson (4 and 2)	1	G McGimpsey	0
G Lesher	0	C Cassells (1 hole)	1
J Sigel	1/2	RN Roderick	1/2
	3		5

First day's aggregate: Great Britain and Ireland, 7 1/2; USA, 4 1/2.

Second Day—Foursomes

USA	Matches	Great Britain and Ireland	Matches
R Gamez and D Martin	1/2	P McEvoy and E O'Connell	1/2
J Sigel and G Lesher	0	R Claydon and C Cassells (3 and 2)	1
D Eger and K Johnson	0	J Milligan and A Hare (2 and 1)	1
P Mickelson and D Yates	0	G McGimpsey and S Dodd (2 and 1)	1
	1/2		3 1/2

Singles

USA	Matches	Great Britain and Ireland	Matches
R Gamez (1 hole)	1	S Dodd	0
D Martin	1/2	A Hare	1/2
G Lesher (3 and 2)	1	R Claydon	0
D Yates (4 and 3)	1	P McEvoy	0
P Mickelson	1/2	E O'Connell	1/2
D Eger (4 and 2)	1	RN Roderick	0
GK Johnson (4 and 2)	1	C Cassells	0
J Sigel	1/2	J Milligan	1/2
	6 1/2		1 1/2

Second day's aggregate: Great Britain and Ireland, 5; USA, 7.
Grand Match aggregate: Great Britain and Ireland, 12 1/2; USA 11 1/2.

Individual Records

Great Britain and Ireland

Name		Year	Played	Won	Lost	Halved
MF Attenborough	Eng	1967	2	0	2	0
CC Aylmer	Eng	1922	2	1	1	0
P Baker	Eng	1985	3	2	1	0
JB Beck	Eng	1928-**(38)-(47)**	1	0	1	0
PJ Benka	Eng	1969	4	2	1	1
HG Bentley	Eng	1934-36-38	4	0	2	2
DA Blair	Scot	1955-61	4	1	3	0
C Bloice	Scot	1985	3	0	2	1
MF Bonallack	Eng	1957-59-61-63-65-67- 69-**71**-73	25	8	14	3
G Brand	Scot	1979	3	0	3	0
OC Bristowe	Eng	(1923)-24	1	0	1	0
A Brodie	Scot	1977-79	8	5	2	1
A Brooks	Scot	1969	3	2	0	1
Hon WGE Brownlow	Eng	1926	2	0	2	0
J Bruen	Ire	1938-49-51	5	0	4	1
JA Buckley	Wales	1979	1	0	1	0
J Burke	Ire	1932	2	0	1	1
AF Bussell	Scot	1957	2	1	1	0
I Caldwell	Eng	1951-55	4	1	2	1
W Campbell	Scot	1930	2	0	2	0
JB Carr	Ire	1947-49-51-53-55-57-59- 61-63-**(65)**-67	20	5	14	1
RJ Carr	Ire	1971	4	3	0	1
DG Carrick	Scot	1983-87	5	0	5	0
IA Carslaw	Scot	1979	3	1	1	1
C Cassells	Eng	1989	3	2	1	0
JR Cater	Scot	1955	1	0	1	0
J Caven	Scot	1922	2	0	2	0
BHG Chapman	Eng	1961	1	0	1	0
R Chapman	Eng	1981	4	3	1	0
MJ Christmas	Eng	1961-63	3	1	2	0
*CA Clark	Eng	1965	4	2	0	2
GJ Clark	Eng	1965	1	0	1	0
*HK Clark	Eng	1973	3	1	1	1
R Claydon	Eng	1989	4	2	2	0
GB Cosh	Scot	1965	4	3	1	0
T Craddock	Ire	1967-69	6	2	3	1
LG Crawley	Eng	1932-34-38-47	6	3	3	0
B Critchley	Eng	1969	4	1	1	2
D Curry	Eng	1987	4	1	3	0
CR Dalgleish	Scot	1981	3	1	2	0
B Darwin	Eng	1922	2	1	1	0
JC Davies	Eng	1973-75-77-79	13	3	8	2
P Deeble	Eng	1977-81	5	1	4	0
FWG Deighton	Scot	(1951)-57	2	0	2	0
SC Dodd	Wales	1989	4	1	1	2
*NV Drew	Ire	1953	1	0	1	0
AA Duncan	Wales	**(1953)**	0	0	0	0
JM Dykes	Scot	1936	2	0	1	1
R Eggo	Eng	1987	2	0	2	0
D Evans	Wales	1981	3	1	1	1
RC Ewing	Ire	1936-38-47-49-51-55	10	1	7	2
GRD Eyles	Eng	1975	4	2	2	0
EW Fiddian	Eng	1932-34	4	0	4	0
J de Forest	Eng	1932	1	0	1	0
R Foster	Eng	1965-67-69-71-73-**(79)-(81)**	17	2	13	2
DW Frame	Eng	1961	1	0	1	0
D Gilford	Eng	1985	1	0	1	0
P Girvan	Scot	1987	3	0	3	0
G Godwin	Eng	1979-81	7	2	4	1
CW Green	Scot	1963-69-71-73-75-**(83)-(85)**	17	4	10	3
RH Hardman	Eng	1928	1	0	1	0
A Hare	Eng	1989	3	2	0	1
R Harris	Scot	**(1922)-23-26**	4	1	3	0
RW Hartley	Eng	1930-32	4	0	4	0
WL Hartley	Eng	1932	2	0	2	0
J Hawksworth	Eng	1985	4	2	1	1
P Hedges	Eng	1973-75	5	0	2	3
CO Hezlet	Ire	1924-26-28	6	0	5	1
GA Hill	Eng	1936-**(55)**	2	0	1	1
Sir EWE Holderness	Eng	1923-26-30	6	2	4	0
TWB Homer	Eng	1973	3	0	3	0
CVL Hooman	Eng	1922-23	3	1**	2	0**
WL Hope	Scot	1923-24-28	5	1	4	0
G Huddy	Eng	1961	1	0	1	0
W Humphreys	Eng	1971	3	2	1	0
IC Hutcheon	Scot	1975-77-79-81	15	5	8	2

Name		Year	Played	Won	Lost	Halved
RR Jack	Scot	1957-59	4	2	2	0
*M James	Eng	1975	4	3	1	0
A Jamieson, Jr	Scot	1926	2	1	1	0
MJ Kelley	Eng	1977-79	7	3	3	1
SD Keppler	Eng	1983	4	0	3	1
*MG King	Eng	1969-73	7	1	5	1
AT Kyle	Scot	1938-47-51	5	2	3	0
DH Kyle	Scot	1924	1	0	1	0
JA Lang	Scot	(1930)	0	0	0	0
JDA Langley	Eng	1936-51-53	6	0	5	1
CD Lawrie	Scot	(1961)-(63)	0	0	0	0
ME Lewis	Eng	1983	1	0	1	0
PB Lucas	Eng	(1936)-47-(49)	2	1	1	0
MSR Lunt	Eng	1959-61-63-65	11	2	8	1
*AWB Lyle	Scot	1977	3	0	3	0
AR McCallum	Scot	1928	1	0	1	0
SM McCready	Ire	1949-51	3	0	3	0
JS Macdonald	Scot	1971	3	1	1	1
P McEvoy	Eng	1977-79-81-85-89	18	5	11	2
G McGimpsey	Ire	1985-89	7	2	3	2
G Macgregor	Scot	1971-75-83-85-87-(91)	14	5	8	1
RC MacGregor	Scot	1953	2	0	2	0
J McHenry	Ire	1987	4	2	2	0
P McKellar	Scot	1977	1	0	1	0
WW Mackenzie	Scot	1922-23	3	1	2	0
SL McKinlay	Scot	1934	2	0	2	0
J McLean	Scot	1934-36	4	1	3	0
EA McRuvie	Scot	1932-34	4	1	2	1
JFD Madeley	Ire	1963	2	0	1	1
LS Mann	Scot	1983	4	2	1	1
B Marchbank	Scot	1979	4	2	2	0
GC Marks	Eng	1969-71-(87)-(89)	6	2	4	0
DM Marsh	Eng	(1959)-71-(73)-(75)	3	2	1	0
GNC Martin	Ire	1928	1	0	1	0
S Martin	Scot	1977	4	2	2	0
P Mayo	Wales	1985-87	4	0	3	1
GH Micklem	Eng	1947-49-53-55-(57)-(59)	6	1	5	0
DJ Millensted	Eng	1967	2	1	1	0
JW Milligan	Scot	1989	4	2	1	1
EB Millward	Eng	(1949)-55	2	0	2	0
WTG Milne	Scot	1973	4	2	2	0
CS Montgomerie	Scot	1985-87	8	2	5	1
JL Morgan	Wales	1951-53-55	6	2	4	0
P Mulcare	Ire	1975	3	2	1	0
GH Murray	Scot	1977	2	1	1	0
SWT Murray	Scot	1963	4	2	2	0
WA Murray	Scot	1923-24-(26)	4	1	3	0
E O'Connell	Ire	1989	4	2	0	2
A Oldcorn	Eng	1983	4	4	0	0
*PA Oosterhuis	Eng	1967	4	1	2	1
R Oppenheimer	Eng	(1951)	0	0	0	0
P Parkin	Wales	1983	3	2	1	0
JJF Pennink	Eng	1938	2	1	1	0
TP Perkins	Eng	1928	2	0	2	0
AH Perowne	Eng	1949-53-59	4	0	4	0
GB Peters	Scot	1936-38	4	2	1	1
AD Pierse	Ire	1983	3	0	2	1
AK Pirie	Scot	1967	3	0	2	1
MA Poxon	Eng	1975	2	0	2	0
D Prosser	Eng	1989	1	0	1	2
*R Rafferty	Ire	1981	4	2	2	0
J Robinson	Eng	1987	4	2	2	0
RN Roderick	Wales	1989	2	0	1	1
AC Saddler	Scot	1963-65-67-(77)	10	3	5	2
Hon M Scott	Eng	1924-**34**	4	2	2	0
R Scott, Jr	Scot	1924	1	1	0	0
PF Scrutton	Eng	1955-57	3	0	3	0
DN Sewell	Eng	1957-59	4	1	3	0
RDBM Shade	Scot	1961-63-65-67	14	6	6	2
G Shaw	Scot	1987	4	1	2	1
DB Sheahan	Ire	1963	4	2	2	0
AE Shepperson	Eng	1957-59	3	1	1	1
AF Simpson	Scot	(1926)	0	0	0	0
JN Smith	Scot	1930	2	0	2	0
WD Smith	Scot	1959	1	0	1	0
AR Stephen	Scot	1985	4	2	1	1
EF Storey	Eng	1924-26-28	6	1	5	0
JA Stout	Eng	1930-32	4	0	3	1
C Stowe	Eng	1938-47	4	2	2	0
HB Stuart	Scot	1971-73-75	10	4	6	0
A Thirlwell	Eng	1957	1	0	1	0
KG Thom	Eng	1949	2	0	2	0

Name		Year	Played	Won	Lost	Halved
MS Thompson	Eng	1983	3	1	2	0
H Thomson	Scot	1936-38	4	2	2	0
CJH Tolley	Eng	1922-23-**24**-26-30-34	12	4	8	0
TA Torrance	Scot	1924-28-30-**32**-34	9	3	5	1
WB Torrance	Scot	1922	2	0	2	0
*PM Townsend	Eng	1965	4	3	1	0
LP Tupling	Eng	1969	2	1	1	0
W Tweddell	Eng	**1928**-(36)	2	0	2	0
J Walker	Scot	1961	2	0	2	0
P Walton	Ire	1981-83	8	6	2	0
*P Way	Eng	1981	4	2	2	0
RH Wethered	Eng	1922-23-26-**30**-34	9	5	3	1
RJ White	Eng	1947-49-51-53-55	10	6	3	1
J Wilson	Scot	1923	2	2	0	0
JC Wilson	Scot	1947-53	4	0	4	0
GB Wolstenholme	Eng	1957-59	4	1	2	1

Notes: Bold Type indicates captain; in brackets, did not play.
*Players who have also played in the Ryder Cup.
**CVL Hooman and J Sweetser in 1922 were all square after 36 holes; instructions to the contrary not being readily available, they played on and Hooman won at the 37th. On all other occasions halved matches have counted as such.

Walker Cup

continued

Individual Records

United States of America

Name	Year	Played	Won	Lost	Halved
*TD Aaron	1959	2	1	1	0
B Alexander	1987	3	2	1	0
DC Allen	1965-67	6	0	4	2
B Andrade	1987	4	2	2	0
ES Andrews	1961	1	1	0	0
D Ballenger	1973	1	1	0	0
R Baxter, jr	1957	2	2	0	0
DR Beman	1959-61-63-65	11	7	2	2
RE Billows	1938-49	4	2	2	0
SE Bishop	1947-49	3	2	1	0
AS Blum	1957	1	0	1	0
J Bohmann	1969	3	1	2	0
M Brannan	1977	3	1	2	0
GF Burns	1975	3	2	1	0
C Burroughs	1985	3	1	2	0
AE Campbell	1936	2	2	0	0
JE Campbell	1957	1	0	1	0
WC Campbell	1951-53-(**55**)-57-65-67-71-75	18	11	4	3
RJ Cerrudo	1967	4	1	1	2
RD Chapman	1947-51-53	5	3	2	0
D Cherry	1953-55-61	5	5	0	0
D Clarke	1979	3	2	0	1
RE Cochran	1961	1	1	0	0
CR Coe	1949-51-53-(**57**)-**59**-61-63	13	7	4	2
R Commans	1981	3	1	1	1
JW Conrad	1955	2	1	1	0
N Crosby	1983	2	1	1	0
BH Cudd	1955	2	2	0	0
RD Davies	1963	2	0	2	0
JW Dawson	1949	2	2	0	0
RB Dickson	1967	3	3	0	0
GT Dunlap Jr	1932-34-36	5	3	1	1
D Edwards	1973	4	4	0	0
HC Egan	1934	1	1	0	0
HC Eger	1989	3	1	2	0
D Eichelberger	1965	3	1	2	0
J Ellis	1973	3	2	1	0
W Emery	1936	2	1	0	1
C Evans Jr	1922-24-28	5	3	2	0
J Farquhar	1971	3	1	2	0
B Faxon	1983	4	3	1	0
R Fehr	1983	4	2	1	1
JW Fischer	1934-36-38-(**65**)	4	3	0	1
D Fischesser	1979	3	1	2	0
MA Fleckman	1967	2	0	2	0
B Fleisher	1969	4	0	2	2
J Fought	1977	4	4	0	0
WC Fownes Jr	**1922**-24	3	1	2	0
F Fuhrer	1981	3	2	1	0
JR Gabrielsen	1977-(**81**)	3	1	2	0
R Gamez	1989	4	3	0	1
RA Gardner	1922-**23**-**24**-**26**	8	6	2	0
RW Gardner	1961-63	5	4	0	1

Name	Year	Played	Won	Lost	Halved
M Giles	1969-71-73-75	15	8	2	5
HL Givan	1936	1	0	0	1
JG Goodman	1934-36-38	6	4	2	0
M Gove	1979	3	2	1	0
J Grace	1975	3	2	1	0
JA Grant	1967	2	2	0	0
AD Gray Jr	1963-65-67	12	5	6	1
JP Guilford	1922-24-26	6	4	2	0
W Gunn	1926-28	4	4	0	0
*F Haas Jr	1938	2	0	2	0
*J Haas	1975	3	3	0	0
J Haas	1985	3	1	2	0
G Hallberg	1977	3	1	2	0
GS Hamer Jr	(1947)	0	0	0	0
LE Harris Jr	1963	4	3	1	0
V Heafner	1977	3	3	0	0
SD Herron	1923	2	0	2	0
S Hoch	1979	4	4	0	0
W Hoffer	1983	2	1	1	0
J Holtgrieve	1979-81-83	10	6	4	0
JM Hopkins	1965	3	0	2	1
R Howe	1989	1	0	1	0
W Howell	1932	1	1	0	0
W Hyndman	1957-59-61-69-71	9	6	1	2
J Inman	1969	2	2	0	0
JG Jackson	1953-55	3	3	0	0
K Johnson	1989	3	1	2	0
HR Johnston	1923-24-28-30	6	5	1	0
RT Jones Jr	1922-24-26-**28-30**	10	9	1	0
AF Kammer	1947	2	1	1	0
M Killian	1973	3	1	2	0
C Kite	1987	3	2	1	0
*TO Kite	1971	4	2	1	1
RE Knepper	(1922)	0	0	0	0
RW Knowles	1951	1	1	0	0
G Koch	1973-75	7	4	1	2
CR Kocsis	1938-49-57	5	2	2	1
G Lesher	1989	4	1	3	0
B Lewis Jr	1981-83-85-87	14	10	4	0
JW Lewis	1967	4	3	1	0
WL Little Jr	1934	2	2	0	0
*GA Littler	1953	2	2	0	0
B Loeffler	1987	3	2	1	0
D Love	1985	3	2	0	1
MJ McCarthy Jr	(1928)-32	1	1	0	0
BN McCormick	1949	1	1	0	0
JB McHale	1949-51	3	2	0	1
RR Mackenzie	1926-28-30	6	5	1	0
MR Marston	1922-23-24-34	8	5	3	0
D Martin	1989	4	1	1	2
L Mattiace	1987	3	2	1	0
B Mayfair	1987	3	3	0	0
E Meeks	1989	1	0	0	1
SN Melnyk	1969-71	7	3	3	1
P Mickelson	1989	4	1	1	2
AL Miller	1969-71	8	4	3	1
L Miller	1977	4	4	0	0
DK Moe	1930-32	3	3	0	0
B Montgomery	1987	2	2	0	0
G Moody	1979	3	1	2	0
GT Moreland	1932-34	4	4	0	0
D Morey	1955-65	4	1	3	0
J Mudd	1981	3	3	0	0
*RJ Murphy	1967	4	1	2	1
JF Neville	1923	1	0	1	0
*JW Nicklaus	1959-61	4	4	0	0
LW Oehmig	**(1977)**	0	0	0	0
FD Ouimet	1922-23-24-26-30-**32-34**-**(36)**-**(38)**-**(47)**-**(49)**	16	9	5	2
HD Paddock Jr	1951	1	0	0	1
*J Pate	1975	4	0	4	0
WJ Patton	1955-57-59-63-65-**(69)**	14	11	3	0
C Pavin	1981	3	2	0	1
M Peck	1979	3	1	1	1
M Pfeil	1973	4	2	1	1
M Podolak	1985	2	1	0	1
SL Quick	1947	2	1	1	0
S Randolph	1985	4	2	1	1
J Rassett	1981	3	3	0	0
F Ridley	1977-**(87)**-**(89)**	3	2	1	0
RH Riegel	1947-49	4	4	0	0
H Robbins Jr	1957	2	0	1	1

Name	Year	Played	Won	Lost	Halved
*W Rogers	1973	2	1	1	0
GV Rotan	1923	2	1	1	0
*EM Rudolph	1957	2	1	0	1
B Sander	1977	3	0	3	0
CH Seaver	1932	2	2	0	0
RL Siderowf	1969-73-75-77-**(79)**	14	4	8	2
J Sigel	1977-79-81-**83**-85-87-89	27	14	8	5
RH Sikes	1963	3	1	2	0
JB Simons	1971	2	0	2	0
*S Simpson	1977	3	3	0	0
CB Smith	1961-63	2	0	1	1
R Smith	1936-38	4	2	2	0
R Sonnier	1985	3	0	1	1
J Sorensen	1987	3	1	1	1
*C Stadler	1975	3	3	0	0
FR Stranahan	1947-49-51	6	3	2	1
*C Strange	1975	4	3	0	1
*H Sutton	1979-81	7	2	4	1
JW Sweetser	1922-23-24-26-28-32-**(67)**-**(73)**	12	7	4**	1**
FM Taylor	1957-59-61	4	4	0	0
D Tentis	1983	2	0	1	1
RS Tufts	**(1963)**	0	0	0	0
WP Turnesa	1947-49-**51**	6	3	3	0
B Tuten	1983	2	1	1	0
EM Tutweiler	1965-67	6	5	1	0
ER Updegraff	1963-65-69-**(75)**	7	3	3	1
S Urzetta	1951-53	4	4	0	0
K Venturi	1953	2	2	0	0
S Verplank	1985	4	3	0	1
GJ Voigt	1930-32-36	5	2	2	1
G Von Elm	1926-28-30	6	4	1	1
D von Tacky	1981	3	1	2	0
*JL Wadkins	1969-71	7	3	4	0
D Waldorf	1985	3	1	2	0
EH Ward	1953-55-59	6	6	0	0
MH Ward	1938-47	4	2	2	0
M West	1973-79	6	2	3	1
J Westland	1932-34-53-**(61)**	5	3	0	2
HW Wettlaufer	1959	2	2	0	0
E White	1936	2	2	0	0
OF Willing	1923-24-30	4	4	0	0
JM Winters Jr	**(1971)**	0	0	0	0
W Wood	1983	4	1	2	1
FJ Wright	1923	1	1	0	0
CR Yates	1936-38-**(53)**	4	3	0	1
D Yates	1989	4	1	2	1
RL Yost	1955	2	2	0	0

Notes: Bold type indicates captain: in brackets, did not play.
*Players who have also played in the Ryder Cup.
**CVL Hooman and J Sweetser in 1922 were all square after 36 holes; instructions to the contrary not being readily available, they played on and Hooman won at the 37th. On all other occasions halved matches have counted as such.

Walker Cup
continued

Eisenhower Trophy (World Amateur Team Championship)

Year	Winners	Runners-up	Venue	Score
1958	Australia	United States	St Andrews	918
(After a tie, Australia won the play-off by two strokes. Australia 222, United States 224)				
1960	United States	Australia	Ardmore, USA	834
1962	United States	Canada	Kawana, Japan	854
1964	Great Britain & Ireland	Canada	Olgiata, Rome	895
1966	Australia	United States	Mexico City	877
1968	United States	Great Britain & Ireland	Melbourne	868
1970	United States	New Zealand	Madrid	857
1972	United States	Australia	Buenos Aires	865
1974	United States	Japan	Dominican Rep.	888
1976	Great Britain & Ireland	Japan	Penina, Portugal	892
1978	United States	Canada	Fiji	873
1980	United States	South Africa	Pinehurst, USA	848
1982	United States	Sweden	Lausanne	859
1984	Japan	United States	Hong Kong	870
1986	Canada	United States	Caracas, Venezuela	860
1988	Great Britain & Ireland	United States	Ullva, Sweden	882
1990	Sweden	New Zealand	Christchurch, New Zealand	279

European Amateur Team Championship

Year	Winner	Second	Venue
1959	Sweden		
1961	Sweden	England	Brussels, Belgium
1963	England	Sweden	Falsterbo, Sweden
1965	Ireland	Scotland	St George's, England
1967	Ireland	France	Turin, Italy
1969	England	W Germany	Hamburg, W Germany
1971	England	Scotland	Lausanne, Switzerland
1973	England	Scotland	Penina, Portugal
1975	Scotland	Italy	Killarney, Ireland
1977	Scotland	Sweden	The Haagsche, Holland
1979	England	Wales	Esbjerg, Denmark
1981	England	Scotland	St Andrews, Scotland
1983	Ireland	Spain	Chantilly, France
1985	Scotland	Sweden	Halmstad, Sweden
1987	Ireland	England	Murhof, Austria
1989	England	Scotland	Royal Porthcawl

Home Internationals

Winners:		Winners:	
1932	Scotland	1962	Tie: England, Ireland, Scotland
1933	Scotland	1963	Tie: England, Ireland, Scotland
1934	Scotland	1964	England
1935	Tie: England, Scotland, Ireland	1965	England
1936	Scotland	1966	England
1937	Scotland	1967	Scotland
1938	England	1968	England
1939-46	No Internationals held	1969	England
1947	England	1970	Scotland
1948	England	1971	Scotland
1949	England	1972	Tie: Scotland, England
1950	Ireland	1973	England
1951	Tie: Ireland, Scotland	1974	England
1952	Scotland	1975	Scotland
1953	Scotland	1976	Scotland
1954	England	1977	England
1955	Ireland	1978	England
1956	Scotland	1979	No Internationals held

Winners:		Winners:	
1957	England	1980	England
1958	England	1981	Scotland
1959	Tie: England, Ireland, Scotland	1982	Scotland
1960	England	1983	Ireland
1961	Scotland	1984	England

1985—At Formby
Winners: England

England beat Wales	11 matches to 4
England beat Scotland	8 matches to 7
England beat Ireland	8½ matches to 6½
Wales beat Scotland	8 matches to 7
Wales beat Ireland	9½ matches to 5½
Ireland beat Scotland	11½ matches to 3½

1986—At Harlech
Winners: Scotland

Scotland beat England	9½ matches to 5½
Scotland beat Ireland	10½ matches to 4½
Scotland beat Wales	10 matches to 5
England beat Wales	9 matches to 6
Ireland beat England	8 matches to 7
Wales halved with Ireland	7½ matches each

1987—At Lahinch
Winners: Ireland

Ireland beat England	6 matches to 4
Ireland beat Scotland	10½ matches to 4½
Ireland beat Wales	8 matches to 7
England beat Scotland	9 matches to 6
England halved with Wales	7 matches each
Scotland beat Wales	6½ matches to 3½

(On the first day the foursomes were abandoned due to bad weather, singles only being played.)

1988—At Muirfield
Winners: England

England beat Wales	11 matches to 4
England beat Scotland	9 matches to 6
England beat Ireland	8 matches to 7
Ireland halved with Wales	7½ matches each
Ireland beat Scotland	10 matches to 5
Wales beat Scotland	8 matches to 7

1989—At Ganton
Winners: England

England beat Ireland	8 matches to 7
England beat Scotland	9 matches to 6
England beat Wales	12 matches to 3
Ireland beat Wales	11 matches to 4
Scotland beat Wales	8 matches to 7
Scotland beat Ireland	8½ matches to 6½

1990—At Conwy
Winners: Ireland

England beat Wales	10 matches to 5
Ireland beat Scotland	9 matches to 6
Scotland beat England	9½ matches to 5½
Ireland beat Wales	11 matches to 4
Wales beat Scotland	8 matches to 7
Ireland beat England	8 matches to 7

St Andrews Trophy (Great Britain and Ireland *v* Continent of Europe)

Match instituted 1956
Trophy presented 1962

Year	Winner	Venue	Result
1956	Great Britain & Ireland	Wentworth	12½-2½
1958	Great Britain & Ireland	St Cloud, France	10-5
1960	Great Britain & Ireland	Walton Heath	13-5
1962	Great Britain & Ireland	Halmstead, Sweden	18-12
1964	Great Britain & Ireland	Muirfield	23-7
1966	Great Britain & Ireland	Bilbao, Spain	19½-10½
1968	Great Britain & Ireland	Portmarnock	20-10
1970	Great Britain & Ireland	La Zoute, Belgium	17½-12½
1972	Great Britain & Ireland	Berkshire	19½-10½
1974	Continent of Europe	Punta Ala, Italy	16-14
1976	Great Britain & Ireland	St Andrews	18½-11½
1978	Great Britain & Ireland	Bremen, Germany	20½-9½
1980	Great Britain & Ireland	Sandwich, R St George's	19½-10½
1982	Continent of Europe	Rosendaelsche, Netherlands	14–10
1984	Great Britain & Ireland	Taunton, Devon	13-11
1986	Great Britain & Ireland	Halmstead, Sweden	14½-9½
1988	Great Britain & Ireland	St Andrews	15½-8½
1990	Great Britain & Ireland	El Saler, Spain	13-11

Ladies' Amateur

Astor Salver
Venue: The Berkshire

Year	Winner	Score	Year	Winner	Score
1981	A Uzielli	148	1986	C Pierce	144
1982	Abandoned after one		1987	V Thomas	145
	round due to weather		1988	J Thornhill	136
1983	L Bayman	148	1989	S Sutton	140
1984	L Bayman	142	1990	{ J Hall / J Morley } tied	144
1985	H Wadsworth	138			

Hampshire Rose
Played annually at North Hants GC

Year	Winner	Year	Winner
1981	J Nicholson	1986	C Hourihane
1982	J Thornhill	1987	J Thornhill
1983	J Pool	1988	J Thornhill
1984	C Caldwell	1989	A MacDonald
1985	A Uzielli	1990	S Keogh

Helen Holm Trophy

Year	Winner	Year	Winner
1981	G Stewart	1986	IC Robertson
1982	W Aitken	1987	E Farquharson
1983	J Connachan	1988	E Farquharson
1984	G Stewart	1989	S Robinson
1985	P Wright	1990	C Lambert

Ladies' Amateur International Tournaments and Matches

Great Britain & Ireland *v* United States (Ladies) Curtis Cup

	Great Britain & Ireland			USA			Venue
1932	Foursomes Singles	0 3¹/₂	3¹/₂	Foursomes Singles	3 2¹/₂	5¹/₂	Wentworth
1934	Foursomes Singles	1¹/₂ 1	2¹/₂	Foursomes Singles	1¹/₂ 5	6¹/₂	Chevy Chase
1936	Foursomes Singles	1¹/₂ 3	4¹/₂	Foursomes Singles	1¹/₂ 3	4¹/₂	Gleneagles
1938	Foursomes Singles	2¹/₂ 1	3¹/₂	Foursomes Singles	¹/₂ 5	5¹/₂	Essex County Club
1948	Foursomes Singles	1 1¹/₂	2¹/₂	Foursomes Singles	2 4¹/₂	6¹/₂	Birkdale
1950	Foursomes Singles	1 ¹/₂	1¹/₂	Foursomes Singles	2 5¹/₂	7¹/₂	Buffalo
1952	Foursomes Singles	2 3	5	Foursomes Singles	1 3	4	Muirfield
1954	Foursomes Singles	0 3	3	Foursomes Singles	3 3	6	Merion
1956	Foursomes Singles	1 4	5	Foursomes Singles	2 2	4	Sandwich, Prince's
1958	Foursomes Singles	2 2¹/₂	4¹/₂	Foursomes Singles	1 3¹/₂	4¹/₂	Brae Burn GC
1960	Foursomes Singles	1 1¹/₂	2¹/₂	Foursomes Singles	2 4¹/₂	6¹/₂	Lindrick
1962	Foursomes Singles	0 1	1	Foursomes Singles	3 5	8	Colorado Springs
1964	Foursomes Singles	3¹/₂ 4	7¹/₂	Foursomes Singles	2¹/₂ 8	10¹/₂	Porthcawl
1966	Foursomes Singles	1¹/₂ 3¹/₂	5	Foursomes Singles	4¹/₂ 8¹/₂	13	Hot Springs
1968	Foursomes Singles	2¹/₂ 5	7¹/₂	Foursomes Singles	3¹/₂ 7	10¹/₂	Newcastle, Co Down
1970	Foursomes Singles	2¹/₂ 4	6¹/₂	Foursomes Singles	3¹/₂ 8	11¹/₂	Brae Burn, USA
1972	Foursomes Singles	3¹/₂ 4¹/₂	8	Foursomes Singles	2¹/₂ 7¹/₂	10	Western Gailes
1974	Foursomes Singles	2¹/₂ 2¹/₂	5	Foursomes Singles	3¹/₂ 9¹/₂	13	San Francisco, Cal.
1976	Foursomes Singles	2 4¹/₂	6¹/₂	Foursomes Singles	4 7¹/₂	11¹/₂	R Lytham and St Annes
1978	Foursomes Singles	2¹/₂ 3¹/₂	6	Foursomes Singles	3¹/₂ 8¹/₂	12	Apawamis, NY

At St Pierre, 6th and 7th June, 1980

First Day–Foursomes

Great Britain & Ireland		United States	
M McKenna and C Nesbitt	½	L Smith and T Moody	½
T Thomas and G Stewart	0	P Sheehan and L Castillo	
		(5 and 3)	1
M Madill and C Caldwell	½	J Oliver and C Semple	½
	1		2

Singles

Great Britain & Ireland		United States	
M McKenna	0	P Sheehan (3 and 2)	1
C Nesbitt	½	L Smith	½
J Connachan	0	B Goldsmith (2 holes)	1
M Madill	0	C Semple (4 and 3)	1
L Moore	½	M Hafeman	½
C Caldwell	0	J Oliver (1 hole)	1
	1		5

Second Day–Foursomes

Great Britain & Ireland		United States	
C Caldwell and M Madill	0	P Sheehan and L Castillo	
		(3 and 2)	1
C Nesbitt and M McKenna	0	L Smith and T Moody (6 and 5)	1
T Thomas and L Moore	0	J Oliver and C Semple (1 hole)	1
	0		3

Singles

Great Britain & Ireland		United States	
M Madill	0	P Sheehan (5 and 4)	1
M McKenna (5 and 4)	1	L Castillo	0
J Connachan	0	M Hafeman (6 and 5)	1
G Stewart (5 and 4)	1	L Smith	0
L Moore (1 hole)	1	B Goldsmith	0
T Thomas	0	C Semple (4 and 3)	1
	3		3

Aggregate: United States, 13; Great Britain and Ireland, 5

At Denver, Colorado, USA, on 5th and 6th August, 1982

First Day–Foursomes

United States		Great Britain & Ireland	
J Inkster and C Semple (5 and 4)	1	IC Robertson and M McKenna	0
K Baker and L Smith	½	K Douglas and J Soulsby	½
A Benz and C Hanlon (2 and 1)	1	G Stewart and J Connachan	0
	2½		½

Singles

Curtis Cup
continued

United States		Great Britain & Ireland	
A Benz (2 and 1)	1	M McKenna	0
C Hanlon (5 and 4)	1	J Connachan	0
M McDougall (2 holes)	1	W Aitken	0
K Baker (7 and 6)	1	IC Robertson	0
J Oliver	0	J Soulsby (2 holes)	1
J Inkster (7 and 6)	1	K Douglas	0
	5		1

Second Day–Foursomes

United States		Great Britain & Ireland	
J Inkster and C Semple (3 and 2)	.1	J Connachan and W Aitken	0
K Baker and L Smith (1 hole)	.1	K Douglas and J Soulsby	0
A Benz and C Hanlon	.0	M McKenna and IC Robertson	
		(1 hole)	1
	2		1

Singles

United States		Great Britain & Ireland	
J Inkster (7 and 6)	1	K Douglas	0
K Baker (4 and 3)	1	G Stewart	0
J Oliver (5 and 4)	1	V Thomas	0
M McDougall (2 and 1)	1	J Soulsby	0
C Semple (1 hole)	1	M McKenna	0
L Smith	0	IC Robertson (5 and 3)	1
	1		1

Aggregate: United States, 14 1/2: Great Britain and Ireland, 3 1/2

At Muirfield on 8th and 9th June, 1984

First Day–Foursomes

Great Britain & Ireland		United States	
C Waite and B New (2 holes)	1	J Pacillo and A Sander	0
J Thornhill and P Grice	1/2	L Smith and J Rosenthal	1/2
M McKenna and L Davies	0	M Widman and H Farr (1 hole)	1
	1 1/2		1 1/2

Singles

Great Britain & Ireland		United States	
J Thornhill	1/2	J Pacillo	1/2
C Waite	0	P Hammel (4 and 2)	1
C Hourihane	0	J Rosenthal (3 and 1)	1
V Thomas (2 and 1)	1	D Howe	0
P Grice (2 holes)	1	A Sander	0
B New	0	M Widman (4 and 3)	1
	2 1/2		3 1/2

Second Day–Foursomes

Curtis Cup

continued

Great Britain & Ireland		United States	
C Waite and B New	0	L Smith and J Rosenthal (3 and 1)	1
J Thornhill and P Grice (2 and 1)	1	M Widman and H Farr	0
V Thomas and C Hourihane	1/2	D Howe and P Hammel	1/2
	1 1/2		1 1/2

Singles

Great Britain & Ireland		United States	
J Thornhill	0	J Pacillo (3 and 2)	1
L Davies (1 hole)	1	A Sander	0
C Waite (5 and 4)	1	L Smith	0
P Grice	0	D Howe (2 holes)	1
B New	0	H Farr (6 and 5)	1
C Hourihane (2 and 1)	1	P Hammel	0
	3		3

Aggregate: Great Britain and Ireland 8 1/2; United States 9 1/2

At Prairie Dunes, Kansas, USA on 1st and 2nd August, 1986

First Day–Foursomes

United States		Great Britain & Ireland	
K Kessler and C Schreyer	0	L Behan and J Thornhill (7 and 6)	1
D Ammaccapane and D Mochrie	0	P Johnson and K Davies (2 and 1)	1
K Gardner and K McCarthy	0	IC Robertson and M McKenna (1 hole)	1
	0		3

Singles

United States		Great Britain & Ireland	
L Shannon	0	P Johnson (1 hole)	1
K Williams	0	J Thornhill (4 and 3)	1
D Ammaccapane	0	L Behan (4 and 3)	1
K Kessler (3 and 2)	1	V Thomas	0
D Mochrie	1/2	K Davies	1/2
C Schreyer (2 and 1)	1	C Hourihane	0
	2 1/2		3 1/2

Second Day–Foursomes

United States		Great Britain & Ireland	
D Ammaccapane and D Mochrie	0	P Johnson and K Davies (1 hole)	1
L Shannon and K Williams	0	L Behan and J Thornhill (5 and 3)	1
K Gardner and K McCarthy	1/2	IC Robertson and M McKenna	1/2
	1/2		2 1/2

Singles

United States		Great Britain & Ireland	
L Shannon	1/2	J Thornhill	1/2
K McCarthy	0	P Johnson (5 and 3)	1
K Gardner (1 hole)	1	L Behan	0
K Williams	0	V Thomas (4 and 3)	1
K Kessler	1/2	K Davies	1/2
C Schreyer	0	C Hourihane (5 and 3)	1
	2		4

Aggregate: Great Britain and Ireland 13, United States 5

At Royal St George's, on 10th and 11th June, 1988

Curtis Cup
continued

First Day–Foursomes

Great Britain & Ireland		United States	
L Bayman and J Wade (2 and 1)	1	T Kerdyk and K Scrivner	0
S Shapcott and K Davies (5 and 4)	1	C Scholefield and C Thompson	0
J Thornhill and V Thomas	1/2	L Shannon and C Keggi	1/2
	2 1/2		1/2

Singles

Great Britain & Ireland		United States	
L Bayman	1/2	T Kerdyk	1/2
J Wade (2 holes)	1	C Scholefield	0
S Shapcott	0	C Thompson (1 hole)	1
K Davies	0	P Sinn (4 and 3)	1
S Lawson (1 hole)	1	P Cornett	0
J Thornhill (3 and 2)	1	L Shannon	0
	3 1/2		2 1/2

Second Day–Foursomes

Great Britain & Ireland		United States	
L Bayman and J Wade	0	T Kerdyk and K Scrivner (1 hole)	1
S Shapcott and K Davies (2 holes)	1	L Shannon and C Keggi	0
J Thornhill and V Thomas (6 and 5)	1	C Scholefield and C Thompson	0
	2		1

Singles

Great Britain & Ireland		United States	
J Wade	0	T Kerdyk (2 and 1)	1
S Shapcott (3 and 2)	1	C Keggi	0
S Lawson	0	K Scrivner (4 and 3)	1
V Thomas (5 and 3)	1	P Cornett	0
L Bayman (1 hole)	1	P Sinn	0
J Thornhill	0	C Thompson (3 and 2)	1
	3		3

Aggregate: Great Britain and Ireland 11, United States 7

For 1990 results see page 133

Individual Records

Great Britain and Ireland

Name		Year	Played	Won	Lost	Halved
Jean Anderson (Donald)	Scot	1948	6	3	3	0
Diane Bailey [Frearson] (Robb)	Eng	1962-72-(84)-(86)-(88)	5	2	2	1
Sally Barber (Bonallack)	Eng	1962	1	0	1	0
Pam Barton	Eng	1934-36	4	0	3	1
Linda Bayman	Eng	1988	4	2	1	1
Baba Beck (Pym)	Ire	(1954)	0	0	0	0
Charlotte Beddows [Watson] (Stevenson)	Scot	1932	1	0	1	0
Lilian Behan	Ire	1986	4	3	1	0
Veronica Beharrell (Anstey)	Eng	1956	1	0	1	0

Name		Year	Played	Won	Lost	Halved
Pam Benka (Tredinnick)	Eng	1966-68	4	0	3	1
Jeanne Bisgood	Eng	1950-52-54-**(70)**	4	1	3	0
Zara Bolton (Davis)	Eng	1948-**(56)**-**(66)**-**(68)**	2	0	2	0
Angela Bonallack (Ward)	Eng	1956-58-60-62-64-66	15	6	8	1
Ita Butler (Burke)	Ire	1966	3	2	1	0
Lady Katherine Cairns	Eng	**(1952)**	0	0	0	0
Carole Caldwell (Redford)	Eng	1978-80	5	0	3	2
Doris Chambers	Eng	**(1934)**-**(36)**-**(48)**	0	0	0	0
Carol Comboy (Grott)	Eng	**(1978)**-**(80)**	0	0	0	0
Jane Connachan	Scot	1980-82	5	0	5	0
Elsie Corlett	Eng	1932-38-**(64)**	3	1	2	0
Diana Critchley (Fishwick)	Eng	1932-34-**(50)**	3	1	2	0
Karen Davies	Wales	1986-88	7	4	1	2
Laura Davies	Eng	1984	2	1	1	0
Helen Dobson	Eng	1990	.3	1	2	0
Kitrina Douglas	Eng	1982	4	0	3	1
Marjorie Draper [Peel] (Thomas)	Scot	1954	1	0	1	0
Mary Everard	Eng	1970-72-74-78	15	6	7	2
Elaine Farquharson	Scot	1990	.4	0	4	0
Daisy Ferguson	Ire	**(1958)**	0	0	0	0
Marjory Ferguson (Fowler)	Scot	1966	1	0	1	0
Elizabeth Price Fisher (Price)	Eng	1950-52-54-56-58-60	12	7	4	1
Linzi Fletcher	Eng	1990	1	0	1	0
Maureen Garner (Madill)	Ire	1980	4	0	3	1
Marjorie Ross Garon	Eng	1936	2	1	0	1
Maureen Garrett (Ruttle)	Eng	1948-**(60)**	2	0	2	0
Philomena Garvey	Ire	1948-50-52-54-56-60	11	2	8	1
Carol Gibbs (Le Feuvre)	Eng	1974	3	0	3	0
Jacqueline Gordon	Eng	1948	2	1	1	0
Molly Gourlay	Eng	1932-34	4	0	2	2
Julia Greenhalgh	Eng	1964-70-74-76-78	17	6	7	4
Penny Grice-Whittaker (Grice)	Eng	1984	4	2	1	1
Julie Hall (Wade)	Eng	1988-90	8	4	4	0
Marley Harris [Spearman] (Baker)	Eng	1960-62-64	6	2	2	2
Dorothea Hastings (Sommerville)	Scot	1958	0	0	0	0
Lady Heathcoat-Amory (Joyce Wethered)	Eng	1932	2	1	1	0
Dinah Henson (Oxley)	Eng	1968-70-72-76	11	3	6	2
Helen Holm (Gray)	Scot	1936-38-48	5	3	2	0
Claire Hourihane	Ire	1984-86-88-90	5	2	2	1
Ann Howard (Phillips)	Eng	1956-68	2	0	2	0
Beverley Huke	Eng	1972	2	0	2	0
Kathryn Imrie	Scot	1990	4	1	3	0
Anne Irvin	Eng	1962-68-70-76	12	4	7	1
Bridget Jackson	Eng	1958-64-68	8	1	6	1
Patricia Johnson	Eng	1986	4	4	0	0
Catriona Lambert	Scot	1990	4	1	3	0
Susan Langridge (Armitage)	Eng	1964-66	6	0	5	1
Joan Lawrence	Scot	1964	2	0	2	0
Shirley Lawson	Scot	1988	2	1	1	0
Wilma Leburn (Aitken)	Scot	1982	2	0	2	0
Jenny Lee Smith	Eng	1974-76	3	0	3	0
Kathryn Lumb (Phillips)	Eng	1970-72	2	1	1	0
Mary McKenna	Ire	1970-72-74-76-78-80-82-84-86	30	10	16	4
Suzanne McMahon (Cadden)	Scot	1976	4	0	4	0
Sheila Maher (Vaughan)	Eng	1962-64	4	1	2	1
Vanessa Marvin	Eng	1978	3	1	2	0
Moira Milton (Paterson)	Scot	1952	2	1	1	0
Wanda Morgan	Eng	1932-34-36	6	0	5	1
Beverley New	Eng	1984	4	1	3	0
Maire O'Donnell	Ire	**(1982)**	0	0	0	0
Margaret Pickard (Nichol)	Eng	1968-70	5	2	3	0
Diana Plumpton	Eng	1934	2	1	1	0
Elizabeth Pook (Chadwick)	Eng	1966	4	1	3	0
Doris Porter (Park)	Scot	1932	1	0	1	0
Clarrie Reddan (Tiernan)	Ire	1938-48	3	2	1	0
Joan Rennie (Hastings)	Scot	1966	2	0	1	1

Curtis Cup

continued

Name		Year	Played	Won	Lost	Halved
Maureen Richmond (Walker)	Scot	1974	4	2	2	0
Jean Roberts	Eng	1962	1	0	1	0
Belle Robertson (McCorkindale)	Scot	1960-66-68-70-72-(74)-(76)-82-86	24	5	12	7
Claire Robinson (Nesbitt)	Ire	1980	3	0	1	2
Vivien Saunders	Eng	1968	4	1	2	1
Susan Shapcott	Eng	1988	4	3	1	0
Linda Simpson (Moore)	Eng	1980	3	1	1	1
Ruth Slark (Porter)	Eng	1960-62-64	7	3	3	1
Anne Smith [Stant] (Willard)	Eng	1976	1	0	1	0
Frances Smith (Stephens)	Eng	1950-52-54-56-58-60-(62)-(72)	11	7	3	1
Janet Soulsby	Eng	1982	4	1	2	1
Gillian Stewart	Scot	1980-82	4	1	3	0
Tegwen Thomas (Perkins)	Wales	1974-76-78-80	14	4	8	2
Vicki Thomas (Rawlings)	Wales	1982-84-86-88-90	10	5	3	2
Muriel Thomson	Scot	1978	3	2	1	0
Jill Thornhill	Eng	1984-86-88	12	6	2	4
Angela Uzielli (Carrick)	Eng	1978	1	0	1	0
Jessie Valentine (Anderson)	Scot	1936-38-50-52-54-56-58	13	4	9	0
Helen Wadsworth	Wales	1990	2	0	2	0
Claire Waite	Eng	1984	4	2	2	0
Mickey Walker	Eng	1972	4	3	0	1
Pat Walker	Ire	1934-36-38	6	2	3	1
Verona Wallace-Williamson	Scot	**(1938)**	0	0	0	0
Nan Wardlaw (Baird)	Scot	1938	1	0	1	0
Enid Wilson	Eng	1932	2	1	1	0
Janette Wright (Robertson)	Scot	1954-56-58-60	8	3	5	0
Phyllis Wylie (Wade)	Eng	1938	1	0	0	1

Bold print: captain; bold print in brackets: non-playing captain
Maiden name in parentheses, former surname in square brackets

United States of America

Player	Year	Played	Won	Lost	Halved
Roberta Albers	1968	2	1	0	1
Danielle Ammaccapane	1986	3	0	3	0
Kathy Baker	1982	4	3	0	1
Barbara Barrow	1976	2	1	0	1
Beth Barry	1972-74	5	3	1	1
Larua Baugh	1972	4	2	1	1
Judy Bell	1960-62-**(86)**-**(88)**	2	1	1	0
Peggy Kirk Bell (Kirk)	1950	2	1	1	0
Amy Benz	1982	3	2	1	0
Patty Berg	1936-38	4	1	2	1
Barbara Fay Boddie (White)	1964-66	8	7	0	1
Jane Booth (Bastanchury)	1970-72-74	12	9	3	0
Mary Budke	1974	3	2	1	0
Brandie Burton	1990	3	3	0	0
JoAnne Carner (Gunderson)	1958-60-62-64	10	6	3	1
Lori Castillo	1980	3	2	1	0
Leona Cheney (Pressler)	1932-34-36	6	5	1	0
Sis Choate	**(1974)**	0	0	0	0
Peggy Conley	1964-68	6	3	1	2
Mary Ann Cook (Downey)	1956	2	1	1	0
Patricia Cornett	1978-88	4	1	2	1
Jean Crawford (Ashley)	1962-66-68-**(72)**	8	6	2	0
Clifford Ann Creed	1962	2	2	0	0
Grace Cronin (Lenczyk)	1948-50	3	2	1	0
Carolyn Cudone	1956-**(70)**	1	1	0	0
Beth Daniel	1976-78	8	7	1	0
Virginia Dennehy	**(1958)**	0	0	0	0
Mary Lou Dill	1968	3	1	1	1
Alice Dye	1970	2	1	0	1
Heather Farr	1984	3	2	1	0
Jane Fassinger	1970	1	0	1	0

Player	Year	Played	Won	Lost	Halved
Mary Lena Faulk	1954	2	1	1	0
Carol Sorensen					
Flenniken (Sorensen)	1964-66	8	6	1	1
Edith Flippin (Quier)	**(1954)-(56)**	0	0	0	0
Kim Gardner	1986	3	1	1	1
Charlotte Glutting	1934-36-38	5	3	1	1
Vicki Goetze	1990	4	3	1	0
Brenda Goldsmith	1978-80	4	2	2	0
Aniela Goldthwaite	1934-**(52)**	1	0	1	0
Joanne Goodwin	1960	2	1	1	0
Mary Hafeman	1980	2	1	0	1
Shelley Hamlin	1968-70	8	3	3	2
Penny Hammel	1984	3	1	1	1
Nancy Hammer (Hager)	1970	2	1	1	0
Cathy Hanlon	1982	3	2	1	0
Beverley Hanson	1950	2	2	0	0
Patricia Harbottle					
(Lesser)	1954-56	3	2	1	0
Helen Hawes	**(1964)**	0	0	0	0
Kathryn Hemphill	1938	1	0	0	1
Helen Hicks	1932	2	1	1	0
Carolyn Hill	1978	2	0	0	2
Cindy Hill	1970-74-76-78	14	5	6	3
Opel Hill	1932-34-36	6	2	3	1
Marion Hollins	**(1932)**	0	0	0	0
Dana Howe	1984	3	1	1	1
Juli Inkster	1982	4	4	0	0
Ann Casey Johnstone	1958-60-62	4	3	1	0
Mae Murray Jones					
(Murray)	1952	1	0	1	0
Caroline Keggi	1988	3	0	2	1
Tracy Kerdyk	1988	4	2	1	1
Kandi Kessler	1986	3	1	1	1
Dorothy Kielty	1948-50	4	4	0	0
Dorothy Kirby	1948-50-52-54	7	4	3	0
Martha Kirouac					
(Wilkinson)	1970-72	8	5	3	0
Nancy Knight (Lopez)	1976	2	2	0	0
Bonnie Lauer	1974	4	2	2	0
Marjorie Lindsay	1952	2	1	1	0
Patricia Lucey					
(O'Sullivan)	1952	1	0	1	0
Mari McDougall	1982	2	2	0	0
Barbara McIntire	1958-60-62-64-66-72-**(76)**	16	6	6	4
Lucile Mann (Robinson)	1934	1	0	1	0
Debbie Massey	1974-76	5	5	0	0
Marion Miley	1938	2	1	0	1
Dottie Mochrie (Pepper)	1986	3	0	2	1
Evelyn Monsted	**(1968)**	0	0	0	0
Terri Moody	1980	2	1	0	1
Karen Noble	1990	4	2	2	0
Judith Oliver	1978-80-82	8	5	1	2
Maureen Orcutt	1932-34-36-38	8	5	3	0
Joanne Pacillo	1984	3	1	1	1
Estelle Page (Lawson)	1938-48	4	3	1	0
Katie Peterson	1990	3	3	0	0
Margaret Platt	1990	2	0	2	0
Frances Pond (Stebbins)	**(1938)**	0	0	0	0
Dorothy Germain Porter	1950-**(66)**	2	1	0	1
Phyllis Preuss	1962-64-66-68-70-**(84)**	15	10	4	1
Betty Probasco	**(1982)**	0	0	0	0
Mildred Prunaret	**(1960)**	0	0	0	0
Polly Riley	1948-50-52-54-56-58-**(62)**	10	5	5	0
Barbara Romack	1954-56-58	5	3	2	0
Jody Rosenthal	1984	3	2	0	1
Anne Sander [Welts]					
[Decker] (Quast)	1958-60-62-66-68-74-84-90	22	11	7	4
Cindy Scholefield	1988	3	0	3	0
Cindy Schreyer	1986	3	1	2	0
Kathleen McCarthy					
Scrivner (McCarthy)	1986-88	6	2	3	1
Leslie Shannon	1986-88-90	6	0	4	2
Patty Sheehan	1980	4	4	0	0
Pearl Sinn	1988	2	1	1	0
Grace De Moss Smith					
(De Moss)	1952-54	3	1	2	0
Lancy Smith	1972-78-80-82-84	16	7	5	4
Margaret Smith	1956	2	2	0	0
Hollis Stacy	1972	2	0	1	1
Claire Stancik (Doran)	1952-54	4	4	0	0

Curtis Cup

continued

Player	Year	Played	Won	Lost	Halved
Judy Street (Eller)	1960	2	2	0	0
Louise Suggs	1948	2	0	1	1
Nancy Roth Syms (Roth)	1964-66-76-**(80)**	9	3	5	1
Carol Thompson (Semple)	1974-76-80-82-90	17	9	6	2
Noreen Uihlein	1978	3	1	1	1
Virginia Van Wie	1932-34	4	3	0	1
Glenna Collett Vare (Collett)	1932-**(34)**-36-38-**48**-**(50)**	7	4	2	1
Jane Weiss (Nelson)	1956	1	0	1	0
Robin Weiss	1990	3	3	0	0
Donna White (Horton)	1976	2	2	0	0
Mary Anne Widman	1984	3	2	1	0
Kimberley Williams	1986	3	0	3	0
Helen Sigel Wilson (Sigel)	1950-66-**(78)**	2	0	2	0
Joyce Ziske	1954	1	0	1	0

Bold print: captain; bold print in brackets: non-playing captain.
Maiden name in parenthesis; former surname in square brackets.

Curtis Cup

continued

Commonwealth Tournament (Ladies)

Year	Winner	Venue
1959	Great Britain	St Andrews
1963	Great Britain	Royal Melbourne, Australia
1967	Great Britain	Ancaster, Ontario, Canada
1971	Great Britain	Hamilton, New Zealand
1975	Great Britain	Ganton, England
1979	Canada	Lake Karrinup, Perth, Australia
1983	Australia	Glendale, Edmonton, Canada
1987	Canada	Christchurch, New Zealand

European Ladies' Amateur Team Championship

Year	Winner	Second	Venue
1967	England	France	Penina, Portugal
1969	France	England	Tylosand, Sweden
1971	England	France	Ganton, England
1973	England	France	Brussels, Belgium
1975	France	Spain	Paris, France
1977	England	Spain	Sotogrande, Spain
1979	Ireland	Germany	Hermitage, Ireland
1981	Sweden	France	Troia, Portugal
1983	Ireland	England	Waterloo, Belgium
1985	England	Italy	Stavanger, Norway
1987	Sweden	Wales	Turnberry, Scotland
1989	France	England	Pals, Spain

Vagliano Trophy—Great Britain & Ireland v Europe (Ladies)

Played for biennially between teams of women amateur golfers representing the British Isles and Europe. (From 1947 to 1957 was between the British Isles and France.)

Year	Winner	Result	Venue
1959	Great Britain & Ireland	12-3	Wentworth
1961	Great Britain & Ireland	8-7	Villa d'Este
1963	Great Britain & Ireland	20-10	Muirfield
1965	Continent of Europe	17-13	Cologne
1967	Continent of Europe	15½-14½	R Lytham and St Anne's
1969	Continent of Europe	16-14	Chantilly
1971	Great Britain & Ireland	17½-12½	Worplesdon
1973	Great Britain & Ireland	20-10	Eindhoven
1975	Great Britain & Ireland	13½-10½	Muirfield
1977	Great Britain & Ireland	15½-8½	Malmo
1979	Halved	12-12	R Porthcawl
1981	Continent of Europe	14-10	P de Hierro
1983	Great Britain & Ireland	14-10	Woodhall Spa
1985	Great Britain & Ireland	14-10	Hamburg
1987	Great Britain & Ireland	15-9	The Berkshire
1989	Great Britain & Ireland	14½-9½	Venice

Women's Home Internationals

Year	Winner	Venue	Year	Winner	Venue
1948	England	R Lytham and St Annes	1969	England / Scotland	Western Gailes
1949	Scotland	Harlech	1970	England	Killarney
1950	Scotland	Newcastle Co Down	1971	England	Longniddry
1951	Scotland	Broadstone	1972	England	R Lytham and St Annes
1952	Scotland	Troon	1973	England	Harlech
1953	England	Porthcawl	1974	England / Scotland / Ireland	Sandwich, Princes
1954	England	Ganton			
1955	England / Scotland	Western Gailes	1975	England	Newport
1956	Scotland	Sunningdale	1976	England	Troon
1957	Scotland	Troon	1977	England	Cork
1958	England	Hunstanton	1978	England	Moortown
1959	England	Hoylake	1979	Scotland / Ireland	Harlech
1960	England	Gullane			
1961	Scotland	Portmarnock	1980	Ireland	Cruden Bay
1962	Scotland	Porthcawl	1981	Scotland	Portmarnock
1963	England	Formby	1982	England	Burnham and Barrow
1964	England	Troon	1983	*Matches abandoned due to weather*	
1965	England	Portrush	1984	England	Gullane
1966	England	Woodhall Spa	1985	England	Waterville
1967	England	Sunningdale	1986	Ireland	Whittington Barracks
1968	England	Porthcawl			

At Ashburnham, Dyfed, 1987

England beat Scotland	5½ matches to 3½
England beat Ireland	5½ matches to 3½
England beat Wales	6 matches to 3
Scotland beat Ireland	6 matches to 3
Scotland beat Wales	7 matches to 2
Ireland beat Wales	8 matches to 1

Result: England 3; Scotland 2; Ireland 1; Wales 0

At Barassie, Ayrshire, 1988

Scotland beat England	5¹/₂ matches to 3¹/₂
Scotland beat Ireland	5 matches to 4
Scotland beat Wales	7¹/₂ matches to 1¹/₂
England beat Ireland	6¹/₂ matches to 2¹/₂
England beat Wales	7 matches to 2
Ireland halved with Wales	4¹/₂ matches each

Result: England 2; Scotland 3; Ireland 0; Wales 0

At Westport, Ireland, 1989

Scotland beat Ireland	7 matches to 2
England beat Wales	6¹/₂ matches to 2¹/₂
Scotland beat Wales	5 matches to 4
England beat Ireland	5¹/₂ matches to 3¹/₂
England beat Scotland	8 matches to 1
Ireland beat Wales	6 matches to 3

Result: England 3; Scotland 2; Ireland 1; Wales 0

At Hunstanton, Norfolk, 1990

England halved with Ireland	4 matches each
Scotland beat Wales	5 matches to 4
Scotland beat Ireland	5 matches to 4
England beat Wales	6 matches to 3
Ireland halved with Wales	4 matches each
Scotland beat England	6 matches to 3

Result: Scotland 3; England 1; Ireland 1; Wales 0

Women's World Amateur Team Championship (Espirito Santo Trophy)

Year	Winners	Runners-up	Venue	Score
1964	France	United States	St Germain	588
1966	United States	Canada	Mexico	580
1968	United States	Australia	Melbourne	616
1970	United States	France	Madrid	598
1972	United States	France	Buenos Aires	583
1974	United States	Great Britain, South Africa	Dominican Republic	620
1976	United States	France	Vilamoura, Portugal	605
1978	Australia	Canada	Fiji	596
1980	United States	Australia	Pinehurst, USA	588
1982	United States	New Zealand	Geneva, Switzerland	579
1984	United States	France	Hong Kong	585
1986	Spain	France	Caracas, Venezuela	580
1988	United States	Sweden	Drottningholm, Sweden	587
1990	United States	New Zealand	Christchurch, New Zealand	585

Juniors and Youths

Boys' Amateur Championship

Year	Winner	Runner-up	Venue	By
1921	ADD Mathieson	GH Lintott	Ascot	37th hole
1922	HS Mitchell	W Greenfield	Ascot	4 and 2
1923	ADD Mathieson	HS Mitchell	Dunbar	3 and 2
1924	RW Peattie	P Manuevrier	Coombe Hill	2 holes
1925	RW Peattie	A McNair	Barnton	4 and 3
1926	EA McRuvie	CW Timmis	Coombe Hill	1 hole
1927	EW Fiddian	K Forbes	Barnton	4 and 2
1928	S Scheftel	A Dobbie	Formby	6 and 5
1929	J Lindsay	J Scott-Riddell	Barnton	6 and 4
1930	J Lindsay	J Todd	Fulwell	9 and 8
1931	H Thomson	F McGloin	Killermont	5 and 4
1932	IS MacDonald	LA Hardie	R Lytham and St Annes	2 and 1
1933	PB Lucas	W McLachlan	Carnoustie	3 and 2
1934	RS Burles	FB Allpass	Moortown	12 and 10
1935	JDA Langley	R Norris	Balgownie, Ab'deen	6 and 5
1936	J Bruen	W Innes	Birkdale	11 and 9
1937	IM Roberts	J Stewart	Bruntsfield	8 and 7
1938	W Smeaton	T Snowball	Moor Park	3 and 2
1939	SB Williamson	KG Thom	Carnoustie	4 and 2
1940-45	*Suspended during War*			
1946	AFD MacGregor	DF Dunstan	Bruntsfield	7 and 5
1947	J Armour	I Caldwell	Hoylake	5 and 4
1948	JD Pritchett	DH Reid	Barasssie	37th hole
1949	H MacAnespie	NV Drew	St Andrews	3 and 2
1950	J Glover	I Young	R Lytham and St Annes	2 and 1
1951	N Dunn	MSR Lunt	Prestwick	6 and 5
1952	M Bonallack	AE Shepperson	Formby	37th hole
1953	AE Shepperson	AT Booth	Dunbar	6 and 4
1954	AF Bussell	K Warren	Hoylake	38th hole
1955	SC Wilson	BJK Aitken	Barassie	39th hole
1956	JF Ferguson	CW Cole	Sunningdale	2 and 1
1957	D Ball	J Wilson	Carnoustie	2 and 1
1958	R Braddon	IM Stungo	Moortown	4 and 3
1959	AR Murphy	EM Shamash	Pollok	3 and 1
1960	P Cros	PO Green	Olton	5 and 3
1961	FS Morris	C Clark	Dalmahoy	3 and 2
1962	PM Townsend	DC Penman	R Mid-Surrey	1 hole
1963	AHC Soutar	DI Rigby	Prestwick	2 and 1
1964	PM Townsend	RD Gray	Formby	9 and 8
1965	GR Milne	DK Midgley	Gullane	4 and 2
1966	A Phillips	A Muller	Moortown	12 and 11
1967	LP Tupling	SC Evans	Western Gailes	4 and 2
1968	SC Evans	K Dabson	St Annes Old Links	3 and 2
1969	M Foster	M Gray	Dunbar	37th hole
1970	ID Gradwell	JE Murray	Hillside	1 hole
1971	H Clark	G Harvey	Barassie	6 and 5
1972	G Harvey	R Newsome	Moortown	7 and 5
1973	DM Robertson	S Betti	Blairgowrie	5 and 3
1974	TR Shannon	A Lyle	Hoylake	10 and 9
1975	B Marchbank	A Lyle	Bruntsfield	1 hole
1976	M Mouland	G Hargreaves	Sunningdale	6 and 5
1977	I Ford	CR Dalgleish	Downfield	1 hole
1978	S Keppler	M Stokes	Seaton Carew	3 and 2
1979	R Rafferty	D Ray	Barassie	6 and 5
1980	D Muscroft	A Llyr	Formby	7 and 6
1981	J Lopez	R Weedon	Gullane	4 and 3
1982	M Grieve	G Hickman	Burnham and Barrow	37th hole
1983	JM Olazabal	M Pendaries	Glenbervie	6 and 5

Year	Winner	Runner-up	Venue	By
1984	L Vannett	A Mednick	Royal Porthcawl	2 and 1
1985	J Cook	W Henry	Barnton	5 and 4
1986	L Walker	G King	Seaton Carew	5 and 4
1987	C O'Carrol	P Olsson	Barassie	3 and 1
1988	S Pardoe	D Haines	Formby	3 and 2
1989	C Watts	C Fraser	Nairn	5 and 3
1990	M Welch	M Ellis	Hunstanton	3 and 1

Boys' Amateur Championship

continued

Boys' Internationals
England v Scotland

Year	Winner	Result	Venue
1946	England	8½-3½	Bruntsfield
1947	England	7-5	Hoylake
1948	England	9-3	Barassie
1949	Scotland	8-4	St Andrews
1950	Scotland	8½-3½	R Lytham and St Annes
1951	England	7-5	Prestwick
1952	England	6½-5½	Formby
1953	Scotland	7-5	Dunbar
1954	England	6½-5½	Hoylake
1955	Scotland	9-3	Barassie
1956	England	7½-4½	Sunningdale
1957	Scotland	7½-4½	Carnoustie
1958	England	7-5	Moortown
1959	England	8½-3½	Pollok
1960	England	10-2	Olton
1961	Scotland	7-5	Dalmahoy
1962	England	6½-5½	R Mid-Surrey
1963	Scotland	9-3	Prestwick
1964	England	9-3	Formby
1965	England	10-5	Gullane
1966	England	12-3	Moortown
1967	Scotland	8-7	Western Gailes
1968	England	10-5	St Annes Old Links
1969	England	12-3	Dunbar
1970	England	12-3	Hillside
1971	Halved	7½-7½	Barassie
1972	England	13½-1½	Moortown
1973	England	9-6	Blairgowrie
1974	England	11-4	Liverpool
1975	England	9½-5½	Bruntsfield
1976	Scotland	8-7	Sunningdale
1977	England	8-7	Downfield
1978	Scotland	8½-6½	Seaton Carew
1979	England	11-4	Barassie
1980	England	9-6	Formby
1981	Halved	7½-7½	Gullane
1982	England	8-7	Burnham & Berrow
1983	England	8-7	Glenbervie
1984	England	9½-5½	Porthcawl
1985	England	10-5	Barnton
1986	Scotland	8½-6½	Seaton Carew
1987	Scotland	8-7	Barassie
1988	England	11-4	Formby
1989	England	8-7	Nairn
1990	Scotland	10½-4½	Hunstanton

Wales v Ireland

Year	Winner	Result	Venue
1972	Ireland	5-4	Moortown
1973	Ireland	5½-3½	Blairgowrie
1974	Wales	5-4	Hoylake
1975	Wales	6½-2½	Bruntsfield
1976	Wales	7½-1½	Sunningdale
1977	Ireland	6½-5½	Downfield
1978	Wales	8-4	Seaton Carew
1979	Ireland	9½-2½	Barassie
1980	Wales	6½-5½	Formby
1981	Ireland	8-4	Gullane
1982	Wales	9-3	Burnham & Berrow
1983	Ireland	7-5	Glenbervie
1984	Wales	6½-5½	Porthcawl
1985	Ireland	11½-3½	Barnton
1986	Ireland	8½-6½	Seaton Carew
1987	Wales	10½-4½	Barassie
1988	Wales	8-7	Formby
1989	Wales	10½-4½	Nairn
1990	Ireland	8½-6½	Hunstanton

R & A Trophy

This trophy is played between the winners of the England v Scotland and Wales v Ireland International Matches and was introduced in 1985.

Year	Winner	Result	Venue
1985	{ England Ireland } tie	7½-7½	Barnton
1986	Ireland	8½-6½	Seaton Carew
1987	Scotland	10½-4½	Barassie
1988	England	14-1	Formby
1989	England	11½-3½	Nairn
1990	Scotland	12½-2½	Hunstanton

British Youths' Open Amateur Championship

Year	Winner	Club/Country	Venue	Score
1954	JS More	Swanston, Edinburgh	Erskine	287
1955	B Stockdale	Royal Lytham St Annes	Pannal	297
1956	AF Bussell	Coxmoor	Barnton	287
1957	G Will	St Andrews	Pannal	290
1958	RH Kemp	Glamorganshire	Dumfries and County	281
1959	RA Jowle	Moseley	Pannal	286
1960	GA Caygill	Sunningdale	Pannal	279
1961	JS Martin	Kilbirnie Place	Bruntsfield	284
1962	GA Caygill	Sunningdale	Pannal	287
1963	AJ Low	St Andrews University	Pollok	283
1964	BW Barnes	Burnham and Berrow	Pannal	290
1965	PM Townsend	Porters Park	Cosforth Park	281
1966	PA Oosterhuis	Dulwich and Sydenham	Dalmahoy (54 holes)	219
1967	PJ Benka	Addington	Copt Heath	278
1968	PJ Benka	Addington	Ayr Belleisle	281
1969	JH Cook	Calcot Park	Lindrick	289
1970	B Dassu	Italy	Barnton	276
1971	P Elson	Coventry	Northamptonshire	277
1972	AH Chandler	Regent Park	Glasgow Gailes	281
1973	SC Mason	Goring and Streatley	Southport and Ainsdale	284
1974	DM Robertson	Dunbar	Downfield	284
1975	N Faldo	Welwyn Garden City	Pannal	278
1976	ME Lewis	Henbury	Gullane	277
1977	A Lyle	Hawkstone Park	Moor Park	285
1978	B Marchbank	Auchterarder	East Renfrewshire	278

Year	Winner	Club/Country	Venue	Score
1979	G Brand Jr	Knowle	Woodhall Spa	291
1980	G Hay	Hilton Park	Troon	303
1981	T Antevik	Sweden	West Lancashire	290
1982	AP Parkin	Newtown	St Andrews New	280
1983	P Mayo	Newport	Sunningdale	290
1984	R Morris	Padeswick and Buckley	Blairgowrie	281
1985	JM Olazabal	Spain	Ganton	281
1986	D Gilford	GB	Carnoustie	283
1987	J Cook / O Nordberg } tie	GB / Sweden	Hollinwell	283
(Cook won play-off)				
1988	C Cassells / C Cevaer } tie	Murcar / France	Royal Aberdeen	275
(Cevaer won play-off)				
1989	M Smith / A Coltart } tie	Brokenhurst Manor / Thornhill	Ashburnham	285
(Smith won play-off)				
1990	M Gronberg	Sweden	Southerness	275

British Youths' Open Amateur Championship continued

Youths' Internationals
England *v* Scotland

Year	Winner	Result	Venue
1955	England	13-5	Pannal
1956	Scotland	+17 holes	Burgess
1957	*Not played*		
1958	England	+4 holes	Dumfries & County
1959	Scotland	12-6	Pannal
1960	Scotland	11½-6½	Pannal
1961	England	11½-6½	Bruntsfield
1962	England	9½-8½	Pannal
1963	Scotland	9-6	Pollok
1964	Scotland	9-6	Pannal
1965	Scotland	10½-3½	Northumberland
1966	England	9½-5½	Dalmahoy
1967	Halved	7½-7½	Copt Heath
1968	Scotland	8½-6½	Ayr Belleisle
1969	England	8½-6½	Lindrick
1970	Scotland	8½-6½	Barnton
1971	England	11-4	Northampton County
1972	England	11-4	Glasgow Gailes
1973	England	10-5	Southport & Ainsdale
1974	England	9-6	Downfield
1975	Scotland	11-4	Pannal
1976	England	8½-6½	Gullane
1977	Scotland	9½-5½	Moor Park
1978	Scotland	8½-6½	East Renfrewshire
1979	Halved	7½-7½	Woodhall Spa
1980	Scotland	9-6	Troon
1981	Scotland	8-7	West Lancs
1982	Halved	7½-7½	St Andrews New
1983	Scotland	8½-6½	Sunningdale
1984	Scotland	9-6	Blairgowrie
1985	Halved	7½-7½	Ganton
1986	Scotland	8-7	Carnoustie
1987	England	9½-5½	Hollinwell
1988	England	10-5	R. Aberdeen
1989	England	9-6	Ashburnham
1990	Scotland	9-6	Southerness

Great Britain & Ireland *v* Continent of Europe, Youths (EGA Trophy)

Year	Winner	Result	Venue
1967	Great Britain & Ireland	8-7	Copt Heath
1968	Great Britain & Ireland	11-4	Ayr Belleisle
1969	Great Britain & Ireland	13^1/$_2$-1^1/$_2$	Lindrick
1970	Great Britain & Ireland	10^1/$_2$-4^1/$_2$	Barnton
1971	Great Britain & Ireland	10-5	Northampton County
1972	Great Britain & Ireland	11^1/$_2$-3^1/$_2$	Glasgow Gailes
1973	Great Britain & Ireland	10-5	Southport & Ainsdale
1974	Great Britain & Ireland	10-5	Downfield
1975	Great Britain & Ireland	9-6	Pannal
1976	Great Britain & Ireland	17-13	Chantilly
1977	Great Britain & Ireland	11^1/$_2$-3^1/$_2$	Moor Park
1978	Great Britain & Ireland	12^1/$_2$-2^1/$_2$	East Renfrewshire
1979	Great Britain & Ireland	12-3	Woodhall Spa
1980	Continent of Europe	13-11	Lunds Akademiska
1981	Great Britain & Ireland	7^1/$_2$-4^1/$_2$	West Lancs
(Singles curtailed owing to weather)			
1982	Great Britain & Ireland	7^1/$_2$-4^1/$_2$	St Andrews New
1983	Great Britain & Ireland	11-13	Punta Ala, Italy
1984	Halved	6-6	Blairgowrie
1985	Great Britain & Ireland	8-4	Ganton
1986	Great Britain & Ireland	13^1/$_2$-10^1/$_2$	Bilbao, Spain
1987	Continent of Europe	7-5	Hollinwell
1988	Great Britain & Ireland	13^1/$_2$-10^1/$_2$	Copenhagen, Denmark
1989	Great Britain & Ireland	8^1/$_2$-3^1/$_2$	Ashburnham
1990	Great Britain & Ireland	14^1/$_2$-9^1/$_2$	Oporto, Portugal

English Boys Amateur Open Stroke Play Championship

(formerly Carris Trophy)

Year	Winner	Score	Year	Winner	Score
1935	R Upex	75	1966	A Black	151
1936	JDA Langley	152	1967	RF Brown	147
1937	RJ White	149	1968	P Dawson	149
1938	IP Garrow	147	1969	ID Gradwell	150
1939	CW Warren	149	1970	MF Foster	146
1946	AH Perowne	158	1971	RJ Evans	146
1947	I Caldwell	159	1972	L Donovan	143
1948	I Caldwell	152	1973	S Hadfield	148
1949	PB Hine	148	1974	KJ Brown	304
1950	J Glover	144	1975	A Lyle	270
1951	I Young	154	1976	H Stott	285
1952	N Thygesen	150	1977	R Mugglestone	293
1953	N Johnson	148	1978	J Plaxton	144
1954	K Warren	149	1979	P Hammond	288
1955	ID Wheater	151	1980	MP McLean	290
1956	G Maisey	141	1981	D Gilford	290
1957	G Maisey	145	1982	M Jarvis	298
1958	J Hamilton	149	1983	P Baker	288
1959	RT Walker	152	1984	J Coe	283
1960	PM Baxter	150	1985	P Baker	286
1961	DJ Miller	143	1986	G Evans	292
1962	FS Morris	145	1987	D Bathgate	289
1963	EJ Threlfall	147	1988	P Page	284
1964	PM Townsend	148	1989	I Garbutt	285
1965	G McKay	145	1990	M Welch	276

Peter McEvoy Trophy
Venue: Copt Heath

Year	Winner
1984	W Henry
1985	A Morley
1986	C Mitchell
1987	W Henry
1988	P Sefton
1989	D Bathgate
1990	P Sherman

Scottish Boys' Championship

Year	Winner	Runner-up	Venue	By
1960	L Carver	S Wilson	North Berwick	6 and 5
1961	K Thomson	G Wilson	North Berwick	10 and 8
1962	HF Urquhart	S MacDonald	North Berwick	3 and 2
1963	FS Morris	I Clark	North Berwick	9 and 8
1964	WR Lockie	MD Cleghorn	North Berwick	1 hole
1965	RL Penman	J Wood	North Berwick	9 and 8
1966	J McTear	DG Greig	North Berwick	4 and 3
1967	DG Greig	I Cannon	North Berwick	2 and 1
1968	RD Weir	M Grubb	North Berwick	6 and 4
1969	RP Fyfe	IP Doig	North Berwick	4 and 2
1970	S Stephen	M Henry	North Berwick	38th hole
1971	JE Murray	AA Mackay	North Berwick	4 and 3
1972	DM Robertson	G Cairns	North Berwick	9 and 8
1973	R Watson	H Alexander	North Berwick	8 and 7
1974	DM Robertson	J Cuddihy	North Berwick	6 and 5
1975	A Brown	J Cuddihy	North Berwick	6 and 4
1976	B Marchbank	J Cuddihy	Dunbar	2 and 1
1977	JS Taylor	GJ Webster	Dunbar	3 and 2
1978	J Huggan	KW Stables	Dunbar	2 and 1
1979	DR Weir	S Morrison	West Kilbride	5 and 3
1980	R Gregan	AJ Currie	Dunbar	2 and 1
1981	C Stewart	G Mellon	Dunbar	3 and 2
1982	A Smith	J White	Dunbar	39th hole
1983	C Gillies	C Innes	Dunbar	38th hole
1984	K Buchan	L Vannet	Dunbar	2 and 1
1985	AD McQueen	FJ McCulloch	Dunbar	1 hole
1986	AG Tait	EA McIntosh	Dunbar	6 and 5
1987	AJ Coltart	SJ Bannerman	Dunbar	37th hole
1988	CA Fraser	F Clark	Dunbar	9 and 8
1989	M King	D Brolls	Dunbar	8 and 7
1990	B Collier	D Keeney	West Kilbride	2 and 1

Scottish Boys' Open Amateur Stroke Play Championship

Year	Winner	Club	Venue	Score
1970	D Chillas	R Aberdeen	Carnoustie	298
1971	JE Murray	Baberton	Lanark	274
1972	S Martin	Downfield	Montrose	280
1973	S Martin	Carnoustie	Barnton	284
1974	PW Gallacher	Peebles	Lundin Links	290
1975	A Webster	Edzell	Kilmarnock Barassie	286

Year	Winner	Club	Venue	Score
1976	A Webster	Edzell	Forfar	292
1977	{ J Huggan } tie { L Mann }	Winterfield	Renfrew	303
1978	R Fraser	Hilton Park	Arbroath	283
1979	L Mann	Carnoustie	Stirling	289
1980	ASK Glen	Ormesson (France)	Forfar	288
1981	J Gullen	Tillicoultry	Bellshill	296
1982	D Purdie	Turriff	Monifieth	296
1983	L Vannet	Carnoustie	Barassie	286
1984	K Walker	Royal Burgess	Carnoustie	280
1985	G Matthew	Melrose	Baberton	297
1986	G Cassells	Cruden Bay	Edzell	294
1987	C Ronald	Torrance House	Lanark	287
1988	M Urquhart	Inverness	Dumfries and County	280
1989	C Fraser	Burntisland	Stirling	282
1990	N Archibald	Kingsknowe	Monifieth	292

Scottish Boys' Open Amateur Stroke Play Championship

continued

West of Scotland Boys' Championship

Year	Winner	Year	Winner
1981	S Thompson	1986	G King
1982	P Girvan	1987	C Ronald
1983	G Collinson	1988	M King
1984	G Orr	1989	S Dundas
1985	F O'Callaghan	1990	D Keeney

Welsh Boys' Championship

Year	Winner	Runner-up	Venue	By
1960	C Gilford	JL Toye	Llandrindod Wells	5 and 4
1961	AR Porter	JL Toye	Llandrindod Wells	3 and 2
1962	RC Waddilove	W Wadrup	Harlech	20th hole
1963	G Matthews	R Witchell	Penarth	6 and 5
1964	D Lloyd	M Walters	Conway	2 and 1
1965	G Matthews	DG Lloyd	Wenvoe Castle	7 and 6
1966	J Buckley	DP Owen	Holyhead	4 and 2
1967	J Buckley	DL Stevens	Glamorganshire	2 and 1
1968	J Buckley	C Brown	Maesdu	1 hole
1969	K Dabson	P Light	Glamorganshire	5 and 3
1970	P Tadman	A Morgan	Conway	2 and 1
1971	R Jenkins	TJ Melia	Ashburnham	3 and 2
1972	MG Chugg	RM Jones	Wrexham	3 and 2
1973	R Tate	N Duncan	Penarth	2 and 1
1974	D Williams	S Lewis	Llandudno	5 and 4
1975	G Davies	PG Garrett	Glamorganshire	20th hole
1976	JM Morrow	MG Mouland	Caernarvonshire	1 hole
1977	JM Morrow	MG Mouland	Glamorganshire	2 and 1
1978	JM Morrow	A Laking	Harlech	2 and 1
1979	P Mayo	M Hayward	Penarth	24th hole
1980	A Llyr	DK Wood	Llandudno (Maesdu)	2 and 1
1981	M Evans	P Webborn	Pontypool	5 and 4
1982	CM Rees	KH Williams	Prestatyn	2 holes
1983	MA Macara	RN Roderick	Radyr	1 hole
1984	GA Macara	D Bagg	Llandudno	1 hole
1985	B Macfarlane	R Herbert	Cardiff	1 hole
1986	C O'Carroll	GA Macara	Rhuddlan	1 hole
1987	SJ Edwards	A Herbert	Abergavenny	19th hole
1988	C Platt	P Murphy	Holyhead	2 and 1
1989	R Johnson	RL Evans	Southerndown	2 holes
1990	M Ellis	C Sheppard	Llandudno (Maesdu)	3 and 2

European Boys' Team Championship

Year	Winner	Venue
1980	Spain	El Prat Golf Club, Barcelona
1981	England	Olgiata Golf Club, Rome
1982	Italy	Frankfurt Golf Club, West Germany
1983	Sweden	Helsinki Golf Club, Finland
1984	Scotland	Royal St George's Golf Club, England
1985	England	Troia Golf Club, Portugal
1986	England	Turin Golf Club, Italy
1987	Scotland	Chantilly Golf Club, France
1988	France	Renfrew Golf Club, Scotland
1989	England	Lyckoma, Sweden
1990	Spain	Reykjavik, Iceland

Great Britain & Ireland *v* Continent of Europe, Boys (Jacques Leglise Trophy)

Year	Winner	Result	Venue
1958	Great Britain & Ireland	11$^{1}/_{2}$-$^{1}/_{2}$	Moortown
1959	Great Britain & Ireland	7-2	Pollok
1960	Great Britain & Ireland	8-7	Olton
1961	Great Britain & Ireland	11-4	Dalmahoy
1962	Great Britain & Ireland	11-4	Mid-Surrey
1963	Great Britain & Ireland	12-3	Prestwick
1964	Great Britain & Ireland	12-1	Formby
1965	Great Britain & Ireland	12-1	Gullane
1966	Great Britain & Ireland	10-2	Moortown
1967-76	*Not played*		
1977	Continent of Europe	7-6	Downfield
1978	Continent of Europe	7-6	Seaton Carew
1979	Great Britain & Ireland	9$^{1}/_{2}$-2$^{1}/_{2}$	Barassie
1980	Great Britain & Ireland	7-5	Formby
1981	Great Britain & Ireland	8-4	Gullane
1982	Great Britain & Ireland	11-1	Burnham & Berrow
1983	Great Britain & Ireland	6$^{1}/_{2}$-5$^{1}/_{2}$	Glenbervie
1984	Great Britain & Ireland	6$^{1}/_{2}$-5$^{1}/_{2}$	Porthcawl
1985	Great Britain & Ireland	7$^{1}/_{2}$-4$^{1}/_{2}$	Barnton
1986	Continent of Europe	8$^{1}/_{2}$-3$^{1}/_{2}$	Seaton Carew
1987	Great Britain & Ireland	7$^{1}/_{2}$-4$^{1}/_{2}$	Barassie
1988	Great Britain & Ireland	5$^{1}/_{2}$-2$^{1}/_{2}$	Formby
1989	Great Britain & Ireland	7$^{1}/_{2}$-4$^{1}/_{2}$	Nairn
1990	Great Britain & Ireland	10-2	Hunstanton

Girls' British Open Amateur Championship

Year	Winner	Runner-up	Venue	By
1960	S Clarke	AL Irvin	Barassie	2 and 1
1961	D Robb	J Roberts	Beaconsfield	3 and 2
1962	S McLaren-Smith	A Murphy	Foxton Hall	2 and 1
1963	D Oxley	B Whitehead	Gullane	2 and 1
1964	P Tredinnick	K Cumming	Camberley Heath	2 and 1
1965	A Willard	A Ward	Formby	3 and 2
1966	J Hutton	D Oxley	Troon Portland	20th hole
1967	P Burrows	J Hutton	Liphook	2 and 1
1968	C Wallace	C Reybroeck	Leven	4 and 3
1969	J de Witt Puyt	C Reybroeck	Ilkley	2 and 1
1970	C Le Feuvre	Michelle Walker	North Wales	2 and 1
1971	J Mark	Maureen Walker	North Berwick	4 and 3
1972	Maureen Walker	S Cadden	Norwich	2 and 1
1973	AM Palli	N Jeanson	Northamptonshire	2 and 1
1974	R Barry	T Perkins	Dunbar	1 hole
1975	S Cadden	L Isherwood	Henbury	4 and 3
1976	G Stewart	S Rowlands	Pyle and Kenfig	5 and 4
1977	W Aitken	S Bamford	Formby Ladies	2 and 1
1978	M L de Lorenzi	D Glenn	Largs	2 and 1
1979	S Lapaire	P Smilie	Edgbaston	19th hole
1980	J Connachan	L Bolton	Wrexham	2 holes
1981	J Connachan	P Grice	Woodbridge	20th hole
1982	C Waite	M Mackie	Edzell	6 and 5
1983	E Orley	A Walters	Leeds	7 and 6
1984	C Swallow	E Farquharson	Maesdu	1 hole
1985	S Shapcott	E Farquharson	Hesketh	3 and 1
1986	S Croce	S Bennett	West Kilbride	5 and 4
1987	H Dobson	S Croce	Barnham Broom	19th hole
1988	A Macdonald	J Posener	Pyle and Kenfig	3 and 2
1989	M McKinlay	S Eriksson	Carlisle	19th hole
1990	S Cavalleri	E Valera	Penrith	5 and 4

English Girls' Championship

Year	Winner	Runner-up	Venue	By
1964	S Ward	P Tredinnick	Wollaton Park	2 and 1
1965	D Oxley	A Payne	Edgbaston	2 holes
1966	B Whitehead	D Oxley	Woodbridge	1 hole
1967	A Willard	G Holloway	Burhill	1 hole
1968	K Phillips	C le Feuvre	Harrogate	6 and 5
1969	C le Feuvre	K Phillips	Hawkstone Park	2 and 1
1970	C le Feuvre	M Walker	High Post	2 and 1
1971	C Eckersley	J Stevens	Liphook	4 and 3
1972	C Barker	R Kelly	Trentham	4 and 3
1973	S Parker	S Thurston	Lincoln	19th hole
1974	C Langford	L Harrold	Knowle	2 and 1
1975	M Burton	R Barry	Formby	6 and 5
1976	H Latham	D Park	Moseley	3 and 2
1977	S Bamford	S Jolly	Chelmsford	21st hole
1978	P Smillie	J Smith	Willesley Park	3 and 2
1979	L Moore	P Barry	Cirencester	1 hole
1980	P Smillie	J Soulsby	Kedleston Park	3 and 2
1981	J Soulsby	C Waite	Worksop	7 and 5
1982	C Waite	P Grice	Wilmslow	3 and 2
1983	P Grice	K Mitchell	West Surrey	2 and 1
1984	C Swallow	S Duhig	Bath	3 and 1
1985	L Fairclough	K Mitchell	Coventry	6 and 5
1986	S Shapcott	N Way	Huddersfield	7 and 6
1987	S Shapcott	S Morgan	Sandy Lodge	1 hole
1988	H Dobson	S Shapcott	Long Ashton	1 hole
1989	H Dobson	A MacDonald	Edgbaston	3 and 1
1990	C Hall	J Hockley	Bolton Old Links	20th hole

Irish Girls' Championship

Year	Winner	Runner-up	Venue	By
1961	M Coburn	C McAuley	Portrush	6 and 5
1962	P Boyd	P Atkinson	Elm Park	4 and 3
1963	P Atkinson	C Scarlett	Donaghadee	8 and 7
1964	C Scarlett	A Maher	Milltown	6 and 5
1965	V Singleton	P McKenzie	Ballycastle	7 and 6
1966	M McConnell	D Hulme	Dun Laoghaire	3 and 2
1967	M McConnell	C Wallace	Portrush	6 and 5
1968	C Wallace	A McCoy	Louth	3 and 1
1969	EA McGregor	M Sheenan	Knock	6 and 5
1970	EA McGregor	J Mark	Greystones	3 and 2
1971	J Mark	C Nesbitt	Belfast	3 and 2
1972	P Smyth	M Governey	Elm Park	1 hole
1973	M Governey	R Hegarty	Mullingar	3 and 1
1974	R Hegarty	M Irvine	Castletroy	2 holes
1975	M Irvine	P Wickham	Carlow	2 and 1
1976	P Wickham	R Hegarty	Castle	5 and 3
1977	A Ferguson	R Walsh	Birr	3 and 2
1978	C Wickham	B Gleeson	Killarney	1 hole
1979	L Bolton	B Gleeson	Milltown	3 and 2
1980	B Gleeson	L Bolton	Kilkenny	5 and 3
1981	B Gleeson	E Lynn	Donegal	1 hole
1982	D Langan	S Lynn	Headfort	5 and 4
1983	E McDaid	S Lynn	Ennis	20th hole
1984	S Sheehan	L Tormey	Thurles	6 and 4
1985	S Sheehan	D Hanna	Laytown/Bettystown	5 and 4
1986	D Mahon	T Eakin	Mallow	4 and 3
1987	V Greevy	B Ryan	Galway	8 and 7
1988	L McCool	P Gorman	Courtown	3 and 2
1989	A Rogers	R MacGuigan	Athlone	2 and 1
1990	G Doran	L McCool	Royal Portrush	3 and 1

Scottish Girls' Open Stroke Play Championship

Year	Winner	Venue
1960	J Greenhalgh	Ranfurly Castle
1961	D Robb	Whitecraigs
1962	S Armitage	Dalmahoy
1963	A Irvin	Dumfries
1964	M Nuttall	Dalmahoy
1965	I Wylie	Carnoustie
1966	J Smith	Douglas Park
1967	J Bourassa	Dunbar
1968	K Phillips	Dumfries
1969	K Phillips	Prestonfield
1970	B Huke	Leven
1971	B Huke	Dalmahoy
1972	L Hope	Troon, Portland
1973	G Cadden	Edzell
1974	S Lambie	Stranraer
1975	S Cadden	Lanark
1976	S Cadden	Prestonfield
1977	S Cadden	Edzell
1978	J Connachan	Peebles
1979	A Gemmill	Troon, Portland
1980	J Connachan	Kirkcaldy
1981	K Douglas	Downfield
1982	J Rhodes	Dumfries & Galloway
1983	S Lawson	Largs
1984	S Lawson	Dunbar
1985	K Imrie	Ballater
1986	K Imrie	Dumfries and County
1987	K Imrie	Douglas Park
1988	C Lambert	Baberton
1989	C Lambert	Dunblane New
1990	J Moodie	Royal Troon

Scottish Girls' Close Amateur Championship

Year	Winner	Runner-up	Venue	By
1960	J Hastings	A Lurie	Kilmacolm	6 and 4
1961	I Wylie	W Clark	Murrayfield	3 and 1
1962	I Wylie	U Burnet	West Kilbride	3 and 1
1963	M Norval	S MacDonald	Carnoustie	6 and 4
1964	JW Smith	C Workman	West Kilbride	2 and 1
1965	JW Smith	I Walker	Leven	7 and 5
1966	J Hutton	F Jamieson	Arbroath	2 holes
1967	J Hutton	K Lackie	West Kilbride	4 and 2
1968	M Dewar	J Crawford	Dalmahoy	2 holes
1969	C Panton	A Coutts	Edzell	23rd hole
1970	M Walker	L Bennett	Largs	3 and 2
1971	M Walker	S Kennedy	Edzell	1 hole
1972	G Cadden	C Panton	Stirling	3 and 2
1973	M Walker	M Thomson	Cowal, Dunoon	1 hole
1974	S Cadden	D Reid	Arbroath	3 and 1
1975	W Aitken	S Cadden	Leven	1 hole
1976	S Cadden	D Mitchell	Dumfries and County	4 and 2
1977	W Aitken	G Wilson	West Kilbride	2 holes
1978	J Connachan	D Mitchell	Stirling	7 and 5
1979	J Connachan	G Wilson	Dunbar	3 and 1
1980	J Connachan	P Wright	Dumfries and County	21st hole
1981	D Thomson	P Wright	Barassie	2 and 1
1982	S Lawson	D Thomson	Montrose	1 hole
1983	K Imrie	D Martin	Leven	2 and 1
1984	T Craik	D Jackson	Peebles	3 and 2
1985	E Farquharson	E Moffat	West Kilbride	2 holes
1986	C Lambert	F McKay	Nairn	4 and 3
1987	S Little	L Moretti	Stirling	3 and 2
1988	J Jenkins	F McKay	Dumfries and County	4 and 3
1989	J Moodie	V Melvin	Kilmacolm	19th hole
1990	M McKay	J Moodie	Duff House Royal	3 and 2

West of Scotland Girls' Championship

Year	Winner	Year	Winner
1981	S Lawson	1986	L Lundie
1982	S Lawson	1987	A Ferguson
1983	A Johnson	1988	A Ferguson
1984	D Jackson	1989	J Risby
1985	K Fitzgerald	1990	J Moodie

Welsh Girls' Amateur Championship

Year	Winner	Runner-up	Venue	By
1960	A Hughes	D Wilson	Llandrindod Wells	6 and 4
1961	J Morris	S Kelly	North Wales	3 and 2
1962	J Morris	P Morgan	Southerndown	4 and 3
1963	A Hughes	A Brown	Conway	8 and 7
1964	A Hughes	M Leigh	Holyhead	5 and 3
1965	A Hughes	A Reardon-Hughes	Swansea Bay	19th hole
1966	S Hales	J Rogers	Prestatyn	1 hole
1967	E Wilkie	L Humphreys	Pyle and Kenfig	1 hole
1968	L Morris	J Rogers	Portmadoc	1 hole
1969	L Morris	L Humphreys	Wenvoe Castle	5 and 3
1970	T Perkins	P Light	Rhuddlan	2 and 1
1971	P Light	P Whitley	Glamorganshire	4 and 3
1972	P Whitley	P Light	Llandudno (Maesdu)	2 and 1
1973	V Rawlings	T Perkins	Whitchurch	19th hole
1974	L Isherwood	S Rowlands	Wrexham	4 and 3
1975	L Isherwood	S Rowlands	Swansea Bay	1 hole

Welsh Girls'
Amateur
Championship
continued

Year	Winner	Runner-up	Venue	By
1976	K Rawlings	C Parry	Rhuddlan	5 and 4
1977	S Rowlands	D Taylor	Clyne	7 and 5
1978	S Rowlands	G Rees	Abergele	3 and 2
1979	M Rawlings	J Richards	St Mellons	19th hole
1980	K Davies	M Rawlings	Vale of Llangollen	19th hole
1981	M Rawlings	F Connor	Radyr	4 and 3
1982	K Davies	K Beckett	Wrexham	6 and 5
1983	N Wesley	J Foster	Whitchurch	4 and 2
1984	J Foster	J Evans	Pwllheli	6 and 5
1985	J Foster	S Caley	Langland Bay	6 and 5
1986	J Foster	L Dermott	Holyhead	3 and 2
1987	J Lloyd	S Bibbs	Cardiff	2 and 1
1988	L Dermott	A Perriam	Builth Wells	2 holes
1989	L Dermott	N Stroud	Carmarthen	4 and 2
1990	L Dermott	N Stroud	Padeswood and Buckley	6 and 4

European Girls' Team Championship

Year	Winner	Second	Venue
1990	Sweden	England	Shannon, Ireland

Girls' Home Internationals: Stroyan Cup

Year	Winner	Venue
1966	Scotland	Troon (Portland)
1967	England	Liphook
1968	England	Leven
1969	England	Ilkley
1970	England	North Wales
1971	England	North Berwick
1972	Scotland	Royal Norwich
1973	Scotland	Northamptonshire County
1974	England	Dunbar
1975	England	Henbury
1976	Scotland	Pyle and Kenfig
1977	England	Formby Ladies
1978	England	Largs
1979	England	Edgbaston
1980	England	Wrexham
1981	England	Woodbridge
1982	England	Edzell
1983	England	Alwoodley
1984	Scotland	Llandudno (Maesdu)
1985	England	Hesketh GC
1986	England	West Kilbride

1987 at Barnham Broom

England beat Scotland	6 1/2-1/2
England beat Ireland	7-0
England beat Wales	6-1
Scotland beat Ireland	4-3
Ireland beat Wales	4 1/2-2 1/2
Wales beat Scotland	4-3

Result: England 3; Ireland 1; Scotland 1; Wales 1

1988 at Pyle and Kenfig

England beat Ireland	4-3
England beat Wales	4-3
England halved with Scotland	3^1/$_2$-3^1/$_2$
Ireland beat Wales	4-3
Ireland beat Scotland	5-2
Wales beat Scotland	4-3

Result: England 3; Ireland 2; Scotland 1; Wales 1

1989 at Carlisle

Ireland beat Scotland	4^1/$_2$-2^1/$_2$
England beat Wales	4-3
Ireland beat Wales	4^1/$_2$-2^1/$_2$
England beat Scotland	5-2
Scotland beat Wales	4-3
England beat Ireland	4^1/$_2$-2^1/$_2$

Result: England 3; Ireland 2; Scotland 1; Wales 0

1990 at Penrith

England beat Wales	7-2
Ireland beat Scotland	6-3
England beat Scotland	8-1
Ireland beat Wales	9-0
England beat Ireland	7^1/$_2$-1^1/$_2$
Scotland beat Wales	7-2

Result: England 3; Ireland 2; Scotland 1; Wales 0

Irish Youths' Open Amateur Championship

Year	Winner	Venue	Score
1980	J McHenry	Clandeboye	296
1981	J McHenry	Westport	303
1982	K O'Donnell	Mullingar	286
1983	P Murphy	Cork	287
1984	JC Morris	Bangor	292
1985	J McHenry	Co Sligo	287
1986	JC Morris	Carlow	280
1987	C Everett	Killarney	300
1988	P McGinley	Malone	283
1989	A Mathers	Athlone	280
1990	D Errity	Dundalk	293

Scottish Youths' Open Amateur Stroke Play Championship

Year	Winner	Club	Venue	Score
1979	A Oldcorn	Ratho Park	Dalmahoy	217
1980	G Brand, Jr	Knowle	Monifieth and	
			Ashludie	281
1981	S Campbell	Cawder	Cawder and Keir	279
1982	LS Mann	Carnoustie	Leven and Scoonie	270
1983	A Moir	McDonald	Mortonhall	284
1984	B Shields	Bathgate	Eastwood, Renfrew	280
1985	H Kemp	Cawder	East Kilbride	282
1986	A Mednick	Sweden	Cawder	282
1987	K Walker	Royal Burgess	Bogside	291
1988	P McGinley	Grange	Ladybank &	
			Glenrothes	281
1989	J Mackenzie	West Linton	Longniddry	281
1990	S Bannerman	Cruden Bay	Portpatrick and	213
			Stranraer	(54 holes)

Ulster Youths' Open Amateur Championship

Year	Winner	Year	Winner
1981	M Windebank	1986	DA Mulholland
1982	G Hamill	1987	J Carvill
1983	M Froggatt	1988	G McAllister
1984	G Clarke	1989	G Moore
1985	J Carvill	1990	N Crawford

European Youths' Team Championship

Year	Winner	Second	Venue
1990	Italy	Sweden	Turin, Italy

County and District Championships

Aberdeenshire Ladies' Championship

Year	Winner	Year	Winner
1981	CA Stewart	1986	E Farquharson
1982	P Wright	1987	E Farquharson
1983	E Farquharson	1988	L Urquhart
1984	J Self	1989	J Forbes
1985	P Wright	1990	E Farquharson

Angus Amateur Championship

Year	Winner
1988	D Downie
1989	T Peebles
1990	D Leith

Angus Ladies' Championship

Year	Winner	Year	Winner
1981	K Sutherland	1986	F Farquharson
1982	K Imrie	1987	F Farquharson
1983	K Imrie	1988	C Hay
1984	K Imrie	1989	C Hope
1985	M Mackie	1990	K Sutherland

Argyll and Bute Amateur Championship

Year	Winner	Year	Winner
1981	M Cannon	1986	G Tyre
1982	J Ewing	1987	S Campbell
1983	G Tyre	1988	G Bolton
1984	D MacIntyre	1989	G Tyre
1985	G Reynolds	1990	G Reynolds

Ayrshire Amateur Championship

Year	Winner	Year	Winner
1981	D Murdoch	1986	G Armstrong
1982	C Evans	1987	B Gemmell
1983	L Crawford	1988	G Blair
1984	J Milligan	1989	D Hawthorn
1985	P Girvan	1990	R Crawford

Ayrshire Ladies' Championship

Year	Winner	Year	Winner
1981	A Gemmill	1986	A Gemmill
1982	A Gemmill	1987	A Gemmill
1983	A Gemmill	1988	M Wilson
1984	A Gemmill	1989	A Gemmill
1985	J Leishman	1990	C Gibson

Bedfordshire Amateur Championship

Year	Winner	Year	Winner
1981	C Beard	1986	M Wharton
1982	A Rose	1987	P Wharton
1983	A Rose	1988	P Wharton
1984	M Stokes	1989	C Staroscik
1985	R Harris	1990	D Charlton

Bedfordshire Ladies' Championship

Year	Winner	Year	Winner
1981	S Kiddle	1986	C Westgate
1982	S Kiddle	1987	S White
1983	S White	1988	S Cormack
1984	S White	1989	T Gale
1985	S White	1990	C Cummings

Berks, Bucks and Oxfordshire Amateur Championship

Year	Winner	Year	Winner
1981	M Rapley	1986	D Lane
1982	D Lane	1987	F George
1983	M Orris	1988	F George
1984	N Webber	1989	H Bareham
1985	M Rapley	1990	S Barwick

Berkshire Ladies' Championship

Year	Winner	Year	Winner
1981	A Uzielli	1986	A Uzielli
1982	C Caldwell	1987	A Uzielli
1983	A Uzielli	1988	T Smith
1984	A Uzielli	1989	L Walton
1985	A Uzielli	1990	A Uzielli

Border Counties Ladies' Championship

Year	Winner	Year	Winner
1981	A Hunter	1986	S Gallacher
1982	S Simpson	1987	S Simpson
1983	E White	1988	A Hunter
1984	S Gallacher	1989	A Fleming
1985	S Gallacher	1990	J Anderson

Border Golfers' Association Amateur Championship

Year	Winner	Year	Winner
1981	P Gallagher	1986	L Wallace
1982	D Campbell	1987	D Ballantyne
1983	B Reid	1988	W Renwick
1984	A Turnbull	1989	A Turnbull
1985	L Wallace	1990	M Thomson

Bucks Ladies' Championship

Year	Winner	Year	Winner
1981	J Warren	1986	A Tyreman
1982	J Warren	1987	C Watson
1983	G Bonallack	1988	C Hourihane
1984	J Warren	1989	C Hourihane
1985	E Franklin	1990	C Watson

Caernarfonshire and District Amateur Championship

Year	Winner	Year	Winner
1981	W Jones	1985	M Macara
1982	D McLean	1986	R Roberts
1983	{ J Parry / W Jones	1987	D McLean
		1988	D McLean
1984	S Owen	1989	W Jones
		1990	D McLean

Caernarfonshire Amateur Championship Cup

Year	Winner
1989	M Sheppard
1990	I Jones

Caernarvonshire and Anglesey Ladies' Championship

Year	Winner	Year	Winner
1981	S Jump	1986	S Turner
1982	F Connor	1987	S Roberts
1983	S Roberts	1988	S Turner
1984	S Jump	1989	S Roberts
1985	A Lewis	1990	S Roberts

Cambridge Area GU Amateur Championship

Year	Winner	Year	Winner
1981	M Seaton	1986	J Miller
1982	R Guy	1987	R Claydon
1983	J Gray	1988	R Claydon
1984	N Hughes	1989	B Jackson
1985	D Wood	1990	G Stevenson

Cambridgeshire and Hunts Ladies' Championship

Year	Winner	Year	Winner
1981	J Walter	1986	J Walter
1982	J Walter	1987	R Farrow
1983	J Walter	1988	S Meadows
1984	J Walter	1989	J Hatcher
1985	J Walter	1990	J Walter

Channel Islands Ladies' Championship

Year	Winner	Year	Winner
1981	L Cummins	1986	V Bougourd
1982	V Bougourd	1987	L Cummins
1983	D Heaton	1988	L Cummins
1984	E Roberts	1989	L Cummins
1985	L Cummins	1990	L Cummins

Cheshire Amateur Championship

Year	Winner	Year	Winner
1981	C Harrison	1986	P Bailey
1982	C Smethurst	1987	P Jones
1983	C Smethurst	1988	P Bailey
1984	I Spencer	1989	P Bailey
1985	C Harrison	1990	J Berry

Cheshire Ladies' Championship

Year	Winner	Year	Winner
1981	A Briggs	1986	J Hill
1982	H Latham	1987	S Robinson
1983	H Latham	1988	J Morley
1984	J Hill	1989	J Morley
1985	L Percival	1990	J Morley

Clackmannanshire Amateur Championship

Year	Winner
1988	R Stewart
1989	J Gullen
1990	P MacLeod

Cornwall Amateur Championship

Year	Winner	Year	Winner
1981	J Hirst	1986	R Simmons
1982	M Edmunds	1987	P Clayton
1983	M Edmunds	1988	P Clayton
1984	R Simmons	1989	C Phillips
1985	C Phillips	1990	M Edmunds

Cornwall Ladies' Championship

Year	Winner	Year	Winner
1981	L Moore	1986	J Ryder
1982	S Cann	1987	J Ryder
1983	J Ryder	1988	S Currie
1984	J Fernleigh	1989	S Currie
1985	J Fern	1990	S Currie

County Champions' Tournament (England)

Formerly President's Bowl

Year	Winner	Year	Winner
1962	{ G Edwards, Cheshire	1976	R Brown, Devon
	{ A Thirwell, Northumberland	1977	M Walls, Cumbria
1963	{ M Burgess, Sussex	1978	I Simpson, Notts
	{ R Foster, Yorks	1979	N Burch, Essex
1964	M Attenborough, Kent	1980	D Lane, Berks, Bucks and Oxon
1965	M Lees, Lincs	1981	M Kelly, Yorks
1966	R Stephenson, Middx	1982	P Deeble, Northumberland
1967	P Benka, Surrey	1983	N Chesses, Warwickshire
1968	G Hyde, Sussex	1984	{ N Briggs, Herts
1969	A Holmes, Herts		{ P McEvoy, Warwickshire
1970	M King, Berks, Bucks and Oxon	1985	P Robinson, Herts
1971	M Lee, Yorks	1986	A Gelsthorpe, Yorks
1972	P Berry, Glos	1987	{ F George, Berks, Bucks & Oxon
1973	A Chandler, Lancs		{ D Fay, Surrey
1974	{ G Hyde, Sussex	1988	R Claydon, Cambridge
	{ A Lyle, Shrops & Hereford	1989	R Willison, Middlesex
1975	N Faldo, Herts	1990	{ P Streeter, Lincs
			{ R Sloman, Kent

Cumbria Amateur Championship

Formerly Cumberland and Westmorland Amateur Championship

Year	Winner	Year	Winner
1981	J Kirkpatrick	1986	M Ruddick
1982	E Gulliksen	1987	J Longcake
1983	A Drabble	1988	G Waters
1984	M Lowe	1989	G Winter
1985	J Longcake	1990	G Winter

Cumbria Ladies' Championship

Year	Winner	Year	Winner
1981	D Thomson	1986	H Porter
1982	D Thomson	1987	J McColl
1983	P Brumwell	1988	D Thomson
1984	D Thomson	1989	S Tuck
1985	J Currie	1990	S Tuck

Denbighshire and Flintshire Ladies' Championship

Year	Winner	Year	Winner
1981	E Higgs	1986	S Thomas
1982	K Davies	1987	S Thomas
1983	E Davies	1988	S Thomas
1984	C Ellis	1989	S Thomas
1985	E Davies	1990	L Dermott

Derbyshire Amateur Championship

Year	Winner	Year	Winner
1981	R Hall	1986	J Feeney
1982	R Davenport	1987	R Green
1983	R Davenport	1988	N Wylde
1984	G Shaw	1989	P Eastwood
1985	R Davenport	1990	R Fletcher

Derbyshire Ladies' Championship

Year	Winner	Year	Winner
1981	A Howe	1986	E Robinson
1982	V McWilliams	1987	E Clark
1983	J Williams	1988	A Howe
1984	J Williams	1989	D Andrews
1985	L Holmes	1990	D Andrews

Derbyshire Match-Play Championship

Year	Winner	Year	Winner
1981	N Rowland	1986	J Feeney
1982	M Higgins	1987	G Shaw
1983	G Shaw	1988	M Higgins
1984	G Shaw	1989	G Shaw
1985	C Ibbotson	1990	R Fletcher

Derbyshire Open Championship

Year	Winner	Year	Winner
1981	R Davenport (Am)	1986	N Furniss (Am)
1982	R Davenport (Am)	1987	S Smith
1983	C Radford (Am)	1988	G Shaw
1984	J Feeney (Am)	1989	D Clark (Am)
1985	M McLean	1990	M Deeley

Derbyshire Professional Championship

Year	Winner	Year	Winner
1981	J Lower	1986	J Lower
1982	A Wardle	1987	A Skingle
1983	P Seal	1988	M McLean
1984	W Bird	1989	N Hallam
1985	J Turnbull	1990	M Deeley

Devon Amateur Championship

Year	Winner	Year	Winner
1981	M Jewell	1986	P Newcombe
1982	M Symons	1987	J Langmead
1983	A Richards	1988	J Langmead
1984	J May	1989	R Barrow
1985	J Langmead	1990	G Milne

Devon Ladies' Championship

Year	Winner	Year	Winner
1981	C Stephens	1986	J Hurley
1982	J Hurley	1987	G Jenkinson
1983	J Hurley	1988	J Hurley
1984	J Hurley	1989	S Germain
1985	L Lines	1990	V Holloway

Devon Open Championship

Year	Winner	Year	Winner
1981	D Sheppard	1986	P Newcombe
1982	M Jewell (Am)	1987	G Milne
1983	T Valentine	1988	D Sheppard
1984	M Symons	1989	D Sheppard
1985	A MacDonald	1990	G Tomkinson

Dorset Amateur Championship

Year	Winner	Year	Winner
1981	R Hearn	1986	A Lawrence
1982	R Miles	1987	A Lawrence
1983	R Miles	1988	A Lawrence
1984	J Gordon	1989	A Lawrence
1985	J Bloxham	1990	P McMullen

Dorset Ladies' Championship

Year	Winner	Year	Winner
1981	R Page	1986	H Delew
1982	B Langley	1987	J Sugden
1983	J Sugden	1988	H Delew
1984	S Lowe	1989	T Loveys
1985	S Lowe	1990	T Loveys

Dumfriesshire Ladies' Championship

Year	Winner	Year	Winner
1981	E Hill	1986	M McKerrow
1982	B Hill	1987	M McKerrow
1983	D Hill	1988	D Douglas
1984	D Hill	1989	D Douglas
1985	R Morrison	1990	L Armstrong

Dumbartonshire Amateur Championship

Year	Winner	Year	Winner
1981	J Graham	1986	D Carrick
1982	D Carrick	1987	D Shaw
1983	D Carrick	1988	J Laird
1984	T Eckford	1989	D Shaw
1985	S Miller	1990	J Kinloch

Dumbartonshire Amateur Match Play Championship

Year	Winner	Year	Winner
1981	G Jack	1986	W Thom
1982	C White	1987	A Brodie
1983	G Millar	1988	R Blair
1984	R Fraser	1989	C Stewart
1985	D Carrick	1990	D Shaw

Dumbartonshire and Argyll Ladies' Championship

Year	Winner	Year	Winner
1981	V McAlister	1986	J Kinloch
1982	V McAlister	1987	S McDonald
1983	V McAlister	1988	V McAlister
1984	V McAlister	1989	M McKinlay
1985	V McAlister	1990	M McKinlay

Durham Amateur Championship

Year	Winner	Year	Winner
1981	D Hawkins	1986	H Ashby
1982	J Ellwood	1987	P Highmoor
1983	M Ure	1988	J Ellwood
1984	M Ure	1989	G Bell
1985	A Robertson	1990	R Walker

Durham Ladies' Championship

Year	Winner	Year	Winner
1981	C Barker	1986	L Chesterton
1982	P Hunt	1987	B Mansfield
1983	P Hunt	1988	L Chesterton
1984	B Mansfield	1989	L Still
1985	M Scullan	1990	B Mansfield

East Anglian Ladies' Championship

Year	Winner
1986	J Walter
1987	J Walter
1988	R Farrow
1989	W Fryer
1990	J Sheldrick

East Anglian Open Championship

Year	Winner	Year	Winner
1981	F Hill	1986	M Stokes
1982	R Mann	1987	*Not played*
1983	R Mann	1988	P Kent
1984	{ M Stokes / K Ashdown } tie	1989	R Mitchell
1985	C Platts	1990	N Wichelow

East Lothian Ladies' Championship

Year	Winner	Year	Winner
1981	A Ferguson	1986	P Lees
1982	*Null and void*	1987	J Ford
1983	M Thomson	1988	C Lugton
1984	M Ferguson	1989	C Lugton
1985	M Ferguson	1990	C Lambert

East of Ireland Open Amateur Championship

Year	Winner	Year	Winner
1981	D Branigan	1986	P Hogan
1982	M Sludds	1987	P Rayfus
1983	A Morrow	1988	G McGimpsey
1984	B Reddan	1989	D Clarke
1985	F Ronan	1990	D O'Sullivan

Eastern Division Ladies' Championship (Scotland)

Year	Winner	Year	Winner
1981	E Kimmen	1986	J Harrison
1982	J Bald	1987	A Rose
1983	J Marshall	1988	J Ford
1984	L Hope	1989	H Rose
1985	L Bennett	1990	A Hendry

East of Scotland Open Amateur Stroke Play

Year	Winner	Year	Winner
1981	K Gray	1986	S Knowles
1982	G Macgregor	1987	T Cochrane
1983	S Stephen	1988	C Everett
1984	S Stephen	1989	K Hird
1985	A McQueen	1990	G Lawrie

East Region PGA Championship

Year	Winner
1987	{ J Pinsent / P Kent } tie
1988	L Farmer
1989	*Not played*
1990	R Mann

Essex Ladies' Championship

Year	Winner	Year	Winner
1981	P Jackson	1986	S Moorcroft
1982	A Bonallack	1987	M King
1983	E Boatman	1988	W Dicks
1984	S Barber	1989	A MacDonald
1985	S Barber	1990	S Bennett

Essex Amateur Championship

Year	Winner	Year	Winner
1981	C Davies	1986	M Davis
1982	C Laurence	1987	V Cox
1983	M Davis	1988	R Scott
1984	M Stokes	1989	V Cox
1985	D Wood	1990	*Null and void*

Fife Amateur Championship

Year	Winner	Year	Winner
1981	D Ross	1986	D Spriddle
1982	D Weir	1987	S Meiklejohn
1983	T Cochrane	1988	A Mathers
1984	C Birrell	1989	D Spriddle
1985	D Weir	1990	D Spriddle

Fife County Ladies' Championship

Year	Winner	Year	Winner
1981	J Bald	1986	L Bennett
1982	J Bald	1987	L Bennett
1983	R Scott	1988	J Lawrence
1984	E Hunter	1989	J Ford
1985	L Bennett	1990	J Lawrence

Galloway Ladies' Championship

Year	Winner	Year	Winner
1981	M Clements	1986	M Wright
1982	M Clements	1987	M Wright
1983	S McDonald	1988	M Wright
1984	S McDonald	1989	F Rennie
1985	M Wright	1990	F Rennie

Glamorgan Amateur Championship

Year	Winner	Year	Winner
1981	T Melia	1986	L Price
1982	T Melia	1987	RN Roderick
1983	P Bloomfield	1988	I Booth
1984	RN Roderick	1989	B Knight
1985	R Brown	1990	P Bloomfield

Glamorgan County Ladies' Championship

Year	Winner	Year	Winner
1981	T Thomas	1986	P Johnson
1982	M Rawlings	1987	V Thomas
1983	T Thomas	1988	V Thomas
1984	J Foster	1989	V Thomas
1985	P Johnson	1990	A Perriam

Glasgow Match Play Championship

Year	Winner	Year	Winner
1981	D Carrick	1986	G Shaw
1982	B Pearson	1987	S Dixon
1983	B Pearson	1988	J Finnigan
1984	I Carslaw	1989	L McLaughlin
1985	S Savage	1990	C Barrowman

Glasgow Stroke Play Championship

Year	Winner
1984	I Carslaw
1985	I Carslaw
1986	A Maclaine
1987	S Machin
1988	D Martin
1989	G Shaw
1990	H Kemp

Gloucestershire Amateur Championship

Year	Winner	Year	Winner
1981	J Durbin	1986	R Broad
1982	D Ray	1987	M Bessell
1983	D Rollo	1988	J Webber
1984	C Robinson	1989	R Broad
1985	D Carroll	1990	D Hares

Gloucestershire Ladies' Championship

Year	Winner	Year	Winner
1981	K Douglas	1986	S Shapcott
1982	K Douglas	1987	R Page
1983	K Douglas	1988	S Elliott
1984	K Douglas	1989	S Elliott
1985	C Griffiths	1990	M Mayes

Gwent Amateur Championship

Formerly Monmouthshire Amateur Championship

Year	Winner	Year	Winner
1981	A Disley	1986	G Hughes
1982	P Mayo	1987	M Bearcroft
1983	N Davies	1988	A Williams
1984	P Mayo	1989	P Glyn
1985	M Brimble	1990	M Hayward

Hampshire, Isle of Wight and Channel Islands Open Championship

Year	Winner	Year	Winner
1981	B Winteridge (Am)	1986	M Desmond
1982	J Hay	1987	T Healey
1983	J Hay	1988	K Bowden
1984	M Desmond	1989	J Coles
1985	I Young	1990	R Watkins

Hampshire, Isle of Wight and Channel Islands Amateur Championship

Year	Winner	Year	Winner
1981	B Winteridge	1986	R Eggo
1982	B Winteridge	1987	A Mew
1983	K Weeks	1988	S Richardson
1984	R Eggo	1989	M Smith
1985	R Alker	1990	M Wiggett

Hampshire Ladies' Championship

Year	Winner	Year	Winner
1981	S Pickles	1986	C Hayllar
1982	A Wells	1987	C Stirling
1983	C Hayllar	1988	C Stirling
1984	C Mackintosh	1989	S Pickles
1985	C Stirling	1990	A MacDonald

Hampshire Professional Match Play Championship

Year	Winner
1984	J Hay
1985	P Dawson
1986	K Bowden
1987	M Desmond
1988	K Bowden
1989	I Young
1990	K Bowden

Hampshire Professional Stroke Play Championship

Year	Winner	Year	Winner
1981	J Grant	1986	M Desmond
1982	J Garner	1987	T Healy
1983	I Pinner	1988	G Stubbington
1984	G Stubbington	1989	J Coles
1985	T Healy	1990	S Watson

Herts Amateur Championship

Year	Winner	Year	Winner
1981	R Mitchell	1986	P Cherry
1982	J Ambridge	1987	A Clark
1983	C McKay	1988	J Ambridge
1984	N Briggs	1989	S Hankin
1985	P Robinson	1990	N Leconte

Herts Ladies' Championship

Year	Winner	Year	Winner
1981	V Pearson	1986	T Jeary
1982	N McCormack	1987	H Kaye
1983	E Provan	1988	T Jeary
1984	K Hurley	1989	H Kaye
1985	H Kaye	1990	S Allison

Isle of Wight Ladies' Championship

Year	Winner	Year	Winner
1981	G Wright	1986	M Ankers
1982	G Wright	1987	M Ankers
1983	G Wright	1988	M Butler
1984	M Butler	1989	M Ankers
1985	G Wright	1990	M Ankers

Kent Amateur Championship

Year	Winner	Year	Winner
1981	M McLean	1986	M Lawrence
1982	S Baldwin	1987	L Batchelor
1983	M Lawrence	1988	W Hodkin
1984	M Lawrence	1989	S Green
1985	J Simmance	1990	R Sloman

Kent Ladies' Championship

Year	Winner	Year	Winner
1981	J Guntrip	1986	C Caldwell
1982	S Hedges	1987	L Bayman
1983	J Guntrip	1988	C Caldwell
1984	S Kitchen	1989	S Sutton
1985	L Bayman	1990	H Wadsworth

Kent Open Championship

Year	Winner	Year	Winner
1983	G Potter	1987	M Goodin
1984	R Cameron	1988	J Bennett
1985	G Will	11989	R Cameron
1986	J Bennett	1990	S Barr

Kent Professional Championship

Year	Winner
1985	J Bennett
1986	P Mitchell
1987	S Barr
1988	R Cameron
1989	P Lyons
1990	R Cameron

Lanarkshire Amateur Championship

Year	Winner	Year	Winner
1981	G Banks	1986	W Bryson
1982	G Jones	1987	S Henderson
1983	R Lynch	1988	G Jones
1984	W Bryson	1989	J Taylor
1985	J Reid	1990	G Shanks

Lanarkshire Ladies' County Championship

Year	Winner	Year	Winner
1981	E Dunn	1986	J Scott
1982	W Norris	1987	A Hendry
1983	S Roy	1988	F McKay
	(née Needham)	1989	K Dallas
1984	S Roy	1990	A Hendry
1985	P Hutton		

Lancashire Amateur Championship

Year	Winner	Year	Winner
1981	M Wild	1986	M Wild
1982	A Squires	1987	T Foster
1983	M Wallis	1988	M Kingsley
1984	S Birtwell	1989	R Bardsley
1985	R Bardsley	1990	T Foster

Lancashire Ladies' Championship

Year	Winner	Year	Winner
1981	A Brown	1986	J Collingham
1982	G Costello		(née Melville)
1983	J Melville	1987	J Collingham
1984	A Goucher	1988	L Fairclough
1985	A Bromilow	1989	C Blackshaw
		1990	L Fairclough

Lancashire Open Championship

Year	Winner	Year	Winner
1981	D Durnian	1986	T Foster (Am)
1982	S Hadfield	1987	S Hamer (Am)
1983	S Hamer (Am)	1988	P Wesselingh
1984	R Longworth	1989	M Jones
1985	R Green	1990	P Allan

Leicestershire and Rutland Amateur Championship

Year	Winner	Year	Winner
1981	E Hammond	1986	I Middleton
1982	C Gotla	1987	G Marshall
1983	T Stephens	1988	A Martinez
1984	A Martinez	1989	J Cayless
1985	E Hammond	1990	D Gibson

Leicestershire and Rutland Open Championship

Year	Winner	Year	Winner
1981	S Adams (Am)	1986	R Stephenson
1982	I Middleton	1987	*Not played*
1983	E Feasey (Am)	1988	D Gibson
1984	S Sherratt	1989	R Adams
1985	R Adams	1990	R Larratt

Leicestershire and Rutland Ladies' Championship

Year	Winner	Year	Winner
1981	R Reed	1986	V Davis
1982	P Gray	1987	M Page
1983	R Reed	1988	A Walters
1984	P Martin	1989	M Page
1985	A Waters	1990	R Reed

Lincolnshire Amateur Championship

Year	Winner	Year	Winner
1981	L Brumpton	1986	J Purdy
1982	S Graves	1987	P Stenton
1983	P Stenton	1988	P Streeter
1984	J Purdy	1989	J Payne
1985	J Robinson	1990	P Streeter

Lincolnshire Ladies' Championship

Year	Winner	Year	Winner
1981	R Broughton	1986	A Johns
1982	B Hicks	1987	H Dobson
1983	B Hicks	1988	H Dobson
1984	A Burtt	1989	H Dobson
1985	H Dobson	1990	A Johns

Lincolnshire Open Championship

Year	Winner	Year	Winner
1981	P Davies	1986	G Stafford
1982	T Squires	1987	S Dickinson (Am)
1983	S Dickinson (Am)	1988	J Heib
1984	J Taylor	1989	A Hare
1985	A Carter	1990	A Butler (Am)

Lothians Amateur Championship

Year	Winner	Year	Winner
1981	B Dunlop	1986	S Smith
1982	R Bradley	1987	D Kirkpatrick
1983	A Roy	1988	B Shields
1984	P Smith	1989	K Hastings
1985	S Easingwood	1990	S Middleton

Manx Amateur Championship

Year	Winner	Year	Winner
1981	G Kelly	1986	A Cain
1982	J Sutton	1987	J Sutton
1983	J Sutton	1988	G Kelly
1984	J Sutton	1989	G Ashe
1985	J Sutton	1990	M Pugh

Middlesex Amateur Championship

Year	Winner	Year	Winner
1981	G Homewood	1986	A Rogers
1982	M Weir	1987	R Willison
1983	G Homewood	1988	A Rogers
1984	R Willison	1989	R Willison
1985	R Willison	1990	A Rogers

Middlesex Ladies' Championship

Year	Winner
1984	C Nelson
1985	C Nelson
1986	A Gems
1987	A Gems
1988	S Keogh
1989	S Keogh
1990	S Keogh

Middlesex Open Championship

Year	Winner
1983	N Wichelow
1984	L Fickling
1985	P Golding
1986	*Not played*
1987	L Fickling
1988	L Fickling
1989	L Fickling
1990	R Willison (Am)

Midland Ladies' Championship

Year	Winner
1984	L Waring
1985	L Waring
1986	J Collingham
1987	S Roberts
1988	S Roberts
1989	R Bolas
1990	J Hockley

Midland Masters

Year	Winner
1988	B Waites
1989	C Haycock
1990	J King

Midland Professional Stroke Play Championship

Year	Winner	Year	Winner
1981	D Stewart	1986	A Skingle
1982	P Elson	1987	M Mouland
1983	A Minshall	1988	G Farr
1984	M Mouland	1989	J Higgins
1985	K Hayward	1990	G Stafford

Midland Professional Match Play Championship

Year	Winner	Year	Winner
1981	P Elson	1986	J Higgins
1982	P Elson	1987	K Hayward
1983	P Ackerley	1988	J Higgins
1984	P Elson	1989	K Hayward
1985	D Ridley	1990	G Farr

Midland Counties Amateur Stroke Play Championship

Year	Winner	Year	Winner
1981	P Baxter	1986	G Wolstenholme
1982	N Chesses	1987	C Suneson
1983	C Banks	1988	A Hare
1984	K Valentine	1989	J Cook
1985	M Hassall	1990	J Bickerton

Midlothian Ladies' Championship

Year	Winner	Year	Winner
1981	MF Allen	1986	J Marshall
1982	S Little	1987	M Stavert
1983	J Marshall	1988	M Stavert
1984	F de Vries	1989	E Bruce
1985	F de Vries	1990	E Jack

Mid-Wales Ladies' Championship

Year	Winner
1987	A Hubbard
1988	S James
1989	S Wilson
1990	P Morgan

Monmouthshire Ladies' Championship

Year	Winner	Year	Winner
1981	K Beckett	1986	H Buckley
1982	M Davis	1987	H Buckley
1983	K Beckett	1988	H Armstrong
1984	J Lapthorne	1989	B Chambers
1985	P Lord	1990	W Wood

Norfolk Amateur Championship

Year	Winner	Year	Winner
1981	M Few	1986	I Sperrin
1982	D Rains	1987	N Williamson
1983	M Sperrin	1988	N Williamson
1984	T Hurrell	1989	N Williamson
1985	C Lamb	1990	P Little

Norfolk Ladies' Championship

Year	Winner	Year	Winner
1981	A Davies	1986	N Clarke
1982	V Cooper	1987	A Davies
1983	M Davies	1988	L Elliott
1984	L Elliott	1989	T Keeley
1985	M Whybrow	1990	T Ireland

Norfolk Professional Championship

Year	Winner	Year	Winner
1981	S Beckham	1986	M Spooner
1982	R Page	1987	M Elsworthy
1983	R Foster	1988	M Few
1984	M Elsworthy	1989	M Few
1985	M Spooner	1990	M Few

Norfolk Open Championship

Year	Winner	Year	Winner
1981	J Parkhill	1986	M Spooner
1982	R Page	1987	M Elsworthy
1983	R Foster	1988	M Few
1984	M Elsworthy	1989	M Few
1985	T Hurrell	1990	A Brydon

Northamptonshire Amateur Championship

Year	Winner	Year	Winner
1981	M Haddon	1986	M Scott
1982	S McDonald	1987	D Jones
1983	D Warren	1988	D Ellson
1984	M Scott	1989	N Goodman
1985	M McNally	1990	A Print

Northamptonshire Ladies' Championship

Year	Winner	Year	Winner
1981	J Dicks	1986	P Le Vai
1982	P Coles	1987	J Kendrick
1983	J Dicks	1988	A Duck
1984	A Duck	1989	C Gibbs
1985	A Duck	1990	C Gibbs

Northern (England) Professional Championship

Year	Winner	Year	Winner
1981	B Evans	1986	D Stirling
1982	H Muscroft	1987	S Rolley
1983		1988	K Waters
1984		1989	S Bottomley
1985	A Murray	1990	J Morgan

Northern Counties (Scotland) Ladies' Championship

Year	Winner	Year	Winner
1981	S Ross	1986	F McKay
1982	G Stewart	1987	I McIntosh
1983	L Anderson	1988	I McIntosh
1984	J Buist	1989	E Fiskin
1985	A Shannon	1990	F McKay

North of Ireland Open Amateur Championship

Year	Winner	Year	Winner
1981	D Long	1986	D Ballantine
1982	D Long	1987	A Pierse
1983	T Hoey	1988	N Anderson
1984	G McGimpsey	1989	N Anderson
1985	I Elliott	1990	D Clarke

Northern Scottish Open Championship

Year	Winner	Year	Winner
1981	A Thomson	1986	R Weir
1982	T Minshall	1987	A Hunter
1983	D Cooper	1988	D Huish
1984	D Huish	1989	C Brooks
1985	B Barnes	1990	C Brooks

Northern Women's Championship

Year	Winner	Year	Winner
1981	A Brown	1986	L Fairclough
1982	C Swallow	1987	S Robinson
1983	C Hall	1988	K Tebbet
1984	C Hall	1989	L Fletcher
1985	C Hall	1990	L Fairclough

Northumberland Amateur Championship

Year	Winner	Year	Winner
1981	D George	1986	D Martin
1982	P Deeble	1987	K Fairbairn
1983	P Deeble	1988	J Metcalfe
1984	J Straker	1989	J Metcalfe
1985	D Faulder	1990	K Fairbairn

Northumberland Ladies' Championship

Year	Winner	Year	Winner
1981	E Elliot	1986	C Hall
1982	M Pickard	1987	C Breckon
1983	J Soulsby	1988	D Glenn
1984	C Hall	1989	D Glenn
1985	C Hall	1990	L Fletcher

Northern Division Ladies' Championship (Scotland)

Year	Winner	Year	Winner
1981	F McNab	1987	A Murray
1982	G Stewart		(née Shannon)
1983	G Stewart	1988	K Imrie
1984	P Wright	1989	S Wood
1985	A Shannon	1990	K Imrie
1986	C Middleton		

North of Scotland Open Amateur Stroke Play Championship

Year	Winner	Year	Winner
1981	N Grant	1986	S Cruickshank
1982	I Hutcheon	1987	S McIntosh
1983	D Kryzanowski	1988	K Hird
1984	J Macdonald	1989	G Hickman
1985	J Macdonald	1990	S McIntosh

Nottinghamshire Amateur Championship

Year	Winner	Year	Winner
1981	C Banks	1986	G Krause
1982	C Banks	1987	R Sallis
1983	T Estrop	1988	C Banks
1984	G Krause	1989	P Shaw
1985	M Scothern	1990	L White

Nottinghamshire Ladies' Championship

Year	Winner	Year	Winner
1981	K Horberry	1986	C Palmer
1982	K Horberry	1987	M Elswood
1983	M Elswood	1988	A Ferguson
1984	M Elswood	1989	A Peters
1985	K Horberry	1990	L Broughton

Nottinghamshire Open Championship

Year	Winner	Year	Winner
1981	C Banks (Am)	1986	B Waites
1982	B Waites	1987	C Hall
1983	C Banks (Am)	1988	C Banks (Am)
1984	CD Hall	1989	P Hinton
1985	C Jepson	1990	C Hall

One-Armed Championship

Year	Winner	Year	Winner
1981	A Robinson	1986	M O'Grady
1982	M O'Grady	1987	J Cann
1983	A Robinson	1988	Q Talbot
1984	A Robinson	1989	A Robinson
1985	A Robinson	1990	D Parsons

Oxfordshire Ladies' Championship

Year	Winner	Year	Winner
1981	N Sparks	1986	T Craik
1982	M Glennie	1987	T Craik
1983	M Glennie	1988	T Craik
1984	T Craik	1989	L King
1985	N Sparks	1990	N Sparks

Perth and Kinross Ladies' Championship

Year	Winner	Year	Winner
1981	J Aitken	1986	I Shannon
1982	J Aitken	1987	F Anderson
1983	F Anderson	1988	V Pringle
1984	E Aitken	1989	A Sharp
1985	A Guthrie	1990	S Mailer

Perth and Kinross Amateur Stroke Play Championship

Year	Winner	Year	Winner
1981	A Campbell	1986	C Bloice
1982	M Niven	1987	B Grieve
1983	E Lindsay	1988	E Lindsay
1984	G Lowson	1989	A Campbell
1985	G Lowson	1990	G Smith

Renfrewshire Amateur Championship

Year	Winner	Year	Winner
1981	D Howard	1986	I Riddell
1982	A Hunter	1987	D Howard
1983	G Thomson	1988	E Grey
1984	D Howard	1989	R Clark
1985	J McDonald	1990	R Clark

Renfrewshire County Ladies' Championship

Year	Winner	Year	Winner
1981	W Aitken	1986	S Lawson
1982	W Aitken	1987	S Lawson
1983	JL Hastings	1988	S Lawson
1984	Dr A Wilson	1989	D Jackson
1985	S Lawson	1990	D Jackson

Scottish Area Team Championship

Year	Winner	Year	Winner
1981	Stirlingshire	1986	Ayrshire
1982	Renfrewshire	1987	Lothians
1983	Lothians	1988	Lothians
1984	Glasgow	1989	Lanarkshire
1985	Lothians	1990	North East

Scottish Champion of Champions

Year	Winner	Year	Winner
1970	A Horne	1981	I Hutcheon
1971	D Black	1982	G Macgregor
1972	R Strachan	1983	D Carrick
1973	*Not held*	1984	S Stephen
1974	M Niven	1985	I Brotherston
1975	A Brodie	1986	I Hutcheon
1976	A Brodie	1987	G Shaw
1977	V Reid	1988	I Hutcheon
1978	D Greig	1989	J Milligan
1979	B Marchbank	1990	J Milligan
1980	I Hutcheon		

Scottish Foursomes Tournament–*Glasgow Evening Times* Trophy

Year	Winner	Year	Winner
1981	Duddingston	1986	Hamilton
1982	Haggs Castle	1987	Drumpellier
1983	Haggs Castle	1988	Irvine Ravenspark
1984	Royal Musselburgh	1989	Cochrane Leith
1985	East Renfrewshire	1990	Dunblane New

Scottish Ladies' County Championship

Year	Winner	Year	Winner
1981	Northern Counties	1986	Aberdeenshire
1982	Renfrewshire	1987	Renfrewshire
1983	Lanarkshire	1988	Lanarkshire
1984	Lanarkshire	1989	Lanarkshire
1985	East Lothian	1990	East Lothian

Scottish Ladies' Foursomes

Year	Winner	Year	Winner
1981	Baberton	1986	Blairgowrie
1982	Aberdour	1987	Baberton
1983	Hamilton	1988	Gullane
1984	Gullane	1989	Gullane
1985	*No Championship*	1990	Gullane

Shropshire and Herefordshire Amateur Championship

Year	Winner	Year	Winner
1981	J Wilson	1986	C Bufton
1982	N Kelly	1987	R Dixon
1983	P Baker	1988	S Thomas
1984	P Baker	1989	M Welch
1985	P Baker	1990	M Welch

Shropshire Ladies' Championship

Year	Winner	Year	Winner
1981	S Pidgeon	1986	S Pidgeon
1982	S Pidgeon	1987	S Pidgeon
1983	C Gauge	1988	A Jackson
1984	A Johnson	1989	C Gauge
1985	A Johnson	1990	J Marvell

Somerset Amateur Championship

Year	Winner	Year	Winner
1981	J Clifford	1986	C Edwards
1982	B Reeves	1987	G Hickman
1983	D Huxtable	1988	C Edwards
1984	C Edwards	1989	C Edwards
1985	P Hare	1990	C Edwards

Somerset Ladies' Championship

Year	Winner	Year	Winner
1981	B New	1986	K Nicholls
1982	B New	1987	K Nicholls
1983	B New	1988	C Whiting
1984	M Perriam	1989	K Nicholls
1985	K Nicholls	1990	K Nicholls

South-Eastern Ladies' Championship

Year	Winner	Year	Winner
1981	C Caldwell	1986	S Moorcroft
1982	J Nicholson	1987	N Way
1983	L Davies	1988	C Stirling
1984	L Davies	1989	A MacDonald
1985	J Thornhill	1990	A MacDonald

South Region PGA Championship

Formerly Southern (England) Professional Championship

Year	Winner	Year	Winner
1981	P Milton	1986	P Mitchell
1982	D McClelland	1987	*Not played*
1983	M McLean	1988	J Spence
1984	M McLean	1989	W Grant
1985	C Mason	1990	*Not played*

South of Ireland Open Amateur Championship

Year	Winner	Year	Winner
1981	P O'Rourke	1986	J McHenry
1982	M Maurice	1987	B Reddan
1983	AJC Morrow	1988	MA Gannon
1984	N Anderson	1989	S Keenan
1985	P O'Rourke	1990	D Clarke

South of Scotland Championship

Year	Winner	Year	Winner
1981	D James	1986	I Semple
1982	I Brotherston	1987	I Brotherston
1983	I Brotherston	1988	A Coltart
1984	D Ireland	1989	V Reid
1985	I Brotherston	1990	B Kerr

Southern Division Ladies' Championship (Scotland)

Year	Winner	Year	Winner
1981	A Gallagher	1986	M Wright
1982	A Hunter	1987	M Wright
1983	S McDonald	1988	S Simpson
1984	F Rennie	1989	F Rennie
1985	S Simpson	1990	F Rennie

South of Scotland Ladies' Championship

Year	Winner	Year	Winner
1981	A Barclay	1986	F Rennie
1982	D Hill	1987	S McDonald
1983	S McDonald	1988	M Wright
1984	M Wright	1989	M Wright
1985	F Rennie	1990	M Wright

South-Western Ladies' Championship

Year	Winner	Year	Winner
1981	L Moore	1986	K Nicholls
1982	L Moore	1987	J Fernley
1983	P Johnson	1988	V Thomas
1984	P Johnson	1989	C Hall
1985	S Shapcott	1990	V Thomas

South-Western Counties Amateur Championship

Year	Winner	Year	Winner
1981	P Newcombe	1986	C Phillips
1982	D Ray	1987	P Newcombe
1983	C Edwards	1988	J Langmead
1984	M Blaber	1989	K Jones
1985	C Phillips	1990	S Amor

Staffordshire Amateur Championship

Year	Winner	Year	Winner
1981	M Hassall	1986	M Scarrett
1982	A Stubbs	1987	M Hassall
1983	M Hassall	1988	P Sweetsur
1984	M Hassall	1989	C Poxon
1985	M Hassall	1990	P Sweetsur

Staffordshire Ladies' Championship

Year	Winner	Year	Winner
1981	J Brown	1986	A Booth
1982	J Brown	1987	D Christison
1983	D Christison	1988	D Boyd
1984	D Boyd	1989	R Bolas
1985	L Hackney	1990	R Bolas

Staffordshire Open Championship

Year	Winner	Year	Winner
1981	J Rhodes	1986	J Higgins
1982	A Stubbs (Am)	1987	J Annable
1983	C Poxon (Am)	1988	J Rhodes
1984	D Gilford	1989	M Passmore
1985	J Annable	1990	J Rhodes

Staffordshire and Shropshire Stroke Play Championship

Year	Winner	Year	Winner
1981	A Griffiths	1986	A Minshall
1982	A Griffiths	1987	J Higgins
1983	A Griffiths	1988	J Annable
1984	A Minshall	1989	J Higgins
1985	A Stubbs	1990	G Farr

Stirlingshire Amateur Championship

Year	Winner	Year	Winner
1981	A Liddle	1986	R Godfrey
1982	A Liddle	1987	S Lee
1983	C Gillies	1988	H Anderson
1984	G Barrie	1989	S Russell
1985	W Fleming	1990	K Goodwin

Stirling and Clackmannan County Ladies' Championship

Year	Winner	Year	Winner
1981	E Miskimmin	1986	S Michie
1982	*Null and void*	1987	J Harrison
1983	J Harrison	1988	J Harrison
1984	W McCallum	1989	J Abernethy
1985	S Michie	1990	A Rose

Suffolk Amateur Championship

Year	Winner	Year	Winner
1981	P Buckle	1986	M Clark
1982	C Lloyd	1987	C Coulton
1983	M Turner	1988	J Whitby
1984	S Goodman	1989	M Turner
1985	R Barrell	1990	J Booth

Suffolk Ladies' Championship

Year	Winner	Year	Winner
1981	D Marriott	1986	J Wade
1982	D Marriott	1987	W Day
1983	D Marriott	1988	S Dawson
1984	Dr J Gibson	1989	J Hall
1985	Dr J Gibson	1990	J Hall

Suffolk Open Championship

Year	Winner	Year	Winner
1981	P Buckle (Am)	1986	S Beckham
1982	R Mann	1987	M Turner
1983	S Whymark	1988	J Maddock
1984	J Marks	1989	M Elsworthy
1985	K Preston	1990	S Crosby (Am)

Suffolk Professional Championship

Year	Winner	Year	Winner
1981	M Elsworthy	1986	R Mann
1982	M Elsworthy	1987	S Beckham
1983	R Mann	1988	S Whymark
1984	R Mann	1989	S Whymark
1985	S Beckham	1990	R Mann

Surrey Amateur Championship

Year	Winner	Year	Winner
1981	S Keppler	1986	B White
1982	R Boxall	1987	J Paramor
1983	C Lashford	1988	A Carter
1984	P Talbot	1989	T Lloyd
1985	G Walmsley	1990	J Good

Surrey Ladies' Championship

Year	Winner	Year	Winner
1981	J Thornhill	1986	S Prosser
1982	J Thornhill	1987	W Wooldridge
1983	J Thornhill	1988	C Bailey
1984	J Thornhill	1989	J Thornhill
1985	J Nicolson	1990	W Wooldridge

Sussex Amateur Championship

Year	Winner	Year	Winner
1981	N Mitchell	1986	A Schofield
1982	D Sewell	1987	D Fay
1983	P Scarles	1988	D Alderson
1984	J Spence	1989	P Hurring
1985	M Jarvis	1990	D Arnold

Sussex Ladies' Championship

Year	Winner	Year	Winner
1981	C Larkin	1986	M Cornelius
1982	C Larkin	1987	K Mitchell
1983	M Gallagher	1988	M Cornelius
1984	C Rolph	1989	M Cornelius
1985	N Way	1990	M Cornelius

Sussex Open Championship

Year	Winner	Year	Winner
1981	J Pinsent (Am)	1986	C Giddins
1982	C Jones	1987	B Barnes
1983	C Giddins	1988	S Rolley
1984	J Dodds (Am)	1989	M Groombridge (Am)
1985	J Spence (Am)	1990	*Not played*

Ulster Professional Championship

Year	Winner	Year	Winner
1981	P Leonard	1986	W Todd
1982	P Leonard	1987	W Todd
1983	R Campbell	1988	J Heggarty
1984	D Carson	1989	D Feherty
1985	D Jones	1990	J Heggarty

Warwickshire Ladies' Championship

Year	Winner	Year	Winner
1981	J Evans	1986	T Hammond
1982	T Hammond	1987	M Button
1983	T Hammond	1988	S Morgan
1984	M Stevens	1989	S Morgan
1985	S Seville	1990	S Morgan

Warwickshire Amateur Championship

Year	Winner	Year	Winner
1981	B Wilkes	1986	P Downes
1982	A Roach	1987	W Bladon
1983	N Chesses	1988	A Allen
1984	P McEvoy	1989	J Cook
1985	C Suneson	1990	J Cook

Warwickshire Stroke Play Championship

Year	Winner
1984	A Bownes
1985	P Elson
1986	P Elson
1987	P Elson
1988	C Wicketts
1989	T Rouse
1990	N McEwan

Warwickshire Professional Championship

Year	Winner	Year	Winner
1981	PJ Weaver	1986	P Elson
1982	N Selwyn-Smith	1987	P Elson
1983	PJ Weaver	1988	C Wicketts
1984	A Bownes	1989	T Rouse
1985		1990	N McEwan

Warwickshire Open Championship

Year	Winner	Year	Winner
1981	T Allen (Am)	1986	P Weaver
1982	T Allen (Am) / P Downes (Am)	1987	P Weaver
1983	P Weaver	1988	T Allen (Am)
1984	P Broadhurst	1989	T Allen
1985	J Gould	1990	M Biddle (Am)

Welsh Team Championship

Year	Winner	Year	Winner
1981	Radyr	1986	Pontnewydd
1982	Newport	1987	Llandudno (Maesdu)
1983	Pontypridd	1988	Ashburnham
1984	Whitchurch	1989	Cardiff
1985	Whitchurch	1990	Whitchurch

Welsh Ladies' Team Championship

Year	Winner	Year	Winner
1981	Porthcawl	1986	Porthcawl
1982	St David's	1987	Whitchurch
1983	Llandudno (Maesdu)	1988	Pennard
1984	Monmouthshire	1989	Llandudno (Maesdu)
1985	Llandudno (Maesdu)	1990	Llandudno (Maesdu)

West of Ireland Open Amateur Championship

Year	Winner	Year	Winner
1981	D Branigan	1986	P Rayfus
1982	A Pierse	1987	N McGrane
1983	C Glasgow	1988	G McGimpsey
1984	G McGimpsey	1989	P McInerney
1985	J Feeney	1990	N Goulding

West of Scotland Close Amateur Championship

Year	Winner	Year	Winner
1981	D Howard	1986	S Savage
1982	G Shaw	1987	R Jenkins
1983	D Murdoch	1988	G King
1984	W Erskine	1989	G Lawrie
1985	S Savage	1990	B Smith

Western Division Ladies' Championship (Scotland)

Year	Winner	Year	Winner
1981	W Aitken	1986	S Lawson
1982	S Lawson	1987	A Hendry
1983	S Lawson	1988	S Lawson
1984	Dr A Wilson	1989	K Dallas
1985	I Robertson	1990	S Spiewak

West Region PGA Championship

Previously West of England Professional Championship

Year	Winner	Year	Winner
1981	G Brand Jr	1986	S Little
1982	G Smith	1987	A Sherborne
1983	G Marks	1988	M Thomas
1984	M Thomas	1989	G Laing
1985	D Sheppard	1990	P Price

Wigtownshire Championship

Year	Winner	Year	Winner
1981	J Young	1986	A Cunningham
1982	Dr R Douglas	1987	J Burns
1983	K Hardie	1988	K Hardie
1984	A Burns	1989	D Taylor
1985	M Gibson	1990	R Burns

Wiltshire Amateur Championship

Year	Winner	Year	Winner
1981	J Fleming	1986	G Clough
1982	B McCallum	1987	RE Searle
1983	D Kingsman	1988	G Clough
1984	N Garfoot	1989	A Burch
1985	S Amor	1990	N Williams

Wiltshire Ladies' Championship

Year	Winner	Year	Winner
1981	C Waite	1986	S Marks
1982	F Dawson	1987	J Lawrence
1983	C Waite	1988	S Sutton
1984	V Morgan	1989	J Lawrence
1985	C Waite	1990	M Johnston

Wiltshire Professional Championship

Now known as the "Hills" Wiltshire Pro Champ

Year	Winner	Year	Winner
1981	G Smith	1986	B Sandry
1982	R Emery	1987	G Laing
1983	I Bolt	1988	R Emery
1984	G Laing	1989	G Emerson
1985	G Laing	1990	G Clough

Worcestershire Amateur Championship

Year	Winner	Year	Winner
1981	M Reynard	1986	D Eddiford
1982	D Eddiford	1987	D Prosser
1983	T Shingler	1988	D Prosser
1984	T Martin	1989	S Braithwaite
1985	S Pimley	1990	D Eddiford

Worcestershire Stroke Play Championship

Year	Winner
1984	G Mercer
1985	K Hayward
1986	D Dunk
1987	K Hayward
1988	C Hancock
1989	K Hayward
1990	K Hayward

Worcestershire Ladies' Championship

Year	Winner	Year	Winner
1981	J Blaymire	1986	K Cheetham
1982	J Blaymire	1987	L Waring
1983	S Nicklin	1988	J Blaymire
1984	S Nicklin	1989	L Waring
1985	L Waring	1990	J Deeley

Worcestershire Open Championship

Year	Winner	Year	Winner
1981	W Firkins	1986	W Painter (Am)
1982	M Reynard (Am)	1987	K Hayward
1983	A Hill	1988	D Eddiford
1984	K Hayward	1989	K Hayward
1985	D Eddiford	1990	J Bickerton

Worcestershire Professional Championship

Year	Winner	Year	Winner
1981	R Livingston	1986	D Dunk
1982	W Firkins	1987	G Mercer
1983	K Hayward	1988	C Hancock
1984	K Hayward	1989	K Hayward
1985	K Hayward	1990	K Hayward

Yorkshire Amateur Championship

Year	Winner	Year	Winner
1981	M Kelley	1986	A Gelsthorpe
1982	S East	1987	R Roper
1983	J Plaxton	1988	S Field
1984	J Whiteley	1989	G Harland
1985	S Field	1990	P Wood

Yorkshire Amateur Stroke Play Championship

Year	Winner
1986	P Hall
1987	{ P Hall / RM Roper } tied
1988	C Rawson
1989	S East
1990	L Walker

Yorkshire Ladies' Championship

Year	Winner	Year	Winner
1981	P Grice	1986	P Smillie
1982	P Grice	1987	J Copley
1983	P Grice	1988	J Furby
1984	A Nicholas	1989	K Firth
1985	A Farmery	1990	N Buxton

Yorkshire Professional Championship

Year	Winner	Year	Winner
1981	G Townhill	1986	M Ingham
1982	M Mackenzie	1987	D Stirling
1983	P Cowen	1988	M Higginbottom
1984	D Hutchinson	1989	D Stirling
1985	B Jagger	1990	D Stirling

THE
ROYAL &
ANCIENT

BOOK OF

GOLF
RECORDS

Edited by Laurence Viney

In 600 pages this is the exhaustive record of all Amateur and Professional golf championships played at National, Regional and County level in the UK and Ireland and at National level in Europe.

*

In addition the winners of all the US majors and the US Amateur and Ladies Open and Amateur Championships are recorded.

*

The winners of the Australian, Canadian, New Zealand and South African Open and Amateur Championships and the Japanese Open are included.

*

This will be an invaluable addition to all serious golf libraries.

*

Available from all good bookshops, price £25.

*

In case of difficulties please send a cheque for £27 (including post and packing) payable to **Macmillan Press Ltd** to Section 12, Stockton House, 1 Melbourne Place, London WC2B 4LF.

Part III
Who's Who in Golf

British Isles Players

Explanations of abbreviations used

Cls	Club membership
PRO	Professional
AM	Amateur
Maj	The Open, US Open, USPGA, US Masters (men) Ladies British Open, US Women's Open, USLPGA (ladies)
Chp	Amateur Championship or Ladies British Open Amateur (or, within text, any championship)
Nat	The player's national championship
Trn	Tournament(s)
Oth	Other national championship or tournament
Reg	Regional tournaments
Int	International team appearances
Eur	European Tour or general European tournament(s)
US	Tournament(s) in United States or Canada
RoW	Tournament(s) in the rest of the world
Sen	Senior
Jun	Junior
Mis	Miscellaneous information
r/u	runner up
s/f	semi-finalist
tied	A lost play-off after first place tie
Eur(L) T Ch	European (Ladies) Amateur Team Championship

Captaincy is indicated by the year printed in **bold** type; years in bold type within brackets indicate non-playing captain.

Aitken, Wilma
See Leburn

Alliss, Peter
Born Berlin on 28th February, 1931. Turned Professional 1946

PRO
Eur   Spanish Open 1956-58. Italian Open, Portuguese Open 1958.
Trn   Daks 1954; Dunlop 1955; PGA Close 1957; Dunlop 1959; Sprite 1960 (shared). PGA Close 1962; Daks 1963 (shared); Swallow-Penfold, Esso Golden 1964; PGA Close, Jeyes 1965; Martini (shared), Rediffusion 1966; Agfa-Gevaert 1967; Piccadilly 1969; Sunningdale Foursomes 1958-61; Wentworth Pro-Am Foursomes 1959
Oth   British Assistants 1952
RoW   Brazilian Open 1961
Reg   West of England Open Professional 1956-58-62-66
Int   Ryder Cup 1953-57-59-61-63-65-67-69; UK v Europe 1954-55-56; England in World Cup 1954-55-57-58-59-61-62-64-66-67; Home International **1967**

Mis   Vardon Trophy 1964-66; PGA Captain 1962-87; Author, TV commentator
AM
Jun Int England Boys 1946

Anderson, Fiona
Born Perth on 24th August, 1954
Cls   Blairgowrie
Nat   Scottish Ladies Amateur 1987. r/u 1980-83-88
Reg   North of Scotland Ladies 1977. Scottish Universities Champion 1975
Int   Vagliano Trophy 1987. (Scotland) Home Int 1977-79-80-81-83-84-86-87-88-89-90; (Eur L T Ch) 1979-83-87

Anderson, Jessie
See Valentine

Anstey, Veronica
See Beharrell

Armitage, Susan
See Langridge

Attenborough, Michael F
Born Britford, nr Salisbury in October, 1939

Cls	Chislehurst, Royal St George's, Royal & Ancient
Oth	Scandinavian Amateur 1965
Trn	Hampshire Hog 1960. President's Putter 1962-66. County Champion of Champions 1964. Duncan Putter 1966. Prince of Wales Challenge Cup 1969
Reg	Kent Amateur 1963-64-65
Int	Walker Cup 1967. GB v Europe 1966-68. England (Home Int) 1964-66-67-68; (Eur T Ch) 1967
Mis	Captain of Royal & Ancient 1989/90

Bailey, Diane
[Frearson], (*née* Robb)
Born Wolverhampton on 31st August, 1943

Cls	Enville (Hon), Reigate Heath, Betchworth Park
Chp	British Ladies Amateur r/u 1961
Trn	Worplesdon Mixed Foursomes 1971. Avia Foursomes 1972
Reg	Staffordshire Ladies 1961. Lincolnshire Ladies 1966-67. Midland Ladies 1966
Int	Curtis Cup 1962-72-(**84**)-(**86**)-(**88**). Vagliano Trophy 1961-(**83**)-(**85**). Espirito Santo 1968. England (Home Int) 1961-62-71. Commonwealth Team Ch (**1983**).
Mis	Surrey Ladies County Captain 1981-2
Jun	British Girls 1961. Scottish Girls Open Stroke Play 1959-61
Int	England Girls 1957-61

Baker, Peter
Born 7th October, 1967. Turned Professional 1986

PRO	
Eur	Benson & Hedges International 1988
Oth	UAP U25 European Open 1990
Mis	Rookie of the Year 1987
AM	
Nat	English Open Amateur Stroke Play 1985 (shared)
Reg	Shropshire & Herefordshire Amateur 1983-84-85
Int	Walker Cup 1985; GBI v Europe 1986; England (Home Int) 1985
Jun	Carris Trophy 1983-85

Bannerman, Harry
Born Aberdeen on 5th March, 1942. Turned Professional 1965

PRO	
Oth	Scottish Professional 1967-72. Northern Scottish Open 1967-69-72. East of Scotland PGA Match Play 1969. Scottish Coca Cola 1976
Int	Ryder Cup 1971. Scotland in World Cup 1967-72; in Double Diamond 1972-74
Mis	Frank Moran Trophy 1972
AM	
Reg	North of Scotland Stroke Play 1962; North-East Scotland Stroke Play 1963-64-65
Jun Int	Scottish Boys 1959

Barber, Sally (*née* Bonallack)
Born Chigwell, Essex on 9th April, 1938. Turned Professional 1979. Reinstated Amateur 1982

AM	
Cls	Thorpe Hall, Thorndon Park, Hunstanton (Hon), Killarney (Hon)
Nat	English Ladies Amateur 1968; r/u 1970-71
Oth	German Ladies 1958
Trn	Astor Salver 1972; Avia Foursomes 1976

Reg	Essex Ladies 1958-59-60-61-62-63-66-67-70-71; London Foursomes 1984
Int	Curtis Cup 1962; Vagliano Trophy 1961-69; England (Home Int) 1960-61-62-63-68-70-72-**77**-(**78**) (Eur L T Ch) 1969-71

Barnes, Brian
Born Addington, Surrey on 3rd June, 1945. Turned Professional 1964

PRO	
Eur	Agfacolor 1969; Martini International 1972; Dutch Open 1974; French Open 1975; Sun Alliance PGA Match Play 1976; Spanish Open, Greater Manchester Open 1978; Italian Open, Portuguese Open 1979; Tournament Players Chp 1981
Oth	Scottish Professional 1981-82; Coca Cola Young Professionals 1969; East of Scotland Professional 1975; Northern Scottish Open 1978; PGA Club Professional Chp 1990
RoW	Flame Lily (Rhodesia) 1967; Australian Masters 1970; Zambian Open 1979-81; Kenya Open 1981
Int	Ryder Cup 1969-71-73-75-77-79; Hennessy–Cognac Cup 1974-76-78-80; v South Africa; Scotland in World Cup 1974-75-76-77; in Double Diamond 1972-73-74-75-76-77; in PGA Cup 1990
AM	
Reg	Somerset Amateur 1964; South Western Counties Amateur 1964
Jun	British Youths 1964
Int	English Youths 1964

Bayman, Linda (*née* Denison-Pender)
Born 10th June, 1948

Nat	English Ladies Amateur 1983; Ladies British Amateur Stroke Play 1987
Trn	Avia Foursomes 1969-71-73-79-80; Worplesdon Mixed Foursomes 1980-84; Astor Salver 1983-84; Critchley Salver 1984
Reg	Kent Ladies 1968-72-73-78
Int	Curtis Cup 1988; Vagliano Trophy 1971-73-85-87; Espirito Santo 1988; England (Home Int) 1971-72-73-83-84-85-87-88; Eur L T Ch 1983-85-87
Jun	Kent Girls 1966
Mis	Avia Woman Golfer of the Year 1987; Doris Chambers Trophy 1987-88; Angus Trophy 1987

Beck, Mrs JB (*née* Pim)
Born Cantibeely, Co Dublin on 1st July, 1901

Cls	Royal Portrush, The Berkshire, Prince's
Nat	Irish Ladies 1938, r/u 1949
Oth	Ladies Veteran 1952-55-56-59
Int	Curtis Cup (**1954**); LGU team to South Africa **1951**. Ireland (Home Int) 1926 to 1950-56
Mis	Irish hockey internationalist 1920

Behan, Lillian
Born Co Kildare on 12th January 1965. Turned Professional 1986

AM	
Chp	Ladies British Open Amateur 1985
Trn	The Curragh Scratch Cup 1986
Int	Curtis Cup 1986; Vagliano Trophy 1985; Ireland (Home Int) 1984-85-86; (Eur L T Ch) 1985

Beharrell, John Charles
Born Solihull, Warwickshire on 2nd May, 1938

Cls	Royal & Ancient, Edgbaston, Aldeburgh. Hon member of Little Aston, Blackwell, Handsworth
Chp	Amateur Champion 1956

Trn   Antlers Royal Mid-Surrey 1960.
Reg   Central England Mixed Foursomes 1956-57-75
Int   GB v Europe 1956; v Professionals 1956. England
      (Home Int) 1956
Jun Int English Boy 1955

Beharrell, Veronica (*née* Anstey)
Born Birmingham on 14th January, 1935

Cls   Edgbaston (Hon), Little Aston
Oth   Australian Ladies, New Zealand Ladies 1955; Victoria
      Ladies Open 1955
Reg   Warwickshire Ladies 1955-56-57-58-60-71-72-75;
      Central England Mixed Foursomes 1957-75
Int   Curtis Cup 1956. England (Home Int) 1955-56-58-
      (61)
Jun Int English Girls 1953

Bembridge, Maurice
*Born Worksop on 21st February, 1945. Turned
Professional 1960*

PRO
Maj   Leading British player in Open 1968 (5th)
Eur   PGA Match Play, Sumrie 1969; Dunlop Masters 1971;
      Martini 1973; Piccadilly Medal, Viyella PGA, Double
      Diamond Individual 1974; German Open 1975;
      Benson and Hedges International 1979
RoW   Kenya Open 1968-69-70; Caltex (New Zealand) 1970;
      Lusaka Open 1972
Oth   British Assistants 1967
Int   Ryder Cup 1969-71-73-75; GB v South Africa 1976;
      England in Double Diamond 1973-74-75; in World
      Cup 1974-75
Mis   His 63 in the qualifying round for the 1967 Open
      equals the lowest recorded; second in Order of Merit
      1973; scored 64 in last round US Masters 1974
      equalling record; his inward half of 30 also equalled
      the record

Benka, Peter
Born London on 18th September, 1946

Cls   Addington, West Sussex
Nat   Scottish Open Amateur Stroke Play r/u 1969
Oth   Dutch Amateur 1972
Trn   County Champion of Champions 1967; Sunningdale
      Foursomes 1969; St George's Challenge Cup 1969.
      Mullingar Trophy 1970; St George's Hill Trophy 1971-
      75.
Reg   Surrey Amateur 1967-68
Int   Walker Cup 1969; GBI v Europe 1970; England (Home
      Int) 1967-68-69-70; (Eur T Ch) 1969
Jun   British Youths 1967-68.
Int   Boys 1964; Youths 1966-67-68

Bennett, Stephen
*Born Cleethorpes on 23rd April, 1959. Turned
Professional 1979*

PRO
Eur   Tunisian Open 1985
RoW   Zimbabwe Open 1986
Reg   Lincolnshire Open 1979
AM
Reg   Lincolnshire Amateur 1977-78

Bentley, Arnold Lewis
Born Southport on 11th June, 1911

Cls   Royal & Ancient, Hesketh (Hon), Royal Birkdale
Nat   English Amateur 1939

Int   England (Home Int) 1936-37; v France 1937-39
Mis   Played for British Seniors 1969
Jun Int Boys 1928

Bentley, Harry Geoffrey
Born Manchester on 13th October, 1907

Cls   Royal & Ancient, Hesketh (Hon), Le Touquet
Nat   English Amateur 1936, r/u 1954; Irish Open Amateur
      1934
Oth   French Amateur 1931-32; German Amateur 1933-37-
      38-39; Italian Amateur 1954
Trn   St George's Challenge Cup 1932; Prince of Wales
      Cup 1935
Reg   Lancashire Amateur 1931-32-39
Int   Walker Cup 1934-36-38; GBI v Professionals 1930-31-
      32-34-35; England (Home Int) 1931 to 38; 47; v France
      1934-36-37-38-39-**54**
Mis   Chairman, Walker Cup selectors 1953; British Seniors
      Captain 1967; Leading Amateur in French, Belgian,
      German, Czechoslovakian Opens 1935

Bisgood, Jeanne, CBE
Born Richmond, Surrey on 11th August, 1923

Cls   Parkstone (Hon)
Nat   English Ladies 1951-53-57
Oth   Swedish Ladies 1952; Italian Ladies, German Ladies
      1953; Portuguese Ladies 1954; Norwegian Ladies
      1955.
Trn   Astor Salver 1951-52-53; Roehampton Gold Cup
      1951-52-53. Daily Graphic Cup 1945-51
Reg   South Eastern Ladies 1950-52; Surrey Ladies 1951-
      53-69
Int   Curtis Cup 1950-52-54-(**70**); England (Home Int)
      1949-50-51-52-53-54-56-58

Bloice, Cecil
Born Aberfeldy on 30th July, 1954

Reg   Perth & Kinross Amateur Stroke Play 1986
Int   Walker Cup 1985; Scotland (Home Int) 1985-86

Bolton, Zara (*née* Davies)
Born London on 16th March, 1914

Cls   Hon Member of Royal Portrush, Bishop's Stortford,
      Maccauvlei, County Down, Castlerock, Ballycastle
Nat   English Ladies r/u 1948
Reg   Ulster Scratch Cup 1947-48-49-50-56-60; Herts
      Ladies 1935; Kent Ladies 1948
Int   Curtis Cup 1948-(**56**)-(**66**)-(**68**); GBI v France 1948;
      GB Commonwealth Team (**1967**); LGU team to
      South Africa 1951; England (Home Int) 1939-49-50-
      51-**55**-56

Bonallack, Michael Francis, OBE
Born Chigwell on 31st December, 1934

Cls   Thorpe Hall, Pine Valley, Elie.
Maj   Leading Amateur in Open 1968-71
Chp   Amateur Champion 1961-65-68-69-70; s/f 1958-72-77
Nat   English Amateur 1962-63-65-67-68; r/u 1959; English
      Open Amateur Stroke Play 1964-68-69 (tied)-71; r/u
      1959-66-67
Trn   Berkshire Trophy 1957-61-65-68-70-71 (shared);
      Hampshire Hog 1957-79; Worplesdon Mixed
      Foursomes 1958; Sunningdale Foursomes 1959; Golf
      Illustrated Gold Vase 1961 (shared)-67 (shared)-68-69
      (shared)-71-75; Scrutton Jug 1961-64-66-68-70-71;
      Lytham Trophy 1965 (shared)-72; Antlers Royal Mid-
      Surrey 1964; St George's Challenge Cup 1965-68-81;
      Prince of Wales Challenge Cup 1967

Reg Essex Amateur 1954-57-59-60-61-63-64-68-69-70-72;
Essex Open 1969; East Anglian Open 1973
Int Walker Cup 1957-59-61-63-65-67-**69-71**-73;
GB Commonwealth Team 1959-63-**67-71**-**(75)**;
Eisenhower Trophy 1960-62-64-66-**68** (individual
winner, shared)-**70-72**; v Professionals 1957-58-59-60;
v Europe 1958-60-62-64-66-68-70-72. England
(Home Int) 1957 to 72-74 (**1962** to **67**); (Eur T Ch)
1959-61-63-65-67-69-71
Jun British Boys 1952
Mis AGW Trophy 1968; Bobby Jones Award 1972; PGA
Chairman 1976; Chairman Golf Foundation 1977;
President English Golf Union 1982. Best equal
individual score Eisenhower Trophy 1968. Chairman
Royal & Ancient Selection Committee 1975 to 1979;
Secretary to Royal & Ancient since 1983

Bonallack, Angela (née Ward)
Born Birchington on 7th April, 1937

Cls Prince's, Thorpe Hall, St Rule
Chp Ladies British Open Amateur r/u 1962-74
Nat English Ladies 1958-63, r/u 1960-62-72. British Ladies
r/u 1962-74
Oth Swedish Ladies, German Ladies 1955; Scandinavian
Ladies 1956; Portuguese Ladies 1957
Trn Astor Salver 1957-58-60-61-66; Worplesdon Mixed
Foursomes 1958; Kayser-Bondor Foursomes 1958
(shared); Astor Prince's 1968; Avia Foursomes 1976;
Roehampton Gold Cup 1980.
Reg Essex Ladies 1968-69-73-74-76-77-78-82; South East
Ladies 1957-65; Kent Ladies' 1955-56-58
Int Curtis Cup 1956-58-60-62-64-66. Vagliano Trophy
1959-61-63. England (Home Int) 1956 to 1964; 1966-72
Jun British Girls 1955
Mis Leading amateur Colgate European Ladies' Open
1975-76

Bousfield, Kenneth
*Born Marston Moor on 2nd October, 1919. Turned
Professional 1938*

Eur German Open 1955-59. Swiss Open, Belgian Open
1958; Portuguese Open 1960-61
Trn News Chronicle 1951; PGA Match Play 1955. PGA
Close 1955; Yorkshire Evening News 1956 (shared);
Dunlop 1957. Sprite 1959. Irish Hospitals 1960
(shared); Swallow-Penfold 1961
Oth Gleneagles Pro-Am 1964.
Reg Southern England Professional 1951-57-74. Pringle
Seniors 1972
Int Ryder Cup 1949-51-55-57-59-61; England in World
Cup 1956-57

Brand, Gordon J.
*Born Cambridge on 6th August, 1955. Turned
Professional 1976*

PRO
Maj Open r/u 1986
Eur Volvo Belgian Open 1989
RoW Ivory Coast Open 1981; Nigerian Open 1983;
Nigerian Open, Ivory Coast Open 1986; Zimbabwe
Open 1987; Ivory Coast Open 1988; Zambian Open
1990
Int Ryder Cup 1983; Nissan Cup 1986; England in World
Cup 1983; Dunhill Cup 1986-87 (winners)
Mis Tooting Bec Cup 1981-86; Braid-Taylor Memorial
Medal 1986; Headed Safari Tour Order of Merit 1983,
1986, 1987
AM
Int GBI v Europe 1976; England (Home Int) 1976

Brand, Gordon Jr
*Born Burntisland, Fife on 19th August, 1958. Turned
Professional 1981*

Cls Hon member of Woodhall Spa, Knowle
PRO
Eur Coral Classic, Bob Hope British Classic 1982; Celtic
International, Panasonic European Open 1984; KLM
Dutch Open, Scandinavian Enterprise Open 1987;
Benson & Hedges International 1989
RoW South Australian Open 1988
Oth PGA Qualifying School winner 1981
Int Ryder Cup 1987-89; Nissan Cup 1985; Kirin Cup
1988; Four Tours World Chp 1989; Scotland in World
Cup 1984-85-88-89-90; in Dunhill Cup 1985-86-87
(r/u)-88-89.
Mis Rookie of the Year 1982; AGW Trophy 1982
AM
Nat English Open Amateur Stroke Play 1978; Scottish
Open Amateur Stroke Play 1980
Oth Swedish Open Amateur Stroke Play 1979;
Portuguese Amateur 1981
Trn Golf Illustrated Gold Vase 1980; Sunningdale
Foursomes 1981
Reg Gloucestershire Amateur 1977; South-Western
Counties Amateur 1977-78
Int Walker Cup 1979; Eisenhower Trophy 1978-80;
GB v Europe 1978-80; Scotland (Home Int) 1978-80;
v England 1979; v Italy 1979; v France 1980-81;
v Belgium 1980; (Eur T Ch) 1979
Jun British Youths 1979; Scottish Youths 1980
Int Youths 1977-78-79

Branigan, Declan
Born Drogheda, Ireland on 22nd July, 1948

Cls Laytown and Bettystown
Nat Irish Amateur 1976-81
Reg West of Ireland Open Amateur 1976-81. East of
Ireland Open Amateur 1981
Int Ireland (Home Int) 1975-76-77-80-86; (Eur T Ch)
1977-81; v France, West Germany, Sweden 1976
Jun Irish Youths 1969

Briggs, Audrey (née Brown)
Born Kent on 31st January, 1945

Cls Royal Liverpool
Nat Welsh Ladies 1970-71-73-74, r/u 1978-79-80-81
Reg Sussex Ladies 1969. Cheshire Ladies 1971-73-76-80-
81. North of England Ladies 1976
Int Vagliano Trophy 1971-73. Wales (Home Int) 1969 to
84, (Eur L T Ch) 1969-71-73-75-77-79-81-83; Fiat
Trophy 1978-79-80

Broadhurst, Paul
*Born Staffordshire on 14th August, 1965. Turned
Professional 1988*

Maj Leading amateur in Open 1988
PRO
Eur Crédit Lyonnais Cannes Open 1989; Motorola Classic
1990
Mis Rookie of the Year 1989
AM
Trn Lytham Trophy 1988
Int (GBI) v Europe 1988. England (Home Int) 1986-87.

Brodie, Allan
Born Glasgow on 25th September, 1947

Cls	Balmore (Hon), Glasgow
Chp	Amateur s/f 1976
Nat	Scottish Amateur 1977; r/u 1973. Scottish Open Amateur Stroke Play r/u 1970
Trn	Tennant Cup 1972-80; Golf Illustrated Gold Vase 1976
Reg	West of Scotland Open Amateur 1974; Dunbartonshire Amateur Stroke Play 1975-76
Int	Walker Cup 1977-79; Eisenhower Trophy 1978; GBI v Europe 1974-76-78-80; Scotland (Home Int) 1970-72-73-74-75-76-77-78-80; (Eur T Ch) 1973-77-79; v Belgium, Spain 1977; v France 1978; v England, Italy 1979
Jun Int	Youths 1966-67

Brooks, Colin
Born Edinburgh on 14th July, 1965

PRO	
Eur	Barnham Broom Challenge 1990
Oth	Scottish Assistants 1989; British Assistants 1989; Scottish U25s 1989
AM	
Nat	Scottish Amateur 1986
Trn	Tennant Cup 1985. Gran Primo 1986.
Reg	West of Scotland Open Amateur Stroke Play 1986
Int	GBI v Europe 1986; Scotland (Home Int) 1984-85

Brown, Audrey
See Briggs

Brown, Julie
Born Stoke-on-Trent on 26th December, 1963.

PRO	
Eur	LBS Ladies German Open 1985
AM	
Chp	Ladies British Open Amateur r/u 1984
Reg	Staffordshire Ladies 1982-83
Int	Vilmorin Cup 1984; England (Home Int) 1984

Brown, Kenneth
Born Harpenden, Herts on 9th January, 1957. Turned Professional 1974

Eur	Carrolls Irish Open 1978; KLM Dutch Open 1983; Glasgow Classic 1984; Four Stars Pro-Celebrity 1985
US	Southern Open 1987
RoW	Kenya Open 1983
Oth	Hertfordshire Open 1975
Int	Ryder Cup 1977-79-83-85-87; Hennessy-Cognac Cup 1978-84; Kirin Cup 1987; Scotland in Double Diamond 1977; Scotland in World Cup 1977-78-79-83
Mis	Tooting Bec Cup 1980
Jun	Carris Trophy 1974
Int	Boys 1974

Buckley, James A
Born Ontario, Canada on 14th September, 1950. Turned Professional 1969. Reinstated Amateur 1976

Cls	Abergele, Killarney (Hon)
Nat	Welsh Amateur 1968. Welsh Amateur Stroke Play 1968-77, r/u 1978. Welsh Close 1969. Welsh Professional Championship 1971-72
Reg	Denbighshire Amateur 1967-68-76-78. North Wales Professional (as Amateur) 1976
Int	Walker Cup 1979. Wales (Home Int) 1967-68-69-76-77-78; (Eur T Ch) 1967-69; v Denmark 1976-77
Jun	Welsh Boys 1966-67-68

Burke, Ita
See Butler

Bussell, Alan Francis
Born Glasgow on 25th February, 1937

Cls	Whitecraigs (Hon), Coxmoor (Hon), Chevin
Chp	Amateur s/f 1957
Trn	Antlers Royal Mid-Surrey 1956. Golf Illustrated Gold Vase 1959
Reg	Nottinghamshire Amateur 1959-60-62-63-64-68-69. Nottinghamshire Open 1960-62. Nottinghamshire Match Play 1960-62. Renfrewshire Amateur 1955
Int	Walker Cup 1957. GB v Europe 1956-62; v Professionals 1956-57-59. Scotland (Home Int) 1956-57-58-61; v Scandinavia 1956-60
Jun	British Boys 1954. Boy International 1954. British Youths 1956. Youth International 1954-55-56

Butler, Ita (*née* Burke)
Born Nenagh, Co Tipperary

Cls	Hon member of Elm Park, Killarney, Woodbrook, Nenagh
Nat	Irish Ladies r/u 1972-78
Reg	Leinster Ladies three times. Munster and Midland Ladies twice
Int	Curtis Cup 1966. World Team Championship 1966. Vagliano Trophy 1965. Ireland (World Cup) 1964; (Home Int) 1962-63-64-65-66-68-71-72-73-76-77-78-79; (Eur T Ch) 1967; Fiat Trophy 1978

Butler, Peter J
Born Birmingham on 25th March, 1932. Turned Professional 1948

Tls	French Open 1968. Colombian Open 1975
Trn	Swallow-Penfold 1959. Yorkshire Evening News 1962; PGA Close 1963. Bowmaker 1963-67. Cox Moore 1964. PGA Match Play r/u 1964-75. Martini 1965. Piccadilly 1965-67. Penfold, Wills 1968. RTV 1969. Classic International 1971. Sumrie 1974 Evian International 1963. Grand Bahama Invitation Open 1971-72
Reg	Midland Open 1956-58-60-65-69. Midland Professional 1961.
Oth	Gleneagles Pro-Am 1963. Sunningdale Foursomes 1974
Int	Ryder Cup 1965-69-71-73. England in World Cup. 1969-70-73. England in Double Diamond 1971-72-76. GBI v Europe 1976
Mis	Equal lowest round in British events of 61. Second in Order of Merit 1968. PGA Captain 1972

Cadden, Suzanne
See McMahon

Caldwell, Ian
Born Streatham on 17th May, 1930

Cls	Royal & Ancient, Sunningdale, Walton Heath
Nat	English Amateur 1961
Trn	Prince of Wales Challenge Cup 1950-51-52. Boyd Quaich 1954.
Reg	Surrey Amateur 1961
Int	Walker Cup 1951-55. GB Commonwealth Team 1954. GBI v Europe 1955. England (Home Int) 1950-51-52-53-54-55-56-57-61
Jun	Carris Trophy 1947-48

Caldwell, Carole (*née* Redford)
Born Kingston, Surrey on 23rd April, 1949

Cls	Canterbury (Hon)
Trn	Newmark-Avia International 1973. Roehampton Gold Cup 1973-75-78; Hampshire Rose 1973, 1984; Avia Foursomes 1974; Critchley Salver 1974; Canadian Ladies Foursomes 1978; London Foursomes 1984
Oth	Portuguese Ladies 1980
Reg	South Eastern Ladies 1973-78. Kent Ladies 1970-75-77-86. Berkshire Ladies 1982
Int	Curtis Cup 1978-80; Vagliano Trophy 1973; England (Home Int) 1973-78-79-80
Mis	Playing captain of LGU U-23 team to tour Canada 1973. Lost at 27th hole in first round of American Ladies Amateur 1978

Carr, Joseph B
Born Dublin on 18th February, 1922

Cls	Sutton (Hon)
Maj	Leading Amateur in Open 1956-58
Chp	Amateur Champion 1953-58-60, r/u 1968 s/f 1952-54.
Nat	Irish Amateur 1954-57-63-64-65-67, r/u 1951-59. Irish Open Amateur 1946-50-54-56, r/u 1947-48-51; US Amateur s/f 1961
Trn	Golf Illustrated Gold Vase 1951. Gleneagles Saxone 1955. Berkshire Trophy 1959. Formby Hare 1962. Mullingar Trophy 1963. Antlers Royal Mid-Surrey 1970
Reg	South of Ireland Open Amateur 1948-66-69. East of Ireland Open Amateur 1941-43-45-46-48-56-57-58-60-61-64-69. West of Ireland Open Amateur 1946-47-48-51-53-54-56-58-60-61-62-66.
Int	Walker Cup 1947-49-51-53-55-57-59-61-**63**-(**65**)-67. GBI v Europe 1954-56-**64**-**66**-68. Eisenhower Trophy 1958-60-(**64**)-(**66**). Ireland (Home Int) 1947 to 1969 (Eur T Ch) 1965-67-69
Mis	AGW Trophy 1953. Bobby Jones Award 1961. Walter Hagen Award 1967

Carr, Roderick J
Born 27th October, 1950. Turned Professional 1971. Reinstated Amateur 1983

Trn	Antlers Royal Mid-Surrey 1970.
Reg	East of Ireland Open Amateur 1970. West of Ireland Open Amateur 1971. Turnberry Pro-Am 1970
Int	Walker Cup 1971. Ireland (Home Int) 1970-71; (Eur T Ch) 1971
Jun	Youth International 1970-71
Mis	Leading Amateur South African Open 1971

Carrick, David
Born Glasgow on 28th January, 1957

Nat	Scottish Amateur 1985. Scottish Open Amateur Stroke Play 1987
Trn	Scottish Champion of Champions 1983. Glasgow Amateur 1980-81
Reg	Dunbartonshire Amateur 1979-80-82-83
Int	Walker Cup 1983-87. GBI v Europe 1986. Scotland (Home Int) 1981 to 1989; v Italy 1988; v France 1989; (Eur T Ch) 1989; v West Germany 1987
Mis	Braid Panton Trophy 1987

Carslaw, Iain Alexander
Born Glasgow on 4th October, 1949

Cls	Williamwood (Hon), Walton Heath
Chp	Amateur s/f 1976
Nat	Scottish Amateur 1978
Trn	Tennant Cup 1978. Golf Illustrated Gold Vase 1982

Reg	Glasgow County Match Play 1977-78-79-80. Glasgow Amateur 1978
Int	Walker Cup 1979. GB v Europe 1978. Scotland (Home Int) 1976-77-78-80-81; (Eur T Ch) 1977-79; v Spain 1977; v Belgium 1978; v France 1978-83; in Fiat Trophy 1978; v Italy 1979; v England 1979; in Moroccan International 1979
Jun Int	Boys 1967. Youths 1971

Cassells, Craig
Turned Professional 1990

Chp	Amateur r/u 1989; s/f 1990
Reg	South-East of Scotland Amateur 1989
Int	Walker Cup 1989; England (Home Int) 1989; GBI v Europe 1990

Cater, John Robert
Born Edinburgh, 1919

Cls	Williamwood (Hon), Royal & Ancient, Elie
Chp	Amateur s/f 1952
Trn	Gleneagles Silver Tassie 1952
Reg	West of Scotland Amateur 1951-55. Glasgow County 1957
Int	Walker Cup 1955. Scotland (Home Int) 1952-53-54-55-56; v South Africa 1954; v Scandinavia 1956
Mis	Captain of Royal & Ancient 1986/87

Chadwick, Elizabeth
See Pook

Chapman, Roger
Born in Nakuru, Kenya on 1st May, 1959. Turned Professional 1981

PRO	
RoW	Zimbabwe Open 1988
Trn	Sunningdale Open Foursomes 1986
AM	
Nat	English Amateur 1979
Trn	Duncan Putter (shared), Lytham Trophy 1981; Sunningdale Open Foursomes 1979
Int	Walker Cup 1981; GBI v Europe 1980; England (Home Int) 1980-81; (Eur T Ch) 1981

Christmas, Martin J
Born 1939

Cls	West Sussex, Addington
Chp	Amateur s/f 1961-64-65
Nat	English Amateur r/u 1960. English Open Amateur Stroke Play r/u 1960
Trn	Gleneagles Pro-Am 1961. Wentworth Pro-Am Foursomes 1962
Ove	Belgian Open Amateur 1976
Reg	Sussex Amateur 1962
Int	Walker Cup 1961-63. Eisenhower Trophy 1962. GBI v Europe 1960-62-64. England (Home Int) 1960-61-62-63-64

Chugg, Pamela Mary (*née* Light)
Born Cardiff on 10th May, 1955. Turned Professional 1979. Reinstated Amateur 1986

Cls	Whitchurch (Cardiff)
Nat	Welsh Ladies 1978. Welsh Ladies Open Stroke Play 1976
Reg	South Western Ladies 1976-78
Int	Wales (Home Int) 1972-73-74-75-76-77-78-86-87-88; (Eur L T Ch) 1973-75-77-87
Jun	Welsh Girls 1970. Girl International 1969-70-71-72-73
Mis	Captain of Welsh Juniors 1988

Clark, Clive Anthony
Born Winchester, Hants on 27th June, 1945. Turned Professional 1965

Maj	Open (tied) 3rd 1967 (leading British player)
Tls	Danish Open 1966
Chp	Amateur r/u 1965.
Nat	English Amateur r/u 1965. English Open Amateur Stroke Play 1965 (tied)
Trn	Lytham Trophy 1965 (tied). Golf Illustrated Gold Vase, Scrutton Jug 1965. Bowmaker, Agfa-Gevaert 1968. John Player Trophy 1970. Sumrie 1974
Oth	Sunningdale Foursomes 1974-76
Int	Walker Cup 1965. GBI v Europe 1964. England (Home Int) 1964-65. Ryder Cup 1973
Mis	Lost play-off for 1972 French Open. Braid-Taylor Memorial Medal; TV commentator.

Clark, Gordon James
Born Newcastle-upon-Tyne on 15th April, 1933. Turned Professional 1974. Reinstated Amateur 1983

Chp	Amateur Champion 1964; s/f 1967
Nat	English Amateur r/u 1961. Scottish Open Amateur Stroke Play 1973 (tied)
Oth	Portuguese Amateur 1974
Reg	Northumberland Amateur 1956-71. Northumberland Amateur Stroke Play 1967-72
Int	Walker Cup 1965. GBI v Europe 1964-66. England (Home Int) 1961-64-65-66-67-68-71; (Eur T Ch) 1961-65
Jun	English Boy International 1950

Clark, Howard K
Born Leeds on 26th August, 1954. Turned Professional October 1973

PRO

Eur	Portuguese Open, Madrid Open 1978; Cepsa Madrid Open, Whyte & Mackay PGA Championship 1984; Jersey Open, Glasgow Open 1985; Cepsa Madrid Open, Peugeot Spanish Open 1986; Moroccan Open, PLM Open 1987; English Open 1988
Oth	U-25 TPD 1976
Int	Ryder Cup 1977-81-85-87-89; Nissan Cup 1985-86; Hennessy-Cognac Cup 1978-84; England in World Cup 1978-84-85 (individual winner)-87; Dunhill Cup 1985-86-87 (winners)-89-90(r/u)

AM

Chp	Amateur s/f 1973
Reg	Yorkshire Amateur 1973
Int	Walker Cup 1973; England (Home Int) 1973
Jun	British Boys 1971
Int	Boys 1969-71; Youths 1971-72-73

Claydon, Russell
Born on 19th November 1965. Turned Professional 1989

Maj	Leading amateur in Open 1989

AM

Nat	English Amateur 1988
RoW	Australian Masters r/u 1989
Trn	St George's Challenge Cup 1986; Berkshire Trophy 1988; St Andrews Links Trophy 1989; Sunningdale Open Foursomes 1989
Reg	Cambridge Amateur 1987-88
Oth	UAP U-25 European Open r/u 1988
Int	Walker Cup 1989; England (Home Int) 1988 (Eur T Ch) 1989
Mis	Rookie of the Year 1990

Coles, Neil, MBE
Born London on 26th September, 1934. Turned Professional 1950

Maj	Open 3rd 1961; r/u 1973; leading British player 1975 (7th)
Eur	German Open 1971. Spanish Open 1973
Trn	Ballantine 1961. Senior Service 1962. Daks 1963 (tied)-64-70-71 (tied). Martini 1963 (tied). Engadine Open 1963. Bowmaker 1964-70. PGA Match Play 1964-65-73, r/u 1966-72-78. Carrolls 1965-71. Pringle, Dunlop Masters 1966. Sumrie 1970-73. Shell BP Italy, Walworth Aloyco Italy 1970; Penfold 1971. Sunbeam 1972. Wills 1974. Penfold PGA 1976. Tournament Players' Championship 1977. Sanyo Open 1982
Oth	British Assistants 1956. Sunningdale Foursomes 1962-67-80. Wentworth Pro-Am Foursomes 1963-70. Southern England Professionals 1970
Int	Ryder Cup 1961-63-65-67-69-71-73-77. England in World Cup 1963-68. England in Double Diamond 1971-73-75-76-77. Hennessy-Cognac Cup 1974-76-78-80
Mis	Harry Vardon Trophy 1963-70. Second in Order of Merit 1987
Sen	Seniors British Open 1987. PGA Seniors Chp 1985-86-87-89

Collingham, Janet (*née* Melville)
Born Barrow-in-Furness on 16th March, 1958

Cls	Notts Ladies
Chp	Ladies British Open Amateur 1987
Nat	Ladies British Open Amateur Stroke Play 1978
Trn	Worplesdon Mixed Foursomes 1979. Northern Foursomes 1977-78. Mary McCalley Trophy 1980
Reg	Highland Open 1978. Midland Ladies 1986. Lancashire Champion 1983-86
Int	Vagliano Trophy 1979-87. England (Home Int) 1978-79-81-84-86-87 (Eur L T Ch) 1979. Girls International 1976-(81)
Mis	Varsity Athlete in golf at Florida International University 1980-81; Duncan Salver 1978

Connachan, Jane
Born Haddington, East Lothian on 25th February, 1964. Turned Professional 1984

Cls	Royal Musselburgh (Hon)

PRO

Eur	Jersey Open 1984; British Olivetti, 415/Vantage European Match Play 1985; British Olivetti 1987; Expedier Ladies European Open 1989

AM

Nat	Scottish Ladies 1982; Ladies British Open Amateur Stroke Play 1982, r/u 1981-83
Trn	Helen Holm Trophy 1983
Reg	East Lothian Ladies 1978-79
Int	Curtis Cup 1980-82; Espirito Santo 1980-82; Vagliano Trophy 1981-83; Commonwealth Trn 1983; Scotland (Home Int) 1979-80-81-82-83; (Eur L T Ch) 1983
Jun	Scottish Girls 1978-79-80; Scottish Girls Open Stroke Play 1978-80; British Girls 1980-81; Australian Girls 1982; Australian Junior Chp 1982
Int	Girls 1976-77-78-79-80; Eur Junior Ladies 1983
Mis	Avia Golfer of the Year 1982; Dinwiddy Trophy 1979; Duncan Salver 1982; Angus Trophy 1982; Taunton Trophy 1982

Cosh, Gordon B
Born Glasgow on 26th March, 1939

Cls	Troon, Royal Aberdeen, Bruntsfield Links. Hon member of Cowglen, Killarney
Nat	Scottish Amateur 1968, r/u 1965. Scottish Open Amateur Stroke Play r/u 1968
Trn	Newlands Trophy 1980
Reg	West of Scotland Amateur 1961-64-65-66. Glasgow County Match Play 1965-66. Glasgow Amateur 1969. Glasgow County Stroke Play 1972-74
Int	Walker Cup 1965. Eisenhower Trophy 1966-68. GB Commonwealth Team 1967. GBI v Europe 1966-68. Scotland (Home Int) 1964-65-66-67-68-69; (Eur T Ch) 1965-**69**
Jun Int	Youths 1959-60

Craddock, Tom
Born Malahide on 16th December, 1931

Cls	Malahide, Donabate, Sutton, The Island Malahide, Malone, Woodbrook, Mullingar, Carlow, Howth, Tara, Killarney
Nat	Irish Amateur 1959, r/u 1965. Irish Open Amateur 1958
Trn	Lytham Trophy 1969
Reg	East of Ireland Open Amateur 1959-65-66
Int	Walker Cup 1967-69. Ireland (Home Int) 1955-56-57-58-59-60-65-66-67-69; (Eur T Ch) 1967-71

Critchley, Bruce
Born 9th December, 1942

Cls	Sunningdale, Killarney (Hon)
Chp	Amateur s/f 1970
Trn	Worplesdon Mixed Foursomes 1961. Sunningdale Foursomes 1964. Hampshire Hog 1969. Antlers Royal Mid-Surrey 1974
Reg	Surrey Amateur 1969
Int	Walker Cup 1969. GBI v Europe 1970. England (Home Int) 1962-69-70; (Eur T Ch) 1969
Mis	TV commentator. Co-founder annual match at Deal between former Ryder Cup v Walker Cup Players

Critchley, Diana Lesley *(née* Fishwick)
Born London on 12th April, 1911

Cls	North Foreland, Bramley, Canterbury, Sunningdale, Sunningdale Ladies
Chp	British Ladies 1930.
Nat	English Ladies 1932-49, r/u 1929
Oth	French Ladies 1932. German Ladies 1936-38. Belgian Ladies 1938. Dutch Ladies 1946. Florida (USA) West Coast 1933
Trn	Sunningdale Foursomes 1934
Reg	Kent Ladies 1934. Surrey Ladies 1936-46
Int	Curtis Cup 1932-34-(**50**). GBI v France 1931-32-33-34-(**48**); v Canada 1934-50. England (Home Int) 1930-31-32-33-35-36-47
Jun	British Girls 1927-28
Mis	Chairman of ELGA Selection Committee 1967-68-69-70. LGU International Selector 1970-71-72-73. Member LGU Team to tour South Africa 1933

Curry, David H
Born 6th July, 1963

Chp	Amateur Champion 1986
Trn	Selborne Salver 1984
Int	England (Home Int) 1984-86-87. v France 1988. (GBI) v Europe 1986-88. Walker Cup 1987

Dalgleish, Colin R
Born Glasgow on 24th September, 1960

Cls	Helensburgh (Hon), Millstone Mills (Hon)
Nat	Scottish Amateur 1981
Trn	Tennant Cup 1983-88
RoW	East of India Amateur 1981. Indian Amateur r/u 1981. Lake Macquarie International Stroke-Play Champion (Australia) 1983
Oth	Scottish Universities Champion 1983
Int	Walker Cup 1981. Scotland (Home Int) 1981-82-83; v France 1982; (Eur T Ch) 1981-83. GB v Europe 1982. Europe v South America 1982
Jun	International Junior Masters 1977. Belgian Junior Championship 1980. British Boys r/u 1977. British Youths r/u 1979-82. Boy International 1976-77-78. Youth International 1979-80-81-82

Darcy, Eamonn
Born Delgany on 7th August, 1952. Turned Professional 1969

Eur	Spanish Open 1983; Belgian Open 1987; Desert Classic 1990
Trn	Sumrie 1976-78. Greater Manchester Open 1977
RoW	Air New Zealand Open 1980. Cock o' the North Open 1981. Kenya Open 1982. Mufulira Open 1984. West Lakes Classic (Aus) 1981
Oth	Irish Dunlop 1976. Cacharel World Under-25 1976. Irish Match Play 1981
Int	Ryder Cup 1975-77-81-87. Ireland in Double Diamond 1975-76-77. Ireland in World Cup 1976-77-83-84-85-87. GBI v Europe 1976; v South Africa 1976. Hennessy-Cognac Cup 1976-84. Dunhill Cup 1987-88 (winners)
Mis	Second in Order of Merit 1976

Davies, John C
Born London on 14th February, 1948

Cls	Mid-Surrey, Sunningdale, Royal Cinque Ports, Killarney
Chp	Amateur r/u 1976.
Nat	English Amateur r/u 1971-76. English Open Amateur Stroke Play r/u 1977
Trn	Berkshire Trophy 1969-71 (tied). Royal St George's Challenge Cup 1972-73-74-75-76-77. Sunningdale Foursomes 1968-72. Antlers Royal Mid-Surrey 1969-75-77. Golf Illustrated Gold Vase 1973-77. Prince of Wales Cup 1975. Berkhamsted Trophy 1976-78-79
Oth	Second equal in South African Open Amateur Stroke Play 1974
Reg	Surrey Amateur 1971-72-77
Int	Walker Cup 1973-75-77-79. Eisenhower Trophy 1974-76 (winners). GBI v Europe 1972-74-76-78; England (Home Int) 1969-70-71-72-73-74-78; (Eur T Ch) 1973-75-77
Mis	Member of European Team to tour South Africa 1974

Davies, Karen L
Born 19th June, 1965. Turned Professional 1988

Oth	Florida State Tournament 1985. South-Eastern USA Championship 1985
Int	Curtis Cup 1986-88. Wales (Home Int) 1981-82-83 (Eur L U-22) 1981-82-83-84-85-86; (Eur L T Ch) 1987, Commonwealth Team 1987
Jun	Welsh Girls 1980-82

Davies, Laura
Born Coventry on 5th October, 1963. Turned Professional 1985

Maj	Ladies British Open 1986, r/u 1987. US Women's Open 1987
PRO	
Eur	Belgian Ladies Open 1985; McEwan's Lager Classic, Greater Manchester Tournament 1986; Italian Open 1987; Italian Open, Ford Ladies Classic, Biarritz Ladies Open 1988. Laing Charity Ladies Classic 1989
US	Tucson Open, Toledo Classic 1988; Lady Keystone Open 1989
Int	Solheim Cup 1990
Mis	Order of Merit leader 1985-86
AM	
Nat	Welsh Open Stroke Play 1984
Oth	English Intermediate 1983
Trn	London Foursomes 1981.
Reg	South-Eastern Champion 1983-84
Int	Curtis Cup 1984; Vilmorin Cup 1984; England (Home Int) 1983-84
Jun	Surrey Girls 1982

Davies, Pamela
See Large

Davies, Zara
See Bolton

Davis, Mark
Born 4th July, 1964. Turned Professional 1986

Nat	English Open Amateur Stroke Play 1984
Trn	Golf Illustrated Gold Vase 1985. Prince of Wales Cup 1983. Lagonda Trophy 1984
Reg	Essex Amateur 1983
Int	England (Home Int) 1984-85

Dawson, Peter
Born Doncaster on 9th May, 1950. Turned Professional 1970

PRO	
Trn	Double Diamond Individual 1975
Int	Ryder Cup 1977. England in World Cup 1977. England in Double Diamond 1977
AM	
Nat	English Amateur r/u 1969
Int	England (Home Int) 1969
Jun	Carris Trophy 1968
Int	Boys 1967; Youths 1969-70
Mis	Plays left-handed

De Bendern, Count John (John de Forest)
Born 1907

Cls	Royal & Ancient, Sunningdale, Addington, Lausanne
Chp	Amateur Champion 1932, r/u 1931
Oth	Austrian Amateur 1937. Czechoslovakian Amateur 1937
Reg	Surrey Amateur 1931-49
Int	Walker Cup 1932. England (Home Int) 1931

Deeble, Peter George
Born Alnwick on 27th February, 1954

Cls	Alnmouth, Alnwick, Hon member of Ponteland, Hexham, Rothbury, Washington, Tynedale
Nat	English Amateur 1976-80
Trn	Antlers Royal Mid-Surrey 1976. Lytham Trophy 1977. Berkhamsted Trophy 1975. County Champion of Champions 1982

Reg	Northumberland Amateur 1975-82-83. Northumberland Stroke Play 1973-75-77-78-79. Northumberland and Durham Open 1976
Int	Walker Cup 1977-81. GBI v Europe 1978. Europe v South America 1980. GB in Colombian International 1978. England (Home Int) 1975-76-77-78-80-81-83; (Eur T Ch) 1979-81; v Scotland 1979; v France 1982. England in Fiat Trophy 1980
Jun Int	Boys 1970-71. Youths 1973-75-76

Deighton, Dr FWG
Born Glasgow on 21st May, 1927

Cls	Royal & Ancient, Western Gailes, Elie, Glasgow, Hilton Park (Hon), North Hants
Nat	Scottish Amateur 1956-59
Trn	Edward Trophy 1954. Gleneagles Silver Tassie 1956. Tennant Cup 1958-60-64
Oth	Boyd Quaich 1947 (tied). Royal & Ancient Silver Cross 1953-60-63-70-73. Royal Medal 1956-59-61-63-66-73. Glennie Medal 1956-58-59-60-66-70-73
Reg	West of Scotland Amateur 1959. Dunbartonshire Amateur 1949-50-53-54. Glasgow Amateur 1951-55
Int	Walker Cup 1951-57. GB Commonwealth Team 1954-59. GBI v Professionals 1956-57. Scotland (Home Int) 1950-52-53-56-58-59-60; v South Africa 1954; v New Zealand 1954; v Scandinavia 1956
Mis	Member of British Touring Team to South Africa 1952

Dobson, Helen
Born 25th February, 1971. Turned Professional 1990

Cls	Seacroft
Chp	Ladies British Open Amateur 1989
Nat	Ladies British Open Amateur Stroke Play 1989
Oth	World Fourball (with Elaine Farquharson) 1989
Int	Curtis Cup 1990; Vagliano Trophy 1989; England (Home Int) 1987-88-89; (Eur L T Ch) 1989
Jun	British Girls 1987; English Girls 1988
Int	English Girls 1988

Dodd, Stephen
Born Cardiff, on 15th July, 1966. Turned Professional 1990

Cls	Brynhill
Chp	Amateur Champion 1989
Nat	Welsh Amateur 1989
Trn	Silver Dragon, WI Tucker Trophy 1987; Duncan Putter, Carad Trophy, Cardiff Feathers, Golden Lamp 1988
Int	Walker Cup 1989; Wales (Home Int) 1985-87-88-89, (Eur T Ch) 1987

Douglas, Kitrina
Born Bristol on 6th September, 1960. Turned Professional 1984

Maj	Ladies British Open 3rd 1990
PRO	
Eur	Ford Classic, Swedish Ladies Open, Rookie of the Year 1984; Mitsubishi Colt Cars, Jersey Open 1986; Hennessy-Cognac Ladies Cup 1987; St Moritz Ladies Classic, Godiva European Masters 1989
AM	
Chp	British Ladies 1982
Oth	Portuguese Champion 1983
Trn	Critchley Salver 1983
Reg	Gloucestershire Champion 1980-81-82-83-84
Int	Curtis Cup 1982. Vagliano Trophy 1983. England (Home Int) 1981-82. Eur L T Ch 1983
Jun	Scottish Girls Stroke-Play 1981

Dowling, Deborah
Born Wimbledon on 26th July, 1962. Turned Professional 1981

Reg	Surrey Champion 1980
Int	England (Home Int) 1981 (Eur L T Ch) 1981
Eur	Jersey Open, Woodhall Hills 1983. Portuguese Ladies Open 1985. Eastleigh Classic 1986. Laing Ladies Classic 1986. Bloor Homes Eastleigh Classic 1989

Downes, Paul
Born Coventry on 27th September, 1959

Cls	Coventry (Hon)
Nat	English Amateur 1978. English Amateur Stroke Play 1982
Trn	Berkshire Trophy 1980
Oth	Leading Amateur Malaysian Dunlop Masters 1977. Leading Amateur Singapore Open Championship 1978
Reg	Midland Open Amateur Stroke Play 1976-77-80. Warwickshire Match Play 1977-82. Warwickshire Open 1982
Int	England (Home Int) 1976-77-78-80-81-82; (Eur T Ch) 1977-79-81. GBI v Europe 1980
Jun Int	Boys 1974-75-76-77. Youths 1976-77-78-79-80-81

Drew , Norman Vico
Born Belfast on 25th May, 1932. Turned Professional 1958

PRO

Trn	Yorkshire Evening News, Irish Dunlop 1959
Oth	Irish Professional 1959; Ulster Professional 1966-72
Int	Ryder Cup 1959; Ireland in World Cup 1960-61

AM

Nat	Irish Open Amateur 1952-53
Reg	North of Ireland Open Amateur 1950-52; East of Ireland Open Amateur 1952
Int	Walker Cup 1953; Ireland (Home Int) 1952-53

Duncan, Colonel Anthony Arthur, OBE
Born Cardiff on 10th December, 1914

Cls	Royal & Ancient, Southerndown, Hindhead, Royal Porthcawl
Chp	Amateur r/u 1939.
Nat	Welsh Amateur 1938-48-52-54, r/u 1933
Trn	Worplesdon Mixed Foursomes 1946-47. Hampshire Hog 1959. President's Putter 1948-58
Int	Walker Cup 1953. Wales (Home Int) 1933-34-36-38-47-48-49-50-51-52-53-54-55-56-57-58-59
Mis	Chairman Walker Cup Selection Committee 1954-55. Won all six matches in 1956 Home Internationals. President Oxford and Cambridge Golfing Society 1979-83

Easingwood, Stephen
Born Edinburgh on 23rd June 1965

Cls	Dunbar
Nat	Scottish Amateur Stroke Play 1988
Trn	Edward Trophy 1987
Reg	Lothians Champion 1985, South-East District Champion 1987-88, Craigmillar Park Open 1986
Int	Scotland (Home Int) 1986-87-88; v France 1987; v Italy 1988-90
Jun	Scottish Boys v England 1982. Scottish Youths 1983-86
Mis	Braid Panton Trophy 1988

Eggo, Bobby
Born 5th July, 1961

Nat	English Amateur Stroke Play 1988
Trn	Hampshire Hog 1986. Golf Illustrated Gold Vase 1986
Reg	Channel Islands Amateur 1984
Int	Walker Cup 1987. England (Home Int) 1986-87-88; v France 1988. (GBI) v Europe 1988

Evans, Albert David
Born Newton, Brecon, South Wales on 28th August, 1911

Cls	Royal & Ancient, Royal Porthcawl. Hon member of Brecon, Ross-on-Wye, Hereford, Worcestershire, Builth Wells, Pennard, Monmouth, Killarney
Chp	Welsh Amateur 1949-61
Reg	Herefordshire Amateur 1938-46-49-51-53-54-55-59-60-61-62. Breconshire Amateur 1929-31-32-33-34-37
Int	Wales (Home Int) 1931-32-33-34-35-38-39-47-48-49-50-51-52-53-54-55-56-**60-61-62-63-64-65**; v Australia 1954
Mis	Walker Cup Selector 1964-75

Evans, Duncan
Born Crewe on 23rd January, 1959

Cls	Hon member of Leek, Conway, Holyhead, Royal Porthcawl, Westwood
Chp	Amateur 1980.
Nat	Welsh Amateur Stroke Play Championship 1981, r/u 1980
Reg	Staffordshire Amateur 1979. Aberconwy Trophy 1981
Int	GBI v Europe. Europe v South America 1980. Wales (Home Int) 1978-80; v Ireland 1979; in Fiat Trophy 1980. Walker Cup 1981; (Eur T Ch) 1981
Jun Int	Youths 1980

Evans, Hugh
Born Swansea on 19th May, 1957

Cls	Langland Bay
Nat	Welsh Amateur Stroke Play 1978
Trn	Duncan Putter 1979
Reg	Glamorgan County Champion 1978
Int	Wales (Home Int) 1976-77-78-79-80-81-84-85-87-88; (Eur T Ch) 1979-81
Mis	Glamorgan County 1974 to 82; **83**-84-**85**-86-87-88

Everard, Mrs D Mary
Born Sheffield on 8th October, 1942

Cls	Hallamshire (Hon), Woodhall Spa (Hon), Kilton Forest (Hon), Lindrick
Maj	Ladies British Open r/u 1977
Chp	Ladies British Open Amateur r/u 1967
Nat	Ladies British Open Amateur Stroke Play 1970-77, r/u 1971-73; English Ladies 1972, r/u 1964-77
Trn	Astor Salver 1967-68-78. Hovis Ladies 1967. Roehampton Gold Cup 1970. Sunningdale Foursomes 1973. Hoylake Mixed Foursomes 1965-67-71-76. Avia Foursomes 1978
Reg	North of England Ladies 1972. Yorkshire Ladies 1964-67-72-73-77
Int	Curtis Cup 1970-72-74-78. Vagliano Trophy 1967-69-71-73. GB Commonwealth Team 1971. World Team Championship 1968-**72**-78, England (Home Int) 1964-67-70-72-73-77-78; (Eur LT Ch) 1967-71-73-77
Mis	Member of British team to tour Australia 1973. Captain English team to tour Kenya 1973

Everett, Craig
Born Glasgow on 31st January, 1968

Cls	Cambuslang
Nat	Scottish Amateur 1990
Trn	Cameron Corbett Vase 1988; Leven Gold Medal 1988
Reg	East of Scotland Open Amateur 1988
Int	Scotland (Home Int) 1988-89-90; v Italy 1988-90; v France 1989; (Eur T Ch) 1989; Nixdorf Nations Cup 1989; v Sweden 1990
Jun	Irish Youths Open 1987; Scottish Boys Stroke Play r/u 1985
Int	Scottish Boys 1985; Scottish Youths 1987-88; British Boys 1985; British Youth 1988

Faldo, Nicholas Alexander, MBE
Born Welwyn Garden City on 18th July, 1957. Turned Professional 1976

PRO	
Maj	Open Championship 1987-90; 3rd 1988; US Open r/u 1988 (tied) 3rd 1990; US Masters 1989
Eur	Colgate PGA 1978; Sun Alliance PGA 1980; Sun Alliance 1981; Haig Whisky TPC 1982; French Open, Martini International, Lawrence Batley International, Car Care Plan International, Ebel Swiss Open European Masters 1983; Car Care Plan International 1984; Peugeot Spanish Open 1987; Peugeot French Open, Volvo Masters 1988; Volvo PGA, Dunhill British Masters, Peugeot French Open, Suntory World Match Play 1989
US	Heritage Classic 1984
RoW	ICL International 1979; Johnnie Walker Asian Classic 1990
Oth	Skol Lager 1977
Int	Ryder Cup 1977-79-81-83-85-87-89; Nissan Cup 1986; Kirin Cup 1987-88; Hennessy-Cognac Cup 1978-80-82-84; England in World Cup 1977; in Double Diamond 1977; in Dunhill Cup 1985-86-87 (winners)-88-90; Four Tours Chp 1990
Mis	Rookie of the Year 1977; Harry Vardon Trophy 1983; AGW Trophy 1983; Braid-Taylor Memorial Medal 1983-84-87-88-90; BBC Sports Personality of the Year 1989; USPGA Player of the Year 1990
AM	
Nat	English Amateur 1975
Trn	Berkshire Trophy, Scrutton Jug, County Champion of Champions 1975
Reg	Hertfordshire Amateur 1975
Oth	South African GU Special Stroke Chp 1975
Int	GB Commonwealth Trn 1975; England (Home Int) 1975
Jun	British Youths 1975
Int	Boys 1974; Youths 1975

Farquharson, Elaine
Born Aberdeen on 21st March, 1968

Cls	Deeside
Chp	Ladies British Open Amateur r/u 1989
Nat	Scottish Ladies 1990
Oth	World Fourball (with Helen Dobson) 1989
Trn	Helen Holm Trophy 1987
Reg	Aberdeenshire Ladies 1983-86-87
Int	Curtis Cup 1990; Vagliano Trophy 1989; Scotland (Home Int) 1987-88-89-90; (Eur L T Ch) 1989
Jun	British Girls r/u 1984-85; Scottish Girls 1985;
Int	Scottish Girls 1982-84-85; Eur Jun L T Ch 1986-88

Faulkner, Max
Born Bexhill, Sussex on 29th July, 1916. Turned Professional June 1933

Maj	Open Champion 1951
Eur	Spanish Open 1952-53-57. Portuguese Open 1968
Trn	Dunlop Southport 1946. Dunlop 1949-52. Penfold Foursomes 1949. Lotus 1949. Dunlop Masters 1951. PGA Match Play 1953. Irish Hospitals 1959
Reg	West of England Open Professional 1947. Southern England Professional 1964.
Oth	Sunningdale Open Foursomes 1964; Pringle Seniors 1968-70
Int	Ryder Cup 1947-49-51-53-57

Feherty, David
Born in Bangor, NI on 13th August, 1958. Turned Professional 1976

Eur	Italian Open, Bells Scottish Open 1986; BMW International Open 1989
RoW	ICL International 1984; Lexington PGA 1988
Int	Ireland; Dunhill Cup 1986-90 (winners); World Cup 1990; Four Tours World Chp 1990
Mis	Braid-Taylor Memorial Medal 1989

Ferguson, Marjory (née Fowler)
Born North Berwick on 15th May, 1937

Cls	North Berwick, Gullane, Killarney (Hon)
Nat	Scottish Ladies r/u 1966-71
Oth	Portuguese Ladies 1960
Reg	East of Scotland Ladies 1959-60-62-75. East Lothian Ladies 1957-58-59-60-61-62-63-64-66-67-69-74-81
Int	Curtis Cup 1966. Vagliano Trophy 1965. Scotland (Home Int) 1959-62-63-64-65-66-67-69-70; (Eur L T Ch) 1965-67-71

Le Feuvre, Carol
See Gibbs

Fiddian, Eric Westwood
Born Stourbridge on 28th March, 1910

Cls	Stourbridge, Handsworth, Lindrick
Chp	Amateur r/u 1932.
Nat	English Amateur 1932, r/u 1935. Irish Open Amateur r/u 1933
Reg	Worcestershire Amateur 1928-30-50. Midland Counties 1931
Int	Walker Cup 1932-34. England (Home Int) 1929-30-31-32-33-34-35
Jun	Boys 1927.
Int	English Boys 1926-27
Mis	Had two holes-in-one in the Final of 1933 Irish Open Amateur

Fishwick, Diana Lesley
See Critchley

Fletcher, Linzi
Born on 21st January, 1968

Cls	Alnmouth
Nat	English Ladies r/u 1990; English Womens Intermediate 1990
Trn	Critchley Salver 1989; Wentworth Scratch Trophy 1990
Int	Curtis Cup 1990; England (Home Int) 1989-90

Foster, Rodney
Born Shipley, Yorkshire on 13th October, 1941

Cls Royal & Ancient Hon member of Bradford, Halifax, Leeds, West Bowling, Ilkley, East Bierley
Chp Amateur s/f 1962-65
Nat English Amateur r/u 1964. English Open Amateur Stroke Play 1969 (tied)-70, r/u 1965
Trn Berkshire Trophy 1964. Lytham Trophy 1967-68. County Champion of Champions 1963 (tied)
Reg Yorkshire Amateur 1963-64-65-67-70
Int Walker Cup 1965-67-69-71-73-(**79**). GBI v Europe 1964-66-68-70-(**80**). Eisenhower Trophy 1964-70-(**80**). GB Commonwealth Team 1967-71. England (Home Int) 1963-64-66-67-68-69-70-71-72-(**76**)-(**77**)-(**78**); (Eur T Ch) 1963-65-67-69-71-73-(**77**)
Jun Int Boys 1959. Youths 1959

Fowler, Marjory
See Ferguson

Francis, Craig
Born London on 18th March, 1950

Cls Sunningdale, Lyford Cay, Geneva, Lausanne
Oth Luxembourg Amateur 1972-75-82. Swiss Amateur 1973-74-77. Swiss Amateur Stroke Play 1982. Belgian Amateur 1975. Italian Amateur 1982, r/u 1972-81. Dutch Amateur r/u 1976

Frearson, Diane
See Bailey

Furby, Joanne
Born 13th May, 1969. Turned Professional 1989

Cls Masham
Chp British Ladies 1988
Nat English Ladies 1987.
Reg Yorkshire Ladies 1988
Int England (Home Int) 1987-88; (Eur L T Ch) 1987

Gallacher, Bernard
Born Bathgate on 9th February, 1949. Turned Professional 1967

PRO
Eur Spanish Open 1977; French Open 1979
Trn Schweppes, Wills 1969; Martini International 1971; Carrolls International, Dunlop Masters 1974; Dunlop Masters 1975; Tournament Players Chp 1980; Greater Manchester Open 1981; Martini International; Jersey Open 1982; Jersey Open 1984
Oth Scottish Professional 1971-73-74-77; Coca-Cola Young Professionals 1973
RoW Zambia Eagle Open, Zambia Cock o' the North 1969; Mufulira Open 1970
Int Ryder Cup 1969-71-73-75-77-79-81-83-(**91**); Hennessy-Cognac Cup 1974-78-82-84; Scotland in World Cup 1969-71-74-82-83; in Double Diamond 1971-72-73-74-75-76-77; v South Africa 1976
Mis Rookie of the Year 1968; Harry Vardon Trophy 1969 (then youngest winner); Scottish Sportsman of the Year 1969; Frank Moran Trophy 1973

AM
Nat Scottish Open Amateur Stroke Play 1967
Int Scotland (Home Int) 1967
Jun Int Boys 1965-66

Gannon, Mark Andrew
Born Drogheda, Ireland on 15th July, 1952

Cls Co Louth (Hon)
Nat Irish Amateur 1977, r/u 1974-79
Trn Mullingar Trophy 1973

Reg South of Ireland Open Amateur 1973. West of Ireland Open Amateur 1974. East of Ireland Open Amateur 1978
Int GBI v Europe 1974-78. Ireland (Home Int) 1973-74-77-78-80; (Eur T Ch) 1979-81; v France, West Germany and Sweden 1978-80; in Fiat Trophy 1979
Jun Irish Boys 1968. Irish Youths 1971-72.
Int Youths 1971

Garner, Maureen (*née* Madill)
Born Coleraine, Co Derry on 1st February, 1958. Turned Professional 1986

Cls Hon member of Portstewart, Royal Portrush, Milltown, Co Down, Brancepeth Castle, Delamere Forest
Chp Ladies British Amateur 1979
Nat Ladies British Open Amateur Stroke Play 1980. Irish Foursomes 1980
Maj Avia Foursomes 1980-85.
Reg North-West Scratch Cup 1978. Ulster Ladies 1980
Int Curtis Cup 1980. Vagliano Trophy 1979-81-85. GB Commonwealth Team 1979. World Team Championship 1980. Ireland (Home Int) 1978-79-80-81-82-83; (Eur LT Ch) 1979-81-83
Jun Int Girls 1972-73-74-75-76

Garrett, Maureen (*née* Ruttle)
Born 22nd August, 1922

Oth French Ladies 1964
Int Curtis Cup **1960**. England (Home Int) **1960**. Vagliano Trophy **1961**
Mis LGU President 1982-85. Bobby Jones Award 1983

Garvey, Philomena K
Born Drogheda, Co Louth on 26th April, 1927. Turned Professional 1964, subsequently reinstated Amateur

Cls Co Down, Co Louth, Portrush, Milltown
Chp British Ladies 1957, r/u 1946-53-60-63.
Nat Irish Ladies 1946-47-48-50-51-53-54-55-57-58-59-60-62-63-70
Trn Worplesdon Mixed Foursomes 1955
Reg Munster Ladies 1951
Int Curtis Cup 1948-50-52-54-56-60. GBI v France 1949-51-53-55; v Belgium 1951-53. Vagliano Trophy 1959-63. Ireland (Home Int) 1947-48-49-50-51-52-53-54-55-56-59-60-61-62-63-69; v Australia 1950
Mis Quarter-finalist US Ladies 1950.

Gemmill, Alison
Born 13th September, 1958

Nat Scottish Ladies 1981-85
Trn Helen Holm Trophy 1988
Reg Ayrshire Champion 1980-81-82-83-84-86
Int Scotland (Home Int) 1981-82-84-85-86-87-88-89; (Eur L T Ch) 1981
Jun Scottish Girls Stroke Play 1979

Gibbs, Carol (*née* Le Feuvre)
Born Jersey on 18th October, 1951

Cls Jersey, Lee-on-the-Solent
Nat English Ladies r/u 1973
Oth Dutch Ladies 1972
Trn Avia Foursomes 1974
Reg Jersey Ladies 1966-67-68. Hampshire Ladies 1970-71-72-73-74-76. South-Eastern Ladies 1974
Int Curtis Cup 1974. Vagliano Trophy 1973. England (Home Int) 1971-72-73-74; (Eur LT Ch) 1973

Jun	English Girls 1969-70. British Girls 1970.
Int	English Girls 1968-69-70
Mis	Member of LGU Team to tour Australia 1973, and Under-25 team to tour Canada 1973

Gilford, David
Born 14th September, 1965. Turned Professional 1986

PRO	
Oth	Silvermere Satellite Trophy 1987
AM	
Nat	English Amateur 1984
Trn	Lagonda Trophy 1986
Int	Walker Cup 1985. GBI v Europe 1986. England (Home Int) 1983-84-85
Jun	British Youths 1986. Carris Trophy 1981

Girvan, Paul
Born Ayr on 2nd October, 1965. Turned Professional 1988

Reg	Ayrshire Champion 1985
Int	Walker Cup 1987. Scotland (Home Int) 1986

Glover, John
Born Belfast on 3rd March, 1933

Cls	Killarney (Hon), New Club, St Andrews
Trn	Formby Hare 1963
Oth	British Universities 1954-55
Reg	Lancashire Amateur 1970
Int	Ireland (Home Int) 1951-52-53-55-59-60-62-70
Jun	Boy Champion 1950. Carris Trophy 1950
Mis	Secretary Royal & Ancient Rules of Golf Committee

Godwin, Geoffrey Frank
Born Wanstead on 28th July, 1950

Cls	Thorndon Park
Trn	St George's Challenge Cup 1979. Prince of Wales Challenge Cup 1979. Hampshire Hog 1978
Reg	Essex Amateur 1978-80
Int	Walker Cup 1979-81. Europe v South America 1978. England (Home Int) 1976-77-78-80-81; (Eur T Ch) 1979-81; v Scotland 1979; v France 1982

Gorry, Mary Philomena
Born Baltinglass, Co Wicklow on 11th June, 1952

Cls	Baltinglass (Hon), Grange (Hon)
Nat	Irish Ladies 1975-78
Trn	Hermitage Scratch Cup 1978
Reg	South of Ireland Scratch Cup 1975-78-80. Irish Midland Ladies 1974-79. Leinster Ladies 1977-79. Ulster Ladies 1979. Connaught Ladies 1979
Int	Vagliano Trophy 1977. Ireland (Home Int)1971-72-73-74-75-76-77-78-79-80-**88**-(**90**); (Eur LT Ch) 1971-73-75-77-79; in Fiat Trophy 1978
Jun Int	Girls 1970
Mis	Irish Lady Golfer of the Year 1977-78. Non-playing captain of Irish team for European Ladies' Junior Championship 1983

Green, Charles Wilson
Born Dumbarton on 2nd August, 1932

Cls	Dumbarton, Cardross, Helensburgh
Maj	Leading amateur in Open 1962
Nat	Scottish Amateur 1970-82-83, r/u 1971-80. Scottish Open Amateur Stroke Play 1975, 1984, r/u 1967-83. British Seniors 1988-90
Trn	Lytham Trophy 1970 (tied)-74. Eden Tournament

	1959. Tennant Cup 1968-70-75. Edward Trophy 1968-73-74-75
Reg	West of Scotland Amateur 1962-70-79. Dunbartonshire Amateur 1960-67-68-73-77. Dunbartonshire Match Play 1965-67-69-71-74. Glasgow Amateur 1979
Int	Walker Cup 1963-69-71-73-75-(**83**)-(**85**); GBI v Scandinavia 1962; v Europe 1962-66-68-70-72-74-76. Eisenhower Trophy 1970-**72**-84-86. GB Commonwealth Team 1971. Scotland (Home Int) 1961-62-63-64-65-67-68-69-70-71-72-73-74-75-76-77-78-(**80**); v Australia 1964, (Eur T Ch) 1965-67-69-71-73-75-77-**79**-81-83; v Belgium 1973-75-77-78; v Spain 1977; v Italy 1979; v England 1979
Mis	Frank Moran Trophy 1974. British Selector 1980. Scottish Sports Photographer Award 1983

Greenhalgh, Julia
Born Bolton on 6th January, 1941

Cls	Hon member of Pleasington, Killarney, Ganton, Hermitage
Chp	Ladies British Open Amateur r/u 1978
Nat	British Ladies Stroke Play 1974-75. Runner-up British English Ladies 1966-79. Welsh Ladies Open Amateur Stroke Play 1977
Trn	Astor Salver 1969-79. Hermitage Cup 1977. Hampshire Rose 1977. Sunningdale Foursomes 1978
Oth	New Zealand Ladies 1963
Reg	Lancashire Ladies 1961-62-66-68-73-75-76-77-78. Northern Ladies 1961-62
Int	Curtis Cup 1964-70-74-76-78. Vagliano Trophy 1961-65-75-77. GB Commonwealth Team 1963-75. World Team 1970-**74**-78. England (Home Int) 1960-61-63-66-69-70-71-76-77-78; (Eur L T Ch) 1971-75-77-79
Jun	Scottish Girls Open Stroke Play 1960. Girl International 1957-58-59
Mis	Leading Amateur (4th) in Australian Wills Ladies Open Stroke Play 1974. Daks Woman Golfer of the Year 1974. Taunton Trophy 1975-77. Doris Chambers Trophy 1977

Gregson, Malcolm Edward
Born Leicester on 15th August, 1943. Turned Professional 1961

Trn	Schweppes 1967. RTV 1967. Daks 1967-68. Martini 1967 (tied). Sumrie 1972
RoW	Zambia Cock o' the North 1974. Gambian Open 1981
Oth	Pannal Foursomes 1964. British Assistants 1964
Int	Ryder Cup 1967. England in World Cup 1967. GBI v France 1966. Sumrie 1972 England in Double Diamond 1971
Mis	Harry Vardon Trophy 1967
Am	Boy International 1959-60

Greig, David G
Born Broughty Ferry on 24th January, 1950

Cls	Carnoustie (Hon), Caledonia
Nat	Scottish Amateur 1975
Oth	Boyd Quaich 1972. British Universities Stroke Play 1969
Reg	Angus Stroke Play 1978. Angus Match Play 1978. Scottish Counties Champion of Champions 1978. East of Scotland Open Amateur 1980
Int	GB Commonwealth Team 1975. Scotland (Home Int) 1972-73-75
Jun	Scottish Boys 1967. Boy International 1967. Youth International 1969-71

Grice-Whittaker, Penny
Born Sheffield on 11th September, 1964. Turned Professional 1985

Nat	English Intermediate Champion 1984. English Stroke Play 1984
Eur	Belgian Open 1986
Reg	Yorkshire Champion 1981-82-83. Northern Foursomes 1984
Int	Curtis Cup 1984. England (Home Int) 1983-84. (Eur L T Ch) 1983. Vilmorin Trophy 1984. Espirito Santo 1984
Jun	English Girls 1983

Hall, Julie (*née* Wade)
Born on 10th March 1967

Cls	Felixstowe Ferry
Chp	Ladies British Open Amateur 1990
Nat	English Ladies Stroke Play 1987; English Ladies 1988, r/u British Ladies Amateur Stroke Play 1988
Oth	World Fourball Chp (with Helen Wadsworth) 1987
Trn	Astor Salver 1990
Int	Curtis Cup 1988-90; England (Home Int) 1987-88-89-90, (Eur L T Ch) 1987-89; GBI Espirito Santo 1988-90, Vagliano Trophy 1989

Hargreaves, Jack
Born Fleetwood on 12th February, 1914. Turned Professional 1930

Maj	Open 3rd 1948
Trn	Spalding 1951. Swallow-Harrogate 1953. Goodwin Foursomes 1953
Reg	Midland Professional 1952-60
Int	Ryder Cup 1951
Mis	Secretary Midland PGA. Captain PGA 1977

Harris, Marley [Spearman] (*née* Baker)
Born on 11th January, 1928

Cls	Sudbury
Chp	British Ladies 1961-62.
Nat	English Ladies 1964
Trn	Spalding Ladies 1956; Worplesdon Mixed Foursomes r/u 1956-64; Kayser-Bondor Foursomes 1958 (tied); London Ladies Foursomes 1960; Astor Salver 1964-65; Astor Princes' Trophy 1964-65; Sunningdale Foursomes, Casa Pupo Foursomes, Roehampton Gold Cup, Hovis Ladies 1965
RoW	New Zealand Ladies Stroke Play 1963
Reg	Middlesex Ladies 1955-56-57-58-59-61-64-65. South-East Ladies 1956-58-61
Int	Curtis Cup 1960-62-64. Vagliano Trophy 1959-61. GB Commonwealth Team 1959-63. England (Home Int) 1955 to 65
Mis	AGW Trophy 1962. Non-playing captain English Team European Team Championship 1971

Hastings, Joan
See Rennie

Hastings, Dorothea (*née* Sommerville)
Born Glasgow on 21st June, 1934

Cls	Haggs Castle (Hon), Troon Ladies (Hon), Erskine
Nat	Scottish Ladies 1958, r/u 1960
Reg	West of Scotland Ladies 1961. Renfrewshire Ladies 1956-57-58-59-61-63-83
Int	Curtis Cup 1958. Vagliano Trophy 1963. Scotland (Home Int) 1955 to 1963
Jun	Junior International 1953. Junior Tour of Australasia 1955

Hawksworth, John
Born 27th March, 1961. Turned Professional 1986

PRO	
Trn	Peugeot-Talbot Assistants Championship 1987. Broadstone Satellite 1988
AM	
Trn	Berkhamsted Trophy 1983. Hampshire Hog 1984. Lytham Trophy 1984
Int	Walker Cup 1985. England (Home Int) 1984-85

Heathcoat-Amory, Lady
(*née* Joyce Wethered)
Born 17th November, 1901

Cls	Worplesdon
Chp	British Ladies 1922-24-25-29, r/u 1921.
Nat	English Ladies 1920-21-22-23-24
Trn	Worplesdon Mixed Foursomes 1922-23-27-28-31-32-33-36. Sunningdale Foursomes 1935-36
Reg	Surrey Ladies 1921-22-24-29-32
Int	Curtis Cup 1932. GBI v France 1931. England (Home Int) 1921-22-23-24-25-29
Mis	Forfeited Amateur status and toured USA in 1935. Reinstated as Amateur after the war

Hedges, Peter J
Born 30th March, 1947

Cls	Langley Park (Hon), Royal Cinque Ports, Addington, Wildernesse, Royal & Ancient
Nat	English Open Amateur Stroke Play 1976
Trn	Royal St George's Challenge Cup 1970. Prince of Wales Challenge Cup 1972-73-74-77. Berkshire Trophy 1973-76-78. Golf Illustrated Gold Vase 1974. Scrutton Jug 1976
Reg	Kent Amateur 1968-71-79. Kent Open 1970-74
Int	Walker Cup 1973-75. GBI v Europe 1974-76 Eisenhower Trophy 1974. England (Home Int) 1970-73-74-75-76-77-78-82; (Eur T Ch) 1973-75-77
Jun	Youth International 1968
Mis	Member of European Team to tour South Africa 1974

Hedges, Susan Claire (*née* Whitlock)
Born Beckenham, Kent on 8th May, 1947

Cls	Wrotham Heath (Hon), Royal Cinque Ports, Langley Park
Maj	Ladies British Open 3rd 1979
Nat	Welsh Ladies Open Amateur Stroke Play 1978. English Ladies r/u 1979
Oth	Belgian Ladies 1974. Luxembourg Ladies 1976-77. Zaire Ladies 1980
Reg	Kent Ladies 1976-79; Central England Mixed Foursomes 1977-81; Hoylake Mixed Foursomes 1982
Int	Vagliano Trophy 1979. GB Commonwealth Team 1979. England (Home Int) 1979; (Eur L T Ch) 1979
Mis	Smyth Salver 1979

Henson, Dinah (*née* Oxley)
Born Dorking on 17th October, 1948

Cls	Hon member of West Byfleet, Killarney, Fairfield, US
Chp	British Ladies 1970.
Nat	English Ladies 1970-71, r/u 1968. British Ladies Stroke Play r/u 1969
Trn	Wills Ladies 1969-70-71. Worplesdon Mixed Foursomes 1968-77. Newmark International 1975 (tied)-77
Reg	Surrey Ladies 1967-70-71-76
Int	Curtis Cup 1968-70-72-76. Vagliano Trophy 1967-69-71. World Team 1970. GB Commonwealth Team 1967-71. England (Home Int) 1967-68-69-70-75-76-77-78; (Eur L T Ch) 1971-77

Jun British Girls 1963. English Girls 1965. French Girls
1969. Girl International 1964-65-66
Mis Daks Woman Golfer of the Year 1970. Leading
Amateur Colgate European Ladies Open 1974

Hetherington, Jean (*née* McClure)
See Holmes

Hill, George Alec, DSO
Born Northwood, Middlesex in 1908

Cls Royal & Ancient, Royal St George's, Hon Company of
Edinburgh Golfers, Sandy Lodge
Int Walker Cup 1936-(**55**). England (Home Int) 1936-37
Jun Boy International 1926
Mis Chairman R & A Championship Committee 1955.
Chairman Rules of Golf Committee 1958-59. Captain
Royal & Ancient 1964/65

Hoey, T Brian C

Nat Irish Amateur 1984
Reg North of Ireland Amateur 1979-83
Int Ireland (Home Int) 1970-71-72-73-77-84

Holmes, Jean [Hetherington]
(*née* McClure)
Born Wanstead, Essex on 17th August, 1923

Cls Wanstead, Hunstanton, Thorndon Park
Chp British Ladies 1946, r/u 1958.
Nat English Ladies 1966
Reg Nottinghamshire Ladies 1949-50-51. Essex Ladies
1956-57
Int England (Home Int) 1957-66-(**67**)

Homer, Trevor Walter Brian
*Born Bloxworth on 8th September, 1943. Turned
Professional July 1974. Reinstated as Amateur in 1978*

Chp Amateur Champion 1972-74
Trn Leicestershire Fox 1972. Harlech Gold Cross 1970
Int Walker Cup 1973. Eisenhower Trophy 1972.
GBI v Europe 1972. England (Home Int) 1972-73; (Eur
T Ch) 1973

Hope, Lesley Alexandra
Born Gullane, East Lothian on 22nd May, 1955

Cls Gullane Ladies, Catterick
Nat Scottish Ladies Amateur 1975, r/u 1979
Reg East of Scotland Ladies 1977-78
Int Scotland (Home Int) 1975-76-80-84-85-86-87-(**88**)-
(**89**)-(**90**); (Eur LT Ch) 1975-77-79; in Fiat Trophy
1979

Horton, Tommy
*Born St Helens, on 16th June, 1941. Turned
Professional 1957*

Trn RTV 1968. PGA Match Play 1970. Gallaher Ulster
1971. Piccadilly 1972. Penfold 1974. Uniroyal
International 1976. Dunlop Masters 1978
RoW South African Open 1970. Nigerian Open 1973.
Zambian Open 1977. Tobago Open 1975. Gambian
Open 1975
Int Ryder Cup 1975-77. GBI v France 1966. England in
World Cup 1976. England in Double Diamond 1971-
74-75-76-77. GBI v Europe 1974-76
Mis Second in Order of Merit 1967. PGA Captain 1978;
Braid-Taylor Memorial Medal 1976-77

Hourihane, Claire
Born 18th February, 1958

Cls Woodbrook
Nat Irish Ladies 1983-84-85-87; r/u 1980. British Ladies
Stroke Play 1986; r/u 1990
Trn South Atlantic (USA) 1983; Hampshire Rose 1986
Reg South Ireland Cup 1977. Leinster Ladies 1980
Int Curtis Cup 1984-86-88-90. Vagliano Trophy 1981-83-
85-87-89. Ireland (Home Int) 1979 to 1990. (Eur LT
Ch) 1981-83-85-87-89. Espirito Santo 1986-90

Howard, Ann (*née* Phillips)
Born Prestwich on 22nd October, 1934

Cls Whitefield (Hon), Royal Birkdale, Castletown
Oth Danish Ladies 1955
Reg Lancashire Ladies 1957. Manx Ladies 1977-78
Int Curtis Cup 1956-68. GBI v France and Belgium 1955-
57. England (Home Int) 1953-54-55-56-(**79**)-(**80**).
Senior European (**1981**)
Jun British Girls 1952

Huggan, Shirley Margaret (*née* Lawson)
Born Glasgow on 16th September, 1964

Cls Eastwood, Rock Ridge, USA
Nat Scottish Ladies Amateur 1988-89 r/u 1990; Taunton
Trophy 1987
Reg West of Scotland Ladies 1986-88; Renfrewshire Ladies
1985-86-87-88
Int Curtis Cup 1988; Scotland (Home Int) 1985-86-87-88-
89; (Eur LT Ch) 1985-87-89; GBI Vagliano Trophy
1989
Jun Scottish Girls 1982; Scottish Girls Stroke Play 1983-
84; r/u 1982-85
Int Girls 1980-81-82

Huggett, Brian George Charles, MBE
*Born Porthcawl on 18th November, 1936. Turned
Professional 1951*

Maj Open r/u 1965. 3rd 1962
Eur Dutch Open 1962. German Open 1963. Portuguese
Open 1974
Trn Cox-Moore 1963. Smart-Weston 1965. Sumrie
1968-72. PGA Close 1967. Martini 1967 (tied)-68.
Shell Winter Tournament 1967-68. PGA Match Play
1968, r/u 1977. Daks 1969-71 (tied). Bowmaker 1969
(tied). Carrolls 1970. Dunlop Masters 1970. British
Airways-Avis 1978
RoW Singapore International 1962. Algarve Open 1970
Oth Sunningdale Foursomes 1957. British Assistants 1958.
Gleneagles Pro-Am 1961-65. Turnberry Pro-Am
1968. Welsh Professional 1978
Reg East Anglian Open 1962-67
Int Ryder Cup 1963-67-69-71-73-75-(**77**). Wales in World
Cup 1963-64-65-68-69-70-71-76-79. Wales in Double
Diamond 1971-72-73-74-75-76-77. GBI v Europe 1974-
78
Mis Vardon Trophy 1968. 1972

Hughes, Ann
See Johnson

Huke, Beverly Joan Mary
*Born Great Yarmouth on 10th May, 1951. Turned
Professional 1978*

Cls Cotswold Hills (Hon), Windmill Hill (Hon), Leighton
Buzzard, Panmure Barry
Chp British Ladies r/u 1971.
Nat English Ladies 1975

Eur Carlsberg (Ballater) 1979. Carlsberg (Rosemount) 1980. NABS Pro-Am 1st Pro Individual 1981. Brickendon Grange and Stourbridge Pro-Am 1983; Lark Valley Classic 1983 (shared); White Horse Whisky Challenge Trophy 1983. Trusthouse Forte Classic 1985. German Ladies Open 1984. Wester Volkswagen Classic 1986

Trn Roehampton Gold Cup 1971. Renfrew Rose Bowl 1976-77-78. Helen Holm Trophy 1977

Reg Gloucestershire Ladies 1972. Angus Ladies 1976

Int Curtis Cup 1972. Vagliano Trophy 1971-75. England (Home Int) 1971-72-75-76-77; (Eur L T Ch) 1975-77

Jun Scottish Girls Open Stroke Play 1970-71. Girl International 1966-67-68

Mis Chairman WPGET 1988

Humphreys, Warren
Born Kingston, Surrey on 1st April, 1952. Turned Professional 1971

PRO

Eur Portuguese Open 1985

Mis Accles & Pollock Award 1972

AM

Nat English Amateur 1971

Trn Sunningdale Foursomes 1968; Antlers Royal Mid-Surrey 1969; Duncan Putter 1971; Lytham Trophy 1971

Int Walker Cup 1971; GBI v Europe 1970; England (Home Int) 1970-71; (Eur T Ch) 1971

Jun Int Boys 1967-68-**69**; Youths 1969-70-71

Hunt, Bernard John, MBE
Born Atherstone on 2nd February, 1930. Turned Professional 1946

Maj Open 3rd 1960; leading British player (4th) 1964

Eur Belgian Open 1957; German Open 1961; French Open 1967

Trn Spalding, Goodwin Foursomes, Gleneagles-Saxone 1953; Goodwin Foursomes 1954; Irish Hospitals 1956; Bowmaker 1958 (shared); Martini, Daks 1961; Carrolls, Swallow-Penfold, Smart-Weston, Gevacolour, Dunlop Masters 1963; Rediffusion 1964; Dunlop Masters, Gallaher Ulster 1965; Piccadilly 1966; Gallaher Ulster 1967; Penfold, Sumrie, Agfacolor 1970; Wills 1971; Sumrie 1973

Reg Southern England Professional 1959-60-62-67; West of England Open Professional 1960-61

Oth British Assistants 1953; Algarve Open, BP Italy 1969

RoW Egyptian Open 1956; Brazilian Open 1962

Int Ryder Cup 1953-57-59-61-63-65-67-69-(**73**)-(**75**); England in World Cup 1958-59-60-62-63-64-68; in Double Diamond 1971-72-73

Mis Harry Vardon Trophy 1958-60-65

Hutcheon, Ian C
Born Monifieth, Angus on 22nd February, 1942

Cls Monifieth (Hon), Grange and Dundee (Hon)

Nat Scottish Amateur 1973. Scottish Open Amateur Stroke Play 1971-74-79

Trn Tennant Cup 1976; Lytham Trophy 1980; Scottish Champion of Champions 1980-81-86-88; Leven Gold Medal 1981-82

Oth North of Spain Stroke Play 1972

Reg Scottish Central District Amateur 1972. Angus Match Play 1965-70-72. Angus Stroke Play 1968-71-72-74. North of Scotland District Amateur Stroke Play 1975-76-82

Int GBI v Europe 1974-76. Eisenhower Trophy 1974-76 (winners and joint winning individual)-80. Scotland

(Home Int) 1971-72-73-74-75-76-77-78-80; (Eur T Ch) 1973-75-77-79-81; v Spain 1972-77; v Belgium 1973-75-77-78-80; v France 1978-80-81; v Italy 1979; in Fiat Trophy 1979. GBI in Dominican International 1973. Walker Cup 1975-77-79-81. GBI in Colombian International 1975. GB Commonwealth Team 1975

Mis Frank Moran Trophy 1976

Imrie, Kathryn
Born Southend on 8th June 1967. Turned Professional 1990

Cls Monifieth

Maj Leading Amateur in Ladies British Open 1988 (Smyth Salver)

Trn St Rule Trophy 1985; Riccarton Rosebowl 1985; Roehampton Gold Cup 1990

Reg Highland Open 1985; North of Scotland Ladies Amateur 1988-90; Northern Counties Ladies Open Stroke Play 1986-87-88-89; Angus Ladies 1982-83-84-85

Int Curtis Cup 1990; Vagliano Trophy 1989; Scotland (Home Int) 1984-88-89; (Eur L T Ch) 1987-89

Mis Taunton Trophy 1986; winner of two NCAA events whilst at University of Arizona (1985-89)

Jun Scottish Girls Open Stroke Play 1985-86-87

Irvin, Ann Lesley
Born 11th April, 1943

Cls Lytham (Hon), Lytham Green Drive (Hon)

Chp British Ladies 1973, r/u 1969.

Nat English Ladies 1967-74. British Ladies Stroke Play 1969.

Trn Roehampton Gold Cup 1967-68-69-72-76. Hovis Ladies 1966-68-70. Avia Foursomes 1968

Reg Northern Ladies 1963-64. Lancashire Ladies 1965-67-69-71-72-74. Northern Foursomes Championship 1973

Int Curtis Cup 1962-68-70-76. Vagliano Trophy 1961-63-65-67-69-71-73-75. GB Commonwealth Team 1967-75. England (Home Int) 1962-63-65-67-68-69-70-71-72-73-75; (Eur L T Ch) 1965-67-69-71-73-75

Jun French Girls 1963.

Int Girls 1960-61; British Girls 1961

Mis Daks Woman Golfer of the Year 1968-69. Captain of British Team to tour Australia 1973. Lancashire 1981. County Captain 1979. England Junior Captain. 1981-82. International Selector 1981-82. England Selector 1981-82. County Selector and Junior Organiser

Jack, Robert Reid
Born Cumbernauld on 17th January, 1924

Cls Dullatur

Maj Leading Amateur in Open 1959

Chp Amateur Champion 1957. Scottish Amateur 1955

Nat Scottish Amateur 1955

Trn Edward Trophy 1959. Tennant Cup 1961

Oth Royal & Ancient Royal Medal 1965-67. Silver Cross 1956-66. Glennie Medal 1965

Reg Glasgow Amateur 1953-54-58. Dunbartonshire Match Play 1949

Int Walker Cup 1957-59. Eisenhower Trophy 1958. GB Commonwealth Team 1959. GBI v Europe 1956. Scotland (Home Int) 1950-51-54-55-56-57-58-59-61; v Scandinavia 1956-58

Jacklin, Tony, CBE
Born Scunthorpe on 7th July, 1944. Turned Professional 1962

PRO
Maj Open 1969, 3rd 1971-72; US Open 1970
Eur Blaxnit 1966; Pringle, Dunlop Masters 1967; Wills, Lancôme Trophy 1970; Benson & Hedges Festival 1971; Viyella PGA Close 1972; Dunlop Masters, Italian Open 1973; Scandinavian Enterprise Open 1974; Kerrygold International Classic 1976; German Open 1979; Jersey Open 1981; Sun Alliance PGA 1982
Oth British Assistants 1964; English Professional 1977
US Greater Jacksonville Open 1972
RoW Kimberley 1966 (shared); Forest Products, New Zealand, New Zealand PGA 1967; Dunlop International Australia 1972; Los Lagartos Open 1973-74; Venezuelan Open 1979
Int Ryder Cup 1967-69-71-73-75-77-79-**(83)**-**(85)**-**(87)**-**(89)**; Hennessy-Cognac 1976; England in World Cup 1966-70-71-72; in Double Diamond 1972-73-74-76-77
Mis Rookie of the Year 1963; Hon Life President PGA; first British player since Harry Vardon to hold Open and US Open simultaneously; Braid-Taylor Memorial Medal 1969-70-71-72
AM
Reg Lincolnshire Open 1961

Jackson, Barbara Amy Bridget
Born Birmingham on 10th July, 1936

Cls Royal St David's, Edgbaston. Hon member of Handsworth, Hunstanton, Killarney
Chp British Ladies r/u 1964.
Nat English Ladies 1956, r/u 1958
Trn Fairway and Hazard Foursomes 1954. Kayser Bondor Foursomes 1962. Avia Foursomes 1967. Worplesdon Mixed Foursomes 1960. Astor Prince's 1963
Oth German Ladies 1956. Canadian Ladies 1967
Reg Midland Ladies 1954-56-57-58-59-60-69. Staffordshire Ladies 1954-56-57-58-59-63-64-67-69-76
Int Curtis Cup 1958-64-68. Vagliano Trophy 1959-63-65-67-**(73)**-**(75)**. GB Commonwealth Team 1959-67. GBI v Belgium 1957; v France 1957. World Team Championship 1964. England (Home Int) 1955-56-57-58-59-63-64-65-66-**(73)**-**(74)**; (Eur L T Ch) **(1975)**; v France 1964-66
Jun British Girls 1954
Mis LGU International Selector 1983. English and GBI Selector 1983 to 1988. Chairman of English Ladies Association 1970-71

Jacobs, John Robert Maurice
Born Lindrick, Yorkshire on 14th March, 1925. Turned Professional 1947

Eur Dutch Open 1957
RoW South African Match Play 1957
Int Ryder Cup 1955-**(79)**-**(81)**. GBI v Continent 1954-55-58
Mis Former PGA Tournament Director-General. TV commentator. Coach to many International Teams

James, Mark H
Born Manchester on 28th October, 1953. Turned Professional 1975

PRO
Maj Open 3rd 1981
Eur Sun Alliance Match Play 1978; Welsh Classic, Carroll's Irish Open 1979; Carroll's Irish Open, Italian Open 1980; Tunisian Open 1983; GSI Open 1985; Benson & Hedges International 1986; Peugeot

Spanish Open 1988; Karl Litten Desert Classic, AGF Open, NM English Open 1989; Dunhill British Masters, English Open 1990
RoW Lusaka Open 1977; Sao Paulo Open 1981; South African TPC 1988
Int Ryder Cup 1977-79-81-89; Hennessy-Cognac 1976-78-80-82 (individual winner)-84; World Cup 1978-79-82-84-87-88-90; Dunhill Cup 1988-89-90 (r/u); Kirin Cup 1988; Four Tours World Chp 1989-90
Mis Tooting Bec Cup 1976; Braid-Taylor Memorial Medal 1976-79-81; Rookie of the Year 1976
AM
Chp Amateur r/u 1975
Nat English Amateur 1974
Trn Leicestershire Fox 1974
Int Walker Cup 1975; England (Home Int) 1974-75; (Eur T Ch) 1975
Jun
Int (England) Boys 1971; Youths 1974-75

Johnson, Ann (*née* Hughes)
Born Llandudno, Gwynedd on 18th October, 1946

Cls Ludlow, Killarney (Hon)
Chp Welsh Ladies 1966-72-75, r/u 1969-76
Reg Caernarvonshire and Anglesey Ladies 1964-68-69-72-78
Int Wales (Home Int) 1964-66-67-68-69-70-71-72-73-74-75-76-78-79; (Eur L T Ch) 1965-67-69-71-75-79
Jun Welsh Girls 1960-63-64-65. Girl International 1965

Johnson, Patricia (Trish)
Born Bristol on 17th January, 1966. Turned Professional 1987

PRO
Eur McEwan's Wirral Classic, Bloor Homes Eastleigh Classic, Woolmark Match Play 1987; Hennessy Cup, Bloor Homes Eastleigh Classic, European Open 1990
US LPGA Qualifying School 1987
Int Solheim Cup 1990
AM
Nat English Ladies 1985. English Ladies Stroke Play 1985
Trn Roehampton Gold Cup 1986
Reg South-Western Ladies 1984
Int Curtis Cup 1986; England (Home Int) 1984-85
Jun Devon Girls 1982
Mis Woolmark Order of Merit leader 1990

Jones, Emyr O
Born 28th January, 1965

Chp Welsh Amateur 1985
Maj Wales (Home Int) 1983-85-86

Jones, John Roger
Born Old Colwyn, Denbighshire on 14th June, 1944

Cls Langland Bay (Hon)
Nat Welsh Amateur Stroke Play 1972-73-82, r/u 1983. Welsh Amateur Championship 1983
Trn Harlech Gold Cross 1976
Reg Denbighshire Amateur 1969-71. Caernarfonshire and Anglesey Amateur 1970 (tied)-72-74-75. Glamorgan Amateur 1977-79. North Wales Amateur 1976. Carmarthenshire Amateur 1979-80. Landsdowne Trophy (Channel League) Stroke Play 1979-80-83
Int Wales (Home Int) 1970-72-73-77-78-80-81-82-83; (Eur T Ch) 1973-79-81-83; v Denmark 1976-80; v Ireland 1979; v Switzerland 1980; v Spain 1980; in Asian Team Championship 1979

Jones, Keith Glyn
Born Brentwood on 19th July, 1969

Cls	Worplesdon, The Berkshire, Lansdown
Nat	Welsh Amateur 1988
Reg	Bristol Open 1988. Whitchurch Silver Dragon 1988. WI Tucker Trophy 1988
Int	Wales (Home Int) 1988
Jun	Prince of Wales Trophy 1988

Jones, Stephen P
Born 30th January, 1961

Nat	Welsh Amateur 1981
Int	Wales (Home Int) 1981-82-83-84-85-86

Kelley, Michael John
Born Scarborough on 6th February, 1945

Cls	Ganton, Hon member of Scarborough North Cliff, Bridlington, Bradford
Trn	Lytham Trophy 1976. Antlers Royal Mid-Surrey 1972
Reg	Yorkshire Amateur 1969-74-81. Yorkshire Open 1969-75. Champion of Champions 1981
Int	Walker Cup 1977-79. Eisenhower Trophy 1976 (winners). GBI v Europe 1976-78-82; GBI in Colombian International 1978. England (Home Int) 1974-75-76-77-78-80-81-82-**88**; (Eur T Ch) 1977-79; v France 1982
Jun Int	Boys 1962. Youths 1965-66

Keppler, Steven D
Born 17th February, 1961

Trn	Berkshire Trophy 1982. Golf Illustrated Gold Vase 1983
Reg	Surrey Amateur 1981
Int	Walker Cup 1983. England (Home Int) 1982-83

King, Michael
Born London on 15th February, 1950. Turned Professional 1974

PRO	
Eur	Tournament Players Chp 1979
Int	Ryder Cup 1979; England in World Cup 1979
AM	
Trn	St George's Hill Trophy 1970; County Champion of Champions 1970; Sunningdale Foursomes 1972; Lytham Trophy 1973 (shared)
Reg	Berks, Bucks & Oxon Amateur 1968-69-70-73-74; Berks, Bucks & Oxon Open 1968-73
Int	Walker Cup 1969-73; GB Commonwealth Trn 1971; v Europe 1972; England (Home Int) 1971-72-73; (Eur T Ch) 1971-73

King, Samuel Leonard
Born Godden Green, Sevenoaks, Kent on 27th March, 1911

Maj	Open 3rd 1939
Trn	Daily Mail 1937. Yorkshire Evening News 1944-49
Oth	British Assistants 1933. Dunlop-Southern 1936-37. Sunningdale Foursomes 1948. Teachers Senior 1961-62
Int	Ryder Cup 1937-47-49. England 1934-36-37-38

Kyle, Alexander Thomson
Born Hawick on 16th April, 1907

Cls	Royal & Ancient, Easingwold, Sandmoor, Moortown, Harrogate, Knaresborough, Peebles, Fulford (Hon)
Chp	Amateur Champion 1939.
Nat	Irish Open Amateur r/u 1946. English Open Amateur Stroke Play r/u 1952
Trn	Newlands Trophy 1930

Reg	Borders Amateur 1929-30. Yorkshire Amateur 1935-36
Int	Walker Cup 1938-47-51. GBI v South Africa 1952. Scotland (Home Int) 1938-47-49-50-51-52-53
Mis	Played for British Seniors 1969-75

Lambert, Catriona
Born on 25th August, 1969

Cls	North Berwick
Trn	Roehampton Gold Cup 1989; Helen Holm Trophy 1990; British Universities Womens Chp 1990
Int	Curtis Cup 1990; Vagliano Trophy 1989; Scotland (Home Int) 1989-90; (Eur L T Ch) 1989
Jun	Scottish Girls 1986; Scottish Girls Open Stroke Play 1988-89, r/u 1987

Lane, Barry
Born Hayes, Middlesex on 21st June, 1960. Turned Professional 1976

Eur	Equity & Law Challenge 1987. Scottish Open 1988
RoW	Jamaica Open 1983
Int	(England) Dunhill Cup 1988. World Cup 1988

Langley, John DA
Born Northwood, Middlesex on 25th April, 1918. Turned Professional 1990

Cls	Sunningdale, Burnham (Hon), Swinley Forest, Fulwell (Hon), Metropolitan (Aus)
Nat	English Amateur 1950, r/u 1936
Trn	Golf Illustrated Gold Vase 1952-53. St George's Hill Trophy 1952
Int	Walker Cup 1936-51-53. England (Home Int) 1950-51-52-53; v France 1950-52
Jun	British Boys 1935. Carris Trophy 1936
Int	Boys 1932-33-34-35
Mis	Chairman Royal & Ancient Selection Committee 1967 to 1969

Langmead, Jonathan
Born 3rd November, 1967. Turned Professional 1990

Chp	English Amateur 1986
Int	England (Home Int) 1986
Jun Int	Youths 1987

Langridge, Susan (*née* Armitage)
Born Huddersfield on 5th April, 1943

Cls	Walsall, Whittington Barracks (Hon)
Reg	Midland Ladies 1961-65
Int	Curtis Cup 1964-66. Vagliano Trophy 1963-65-67. England (Home Int) 1963-64-65-66-67
Jun	Scottish Girls Open Stroke Play 1962

Large, Pamela (*née* Davies)
Born Coventry on 12th April, 1930

Cls	Coventry (Hon)
Nat	English Ladies 1952, r/u 1950
Reg	Midland Ladies 1952. Warwickshire Ladies 1952
Int	England (Home Int) 1950-51-52; v Australia 1950
Jun	British Girls 1949
Mis	Captain English Ladies (Home Int) Team 1981-82

Lawrence, Joan B
Born Kinghorn, Fife on 20th April, 1930

Cls	Hon member of Dunfermline, Aberdour, Killarney
Chp	Scottish Ladies 1962-63-64, r/u 1965. Scottish Veteran Ladies Champion 1982
Reg	East of Scotland Ladies 1971-72. Fife Ladies 1953-57-58-59-60-61-62-63-64-65-67-68-69

Int	Curtis Cup 1964. World Team Champion 1964. GB Commonwealth Team **1971**. Vagliano Trophy 1963-65. Scotland (Home Int) 1959 to 70-(**77**); (Eur L T Ch) 1965-67-**69**-71-(**77**)
Jun	Girl International 1949
Mis	LGU International Selector 1973-74-75-76-80-81-82-83. Treasurer Scottish Ladies Golfing Association from 1980. Chairman of LGU Executive 1989

Leburn, Wilma (née Aitken)
Born 24th January, 1959

Trn	Helen Holm Trophy 1978-80-82. Avia Foursomes 1982
Reg	West of Scotland 1978-80-81. Renfrewshire Champion 1978-79-80-81-82
Int	Curtis Cup 1982. Vagliano Trophy 1981-83. Scotland (Home Int) 1978-79-80-81-82-83. Vilmorin Cup 1979. (Eur L T Ch) 1979-81-83.
Jun	Scottish Girls 1975-77. West of Scotland Girls 1977. British Girls 1977
Int	Scottish Girls 1975-77-78

Lee, Robert
Born in London on 12th October, 1961. Turned Professional 1982

Eur	Cannes Open 1985. Portuguese Open 1987
RoW	Brazilian Open 1984-5

Lee-Smith, Jenny
Born Newcastle-upon-Tyne on 2nd December, 1948. Turned Professional 1977

Maj	Ladies British Open 1976 (as amateur)
PRO	
Eur	Carlsberg 1979; Carlsberg, Robert Windsor Trn, Volvo Swedish International, Manchester Evening News Classic 1980; Sports Space Trn, McEwan's Lager Welsh Classic, Lambert & Butler Match Play 1981; Ford Classic 1982; British Olivetti 1984
AM	
Nat	Ladies British Open Amateur Stroke Play 1976
Trn	Wills Match Play 1974; Newmark 1976; Hoylake Mixed Foursomes 1969
Reg	Northumberland Ladies 1972-73-74
Int	Curtis Cup 1974-76; Espirito Santo 1976; GB Commonwealth Trn 1975; Colombian International 1975; England (Home Int) 1973-74-75-76; (Eur L T Ch) 1975
Mis	Daks Woman Golfer of the Year 1976

Lees, Arthur
Born Sheffield on 21st February, 1908

Eur	Irish Hospitals 1939
Trn	Dunlop Masters 1947. Penfold 1951-53
Oth	Midland Professional 1948-49. Southern England Professional 1956. Wentworth Pro-Am Foursomes 1957. Teachers Seniors 1959
Int	Ryder Cup 1947-49-51-55. England 1938

Lewis, Malcolm Elvet
Born Bristol on 8th January 1959

Cls	Newport, Royal & Ancient, Henbury (Hon)
Maj	Leading amateur in Open, 1982
Oth	Greek Amateur 1979; India Amateur 1981; Dutch International Amateur 1982
Trn	British Universities Stroke Play 1978-79-80; British Universities Match Play 1980-81; Boyd Quaich 1980-82

Reg	Gloucestershire Amateur 1980; East of India 1982
Int	Walker Cup 1983; England (Home Int) 1980-81-82; v France 1982
Jun	British Youths 1976
Int	Boys 1975-76; Youths 1976-77-78-80; Universities 1978-82

Light, Pamela Mary
See Chugg

Llewellyn, David
Born Dover on 18th November, 1951. Turned Professional 1968

Eur	Biarritz Open 1988.
Oth	Vernons Open 1987; Motorola Classic 1989
RoW	Kenya Open 1972. Ivory Coast Open 1985. Zambian Open 1988
Int	Wales in World Cup 1974-85-87 (winners)-88. Dunhill Cup 1985-88
Mis	Rookie of the Year 1971

Longmuir, Bill
Born Essex on 10th June, 1953. Turned Professional 1968

RoW	Nigerian Open 1976-80-85. Ivory Coast Open 1983; Southlands Classic (NZ) 1976
Mis	Tooting Bec Cup 1979

Lucas, Percy Belgrave, CBE, DSO, DFC
Born Sandwich Bay, Kent on 2nd September, 1915

Cls	Sandy Lodge, Walton Heath, Prince's, Royal West Norfolk
Trs	Berkshire Trophy 1947-49. St George's Challenge Cup 1947. Prince of Wales Challenge Cup 1947. President's Putter 1949
Reg	Herts Amateur 1946-47
Int	Walker Cup 1936-47-(**49**). GBI v Professionals 1935. England (Home Int) 1936-48-**49**; v France 1936-47
Jun	British Boys 1933.
Int	Boys 1930-31-32-33
Mis	President Golf Foundation 1963 to 1966. President National Golf Clubs Advisory Association 1963 to 1969. President Association of Golf Club Secretaries 1968 to 1974. Member UK Sports Council 1971 to 1983

Lugton, Constance J, MVO
Born Edinburgh on 17th November, 1936

Cls	Gullane Ladies, Musselburgh
Nat	Scottish Ladies Amateur 1977, r/u 1972
Reg	East of Scotland Ladies 1974, East Lothian Ladies 1965-68-70-71-72-73-76-77-80
Int	Scotland (Home Int) 1965-68-72-73-(**75**)-(**76**)-77-78-80 (Eur LT Ch) 1977
Jun	Girl International 1955

Lumb, Kathryn (née Phillips)
Born Bradford on 24th February, 1952

Cls	Hon member of Bradford, West Bowling, Killarney, Filton
Reg	Central England Mixed Foursomes 1966-70. Yorkshire Ladies 1968-69
Int	Curtis Cup 1970-72. Vagliano Trophy 1969-71. England (Home Int) 1968-69-70-71; (Eur L T Ch) 1969
Jun	English Girls 1968. Scottish Girls Open Stroke Play 1968-69. French Girls 1970.
Int	Girls 1967-68-69

Lunt, Michael Stanley Randle
Born Birmingham on 20th May, 1935

Cls	Royal & Ancient, Walton Heath, St Enodoc, Hon member of Blackwell, Royal St David's, Moseley, Edgbaston, Stourbridge, Willesley Park, Kibworth, Handsworth, King's Norton, Dudley
Chp	Amateur Champion 1963, r/u 1964
Nat	English Amateur 1966, r/u 1962. English Open Amateur Stroke Play r/u 1961
Trn	Golf Illustrated Gold Vase 1958, Harlech Gold Cross 1959-61-64-65-66-67. Leicestershire Fox 1966
Reg	Midland Counties Amateur 1960-62
Int	Walker Cup 1959-61-62-65. Eisenhower Trophy 1964 GB Commonwealth Team 1963. England (Home Int) 1956-57-58-59-60-62-63-64-66-(72)-(73)-(74)-(75). (Eur T Ch) (1973)-(75)
Jun	Boy International 1949-50-51-52
Mis	AGW Trophy 1963. President Midland Counties Golf Association 1978 to 1980

Lyle, Alexander Walter Barr (Sandy), MBE
Born Shrewsbury on 9th February, 1958. Turned Professional 1977

PRO

Maj	Open Champion 1985. US Masters 1988
Eur	Jersey Open, Scandinavian Enterprise Open, European Open 1979; Coral Classic 1980; French Open, Lawrence Batley International 1981; Lawrence Batley International 1982; Madrid Open 1983; Italian Open, Lancôme Trophy 1984; Benson & Hedges International 1985; German Masters 1987; Dunhill British Masters, Suntory World Match Play 1988
US	Greater Greensboro Open 1986; Tournament Players Championship 1987; Phoenix Open, Greater Greensboro Open 1988
Oth	PGA Qualifying School winner 1977; Scottish Professional Chp 1979
RoW	Nigerian Open 1978; Casio World Open, Kapalua International (Hawaii) 1984
Int	Ryder Cup 1979-81-83-85-87; Nissan Cup 1985-86, Kirin Cup 1987-88; Hennessy-Cognac Cup 1980-84; Scotland in World Cup 1979-80 (Individual Winner) - 87(r/u); Dunhill Cup 1985-86-87 (r/u)-88-89-90
Mis	Rookie of the Year 1978; Harry Vardon Trophy 1979-80-85; AGW Trophy 1980-88; Tooting Bec Cup 1982-88; Braid-Taylor Memorial Medal 1985; Frank Moran Trophy 1985; Golfer's Handbook Golfer of the Year 1985

AM

Nat	English Open Amateur Stroke Play 1975-77
Trn	County Champion of Champions 1974; Hampshire Hog, Berkshire Trophy, Scrutton Jug, Berkhamsted Trophy 1977
Reg	Midland Amateur, Shropshire & Herefordshire Amateur 1974; Midland Open 1975; Shropshire & Herefordshire Amateur 1976
Int	Walker Cup 1977; GB Commonwealth Trn 1975; GBI v Europe 1976; England (Home Int) 1975-76-77, (Eur T Ch) 1977
Jun	Carris Trophy 1975; British Youths 1977; r/u British Boys 1974-75
Int	Boys 1972-73-74-75
Mis	In 1975 represented England in Boy, Youth and Full Internationals.

Macara, Michael
Born 31st October, 1965

Cls	Maesdu
Chp	Amateur r/u 1990
Nat	Welsh Amateur Stroke Play 1985-87
Int	Wales (Home Int) 1983-84-85-87

McAllister, Stephen
Born Paisley on 16th February, 1962. Turned Professional 1983

Eur	Vinho Verde Atlantic Open, KLM Dutch Open 1990
Int	Scotland: Dunhill Cup 1990

McCann, Catherine (née Smye)
Born Clonmel, Co Tipperary in 1922

Cls	Tullamore
Chp	British Ladies 1951.
Nat	Irish Ladies 1949-61, r/u 1947-52-57-60
Reg	Munster Ladies 1958, Irish Midland Ladies 1952-57-58
Int	Curtis Cup 1952. Ireland (Home Int) 1947-48-49-50-51-52-53-54-56-57-58-60-61-62; v New Zealand 1953; v Canada 1953

McClure, Jean
See Holmes

McCorkindale, Isabella
See Robertson

Macdonald, JS
Born St Andrews on 9th July, 1944

Cls	Elgin, Baberton, Killarney (Hon), Frigate Bay (Hon)
Nat	Scottish Amateur Open Stroke Play 1969. English Open Amateur Stroke Play r/u 1970-71.
Oth	Kuwait Open Champion 1977
Trn	Boyd Quaich 1963-65. British Universities 1965
Reg	South East Scotland Amateur 1969-71. North of Scotland Open Amateur Stroke Play 1984-85
Int	Walker Cup 1971. GBI v Europe 1970. Scotland (Home Int) 1969-70-71-72; (Eur T Ch) 1971; v Belgium 1973
Jun Int	Boys 1961. Youths 1962-64-65

McEvoy, Peter
Born London on 22nd March, 1953

Cls	Copt Heath (Hon)
Maj	Open leading amateur 1978-79
Chp	Amateur Champion 1977-78, r/u 1987
Nat	English Open Amateur Stroke Play 1980 (tied), r/u 1978. English Amateur r/u 1980
Trn	Duncan Putter 1978-80-87; Scrutton Jug 1978-80-85; Lytham Trophy 1979; Selborne Salver 1979-80; Leicestershire Fox 1976; Lagonda Trophy 1980; Berkshire Trophy 1985; County Champion of Champions 1984 (shared); Berkhamsted Trophy 1986; Hampshire Hog 1989
Oth	British Universities Stroke Play 1973
Reg	Warwickshire Match Play 1973-75-81; Warwickshire Amateur 1974-76-77-80-84; Warwickshire Open 1973-74; West of England Open Amateur Stroke Play 1977-80-83-85; Midland Open Amateur Stroke Play 1978; Midland Scratch Cup (Ireland) 1982-83-84-88
Int	Walker Cup 1977-79-81-85-89; Eisenhower Trophy 1978-80-84-86-88 (winners); GBI v Europe 1978-80-84-86-88; England (Home Int) 1977-78-80-81-83-84-85-86-87-88-89; v Scotland 1979; (Eur T Ch) 1977-79-81-83-85-87-89; in Fiat Trophy 1980; v France 1982-84-86-88-90; v Spain 1985-87-89
Jun	Youth International 1974
Mis	Only British amateur to complete 72 holes in US Masters (1978); AGW Trophy 1978

McGimpsey, Garth M
Born 17th July, 1955

Cls	Bangor, Royal Portrush, Royal Co Down
Chp	Amateur Champion 1985, s/f 1989
Nat	Irish Close Champion 1985; Irish Amateur 1988
Reg	North of Ireland Champion 1978-84, West of Ireland Champion 1984-88, East of Ireland Champion 1988 r/u 1979-80
Int	Walker Cup 1985-89. GBI v Europe 1984-86-88. Eisenhower Trophy 1984-86-88 (winners). Ireland (Home Int) 1978-80-81-82-83-84-85-86-87-88. (Eur T Ch) 1981
Mis	Irish long-driving champion 1977; UK long-driving champion 1979

Macgregor, George
Born Edinburgh on 19th August, 1944

Cls	Glencorse, Killarney (Hon), West Linton (Hon)
Nat	Scottish Open Amateur Stroke Play 1982. r/u 1975-79-80
Trn	Lytham Trophy 1975. Leven Gold Medal 1987
Reg	Lothians Amateur 1968. South-East Scotland Amateur 1972-75-79-80-81. East of Scotland Open Amateur 1979-82
Int	Walker Cup 1971-75-83-85-87-(91). GBI v Europe 1970-74. GB Commonwealth Team 1971-75. Scotland (Home Int) 1969-70-71-72-73-74-75-76-80-81-82-83-84-85-86-87; (Eur T Ch) 1971-73-75-81-83; v Belgium 1973-75-80; v England 1979; v France 1981-82; Scotland v Sweden 1983
Jun Int	Youths 1964-65-66
Mis	Leading Amateur Wills PGA Open 1970-71

McHenry, John
Born Cork on 14th March, 1964. Turned Professional 1987

PRO	
Eur	Boggi Open, Rolex Pro-Am 1990
AM	
Nat	Irish Amateur 1986
Reg	South of Ireland 1986
Int	Walker Cup 1987. Ireland (Home Int) 1985-86.

Macintosh, Keith William
Born Cardross, Dunbartonshire on 21st June, 1949

Cls	Cardross (Hon), Glasgow
Nat	Scottish Amateur 1979. Scottish Open Amateur Stroke Play r/u 1978 (tied)
Oth	Belgian Open Amateur 1980
Trn	Scottish Universities 1969. Cameron Corbett Vase 1979. Cadzow Cup 1968
Reg	Glasgow District Amateur 1973. Dunbartonshire Match Play 1980
Int	GBI v Europe 1980. Scotland (Home Int) 1980; v England 1979; v France 1980; v Belgium 1980; in Fiat Trophy 1980. Moroccan Amateur Team Champion 1980. Simon Bolivar Trophy 1979
Jun Int	Youths 1964

McKellar, Paul James
Born Clarkston, Glasgow on 6th April, 1956

Cls	East Renfrewshire (Hon)
Chp	Amateur r/u 1978, s/f 1977
Nat	Scottish Open Amateur Stroke Play 1977. Scottish Amateur r/u 1977-79
Reg	West of Scotland Close 1980
Int	Walker Cup 1977. GBI v Europe 1978. Europe v South America 1979. Scotland (Home Int) 1976-77-78; v Belgium 1978; v France 1978; v England 1979; in Caracas International 1979
Jun Int	Youths 1974-75-76-77-(**78**)-(**79**)

McKenna, Mary A
Born Dublin on 29th April, 1949

Cls	Donabate
Nat	British Ladies Open Amateur Stroke Play 1979, r/u 1976. Irish Ladies 1969-72-74-77-79-81-82-89, r/u 1968-73-76. Irish Women's Close Ch 1981
Trn	Dorothy Grey Stroke Play 1970-71-73. Players No 6 Cup 1971-72-74. Avia Foursomes 1977-84-86. Hermitage Scratch Cup 1975-79
Reg	South of Ireland Scratch Cup 1973-74-76-79
Int	Curtis Cup 1970-72-74-76-78-80-82-84-86. Vagliano Trophy 1969-71-73-75-77-79-81-85-87. World Team Championship 1970-74-76-**86**. Ireland (Home Int) 1968 to 1990; (Eur L T Ch) 1969-71-73-75-77-79-81-83-85-87; in Fiat Trophy 1979
Mis	Semi-finalist US Women's Western 1972, Broadmoor Tournament 1972 and US Women's Amateur 1980. Captain of LGU Touring Team to South Africa 1974. Leading Amateur Colgate European LPGA 1977 (tied)-79. Daks Woman Golfer of the Year 1979 Smyth Salver 1984. Taunton Trophy 1976

McLean, David
Born Holyhead on 30th January, 1947

Cls	Holyhead, Baron Hill, Killarney
Nat	Welsh Amateur 1973-78. Welsh Amateur Stroke Play 1975-79
Trn	Duncan Putter 1982
Reg	North Wales Amateur 1971-75-77-81. Caernarfonshire Amateur 1966-68-69-70 (tied)-77-79-81-82. Anglesey Amateur 1965-67-68-69-70-72-73-74-76-78-79-80-81-82
Int	Wales (Home Int) 1968-69-70-71-72-73-74-75-76-77-78-80-81-82-83-85-86-88; (Eur T Ch) 1975-77-79-81-83; v France 1975-76; v Denmark 1976-80-82; v Ireland 1979; v Spain 1980; v Austria 1982; v Switzerland 1980-82; in Fiat Trophy 1978-79; in Asian Team Championship 1979

McMahon, Suzanne (née Cadden)
Born Old Kilpatrick, Dunbartonshire on 8th October, 1957

Cls	Troon
Chp	British Ladies r/u 1975. British Ladies Stroke Play r/u 1975
Nat	Scottish Ladies Foursomes 1972
Reg	Dunbartonshire Ladies 1976-77-79
Int	Curtis Cup 1976. Vagliano Trophy 1975. Scotland (Home Int) 1974-75-76-77-79; (Eur L T Ch) 1975
Jun	Scottish Girls 1974-76. Scottish Girls Open Stroke Play 1976-77. British Girls 1975. Girl International 1972-73-74-75-76. World Junior Championship 1973
Mis	Daks Woman Golfer of the Year 1975

Madill, Maureen
See Garner

Maher, Sheila (née Vaughan)
Born Whiston, Liverpool on 9th March, 1942

Cls	Huyton and Prescot
Reg	Lancashire Ladies 1958-63-64
Int	Curtis Cup 1962-64. Vagliano Trophy 1961-65. GB Commonwealth Team 1963. England (Home Int) 1960-61-62-63-64
Jun	British Girls 1959.
Int	England Girls 1956-57-58-59
Mis	In 1963 on tour of Australasia as member of GB Commonwealth Team, tied first in Australian Ladies Foursomes, won New Zealand Ladies Foursomes and won New Zealand Junior Stroke Play

Mann, Lindsay S
Born 28th February, 1962

Trn	Tennant Cup 1982
Int	Walker Cup 1983. Scotland (Home Int) 1982-83

Marchbank, Brian
Born Perth on 20th April, 1958. Turned Professional 1979

PRO	
Eur	Equity & Law Challenge 1990
AM	
Nat	English Open Amateur Stroke Play r/u 1979
Trn	Lytham Trophy 1978. Scottish Champion of Champions 1979
Int	Walker Cup 1979. GBI v Europe 1976-78. Eisenhower Trophy 1978. Scotland (Home Int) 1978; (Eur T Ch) 1979; v Italy 1979
Jun	British Boys 1975. Scottish Boys 1976. British Youths 1978.
Int	Boys 1973-74-75. Youths 1976-77-78-79

Marks, Geoffrey C
Born Hanley, Stoke-on-Trent, in November, 1938

Cls	Hon member of Trentham, Trentham Park, Greenway Hall, Killarney, Walsall, Newcastle, Trevose, Stone. Royal & Ancient
Chp	Amateur s/f 1968-75
Nat	English Open Amateur Stroke Play r/u 1973-75
Trn	Scrutton Jug 1967. Prince of Wales Challenge Cup 1968. Leicestershire Fox 1968. Lytham Trophy 1970 (tied). Harlech Gold Cup 1974. Homer Salver 1977
Reg	Midland Amateur 1967. Staffordshire Amateur 1959-60-63-66-67-68-69-73
Int	Walker Cup 1969-71-**87**. Eisenhower Trophy 1970. GBI v Europe 1968-70. England (Home Int) 1963-67-68-69-70-71-74-75-(**80**)-(**81**)-(**82**)-(**83**); (Eur T Ch) 1967-69-71-75. GB Commonwealth Team 1975. GBI in Colombian International 1975
Jun Int	Boys 1955-56. Youths 1957-58-59-60
Mis	England Selector 1980-81-82-83 (chairman)

Marsh, Dr David Max
Born Southport on 29th April, 1934

Cls	Royal & Ancient, Hon member of Southport and Ainsdale, Ormskirk, West Lancashire, Worlington and Newmarket, Hillside, Clitheroe, Whalley
Nat	English Amateur 1964-70
Trn	Antlers Royal Mid-Surrey 1964-66. Formby Hare 1968. Boyd Quaich 1957
Int	Walker Cup 1959-71-(**73**)-(**75**); GBI v Europe 1958-(**72**)-(**74**). GBI v Professionals 1959. England (Home Int) 1956-57-58-59-60-64-65-66-**68**-**69**-**70**-**71**-72; (Eur T Ch) 1971
Jun Int	Boys 1951
Mis	EGU Selector 1974. British Selector 1975. Chairman Royal & Ancient Selection Committee 1979-83. President EGU 1987. Captain of Royal & Ancient 1990/91

Martin, Steve W
Born Dundee on 21st December, 1955. Turned Professional 1977

PRO	
Int	Scotland in World Cup 1980
AM	
Nat	Scottish Open Amateur Stroke Play 1976
Trn	Tennant Cup 1977
Reg	Central District Amateur 1973. Angus Amateur 1973. East of Scotland Open Amateur Stroke Play 1976.

Int	Walker Cup 1977. Eisenhower Trophy 1976 (winning team). GBI v Europe 1976. Scotland (Home Int) 1975-76-77; (Eur T Ch) 1977; v Belgium 1977; v Spain 1977
Jun	Scottish Boys Stroke Play 1972-73.
Int	Boys 1972-73. Youths 1973-75-76-77

Marvin, Vanessa Price
Born Cosford on 30th December, 1954. Turned Professional 1978

Cls	Easingwold (Hon)
PRO	
Eur	Carlsberg Trn 1979
AM	
Chp	British Ladies Amateur r/u 1977
Nat	English Ladies Amateur 1977-78.
Trn	Hampshire Rose 1975-78 (tied). Roehampton Gold Cup 1976. Newmark-Avia 1978
Reg	Yorkshire Ladies 1975-78. North of England Ladies 1975
Int	Curtis Cup 1978. Vagliano Trophy 1977. England (Home Int) 1977-78; (Eur L T Ch) 1977; in Fiat Trophy 1978
Mis	Leading amateur Colgate European LPGA 1977. Daks Woman Golfer of the Year 1978.

Mayo, Paul M
Born Newport, Gwent on 6th January, 1963. Turned Professional 1988

PRO	
Nat	Welsh PGA 1990
AM	
Maj	Leading Amateur in Open 1987
Chp	Amateur Champion 1987
Nat	Welsh Amateur 1987
Reg	Gwent Amateur 1982
Int	Walker Cup 1985-87; GBI v Europe 1986; Wales (Home Int) 1982-87
Jun	British Youths 1983; Welsh Boys 1979

Melia, Terry J
Born Wrexham on 7th July, 1955

Cls	Cardiff
Nat	Welsh Amateur 1979. Welsh Amateur Stroke Play 1980
Reg	Glamorgan County 1981-82
Int	Wales (Home Int) 1976-77-78-80-81-82; (Eur T Ch) 1977-79; v Denmark 1976-80; v Ireland 1979; v Switzerland 1980; v Spain 1980; v S America 1979

Milligan, James W
Born Irvine on 15th June, 1963

Cls	Kilmarnock (Barassie)
Nat	Scottish Amateur 1988
Trn	Scottish Champion of Champions 1989-90
Int	Walker Cup 1989; Scotland (Home Int) 1986-87-88-89-90; v West Germany 1987; v Italy 1988-90; v Sweden 1990; GBI v Europe 1988-90; World Cup (Eisenhower) 1988 (winners)-90
Jun	Scottish Youths 1984

Milne, William TG
Born Perth on 13th July, 1951. Turned Professional 1973

Trn	Newlands Trophy 1972
Reg	North of Scotland Stroke Play 1971. Perthshire Stroke Play 1973
Int	Walker Cup 1973. Scotland (Home Int) 1972-73; (Eur T Ch) 1973; v Belgium 1973
Jun	Scotland Youth International 1970-71-72
Mis	Won Lusaka Eagle Open 1974 and Northern Scottish Open 1974-75

Milton, Moira (née Paterson)
Born 18th December, 1923

Cls	Turnhouse, Hon Member of Gullane, Lenzie, Maccauvlei
Chp	British Ladies 1952.
Nat	Scottish Ladies r/u 1951
Reg	Dunbartonshire Ladies 1949. Midlothian Ladies 1962
Int	Curtis Cup 1952. GBI v France 1949-50; v Belgium 1950. Scotland (Home Int) 1949-50-51-52; v Australia 1951; v South Africa 1951. (Eur LT Ch) (1973)
Mis	Member of LGU Team to South Africa 1951.

Montgomerie, Colin S
Born Glasgow on 23rd June, 1963. Turned Professional 1987

PRO	
Eur	Portuguese Open 1989
Int	Scotland in Dunhill Cup 1988; in World Cup 1988
Mis	Rookie of the Year 1988
AM	
Chp	Amateur r/u 1984
Nat	Scottish Open Amateur Stroke Play 1985; Scottish Amateur 1987
Int	Walker Cup 1985-87; Eisenhower Trophy 1984-86; GBI v Europe 1986; Scotland (Home Int) 1984-85-86 (Eur T Ch) 1985; v Sweden 1984-86; v France 1985

Montgomerie, John Speir
Born Cambuslang on 7th August, 1913

Cls	Royal & Ancient, Cambuslang, Kilmarnock (Barassie), Pollok
Nat	Scottish Amateur 1957
Reg	Lanarkshire Amateur 1951-54
Int	Scotland (Home Int) 1957-(62)-(63); v Scandinavia 1958
Mis	Non-playing captain Scottish Team (Eur T Ch) 1965. Walker Cup Selector 1957 to 1965. President Scottish Golf Union 1965-66

Moore, Linda
See Simpson

Morgan, John
Born Oxford on 3rd September, 1943. Turned Professional 1968

Eur	Jersey Open 1986
RoW	Nigerian Open 1979. Lusaka Open 1979. Ivory Coast 1982

Morgan, John Llewellyn
Born Llandrindod Wells on 23rd June, 1918

Cls	Llandrindod Wells, Sutton Coldfield, Builth Wells, Little Aston, Aberystwyth, Killarney, St Deiniol, Ashburnham
Nat	Welsh Amateur 1950-51, r/u 1952
Trn	Berkshire Trophy 1953. Duncan Putter 1968. Harlech Gold Cross 1951-55
Sen	British Seniors 1974
Reg	Midlands Amateur 1949-50-52. Midlands Open 1950. Warwickshire Amateur 1951
Int	Walker Cup 1951-53-55. Wales (Home Int) 1948-49-50-51-52-53-54-56-57-58-59-60-61-62-63-64-66-67. (Eur T Ch) 1965
Mis	Professional for 4 years subsequently reinstated as Amateur

Morgan, Wanda
Born Lymm, Cheshire on 22nd March, 1910

Cls	Hon life member of Canterbury, Westgate, St Enodoc, Herne Bay, Belmont, Chestfield, Rochester and Cobham Park, Cooden Beach, Littlestone, Prince's, Seasalter, Barnehurst.
Chp	British Ladies 1935, r/u 1931.
Nat	English Ladies 1931-36-37
Trn	Sunningdale Foursomes 1948. Worplesdon Mixed Foursomes 1948. Fairway and Hazard Foursomes 1956. Daily Graphic 1941-42
Reg	Kent Ladies 1930-31-33-35-36-37-53
Int	Curtis Cup 1932-34-36. GBI v France 1932-33-34-35-36-37; v Canada 1934. England (Home Int) 1931-32-33-34-35-36-37-53

Mosey, Ian
Born Keighley on 29th August, 1951. Turned Professional 1972

Maj	Monte Carlo Open 1984
Oth	Merseyside International 1980.
RoW	Kalahari Classic 1980. Holiday Inns, SA 1981

Mouland, Mark
Born Wales on 23rd April, 1961. Turned Professional 1981

PRO	
Eur	Car Care Plan International 1986. KLM Open 1988
Reg	Midland Professional Stroke Play 1984
Int	Wales: in Dunhill Cup 1986-87-88-89-90; World Cup 1988-89-90; Kirin Cup 1988
AM	
Jun	British Boys 1976

Mulcare, Pat
Born Ballybunion, 1945

Cls	Woodbrook (Hon), Dublin (Hon)
Maj	East of Ireland Open Amateur 1971-72-73. South of Ireland Open Amateur 1971
Int	Walker Cup 1975. Ireland (Home Int) 1968-69-70-71-72-73-74-78-80; (Eur T Ch) 1975-79; v France, West Germany and Sweden 1978-80

Murray, Gordon H
Born Paisley on 19th December, 1936

Cls	Fereneze (Hon)
Nat	Scottish Amateur 1974-76, r/u 1975; Scottish Stroke Play 1983
Reg	West of Scotland Amateur 1971-73-76-78
Int	Walker Cup 1977. GBI v Europe 1978. Scotland (Home Int) 1973-74-75-76-77-78-83 (Eur T Ch) 1975-77; v Spain 1974-77; v Belgium 1975-77

Murray, Stuart
Born Paisley on 10th November, 1933. Turned Professional 1963

Nat	Scottish Amateur 1962, r/u 1961
Trn	Tennant Cup 1963. Edward Trophy 1960-61
Reg	West of Scotland Amateur 1958. Renfrewshire Amateur 1958-59. Glasgow Amateur 1960. Hampshire Amateur 1963. Midland Professional 1964-67-68. Middlesex Open 1973
Int	Walker Cup 1963. GB Commonwealth Team 1963 GBI v Europe. 1958-62. Scotland (Home Int) 1959-60-61-62-63, v Scandinavia 1960

Needham, Sandra Claire
See Roy

Nesbitt, Claire
See Robinson

New, Beverley Jayne
Born Bristol on 30th July, 1960. Turned Professional 1984

PRO
Eur   Broadway Group Wirral Classic 1988
RoW   Thailand Ladies Open 1987; Malaysian Ladies Open 1988
AM
Nat   English Ladies 1980; Welsh Ladies Stroke Play r/u 1979
Trn   Hampshire Rose 1980; WPGA United Friendly Insurance Trn, Worplesdon Mixed Foursomes 1982; Roehampton Gold Cup, Worplesdon Mixed Foursomes, Martin Bowl 1983
Reg   Somerset Ladies 1979-80-81-82-83; Bristol & District Open 1983
Int   Curtis Cup 1984; Vagliano Trophy 1983; England (Home Int) 1980-81-82-83; (Eur L T Ch) 1981-83; Fiat Trophy 1980
Mis   Doris Chambers Trophy 1983

Nichol, Margaret
See Pickard

Nicholas, Alison
Born Gibraltar on 6th March, 1962. Turned Professional 1984

PRO
Maj   Ladies British Open 1987, 3rd 1988
Eur   Laing Charity Classic 1987; Variety Club Classic, British Olivetti, Guernsey Open 1988; Lufthansa German Open, Gislaved Open 1989; Variety Club Classic 1990
Int   Solheim Cup 1990
AM
Nat   Ladies British Open Amateur Stroke Play 1983
Reg   Yorkshire Ladies 1984; Northern Foursomes 1983
Jun   North of England Girls 1982-83
Mis   Taunton Trophy 1983; Duncan Salver 1983

O'Connell, Eoghan
Turned Professional 1990

PRO
Eur   Swedish Match Play, Torras Hostench-El Prat 1990
AM
Int   Walker Cup 1989; Eisenhower Trophy 1988 (winners); GBI v Europe 1988; Ireland (Home Int) 1985; (Eur T Ch) 1989

O'Connor, Christy
Born Galway on 21st December, 1924

Maj   Open r/u 1965, 3rd 1958-61.
Trn   Swallow-Penfold 1955. Dunlop Masters 1956-59. Spalding 1955 (tied). PGA Match Play 1957. Daks 1959. Ballantine 1960. Irish Hospitals 1960-62. Carling-Caledonian 1961. Martini 1963 (tied)-64. Jeyes 1964. Carrolls 1964-66-67-72. Senior Service 1965; Gallaher Ulster 1966-68-69. Alcan International 1968 (tied). Bowmaker 1970. John Player Classic 1970.
Oth   Ulster Professional 1953-54. Irish Professional 1958-60-61-62-63-65-66-71-75-77. Irish Dunlop 1962-65-66-67. Gleneagles Pro-Am 1962. Southern Ireland Professional 1969-76. Sean Connery Pro-Am 1970.
Sen   PGA Seniors 1976-77-79-81-82. World Seniors 1976-77
Int   Ryder Cup 1955-57-59-61-63-65-67-69-71-73. GBI v Commonwealth 1956. Ireland in World Cup 1956-57-58 (winners) -59-60-61-62-63-64-66-67-68-69-71-75. Ireland in Double Diamond 1971-72-73-74-75-76-77
Mis   Harry Vardon Trophy 1961-62. Second in order of Merit 1964 (equal)-65-66-69-70. AGW Trophy 1977

O'Connor, Christy, Jr
Born Galway on 19th August, 1948. Turned Professional 1965

Maj   Open 3rd 1985
Eur   Martini 1975 (tied). Carrolls Irish Open 1975. Sumrie 1976-78
Oth   Irish Dunlop 1974. Carrolls Irish Match Play 1975-77
RoW   Zambian Open 1974
Int   Ryder Cup 1975-89. Ireland in Double Diamond 1972-74-76-77. Ireland in World Cup 1974-75-78-85-89. Hennessy-Cognac 1974-84. GBI v South Africa 1976. Dunhill Cup 1985-89
Mis   Braid Taylor Memorial Medal 1976-83. Tooting Bec Cup 1985

Oldcorn, Andrew
Born Bolton on 31st March, 1960. Turned Professional 1983

Nat   English Amateur 1982
Int   Walker Cup 1983. England (Home Int) 1982-83
Jun   Scottish Youths Stroke Play 1979

O'Leary, John E
Born Dublin on 19th August, 1949. Turned Professional 1970

PRO
Trn   Sumrie 1975. Greater Manchester Open 1976. Carrolls Irish Open 1982; Irish Dunlop 1972
RoW   Holiday Inns (Swaziland) 1975
Int   Ryder Cup 1975. Ireland in World Cup 1972-80-82. Ireland in Double Diamond 1972-73-74-75-76-77. GBI v Europe 1976-78-82
AM
Reg   South of Ireland Amateur 1970.
Int   Ireland (Home Int) 1969-70; (Eur T Ch) 1969
Jun Int   Youths 1970

Oosterhuis, Peter A
Born London on 3rd May, 1948. Turned Professional November 1968

PRO
Maj   Open r/u 1974-82; leading British player 1975 (7th), 1978 (6th) US Masters 3rd 1973
Eur   Agfacolor, Sunbeam Pro-Am, Piccadilly 1971; Penfold 1972; French Open, Piccadilly, Viyella PGA 1973; French Open, Italian Open 1974
US   Canadian Open 1981
RoW   General Motors South Africa 1970; Transvaal Open, Schoeman Park, Rhodesian Dunlop Masters 1971; Glen Anil Classic 1972; Rothman's Match Play South Africa, Maracaibo Open 1973; El Paraiso Open 1974
Oth   Sunningdale Foursomes 1969; Coca-Cola Young Professionals 1970-72
Reg   Southern England Professional 1971
Int   Ryder Cup 1971-73-75-77-79-81; England in World Cup 1971-73, in Double Diamond 1973-74
Mis   Rookie of the Year 1969; Harry Vardon Trophy 1971-72-73-74; AGW Trophy 1973-74
AM
Trn   Berkshire Trophy 1966
Int   Walker Cup 1967; Eisenhower Trophy 1968; England (Home Int) 1966-67-68
Jun   British Youths 1966
Int   Boys 1964-65; Youths 1966-67-68

O'Reilly, Therese (*née* Moran)
Born 29th January, 1954

Cls	Grange
Nat	Irish Ladies' Amateur 1986
Reg	Leinster Ladies 1975-78. Irish Midland Ladies 1974
Int	Ireland (Home Int) 1977-78-86-88; (Eur L T Ch) 1988

O'Sullivan, Denis

Nat	Irish Amateur 1985
Int	Ireland (Home Int) 1985-86-87

O'Sullivan, Dr William M
Born Killarney on 13th March, 1911

Cls	Waterville, Hon member of Killarney, Dooks, Tralee, Muskerry, Cork, Ballybunion
Chp	Irish Open Amateur 1949, r/u 1936-53. Irish Amateur r/u 1940
Int	Ireland (Home Int) 1934-35-36-37-38-47-48-49-50-51-53-54. President Golfing Union of Ireland 1959-60

Oxley, Dinah
See Henson

Panton, Catherine Rita
Born Bridge of Allan, Stirlingshire on 14th June, 1955. Turned Professional 1978

Cls	Glenbervie (Hon), Pitlochry (Hon), Silloth (Hon), South Herts
PRO	
Eur	Carlsberg Tournament 1979. State Express Ladies Championship 1979. Elizabeth Ann Classic 1980. European Ladies Champion 1981. Moben Kitchens Classic 1982. Qualified for USLPGA Tour, January 1983. Smirnoff Irish Classic, UBM Northern Classic 1983, Dunham Forest Pro-Am 1983. McEwans Wirral Caldy Classic 1985. Delsjö Open 1985. Portuguese Open 1986-87. Scottish Open 1988
AM	
Chp	Ladies British Open Amateur 1976
Reg	East of Scotland Ladies 1976
Int	World Team Championship 1976. Vagliano Trophy 1977. Scotland (Home Int) 1972-73-76-77-78; (Eur L T Ch) 1973-77
Jun	Scottish Girls 1969. Girl Int 1969-70-71-72-73
Mis	Scottish Sportswoman of the Year 1976. Member of LGU under-25 team to tour Canada 1973

Panton, John, MBE
Born Pitlochry, Perthshire on 9th October, 1916. Turned Professional 1935

Maj	Leading British player in 1956 Open (5th)
Trn	Silver King 1950. Daks 1951. North-British-Harrogate 1952. Goodwin Foursomes 1952. Yorkshire Evening News 1954. PGA Match Play 1956, r/u 1968
Eur	Woodlawn Invitation Open (Germany) 1958-59-60
Oth	West of Scotland Professional 1947-48-52-54-55-61-63. Scottish Professional 1948-49-50-51-54-55-59-66 (tied). Northern Open 1948-51-52-56-59-60-62. West of Scotland PGA Match Play 1954-55-56-64. Goodwin Foursomes 1952. Gleneagles-Saxone 1956.
Sen	Pringle Seniors 1967-69. World Seniors 1967
Int	Ryder Cup 1951-53-61. Scotland in World Cup 1955-56-57-58-59-60-62-63-64-65-66-68
Mis	Harry Vardon Trophy 1951. AGW Trophy 1967. Hon Professional to Royal & Ancient from 1988

Parkin, Philip
Born Doncaster on 12th December, 1961. Turned Professional 1984

PRO	
Int	Wales in World Cup 1984-89; Dunhill Cup 1985-86-87-89-90; Hennessy-Cognac Cup 1984
Mis	Rookie of the Year 1984
AM	
Chp	Amateur Champion 1983
Int	Walker Cup 1983. Wales (Home Int) 1980-81-82.
Jun	British Youths 1982

Paterson, Moira
See Milton

Peel, Marjorie
See Draper

Perkins, Tegwen
See Thomas

Perowne, Arthur Herbert
Born Norwich on 21st February, 1930

Cls	Royal Norwich, Hunstanton, West Norfolk
Chp	English Open Amateur Stroke Play 1958
Oth	Swedish Amateur 1974
Trn	Berkshire Trophy 1958 (tied)
Reg	East Anglia Open 1952. Norfolk Amateur 1948-51-52-53-54-55-56-57-58-60-61. Norfolk Open 1964
Int	Walker Cup 1949-53-59. Eisenhower Trophy 1958. GBI v Denmark 1955; v Professionals 1956-58. England (Home Int) 1947-48-49-50-51-53-54-55-57; v France 1950-54-56-59; v Sweden 1947; v Denmark 1947
Jun	Carris Trophy 1946
Int	Boys 1946

Phillips, Ann
See Howard

Phillips, Kathryn
See Lumb

Pickard, Margaret (*née* Nichol)
Born on 25th April, 1938

Cls	Alnmouth (Hon)
Nat	English Ladies 1960, r/u 1957-67
Reg	Northern Ladies 1957-58. Northumberland Ladies 1956-57-58-61-62-64-65-66-67-69-70-71-76-77-82
Int	Curtis Cup 1968-70. Vagliano Trophy 1959-61-67. England (Home Int) 1957-58-59-60-61-67-69-(83). (Eur L T Ch) (1983)

Pierse, Arthur D'Arcy
Born Dublin on 30th April, 1952

Reg	West of Ireland Open Amateur 1980-82. North of Ireland Amateur 1987. East of Ireland 1979
Int	Walker Cup 1983, GBI v Europe 1980-82. Ireland (Home Int) 1976-77-78-80-81-82-83-84-85-87-88 (Eur T Ch) 1981. Eisenhower Trophy 1982

Pirie, Alex Kemp
Born Aberdeen on 21st June, 1942

Cls	Hazelhead (Hon), Cruden Bay
Nat	Scottish Amateur r/u 1972-74
Trn	Eden Tournament 1963.

Reg Northern Scottish Open 1970. West of Scotland Open
Amateur 1972. East of Scotland Open Amateur Stroke
Play 1975. North East Scotland Match Play 1964-66-
67-68-71-73. Aberdeenshire Stroke Play 1966-68
Int Walker Cup 1967. GBI v Europe 1970. Scotland (Home
Int) 1966-67-68-69-70-71-72-73-74-75; (Eur T Ch)
1967-69; v Belgium 1973-75; v Spain 1974

Polland, Eddie
*Born Newcastle, Co Down on 10th June, 1947. Turned
Professional 1967*

Eur Spanish Open 1976-80
Trn Penfold 1973. Sun Alliance PGA Match Play 1975.
Irish Dunlop 1973-75. Irish Professional 1974. Carrolls
Irish Match Play 1974. Ulster Professional 1976
Int Ryder Cup 1973. Ireland in World Cup 1973-74-76-
77-78-79. Ireland in Double Diamond 1972-73-74-75-
76-77. GB v Europe 1974-76-78-80; v South Africa 1976

Pook, Elizabeth (*née* Chadwick)
Born Inverness on 4th April, 1943

Cls Mendip
Chp British Ladies 1966-67.
Nat English Ladies r/u 1963
Reg Central England Mixed Foursomes 1962-63-64 North
of England Ladies 1965-66-67. Cheshire Ladies 1963-
64-65-66-67
Int Curtis Cup 1966. GB Commonwealth 1967.
GBI v Europe 1963-67. England (Home Int) 1963-65-
66-67; (Eur L T Ch) 1967; v France 1965
Jun Girl International 1961

Porter, Ruth
See Slark

Power, Eddie
Born Waterford on 17th January, 1965

Cls Tramore (Hon) Enniscorthy (Hon)
Nat Irish Amateur 1987, r/u 1983
Int Ireland (Home Int) 1987-88
Jun Boy International 1982. Youth International 1984-86.
European Boys 1982. Junior World Cup 1982

Price Fisher, Elizabeth
*Born London on 17th January, 1923. Turned Professional
1968, reinstated as Amateur 1971*

Cls Hankley Common, Farnham, Berkshire
Chp British Ladies 1959, r/u 1954-58.
Nat English Ladies r/u 1947-54-55
Oth Danish Ladies 1952. Portuguese Ladies 1964
Trn Spalding Ladies 1955-59. Astor Salver 1955-56-59.
Fairway and Hazard Foursomes 1954-60. Kayser
Bondor Foursomes 1958 (tied). Roehampton Gold
Cup 1960. Central England Mixed Foursomes 1971-
76-82
Reg South Eastern Ladies 1955-59-60-69. Surrey Ladies
1954-55-56-57-58-59-60
Int Curtis Cup 1950-52-54-56-58-60. Vagliano Trophy
1959. GBI v Canada 1950-54-58; v France 1953-55-57;
v Belgium 1953-55-57. GB Commonwealth Team
1955-59. England (Home Int) 1948-51-52-53-54-55-
56-57-58-59-60
Mis AGW Trophy 1952.

Rafferty, Ronan
*Born Newry on 13th January, 1964. Turned Professional
1981*

PRO
Eur Equity & Law Challenge 1988; Lancia Italian Open,
Scandinavian Enterprise Open, Volvo Masters 1989,
PLM Open, Swiss Open 1990
RoW Venezuelan Open 1982; South Australian Open, New
Zealand Open 1987; Australian Match Play 1988;
Coca-Cola Classic (Aust) 1990
Int Ryder Cup 1989; Kirin Cup 1988; Four Tours World
Chp 1989-90; GBI v Australia 1988; Hennessy-Cognac
1984; Ireland in World Cup 1983-84-87-88; Dunhill
Cup 1986-87-88(winners)-89-90 (winners)
Mis Harry Vardon Trophy 1989
AM
Nat Irish Amateur 1980; English Amateur Open Stroke
Play 1980(tied)
Int Walker Cup 1981; Eisenhower Trophy 1980;
GBI v Europe 1980; Ireland (Home Int) 1980; v Wales
1979; v France, Germany, Sweden 1980; Fiat Trophy
1980; (Eur T Ch) 1981
Jun British Boys 1979; Irish Youths 1979; Ulster Youths
1979
Int Boys 1978-79; Youths 1979-80

Rawlings, Mandy
Born Bargoed, Glamorganshire on 15th June, 1964

Cls Bargoed, Whitchurch, Radyr (Hon)
Nat Welsh Ladies 1980-81
Int Wales (Home Int) 1978-79-80; in Fiat Trophy 1980.
Girls International 1981. Senior International 1981-83-
84. Vagliano Trophy 1981
Jun Welsh Girls 1979-81. Girl International 1976-77-78-
79-80. De Beers Ch 1980

Rawlings, Vicki
See Thomas

Reddan, Clarrie (*née* Tiernan)
Born Drogheda on 3rd July, 1916

Cls Co Louth
Chp British Ladies r/u 1949
Nat Irish Ladies 1936, r/u 1946-48.
US New Jersey State Ladies 1937. Canadian Ladies r/u
1938
Int Curtis Cup 1938-48. GBI v Canada 1938. Ireland
(Home Int) 1935-36-37-38-39-47-48-49

Redford, Carole
See Caldwell

Rees, Christopher
Nat Welsh Amateur 1986
Int Wales (Home Int) 1986-88
Jun Welsh Boys 1982

Reid, Dale
*Born Ladybank, Fife on 20th March, 1959. Turned
Professional 1979*

PRO
Eur Carlsberg (Coventry) 1980. Carlsberg (Gleneagles),
Moben Kitchens 1981. Guernsey Open 1982. United
Friendly, International Classic 1983. Caldy Classic
1983. UBM Classic, JS Bloor Classic 1984. Ulster
Volkswagen Classic, Brend Hotels International 1985.
British Olivetti 1986. Volmac Open, European Open,
Bowring Scottish Ladies Open, Volkswagen Classic
1987. European Open, Toshiba Players Chp 1988.

Oth	Sunningdale Foursomes (with Corinne Dibnah) 1990
Int	Solheim Cup 1990
Mis	Order of Merit winner 1984-87
AM	
Int	Scotland (Home Int) 1978
Jun	Fife Girls 1973-75. Scottish Girls International 1974-75-76-77

Rennie, Joan Kerr (née Hastings)
Born Troon on 29th May, 1941

Cls	Aberdeen Ladies, Hon member of Troon Bentinck, Kilmarnock (Barassie), Troon Municipal
Nat	Scottish Ladies 1967, r/u 1968
Reg	Ayrshire Ladies 1960-61-63-64-66-67. Aberdeenshire Ladies 1980
Int	Curtis Cup 1966. Vagliano Trophy 1961-67. Scotland (Home Int) 1961-65-66-67-71-72; (Eur L T Ch) 1973
Jun	Scottish Girls 1980.
Int	Girls 1957-58-59

Richmond, Maureen (née Walker)
Born Kilmacolm on 22nd April, 1955

Cls	Kilmacolm (Hon), Troon, Shiskine (Hon)
Int	Curtis Cup 1974. Vagliano Trophy 1975. Scotland (Home Int) 1972-73-74-75-77-78; (Eur L T Ch) 1973-75
Jun	British Girls 1972. Scottish Girls 1970-71-73.
Int	Girls International 1969-70-71-72-73
Mis	Member of LGU Under-25 Team to tour Canada 1973.

Robb, Diane
See Bailey

Roberts, Sharon
Born Penmaenmawr on 8th June, 1964

Cls	Llandudno (Maesdu)
Nat	Welsh Ladies Amateur 1984-88-90 r/u 1987
Trn	Keighley Open 1987. Birkdale Open 1988
Reg	Midlands Match Play 1987-88
Int	Wales (Home Int) 1983-84-85-86-87-88-89-90; (Eur L T Ch) 1983-87.

Robertson, Isabella (Belle), MBE
Born Southend, Argyll, on 11th April, 1936

Cls	Dunaverty (Hon)
Maj	Ladies British Open: leading amateur (Smyth Salver); r/u 1980-81
Chp	Ladies British Open Amateur 1981; r/u 1959-65-70
Nat	Ladies British Open Amateur Stroke Play 1971-72-85; Scottish Ladies 1965-66-71-72-78-80; r/u 1959-63-70
Oth	New Zealand Ladies Match Play 1971
Trn	Sunningdale Foursomes 1960; Avia Foursomes 1972-81-84-86; Helen Holm Trophy 1973-79-86; Players No 6 Cup 1973-76; Roehampton Gold Cup 1978 (tied)-79-81-82
Reg	West of Scotland Ladies 1957-64-66-69; Dunbartonshire Ladies 1958 to 1963, 1965-66-68-69-78
Int	Curtis Cup 1960-66-68-70-72-(**74**)-(**76**)-82-86; Vagliano Trophy 1959-63-65-69-71-81; Espirito Santo 1964-66-**68**-72-80-82; GB Commonwealth Team 1971-(**75**); Scotland (Home Int) 1958 to 1966, 69-72-73-78-80-81-82 (Eur L T Ch) 1965-**67**-69-71-73-81-83; Fiat Trophy 1978-80
Mis	Daks Woman Golfer of the Year 1971-81; Frank Moran Trophy 1971; leading qualifier in US Ladies Amateur 1978; Scottish Sportswoman of the Year 1968-71-78-81; Avia Golfer of the Year 1985

Robertson, Janette
See Wright

Robinson, Claire (née Nesbitt)
Born 7th March, 1953

Nat	Irish Ladies Amateur 1976-80
Reg	Ulster Ladies 1976-78
Int	Curtis Cup 1980. Vagliano Trophy 1979. Ireland (Home Int) 1974 to 81. (Eur L T Ch) 1975-77-79

Robinson, Jeremy
Born 21st January, 1966. Turned Professional 1987

PRO	
Eur	Old Links Satellite 1989
AM	
Nat	English Amateur Stroke Play (Brabazon Trophy) 1987
Trn	Lagonda Trophy 1985
Int	Walker Cup 1987. England (Home Int) 1986

Roderick, R Neil
Born Swansea on 8th March, 1966. Turned Professional 1990

Cls	Pontardawe
Nat	Welsh Amateur Stroke Play 1984-88. English Open Amateur Stroke Play 1989
Trn	Tenby Eagle 1988. Harlech Gold Cross 1986. Southerndown Silver Ram 1984-85-86. Worplesdon Mixed Foursomes 1986. Duncan Putter 1989
Int	Walker Cup 1989. Wales (Home Int) 1983-84-85-86-87-88. GBI v Europe 1988
Jun	Welsh Boys 1982-83

Roper, Roger
Born 15th April, 1962

| Nat | English Open Amateur Stroke Play 1985 (shared) |
| Int | England (Home Int) 1984-85-86-87 |

Roy, Sandra Clair (née Needham)
Born Bishopton, Renfrewshire on 8th March, 1946

Cls	Cawder (Hon), Machrihanish (Hon), Troon
Nat	Scottish Ladies 1976
Trn	Helen Holm Trophy 1974
Reg	West of Scotland Ladies 1967-71-72-73-75. Lanarkshire Ladies 1969-72-73-77-83-84
Int	Vagliano Trophy 1973-75, Scotland (Home Int) 1969-71-72-73-74-75-76-83; (Eur L T Ch) 1969-75-77
Mis	Member of LGU team to tour South Africa 1974

Russell, David J
Born Birmingham on 2nd May, 1954. Turned Professional 1973

| Eur | Car Care Plan International 1985 |

Saddler, AC
Born Forfar, Angus on 11th August, 1935

Cls	Forfar, Carnoustie
Nat	Scottish Amateur r/u 1960
Trn	Berkshire Trophy 1962
Int	Walker Cup 1963-65-67-(**77**) Eisenhower Trophy 1962-(**76**) (winners)-78. GB Commonwealth Team 1959-63-67; v Europe 1960-62-66-(**76**)-(**78**); v Professionals 1959-61. Scotland (Home Int) 1959-60-61-62-63-65-(**74**)-(**75**)-(**76**)-(**77**); (Eur T Ch) (**1975**)-(**77**)

Saunders, Vivien Inez
Born Sutton on 24th November, 1946. Turned Professional 1969

PRO	
Maj	Ladies British Open 1977
Trn	Avia Foursomes 1978; Keighley Trophy 1981; British Car Auctions 1980
US	1969 First European to qualify for LPGA tour
RoW	Schweppes-Tarax Open (Australia), Chrysler Open (Australia) 1973
Mis	Founder WPGA & Chairman 1978-79
AM	
Chp	Ladies British Open Amateur r/u 1966
Trn	Avia Foursomes 1967
Int	Curtis Cup 1968; Vagliano Trophy 1967; GB Commonwealth Team 1967; England (Home Int) 1967-68 (Eur L T Ch) 1967; v France 1966-67
Jun Int	Girls 1964-65-66-67

Sewell, Douglas
Born Woking on 19th November, 1929. Turned Professional 1960

PRO	
Trn	Martini International 1970 (shared); Wentworth Pro-Am Foursomes 1968
Reg	West of England Open Professional 1968-70
AM	
Nat	English Amateur 1958-60; English Open Amateur Stroke-Play 1957-59
Trn	Scrutton Jug 1959; Golf Illustrated Gold Vase 1960; Sunningdale Foursomes 1959
Reg	Surrey Amateur 1954-56-58
Int	Walker Cup 1957-59; Eisenhower Trophy 1960; GB Commonwealth Team 1959; England (Home Int) 1956-57-58-59-60

Shapcott, Susan
Born 2nd November, 1969. Turned Professional 1989

Cls	Knowle
Chp	Ladies British Open Amateur r/u 1987
Nat	English Women's Stroke Play 1986. Welsh Open Amateur Stroke Play 1987-88. English Ladies Close r/u 1986
Reg	Gloucestershire Ladies 1986
Int	Curtis Cup 1988. England (Home Int) 1986-88
Mis	Dinwiddy Trophy 1985-87
Jun	British Girls 1985. English Girls 1986-87

Shaw, Graeme
Born Glasgow on 6th June, 1960

Cls	Haggs Castle
Reg	Glasgow Amateur 1986. Scottish Champion of Champions 1987
Int	Walker Cup 1987. (Scotland) Home Int 1984-86-87-88-90; v West Germany 1987

Sheahan, Dr David B
Born Southsea, England on 25th February, 1940

Cls	Grange
Nat	Irish Amateur 1961-66-70
Trn	Jeyes Professional 1962 (as an Amateur)
Oth	Boyd Quaich 1962
Int	Walker Cup 1963. GBI v Europe 1962-64. Ireland (Home Int) 1961-62-63-64-65-66-67-70; (Eur T Ch) 1965-67 (winners on both occasions)

Shepperson, AE
Born Sutton-in-Ashfield on 8th April, 1936

Cls	Coxmoor (Hon), Notts
Nat	English Open Amateur Stroke Play r/u 1958-62
Trn	President's Putter 1957
Reg	Nottinghamshire Amateur 1955-58-61-65. Nottinghamshire Open 1955-58
Int	Walker Cup 1957-59. England (Home Int) 1956-57-58-59-60-62
Jun	British Boys 1953

Simpson, Linda (*née* Moore)
Born 7th October, 1961

Reg	Cornwall Ladies 1979-80-81. South-West Ladies 1981
Int	Curtis Cup 1980. England (Home Int) 1979-80. (Eur L T Ch) 1981

Sinclair, Alexander
Born West Kilbride, Ayrshire on 6th July, 1920

Cls	Royal & Ancient, Hon member of West Kilbride, Drumpellier, Bothwell Castle, Royal Troon
Trn	Newlands Trophy 1950
Oth	Royal & Ancient Silver Cross 1972. Royal Medal 1977. Scottish Open Amateur Seniors 1979
Reg	West of Scotland Amateur 1950. Lanarkshire Amateur 1952-59-61. Glasgow Amateur 1961
Int	Scotland (Home Int) 1950-(66)-(67). (Eur T Ch) (1967)
Mis	Chairman R & A Selection Committee from 1969 to 1975. Leading Amateur (joint second) in Northern Open 1948. President Scottish Golf Union 1976-78. Frank Moran Trophy 1978. Chairman R & A Amateur Status Committee 1979-81. President European Golf Association 1981-82-83. Captain of Royal & Ancient 1988/89

Slark, Ruth (*née* Porter)
Born Chesterfield on 6th May, 1939

Cls	Long Ashton (Hon), Bath, Burnham and Berrow, Reigate Heath, Walton Heath
Nat	English Ladies 1959-61-65, r/u 1978
Oth	Australian Ladies r/u 1963
Trn	Astor Prince's 1961. Fairway and Hazard Foursomes 1958. Roehampton Gold Cup 1963. Astor Salver 1962-63. Hovis Ladies 1966 (tied). Avia Foursomes 1968
Reg	South Western Ladies 1956-57-60-61-62-64-65-66-67-69-72-77-79. Gloucestershire Ladies 1957-59-61-62-63-64-66-67-69-73-74-75-76-77
Int	Curtis Cup 1960-62-64. Vagliano Trophy 1959-61-65. GB Commonwealth Team 1963. World Team Ch 1964-66. England (Home Int) 1959-60-61-62-64-65-66-68-75-78; (Eur L T Ch) 1965
Jun	British Girls 1956. Scottish Girls Open Stroke Play 1958. Girls International 1955-56-57
Mis	Taunton Trophy 1978

Smith, Anne [Stant], (*née* Willard)
Born Calcutta, India on 23rd May, 1950

Cls	Walsall, Hon member of Gorleston, Purdis Heath (Ipswich), Ganton, Beau Desert
Nat	British Ladies Stroke Play 1973
Trn	Sunningdale Foursomes 1970. Central England Mixed Foursomes 1968. Hoylake Mixed Foursomes 1978
Reg	Suffolk Ladies 1967-69-70-71. Midland Ladies 1973-75. Staffordshire Ladies 1975-78-79, r/u 1977

Int	Curtis Cup 1976. Vagliano Trophy 1975. GB Commonwealth Team 1975. England (Home Int) 1974-75-76; (Eur L T Ch) 1975
Jun	British Girls 1965. English Girls 1967. Girl International 1965-66-67-68
Mis	Member of LGU Touring Team to South Africa 1974

Smith, William Dickson
Born Glasgow on 2nd February, 1918

Cls	Prestwick (Hon), Royal & Ancient, Royal Troon, Selkirk (Hon), Southerness, Gullane
Maj	Leading amateur (5th) in Open 1957
Nat	Scottish Amateur 1958. Scottish Senior Open Amateur 1983
Oth	Indian Open Amateur 1945. Portuguese Open Amateur 1967-70.
Trn	Worplesdon Mixed Foursomes 1957. Royal & Ancient Royal Medal 1971
Reg	Border Amateur 1949-51-57-63. Dumfriesshire Amateur 1956
Int	Walker Cup 1959. GBI v Europe 1958. Scotland (Home Int) 1957-58-59-60-63-(83); v Scandinavia 1958-60

Smye, Catherine
See McCann

Smyth, Des
Born Drogheda on 12th February, 1953. Turned Professional 1973

PRO	
Trn	PGA Match Play 1979. Newcastle Brown 900, Greater Manchester Open 1980. Coral Classic 1981. Sanyo Open 1983. Jersey Open 1988
Oth	Irish PGA 1979-90. Carrolls Irish Match Play, Irish Dunlop 1980
Int	Ryder Cup 1979-81. Ireland in World Cup 1979-80-82-83-88-89. Hennessy-Cognac Cup 1980-82-84. Dunhill Cup 1985-86-87-88 (winners)
AM	
Int	Ireland (Home Int) 1972-73; (Eur T Ch) 1973

Sommerville, Dorothea
See Hastings

Soulsby, Janet
Born Corbridge on 25th December, 1964. Turned Professional 1985

Nat	Ladies British Open Amateur Stroke Play 1981
Reg	Northumberland Ladies 1983
Int	Curtis Cup 1982
Mis	Taunton Trophy, Duncan Salver, Dinwiddy Trophy 1981

Spearman, Marley
See Harris

Squirrell, Hew Crawford
Born Cardiff on 15th August, 1932

Cls	Hon member of Cardiff, Moseley, Killarney
Nat	Welsh Amateur 1958-59-60-64-65, r/u 1962-71
Trn	Antlers Royal Mid-Surrey 1959-61. Hampshire Hog 1961. Berkhamsted Trophy 1960-63. Boyd Quaich 1955
Reg	Glamorgan Amateur 1959-65. Herts Amateur 1963-73
Int	Wales (Home Int) 1955-56-57-58-59-60-61-62-63-64-65-66-67-68-**69-70-71**-73-74-75; (Eur T Ch) 1965-67-69-71-75; v France 1975
Mis	Deputy-Director Golf Foundation

Stant, Anne
See Smith

Stephen, Alexander R (Sandy)
Born St Andrews on 8th January, 1954. Turned Professional 1985

Cls	Lundin (Hon), Muckhart (Hon), Broomieknowe
PRO	
Trn	Scottish Professional Chp 1988
AM	
Nat	Scottish Amateur 1971
Trn	Scottish Champion of Champions 1984. Leven Gold Medal 1984
Reg	North of Scotland Open Amateur 1972-77. Fife Amateur 1973. Lothians Amateur 1978; East of Scotland Open Amateur 1974-77-83-84. West of Scotland Open Amateur 1975.
Int	Walker Cup 1985. GBI v Europe 1972. Scotland (Home Int) 1971-72-73-74-75-76-77-84-85; (Eur T Ch) 1975; v Spain 1974; v Belgium 1975-77-78.
Jun	Scottish Boys 1970.
Int	Boys 1970-71. Youths 1972-73-74-75
Mis	Finished third in World Boys International Trophy (USA) 1970

Stevens, David Llewellyn
Born Church Village, Glamorgan on 14th April, 1950

Cls	Llantrisant and Pontyclun, Southerndown, Killarney (Hon)
Nat	Welsh Amateur Stroke Play 1969. Welsh Amateur 1977-80
Reg	Glamorgan Amateur 1974-76-80
Int	Wales (Home Int) 1968-69-70-74-75-76-78-80-82; (Eur T Ch) 1969-77; v France 1976; v Denmark 1977; in Fiat Trophy 1980

Stewart, Gillian
Born Inverness on 21st October, 1958. Turned Professional 1985

Cls	Inverness (Hon), Nairn
PRO	
Eur	IBM European Open 1984 (as amateur). Ford Ladies Classic 1985-87
AM	
Nat	Scottish Ladies 1979-83-84. Ladies British Open Amateur r/u 1982
Trn	Helen Holm Trophy 1981-84
Reg	Northern Counties Ladies 1976-78-82. North of Scotland Ladies 1975-78-80-82-83.
Int	Curtis Cup 1980-82. GB Commonwealth Team 1979-83. Vagliano Trophy 1979-81-83. World Cup 1982-84. Scotland (Home Int) 1979-80-81-82-83-84; (Eur L T Ch) 1979-81-83.
Jun	British Girls 1976. Scottish U-19 Stroke Play Champion 1975
Int	Girls 1975-76-77
Mis	Member of Scottish team which won the 1980 European Junior Team Championship. Avia Golfer of the Year 1984.

Storey, Eustace Francis
Born Lancaster on 30th August, 1901

Cls	Swinley Forest
Maj	Leading Amateur in Open Championship 1938
Chp	Amateur Championship r/u 1924
Trn	Worplesdon Mixed Foursomes 1938-48. President's Putter 1926 (tied)
Int	Walker Cup 1924-26-28. England (Home Int) 1924-25-26-27-28-30-36; v France 1936

Stuart, Hugh Bannerman
Born Forres on 27th June, 1942

Cls	Forres (Hon), Murcar (Hon)
Chp	Amateur s/f 1974
Nat	Scottish Amateur 1972, r/u 1970-76
Reg	North of Scotland Amateur 1967-74. Moray Amateur 1960. Nairnshire Amateur 1966
Int	Walker Cup 1971-73-75. GB Commonwealth Team 1971. Eisenhower Trophy 1972. GBI v Europe 1968-72-74. Scotland (Home Int) 1967-68-70-71-72-73-74-76; (Eur T Ch) 1969-71-73-75; v Belgium 1973-75
Jun	Scottish Boys 1959.
Int	Boys 1959
Mis	Won all his matches in 1971 Walker Cup. Member of European Team to tour South Africa 1974

Swallow, Carole
Born 14th August, 1967. Turned Professional 1985

Nat	Welsh Ladies Open Amateur Stroke Play 1985
Int	England (Eur L T Ch) 1985; (Home Int) 1985
Jun	British Girls 1984. English Girls 1984
Mis	Dinwiddy Trophy 1984

Thirlwell, Alan
Born 8th August, 1928

Cls	Gosforth, Formby
Chp	Amateur r/u 1958-72.
Nat	English Amateur 1954-55, r/u 1963. English Open Amateur Stroke Play r/u 1964
Trn	County Champion of Champions 1962. Wentworth Pro-Am Foursomes 1960-61-68
Reg	Northumberland Amateur 1952-55-62-64. Northumberland and Durham Open 1960
Int	Walker Cup 1957. GB Commonwealth Team 1954-63. GBI v Europe 1956-58; v Denmark 1955; v Professionals 1963. England (Home Int) 1951-52-54-55-56-57-58-59-63-64; v France 1954-56-59
Mis	Canadian Amateur s/f 1957. EGU Selector 1974 to 1977. Secretary CONGU

Thom, Kenneth Gordon
Born 1st March, 1922

Cls	Hendon
Nat	English Amateur r/u 1946
Reg	Middlesex Amateur 1947-48
Int	Walker Cup 1949. England (Home Int) 1947-48-49-53
Jun	Boy International 1939

Thomas, David C
Born Newcastle-upon-Tyne on 16th August, 1934. Turned Professional 1949

Maj	Open r/u 1958 (tied), r/u 1966
Eur	Belgian Open 1955. Dutch Open 1958. French Open 1959
Trn	Esso Golden 1961 (tied)-62-66. PGA Match Play, Olgiata Trophy (Rome) 1963. Silentnight 1965 (tied). Penfold-Swallow, Jeyes 1966. Penfold 1968 (tied). Graham Textiles 1969. Pains-Wessex 1969
RoW	Caltex (NZ) 1958-59.
Oth	British Assistants 1955. Wentworth Pro-Am Foursomes 1960-61
Int	Ryder Cup 1959-63-65-67. Wales in World Cup 1957-58-59-60-61-62-63-66-67-69-70. Wales in Double Diamond 1972-73
Mis	Won qualifying competition for US Open 1964

Thomas, Tegwen (née Perkins)
Born Cardiff on 2nd October, 1955

Cls	Wenvoe Castle, Porthcawl, Pennard
Nat	Welsh Ladies Amateur 1976-77. Welsh Ladies Open Amateur Stroke Play 1980. British Ladies Amateur Stroke Play r/u 1974
Trn	Wills Match Play 1973. Avia Foursomes 1977. Worplesdon Mixed Foursomes 1973-78
Reg	South-Western Ladies 1973-74-76. Glamorganshire Ladies 1972-74-75-77-78-80-81-83
Int	Curtis Cup 1974-76-78-80. Vagliano Trophy 1973-75-77-79. World Team Championship 1974. GB Commonwealth Team 1975-79. GBI in Colombian International 1977-79. Wales (Home Int) 1972 to 84; (Eur L T Ch) 1975-77-79-81-83; in Fiat Trophy 1978.
Jun	Welsh Girls 1970.
Int	Girls 1970-71-72-73
Mis	Member of LGU Team to tour South Africa 1974. First Welsh player in Curtis Cup Team. In 1976 became first Welsh Woman player to win all matches in Home Internationals. Daks Woman Golfer of the Year 1976 (joint). Taunton Trophy 1974. Duncan Salver 1974-76. Dinwiddy Trophy 1973-74

Thomas, Vicki (née Rawlings)
Born Northampton on 27th October, 1954

Cls	Pennard
Nat	Welsh Ladies Amateur 1979-82-83-85-86-87. British Ladies Amateur Stroke Play 1990, r/u 1979. Welsh Ladies Open Stroke Play 1981-82-89, r/u 1980
Trn	Roehampton Gold Cup 1983-85. Cotswold Gold Vase 1983. Keithley Trophy 1983. Sunningdale Foursomes 1989
Reg	Glamorganshire Ladies 1970-71-79
Int	Curtis Cup 1982-84-86-88-90. GB Commonwealth Team 1979-83-87. Vagliano Trophy 1979-83-85-87-89. Espirito Santo 1990; Wales (Home Int) 1971 to 1990; (Eur L T Ch) 1973-75-77-79-81-83-87.
Jun	Welsh Girls 1973.
Int	Girls 1969-70-71-72-73
Mis	Taunton Trophy 1979, Smyth Salver 1986

Thompson, Martyn S
Born 27th January, 1964

Chp	Amateur Champion 1982
Int	Walker Cup 1983. England (Home Int) 1982

Thomson, James Allan
Born Prestwick on 2nd May 1958

Cls	Ayr Belleisle
Nat	Scottish Amateur 1989; r/u 1981-86; s/f 1983-88
Reg	West of Scotland Amateur 1985
Int	Scotland (Home Int) 1981-82-83-84-85-86-87-88-89-90; v West Germany 1987; v Italy 1988-90; v Sweden 1990

Thomson, Muriel
Born Aberdeen on 12th December, 1954. Turned Professional 1979

PRO	
Eur	Carlsberg, Viscount Double Glazing, Barnham Broom 1980; Elizabeth Ann Classic 1981; Guernsey Open, Sands International 1984; Laing Ladies Classic 1985; Irish Open, Ford Ladies Classic 1986
Mis	Order of Merit winner 1980-83; Frank Moran Trophy 1981
AM	
Nat	Scottish Ladies r/u 1977
Trn	Helen Holm Trophy 1975-76; Canadian Ladies Foursomes 1978

Reg North of Scotland Ladies 1973-74; Aberdeenshire
Ladies 1977
Int Curtis Cup 1978; Vagliano Trophy 1977; Espirito
Santo 1978; GBI in Colombian International 1979;
Scotland (Home Int) 1974-75-76-77-78; (Eur L T Ch)
1975-77

Thornhill, Jill
Born 18th August, 1942

Cls Walton Heath, Silloth-on-Solway
Chp Ladies British Open Amateur 1983
Nat English Ladies 1986, r/u 1974. Ladies British Open
Amateur Stroke Play r/u 1987
Trn Avia Foursomes 1970-83. Astor Salver 1972-75.
Newmark International 1974. Worplesdon Mixed
Foursomes 1975. Hampshire Rose 1982-87
Eur Belgian Ladies 1967
Reg South Eastern Ladies 1964-64-85. Surrey Ladies
1962-64-65-73-74-77-78-81-82-83-84
Int Curtis Cup 1984-86-88-(**90**). Vagliano Trophy 1965-
83-85-87-(**90**). England (Home Int) 1964-65-74-82-83-
84-85-86 -87-88. Commonwealth Team Ch 1983;
(Eur L T Ch) 1983. Avia Golfer of the Year 1983
Mis Doris Chambers Trophy 1986

Tiernan, Clarrie
See Reddan

Torrance, Sam
*Born Largs, Ayrshire on 24th August, 1953. Turned
Professional 1970*

PRO
Eur Piccadilly Medal, Martini International 1976; Carrolls
Irish Open 1981; Spanish Open, Portuguese Open
1982; Scandinavian Enterprise Open, Portuguese
Open 1983; Tunisian Open, Benson & Hedges
International, Sanyo Open 1984; Monte Carlo Open
1985; Lancia Italian Open 1987; German Masters
1990
Oth U-25 Match Play 1972; Scottish Uniroyal 1975; Scottish
Professional 1978-80
RoW Zambian Open 1975; Colombian Open 1979;
Australian PGA 1980
Int Ryder Cup 1981-83-85-87-89; Hennessy-Cognac
Cup 1976-80-82-84; Nissan Cup 1985; Scotland in
World Cup 1976-78-82-84-85-87-89-90; Double
Diamond 1973-76-77; Dunhill Cup 1985-86-87-89-90
Mis Rookie of the Year 1972; Tooting Bec Cup 1984
AM
Jun Int Scottish Boys 1970

Townsend, Peter Michael Paul
*Born Cambridge on 16th September, 1946. Turned
Professional 1966*

PRO
Eur Dutch Open 1967; Swiss Open, Carrolls Irish Match
Play 1971; Carrolls Irish Match Play 1976; Irish
Dunlop 1977
Oth PGA Close, Coca-Cola Young Professionals 1968
US Chesterfield 1968
RoW Western Australia Open 1968; Caracas Open 1969;
Walworth Aloyco 1971; Los Lagaratos Open 1972;
ICL International (South Africa) 1975; Moroccan
Grand Prix, Los Lagaratos Open, Caribbean Open,
Zambian Open 1978; Laurent Perrier 1981
Int Ryder Cup 1969-71; Hennessy-Cognac 1974;
England in World Cup 1969-74; in Double Diamond
1971-72-74
AM
Nat English Open Amateur Stroke Play 1966

Trn Duncan Putter 1965; Mullingar Trophy 1965-66;
Lytham Trophy 1966; Golf Illustrated Golf Vase 1966;
Prince of Wales Challenge Cup 1966; St George's
Challenge Cup 1966; Berkhamsted Trophy 1966
Reg Herts Amateur 1964
Int Walker Cup 1965; Eisenhower Trophy 1966;
GBI v Europe 1966; England (Home Int) 1965-66
Jun British Boys 1962-64; British Youths 1965
Int Boys 1961-62-63-64; Youths 1965
Mis Captain PGA 1984

Tucker, William Iestyn
Born Nantyglo, Monmouth on 9th December, 1926

Cls Monmouthshire, Brecon, Killarney, Morlais Castle,
Tredegar and Rhymney, Pontynewydd, Llantrisant,
Radyr, Whitehall
Nat Welsh Amateur 1933-36, r/u 1951-56-64-67-75-76.
Welsh Amateur Stroke Play 1976
Trn Duncan Putter 1960-61 (tied)-63-69-76
Reg Monmouthshire Amateur 1949, 1952 to 63, 1967-69-
74. Gwent Amateur 1976
Int Wales (Home Int) 1949 to 72, 1974-75; (Eur T Ch)
1965-67-69-75; v Australia 1953; v France 1975.
Captain Welsh Team 1966-67-68

Uzielli, Angela (*née* Carrick)
Born Swanton Morley, Norfolk on 1st February, 1940

Cls Berkshire (Hon),
Chp British Ladies Open Amateur 1977.
Nat English Ladies Amateur r/u 1976 English Ladies 1990
Trn Astor Salver 1971-73 (tied)-77-81. Roehampton Gold
Cup 1977. Avia Foursomes 1982. Hampshire Rose
1985
Reg Berkshire Ladies 1976-77-78-79-80-81-83
Int Curtis Cup 1978. Vagliano Trophy 1977. England
(Home Int) 1976-77-78-90; (Eur L T Ch) 1977
Sen British Ladies Senior 1990
Mis Daks Woman Golfer of the Year 1977; Daily
Telegraph Woman Golfer of the Year 1990

Valentine, Jessie, MBE (*née* Anderson)
Born Perth on 18th March, 1915. Turned Professional 1960

Cls Hon member of Craigie Hill, St Rule, Hunstanton,
Blairgowrie, Murrayshall
Chp British Ladies 1937-55-58, r/u 1950-57.
Nat Scottish Ladies 1938-39-51-53-55-56, r/u 1934-54
Oth New Zealand Ladies 1935. French Ladies 1936
Trn Spalding Ladies 1957. Kayser Bondor Foursomes
1959-61. Worplesdon Mixed Foursomes 1963-64-65
Reg East of Scotland Ladies 1936-38-39-50
Int Curtis Cup 1936-38-50-52-54-56-58. GBI v France
1935-36-38-39-47-49-51-55; v Belgium 1949-51-54-55;
v Canada 1938-50. GB Commonwealth Team 1953-
55-(**59**). Scotland (Home Int) 1934-35-36-37-38-39-
47-49-50-51-52-53-54-55-56-57-58
Jun British Girls 1933
Mis Canadian Ladies s/f 1938. Member of LGU Team to
Australia and New Zealand 1935. Frank Moran
Trophy 1967

Vaughan, Sheila
See Maher

Wade, Julie
See Hall

Wadsworth, Helen Elizabeth
Born on the Gower, Swansea on 7th April, 1964

Cls	Royal Cinque Ports
Chp	British Ladies Open Amateur r/u 1990 s/f 1988
Nat	Welsh Ladies Open Amateur Stroke Play 1986
Oth	World Fourball Chp with Julie Hall 1987
Trn	Astor Salver, Wentworth Scratch Trophy 1985.
Reg	Kent Ladies 1990
Int	Curtis Cup 1990. Wales (Home Int) 1987-88-89-90; (Eur L T Ch) 1985-87-89
Jun	South-East Girls 1981
Int	Wales (Jun Eur T Ch) 1983
Mis	Leading amateur, Ladies European Open 1990

Waite, Claire
Born Marlborough on 4th November, 1964. Turned Professional 1985

Nat	English Ladies 1984. British Ladies Stroke Play 1984
Oth	Australian Stroke Play Team 1982. South Atlantic (USA) 1984. Trans National (USA) 1984
Reg	Wiltshire Ladies 1980-81-83
Int	Curtis Cup 1984. Vagliano Trophy 1983. Commonwealth Trn 1983. Espirito Santo 1984. England (Home Int) 1981-82-83. (Eur L T Ch) 1983
Jun	British Girls 1982.
Int	English Girls 1982
Mis	Avia Golfer of the Year 1984

Waites, Brian J
Born Bolton on 1st March, 1940. Turned Professional 1957

Eur	Tournament Players' Championship 1978. Car Care Plan International 1982
RoW	Kenya Open 1980. Mufulira Open (Zambia) 1980-82. Cock o' the North (Zambia) Open 1985
Reg	Midland Open 1971-76-81. Midland Professional Stroke Play 1972-77-78-79. Midland Professional Match Play 1972-73-74.
Int	Ryder Cup 1983. GBI v Europe 1980. Hennessy-Cognac Cup 1984. England in World Cup 1980-82-83
Sen	PGA Seniors 1990

Walker, Carole Michelle (Mickey)
Born Alwoodley, nr Leeds on 17th December, 1952. Turned Professional 1973

PRO

Maj	Ladies British Open r/u 1979
Eur	Carlsberg 1979; Lambert & Butler Match Play 1980; Carlsberg 1981; Sands International 1983; Baume-Mercier Classic, Lorne Stewart Match Play 1984
Oth	Sunningdale Foursomes 1982
Int	Solheim Cup (1990)

AM

Chp	Ladies British Open Amateur 1971-72; r/u 1973
Nat	Ladies British Open Amateur Stroke Play r/u 1972; English Ladies 1973
Oth	Portuguese Ladies Amateur, US Trans-Mississippi 1972; Spanish Ladies Amateur 1973
Trn	Hovis Ladies 1972
Int	Curtis Cup 1972; GB Commonwealth Team 1971; Espirito Santo 1972; Vagliano Trophy 1971; England (Home Int) 1970-72 (Eur L T Ch) 1971-73
Jun	French Girls U-22 Open 1971
Int	English Girls 1969-70-71
Mis	AGW Trophy 1972; Daks Women Golfer of the Year 1972; Duncan Salver 1972

Walker, Mrs JB, MBE
Born Ireland on 21st June, 1896

Cls	Gosforth, Hon member of Troon, Island, Malahide, Alnmouth, Foxton Hall
Nat	Irish Ladies 1930, r/u 1934
Oth	Australian Ladies 1935. New Zealand Ladies r/u 1935
Reg	Ayrshire Ladies 1934-37-38
Int	Curtis Cup 1934-36-38. GBI v France 1935-38-39; v Canada 1938. Ireland (Home Int) 1928 to 38-48
Mis	Two holes-in-one in the same week

Walker, James
Born Bartonholme, by Irvine, on 11th February, 1921

Cls	Irvine Bogside
Chp	Amateur Championship r/u 1961
Nat	Scottish Amateur 1961
Reg	West of Scotland Amateur 1954. Ayrshire Amateur 1956 (tied)
Int	Walker Cup 1961. GBI v Europe 1958-60; vProfessionals 1958-60. Scotland (Home Int) 1954-55-57-58-60-61-62-63

Walker, Kenneth
Born Edinburgh on 1st December, 1966

Nat	Scottish Open Amateur Stroke Play 1986
Trn	Edward Trophy 1984
Oth	Scottish Universities Individual 1985
Int	Scotland (Home Int) 1986

Walker, Maureen
See Richmond

Walton, Philip
Born Dublin on 28th March, 1962. Turned Professional 1983

PRO

Eur	French Open 1990
Trn	Irish Professional 1989
Int	Dunhill Cup 1989-90 (winners)

AM

Nat	Scottish Open Amateur Stroke Play 1981. Irish Amateur 1982
Int	Walker Cup 1981-83. Ireland (Home Int) 1980-81; (Eur T Ch) 1981

Ward, Angela
See Bonallack

Ward, Charles Harold
Born Birmingham on 16th September, 1911

Maj	Open 3rd 1948-51, leading British player (4th) 1946
Trn	Daily Mail Victory 1945. Silver King (tied), Yorkshire Evening News 1948. Spalding, North British-Harrogate, Dunlop Masters 1949. Daily Mail 1950. Dunlop, Lotus 1951. PGA Close 1956
Oth	West of England Open Professional 1937. Daily Telegraph Pro-Am 1947-48. Midland Professional 1933-34-50-53-55-63. Midland Open 1949-51-52-54-57
Int	Ryder Cup 1947-49-51
Mis	Vardon Trophy 1948-49

Way, Paul
Born Kingsbury, Middlesex on 12th March, 1963. Turned Professional 1981

PRO
Eur   KLM Dutch Open 1982. Whyte & McKay PGA 1985. European Open 1987
RoW   South African Charity Classic 1985
Int   Ryder Cup 1983-85. England in World Cup 1985. Dunhill Cup 1985

AM
Nat   English Open Amateur Stroke Play 1981
Int   Walker Cup 1981

Weeks, Kevin

Nat   English Amateur 1987
Int   England (Home Int) 1987-88; v France 1988

Wethered, Joyce
See Lady Heathcoat-Amory

White, Ronald James
Born Wallasey on 9th April, 1921

Cls   Hon member of Royal Birkdale, Woolton, Buxton and High Peak, Killarney
Nat   English Amateur 1949 r/u, 1953. English Open Amateur Stroke Play 1950-51
Trn   Golf Illustrated Gold Vase 1949. Daily Telegraph Pro-Am 1947-49
Sen   British Seniors Open Amateur 1978-79
Reg   Lancashire Amateur 1948
Int   Walker Cup 1947-49-51-53-55. England (Home Int) 1947-48-49-53; France 1947-48
Jun   Carris Trophy 1937
Int   Boys 1936-37-38

Whitlock, Susan
See Hedges

Willard, Anne
See Smith

Wilson, Enid
Born Stonebroom, nr Alfreton, Derbyshire on 15th March, 1910

Cls   Hon member of Notts, Sherwood Forest, Chesterfield, Bramley, Sandy Lodge, Knole Park, North Hants, Crowborough
Chp   British Ladies 1931-32-33.
Nat   English Ladies 1928-30, r/u 1927; US Ladies Amateur s/f 1931-33
Trn   Roehampton Gold Cup 1930
Reg   Midland Ladies 1926-28-29-30. Derbyshire Ladies 1925-26. Cheshire Ladies 1933
Int   Curtis Cup 1932. England (Home Int) 1928-29-30
Jun   British Girls 1925

Winchester, Roger
Born 28th March, 1967. Turned Professional 1990

Chp   English Amateur 1985
Int   England (Home Int) 1985-87-89. Youth (GBI) v Europe 1987

Wood, David K
Born 27th March, 1963

Nat   Welsh Amateur 1982
Trn   Lytham Trophy 1987
Int   Wales (Home Int) 1982-83-84-85-86-87

Woosnam, Ian
Born Oswestry on 2nd March, 1958. Turned Professional 1976

PRO
Maj   Open 3rd 1986; US Open r/u 1989
Eur   Swiss Open 1982; Silk Cut Masters 1983; Scandinavian Enterprise Open 1984; Lawrence Batley TPC 1986; Jersey Open, Cepsa Madrid Open, Bell's Scottish Open, Lancôme Trophy, Suntory World Match Play 1987; Volvo PGA, Carrolls Irish Open, Panasonic European Open 1988; Carrolls Irish Open 1989; Mediterranean Open, Monte Carlo Open, Bell's Scottish Open, Suntory World Match Play, Epson Grand Prix 1990
Oth   News of the World U-23 Match Play 1979; Cacharel U-25 Chp 1982
RoW   Zambian Open 1985; Kenya Open 1986; Hong Kong Open 1987
Int   Ryder Cup 1983-85-87-89; Nissan Cup 1985-86; Kirin Cup 1987; Four Tours World Chp 1989-90; GBI v Australia 1988; Hennessy-Cognac Cup 1982-84; Wales in World Cup 1980-82-83-84-85-87 (winners; also individual winner)-90; in Dunhill Cup 1985-86-87-88-89-90
Mis   Harry Vardon Trophy 1987-90
AM
Reg   Shropshire & Herefordshire Amateur 1975

Wright, Janette (née Robertson)
Born Glasgow on 7th January, 1935

Cls   Hon member of Lenzie, Troon, Cruden Bay, Aboyne, St Rule
Nat   Scottish Ladies 1959-60-61-73, r/u 1958
Trn   Kayser Bondor Foursomes 1958 (tied)-61. Worplesdon Mixed Foursomes 1959
Reg   North of Scotland Ladies 1970. Lanarkshire Ladies 1954-55-56-57-58-59. West of Scotland Ladies 1956-58-59
Int   Curtis Cup 1954-56-58-60. Vagliano Trophy 1959-61. GBI v France 1957; v Belgium 1957; v Canada 1954. GB Commonwealth Team 1959. Scotland (Home Int) 1952-53-54-55-56-57-58-59-60-61-63-65-66-67-73-(**78**)-(**79**)-(**80**). (Eur L T Ch) 1965-73-(**79**)
Jun   British Girls 1950.
Int   Girls 1950-51-52-53

Overseas Players

See page 328 for list of abbreviations

Aaron, Tommy
Born Gainesville, Georgia, USA on 22nd February, 1937.
Turned Professional 1961

PRO
Maj US Masters 1973; USPGA r/u 1972
Eur Lancôme Trophy 1972
US   Canadian Open 1969; Georgia-Pacific Atlanta Golf
        Classic 1970
Int Ryder Cup 1969-73
AM
Nat US Amateur r/u 1958
Int Walker Cup 1959

Alcott, Amy
Born Kansas City, Missouri, USA on 22nd February, 1956.
Turned Professional 1975

PRO
Maj US Women's Open 1980, 3rd 1984; USLPGA r/u 1988
US   27 LPGA wins to end of 1988; Boston Five Classic
        1989
Mis Gatorade Rookie of the Year 1975; Vare Trophy, Golf
        Magazine Player of the Year 1980; Founders Cup
        1986
AM
Jun USGA Girls 1973

Alfredsson, Helen
Born on 9th April, 1965. Turned Professional 1989

Maj Ladies British Open 1990
PRO
Int Solheim Cup 1990
Mis Rookie of the Year 1989
AM
Nat Swedish Ladies 1986-87-88; Swedish Ladies Open
        Stroke Play 1988
Int Sweden (Eur L T Ch) 1983-85-87 (winners)

Aoki, Isao
*Born Abiko, Chiba, Japan on 31st August, 1942. Turned
Professional 1964*

Eur World Match Play Chp 1978. European Open 1983
RoW Japan PGA 1973-81-86; Japan Open 1983-87.
        Hawaiian Open 1983; Dunlop Jap International 1987;
        Tokai Classic, Casio World Open, Coca Cola Classic
        (Aust) 1989; Mitsubishi Gallant 1990
Int Japan v US 1982-83-84. Dunhill Cup 1985. Nissan Cup
        1985. Kirin Cup 1987

Azinger, Paul William
Born Holyoke Massachusetts, USA on 6th January, 1960.
Turned Professional 1981

Maj Open r/u 1987; USPGA r/u 1988
Eur BMW International Open 1990
US   1987-three; 1988-one; 1989-one (Great Hartford
        Open)
Int Ryder Cup 1989. World Cup 1989
Mis USPGA Player of the Year 1987

Baiocchi, Hugh
Born Johannesburg, South Africa on 17th August, 1946.
Turned Professional 1971

PRO
Eur Swiss Open 1973; Dutch Open 1975; Scandinavian
        Enterprise Open 1976; PGA Match Play 1977; Swiss
        Open 1979; State Express Classic 1983
RoW South African Open 1978; South African PGA 1980;
        Western Province Open, SA International Classic
        1973; Transvaal Open 1974-76; Rhodesian Dunlop
        Masters, Swaziland Holiday Inns, 1976; Zimbabwe
        Open, Vaal Reefs Open 1980; Twee Jongegezellen
        Masters 1989
Int South Africa in World Cup 1973-77-79; Hennessy-
        Cognac Cup 1982
Mis Captain SA PGA 1978-79
AM
Nat South African Amateur 1970
Oth Brazilian Amateur 1968

Baker, Kathy
*Born Albany, New York, USA on 20th March, 1961. Turned
Professional 1983.*

PRO
Maj US Women's Open 1985
AM
Int Curtis Cup 1982; Espirito Santo 1982 (winners)

Baker-Finch, Ian
*Born Nambour, Queensland, Australia on 24th October,
1960. Turned Professional 1979*

Eur Scandinavian Open 1985
US   Colonial National Invitation 1989
RoW Australian Match Play 1987; Australian Masters 1988;
        Western Australian Open, NSW Open, Queensland
        PGA 1984; Victoria Open 1985; Golf Digest 1987;
        Pocari Sweat Open 1988
Int Nissan Cup 1986; Kirin Cup 1987-88; Four Tours
        World Chp 1990 (winners)

Ballesteros, Severiano
Born Pedreña, Spain on 9th April, 1957. Turned Professional 1974

Maj Open Champion 1979-84-88; r/u 1976. US Open 3rd 1987. US Masters 1980-83 r/u 1985-87; 3rd 1982
Eur Dutch Open, Lancôme Trophy 1976; French Open, Uniroyal International, Swiss Open 1977; Martini International, German Open, Scandinavian Enterprise Open, Swiss Open 1978; English Classic 1979; Madrid Open, Martini International, Dutch Open 1980; Scandinavian Enterprise Open, Spanish Open, Suntory World Match Play 1981; Madrid Open, French Open, Suntory World Match Play 1982; Sun Alliance PGA, Irish Open, Lancôme Trophy 1983. Suntory World Match Play 1984; Irish Open, French Open, Sanyo Open, Spanish Open, Suntory World Match Play 1985; British Masters, Irish Open, Monte Carlo Open, French Open, Dutch Open, Lancôme Trophy (tied) 1986; Suze Open 1987; Open de Baleares, Scandinavian Enterprise Open, German Open, Lancôme Trophy 1988. Cepsa Madrid Open; Epson Grand Prix; Ebel European Masters-Swiss Open 1989; Open de Baleares 1990
US Greater Greensboro Open 1978; Westchester Classic 1983; USF&G Classic 1985; Westchester Classic 1988
RoW Japanese Open, Dunlop Phoenix , Otago Classic 1977; Japanese Open, Kenya Open 1978; Dunlop Phoenix, Australian PGA 1981; Visa Taiheiyo Masters 1988
Int Ryder Cup 1979-83-85-87-89; Hennessy-Cognac Cup 1976-78; Spain in World Cup 1975-76(winners)-77(winners); Dunhill Cup 1985-86-88
Mis Harry Vardon Trophy 1976-77-78-86-88; AGW Trophy 1979; Ritz Club Golfer of the Year 1988

Barber, Miller
Born Shreveport, Louisiana, USA on 31st March, 1931. Turned Professional 1958

US 11 wins 1964-78
Sen US Seniors PGA 1981. US Seniors Open 1982-84-85.US Sen Tour 24 wins 1981-89
Int Ryder Cup 1969-71

Bean, Andy
Born Lafayette, Georgia on 13th March, 1953. Turned Professional 1975

Maj Open r/u 1983, USPGA r/u 1980-89, 3rd 1985
US 11 wins 1977-86
Int Ryder Cup 1979-87

Beck, Chip
Born Fayetteville, North Carolina, USA on 12th September, 1956. Turned Professional 1978

Maj US Open r/u 1986-89
US Los Angeles Open, USF & G Classic 1988; Buick Open 1990
Int Ryder Cup 1989, Dunhill Cup 1988
Mis Vardon Trophy 1988

Beman, Deane R
Born Washington, DC, USA on 22nd April, 1938. Turned Professional 1987

Maj US Open r/u 1969, leading amateur 1962
PRO
US Texas Open 1969; Greater Milwaukee Open; Quad Cities Open 1972; Shrine-Robinson Classic 1973
Mis Commissioner of US PGA Tour since 1974; Herb Graffis Award 1987
AM
Chp Amateur Champion 1959

Nat US Amateur 1960-63, r/u 1966
Reg Eastern Amateur 1960-61-63-64
Int Walker Cup 1959-61-63-65; Eisenhower Trophy 1960(winners)-62(winners)-64-66(r/u)

Berg, Patty
Born Minneapolis, USA on 13th February, 1918. Turned Professional 1940 (Founder member of LPGA)

PRO
Maj US Women's Open 1946, r/u 1957
US 57 LPGA wins 1941-62 (incl Western Open 1941-48-51-55-57-58; Titleholders Chp 1948-53-55-57)
Mis Leading money winner 1954-55-57; Bobby Jones Award 1963; Ben Hogan Award 1975; first President of USLPGA; LPGA Hall of Fame 1951; World Golf Hall of Fame 1974; Founder's Cup 1981; Old Tom Morris Award 1986
AM
Nat US Ladies Amateur 1938
Reg Western Amateur 1938
Trn 29 amateur wins 1934-40
Int Curtis Cup 1936-38

Bevione, Isa
See Goldschmid

Bland, John
Born Johannesburg, South Africa on 22nd September, 1945. Turned Professional 1970

Eur Benson & Hedges International 1983; Suze Cannes Open 1986
RoW South African PGA 1977; 13 trn wins in Southern Africa 1970-88; Tournament of Champions 1988; Minolta Match Play 1990.
Int South Africa in World Cup 1975; Hennessy-Cognac Cup 1982

Boros, Julius
Born Fairfield, Connecticut on 3rd March, 1920. Turned Professional 1950

Maj US Open 1952-63, r/u 1956, 3rd 1958-60; USPGA 1968; US Masters 3rd 1963
US 15 wins 1952-1968
Sen USPGA Seniors 1971-77; Legends of Golf 1979
Int Ryder Cup 1959-63-65-67; USA in World Cup 1953-68(r/u)
Mis US leading money winner 1952-55; USPGA Player of the Year 1952-63

Bradley, Pat
Born Westford, Massachusetts, USA on 24th March, 1951. Turned Professional 1974

Maj US Women's Open 1981, 3rd 1989; USLPGA 1986, 3rd 1984-85
US 26 LPGA wins 1976 to 1990
RoW Colgate Far East Open 1975
Int Solheim Cup 1990
Mis Rolex Player of the Year 1986; Vare Trophy 1986; Mazda-LPGA Series 1983-86; Golf Magazine Player of the Year 1986

Burke, Jack, Jr
Born Fort Worth, Texas, USA in January, 1923. Turned Professional 1940

Maj USPGA 1956; US Masters 1956, r/u 1952
US 15 wins 1950-63
Int Ryder Cup 1951-53-55-**57**-59-**(73)**
Mis USPGA Player of the Year 1956

Calcavecchia, Mark
Born Laurel, Nebraska, USA on 12th June, 1960. Turned Professional 1981

Maj	Open Champion 1989; US Masters r/u 1988
US	WSW Golf Classic 1986 Honda Classic 1987, Bank of Boston Classic 1988; Phoenix Open, Nissan Los Angeles Open, Spalding Invitational Pro-Am 1989
Int	Ryder Cup 1987-89; Dunhill Cup 1989 (winners) -90; Kirin Cup 1987; Four Tours World Chp 1990

Campbell, William Cammack
Born West Virginia, USA on 5th May, 1923

Chp	Amateur r/u 1954
Nat	US Amateur 1964
Oth	Canadian Amateur r/u 1952-54-65; Mexican Amateur 1956
Reg	North & South Amateur 1950-53-57-67. Tam O'Shanter World Amateur 1948-49. Ontario Amateur 1967
Sen	USGA Seniors 1979-80. US Seniors Open r/u 1980
Int	Walker Cup 1951-53-**55**-57-65-67-71-75. Eisenhower Trophy 1964-**(68)**
Mis	Bobby Jones Award 1956. President USGA 1983. Captain Royal & Ancient 1987/88

Canizares, José Maria
Born Madrid on 18th February, 1947. Turned Professional 1967

Eur	Lancia D'Oro 1972; Avis Jersey Open; Bob Hope British Classic 1980; Italian Open 1981; Bob Hope British Classic 1983; Benson & Hedges Trophy (with Tania Abitbol) 1990
RoW	Kenya Open 1984
Int	Ryder Cup 1981-83-85-89; Hennessy-Cognac Cup 1974-76-78-80-82-84; Spain in World Cup 1974-80-82(winners)-83-84(winners; individual winner)-85-87-89; Dunhill Cup 1985-87-89-90; Double Diamond 1974

Caponi, Donna
Born Detroit, Michigan, USA on 29th January, 1945. Turned Professional 1965

Maj	US Women's Open 1969-70. USLPGA 1979-81
Eur	Colgate European Open 1975
US	24 LPGA wins 1969-81
Mis	LA Times Woman Golfer of the Year 1970

Carner, JoAnne *(née Gunderson)*
Born Kirkland, Washington, USA on 4th April, 1939. Turned Professional 1970

PRO	
Maj	US Women's Open 1971-76, r/u 1975-78-82-83-87 (tied); USLPGA r/u 1974-82
US	42 LPGA wins 1970-85
RoW	Australian Ladies Open 1975
Mis	Rolex Player of the Year 1974-81-82; Vare Trophy 1974-75-81-82-83; Gatorade Rookie of the Year 1970; Golf Magazine Player of the Year 1974-81-82; LPGA Hall of Fame 1982; World Golf Hall of Fame 1985; Bobby Jones Award 1981
AM	
Nat	US Ladies Amateur 1957-60-62-66-68, r/u 1956-64
Trn	LPGA Burdine's Invitational 1969 (as amateur)
Reg	Western Ladies Open Amateur 1959
Int	Curtis Cup 1958-60-62-64
Jun	US Girls 1956

Casper, Billy
Born in San Diego, California, USA on 24th June, 1931. Turned Professional 1954

Maj	US Open 1959-66; USPGA r/u 1958-65-71; US Masters 1970, r/u 1969
Eur	Lancôme Trophy 1974; Italian Open 1975
Oth	Lancia D'Oro 1974
US	51 wins 1956-75; Canadian Open 1967
RoW	Moroccan Grand Prix 1973-75; Mexican Open 1977
Sen	Arizona Classic 1987
Int	Ryder Cup 1961-63-65-67-69-71-73-75-**(79)**
Mis	Vardon Trophy 1960-63-65-66-68; leading money winner 1966-68. USPGA Player of the Year 1966-70; Byron Nelson Award 1966-68-70. World Golf Hall of Fame 1978; USPGA Hall of Fame 1982

Charles, Robert J (Bob)
Born Carterton, New Zealand on 14th March, 1936. Turned Profesional 1960

PRO	
Maj	Open Champion 1963, r/u 1968-69; US Open 3rd 1964-70; USPGA r/u 1968
Eur	Bowmaker 1961; Engadine Open, Swiss Open, Daks 1962; Piccadilly World Match Play 1969, r/u 1968; John Player Classic, Dunlop Masters 1972; Scandinavian Enterprise Open 1973; Swiss Open 1974
US	4 wins 1963-74; Canadian Open 1968
RoW	New Zealand Open 1954 (as amateur)-66-70-73, r/u 1974; New Zealand Professional 1961-79-80; 17 other trn wins in New Zealand 1961-78; South African Open 1973
Sen	Volvo Seniors British Open 1989. US Sen Tour 7 wins 1989
Int	New Zealand in World Cup 1962 to 1968, 1971-72; Dunhill Cup 1985-86
Mis	First New Zealander and first left-handed player to win the Open
AM	
Int	Eisenhower Trophy 1960

Coe, Charles R
Born Oklahoma City, USA on 26th October, 1923

Maj	US Masters r/u 1961
Chp	Amateur r/u 1951
Nat	US Amateur 1949-58; r/u 1959
Reg	Western Amateur 1950
Int	Walker Cup 1949-51-53-**(57)**-**59**-61-63. Eisenhower Trophy 1960
Mis	Bobby Jones Award 1964

Cole, Robert
Born Springs, South Africa on 11th May, 1948. Turned Professional 1966

PRO	
Maj	Open 3rd 1975
US	Buick Open 1977
RoW	South African Open 1974-80; Dunlop Masters (SA) 1969; Natal Open 1969-70-72; Cape Classic 1970; Transvaal Open 1972; Rhodesian Masters 1972; Vavasseur (SA) 1974
Int	South Africa in World Cup 1969-74 (winners; individual winner)-76
AM	
Chp	Amateur 1966
Nat	English Open Amateur Stroke Play r/u 1966
Int	Eisenhower Trophy 1966

Couples, Fred
Born Seattle, Washington, USA on 3rd October, 1959.
Turned Professional 1980

Maj US Open leading amateur 1978; USPGA, r/u 1990, 3rd 1982
US Kemper Open 1983; Tournament Players Chp 1984; Byron Nelson Classic 1987; Los Angeles Open 1990
Int Ryder Cup 1989; Four Tours World Chp 1990 (individual winner)

Crenshaw, Ben
Born Austin, Texas, USA on 11th January, 1952. Turned Professional 1973

PRO
Maj Open r/u 1978-79, 3rd 1980; US Open leading amateur 1970, 3rd 1975; USPGA r/u 1979; US Masters 1984, r/u 1976-83, 3rd 1989
Eur Carrolls Irish Open 1976
US 14 wins 1973 to 1990
RoW Australian Open r/u 1978; Mexican Open 1982
Int Ryder Cup 1981-83-87; US in World Cup 1972-87-88(winners; individual winner); Kirin Cup 1988
Mis Rookie of the Year 1974; Byron Nelson Award 1976
AM
Trn NCAA Chp 1971-72(shared)-73
Int Eisenhower Trophy 1972(winners)

Crosby, Nathaniel
Born Los Angeles, California, USA on 29th October, 1961.
Turned Professional 1984

Nat US Amateur 1981
Int Walker Cup 1983. Eisenhower Trophy 1982 (winners)

Daniel, Beth
Born Charleston, South Carolina, USA on 14th October, 1956. Turned Professional October, 1978

Maj USLPGA 1990, r/u 1984
PRO
US 25 LPGA wins 1979 to 1990
RoW World Ladies Championship (Japan) 1979
Mis USLPGA Rookie of the Year 1979. USLPGA leading money winner 1980. Rolex Player of the Year 1980. Vare Trophy 1989. Order of Merit winner 1990
AM
Nat US Women's Amateur 1975-77
Int Curtis Cup 1976-78

Davies, Richard
Born USA on 29th October, 1930

Maj US Open leading amateur 1963
Chp Amateur Champion 1962
Int Walker Cup 1963

Davis, Rodger
Born Sydney, New South Wales, Australia on 18th May, 1951. Turned Professional 1974

Maj Open r/u 1987
Eur State Express Classic 1981; Whyte & Mackay PGA 1986; Wang Four Stars 1988; Spanish Open, Wang Four Stars 1990
RoW Australian Open 1986; South Australia Open 1978; Victoria Open 1979; New South Wales Open 1989
Int World Cup 1985-87; Dunhill Cup 1986 (winners)-87-88-90; Nissan Cup 1986; Kirin Cup 1987-88, Four Tours World Chp 1990 (winners)

Decker, Anne
See Sander

Dibnah, Corinne
Born Brisbane, Australia on 29th July, 1962. Turned Professional 1984

Maj Ladies British Open 1988
PRO
Trn Trusthouse Forte Ladies Classic, Kristianstad Open 1986; Guernsey Open, Spanish Open 1987; Eastleigh Classic 1988; Paris Ladies Masters 1990
Oth Sunningdale Foursomes (with Dale Reid) 1990
AM
Nat Australian Ladies 1981. New Zealand Champion 1983
Int Commonwealth Tournament 1983 (winners)

Dickson, Robert B
Born McAlester, Oklahoma, USA on 25th January, 1944. Turned Professional 1968

PRO
US 2 wins 1968-73
AM
Chp Amateur Champion 1967
Nat US Amateur 1967
Int Walker Cup 1967
Mis One of only four to win British and US Amateur titles in the same year. Bobby Jones Award 1968.

Fernandez, Vicente
Born Corrientes, Argentina on 5th May, 1946. Turned Professional 1964

Eur Dutch Open 1970; Benson & Hedges 1975; Colgate PGA 1979; Tenerife Open 1990
RoW Argentine Open 1968-69-81; Maracaibo Open 1972; Brazil Open 1977-83-84
Int World Cup 1970-72-78-84-85. Dunhill Cup 1986-88-89-90. Hennessy-Cognac 1982

Finsterwald, Dow
Born Athens, Ohio, USA on 6th September, 1929. Turned Professional 1951

Maj US Open 3rd 1960; USPGA 1958; r/u 1957; US Masters r/u 1962 (tied), 3rd, 1960
US 11 wins 1955-63; Canadian Open 1956
Int Ryder Cup 1957-59-61-63-(77)
Mis Vardon Trophy 1957; USPGA Player of the Year 1958

Floyd, Ray
Born Fort Bragg, North Carolina, USA on 4th September, 1942. Turned Professional 1961

Maj Open r/u 1978; 3rd 1981; US Open 1986; US Masters 1976, r/u 1985-90; USPGA 1969-82, r/u 1976
US 19 wins 1963-86
RoW Brazilian Open 1978
Int Ryder Cup 1969-75-77-83-(89). Dunhill Cup 1985-86. Nissan Cup 1985
Mis Rookie of the Year 1963. World Golf Hall of Fame 1989

Ford, Doug
Born West Haven, Connecticut, USA on 6th August, 1922. Turned Professional 1949

Maj US Masters 1957; r/u 1958. USPGA 1955
US 15 wins 1955-62; Canadian Open 1959-63
Sen 1987-one
Int Ryder Cup 1955-57-59-61
Mis USPGA Player of the Year 1955

Frost, David
Born Cape Town, South Africa on 11th September, 1959

Eur   Cannes Open 1984
RoW   South African Open 1986; Sun City Challenge 1988-90
US   1988-one; 1989-one (NEC World Series); 1990-one
(USF & G Classic)

Garrido, Antonio
Born Madrid on 2nd February, 1944. Turned Professional 1961

Eur   Benson & Hedges International 1977. Standard Four
Stars National 1986. Madrid Open 1977. Spanish
Open 1972. Tunisian Open 1982
Int   Ryder Cup 1979. Spain in World Cup 1977(winners)-
78-79. Hennessy-Cognac Cup 1976-78-80-82-84.
Double Diamond 1976

Geddes, Jane
*Born Huntingdon, New York, USA on 5th February, 1960.
Turned Professional 1983*

Maj   Ladies British Open 1989; US Women's Open 1986;
USLPGA 1987
US   Boston Five Classic 1986; Women's Kemper Open,
GNA Glendale Federal Classic, LPGA Championship,
Toledo Classic, Boston Five Classic 1987
RoW   Australian Women's Masters 1990

Giles, Marvin

Maj   US Open leading amateur 1973
Chp   Amateur Champion 1975
Nat   US Amateur Champion 1972, r/u 1967-68-69
Int   Walker Cup 1969-71-73-75. Eisenhower Trophy
(winners) 1968-70-72

Goldschmid, Isa (*née* Bevione)
Born Italy

Nat   Italian Ladies' Close 1947-51-53-54-55-56-57-
58-59-60-61-62-63-64-65-66-67-69-71-73-74. Italian
Ladies' Open 1952-57-58-60-61-63-64-67-68-69
Oth   Spanish Ladies 1952. French Ladies 1975
Trn   Kayser Bondor 1963
Int   Vagliano Trophy 1959-61-63-65-67-69-71-73-(**77**) Eur
v United States 1968. Italy in Espirito Santo 1964-66-
68-70-72

Grady, Wayne
*Born Brisbane, Queensland, Australia on 26th July, 1957.
Turned Professional 1978*

Maj   Open r/u 1989 (tied); USPGA 1990
Eur   German Open 1984
US   Westchester Classic 1989
RoW   West Lakes Classic (Aust) 1978
Int   Australia in World Cup 1978-83-89 (winners); Nissan
Cup 1985; Four Tours Chp 1990 (winners); Dunhill
Cup 1989-90

Graham, David
*Born Windsor, Tasmania on 23rd May, 1946. Turned
Professional 1962*

Maj   Open 3rd 1985; US Open 1981; USPGA 1979
Eur   French Open 1970; Piccadilly World Match Play 1976;
Lancôme Trophy 1982
US   6 wins 1972-83
RoW   Australian Open 1977, r/u 1972; Australian Wills
Masters 1975; Thailand Open, Victoria Open,
Tasmanian Open, Yomiuri Open 1970; Caracas Open,
Japanese Airlines 1971; Chunichi Crowns (Japan)
1976; West Lakes Classic (Aust), New Zealand Open
1979; Queensland Open 1987

Graham, Lou
*Born Nashville, Tennessee, USA on 7th January, 1938.
Turned Professional 1962*

Maj   US Open 1975; r/u 1977
US   1967-one. 1972-one. 1979-three.
Int   Ryder Cup 1973-75-77. World Cup 1975 (winners)

Green, Hubert
*Born Birmingham, Alabama, USA on 18th December, 1946.
Turned Professional 1970*

Maj   US Open 1977. US Masters r/u 1978. USPGA 1985
Eur   Carrolls Irish Open 1977
US   16 wins 1971-84
RoW   Dunlop Phoenix (Japan) 1975
Int   Ryder Cup 1977-79-85. USA in World Cup 1977
Mis   Rookie of the Year 1971

Green, Ken
*Born Danbury, Connecticut, USA on 23rd July 1958.
Turned Professional 1979*

US   Buick Open 1985; The International 1986; Canadian
Open, Greater Milwaukee Open 1988; Greater
Greensboro Open 1989
RoW   Hong Kong Open 1990
Int   Ryder Cup 1989

Guadagnino, Kathy
See Baker

Gunderson, JoAnne
See Carner

Härdin Christian
Born Sweden

Chp   Amateur Champion 1988
Nat   Nordic Men's Open 1985
Int   (Eur) v GBI 1988

Harper, Chandler
*Born Portsmouth, Virginia, USA on 10th March, 1914.
Turned Professional 1934*

Maj   USPGA 1950
US   Won over 20 tournaments. Ten times Virginia Open
Champion.
Sen   National Seniors 1965 World Senior Professional,
USPGA Seniors 1968.
Int   Ryder Cup 1955
Mis   Elected to USPGA Hall of Fame 1969. In 1941 scored
round of 58 (29-29) on 6100 yards, Portsmouth,
Virginia

Hayes, Dale
*Born Pretoria, South Africa on 1st July, 1952. Turned
Professional 1970*

PRO
Eur   Spanish Open 1971; Swiss Open 1975; Italian Open,
French Open 1978; Spanish Open 1979
Oth   Coca-Cola Young Professionals 1974; PGA U-25 1975
RoW   South African Open 1976, leading amateur 1969;

South African PGA 1974-75-76; 12 wins in Southern Africa 1970-76; Brazilian Open 1970; Bogota Open 1979

Int	South Africa in World Cup 1974(winners)-76
Mis	Accles & Pollock Award 1973; Harry Vardon Trophy 1975
AM	
Nat	South African Amateur Stroke Play 1969-70
Oth	English Open Amateur Stroke Play r/u 1969; German Amateur 1969; Scottish Open Amateur Stroke Play 1970
Int	Eisenhower Trophy 1970(r/u individual)
Jun	World Junior Chp 1969

Haynie, Sandra
Born Fort Worth, Texas, USA on 4th June 1943. Turned Professional 1961

Maj	US Open 1965-74, r/u 1963-70-82; USLPGA 1974, r/u 1975-83
US	42 LPGA wins 1962-82
Mis	Rolex Player of the Year 1970; LPGA Hall of Fame 1977

Henning, Harold
Born Johannesburg, South Africa on 3rd October, 1934. Turned Professional 1953

Maj	Open 3rd 1960-70.
Trn	Daks 1958 (tied). Yorkshire Evening News 1958 (tied). Spalding 1959 (tied). Sprite 1960. Pringle 1964
Nat	South African Open 1957-62. South African PGA 1965-66-67-72
Eur	Italian Open 1957. Swiss Open 1960-64. Danish Open 1960-64-65. German Open 1965.
RoW	Malaysian Open 1966
US	2 wins 1966-70
Oth	Transvaal Open 1957. Natal Open 1957. Western Province Open 1957-59. Cock o' the North 1959. Engadine Open 1966. South African International Classic 1972. ICL International (SA) 1980
Int	South Africa in World Cup 1957-58-59-61-65 (winners)-66-67-69-70-71

Hogan, Ben W
Born Dublin, Texas, USA on 13th August, 1912. Turned Professional 1929

Maj	Open Champion 1953; US Open 1948-50-51-53; r/u 1955-56. USPGA 1946-48. US Masters 1951-53; r/u 1942-46-54-55
US	57 wins 1938-59
Int	Ryder Cup 1947-49-51-(67). World Cup 1956 (winners and individual winner)-58
Mis	USPGA Player of the Year 1948-50-51-53. US leading money winner 1940-41-42-46-48. Sportsman of the Decade Award 1946-56. Had a serious car crash in 1949 which seemed likely to prevent him playing golf again but returned to win more major victories. In 1965 was named the greatest professional of all time by US golf writers. Bobby Jones Award 1976

Hyndman, William III
Born 25th December, 1915

Chp	Amateur r/u 1959-69-70
Nat	US Amateur r/u 1955
Sen	US Seniors 1973
Int	Walker Cup 1957-59-61-71. Eisenhower Trophy 1958-60

Inkster, Juli
Born Santa Cruz, California, USA on 24th June, 1960. Turned Professional 1983

Maj	USLPGA 3rd 1986
PRO	
US	13 wins 1983-89
AM	
Nat	US Ladies Amateur 1980-81-82
Int	Curtis Cup 1982; World Cup 1980-82

Irwin, Hale
Born Joplin, Montana, USA on 3rd June, 1945. Turned Professional 1968

Maj	Open r/u 1983; US Open 1974-79-90, 3rd 1975
Eur	Piccadilly World Match Play 1974-75
US	19 wins 1971 to 1990
RoW	Australian PGA 1978. South African PGA 1978. Bridgestone 1981
Int	Ryder Cup 1975-77-79-81. USA in World Cup 1974-79 (winners and individual winner)

January, Don
Born Plainview, Texas, USA on 20th November, 1929. Turned Professional 1955

Maj	USPGA 1967; r/u 1961-76
US	11 wins 1956-76
Sen	US Sen Tour 22 wins 1980-87
Int	Ryder Cup 1965-67

Kennedy, Edwina
Born 10th June, 1959

Nat	Ladies British Amateur 1978.
Oth	Canadian Ladies Amateur 1980
Int	World Cup 1978 (winners) 80-84-86. Commonwealth Tournament 1979-83-87

King, Betsy
Born Reading, Pennsylvania, USA on 13th August, 1955. Turned Professional 1977

Maj	Ladies British Open 1985, r/u 1984; US Woman's Open 1989-90, 3rd 1986; USLPGA r/u 1987
US	23 LPGA wins 1984-90
Int	Solheim Cup 1990
Mis	Golf Magazine Player of the Year 1984-89; Founder's Cup 1989; Rolex Player of the Year 1984-89

Kite, Tom
Born Austin, Texas, USA on 9th December, 1949. Turned Professional 1972

PRO	
Maj	Open r/u 1978; US Masters r/u 1983-86, 3rd 1977
US	14 wins 1976 to 1990
RoW	Auckland Classic (NZ) 1974
Int	Ryder Cup 1979-81-83-85-87-89; Kirin Cup 1987(individual winner); Dunhill Cup 1989(winners)-90; World Cup 1984-85
Mis	Rookie of the Year 1973; Vardon Trophy 1981-82; Arnold Palmer Award 1981-89; Bobby Jones Award 1979; Golf Writers Player of the Year 1981; USPGA Player of the Year 1989
AM	
Chp	Amateur s/f 1971
Nat	US Amateur r/u 1970
Trn	NCAA Chp 1972(shared)
Int	Walker Cup 1971; Eisenhower Trophy 1970(winners)

Knight, Nancy
See Lopez

Kuramoto, Masahiro
Born Hiroshima City, Hiroshima, Japan on 9th September, 1955. Turned Professional 1981

RoW	Japan Amateur 1975-77-80. Japan PGA 1982
RoW	14 wins in Japan 1983-88
Int	Dunhill Cup 1985; Four Tours World Chp 1990

Lacoste, Catherine
See Prado

Langer, Bernhard
Born Anhausen, Germany on 27th August, 1957. Turned Professional 1972

Maj	Open r/u 1981-84, 3rd 1985-86; US Masters 1985
Eur	Dunlop Masters 1980; German Open, Bob Hope Classic 1981; German Open 1982; Italian Open, Glasgow Golf Classic, St Mellion TPC 1983; French Open, Dutch Open, Irish Open, Spanish Open 1984; German Open, European Open 1985; Lancôme Trophy(shared), German Open 1986; Whyte & Mackay PGA, Irish Open 1987; Epson Grand Prix 1988; Peugeot Spanish Open, German Masters 1989; Cepsa Madrid Open, Austrian Open 1990
Oth	German Close Professional, Cacherel U-25 Chp 1979; Belgian Classic 1987
US	Sea Pines Heritage Classic 1985
RoW	Colombian Open 1980; Johnnie Walker Tournament, Casio World Open 1983; Australian Masters, Sun City Challenge 1985
Int	Ryder Cup 1981-83-85-87-89; Hennessy-Cognac Cup 1976-78-80-**82**; Germany in World Cup 1976-77-78-79-80-90 (winners); Four Tours World Chp 1989-90; Nissan Cup 1985-86, Kirin Cup 1987
Mis	Harry Vardon Trophy 1981-84; AGW Trophy 1981. Ritz Club Trophy 1985

Lewis, Bob

Nat	US Amateur r/u 1980
Int	Walker Cup 1981-83-85-87. Eisenhower Trophy (winners) 1982

Littler, Gene
Born San Diego, California, USA on 21st July, 1930. Turned Professional 1954

PRO	
Maj	US Open 1961, r/u 1954; USPGA r/u 1977; US Masters r/u 1970(tied)
US	26 wins 1955-1977; Canadian Open 1965
RoW	Taiheiyo Pacific Masters 1974-75; Australian Masters 1980; Yellow Pages (SA) 1977
Sen	1987-two
Int	Ryder Cup 1961-63-65-67-69-71-75
Mis	Byron Nelson Award 1959; Bobby Jones Award, Ben Hogan Award 1973; USPGA Hall of Fame 1982
AM	
Nat	US Amateur 1953
Int	Walker Cup 1953

Lopez, Nancy
Born Torrance, California, USA on 6th January, 1957. Turned Professional July, 1977

Maj	US Women's Open r/u 1975(leading amateur)-77-89; USLPGA 1978-85-89
PRO	
Eur	Colgate European 1978-79
US	43 LPGA wins 1978-90

RoW	Colgate Far East 1978
Int	Solheim Cup 1990
Mis	Rolex Player of the Year 1978-79-85-88; Vare Trophy 1978-79-85; Mazda-LPGA Series 1985; Gatorade Rookie of the Year 1978; Powell Award 1987; Golf Magazine Player of the Year 1978-79-85; LPGA Hall of Fame 1987; World Golf Hall of Fame 1989
AM	
Oth	Mexican Ladies Amateur 1975
Int	Curtis Cup 1976; Espirito Santo 1976(winners)
Jun	US Girls 1972-74

de Lorenzi, Marie-Laure
Born Biarritz, France on 21st January 1961. Turned Professional 1986

PRO	
Maj	Ladies British Open 3rd 1989
Eur	BMW Ladies German Open, Belgian Ladies Godiva Open 1987; French Open, Volmac Open, Hennessy Ladies Cup, Gothenburg Ladies Open, Laing Charity Classic, Woolmark Match Play Chp, Qualitair Ladies Spanish Open, Benson & Hedges Trophy (with M McNulty) 1988; Ford Ladies Classic, Hennessy Ladies Cup, BMW Ladies Classic 1989; Ford ladies Classic 1990
Int	Solheim Cup 1990
Mis	Woolmark Order of Merit winner 1988-89
AM	
Nat	French Close Chp 1983
Oth	Spanish Ladies 1978-80-83
Int	France (Eur L T Ch) 1977-83; Vagliano Trophy 1983
Jun	French Girls 1976; British Girls 1978
Mis	Doris Chambers Trophy 1982-85; Angus Trophy 1980

McCumber, Mark
Born Jacksonville, Florida, USA on 7th September, 1951. Turned Professional 1974

Maj	US Open r/u 1989
US	Doral-Eastern Open 1979; Western Open 1983; Pensacola Open 1983; Doral-Eastern Open 1985; Anheuser-Busch Classic 1987; Tournament Players Championship 1988. Beatrice Western Open 1989
Int	Ryder Cup 1989. Dunhill Cup 1988

McGuire, Marnie
Born New Zealand

Nat	Ladies British Amateur 1986

McIntire, Barbara

Maj	US Women's Open r/u 1956
Chp	Ladies British Amateur 1960
Nat	US Ladies Amateur 1959-64
Int	Curtis Cup 1958-60-62-64-66-72

McNulty, Mark
Born Zimbabwe on 25th October, 1953. Turned Professional 1977

Maj	Open r/u 1990
Eur	Greater Manchester Open 1979; German Open 1980; Portuguese Open 1986; German Open, 4 Stars Pro-Celebrity, Dunhill Masters 1987; Cannes Open, Benson & Hedges Trophy (with Maine-Laure de Lorenzi) 1988; Torres Monte Carlo Open 1989; Cannes Open, German Open 1990
RoW	SA Open 1987, SA Masters 1982-86; 19 wins 1980-89; Malay Open 1980

Mahaffey, John Drayton
Born Kerrville, Texas, USA on 9th May, 1948. Turned Professional 1971

PRO
Maj	US Open leading Amateur 1970, r/u 1975;
US	8 wins 1973-86; St Jude Classic 1989; USPGA 1978
Int	Ryder Cup 1979, US in World Cup 1978 (winners; individual winner) 1979 (winners)

AM
Trn	NCAA Champion 1970

Marsh, Graham, MBE
Born Kalgoorlie, Western Australia on 14th January, 1944. Turned Professional 1968

Eur	Swiss Open 1970; German Open 1972; Sunbeam Electric 1973; Benson & Hedges International 1976; Colgate World Match Play, Lancôme Trophy 1977; Dutch Open, Dunlop Masters 1979; Benson & Hedges International 1980; European Open 1981; Dutch Open 1985
US	1977-one
RoW	Watties Open (NZ) 1970; Indian Open, Spalding Masters (NZ) 1971; Indian Open, Thailand Open 1973; Malaysian Open 1974; Malaysian Open 1975; Western Australian Open 1976; 17 wins in Japan 1972-81; Sapporo-Tokyu Open (Jap) 1989; Tokai Classic 1990
Int	Dunhill Cup 1985(winners); Nissan Cup 1986; Kirin Cup 1987
Mis	USPGA Rookie of the Year 1977; Australian Sportsman of the Year 1977

Massey, Debbie
Born Grosse Pointe, Michigan, USA on 5th November 1950. Turned Professional 1977.

Maj	Ladies British Open 1980-81; US Women's Open leading amateur 1974; USLPGA 3rd 1983

PRO
US	Mizuno Japan Classic 1977; Wheeling Classic 1979
Mis	Gatorade Rookie of the Year 1977

AM
Oth	Canadian Ladies Amateur 1974-75-76
Reg	Western Amateur 1972-75; Eastern Amateur 1975
Int	Curtis Cup 1974-76; Espirito Santo 1976
Mis	Doris Chambers Trophy 1976; Angus Trophy 1976

Melnyk, Steve
Born Brunswick, Georgia, USA on 26th February, 1947. Turned Professional 1971

AM
Maj	Open leading amateur 1970; US Masters leading amateur 1970
Chp	Amateur 1971
Nat	US Amateur 1969
Reg	Western Amateur 1969. Eastern Amateur 1970
Int	Walker Cup 1969-71
Mis	US Amateur Golfer of the Year 1969

Middlecoff, Cary
Born Halls, Tennessee, USA on 6th January, 1921. Turned Professional 1947

Maj	US Open 1949-56, r/u 1957; USPGA r/u 1955; US Masters 1955, r/u 1948
US	37 wins 1947-61
Int	Ryder Cup 1953-55-59; World Cup 1959
Mis	Byron Nelson Award 1955; Vardon Trophy 1956; USPGA Hall of Fame 1974; World Golf Hall of Fame 1986

Miller, Johnny Lawrence
Born San Francisco, USA on 29th April, 1947. Turned Professional 1969

Maj	Open Champion 1976, r/u 1973, 3rd 1975; US Open 1973, leading amateur 1966; US Masters r/u 1971-75
Eur	Lancôme Trophy 1973-79
US	21 wins 1971-87
RoW	Dunlop Phoenix International (Japan) 1974. Otago Classic (NZ) 1972
Int	Ryder Cup 1975-81; World Cup 1973 (winners; individual winner)-75 (winners; individual winner)-80; v Japan 1983
Mis	USPGA Player of the Year 1974. US leading money winner 1974

Mize, Larry Hogan
Born Augusta, Georgia, USA on 23rd September, 1958. Turned Professional 1980

Maj	US Masters 1987
US	Memphis Classic 1983
RoW	Casio World Open (Jap) 1988. Dunlop Phoenix 1989-90
Int	Ryder Cup 1987

Muntz, Rolf
Born Voorschoten, Netherlands on 26th March, 1969

Cls	Toxandria
Chp	Amateur Champion 1990
Nat	Dutch Open Amateur 1989
Trn	Lancôme Trophy 1988-89
Int	Europe v GBI 1990; Dutch National Team 1989-90
Jun	Dutch Junior Match Play, Dutch Junior Stroke Play 1989; Dutch International Junior Open 1989
Int	Dutch Boys 1986-87

Nagle, Kelvin DG
Born North Sydney, Australia on 21st December, 1920. Turned Professional 1946

Maj	Open Champion 1960, r/u 1962; US Open r/u 1965 (tied)
Eur	Irish Hospitals, Dunlop, French Open 1961. Bowmaker 1962-65. Esso Golden 1963-67
US	Canadian Open 1964
RoW	Australian Open 1959. Australian Professional 1949-54-58-59-65-68. New Zealand Professional 1957-58-60-70-73-74-75. New Zealand Open 1957-58-62-64-67-68-69. In New Zealand BP 1968; Caltex 1969, Garden City, 1969, Otago Charity Classic 1970-76. Stars Travel 1970. In Australia: West End 1968-72-74, New South Wales Open 1968. Victoria Open 1969, NBN Newcastle 1970, New South Wales Professional 1971, South Coast Open 1975, Western Australia PGA 1977
Sen	World Seniors 1971-75; British Seniors 1971-73-75 (winners)
Int	Australia in World Cup 1954 (winners) 55-58-59-(winners)-60-61-62-65-66
Mis	Honorary Member of Royal & Ancient.

Nakajima, Tsuneyuki
Born Kiryu City, Gumma, Japan on 20th October, 1954. Turned Professional 1975

Maj	USPGA 3rd 1988
RoW	Japan Amateur 1973. Japan Open 1985-86. Japan PGA 1983-84-86; 12 wins 1984-87
Int	Dunhill Cup 1986. Nissan Cup 1986(individual winner). Kirin Cup 1987-88.

Nelson, Byron
Born Fort Worth, Texas, USA on 4th February, 1912.
Turned Professional 1932

Maj	US Open 1939; r/u 1946; USPGA 1940-45, r/u 1939-41-44; US Masters 1937-42, r/u 1941-47
Eur	French Open 1955
US	54 wins 1935-one 1936-one 1937-two 1938-two 1939-three 1940-two 1941-three 1942-three 1944-six 1945-fifteen 1946-five
Int	Ryder Cup 1937-47
Mis	Vardon Trophy 1939; leading money winner 1944-45; USPGA Hall of Fame 1953; World Golf Hall of Fame 1974; Bobby Jones Award 1974; 11 consecutive tour wins March-August 1945, and 18 for the year.

Nelson, Larry Gene
Born Fort Payne, Alabama, USA on 10th September, 1947.
Turned Professional 1971

Maj	US Open 1983. USPGA 1981-87.
US	4 wins 1979-88
RoW	Suntory Open (Japan) 1989
Int	Ryder Cup 1979-81-87

Neumann, Liselotte
Born Finspang, Sweden on 20th May, 1966. Turned Professional 1985

PRO	
Maj	US Women's Open 1988
Eur	5 wins 1985-88
RoW	Singapore Open 1987
Int	Solheim Cup 1990
AM	
Nat	Swedish Ladies Open 1981-82; Swedish Ladies Match Play 1984
Int	Sweden (Eur L T Ch) 1983. Espirito Santo 1982-84

Newton, Jack
Born Sydney, Australia on 30th January, 1950. Turned Professional 1969

Maj	Open r/u 1975 (tied); US Masters r/u 1980
Nat	Australian Open 1979
Eur	Benson & Hedges Festival 1972. Benson & Hedges PGA Match Play 1974. Sumrie 1975. Dutch Open 1972
US	1978-one
RoW	City of Auckland Classic (NZ) 1972. Amoco Forbes (Aust) 1972. Nigerian Open 1974. Cock o' the North (Zambia) 1976. Mufulira Open 1976. New South Wales Open 1976-79
Mis	Seriously injured on tarmac by aeroplane propeller accident 1983

Nicklaus, Jack William
Born Columbus, Ohio, USA on 21st January, 1940. Turned Professional 1961

Maj	Open Champion 1966-70-78, r/u 1964-67-72-76-79, 3rd 1963-74-75; US Open 1962-67-72-80, r/u 1960 (leading amateur)-68-71(tied)-82, leading amateur (4th) 1961; USPGA 1963-71-73-75-80, r/u 1964-65-74-83, 3rd 1967-77; US Masters 1963-65-66-72-75-86, r/u 1964-71-77-81, 3rd 1973-76
PRO	
Eur	Piccadilly World Match Play 1970, r/u 1966-71
US	71 wins 1962-84; World Series 1962-63-67-70-76
RoW	Australian Open 1964-68-71-75-76-78; Dunlop International (Aust) 1971

Sen	US Sen Tour 2 wins 1990
Int	Ryder Cup 1969-71-73-75-77-81-(83)-(87); World Cup 1963(winners; individual winner) -64(winners; individual winner) -65-66(winners) -67(winners) -71(winners; individual winner) -73(winners)
Mis	Rookie of the Year 1962; USPGA Player of the Year 1967-72-73-75-76; leading money winner 1964-65-67-71-72-73-75-76; Byron Nelson Award 1964-65-67-72-73; Bobby Jones Award 1975; Walter Hagen Award 1980; World Golf Hall of Fame 1974; US Sportsman of the Year 1978; Card Walker Award 1983; Honorary Member of Royal & Ancient
AM	
Nat	US Amateur 1959-61
Trn	NCAA Chp 1961
Int	Walker Cup 1959-61; Eisenhower Trophy 1960(winners; individual winner)

Norman, Greg
Born Mt Isa, Queensland, Australia on 10th February, 1955.
Turned Professional 1976

Maj	Open Champion 1986, r/u 1989(tied); US Open r/u 1984(tied); USPGA r/u 1986; US Masters r/u 1986-1987(tied), 3rd 1989
Eur	Martini 1977; Martini 1979; Scandinavian Enterprise Open, French Open, Suntory World Match Play 1980; Martini, Dunlop Masters 1981; Dunlop Masters, Benson & Hedges International, State Express Classic 1982; Suntory World Match Play 1983; European Open, Suntory World Match Play 1986; Italian Open 1988
US	Kemper Open, Canadian Open 1984; Panasonic-Las Vegas Invitational, Kemper Open 1986; MCI Heritage Classic 1988; The International, Greater Milwaukee Open 1989; Doral Ryder Open 1990
RoW	Australian Open 1980-85; Australian Masters 1984-87-89; Australian PGA 1984-85; Australian TPC 1988-89; West Lakes Classic (Aust) 1976; South Seas Classic (Fiji), NSW Open 1978; Hong Kong Open 1979; NSW Open, Hong Kong Open 1983; Victoria Open 1984; NSW Open, Queensland Open, South Australian Open, Western Australian Open 1986; ESP Open, Palm Meadows Cup 1988; Chunichi Crowns 1989
Int	Australia in World Cup 1976-78; Dunhill Cup 1985(winners)-1986(winners)-87-88-89-90; Nissan Cup 1985-86, Kirin Cup 1987; test match v GBI 1988
Mis	Harry Vardon Trophy 1982; Arnold Palmer Award 1986; Mary Bea Porter Award 1988; Vardon Trophy 1989

North, Andy
Born Thorp, Wisconsin, USA on 9th March, 1950. Turned Professional 1972

Maj	US Open 1978-85
US	1 win 1977
Int	US in World Cup 1978

Okamoto, Ayako
Born Hiroshima, Japan on 2nd April, 1951. Turned Professional 1976

Maj	Ladies British Open 1984; US Women's Open r/u 1987 (tied), 3rd 1986; USLPGA r/u 1989, 3rd 1986-87-88
Eur	German Open 1990
US	15 wins 1982-89
Mis	Rolex Player of the Year 1987; Mazda-LPGA Series 1984-87

Olazabal, José Maria
Born Fuenterrabia, Spain on 5th February, 1966. Turned Professional 1985

PRO
Eur   Ebel European Masters -Swiss Open, Sanyo Open 1986; Volvo Belgian Open, German Masters 1988; Tenerife Open, KLM Dutch Open 1989; Benson & Hedges International, Carrolls Irish Open, Lancôme Trophy 1990
US   NEC World Series 1990; Wild Coast Skins Game 1990
RoW   Japanese Masters 1989
Int   Ryder Cup 1987-89; Kirin Cup 1987; Spain in Dunhill Cup 1986-87-88-89; Four Tours World Chp 1989; World Cup 1989.
Mis   PGA Qualifying School winner 1985
AM
Chp   Amateur 1984
Nat   Spanish Open Amateur 1983
Oth   Italian Open Amateur 1983
Jun   British Boys 1983; Belgian International Youths Chp 1984; British Youths 1985

O'Meara, Mark
Born Goldsboro, North Carolina, USA on 13th January, 1957. Turned Professional 1980

PRO
Maj   Open 3rd 1985; US Open 3rd 1988
Eur   Lawrence Batley International 1987
US   Greater Milwaukee Open 1984; Bing Crosby Pro-Am, Hawaiian Open 1985; AT&T Pebble Beach National Pro-Am 1989; Texas Open 1990
RoW   Kapalua International, Fuji Sankei Classic (Jap) 1985; Australian Masters 1986
Int   Ryder Cup 1985-89; Nissan Cup 1985; Dunhill Cup 1985-86-87; US v Japan 1984
Mis   Rookie of the Year 1981
AM
Nat   US Amateur 1979
Oth   Mexican Amateur 1979

Ozaki, Masashi
Born Kaiman Town, Tokushima, Japan on 24th January, 1947. Turned Professional 1980

RoW   Japan Open 1974-88-89; Japan PGA 1971-74-89; Japan Match Play 1989; Japan tour 24 wins 1984-90
Int   Nissan Cup 1986; Kirin Cup 1987; Four Tours World Chp 1989

Palmer, Arnold
Born Latrobe, Pennsylvania, USA on 10th September, 1929. Turned Professional 1954

PRO
Maj   Open Champion 1961-62, r/u 1960; US Open 1960, r/u 1962-63(tied)-66(tied)-67, 3rd 1972; USPGA r/u 1964-68-70; US Masters 1958-60-62-64, r/u 1961-65, 3rd 1959
Eur   Piccadilly World Match Play 1964-67; Lancôme Trophy 1971; Penfold PGA, Spanish Open 1975
US   61 wins 1956-four 1957-four 1958-two 1959-three 1960-six 1961-five 1962-six 1963-seven 1964-one 1965-one 1966-four 1967-four 1968-two 1969-two 1970-one 1971-four 1973-one. Canadian Open 1955; Canadian PGA 1980
RoW   Australian Open 1966
Int   Ryder Cup 1961-63-65-67-71-73-(**75**); World Cup 1960-62-63-64-66-67 (winners each year; individual winner 1967)
Mis   USPGA Player of the Year 1960-62; Vardon Trophy

1961-62-64-67; leading money winner 1958-60-62-63; Byron Nelson Award 1957-60-61-62-63; World Golf Hall of Fame 1974; USPGA Hall of Fame 1980; Bobby Jones Award 1971; William Richardson Award 1970; Walter Hagen Award 1981; Old Tom Morris Award 1983; Honorary Member of Royal & Ancient
AM
Nat   US Amateur 1954

Parry, Craig
Born Sunshine, Victoria, Australia on 12th January, 1966. Turned Professional 1985

Eur   Wang Four Stars National Pro-Celebrity, German Open 1989
US   Canadian TPC 1987
RoW   NSW Open, South Australian PGA 1987; Bridgestone Open 1989
Int   Kirin Cup 1988; Four Tours World Chp 1990 (winners)

Pate, Jerry
Born Macon, Georgia, USA on 16th September, 1953. Turned Professional 1975

PRO
Maj   US Open 1976; r/u 1979; USPGA 1978; US Masters 3rd 1982
US   4 wins 1977-82; Canadian Open 1976
RoW   Taiheiyo Pacific Masters 1976; Brazilian Open 1980
Int   USA in World Cup 1976
Mis   Rookie of the Year 1976
AM
Nat   US Amateur 1974
Int   Walker Cup 1975

Pavin, Corey
Born Oxnard, California, USA on 16th November, 1959. Turned Professional 1981

PRO
Eur   German Open 1983.
US   7 wins 1984-88
RoW   SA PGA 1983
Int   Nissan Cup 1985
AM
Int   Walker Cup 1981

Peete, Calvin
Born Detroit, USA on 18th July, 1943. Turned Professional 1971

Maj   USPGA 3rd 1982
US   12 wins 1979-86
Oth   Vardon Trophy 1984
Int   Ryder Cup 1983-85. Nissan Cup 1985-86
Mis   Ben Hogan Award 1984

Pinero, Manuel
Born Badajoz, Spain on 1st September, 1952. Turned Professional 1968

Eur   Madrid Open 1974; Swiss Open 1976; Penfold PGA 1977; English Classic 1980; Madrid Open, Swiss Open 1981; European Open 1982; Cepsa Madrid Open, Italian Open 1985
Oth   Spanish Professional 1972-73
Int   Ryder Cup 1981-85; Hennessy-Cognac Cup 1974-76-78-80-82; Spain in World Cup 1974-76(winners)-78-79-80-82(winners; individual winner)-83-85-88; Dunhill Cup 1985

Player, Gary
*Born Johannesburg, South Africa on 1st November, 1935.
Turned Professional 1953*

Maj	Open Champion 1959-68-74, 3rd 1967; US Open 1965, r/u 1958-79; USPGA 1962-72, r/u 1969; US Masters 1961-74-78, r/u 1962(tied)-65, 3rd 1970
Eur	Dunlop 1956; Piccadilly World Match Play 1965-66-68-71-73; Ibergolf European Chp 1974; Lancôme Trophy 1975
US	21 wins 1958-78; World Series 1965-68-72
RoW	South African Open 1956-60-65-66-67-68-69-72-75-76-77-79-81; South African PGA 1968-79-81; South African Masters 1959-60-64-67-71-72-73-74-76-76(2)-79; Australian Open 1958-62-63-65-69-70-74; Australian PGA 1957; Brazilian Open 1972-74; Chile Open 1980; Ivory Coast Open 1980; Transvaal Open 1959-60-62-66; Natal Open 1958-60-66-68; Western Province Open 1968-71-72; General Motors (SA) 1971-75-76; Rothmans Match Play (SA) 1973; International Classic (SA) 1974; ICL International (SA) 1977; Johannesburg International, Sun City Classic 1979; Wills Masters (Aust) 1968; Dunlop International (Aust) 1970; Japan Airlines Open 1972
Sen	USGA Senior Open 1987-88; Senior TPC 1987; Volvo Seniors British Open 1988-90
Int	South Africa in World Cup 1956-57-58-59-60-62-63-64-65(winners; individual winner) -66-67-68-71-72-73-77(individual winner)
Mis	US leading money winner 1961; Bobby Jones Award 1966; World Golf Hall of Fame 1974; William Richardson Award 1976; SA PGA captain 1977, president 1978

Ploujoux, Philippe
Born La Bouille, Seine Maritime, France on 20th February, 1955

Chp	Amateur Champion 1981
Nat	French Amateur Close Match Play 1977
Oth	International Moroccan Stroke Play 1977
Int	Continental Team (St Andrews Trophy) five times (including winners) 1982) Continental Youth Team four times. Represented France more than fifty times
Jun	French Youths Match Play 1972-73-74-75-76. French Boys 1969-70

Pohl, Dan
*Born Mt Pleasant, Michigan, USA on 1st April, 1955.
Turned Professional 1977*

PRO	
Maj	US Open 3rd 1982; US Masters r/u 1982
US	2 wins 1986
Int	Ryder Cup 1987
AM	
Reg	Michigan State Champion 1975-77

Prado, Catherine (née Lacoste)
Born Paris on 27th June, 1945

Maj	US Women's Open 1967
Chp	Ladies British Open Amateur 1969
Nat	French Ladies Open Amateur 1967-69-70-72. French Ladies Close Amateur 1968-69
Oth	US ladies' Amateur 1969; Spanish Ladies Amateur 1969-72-76
Reg	Western Ladies Amateur 1968
Trn	Astor Princes' 1966; Worplesdon Foursomes 1967; Hovis 1969
Int	Espirito Santo 1964 (winners; individual winner)-68 (individual winner)
Mis	Doris Chambers Trophy 1967-69; First amateur, first non-American and youngest player at that time to win the US Women's Open

Price, Nick
Born Durban, South Africa on 28th January, 1957. Turned Professional 1977

Maj	Open r/u 1982-1988
Eur	Swiss Open 1980; Lancôme Trophy 1985
US	World Series 1983
RoW	South African Masters 1980; Vaal Reefs Open (SA) 1982; ICL International (SA) 1985; South Australian Open 1989

Quast, Anne
See Sander

Randolph, Sam
*Born Santa Barbara, California, USA on 13th May 1964.
Turned Professional 1987*

PRO	
US	1987-one (Bank of Boston Classic)
AM	
Nat	US Amateur 1985
Int	Walker Cup 1985

Rawls, Betsy
*Born Spartanburg, South Carolina, USA on 4th May, 1928.
Turned Professional 1951*

Maj	US Women's Open 1951-53-57-60, r/u 50(as amateur)-61; USLPGA 1959-69
US	55 LPGA wins 1951-72 (incl Western Open 1952-59)
Mis	Vare Trophy 1959; LPGA Hall of Fame 1960; World Golf Hall of Fame 1987; Patty Berg Award 1980

Reid, Mike
Born Bainbridge, Maryland, USA on 1st July, 1954. Turned Professional 1976

Maj	US Open leading amateur 1976; USPGA r/u 1989
US	Seiko Tucson Open 1987; NEC World Series 1988
RoW	Casio World Open 1990
Int	World Cup 1980

Rivero, José
Born Spain on 20th September, 1955. Turned Professional 1973

Eur	Lawrence Batley International 1984. French Open 1987. Monte Carlo Open 1988
Int	Ryder Cup 1985-87. World Cup 1984 (winners)-87-88-90. Dunhill Cup 1986-87-88-90. Kirin Cup 1988

Rogers, William Charles (Bill)
Born Waco, Texas, USA on 10th September, 1951. Turned Professional 1974

PRO	
Maj	Open Champion 1981; US Open r/u 1981, 3rd 1982
Eur	Suntory World Match Play 1979
US	1978-one, 1981-three, 1983-one
Oth	Pacific Masters 1977
RoW	Suntory Open (Jap) 1980; NSW Open, Australian Open, Suntory Open (Jap) 1981
Int	Ryder Cup 1981
Mis	USPGA Player of the Year 1981
AM	
Int	Walker Cup 1973

Rosenthal, Jody
Born Minneapolis, Minnesota, USA on 18th October, 1962.
Turned Professional 1985

PRO
US   United Virginia Bank Classic, du Maurier Classic 1987
Mis   Gatorade Rookie of the Year 1986
AM
Chp   Ladies British Open Amateur 1984
Int   Curtis Cup 1984; Espirito Santo 1984(winners)

St Sauveur, Vicomtesse de
See Segard

Sander, Anne [Welts] [Decker] (*née Quast*)

Chp   Ladies British Open Amateur 1980.
Nat   US Ladies Amateur 1958-61-63, r/u 1965-68-73
Int   Curtis Cup 1958-60-62-66-68-74-84-90; Espirito
        Santo 1966(winners)-68(winners)
Mis   Doris Chambers Trophy 1973-74; Angus Trophy
        1974

Sarazen, Gene
Born Harrison, New York, USA on 27th February, 1902.
Turned Professional 1920

Maj   Open Champion 1932, r/u 1928, 3rd 1931-33; US
        Open 1922-32, r/u 1934-40; USPGA 1922-23-33, r/u
        1930; US Masters 1935
Eur   North of England Professional 1923
US   1922-one 1925-one 1927-two 1928-two 1930-two
        1935-one 1936-one 1937-two 1938-one 1939-one
        1941-one; USPGA Seniors 1954-58
RoW   Australian Open 1936
Int   Ryder Cup 1927-29-31-33-35-37
Mis   PGA Hall of Fame 1940; World Golf Hall of Fame
        1974; William Richardson Award 1966; Old Tom
        Morris Award 1988; one of the few to win the Open
        and the US Open in the same year; Honorary
        Member of the Royal & Ancient

Segard, Mme Patrick [De St Sauveur] (*née Lally Vagliano*)

Chp   British Ladies 1950.
Trn   Worplesdon Foursomes 1962. Avia Foursomes 1966.
        Kayser-Bondor Foursomes 1960
Nat   French Ladies' Open 1948-50-51-52. French Ladies'
        Close 1939-46-49-50-51-54
Oth   Swiss Ladies 1949-65. Luxembourg Ladies 1949.
        Italian Ladies 1949-51. Spanish Ladies 1951
Int   France 1937-38-39-47-48-49-50-51-52-53-54-55-
        56-57-58-59-60-61-62-63-64-65-70. Vagliano Trophy
        1959-61-63-65-(75)
Jun   British Girls 1937
Mis   Chairman of The Women's Committee of World
        Amateur Golf Council 1964 to 1972

Semple, Carol
See Thompson

Senior, Peter
Born Singapore on 31st July, 1959. Turned Professional 1978

Eur   PLM Open 1986; Monte Carlo Open 1987; Panasonic
        European Open 1990
RoW   Australian Open, Australian PGA 1989; Queensland
        Open, New South Wales PGA 1984; New South Wales
        PGA, Rich River Classic, (South Australian Open

1979). Queensland PGA 1987. Johnnie Walker Classic
1989
Int   Australia in Dunhill Cup 1987. Kirin Cup 1987; World
        Cup 1988-90. Four Tours World Chp 1990 (winners).

Sheehan, Patty
Born Middlebury, Vermont, USA on 27th October, 1956.
Turned Professional 1980

PRO
Maj   US Women's Open r/u 1983-88; USLPGA 1983-84, r/u
        1986
US   24 LPGA wins 1981-90
Int   Solheim Cup 1990
Mis   Founders Cup 1985
AM
Int   Curtis Cup 1980

Siderowf, Dick
Maj   US Open leading amateur 1968
Chp   Amateur Champion 1973-76
Oth   Canadian Amateur 1971
Int   Walker Cup 1969-73-75-77-(79). Eisenhower Trophy
        1968-76

Sigel, Jay
Chp   Amateur Champion 1979
Nat   US Amateur 1982-83
Int   Walker Cup 1977-79-81-83-85-87-89
Mis   Most wins (14) in Walker Cup matches

Simpson, Scott William
Born San Diego, California, USA on 17th September, 1955.
Turned Professional 1977

PRO
Maj   US Open 1987
US   1980-one. 1984-one. 1987-one (Greater Greensboro
        Open). Bell South Atlanta Classic 1989
RoW   1984-two (Chunichi Crowns, Dunlop Phoenix)
Int   Ryder Cup 1987. Kirin Cup 1987
AM
Trn   NCAA Chp 1976-77

Sluman, Jeff
Born Rochester, New York, USA on 11th September, 1957.
Turned Professional 1980

Maj   USPGA 1988
Oth   Belgian Classic 1989

Snead, Samuel Jackson
Born Hot Springs, Virginia, USA on 27th May, 1912. Turned Professional 1934

Maj   Open Champion 1946; US Open r/u 1937-47-49-53;
        USPGA 1942-49-51, r/u 1938-40, 3rd 1974; US
        Masters 1949-52-54, r/u 1939-57
US   84 wins 1936-65; Canadian Open 1938-40-41
Sen   USPGA Seniors 1964-65-67-70-72-73 World Senior
        Professional 1964-65-70-72-73
Int   Ryder Cup 1937-47-49-51-53-55-59-(69); USA in
        World Cup 1954-56-57-58-59-60-61-62; (winners 56-
        60-61-62; individual winner 1961)
Mis   US leading money winner 1938-49-50. USPGA Player
        of the Year 1949. Oldest professional to win a major
        tournament 1965. Unofficially credited with 164
        victories (including 84 official USPGA tournaments) in
        his long career of which full details are not available.
        Finished 2nd equal in a 1974 USPGA tournament
        aged 61 and 3rd equal in 1974 USPGA Championship
        aged 62. 24 holes-in-one

Somerville, Charles Ross
Born London, Ontario, Canada on 4th May, 1903

Nat Canadian Amateur 1926-28-30-31-35-37; r/u 1924-25-34-38
Oth US Amateur 1932
Reg Ontario Amateur 1927-28-29-37. Manitoba Amateur 1926. Canadian Seniors 1960-61 (tied)-65-66 (tied)
Mis President Royal Canadian Golf Association 1957

Stacy, Hollis
Born Savannah, Georgia, USA on 16th March, 1954.
Turned Professional 1974

PRO
Maj US Women's Open 1977-78-84; r/u 1980
US 14 wins 1977-85
AM
Int Curtis Cup 1972
Jun US Girls 1969-70-71

Stadler, Craig
Born San Diego, California, USA on 2nd June, 1953.
Turned Professional 1975

PRO
Maj US Masters 1982, 3rd 1988
Eur Scandinavian Enterprise Open 1990
US 1980-two. 1981-one. 1982-three. 1984-one
Int Ryder Cup 1983-85
Mis Arnold Palmer Award 1982
AM
Nat US Amateur 1973
Int Walker Cup 1975

Stephenson, Jan
Born Sydney, NSW, Australia on 22nd December, 1951.
Turned Professional 1973

Chp US Women's Open 1983. LPGA 1982
Nat Australian Ladies Open 1973-77
US 13 wins 1976-86; 1987-two

Stewart, Payne
Born Springfield, Missouri, USA on 30th January, 1957.
Turned Professional 1979

Maj Open r/u 1985-90; USPGA 1989
US 1982-two 1986-one 1987-one 1989-one (MCI Heritage Classic) 1990-two (MCI Heritage Classic, Byron Nelson Classic)
RoW Indian Open, Indonesian Open 1981; Tweed Head Classic (Aust) 1982; Jun Classic (Jap) 1985
Int Ryder Cup 1987-89; Nissan Cup 1986; Kirin Cup 1988; Four Tours World Chp 1990; World Cup 1990 (individual winner)

Stockton, Dave
Born San Bernardino, California, USA on 2nd November, 1941. Turned Professional 1964

Maj US Open r/u 1978. USPGA 1970-76. US Masters r/u 1974.
US 1967-two. 1968-two. 1971-one. 1973-one. 1974-three 9 wins 1967-74
Int Ryder Cup 1971-77-(91). World Cup 1970-76

Stranahan, Frank R
Born Toledo, Ohio, USA on 5th August, 1922. Turned Professional 1954

Maj Open r/u 1947-53, leading amateur 1947-49-50-51-53
PRO
US 1955-one 1958-one

AM
Chp Amateur 1948-50, r/u 1952
Nat US Amateur r/u 1950
Oth Mexican Amateur 1946-48-51; Canadian Amateur 1947-48
Reg North & South Amateur 1946-49-52; Western Amateur 1946-49-51-53; Tam o' Shanter All-American Amateur 1948-49-50-51-52-53; Tam o' Shanter World Amateur 1950-51-52-53-54
Int Walker Cup 1947-49-51

Strange, Curtis
Born Norfolk, Virginia, USA on 20th January, 1955. Turned Professional 1976

PRO
Maj US Open 1988-89, 3rd 1984; USPGA r/u 1989; US Masters r/u 1985
Oth Canadian Open 1985-87
US 14 wins 1979-88
RoW Palm Meadows Cup (Aus) 1989
Int Ryder Cup 1983-85-87-89. Dunhill Cup 1985-87-88-89(winners)-90. Nissan Cup 1985. Kirin Cup 1987-88
Mis Arnold Palmer Award 1985-87. USPGA Player of the Year 1988
AM
Int Walker Cup 1975; Eisenhower Trophy 1974

Streit, Marlene Stewart
Born Cereal, Alberta, Canada on 9th March, 1934

Chp Ladies British Amateur 1953
Nat Canadian Ladies' Open 1951-54-55-56-58-59-63-68-72-73. Canadian Ladies' Close 1951 to 1957, 1963-68
Oth US Ladies Amateur 1956; r/u 1966. Australian Ladies 1963
Reg Ontario Provincial 1951-56-57-58. US North and South Ladies 1956
Int Canadian Commonwealth Team 1959-63-**79**
Mis Canadian Athlete of the Year 1951-53-56. Canadian Woman Athlete of the Year 1951-53-56-60-63

Suggs, Louise
Born Atlanta, Georgia, USA on 7th September, 1923.
Turned Professional 1948 (Founder Member of LPGA)

PRO
Maj US Women's Open 1949-52, r/u 1951-55-58-59-63; USLPGA 1957, r/u 1955-60-61-63
US 50 LPGA wins 1949-62 (incl Titleholders Chp 1946(as amateur)-54-56-59; Western Open 1946-47(both as amateur)-49-53
Mis Leading money winner 1953-60; Vare Trophy 1957; LPGA Hall of Fame 1951; World Golf Hall of Fame 1979
AM
Chp British Ladies 1948
Nat US Ladies Amateur 1947
Int Curtis Cup 1948

Sutton, Hal
Born Shreveport, Louisiana, USA on 28th April, 1958.
Turned Professional 1981

Maj USPGA 1983
US 1982-one 1983-one 1985-two 1986-two
Int Ryder Cup 1985-87; Nissan Cup 1986; v Japan 1983
Mis Arnold Palmer Award 1983; Golf Writers Player of the Year 1983; USPGA Player of the Year 1983
AM
Nat US Amateur 1980
Int Walker Cup 1979-81

Thompson, Carol

Chp British Ladies 1974.
Nat US Ladies' Amateur 1973
Trn Newmark International 1975 (tied), r/u 1974
Int Curtis Cup 1974-77-80-82-90. World Team
Championship 1974(winners)-80 (winners)

Thomson, Peter W, CBE
*Born Melbourne, Australia on 23rd August, 1929. Turned
Professional 1949*

Maj Open Champion 1954-55-56-58-65, r/u 1952-53-57.
3rd 1969
Eur PGA Match Play 1954; Yorkshire Evening News 1957;
Dunlop, Daks(shared) 1958; Italian Open, Spanish
Open 1959; German Open, Yorkshire Evening News,
Bowmaker, Daks 1960; PGA Match Play, Yorkshire
Evening News, Esso Golden(shared), Dunlop
Masters 1961; Martini International, Piccadilly 1962;
Daks 1965; PGA Match Play 1966; Alcan International,
PGA Match Play, Esso Golden(tied) 1967; Dunlop
Masters 1968; Martini International 1970(shared);
Wills 1972
US 1956-one 1957-one
RoW Australian Open 1951-67-72, r/u 1950, leading
amateur 1948; Australian Professional 1967; New
Zealand Open 1950-51-53-55-59-60-61-65-71; New
Zealand Professional 1953; Hong Kong Open 1960-
65-67; India Open 1963-76; Philippines Open 1964;
New Zealand Caltex 1967; Victorian Open 1973
Int Australia in World Cup 1953-54(winners)-55-56-67-
59(winners)-60-61-62-65-69
Mis World Golf Hall of Fame 1988. Honorary Member of
Royal & Ancient

Trevino, Lee
*Born Dallas, Texas, USA on 1st December, 1939. Turned
Professional 1961*

Maj Open Champion 1971-72, r/u 1980, 3rd 1970; US
Open 1968-71; USPGA 1974-84, r/u 1985
Eur Benson & Hedges International, Lancôme Trophy
1978; Lancôme Trophy 1980; Dunhill British Masters
1985
US 27 wins 1968-one 1969-one 1970-two 1971-three
1972-three 1973-two 1974-one 1975-one 1976-one
1978-one 1980-three 1981-one; World Series 1974;
Canadian Open 1971-77-79; Canadian PGA 1979-83
RoW Chrysler Classic (Aust) 1973; Mexican Open 1975;
Moroccan Grand Prix 1977
Sen US Sen Tour 6 wins 1990; USGA Senior Open 1990
Int Ryder Cup 1969-71-73-75-79-81-(**85**); World Cup
1968-69(winners; individual winner) -70-71(winners)
-74
Mis Rookie of the Year 1967; leading money winner 1970;
USPGA Player of the Year 1971; Vardon Trophy 1970-
71-72-74-80; Byron Nelson Award 1971; Ben Hogan
Award 1981; World Golf Hall of Fame 1981; William
Richardson Award 1985

Tway, Bob
*Born Oklahoma City, USA on 4th May, 1959. Turned
Professional 1981*

Maj USPGA 1986
US 1986-three 1989-one 1990-one (Las Vegas
Invitational)
Oth Paris Open 1989
Int Nissan Cup 1986
Mis USPGA Player of the Year 1986

Vagliano, Lally
See Segard

Van Donck, Flory
*Born Tervueren, Brussels, Belgium on 23rd June, 1912.
Turned Professional 1934*

Maj Open r/u 1956-59
Trn PGA Match Play r/u 1947-52; Silver King 1951-53;
North British Harrogate 1951; South of England
Professional 1952; Yorkshire Evening News 1953
Nat Belgian Open 1939-46-47-53-56, r/u 1935-51;
Belgian Professional 1935-38-39-52-53-54-55-56-
57-59-60-63-64-65-66-68
Eur Dutch Open 1936-37-46-51-53; Italian Open 1938-47-
53-55; Swiss Open 1953-55; French Open 1954-57-
58; German Open 1953-56; Portuguese Open 1955;
Danish Open 1959
RoW Uruguay Open 1954; Venezuelan Open 1957
Int Belgium in World Cup 1954 to 1970, 1972-79
(individual winner 1960); Europe v GBI 1954-55-56-58
Mis Harry Vardon Trophy 1953

Varangot, Brigitte
Born Biarritz, France on 1st May, 1940

Chp Ladies British Open Amateur 1963-65-68
Nat French Ladies Open Amateur 1961-62-64-65-66-73,
r/u 1960-63-67-70; French Ladies Close Amateur
1959-61-63-70
Oth Italian Ladies 1970
Trn Kayser-Bondor Foursomes; Casa Pupo Foursomes
1965; Avia Foursomes 1966-73
Int France in Vagliano Trophy 1959-61-63-65-69-71;
Espirito Santo 1964(winners)-66-68-70-72-74

Verplank, Scott
*Born Dallas, Texas, USA on 9th July, 1964. Turned
Professional 1986*

PRO
US Buick Open 1988
AM
Nat US Amateur 1984
US Western Open (USPGA circuit) 1985
Trn NCAA Chp 1986
Reg Western Amateur 1984
Int Walker Cup 1985

De Vicenzo, Roberto
*Born Buenos Aires, Argentina on 14th April, 1923. Turned
Professional 1938*

Maj Open Champion 1967, r/u 1950, 3rd 1948-49-56-60-
64-69; US Masters r/u 1968
Eur Belgian Open, Dutch Open, French Open 1950;
French Open 1960; French Open, German Open
1964; Spanish Open 1966
US 1951-two 1953-one 1957-two 1966-one
RoW Argentine Open 1944-49-51-52-58-65-67-70-74;
Argentine Professional 1944-45-47-48-49-51-52; Chile
Open 1946; Colombia Open 1947; Uruguay Open
1949; Mexican Open 1951; Panama Open 1952;
Mexican Open 1953; Jamaican Open 1956; Brazilian
Open, Jamaican Open 1957; Brazilian Open 1960-63-
64; Bogota Open 1969; Panama Open, Brazilian
Open, Caracas Open 1973; Panama Open 1974
Sen USPGA Seniors 1974; World Senior Professional
1974; Legends of Golf 1979; US Senior Open 1980
Int Argentina in World Cup 1953(winners) -54-55-
62(individual winner) -63-64-65-66-68-69-70
(individual winner) -71-72-73-74; Mexico in World
Cup 1956-59-60-61
Mis Bobby Jones Award 1970; William Richardson Award
1971; Walter Hagen Award 1979; USPGA Hall of
Fame 1979; World Golf Hall of Fame 1989; Honorary
Member of the Royal & Ancient.

Wadkins, Lanny
Born Richmond, Virginia, USA on 5th December, 1949.
Turned Professional 1971

PRO
Maj US Open r/u 1986; USPGA 1977, r/u 1982-84-87, 3rd 1973; US Masters 3rd 1990
US 19 wins 1972-90; World Series 1977
RoW Victoria PGA (Aust) 1978
Int Ryder Cup 1977-79-83-85-87-89; World Cup 1977-84-85; v Japan 1982-83; Nissan Cup 1985; Kirin Cup 1987
Mis USPGA Player of the Year 1985; Rookie of the Year 1972
AM
Nat US Amateur 1970
Reg Western Amateur 1970; Southern Amateur 1968-70; Eastern Amateur 1969
Int Walker Cup 1969-71; Eisenhower Trophy 1970(winners)

Ward, Harvie
Born Tarboro, North Carolina, USA in 1926. Turned Professional 1973

Chp Amateur Champion 1952; r/u 1953
Nat US Amateur 1955-56
Oth Canadian Amateur 1964
Trn NCAA Chp 1949
Reg North and South Amateur 1948
Int Walker Cup 1953-55-59

Watson, Tom
Born Kansas City, Missouri, USA on 4th September, 1949.
Turned Professional 1971

Maj Open Champion 1975-77-80-82-83, r/u 1984; US Open 1982, r/u 1983-87, 3rd 1980; USPGA r/u 1978; US Masters 1977-81, r/u 1978-79-84
US 32 wins 1974-one 1975-one 1977-three 1978-five 1979-five 1980-five 1981-four 1982-two 1984-three 1987-one; World Series 1975-80
RoW Phoenix Open (Jap) 1980
Int Ryder Cup 1977-81-83-89; v Japan 1982-84
Mis Vardon Trophy 1977-78-79; leading money winner 1977-78-79-80-84; USPGA Player of the Year 1977-78-79-80-84; Bobby Jones Award 1986; World Golf Hall of Fame 1988

Weiskopf, Tom
Born Massillon, Ohio, USA on 9th November, 1942. Turned Professional 1964

Maj Open Champion 1973; US Open r/u 1976; 3rd 1973-77; USPGA 3rd 1975; US Masters r/u 1969-72-74-75
Eur Piccadilly World Match Play 1972
US 1968-two 1971-two 1972-one 1973-three 1975-one 1977-one 1978-one 1982-one World Series 1973; Canadian Open 1973-75
RoW South African PGA 1973; Argentine Open 1979
Int Ryder Cup 1973-75; USA in World Cup 1972

Welts, Anne
See Sander

Whitworth, Kathy
Born Monahans, Texas, USA on 27th September, 1939.
Turned Professional 1959

Maj US Open r/u 1971; USLPGA 1967-71-75, r/u 1968-70
US 88 LPGA wins 1962-85 (incl Titleholder's Chp 1965-66; Western Open 1967)
Int Solheim Cup (1990)
Mis Rolex Player of the Year 1966-67-68-69-71-72-73. Vare Trophy 1965-66-67-69-70-71-72. William Richardson Award 1986; Woman Athlete of the Year 1965-66; LPGA Hall of Fame; World Golf Hall of Fame 1982; Powell Award 1986; Patty Berg Award 1987

Wright, Mary Kathryn (Mickey)
Born San Diego, California, USA on 14th February, 1935.
Turned Professional 1954

Maj US Open 1958-59-61-64, r/u 1968, leading amateur 1954; USLPGA 1958-60-61-63, r/u 1964-66
PRO
US 82 LPGA wins 1956-73 (incl Titleholders Chp 1961-62; Western Open 1962-63-66; 13 wins in 1963)
Mis Leading money winner 1961-62-63-64; Vare Trophy 1960-61-62-63-64; LPGA Hall of Fame 1964; World Golf Hall of Fame 1976; Woman Athlete of the Year 1963-64

Yates, Charles Richard
Born Atlanta, Georgia, USA on 9th September, 1913

Maj US Masters leading amateur 1934-39-40
Chp Amateur Champion 1938
Reg Western Amateur 1935.
Int Walker Cup 1936-38-(83)

Zoeller, Frank Urban (Fuzzy)
Born New Albany, Indiana, USA on 11th November, 1951.
Turned Professional 1973

Maj US Open 1984; USPGA r/u 1981; US Masters 1979
US 1979-two 1983-two 1985-one 1986-three
Int Ryder Cup 1979-83-85
Mis Ben Hogan Award 1986

British Isles International Players, Professional Men

Since 1979 the 'Great Britain and Ireland' team format for the Ryder Cup match against the United States has been widened to include professionals from the Continent of Europe.

Adams, J
(Scotland): v England 1932-33-34-35-36-37-38; v Wales 1937-38; v Ireland 1937-38. (GBI): v America 1947-49-51-53

Ainslie, T
(Scotland): v Ireland 1936

Alliss, Percy
(England): v Scotland 1932-33-34-35-36-37; v Ireland 1932-38; v Wales 1938. (GBI): v France 1929; v America 1929-31-33-35-37

Alliss, Peter
(England): in Canada Cup 1954-55-57-58-59-61-62-64-66; in World Cup 1967. (GBI): v America 1953-57-59-61-63-65-67-69

Anderson, Joe
(Scotland): v Ireland 1932

Anderson, W
(Scotland): v Ireland 1936; v England 1937; v Wales 1937

Ayton, LB
(Scotland): v England 1910-12-13-33-34

Ayton, JB, jr
(Scotland): v England 1937. (GBI): v America 1949

Ballantine, J
(Scotland): v England 1932-36

Ballingall, J
(Scotland): v England 1938; Ireland 1938; v Wales 1938

Bamford, BJ
(England): in Canada Cup 1961

Bannerman, H
(Scotland): in World Cup 1967-72. (GBI): v America 1971

Barber, T
(England): v Ireland 1932-33

Barnes, BW
(Scotland): in World Cup 1974-75-76-77. (GBI): v America 1969-71-73-75-77-79; v Europe 1974-76-78-80; v South Africa 1976

Batley, JB
(England): v Scotland 1912

Beck, AG
(England): v Wales 1938; v Ireland 1938

Bembridge, M
(England): in World Cup 1974-75. (GBI): v America 1969-71-73-75; v South Africa 1976

Boomer, A
(England): (GBI): v America 1926-27-29

Bousfield, K
(England): in Canada Cup 1956-57. (GBI): v America 1949-51-55-57-59-61

Boxall, R
(England): in Dunhill Cup 1990; in World Cup 1990

Boyle, HF
(Ireland): in World Cup 1967. (GBI): v America 1967

Bradshaw, H
(Ireland): in Canada Cup 1954-55-56-57-58-59; v Scotland 1937-38; v Wales 1937; v England 1938. (GBI): v America 1953-55-57

Braid, J
(Scotland): v England 1903-04-05-06-07-09-10-12. (GBI): v America 1921

Branch, WJ
(England): v Scotland 1936

Brand, G, jr
(Scotland): in World Cup 1984-85-88-89-90; in Dunhill Cup 1985-86-87-88-89; (Eur): in Nissan Cup 1985; Kirin Cup 1988; Four Tours World Chp 1989; (GBI): v America 1987-89; v Australia 1988

Brand, GJ
(England): in World Cup 1983; in Dunhill Cup 1986-87 (winners). (GBI): v America 1983; (Eur) Nissan Cup 1986

Brown, EC
(Scotland): in Canada Cup 1954-55-56-57-58-59-60-61-62-65-66; in World Cup 1987-68. (GBI): v America 1953-55-57-59

Brown, K
(Scotland): in World Cup 1977-78-79-83. (GBI): v America 1977-79-83-85-87; v Europe 1978; (Eur) Kirin Cup 1987

Burns, S
(Scotland): v England 1932. (GBI): v America 1929

Burton, J
(England): v Ireland 1933

Burton, R
(England): v Scotland 1935-36-37-38; v Ireland 1938; v Wales 1938. (GBI): v America 1935-37-49

Busson, JH
(England): v Scotland 1938

Busson, JJ
(England): v Scotland 1934-35-36-37. (GBI): v America 1935

Butler, PJ
(England): in World Cup 1969-70-73. (GBI): v America 1965-69-71-73; v Europe 1976

Callum, WS
(Scotland): v Ireland 1935

Campbell, J
(Scotland): v Ireland 1936

Carrol, LJ
(Ireland): v Scotland 1937-38; v Wales 1937; v England 1938

Cassidy, J
(Ireland): v England 1933; v Scotland 1934-35

Cassidy, D
(Ireland): v Scotland 1936-37; v Wales 1937

Cawsey, GH
(England): v Scotland 1906-07

Caygill, GA
(England): (GBI): v America 1969

Clark, C
(England): (GBI): v America 1973

Clark, HK
(England): in World Cup 1978-84-85-87; in Dunhill Cup 1985-86-87 (winners)-89-90 (r/u). (GBI): v America 1977-81-85-87-89; v Australia 1988; v Europe 1978-84. (Eur): in Nissan Cup 1985

Coles, NC
(England): in Canada Cup 1963; in World Cup 1968. (GBI): v America 1961-63-65-67-69-71-73-77; v Europe 1974-76-78-80

Collinge, T
(England): v Scotland 1937

Collins, JF
(England): v Scotland 1903-04

Coltart, F
(Scotland): v England 1909

Compston, A
(England): v Scotland 1932-35; v Ireland 1932. (GBI): v America 1926-27-29-31; v France 1929

Cotton, TH
(England): (GBI): v America 1929-37-47; v France 1929

Cox, S
(Wales): in World Cup 1975

Cox, WJ
(England): v Scotland 1935-36-37. (GBI): v America 1935-37

Curtis, D
(England): v Scotland 1934-38; v Ireland 1938; v Wales 1938

Dabson, K
(Wales): in World Cup 1972

Dailey, A
(Scotland): v England 1932-33-34-35-36-38; v Ireland 1938; v Wales 1938. (GBI): v America 1933

Daly, F
(Ireland): v Scotland 1936-37-38; v England 1938; v Wales 1937; in Canada Cup 1954-55. (GBI): v America 1947-49-51-53

Darcy, E
(Ireland): in World Cup 1976-77-83-84-85-87; Dunhill Cup 1987-88 (winners). (GBI): v America 1975-77-81-87; v Europe 1976-84; v South Africa 1976

Davies, R
(Wales): in World Cup 1968

Davies, WH
(England): v Scotland 1932-33; v Ireland 1932-33. (GBI): v America 1931-33

Davis, W
(Scotland): v Ireland 1933-34-35-36-37-38; v England 1937-38; v Wales 1937-38

Dawson, P
(England): in World Cup 1977. (GBI): v America 1977

De Foy, CB
(Wales): in World Cup 1971-73-74-75-76-77-78

Denny, CS
(England): v Scotland 1936

Dobson, T
(Scotland): v England 1932-33-34-35-36-37; v Ireland 1932-33-34-35-36-37-38; v Wales 1937-38

Don, W
(Scotland): v Ireland 1935-36

Donaldson, J
(Scotland): v England 1932-35-38; v Ireland 1937; v Wales 1937

Dornan, R
(Scotland): v Ireland 1932

Drew, NV
(Ireland): in Canada Cup 1960-61. (GBI): v America 1959

Duncan, G
(Scotland): v England 1906-07-09-10-12-13-32-34-35-36-37. (GBI): v America 1921-26-27-29-31

Durnian, D
(England): in World Cup 1989; in Dunhill Cup 1989

Durward, JG
(Scotland): v Ireland 1934; v England 1937

Easterbrook, S
(England): v Scotland 1932-33-34-35-38; v Ireland 1933. (GBI): v America 1931-33

Edgar, J
(Ireland): v Scotland 1938

Fairweather, S
(Ireland): v England 1932; v Scotland 1933. (Scotland): v England 1933-35-36; v Ireland 1938; v Wales 1938

Faldo, NA
(England): in World Cup 1977; in Dunhill Cup 1985-86-87 (winners) -88. (GBI): v America 1977-79-81-83-85-87-89; v Europe 1978-80-82-84; v Rest of World 1982. (Eur) Nissan Cup 1986. Kirin Cup 1987; Four Tours World Chp 1990

Fallon, J
(Scotland): v England 1936-37-38; v Ireland 1937-38; v Wales 1937-38. (GBI): v America 1955

Faulkner, M
(England): (GBI): v America 1947-49-51-53-57

Feherty, D
(Ireland): in World Cup 1990; in Dunhill Cup 1985-86-90 (winners); (Eur): in Four Tours World Chp 1990

Fenton, WB
(Scotland): v England 1932; v Ireland 1932-33

Fernie, TR
(Scotland): v England 1910-12-13-33

Foster, M
(England): in World Cup 1976. (GBI): v Europe 1976

Gadd, B
(England): v Scotland 1933-35-38; v Ireland 1933-38; v Wales 1938

Gadd, G
(England): (GBI): v America 1926-27

Gallacher, BJ
(Scotland): in World Cup 1969-71-74-82-83. (GBI): v America 1969-71-73-75-77-79-81-83-91 (Captain); v Europe 1974-78-82-84; v South Africa 1976; v Rest of World 1982

Garner, JR
(England): (GBI): v America 1971-73

Gaudin, PJ
(England): v Scotland 1905-06-07-09-12-13

Good, G
(Scotland): v England 1934-36

Gould, H
(Wales): in Canada Cup 1954-55

Gow, A
(Scotland): v England 1912

Grabham, C
(Wales): v England 1938; v Scotland 1938

Grant, T
(Scotland): v England 1913

Gray, E
(England): v Scotland 1904-05-07

Green, E
(England): (GBI): v America 1947

Green, T
(England): v Scotland 1935. (Wales): v Scotland 1937-38;
v Ireland 1937; v England 1938

Greene, C
(Ireland): in Canada Cup 1965

Gregson, M
(England): in World Cup 1967. (GBI): v America 1967

Haliburton, TB
(Scotland): v Ireland 1935-36-38; v England 1938; v Wales
1938; in Canada Cup 1954. (GBI): v America 1961-63

Hamill, J
(Ireland): v Scotland 1933-34-35; v England 1932-33

Hargreaves, J
(England): (GBI): v America 1951

Hastings, W
(Scotland): England 1937-38; v Wales 1937-38; v Ireland
1937-38

Havers, AG
(England): v Scotland 1932-33-34; v Ireland 1932-33.
(GBI): v America 1921-26-27-31-33; v France 1929

Healing, SF
(Wales): v Scotland 1938

Hepburn, J
(Scotland): v England 1903-05-06-07-09-10-12-13

Herd, A
(Scotland): v England 1903-04-05-06-09-10-12-13-32

Hill, EF
(Wales): v Scotland 1937-38; v Ireland 1937;
v England 1938

Hitchcock, J
(England): (GBI): v America 1965

Hodson, B
(England): v Ireland 1933. (Wales): v Scotland 1937-38;
v Ireland 1937; v England 1938. (GBI): v America 1931

Holley, W
(Ireland): v Scotland 1933-34-35-36-38;
v England 1932-33-38

Horne, R
(England): (GBI): v America 1947

Horton, T
(England): in World Cup 1976. (GBI): v Europe 1974-76;
v America 1975-77

Houston, D
(Scotland): v Ireland 1934

Huggett, BGC
(Wales): in Canada Cup 1963-64-65; in World Cup 1968-
69-70-71-76-79. (GBI): v America 1963-67-69-71-73-75;
v Europe 1974-78

Huish, D
(Scotland): in World Cup 1973

Hunt, BJ
(England): in Canada Cup 1958-59-60-62-63-64; in World
Cup 1968. (GBI): v America 1953-57-59-61-63-65-67-69

Hunt, GL
(England): in World Cup 1972-75. (GBI): v Europe 1974;
v America 1975

Hunt, Geoffrey M
(England): (GBI): v America 1963

Hunter, W
(Scotland): v England 1906-07-09-10

Hutton, GC
(Scotland): v Ireland 1936-37; v England 1937-38;
v Wales 1937

Ingram, D
(Scotland): in World Cup 1973

Jacklin, A
(England): in Canada Cup 1966; in World Cup 1970-71-72.
(GBI): v America 1967-69-71-73-75-77-79-83 (captain)
-85(captain) -87(captain) -89(captain); v Europe 1976-82; v
Rest of World 1982

Jackson, H
(Ireland): in World Cup 1970-71

Jacobs, JRM
(England): (GBI): v America 1955

Jagger, D
(England): (GBI): v Europe 1976

James, G
(Wales): v Scotland 1937; v Ireland 1937

James, MH
(England): in World Cup 1978-79-82-84-87-88; in Dunhill
Cup 1988-89-90 (r/u). (GBI): v America 1977-79-81-89; v
Europe 1978-80-82; v Rest of World 1982; v Australia 1988;
(Eur): Kirin Cup 1988; Four Tours World Chp 1989-90

Jarman, EW
(England): v Scotland 1935. (GBI): v America 1935

Job, N
(England): (GBI): v Europe 1980

Jolly, HC
(England): (GBI): v America 1926-27; v France 1929

Jones, DC
(Wales): v Scotland 1937-38; v Ireland 1937; v England 1938

Jones, E
(Ireland): in Canada Cup 1965

Jones, R
(England): v Scotland 1903-04-05-06-07-09-10-12-13

Jones, T
(Wales): v Scotland 1936; v Ireland 1937; v England 1938

Kenyon, EWH
(England): v Scotland 1932; v Ireland 1932

King, M
(England): in World Cup 1979. (GBI): v America 1979

King, SL
(England): v Scotland 1934-36-37-38; v Wales 1938;
v Ireland 1938. (GBI): v America 1937-47-49

Kinsella, J
(Ireland): in World Cup 1968-69-72-73

Kinsella, W
(Ireland): v Scotland 1937-38; v England 1938

Knight, G
(Scotland): v England 1937

Lacey, AJ
(England): v Scotland 1932-33-34-36-37-38; v Ireland
1932-33-38; v Wales 1938. (GBI): v America 1933-37

Laidlaw, W
(Scotland): v England 1935-36-38; v Ireland 1937;
v Wales 1937

Lane, B
(England): in World Cup 1988; in Dunhill Cup 1988

Lees, A
(England): v Scotland 1938; v Wales 1938; v Ireland 1938.
(GBI): v America 1947-49-51-55

Llewellyn, D
(Wales): in World Cup 1974-85-87 (winners)-88; in Dunhill
Cup 1985-88. (GBI): v Europe 1984

Lloyd, F
(Wales): v Scotland 1937-38; v Ireland 1937;
v England 1938

Lockhart, G
(Scotland): v Ireland 1934-35

Lyle, AWB
(Scotland): in World Cup 1979-80-87; in Dunhill Cup 1985-
86-87-88-89-90. (GBI): v America 1979-81-83-85-87; v
Europe 1980-82-84; v Rest of World 1982; v Australia 1988.
(Eur): in Nissan Cup 1985-86; Kirin Cup 1987.

McCartney, J
(Ireland): v Scotland 1932-33-34-35-36-37-38;
v England 1932-33-38; v Wales 1937

McCulloch, D
(Scotland): v England 1932-33-34-35-36-37;
v Ireland 1932-33-34-35

McDermott, M
(Ireland): v England 1932; v Scotland 1932

McDowall, J
(Scotland): v England 1932-33-34-35-36;
v Ireland 1933-34-35-36

McEwan, P
(Scotland): v England 1907

McIntosh, G
(Scotland): v England 1938; v Ireland 1938;
v Wales 1938

McKenna, J
(Ireland): v Scotland 1936-37-38; v Wales 1937-38;
v England 1938

McKenna, R
(Ireland): v Scotland 1933-35; v England 1933

McMillan, J
(Scotland): v England 1933-34-35; v Ireland 1933-34

McMinn, W
(Scotland): v England 1932-33-34

McNeill, H
(Ireland): v England 1932

Mahon, PJ
(Ireland): v Scotland 1932-33-34-35-36-37-38;
v Wales 1937-38; v England 1932-33-38

Martin, J
(Ireland): in Canada Cup 1962-63-64-66;
in World Cup 1970. (GBI): v America 1965

Martin, S
(Scotland): in World Cup 1980

Mason, SC
(England): in World Cup 1980. (GBI): v Europe 1980

Mayo, CH
(England): v Scotland 1907-09-10-12-13

Mills, RP
(England): (GBI): v America 1957

Mitchell, A
(England): v Scotland 1932-33-34. (GBI): v America
1921-26-29-31-33

Moffitt, R
(England): (GBI): v America 1961

Montgomerie, C
(Scotland): in World Cup 1988; in Dunhill Cup 1988

Mouland, M
(Wales): in World Cup 1988-89-90; in Dunhill Cup 1986-87-
88-89. (Eur): Kirin Cup 1988.

Mouland, S
(Wales): in Canada Cup 1965-66; in World Cup 1967

O'Brien, W
(Ireland): v Scotland 1934-36-37; v Wales 1937

Ockenden, J
(England): (GBI): v America 1921

O'Connor, C
(Ireland): in Canada Cup 1956-57-58-59-60-61-62-63-64-66;
in World Cup 1967-68-69-71-73. (GBI): v America 1955-57-
59-61-63-65-67-69-71-73

O'Connor, C, jr
(Ireland): in World Cup 1974-75-78-85-89; in Dunhill Cup
1985-89. (GBI): v Europe 1974-84; v America
1975-89; v South Africa 1976

O'Connor, P
(Ireland): v Scotland 1932-33-34-35-36; v England 1932-33

Oke, WG
(England): v Scotland 1932

O'Leary, JE
(Ireland): in World Cup 1972-80-82. (GBI): v America 1975;
v Europe 1976-78-82; v Rest of World 1982

O'Neill, J
(Ireland): v England 1933

O'Neill, M
(Ireland): v Scotland 1933-34; v England 1933

Oosterhuis, PA
(England): in World Cup 1971. (GBI): v America 1971-73-
75-77-79-81; v Europe 1974

Padgham, AH
(England): v Scotland 1932-33-34-35-36-37-38; v Ireland
1932-33-38; v Wales 1938. (GBI): v America 1933-35-37

Panton, J
(Scotland): in Canada Cup 1955-56-57-58-59-60-61-62-63-
64-65-66; in World Cup 1968. (GBI): v America 1951-53-61

Park, J
(Scotland): v England 1909

Parkin, P
(Wales): in World Cup 1984-89; in Dunhill Cup 1985-86-87-89-90. (GBI): v Europe 1984

Patterson, E
(Ireland): v Scotland 1933-34-35-36; v England 1933; v Wales 1937

Perry, A
(England); v Ireland 1932; v Scotland 1933-36-38. (GBI): v America 1933-35-37

Pickett, C
(Wales): v Scotland 1937-38; v Ireland 1937; v England 1938

Platts, L
(Wales): (GBI): v America 1965

Polland, E
(Ireland): in World Cup 1973-74-76-77-78-79. (GBI): v America 1973; v Europe 1974-76-78-80; v South America 1976

Pope, CW
(Ireland): v England 1932; v Scotland 1932

Rafferty, R
(Ireland): in World Cup 1983-84-87-88-90; in Dunhill Cup 1986-87-88 (winners)-89-90 (winners); (GBI): v Europe 1984; v Australia 1988. (Eur): v America 1989; Kirin Cup 1988; Four Tours World Chp 1989-90

Rainford, P
(England): v Scotland 1903-07

Ray, E
(England): v Scotland 1903-04-05-06-07-09-10-12-13. (GBI): v America 1921-26-27

Rees, DJ
(Wales): v Scotland 1937-38; v Ireland 1937; England 1938; in Canada Cup 1954-56-57-58-59-60-61-62-64. (GBI): v America 1937-47-49-51-53-55-57-59-61

Reid, W
(England): v Scotland 1906-07

Renouf, TG
(England): v Scotland 1903-04-05-10-13

Ritchie, WL
(Scotland): v England 1913

Robertson, F
(Scotland): v Ireland 1933; v England 1938

Robertson, P
(Scotland): v England 1932; v Ireland 1932-34

Robson, F
(England): v Scotland 1909-10. (GBI): v America 1926-27-29-31

Roe, M
(England): in World Cup 1989

Rowe, AJ
(England): v Scotland 1903-06-07

Sayers, B, jr
(Scotland): v England 1906-07-09

Scott, SS
(England): (GBI): v America 1955

Seymour, M
(England): v Scotland 1932-33; v Ireland 1932-33. (Scotland): v Ireland 1932

Shade, RDBM
(Scotland): in World Cup 1970-71-72

Sherlock, JG
(England): v Scotland 1903-04-05-06-07-09-10-12-13. (GBI): v America 1921

Simpson, A
(Scotland): v England 1904

Smalldon, D
(Wales): in Canada Cup 1955-56

Smith, CR
(Scotland): v England 1903-04-07-09-13

Smith, GE
(Scotland): v Ireland 1932

Smyth, D
(Ireland): in World Cup 1979-80-82-83-88-89; in Dunhill Cup 1985-86-87-88 (winners). (GBI): v America 1979-81; v Europe 1980-82-84; v Rest of World 1982

Snell, D
(England): in Canada Cup 1965

Spark, W
(Scotland): v Ireland 1933-35-37; v England 1935; v Wales 1937

Stevenson, P
(Ireland): v Scotland 1933-34-35-36-38; v England 1933-38

Sutton, M
(England): in Canada Cup 1955

Taylor, JH
(England): v Scotland 1903-04-05-06-07-09-10-12-13. (GBI): v America 1921

Taylor, JJ
(England): v Scotland 1937

Taylor, Josh
(England): v Scotland 1913. (GBI): v America 1921

Thomas, DC
(Wales): in Canada Cup 1957-58-59-60-61-62-63-66; in World Cup 1967-69-70. (GBI): v America 1959-63-65-67

Thompson, R
(Scotland): v England 1903-04-05-06-07-09-10-12

Tingey, A
(England): v Scotland 1903-05

Torrance, S
(Scotland): in World Cup 1976-78-82-84-85-87-89-90; in Dunhill Cup 1985-86-87-89-90. (GBI): v Europe 1976-78-80-82-84; v America 1981-83-85-87-89; v Rest of World 1982. (Eur): in Nissan Cup 1985

Townsend, P
(England): in World Cup 1969-74. (GBI): v America 1969-71; v Europe 1974

Twine, WT
(England): v Ireland 1932

Vardon, H
(England): (GBI): v America 1921

Vaughan, DI
(Wales): in World Cup 1972-73-77-78-79-80

Waites, BJ
(England): in World Cup 1980-82-83. (GBI): v Europe 1980-82-84; v Rest of World 1982; v America 1983

Walker, RT
(Scotland): in Canada Cup 1964

Wallace, L
(Ireland): v England 1932; v Scotland 1932

Walton P
(Ireland): in Dunhill Cup 1989-90 (winners)

Ward, CH
(England): v Ireland 1932. (GBI): v America 1947-49-51

Watt, T
(Scotland): v England 1907

Watt, W
(Scotland): v England 1912-13

Way, P
(England): in Dunhill Cup 1985; in World Cup 1985.
(GBI): v America 1983-85

Weetman, H
(England): in Canada Cup 1954-56-60. (GBI): v America
1951-53-55-57-59-61-63

Whitcombe, CA
(England): v Scotland 1932-33-34-35-36-37-38;
v Ireland 1933. (GBI): v America 1927-29-31-33-35-37;
v France 1929

Whitcombe, EE
(England): v Scotland 1938; v Wales 1938; v Ireland 1938

Whitcombe, ER
(England): v Scotland 1932; v Ireland 1933.
(GBI): v America 1926-29-31-35; v France 1929

Whitcombe, RA
(England): v Scotland 1933-34-35-36-37-38.
(GBI): v America 1935

White, J
(Scotland): v England 1903-04-05-06-07-09-12-13

Wilcock, P
(England): in World Cup 1973

Will, G
(Scotland): in Canada Cup 1963; in World Cup 1969-70.
(GBI): v America 1963-65-67

Williams, K
(Wales): v Scotland 1937-38; v Ireland 1937;
v England 1938

Williamson, T
(England): v Scotland 1904-05-06-07-09-10-12-13

Wilson, RG
(England): v Scotland 1913

Wilson, T
(Scotland): v England 1933-34; v Ireland 1932-33-34

Wolstenholme, GB
(England): in Canada Cup 1965

Wood, N
(Scotland): in World Cup 1975. (GBI): v America 1975

Woosnam, I
(Wales): in World Cup 1980-82-83-84-85-87 (winners)-90;
Dunhill Cup 1985-86-87-88-89-90. (GBI): v Europe 1982-84;
v Rest of World 1982; v America 1983-85-87-89; v Australia
1988. (Eur): in Nissan Cup 1985-86. Kirin Cup 1987; Four
Tours World Chp 1989-90

British Isles International Players, Amateur Men

Abbreviations:

Com Trnmt   Commonwealth Tournament
Eur T Ch   played in European Team Championship for home country;
Home Int   played in Home International matches

Adams, MPD
(Wales): Home Int 1969-70-71-72-75-76-77; Eur T Ch 1971

Aitken, AR
(Scotland): v England 1906-07-08

Alexander, DW
(Scotland): Home Int 1958; v Scandinavia 1958

Allison, A
(Ireland): v England 1928; v Scotland 1929

Anderson, N
(Ireland): Home Int 1985-86-87-88-89-90. Eur T Ch 1989.
(GBI): v Europe 1988

Anderson, RB
(Scotland): v Scandinavia 1960-62; Home Int 1962-63

Andrew, R
(Scotland): v England 1905-06-07-08-09-10

Armour, A
(Scotland): v England 1922

Armour, TD
(GBI): v America 1921

Ashby, H
(England): Home Int 1972-73-74. (GBI): in Dominican Int
1973. (GBI): v Europe 1974

Atkinson, HN
(Wales): v Ireland 1913

Attenborough, M
(England): Home Int 1964-66-67-68; Eur T Ch 1967.
(GBI): v Europe 1966-68; v America 1967

Aylmer, CC
(England): v Scotland 1911-22-23-24. (GBI): v America
1921-22

Babington, A
(Ireland): v Wales 1913

Baker, P
(England): Home Int 1985. (GBI): v America 1985;
v Europe 1986

Baker, RN
(Ireland): Home Int 1975

Ball, J
(England): v Scotland 1902-03-04-05-06-07-08-09-10-11-12

Bamford, JL
(Ireland): Home Int 1954-56

Banks, C
(England): Home Int 1983

Banks, SE
(England): Home Int 1934-38

Bannerman, S
(Scotland): Home Int 1988; v Sweden 1990

Bardsley, R
(England): Home Int 1987; v France 1988

Barker, HH
(England): v Scotland 1907

Barnett, A
(Wales): Home Int 1989-90

Barrie, GC
(Scotland): Home Int 1981-83

Barry, AG
(England): v Scotland 1906-07

Bathgate, D
(England): Home Int 1990

Bayliss, RP
(England): v Ireland 1929; Home Int 1933-34

Bayne, PWGA
(Wales): Home Int 1949

Beamish, CH
(Ireland): Home Int 1950-51-53-56

Beck, JB
(England): v Scotland 1926-30; Home Int 1933.
(GBI): v America 1928-38 (Captain) -47 (Captain)

Beddard, JB
(England): v Wales/Ireland 1925; v Ireland 1929;
v Scotland 1927-28-29

Beharrell, JC
(England): Home Int 1956

Bell, HE
(Ireland): v Wales 1930; Home Int 1932

Bell, RK
(England): Home Int 1947

Benka, PJ
(England): Home Int 1967-68-69-70: Eur T Ch 1969.
(GBI): v America 1969; v Europe 1970

Bennett, H
(England): Home Int 1948-49-51

Bennett, S
(England): v Scotland 1979

Bentley, AL
(England): Home Int 1936-37; v France 1937-39

Bentley, HG
(England): v Ireland 1931; v Scotland 1931. Home Int 1932-33-34-35-36-37-38-47; v France 1934-35-36-37-39-54.
(GBI): v America 1934-36-38

Berry, P
(England): Home Int 1972. (GBI): v Europe 1972

Bevan, RJ
(Wales): Home Int 1964-65-66-67-73-74

Beveridge, HW
(Scotland): v England 1908

Birtwell, SG
(England): Home Int 1968-70-73

Black, D
(Scotland): Home Int 1966-67

Black, FC
(Scotland): Home Int 1962-64-65-66-68; v Scandinavia 1962; Eur T Ch 1965-67. (GBI): v Europe 1966

Black, GT
(Scotland): Home Int 1952-53; v South Africa 1954

Black, JL
(Wales): Home Int 1932-33-34-35-36

Black, WC
(Scotland): Home Int 1964-65

Blackwell, EBH
(Scotland): v England 1902-04-05-06-07-09-10-12-23-24-25

Blair, DA
(Scotland): Home Int 1948-49-51-52-53-55-56-57;
v Scandinavia 1956-58-62. (GBI): v America 1955-61;
in Com Tnmt 1954

Blakeman, D
(England): Home Int 1981; v France 1982

Bloice, C
(Scotland): Home Int 1985-86. (GBI): v America 1985

Bloxham, JA
(England): Home Int 1966

Blyth, AD
(Scotland): v England 1904

Bonallack,MF
(England): Home Int 1957-58-59-60-61-62-63-64-65-66-67-68-69-70-71-72-73-74; Eur T Ch 1969-71. (GBI): v America 1957-59-61-63-65-67-69 (Captain) -71 (Captain) -73;
v Europe 1958-62-64-66-68-70-72; in Com Tnmt 1959-63-67-71; in World Team Ch 1960-62-64-66-68-70-72

Bonnell, DJ
(Wales): Home Int 1949-50-51

Bookless, JT
(Scotland): v England 1930-31; v Ireland 1930;
v Wales 1931

Bottomley, S
(England): Home Int 1986

Bourn, TA
(England): v Ireland 1928; v Scotland 1930;
Home Int 1933-34; v France 1934. (GBI): v Australia 1934

Bowen, J
(Ireland): Home Int 1961

Bowman, TH
(England): Home Int 1932

Boxall, R
(England): Home Int 1980-81-82; v France 1982

Boyd, HA
(Ireland): v Wales 1913-23

Bradshaw, AS
(England): Home Int 1932

Bradshaw, EI
(England): v Scotland 1979; Eur T Ch 1979

Braid, H
(Scotland): v England 1922-23

Bramston, JAT
(England): v Scotland 1902

Brand, GJ
(England): Home Int 1976. (GBI) v Europe 1976

Brand, G
(Scotland): Home Int 1978-80; v England 1979;
Eur T Ch 1979; v Italy 1979; v Belgium 1980; v France 1980.
(GBI): v Europe 1978-80; in World Team Ch 1978-80;
v America 1979; v France 1981

Branigan, D
(Ireland): Home Int 1975-76-77-80-81-82-86; Eur T Ch 1977-81; v West Germany, France, Sweden 1976

Bretherton, CF
(England): v Scotland 1922-23-24-25; v Wales/Ireland 1925

Briscoe, A
(Ireland): v England 1928-29-30-31; v Scotland 1929-30-31;
v Wales 1929-30-31; Home Int 1932-33-38

Bristowe, OC
(GBI): v America 1923-24

Broad, RD
(Wales): v Ireland 1979; Home Int 1980-81-82-84;
Eur T Ch 1981

Broadhurst, P
(England): Home Int 1986-87; v France 1988. (GBI) v Europe 1988

Brock, J
(Scotland) v Ireland 1929; Home Int 1932

Brodie, Allan
(Scotland): Home Int 1970-72-73-74-75-76-77-78-80; Eur T Ch 1973-77-79; v England 1979; v Italy 1979; v Belgium 1977; v Spain 1977; v France 1978. (GBI): v America 1977-79; v Europe 1974-76-78-80;in World Team Ch 1978

Brodie, Andrew
(Scotland): Home Int 1968-69; v Spain 1974

Bromley-Davenport, E
(England): Home Int 1938-51

Brooks, A
(Scotland): Home Int 1968-69; Eur T Ch 1969.
(GBI): v America 1969

Brooks, CJ
(Scotland): Home Int 1984-85. (GBI): v Europe 1986

Brotherton, IR
(Scotland): Home Int 1984-85

Brough, S
(England): Home Int 1952-55-59-60; v France 1952-60.
(GBI): v Europe 1960

Brown, CT
(Wales): Home Int 1970-71-72-73-74-75-77-78-80-88
(captain); Eur T Ch 1973; v Denmark 1977-80;
v Ireland 1979; v Switzerland, Spain 1980

Brown, D
(Wales): v Ireland 1923-30-31; v England 1925; v Scotland
1931

Brown, JC
(Ireland): Home Int 1933-34-35-36-37-38-48-52-53

Brownlow, Hon WGE
(GBI): v America 1926

Bruen, J
(Ireland): Home Int 1937-38-49-50. (GBI): v America
1938-49-51

Bucher, AM
(Scotland): Home Int 1954-55-56; v Scandinavia 1956

Buckley, JA
(Wales): Home Int 1967-68-69-76-77-78; Eur T Ch 1967-69;
v Denmark 1976-77. (GBI): v America 1979

Burch, N
(England): Home Int 1974

Burgess, MJ
(England): Home Int 1963-64-67; Eur T Ch 1967

Burke, J
(Ireland): v England 1929-30-31; v Wales 1929-30-31;
v Scotland 1930-31; Home Int 1932-33-34-35-36-37-38-47-
48-49. (GBI): v America 1932

Burns, M
(Ireland): Home Int 1973-75-83

Burnside, J
(Scotland): Home Int 1956-57

Burrell, TM
(Scotland): v England 1924

Bussell, AF
(Scotland): Home Int 1956-57-58-61; v Scandinavia
1956-60. (GBI): v America 1957; v Europe 1956-62

Butterworth, JR
(England): v France 1954

Cairnes, HM
(Ireland): v Wales 1913-25; v England 1904; v Scotland
1904-27

Caldwell, I
(England): Home Int 1950-51-52-53-54-55-56-57-58-59-61;
v France 1950. (GBI): v America 1951-55

Calvert, M
(Wales): Home Int 1983-84-86-87-89

Cameron, D
(Scotland): Home Int 1938-51

Campbell, Bart, Sir Guy C
(Scotland): v England 1909-10-11

Campbell, HM
(Scotland): Home Int 1962-64-68; v Scandinavia 1962;
v Australia 1964; Eur T Ch 1965.(GBI): v Europe 1964

Campbell, JGS
(Scotland): Home Int 1947-48

Campbell, W
(Scotland): v Ireland 1927-28-29-30-31; v England 1928
-29-30-31; v Wales 1931; Home Int 1933-34-35-36.
(GBI): v America 1930

Cannon, JHS
(England): v Ireland/Wales 1925

Cannon, JM
(Scotland): Home Int 1969; v Spain 1974

Carman, A
(England): v Scotland 1979; Home Int 1980

Carr, FC
(England): v Scotland 1911

Carr, JB
(Ireland): Home Int 1947-48-49-50-51-52-53-54-55-56-57-
58-59-60-61-62-63-64-65-66-67-68-69; Eur T Ch 1965-67-
69. (GBI): v America 1947-49-51-53-55-57-59-61-63-65
(Captain) -67 (Captain); v Europe 1954-56-64-66-68;
in World Team Ch 1958-60

Carr, JJ
(Ireland): Home Int 1981-82-83

Carr, JP
(Wales): v Ireland 1913

Carr, JR
(Ireland): v Wales 1930-31; v England 1931; Home Int 1933

Carr, R
(Ireland): Home Int 1970-71; Eur T Ch 1971.
(GBI): v America 1971

Carrgill, PM
(England): Home Int 1978

Carrick, DG
(Scotland): Home Int 1981-82-83-84-85-86-87-88-89; v West
Germany 1987; v Italy 1988; v France 1989; Eur T Ch 1989.
(GBI): v America 1983-87; v Europe 1986

Carroll, CA
(Ireland): v Wales 1924

Carroll, JP
(Ireland): Home Int 1948-49-50-51-62

Carroll, W
(Ireland): v Wales 1913-23-24-25; v England 1925;
v Scotland 1929; Home Int 1932

Carslaw, LA
(Scotland): Home Int 1976-77-78-80-81; Eur T Ch 1977-79;
v England 1979; v Italy 1979; v Spain 1977;
v Belgium 1978; v France 1978. (GBI): v Europe 1978;
v America 1979

Carvill, J
(Ireland): Home Int 1989; Eur T Ch 1989. (GBI): v Europe
1990

Cashell, BG
(Ireland): Home Int 1978; v France, West Germany, Sweden
1978

Cassells, C
(England): Home Int 1989

Castle, H
(England): v Scotland 1903-04

Cater, JR
(Scotland): Home Int 1952-53-54-55-56. (GBI): v America
1955

Caul, P
(Ireland): Home Int 1968-69-71-72-73-74-75

Caven, J
(Scotland): v England 1926. (GBI): v America 1922

Chapman, BHG
(England): Home Int 1961-62. (GBI): v America 1961;
v Europe 1962

Chapman, JA
(Wales): v Ireland 1923-29-30-31; v Scotland 1931;
v England 1925

Chapman, R
(Wales): v Ireland 1929; Home Int 1932-34-35-36

Chapman, R
(England): v Scotland 1979; Home Int 1980-81; Eur T Ch 1981. (GBI): v Europe 1980; v America 1981

Charles, WB
(Wales): v Ireland 1924

Chillas, D
(Scotland): Home Int 1971

Christmas, MJ
(England): Home Int 1960-61-62-63-64. (GBI): v America 1961-63; v Europe 1962-64; in World Team Ch 1962

Clark, CA
(England): Home Int 1964. (GBI): v Europe 1964; v America 1965

Clark, D
(Ireland): Home Int 1987-89. (GBI): v Europe 1990

Clark, GJ
(England): Home Int 1961-64-66-67-68-71. (GBI): v Europe 1964-66; v America 1965.

Clark, HK
(England): Home Int 1973. (GBI): v America 1973

Clark, MD
(Wales): v Ireland 1947

Clay, G
(Wales): Home Int 1962

Claydon, R
(England): Home Int 1988; Eur T Ch 1989: (GBI): v America 1989

Cleary, T
(Ireland): Home Int 1976-77-78-82-83-84-85-86; v Wales 1979; v France, West Germany, Sweden 1976

Clement, G
(Wales): v Ireland 1979

Cochran, JS
(Scotland): Home Int 1966

Colt, HS
(England): v Scotland 1908

Coltart, A
(Scotland): Home Int 1988-89-90; Eur T Ch 1989; v Sweden 1990; v Italy 1990; Nixdorf Nations Cup 1990; (GBI): v Europe 1990; World Cup 1990

Cook, J
(England): Home Int 1989-90

Cook, JH
(England): Home Int 1969

Corridan, T
(Ireland): Home Int 1983-84

Corcoran, DK
(Ireland): Home Int 1972-73; Eur T Ch 1973

Cosh, GB
(Scotland): Home Int 1964-65-66-67-68-69; Eur T Ch 1965-69. (GBI): v America 1965; v Europe 1966-68; in Com Tnmt 1967; in World Team Ch 1966-68

Coulter, JG
(Wales): Home Int 1951-52

Coutts, FJ
(Scotland): Home Int 1980-81-82; Eur T Ch 1981; v France 1981-82

Cox, S
(Wales): Home Int 1970-71-72-73-74; Eur T Ch 1971-73

Crabbe, JL
(Ireland): v Wales 1925; v Scotland 1927-28

Craddock, T
(Ireland): Home Int 1955-56-57-58-59-60-67-68-69-70; Eur T Ch 1971. (GBI): v America 1967-69

Craigan, RM
(Ireland): Home Int 1963-64

Crawford, D
(Scotland): Home Int 1990

Crawley, LG
(England): v Ireland 1931; v Scotland 1931; Home Int 1932-33-34-36-37-38-47-48-49-54-55; v France 1936-37-38-49. (GBI): v America 1932-34-38-47

Critchley, B
(England): Home Int 1962-69-70; Eur T Ch 1969. (GBI): v America 1969; v Europe 1970

Crosbie, GF
(Ireland): Home Int 1953-55-56-57-88 (captain)

Crowley, M
(Ireland): v England 1928-29-30-31; v Wales 1929-31; v Scotland 1929-30-31; Home Int 1932

Cuddihy, J
(Scotland): Home Int 1977

Curry, DH
(England): Home Int 1984-86-87; v France 1988. (GBI): v Europe 1986-88 v America 1987

Dalgleish, CR
(Scotland): Home Int 1981-82-83-89; v France 1982; Eur T Ch 1981; Nixdorf Nations Cup 1989. (GBI): v America 1981

Darwin, B
(England): v Scotland 1902-04-05-08-09-10-23-24. (GBI): v America 1922

Davies, EN
(Wales): Home Int 1959-60-61-62-63-64-65-66-67-68-69-70-71-72-73-74; Eur T Ch 1969-71-73

Davies, JC
(England): Home Int 1969-71-72-73-74-78; Eur T Ch 1973-75-77. (GBI): v Europe 1972-74-76-78; v America 1973-75-77-79; in World Team Ch 1974-76

Davies, FE
(Ireland): v Wales 1923

Davies, G
(Wales): v Denmark 1977; Home Int 1981-82-83

Davies, HE
(Wales): Home Int 1933-34-36

Davies, M
(England): Home Int 1984-85

Davies, TJ
(Wales): Home Int 1954-55-56-57-58-58-60

Davison, C
(England): Home Int 1989

Dawson, JE
(Scotland): v Ireland 1927-29-30-31; v England 1930-31; v Wales 1931; Home Int 1932-33-34-37

Dawson, M
(Scotland): Home Int 1963-65-66

Dawson, P
(England): Home Int 1969

Deboys, A
(Scotland): Home Int 1956-59-60; v Scandinavia 1960

Deeble, P
(England): Home Int 1975-76-77-78-80-81-83-84;
v Scotland 1979; Eur T Ch 1979-81. (GBI): v America 1977-81; v Europe 1978; v France 1982; in Colombian Int 1978

Deighton, FWG
(Scotland): Home Int 1950-52-53-56-57-58-59-60.
(GBI): v America 1951-57; v South Africa 1952;
in Com Tnmt 1954-59

Denholm, RB
(Scotland): v Ireland 1929-31; v Wales 1931; v England 1931; Home Int 1932-33-34-35

Dewar, FG
(Scotland): Home Int 1952-53-55

Dick, CE
(Scotland): v England 1902-03-04-05-09-12

Dickson, HM
(Scotland): v Ireland 1929-31

Dickson, JR
(Ireland): Eur T Ch 1977; Home Int 1980

Disley, A
(Wales): Home Int 1976-77-78; v Denmark 1977;
v Ireland 1979

Dodd, SC
(Wales):Home Int 1985-57-88-89. (GBI): v America 1989

Donellan, B
(Ireland): Home Int 1952

Dowie, A
(Scotland): Home Int 1949

Downes, P
(England): Home Int 1976-77-78-80-81-82;
Eur T Ch 1977-79-81. (GBI): v Europe 1980

Downie, JJ
(England): Home Int 1974

Draper, JW
(Scotland): Home Int 1954

Drew, NV
(Ireland): Home Int 1952-53. (GBI): v America 1953

Duffy, I
(Wales): Home Int 1975

Duncan, AA
(Wales): Home Int 1933-34-36-38-47-48-49-50-51-52-53-54-55-56-57-58-59. (GBI): v America (Captain) 1953

Duncan, GT
(Wales): Home Int 1952-53-54-55-56-57-58

Duncan, J, jr
(Wales): v Ireland 1913

Duncan, J
(Ireland): Home Int 1959-60-61

Dunn, NW
(England): v Ireland 1928

Dunn, P
(Wales): Home Int 1957-58-59-60-61-62-63-65-66

Dunne, E
(Ireland): Home Int 1973-74-76-77; v Wales 1979;
Eur T Ch 1975

Durrant, RA
(England): Home Int 1967; Eur T Ch 1967

Dykes, JM
(Scotland): Home Int 1934-35-36-48-49-51.
(GBI): v America 1936

Easingwood, SR
(Scotland): Home Int 1986-87-88-90; v Italy 1988-90; v France 1989; Eur T Ch 1989

Eaves, CH
(Wales): Home Int 1935-36-38-47-48-49

Edwards, B
(Ireland): Home Int 1961-62-64-65-66-67-68-69-73

Edwards, M
(Ireland): Home Int 1956-57-58-60-61-62

Edwards, TH
(Wales): Home Int 1947

Egan, TW
(Ireland): Home Int 1952-53-59-60-62-67-68;
Eur T Ch 1967-69

Eggo, R
(England): Home Int 1986-87-88-89-90; v France 1988.
(GBI): v America 1987; v Europe 1988

Elliot, A
(Scotland): Home Int 1989; v France 1989; Eur T Ch 1989

Elliot, C
(Scotland): Home Int 1982

Elliot, IA
(Ireland): Home Int 1975-77-78; Eur T Ch 1975,
v France, West Germany, Sweden 1978

Ellis, HC
(England): v Scotland 1902-12

Ellison, TF
(England): v Scotland 1922-25-26-27

Emerson, T
(Wales): Home Int 1932

Emery, G
(Wales): v Ireland 1925; Home Int 1933-36-38

Errity, D
(Ireland): Home Int 1990

Evans, AD
(Wales): v Scotland 1931-35; v Ireland 1931; Home Int 1932-33-34-35-38-47-49-50-51-52-53-54-55-56-61

Evans, C
(Wales): Home Int 1990

Evans, Duncan
(Wales): Home Int 1978-80-81; v Ireland 1979;
Eur T Ch 1981. (GBI) v Europe 1980; v America 1981

Evans, G
(England): Home Int 1961

Evans, G
(England): Home Int 1990. (GBI) World Cup 1990

Evans, HJ
(Wales): Home Int 1976-77-78-80-81-84-85-87-88;
v France 1976; v Denmark 1977-80; v Ireland 1979;
Eur T Ch 1979-81; v Switzerland, Spain 1980

Evans, M Gear
(Wales): v Ireland 1930-31; v Scotland 1931

Everett, C
(Scotland): Home Int 1988-89-90; v Italy 1988-90;
v France 1989; Eur T Ch 1989; Nixdorf Nations Cup 1989-90; v Sweden 1990;

Ewing, RC
(Ireland): Home Int 1934-35-36-37-38-47-48-49-50-51-53-54-55-56-57-58. (GBI): v America 1936-38-47-49-51-55

Eyles, GR
(England): Home Int 1974-75; Eur T Ch 1975. (GBI): v America 1975; v Europe 1974; in World Team Ch 1974

Fairbairn, KA
(England): Home Int 1988

Fairchild, CEL
(Wales): v Ireland 1923; v England 1925

Fairchild, LJ
(Wales): v Ireland 1924

Fairlie, WE
(Scotland): v England 1912

Faldo, N
(England): Home Int 1975. (GBI): in Com Tnmt 1975

Fanagan, J
(Ireland): Home Int 1989-90

Farmer, JC
(Scotland): Home Int 1970

Ferguson, M
(Ireland): Home Int 1952

Ferguson, WJ
(Ireland): Home Int 1952-54-55-58-59-61

Fergusson, S Mure
(Scotland): v England 1902-03-04

Ffrench, WF
(Ireland): v Scotland 1929; Home Int 1932

Fiddian, EW
(England): v Scotland 1929-30-31; v Ireland 1929-30-31; Home Int 1932-33-34-35; v France 1934. (GBI): v America 1932-34

Fitzgibbon, JF
(Ireland): Home Int 1955-56-57

Fitzsimmons, J
(Ireland): Home Int 1938-47-48

Flaherty, JA
(Ireland): Home Int 1934-35-36-37

Flaherty, PD
(Ireland): Home Int 1967; Eur T Ch 1967-69

Fleming, J
(Scotland): Home Int 1987

Fleury, RA
(Ireland): Home Int 1974

Flockhart, AS
(Scotland): Home Int 1948-49

Fogarty, GN
(Ireland): Home Int 1956-58-63-64-67

Fogg, HN
(England): Home Int 1933

Forest, J de (now Count J de Bendern)
(England): v Ireland 1931; v Scotland 1931. (GBI): v America 1932

Foster, MF
(England): Home Int 1973

Foster, R
(England): Home Int 1963-64-66-67-68-69-70-71-72; Eur T Ch 1967-69-71-73. (GBI): v Europe 1964-66-68-70; v America 1965-67-69-71-73-79 (Captain) -81 (Captain); in Com Tnmt 1967-71; in World Team Ch 1964-70

Fowler, WH
(England): v Scotland 1903-04-05

Fox, SJ
(England): Home Int 1956-57-58

Frame, DW
(England): Home Int 1958-59-60-61-62-63. (GBI): v America 1961

Francis, F
(England): Home Int 1936; v France 1935-36

Frazier, K
(England): Home Int 1938

Froggatt, P
(Ireland): Home Int 1957

Fry, SH
(England): v Scotland 1902-03-04-05-06-07-09

Gairdner, JR
(Scotland): v England 1902

Gallacher, BJ
(Scotland): Home Int 1967

Galloway, RF
(Scotland): Home Int 1957-58-59; v Scandinavia 1958

Gannon, MA
(Ireland): Home Int 1973-74-77-78-80-81-83-84-87-88-89-90; v France, West Germany, Sweden 1978-80; Eur T Ch 1979-81-89. (GBI): v Europe 1974-78

Garbutt, I
(England): Home Int 1990

Garner, PF
(England): Home Int 1977-78-80; v Scotland 1979

Garnet, LG
(England): v France 1934. (GBI): v Australia 1934

Garson, R
(Scotland): v Ireland 1928-29

Gent, J
(England): v Ireland 1930; Home Int 1938

Gibb, C
(Scotland): v England 1927; v Ireland 1928

Gibson, WC
(Scotland): Home Int 1950-51

Gilford, CF
(Wales): Home Int 1963-64-65-66-67

Gilford, D
(England): Home Int 1983-84-85. (GBI): v America 1985; v Europe 1986

Gill, WJ
(Ireland): v Wales 1931; Home Int 1932-33-34-35-36-37

Gillies, HD
(England): v Scotland 1908-25-26-27

Girvan, P
(Scotland): Home Int 1986; West Germany 1987. (GBI): v America 1987

Glossop, R
(Wales): Home Int 1935-37-38-47

Glover, J
(Ireland): Home Int 1951-52-53-55-59-60-70

Godwin, G
(England): Home Int 1976-77-78-80-81; v Scotland 1979; v France 1982; Eur T Ch 1979-81. (GBI): v America 1979-81

Goulding, N
(Ireland): Home Int 1988-89-90

Graham, AJ
(Scotland): v England 1925

Graham, J
(Scotland): v England 1902-03-04-05-06-07-08-09-10-11

Graham, JSS
(Ireland): Home Int 1938-50-51

Gray, CD
(England): Home Int 1932

Green, CW
(Scotland): Home Int 1961-62-63-64-65-67-68-69-70-71-72-73-74-75-76-77-78; Eur T Ch 1965-67-69-71-73-75-77-79; v Scandinavia 1962; v Belgium 1973-75-77-78; v Spain 1977; v Italy 1979; v England 1979. (GBI): v Europe 1962-66-68-70-72-74-76; v America 1963-69-71-73-75-83 (Captain) -85 (Captain) in Com Tnmt 1971; in World Team Ch 1970-72

Green, HB
(England): v Scotland 1979

Green, PO
(England): Home Int 1961-62-63. (GBI): in Com Tnmt 1963

Greene, R
(Ireland): Home Int 1933

Greig, DG
(Scotland): Home Int 1972-73-75. (GBI): in Com Tnmt 1975

Greig, K
(Scotland): Home Int 1933

Griffiths, HGB
(Wales): v Ireland 1923-24-25

Griffiths, HS
(Wales): v England 1958

Griffiths, JA
(Wales): Home Int 1933

Guild, WJ
(Scotland): v England 1925-27-28; v Ireland 1927-28

Hales, JP
(Wales): v Scotland 1963

Hall, AH
(Scotland): Home Int 1962-66-69

Hall, D
(Wales): Home Int 1932-37

Hall, K
(Wales): Home Int 1955-59

Hambro, AV
(England): v Scotland 1905-08-09-10-22

Hamilton, CJ
(Wales): v Ireland 1913

Hamilton, ED
(Scotland): Home Int 1936-37-38

Hamer, S
(England): Home Int 1983-84

Hanway, M
(Ireland): Home Int 1971-74

Hardman, RH
(England): v Scotland 1927-28. (GBI): v America 1928

Hare, A
(England): Home Int 1988; Eur T Ch 1989. (GBI) v America 1989

Hare, WCD
(Scotland): Home Int 1953

Harrhy, A
(Wales): Home Int 1988-89

Harrington, J
(Ireland): Home Int 1960-61-74-75-76; Eur T Ch 1975; v Wales 1979

Harrington, P
(Ireland): Home Int 1990

Harris, IR
(Scotland): Home Int 1955-56-58-59

Harris, R
(Scotland): v England 1905-08-10-11-12-22-23-24-25-26-27-28 (GBI): v America 1922 (Captain) -23 (Captain) -26 (Captain)

Harrison, JW
(Wales): Home Int 1937-50

Hartley, RW
(England): v Scotland 1926-27-28-29-30-31; v Ireland 1928-29-30-31; Home Int 1933-34-35. (GBI): v America 1930-32

Hartley, WL
(England): v Ireland/Wales 1925; v Scotland 1927-31; v Ireland 1928-31; Home Int 1932-33; v France 1935. (GBI): v America 1932

Hassall, JE
(England): v Scotland 1923; v Ireland/Wales 1925

Hastings, JL
(Scotland): Home Int 1957-58; v Scandinavia 1958

Hawksworth, J
(England): Home Int 1984-85. (GBI): v America 1985

Hay, G
(Scotland): v England 1979; Home Int 1980-88-90; v Belgium 1980; v France 1980-82-89; v Italy 1988. (GBI): v Europe 1986

Hay, J
(Scotland): Home Int 1972

Hayes, JA
(Ireland): Home Int 1977

Hayward, CH
(England): v Scotland 1925; v Ireland 1928

Healy, TM
(Ireland): v Scotland 1931; v England 1931

Heather, D
(Ireland): Home Int 1976; v France, West Germany, Sweden 1976

Hedges, PJ
(England): Home Int 1970-73-74-75-76-77-78-82-83; Eur T Ch 1973-75-77. (GBI): v America 1973-75; v Europe 1974-76; in World Team Ch 1974

Hegarty, J
(Ireland): Home Int 1975

Hegarty, TD
(Ireland): Home Int 1957

Helm, AGB
(England): Home Int 1948

Henderson, J
(Ireland): v Wales 1923

Henderson, N
(Scotland): Home Int 1963-64

Henriques, GLQ
(England): v Ireland 1930

Henry, W
(England): Home Int 1987; v France 1988

Herlihy, B
(Ireland): Home Int 1950

Herne, KTC
(Wales): v Ireland 1913

Heverin, AJ
(Ireland): Home Int 1978; v France, West Germany, Sweden 1978

Hezlet, CO
(Ireland): v Wales 1923-25-27-29-31; v Scotland 1927-28-29-30-31; v England 1929-30-31. (GBI): v America 1924-26-28; v South Africa 1927

Higgins, L
(Ireland): Home Int 1968-70-71

Hill, GA
(England): Home Int 1936-37. (GBI): v America 1936-55 (Captain)

Hilton, HH
(England): v Scotland 1902-03-04-05-06-07-09-10-11-12

Hird, K
(Scotland): Home Int 1987-88-89; Nixdorf Nations Cup 1989; v Italy 1990

Hoad, PGJ
(England): Home Int 1978; v Scotland 1979

Hodgson, C
(England): v Scotland 1924

Hoey, TBC
(Ireland): Home Int 1970-71-72-73-77-84; Eur T Ch 1971-77

Hogan, P
(Ireland): Home Int 1985-86-87-88

Holderess, Sir EWE
(England): v Scotland 1922-23-24-25-26-28. (GBI): v America 1921-23-26-30

Holmes, AW
(England): Home Int 1962

Homer, TWB
(England): Home Int 1972-73; Eur T Ch 1973. (GBI): v America 1973; v Europe 1972; in World Team Ch 1972

Homewood, G
(England): Home Int 1985

Hooman, CVL
(England): v Scotland 1910-22. (GBI): v America 1922-23

Hope, WL
(Scotland): v England 1923-25-26-27-28-29. (GBI): v America 1923-24-28

Horne, A
(Scotland): Home Int 1971

Hosie, JR
(Scotland): Home Int 1936

Houston, G
(Wales): Home Int 1990

Howard, DB
(Scotland): v England 1979; Home Int 1980-81-82-83; v Belgium 1980; v France 1980-81; Eur T Ch 1981. (GBI): v Europe 1980.

Howell, HR
(Wales): v Ireland 1923-24-25-29-30-31; v England 1925; v Scotland 1931; Home Int 1932-34-35-36-37-38-47

Howell, H Logan
(Wales): v Ireland 1925

Huddy, G
(England): Home Int 1960-61-62. (GBI): v America 1961

Huggan, J
(Scotland): Home Int 1981-82-83-84; v France 1982; Eur T Ch 1981

Hughes, I
(Wales): Home Int 1954-55-56

Hulme, WJ
(Ireland): Home Int 1955-56-57

Humphrey, JG
(Wales): v Ireland 1925

Humphreys, AR
(Ireland): v England 1957

Humphreys, DI
(Wales): Home Int 1972

Humphreys, W
(England): Home Int 1970-71; Eur T Ch 1971. (GBI): v Europe 1970; v America 1971

Hunter, NM
(Scotland): v England 1903-12

Hunter, WI
(Scotland): v England 1922

Hutcheon, I
(Scotland): Home Int 1971-72-73-74-75-76-77-78-80; v Belgium 1973-75-77-78-80; v Spain 1977; v France 1978-80-81; v Italy 1979; Eur T Ch 1973-75-77-79-81. (GBI): v Europe 1974-76; v America 1975-77-79-81; in World Team Ch 1974-76-80; in Com Tnmt 1975; in Dominican Int 1973; in Colombian Int 1975

Hutchings, C
(England): v Scotland 1902

Hutchinson, HG
(England): v Scotland 1902-03-04-06-07-09

Hutchison, CK
(Scotland): v England 1904-05-06-07-08-09-10-11-12

Hyde, GE
(England): Home Int 1967-68

Illingworth, G
(England): v Scotland 1929; v France 1937

Inglis, MJ
(England): Home Int 1977

Isitt, GH
(Wales): v Ireland 1923

Jack, RR
(Scotland): Home Int 1950-51-54-55-56-57-58-59-61; v Scandinavia 1958. (GBI): v America 1957-59; v Europe 1956; in World Team Ch 1958; in Com Tnmt 1959

Jack, WS
(Scotland): Home Int 1955

Jacob, NE
(Wales): Home Int 1932-33-34-35-36

James, D
(Scotland): Home Int 1985

James, M
(England): Home Int 1974-75; Eur T Ch 1975 (GBI): v America 1975

James, RD
(England): Home Int 1974-75

Jameson, JF
(Ireland): v Wales 1913-24

Jamieson, A, jr
(Scotland): v England 1927-28-31; v Ireland 1928-31; v Wales 1931; Home Int 1932-33-36-37. (GBI): v America 1926

Jamieson, D
(Scotland): Home Int 1980

Jenkins, JLC
(Scotland): v England 1908-12-22-24-26-28; v Ireland 1928. (GBI): v America 1921

Jermine, JG
(Wales): Home Int 1972-73-74-75-76-82; Eur T Ch
1975-77; v France 1975

Jobson, RH
(England): v Ireland 1928

Johnson, R
(Wales): Home Int 1990

Johnson, TWG
(Ireland): v England 1929

Johnston, JW
(Scotland): Home Int 1970-71

Jones, A
(Wales): Home Int 1989-90

Jones, DK
(Wales): Home Int 1973

Jones, EO
(Wales): Home Int 1983-85-86

Jones, JG Parry
(Wales): Home Int 1959-60

Jones, JL
(Wales): Home Int 1933-34-36

Jones, JR
(Wales): Home Int 1970-72-73-77-78-80-81-82-83-84-85;
Eur T Ch 1973-79-81; v Denmark 1976-80; v Ireland
1979; v Switzerland, Spain 1980; v Ireland 1979

Jones, JW
(England): Home Int 1948-49-50-51-52-54-55

Jones, KG
(Wales): Home Int 1988

Jones, MA
(Wales): Home Int 1947-48-49-50-51-53-54-57

Jones, Malcolm F
(Wales): Home Int 1933

Jones, SP
(Wales): Home Int 1981-82-83-84-85-86-88-89

Kane, RM
(Ireland): Home Int 1967-68-71-72-74-78; Eur T Ch
1971-79; v Wales 1979. (GBI): v Europe 1974

Kearney, K
(Ireland): Home Int 1988-89-90

Keenan, S
(Ireland): Home Int 1989

Kelleher, WA
(Ireland): Home Int 1962

Kelley, MJ
(England): Home Int 1974-75-76-77-78-80-81-82-88
(Captain); v France 1982; Eur T Ch 1977-79. (GBI): v
America 1977-79; v Europe 1976-78; in World Team Ch
1976; in Colombian Int 1978

Kelley, PD
(England): Home Int 1965-66-68

Kelly, NS
(Ireland): Home Int 1966

Keppler, SD
(England): Home Int 1982-83; v France 1982.
(GBI): v America 1983

Kilduff, AJ
(Ireland): v Scotland 1928

Killey, GC
(Scotland): v Ireland 1928

King, M
(England): Home Int 1969-70-71-72-73; Eur T Ch 1971-73
(GBI): v America 1969-73; v Europe 1970-72; in Com Tnmt
1971

Kissock, B
(Ireland): Home Int 1961-62-74-76; v France, West
Germany, Sweden 1978

Kitchin, JE
(England): v France 1949

Knight, B
(Wales): Home Int 1986

Knipe, RG
(Wales): Home Int 1953-54-55-56

Knowles, S
(Scotland): Home Int 1990

Knowles, WR
(Wales): v England 1948

Kyle, AT
(Scotland): Home Int 1938-47-49-50-51-52-53.
(GBI): v America 1938-47-51; v South Africa 1952

Kyle, D
(Scotland): v England 1924-30. (GBI): v America 1924

Kyle, EP
(Scotland): v England 1925

Laidlay, JE
(Scotland): v England 1902-03-04-05-06-07-08-09-10-11

Lake, AD
(Wales): Home Int 1958

Lang, JA
(Scotland): v England 1929-31; v Ireland 1929-30-31;
v Wales 1931. (GBI): v America 1930

Langley, JDA
(England): Home Int 1950-51-52-53; v France 1950.
(GBI): v America 1936-51-53

Langmead, J
(England): Home Int 1986

Lassen, EA
(England): v Scotland 1909-10-11-12

Last, CN
(Wales): Home Int 1975

Laurence, C
(England): Home Int 1983-84-85

Lawrie, CD
(Scotland): Home Int 1949-50-55-56-57-58; v Scandinavia
1958. (GBI): v South Africa 1952; v America 1961
(Captain) -63 (Captain)

Lawrie, G
(Scotland): Home Int 1990

Layton, EN
(England): v Scotland 1922-23-26; v Ireland/Wales 1925

Lee, IGF
(Scotland): Home Int 1958-59-60-61-62; v Scandinavia 1960

Lee, JN
(Wales): Home Int 1988-89

Lee, M
(England): Home Int 1950

Lee, MG
(England): Home Int 1965

Lehane, N
(Ireland): Home Int 1976; v France, West Germany,
Sweden 1976

Lewis, DH
(Wales): Home Int 1935-36-37-38

Lewis, DR
(Wales): v Ireland 1925-29-30-31; v Scotland 1931;
Home Int 1932-34

Lewis, ME
(England): Home Int 1980-81-82; v France 1982.
(GBI): v America 1983

Lewis, R Cofe
(Wales): v Ireland 1925

Leyden, PJ
(Ireland): Home Int 1953-55-56-57-59

Lincoln, AC
(England): v Scotland 1907

Lindsay, J
(Scotland): Home Int 1933-34-35-36

Lloyd, HM
(Wales): v Ireland 1913

Lloyd, RM de
(Wales): v Scotland 1931; v Ireland 1931; Home Int
1932-33-34-35-36-37-38-47-48

Llyr, A
(Wales): Home Int 1984-85

Lockhart, G
(Scotland): v England 1911-12

Lockley, AE
(Wales): Home Int 1956-57-58-62

Logan, GW
(England): Home Int 1973

Long, D
(Ireland): Home Int 1973-74-80-81-82-83-84;
v Wales 1979; Eur T Ch 1979

Low, AJ
(Scotland): Home Int 1964-65; Eur T Ch 1965

Low, JL
(Scotland): v England 1904

Lowe, A
(Ireland): v Wales 1924; v England 1925-28; v Scotland
1927-28

Lowson, G
(Scotland): Home Int 1989-90; v Sweden 1990

Lucas, PB
(England): Home Int 1936-48-49; v France 1936.
(GBI): v America 1936-47-49 (Captain)

Lunt, MSR
(England): Home Int 1956-57-58-59-60-62-63-64-66.
(GBI): v America 1959-61-63-65; v Europe 1964;
in Com Tnmt 1963; in World Team Ch 1964

Lunt, S
(England): Home Int 1932-33-34-35; v France 1934-35-39

Lygate, M
(Scotland): Home Int 1970-75-88 (Captain); Eur T Ch 1971

Lyle, AWB
(England): Home Int 1975-76-77; Eur T Ch 1977.
(GBI): v America 1977; in Com Tnmt 1975; v Europe 1976

Lyon, JS
(England): Home Int 1937-38

Lyons, P
(Ireland): Home Int 1986

McAllister, SD
(Scotland): Home Int 1983

Macara, MA
(Wales): Home Int 1983-84-85-87-89-90

McArthur, W
(Scotland): Home Int 1952-54

McBeath, J
(Scotland): Home Int 1964

McBride, D
(Scotland): Home Int 1932

McCallum, AR
(Scotland): v England 1929. (GBI): v America 1928

McCarrol, F
(Ireland): Home Int 1968-69

McCart, DM
(Scotland): Home Int 1977; v Belgium 1978

McCarthy, L
(Ireland): Home Int 1953-54-55-56

McConnell, FP
(Ireland): v Wales 1929-30-31; v England 1929-30-31;
v Scotland 1930-31; Home Int 1934

McConnell, RM
(Ireland): v Wales 1924-25-29-30-31; v England 1925-28-29-
30-31; v Scotland 1927-28-29-31; Home Int 1934-35-36-37

McConnell, WG
(Ireland): v England 1925

McCormack, JD
(Ireland): v Wales 1913-24; v England 1928, Home Int 1932-
33-34-35-36-37

McCrea, WE
(Ireland): Home Int 1965-66-67; Eur T Ch 1965

McCready, SM
(Ireland): Home Int 1947-49-50-52-54. (GBI): v America
1949-51

McDaid, B
(Ireland): v Wales 1979

MacDonald, GK
(Scotland): Home Int 1978-81-82; v England 1979; v France
1981-82

McDonald, H
(Scotland): Home Int 1970

Macdonald, JS
(Scotland): Home Int 1969-70-71-72; v Belgium 1973;
Eur T Ch 1971. (GBI): v Europe 1970; v America 1971

McEvoy, P
(England): Home Int 1976-77-78-80-81-83-84-85-86-87-88-
89; v Scotland 1979; v France 1982-88; Eur T Ch 1977-79-
81-89; (GBI): v America 1977-79-81-85-89; v Europe 1978-
80-86-88; in World Cup 1978-80-88 (winners)

Macfarlane, CB
(Scotland): v England 1912

McGimpsey, G
(Ireland): Home Int 1978-80-81-82-83-84-85-86-87-88-89-
90; v Wales 1979; Eur T Ch 1981-89. (GBI): v America 1985-
89; v Europe 1986-88-90; World Cup 1988 (winners)

McGinley, P
(Ireland): Home Int 1989-90

Macgregor, A
(Scotland): v Scandinavia 1956

Macgregor, G
(Scotland): Home Int 1969-70-71-72-73-74-75-76-80-81-82-
83- 84-85-86-87; v Belgium 1973-75-80; v England 1979;
Eur T Ch 1971-73-75-81. (GBI): v Europe 1970-74; v America
1971-75-83-85-87-91 (Captain); in Com Tnmt 1971-75; v
France 1981-82

MacGregor, RC
(Scotland): Home Int 1951-52-53-54. (GBI): v America 1953

McHenry, J
(Ireland): Home Int 1985-86. (GBI): v America 1987

McInally, H
(Scotland): Home Int 1937-47-48

McInally, RH
(Ireland): Home Int 1949-51

McIntosh, E
(Scotland): Home Int 1989

Macintosh, KW
(Scotland): v England 1979; Home Int 1980; v France 1980; v Belgium 1980. (GBI): v Europe 1980

McKay, G
(Scotland): Home Int 1969

McKay, JR
(Scotland): Home Int 1950-51-52-54

McKellar, PJ
(Scotland): Home Int 1976-77-78; v Belgium 1978; v France 1978; v England 1979. (GBI): v America 1977; v Europe 1978

Mackenzie, F
(Scotland): v England 1902-03

MacKenzie, S
(Scotland): Home Int 1990

Mackenzie, WW
(Scotland): v England 1923-26-27-29; v Ireland 1930. (GBI): v America 1922-23

Mackeown, HN
(Ireland): Home Int 1973; Eur T Ch 1973

Mackie, GW
(Scotland): Home Int 1948-50

McKinna, RA
(Scotland): Home Int 1938

McKinlay, SL
(Scotland): v England 1929-30-31; v Ireland 1930; v Wales 1931; Home Int 1932-33-35-37-47. (GBI): v America 1934

McKinnon, A
(Scotland): Home Int 1947-52

McLean, D
(Wales): Home Int 1968-69-70-71-72-73-74-75-76-77-78-80-81-82-83-85-86-88-90; Eur T Ch 1975-77-79-81; v France 1975-76; v Denmark 1976-80; v Ireland 1979; v Switzerland, Spain 1980

McLean, J
(Scotland): Home Int 1932-33-34-35-36. (GBI): v America 1934-36; v Australia 1934

McLeod, AE
(Scotland): Home Int 1937-38

McLeod, WS
(Scotland): Home Int 1935-37-38-47-48-49-50-51

McMenamin, E
(Ireland): Home Int 1981

McMullan, C
(Ireland): Home Int 1933-34-35

McNair, AA
(Scotland): v Ireland 1929

MacNamara, L
(Ireland): Home Int 1977-83-84-85-86-87-88-89-90; Eur T Ch 1977

McRuvie, EA
(Scotland): v England 1929-30-31; v Ireland 1930-31; v Wales 1931; Home Int 1932-33-34-35-36. (GBI): v America 1932-34

McTear, J
(Scotland): Home Int 1971

Madeley, JFD
(Ireland): Home Int 1959-60-61-62-63-64. (GBI): v Europe 1962; v America 1963

Mahon, RJ
(Ireland): Home Int 1938-52-54-55

Maliphant, FR
(Wales): Home Int 1932

Malone, B
(Ireland): Home Int 1959-64-69-71-75; Eur T Ch 1971-75

Manford, GC
(Scotland): v England 1922-23

Manley, N
(Ireland): v Wales 1924; v England 1928; v Scotland 1927-28

Mann, LS
(Scotland): Home Int 1982-83. (GBI): v America 1983

Marchbank, B
(Scotland): Home Int 1978; v Italy 1979; Eur T Ch 1979. (GBI): v Europe 1976-78; in World Team Ch 1978; v America 1979

Marks, GC
(England): Home Int 1963-67-68-69-70-71-74-75-82; Eur T Ch 1967-69-71-75. (GBI): v Europe 1968-70; v America 1969-71-87 (Captain); in World Team Ch 1970; in Com Tnmt 1975; in Colombian Int 1975. Non playing captain v France 1982

Marren, JM
(Ireland): v Wales 1925

Marsh, DM
(England): Home Int 1956-57-58-59-60-64-66-68-69-70-71-72; Eur T Ch 1971. (GBI): v Europe 1958; v America 1959-71-73 (Captain) -75 (Captain)

Marshman, A
(Wales): Home Int 1952

Marston, CC
(Wales): v Ireland 1929-30-31; v Scotland 1931

Martin, DHR
(England): Home Int 1938; v France 1934-49

Martin, GNC
(Ireland): v Wales 1923-29; v Scotland 1928-29-30; v England 1929-30. (GBI): v America 1928

Martin, S
(Scotland): Home Int 1975-76-77; Eur T Ch 1977; v Belgium 1977; v Spain 1977. (GBI): v America 1977; v Europe 1976; in World Team Ch 1976

Mason, SC
(England): Home Int 1973

Mathias-Thomas, FEL
(Wales): v Ireland 1924-25

Matthews, RL
(Wales): Home Int 1935-37

Maxwell, R
(Scotland): v England 1902-03-04-05-06-07-09-10

Mayo, PM
(Wales): Home Int 1982-87. (GBI): v America 1985-87

Meharg, W
(Ireland): Home Int 1957

Melia, TJ
(Wales): Home Int 1976-77-78-80-81-82; v Ireland 1979;
Eur T Ch 1977-79; v Denmark 1976-80; v Switzerland,
Spain 1980

Mellin, GL
(England): v Scotland 1922

Melville, LM Balfour
(Scotland): v England 1902-03

Melville, TE
(Scotland): Home Int 1974

Menzies, A
(Scotland): v England 1925

Metcalfe, J
(England): Home Int 1989. (GBI) v Europe 1990

Micklem, GH
(England): Home Int 1947-48-49-50-51-52-53-54-55.
(GBI): v America 1947-49-53-55-57 (Captain) -59 (Captain);
in World Team 1958

Mill, JW
(Scotland): Home Int 1953-54

Millensted, DJ
(England): Home Int 1966; Eur T Ch 1967. (GBI): v America
1967; in Com Tnmt 1967

Miller, AC
(Scotland): Home Int 1954-55

Miller, MJ
(Scotland): Home Int 1974-75-77-78; v Belgium 1978;
v France 1978

Milligan, JW
(Scotland): Home Int 1986-87-88-89-90; v West Germany
1987; v Italy 1988-90; v France 1989; Eur T Ch 1989; Nixdorf
Nations Cup 1989; v Sweden 1990. (GBI): v Europe 1988;
World Cup 1988 (winners)-90. (GBI): v America 1989

Mills, ES
(Wales): Home Int 1957

Millward, EB
(England): Home Int 1950-52-53-54-55. (GBI): v America
1949-55

Milne, WTG
(Scotland): Home Int 1972-73; Eur T Ch 1973;
v Belgium 1973. (GBI): v America 1973

Mitchell, A
(England): v Scotland 1910-11-12

Mitchell, CS
(England): Home Int 1975-76-78

Mitchell, FH
(England): v Scotland 1906-07-08

Mitchell, JWH
(Wales): Home Int 1964-65-66

Moffat, DM
(England): Home Int 1961-63-67; v France 1959-60

Moir, A
(Scotland): Home Int 1983-84

Montgomerie, CS
(Scotland): Home Int 1984-85-86; v West Germany 1987.
(GBI): v America 1985-87; v Europe 1986

Montgomerie, JS
(Scotland): Home Int 1957; v Scandinavia 1958

Montgomerie, RH de
(England): v Scotland 1908 v Wales/Ireland 1925;
v South Africa 1927. (GBI): v America 1921

Moody, JV
(West): Home Int 1947-48-49-51-56-58-59-60-61

Moody, PH
(England): Home Int 1971-72. (GBI): v Europe 1972

Moore, GJ
(Ireland): v England 1928; v Wales 1929

Morgan, JL
(Wales): 1948-49-50-51-52-53-54-55-56-57-58-59-60-61-62-
64-68. (GBI): v America 1951-53-55

Morris, FS
(Scotland): Home Int 1963

Morris, MF
(Ireland): Home Int 1978-80-82-83-84; v Wales 1979;
Eur T Ch 1979; v France, West Germany, Sweden 1980

Morris, R
(Wales): Home Int 1983-86-87

Morris, TS
(Wales): v Ireland 1924-29-30

Morrison, JH
(Scotland): v Scandinavia 1960

Morrison, JSF
(England): v Ireland 1930

Morrow, AJC
(Ireland): Home Int 1975-83

Morrow, JM
(Wales): v Ireland 1979; Home Int 1980-81; Eur T Ch
1979-81; v Denmark, Switzerland, Spain 1980

Mosey, IJ
(England): Home Int 1971

Moss, AV
(Wales): Home Int 1965-66-68

Mouland, MG
(Wales): Home Int 1978-81; v Ireland 1979; Eur T Ch 1979

Moxon, GA
(Wales): v Ireland 1929-30

Mulcare, P
(Ireland): Home Int 1968-69-70-71-72-74-78-80; v France,
West Germany, Sweden 1978-80; Eur T Ch 1975-79.
(GBI): v Europe 1972; v America 1975

Mulholland, D
(Ireland): Home Int 1988

Munn, E
(Ireland): v Wales 1913-23-24; v Scotland 1927

Munn, L
(Ireland): v Wales 1913-23-24; Home Int 1936-37

Munro, RAG
(Scotland): Home Int 1960

Murdoch, D
(Scotland): Home Int 1964

Murphy, AR
(Scotland): Home Int 1961-65-67

Murphy, P
(Ireland): Home Int 1985-86

Murray, GH
(Scotland): Home Int 1973-74-75-76-77-78-83; v Spain
1974-77; v Belgium 1975-77; Eur T Ch 1975-77.
(GBI): v America 1977; v Europe 1978

Murray, SWT
(Scotland): Home Int 1959-60-61-62-63; v Scandinavia
1960. (GBI): v Europe 1958-62; v America 1963

Murray, WA
(Scotland): v England 1923-24-25-26-27. (GBI): v America
1923-24

Murray, WB
(Scotland): Home Int 1967-68-69; Eur T Ch 1969

Muscroft, R
(England): Home Int 1986

Nash A
(England): Home Int 1988-89

Neech, DG
(England): Home Int 1961

Neill, JH
(Ireland): Home Int 1938-47-48-49

Neill, R
(Scotland): Home Int 1936

Nestor, JM
(Ireland): Home Int 1962-63-64

Nevin, V
(Ireland): Home Int 1960-63-65-67-69-72;
Eur T Ch 1967-69-73

Newey, AS
(England): Home Int 1932

Newman, JE
(Wales): Home Int 1932

Newton, H
(Wales): v Ireland 1929

Nicholson, J
(Ireland): Home Int 1932

Noon, GS
(Wales): Home Int 1935-36-37

Noon, J
(Scotland): Home Int 1987

O'Boyle, P
(Ireland): Eur T Ch 1977

O'Brien, MD
(Ireland): Home Int 1968-69-70-71-72-75-76-77; Eur T
Ch 1971; v France, West Germany, Sweden 1976

O'Carroll, C
(Wales): Home Int 1989-90

O'Connell, A
(Ireland): Home Int 1967-70-71-71

O'Connell, E
(Ireland): Home Int 1985; Eur T Ch 1989. (GBI): v Europe
1988; World Cup 1988 (winners). (GBI): v America 1989

O'Leary, JE
(Ireland): Home Int 1969-70; Eur T Ch 1969

O'Neill, JJ
(Ireland): Home Int 1968

Oldcorn, A
(England): Home Int 1982-83. (GBI): v America 1983

Oosterhuis, PA
(England): Home Int 1966-67-68. (GBI): v America 1967;
v Europe 1968; in World Team Ch 1968

Oppenheimer, RH
(England): v Ireland 1928-29-30; v Scotland 1930.
(GBI): v America 1957 (Captain)

O'Rourke, P
(Ireland): Home Int 1980-81-82-84-85

O'Sullivan, D
(Ireland): Home Int 1985-86-87

O'Sullivan, DF
(Ireland): Home Int 1976; Eur T Ch 1977

O'Sullivan, WM
(Ireland): Home Int 1934-35-36-37-38-47-48-49-50-51-53-54

Osgood, TH
(Scotland): v England 1925

Owen, JB
(Wales): Home Int 1971

Owens, GF
(Wales): Home Int 1960-61

Ownes, GH
(Ireland): Home Int 1935-37-38-47

Palferman, H
(Wales): Home Int 1950-53

Palmer, DJ
(England): Home Int 1962-63

Parfitt, RWM
(Wales): v Ireland 1924

Parkin, AP
(Wales): Home Int 1980-81-82. (GBI): v America 1983

Parry, JR
(Wales): Home Int 1966-75-76-77; v France 1976

Patey, IR
(England): Home Int 1952; v France 1948-49-50

Patrick, KG
(Scotland): Home Int 1937

Patterson, AH
(Ireland): v Wales 1913

Pattinson, R
(England): Home Int 1949

Payne, J
(England): Home Int 1950-51

Payne, J
(England): Home Int 1989-90. (GBI) v Europe 1990

Pearson, AG
(GBI): v South Africa 1927

Pearson, MJ
(England): Home Int 1951-52

Pease, JWB (*later* Lord Wardington)
(England): v Scotland 1903-04-05-06

Pennink, JJF
(England): Home Int 1937-38-47; v France 1937-38-39.
(GBI): v America 1938

Perkins, TP
(England): v Scotland 1927-28-29. (GBI): v America 1928

Perowne, AH
(England): Home Int 1947-48-49-50-51-53-54-55-57.
(GBI): v America 1949-53-59; in World Team Ch 1958

Peters, GB
(Scotland): Home Int 1934-35-36-37-38. (GBI): v America
1936-38

Peters, JL
(Wales): Home Int 1987-88-89

Phillips, LA
(Wales): v Ireland 1913

Pierse, AD
(Ireland): Home Int 1976-77-78-80-81-82-83-84-85-87-88;
v Wales 1979; v France, West Germany, Sweden 1980;
Eur T Ch 1981. (GBI): v Europe 1980; v America 1983

Pinch, AG
(Wales): Home Int 1969

Pirie, AK
(Scotland): Home Int 1966-67-68-69-70-71-72-73-74-75;
Eur T Ch 1967-69; v Belgium 1973-75; v Spain 1974.
(GBI): v America 1967; v Europe 1970

Plaxton, J
(England): Home Int 1983-84

Pollin, RKM
(Ireland): Home Int 1971; Eur T Ch 1973

Pollock, VA
(England): v Scotland 1908

Povall, J
(Wales): Home Int 1960-61-62-63-65-66-67-68-69-70-71-72-
73-74-75-76-77; Eur T Ch 1967-69-71-73-75-77; v France
1975-76; v Denmark 1976, (GBI): v Europe 1962

Powell, WA
(England): v Scotland 1923-24; v Wales/Ireland 1925

Power, E
(Ireland): Home Int 1987-88

Power, M
(Ireland): Home Int 1947-48-49-50-51-52-54

Poxon, MA
(England): Home Int 1975-76; Eur T Ch 1975.
(GBI): v America 1975

Pressdee, RNG
(Wales): Home Int 1958-59-60-61-62

Pressley, J
(Scotland): Home Int 1947-48-49

Price, JP
(Wales): Home Int 1986-87-88

Prosser, D
(England): Eur T Ch 1989

Pugh, RS
(Wales): v Ireland 1923-24-29

Purcell, J
(Ireland): Home Int 1973

Raeside, A
(Scotland): v Ireland 1929

Rafferty, R
(Ireland): v Wales 1979; Home Int 1980-81; v France, West
Germany, Sweden 1980; Eur T Ch 1981. (GBI): v Europe
1980; in World Team Ch 1980; v America 1981

Rainey, WHE
(Ireland): Home Int 1962

Rawlinson, D
(England): Home Int 1949-50-52-53

Ray, D
(England): Home Int 1982; v France 1982

Rayfus, P
(Ireland): Home Int 1986-87-88

Reade, HE
(Ireland): v Wales 1913

Reddan, B
(Ireland): Home Int 1987

Rees, CN
(Wales): Home Int 1986-88-89

Rees, DA
(Wales): Home Int 1961-62-63-64

Renfrew, RL
(Scotland): Home Int 1964

Renwick, G, jr
(Wales): v Ireland 1923

Revell, RP
(England): Home Int 1972-73; Eur T Ch 1973

Ricardo, W
(Wales): v Ireland 1930-31; v Scotland 1931

Rice, JH
(Ireland): Home Int 1947-52

Rice-Jones, L
(Wales): v Ireland 1924

Richards, PM
(Wales): Home Int 1960-61-62-63-71

Richardson, S
(England): Home Int 1986-87-88

Risdon, PWL
(England): Home Int 1935-36

Robb, J, jr
(Scotland): v England 1902-03-05-06-07

Robb, WM
(Scotland): Home Int 1935

Roberts, AT
(Scotland): v Ireland 1931

Roberts, G
(Scotland): Home Int 1937-38

Roberts, GP
(England): Home Int 1951-53; v France 1949

Roberts, HJ
(England): Home Int 1947-48-53

Roberts, J
(Wales): Home Int 1937

Roberts, SB
(Wales): Home Int 1932-33-34-35-37-38-47-48-49-50-51-
52-53-54

Roberts, WJ
(Wales): Home Int 1948-49-50-51-52-53-54

Robertson, A
(England): Home Int 1986-87; v France 1988

Robertson, CW
(Ireland): v Wales 1930; v Scotland 1930

Robertson, DM
(Scotland): Home Int 1973-74; v Spain 1974

Robertson-Durham, JA
(Scotland): v England 1911

Robinson, J
(England): v Ireland 1928

Robinson, J
(England): Home Int 1986. (GBI): v America 1987

Robinson, S
(England): v Scotland 1925; v Ireland 1928-29-30

Roderick, RN
(Wales): Home Int 1983-84-85-86-87-88. (GBI) v Europe
1988. (GBI): v America 1989

Rolfe, B
(Wales): Home Int 1963-65

Roobottom, EL
(Wales): Home Int 1967

Roper, HS
(England): v Ireland 1931; v Scotland 1931

Roper, MS
(Wales): v Ireland 1979

Roper, R
(England): Home Int 1984-85-86-87

Rothwell, J
(England): Home Int 1947-48

Rutherford, DS
(Scotland): v Ireland 1929

Rutherford, R
(Scotland): Home Int 1938-47

Saddler, AC
(Scotland): Home Int 1959-60-61-62-63-64-66; Eur T Ch 1965-67. (GBI): v Europe 1960-62-64—66; v America 1963-65-67-77 (Captain); in Com Tnmt 1959-63-67; in World Team Ch 1962

Sandywell, A
(England): Home Int 1990

Scannel, BJ
(Ireland): Home Int 1947-48-49-50-51-53-54

Scott, KB
(England): Home Int 1937-38; v France 1938

Scott, Hon M
(England): v Scotland 1911-12-23-24-25-26. (GBI): v America 1924-34 (Captain); v Australia 1934

Scott, Hon O
(England): v Scotland 1902-05-06

Scott, R, jr
(Scotland): v England 1924-28. (GBI): v America 1924

Scratton, EWHB
(England): v Scotland 1912

Scroggie: FH
(Scotland): v England 1910

Scrutton, PF
(England): Home Int 1950-55. (GBI): v America 1955-57

Sewell, D
(England): Home Int 1956-57-58-59-60. (GBI): v America 1957-59; in Com Tnmt 1959; in World Team Ch 1960

Shade, RDBM
(Scotland): Home Int 1957-60-61-62-63-64-65-66-67-68; v Scandinavia 1960-62; Eur T Ch 1965-67. (GBI): v America 1961-63-65-67; v Europe 1962-64-66-68; in World Team Ch 1962-64-66-68; in Com Tnmt 1963-67

Shaw, G
(Scotland): Home Int 1984-86-87-88-90; v West Germany 1987. (GBI): v America 1987

Sheals, HS
(Ireland): v Wales 1929; v England 1929-30-31; v Scotland 1930; Home Int 1932-33

Sheahan, D
(Ireland): Home Int 1961-62-63-64-65-66-67-70. (GBI): v Europe 1962-64-67; v America 1963

Sheilds, B
(Scotland):Home Int 1986

Sheppard, M
(Wales): Home Int 1990

Shepperson, AE
(England): Home Int 1956-57-58-59-60-62. (GBI): v America 1957-59

Sherborne, A
(England): Home Int 1982-83-84

Shingler, TR
(England): Home Int 1977

Shorrock, TJ
(England): v France 1952

Simcox, R
(Ireland): v Wales 1930-31; v Scotland 1930-31; v England 1931; Home Int 1932-33-34-35-36-38

Simpson, AF
(Scotland): v Ireland 1928; v England 1927

Simpson, JG
(Scotland): v England 1906-07-08-09-11-12-22-24-26. (GBI): v America 1921

Sinclair, A
(Scotland): Home Int 1950

Slark, WA
(England): Home Int 1957

Slater, A
(England): Home Int 1955-62

Slattery, B
(Ireland): Home Int 1947-48

Sludds, MF
(Ireland): Home Int 1982

Smith, Eric M
(England): v Ireland 1931; v Scotland 1931

Smith, Everard
(England): v Scotland 1908-09-10-12

Smith, GF
(England): v Scotland 1902-03

Smith, JN
(Scotland): v Ireland 1928-30-31; v England 1929-30-31; v Wales 1931; Home Int 1932-33-34. (GBI): v America 1930

Smith, JR
(England): Home Int 1932

Smith, LOM
(England): Home Int 1963

Smith, VH
(Wales): v Ireland 1924-25

Smith, W
(England): Home Int 1972. (GBI): v Europe 1972

Smith, WD
(Scotland): Home Int 1957-58-59-60-63; v Scandinavia 1958-60. (GBI): v Europe 1958; v America 1959

Smyth, D
(Ireland): Home Int 1972-73; Eur T Ch 1973

Smyth, DW
(Ireland): v Wales 1923-30; v England 1930; v Scotland 1931; Home Int 1933

Smyth, HB
(Ireland): Home Int 1974-75-76-78; Eur T Ch 1975-79; v France, West Germany, Sweden 1976. (GBI): v Europe 1976

Smyth, V
(Ireland): Home Int 1981-82

Snowdon, J
(England): Home Int 1934

Soulby, DEB
(Ireland): v Wales 1929-30; v England 1929-30; v Scotland 1929-30

Spiller, EF
(Ireland): v Wales 1924; v England 1928; v Scotland 1928-29

Squirrell, HC
(Wales): Home Int 1955-56-57-58-59-60-61-62-63-64-65-66-67-68-69-70-71-73-74-75; Eur T Ch 1967-69-71-75; v France 1975

Staunton, R
(Ireland): Home Int 1964-65-72; Eur T Ch 1973

Steel, DMA
(England): Home Int 1970

Stephen, AR
(Scotland): Home Int 1971-72-73-74-75-76-77-84-85; Eur T Ch 1975; v Spain 1974; v Belgium 1975-77-78. (GBI): v Europe 1972; v America 1985

Stevens, DI
(Wales): Home Int 1968-69-70-74-75-76-77-78-80-82; Eur T Ch 1969-77; v France 1976; v Denmark 1977

Stevens, LB
(England): v Scotland 1912

Stevenson, A
(Scotland): Home Int 1949

Stevenson, JB
(Scotland): v Ireland 1931; Home Int 1932-38-47-49-50-51

Stevenson, JF
(Ireland): v Wales 1923-24; v England 1925

Stevenson, K
(Ireland): Home Int 1972

Stockdale, B
(England): Home Int 1964-65

Stoker, K
(Wales): v Ireland 1923-24

Stokoe, GC
(Wales): v England 1925; v Ireland 1929-30

Storey, EF
(England): v Scotland 1924-25-26-27-28-30; Home Int 1936; v France 1936. (GBI): v America 1924-26-28

Stott, HAN
(England): Home Int 1976-77

Stout, JA
(England): v Scotland 1928-29-30-31; v Ireland 1929-31. (GBI): v America 1930-32

Stowe, C
(England): Home Int 1935-36-37-38-47-49-54; v France 1938-39-49. (GBI): v America 1938-47

Strachan, CJL
(Scotland): Home Int 1965-66-67; Eur T Ch 1967

Straker, R
(England): Home Int 1932

Stuart, HB
(Scotland): Home Int 1967-68-70-71-72-73-74-76; Eur T Ch 1969-71-73-75; v Belgium 1973-75. (GBI): v Europe 1968-72-74; v America 1971-73-75; in Com Tnmt 1971; in World Team Ch 1972

Stuart, JE
(Scotland): Home Int 1959

Stubbs, AK
(England): Home Int 1982

Suneson, C
(England): Home Int 1988; Eur T Ch 1989

Sutherland, DMG
(England): Home Int 1947

Sutton, W
(England): v Scotland 1929-31; v Ireland 1929-30-31

Symonds, A
(Wales): v Ireland 1925

Taggart, J
(Ireland): Home Int 1953

Tait, AG
(Scotland): Home Int 1987-88-89; Nixdorf Nations Cup 1989

Tate, JK
(England): Home Int 1954-55-56

Taylor, GN
(Scotland): Home Int 1948

Taylor, HE
(England): v Scotland 1911

Taylor, JS
(Scotland): v England 1979; Home Int 1980; v Belgium 1980; v France 1980

Taylor, LG
(Scotland): Home Int 1955-56

Taylor, TPD
(Wales): Home Int 1963

Thirlwell, A
(England): Home Int 1951-52-54-55-56-57-58-63-64. (GBI): v Europe 1956-58-64; v America 1957; in Com Tnmt 1953-64

Thirsk, TJ
(England): v Ireland 1929; Home Int 1933-34-35-36-37-38; v France 1935-36-37-38-39

Thom, KG
(England): Home Int 1947-48-49-53. (GBI): v America 1949

Thomas, I
(England): Home Int 1933

Thomas, KR
(Wales): Home Int 1951-52

Thompson, ASG
(England): Home Int 1935-37

Thompson, MS
(England): Home Int 1982. (GBI): v America 1983

Thomson, AP
(Scotland): Home Int 1970; Eur T Ch 1971

Thomson, H
(Scotland): Home Int 1934-35-36-37-38. (GBI): v America 1936-38

Thomson, JA
(Scotland): Home Int 1981-82-83-84-85-86-87-88-89; v West Germany 1987; v Italy 1988-90; v Sweden 1990

Thorburn, K
(Scotland): v England 1928; v Ireland 1927

Timbey, JC
(Ireland): v Scotland 1928-31; v Wales 1931

Timmis, CW
(England): v Ireland 1930; Home Int. 1936-37

Tipping, EB
(England): v Ireland 1930

Tipple, ER
(England): v Ireland 1928-29; Home Int 1932

Tolley, CJH
(England): v Scotland 1922-23-24-25-26-27-28-29-30;
Home Int 1936-37-38; v Ireland/Wales 1925; v France 1938.
(GBI): v America 1921-22-23-24 (Captain) -26-30-34;
v South Africa 1927

Tooth, EA
(Wales): v Ireland 1913

Torrance, TA
(Scotland): v England 1922-23-25-26-28-29—30; Home Int
1933. (GBI): v America 1924-28-30-32 (Captain) -34

Torrance, WB
(Scotland): v England 1922-23-24-26-27-28-30; v Ireland
1928-29-30. (GBI): v America 1922

Townsend, PM
(England): Home Int 1965-66. (GBI): v America 1965;
v Europe 1966; in World Team Ch 1966

Toye, JL
(Wales): Home Int 1963-64-65-66-67-69-70-71-72-73-74-
76-78; Eur T Ch 1971-73-75-77; v France 1975

Tredinnick, SV
(England): Home Int 1950

Tucker, WI
(Wales): Home Int 1949-50-51-52-53-54-55-56-57-58-59-
60-61-62-63-64-65-66-67-68-69-70-71-72-74-75; Eur
T Ch 1967-69-75; v France 1975

Tulloch, W
(Scotland): v England 1929-30-31; v Ireland 1930-31;
v Wales 1931; Home Int 1932

Tupling, LP
(England): Home Int 1969; Eur T Ch 1969.
(GBI): v America 1969

Turnbull, CH
(Wales): v Ireland 1913-25

Turner, A
(England): Home Int 1952

Turner, GB
(Wales): Home Int 1947-48-49-50-51-52-55-56

Tweddell, W
(England): v Scotland 1928-29-30; Home Int 1935.
(GBI): v America 1928 (Captain) -36 (Captain)

Twynholm, S
(Scotland): Home Int 1990. Nixdorf Nations Cup 1990

Vannet, L
(Scotland): Home Int 1984

Waddell, G
(Ireland): v Wales 1925

Walker, J
(Scotland): Home Int 1954-55-57-58-60-61-62-63; v
Scandinavia 1958-62. (GBI): v Europe 1958-60; v America
1961

Walker, KH
(Scotland): Home Int 1985-86

Walker, MS
(England): v Ireland/Wales 1925

Walker, RS
(Scotland): Home Int 1935-36

Wallis, G
(Wales): Home Int 1934-36-37-38

Walls, MPD
(England): Home Int 1980-81-85

Walters, EM
(Wales): Home Int 1967-68-69; Eur T Ch 1969

Walton, AR
(England): Home Int 1934-35

Walton, P
(Ireland): v Wales 1979: Home Int 1980-81; v France,
Germany, Sweden 1980; Eur T Ch 1981. (GBI): v America
1981-83

Warren, KT
(England): Home Int 1962

Watt, A
(Scotland): Home Int 1987

Way, P
(England): Home Int 1981; Eur T Ch 1981,
(GBI): v America 1981.

Webster, A
(Scotland): Home Int 1978

Webster, F
(Ireland): Home Int 1949

Weeks, K
(England): Home Int 1987-88; v France 1988

Welch, L
(Ireland): Home Int 1936

Wemyss, DS
(Scotland): Home Int 1937

Werner, LE
(Ireland): v Wales 1925

West, CH
(Ireland): v England 1928; Home Int 1932

Wethered, RH
(England): v Scotland 1922-23-24-25-26-27-28-29-30.
(GBI): v America 1921-22-23-26-30 (Captain) -34

White, L
(England): Home Int 1990

White, RJ
(England): Home Int 1947-48-49-53-54.
(GBI): v America 1947-49-51-53-55

Whyte, AW
(Scotland): Home Int 1934

Wiggett, M
(England): Home Int 1990

Wilkie, D
(Scotland): Home Int 1962-63-65-67-68

Wilkie, G
(Scotland): v England 1911

Wilkie, GT
(Wales): Home Int 1938

Wilkinson, S
(Wales): Home Int 1990

Willcox, FS
(Wales): v Scotland 1931; v Ireland 1931

Williams, DF
(England): v Scotland 1979

Williams KH
(Wales): Home Int 1983-84-85-86-87

Williams, PG
(Wales): v Ireland 1925

Williamson, SB
(Scotland): Home Int 1947-48-49-51-52

Willison, R
(England): Home Int 1988-89-90; Eur T Ch 1989. (GBI) v Europe 1990. World Cup 1990

Wills, M
(Wales): Home Int 1990

Wilson, F
(Scotland): Home Int 1985

Wilson, J
(Scotland): v England 1922-23-24-26. (GBI): v America 1923

Wilson, JC
(Scotland): Home Int 1947-48-49-51-52-53. (GBI): v America 1947-53; v South Africa 1952; in Com Tnmt 1954

Wilson, P
(Scotland): Home Int 1976; Belgium 1977

Winchester, R
(England): Home Int 1985-87-89

Winfield, HB
(Wales): v Ireland 1913

Wise, WS
(England): Home Int 1947

Wolstenholme, G
(England): Home Int 1953-55-56-57-58-59-60 (GBI): v America 1957-59; in World Team Ch 1958-60; in Com Tnmt 1959

Wolstenholme, G
(England): Home Int 1988-89-90; v France 1988

Wood, DK
(Wales): Home Int 1982-83-84-85-86-87

Woollam, J
(England): Home Int 1933-34-35; v France 1935

Woolley, FA
(England): v Scotland 1910-11-12

Woosnam, I
(Wales): v France 1976

Worthington, JS
(England): v Scotland 1905

Wright, I
(Scotland): Home Int 1958-59-60-61; v Scandinavia 1960

Yeo, J
(England): Home 1971

Young, D
(Ireland): Home Int 1969-70-77

Young, ID
(Scotland): Home Int 1981-82; v France 1982

Young, JR
(Scotland): Home Int 1960-61-65; v Scandinavia 1960. (GB): v Europe 1960

Zacharias, JP
(England): Home Int 1935

Zoete, HW de
(England): v Scotland 1903-04-06-07

British Isles International Players, Amateur Ladies

Abbreviations:

Eur L T Ch   played in European Ladies Amateur Team Championship
Home Int   played in Home International matches
CW   played in Commonwealth International
Previous surnames are shown in brackets.

Aitken, E (Young)
(Scotland): Home Int 1954

Alexander, M
(Ireland): Home Int 1920-21-22-30

Allen, F
(England): Home Int 1952

Allington Hughes, Miss
(Wales): Home Int 1908-09-10-12-14-22-25

Anderson, E
(Scotland): Home Int 1910-11-12-21-25

Anderson, F
(Scotland): Home Int 1977-79-80-81-83-84-86-87-88-89-90;
Eur L T Ch 1987. (GBI): in Vagliano Trophy 1987

Anderson, H
(Scotland): Home Int 1964-65-68-69-70-71; Eur L T Ch 1969.
(GBI): in Vagliano Trophy 1969

Anderson, J (Donald)
(Scotland): Home Int 1947-48-49-50-51-52-53. (GBI): in
Curtis Cup in 1948-50-52

Anderson, L.
(Scotland): Home Int 1986-87-88-89; Eur L T Ch 1987-89

Anderson, VH
(Scotland): Home Int 1907

Arbuthnot, M
(Ireland): Home Int 1921

Archer, A (Rampton)
(England): Home Int 1968 (Captain)

Armstrong, M
(Ireland): Home Int 1906

Ashcombe, Lady
(Wales): Home Int 1950-51-52-53-54

Aubertin, Mrs
(Wales): Home Int 1908-09-10

Bailey, D [Frearson] (Robb)
(England): Home Int 1961-62-71; Eur L T Ch 1968. (GBI): in
Curtis Cup 1962-72-84 (Captain)-86(Captain)-88(Captain);
in Vagliano Trophy 1961-83(Captain)-85(Captain);
CW 1983

Baker, J
(Wales): Home Int 1990

Bald, J
(Scotland): Home Int 1968-69-71; Eur L T Ch 1969

Barber, S (Bonallack)
(England): Home Int 1960-61-62-68-70-72-77-78 (Captain);
Eur L T Ch 1969-71. (GBI): in Curtis Cup 1962; in Vagliano
Trophy 1961-63-69

Barclay, C (Brisbane)
(Scotland): Home Int 1953-61-68

Bargh Etherington, B (Whitehead)
(England): Home Int 1974

Barlow, Mrs
(Ireland): Home Int 1921

Barron, M
(Wales): Home Int 1929-30-31-34-35-36-37-38-39-47-48-49-
50-51-52-53-54-55-56-57-58-60-61-62-63

Barry, L
(England): Home Int 1911-12-13-14

Barry, P
(England): Home Int 1982

Barton, P
(England): Home Int 1935-36-37-38-39. (GBI): in Curtis Cup
1934-36

Bastin, G
(England): Home Int 1920-21-22-23-24-25

Bayliss, Mrs
(Wales): Home Int 1921

Bayman, L (Denison Pender)
(England): Home Int 1971-72-73-83-84-85-87-88; Eur L T Ch
1985-87-89. (GBI) in Curtis Cup 1988; in Vagliano Trophy
1971-85-87; in Espirito Santo 1988

Baynes, Mrs CE
(Scotland): Home Int 1921-22

Beck, B (Pim)
(Ireland): Home Int 1930-31-32-33-34-36-37-47-48-49-50-
51-52-53-54-55-56-58-59-61

Beckett, J
(Ireland): Home Int 1962-66-67-68; Eur L T Ch 1967

Beddows, C [Watson] (Stevenson)
(Scotland): Home Int 1913-14-21-22-23-27-29-30-31-32-33-
34-35-36-37-39-47-48-49-50-51. (GBI): in Curtis Cup 1932

Behan, L
(Ireland): Home Int 1984-85-86. (GBI): in Curtis Cup 1986; in Vagliano Trophy 1985

Beharrell, V (Anstey)
(England): Home Int 1955-56-57-61(Captain). (GBI): in Curtis Cup 1956

Benka, P (Tredinnick)
(England): Home Int 1967. (GBI): in Curtis Cup 1966-68; in Vagliano Trophy 1967

Bennett, L
(Scotland): Home Int 1977-80-81

Benton, MH
(Scotland): Home Int 1914

Birmingham, M
(Ireland): Home Int 1967(Captain)

Bisgood, J
(England) Home Int 1949-50-51-52-53-54-56-58. (GBI): in Curtis Cup 1950-52-54-70(Captain)

Blair, N (Menzies)
(Scotland): Home Int 1955

Blake, Miss
(Ireland): Home Int 1931-32-34-35-36

Blaymire, J
(England): Home Int 1971-88-89(Captain)

Bloodworth, D (Lewis)
(Wales): Home Int 1954-55-56-57-60

Boatman, EA (Collis)
(England): Home Int 1974-80-84 (Captain)-85 (Captain)-90 (Captain); Eur L T Ch 1985 (Captain)-87 (Captain). (GBI): CW 1987 (Captain)

Bolton, L
(Ireland): Home Int 1981-82-88-89

Bolton, Z (Bonner Davis)
(England): Home Int 1939-48-49-50-51-55-(Captain)-56. (GBI): in Curtis Cup 1948-56(Captain)-66(Captain)-68(Captain);CW 1967

Bonallack, A (Ward)
(England): Home Int 1956-57-58-59-60-61-62-63-64-65 (Captain)-66-72. (GBI): in Curtis Cup 1956-58-60-62-64-66; in Vagliano Trophy 1959-61-63

Bostock, M
(England): Home Int 1954(Captain)

Bourn, Mrs
(England): Home Int 1909-12

Bowhill, M (Robertson-Durham)
(Scotland): Home Int 1936-37-38

Boyd, J
(Ireland): Home Int 1912-13-14

Bradley, K (Rawlings)
(Wales): Home Int 1975-76-77-78-79-82-83

Bradshaw, E
(Ireland): Home Int 1964-66-67-68-69-70-71-74-75-80 (Captain)-81(Captain); Eur L T Ch 1969-71-75. (GBI): in Vagliano Trophy 1969-71

Brandom, G
(Ireland): Home Int 1965-66-67-68; Eur L T Ch 1967. (GBI) in Vagliano Trophy 1967

Brearley, M
(Wales): Home Int 1937-38

Brennan, R (Hegarty)
(Ireland): Home Int 1974-75-76-77-78-79-81

Brice, Mrs
(Ireland): Home Int 1948

Bridges, Mrs
(Wales): Home Int 1933-38-39

Briggs, A (Brown)
(Wales): Home Int 1969-70-71-72-73-74-75-76-77-78-79-80-81(Captain)-82(Captain)-83(Captain)-84; Eur L T Ch 1971-75. (GBI): in Vagliano Trophy 1971-75

Brinton, Mrs
(Ireland): Home Int 1922

Bromley-Davenport, I (Rieben)
(Wales): Home Int 1932-33-34-35-36-48-50-51-52-53-54-55-56

Brook, D
(Wales): Home Int 1913

Brooks, E
(Ireland): Home Int 1953-54-56

Broun, JG
(Scotland): Home Int 1905-06-07-21

Brown, B
(Ireland): Home Int 1960

Brown, E (Jones)
(Wales): Home Int 1947-48-49-50-52-53-57-58-59-60-61-62-63-64-65-66-68-69-70

Brown, Mrs FW (Gilroy)
(Scotland): Home Int 1905-06-07-08-09-10-11-13-21

Brown, J
(Wales): Home Int 1960-61-62-64-65; Eur L T Ch 1965-69

Brown, J
(England): Home Int 1984

Brown, TWL
(Scotland): Home Int 1924-25

Brown, Mrs
(Wales): Home Int 1924-25-27

Brownlow, Miss
(Ireland): Home Int 1923

Bryan-Smith, S
(Wales): Home Int 1947-48-49-50-51-52-56

Burrell, Mrs
(Wales): Home Int 1939

Burton, H (Mitchell)
(Scotland): Home Int 1931-55-56-59(Captain). (GBI): in Vagliano Trophy 1961

Burton, M
(England): Home Int 1975-76

Butler, I (Burke)
(Ireland): Home Int 1962-63-64-65-66-68-70-71-72-73-76-77-78-79-86(Captain)-87(Captain): Eur L T Ch 1967. (GBI): in Curtis Cup 1966; in Vagliano Trophy 1965; in Espirito Santo 1964-66

Byrne, A (Sweeney)
(Ireland): Home Int 1959-60-61-62-63-90 (Captain)

Cadden, G
(Scotland): Home Int 1974-75

Cairns, Lady Katherine
(England): Home Int 1947-48-50-51-52-53-54. (GBI): in Curtis Cup 1952(Captain)

Caldwell, C (Redford)
(England): Home Int 1973-78-79-80. (GBI): in Curtis Cup 1978-80; in Vagliano Trophy 1973

Callen, L
(Ireland): Home Int 1990

Campbell, J (Burnett)
(Scotland): Home Int 1960

Cann, M (Nuttall)
(England): Home Int 1966

Carrick, P (Bullard)
(England): Home Int 1939-47

Caryl, M
(Wales): Home Int 1929

Casement, M (Harrison)
(Ireland): Home Int 1909-10-11-12-13-14

Cautley, B (Hawtrey)
(England): Home Int 1912-13-14-22-23-24-25-27

Chambers, D
(England): Home Int 1906-07-09-10-11-12-20-24-25.
(GBI): in Curtis Cup 1934(Captain)-36(Captain)-38(Captain)

Christison, D
(England): Home Int 1981

Chugg, P (Light)
(Wales): Home Int 1973-74-75-76-77-78-86-87-78; Eur L T
Ch 1975-87

Clark, G (Atkinson)
(England): Home Int 1955

Clarke, Mrs ML
(England): Home Int 1933-35

Clarke, P
(England): Home Int 1981

Clarke, Mrs
(Ireland): Home Int 1922

Clarkson, H (Reynolds)
(Wales): Home Int 1935-38-39

Clay, E
(Wales): Home Int 1912

Clement, V
(England): Home Int 1932-34-35

Close, M (Wenyon)
(England): Home Int 1968-69; Eur L T Ch 1969. (GBI) in
Vagliano Trophy 1969

Coats, Mrs G
(Scotland): Home Int 1931-32-33-34

Cochrane, K
(Scotland): Home Int 1924-25-28-29-30

Collett, P
(England): Home Int 1910

Collingham, J (Melville)
(England): Home Int 1978-79-81-84-86-87; Eur L T Ch 1989.
(GBI): in Vagliano Trophy 1979-87; CW 1987

Colquhoun, H
(Ireland): Home Int 1959-60-61-63

Comboy, C (Grott)
(England): Home Int 1975(Captain)-76(Captain). (GBI): in
Curtis Cup 1978(Captain)-80(Captain); in Vagliano Trophy
1977(Captain)-1979(Captain); in Espirito Santo
1978(Captain); CW 1979

Connachan, J
(Scotland): Home Int 1979-80-81-82-83. (GBI): in Curtis Cup
1980-82; in Vagliano Trophy 1981-83; in Espirito Santo 1980-
82; CW 1983

Coote, Miss
(Ireland): Home Int 1925-28-29

Copley, K (Lackie)
(Scotland): Home Int 1974-75

Corlett, E
(England): Home Int 1927-29-30-31-32-33-35-36-37-38-39.
(GBI): in Curtis Cup 1932-38-64(Captain)

Costello, G
(Ireland): Home Int 1973-84(Captain)-85(Captain)

Cotton, S (German)
(England): Home Int 1967-68; Eur L T Ch 1967. (GBI) in
Vagliano Trophy 1967

Couper, M
(Scotland): Home Int 1929-34-35-36-37-39-56

Cowley, Lady
(Wales): Home Int 1907-09

Cox, Margaret
(Wales): Home Int 1924-25

Cox, Nell
(Wales): Home Int 1954

Craik, T
(Scotland): Home Int 1988

Cramsie, F (Hezlet)
(Ireland): Home Int 1905-06-07-08-09-10-13-20-24

Crawford, I (Wylie)
(Scotland): Home Int 1970-71-72

Cresswell, K (Stuart)
(Scotland): Home Int 1909-10-11-12-14

Critchley, D (Fishwick)
(England): Home Int 1930-31-32-33-35-36-47. (GBI): in
Curtis Cup 1932-34-50(Captain)

Croft, A
(England): Home Int 1927

Cross, M
(Wales): Home Int 1922

Cruickshank, DM (Jenkins)
(Scotland): Home Int 1910-11-12

Crummack, Miss
(England): Home Int 1909

Cuming, Mrs
(Ireland): Home Int 1910

Cunninghame, S
(Wales): Home Int 1922-25-29-31

Cuthell, R (Adair)
(Ireland): Home Int 1908

Dampney, S
(Wales): Home Int 1924-25-27-28-29-30

David, Mrs
(Wales): Home Int 1908

Davidson, B (Inglis)
(Scotland): Home Int 1928

Davies, K
(Wales): Home Int 1981-82-83; Eur L T Ch 1987. (GBI): in
Curtis Cup 1986-88; in Vagliano Trophy 1987; CW 1987

Davies, L
(England): Home Int 1983-84. (GBI): in Curtis Cup 1984;
CW 1987

Davies, P (Griffiths)
(Wales): Home Int 1965-66-67-68-70-71-73; Eur L T Ch 1971

Deacon, Mrs
(Wales): Home Int 1912-14

Denny, A (Barrett)
(England): Home Int 1951

Dering, Mrs
(Ireland): Home Int 1923

Dermott, Lisa
(Wales): Home Int 1987-88-89

Dickson, M
(Ireland): Home Int 1909

Dobson, H
(England): Home Int 1987-88-89; Eur L T Ch 1989. (GBI): in Vagliano Trophy 1989; in Curtis Cup 1990

Dod, L
(England): Home Int 1905

Douglas, K
(England): Home Int 1981-82-83. (GBI): in Curtis Cup 1982; in Vagliano Trophy 1983

Dowling, D
(England): Home Int 1979

Draper, M [Peel] (Thomas)
(Scotland): Home Int 1929-34-38-49-50-51-52-53-54(Captain)-55(Captain)-56-57-58-61(Captain)-62. (GBI): in Curtis Cup 1954; in Vagliano Trophy 1963(Captain)

Duncan, B
(Wales): Home Int 1907-08-09-10-12

Duncan, M
(Wales): Home Int 1922-23-28-34

Duncan, MJ (Wood)
(Scotland): Home Int 1925-27-28-39

Durlacher, Mrs
(Ireland): Home Int 1905-06-07-08-09-10-14

Durrant, B [Green] (Lowe)
(England): Home Int 1954

Dwyer, Mrs
(Ireland): 1928

Eakin, P (James)
(Ireland): Home Int 1967

Eakin, T
(Ireland): Home Int 1990

Earner, M
(Ireland): Home Int 1960-61-62-63-70

Edwards, E
(Wales): Home Int 1949-50

Edwards, J
(Wales): Home Int 1932-33-34-36-37

Edwards, J (Morris)
(Wales): Home Int 1962-63-66-67-68-69-70-77(Captain)-78 (Captain)-79(Captain); Eur L T Ch 1967-69

Ellis, E
(Ireland): Home Int 1932-35-37-38

Ellis Griffiths (Mrs)
(Wales): Home Int 1907-08-09-12-13

Emery, MJ
(Wales): Home Int 1928-29-30-31-32-33-34-35-36-37-38-47

Evans, H
(England): Home Int 1908

Evans, N
(Wales): Home Int 1908-09-10-13

Everard, M
(England): Home Int 1964-67-69-70-72-73-77-78; Eur L T Ch 1967-71-77. (GBI): in Curtis Cup 1970-72-74-78; in Vagliano Trophy 1967-69-71-73; in Espirito Santo 1968-72-78; CW 1971

Fairclough, L
(England): Home Int 1988-89-90; Eur L T Ch 1989. (GBI): Vagliano Trophy 1989

Falconer, V (Lamb)
(Scotland): Home Int 1932-36-37-47-48-49-50-51-52-53-54-55-56

Fallon, Gaynor, Z
(Ireland): Home Int 1952-53-54-55-56-57-58-59-60-61-62-63-64-65-68-69-70-72 (Captain). (GBI): in Espirito Santo 1964

Farie-Anderson, J
(Scotland): Home Int 1924

Farquharson, E
(Scotland): Home Int 1987-88-89-90; Eur L T Ch 1989. (GBI): in Vagliano Trophy 1989; in Curtis Cup 1990

Ferguson, A
(Ireland): Home Int 1989

Ferguson, D
(Ireland): Home Int 1927-28-29-30-31-32-34-35-36-37-38-61 (Captain). (GBI): in Curtis Cup 1958(Captain)

Ferguson, M (Fowler)
(Scotland): Home Int 1959-62-63-64-65-66-67-69-70-85; Eur L T Ch 1965-67-71. (GBI): in Curtis Cup 1966; in Vagliano Trophy 1965

Ferguson R (Ogden)
(England): Home Int 1957

Fitzgibbon, M
(Ireland): Home Int 1920-21-29-30-31-32-33

FitzPatrick, O (Heskin)
(Ireland): Home Int 1967

Fletcher, L
(England): Home Int 1989-90. (GBI) in Curtis Cup 1990

Fletcher, P (Sherlock)
(Ireland): Home Int 1932-34-35-36-38-39-54-55-66(Captain)

Forbes, J
(Scotland): Home Int 1985-86-87-88-89; Eur L T Ch 1987-89

Foster, C
(England): Home Int 1905-06-09

Foster, J
(Wales): Home Int 1984-85-86-87; Eur L T Ch 1987

Fowler, J
(England): Home Int 1928

Franklin Thomas, E
(Wales): Home Int 1909

Freeguard, C
(Wales): Home Int 1927

Furby, J
(England): Home Int 1987-88; Eur L T Ch 1987

Fyshe, M
(England): Home Int 1938

Gallagher, S
(Scotland): Home Int 1983-84

Gardiner, A
(Ireland): Home Int 1927-29

Garfield Evans, PR (Whittaker)
(Wales): Home Int 1948-49-50-51-52-53-54-55(Captain)-56
(Captain)-57 (Captain)-58(Captain)

Garner, M (Madill)
(Ireland): Home Int 1978-79-80-81-82-83-84-85. (GBI): in
Curtis Cup 1980; in Vagliano Trophy 1979-81-85; in Espirito
Santo 1980; CW 1979

Garon, MR
(England): Home Int 1927-28-32-33-34-36-37-38. (GBI); in
Curtis Cup 1936

Garrett, M (Ruttle)
(England): Home Int 1947-48-50-53-59(Captain)-
60(Captain)-63(Captain). (GBI): in Curtis Cup 1948-
60(Captain); in Vagliano Trophy 1959

Garvey, P
(Ireland): Home Int 1947-48-49-50-51-52-53-54(Captain)-
56-57(Captain) -58(Captain)-59(Captain)-60(Captain)-61-
62-63-68-69. (GBI): in Curtis Cup 1948-50-52-54-56-60; in
Vagliano Trophy 1959-63

Gear Evans, A
(Wales): Home Int 1932-33-34

Gee, Hon. J (Hives)
(England): Home Int 1950-51-52

Gemmill, A
(Scotland): Home Int 1981-82-84-85-86-87-88-89

Gethin Griffith, S
(Wales): Home Int 1914-22-23-24-28-29-30-31-35

Gibb, M (Titterton)
(England): Home Int 1906-07-08-10-12

Gibbs, C (Le Feuvre)
(England): Home Int 1971-72-73-74. (GBI): in Curtis Cup
1974; in Vagliano Trophy 1973

Gibbs, S
(Wales): Home Int 1933-34-39

Gildea, Miss
(Ireland): Home Int 1936-37-38-39

Glendinning, D
(Ireland): Home Int 1937-54

Glennie, H
(Scotland): Home Int 1959

Glover, A
(Scotland): Home Int 1905-06-08-09-12

Gold, N
(England): Home Int 1929-31-32

Gordon, J
403(England): Home Int 1947-48-49-52-53. (GBI): in Curtis
Cup 1948

Gorman, S
(Ireland): Home Int 1976-79-80-81-82

Gorry, Mary
(Ireland): Home Int 1971-72-73-74-75-76-77-78-79-80-88-89
(Captain); Eur L T Ch 1971-75. (GBI): in Vagliano Trophy
1977

Gotto, Mrs C
(Ireland): Home Int 1923

Gotto, Mrs L
(Ireland): Home Int 1920

Gourlay, M
(England): Home Int 1923-24-27-28-29-30-32-33-34-38-57
(Captain). (GBI): in Curtis Cup 1932-34

Gow, J
(Scotland): Home Int 1923-24-27-28

Graham, MA
(Scotland): Home Int 1905-06

Graham, N
(Ireland): Home Int 1908-09-10-12

Granger Harrison, Mrs
(Scotland): Home Int 1922

Grant-Suttie, E
(Scotland): Home Int 1908-10-11-14-22-23

Grant-Suttie, R
(Scotland): Home Int 1914

Green, B (Pockett)
(England): Home Int 1939

Grice-Whittaker, P (Grice)
(England): Home Int 1983-84. (GBI): in Curtis Cup 1984; in
Espirito Santo 1984

Griffith, W
(Wales): Home Int 1981

Griffiths, M
(England): Home Int 1920-21

Greenlees, E
(Scotland): Home Int 1924

Greenlees, Y
(Scotland): Home Int 1928-30-31-33-34-35-38

Guadella, E (Leitch)
(England): Home Int 1908-10-20-21-22-27-28-29-30-33

Gubbins, Miss
(Ireland): Home Int 1905

Hackney, L
(England): Home Int 1990

Haig, J (Mathias Thomas)
(Wales): Home Int 1938-39

Hall, CM
(England): Home Int 1985

Hall, J (Wade)
(England): Home Int 1987-88-89-90; Eur L T Ch 1987-89.
(GBI): in Curtis Cup 1988-90; in Espirito Santo 1988-90; in
Vagliano Trophy 1989

Hall, Mrs
(Ireland): Home Int 1927-30

Hamilton, S (McKinven)
(Scotland): Home Int 1965

Hambro, W (Martin Smith)
(England): Home Int 1914

Hamilton, J
(England): Home Int 1937-38-39

Hammond, T
(England): Home Int 1985

Hampson, M
(England): Home Int 1954

Hanna, D
(Ireland): Home Int 1987-88

Harrington, D
(Ireland): Home Int 1923

Harris, M [Spearman] (Baker)
(England): Home Int 1955-56-57-58-59-60-61-62-63-64-65;
Eur L T Ch 1965-71. (GBI): in Curtis Cup 1960-62-64; in
Vagliano Trophy 1959-61-65; in Espirito Santo 1964

Harrold, L
(England): Home Int 1974-75-76

Hartill, D
(England): Home Int 1923

Hartley, E
(England): Home Int 1964(Captain)

Hartley, R
(Wales): Home Int 1958-59-62

Hastings, D (Sommerville)
(Scotland): Home Int 1955-56-57-58-59-60-61-62-63.
(GBI): in Curtis Cup 1958; in Vagliano Trophy 1963

Hay, J (Pelham Burn)
(Scotland): Home Int 1959

Hayter, J (Yuille)
(England): Home Int 1956

Hazlett, VP
(Ireland): Home Int 1956(Captain)

Healy, B (Gleeson)
(Ireland): Home Int 1980-82

Heathcoat-Amory, Lady (Joyce Wethered)
(England): Home Int 1921-22-23-24-25-29. (GBI): in Curtis Cup 1932(Captain)

Hedges, S (Whitlock)
(England): Home Int 1979. (GBI): in Vagliano Trophy 1979; CW 1979

Hedley Hill, Miss
(Wales): Home Int 1922

Hegarty, G
(Ireland): Home Int 1955-56-64(Captain)

Helme, E
(England): Home Int 1911-12-13-20

Heming Johnson, G
(England): Home Int 1909-11-13

Henson, D (Oxley)
(England): Home Int 1967-68-69-70-75-76-77-78; Eur L T Ch 1971-77. (GBI): in Curtis Cup 1968-70-72-76; in Vagliano Trophy 1967-69-71; in Espirito Santo 1970; CW 1967-71

Heskin, A
(Ireland): Home Int 1968-69-70-72-75-77-82(Captain)-83 (Captain)

Hetherington, Mrs (Gittens)
(England): Home Int 1909

Hewett, G
(Ireland): Home Int 1923-24

Hezlet, Mrs
(Ireland): Home Int 1910

Hickey, C
(Ireland): Home Int 1969-75(Captain)-76(Captain)

Higgins, E
(Ireland): Home Int 1981-82-83-84-85-86-87-88; Eur L T Ch 1987

Hill, J
(England): Home Int 1986

Hill, Mrs
(Wales): Home Int 1924

Hodgson, M
(England): Home Int 1939

Holland, I (Hurst)
(Ireland): Home Int 1958

Holm, H (Gray)
(Scotland): Home Int 1932-33-34-35-36-37-38-47-48-50-51-55-57. (GBI): in Curtis Cup 1936-38-48

Holmes, A
(England): Home Int 1931

Holmes, J [Hetherington] (McClure)
(England): Home Int 1957-66-67(Captain)

Hooman, EM [Gavin]
(England): Home Int 1910-11

Hope, LA
(Scotland): Home Int 1975-76-80-84-85-86-87-88(Captain)-89 (Captain)-90 (Captain)

Hort, K
(Wales): Home Int 1929

Hourihane, C
(Ireland): Home Int 1979 to 1990; Eur L T Ch 1987. (GBI): in Curtis Cup 1984-86-88-90; in Vagliano Trophy 1981-83-85-87-89; in Espirito Santo 1986-90

Howard, A (Phillips)
(England): Home Int 1953-54-55-56-57-58-79(Captain)-80 (Captain). (GBI): in Curtis Cup 1956-58

Huggan, S (Lawson)
(Scotland): Home Int 1985-86-87-88-89; Eur L T Ch 1985-87-89. (GBI): in Curtis Cup 1988, in Vagliano Trophy 1989

Hughes, J
(Wales): Home Int 1967-71-88-89(Captain); Eur L T Ch 1971

Hughes, Miss
(Wales): Home Int 1907

Huke, B
(England): Home Int 1971-72-75-76-77. (GBI): in Curtis Cup 1972; in Vagliano Trophy 1975

Hulton, V (Hezlet)
(Ireland): Home Int 1905-07-09-10-11-12-20-21

Humphreys, A (Coulman)
(Wales): Home Int 1969-70-71

Humphreys, D (Forster)
(Ireland): Home Int 1951-52-53-55-57

Hunter, D (Tucker)
(England): Home Int 1905

Hurd, D [Howe] (Campbell)
(Scotland): Home Int 1905-06-08-09-11-28-30

Hurst, Mrs
(Wales): Home Int 1921-22-23-25-27-28

Hyland, B
(Ireland): Home Int 1964-65-66

Imrie, K
(Scotland): Home Int 1984-85-89. Eur L T Ch 1987-89 (GBI): in Vagliano Trophy 1989; in Curtis Cup 1990

Ingram, E (Lever)
(Wales): Home Int 1947-48-49-50-51-52-53-54-55-56-57-58-64-65

Irvin, A
(England): Home Int 1962-63-65-67-68-69-70-71-72-73-75; Eur L T Ch 1965-67-69-71. (GBI): in Curtis Cup 1962-68-70-76; in Vagliano Trophy 1961-63-65-67-69-71-73-75; in Espirito Santo 1982(Captain); CW 1967-75

Irvine, Miss
(Wales): Home Int 1930

Isaac, Mrs
(Wales): Home Int 1924

Isherwood, L
(Wales): Home Int 1972-76-77-78-80-86-88-89-90

Jack, E (Philip)
(Scotland): Home Int 1962-63-64-81(Captain)-82(Captain)

Jackson, B
(Ireland): Home Int 1937-38-39-50

Jackson, B
(England): Home Int 1955-56-57-58-59-63-64-65-66-73
(Captain)-74(Captain). (GBI): in Curtis Cup 1958-64-68; in
Vagliano Trophy 1959-63-65-67-73(Captain)-75(Captain);
Espirito Santo 1964; CW in 1959-67

Jackson, D
(Scotland): Home Int 1990

Jackson, Mrs H
(Ireland): Home Int 1921

Jackson, J
(Ireland): Home Int 1912-13-14-20-21-22-23-24-25-27-28-
29-30

Jackson, Mrs L
(Ireland): Home Int 1910-12-14-20-22-25

Jameson, S (Tobin)
(Ireland): Home Int 1913-14-20-24-25-27

Jenkin, B
(Wales): Home Int 1959

Jenkins, J (Owen)
(Wales): Home Int 1953-56

John, J
(Wales): Home Int 1974

Johns, A
(England): Home Int 1987-88-89

Johnson, A (Hughes)
(Wales): Home Int 1964-66-67-68-69-70-71-72-73-74-75-76-
78-79-85; Eur L T Ch 1965-67-69-71

Johnson, J (Roberts)
(Wales): Home Int 1955

Johnson, M
(England): Home Int 1934-35

Johnson, R
(Wales): Home Int 1955

Johnson, T
(England): Home Int 1984-85-86; Eur L T Ch 1985. (GBI): in
Curtis Cup 1986; in Vagliano Trophy 1985; in Espirito Santo
1986

Jones, A (Gwyther)
(Wales): Home Int 1959

Jones, K
(Wales): Home Int 1959(Captain)-1960(Captain)-
61(Captain)

Jones, M (De Lloyd)
(Wales): Home Int 1951

Jones, Mrs
(Wales): Home Int 1932-35

Justice, M
(Wales): Home Int 1931-32

Kaye, H (Williamson)
(England): Home Int 1986(Captain)-87(Captain)

Keenan, D
(Ireland): Home Int 1989

Keiller, G [Style]
(England): Home Int 1948-49-52

Kelway Bamber, Mrs
(Scotland): Home Int 1923-27-33

Kennedy, D (Fowler)
(England): Home Int 1923-24-25-27-28-29

Kennion, Mrs (Kenyon Stow)
(England) Home Int 1910

Kerr, J
(Scotland): Home Int 1947-48-49-54

Kidd, Mrs
(Ireland): Home Int 1934-37

King Mrs
(Ireland): Home Int 1923-25-27-29

Kinloch, Miss
(Scotland): Home Int 1913-14

Kirkwood, Mrs
(Ireland): Home Int 1955

Knight, Mrs
(Scotland): Home Int 1922

Kyle, B [Rhodes] (Norris)
(England): Home Int 1937-38-39-48-49

Kyle, E
(Scotland): Home Int 1909-10

Laing, A
(Scotland): Home Int 1966-67-70-71-73(Captain)-
74(Captain); Eur L T Ch 1967. (GBI): in Vagliano Trophy 1967

Lambert, C
(Scotland): Home Int 1989-90; Eur L T Ch 1989. (GBI): in
Curtis Cup 1990

Lambert, S (Cohen)
(England): Home Int 1979-80. (GBI): in Vagliano Trophy
1979

Lambie, S
(Scotland): Home Int 1976

Laming Evans, Mrs
(Wales): Home Int 1922-23

Langford, Mrs
(Wales): Home Int 1937

Langridge, S (Armitage)
(England): Home Int 1963-64-65-66; Eur L T Ch 1965. (GBI):
in Curtis Cup 1964-66; in Vagliano Trophy 1963-65

Large, P (Davies)
(England): Home Int 1951-52-81(Captain)-82(Captain)

Larkin, C (McAuley)
(Ireland): Home Int 1966-67-68-69-70-71-72; Eur L T Ch
1971

Latchford, B
(Ireland): Home Int 1931-33

Latham Hall, E (Chubb)
(England): Home Int 1928

Lauder, G
(Ireland): Home Int 1911

Lauder, R
(Ireland): Home Int 1911

Lawrence, JB
(Scotland): Home Int 1959-60-61-62-63-64-65-66-67-68-69-
70-77(Captain); Eur L T Ch 1965-67-69-71. (GBI): in Curtis
Cup 1964; in Vagliano Trophy 1963-65; in Espirito Santo
1964; CW 1971

Lawson, H
(Wales): Home Int 1989-90

Lebrun, W (Aitken)
(Scotland): Home Int 1978-79-80-81-82-83-85. (GBI): in
Curtis Cup 1982; in Vagliano Trophy 1981-83

Leaver, B
(Wales): Home Int 1912-14-21

Lee Smith, J
(England): Home Int 1973-74-75-76. (GBI): in Curtis Cup 1974-76; in Espirito Santo 1976; CW 1975

Leete, Mrs IG
(Scotland): Home Int 1933

Leitch, C
(England): Home Int 1910-11-12-13-14-20-21-22-24-25-27-28

Leitch, M
(England): Home Int 1912-14

Llewellyn, Miss
(Wales): Home Int 1912-13-14-21-22-23

Lloyd, J
(Wales): Home Int 1988

Lloyd, P
(Wales): Home Int 1935-36

Lloyd Davies, VH
(Wales): Home Int 1913

Lloyd Roberts, V
(Wales): Home Int 1907-08-10

Lloyd Williams, Miss
(Wales): Home Int 1909-10-12-14

Lobbett, P
(England): Home Int 1922-24-27-29-30

Lowry, Mrs
(Ireland): Home Int 1947

Luckin, B (Cooper)
(England): Home Int 1980

Lugton, C
(Scotland): Home Int 1968-72-73-75(Captain)-76(Captain)-77-78-80

Lumb, K (Phillips)
(England): Home Int 1968-69-70-71; Eur L T Ch 1969. (GBI): Curtis Cup 1972; in Vagliano Trophy 1969-71

Lyons, T (Ross Steen)
(England): Home Int 1959. (GBI): in Vagliano Trophy 1959

MacAndrew, F
(Scotland): Home Int 1913-14

Macbeth, M (Dodd)
(England): Home Int 1913-14-20-21-22-23-24-25

MacCann, K
(Ireland): Home Int 1984-85-86

MacCann, K (Smye)
(Ireland): Home Int 1947-48-49-50-51-52-53-54-56-57-58-60-61-62-64-65(Captain)

McCarthy, A
(Ireland): Home Int 1951-52

McCarthy, D
(Ireland): Home Int 1988-90

McCulloch, J
(Scotland): Home Int 1921-22-23-24-27-29-30-31-32-33-35-60(Captain)

McDaid, E (O'Grady)
(Ireland): Home Int 1959

McDaid, ER
(Ireland): Home Int 1987-88-89-90; Eur L T Ch 1987

Macdonald, F
(England): Home Int 1990

Macdonald, K
(Scotland): Home Int 1928-29

MacGeach, C
(Ireland): Home Int 1938-39-48-49-50

McGreevy, V
(Ireland): Home Int 1987-90

McIntosh, B (Dixon)
(England): Home Int 1969-70; Eur L T Ch 1969. (GBI): in Vagliano Trophy 1969

McIntyre, J
(England): Home Int 1949-54

MacKean, Mrs
(Wales): Home Int 1938-39-47

McKenna, M
(Ireland): Home Int 1968 to 1990; Eur L T Ch 1969-71-75-87. (GBI): in Curtis Cup 1970-72-74-76-78-80-82-84-86; in Vagliano Trophy 1969-71-73-75-77-79-81-85-87; in Espirito Santo 1970-74-76-86(Captain)-90(Captain)

Mackenzie, A
(Scotland): Home Int 1921

McKinlay, M
(Scotland): Home Int 1990

McLarty, E
(Scotland): Home Int 1966(Captain)-67(Captain)-68(Captain)

McMahon, S (Cadden)
(Scotland): Home Int 1974-75-76-77-79. (GBI): in Curtis Cup 1976; in Vagliano Trophy 1975

McNair, W
(England): Home Int 1921

McNeil, K
(Scotland): Home Int 1969(Captain)-70(Captain)

McNeile, CL
(Ireland): Home Int 1906

McQuillan, Y
(Ireland): Home Int 1985-86

MacTier, Mrs
(Wales): Home Int 1927

Madeley, M (Coburn)
(Ireland): Home Int 1964-69; Eur L T Ch 1969

Madill, Mrs
(Ireland): Home Int 1920-24-25-27-28-29-33

Magill, J
(Ireland): Home Int 1907-11-13

Maher, S (Vaughan)
(England): Home Int 1960-61-62-63-64. (GBI): in Curtis Cup 1962-64; in Vagliano Trophy 1961; CW 1963

Mahon, D
(Ireland): Home Int 1989-90

Main, M (Farquhar)
(Scotland): Home Int 1950-51

Maitland, M
(Scotland): Home Int 1905-06-08-12-13

Mallam, Mrs S
(Ireland): Home Int 1922-23

Marks, Mrs T
(Ireland): Home Int 1950

Marks, Mrs
(Ireland): Home Int 1930-31-33-35

Marley, MV (Marley)
(Wales): Home Int 1921-22-23-30-37

Marr, H (Cameron)
(Scotland): Home Int 1927-28-29-30-31

Martin, P [Whitworth Jones] (Low)
(Wales): Home Int 1948-50-56-59-60-61

Marvin, V
(England): Home Int 1977-78; Eur L T Ch 1977. (GBI): in
Curtis Cup 1978; in Vagliano Trophy 1977

Mason, Mrs
(Wales): Home Int 1923

Mather, H
(Scotland): Home Int 1905-09-12-13-14

Mellis, Mrs
(Scotland): Home Int 1924-27

Menton, D
(Ireland): Home Int 1949

Menzies, M
(Scotland): Home Int 1962(Captain)

Merrill, J (Greenhalgh)
(England): Home Int 1960-61-63-66-69-70-71-75-76-77-78;
Eur L T Ch 1971-77. (GBI): in Curtis Cup 1964-70-74-76-78;
in Vagliano Trophy 1961-65-75-77; in Espirito Santo 1970-
74(Captain)-78; CW 1963

Millar, D
(Ireland): Home Int 1928

Milligan, J (Mark)
(Ireland): Home Int 1971-72-73

Mills, I
(Wales): Home Int 1935-36-37-39-47-48

Milton, M (Paterson)
(Scotland): Home Int 1948-49-50-51-52. (GBI): in Curtis Cup
1952

Mitchell, J
(Ireland): Home Int 1930

Moodie, J
(Scotland): Home Int 1990

Mooney, M
(Ireland): Home Int 1972-73; Eur L T Ch 1971. (GBI): in
Vagliano Trophy 1973

Moorcroft, S
(England): Home Int 1985-86; Eur L T Ch 1985-87

Moore, S
(Ireland): Home Int 1937-38-39-47-48-49-68(Captain)

Moran, V (Singleton)
(Ireland): Home Int 1970-71-73-74-75; Eur L T Ch 1971-75

Morant, E
(England): Home Int 1906-10

Morgan, S
(England): Home Int 1989; Eur L T Ch 1989

Morgan, W
(England): Home Int 1931-32-33-34-35-36-37. (GBI): in
Curtis Cup 32-34-36

Morgan, Miss
(Wales): Home Int 1912-13-14

Moriarty, M (Irvine)
(Ireland): Home Int 1979

Morley, J
(England): Home Int 1990

Morris, L (Moore)
(England): Home Int 1912-13

Morris, Mrs de B
(Ireland): Home Int 1933

Morrison, G (Cheetham)
(England): Home Int 1965-69(Captain). (GBI): in Vagliano
Trophy 1965

Morrison, G (Cradock-Hartopp)
(England): Home Int 1936

Mountford, S
(Wales): Home Int 1989-90

Murray, Rachel
(Ireland): Home Int 1952

Murray, S (Jolly)
(England): Home Int 1976

Musgrove, Mrs
(Wales): Home Int 1923-24

Myles, M
(Scotland): Home Int 1955-57-59-60-67

Neill-Fraser, M
(Scotland): Home Int 1905-06-07-08-09-10-11-12-13-14

Nes, K (Garnham)
(England): Home Int 1931-32-33-36-37-38-39

Nevile, E
(England): Home Int 1905-06-08-10

New, B
(England): Home Int 1980-81-82-83. (GBI): in Curtis Cup
1984; in Vagliano Trophy 1983

Newell, B
(England): Home Int 1936

Newman, L
(Wales): Home Int 1927-31

Newton, B (Brown)
(England): Home Int 1930-33-34-35-36-37

Nicholls, M
(Wales): Home Int 1962(Captain)

Nicholson, J (Hutton)
(Scotland): Home Int 1969-70; Eur L T Ch 1971; CW 1971

Nicholson, Mrs WH
(Scotland): Home Int 1910-13

Nimmo, H
(Scotland): Home Int 1936-38-39

Norris, J (Smith)
(Scotland): Home Int 1966-67-68-69-70-71-72-75-76-77-78-
79-83(Captain)-84(Captain)-84(Captain); Eur L T Ch 1971.
(GBI): in Vagliano Trophy 1977

Norwell, I (Watt)
(Scotland): Home Int 1954

Nutting, P (Jameson)
(Ireland): Home Int 1927-28

O'Brien, A
(Ireland): Home Int 1969

O'Brien Kenney, S
(Ireland): Home Int 1977-78-83-84-85-86

O'Donnell, M
(Ireland): Home Int 1974-77(Captain)-78(Captain)-79
(Captain); Eur L T Ch 1980(Captain). (GBI): in Curtis Cup
1982; in Vagliano Trophy 1981(Captain)

O'Donohoe, A
(Ireland): Home Int 1948-49-50-51-53-73(Captain)-74
(Captain)

O'Hare, S
(Ireland): Home Int 1921-22

O'Reilly, T (Moran)
(Ireland): Home Int 1977-78-86-88; Eur L T Ch 1987

O'Sullivan, A
(Ireland): Home Int 1982-83-84

O'Sullivan, P
(Ireland): Home Int 1950-51-52-53-54-55-56-57-58-59-60-
63-64-65-66-67-69 (Captain)-70(Captain)-71(Captain); Eur L
T Ch 1971(Captain)

Oliver, M (Jones)
(Wales): Home Int 1955-60-61-62-63-64-65-66.
(GBI): in Espirito Santo 1964

Ormsby, Miss
(Ireland): Home Int 1909-10-11

Orr, P (Boyd)
(Ireland): Home Int 1971

Orr, Mrs
(Wales): Home Int 1924

Owen, E
(Wales): Home Int 1947

Panton, C
(Scotland): Home Int 1972-73-76-77-78. (GBI): in Vagliano
Trophy 1977; in Espirito Santo 1976

Park, Mrs
(Scotland): Home Int 1952

Parker, S
(England): Home Int 1973

Patey, Mrs
(Scotland): Home Int 1922-23

Pearson, D
(England): Home Int 1928-29-30-31-32-34

Percy, G (Mitchell)
(Scotland): Home Int 1927-28-30-31

Perriam, A
(Wales): Home Int 1988-90

Phelips, M
(Wales): Home Int 1913-14-21

Phillips, ME
(England): Home Int 1905

Phillips, Mrs
(Wales): Home Int 1921

Pickard, M (Nichol)
(England): Home Int 1958-59-60-61-67-69-83(Captain).
(GBI): in Curtis Cup 1968-70; in Vagliano
Trophy 1959-61-67

Pim, Mrs
(Ireland): Home Int 1908

Pook, E (Chadwick)
(England): Home Int 1963-65-66-67; Eur L T Ch 1967.
(GBI): in Curtis Cup 1966; in Vagliano Trophy 1963-67;
CW 1967

Porter, D (Park)
(Scotland): Home Int 1922-25-27-29-30-31-32-33-34-35-37-
38-47-48. (GBI): in Curtis Cup 1932

Porter, M (Lazenby)
(England): Home Int 1931-32

Powell, M
(Wales): Home Int 1908-09-10-12

Price, M (Greaves)
(England): Home Int 1956(Captain)

Price Fisher, E (Price)
(England): Home Int 1948-51-52-53-54-55-56-57-58-59-60.
(GBI): in Curtis Cup 1950-52-54-56-58-60; in Vagliano
Trophy 1959; CW 1959

Proctor, Mrs
(Wales): Home Int 1907

Provis, I (Kyle)
(Scotland): Home Int 1910-11

Purcell, E
(Ireland): Home Int 1965-66-67-72-73

Purvis-Russell-Montgomery, C
(Scotland): Home Int 1921-22-23-25-28-29-23-31-32-33-34-
35-36-37-38-39-47-48-49-50-52

Pyman, B
(Wales): Home Int 1925-28-29-30-32-33-34-35-36-37-38

Rabbidge, R
(England): Home Int 1931

Rawlings, M
(Wales): Home Int 1979-80-81-83-84-85-86-87.
(GBI): in Vagliano Trophy 1981

Rawlinson, T (Walker)
(Scotland): Home Int 1970-71-73-76. (GBI): in Vagliano
Trophy 1973

Read, P
(England): Home Int 1922

Reddan, C (Tiernan)
(Ireland): Home Int 1935-36-38-39-47-48-49. (GBI): in Curtis
Cup 1938-48

Reddan, MV
(Ireland): Home Int 1955

Reece, P (Millington)
(England): Home Int 1966(Captain)

Rees, G
(Wales): Home Int 1981

Rees, MB
(Wales): Home Int 1927-31

Reid, A (Lurie)
(Scotland) Home Int 1960-61-62-63-64-66. (GBI): in Vagliano
Trophy 1961

Reid, A (Kyle)
(Scotland): Home Int 1923-24-25

Reid, D
(Scotland): Home Int 1978-79

Remer, H
(England): Home Int 1909

Rennie, J (Hastings)
(Scotland): Home Int 1961-65-66-67-71-72; Eur L T Ch 1967.
(GBI): in Curtis Cup 1966; in Vagliano Trophy 1961-67

Rhys, J
(Wales): Home Int 1979

Rice, J
(Ireland): Home Int 1924-27-29

Richards, J
(Wales): Home Int 1980-82-83-85

Richards, S
(Wales): Home Int 1967

Richardson, Mrs
(England): Home Int 1907-09

Richmond, M (Walker)
(Scotland): Home Int 1972-73-74-75-77-78. (GBI): in Curtis
Cup 1974; in Vagliano Trophy 1975

Rieben, Mrs
(Wales): Home Int 1927-28-29-30-31-32-33

Rigby, F (Macbeth)
(Scotland): Home Int 1912-13

Ritchie, C (Park)
(Scotland): Home Int 1939-47-48-51-52-53-64(Captain)

Roberts, B
(Wales): Home Int 1984(Captain)-85(Captain)-86(Captain)

Roberts, E (Pentony)
(Ireland): Home Int 1932-33-34-35-36-39

Roberts, E (Barnett)
(Ireland): Home Int 1961-62-63-64-65; Eur L T Ch 1964

Roberts, G
(Wales): Home Int 1949-52-53-54

Roberts, M (Brown)
(Scotland): Home Int 1965(Captain). (GBI): in Espirito Santo 1964

Roberts, P
(Wales): Home Int 1950-51-53-55-56-57-58-59-60-61-62-63-64(Captain)-65 (Captain)-66(Captain)-67(Captain)-68-69-70; Eur L T Ch 1965-67-69. (GBI) in Espirito Santo 1964

Roberts, S
(Wales): Home Int 1983-84-85-86-87-88-89-90; Eur L T Ch 1983-87

Robertson, B (McCorkindale)
(Scotland): Home Int 1958-59-60-61-62-63-64-65-66-69-72-73-78-80-81-82-84 -85-86; Eur L T Ch 1965-67(Captain)-69-71(Captain). (GBI): in Curtis Cup 1960-66-68-70-72-74 (Captain)-76(Captain)-82-86; in Vagliano Trophy 1959-63-69-71-81-85; in Espirito Santo 1959-63-69-71-81-85; CW 1971-75(Captain)

Robertson, D
(Scotland): Home Int 1907

Robertson, E
(Scotland): Home Int 1924

Robertson, G
(Scotland): Home Int 1907-08-09

Robinson, C (Nesbitt)
(Ireland): Home Int 1974-75-76-77-78-79-80-81. (GBI): in Curtis Cup 1980; in Vagliano Trophy 1979

Robinson, R (Bayly)
(Ireland): Home Int 1947-56-57

Robinson, S
(England): Home Int 1989

Roche, Mrs
(Ireland): Home Int 1922

Rogers, J
(Wales): Home Int 1972

Rose, A
(Scotland): Home Int 1990

Roskrow, M
(England): Home Int 1948-50

Ross, M (Hezlet)
(Ireland): Home Int 1905-06-07-08-11-12

Roy, S (Needham)
(Scotland): Home Int 1969-71-72-73-74-75-76-83. (GBI): in Vagliano Trophy 1973-75

Rudgard, G
(England): Home Int 1931-32-50-51-52

Rusack, J
(Scotland): Home Int 1908

Sabine, D (Plumpton)
(England): Home Int 1934-35. (GBI): in Curtis Cup 1934

Saunders, V
(England): Home Int 1967-68; Eur L T Ch 1967. (GBI): in Curtis Cup 1968; in Vagliano Trophy 1967; CW 1967

Scott Chard, Mrs
(Wales) Home Int 1928-30

Seddon, N
(Wales): Home Int 1962-63-74(Captain)-75(Captain)-76 (Captain)

Selkirk, H
(Wales): Home Int 1925-28

Shapcott, A
(England): Home Int 1989

Shapcott, S
(England): Home Int 1986-88; Eur L T Ch 1987. (GBI): in Curtis Cup 1988; in Vagliano Trophy 1987; CW 1987; in Espirito Santo 1988

Shaw, P
(Wales): Home Int 1913

Sheldon, A
(Wales): Home Int 1981

Sheppard, E (Pears)
(England): Home Int 1947

Simpson, L (Moore)
(England): Home Int 1979-80

Singleton, B (Henderson)
(Scotland): Home Int 1939-52-53-54-55-56-57-58-60-61-62-63-64-65

Slade, Lady
(Ireland): Home Int 1906

Slark, R (Porter)
(England): Home Int 1959-60-61-62-64-65-66-68-78; Eur L T Ch 1965. (GBI): in Curtis Cup 1960-62-64; in Vagliano Trophy 1959-61-65; in Espirito Santo 1964-66(Captain); CW 1963

Slocombe, E (Davies)
(Wales): Home Int 1974-75

Smalley, Mrs A
(Wales): Home Int 1924-25-31-32-33-34

Smillie, P
(England): Home Int 1985-86

Smith, A [Stant] (Willard)
(England): Home Int 1974-75-76. (GBI): in Curtis Cup 1976; in Vagliano Trophy 1975; CW 1959-63

Smith, F (Stephens)
(England): Home Int 1947-48-49-50-51-52-53-54-55-59-62 (Captain)-71(Captain) -72(Captain). (GBI): in Curtis Cup 1950-52-54-56-58-60-62(non-playing Captain)-72 (non-playing Captain); in Vagliano Trophy 1959-71; CW 1959-63

Smith, Mrs L
(Ireland): Home Int 1913-14-21-22-23-25

Smythe, M
(Ireland): Home Int 1947-48-49-50-51-52-53-54-55-56-58-59-62(Captain)

Sowter, Mrs
(Wales): Home Int 1923

Speir, M
(Scotland): Home Int 1957-64-68-71(Captain)-72(Captain)

Starrett, L (Malone)
(Ireland): Home Int 1975-76-77-78-80

Stavert, M
(Scotland): Home Int 1979

Steel, Mrs DC
(Scotland): Home Int 1925

Steel, E
(England): Home Int 1905-06-07-08-11

Stewart, G
(Scotland): Home Int 1979-80-81-82-83-84; Eur L T Ch 1982-84. (GBI): in Curtis Cup 1980-82; in Vagliano Trophy 1979-81-83; CW 1979-83

Stewart, L (Scraggie)
(Scotland): Home Int 1921-22-23

Stocker, J
(England): Home Int 1922-23

Stockton, Mrs
(Wales): Home Int 1949

Storry, Mrs
(Wales): Home Int 1910-14

Stroud, N
(Wales): Home Int 1989

Stuart, M
(Ireland): Home Int 1905-07-08

Stuart-French, Miss
(Ireland): Home Int 1922

Sugden, J (Machin)
(England): Home Int 1953-54-55

Summers, M (Mackie)
(Scotland): Home Int 1986

Sumpter, Mrs
(England): Home Int 1907-08-12-14-24

Sutherland Pilch, R (Barton)
(England): Home Int 1947-49-50-58(Captain)

Swallow, C
(England): Home Int 1985; Eur L T Ch 1985

Tamworth, Mrs
(England): Home Int 1908

Taylor, I
(Ireland): Home Int 1930

Teacher, F
(Scotland): Home Int 1908-09-11-12-13

Tebbet, K
(England): Home Int 1990

Temple, S
(England): Home Int 1913-14

Temple Dobell, G (Ravenscroft)
(England): Home Int 1911-12-13-14-20-21-25-30

Thomas, C (Phipps)
(Wales): Home Int 1959-63-64-65-66-67-68-69-70-71-72-73-76-77-80

Thomas, I
(Wales): Home Int 1910

Thomas, O
(Wales): Home Int 1921

Thomas, S (Rowlands)
(Wales): Home Int 1977-82-84-85

Thomas, T (Perkins)
(Wales): Home Int 1972-73-74-75-76-77-78-79-80-81-82-83-84; Eur L T Ch 1975. (GBI): in Curtis Cup 1974-76-78-80; in Vagliano Trophy 1973-75-77-79; in Espirito Santo 1979; CW 1975-79

Thomas, V (Rawlings)
(Wales): Home Int 1971 to 1990; Eur L T Ch 1975-87. (GBI): in Curtis Cup 1982-84-86-88-90; in Vagliano Trophy 1979-83 -85-87-89; CW 1979-83-87. Espirito Santo 1990

Thompson, M
(Wales): Home Int 1937-38-39

Thompson, M (Wallis)
(England): Home Int 1948-49

Thompson, M
(Scotland): Home Int 1949

Thomson, D
(Scotland): Home Int 1982-83-85-87

Thomson, M
(Scotland): Home Int 1907

Thomson, M
(Scotland): Home Int 1974-75-76-77-78; Eur L T Ch 1978. (GBI): in Curtis Cup 1978; in Vagliano Trophy 1977

Thornhill, J (Woodside)
(England): Home Int 1965-74-82-83-84-85-86-87-88; Eur L T Ch 1965-85-87. (GBI): in Curtis Cup 1984-86-88; in Vagliano Trophy 1965-83-85-87-89(Captain); CW 1983-87

Thornhill, Miss
(Ireland): Home Int 1924-25

Thornton, Mrs
(Ireland): Home Int 1924

Todd, Mrs
(Ireland): Home Int 1931-32-34-35-36

Thomlinson, J [Evans] (Roberts)
(England): Home Int 1962-64. (GBI): in Curtis Cup 1962; in Vagliano Trophy 1963

Treharne, A [Mills]
(Wales): Home Int 1952-61

Turner, B
(England): Home Int 1908

Turner, S (Jump)
(Wales): Home Int 1982-84-85-86

Tynte, V
(Ireland): Home Int 1905-06-08-09-11-12-13-14

Uzielli, A (Carrick)
(England): Home Int 1976-77-78-90; Eur L T Ch 1977. (GBI): in Curtis Cup 1978; in Vagliano Trophy 1977

Valentine, J (Anderson)
(Scotland): Home Int 1934-35-36-37-38-39-47-49-50-51-52-53-54-55-56 (Captain)-57-58. (GBI): in Curtis Cup 1938-48-50-52-54-56-58; CW 1959

Valentine, P (Whitley)
(Wales): Home Int 1973-74-75-77-78-79-80-90 (Captain)

Veitch, F
(Scotland): Home Int 1912

Wadsworth, H
(Wales): Home Int 1987-88-89-90; Eur L T Ch 1987-90. (GBI): in Curtis Cup 1990

Waite, C
(England): Home Int 1981-82-83-84, Eur L T Ch 1985. (GBI): in Curtis Cup 1984; in Vagliano Trophy 1983; in Espirito Santo 1984; CW 1983

Wakelin, H
(Wales): Home Int 1955

Walker, B (Thompson)
(England): Home Int 1905-06-07-08-09-11

Walker, M
(England): Home Int 1970-72; Eur L T Ch 1971. (GBI): in Curtis Cup 1972; in Vagliano Trophy 1971; CW 1971

Walker, P
(Ireland): Home Int 1928-29-30-31-32-33-34-35-36-37-38-39-48. (GBI): in Curtis Cup 1934-36-38

Walker-Leigh, F
(Ireland): Home Int 1907-08-09-11-12-13-14

Wallace-Williamson, V
(Scotland): Home Int 1932. (GBI): in Curtis Cup 1938 (Captain)

Walsh, R
(Ireland): Home Int 1987

Walter, J
(England): Home Int 1974-79-80-82-86

Wardlaw, N (Baird)
(Scotland): Home Int 1932-35-36-37-38-39-47-48. (GBI): in Curtis Cup 1938

Watson, C (Nelson)
(England): Home Int 1982

Webster, S (Hales)
(Wales): Home Int 1968-69-72

Wesley, N
(Wales): Home Int 1986

Westall, S (Maudsley)
(England): Home Int 1973

Weston, R
(Wales): Home Int 1927

Whieldon, Miss
(Wales): Home Int 1908

Wickham, C
(Ireland): Home Int 1983-89

Wickham, P
(Ireland): Home Int 1976-83-87; Eur L T Ch 1987

Williams, M
(Wales): Home Int 1936

Wlliamson, C (Barker)
(England): Home Int 1979-80-81

Willock-Pollen, G
(England): Home Int 1907

Wilson, A
(Scotland): Home Int 1973-74-85 (Captain)

Wilson, E
(England): Home Int 1928-29-30. (GBI): in Curtis Cup 1932

Wilson, Mrs
(Ireland): Home Int 1931

Wilson Jones, D
(Wales): Home Int 1952

Winn, J
(England): Home Int 1920-21-23-25

Wooldridge, W (Shaw)
(Scotland): Home Int 1982

Wragg, M
(England): Home Int 1929

Wright, J (Robertson)
(Scotland): Home Int 1952-53-54-55-56-57-58-59-60-61-63-65-67-73-78 (Captain)-79(Captain)-80(Captain)-86(Captain); Eur L T Ch 1965. (GBI): in Curtis Cup 1954-56-58-60; in Vagliano Trophy 1959-61-63; CW 1959

Wright, M
(Scotland): Home Int 1990

Wright, N (Cook)
(Wales): Home Int 1938-47-48-49-51-52-53-54-57-58-59-60-62-63-64-66-67-68-71 (Captain)-72(Captain)-73(Captain); Eur L T Ch 1965-71 (Captain). (GBI): in Espirito Santo 1964

Wright, P
(Scotland): Home Int 1981-82-83-84; Eur L T Ch 1987. (GBI): in Vagliano Trophy 1981

Wylie, P (Wade)
(England): Home Int 1934-35-36-37-38-47. (GBI): in Curtis Cup 1938

Association of Golf Writers

(L) = Life member
(H) = Honorary member

Adams, Jack
Daily Record

Andrew, Harry H

(L) Baker, John E

Ballantine, John

Bisher, Firman
Atlanta Journal Constitution,

Blackstock, Dixon
Sunday Mail, Glasgow

Blighton, Bill
Today

Blomquist, Jan
Golf Digest Sverige

Bolze, Gerd A

Booth, Alan

Bowden, Ken

Britten, Mike

(H) Butler, Frank

Caird, Douglas

Callander, Colin
Golf Monthly

Campbell, John G
The Daily Telegraph

Campbell, Malcolm

Chapman, Jeremy
The Sporting Life

Clark, Bill
Sunday Mirror, Belfast

Clough, Frank
The Sun

Coffman, Ron
Golf World

Creighton, Brian
Reuters

Dabell, Norman

Davies, Bob
Shropshire Star

Davies, David
The Guardian

Davies, Patricia

Dobereiner, Peter

Dodd, Richard
The Yorkshire Post

Donald, Peter

Ebbinge, Jan B
Dutch Golf Wegener Tijl

(L) Edwards, Leslie

Elliott, Bill
The Daily Star

Ellison, Stanley
Turf Management

Elsey, Neil
Golf Illustrated Weekly

Farquharson, Colin
Press and Journal, Aberdeen

(H) Fenton, John
BBC Radio

Ferrie, Kevin
Dundee Courier

Ferrier, Bob
Elite World of Sport Ltd

Figar, Jose
Adesport, Madrid

Fraser, Alan
The Independent

Frederick, Adrian

Garrod, Mark
Press Association

Gilleece, Dermot
The Irish Times

Glover, Tim
The Independent

Goodner, Ross
Golf Digest, USA

Green, Bob
The Associated Press, New York

Green, Robert
Golf World

Grimsley, Will

Hamilton, David
Golf Illustrated Weekly

Hamilton, Eddie

Hardy, Martin
Daily Express

Haslam, Peter
Golf World

(L) Hart, Maurice

Hedley, Alan
The Journal, Newcastle-upon-Tyne

Hennessy, John
The Times

Herron, Allan
The People

Higgs, Peter
Mail on Sunday

Hopkins, John
The Sunday Times

(L) Huggins, Percy

Ingham, John

Jacobs, Raymond
Glasgow Herald

Jenkins, Bob
Sunday Post, Glasgow

Jenkins, Dan
Golf Digest, USA

Johnson, Bill
Bolton Evening News

Kahn, Elizabeth

Lafaurie, André-Jean
Golf European, Paris

Laidlaw, Renton
Evening Standard

Lawrenson, Derek
Birmingham Post and Mail

(L) Lincoln, Stanley

McDonnell, Michael
Daily Mail

(H) McKinlay, S L

Macniven, Ian
Edinburgh Evening News

MacVicar, Jock
Scottish Daily Express

Mackie, Keith

Magowan, Jack
Belfast Telegraph

Mair, Norman
The Observer

Mair, Lewine
The Daily Telegraph

Maitland, Bobby
Scottish Daily Express

Mancinelli, Piero
Parliamo di Golf, Milan

Mearing, Paddy

Miró, Miguel
Diario Deportivo, Madrid

Moody, John

Morgan, John
Home Counties Golfer

Moseley, Ron
Press Association

Mossop, James
Sunday Express

Mulqueen, Charles
Cork Examiner

Nicol, Alister
Daily Record

Oakley, John

Ortega, Jesús Ruiz
Golf, Madrid

Ostermann, Ted
Golf Vertrieb, Hamburg

Pargeter, John

Pastor, Nuria
La Vanguardia, Barcelona

Pinner, John
Golf World Wales

(H) Place, Tom
US Tour, Ponte Vedra Beach, Florida

Platts, Mitchell
The Times

Plumridge, Chris
The Sunday Telegraph

Price, Charles

Price-Fisher, Elizabeth

Ramsey, Tom
News Limited Australia, North Sydney

Redmond, John
Irish Press

Reece, John K

Riach, Ian
Scottish Sunday Express

Richardson, Gordon

Robertson, Bill
Today's Golfer

Robertson, Jack
Evening Times, Glasgow

Rodrigo, Robert (Bob Rodney)

Ross, John M
American Golf Magazine

Ruddy, Pat
Golfers Companion

Ryde, Peter

St John, Lauren

(L) Scatchard, Charles

Seitz, Nick
Golf Digest/Tennis, USA

Severino, Dick
Golf Features Service, San Diego

Simpson, Gordon
Press Association, Glasgow

Skelton, Ronald
Dundee Courier

Smart, Chris
Mid-Glamorgan Press Agency

Smith, Colm
Independent Newspapers, Dublin

Sommers, Robert
US Golf Association

Spander, Art
San Francisco Examiner

Steel, Donald

Stobbs, John
Golf and Greenkeeping

Taylor, Dick
Golf World, USA

(H) Thornberry, Henry W

(H) Ullyett, Roy
Daily Express

Van Esbeck, Edmund
The Irish Times

Ward, Barry E
Golfing Life

Whitbread, John S
Surrey Herald Newspapers

White, Gordon S

Williams, Michael
The Daily Telegraph

(L) Wilson, Enid

Wilson, Mark
PGA European Tour, Wentworth

Wind, Herbert Warren
The New Yorker

Wright, Ben

Zachrisson, Goran

British Association of Golf Course Architects

Full Members

J Hamilton Stutt	Hamilton Stutt & Co, Bergen, 12 Bingham Ave, Poole, Dorset BW14 8NE *Tel* (0202) 708406
Donald Harradine, Peter Harradine	CH 6987, Caslano, Switzerland *Tel* (091) 711561
Fred Hawtree, Martin Hawtree, Simon Gidman	Hawtree & Son, 5 Oxford Street, Woodstock, Oxford OX7 1TQ *Tel* (0993) 811976
Tom McAuley	38 Moira Drive, Bangor, Co Down, N Ireland BT20 4RW *Tel* (0247) 465953
Donald Steel	Donald Steel & Co Ltd, The Forum, Stirling Road, Chichester, West Sussex, PO19 2EN *Tel* (0243) 531901

Provisional Members

Peter Bellchambers, Steven Macfarlane	Hawtree & Son, 5 Oxford Street, Woodstock, Oxford OX7 1TQ *Tel* (0993) 811976
Jeremy Pern	13 Lotissement des Chênes, Aussonne 31700, Blagnac (Toulouse), France *Tel* 61 85 09 02
Stephan Quenouille	c/o Tom McAuley, 38 Moira Drive, Bangor, Co Down, N'Ireland BT20 4RW *Tel* (0247) 465953
Alistair Rae	26 Tannoch Road, Uplawmoor, Glasgow G78 4AD *Tel* (050 585) 371
Cameron Sinclair	21 Lauds Road, Crick, Northamptonshire NN6 7TJ

Overseas Members

R Berthet (Provisional)	Château du Tremblay, s/Mauldre, 78490 Montfort L'Amaury, France *Tel* (1)34879200
Tjasa Gregoric (Provisional)	Kobilarna Lipica, 66 210 Sezatia, Yugoslavia
Eddie Hackett	28 Ailesbury Drive, Dublin 4, Eire *Tel* (1) 691592
Joan Dudok van Heel	Beukenlaan 4, B-1640, St Genesius-Rode, nr Brussels, Belgium *Tel* (02) 3583387
Gerard Jol (Provisional)	Landschapsarchitekt bnt, Middenduinerweg 75, 2082 LC Santpoort, Netherlands *Tel* (023) 376449
Pier Mancinelli	21 Via Achille Papa 00195, Rome, Italy *Tel* (06) 36036-35
Kurt Rossknecht (Provisional)	Dennenmoos 5a, 8990 Lindau-Bad, Schachen, Germany *Tel* (08382) 230 05
Jan Sederholm	K Kristoffersweg 3A, S 253 34 Helsingborg, Sweden *Tel* (042) 371 84

Honorary Member

GS Cornish	Fiddlers Green, Amherst, Mass 01002, USA

Golfing Hotel Compendium

The Golfing hotel compendium continues to increase in size and is a comprehensive source of information for golfers wishing to find the most comfortable place to stay at or close to some of the finest courses in the country. This section has been compiled from the premier hotels of the British Isles which include golf among their many attractions.

If readers wish especially to recommend an establishment which is not listed in this section of the Royal & Ancient Golfer's Handbook *the editors will be happy to be advised.*

England

South West

Allhays Country House Hotel
Talland Bay, Near Looe, Cornwall PL13 2JB.
Tel (0503) 72434   *Fax* (0503) 72929
3-crown commended country house hotel. The perfect place to relax after a game at one of the Four courses close by. Excellent food and wines. A warm welcome and personal attention at all times.

The Anchorage Hotel
The Quay, Instow, Bideford, North Devon.
Tel (0271) 860655
Golf parties catered for, any number from two to thirty two. We arrange every aspect of your holiday. Concessionary green fees at Saunton and Royal North Devon – starting times guaranteed. Come and be pampered at Devon's No 1 golf hotel. (See advertisement page 419 for further details.)

Atlantic Hotel
Dane Road, Newquay, Cornwall.
Tel (0637) 872244
The Atlantic provides a complete holiday environment. We are conveniently located for visiting the fine local beaches, the town and Newquay Golf Course where golfing guests can take advantage of special reduced green fees. Three swimming pools, three spa baths, four solariums, two saunas, two tennis/squash courts, 9-hole putting green. (See advertisement page 429 for further details.)

Bodmin Golf and Country Club
Bodmin, Cornwall.
Tel (0208) 73600
Accommodation now under construction. Anticipating completion Summer 1991. Please phone for confirmation. (See advertisement pages 17 and 21 for further details.)

Budock Vean Golf and Country House Hotel
Mawnan Smith, Falmouth, Cornwall TR11 5LG.
Tel (0326) 250288 *Fax* (0326) 250892
Challenging 9-hole (18 tee) private golf course set in sub-tropical grounds, free to guests. Excellent amenities, luxurious surroundings, top quality service and cuisine. Associate to Treglos Hotel, Padstow. (See advertisement page 419 for further details.)

Burnham & Berrow Golf Club
St Christopher's Way, Burnham-on-Sea, Somerset TA8 2PE.
Tel (0278) 785760
18-hole championship links golf course and 9-hole course. (See advertisement page 423 for further details.)

Commodore Hotel AA/RAC 3-star
Beach Road, Sand Bay, Kewstoke, Weston Super Mare, Somerset BS22 9UZ.
Tel (0934) 415778 *Fax* (0934) 636483
Peaceful and stylish haven dedicated to fine food and service. Reduced green fees at both Weston/Worlebury clubs. Special break/party rates. RAC merit awarded for cuisine and service.

The Coombe Bank Hotel
Landscore Road, Teignmouth, Devon TQ14 9JL.
Tel (0626) 772369
Devon golfing holidays. Four different courses. Societies welcome. From only 135 inclusive.

Country Castle Hotel
Lamellion, Liskeard, Cornwall PL14 4EB.
Tel (0579) 42694
Small country house hotel with gourmet cuisine situated between St Mellion, Looe Birkdown, Bodmin and Lostwithiel golf courses.

Culloden House Hotel
Westward Ho! Devon.
Tel (0237) 479 421
The Golfer's hotel – run by golfers for golfers. All-in package includes green fees (choice of eight courses). Full English breakfast, home cooking for your dinner (four couses of course).

The Dormy Hotel and Leisure Club
New Road, Ferndown, Dorset BH22 8ES.
Tel (0202) 872121
De Vere 4-star hotel adjacent to Ferndown Golf Course, offering sporting and leisure activities combined with a high standard of accommodation and cuisine. (See advertisement page 421 for further details.)

Gleneagles Hotel RAC 3-star
Asheldon Road, Wellswood, Torquay TQ1 2QS.
Tel (0803) 293637
42 bedrooms all en suite with sun balconies, colour TV, telephone and room service. Heated pool, jacuzzi, solarium, superb cocktail lounge and poolside restaurant. Four golf courses close by. (See advertisement page 423 for further details.)

Gloucester Hotel and Country Club
Robinswood Hill, Matson Lane, Gloucester GL19 4JE.
Tel (0452) 25653
Extensive leisure facilities including indoor swimming pool, sauna, gymnasium, solarium. Squash courts, tennis courts, snooker, pool, skittles Championship dry ski slopes. Full 18-hole, and 9-hole par 3 courses.

The Greenway
Shurdington, Cheltenham, Gloucestershire GL51 5UG.
Tel (0242) 862352 *Fax* (0242) 862780
16th-century country house hotel set in formal gardens and surrounded by hundreds of acres of parkland. Convenient for Lilley Brook, Cotswold Hills, Cirencester and Broadway golf clubs.

Hotel California
Pentire Crescent, Newquay TR7 1PU.
Tel (0637) 879292 *Fax* (0637) 875611
Situated among glorious scenic views overlooking the River Gannel Estuary. Our excellent hotel offers unsurpassed facilities. All bedrooms have private bathroom, colour TV, video and direct dial telephone. Indoor and outdoor heated pools, gymnasium, squash and tennis courts. Green Fee concessions on local course. (See advertisement page 419 for further details.)

Hotel Collingwood
11 Priory Road, Bournemouth BH2 5DF.
Tel (0202) 557575
Situated in central Bournemouth with nine golf courses within 6 miles. Tee times arranged. Parking, indoor pool, leisure centre, snooker, nightly entertainment. Early breakfast, late evening meal available from £33.00. Also dinner and Bed and Breakfast.

Hotel Penarvor
Crooklets Beach, Bude, Cornwall EX23 8NE.
Tel (0288) 352036 *Fax* (0288) 355027
150 yards from golf course. 50 yards from beach. Enjoy the best of both worlds. The Hotel Penarvor is truly luxury by the sea. All rooms en suite. Colour TV, tea and coffee-making facilities. Golfing holidays a speciality.

Langstone Cliff Hotel
Dawlish, Devon EX7 0NA.
Tel (0626) 865155
64-bedroom hotel overlooking the sea. Set in grounds of 19 acres. Indoor and outdoor heated swimming pool, snooker, table tennis, hard court tennis. Six 18-hole golf courses within 12 miles.

Lansdown Grove Hotel
Lansdown, Bath BA1 5EH.
Tel (0225) 315891
An attractive hotel overlooking historic Bath. 45 en suite bedrooms with TV, telephone, mini-bar and tea/coffee-making facilities. Excellent restaurant. Five local golf courses. A Best Western Hotel. AA/RAC 3-star.

The Manor House Hotel
Moretonhampstead, Devon TQ13 8RE.
Tel (0647) 40355

18-hole championship golf course with its own Jacobean-style country house hotel on the edge of Dartmoor National Park. Par 3 course, undercover driving bay. Professional tuition available. Golf fully inclusive in room rate. (See advertisement page 423 for further details.)

Penmere Manor Hotel
Mongleath Road, Falmouth, Cornwall.
Tel (0326) 314545

A Georgian country house in five acres of gardens and woodland. Indoor and outdoor pools, jacuzzi, gym, sauna, croquet and three-quarter size snooker. Excellent cuisine and wines. Golf available on fourteen Cornish courses at special rates.

Pentire Rocks Hotel
New Polzeath, North Cornwall PL27 6US.
Tel (0208) 862213/862259

Family run 2-star hotel, 16 en suite bedrooms, TV, direct dial telephones. Heated outdoor swimming pool. Off season breaks from 60 for two days. 170 per week – bed, breakfast and evening meal. Close to St Enodoc Golf Club.

Poolway House Hotel & Restaurant
Gloucester Road, Coleford, Gloucester GL16 8BN.
Tel (0594) 33937

Five local golf courses including St Pierre and 'Rolls' of Monmouth. Family run, ETB 4-crown, 16th-century oak beamed manor. Offers excellent cuisine and modern facilities, 300 yards from town centre. Licensed. 1991 Breaks from £31.00 (includes Bed, Breakfast and evening meal) per person, per night.

Port Gaverne Hotel
Nr Port Isaac, Cornwall PL29 3SQ.
Tel (0208) 880 244 *Fax* (0208) 880 151

Courses within 10 minutes drive of hotel are:– St Enodoc Golf Club at Rock and Bowood Park Golf Club opening 1st April at Lan Teglos. Early 17th-century Cornish coastal inn with an international reputation and staff who know how to care.

Preston House Hotel
Saunton, Braunton, North Devon EX33 1LG.
Tel (0271) 890475 *Fax* (0271) 890555

A beautiful Edwardian country house hotel overlooking the Atlantic. All 15 bedrooms en suite some with spa baths. Elegant restaurant and cocktail bar – open all hours. Two informal lounges, sauna, solarium and spa bath. Half mile Saunton Golf Club.

Rose & Crown Hotel
Harnham Road, Salisbury, Wiltshire SP2 8JQ.
Tel (0722) 327908

A 13th-century inn set in beautiful rose garden on banks of River Avon overlooking Salisbury Cathedral. All rooms with full facilities. A modern extension of olde worlde oak beams. Bars and popular restaurant.

Royal York & Faulkner Hotel
Esplanade, Sidmouth, Devon EX10 8AZ.
Tel (0395) 513043

AA/RAC 2-star, Ashley Courtenay, ETB 4-crowns approved. All rooms en suite. Health complex. Indoor short mat bowls. Reduced green fees. Central location to East Devon courses. BARGAIN BREAKS; half-board inclusive from £23.00 per person Brochure and Tariff on request.

St Andrews Hotel
The Terrace, Port Isaac, Cornwall PL29 3SG.
Tel (0208) 880 240

A family run hotel with en suite rooms, magnificent views of the north Cornwall coast, ample parking, and within half hour's drive of at least six golf courses, some new for 1991. 20% discount available.

St Mellion Hotel
St Mellion Golf & Country Club St Mellion, Saltash, Cornwall PL12 6SD.
Tel (0579) 50101

Modern hotel situated next to the St Mellion complex. 24 rooms. AA/RAC 3-star. Two golf courses (the Nicklaus and the Old), indoor pool, tennis, squash and badminton courts.

Slipway Hotel & Restaurant
Harbour Front, Port Isaac, Cornwall PL29 3RH.
Tel (0208) 880264

16th-century hotel, 10 rooms, most en suite. Restaurant famed for fresh local seafood dishes. Golf – 27-hole championship course – St Enodoc 4 miles – three other 18-hole courses within 10 miles. (See advertisement page 423 for further details.)

Tewkesbury Park Hotel Golf and Country Club
Lincoln Green Lane, Tewkesbury, Gloucestershire GL20 7DN.
Tel (0684) 295405

This 82-bedroom hotel with modern facilities is surrounded by its own 18-hole course. It also offers heated indoor pool, sauna, whirlpool, steam room, multi-gym, snooker, squash and all-weather tennis courts.

Trevose Golf and Country Club
Constantine Bay, Padstow, Cornwall PL28 8JB.
Tel (0841) 520208   *Fax* (0841) 521057
Located on the north coast of Cornwall, Trevose offers an idyllic golfing paradise. 18 and 9-hole courses. Three tennis courts, swimming pool. Self-catering accommodation and restaurant. Brochure on request.

Twinbrook Park
Swanpool Road, Falmouth, Cornwall TR11 5BH.
Tel (0326) 313727
The Park is secluded and appeals to golfers/ families who prefer a quiet holiday. Detached self-catering chalets, adjacent Falmouth Golf Club, 800 metres beach. Facilities include indoor pool, lounge bar and shop. Telephone for brochure.

Whitsand Bay Hotel Golf & Country Club
Portwrinkle, Crafthole, By Torpoint, Cornwall PL11 3BU.   *Tel* (0503) 30276
Spectacularly sited 18-hole uncrowded golf course, overlooking the ocean in Cornish fishing hamlet, with 1st tee 100 yards from front door. Leisure complex, heated indoor swimming pools, sauna, solarium, massage/beauty salons.

Yeoldon House Hotel
Durrant Lane, Northam, Bideford, Devon EX39 2RL.   *Tel* (0237) 474400
Play the oldest course in England: Royal North Devon. We take pride in our excellent cuisine and fine wines. Our rooms are comfortable and perfect to rest those well golfed bones. Societies and parties of any number welcome. (See advertisement page 421 for further details.)

The York House Inn
The Avenue, Minehead, Somerset TA24 5AN.
Tel (0643) 705151
Fully licensed hotel with good food and comfortable rooms all en suite. Only 5 minutes drive to Minehead and West Somerset Golf Course. Level links between Exmoor and Sea.

South East

Ashdown Forest Hotel
Chapel Lane, Forest Row, East Sussex.
Tel (0342) 82 4866
Family owned and run hotel offering comfortable accommodation and good food and wines. Royal Ashdown Forest New Course operated by hotel exclusively for residents and visitors.

The Clarendon Hotel
Beach Street, Deal CT14 6HY.
Tel (0304) 374748
Family run seafront hotel offering traditional English cooking and real ales. Entertainment throughout year. Fishing and golfing outings arranged. Bedrooms: 3 single, 4 double and 8 twin. Bed and breakfast 18 single, 30 double or twin. (See advertisement page 429 for further details.)

The Colbern Hotel
South Terrace, Seafront, Littlehampton, West Sussex BN17 5LQ.
Tel (0903) 714270
Small and friendly licensed hotel overlooking the sea, near to Littlehampton and Ham Manor golf courses. ETB 3-crowns and RAC acclaimed. All rooms have private WC and shower, television, radio, plus tea and coffee-making facilities.

Cooden Resort Hotel
Cooden Beach, Bexhill-on-Sea, East Sussex TN39 4TT.
Tel (0424) 32281
Situated on the beach just 200 yards from mainline station and adjacent to golf club. Indoor health club, Sovereign bar, candlelit dinners in grill room. All rooms with bath/shower, TV, direct dial telephone. Ideal for conferences.

Five Sumner Place Hotel
5 Sumner Place, London SW7 3EE.
Tel 071-584 7586
Fax 071-823 9962
Delightful hotel situated close to South Kensington and Knightsbridge, within walking distance of Harrods. All rooms luxuriously appointed complete with en suite facilities, telephone, colour TV and full buffet breakfast. The hotel is located on a direct tube link with London's Heathrow Airport. Brochure available. (See advertisement page 425 for further details.)

Hanbury Manor
Thundridge, Nr Ware, Herts SG12 0SD.
Tel (0920) 487722
Hanbury Manor, a 98-bedroomed country house hotel – is set amidst an 18-hole championship golf course designed by Jack Nicklaus II. The course is complemented by an extensive spa offering two squash courts, indoor swimming pool, gymnasium, tennis courts, dance studio and beauty studios.

Hope Anchor Hotel
Watch Bell Street, Rye, East Sussex TN31 7HA.
Tel (0797) 222216 (Reservations) 223973 (Guests)
Family run hotel with a super dining room. We cater for golfers' needs, ie early morning calls and breakfasts, and drying out facilities. Golf societies welcome. Other activities in our area: wind surfing, tennis, squash and swimming all close by.

Horsted Place
at East Sussex National Golf Club
Little Horsted, Uckfield, East Sussex TN22 5TS.
Tel (0825) 75581
17-suite country house hotel located on 1,000-acre East Sussex National Golf Club. 45 miles south of London. Two 18-hole championship courses, 3-hole teaching academy, two driving ranges, putting and chipping greens.

Lansdowne Hotel
King Edward's Parade, Eastbourne, East Sussex BN21 4EE.
Tel (0323) 25174   *Fax* (0323) 39721
Play 36 holes a day on choice of courses; we book your tee-off time. Two nights with green fees, light lunch at club and use of our drying room. 13 January to 28 February 101; 1 March to 31 March 110; 1 April to 31 May 116; 1 June to 30 September 120; 1 October to 19 December 122. Extra days pro rata. (See advertisement page 421 for further details.)

Lythe Hill Hotel
Petworth Road, Haslemere, Surrey GU27 3BQ.
Tel (0428) 651251
A luxurious, privately owned country hotel with two superb restaurants and beautifully appointed bedrooms and suites situated in four acres of parkland gardens in the Surrey hills. Tennis, sauna and croquet in the grounds and four excellent golf courses within 10 miles: Old Thorns, Hindhead, Liphook and Cowdray Park. Special weekend bargain breaks available.

Oakfield Hotel
11 The Vale, Broadstairs, Kent CT10 1RB
Tel (0843) 62506
A small licensed hotel centrally situated and well known for its good food and friendliness. Open all year. Own car park. Choice of golf courses including Princes at Sandwich. Groups and individuals welcome. (See advertisement page 425 for further details.)

Old Thorns Golf Course, Hotel and Restaurants
Old Thorns, Longmoor Road, Liphook, Hampshire GU30 7PE.
Tel (0428) 724555
Old Thorns is a rare combination of an 18-hole championship golf course. European and Japanese restaurants, hotel and leisure centre set in 400 acres of magnificent Hampshire countryside.

Quinns Hotel
48 Sheen Road, Richmond, Surrey TW9 1AW.
Tel 081-940 5444
Very quiet and centrally located hotel close to many sporting venues. Standard and en suite rooms available all with radio, intercom, colour TV. Car parking in own grounds. Unbeatable rates available.

The Cottage – Royal Eastbourne Golf Club
Paradise Drive, Eastbourne BN20 8BP.
Tel (0323) 29738
The cottage is situated near the 1st tee of the long course. The accommodation consists of two twin-bedded rooms, lounge, kitchen and bathroom. Parking on the premises. From 450 per week including golf. (See advertisement page 429 for further details.)

Royal Oak Hotel
High Street, Sevenoaks, Kent
Tel (0732) 451109
The 17th-century coaching inn. This historic Sevenoaks hotel completed major refurbishment in May 1990. The Royal Oak Restaurant offers English country cooking at its best.

Savoy Hotel and Restaurant
Grange Road, Ramsgate, Kent.
Tel (0843) 592637
Excellent facilities, continental cuisine, well stocked cellar. Ideally sited overlooking town and harbour, ideal for major golf courses and continental ferries. Easy access via M2/M20. Inclusive weekend packages available. Recently refurbished and extended: Resident Proprietor.

Golf

On a 200 acre country estate

Our 6,402 yard Championship golf course [j]ust the beginning of the perfect, relaxing break [fr]om the daily routine.

The Selsdon Park Hotel offers guests [en]joying a golfing holiday, or weekend, [an] unparalleled opportunity to [pl]ay – even after the round is [co]mpleted.

The Tropical Leisure Complex, for [ex]ample, has a sauna, jacuzzi, gymnasium, [ste]am room, solarium and swimming pool.

Selsdon Park also offers fine cuisine in the surroundings you'd expect of a 170 bedroom, four star hotel. Plus excellent facilities for tennis, squash, croquet, putting, boules, jogging and snooker. All of which helps make Selsdon Park Hotel the perfect place to play golf. Reserve now.

Selsdon Park is 30 minutes from London and just 10 minutes from junction 6 of the M25.

SELSDON PARK HOTEL

[S]anderstead, South Croydon, Surrey CR2 8YA Tel: 081-657 8811 Fax: 081-651 6171 Telex: 945003

[P]lease see entry on page 428

Selsdon Park Hotel
Sanderstead, Croydon, Surrey CR2 8YA.
Tel 081-657 8811   *Telex* 945003
Fax 081-651 6171
Traditional country house set in 200 acres of parkland with an 18-hole championship course. Green fee players welcome. Residents' exclusive tropical leisure complex. (See advertisement page 427 for further details.)

Thames Lodge Hotel
Thames Street, Staines, Middlesex TW18 4SF.   *Tel* (0784) 464433
Enjoying a lovely riverside position by the Thames, this Victorian hotel has a fine reputation for food and accommodation. 44 bedrooms all with private bath, central heating. Car parking. Junction 13 on M25 or A30 Staines. (See advertisement page 425 for further details.)

East Anglia

Abbotsley Golf Hotel
Eynesbury Hardwicke, St Neots, Cambridgeshire.
Tel (0480) 74000
Cosy moated country house amidst picturesque golf course. Delightful bedrooms and galleried dining room. Surrounding court yard of award winning gardens. Internationally renowned golf schools with Vivien Saunders. Squash and golf range. (See advertisement page 429 for further details.)

The Angel Hotel
Bury St Edmunds, Suffolk IP33 1LT.
Tel (0284) 753926
An imposing country town hotel, with traditionally high standards of cuisine, service and comfort. 40 bedrooms all with private bath, colour TV, direct dial phone and facilities for exceeding the hotel's 3-star status.

Anglia Court Hotel
5 Runton Road, Cromer, Norfolk NR27 9AR.
Tel (0263) 512443
Golf at Royal Cromer and Sheringham courses. Friendly 1-star hotel. En suite rooms, excellent cuisine. Two to five day breaks arranged for golfers by golfers. Special rates for party bookings. Write or telephone NOW for details.

Barnham Broom Hotel
Golf & Leisure Centre, Honingham Road, Barnham Broom, Norwich, Norfolk NR9 4DD.
Tel (060 545) 393   *Fax* (060 545) 8224
East Anglia's top Conference and Leisure Centre lies in 250 acres of countryside. 52 fully equipped bedrooms include family rooms, served by Flints Restaurant and sports snack bar. Four squash courts, snooker, heated indoor swimming pool with spa jets, tennis and 36-hole golf. Golfing Getaway 128. (See advertisement page 433 for further details.)

Hintlesham Hall
Hintlesham, Ipswich, Suffolk IP8 3NS.
Tel (047 387) 671
Luxurious 16th-century country hotel set in its own park. Offering superb hospitality, food and accommodation. 18-hole championship length golf course, designed by Hawtree, opening 1991. AA 3 Red Stars, RAC Blue Ribbon. (See advertisement page 431 for further details.)

Le Strange Arms Hotel
Golf Course Road, Old Hunstanton, Norfolk PE36 6JJ.
Tel (0485) 534411
Country house hotel with lawns sweeping down to the beach. 40 bedrooms with private facilities, colour TV. Snooker room, fine restaurant, themed pub. Near to Hunstanton, Royal West Norfolk and Kings Lynn courses.

The Links Country Park Hotel & Golf Club
West Runton, Cromer, Norfolk NR27 9QH.
Tel (0263) 75691   *Fax* (0263) 758264
The hotel is privately owned and run, situated in 35 acres of its own grounds. Superb 9-hole golf course, with tight hilly fairways and tricky greens. Other leisure facilities are a large heated indoor swimming pool, tennis court, sauna and solarium. (All leisure facilities FREE to residents.) The renowned golf courses of Sheringham, Cromer and Hunstanton are nearby, making the 'Links' an ideal base. (See advertisement page 431 for further details.)

The Linksway Hotel
Golf Course Road, Old Hunstanton, Norfolk PE36 6JE.
Tel (0485) 532209
Set in secluded gardens, overlooking stanton's 1st fairway – The ideal location. 'Good Food', 'Good Wine' and a 'Hearty' welcome. All rooms fully en suite, heated indoor swimming pool and spa pool and cocktail bar.

Morston Hall
Morston, Holt, North Norfolk NR25 7AA.
Tel (0263) 741041
17th-century house, luxurious rooms en suite in peaceful surroundings. Individual cuisine, from fresh ingredients and local seafood. A good base for Hunstanton, Brancaster, Sheringham and Cromer golf clubs. Good Hotel Guide listed – very civilised hotel.

Thorpeness Golf Club Hotel
Thorpeness, Near Leiston, Suffolk IP16 4NH.
Tel (0728) 452176
Modern luxury hotel adjoining the club house on one of East Anglia's finest 18-hole courses. Situated on the lovely, unspoiled Suffolk coast. Ideal too for non-golfers. (See advertisement page 431 for further details.)

White Horse Hotel
Station Road, Leiston, Suffolk IP16 4HD.
Tel (0728) 830694   *Fax* (0728) 833105
Close to three excellent courses in the heart of Suffolk heritage coast. Friendly bars, excellent food, 12 rooms, 9 en suite, all with TV and telephone. Bargain weekend breaks all year.

East Midlands

Belton Woods Hotel and Country Club
Belton, Nr Grantham, Lincolnshire NG32 2LN
Tel (0476) 593200
A magnificent new hotel, golf and leisure development set in 475 acres of glorious countryside. Two challenging 18-hole golf courses, 9-hole course, driving range, putting green and tennis courts. Due to open January 1991.

Broomhill Hotel
Holdenby Road, Spratton, Northampton NN6 8LD.
Tel (0604) 845959
Fax (0604) 845834
A 4-crown country house hotel set within sixteen acres of private parkland, Broomhill offers excellent cuisine, luxury en suite bedrooms with panoramic views, heated outdoor swimming pool and all-weather tennis court.
Northamptonshire County Golf Course 3 miles.

Farthingstone Hotel Golf & Leisure Centre
Farthingstone, Towcester, Northamptonshire NN12 8HA.
Tel (0327) 36291
Set in glorious wooded countryside, just 90 minutes outside London. Farthingstone Hotel offers 15 superb en suite rooms, upon a challenging 18-hole golf course, with squash courts, full size snooker tables, and a carvery restaurant. (See advertisement page 443 for further details.)

The Grange and Links Hotel
Sea Lane, Sandilands, Sutton-on-Sea, Lincolnshire.
Tel (0507) 441334
3-star 30-bedroom hotel with own 18-hole links course. Two tennis courts, snooker room, ballroom. Renowned for good food, friendliness, comfort and service. Within easy reach are Seacroft and Woodhall Spa golf clubs.

North Shore Hotel and Golf Course
North Shore Road, Skegness, Lincolnshire.
Tel (0754) 3298
The hotel is in a unique position of having its own 18-hole golf course situated on Lincolnshire's east coast. The course designed in 1910 suits all classes of golf enthusiast.

Staverton Park Hotel & Golfing Complex
Staverton, Daventry, Northamptonshire NN11 6JT.
Tel (0327) 705911/300387
Fax (0327) 300821
You are guaranteed the best in quality and service at the Staverton Park Hotel, a superb new 3-star hotel built around an established American style all-weather course which provides interest for novice and skilled players alike. (See advertisement page 435 for further details.)

The Swallow Hotel
Carter Lane East, South Normanton, Derbyshire.
Tel (0773) 812000
The Swallow Hotel at South Normanton is conveniently located at Junction 28 off the M1. This 4-star hotel with leisure facilities is close to Hollinwall Golf Course as well as other local courses.

Whipper-In Hotel
The Market Place, Oakham, Rutland.
Tel (0572) 756971

The Whipper-In is a 17th-century hotel which sits in the market square of historic Oakham. It is furnished throughout with antiques, old prints and pictures. Fresh flowers are on display. Log fires burn in the lounges and bar.

West Midlands

Castle Hotel
**Ladybank, Tamworth,
Staffordshire B79 7NB.**
Tel (0827) 57181

Lying in the shadows of historic Tamworth Castle in the centre of this ancient town. Located in the Midlands with easy access to A5, M42 and access to M6 and M5. 5 miles from Belfry Golf Centre.

Hawkstone Park
**Weston-Under-Redcastle, Shrewsbury,
Shropshire SY4 5UY.**
Tel (093924) 611
Fax (093924) 311

Where Sandy Lyle learned his game. Two 18-hole parkland golf courses. Hawkstone 6465 yards surrounded by hills and antiquities, and Weston 5368 yards. Busy 3-star hotel with 59 rooms all en suite. Located 14 miles north of Shrewsbury on A49. It is advisable to book tee times in advance. Open all year to non-residents.

Hill Valley Golf Hotel
**Hill Valley Golf & Country Club, Terrick
Road, Whitchurch, Shropshire SY13 4JZ.**
Tel (0948) 3584

The Complex has twin-bedded motel accommodation. All rooms have bathroom en suite, colour TV, tea and coffee-making facilities. Two golf courses, squash, tennis and snooker.

Hollies Hotel
**Chester Road, Whitchurch, Shropshire
SY13 1LZ.**
Tel (0948) 2184

Play Hill Valley, Hawkstone Park, Market Drayton. All tee times in advance. All rooms en suite, tea/coffee-making and colour TV. Bed, breakfast, dinner – Golf, from 40.

Lea Marston Hotel and Leisure Complex Ltd
**Haunch Lane, Lea Marston, Nr Kingsbury,
North Warwickshire B76 0BY.**
Tel (0675) 470468

Country hotel set in 20 acres 'Greenbelt' 1 mile J9 M42. 2 miles Belfry Golf Centre. 32-bay driving range, 9-hole golf course, crown green bowling, tennis, health suite, meetings/conferences, banqueting, restaurant. 165 car parking.

Sutton Court Hotel
**60-66 Lichfield Road, Sutton Coldfield,
West Midlands B74 2NA.**
Tel 021-355 6071

Privately owned 3-star hotel, 64 individually designed bedrooms and court yard restaurant enjoying a fine reputation for international cuisine. Eight golf courses within 15 minutes drive, including Belfry Ryder Cup Course.

The Talbot Hotel
**West Street, Leominster,
Herefordshire HR6 8EP.**
Tel (0568) 6347

An old coaching house hotel with parts dating from 15th-century, situated in the small ancient market town of Leominster. Beamed bars, log fire and friendly staff all help to make your break enjoyable. Golfing at Leominster 18-hole golf course. Handicap certificate not required.

Telford Hotel Golf and Country Club
**Great Hay, Sutton Hill, Telford,
Shropshire TF7 4DT.**
Tel (0952) 585642

Overlooking the Ironbridge Gorge and encompassed by its own 9 and 18-hole golf courses, this hotel offers comfort and style in addition to extensive leisure facilities featuring swimming, snooker and squash. (See advertisement page 439 for further details.)

Welcombe Hotel and Golf Course
**Warwick Road, Stratford-upon-Avon,
Warwickshire CV37 0NR.**
Tel (0789) 295252

A 4-star Jacobean-style mansion set within its own 6,202 yards private golf course. A newly created club house and pro's shop within the hotel's 157 acres enhances the parkland course.

Yorkshire & Humberside

Aldwark Manor Hotel
Aldwark Near Alne, York YO6 2NF.
Tel (03473) 8146
Victorian country house hotel set in 98 acres of parkland with its own 9-hole golf course. 15 luxury bedrooms, excellent cuisine. Special two day breaks. 12 miles north of York. Ideal base for golfing holiday or touring North Yorkshire.

Dean Court Hotel
Duncombe Place, York YO1 2EF.
Tel (0904) 625082
Located in the heart of York immediately opposite the Minster. This privately owned hotel offers personal service, a unique ambiance and the comfort of guests' needs are our main priority. (Host Mrs Kay McLeod.) (See advertisement page 439 for further details.)

Downe Arms
Wykeham, Scarborough, North Yorkshire YO13 9QB. *Tel* (0723) 862471
Situated on A170, 6 miles from Ganton and Scarborough. Rooms en suite, colour TV and tea-making facilities. Bars and restaurant. Ring Philip Mort for reservations.

Golden Lion Hotel
Market Square, Leyburn, North Yorks DL8 5AS.
Tel (0969) 22161
Small but comfortable hotel in centre of market town in the heart of Yorkshire Dales. Close to seven golf courses. We specialise in good food and comfortable rooms.

Harewood Arms Hotel
Harrogate Road, Harewood, Nr Leeds, West Yorkshire LS17 9LH.
Tel (0532) 886566   *Fax* (0532) 886064
Ideally located for businessmen and tourists. 7 miles from the commercial centre of Leeds and 7 miles from the Spa town of Harrogate. The hotel is conveniently situated for discovering the charm of the Yorkshire Dales, with an abundance of things to see and do. (See advertisement page 441 for further details.)

Rotherham Moat House Hotel
102-104 Moorgate Road, Rotherham, South Yorks S60 2BG.
Tel (0709) 364902
Friendly 4-star hotel close to M1 and M18. 83 en suite bedrooms with colour TV, tea and coffee-making facilities. Superb restaurant, public bar, leisure club and ample parking. Good golf courses nearby including Lindrick.

North West

Alma Lodge
149 Buxton Road, Stockport, Greater Manchester.
Tel 061-483 4431
Located on the southern edge of Stockport, within easy access to M63, M56, M6 and M62. 58 bedrooms with one suite, all rooms have radio, colour TV, direct dial telephone, hairdryer, tea and coffee-making facilities, etc. Extensive car park. 7 miles from Manchester Airport.

Appleby Manor Country House Hotel
Roman Road, Appleby-in-Westmorland, Cumbria CA16 6JD.
Tel (07683) 51571
Swim, bubble and golf! Enjoy your par 68 on Appleby's 18 moorland holes (5895 yards), then return to your favourite country house hotel for a refreshing swim and a relaxing jacuzzi in the indoor leisure club. Mouth watering meals, too! (See advertisement page 443 for further details.)

Blundellsands Hotel
The Serpentine, Blundellsands, Crosby, Merseyside L23 6TN. 051-924 6515
Situated in a quiet residential area. 43 newly refurbished bedrooms with all modern facilities. The Blundellsands is only 5 miles from the M57 with the Royal Birkdale Golf Course just a short drive away. (See advertisement page 437 for further details.)

Brabyns Hotel
Shaftesbury Avenue, Blackpool, Lancs FY2 9QQ.
Tel (0253) 54263
2-star hotel – open all year. Appointed to high standard. Restaurant offers excellent and varied menus – vegetarian dishes. Choice of golf courses including Royal Lytham. Easy access from M55 – car park. Near Blackpool North Shore.

Calder House Hotel
The Banks, Seascale, Cumbria CA20 1QP.
Tel (09467) 28538
Hotel is adjacent to the 6,416 yards links, Seascale Course, and 100 yards from the beach. Fully furnished double glazed, TV, tea/coffee-making facilities, radio/clock/alarm, direct dial telephone. Fax facilities. Fully licensed. Special Golf Breaks. (See advertisement page 443 for further details.)

Dane Lodge Hotel & Restaurant
Northenden Road, Sale, Cheshire M33 3HB.
Tel 061-973 6666   *Telex* 635091 DANLO
Fax 061-905 2446

A family run hotel giving a warm, friendly atmosphere. All bedrooms are en suite having colour TV, telephone and coffee/tea-making facilities. All sports are well catered for in the area with golf at the fore. Manchester Airport is 10 minutes away.

The Dormy, Lancaster Golf & Country Club Ltd
Ashton Hall, Ashton-with-Stodday, Lancaster LA2 0AJ.
Tel (0524) 751247

Ideal for small parties of up to eighteen persons. For terms and reservations please apply to the secretary. (See advertisement page 437 for further details.)

The Dormy House
Royal Lytham & St Anne's Golf Club, Links Gate, Lytham St Anne's, Lancashire FY8 3LQ.
Tel (0253) 724206

Ideal for small parties wishing to play the championship course. Accommodation for men only. Apply to the secretary. (See advertisement page 435 for further details.)

The Grand Hotel
South Promenade, St Annes-on-Sea, Lancashire FY8 1NB.
Tel (0253) 721288 *Telex* 67481
Fax (0253) 714459

A beautiful Edwardian hotel overlooking the sea front, with 40 individual comfortable bedrooms including four suites, two spa bathrooms and sea view rooms. Elegant restaurant and cocktail bar and informal grand lounge. Within a stroke from Royal Lytham Golf Links. (See advertisement page 437 for further details.)

Holland Hall Hotel
Lafford Lane, Upholland, Lancashire WN8 0QZ.
Tel (0695) 624426

Located minutes away from the M6 motorway, and yet this 17th-century country house is surrounded by the picturesque scenery of South Lancashire. All 34, tastefully furnished bedrooms have bathroom en suite and with two restaurants. We feel sure Holland Hall will be the ideal location.

Metropole Hotel
3 Portland Street, Southport, Merseyside PR8 1LL.
Tel (0704) 536836

RAC/AA 2-star hotel situated within 5 minutes of Royal Birkdale. Fully licensed, full size snooker table, private facilities, special golf terms. Golfing proprietors can assist with golf bookings. Colour brochure on request.

Prince of Wales
Lord Street, Southport PR8 1JS.
Tel (0704) 536688   *Fax* (0704) 543488

Less than an hour's drive from twelve top class golf courses. 98 bedrooms, six suites, two restaurants and famous club house bar. The hotel offers an ideal venue for golfing parties from two to 100 or more. (See advertisement page 435 for further details.)

Shaw Hill Hotel Golf and Country Club
Preston Road, Whittle-Le-Woods, Chorley, Lancashire PR6 7PP.   *Tel* (02572) 69221

RAC/AA 3-star hotel golf and country club. À la carte restaurant. 22 bedrooms, all en suite, overlooking an 18-hole championship course. Special mini break rates available. (See advertisement page 437 for further details.)

The Ship Hotel
The Parade, Parkgate, South Wirral L64 6SA.
Tel 051-336 3931

The Ship Hotel is situated overlooking the Dee Estuary. All bedrooms have private facilities. The Sandpipers Restaurant is renowned for its superb cuisine and friendly service. Pipers Bar is a favourite with locals, serving traditional beers from local brewers.

Shrigley Hall Hotel Golf & Country Club
Shrigley Park, Pott Shrigley, Nr Macclesfield, Cheshire SK10 5SB.
Tel (0625) 575757

4-star country house on the edge of the Peak District, with magnificent views over the 18-hole course to the Cheshire plain below. Adjoining leisure club has swimming pool, squash, snooker, tennis, steam, sauna and solaria.

The Swan
Bucklow Hill, Nr Knutsford, Cheshire WA16 6RD.
Tel (0565) 830295

Well located M6 (J19), M56 (J7) this 70-bedroom 3-star hotel renowned for its cuisine, adjacent to Mere Golf and Country Club, welcomes golfers. Bargain breaks and golf packages.

Isle of Man

Castletown Golf Links Hotel
Derbyhaven, Castletown, Isle of Man.
Tel (0624) 822201
Situated on our own peninsula, our championship golf course of 6,700 yards, with all holes having sea views, is a real test of links golf. The hotel facilities are of a luxurious 3-star standard. (See advertisement page 439 for further details.)

North East

Braeside Guest House
26 Western Hill, (Near Polytechnic), Sunderland SR2 7PH. *Tel* 091-565 4801
Small friendly guest house 2-crown ETB. Theme bedrooms, attractive Victorian lounge, en suite available extra. Tees reserved top local courses; courier accompanies you to different courses daily. Club handicap required. 160 weekly including golf fees. (See Monkwearmouth College page 441 for further details.)

Holmedale Hotel
106 Park Avenue, Whitley Bay, Tyne and Wear NE26 1DN. *Tel* 091-253 1162
Ten golf courses within 10 miles. A family run hotel. Centrally situated. All 18 rooms en suite with tea-making facilities, colour TV, direct dial telephones. TV lounge and fully licensed bar and restaurant. Special weekend rates. (See advertisement page 441 for further details.)

Sheraton Slaley Hall Hotel Golf and Country Club
Slaley, Hexham, Northumberland NE47 0BY.
Tel (0434) 673777
5-star hotel set in 600 acres of wood and parkland in which there is an 18-hole championship sized golf course. Facilities include 140 bedrooms. Superb leisure club, choice of restaurants. Weekend packages available.

Washington Moat House Hotel
Stone Cellar Road, Washington, Tyne and Wear NE37 1PH. *Tel* 091-417 2626
Everything for the golfer, championship 18-hole course, 9-hole par 3, 21-bay floodlit driving range and well stocked pro shop. Hotel accommodation offers superbly appointed bedrooms, restaurant and bars. Snooker, squash and leisure centre with pool.

Scotland

South

Buccleuch and Queensberry Hotel
Drumlanrig Street, Thornhill, Dumfriesshire DG3 5LU. *Tel* (0848) 30215
A warm and friendly hotel. Thornhill Golf Course close by – SSS 70 6124 yards. Other courses within driving distance. Salmon and trout fishing also available. Twelve rooms, nine en suite. Car parking. Highly recommended. AA/RAC listed. (See advertisement page 445 for further details.)

Cally Palace Hotel
Gatehouse of Fleet, Dumfries & Galloway DG7 2DL. *Tel* (0557) 814341
Within the 100-acre policy we provide a tennis court, croquet lawn, putting green, boating/fishing loch, indoor swimming pool, jacuzzi, sauna and solarium. We also provide free golf on three local courses.

Clonyard House Hotel
Colvend, Dalbeattie, Kirkshire DG5 4QW.
Tel (055) 663 372
Family run country hotel in quiet grounds. Excellent restaurant, also informal meals in our lively bar. Ground floor rooms with facilities including direct dial telephones. Four golf courses within a 10 mile radius.

The Fernhill Golf Hotel
Heugh Road, Portpatrick, Nr Stranraer DG9 8TD.
Tel (077 681) 220 *Fax* (077 681) 596
Golf package holidays available throughout the year in this 3-star AA and RAC hotel. Concession golf at the scenic Portpatrick Club and championship Stranraer. Send for illustrated coloured brochure.

Golf Hotel
34 Dirleton Avenue, North Berwick, East Lothian EH39 4BH.
Tel (0620) 2202
Family run hotel ideal for golfers wishing to play any of East Lothian's sixteen courses. Starting times arranged. Lounge bar, TV lounge, rooms with private bathroom and colour TV.

Greywalls
Muirfield, Gullane, East Lothian EH31 2EG.
Tel (0620) 842144
Set in the heart of golf country, ten courses within miles and located overlooking Muirfield. For those who enjoy the best of golf, we provide the best food, comfort and service.

Hopehill House Hotel
off Mayfield Drive, Hawick, Roxburgh.
Tel (0450) 75042
Enjoy the peace and beauty of the Scottish borders. Golf can be arranged at ten courses nearby. Small parties catered for in our comfortable private hotel. En suite available. Close to Scottish knitwear mill shops.

Houstoun House Hotel and Restaurant
Uphall, West Lothian EH52 6JS
Tel (0506) 853831
30 magnificent bedrooms – many with four poster – in this 16th-century house. Excellent dining facilities with only fresh produce used. A central base for your golf holiday. Over 100 courses within one hour's drive. Edinburgh Airport nearby.

Kirroughtree Hotel
Newton Stewart, Galloway, South West Scotland DG8 6AN.
Tel (0671) 2141 *Fax* (0671) 2425
Unlimited free golf at two courses including a championship course. Luxurious country house hotel with finest French cuisine provided by our top continental trained chefs. Please send for details. AA 4-star RAC. (See advertisement page 451 for further details.)

Marine Hotel
Cromwell Road, North Berwick, East Lothian EH39 4LZ.
Tel (0620) 2406
Golfers in North Berwick have a choice of fourteen splendid courses and the superb Marine Hotel overlooks the famous West Links. (See advertisement page 449 for further details.)

Old Waverley Hotel
Princes Street, Edinburgh EH2 2BY.
Tel 031-556 4648
Occupying a prime position on Princes Street, the hotel has unrivalled views across Princes Street Gardens to Edinburgh Castle. Easily accessible to Gullane, Muirfield, Royal Burgess and Bruntsfield.

Peebles Hotel Hydro
Innerleithen Road, Peebles EH45 8LX.
Tel (0721) 20602
Set in 30 acres of private grounds with its own leisure centre, tennis courts, squash, riding, putting green, pitch and putt, snooker room, mini-gym and only 1 mile from golf course.

Portpatrick Hotel
Portpatrick, Nr Stranraer, Wigtownshire, Scotland DG9 8TA.
Tel (077 681) 333
This majestic hotel commands one of the most spectacular sea views in Britain. Three excellent golf courses including Portpatrick and Stranraer where special golf packages are available from 45.00 Dinner, Bed and Breakfast per person. (Including free weekday golf.)

Central

Abbotsford Hotel
Corsehill Road, Ayr.   *Tel* (0292) 261506
"Open golf country' Royal Troon, Old Prestwick, Turnberry. Adjacent to Belleisle and Seafield golf courses, all rooms en suite, colour TV and tea-makers. We will undertake all golf bookings and arrange a package that will suit all grades of golfer. Dinner, bed and breakfast from 33. Society rates. Contact Allan Hunter.

The Ardshiel Hotel
Kilkerran Road, Campbeltown, Argyll.
Tel (0586) 52133
A comfortable small hotel within easy reach of golf course and airport. Golfing packages available.

Balbirnie House Hotel
Balbirnie Park, Markinch, by Glenrothes, Fife KY7 6NE.   *Tel* (0592) 610066
Balbirnie is an elegant 18th-century mansion in a 416 acre park. AA/RAC 4-star, 5-crown Highly Commended STB with 30 rooms/suites. Ideally located for Ladybank, St Andrews, Carnoustie and Balbirnie Park on our doorstep.

Balgeddie House Hotel
Balgeddie Way, Glenrothes (North) KY6 3ET.
Tel (0592) 742511 *Fax* (0592) 621702
Beautifully situated in immaculate gardens with panoramic view over Glenrothes. All bedrooms have private bathrooms, satellite TV, telephone, radio, tea-making facilities. Elegant cocktail bar/restaurant – table d'hôte/à la carte menus. Golf packages arranged. AA/RAC 3-star STB 4-crowns.

Ballathie House Hotel
Kinclaven By Stanley, Perthshire, Scotland PH1 4QN.   *Tel* (025 083) 268
Superb country house hotel within own estate. Perth 20 minutes. Blairgowrie 15 minutes (Rosemount). Luxurious house accommodation: Budget Annexe 3-star accommodation. Putting green, tennis, croquet. STB Highly Commended. See main guides. (See advertisement page 445 for further details.)

Buchanan Highland Hotel
Main Street, Drymen, By Loch Lomond, Stirlingshire G63 0BQ
Tel (0360) 60588

This warm traditional hotel enjoys the attractions of a village setting while being only a short trip from Stirling and Glasgow. Facilities include superb leisure club, golf at Buchanan Castle, Strathendrick, Hilton Park and Aberfoyle, can be arranged.

Caledonian Hotel
Dalblair Road, Ayr, Scotland KA7 1UG.
Tel (0292) 269331

Town centre hotel, with private facilities. Restaurants, bars, swimming pool and leisure club. Try our unlimited Golf Packages with guaranteed starting times on any of our eight local courses. Just call for details – (0292) 269331. (See advertisement page 454 for further details.)

Caledonian Thistle Hotel
Union Terrace, Aberdeen AB9 1HE.
Tel (0224) 640233

80-bedroomed, city centre traditional hotel with an excellent reputation for hospitality, service and cuisine. An ideal base for golfers in the Grampian area who wish a 'Little Extra' from their golfing break special weekend. Rates on request.

Carradale Hotel
Carradale, Argyll PA28 6RY.
Tel (058 33) 223

STB 3-crown commended hotel in idyllic fishing village. All rooms en suite with colour TV etc. Golf on 9-hole course next to hotel, or nearby 18-hole Machrihanish. Own squash courts, sauna and solarium.

County Hotel
32 High Street, Banff, Grampian, Scotland AB4 1AE.
Tel (02612) 5353

Small family run Georgian hotel situated in the historical town of Banff, 5 minutes from Duff House Royal Golf Club. Many other 18-hole courses nearby. Excellent food and service. Special discount rates from October–June.

Dalmunzie House Hotel
Spittal O'Glenshee, Blairgowrie, Perthshire PH10 7QG.　*Tel* (025 085) 224

Set in the Highlands with our own 9-hole course, the highest in Britain. This friendly country house offers an ideal base for a golfing holiday with excellent local courses at Blairgowrie, Pitlochry, Alyth and many more. (See advertisement page 454 for further details.)

Darroch Learg Hotel
Braemar Road, Ballater, Grampian AB35 5UX.
Tel (03397) 55443

The Darroch Learg sits in a high position overlooking the River Dee and Grampian mountains. It is a few minutes from the course at Ballater and convenient for others in the north east of Scotland.

Eight Acres Hotel
Sheriff Mill, Elgin, Moray.
Tel (0343) 543077

Modern 3-star hotel set in landscaped grounds. All rooms with private facilities. Full leisure complex offering swimming pool, squash, gymnasium, sauna, sunbeds, table tennis, snooker etc. Ten golf courses available locally. Special golfing breaks available.

Forest Hills Hotel
The Square, Auchtermuchty, Fife, Scotland.
Tel (0337) 28318

This old inn is situated in the village square, surrounded by rich farming country and forests. Only 25 minutes from St Andrews and close to many golf courses. Candle lit restaurant, all modern facilities. STB 3-crowns.

Gleddoch House
Langbank, Renfrewshire PA14 6YE.
Tel (047 554) 711

Country house hotel overlooking the River Clyde within easy reach of Glasgow and airport. Own golf course (par 72 6,300 yards). Pro shop, club house with own restaurant, bar, sauna, squash and horse riding.

Glencoe Hotel
8 Links Parade, Carnoustie, Angus DD7 7JF.
Tel (0241) 53273

This hotel offers breakfast, coffee, tea, bar lunches and dinner to non-residents and is golf orientated to provide meals to suit tee-off times.

Gleneagles Hotel
Auchterarder, Perthshire PH3 1NF.
Tel (07646) 2231

In addition to four championship golf courses, Gleneagles boasts an indoor sports and leisure complex, tennis courts, the Jackie Stewart Shooting School and, of course, the luxury of Scotland's first and foremost 5-star hotel. (See advertisement page 21 for further details.)

443

443

443

The Golf Hotel
Bank Street, Elie, Fife KY9 1EF.
Tel (0333) 330209   *Fax* (0333) 330381
Outstanding value golf packages inclusive of golf on a wide variety of first class links courses. Twenty five courses within half hour drive (St Andrews only 10 miles away). Good food, '19th Hole', comfortable bedrooms and a warm welcome. (See page 447 for further details.)

The Green Park Hotel
Clumie Bridge Road, Pitlochry, Perthshire PH16 5JY.
Tel (0796) 3248
Country house hotel set in own grounds overlooking Loch Faskally. 37 rooms all en suite. Attractive public rooms. Restaurant table d'hôte & bar meals. Easy access to twenty courses within 35 mile radius.

Hafton Country Club Hotel & Lodges
Dunoon, Argyll PA23 8HP.
Tel (0369) 6205   *Fax* (0369) 6845
Luxury Danish lodges in magnificent lochside setting. All fully equipped kitchens, lounge, bath or shower, colour TV, clock/radio alarm and welcome tea tray. Special golf fees at local Cowal Golf Club – Monday to Friday. Send for our brochure. (See advertisement page 453 for further details.)

Hospitality Inn
Annick Road, Irvine, Ayrshire KA11 4LD.
Tel (0294) 74272
Built around a temperature controlled Hawaiian lagoon this modern hotel offers excellent cuisine in surroundings resembling Tangiers in the 30's. Our own 9-hole golf course, putting green and driving range are currently under construction.

Howard Park Hotel
136 Glasgow Road, Kilmarnock, Ayrshire KA3 1UT.
Tel (0563) 31211
A modern, 46-bedroomed hotel in Kilmarnock. All bedrooms are well appointed with private facilities. The hotel has a welcoming cocktail bar and serves table d'hôte and à la carte meals in the Park Restaurant.

Island Hotel
Shore Road, Brodick, Isle of Arran KA27 8AJ.
Tel (0770) 2585
We cook very good fresh food – game birds, Scotch lamb small carefully chosen wine list. Good whiskies. Clean, comfortable bedrooms.

Seven golf courses on the Island, transport can be arranged to these making a nominal charge. Plenty of car parking space. Very friendly people with personal attention at all times. An old fashioned hotel to eat, drink and relax around a coal fire. (See advertisement page 445 for further details.)

The Kenmore Hotel
Kenmore, Perthshire PH15 2NU.
Tel (08873) 205
Fax (08873) 262
Scotland's oldest inn is uniquely situated on the banks of the river and Loch Tay. We offer modern, comfortable rooms, exciting menus, a fine cellar and our own 18-hole, par 69 Taymouth Castle Golf Course. (See advertisement page 449 for further details.)

Keppoch House Hotel
Perth Road, Crieff, Perthshire PH7 3EQ.
Tel (0764) 4341
The Hotel offers excellent en suite accommodation, fine food and is fully licensed. Only 2 minute walk from Crieff Golf Club with 18 and 9-hole courses. Also the choice of twenty courses within a 20 mile radius.

Killiecrankie Hotel
Pass of Killiecrankie, By Pitlochry, Perthshire.
Tel (0796) 3220
In the heart of Highland Perthshire, the Killiecrankie Hotel sits in four acres of woodland and gardens overlooking the river Garry and the Historic Pass of Killiecrankie. Super food and relaxed atmosphere makes it an ideal base for a golf holiday.

King Malcolm Thistle Hotel
Queensferry Road, Dunfermline, Fife KY11 5DS.
Tel (0383) 722611
20 minutes from Edinburgh City centre this modern 3-star hotel with 48 en suite bedrooms, provides an ideal base for visiting East and Central Scotland, Perth, Dundee, St Andrews. Glasgow only one hour's drive away.

Kinloch Hotel
Blackwaterfoot, Isle of Arran.
Tel (077086) 444
Beside the world's only 12-hole golf course. Breathtaking test of links skill. Six other courses nearby. Swimming pool, tennis, sauna, squash court, solarium. Full en suite facilities. Special golfers' rates.

Kirkton Jean's Hotel
47 Main Street, Kirkoswald, Ayrshire.
Tel (06556) 220

Play golf at the famous Turnberry Golf Course, or any of twenty superb golf courses including Royal Troon, Prestwick and five Open qualifying courses all within 35 minutes. Or visit Culzean Castle and National Park which is nearby. This 18th-century coaching inn situated in the heart of the Burns' country, offers nine twin rooms with en suite showers, colour TV and tea and coffee-making facilities.

Letham Grange
Colliston, by Arbroath DD11 4RL.
Tel (024) 189 373   *Fax* (024) 189 414

20-bedroom Victorian mansion, with 18-hole championship standard golf course, first class facilities set in the heartland of golf. Company/ Society golf outings/breaks welcome. (See advertisement page 454 for further details.)

The Lomond Country Inn
Kinnesswood, Near Kinross, Perthshire KY13 7HN.
Tel (0592 84) 253   *Fax* (0592 84) 693

Friendly inn with 12 good en suite bedrooms. Splendidly situated overlooking Loch Leven and central to the great courses of the Eastern Lowlands. We can arrange your itinerary. Fresh food and real ales in our bar and restaurant overlooking the Loch. (See advertisement page 447 for further details.)

Malin Court
Turnberry, Girvan, Ayrshire KA26 9PB.
Tel (0655) 31457   *Fax* (0655) 31072

Malin Court has recently undergone extensive refurbishment. You may dine in our beautiful restaurant with its breathtaking views of the mystical Isle of Arran. All our bedrooms have private en suite bathrooms and exquisite sea views. (See advertisement page 449 for further details.)

Manor Park Hotel
Monkton, By Prestwick Airport, Ayrshire KA9 2RJ.
Tel (0292) 79365

All rooms have private facilities, telephones, TV and tea/coffee-makers. We are 15 minutes from twelve golf courses, three of which are championship. Our restaurant is 'Above Par'.

Mansion House Hotel
The Haugh, Elgin, Moray IV30 1AW.
Tel (0343) 548811

The Mansion House Hotel offers luxurious accommodation in an imposing mansion close by to many of the regions finest courses. With our gym, swimming pool etc we offer a relaxing base for your golfing holiday.

The Marine Highland Hotel
Troon, Ayrshire, Scotland KA10 6HE.
Tel (0292) 314444   *Telex* 777595
Fax (0292) 316922

Magnificent 4-star hotel overlooking 18th fairway of Royal Troon championship course. It comprises 72 bedrooms and suites, leisure and sports club, conference and banqueting centre, two restaurants and three bars.

Nivingston House Hotel
Cleish, Kinross-shire KY13 7LS.
Tel (05775) 216

Nivingston House Hotel, run by Allan Deeson – a golfing enthusiast – is superbly and centrally located for golfers. Driving net and putting available. Ask for details of many other activities, including fishing, shooting and motor-racing. (See advertisement page 445 for further details.)

Old Manor Hotel
Leven Road, Lundin Links, Fife KY8 6AJ.
Tel (0333) 320368

Hotel and restaurant specialising in golfing societies and short breaks for golfers. Overlooking Lundin Links and Leven golf courses.

The Park Hotel
John Street, Montrose, Angus DD10 8RJ.
Tel (0674) 73415   *Telex* 76367
Fax (0674) 77091

A short distance from Montrose Medal Course. Privately owned hotel, 59 bedrooms all with colour TV and most with private bathrooms. (See advertisement page 451 for further details.)

Parkway Hotel
Abbotshall Road, Kirkcaldy, Fife KY2 5PQ.
Tel (0592) 262143

3-star hotel geared to golfers' needs within 30 minutes' drive of 35 courses including Gleneagles and St Andrews. Superb restaurant serving many specialities and well stocked bar. Two night breaks from 62 per person, Dinner, Bed and Breakfast.

Pitlochry Hydro Hotel
Pitlochry, Perthshire PH16 5JH.
Tel (0796) 2666

Pitlochry – the Gateway to the Highlands – has many activities including the famous Festival Theatre and an excellent 18-hole golf course. Within easy distance are courses at Gleneagles and Blairgowrie (Rosemount).

Queen's Hotel
**Marine Parade, Kiln, Dunoon, Argyll
PA23 8HZ.** *Tel* (0369) 4224
22-bedroomed hotel. Two bars one with pool room. Live music on Saturdays. Restaurant, friendly atmosphere. Close to Championship Cowal Golf Course. Member of local tourist board. Golf parties welcome. (See advertisement page 443 for further details.)

The Queens Hotel
Church Street, Inverkeithing, Fife KY11 1LJ.
Tel (0383) 413075 *Fax* (0383) 416761
Compact family run hotel. Ideally situated for all the major golf courses in Edinburgh and the East of Scotland. Only 1 mile from the Forth Road Bridge and 10 miles from Edinburgh. Golf trips organised. (See advertisement page 447 for further details.)

Rescobie Hotel and Restaurant
**Valley Drive, Leslie, Glenrothes,
Fife KY6 3BQ.**
Tel (0592) 742143
A comfortable country house hotel with eight well equipped bedrooms and an established reputation locally for excellent food. Positioned centrally between Carnoustie, Dalmahoy, Gleneagles and St Andrews. There are 100 golf courses within easy driving range.

Riverview Guest House
Edenside, By St Andrews, Scotland.
Tel (0334) 838009
Fax (0334) 838808
Riverview, a new guest house, overlooking the quiet Eden Estuary, within 5 minutes drive of St Andrews. All rooms en suite. Riverview will tailor a short or long stay golfing holiday to your requirements.

Rosemount Golf Hotel
**Golf Course Road, Blairgowrie,
Perthshire PH10 6LJ.**
Tel (0250) 2604
Rosemount (and Lansdowne) close by St Andrews, Ladybank, Carnoustie and 75 others all within easy reach. We have 12 en suite rooms, two self-catering cottages in lovely gardens. AA/RAC 2-star, STB 3-crowns commended.

St Andrews Golf Hotel
St Andrews, Fife KY16 9AS.
Tel (0334) 72611
Fax (0334) 2188
Most comfortable, traditional Scottish hotel (all bedrooms en suite). Fine restaurant. Extensive cellar. On the seafront 200 yards from the 'Old Course'. Let us arrange your golf in Scotland.

St Andrews Old Course Hotel
Old Station Road, St Andrews, Fife KY16 9SP.
Tel (0334) 74371
Adjacent to the famous 17th Road Hole, the hotel has 125 deluxe bedrooms, two restaurants, conference and banqueting facilities for up to 200 and a health spa with a pool, exercise room, steam rooms and a variety of body treatments and massages.

The Scores Hotel
The Scores, St Andrews, Fife, Scotland.
Tel (0334) 72451
Overlooking St Andrews Bay and the Royal & Ancient Club House, this famous 3-star hotel is only yards from the 1st tee of the Old Course. Facilities include 30 en suite bedrooms, restaurant, coffee shop and bars. Golfing packages available.

Stakis Earl Grey Hotel
Earl Grey Place, Dundee DD1 4DE.
Tel (0382) 29271
Luxury hotel located within 45 minutes of fifty major golf courses with St Andrews and Carnoustie on the doorstep. Car park and leisure facilities available. Special golfing holidays available.

Station Hotel
Station Road, Carnoustie, Angus DD7 6AR.
Tel (0241) 52447
Close to Carnoustie championship course, Burnside and Buddon, this hotel is ideal for golfers. Family run, meals temptingly served with ample portions, rooms with shower en suite, colour TV. Public and lounge bars. Friendly atmosphere.

Turnberry Hotel and Golf Courses
Ayrshire KA26 9LT.
Tel (0655) 31000 *Telex* 777779
Fax (0655) 31706
Situated overlooking Scotland's south west Ayrshire coast. Within its 360 acres are a luxury hotel, golf and leisure resort with few equals in the world.

Woodland Holidays in Kincaple
Kincaple Lodge, St Andrews, Fife KY16 9SH.
Tel (0334) 85217
Fax (0334) 77802
Nine Scandinavian lodges in peaceful country setting. Two and a half miles from St Andrews. Ideal base for your self-catering holiday. All linen included, colour TV, tennis court, golf practice area, home cooking available. Further information and colour brochure contact Pam Smith.

North

Alton Burn Hotel
Alton Burn Road, Nairn IV12 5ND.
Tel (0667) 52051
Superb family run hotel overlooking Nairn Golf Course, with many courses a short drive away. All 27 bedrooms – private facilities, teamakers, TV's. Special rates for golfing parties. We can arrange tee times etc for you.

Burghfield House Hotel
Dornoch, Sutherland IV25 3HN.
Tel (0862) 810212
42-bedroom country house hotel a few minutes from the golf course. Superb restaurant. Golf packages on Royal Dornoch and nearby courses.

Clifton House
Nairn, Scotland IV12 4HW.
Tel (0667) 53119 *Fax* (0667) 52836
Having been 'home' to the owner for fifty nine years, Clifton has a high standard to maintain and welcomes all those who appreciate good food and wines. It is small, elegant, charming and very personal.

Columba House Hotel
Manse Road, Kingussie,
Inverness-shire PH21 1JF.
Tel (0540) 661402
Enjoy your favourite sport in the beautiful Spey Valley. Stay in the family run hotel or self-cater in luxury cottages. AA/RAC 2-star. Licensed. Colour brochure. Golf packages. Your comfort and enjoyment is our priority.

Craigard Country House Hotel
Kinchurdy Road, Boat of Garten,
Inverness-shire.
Tel (047 983) 206
Situated overlooking Boat of Garten Golf Course. Small family run country house hotel ideally placed for a golfing holiday. Within easy reach of six local courses. Excellent cuisine served by friendly local staff. Golf packages and parties arranged. (See advertisement page 453 for further details.)

Dornoch Castle
Dornoch, Sutherland IV25 3SD.
Tel (0862) 810216 *Fax* (0862) 810981
Formerly a Bishop's palace, the hotel has 19 bedrooms. The panelled cocktail bar, elegant lounge and Bishop's Room restaurant overlook historic Dornoch Cathedral. AA, RAC, STB commended 3-crowns. (See advertisement page 453 for further details.

Greenlawns
13 Seafield Street, Nairn IV12 4HG.
Tel (0667) 52738
Greenlawns is situated close to golf courses, beaches, bowling greens, tennis/squash courts, swimming pool, riding stables and fishing. Within easy reach of Loch Ness, Cawdor and Brodie Castles, Culloden Battlefield. An ideal centre for touring Northern Scotland.

Royal Golf Hotel
Grange Road, Dornoch, Sutherland IV25 3LG.
Tel (0862) 810283
The Royal Golf Hotel sits in the ideal position overlooking Royal Dornoch Golf Course, one of the ten best natural courses in the world. Club house and 1st tee 25 yards from front door.

Seafield Lodge Hotel
Woodside Avenue, Grantown-on-Spey PH26 3JN.
Tel (0479) 2152   *Fax* (0479) 2340
STB 4-crowns commended. A 2-star hotel run by the resident proprietors Julie and Peter Miller. Too small for coaches, yet large enough to provide a good restaurant and comfortable lounge bar, where a cosmopolitan group of sportsmen congregate. The subject of a major refurbishment, all rooms now boast private bathrooms, colour TV, tea-making equipment and direct dial telephones. Two luxury suites, with sitting rooms and jacuzzis!

Sutherland Arms Hotel
Lairg, Sutherland IV27 4AT.
Tel (0549) 2291
This attractive country hotel is ideal for the golfer – Royal Dornoch offering championship golf in a magnificent coastal setting and the challenging courses at Golspie and Brora are all within a 35 minute drive.

Wales

South & South West

Belle Vue Royal Hotel
The Promenade, Aberystwyth, Dyfed.
Tel (0970) 617558
Fax (0970) 612190
Situated on the seafront overlooking Cardigan Bay. Free golf at Aberystwyth Golf Club (Monday to Friday) available to residents, half green fees at weekends. Getaway breaks available for individuals or parties.

The Cawdor Arms Hotel
Llandeilo, Dyfed,
South West Wales SA19 6EN.
Tel (0558) 823500
Original 18th-century coaching inn set in
beautiful Vale of Towy. Individually furnished
bedrooms all en suite, excellent and imaginative
food. Ashburnham Championship Golf Course
within short distance, Glenhir close by. Fishing
and shooting available. AA/RAC 3-star.

Cliff Hotel (Gwbert) Ltd
Gwbert-on-Sea, Cardigan, Dyfed.
Tel (0239) 613241
AA/RAC 3-star hotel with its many leisure
facilities is surrounded by its own 9-hole course
on cliffs overlooking Cardigan Bay. The 18-hole
Cardigan Golf Course is only half a mile away.

Fairways Hotel
Seafront, Porthcawl,
Mid Glamorgan CF36 3LS.
Tel (065671) 2085/3544
'Fairways' overlooks the Bristol Channel and is
situated within walking distance of the main
shopping centre. 28 en suite bedrooms with colour
TV's, direct dial telephones and many other private
facilities. Near Royal Porthcawl, Pyle & Kenfig, and
Southerndown golf courses (18-hole). Table d'hôte
and full à la carte menu available. Licensed bars.
Five minutes off the M4, junction 27. (See
advertisement page 447 for further details.)

George Hotel
Moor Street, Chepstow, Gwent.
Tel (0291) 625363
A traditional, friendly hotel in a prime position at
the top of Chepstow High Street adjoining the
medieval port wall, and 16th-century town gate.
Located 3 miles from St Pierre Golf Club and
6 miles from Dewstow. All rooms en suite with
colour TV, direct dial telephone and tea and
coffee-making facilities.

Heronston Hotel
Ewenny, Bridgend,
Mid-Glamorgan CF35 5AW.
Tel (0656) 68811
4 miles off M4. Three championship courses
within 3 miles of Hotel. Indoor and outdoor
heated swimming pools with sauna, steam room,
solarium and jacuzzi. Transport can be
arranged to various activities. Special terms for
weekend breaks. (See advertisement page 456
for further details.)

Hildebrand Hotel
Victoria Street, Tenby, South Pembrokeshire,
Dyfed SA70 7DY.
Tel (0834) 2403
The Hildebrand is conveniently situated close to
Tenby Golf Course and South Beach. Your
experienced resident hosts, Veronica and Jim
Martin have looked after golfers and holiday
makers for two decades, so fully appreciate
your requirements.

The King's Head Hotel
Agincourt Square, Monmouth,
Gwent NP5 3DY.
Tel (0600) 2177
Fax (0600) 3545
Golf breaks 145.00 per person. Two-day
package includes: Dinner, room with bath,
English breakfast and green fees. Golf at Rolls of
Monmouth course offers fair test for players of
all standards in parkland surroundings. (See
advertisement page 456 for further details.)

St Pierre Hotel Golf & Country Club
Chepstow, Gwent NP6 6YA
Tel (0291) 625261
14th-century mansion house, comprising
148 bedrooms, en suite facilities and leisure
club including swimming pool, squash,
badminton, tennis, snooker, spa bath, sauna,
steamroom, gymnasium, health and beauty
salon, and crown green bowling with restaurants
and bars.

Wentloog Resort Hotel
Castleton, Nr Cardiff, Gwent CF3 8UQ.
Tel (0633) 680591
Ideally situated 4 minutes from M4 the Wentloog
Resort Hotel is comfortably furnished to a very
high standard. 'Poachers' Restaurant offers high
quality cuisine with a traditional flavour.
Excellent access to several local golf clubs.

North

Bryn Morfydd Hotel
Llanrhaeadr, Nr Denbigh, Clwyd LL16 4NP.
Tel (074578) 280
Country house hotel nestling on the hillside
overlooking the Vale of Clwyd and the Clwydian
range beyond. Residents enjoy free use of our
9-hole course. There are three 18-hole courses
within a 10 mile radius. (See advertisement
page 456 for further details.)

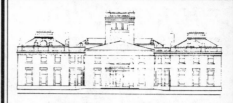

Deganwy Castle Hotel
Deganwy, Conwy, Gwynedd LL31 9DA.
Tel (0492) 583555
Situated within 2 miles of Conwy, North Wales
and Maesdu courses. The hotel has 32 en suite
rooms and a first class reputation for its food and
bars. Special golfing breaks available.

Deucoch Hotel
Abersoch, Pwllheli, Gwynedd LL53 7LD.
Tel (075 881) 2680
AA/RAC 2-star, Ashley Courtenay
recommended. Informal, family run hotel
offering golf packages to include dinner, bed,
breakfast and green fees at Pwllheli, Nefyn,
Porthmadog and Abersoch golf courses.
Bedrooms en suite. Fine collection of rare malt
whiskies.

The Harbour Hotel
Aberdovey, Gwynedd LL35 0EP.
Tel (0654) 767250
A charming family run hotel, painstakingly
restored, in the centre of Aberdovey's
picturesque seafront. The emphasis throughout
is on quality, attention to detail, hospitality and
value for money. Golf parties a speciality.
Quotations on request.

Hotel 70°
**Penmaenhead, Old Colwyn, Colwyn Bay,
Clwyd LL29 9LD.**
Tel (0492) 516555
Fax (0492) 515565
Luxury modern hotel situated on the cliff tops
with breathtaking views. Each of the 44
bedrooms has every modern facility. Superb
award winning restaurant. (See advertisement
page 456 for further details.)

Trearddur Bay Hotel
Trearddur Bay, Holyhead, Anglesey.
Tel (0407) 860 301
Excellent facilities at this prestigeous 3-star
establishment including indoor heated
swimming pool and superb '19th hole' in the
residents bar with over 80 malts and blended

whiskies. Holyhead course 1 mile away plus
three other golf courses within 15 miles. Open
all year.

Trefeddian Hotel
Aberdovey, Gwynedd, Wales LL35 0SB.
Tel (065 472) 213
3-star hotel with 46 rooms all with bath or
shower en suite, central heating, telephone and
colour TV. Indoor pool, putting green, tennis
court, games room. Overlooks the golf links and
sea. Reduced golfers green fee details and hotel
colour brochure sent on request.

Channel Islands

La Place Hotel
Route De L'Isle, La Haule, St Brelade, Jersey.
Tel (0534) 44261
Outdoor swimming pool, sun patio. Soigné
Restaurant/Bar. (See advertisement page 425 for
further details.)

Les Arches Hotel
Archirondel, Gorey, St Martin, Jersey.
Tel (0534) 53839
Fax (0534) 56660
Overlooking France. Private access to beach.
All rooms en suite with TV. One and a half miles
from Royal Jersey Golf Club. Swimming pool,
garden, tennis court, golf net, night club, sauna,
mini-gym and bars.

Ireland

Aghadoe Heights Hotel
Killarney, County Kerry, Ireland.
Tel (064) 31766
Comfort, good food and personalised service
are the keynotes of this luxury 4-star hotel with
its renowned rooftop restaurant. The perfect
golfer's base for playing Ireland's premier
courses such as Killarney, Tralee, Ballybunion
and Waterville.

Buyer's Guide to Good Golfing and Golf Course Maintenance

This compact but informative guide to manufacturers and organisations offering services to Golf Clubs and individual golfers has once again been expanded to include a greater number of categories. The editors do not necessarily endorse the information supplied.

Club Consultancy & Training Courses

Club Management Services
50 Town Street, Duffield, Derby DE6 4GG.
Tel (0332) 840075
Provision of training courses in Golf Club Management. Existing correspondence courses for Secretary/Managers and Stewards. Management consultancy and staff recruitment for golf clubs in Great Britain and in Europe. Expert golf club advisory service.

Course Guides

Above Par Publications
Mill Studio, Crane Mead, Ware, Hertfordshire SG12 9PY.
Tel (0920) 444238   *Fax* (0920) 464464
Publishers of quality 'Course Guides' providing an additional service for the club, a useful and informative handbook for the golfer and a vast and influential audience for the advertiser.

Driving Range Equipment

Range Servant UK Golf Marketing Ltd
8 Chard Close, Woodley, Reading RG5 4HU.
Tel (0734) 695952
Suppliers of machinery for driving ranges and practice areas. Also stance mats and ancillary products. (See advertisement page 463 for further details.)

Universal Materials Co Ltd
5-7 High Street, Dorchester-on-Thames, Oxfordshire OX9 8HH.
Tel (0865) 341580   *Fax* (0865) 341575
Probably the widest choice of mats for driving ranges, winter tees and practice grounds, including the ever-popular 'Astro Turf', together with the Easy-Picker ball harvester and ball washer and the Par T Golf simulator. A consultancy service is also available.

Driving Ranges & Leisure Complexes

Delapre Golf Complex
Eagle Drive, Nene Valley Way, Northampton NN4 0DU.
Tel (0604) 764036
18-hole course SS 70, 2 Par three courses, Pitch and Putt, 44-bay covered driving range. Bar and restaurant facilities. Municipal complex, societies welcome. John Corby golf shop. PGA professional staff available for teaching.

Gosforth Park Golfing Complex Ltd
High Gosforth Park, Newcastle-upon-Tyne.
Tel (091) 236 4480
The Complex has an 18-hole golf course, 30-bay floodlit driving range, 9-hole Pitch and Putt course and putting green. Also pro shop, bar and restaurant. Open to non-members.

Event Organisers

3D Golf Promotion plc
62 Carcluie Crescent, Ayrshire KA7 4SZ.
Tel (0292) 42206/ 43989   *Telex* 776483
Fax (0292) 42617
UK's NO 1 GOLF SPECIALIST PGA approved

organisers of overseas Pro-Am series. Golf Tuition weeks and Golf School series with the UK' S TOP teachers, home and abroad. FULL COLOUR BROCHURE AVAILABLE.

Footwear

Stylo Matchmakers International Ltd
Clayton Wood Bank, Leeds LS16 6RJ.
Tel (0532) 783501
Manufacturers of the Faldo collection of golf shoes, also Stylo Gore-tex and the world famous range of Stylo waterproof shoes. Range includes golf trousers, sweaters, T-shirts, waterproof suits and a range of golf bags.

Golf Accessory Suppliers

Dunlop Golf Division
PO Box 8, Normanton,
West Yorkshire WF6 1YX.
Tel (0924) 896868
Manufacturers of golf balls (Maxfli DDH 500 Tour Ltd MD, Maxfli 65 and Powermax) and golf clubs under the Maxfli brand. A wide range of bags, gloves, holdalls, umbrellas and accessories are also available.

Slazenger Golf Division
P O Box 8, Normanton,
West Yorkshire WF6 1YX.
Tel (0924) 896868
Slazenger manufacture a range of stylish equipment. Balls include 480 Interlok balata, surlyn and two piece. Clubs include Silver Panther, Seve Ballesteros forged irons; Slazenger Persimmon, Black Panther and XTC. Stylish bags, luggage and accessories to complement the range.

Spida Golf
Cornwall House, Falkland Close,
Charter Avenue Industrial Estate,
Canley, Coventry, West Midlands CV4 8AU.
Tel (0203) 464377
Manufacturer of golf bags, headcovers, ball bags and holdalls etc. Supplier of a full range of equipment and accessories – from clubs to tees – in a professionally presented format including specially designed display stands.

Tanaka of Japan
Unit 4, Hambridge Lane Industrial Estate,
Newbury, Berks.
Tel (0635) 550666
High technology wood heads of various materials eg persimmon, graphite, laminates, or 17.4 metals, which can be fitted with various types of shafts and grips, to match forged or investment cast irons. Putters, golf bags and accessories are also available.

Golf Ball Manufacturers

Dunlop Golf Division
P O Box 8, Normanton,
West Yorkshire WF6 1YX.
Tel (0924) 896868
Manufacturers of golf balls (Maxfli DDH 500 Tour Ltd MD, Maxfli 65 and Powermax) and golf clubs under the Maxfli brand. A wide range of bags, gloves, holdalls, umbrellas and accessories are also available.

Kestrel Products Ltd
Unit 34, Cwmdu Estate, Skewen, Neath,
West Glamorgan SA10 6RP.
Tel (0792) 817884   *Fax* (0792) 816585
One piece golf balls and rubber tees for ranges and golf mats. Includes low bounce for crazy golf, mid-compression for ranges and practice and high-compression for higher handicap golfers and up-market ranges.

Slazenger Golf Division
PO Box 8, Normanton, West Yorkshire WF6 1YX.
Tel (0924) 896868
Slazenger manufacture a range of stylish equipment. Balls include 480 Interlok balata, surlyn and two piece. Clubs include Silver Panther, Seve Ballesteros forged irons; Slazenger Persimmon, Black Panther and XTC. Stylish bags, luggage and accessories to complement the range.

Golf Carts, Trolleys and Buggies

Mitsui Machinery Sales (UK) Ltd
Oakcroft Road, Chessington, Surrey KT9 1SA.
Tel 081-397 5111
Suppliers of top selling Yamaha golf car. Available through a national network of distributors. Various schemes include purchase or seasonal hire contracts to clubs, also sales to individuals.

HAWTREE

GOLF COURSE ARCHITECTS
Since 1912

5 OXFORD STREET, WOODSTOCK, OXFORD, OX7 1TQ.
TEL: (0993) 811976 TELEX: 837853 MIMO G FAX: (0993) 812448

Founder Members: British Association of Golf Course Architects.

MACMILLAN GOLF MAILING SERVICE

Macmillan can supply golf club mailing lists, tailored to your requirements and ready-printed on adhesive labels, at a cost of £120 per 1000 addresses.

For further details contact:
Penny Warren
The Macmillan Press Ltd
Stockton House
1 Melbourne Place
London WC2B 4LF
Tel: 071 836 6633   Fax: 071 379 4980

DEREK BURRIDGE
(Wholesale) Limited
General Wholesale Distributors

SUPPLIERS TO GOLF CLUBS AND SOCIETIES
FOR PRIZES AND PRESENTATIONS
AT WHOLESALE TERMS
5-11 Hanbury Road,
Acton, W3 8RF.
Telephone: 081-992-5948 & 7313
Fax: 081-993-4814
Send For Catalogue

Golf Clothing and Rainwear

Sunderland Sportswear Ltd
PO Box 14, Glasgow G2 1ER.
Tel 041-552 3261   *Fax* 041-552 8518
Sunderland Sportswear manufacture high quality golf rainwear in Scotland, all rainsuits are tour tested and guaranteed waterproof, a variety of fabrics including Gore-tex and Vent-x being used. Official supplier to PGA, LPGA and WPGET.

Golf Club & Equipment Manufacturers

Ben Hogan (UK) Ltd
21 Cratfield Road, Bury St Edmunds, Suffolk IP32 7DF.
Tel (0284) 752152   *Fax* (0284) 753114
Hogan continue to expand their range of top quality golf equipment. Balls, woods and irons, including the revolutionary Hogan Edge, an expanded bag and accessory range and sportswear for all ages of golfer, emphasise that Hogan is a total golf company.

Bronty Golf Co Ltd
81 Bradford Road, Stanningley, Pudsey, West Yorks LS28 6AT.
Tel (0532) 577266
Manufacturers of high quality British made custom golf clubs, putters and specialist clubs. Authentic replicas and hickory shafted putters etc. (See advertisement page 463 for further details.)

Browning Sports Ltd
37d Milton Trading Estate, Milton, Abingdon, Oxon OX14 4RT.
Tel (0235) 833939
Browning are established manufacturers of quality clubs, bags and accessories. Club ranges to suit all standards of play include Classic Forged, Tour Class, Mirage, Lady Mirage, DP900, Eclipse and Premier Plus.

Clive Crisell
Unit 4, Moat Lodge Industrial Estate, Stock Chase, Maldon CM9 7AA.
Tel (0621) 858510
Well established company offering specialised services to golfers by manufacturing hand crafted Persimmon woods to suit your personal requirements. Full repair and refurbishment includes regripping, reshafting, loft and lie alterations, regrinding and polishing woods.

(See advertisement page 459 for further details.)

Confidence Golf Ltd
Brook Farm, Linstead Parva, Nr Halesworth, Suffolk IP19 0LA.
Tel (098 685) 332   *Fax* (098 685) 485
Golf club manufacturers offering a range of models across the price and design range from forging to starter set and including two game improvement models. Play with 'Confidence' – you can' t win without it!

J B Halley & Co Ltd
2/3 Charterhouse Square, London EC1M 6ES.
Tel 071-253 5581   *Fax* 071-250 1528
Manufacturers of golf clubs and accessories for over 100 years. Over 90% of our equipment is British made and we supply 76 countries around the world.

Hymec Backspin Ltd
Omega, Gipsy Lane, Wokingham, Berks RG11 2HP.
Tel (0734) 780558
Golf tools and special devices used in golf equipment manufacture.

Pro Drive Golf Ltd
Ocean House, West Quay Road, Southampton SO1 0GY.
Tel (0703) 233030
Manufacturers of the Pro Drive range of golf clubs and accessories. Also sole distributor in UK for the 'Orient Win' shaft from Japan and the 'Alloy 2000' shaft from the USA. Best selling models include Tempest, Powersole, Monaco, Powertrac, Enforcer, Ultimate and Dynamo. (See advertisement page 459 for further details.)

Slazenger Golf Division
P O Box 8, Normanton, West Yorkshire WF6 1YX.
Tel (0924) 896868
Slazenger manufacture a range of stylish equipment. Balls include 480 Interlok balata, surlyn and two piece. Clubs include Silver Panther, Seve Ballesteros forged irons; Slazenger Persimmon, Black Panther and XTC. Stylish bags, luggage and accessories to complement the range.

Slotline Golf Europe Ltd
Largo Road, St Andrews, Fife KY16 8NJ.
Tel (0334) 77017   *Fax* (0334) 75950
Call Free 0800 83 33 77 Manufacturers of INERTIAL and CLASSIC PUTTERS, INERTIAL II,

DOMINATOR, SENIOR MASTER, COPPER CLASSIC and LADY RAMPANT IRONS and WOODS. Free advice and customisation service always available from professional staff.

Spalding Sports UK Ltd
16 Trafalgar Way, Bar Hill, Cambridge CB3 8SQ.
Tel (0954) 781672
Spalding Sports UK Ltd is the UK distributor of the world's largest general sports company. We supply all major golf professionals with a complete range of golfing equipment including the Top Flite and Tour Edition brands.

Swilken Golf Company Ltd
Tom Stewart Works, Tom Stewart Lane, St Andrews, Scotland KY16 8XW.
Tel (0334) 72266
A dedicated Scottish manufacturer which has established itself as a producer of quality golf clubs; Alta, Icon, Vision and Tournament GI in the game improvement range, plus the new TF 270 classic blades. Swilken also distribute Dexter shoes in the UK.

Taylor Made (Great Britain) Ltd
Annecy House, Gastons Wood, Reading Road, Basingstoke, Hants RG24 0TW.
Tel (0256) 479797   *Fax* (0256) 479357
Taylor Made metalwoods continue to be the number one choice of touring professionals. The comprehensive range of metalwoods are complemented by new ICWS and ICW11 irons and putters. New style bags.

Yamaha UK (IMS Ltd)
545-549 Wallisdown Road, Poole, Dorset BH12 5AD.
Tel (0202) 538877
UK distributors for Yamaha golf equipment featuring an extensive range of men's and ladies' graphite clubs, left handed clubs, bags and headcovers.

Golf Course Architects

British Association of Golf Course Architects
Hon Secretary, 5 Oxford Street, Woodstock, Oxford OX7 1TQ.
Tel (0993) 811976
Professional Association of qualified golf course architects officially recognised by the Royal & Ancient and English Golf Union.

Golf Development International NV
(Joan F Dudok Van Heel)
Chaussée de Waterloo 68, B-1640 Rhode St Genese, Belgium.
Tel (02) 358 3387
Architecture, design and construction – supervision of golf courses. Consultancy on golf course and club management. Feasibility studies – promoting and developing the game of golf.

Hamilton Stutt & Co
12 Bingham Avenue, Poole, Dorset BH14 8NE.
Tel (0202) 708406
Founder member of the British Association of Golf Course Architects. One of Europe's most experienced golf architects. Personal attention to each new project - only a limited number accepted each year.

Hawtree
5 Oxford Street, Woodstock, Oxford OX7 1TQ.
Tel (0993) 811976   *Fax* (0993) 812448
Telex 837853 MIMO G
Hawtree celebrates 78 years of golf architectural service throughout the world. (See advertisement page 465 for further details.)

John Jacobs Golf Associates Ltd
68a High Street, Walkern, Stevenage, Herts SG2 7PG.
Tel (0438) 861438   *Fax* (0438) 861788
Golf course architects/consultants offering a complete service from initial concept, through design to project management and on-going maintenance. A highly experienced company whose designs reach across the board from public golf centres to the highly acclaimed Edinburgh course at Wentworth. JJGA also manufactures its own golf driving bay. (See advertisement page 4 for further details.)

Golf Course Maintenance

John Jacobs Golf Associates Ltd
68a High Street, Walkern, Stevenage, Herts SG2 7PG.
Tel (0438) 861438   *Fax* (0438) 861788
The Company is highly experienced in greenkeeping methods, including advice on the choice of grasses most suitable for different

soils and environments. JJGA also provides a full maintenance service to run in parallel with its design and other operations, thus ensuring that courses are kept in the best possible condition at all times. (See advertisement page 4 for further details.)

Ransomes Sims & Jefferies Ltd
Ransomes Way, Ipswich,
Suffolk IP9 3QG.
Tel (0473) 270000
Ransomes offer the widest range of high performance grass cutting and turf maintenance machinery, from the mowing of golf greens, tees and fairways to a comprehensive turf management system from aeration to top dressing. (See advertisement page 32 for further details.)

Watermation Ltd
Tongham Road, Aldershot, Hants GU12 4AA.
Tel (0252) 336838
Manufacturers and installers of top quality golf course irrigation equipment including computer controllers and heavy duty pop-up sprinklers. Installations on hundreds of top quality courses around the UK and mainland Europe.

Golf Course Project Management

International Golfers Club
49 Queen Victoria Street, London EC4N 4SA.
Tel 071-248 4435   *Fax* 071-236 6779
Working with clubs across Europe enabling them to manage their facilities more effectively. Greenkeeping Consultancy in association with BIGGA and our development and consultancy arm, International Leisure Management, geared to meet needs of players, club management and investors. We give professional help from feasibility studies for projects at early stages, through to complete management of golf course and leisure resorts.

International Resort Holdings (Development Services) Ltd
New Lodge, Collingtree Park, Northampton.
Tel (0604) 760182
Golf Course Development Services, Project Management, Design & Build, Grow-in Service, Master Planning, Project Feasibility. (See advertisement page 459 for further details.)

John Jacobs Golf Associates Ltd
68a High Street, Walkern, Stevenage, Herts
SG2 7PG.
Tel (0438) 861438   *Fax* (0438) 861788
The speed of modern golf course construction calls for special skills to ensure that quality is maintained throughout each project and that a client' s interests and investments are protected. JJGA' s project management team was set up for this purpose and with its proven track record can provide a service geared to very high standards of operation. (See advertisement page 4 for further details.)

Golf Financial Services

Golf Plus - Golf Financial Services Ltd
308-314 Kings Road, Reading,
Berkshire RG1 4PA.
Tel (0734) 61022   *Telex* 848511
Fax (0734) 662237
Golf Plus, the credit card designed exclusively for golfers. Approved by the PGA, Golf Plus offers members a comprehensive range of golfing services and benefits through the Golf Plus Club.

Golf Holidays

Meridian Holidays
12-16 Dering Street,
London W1R 9AE.
Tel 071-493 2777
Choose Meridian for over ten years experience in arranging golf holiday packages in Europe. Self-catering or hotel holidays in France, Spain or Portugal with value and style. ABTA/ IATA/ ATOL.

Golf Practice Equipment

Carpetition Limited
14 Kaffir Road, Edgerton, Huddersfield,
West Yorks HD2 2AN.
Tel (0484) 428777
'Tufturf' artificial grass sports surfaces are manufactured by Carpetition Ltd. 'Tufturf' golf tee mats are ideal for practice and may be seen on golf courses throughout the UK and overseas. 'Tufturf' putting material provides ideal indoor putting greens. (See advertisement page 463 for further details.)

Evergreen Products Ltd
Curtis Road, Dorking, Surrey RH4 1XD.
Tel (0306) 881546

The financing, design and building of golf
courses and driving ranges undertaken.
Manufacturers of Portarange golf nets made to
size. Golf mats, frames and artificial greens for
golf courses and driving ranges also
manufactured.

Universal Materials Co Ltd
5-7 High Street, Dorchester-on-Thames,
Oxfordshire OX9 8HH.
Tel (0865) 341580   *Fax* (0865) 341575

Probably the widest choice of mats for driving
ranges, winter tees and practice grounds,
including the ever-popular 'Astro Turf',
together with the Easy-Picker ball harvester and
ball washer and the Par T Golf simulator. A
consultancy service is also available.

Golfing Gifts & Novelties

Another Gift Idea Co
Virginia Mills, Higher Hillgate, Stockport,
Cheshire SK1 3JG.
Tel 061-480 8991

Supply of golfing gifts to golf professionals and
retailers. Portfolio includes exclusive lines from
US, Japan and Far East. Products include the
Sipper, Staco Survivors, Its-a-Lock, and English
bone china figurines.

Baxter Prints
Carseview, Culbowie Crescent, Buchlyvie,
Stirling, Scotland FK8 3NH.
Tel (0360) 85 410   *Fax* (0360) 85 360

Publishers of fine limited and open edition prints
of championship courses of Scotland, England,
Ireland and USA from the original oil paintings of
Graeme W Baxter.

Central Sales and Marketing Ltd
13 Grosvenor Gardens,
London SW1W 0BD.
Tel 071-828 2469

Distributors of Walt Disney golfing goods – club
covers, golf balls and towels. Novelty gifts for
the golfer such as 3-dimensional golf ice cubes,
ice buckets and glasses. New, high quality
designer club covers.

Golfing Tuition

Peter Ballingall Golf School
Barnham Broom Hotel Golf and Country Club
Norwich, Norfolk.
Tel (060 545) 393

Residential golf schools where clients,
regardless of experience, can improve their golf
on a three, four or five day course with Peter
Ballingall, one of the premier teachers of the
game. (See advertisement page 433 for further
details.)

Headwear and Embroidery

David Allan & Co Ltd
(Dept GH) Unit 8, 2 North Avenue,
Clydebank Business Park, Glasgow,
Scotland G81 2DR.
Tel 041-941 3133   *Fax* 041-951 1827

We are the European distributor of Kangol
headwear and offer a complete embroidery
service onto this comprehensive range of
ladies' and gents' hats. The Company also
manufacture casual jackets and sweatshirts.

Irrigation Equipment & Installation

Watermation Ltd
Tongham Road, Aldershot, Hants GU12 4AA.
Tel (0252) 336838

Manufacturers and installers of top quality golf
course irrigation equipment including computer
controllers and heavy duty pop-up sprinklers.
Installations on hundreds of top quality courses
around the UK and mainland Europe.

Professional Bodies

**British Association of Golf Course
Architects**
Hon Secretary, 5 Oxford Street, Woodstock,
Oxford OX7 1TQ.
Tel (0993) 811976

Professional Association of qualified golf course
architects officially recognised by the Royal &
Ancient and English Golf Union.

IRH (DEVELOPMENT SERVICES) LTD

FOR GOLF RELATED PROJECTS WORLDWIDE
- PROJECT MANAGEMENT - MASTER PLANNING -
- DESIGN & BUILD -
GROW-IN SERVICE - PROJECT FEASIBILITY

Contact us at:

EDINBURGH OFFICE:
21 Manor Place
Edinburgh, EH3 7DX
Tel: 031-220 1707
Fax: 031-220 1626

NORTHAMPTON OFFICE:
New Lodge, Collingtree Park
Northampton, NN4 0HT
Tel: 0604 760182
Fax: 0604 765273

Score Cards

Eagle Promotions
93 Church Road, Upper Norwood,
London SE19 2TA.
Tel 081-771 7321
Specialist producers of top quality colour score
cards on behalf of over 450 UK golf clubs. We
have built a reputation for offering a total
service covering all aspects of score card
design.

Suppliers of Golf Awards & Prizes

Derek Burridge Trophies
5-11 Hanbury Road, Acton, London W3 8RF.
Tel 081-992 5948/7313   *Fax* 081-993 4814
The country's leading suppliers of golf prizes.
We offer a vast range of silver plate, crystal,
china, clocks, leather goods and sporting
trophies, all at trade prices. Glass and silver
plate in-house engraving service. (See
advertisement page 465 for further details.)

Trade Suppliers

Golf Equip (GB) Ltd
Gladonian Road, Littlehampton,
West Sussex BN17 6JW.
Tel (0903) 724500
Manufacturers of golf course and range
equipment. Specialist in heavy duty machinery
and mats. All requirements and advice for golf
ranges and practice centres. Trade sales only.
(See advertisement page 463 for further
details.)

Index of Advertisers

Part IV
Clubs and Courses in the British Isles and Europe

1991 Centenary Clubs

Laurence Viney

England

Bedfordshire

Bedfordshire Golf Club started life in 1891 as plain Bedford Golf Club on fields near Brickfield Farm, with the doubtful security of a four-year lease on acreage big enough to provide only 9 holes. By 1895 an alternative site was found in its present course at Biddenham, and an 18-hole course of some 5200 yards was designed, the holes varying in length from 90 to 425 yards. A further 12 acres were soon acquired, all flattish and virtually treeless.

The hazards then, as now, were the hedges bounding the course, the London-Manchester railway (there are many stories of stupendous drives from the 7th tee to be measured in miles), a cart track, a pond (still a water hazard whether there is water in it or not), ditches, turf and sand bunkers. No trees. Not then. Now, several thousand virtually line if not totally enclose every hole.

In the 1920s the Club was asked by the County Golf Union to change its name to Bedfordshire to avoid confusion with another club which had by then established itself.

Captain 1991: M V Macdonald
Secretary: T Nutt
Professional: Gary Buckle

Bolton

The local Bolton newspaper for 25 September 1891 reported that the previous evening 'an influential meeting of Bolton Gentlemen' had taken place at a local hostelry with a view to the formation of a golf club for Bolton. Officials were appointed; the annual subscription fixed at one guinea; and two weeks later the first competition took place on land adjacent to the local cricket club.

The very complete records of the Club indicate that enthusiasm for the game quickly rendered such makeshift facilities unsatisfactory and, before the end of the century, sufficient land

for 9 holes had been rented from a local farmer in Smithills. Difficulties between the farmer and the Club on the relative priorities of a hay crop and good fairways sparked off a search for a suitable area of land which the club might purchase. That objective was achieved by the acquisition of Lostock Park Farm, whence the club moved in 1912.

Despite the attractions and relative proximity of the great Lancashire seaside links the Lostock course is of a golfing quality which has hosted the county championships for both men and ladies as well as county matches. Recent appreciable expenditure on the clubhouse now provides all members of Bolton Golf Club with playing and social facilities of which they are justifiably proud.

Captain 1991: Geoffrey Proffit
Secretary: Harry Cook
Professional: R Longworth

Bolton Old Links

Founded in 1891 as Bolton Golf Club (see above), and closely connected with Bolton Cricket Club, it soon outgrew the available land and moved some 3 miles to the west of the town.

When in 1912 more land was required, there was disagreement and some members bought land about a mile away, taking the name with them. The remaining members bought land adjacent to the existing course and employed Dr Alastair Mackenzie to lay out an excellent moorland course, which is virtually unchanged today, as the Old Links, Bolton. From the course, which rises to 800 feet above sea level, there are magnificent views over the South Lancashire Plain, to the Welsh Mountains and the hills of Derbyshire.

Several professional competitions have been held on this course (SSS 72) and in 1990 it was the venue of the English Girls' Championship. The Club has produced several notable amateurs, and takes pride in its encouragement of juniors.

Captain 1991: D W Johnson, Jr
Secretary: E Monaghan
Professional: P Horridge

Bradford

Founded by the St Andrews Society of Bradford, who were mostly Scots, the Club at first played over 9 holes at Baildon Moor. In 1893 Tom Morris Sr planned 9 more holes for a fee of one guinea plus travel expenses. The Club then changed its name to Bradford and in 1899 moved a few miles to its present site at Hawksworth where a new Clubhouse was opened in 1900 by A J Balfour, MP Leader of the House.

Bradford has played a prominent part in the Yorkshire Union: eight members have been President; Men's and Ladies' teams have each won the county team championships on five occasions, and three men and four lady members have won their county championships.

In national events E A Lassen won the Amateur Championship at Sandwich in 1908, but the outstanding man player from Bradford has been Rodney Foster, who played in five Walker Cups, was twice Captain and represented Great Britain and Ireland for many years. Kathryn Phillips was twice in the Curtis Cup team and Gillian Hickson (Mrs Wilkinson) has done much for county golf and been Chairman of ELGA.

The Club's Hawksworth Trophy, started in 1971, is a leading north country open amateur event, which draws the best players for 36 holes medal play each year.

Captain 1991: Michael Ellison
Secretary: Peter Atkinson
Professional: Sydney Weldon

Bridport & West Dorset

The Bridport & West Dorset Club was formed by a small group of industrialists and professional men in February 1891, Bridport being the capital of the country's net and twine industry in those days.

By 1912 the Club had grown and moved from the west side of the Brit Valley to its present site: a fine 18-hole golf course which was laid out on the east side of the West Bay cliff top. It overlooks West Bay harbour, the River Brit with its reeds and swans, Chesil Beach and the striking East Cliff formation.

One of the most popular features is the 13th hole – as pretty as it is deceptive. The sunken green lies about 70 feet below the tee and is well guarded all around by natural hazards and bunkers. Members call this hole 'Port Coombe'. The 365 yard 16th is famous for the exhibition match in 1952 in which Max Faulkner teed his ball on two tee pegs. His drive not only cleared the dry stone wall which cuts across the fairway some 60 or so yards in front of the flag, but finished 10 feet past the pin. However, 'Bridport is

no pushover,' said Max, 'it takes a good golfer to break the 66 par.'

In 1989, 44 acres of farmland adjoining the course were purchased by the Club, and plans for extending and improving the course and facilities are now in hand.

Captain 1991: Frank Jessop
Secretary: Peter Ridler
Professional: John Parish

Bristol & Clifton

Many of the founder members started to play golf at Clifton Downs Golf Club, a 9-hole municipal course in Bristol, but this was soon to become inconvenient, if not hazardous, to the public. At the inaugural meeting in February 1891, the newly appointed committee were authorised to find a suitable alternative. 100 acres of parkland at Failand were rented for £20 pa with the initial course of 9 holes. Additional land, sufficient to promise 18 holes, was leased in March 1896 and the course remained in that style until 1944 when the remainder of the land was purchased for £7,000.

Requisition of land during the war meant the loss of three holes subsequently replaced in a design by CK Cotton & Co. which reversed the order of play, the old first hole becoming the tenth.

With an SSS of 70 it is a good test of golf and is located in a lovely peaceful setting, complimented by the Clubhouse which retains much of its original character. Trees are a feature of the course and a budget provision for this continues each year.

Captain 1991: Ted Jackson
Managing Secretary: Cdr Peter Woollings RN
Professional: Peter Mawson

Bude & North Cornwall

The first golf course at Bude was built in 1891 by a group of retired admirals, generals and diplomats. The course architect was Tom Dunn, who came down from Scotland to lay out a first-class 18-hole course on land previously known as Summerleaze Downs, owned by Mr Thynne who leased the ground to the Club. A certain amount of opposition came from non-golfers who had previously been allowed free access to the 'Downs'.

In 1893, the Club, in return for a long-term lease, undertook to spend £300 on the erection of a Clubhouse and that a further £200-£300 be spent within a period of five years should the progress of the Club warrant it. While a large

part of the Clubhouse remains the same a number of improvements and extensions have taken place over the years.

Captain 1991: R Thomas
Secretary: PK Brown
Professional: J Yeo

Burnham Beeches

Burnham Beeches Golf Club, the oldest in Buckinghamshire, is set in the beech woods, some 25 miles west of London, which gave the Club its name. It is a setting once described by the golf writer Tom Scott as 'having a dignity and beauty which could hardly be surpassed.'

The Club was founded in October 1891. Most of the first members had fashionable addresses in London – it is estimated that one in ten had a title – but today most of the 700 on the register live within a ten-mile radius and are a more representative cross-section of society. It is very much a 'member's club' with the players in charge of its destiny.

Many people have been involved in the design of the course, including JH Taylor and Fred Hawtree. Today it measures 6463 yards and is a testing par 70 (SSS 71). The record of 64 is held jointly by Harry Flatman and Brian Barnes.

Famous names to have graced the course over the years include the Great Triumvirate of Braid, Taylor and Vardon and other Open winners such as George Duncan and Dick Burton. More recent visitors have included Seve Ballesteros and Bernhard Langer.

President of the Club is Lt. Col. Lord Burnham, whose family has been associated with the course since the 1890s.

Captain (to March 1991): RS Cox
Captain-designate (from April 1991): JJ Wisdom
Manager/Professional: AJ Buckner

Clitheroe

The Club was founded in 1891 and consisted originally of 9 holes. The Club changed the location of the course on several occasions, but in 1930 it purchased the land of the present site. James Braid was engaged to design and construct 16 holes, the other two being the responsibility of the Club's green staff. The new course was opened in July 1932, with a new Clubhouse donated by the brothers R and J Southworth in memory of their father, a founder member.

The Club has prospered over the years and in 1965 some reconstruction work took place to bring the 9th hole back to the vicinity of the Clubhouse. The alterations were celebrated with an exhibition match by Michael Bonallack, Dr David Marsh, Joe Carr and Clive Clark, all of whom

became honorary members.

Popular with visiting societies, the generally undulating terrain with tree-lined fairways, excellent water hazards and extensive rural views provide a delightful testing course, on which the Club has been host to several county and regional championships. The EGU Champion of Champions and President's Trophy Tournaments are to be held here in 1991.

Captain 1991: M Thompson
Secretary: JB Kay
Professional: Peter Geddes

Dewsbury District

Dewsbury was one of several clubs in Yorkshire to be founded in 1891, following a few in previous years. The Club is fortunate, indeed unusual, that it has all its minute books, the first entry being the formation of the Club in a Dewsbury café in October that year.

The owner of the land which the Committee selected, EB Wheatley-Balme, designated an area named 'The Pinnacle' to be used and the following month Old Tom Morris arrived in the town from St Andrews to lay out nine holes. He also made arrangements to sell clubs and balls to new members at 10 per cent discount. No doubt play began directly he had finished, as the intrepid Victorians usually played immediately the positions of the greens had been decided. It was often on common or heathland for which the necessity for cutting grass was minimal.

Nine years later Ted Ray, then at Ganton, planned a further 9 holes which were opened in October 1906.

The first Clubhouse was in a nearby farm. The second, a pavilion, cost £47.10s, and lasted eight years; finally in 1913 the present Clubhouse was built. It has been much extended since.

Captain 1991: Gordon Petrie
Secretary: Peter Croft
Professional: Nigel Hirst

Didsbury Golf Club

Didsbury Golf Club, in Northenden, Manchester, was formed in April 1891, as a 9-hole course; the local station-master's house acted as a clubroom. An early visitor was Harry Vardon, on the occasion of the first 36-hole professional competition in the area in 1894. The club moved to its present site, across the river Mersey in 1885, and purchased the extra land (the famous 'Promised Land') twenty-six years later, for an 18-hole course.

Among the traumas that the Club has survived over the years are a fire which destroyed the Clubhouse in 1907, severe flooding of the course

and Clubhouse in 1931, 1964 and twice in 1973, before the river banks were strengthened, plus the construction of the M63 motorway, which effectively cut the course into two, the parts now joined by a footbridge.

However, the cheerful resilience of Didsbury's members has stood the Club in good stead, and recent expansion has brought the provision of new locker rooms, a new pro's shop, and probably the UK's largest greenkeeping machinery building. Add to this a most scenic parkland course of 6273 yards and Didsbury has a complex of which its forebears of 100 years ago would indeed be proud.

Captain 1991: GB Thomson
Secretary: B Turnbull
Professional: Peter Barber

Ganton

This great course, which has many of the characteristics of a seaside links, is ten miles inland from Scarborough, nestling beneath the Yorkshire Wolds. Many leading championships, tournaments and matches, both national and international have been played at Ganton. It has deep links-style bunkers, much gorse, turf to be envied and a tough finish which daunts the best.

The pattern of holes has remained largely unchanged for many years, although the list of designers and golf architects, who have laid out, altered and adjusted the course over its first six decades, could hardly be more distinguished – Tom Dunn, Harry Vardon, James Braid, Harry Colt, Herbert Fowler, Cecil Hutchison and Kenneth Cotton. Few courses can claim such a heritage.

Ganton is inevitably linked in its early days with two Open Champions, who both cut their teeth as professionals at the Club – Harry Vardon and Ted Ray. Vardon won his first three Opens while attached to Ganton, before his move to South Herts. Although Ray had moved on to Oxhey when he won in 1912 at Muirfield, he followed Vardon at Ganton, remaining there until 1911. Vardon also won the US Championship in 1900 (Ray was second) and was indisputably the best golfer in the world during those years. He brought the Club fame as no one else could have done.

Ganton remains a premier English Club and course. It has been host to many leading events, including the British Men's and Ladies' Amateur Championships, the European Women's Team Championship, the English Amateur (on five occasions) and the 1949 Ryder Cup. In this match the British led 3–1 after the foursomes, but the Americans stormed back taking six singles, several by large margins, to win 7–5, to the dismay of the British. In the English Amateur in 1968

Michael Bonallack contested a remarkable final against Michael Kelley of the home Club, whom he beat 12 & 11. He was round the first 18 holes in 62 with every putt holed.

In its centenary year the British Amateur Championship will be played at Ganton in September for the third time.

Captain 1991: Iain Breese
Secretary: Air Vice-Marshal RG Price
Professional: G Brown

Grange Park, St Helens

In 1891 the Hoylake Professional Jack Morris (nephew of 'Old Tom' of St Andrews) was engaged to lay out 9 holes on land at Grange Park Farm. The course was opened by Sir Henry Seton Karr, MP for St Helens, the first president of the Club. The founder Captain was BB Glover whose grandson George Lacey (a member since 1920) is the club's oldest member.

In 1901 the Club almost died. For payment of £25 it allowed the Royal Lancashire Agricultural Show to be held on the course, but preparing for the show and extensive damage caused by a large attendance during bad weather prevented play during most of the summer and resulted in mass resignations. The restoration of Club and course was led by Dr William Challenor, who in 1905 was elected the first Life Member in recognition of his efforts.

A further 9 holes were added in 1913 and the new 18-hole course was opened by Harry Vardon and Ted Ray.

The new holes were lost in the First World War and the original 9 holes were taken for housing development shortly afterwards, but were replaced by the present course which was leased from Pilkington Brothers Ltd. In 1968 Pilkington sold the course to the Club on generous terms including the payment of a yearly rent of 'a red rose at midsummer', which each year is collected by the Chairman of Pilkington personally from the Club Captain in a ceremony at the Club.

The Club's best known golfer was probably JW (Jackie) Jones, leading Amateur in Bobby Locke's 1952 Open at Lytham and whose invitation to the Masters at Augusta is displayed in the Clubhouse.

Captain 1991: Arthur J Crick
Secretary: David A Wood
Professional: Paul Evans

Hartley Wintney

Hartley Wintney Golf Club was founded in the early 1890s and is a 9-hole parkland course situated close to the centre of the village. From very modest beginnings the history of the Club has

been one of continuous development as golfing needs have grown.

The name Hartley Wintney commemorates the deer that William the Conqueror hunted in the area after 1066; later King John was to pass through the village on his way to a meeting of an early Rules Committee at Runnymede.

Hartley Wintney's 9 holes are fitted neatly into a generally rectangular area of undulating parkland. Apart from the 1st and 10th, each hole is played from a separate tee, providing all categories of golfer with a succession of interesting challenges. The 18 hole yardage exceeds 6000 with a par of 70 and is made up of three par 5s – the longest being 535 yards – ten par 4s and five par 3s of between 139 and 230 yards.

Captain 1991: G Howse
Secretary: BD Powell
Professional: Martin Smith

Henbury

The first meeting at Henbury was in December 1891, but attempts to play the game had been in progress on Coombe Hill before that date. Within a year 48 men and women members were enrolled, making accommodation imperative. The Secretary's report explained how this was achieved: 'An iron hut has been erected on Coombe Hill by public subscription and instead of being in debt, as is the case of most young Clubs, we have in hand a balance of £3 7s 10 d.'

In 1894 two additional fields were acquired with the idea of having separate courses for men and women and to accommodate more players. A new Clubhouse replaced the iron hut at a cost of £119 8s 6d and John Pople of Burnham and Berrow was engaged as Professional. In 1907 the course was extended to 18 holes, but nine were sacrificed in the First World War. They were recovered and redesigned in 1920.

Eleven years later members bought the land and Henbury flourished as a picturesque and accessible Bristol Club, three miles from the city centre and across lovely rolling downs. The old pavilion-type bungalow, a typical English sporting palace, lasted until a new Clubhouse replaced it in 1959. The course is an ample test for all comers at 6059 yards with an SSS of 70.

Captain 1991: Bill Naish
Secretary: John Leeming
Professional: Nick Riley

Hunstanton

The north Norfolk coast has a succession of fine courses instituted in 1891–3, and Hunstanton is recognised as one of the best.

The course was laid out by George Fernie,

who had difficult ground from which to conjure a respectable course. This he achieved in no small measure, to be improved later by James Braid, who decided more bunkers were necessary and placed them with cunning. The present course is little changed from the result of Braid's survey. It is an 'out and in' course with the 9th hole as far from the Clubhouse as one goes, similar to Brancaster just along the coast. The route out is on the land, between the small river Hun, and the second nine generally hug the sea-shore, but with two short holes facing the opposite way from the others to provide variety.

There is ample evidence that Hunstanton is highly regarded by the LGU and other golfing unions. The British Ladies' has been played here on five occasions, the first in 1914 when Cecil Leitch beat Gladys Ravenscroft by 2 & 1. Memorable too was Jessie Valentine's third win in 1958 by 1 hole over Elizabeth Price. The English men have played the Match Play at Hunstanton in 1931 (winner Leonard Crawley), 1951 (Geoffrey Roberts) and 1960, when Doug Sewell beat Martin Christmas at the 41st hole in an epic match . The Brabazon English Stroke Play was here in 1966 (Peter Townsend, just before he turned professional), 1973 (R Revell) and in 1980 which saw the tied result between Peter McEvoy and Ronan Rafferty. Happily the Brabazon returns to Hunstanton this centenary year.

The winners of the English Ladies' Match Play have been Joyce Wethered in 1922, Bridget Jackson 1950, Sally Barber (*née* Bonallack) 1968 and Claire Waite 1984. Both the Mens' and Ladies' Inter-County Championships have been here in 1931 and 1922 respectively.

Hunstanton is not a rival of its near neighbour, the Royal West Norfolk at Brancaster, a few miles along the coast to the west; rather the two are complementary. It is a greener course than Brancaster and less subtle perhaps, but its challenge may well be greater and it is more suited to championships. Together they host the popular Foursomes Tournament for the Grafton-Morrish Cup of the Public Schools Old Boys Golfing Society.

Captain: David C Pull
Secretary: RH Cotton
Professional: J Carter

Kendal Golf Club

The Kendal Club was formed in 1891 and play was over the disused racecourse situated high above the town. The course of 12 holes, beaten firm by much galloping, provided several beautiful greens.

In 1900 there were two Clubs in Kendal – the Kendal Golf Club and the Cunswick Golf Club, sporting a modest 9 holes. Both courses were somewhat inaccessible and in 1897 the

Cunswick Club obtained a lease of about 88 acres of land belonging to the town. There a Clubhouse was erected and membership increased rapidly. Meanwhile the original Club on the racecourse was declining and finally in 1907 closed its course. The younger and more energetic Club absorbed the membership and took the name of Kendal Golf Club.

During its formative years the Club flourished under GE Moser, who was the Club's first President, and BJ Lawlor who had learned his golf at St Andrews and was for a long time the Club's only scratch player.

History records the name of Thomas Haslam who was Secretary from 1901 to 1949 and Treasurer from 1921 to 1952. No amount of work or trouble was too much for him. He probably contributed more to the success of the Club than any other person.

Captain 1991: W Philip
Manager: RE Maunder
Hon Secretary: EF Millar
Professional: D Turner

Kettering

It was due to the initiative and enthusiasm of Dr J Allison, who came to Kettering from Edinburgh, that golf was introduced to Kettering and a golf club formed in the year 1891. Kettering Golf Club was the pioneer club of the county.

Land owned by the Duke of Buccleuch was rented and a 9-hole course was laid out under the advice of Old Tom Morris of St Andrews.

In 1894 the first professional match in the county was contested between JH Taylor who was then commencing his great golfing career and Hugh Kirkaldy, who was the professional to Oxford University. This match was arranged to celebrate the extension of the course to a full 18 holes. In the same year ladies were first admitted to play on the course.

Since those times the Club has developed into one of the most popular courses in the county and in the centenary year will be hosting the County Championship.

Captain 1991: Barry Althorpe
Secretary: John Galt
Professional: Kevin Theobald

Knutsford

Knutsford Golf Club formed in 1891, when Lord Egerton of Tatton allowed a number of his 'lesser neighbours' to play the 9-hole course that he had laid out in his park. The Lords of Tatton continued to be landlords and benefactors of the Club, as well as successive Presidents, until the last Lord Egerton died in 1958, when the members were

fortunate enough to buy both Clubhouse and course from the estate.

In early years the Club was very much 'cap in hand' to the incumbent of the Hall, though increasingly independent after 1909, when the first President died, and the course was moved slightly to be out of sight of the Hall. The Clubhouse, also acquired in 1909, began life as a School for Young Ladies.

The Club is now a private members' Club, with a pleasant and well thought-of 10 holes and active membership in all categories.

Captain 1991: Alan Johnson
Secretary: Derek Francis
Professional: Alan Gillies

Lincoln

Lincoln Golf Club was founded on common land at the Carholme, just west of Lincoln. A 9-hole course was laid out by Willie Park Jr of Musselburgh but in 1903 it was decided to move the course to Torksey, some twelve miles north-west of Lincoln.

JH Taylor, five times Open Champion, was engaged to lay out a 9-hole course. He considered that the land chosen was ideal for making a 'really good sporting course.' Further land was leased and the 18-hole course was formally opened on 12 May 1909.

Numerous alterations and extensions have been made to the course over the years but the overall concept is still today very much as JH Taylor conceived it. The Club and course have always been considered as one of the foremost in Lincolnshire, with many important national and midland events played there. The course measures 6438 yards with an SSS of 71. Membership today totals over 700.

Captain 1991: John Pumfrey
Secretary: Douglas Boag
Professional: Ashley Carter

Lindrick

Lindrick was founded at a meeting in Sheffield in July 1891 and five gentlemen were given the task of 'inspecting grounds that may be considered suitable for a Golf Links'. Later in the month they reported back that they believed Lindrick Common to be the most suitable and it was resolved that the 'Links be opened at Lindrick Common and that the Entrance Fee and Annual Subscription should each be one guinea.'

The original course of 9 holes was laid out by Tom Dunn and were said by Ben Sayers to be 'the longest 9 holes in the United Kingdom' which is perhaps explained by the 3rd being 750 yards long, bogey 8. By 1894 the course was 18 holes

and was nominated as one of the four courses on which the County Championship was to be held, the others being Ganton, Fixby (Huddersfield) and Redcar.

Lindrick has been the scene of many amateur and professional championships and matches, the most memorable being the 1957 Ryder Cup, in which the British team were victorious with a final 7½–4½, having been 1–3 down after the foursomes.

The course is always in demand, the Club having played host to the Ladies' British Open, Dunhill Masters, the Curtis Cup, British Youths, English Seniors and many Yorkshire County mens and ladies championships.

Captain 1991: G Cheetham
Secretary: G Bywater
Professional: P Cowen

Maldon

In November 1891 local dignitaries met at Maldon to form a golf club. Officers were appointed, with EE Bentall as the first Captain, who was later Honorary Secretary for several years. The ground selected for the course was meadowland lying between the Chelmer canal and the tidal river Blackwater on the edge of the historic hamlet of Beeleigh. A 9-hole course measuring 2185 yards was laid out on this convenient site five minutes' walk from Maldon East railway station.

The course was lengthened in 1904 and the greens enlarged, but it remains a 9-hole course with two separate tee positions for each hole. Twice round the 9 holes is today 6197 yards, SSS 69, par 71. The Clubhouse was refurbished in 1979, since when other improvements to the course and Clubhouse have been made.

Maldon has had two long-serving profession-

als, Walter James (1902–35) and Frank Smith (1962–85).

Captain 1991: John Pook
Secretary: GR Bezant

Northwood

The Club was formed in April 1891, soon after Mr CC Forster Dickson had noticed the disused brickfield that was owned by a sand-merchant.

Tom Dunn laid out the first 9 holes for £3.3s and when another 9 holes were added at the turn of the century its most famous hole – the 10th, known as Death and Glory – was retained.

The Club quickly expanded from the early days, when members used a hawthorn tree to hang their hats before a round. Because the Club was relatively close to Harley Street many members came from the medical profession and for a time it was known as the Pill Club.

After laying out 18 holes, erecting the initial Clubhouse and surviving two wars the most significant changes occurred from 1970. A new Clubhouse was built, the operation financed with a new debenture issue, and improvements to Clubhouse and course have been unprecedented in the last twenty years.

Northwood Golf Club is recognised as one of the best parkland courses in Middlesex, a location once known as the Gravel Pit being transformed into 6493 yards of golfing territory where British and US Open champion Tony Jacklin won his first professional title.

Captain 1991: AJ Severn
Secretary RA Bond
Professional: CJ Holdsworth

Painswick

On 1 December 1891 a circular appeared in the *Painswick Annual Register* inviting ladies and gentlemen to join the Painswick Golf Club, which had been formed on 8 October. This is believed to be the first mention of the Club, whose course had been laid out that year by David Brown of Malvern. By the following year, membership had risen to 32 and it was described as a very successful Club. The first recorded competition was the Spring Foursomes held in 1893. This event still takes place, nowadays as a knock-out competition.

The course lies on common land on and around Painswick Beacon, a prehistoric Bronze Age fort, later used by the Romans, stone from which was used to build Gloucester Cathedral in the twelfth century. Evidence of these and other former occupations remain as effective natural hazards.

The first Clubhouse was the Royal William

Hotel, near the existing 9th tee. Later, the Painswick Cemetery Lodge provided shelter for the members and, the present Clubhouse in mellow Cotswold stone was opened in 1985.

Still a comparatively small Club of some 350 members, all its officers are honorary and it has no professional.

Captain 1991: Ron Baldwin
Secretary: Jack May

Pleasington

In September 1890 Fred Marwood of Pleasington Lodge invited George Lowe, the Lytham professional, to lay out an 18-hole course on land alongside the railway at Pleasington. Lowe advised that a start should be made with 9 holes: this advice was accepted the following year and play began and the Club was formed with a membership of 35.

Early on the Club encountered difficulties over land tenure, course maintenance and inadequate Clubhouse facilities; in 1903 the Club was on the point of being closed. However, it recovered to build a new Clubhouse in 1910 and at the same time new land was acquired on which Sandy Herd laid out further holes to provide the full 18.

War in 1914 temporarily halted the Club's progress, but in 1920 and again in 1929 new holes were designed on adjoining land which gave the course more length. At the same time the Clubhouse was extended to provide accommodation for the ladies' section, which had grown rapidly.

Minor changes to the course occurred again in 1933 when the purchase of a small parcel of land near the Clubhouse allowed several holes to be altered to give a length today, following further changes in 1976, of 6417 yards, SSS 71.

Captain 1991: K Hornby
Secretary: L Ingham
Professional: CJ Furey

Ramsey, Isle Of Man

Ramsey was the first golf club to be formed on the island, in September 1891. The original 9-hole links was laid out at Minetown to a design by Tom Morris Sr on which Willie Park Jr set the then record score of 44 in 1892. The course was extended by James Braid in 1928.

The course is now in a parkland setting within the town of Ramsey, a mile and a half from the sea. It is 6019 yards, opens with a par 5 of 515 yards and, unusually, finishes with two par 3s: the 17th has a lake behind the green and the 18th needs a very accurate tee-shot on to a plateau green. The professional record is 65 by Sandy Lyle.

Traditionally Ramsey has always welcomed

visitors, especially to the Golf Week in early August, which opens with the Ramsey Town Cup, which has been played since 1892. Visitors will appreciate the Clubhouse extensions completed last year.

Captain 1991: Denis McGurgan
Secretary: Mrs SJ Burchall
Professional: P Lowrey

Richmond

Richmond Club's first course, of 9 holes, was at the Old Deer Park, but after six weeks the farmer decided golfers and livestock were incompatible and the new Club successfully leased Sudbrook Park, Petersham, from the Crown. Within a year 200 members were playing an 18-hole course which remains substantially unchanged one hundred years on.

The magnificent early Georgian Sudbrook Mansion, built by James Gibbs for the Duke of Argyll in 1723, is as fine a Clubhouse as there is in the country. The 30 feet cube dining room is one of only three in the United Kingdom. The Club appreciates its responsibility for the upkeep of the listed building.

In its early days the Club had many members among the peerage and aristocracy, including five Dukes, three Lords Chancellor, the Bishop of London, King Manuel of Portugal and a Prince of Schleswig Holstein. The Club has enjoyed a long association with the Royal Family; apart from two of the earlier Dukes, King George VI, as Duke of York, was Captain in 1924 and the Queen Mother has long been an Honorary Member, as were Prince and Princess Arthur of Connaught.

Today's membership is strong in representatives of the law, medicine and the City. The Sudbrook Ladies Golfing Association, founded in 1962, is flourishing and there are numerous mixed events available.

An enclosed course such as Richmond is not suitable for staging important tournaments although early on, in 1896, a professional com-

petition attracted JH Taylor, Willie Park, James Braid, Harry Vardon, Alex Herd and Ben Sayers.

Captain 1991: Paul de Biase
Secretary: JF Stocker
Professional: Nick Job

Rochester & Cobham

The Club formed in 1891 and was an amalgamation of two golf clubs, one on the lower marshland area at Higham, and the other at Borstal. The present site at Park Pale, Cobham, was leased to the Club by the Earl of Darnley in the 1920s. To this day, the Earl is the President of the Club even though the course was purchased outright from his estate in 1985.

The present Clubhouse was built in 1980 and the most rewarding feature for the members, apart from the obviously improved facilities, was that the long walk to the then 1st tee on the other side of the motorway (now the 2nd tee) was eliminated. Indeed, before the old A2 road was widened and a bridge provided, members had to cross the A2 Dover Road on foot with clubs on back or trollies in tow, a very dangerous occupation. Amazingly there are no records of any casualties.

The course itself is one of undulating parkland of challenging dimensions and acknowledged as one of Kent's finest. Each hole differs and requires an accurate drive placing to derive the best advantage. The wind direction can vary daily and thus the course presents a different challenge almost every time it is played.

Captain 1991: GR Dyer
Manager: JW Irvine
Professional: Matt Henderson

Rookery Park

Golf was played at Lowestoft before 1891, but that year the Council agreed to lease land on the 'Denes' foreshore for 9 holes.

Unable to obtain a long lease, having to share some of the land with local fishermen drying their nets and lack of protection from the intruding sea encouraged the golfers to move south of the town in 1906, to play on 9 holes laid out at Pakefield. A further 3 holes were added in 1912. James Braid designed more holes after the Second World War and the full 18 were opened with an exhibition match by Braid and Harry Vardon in 1924. A ladies' section and Artisan's Club were started a year later, the Artisan's amalgamating with the Men's Club in the 1960s.

An anti-aircraft battery stationed on the course and part of the land commandeered for allotments during the war meant little golf was possible until rehabilitation in the mid-1950s

when the Club came fully alive again; it lasted until the early 1970s when a relief road was routed through the course. New land had to be purchased and the present course and Clubhouse were opened in 1976.

The new course was designed by Charles Lawrie and renamed Rookery Park Golf Club. There are now 900 members and plans are in hand for 9 more holes to supplement the present 7000 yards 18, with a 9-hole par 3 course in addition for juniors.

Captain 1991: J Corbett
Professional: MJ Elsworthy

Rothbury

In its life the Rothbury Club has played golf in three different areas near the village. The first, soon after its foundation in December 1891, was at Wolves Haugh, west of the village close by the river Coquet; this course soon fell into disuse in favour of one at Whitton Farm on hilly country to the south. Harry Vardon and James Braid played an exhibition match here in 1913. Since 1951 the course has returned to the riverside, with a new layout of holes and a Clubhouse dating from 1967.

Membership never rose above 100 before 1970, but it has increased steadily to the 300 it is today, with active Ladies and Junior sections. The Club has enjoyed long service from several honorary officers, including R Donkin (Captain 1911 and 1934), N Snaith (Treasurer 1913–41) and JR Soulsby (Secretary for 57 years, 1932-79). The oldest playing member, K Davison, joined the Club in 1925.

Captain 1991/Secretary: WT Bathgate

Rugby

While golf was played on the Rugby course in November 1890, the Club itself was not formed until the following year with a membership of 40. The course was laid out on much the same ground as today's, between the LMS main line to the south and the Oxford Canal to the north, with a wide stream in the middle as a hazard at several holes. The nearby Dunsmore Club amalgamated with Rugby in 1916.

In 1941 three holes were commandeered for agriculture, but in 1949 the remaining 15 holes were altered to accommodate 18, under the supervision of James Braid. Eight years later the Clubhouse was rebuilt after a fire and since then new buildings have been added to provide a professional's shop and other amenities.

The course, at 5457 yards, is short by today's standards, with an SSS of 67 and par of 68, but to equal or better them is never easy. Since 1922

only two professionals have served the Club, Jim Beaumont (1922–68) and David Sutherland since. Membership is limited to 550.

Captain 1991: P Duncan
Secretary: B Poxon
Professional: D Sutherland

Sheringham

Sheringham, together with other Clubs on the north Norfolk coast, was founded with the advent of the local railway line. The ubiquitous Tom Dunn laid out 9 holes in 1891, and these were extended to 18 in 1898. Dunn's caddie, Ernest Riseboro, then aged 13, became the Club's professional until he retired in 1956. In his time he did eighteen holes-in-one and there was no hole on the course which he had not holed in two or under! His successor, Michael Leeder, retires this year. Nearly 100 years with only two professionals is a proud record, if not unique. Long service is a characteristic of the Club: Herbert Craske was appointed Clerk in 1903 and continued as Secretary from 1912 to 1973, giving 69 years of sterling service.

The English Ladies' Championship, held at Sheringham in 1920 and 1950, will again be played there this year. The 19-year-old Joyce Wethered won in 1920 when, by own admission, there occurred the well-known 'What train?' story, when she holed a vital putt as a train puffed by. In the early years Taylor, Vardon and Braid played exhibition matches here, while recent pro-am events have included Gary Player, Lee Trevino, Sandy Lyle, and Neil Coles.

Captain 1991: RW Maris
Secretary: MJ Garrett
Professional: MT Leeder

Sidcup

Sidcup Golf Club was instituted in October 1891 and first listed in *The Golfing Annual* of 1892. The first Captain was DT Barker and the first President was Sir John Pender, KCMG,MP. In Centenary Year the President is Maurice L Court.

Originally a 9-hole course, the Club moved to Lamorbey Park in 1910. Records show that the design of the course was influenced by James Braid: he visited the site, made a report, submitted plans and received £5 for his advice. However, he declined an invitation to supervise the construction because he could not spare the time. After the First World War the course became one of the best in southern England. Several of the best known golfing societies were regular visitors, and the Club often hosted the Kent Championships, both amateur and professional.

The first Professional at Lamorbey was Harry Wilson, a Scot from Melrose. He supervised the construction of the course and was to serve Sidcup Golf Club as Professional, Greenkeeper and Secretary for more than 50 years. In 1952 half the course was taken by the Kent Education Committee and two schools were built on the land. Since then the course has been of 9 holes again. Nevertheless, the bunkers and trees combine with the river Shuttle and a lake to make Sidcup a fairly severe test for the serious golfer.

Captain 1991: John S Aughterlony
Secretary: Sandy Watt
Professional: Ross Taylor

Wakefield

The Club was founded in December 1891 and a course of 9 holes was laid out on Heath Common, the home of the Club for the first twenty years. In April 1892 the first ball was driven off by Percy Tew of Heath Hall, the Club's inaugural President. In 1894 the Club helped in the formation of The Yorkshire Union of Golf Clubs and two years later, with GH Peacock, amateur champion, Miss Haigh, ladies champion and the first winners of the team championship, it became the only club in the history of the Union to hold the three county championships in the same year.

In 1911 the Club moved to its present home at Woodthorpe. The course was laid out by Sandy Herd and opened by Lord Eldon; the opening was followed by an exhibition match between James Braid and JH Taylor.

Wakefield produced the Yorkshire Amateur Champion L Butler Smith in 1910 and the Ladies Champion Mrs Harrop in 1919. The foremost player to come from Wakefield was Alan Slater who represented the county 125 and England four times. In 1955 he was a finalist in the Amateur Championship and in 1962 he won the English Amateur Open Stroke Play Championship (Brabazon Trophy) at Woodhall Spa.

Since then AW Clarke played for the English Boys and in 1976 won the Yorkshire Boys' Championship. This feat was repeated in 1989 by S Church.

Captain 1991: PGA Bloomer
Secretary: DT Hall
Professional: IM Wright

Wallasey

Endowed with undulating fairways and sandhills that are an important part of links golf, Wallasey's course was originally laid out by Tom Morris Sr, although alterations have been made during its history by such distinguished golfers as Alex

Herd, Harold Hilton and James Braid. The links provide an interesting and exacting test of golf with a length of 6607 yards and SSS of 73.

Wallasey has been a popular venue for county championships and matches and, among other tournaments, the Club hosted the World Senior Professional Championship in 1958 and 1967.

The first Stableford competition, played at Wallasey on 16 May 1932, was devised by Dr Frank Stableford, a member of the Club for many years. His system of point scoring was born out of frustration of being unable to reach some of the long par 4s in regulation figures when harsh westerly winds made a nonsense of the traditional bogey system of scoring. As a tribute to him, Wallasey holds an annual open 36-hole Stableford competition in which the Stableford Memorial Trophy is competed for.

The Club collection of oil paintings includes the original portrait of Bobby Jones, which has become famous throughout the world.

Captain 1991: JT Thompson
Secretary: JA Sword
Professional/ Mike W Adams

Warkworth

The first suggestion for a course at Warkworth came from a southern visitor, who wrote to the local paper in June 1891 that the dunes near the town were an ideal place to play golf. At once the idea was enthusiastically accepted, a meeting was held and in October Old Tom Morris spent three days laying out 12 holes on land owned by the Duke of Northumberland. The course was reduced to 9 holes in 1914.

A feature of this 9-hole course is a chine which comes into play as a hazard at several holes. Tom Morris christened it 'Wee Killiecrankie'; the name has stuck and the ravine is still referred to as 'The Killie'.

The Club is now flourishing after many troubles following 1945. The Clubhouse has been refurbished and recently extended ready for the Centenary this year. Warkworth, like its neighbours Alnwick and Alnmouth, receives many visitors, especially in holiday times.

Captain 1991: John Krzysiak
Secretary: JW Anderson

West Middlesex

The opening of the West Middlesex Golf Club on 25 April 1891 was marked by a match between the Captain, C Plummer and the Honorary Treasurer,

Dr Common, at the newly formed 12-hole course in the grounds of Twyford Abbey. Founded by Frank Carver as The Ealing Golf Club, it was moved in 1894 to an 18-hole course on land belonging to Lord Jersey near the Uxbridge Road, with a separate 9-hole course for the exclusive use of the Ladies' Club formed in that year.

Reported to be 'the most uneven and broken ground that could be found for miles around', the site was enhanced by a picturesque mill-pond, panoramic views of Hanwell Church and Harrow-on-the-Hill and easy accessibility from London by train, tram or omnibus. WS Marks, formerly of Wimbledon, was appointed as Professional and, in 1895, Lord George Hamilton MP became the first President.

Accommodation for members has developed from two rooms in a cottage (at Twyford) to a wooden pavilion destroyed by fire in 1929 to the present Clubhouse incorporating squash courts, built in 1976. Total membership, which in 1892 stood at 225 is now 700.

Captain 1991: Robert Palmer
Secretary: Patrick Furness
Professional: Lawrence Farmer

West Wilts

West Wilts' original course was set out on Arn Hill to the north of Warminster and consisted of 9 holes with a total length of 1597 yards. The annual subscription was 2s 6d.

In 1906 it was decided to build a new Clubhouse and convert the course into one of 18 holes. JH Taylor was engaged to lay out the new course and, apart from renumbering the holes in 1953 when another Clubhouse was built at the top of the hill, the repositioning of some greens and tees and the introduction of new bunkers, the course he designed has remained much the same to the present day. The medal card today reads 5701 yards, SSS 68 and par 70. The formal opening of the new course and Clubhouse took place in April 1907 and was performed by the Right Hon. AJ Balfour, then Leader of the Opposition.

The growth in membership, from 50 players in 1892 to a total of 580 in 1990, of which 450 are full playing members, has resulted in many improvements to the facilities offered by the Club over the years. Today the course can scarcely be matched for variety and interest by any other course in the west of England.

Captain 1991: Major RE Bradbury
Secretary: Major LR Weaver
Professional: Alan Harvey

Scotland

Alloa

Alloa Golf Club was instituted in May 1891 by local inhabitants interested in forming a Club. Willie Park was invited to inspect two possible venues at Arnsbrae and Gartmorn Moor. Park was unavailable and sent Robert Tait, once a Musselburgh professional, in his place. For a fee of two guineas, Tait's report recommended both sites as satisfactory, but as Gartmorn would cost several hundred pounds to develop and Arnsbrae very little, the committee plumped for a 9-hole course at the latter.

The land was rented from the farmer at £20 per annum and 49 original members paid 10s 6d entry fee, a guinea subscription, (Ladies and Juniors 10s 6d). Thomas Davidson, first winner of the Champions Gold Medal in 1891, also held the course record of 39.

Play continued at Arnsbrae until 1926 when the Club moved to nearby Braehead. In 1936, wishing to extend to 18 holes, the Club leased ground at the Schawpark Estate where James Braid designed a beautiful parkland course.It is now considered one of the best tests of golf in the central belt of Scotland. It will soon be owned by members when the purchase of the land is completed.

Captain 1991: AS Goodwillie
Secretary: AM Frame
Professional: W Bennett

Braehead

There are some who will contest that the Braehead Club came into existence in 1891, as in that year its members belonged to the Alloa Club and continued to do so until 1936. The Alloa Club moved to Braehead in 1927 and, wanting to extend its course to 18 holes, moved again to Schawpark, Sauchie in 1936, where the new course was laid out.

The move caused a schism and a body of Alloa members remained at Braehead and formed the Braehead Club. It would appear that 2036, or possibly 2027, might be more appropriate dates to celebrate Braehead's centenary. However the present membership feels it has equal claim to the 1891 date and is so included. The Club has survived, purchased its ground in 1979 and now has 500 members.

Secretary: June A. Harrison

Brora

Brora in Sutherland is one of several fine natural links courses to be found on the north-east coast of the Scottish Highlands. It began as 9 holes laid out by John Sutherland of Dornoch in 1891. Membership was 82 and there was a separate layout for the Ladies. It was extended to 18 holes in 1896, refined in 1913 when the Ladies' course was discarded and in 1933 the present green

measuring, 6101 yards, was designed by James Braid on the same parcel of land.

Since then the Club has steadily progressed, with a new Clubhouse being built in 1963 when Sunday play was first allowed. Green fees at £10 per day for a delightful links course must be one of the best values available.

Membership is 300. The record by Jim Miller, a Brora member and several times North District Champion, is 61 and the ladies record by another local, Marlene Bokas, is 73.

Captain 1991: R J Wilson
Secretary: H Baillie

Comrie

In March 1891 twenty-five Comrie gentlemen met with a view to forming a golf club in their beautiful village. They approached Col. David Williamson of Lawers regarding the Laggan Braes. He telegraphed a reply: 'Hurrah for Comrie and golf' and agreed an initial lease of £16 per year. The 9-hole course was officially opened by Col. Williamson on 6 June 1891. Over the years and through several different landlords this rent increased until 1962 when, through fundraising efforts and loans from member and friends, the course was purchased from the then owner, Sir David Baird.

In 1891 the annual subscription was 5s for gentlemen and 2s 6d for ladies. It is now £45 for both – Comrie having accorded its lady members equal status.

Comrie is situated in the vale of Strathearn and from the course one can appreciate countless attractions of mountain, forest and river. At one time the view from the 4th green was the frontispiece for the Scottish Tourist Board magazine and posters depicting this were displayed worldwide. A capercaillie recently adopted the Club and for about three years escorted members on their rounds – becoming the excuse for many a muffed shot. The capercaillie is now the official emblem of the Club.

Captain 1991/Secretary: DG McGlashan

Cowal

Cowal Golf Club, at Kirn near Dunoon, was founded as a 9-hole course in October 1891 and laid out by Willie Campbell of Bridge of Weir. The annual subscription of the 80 members was 10s 6d with an entry fee of one guinea.

After a new Clubhouse was built for £200, in 1903, the course was extended under the direction of Willie Auchterlonie of St Andrews. The course commands splendid views of the Firth of Clyde. An early member was Harry Lauder, who presented a cup for annual competition and played an exhibition match with his friend JH Taylor in 1913.

James Braid re-designed the course in 1924–6 and opened it with an exhibition match. The Club was since expanded and the Clubhouse has been twice extended since the Second World War. On the last occasion, in 1975, the well-known Scots International and Walker Cup player, Charlie Green, performed the opening ceremony.

Russell Weir, the Club's Professional, won the PGA Club Professionals Championship in two consecutive years and the European Club Professionals Championship once.

Captain 1991: William Keating
Secretary: J Bruce
Professional: Russell Weir

Crieff

When Old Tom Morris came from St Andrews to play the shot which opened Crieff Golf Club's original course (he had designed it at Ledbowie in 1891), he could hardly have imagined that a century later the Club which he had helped inaugurate would celebrate its hundredth birthday by opening a brand-new £600,000 Centenary Clubhouse using substantial financial assistance from the very Royal & Ancient Golf Club with which he had spent the last quarter century of his working life.

After two moves from that original site the Club is now well and truly established at Ferntower, Crieff, commanding magnificent views over the Strathearn Valley and the Ochil Hills. In 1980 the present 18-hole Ferntower Course (SSS 71) was formed by combining several of the holes from the previous layout with some new ones, thereby releasing the remainder for the creation of the 9-hole Dornock Course (SSS 63).

Captain 1991: David Philips
Secretary: Leslie J Rundle
Professionals: John Stark and David Murchie

Kilmacolm

Like many clubs founded a hundred years ago, Kilmacolm started with 9 holes which were laid out in April and May of 1891, but the course was extended to 18 holes in the autumn of that same year.

The village, deep in the Renfrewshire hills, 17 miles from Glasgow, was then growing rapidly and the Club was an immediate success.

Unlike many Clubs, ladies were welcomed immediately and had free golf until 1895 when charges were introduced – 2s 6d per annum for wives of members.

The first 18-hole course was very short at only

3755 yards, but further ground was acquired, and by 1904 the length was up to 4360 yards. This was still unsatisfactory, but in 1908 Elderslie Estates leased to the Club a magnificent stretch of reclaimed moorland which gave Kilmacolm one of the finest inland courses in Scotland, on which one can play in surroundings of unrivalled natural beauty. The present course measures 5964 yards, par 69, SSS 68.

In 1984 the Club was at last able to purchase the ground. A much needed extension to the Clubhouse is now in hand which will be completed in time for the Centenary events of 1991.

Captain 1991: Colin M Brown
Secretary: RF McDonald
Professional: David Stewart

Kingussie

A 9-hole course was first laid out in 1891 in Glen Gynack, about half a mile north of Kingussie. There has always been some confusion about the exact date of the inception of the course, and indeed the elaborate 21st anniversary celebrations, which included the opening of the Clubhouse (modelled on an English cricket pavilion), took place in 1911. However recent research by the present Captain has established that 1891 is the correct date.

The Club did not stay long on its original site, being forced to move following a dispute with the Estate after only about a season. The members were required to play in a virtual bog near the river Spey for a short while before returning to Glen Gynack once cordial relations had been re-established with the landlord.

In 1906 Harry Vardon was approached to help design a further 9 holes, and as a result an 18-hole layout was in operation by 1908. Two exhibition matches were played by Vardon and Herd during this period, each wining one.

The Club went through a difficult period following the Second World War. It is thriving again now, popular with holidaymakers to the Spey Valley, and 1991 sees the first Pro-Am to be staged at the course.

Captain 1991: Graham MacDonald
Secretary: William Cook

Lundin Ladies

This is one of the few courses, probably the oldest, which is owned and run by a private Ladies' Club, employing its own greenkeeping and Clubhouse staff. Men are allowed to play and can join as Associate members, but are not permitted in the Clubhouse except on special occasions.

The Club began its life playing on a links area, Massney Brae, south of Lundin village. It soon moved to the North Links, separated from Lundin (Men's) Golf Club course by the railway. A further move to the present site, brought about by increasing congestion on the men's course, was made in 1910 when 9 holes, designed by James Braid, were opened. Braid's plans for a further 9 were held in abeyance until after the First World War. The course, which is essentially parkland rather than links, has remained largely unaltered since.

Today the Club thrives with nearly 300 members. It is especially keen and effective in encouraging younger children to play the game: several competitions are organised for them every year.

Captain 1991: Mrs Heather Elliott
Secretary: Mrs HJ Melville

Machrie

Machrie, a splendid links on the far-west island of Islay, was laid out by Willie Campbell in 1891. That May he used his local knowledge to beat Willie Fernie, Open Champion in 1883, 7 & 6 over 36 holes. Far too remote now to attract major events, the Club staged a tournament in 1901, following the Open at Muirfield, with first prize of £100, a vast sum then when the winner of the Open received but £30!

This incentive encouraged all the leading professionals to make the complicated journey to Islay from Muirfield: this involved three trains to Edinburgh, Glasgow and Gourock, a steamer ferry to Tarbert, a coach ride across the Kintyre peninsula to catch the 3-hour ferry to Port Ellen on Islay and another coach for the final three miles to the course. They all thought highly of it. JH Taylor beat Fernie, Vardon (at the 24th) and Herd on his way to the final when he mastered Braid at the 37th and collected the £100. Braid received £40.

After a checkered history the course is now owned by the Machrie Hotel and is being developed successfully as a holiday golf centre for short and long vacations. Cars, planes and faster ferries make the journey easier than a century ago.

Proprietor: Murdo MacPherson

Ireland

North West, Co Donegal

The original 9 holes of the course were laid out by WH Mann and Charles Thompson, Professional at Portrush, added 9 holes at Lisfannon, of which one hole was 515 yards bogey six. The present 18-hole course was established in 1938, designed by E Hackett.

The formation of the Golf Union of Ireland was first suggested at North West and with Portrush, the Clubs became founder members. Situated close to the Buncrana Naval Base, there were many RN members during both wars and the Fleet Shield, a Scratch Cup, reminds the Club of its strong naval association.

Lionel Munn and Eddie Spiller, both Irish Champions, were prominent members for 25 years up to 1939. The Ladies won the ILGU Senior Cup in 1908. An Open Amateur Scratch Cup, started in 1968, was won by Des Smyth in 1972 and Ronan Rafferty, as a 14-year-old, in 1978. Both have since become prominent professionals.

In 1952 severe storms caused much damage to the links which, added to continuous erosion, has meant heavy expenditure. In 1965 a new Clubhouse was built after the old one was destroyed by fire, together with all the Club's early records.

Captain 1991: Cathal Harvey
Secretary: Dudley Coyle
Professional: Seamus McBriarty

Portsalon

This 18-hole links course on the western shore of Lough Swilly in Co Donegal was laid out on land owned by Col Barton, the proprietor of the Portsalon Hotel. The *Golfing Annual 1891–92* says of the new course: 'the golfing fraternity is indebted to Captain M'Laren for the discovery of this new ground and the holes were laid out under the supervision of Mr RA Collingwood of Portrush.' The course was owned by the Portsalon Hotel until 1987 when it was purchased by the Club from the then owner, Mr PC Duffy.

The Club was formed in 1891 with nine founder members and it seems that Mr Collingwood was the leader and spokesman for all at the birth of the Club.

The Irish Ladies' Championship was played at Portsalon in 1905 and 1912.

Captain 1991: Paul Blaney
Secretary: Michael Kerr

Wales

Royal Porthcawl

In 1891 the first course of 9 holes was laid out by Charles Gibson of Westward Ho! The Club's membership grew quickly to 300 in 1896, when more ground to provide another 9 holes was purchased nearby, but with a long walk between the two. Soon afterwards 9 more holes were constructed near the new holes and the original course given over to the Ladies. The layout today is little altered except for minor changes over seventy years by a succession of well-known golf architects: Harry Colt, Hawtree, Braid, Tom Simpson and CK Cotton.

The course is triangular, thus providing fine links holes by the sea and first-class moorland turf inland, with dunes abounding, making it a Championship course of variety, but still with the wind the most constant feature. Unusually for a links course the sea can be seen from every hole.

Porthcawl was added to the Amateur Championship rota as late as 1951 and it has been played there four times since. In 1965 Michael Bonallack won his second title there: against Clive Clark he was six down after thirteen holes in the morning but came back to win 2 & 1. In 1980 Duncan Evans was the first Welshman to be Champion, appropriately at Porthcawl. The Ladies have held the British Amateur Championship here three times: the first winner was Helen Holm, who beat the 17-year-old Pam Barton in the first of the latter's four finals in six years.

In 1964 the USA won the Curtis Cup at Porthcawl $10\frac{1}{2}$–$7\frac{1}{2}$ after the home team had led $3\frac{1}{2}$–$2\frac{1}{2}$ in the foursomes. Numerous other well-known events have been played here, including several Professional competitions, the University match and many Welsh Men's and Ladies' close championships.

Captain 1991: Dr Leo MacMahon
Secretary: AW Woolcott
Professional: G Poor

The following Clubs are also celebrating their centenaries in 1991, but regrettably no information has been received: *England:* Braintree (Essex), Leasowe (Merseyside), Ryton (Tyne & Wear), Shrewsbury (Shropshire). *Scotland:* Askernish (Western Isles), Bearsden (Dunbartonshire), Craigentinny (Midlothian), Inellen (Argyll), Largs (Ayrshire), Skelmorlie (Ayrshire). *Ireland:* Fortwilliam (Belfast), Limerick (Co Limerick).

The need for low-budget courses

Michael Gedye

It would be nice to report that the domestic development of golf, fuelled by rapidly increasing demand and a change in land use policy, had led to a wealth of new courses throughout the British Isles in the last few years. Sadly this is not the case. Although a few notable exceptions have opened their doors recently, the general pattern lags far behind what is required. In 1989, the Royal & Ancient Golf Club of St Andrews published a report which concluded that nearly 700 more golf courses were needed throughout the country by the year 2000 if facilities were to keep pace with demand. That represents an increase of nearly 40 per cent on existing places to play.

To put the figures into perspective, the current world leader in golf course construction is the United States, where more than two new courses open weekly, some 125 in a year. The top performer in Europe is France, where the present golfing boom generates more than one course per week, around 65 per annum. The R & A projection requires an average of 70 new golfing locations each year until the turn of the century; recent performance, however, shows only seventeen 18-hole and eleven 9-hole courses opened in Great Britain during the last five years, an average of five annually. A total of 100 courses were opened in the ten years since 1980, pushing the annual average up to ten although nearly half of these were 9-hole courses. The current trend is for less new development rather than more. Demand, however, is continuing to expand against supply. On the basis that in a normal market economy, products will always be made available where there is sufficient requirement, it is worth considering how the present situation of limited growth against rising interest has been reached and whether too many projects are based on an unsuitable product.

Golf has been one of the major sporting success stories over the last thirty years – not only with improved standards and success at the professional level but in the spread and democratisation of interest throughout the country and, in particular, a realisation that here was a game for all. Even in the period immediately after the Second World War, the British game still clung to the traditions and essentially exclusive nature that pervaded golf in the 1920s and 30s. The outward (or downward) growth of the game, depending on your perspective, came about in recent times for three reasons.

The most significant was television. Effectively entertaining on the small screen, the game grew as sponsors discovered a widening audience, which in turn brought better and more international players to tournaments. The broader audience found a game of infinite variety often played in very beautiful settings, yet within the physical capacity of most at almost any age. This new market looked to a well-established selection of courses to play and visitors' income brought clubs much needed revenue. The third factor in this expansion has been the general increase in leisure time and affluence across a broad cross-section of society and, to some extent, a redistribution of disposable income. This increased interest and demand did not come about, however, through additional facilities. The bulk of the 2000-plus golf courses in the British Isles were in place well before the 1940s. The rising tide of golf has merely served to increase pressure on tee-off times, waiting lists and public playing facilities while new course development has failed to keep pace.

It would be a mistake, though, to assume that golf is lagging far behind demand in all areas of the British Isles. The R & A report suggested that the optimum relationship should be one golf courses to 25,000 people. Areas of relatively low population density such as Scotland, Ireland and Wales already meet this criterion or can improve on it. It is England, mainly in the Midlands and the South, where the problem is acute and where, conversely, suitable land is both at a premium and difficult to develop. It was hoped that recent government legislation covering a 'set-aside' policy for agriculture, which opened the way for conversion of land to golfing use, would ease the problem. But, particularly in areas of high demand, many projects have met resistance in securing planning approval. This is usually related to ancillary buildings and 'country club' facilities rather than the golf course itself. A reasonable argument can be made that a golf course, sympathetically in tune with its environ-

ment, enhances the land and preserves the wildlife habitat. The problems normally occur where the overall concept is one of luxury and the highest quality. Such projects rely on catering, accommodation, convention facilities and possibly real estate sales to generate the income which will offset the considerable investment. It is this aspect of golf club development that worries planners, who tend to see golf as a spoiler rather than a saviour of the countryside. All too often developers only see big as beautiful, albeit, with the expanding market for golf, there is a wider pool of frustrated enthusiasts who do not have the means to buy into a multi-million pound project. The British Isles has a tradition of accessible golf at some of the lowest prices in the world and, although there will always be a market for developments of the highest class, consideration must be given to ways of maintaining golf for all.

If we are to have any hope of meeting the projected need for 700 more courses by the year 2000, which can cater to players across a broad social and financial spectrum, developers and planners must accept the concept of limited-budget courses designed for new golfers. Courses where playing the game would be the only priority – the concept of 'rough golf', an idea supported by the late Henry Cotton – might be one answer. He could see clearly the problems ahead for our growing golf population.

A feature common to many of the world's top courses is their 'natural' appearance, their lack of artificial features. In many cases, these were laid out at a time when major earthmoving was unthinkable and the designer was required to use the land to best advantage much as it lay. The results speak for themselves. Low-budget golf does not have to be dull; a thoughtful architect can create imaginative and interesting holes in harmony with their environment and, equally important, within the playing ability of the likely market.

At the present time, although progress is clearly failing to keep pace with demand, a number of newly opened golf developments are notable for their quality and the comprehensive nature of their facilities.

Probably the most ambitious is the East Sussex National Golf Club at Little Horsted, some 45 miles south of London. Two 18-hole courses of championship length (7099 yards and 7192 yards respectively) have been open since 1989, supported by a teaching academy, members' golf club, the elegant Horsted Place Hotel and, to come, a further hotel and conference complex as part of the golf village.

Another new development with a distinctly transatlantic flavour is Collingtree Park, near Northampton. Former Open and US Open champion Johnny Miller has designed 18 holes full of interest and considerable strategic water. The course also boasts a well-equipped golf academy and shop, mandatory golf carts for all players, with future plans for integral housing and a clubhouse hotel as well as a comprehensive corporate hospitality programme.

In the north, Slaley Hall Golf & Country Club near Hexham, Northumberland, is a further example of a comprehensive multi-purpose development. The 18-hole course, designed by Dave Thomas, is laid out over a wooded country estate which will include a 5-star hotel based on the original stately home, timeshare lodges, holiday villas, conference facilities and a leisure club, plus fishing and shooting.

In Scotland, two new projects have provoked particular attention. Letham Grange, just north of Arbroath and Carnoustie, has 18 holes (6995 yards par 74 from the back tees) running over wooded parkland with an additional, less demanding 18-hole course to follow. The converted Victorian mansion acts as a stylish clubhouse and hotel, there is an indoor arena for tennis in summer and curling in winter and a riding centre planned. The other is Hawkshill, at Newmacher just north of Aberdeen. Designed over farm and heathland, with some areas of evergreen trees and natural wetland wildlife reserves, this is essentially a members' golf club created through the enthusiasm of individuals without the financial support of a major developer. Completed after eleven years of effort and determination, it has already earned praise for both its natural quality and potential.

Other recent arrivals include the third course at Wentworth, the Edinburgh, a demanding test of 6995 yards par 72 with play currently limited to members and their guests. Three more are the Horncastle Golf & Country Club, built on farmland in Lincolnshire with water affecting thirteen holes; Wavendon Golf Club in Buckinghamshire, which has added 18 holes to a previous nine; and the 18 holes of Paxhill Park Golf Club in Sussex.

Present golf course openings include a few luxury multi-purpose developments and a number of other, less ambitious, land conversions but the total is way behind the number required to satisfy the burgeoning demand. The real need is for simple, relatively undemanding facilities built to a low budget, which can cater to the massive market of new golfers looking for somewhere to learn and play both within their golfing capacity and their pocket.

Golf Clubs and Courses in the British Isles and Europe

How to use this section

1. Geographical divisions

Clubs are listed in alphabetical order within counties, which are themselves listed alphabetically. All clubs are now listed under their geographical county and not the county of affiliation. In Scotland, counties are grouped under the recognised Scottish administrative regions. European clubs are in alphabetical order by country, grouped under useful regional headings as a further guide. In addition, all clubs and courses are listed in the index at the back of the book.

2. Explanation of details given

a After the name of the club is the date of foundation (where available).

b Courses are private unless otherwise stated. Many public courses have members' clubs which play over them; information on these clubs can be obtained from the course concerned.

c The address is the postal address of each club or course. If the postal county is different from the one under which the club or course is listed, it will be shown in the address.

d The membership figure denotes the total number of members. The number of lady members (L), the number of juniors (J) and of five day members (5) are sometimes shown separately.

e Telephone numbers for secretaries and professionals are shown if different from the club telephone number.

f Fees: green fees are only quoted for visitors if they are permitted to play unaccompanied by a member. The basic cost per round is shown first, then in brackets, the cost of a weekend and/or Bank Holiday round where this is available to unaccompanied visitors. Green fees for visitors playing with a member are not given. Weekly (W), monthly (M) and fortnightly (F) terms are shown where available. *Green fees quoted are the most up to date supplied by each club.*

3. Abbreviations

V'trs this shows what restrictions (if any) are in force for visitors.
WD Weekdays
WE Weekends
BH Bank Holidays
   (If no days stated, the particular restrictions apply at all times)
U Unrestricted, ie casual visitors may play without restriction on the days stated.
M with a member, ie casual visitors are not allowed. Only visitors playing with a member are permitted on the days stated.
H Handicap certificate required
I Introduction, ie visitors are permitted on the days stated if they have a letter of introduction from their own club, their own club's membership card, or a handicap certificate.
XL No ladies allowed on the days stated
NA No visitors allowed
SOC Recognised Golfing Societies welcome if previous arrangements made with secretary

Information given is as up to date as possible at the time of going to press. Great reliance on the accuracy of this information is placed on details received from club secretaries, for whose assistance we are indebted, but we would be grateful to be notified of any inaccuracies.

County Index

Golf Courses of the UK and Europe

England

Avon

Bath (1880)

Sham Castle, North Road, Bath
BA2 6JG
Tel	(0225) 425182
Mem	650
Sec	PB Edwards (0225) 463834
Pro	P Hancox (0225) 466953
Holes	18 L 6369 yds SSS 70
Recs	Am–65 CS Edwards (1989)
	Pro–68 G Brand (1982)
V'trs	H SOC
Fees	£18 (£22) (1990)
Loc	1½ miles SE of Bath, off A36

Bristol & Clifton (1891)

Beggar Bush Lane, Failand,
nr Clifton, Bristol BS8 3TH
Tel	(0272) 393117/ 393474
Mem	800
Sec	Cdr PA Woollings RN (0272) 393474
Pro	P Mawson (0272) 393031
Holes	18 L 6294 yds SSS 70
Recs	Am–65 P Godsland
	Pro–64 P Oosterhuis
V'trs	WD–UH WE/ BH–MH
Fees	On request
Loc	2 miles W of suspension bridge. 4 miles S of M5 Junction 19

Chipping Sodbury (1954)

The Common, Chipping Sodbury,
Bristol BS17 6PU
Tel	(0454) 312024 (Members)
	(0454) 315822 (Steward)
Mem	750
Sec	KG Starr (0454) 319042
Pro	SC Harris (0454) 314087
Holes	New 18 L 6912 yds SSS 73
	Old 9 L 6194 yds SSS 69
Recs	New Am–66 D Wood (1988)
	Pro–68 J Nicholas (1988)
V'trs	WD–U SOC WE/ BH pm only–M Sat/ Sun am–XL
Fees	New £10 D–£14 (£12 D–£18) Old £2.50
Loc	12 miles NE of Bristol. M4 Junction 18, 5 miles. M5 Junction 14, 9 miles.

Clevedon (1894)

Castle Road, Clevedon BS21 7AA
Tel	(0272) 873140
Mem	700
Sec	Capt (Retd) M Sullivan (0272) 874057
Pro	Miss C Langford (0272) 874704
Holes	18 L 5887 yds SSS 69
Recs	Am–65 S Wyllie
	Pro–67 G Ryall (1987)
V'trs	WD–U H exc Wed am–NA
	WE/ BH–H I NA before 11am
	SOC–Mon only
Fees	£16 (£24)
Loc	Holly Lane, Walton, Clevedon. M5 Junction 19 or 20

Entry Hill (1985)

Public
Entry Hill, Bath BA2 5NA
Tel	(0225) 834248
Pro	T Tapley
Holes	9 L 4206 yds SSS 61
Recs	Am–65 R Blannin (1989),
	I Hulley (1990)
V'trs	WD/ WE–booking only
Fees	18 holes–£6 9 holes–£4
Loc	1 mile S of Bath, off A367
Mis	Entry Hill GC plays here

Filton (1909)

Golf Course Lane, Bristol BS12 7QS
Tel	(0272) 692021
Mem	700
Sec	MJA Hutton (0272) 694169
Pro	JCN Lumb (0272) 694158
Holes	18 L 6042 yds SSS 69
Recs	Am–65 S Hurley
	Pro–66 G Marks
V'trs	WD–U WE/ BH–M
Fees	£16
Loc	4 miles N of Bristol

Fosseway CC (1970)

Charlton Lane, Midsomer Norton,
Bath BA3 4BD
Tel	(0761) 412214
Mem	280
Sec	RF Jones (Mgr)
Holes	9 L 4148 yds SSS 61
Recs	Am–55 M Chedgy (1985)
V'trs	U exc Wed–M after 5pm
	Sun–NA before 1.30pm
Fees	£10 (£15)
Loc	10 miles SW of Bath on A367

Henbury (1891)

Westbury-on-Trym, Bristol
BS10 7QB
Tel	(0272) 500660
Mem	330 85(L) 48(J) 157(5)
Sec	J Leeming (0272) 500044
Pro	N Riley (0272) 502121
Holes	18 L 6039 yds SSS 70
Recs	Am–63 R Tugwell
	Pro–67 B Sandry
V'trs	WD–H WE–M SOC–Tues & Fri
Fees	£16
Loc	3 miles N of Bristol. M5 Junction 17

Knowle (1905)

Fairway, Knowle, Brislington, Bristol
BS4 5DF
Tel	(0272) 776341
Mem	700
Sec	Mrs JD King (0272) 770660
Pro	GM Brand (0272) 779193
Holes	18 L 6016 yds SSS 69
Recs	Am–64 SD Hurley, D Hares
	Pro–64 S Brown
V'trs	WD exc Thurs-H WE/ BH–H
	SOC–Thurs
Fees	£16 D–£20 (£20 D–£25)
Loc	Brislington Hill, 3 miles S of Bristol, off A4

Lansdown (1894)

Lansdown, Bath BA1 9BT
Tel	(0225) 425007
Mem	750
Sec	J Prosser (0225) 422138
Pro	T Mercer (0225) 420242
Holes	18 L 6299 yds SSS 70
Recs	Am–64 P McMullen (1990)
	Pro–65 D Ray (1987)
V'trs	WD/ WE–H SOC
Fees	£14 (£18)
Loc	2 miles NW of Bath, by racecourse. M4 Junction 18, 6 miles

Long Ashton (1893)

Long Ashton, Bristol BS18 9DW
Tel	(0272) 392229
Mem	800
Sec	RE Burniston (0272) 392316
Pro	DP Scanlan (0272) 392265
Holes	18 L 6051 yds SSS 70
Recs	Am–64 A Rogers, J Bickerton
	Pro–65 D Snell

V'trs WD–U H WE/ BH–I H
SOC–Wed
Fees £18 (£25)
Loc 3 miles S of Bristol on B3128

Mangotsfield (1975)

Carsons Road, Mangotsfield, Bristol
BS17 3LW
Tel (0272) 565501
Mem 600
Sec R Tomlin
Pro C Trewin
Holes 18 L 5297 yds SSS 66
V'trs U
Fees £7 (£10)
Loc 6 miles NE of Bristol

Saltford (1904)

Golf Club Lane, Saltford, Bristol
Tel (0225) 873220
Mem 650
Sec V Radnedge (0225) 873513
Pro D Millensted (0225) 872043
Holes 18 L 6081 yds SSS 69
Recs Am–68 S Godfrey
Pro–P Evans
V'trs U
Fees £18 (£22)
Loc 6 miles NW of Bath. 7 miles SE
of Bristol

Shirehampton Park (1907)

Park Hill, Shirehampton, Bristol
BS11 0UL
Tel (0272) 823059
Mem 600
Sec (0272) 822083
Pro B Ellis (0272) 822488
Holes 18 L 5493 yds SSS 67
Recs Am–61 M Bessell (1990)
Pro–63 K Spurgeon (1986)
V'trs WD–UH WE–M
Fees £15
Loc M5 Junction 18, 1¹/₂ miles

Tracy Park (1976)

Tracy Park, Bath Road, Wick, nr
Bristol BS15 5RN
Tel (027582) 2251
Fax (027582) 4288
Mem 1200
Sec Capt J Seymour-Williams
Pro G Aitken (027582) 3521
Holes 27-Avon L 6834 yds SSS 73
Bristol L 6861 yds SSS 73
Cotswold L 6203 yds SSS 70
Recs Am–65 S Pugh
Pro–64 P Pring
V'trs WD/ WE(phone first) SOC
Fees £15 (£20)
Loc 10 miles NW of Bath, off A420.
M4 Junction 18

Weston-super-Mare (1892)

Uphill Road North, Weston-super-
Mare BS23 4NQ
Tel (0934) 621360
Mem 800
Sec (0934) 626968

Pro T Murray (0934) 633360
Holes 18 L 6251 yds SSS 70
Recs Am–67 G Robert
Pro–69 A Lees, WJ Branch
V'trs H SOC
Fees £17.50 (£22) W–£45
Loc Weston-super-Mare

Worlebury (1908)

Monks Hill, Weston-super-Mare
BS22 9SX
Tel (0934) 623214
Mem 640
Sec RT Bagg (0934) 625789
Pro G Marks (0934) 418473
Holes 18 L 5963 yds SSS 69
Recs Am–68 A Deakins,
P Gilpin (1990)
Pro–72 G Marks (1990)
V'trs U SOC–WD
Fees £15 (£25)
Loc 2 miles NE of Weston

Bedfordshire

Aspley Guise & Woburn Sands (1914)

West Hill, Aspley Guise, Milton
Keynes MK17 8DX
Tel (0908) 582264
Mem 530
Sec TE Simpson (0908) 583596
Pro G McCarthy (0908) 582974
Holes 18 L 6248 yds SSS 70
Recs Am–67 M Wharton
Pro–68 P Webster
V'trs WD–H WE/ BH–MH SOC–Wed
& Fri
Fees £15 D–£20
Loc 2 miles W of M1 Junction 13

Beadlow Manor Hotel G & CC

Beadlow, Shefford SG17 5PH
Tel (0525) 60800
Mem 700
Pro (0525) 61292
Holes 18 L 6238 yds SSS 71
9 L 6042 yds SSS 70
Recs Am–71 C Skinner
Pro–66 L Fickling
V'trs UH SOC
Fees On application
Loc 2 miles W of Shefford on A507

Bedford & County (1912)

Green Lane, Clapham, Bedford
MK41 6ET
Tel (0234) 52617
Mem 600
Sec E Bullock
Pro E Bullock (0234) 59189
Holes 18 L 6347 yds SSS 70
Recs Am–66 C Allen (1980)
Pro–66 M King (1978)
V'trs WD–UH WE–M SOC
Fees WD–£20
Loc 2 miles NW of Bedford on A6

Bedfordshire (1891)

Bromham Rd, Biddenham, Bedford
MK40 4AF
Tel (0234) 53241
Mem 600
Sec TA Nutt (0234) 61669
Pro G Buckle (0234) 53653
Holes 18 L 6185 yds SSS 69
Recs Am–64 CM Beard
Pro–65 K Warren
V'trs WD–U (phone first) WE–M
before noon SOC–WD
Fees On application
Loc 1¹/₂ miles NW of Bedford
boundary (A428)

Colworth (1985)

Unilever Research, Sharnbrook,
Bedford MK44 1LQ
Tel (0234) 781781
Mem 350
Sec S Granger
Holes 9 L 2500 yds
Recs Am–57 J Barrett (1988)
V'trs M
Loc 10 miles N of Bedford, off A6

Dunstable Downs (1907)

Whipsnade Road, Dunstable
LU6 2NB
Tel (0582) 604472
Mem 696
Sec PJ Nightingale
Pro M Weldon (0582) 662806
Holes 18 L 6184 yds SSS 70
Recs Am–65 RA Durrant
Pro–65 L Fickling
V'trs WD–H WE–M SOC–Tues &
Thurs
Fees On application
Loc 2 miles SW of Dunstable on
B4541. M1 Junction 11

Griffin (1985)

c/o 3 Hillcrest Avenue, Luton
LU2 7AB
Tel (0582) 415573
Mem 400
Sec Mrs L Weedon (0582) 579511
Holes 9 L 5516 yds SSS 66
Recs Am–73 A Halliday (1987)
V'trs WD–U before 3pm WE/ BH–M
(exc Sun am–NA) SOC
Fees D–£7
Loc 3 miles W of Luton on A505
between Dunstable and
Caddington. M1 Junction 11

John O'Gaunt (1948)

Sutton Park, Sandy, Biggleswade
SG19 2LY
Tel (0767) 260360
Mem 1250
Sec DJ Wallace
Pro R Round (0767) 260094
Holes John O'Gaunt 18 L 6513 yds
SSS 71; Carthagena 18 L
5869 yds SSS 68
Recs Am–64 N Wharton
Pro–67 SC Evans

V'trs WD–U WE–H
Fees £25 (£40)
Loc 3 miles NE Biggleswade on B1040
Mis Advisable phone before visit

Leighton Buzzard (1925)

Plantation Road, Leighton Buzzard
Tel (0525) 373811/ 373812
Mem 600
Sec FJ Clements (0525) 373811
Pro LJ Muncey (0525) 372143
Holes 18 L 5366 yds SSS 68
Recs Am–65 D Horne
V'trs WD exc Tues-U WE/ BH–MH
Fees £17 D–£22
Loc 1 mile N of Leighton Buzzard

Millbrook

Millbrook, Ampthill
Tel (0525) 404683
Mem 250
Sec Mrs M Brackley (0525) 840252
Pro T Devine (0525) 402269
Holes 18 L 6473 yds SSS 72
V'trs WD–U exc Thurs WE–NA before 9.30am
Fees £10 (£15)
Loc Millbrook

Mowsbury (1975)

Public
Kimbolton Road, Bedford MK41 8DQ
Tel (0234) 216374
Sec E Thompson (Mgr)
Pro P Ashwell
Holes 18 L 6514 yds SSS 71
Recs Pro–66
Fees £4 (£6)
Loc 3 miles N of Bedford on B660
Mis Driving range

RAF Henlow (1985)

RAF Henlow, Henlow SG16 6DN
Mem 300
Sec Sgt R Chaytor (0462) 815016 (Ext 2267)
Holes 9 L 5616 yds SSS 67
Recs Am–75 JWG Morgan (1988)
V'trs M
Fees D–£2
Loc 3 miles SE of Shefford on A600

South Beds (1892)

Warden Hill Road, Luton LU2 7AA
Tel (0582) 575201
Mem 750
Sec A Beaton (0582) 591500
Pro E Cogle (0582) 591209
Holes Galley 18 L 6332 yds SSS 71
Warden 9 L 4954 yds SSS 64
V'trs Galley WD–U (Ladies Day–Tues) WE/ BH–H exc comp days–NA. Warden-U SOC
Fees 18 hole:£14 D–£21 (£20 D–£30) 9 hole:£7 (£10)
Loc 3 miles N of Luton on E side of A6

Stockwood Park (1973)

Public
Stockwood Park, London Rd, Luton LU7 4LX
Tel (0582) 413704
Pro D Hunt
Holes 18 L 5567 yds SSS 69
Recs Am–73 RM Harris
Pro–66 T Minshall
Fees £3.40 (£5.10)
Loc 1 mile S of Luton on A6

Tilsworth

Public
Dunstable Rd, Tilsworth, Dunstable
Tel (0525) 210721/ 210722
Pro N Webb
Holes 9 L 2773 yds SSS 35
V'trs U
Fees £4.25 (£5.25)
Loc 2 miles N of Dunstable (A5)

Wyboston Lakes (1978)

Public
Wyboston Lakes, Wyboston MK44 3AL
Tel (0480) 219200
Sec B Chinn (Mgr)
Pro P Ashwell (0480) 212501
Holes 18 L 5721 yds SSS 69
V'trs WD–U SOC WE–booking
Fees £7 (£10)
Loc S of St Neots, off A1 and St Neots by-pass

Berkshire

Bearwood (1986)

Mole Road, Sindlesham RG11 5DB
Tel (0734) 761330
Mem 570
Sec C Dyer OBE (0734) 760060
Pro B Tustin (Mgr) (0734) 760643
Holes 9 L 2814 yds SSS 67
Recs Am–72 J Twamley (1989)
V'trs WD–H before 4pm –M after 4pm WE/ BH–M
Fees 18 holes–£12. 9 holes–£7
Loc 1½ miles N of Arborfield Cross, on B3030. M4 Junction 10
Mis 9 hole pitch & putt

Berkshire (1928)

Swinley Road, Ascot SL5 8AY
Tel (0990) 21495
Mem 935
Sec Maj PD Clarke (0990) 21496
Pro KA Macdonald (0990) 22351
Holes Red 18 L 6369 yds SSS 70 Blue 18 L 6260 yds SSS 70
V'trs WD–I WE/ BH–M
Fees On application
Loc 3 miles from Ascot on A332

Calcot Park (1930)

Calcot, nr Reading
Tel (0734) 427124
Mem 700
Sec SD Chisholm
Pro A Mackenzie (0734) 427797
Holes 18 L 6283 yds SSS 70
Recs Am–66 SA Scott
Pro–63 C Defoy
V'trs WD–U WE/ BH–M
Fees On application
Loc 3 miles W of Reading on A4

Datchet (1890)

Buccleuch Road, Datchet
Tel (0753) 43887
Mem 200 50(L) 25(J) 110(5)
Sec Ms A Perkins
Pro A Greig (0753) 42755
Holes 9 L 5978 yds SSS 69
Recs Am–66 R Blyfield
Pro–63 N Wood
V'trs WD–U before 3pm M-after 3pm WE–M
Fees £15 D–£20
Loc Slough, Windsor 2 miles

Donnington Valley

Oxford Road, Donnington, Newbury RG16 9AG
Tel (0635) 32488
Mem 500
Sec KE Crowe
Pro N Mitchell
Holes 18 L 4215 yds SSS 63
V'trs U
Fees On application
Loc N of Newbury, off Old Oxford road

Downshire (1973)

Public
Easthampstead Park, Wokingham
Tel (0344) 424066
Pro G Legouix
Holes 18 L 6382 yds SSS 70
Recs Am–67 T Smith
Pro–66 M King
V'trs U SOC
Fees Summer–£8.50 Winter–£6.50
Loc Off Nine Mile Ride
Mis Easthampstead GC and Downshire GC play here

East Berkshire (1904)

Ravenswood Ave, Crowthorne
Tel (0344) 772041
Fax (0344) 777378
Mem 700
Sec WH Short
Pro A Roe (0344) 774112
Holes 18 L 6345 yds SSS 70
Recs Am–65 J Davies
Pro–65 N Coles
V'trs H WE/ BH–M SOC
Fees £28
Loc Nr Crowthorne Station

Goring & Streatley (1893)

Rectory Road, Streatley-on-Thames RG8 9QA
Tel   (0491) 872688
Mem   740 115(L) 50(J) 130(5)
Sec   J Menzies (0491) 873229
Pro   R Mason (0491) 873715
Holes 18 L 6275 yds SSS 70
Recs   Am–65 DG Lane
         Pro–65 C DeFoy
V'trs   WD–U WE/ BH–M SOC–WD
Fees   £20
Loc   10 miles NW of Reading on
         A417

Hawthorn Hill (1985)

Public
Drift Road, Hawthorn Hill, Maidenhead SL6 3ST
Tel   (0628) 771030/ 75588/ 26035
Sec   CD Smith
Pro   TJ Hill
Holes 18 L 6212 yds SSS 70
V'trs   U
Fees   £8 (£10)
Loc   4 miles S of Maidenhead on
         A330
Mis   Floodlit driving range

Hurst (1979)

Public
Sandford Lane, Hurst, Wokingham
Tel   (0734) 345143
Pro   G Legouix
Holes 9 L 3015 yds SSS
Fees   Summer–£2.50 Winter–£1.65
Loc   Reading 5 miles. Wokingham
         3 miles

Lavender Park

Public
Swinley Road, Ascot SO5 1BD
Tel   (0344) 884074
Pro   G Casy
Holes 9 L 1104 yds SSS 27
V'trs   U
Fees   £3.10
Loc   W of Ascot on B3017
Mis   Driving range

Maidenhead (1898)

Shoppenhangers Road, Maidenhead SL6 2PZ
Tel   (0628) 24693
Mem   730
Sec   I Lindsay
Pro   C Dell (0628) 24067
Holes 18 L 6360 yds SSS 70
Recs   Am–66 M Briggs (1985),
         L Hawkins (1986)
         Pro–64 AN Walker,
         G Wolstenholme
V'trs   WD–H Fri–M after noon WE–M
Fees   D–£25
Loc   Maidenhead Station ½ mile

Mill Ride

Mill Ride, North Ascot SL5 8LT
Tel   (0344) 885444
Sec   J Deeming
Pro   R Newman (0344) 890433
Holes 18 L 6747 yds SSS 72
V'trs   M
Loc   2 miles W of Ascot

Newbury & Crookham (1873)

Bury's Bank Road, Greenham Common, Newbury RG15 8BZ
Tel   (0635) 40035
Mem   626
Sec   Mrs JR Hearsey
Pro   DW Harris (0635) 31201
Holes 18 L 5880 yds SSS 68
Recs   Am–63 D Rosier (1984)
         Pro–61 M Howell (1986)
V'trs   WD–UH WE–M (recognised
         club members)
Fees   £20
Loc   2 miles SE of Newbury

Reading (1910)

17 Kidmore End Road, Emmer Green, Reading RG4 8SG
Tel   (0734) 472169
Mem   700
Sec   ANH Weekes (0734) 472909
Pro   TP Morrison (0734) 476115
Holes 18 L 6204 yds SSS 70
Recs   Am–65 MG King
         Pro–64 AP Morley
V'trs   Mon–Thurs–UH Fri/ WE/ BH–M
         SOC–Tues–Thurs
Fees   £25
Loc   2 miles N of Reading, off
         Peppard Road (B481)

Royal Ascot (1887)

Winkfield Road, Ascot SL5 7LJ
Tel   (0344) 25175
Mem   600
Sec   J Young
Pro   G Malia (0344) 24656
Holes 18 L 5709 yds SSS 68
Recs   Am–66 K Rixon
V'trs   SOC
Fees   On application
Loc   Bracknell 3 miles. Windsor
         4 miles
Mis   Within boundaries of
         racecourse

The Royal Household

Buckingham Palace, London SW1
Tel   (071) 930 4832
Mem   200
Sec   A Jarred
Holes 9 L 4560 yds SSS 62
V'trs   Strictly by invitation
Loc   Home Park, Windsor Castle

Sonning (1914)

Sonning-on-Thames
Tel   (0734) 693332
Mem   500
Sec   PF Williams
Pro   RT McDougall (0734) 692910
Holes 18 L 6345 yds SSS 70
Recs   Am–65 J Lush
         Pro–65 B Lane
V'trs   WD–U WE–M
Fees   On application
Loc   S of A4, nr Sonning

Swinley Forest (1909)

Coronation Road, Ascot SL9 5LE
Tel   (0344) 20197
Mem   335
Sec   IL Pearce
Pro   RC Parker
Holes 18 L 6001 yds
Recs   Am–64 EF Storey, ER Sermon
         Pro–64 P Alliss
V'trs   M
Loc   S of Ascot

Temple (1909)

Henley Road, Hurley, Maidenhead SL6 5LH
Tel   (0628) 824248
Mem   600
Sec   DW Kirkland (0628) 824795
Pro   A Dobbins (0628) 824254
Holes 18 L 6206 yds SSS 70
Recs   Am–63 S Hodsdon
V'trs   WD–I WE/ BH–M SOC
Fees   £30
Loc   Between Maidenhead and
         Henley on A423. M4 Junction
         8/ 9. M40 Junction 3

West Berkshire (1975)

Chaddleworth, Newbury RG16 0HS
Tel   (04882) 574
Mem   700
Sec   W Richardson
Pro   D Sheppard (04882) 8851
Holes 18 L 7069 yds SSS 74
V'trs   WD–U WE–M SOC
Fees   £20
Loc   On A338 to Wantage. M4
         Junction 14

Winter Hill (1976)

Grange Lane, Cookham SL6 9RP
Tel   (06285) 27613
Mem   800
Sec   GB Charters-Rowe
Pro   P Hedges (06285) 27610
Holes 18 L 6408 yds SSS 71
Recs   Am–70 M Hunt (1983), C Bell
         (1985), K Boulter (1988)
V'trs   WD–U WE–M SOC
Fees   £20
Loc   Maidenhead 3 miles

Buckinghamshire

Abbey Hill (1975)

Public
Monks Way, Two Mile Ash, Milton Keynes MK8 8AA
Tel (0908) 563845
Pro S Harlock
Holes 18 L 6193 yds SSS 69
Recs Am–67 T Mernagh
Pro–67 H Stott
Fees On application
Loc 2 miles S of Stony Stratford. N of Milton Keynes

Beaconsfield (1914)

Beaconsfield HP9 2UR
Tel (0494) 676545
Mem 862
Sec PI Anderson
Pro M Brothers (0494) 676616
Holes 18 L 6487 yds SSS 71
Recs Am–66 D Haines
Pro–63 E Murray
V'trs WD–H WE–NA
Fees £30
Loc 8 miles N of Slough. 2 miles E of Beaconsfield

Buckingham (1914)

Tingewick Road, Buckingham MK18 4AE
Tel (0280) 813282
Mem 680
Sec D Rolph (0280) 815566
Pro T Gates (0280) 815210
Holes 18 L 6082 yds SSS 69
Recs Am–69 PJ Clarke
Pro–67 S Watson
V'trs WD–U WE–M SOC
Fees £18
Loc 1½ miles on Oxford road (A421)

Burnham Beeches (1891)

Burnham, Slough SL1 8EG
Tel (0628) 661150
Mem 670
Sec AJ Buckner (Mgr) (0628) 661448
Pro T Buckner (0628) 661661
Holes 18 L 6463 yds SSS 71
Recs Am–67 M Orris
Pro–64 H Flatman
V'trs WD–I WE/ BH–M
Fees £19.50 D–£29.50
Loc 4 miles W of Slough

Chartridge Park (1989)

Chartridge, Chesham HP5 2TF
Tel (0494) 791772
Mem 500
Sec Mrs A Gibbins
Pro P Gibbins
Holes 9 L 3550 yds SSS 68
Recs Am–74 J Grey (1990)
Pro–68 P Gibbins (1990)
V'trs U SOC
Fees £12

Loc Chartridge, 2 miles NW of Chesham. 6 miles W of M25
Mis Buggies available–£12

Chesham & Ley Hill (1919)

Ley Hill, Chesham HP5 1UZ
Tel (0494) 784541
Mem 384
Sec K Brown (Mgr)
Holes 9 L 5240 yds SSS 66
Recs Am–64 GA Knowes
Pro–65 M Lovegrove
V'trs Mon & Thurs-U Wed-U after noon Fri-U before 1pm –M after 1pm Tues–M after 3pm WE/ BH–M SOC–Thurs only
Fees £12
Loc Chesham 2 miles
Mis Course closed Sun after 2pm from 1st Apr-30th Sept

Chiltern Forest (1921)

Aston Hill, Halton, Aylesbury HP22 5NQ
Tel (0296) 630899 (Clubhouse)
Mem 570
Sec LEA Clark (0296) 631267
Pro C Skeet (0296) 631817
Holes 14 L 6173 yds SSS 70
Recs Am–67 D Ball (1989)
V'trs WD–U WE–M SOC
Fees £15 (1990)
Loc 5 miles SE of Aylesbury, off A4011

Denham (1910)

Tilehouse Lane, Denham UB9 5DE
Tel (0895) 832022
Mem 550
Sec Wg Cdr D Graham
Pro J Sheridan (0895) 832801
Holes 18 L 6439 yds SSS 71
Recs Am–66 DMA Steel
Pro–68 J Sheridan
V'trs Mon-Thurs-I H Fri-Sun/ BH–M
Fees £24 D–£37
Loc 3 miles NW of Uxbridge

Ellesborough (1906)

Butlers Cross, nr Aylesbury HP17 0TZ
Tel (0296) 622375
Mem 780
Sec KM Flint (0296) 622114
Pro P Warner (0296) 623126
Holes 18 L 6310 yds SSS 70
Recs Am–66 N Lucas, NM Allen, P Stevens
Pro–68 G Will
V'trs WE/ BH–M WD–I or H SOC–Wed & Thurs only
Fees On application
Loc 1 mile W of Wendover

Farnham Park (1974)

Public
Park Road, Stoke Poges, Slough SL2 4PJ
Tel (0753) 643332
Sec Mrs M Brooker (Hon)

Pro P Harrison
Holes 18 L 5847 yds SSS 68
Recs Am–69 N Harrison, D Ivall
Pro–68 T Bowers
Fees £6 (£8)
Loc 2 miles N of Slough

Flackwell Heath (1907)

High Wycombe HP10 9PE
Tel (062 85) 20027
Mem 750
Sec JJR Barton (062 85) 20929
Pro B Plucknett (062 85) 23017
Holes 18 L 6150 yds SSS 69
Recs Am–65 P Dougan
Pro–65 J Hoskison, E Murray
V'trs WD–H WE–M SOC–Wed & Thurs
Fees £22
Loc Between High Wycombe & Beaconsfield, off A40. M40 Junction 3 from London. M40 Junction 4 from Oxford

Gerrards Cross (1934)

Chalfont Park, Gerrards Cross SL9 0QA
Tel (0753) 883263
Mem 780
Sec PH Fisher
Pro AP Barr (0753) 885300
Holes 18 L 6295 yds SSS 70
Recs Am–65 JB Berney
Pro–63 AP Barr
V'trs WD–H WE/ BH–M SOC
Fees £25 D–£30
Loc 1 mile from station, off A413

Harewood Downs (1908)

Cokes Lane, Chalfont St Giles HP8 4TA
Tel (0494) 762308
Mem 350
Sec M Cannon (0494) 762184
Pro GC Morris (0494) 764102
Holes 18 L 5958 yds SSS 69
Recs Am–65 AL Parsons
Pro–65 JM Hume
V'trs WD–H WE/ BH–M SOC
Fees On application
Loc Off A413 to Amersham

Hazlemere G & CC (1982)

Penn Road, Hazlemere, High Wycombe HP15 7LR
Tel (0494) 714722
Mem 950
Sec DE Hudson
Pro SR Morvell (0494) 718298
Holes 18 L 5855 yds SSS 68
Recs Pro–65 J Bennett, R Green (1987)
V'trs WD–U WE–booking req SOC–WD
Fees £20 (£25)
Loc 3 miles NE of High Wycombe on B474
Mis Buggies for hire

Iver (1983)

Hollow Hill Lane, Iver SL0 0JJ
Tel   (0753) 655615
Mem   500
Sec   T Notley
Pro   T Notley
Holes 9 L 3107 yds SSS
Recs Am–68 D Sargood (1990)
      Pro–71 T Notley (1989)
V'trs U SOC
Fees 18 holes–£6.50 (£9) 9 holes–£4
      (£5.30)
Loc   1/2 mile from Langley station,
      off Langley Park Road

Ivinghoe (1967)

Wellcroft, Ivinghoe, nr Leighton
Buzzard LU7 9EF
Tel   (0296) 668696
Mem   250
Sec   Mrs SE Garrad (0296) 662478
Pro   PW Garrad
Holes 9 L 4508 yds SSS 62
Recs Am–61 J Dillon (1984)
      Pro–60 R Garrad (1967)
V'trs WD–U WE–U after 8am
Fees 18 holes–£5 (£6.50) 36
      holes–£7 (£8.50)
Loc   Tring 3 miles. Dunstable 4
      miles. M1 Junction 11, 5 miles

Little Chalfont (1981)

Lodge Lane, Little Chalfont, nr
Amersham
Tel   (0494) 764877
Mem   400
Sec   JM Dunne
Pro   B Woodhouse (0494) 762942
Holes 9 L 5852 yds SSS 68
Recs Am–76 D Brown
      Pro–65 S Parker
V'trs U SOC
Fees £7 (£9)
Loc   Station 1/2 mile

Stoke Poges (1908)

Park Road, Stoke Poges SL2 4PG
Tel   (0753) 26385
Mem   700
Sec   RC Pickering
Pro   K Thomas (0753) 23609
Holes 18 L 6654 yds SSS 71
Recs Am–65 BA Price, V Phillips
      Pro–65 J Hudson
V'trs WD–I or H WE/ BH–M
Fees £8 (£14)
Loc   2 miles N of Slough

Stowe (1974)

Stowe, Buckingham MK18 5EH
Tel   (0280) 815566
Mem   300
Sec   Mrs SA Cross (0280) 813650
Holes 9 L 4573 yds SSS 63
V'trs WD/WE 8am-1pm & after 7pm
      –M; School holidays–M SOC
Fees £5
Loc   M1 Junction 16-A5-A43-A413.
      4 miles from Buckingham, on
      A413 to Brackley .

Wavendon Golf Centre (1990)

Lower End Road, Wavendon, Milton
Keynes MK17 8DA
Tel   (0908) 281811
Sec   Mrs C Cheney
Pro   P Saunders
Holes 18 L 5800 yds SSS 66 9 hole
      Par 3
V'trs U
Fees £8 (£10)
Loc   1 1/2 miles from M1 Junction 13
Mis   Driving range

Weston Turville (1974)

New Road, Weston Turville, nr
Aylesbury HP22 5QT
Tel   (0296) 24084
Mem   460
Sec   AK Holden
Pro   G George (0296) 25949
Holes 18 L 6100 yds SSS 69
Recs Am–73 B Duff
V'trs U (exc Sun am) Sat-booking
Fees £8 (£10)
Loc   2 1/2 miles SE of Aylesbury

Wexham Park (1979)

Wexham Street, Wexham, nr Slough
SL3 6NB
Tel   (0753) 663271
Mem   650
Sec   JWE Mulley
Pro   D Morgan (0753) 663425
Holes Wexham 18 L 5836 yds SSS 68
      Old Grange 9 L 2383 yds
      SSS 32
V'trs U SOC–WD
Fees 18 hole:£5.60 (£8) 9 hole:£3.60
      (£4.60)
Loc   2 miles N of Slough
Mis   Further 9 holes opening 1991

Whiteleaf (1904)

Whiteleaf, Aylesbury
Tel   (084 44) 3097
Mem   300
Sec   DG Bullard (0844) 274058
Pro   KS Ward (084 44) 5472
Holes 9 L 2756 yds SSS 66
Recs Am–64 M Copping
      Pro–63 MM Caines
V'trs WD–U WE–M SOC
Fees 18 holes–£15. 36 holes–£20
Loc   Princes Risborough 2 miles

Windmill Hill (1972)

Public
Tattenhoe Lane, Bletchley, Milton
Keynes MK3 7RB
Tel   (0908) 378623
Fax   (0908) 271478
Pro   C Clingan
Holes 18 L 6773 yds SSS 72
Recs Am–69 RJ Long
      Pro–66 C Defoy
V'trs U SOC

Fees £4.50 (£6.30)
Loc   4 miles from M1 Junction 14,
      on A421
Mis   Floodlit driving range

Woburn (1976)

Bow Brickhill, Milton Keynes
Tel   (0908) 370756
Pro   A Hay (0908) 647987
Holes Duke's 18 L 6940 yds SSS 74
      Duchess 18 L 6641 yds SSS 72
Recs Duke's Pro–64 P Mitchell,
      A Murray
V'trs WD–H (by arrangement)
      WE–M
Fees By arrangement
Loc   4 miles W of M1 Junction 13

Cambridgeshire

Abbotsley (1986)

Eynesbury Hardwicke, St Neots
PE19 4XN
Tel   (0480) 215153
Mem   700
Sec   J Wisson
Pro   V Saunders
Holes 18 L 6150 yds SSS 71
Recs Am–72 J Morrow (1987)
      Pro–69 S Whymark (1984)
V'trs WD–U SOC WE–M before
      10am –U after 10am BH–U
Fees £12 (£15)
Loc   2 miles SE of St Neots on
      B1046. 12 miles W of
      Cambridge. M11 Junction 13,
      on to A45
Mis   Floodlit driving range. Hotel.

Cambridgeshire Moat House Hotel (1974)

Bar Hill, Cambridge CB3 8EU
Tel   (0954) 780555
Mem   450
Sec   GW Huggett
Pro   GW Huggett (0954) 780098
Holes 18 L 6734 yds SSS 72
Recs Am–68 P Way
      Pro–68 P Townsend
V'trs I
Fees £18.50 (£25)
Loc   5 miles NW of Cambridge on
      A604
Mis   Buggies for hire

Ely City (1961)

Cambridge Road, Ely CB7 4HX
Tel   (0353) 2751
Mem   750
Sec   GA Briggs
Pro   F Rowden (0353) 3317
      (Touring Pro H Baiocchi)
Holes 18 L 6686 yds SSS 72
Recs Am–68 N Burke
      Pro–66 L Trevino
V'trs WD–H WE–H SOC–Tues-Fri
Fees £20 (£30)
Loc   12 miles N of Cambridge

Girton (1936)

Dodford Lane, Cambridge
Tel	(0223) 276169
Mem	700
Sec	Mrs MA Cornwell
Pro	J Sharkey
Holes	18 L 6085 yds SSS 69
V'trs	WD–U WE/ BH–M SOC
Fees	D–£16 with h'cap certificate. D–£21 without h'cap certificate
Loc	3 miles N of Cambridge (A604)

Gog Magog (1901)

Shelford Bottom, Cambridge
CB2 4AB
Tel	(0223) 247626
Mem	1050
Sec	JE Riches
Pro	I Bamborough (0223) 246058
Holes	Old 18 L 6386 yds SSS 70 New 9 L 5833 yds SSS 68
Recs	Am–64 RW Guy, MT Seaton, DWG Woods, R Claydon Pro–64 G Wolstenholme, PJ Butler
V'trs	WD–I or H WE/ BH–M SOC–Tues & Thurs
Fees	Old–£30 New–£15
Loc	2 miles S of Cambridge on A1307 (A604)

March (1922)

Frogs Abbey, Grange Rd, March
PE15 0YH
Tel	(0354) 52364
Mem	350
Sec	Lt Cdr AJ de Lozey (0354) 54910
Pro	SJ Scott
Holes	9 L 6210 yds SSS 70
Recs	Am–68 JW Kisby
V'trs	H WE–M
Fees	£15
Loc	18 miles E of Peterborough

Orton Meadows (1987)

Public
Ham Lane, Peterborough PE2 0UU
Tel	(0733) 237478
Pro	N Grant
Holes	18 L 5800 yds SSS 68
Recs	Am–71 J Devine (1990) Pro–67 R Mann (1987)
V'trs	U (phone Pro)
Fees	£5 (£7.50)
Loc	2 miles SW of Peterborough on A605
Mis	12 hole pitch & putt

Peterborough Milton (1937)

Milton Ferry, Peterborough
PE6 7AG
Tel	(0733) 380204
Mem	800
Sec	DK Adams (0733) 380489
Pro	NS Bundy (0733) 380793
Holes	18 L 6450 yds SSS 71
Recs	Am–68 MS Herson (1990) Pro–66 J Higgins (1990)
V'trs	WD–U WE–M SOC
Fees	£20
Loc	4 miles W of Peterborough on A47
Mis	Buggies for hire

Ramsey (1964)

4 Abbey Terrace, Ramsey,
Huntingdon PE17 1DD
Tel	(0487) 813573
Mem	750
Sec	R Muirhead (0487) 812600
Pro	BJ Puttick (0487) 813022
Holes	18 L 6145 yds SSS 70
Recs	Am–66 DP Smith (1987) Pro–67 F Kiddie (1989)
V'trs	WD–H WE/ BH–M SOC
Fees	£20
Loc	12 miles SE of Peterborough

St Ives (1923)

St Ives, Huntingdon PE17 4RS
Tel	(0480) 64459
Mem	320
Sec	R Hill IPFA (0480) 68392
Pro	A Headley (0480) 66067
Holes	9 L 6100 yds SSS 69
Recs	Am–67 Fl-Lt CJB Murdoch Pro–61 P Alliss
V'trs	WD–U WE–M
Fees	£12
Loc	5 miles E of Huntingdon

St Neot's (1890)

Crosshall Road, St Neot's PE19 4AE
Tel	(0480) 74311
Mem	600
Sec	RJ Marsden (0480) 72363
Pro	G Bithrey (0480) 76513
Holes	18 L 6027 yds SSS 69
Recs	Am–67 JR Gray Pro–65 M Gallagher, H Flatman
V'trs	H WE–M
Fees	£15 D–£25
Loc	1 mile W of St Neot's on A45
Mis	Buggy £12 D–£20

Thorpe Wood (1975)

Public
Nene Parkway, Peterborough
PE3 6SE
Tel	(0733) 267701
Fax	(0733) 332774
Pro	D Fitton, R Fitton
Holes	18 L 7086 yds SSS 74
Recs	Am–74 N Brownlie, JN Dodd, J Brady Pro–71 R Fitton
V'trs	U
Fees	£5 (£7.50)
Loc	3 miles W of Peterborough, on A47

Channel Islands

Alderney (1969)

Route des Carrières, Alderney
Tel	(048 182) 2835
Mem	520
Sec	AW Barthram
Holes	9 L 2528 yds SSS 33
Recs	Am–29 M Hugman Pro–28 PL Cunningham
V'trs	U
Fees	£8 (£14)
Loc	1 mile E of St Anne

L'Ancresse

L'Ancresse, Guernsey
Tel	(0481) 47408
Mem	315
Sec	M Russell (0481) 55805
Holes	Share L'Ancresse course with Royal Guernsey

La Moye (1902)

La Moye, St Brelade, Jersey
Tel	(0534) 42701
Mem	1250
Sec	P Clash (0534) 43401
Pro	D Melville (0534) 43130
Holes	18 L 6741 yds SSS 72
Recs	Am–69 BJ McCarthy (1987) Pro–62 G Brand Jr
V'trs	IH SOC–9.30–11am and 2.30–4pm WE–after 2.30pm
Fees	£25 (£30) W–£125
Loc	6 miles W of St Helier

Les Mielles

Public
The Mount, Val de la Mare,
St Ouens, Jersey
Tel	(0534) 81947/ 82787
Sec	J Le Brun (Mgr) (0534) 82629
Pro	C Wackeb (0534) 82787
Holes	12 holes Par 3 SSS 36
V'trs	U
Fees	£3.50 (£4)
Loc	Five Mile Road, St Ouens Bay
Mis	Driving range

Royal Guernsey (1890)

L'Ancresse, Guernsey
Tel	(0481) 47022
Mem	1520
Sec	GJ Nicolle (0481) 46523
Pro	N Wood (0481) 45070
Holes	18 L 6206 yds SSS 70
Recs	Am–64 R Eggo (1986) Pro–64 P Cunningham
V'trs	WD–H WE–NA
Fees	£15
Loc	5 miles N of St Peter Port

Royal Jersey (1878)

Grouville, Jersey
Tel	(0534) 54416
Mem	1300
Sec	RC Leader
Pro	T Horton (0534) 52234

Holes	18 L 6051 yds SSS 70
Recs	Am–64 R Harrop (1989)
	Pro–64 P Le Chevalier (1988)
V'trs	WD–H after 10am WE/ BH–H
	after 2.30pm (Winter 12.30pm)
Fees	£25 (£30)
Loc	4 miles E of St Helier

St Clements (1925)

Public

St Clements, Jersey	
Tel	(0534) 21938
Pro	R Marks
Holes	9 L 3972 yds SSS 61
Recs	Am–61 T Gray, B McCarthy
V'trs	U exc Sun am–NA
Fees	D–£9
Loc	1 mile E of St Helier
Mis	Book by telephone

Cheshire

Alderley Edge (1907)

Brook Lane, Alderley Edge SK9 7RU	
Tel	(0625) 585583
Mem	212 90(L) 40(J) 40(5)
Sec	To be appointed
Pro	M Stewart (0625) 584493
Holes	9 L 5836 yds SSS 68
Recs	Am–65 FA Hardy, DJ Austin
	Pro–65 BR Boughey
V'trs	M or H
Fees	£12 (£15)
Loc	12 miles S of Manchester

Astbury (1922)

Peel Lane, Astbury, nr Congleton CW12 4RE	
Tel	(0260) 272772
Mem	600
Sec	T Williams
Pro	SR Bassil
Holes	18 L 6269 yds SSS 70
Recs	Am–65 AJA Hurst (1983)
	Pro–69 I Mosey (1979)
V'trs	WD–H or M WE–M
	SOC–Thurs only
Fees	£12
Loc	1 mile S of Congleton off A34, via Astbury

Birchwood (1979)

Kelvin Close, Birchwood, Warrington	
Tel	(0925) 818819
Mem	1069
Sec	A Jackson
Pro	D Cooper
Holes	18 L 6808 yds SSS 73
Recs	Am–68 P McEwan
	Pro–65 P Affleck
V'trs	U SOC–Mon & Thurs
Fees	£18 (£25)
Loc	M62 Junction 11, 2 miles

Chester (1900)

Curzon Park, Chester CH4 8AR	
Tel	(0244) 675130
Mem	840
Sec	E Butler ACIS (0244) 677760
Pro	G Parton (0244) 671185
Holes	18 L 6487 yds SSS 71
Recs	Am–68 M Weetman
	Pro–66 D Screeton
V'trs	UH SOC
Fees	£16 (£20)
Loc	Chester 1 mile

Congleton (1897)

Biddulph Road, Congleton CW12 3LZ	
Tel	(0260) 273540
Mem	425
Sec	FT Pegg
Pro	JA Colclough (0260) 271083
Holes	9 L 5704 yds SSS 65
Recs	Am–60 M Griffiths (1989)
	Pro–59 N Coles (1968)
V'trs	U
Fees	On application
Loc	1½ miles from Congleton on A527

Crewe (1911)

Fields Road, Haslington, Crewe CW1 1TB	
Tel	(0270) 584227 (Steward)
Mem	601
Sec	DG Elias B.Sc (0270) 584099
Pro	R Rimmer (0270) 585032
Holes	18 L 6202 yds SSS 70
Recs	Am–67 VG McCandless (1990)
	Pro–68 D Cooper, M Roe (1990)
V'trs	WD–U WE/ BH–M SOC
Fees	£15 D–£20
Loc	2 miles NE of Crewe Station, off A534. 5 miles W of M6 Junction 16

Delamere Forest (1910)

Station Road, Delamere, Northwich CW8 2JE	
Tel	(0606) 882807
Mem	400
Sec	L Parkin
Pro	EB Jones (0606) 883307
Holes	18 L 6305 yds SSS 70
Recs	Am–66 B Stockdale
	Pro–63 M Bembridge
V'trs	WD–U WE–2 ball only SOC
Fees	£15 (£20)
Loc	10 miles E of Chester

Eaton (1965)

Eaton Park, Eccleston, Chester CH4 9JF	
Tel	(0244) 671420
Fax	(0244) 671838
Sec	RT Robinson (0244) 680474
Pro	A Mitchell (0244) 680170
Holes	18 L 6446 yds SSS 71
V'trs	I SOC–WD
Fees	On application
Loc	3 miles S of Chester

Ellesmere Port (1971)

Public

Chester Road, Hooton, South Wirral L66 1QH	
Tel	(051) 339 7689
Pro	D Yates
Holes	18 L 6432 yds SSS 71
Recs	Am–66 A Waterhouse
	Pro–67 B Evans, A Caygill
V'trs	SOC–WD WE–Arrange with Pro
Fees	£3.20 (£4)
Loc	9 miles N of Chester on A41

Frodsham (1990)

Simons Lane, Frodsham WA6 6HE	
Tel	(0928) 32159
Mem	450
Sec	EI Roylance
Pro	G Tonge (0928) 39442
Holes	18 L 6289 yds SSS 70
V'trs	WD–U WE/ BH–M SOC
Fees	£16
Loc	9 miles NE of Chester (A56). M56 Junction 12, 2 miles

Helsby (1902)

Tower's Lane, Helsby, Warrington WA6 0JB	
Tel	(0928) 722021
Mem	600
Sec	N Littler
Pro	I Wright (0928) 725457
Holes	18 L 6204 yds SSS 70
Recs	Am–69 D Stallard
	Pro–68 I Wright
V'trs	WE–NA SOC
Fees	£15
Loc	1 mile from M56 Junction 14 to Helsby, off Primrose Lane

Knights Grange (1983)

Public

Grange Lane, Winsford CW7 2PT	
Tel	(06065) 52780
Pro	G Moore (0606) 75476
Holes	9 L 5720 yds SSS 68
V'trs	U SOC
Fees	18 holes–£2.30 (£3)
	9 holes–£1.80 (£2.30)
Loc	Signposted to Knights Grange Sports Complex

Knutsford (1891)

Mereheath Lane, Knutsford	
Tel	(0565) 3355
Mem	210
Sec	D Francis
Pro	A Gillies
Holes	9 L 6288 yds SSS 70
Recs	Am–65 B Stockdale
	Pro–65 D Cooper
V'trs	I exc Wed–NA SOC
Fees	£12 (£18)
Loc	Knutsford ¼ mile

Lymm (1907)

Whitbarrow Road, Lymm WA13 9AN
Tel	(092 575) 2177
Mem	400 100(L) 75(J) 50(5)
Sec	JM Pearson (092 575) 5020
Pro	GJ Williams (092 575) 5054
Holes	18 L 6304 yds SSS 70
Recs	Am–68 CN Brown (1987)
	Pro–69 S Lyle (1987)
V'trs	WD–H WE–M
Fees	£18
Loc	5 miles SE of Warrington

Macclesfield (1889)

The Hollins, Macclesfield
SK11 7EA
Tel	(0625) 23227
Mem	600
Pro	T Taylor (0625) 616952
Holes	12 L 6184 yds SSS 69
Recs	Am–69 RA Johnson,
	B Hodkinson
	Pro–67 M Gregson
V'trs	WD/ BH–I WE–M
Fees	£15
Loc	1 mile SE of Macclesfield

Malkins Bank

Public
Malkins Bank, Sandbach
Tel	(0270) 765931
Pro	D Wheeler
Holes	18 L 6071 yds SSS 69
Recs	Am–71 JR Dabecki (1989)
V'trs	U SOC
Fees	£3.65 (£4.40)
Loc	2 miles S of Sandbach via
	A534/ A533. M6 Junction 17

Mere G & CC (1934)

Mere, Knutsford WA16 6LJ
Tel	(0565) 830155
Mem	375 175(L) 100(J)
Sec	AB Turner
Pro	EP Goodwin (0565) 830219
Holes	18 L 6849 yds SSS 73
Recs	Am–68 CR Smethurst
	Pro–69 N Faldo
V'trs	WE/ BH–NA Wed & Fri–NA
	Mon/ Tues/ Thurs-H SOC
Fees	£30
Loc	1 mile E of M6 Junction 19
Mis	Driving range. Buggies

New Mills (1907)

Shaw Marsh, New Mills, Stockport
Tel	(0663) 743485
Mem	350
Sec	R Tuson (0663) 747205
Pro	A Hoyles (0663) 746161
Holes	9 L 5633 yds SSS 67
Recs	Am–67 G Scattergood
	Pro–66 I Scott
V'trs	WD–U WE–M SOC
Fees	D–£8

Oaklands G & CC (1990)

Forest Road, Tarporley CW6 0JA
Tel	(0829) 733884
Sec	R Hitchin (Hon)
Pro	B Rimmer
Holes	18 L 6473 yds SSS 71
V'trs	U
Fees	£18
Loc	1 mile N of Tarporley on A49
	Warrington road

Poulton Park (1980)

Dig Lane, Cinnamon Brow
Tel	(0925) 812034
Mem	360
Sec	J Reekie
Pro	S McCarthy (0925) 825220
Holes	9 L 4918 metres SSS 66
Recs	Am–66 S Bennett
V'trs	WD–NA 5-6pm WE–NA
	12–2pm
Fees	£12 (£14)
Loc	Off Crab Lane, Fearnhead

Prestbury (1920)

Macclesfield Road, Prestbury,
Macclesfield SK10 4BJ
Tel	(0625) 829388
Mem	725
Sec	AW Wilkinson (Hon) (0625)
	828241
Pro	TW Rastall (0625) 828242
Holes	18 L 6359 yds SSS 71
Recs	Am–66 R Foster, JE Allen
	Pro–68 M Faulkener
V'trs	WD–I WE–M SOC–Thurs
Fees	£20
Loc	2¹/₂ miles NW of Macclesfield

Queen's Park (1985)

Public
Queen's Park Gardens, Crewe
CW2 7SB
Tel	(0270) 666724
Pro	M Williams
Holes	9 L 5370 yds Par 68
V'trs	WD–U WE–U after 8.30am
	SOC
Fees	£2.50 (£3)
Loc	1¹/₄ miles from Crewe, off
	Victoria Avenue

Runcorn (1909)

Clifton Road, Runcorn
Tel	(0928) 572093 (Members)
Mem	375 80(L) 80(J)
Sec	GE Povey OBE JP (0928)
	574214
Pro	G Berry (0928) 564791
Holes	18 L 6035 yds SSS 69
Recs	Am–67 I Rockliffe
V'trs	WD–U exc comp days H SOC
Fees	£14 (£18)
Loc	Runcorn (A557). M56
	Junction 12

Sandbach (1923)

Middlewich Road, Sandbach
CW11 9EA
Tel	(0270) 762117
Mem	215 110(L) 50(J)
Sec	AF Pearson
Holes	9 L 5614 yds SSS 67
Recs	Am–64 K Brooks
V'trs	WD–U WE/ BH–M
Fees	D–£15
Loc	Sandbach 1 mile

Sandiway (1921)

Sandiway CW8 2DJ
Tel	(0606) 882606
Mem	750
Sec	VFC Wood (0606) 883247
Pro	W Laird (0606) 883180
Holes	18 L 6435 yds SSS 72
Recs	Am–67 AE Hill
	Pro–65 D Huish
V'trs	I H
Fees	£25 (£30)
Loc	Chester 15 miles on A556

Shrigley Hall

Shrigley Park, Pott Shrigley,
Macclesfield SK10 5SB
Tel	(0625) 575755
Fax	(0625) 573323
Mem	540
Sec	Mrs S Major
Pro	G Ogden (0625) 575626
Holes	18 L 6305 yds SSS 71
Recs	Am–73 N Green (1990)
	Pro–68 G Ogden (1989)
V'trs	H SOC
Fees	£18 (£27)
Loc	5 miles NE of Macclesfield, off
	A523. M6 Junction 18

The Tytherington (1986)

Macclesfield SK10 2JP
Tel	(0625) 34562
Fax	(0625) 611076
Mem	400
Sec	P Dawson
Pro	S Wilson
Holes	18 L 6737 yds SSS 72
V'trs	U
Fees	£18 D–£26 (£22 D–£32)
Loc	Nr Macclesfield on
	Manchester road

Upton-by-Chester (1934)

Upton Lane, Chester CH2 1EE
Tel	(0244) 381183
Mem	750
Sec	JB Durban
Pro	PA Gardner (0244) 381333
Holes	18 L 5875 yds SSS 68
Recs	Am–62 J Davies
	Pro–66 A Perry
V'trs	U SOC–WD
Fees	£15 (£20)
Loc	Off Liverpool road, nr 'Frog' PH

For list of abbreviations see page 487.

Vicars Cross (1939)

Vicars Cross, Chester CH3 7HN
Tel   (0244) 335174
Mem   650
Sec   DC Chilton
Pro   JA Forsythe (0244) 335595
Holes   18 L 6238 yds SSS 70
V'trs   Mon-Thurs-U Fri/ WE/ BH-M
Fees   £15 D-£18
Loc   2 miles E of Chester on A51

Walton Hall

Public
**Warrington Road, Higher Walton,
Warrington WA4 5LU**
Tel   (0925) 66775
Sec   M Youd
Pro   MJ Slater (0925) 63061
Holes   18 L 6843 yds SSS 73
Recs   Am-70 R Davies (1988)
V'trs   U
Fees   £4.50 (£5.50)
Loc   2 miles S of Warrington

Warrington (1903)

Hill Warren, Appleton
Tel   (0925) 61620
Mem   875
Sec   RO Francis (0925) 61775
Pro   AW Fryer (0925) 65431
Holes   18 L 6305 yds SSS 70
Recs   Am-66 JR Bennett
        Pro-65 EG Lester
V'trs   U SOC-Wed & Thurs
Fees   £9.50 (£14)
Loc   3 miles S of Warrington

Widnes (1924)

Highfield Road, Widnes WA8 7DT
Tel   (051) 424 2440
Mem   800
Sec   MM Cresswell (051) 424 2995
Pro   F Robinson (051) 424 2995
Holes   18 L 5719 yds SSS 68
Recs   Am-64 F Whitfield (1990)
        Pro-64 A Murray
V'trs   WD-U WE-NA on comp days
        SOC-Wed
Fees   £13.50 (£16.50)
Loc   Station ½ mile

Widnes Municipal (1977)

Public
Dundalk Road, Widnes WA8 8BS
Tel   (051) 424 6230
Pro   R Bilton (0295) 65241
Holes   18 L 5612 yds SSS 67
Recs   Am-67 I O'Connor (1989)
V'trs   U
Fees   £2.70 (£3.35)
Mis   St Michael Jubilee Club plays
        here

Wilmslow (1889)

**Great Warford, Mobberley,
Knutsford WA16 7AY**
Tel   (056 587) 2579
Mem   770
Sec   BC Jones (056 587) 2148

Pro   J Nowicki (056 587) 3620
Holes   18 L 6500 yds SSS 71
Recs   Am-68 A O'Connor, TB Taylor
        Pro-64 J O'Leary
V'trs   UH exc Wed-NA before 3pm
Fees   On application
Loc   3½ miles W of Alderley Edge

Cleveland

Billingham (1967)

Sandy Lane, Billingham TS22 5NA
Tel   (0642) 554494/ 533816
Mem   800
Sec   DJ Bruce OBE (0642) 533816
Pro   P Bradley (0642) 557060
Holes   18 L 6430 yds SSS 71
Recs   AM-66 M Ure (1988)
        Pro-65 P Harrison (1988)
V'trs   WD-H after 9am WE/ BH-M
        SOC
Fees   D-£15
Loc   W boundary of Billingham by
        A19, E of bypass

Castle Eden & Peterlee (1927)

Castle Eden, Hartlepool
Tel   (0429) 836220
Mem   650
Sec   P Robinson
Pro   T Jenkins (0429) 836689
Holes   18 L 6297 yds SSS 70
Recs   Am-66 G Border (1987)
V'trs   U
Fees   £15 (£20)
Loc   2 miles S of Peterlee

Cleveland (1887)

Queen Street, Redcar TS10 1BT
Tel   (0642) 483693
Mem   674
Sec   LR Manley (0642) 471798
Pro   D Masey (0642) 483462
Holes   18 L 6707 yds SSS 72
Recs   Am-68 M Watson (1978)
        Pro-70 B Hardcastle (1976)
V'trs   WD-U after 9.30am WE/
        BH-no parties SOC
Fees   £12 (£18)
Loc   S bank of River Tees

Eaglescliffe (1914)

**Yarm Road, Eaglescliffe, Stockton-
on-Tees**
Tel   (0642) 780098
Mem   470
Sec   AH Painter (0642) 780238
Pro   J Munro (0642) 780588
Holes   18 L 6275 yds SSS 70
Recs   Am-67 B Skipper (1985)
        Pro-67 J Munro (1976)
V'trs   H
Fees   £14 (£20)
Loc   3 miles S of Stockton-on-Tees

Hartlepool (1906)

Hart Warren, Hartlepool
Tel   (0429) 274398
Mem   600
Sec   WE Storrow (0429) 870282
Pro   ME Cole (0429) 267473
Holes   18 L 6005 yds SSS 70
Recs   Am-63 G Bell (1990)
        Pro-66 G Brown (1987)
V'trs   WD-U SOC
Fees   £14 (£20)
Loc   N boundary of Hartlepool

Middlesbrough (1908)

**Brass Castle Lane, Middlesbrough
TS8 9EE**
Tel   (0642) 316430
Mem   900
Sec   JM Jackson (0642) 311515
Pro   DJ Jones (0642) 311766
Holes   18 L 6136 yds SSS 69
Recs   Am-67 A Raitt (1990)
        Pro-66 W McColl (1990)
V'trs   U
Fees   D-£16 (£20)
Loc   3 miles S of Middlesbrough

Middlesbrough Municipal (1977)

Public
**Ladgate Lane, Middlesbrough
TS5 7YZ**
Tel   (0642) 315533
Sec   J Dilworth (Hon)
Pro   M Nutter (0642) 315361
Holes   18 L 6314 yds SSS 70
Recs   Am-69 NBJ Fick
        Pro-67 B Gallagher
V'trs   U
Fees   £3.75 (£5)
Loc   3 miles S of Middlesbrough on
        A174
Mis   Floodlit driving range

Saltburn (1894)

Hob Hill, Saltburn-by-the-Sea
Tel   (0287) 622812
Mem   900
Sec   D Becker
Pro   R Broadbent (0287) 24653
Holes   18 L 5846 yds SSS 68
Recs   Am-66
        Pro-62 D Rees
V'trs   H SOC
Fees   £12 (£13.50)

Seaton Carew (1874)

Tees Road, Hartlepool TS25 1DE
Tel   (0429) 266249
Mem   650
Sec   T Waite (0429) 267645
Pro   W Hector
Holes   Old L 6604 yds SSS 72
        Brabazon L 6802 yds SSS 73
Recs   Am-66 M Kelley
        Pro-67 JW Johnson
V'trs   U SOC
Fees   £16 (£20)
Loc   Hartlepool 2 miles

Tees-side (1901)

Acklam Road, Thornaby TS17 7JS
Tel   (0642) 676249
Mem   600
Sec   W Allen (0642) 616516
Pro   K Hall (0642) 673822
Holes   18 L 6472 yds SSS 71
V'trs   WD–U before 4.30pm WE–U
        after 11am BH–M before 11am
        SOC
Fees   D–£10 (D–£14)
Loc   2 miles S of Stockton on A1130.
        1/2 mile from A19 on A1130

Wilton (1949)

Wilton, Redcar TS10 4QY
Tel   (0642) 465265
Mem   700
Sec   DW Lewis (0642) 477570
Pro   AL Maskell
Holes   18 L 6104 yds SSS 69
Recs   Am–64 N Crapper
        Pro–68 S Hunt
V'trs   WD–U Sat–NA Sun/ BH–U SOC
Fees   £10
Loc   3 miles W of Redcar on A174

Cornwall

The Ballpark (1988)

Wheal Dream, Wendron, Helston
TR13 0LX
Tel   (0326) 572518
Fax   (0326) 565236
Sec   JD & MC Robinson (Props)
Holes   18 hole approach course
V'trs   U
Fees   £3
Loc   2 miles N of Helston on B3297
Mis   Pitch & putt

Bodmin G & CC (1991)

Bodmin
Tel   (0208) 73600/ 77325
Sec   J Madhvani (Prop)
Holes   18 L 6137 yds SSS 71 (Course
        open June 1991)
V'trs   H SOC
Fees   On application
Loc   1 mile S of Bodmin, off B3268
Mis   Driving range

Bude & North Cornwall (1891)

Burn View, Bude EX23 8DA
Tel   (0288) 352006
Mem   500 220(L) 60(J)
Sec   PK Brown
Pro   J Yeo
Holes   18 L 6202 yds SSS 70
Recs   Am–67 D Cann
        Pro–70 C Pennington
V'trs   U 9.30-12.30pm, 2-5pm and
        after 6.30pm
Fees   £17 (£25)
Loc   In Bude

Budock Vean Hotel (1922)

Falmouth
Tel   (0326) 250288
Mem   250
Sec   FG Benney (0326) 250060
Holes   9 L 5007 yds SSS 65
Recs   Am–61 RJ Sadler
        Pro–64 D Short
V'trs   H
Fees   £9 (£12)
Loc   Falmouth 5 miles

Cape Cornwall G & CC (1990)

St Just, Penzance TR19 7NL
Tel   (0736) 788611
Mem   220
Sec   M Fraser
Pro   R Hamilton
Holes   18 L 5788 yds SSS
V'trs   WD/ Sat–UH Sun–NA before
        noon SOC
Fees   £10 (£12)
Loc   1 mile W of St Just. 8 miles W of
        Penzance, off A3071

Carlyon Bay (1926)

Carlyon Bay, St Austell
Tel   (072 681) 4250
Mem   600
Sec   CH Farmer
Pro   NJ Sears (072 681) 4228
Holes   18 L 6510 yds SSS 71
Recs   Am–68 A Nash
        Pro–65 N Coles
V'trs   U-book with Pro
Fees   £17.50 (£25)
Loc   2 miles E of St Austell
Mis   Buggies for hire

Culdrose

Royal Naval Air Station, Culdrose
Tel   (0326) 574121 (Ext 7413)
Mem   150
Sec   N Darby (Ext 7543)
Holes   9 L 6412 yds SSS 71
V'trs   M

Falmouth (1928)

Swanpool Road, Falmouth TR11 5BQ
Tel   (0326) 311262
Mem   600
Sec   DJ de C Sizer (Mgr) (0326)
        40525
Pro   D Short (0326) 316229
Holes   18 L 5581 yds SSS 67
Recs   Am–60 JL Gresson (1988)
        Pro–65 G Brand Jr (1981)
V'trs   U SOC
Fees   £15 D–£20 W–£70
Loc   6 miles NW of Falmouth, nr
        Swanpool Beach

Isles of Scilly (1904)

St Mary's, Isles of Scilly TR21 0NF
Tel   (0720) 22692
Mem   380
Holes   9 L 5974 yds SSS 69

Recs   Am–69 M Twynham
V'trs   U Sun–M
Fees   £7 W–£15.50
Loc   Hughtown 1 1/2 miles

Launceston (1928)

St Stephen, Launceston
Tel   (0566) 773442
Mem   900
Sec   BJ Grant
Pro   J Tozer
Holes   18 L 6407 yds SSS 71
Recs   Am–67 C Phillips (1987)
        Pro–64 S Little (1989)
V'trs   WE–NA SOC
Fees   £18
Loc   1 mile N of Launceston, off
        Bude road

Looe (1933)

Bin Down, nr Looe PL13 1PX
Tel   (05034) 239
Mem   550
Sec   G Bond (Gen Mgr)
Pro   A MacDonald
Holes   18 L 5940 yds SSS 68
V'trs   U SOC
Fees   £13.50 (£16)
Loc   3 miles E of Looe

Lostwithiel G & CC (1990)

Lower Polscoe, Lostwithiel PL22 0HQ
Tel   (0208) 873550
Fax   (0208) 873550
Sec   Mrs J Collings
Pro   To be appointed
Holes   18 L 6098 yds Par 72
V'trs   WD–H WE–restricted SOC
Fees   £15 (£20)
Loc   1 mile E of Lostwithiel, off A390
Mis   Driving range

Mullion (1895)

Cury Helston TR12 7BP
Tel   (0326) 240276
Mem   800
Sec   D Watts (0326) 240685
Pro   M Singleton (0326) 241176
Holes   18 L 5610 yds SSS 67
Recs   Am–66 PA Gilbert
        Pro–68 BJ Hunt, P Alliss
V'trs   H (restricted comp days and
        open days) SOC–WD
Fees   £12 W–£40 F–£60
Loc   6 miles S of Helston

Newquay (1890)

Tower Road, Newquay TR7 1LT
Tel   (0637) 872091
Mem   500
Sec   G Binney (0637) 874354
Pro   P Muscroft (0637) 874830
Holes   18 L 6140 yds SSS 69
Recs   Am–63 P Clayton (1989)
        Pro–69 PJ Yeo
V'trs   WD/ Sat–H Sun–H
Fees   £12 (£15) W–£48
Loc   1/2 mile from Newquay

Perranporth (1927)

Budnick Hill, Perranporth TR6 0AB
Tel	(0872) 572454
Mem	550
Sec	PDR Barnes (0872) 573701
Pro	DC Mitchell (0872) 572317
Holes	18 L 6286 yds SSS 72
Recs	Am–65
	Pro–68
V'trs	WD–U WE–H SOC
Fees	D–£15 (D–£18)
Loc	1/2 mile NW of Perranporth

Praa Sands (1971)

Praa Sands, Germoe Cross Roads, Penzance TR20 9TQ
Tel	(0736) 763445
Mem	300
Sec	D & K Phillips (Props)
Pro	P Atherton
Holes	9 L 4036 yds SSS 60
Recs	Am–59 P Lorys
V'trs	U exc Sun am
Fees	£10 W–£60
Loc	7 miles E of Penzance on A394 Penzance-Helston road, at Praa Sands

St Austell (1912)

Tregongeeves, St Austell
Tel	(0726) 74756
Mem	780
Sec	SH Davey
Pro	M Rowe (0726) 68621
Holes	18 L 5981 yds SSS 69
Recs	Am–67 AC Nash
V'trs	SOC exc comp days
Fees	On application
Loc	1 1/2 miles W of St Austell

St Enodoc (1890)

Rock, Wadebridge PL27 6LB
Tel	(020 886) 3216
Mem	1050
Sec	Col L Guy OBE
Pro	NJ Williams (020 886) 2402
Holes	Church 18 L 6207 yds SSS 70
	Holywell 18 L 4165 yds SSS 61
Recs	Am–65 K Jones
	Pro–67 Dai Rees
V'trs	Main course-H SOC Short course-U
Fees	Church £20 W–£112 Holywell £12 W–£56
Loc	Wadebridge 6 miles
Mis	Max handicap 24

St Mellion (1976)

St Mellion, nr Saltash PL12 6SD
Tel	(0579) 50101
Mem	700
Sec	D Webb (Golf Dir)
Pro	A Moore (0579) 50724
Holes	Old 18 L 5927 yds SSS 68
	Jack Nicklaus Course 18 L 6626 yds SSS 72
V'trs	H SOC
Loc	Tamar Bridge
Mis	Buggies. Driving range

Tehidy Park (1922)

Camborne TR14 0HH
Tel	(0209) 842208
Mem	1000
Sec	RD Parry
Pro	J Dumbreck (0209) 842914
Holes	18 L 6241 yds SSS 70
Recs	Am–67 N Rogers (1989)
	Pro–68 J Langmead (1990)
V'trs	H
Fees	£15 (£20)
Loc	3 miles N of Camborne

Tregenna Castle Hotel (1982)

St Ives TR26 2DE
Tel	(0736) 795254 (Ext 121)
Mem	297
Sec	J Goodman
Holes	18 L 3549 yds SSS 57
Recs	Am–62 G Thomas (1989)
	Pro–54 L Knapp (1986)
V'trs	U SOC
Fees	£8 (£9)
Loc	St Ives 1 mile

Trevose (1924)

Constantine Bay, Padstow PL28 8JB
Tel	(0841) 520208 Fax 521057
Mem	960
Sec	P Gammon (Prop)
	GL Grindley (Sec/ Mgr)
Pro	G Alliss (0841) 520261
Holes	18 L 6608 yds SSS 72
	9 L 1367 yds SSS 29
Recs	Am–67 C Phillips
	Pro–66 N Burch
V'trs	H SOC
Fees	On application
Loc	4 miles W of Padstow
Mis	3 & 4 ball starting times restricted all year–phone Club

Truro (1937)

Treliske, Truro TR1 3LG
Tel	(0872) 72640
Mem	900
Sec	BE Heggie (0872) 78684
Pro	NK Bicknell (0872) 76595
Holes	18 L 5347 yds SSS 66
Recs	Am–61 AJ Ring
	Pro–63 M Hoyle
V'trs	U H SOC
Fees	£15 (£20)
Loc	2 miles W of Truro on A390

West Cornwall (1889)

Lelant, St Ives TR26 3DZ
Tel	(0736) 753319
Mem	825
Sec	WS Richards (0736) 753401
Pro	P Atherton (0736) 753177
Holes	18 L 5854 yds SSS 68
Recs	Am–65 MC Edmunds, P Darlington
	Pro–64 G Emerson
V'trs	H
Fees	£12 (£18) W–£30
Loc	2 miles E of St Ives

Whitsand Bay Hotel (1909)

Portwrinkle, Torpoint
Tel	(0503) 30470/ 30276 (Hotel)
Mem	500
Sec	GG Dyer (0503) 30418
Pro	S Poole (0503) 30778
Holes	18 L 5615 yds SSS 68
Recs	Am–62 GG Dyer (1981)
	Pro–62 M Faulkner (1948)
V'trs	U SOC
Fees	£12.50 (£15)
Loc	6 miles W of Plymouth

Cumbria

Alston Moor (1906)

The Hermitage, Alston CA9 3DB
Tel	(0434) 381675
Mem	150
Sec	A Dodd (0434) 381242
Holes	9 L 5380 yds SSS 66
Recs	Am–70 A Rutherford
V'trs	U SOC
Fees	£4 (£5)
Loc	2 miles from Alston on B6277

Appleby (1903)

Appleby
Tel	(076 83) 51432
Mem	600
Sec	BW Rimmer
Holes	18 L 5901 yds SSS 68
Recs	Am–63 K Bush
	Pro–69 SS Scott
V'trs	U
Fees	£10 (£14)
Loc	2 miles SE of Appleby. 1/2 mile N of A66

Barrow (1921)

Rakesmoor Lane, Hawcoat, Barrow-in-Furness
Tel	(0229) 25444
Mem	450 109(L) 85(J)
Sec	I Booth (0229) 835213
Pro	M Booth (0229) 823121
Holes	18 L 6209 yds SSS 70
Recs	Am–66 NL Brooks
V'trs	U
Fees	£10 (£10) W–£25
Loc	Hawcoat

Brampton (Talkin Tarn) (1907)

Brampton
Tel	(069 77) 2255
Mem	750
Sec	IJ Meldrum (0228) 23155
Pro	S Harrison (069 77) 2000
Holes	18 L 6420 yds SSS 71
Recs	Am–70 N Johnstone (1988)
V'trs	U
Fees	£7 (£9) W–£24
Loc	B6413, 1 mile SE of Brampton

Carlisle (1908)

Aglionby, Carlisle
Tel (0228) 513303
Mem 870
Sec J Hook
Pro JS More (0228) 513241
Holes 18 L 6278 yds SSS 70
Recs Am–65 M Ruddick (1989)
Pro–65 D Pearce (1988)
V'trs WD–U after 9.30am & 1.30pm
Tues pm/ comp days–NA
Sat–M after 10am & 2.30pm
Sun–U SOC–Mon/ Wed/ Fri
Fees £20 (£25)
Loc ½ mile E of M6 Junction 43, on A69

Cockermouth (1896)

Embleton, Cockermouth
Tel (07687) 76223
Mem 539
Sec RD Pollard (0900) 822650
Holes 18 L 5496 yds SSS 67
Recs Am–65 S Gabb
V'trs WD–U before 5pm exc Wed
Sun–NA before 11am and
2–2.30pm SOC
Fees £8 (£10)
Loc 4 miles E of Cockermouth

The Dunnerholme (1905)

Askam-in-Furness
Tel (0229) 62675
Mem 425
Sec JH Mutton (0229) 62979
Holes 10 L 6181 yds SSS 69 (18 tees)
Recs Am–68 H Bayliff
Pro–70 JB Ball
V'trs U
Fees £8 (£10)
Loc 6 miles N of Barrow on A595, Whitehaven-Workington road

Furness (1872)

Walney Island, Barrow-in-Furness
Tel (0229) 41232
Mem 700
Sec PF Duignan
Pro K Bosward
Holes 18 L 6363 yds SSS 71
Recs Am–67 A Miles (1986)
Pro–65 A Chandler, GJ Brand (1984)
V'trs U
Fees £10 (£10)
Loc Walney Island

Grange Fell (1952)

Cartmel Road, Grange-over-Sands LA11 6HB
Tel (05395) 32536
Mem 260
Sec JB Asplin (05395) 32021
Holes 9 L 4826 metres SSS 66
Recs Am–68 GB Wolstenholme
AI Bremner, N Bremner,
D Airey, G Park
Pro–66 F Robinson
V'trs U
Fees £10 (£15)

Grange-over-Sands (1919)

Meathop Road, Grange-over-Sands LA11 6QX
Tel (05395) 33180
Mem 255 95(L) 25(J)
Sec JR Green (05395) 32717
Holes 18 L 5660 yds SSS 68
Recs Am–64 S McMillan
Pro–67 G Cuthbert
V'trs U SOC
Fees £10 D–£15 (£15 D–£20)
Loc Grange station ½ mile

Kendal (1891)

The Heights, Kendal
Tel (0539) 724079
Mem 460
Sec R Maunder (Sec/ Mgr)
EF Millar (Hon)
Pro D Turner (0539) 723499
Holes 18 L 5550 yds SSS 67
Recs Am–63 J Brennand
Pro–63 P Tupling, GC Norton
V'trs U H SOC
Fees £12 (£16)

Keswick (1978)

Threlkeld Hall, nr Keswick CA12 4HH
Tel (07687) 79324
Mem 670
Sec DS Cowen (07687) 72147
Holes 18 L 6175 yds SSS 72
Recs Am–71 BD Airey (1987)
Pro–69 I Clark (1984)
V'trs U SOC
Fees £10 (£15)
Loc 4 miles E of Keswick (A66)

Kirkby Lonsdale

Casterton Road, Kirkby Lonsdale
Mem 130 30(L) 20(J)
Sec P Jackson (0468) 72085
Holes 9 L 4058 yds SSS 60
V'trs U
Fees £3
Loc 1 mile on Sedbergh road

Maryport (1905)

Bankend, Maryport CA15 6PA
Tel (0900) 812605
Mem 380
Sec NH Cook (0900) 815652
Holes 18 L 6272 yds SSS 71
V'trs U SOC
Fees D–£8 (£10) Mon-Fri–£30
Loc 1 mile N of Maryport, off B5300

Penrith (1890)

Salkeld Road, Penrith CA11 8SG
Tel (0768) 62217/ 65429
Mem 850
Sec J Carruthers (0768) 62217
Pro CB Thomson (0768) 62217
Holes 18 L 6026 yds SSS 69
Recs Am–64 JM Nutter
Pro–65 K Bousfield

V'trs H WE/ BH–10.06-11.30am & after 3pm
Fees £15 (£20)
Loc ½ mile E of Penrith

St Bees (1931)

Rhoda Grove, Rheda, Frizington CA26 3TE
Tel (0946) 812105
Mem 325
Sec JB Campbell
Holes 9 L 5097 yds SSS 65
Recs Am–66 M Pink (1990)
V'trs U
Fees £8 (£10)
Loc 4 miles S of Whitehaven

Seascale (1893)

The Banks, Seascale CA20 1QL
Tel (094 67) 28202/ 28800
Mem 550
Sec C Taylor (094 67) 28202
Holes 18 L 6416 yds SSS 71
Recs Am–67 D Weston, ID Stavert,
G Shuttleworth (1987)
Pro–68 EC Anderson
V'trs U SOC
Fees £15 (£18)
Loc 15 miles S of Whitehaven

Sedbergh (1896)

The Riggs, Sedbergh
Mem 100
Sec AD Lord (05396) 20993
Holes 9 L 2067 yds SSS 61
Recs Am–64 S Gardner
V'trs U
Fees £4
Loc 1 mile S of Sedbergh at Millthorp

Silecroft (1903)

Silecroft, Millom LA18 4AG
Tel (0229) 774250
Mem 370
Sec M O'N Wilson JP (0229) 774160
Holes 9 L 5712 yds SSS 68
Recs Am–68 D Temple
V'trs WD–U WE/ BH–often restricted
until 5.30pm SOC
Fees D–£8
Loc 3 miles N of Millom towards shore

Silloth-on-Solway (1892)

Silloth, nr Carlisle CA5 4AD
Tel (0965) 31179
Mem 600
Sec GS Hartley, G Lowther
Holes 18 L 6343 yds SSS 70
Recs Am–66 C Wallace, DL Watson
V'trs U H SOC
Fees D–£11 (D–£16) 5D–£40
Loc Silloth, 22 miles W of Carlisle

Stoneyholme (1974)

Public
St Aidan's Road, Carlisle CA7 1LS
Tel   (0228) 34856
Pro   S Ling
Holes 18 hole course
Recs   Am–64
V'trs U
Fees   £4.50 (£5)
Loc   1 mile E of Carlisle

Ulverston (1894)

Bardsea Park, Ulverston
Tel   (0229) 52824
Mem   700
Sec   D Weston (0229) 52963
Pro   MR Smith (0229) 52806
Holes 18 L 6122 yds SSS 69
Recs   Am–66 AJ Edwards (1989)
          Pro–71 JA Raisbeck
V'trs H or I SOC
Fees   Summer £16 (£20) Winter £12
          (£15)
Loc   1 1/2 miles SW of Ulverston on
          A5087

Windermere (1891)

Cleabarrow, Windermere LA23 3NB
Tel   (096 62) 3123
Mem   899
Sec   KR Moffat
Pro   WSM Rooke (096 62) 3550
Holes 18 L 5006 yds SSS 65
Recs   Am–58 P Chapman (1988)
          Pro–58 D Cooper (1990)
V'trs H SOC
Fees   £16 (£23)
Loc   1 1/2 miles E of Bowness

Workington (1922)

Branthwaite Road, Workington
Tel   (0900) 603460
Mem   500 125(L) 100(J)
Sec   JK Walker (0900) 605420
Pro   N Summerfield
Holes 18 L 6252 yds SSS 70
Recs   Am–65 A Drabble
V'trs H SOC
Fees   £10 (£15)
Loc   2 miles E of Workington

Derbyshire

Alfreton (1892)

Oakerthorpe, Alfreton
Tel   (0773) 832070
Mem   300
Sec   D Tomlinson (0246) 862661
Holes 9 L 5074 yds SSS 65
Recs   Am–62 S Kyte
          Pro–65 J Smith
V'trs WD exc Mon–U before 4.30pm
          –M after 4.30pm WE/ Mon–M
          SOC
Fees   £8 (£10) (1990)
Loc   Alfreton

Allestree Park (1949)

Public
Allestree Hall, Allestree, Derby
Tel   (0332) 550616
Pro   RG Brown
Holes 18 L 5749 yds SSS 68
Recs   Am–66 J McCann
V'trs U WE–booking req SOC
Fees   £3.50 (£4.60)
Loc   2 miles N of Derby on A6

Ashbourne (1910)

Clifton, Ashbourne
Tel   (0335) 42078
Mem   350
Sec   NPA James (0335) 42077
Holes 9 L 5388 yds SSS 66
V'trs U SOC
Fees   £6 (£8)
Loc   2 miles W of Ashbourne on
          A515 Litchfield road

Bakewell (1899)

Station Road, Bakewell DE4 1GB
Tel   (0629) 812307
Mem   205 67(L) 40(J)
Sec   T Turner
Pro   TE Jones
Holes 9 L 5840 yds SSS 68
Recs   Am–63 W Hudson
V'trs WD–U WE/ BH–M
Fees   £8
Loc   1/2 mile NE of Bakewell and A6

Blue Circle (1985)

Cement Works, Hope S30 2RP
Tel   (0433) 20317
Mem   116
Sec   DS Smith
Holes 9 L 5252 yds SSS 66
Recs   Am–69 B Harper
V'trs NA
Loc   Hope Valley

Breadsall Priory Hotel G & CC (1976)

Moor Road, Morley, Derby DE7 6DL
Tel   (0332) 832235
Mem   782
Sec   A Busman (Gen Mgr)
Pro   A Smith (0332) 834425
Holes 18 L 6202 yds SSS 70
Recs   Am–66 A Thomas
          Pro–66 M Glynn, DJ Russell
V'trs WD–U SOC–WD only
Fees   £22
Loc   A61 Breadsall, left into Croft
          Lane, left into Rectory Lane,
          right on to Moor Road

Buxton & High Peak (1887)

Townend, Buxton SK17 7JB
Tel   (0298) 23453
Mem   450
Sec   B Webb
Pro   A Hoyles (0298) 23112
Holes 18 L 5954 yds SSS 69

Recs   Am–63 N Hallam
          Pro–66 P Anderson, P Norton
V'trs U
Fees   £15 (£20)
Loc   NE boundary of Buxton (A6)

Cavendish (1925)

Gadley Lane, Buxton SK17 6XD
Tel   (0298) 23494
Mem   725
Sec   DN Doyle-Davidson (0298)
          23256
Pro   J Nolan (0298) 25052
Holes 18 L 5833 yds SSS 68
Recs   Am–65 J Slack (1983)
          Pro–63 I Buckley (1988)
V'trs U H SOC–by prior
          arrangement with Pro
Fees   £20 (£30)
Loc   3/4 mile W of Buxton Station. St
          John's Road (A53)

Chapel-en-le-Frith (1905)

**The Cockyard, Manchester Road,
Chapel-en-le-Frith, Stockport
SK12 6UH**
Tel   (0298) 812118
Mem   645
Sec   JW Dranfield (0298) 813943
Pro   DJ Cullen
Holes 18 L 6089 yds SSS 69
V'trs U
Fees   £12 (£20)
Loc   Stockport 13 miles on A6
          (B5470)

Chesterfield (1897)

Walton, Chesterfield S42 7LA
Tel   (0246) 279256
Mem   551
Sec   AW Bonsall (0246) 590330
Pro   M McLean (0246) 276297
Holes 18 L 6326 yds SSS 70
Recs   Am–65 I Wyatt
          Pro–66 K Nagle, B Hutchison
V'trs WD–U H WE–M SOC
Fees   £15–£20
Loc   2 miles SW of Chesterfield on
          A263

Chesterfield Municipal (1934)

Public
**Murray House, Crow Lane,
Chesterfield S41 0EQ**
Tel   (0246) 273887
Pro   J Delany
Holes 18 L 6013 yds SSS 69
V'trs U
Fees   £3.50 (£4.50)
Loc   1/4 mile past Chesterfield
          station
Mis   Tapton Park Club plays here

Chevin (1894)

Duffield, Derby
Tel   (0332) 841864
Mem   500 100(L) 90(J) 70(5)
Sec   CP Elliott

For list of abbreviations see page 487.

Pro	W Bird (0332) 841112
Holes	18 L 6057 yds SSS 69
Recs	Am–65 C Radford (1987)
	Pro–65 DJ Russell (1985)
V'trs	WD–U WE–M SOC exc Sat
Fees	£22
Loc	5 miles N of Derby on A6

Derby (1923)

Public

Shakespeare Street, Sinfin, Derby DE2 9HD

Tel	(0332) 766323
Pro	RG Brown (0332) 766462
Holes	18 L 6144 yds SSS 69
Recs	Am–66
V'trs	U
Fees	£3.50 (£4.50)

Erewash Valley (1905)

Stanton-by-Dale, nr Ilkeston

Tel	(0602) 323258
Mem	450
Sec	D Knowles (0602) 322984
Pro	MJ Ronan (0602) 324667
Holes	18 L 6487 yds SSS 71
Recs	Am–67 R Claydon
	Pro–68 MJ Ronan
V'trs	WE/ BH–NA before noon SOC–WD
Fees	On application
Loc	Between Nottingham and Derby. M1 Junction 25

Glossop & District (1894)

Sheffield Road, Glossop

Tel	(045 74) 3117
Mem	250
Sec	J Dickson (045 74) 62713
Pro	C Wadsworth
Holes	11 L 5716 yds SSS 68
Recs	Am–66 DM Pike
	Pro–68 S Sewgolum
V'trs	U SOC
Fees	£6 (£7)
Loc	1 mile E of Glossop, off A57

Ilkeston (1929)

Public

Peewit West End Drive, Ilkeston

Tel	(0602) 304550
Holes	9 L 4116 yds SSS 60
V'trs	U
Fees	£4
Loc	1/2 mile E of Ilkeston

Kedleston Park (1947)

Kedleston, Derby DE6 4JD

Tel	(0332) 840035
Mem	853
Sec	K Wilson
Pro	J Hetherington (0332) 841685
Holes	18 L 6643 yds SSS 72
Recs	Am–65 M Betteridge
	Pro–66 J Lower
V'trs	U
Fees	£20 (£25)
Loc	4 miles N of Derby. NT signs to Kedleston Hall

Matlock (1907)

Chesterfield Road, Matlock DE4 5LF

Tel	(0629) 582191
Mem	375 67(L) 60(J) 115(5)
Sec	AJ Box
Pro	M Deeley (0629) 584934
Holes	18 L 5984 yds SSS 69
V'trs	WD–U WE/ BH–M SOC–WD
Fees	D–£20 W–£80 M–£160
Loc	1 1/2 miles NE of Matlock (A632)

Mickleover (1923)

Uttoxeter Road, Mickleover

Tel	(0332) 513339 (Clubhouse)
Mem	650
Sec	D Rodgers
Pro	P Wilson (0332) 518662
Holes	18 L 5708 yds SSS 68
Recs	Am–64 CRJ Ibbotson
	Pro–63 A Skingle
V'trs	U SOC–Tues & Thurs
Fees	£13 (£15)
Loc	3 miles W of Derby on A516/B5020

Ormonde Fields

Nottingham Road, Codnor, Ripley

Tel	(0773) 742987
Mem	660
Sec	RN Walters
Pro	S Betteridge
Holes	18 L 6011 yds SSS 69
V'trs	U SOC
Fees	£10 (£15)
Loc	A610 Ripley to Nottingham road. M1 Junction 26, 5 miles

Pastures (1969)

Pastures Hospital, Mickleover

Tel	(0332) 513921 (Ext 348)
Mem	320
Sec	S McWilliams
Holes	9 L 5005 yds SSS 64
Recs	Am–62 C Whyatt (1989)
V'trs	M SOC–WD
Loc	4 miles W of Derby

Shirland (1977)

Lower Delves, Shirland DE5 6AU

Tel	(0773) 834935
Mem	500
Sec	G Brassington (0246) 852816
Pro	NB Hallam (0773) 834935
Holes	18 L 6072 yds SSS 69
Recs	Am–67 R Skingle (1990)
	Pro–71 NB Hallam (1987)
V'trs	WD–U WE–U after 3pm SOC
Fees	£10 (£18) (1990)
Loc	1 mile N of Alfreton, off A61 by Shirland Church

Sickleholme (1898)

Bamford, Sheffield S30 2BH

Tel	(0433) 51306
Mem	250 100(L) 72(J) 80(5)
Sec	WT Scott
Pro	PH Taylor
Holes	18 L 6064 yds SSS 69

Recs	Am–63 IL Fletcher
	Pro–65 AP Highfield
V'trs	U exc Wed am
Fees	£15 (£20) 1989 prices
Loc	W of Sheffield, between Hathersage and Hope (A625)

Stanedge (1934)

Walton Hay Farm, nr Chesterfield

Tel	(0246) 566156
Mem	300
Sec	W Tyzack (0246) 276568
Holes	9 L 4867 yds SSS 64
Recs	Am–64 W Steel Jr (1982)
	Pro–65 A Skingle (1987)
V'trs	WD–U before 2pm –M after 2pm Sat–M Sun–NA before 4pm –M after 4pm
Fees	£10
Loc	5 miles SW of Chesterfield, off B5057

Devon

Axe Cliff (1893)

Squires Lane, Axmouth, Seaton EX12 4AB

Tel	(0297) 24371
Mem	400
Sec	YG Keep
Holes	18 L 5057 yds SSS 65
Recs	Am–65 P Cricard
V'trs	U H SOC
Fees	£12
Loc	Axmouth 3/4 mile, nr Yacht Club at Axmouth Bridge

Bigbury (1923)

Bigbury, Kingsbridge TQ7 4BB

Tel	(0548) 810207
Mem	850
Sec	BJ Perry (0548) 810557
Pro	S Lloyd (0548) 810412
Holes	18 L 6076 yds SSS 69
Recs	Am–65 CS Yeoman
	Pro–67 S Lloyd
V'trs	I H SOC
Fees	D–£16
Loc	Plymouth 15 miles

Chulmleigh (1976)

Leigh Road, Chulmleigh EX18 7BL

Tel	(0769) 80519
Mem	150
Sec	PN Callow
Pro	M Blackwell
Holes	Summer 18 L 1440 yds Winter 9 L 2372 yds
Recs	Am–52 H Gillibrand
	Pro–53 M Blackwell
V'trs	U
Fees	£4 D–£6
Loc	1 mile N of A377 Barnstaple-Crediton road

Churston (1890)

Churston, Brixham
Tel	(0803) 842218
Mem	640
Sec	AM Chaundy (0803) 842751
Pro	R Penfold (0803) 842894
Holes	18 L 6201 yds SSS 70
Recs	Am–64 RHP Knott
	Pro–67 JM Green
V'trs	U (recognised club members)
	Tues am–NA
Fees	£20 (£25)
Loc	Torquay 5¼ miles

Dinnaton (1989)

Ivybridge PL21 9HU
Tel	(0752) 892512
Mem	175
Sec	R Alexander
Pro	T Elsey
Holes	9 L 2200 yds SSS 48 9 hole
	Par 3
V'trs	U H SOC
Fees	D–£6 (D–£7.50)
Loc	12 miles SE of Plymouth, off
	A38/ B3213
Mis	Floodlit driving range

Downes Crediton (1976)

Hookway, Crediton EX17 3PT
Tel	(036 32) 3991
Mem	700
Sec	WJ Brooks (036 32) 3025
Pro	H Finch (036 32) 4464
Holes	18 L 5868 yds SSS 68
V'trs	H
Fees	£15 (£20)
Loc	Off A377, on Exeter side of
	Crediton

East Devon (1902)

North View Road, Budleigh Salterton EX9 6DQ
Tel	(039 54) 2018
Mem	850
Sec	JC Tebbet (039 54) 3370
Pro	T Underwood (039 54) 5195
Holes	18 L 6214 yds SSS 70
Recs	Am–65 R Winchester
	Pro–64 G Ryall
V'trs	H SOC
Fees	£20 (£25)
Loc	12 miles SE of Exeter

Elfordleigh Hotel G & CC (1932)

Elfordleigh, Plympton, Plymouth
Tel	(0752) 336428
Mem	300
Sec	Mrs P Parfitt
Pro	R Troak
Holes	9 L 5759 yds SSS 68
V'trs	WD–U WE–phone first
Fees	£15
Loc	4 miles E of Plymouth

Exeter G & CC (1895)

Countess Wear, Exeter EX2 7AE
Tel	(039 287) 4139
Mem	896
Sec	CHM Greetham
Pro	M Rowett (039 287) 5028
Holes	18 L 5993 yds SSS 69
Recs	Am–63 G Milne (1988)
	Pro–62 I Sparks (1990)
V'trs	WD–U WE–I SOC–Thurs only
Fees	£20

Holsworthy (1937)

Kilatree, Holsworthy
Tel	(0409) 253177
Mem	575
Sec	B Megson
Holes	18 L 6012 yds SSS 69
Recs	Am–66 A Ramsey
	Pro–67 G Ryall, R Troake
V'trs	WD–U Sun–U after noon
Fees	£10 W–£40
Loc	1 mile W of Holsworthy

Honiton (1896)

Middlehills, Honiton EX14 8TR
Tel	(0404) 44422
Mem	820
Sec	J Carter
Pro	(0404) 42943
Holes	18 L 5931 yds SSS 68
Recs	Am–71
	Pro–69 J Langmead
V'trs	U (recognised club member)
	BH–NA SOC
Fees	£16 (£20)
Loc	1 mile S of Honiton. M5
	Junction 25

Hurdwick (1990)

Tavistock Hamlets, Tavistock PL19 8PZ
Tel	(0822) 612746
Mem	100
Sec	Maj RW Cullen (Mgr)
Holes	18 L 4600 yds Par 67
	(Executive Course)
V'trs	U SOC
Fees	£12 D–£20 (£15 D–£25)
Loc	1 mile N of Tavistock, on
	Brentor Church road

Ilfracombe (1892)

Hele Bay, Ilfracombe EX34 9RT
Tel	(0271) 862176
Mem	637
Sec	RC Beer
Pro	D Hoare (0271) 863328
Holes	18 L 5872 yds SSS 68
Recs	Am–66 B Austin (1990)
V'trs	H SOC WD–NA 12-2pm WE/
	BH–U after 10am –NA 12-2pm
Fees	£15 (£17) 5D–£60
Loc	Between Ilfracombe and
	Combe Martin

Libbaton (1990)

High Bickington, Umberleigh EX37 9BS
Tel	(0769) 60269
Mem	250
Sec	JH Brough
Pro	JN Phillips (0769) 60167
Holes	18 L 5812 yds SSS 68
V'trs	U SOC
Fees	£10 Sun–£11
Loc	1 mile S of High Bickington on
	B3217. M5 Junction 27
Mis	Floodlit driving range

Manor House Hotel (1929)

Moretonhampstead TQ13 8RE
Tel	(0647) 40355
Fax	(0647) 40961
Mem	250
Sec	R Lewis
Pro	R Lewis
Holes	18 L 6016 yds SSS 69
Recs	Am–68 G Milne (1989)
	Pro–65 G Emerson (1985)
V'trs	U H SOC
Fees	£18 (£25)
Loc	15 miles SW of Exeter on
	B3212 to Princetown. M5
	Junction 31
Mis	Driving range

Newton Abbot (Stover) (1930)

Newton Abbot TQ12 6QQ
Tel	(0626) 52460
Mem	861
Sec	R Smith
Pro	M Craig (0626) 62078
Holes	18 L 5886 yds SSS 68
Recs	Am–63 M Pym (1989)
	Pro–67 B Barnes (1977)
V'trs	H SOC–Thurs
Fees	D–£17
Loc	3 miles N of Newton Abbot on
	A382

Okehampton (1913)

Okehampton EX20 1EF
Tel	(0837) 52113
Mem	500
Sec	S Chave
Pro	P Blundell (0837) 53541
Holes	18 L 5300 yds SSS 67
Recs	Am–67 MS Moore
	Pro–H Finch
V'trs	H SOC
Fees	On application
Loc	S boundary of Okehampton,
	signposted from traffic lights

Royal North Devon (1864)

Golf Links Road, Westward Ho! EX39 1HD
Tel	(023 72) 473824
Mem	900
Sec	EJ Davies (023 72) 473817
Pro	G Johnston (023 72) 477598
Holes	18 L 6644 yds SSS 72

Recs	Am–66 D Boughey
	Pro–66 P Dawson, KDG Nagle,
	MF Foster
V'trs	On request
Fees	£14 (£18)
Loc	Bideford 2 miles

Saunton (1897)

Saunton, nr Braunton

Tel	(0271) 812436
Mem	1080
Sec	WE Geddes
Pro	JA McGhee (0271) 812013
Holes	East 18 L 6703 yds SSS 73
	West 18 L 6356 yds SSS 71
Recs	East Am–66 PH Watts
	Pro–69 B Huggett West Am–67
	ME Jewell Pro–69 P Berry
V'trs	U H
Fees	On application
Loc	9 miles W of Barnstaple

Sidmouth (1889)

Cotmaton Road, Sidmouth EX10 8SX

Tel	(0395) 513023
Mem	700
Sec	DE Matthews (0395) 513451
Pro	M Kemp (0395) 516407
Holes	18 L 5188 yds SSS 65
Recs	Am–59 N Winchester
	Pro–64 E Murray
V'trs	U SOC
Fees	D–£10 (£12) W–£40
Loc	½ mile W of Sidmouth.
	12 miles SE of M5 Junction 30

Staddon Heights (1895)

Plymstock, Plymouth PL9 9SP

Tel	(0752) 402475
Mem	620
Sec	MG Holliday
Pro	J Cox (0752) 492630
Holes	18 L 5861 yds SSS 68
Recs	Am–64 R Clark, D Roberts
	Pro–67 J Langmead
V'trs	WE–H SOC–WD
Fees	D–£12 (D–£15) 5D–£40
	Summer £30 Winter

Tavistock (1890)

Down Road, Tavistock PL19 9AQ

Tel	(0822) 612049
Mem	625
Sec	BG Steer (0822) 612344
Pro	R Hall (0822) 612316
Holes	18 L 6250 yds SSS 70
Recs	Am–66 MG Symons (1981)
	Pro–69 S Chadwick, N Bicknell
	(1981)
V'trs	U SOC–WD
Fees	£15 (£18)
Loc	Whitchurch Down

Teignmouth (1924)

Teignmouth TQ14 9NY

Tel	(0626) 773614
Mem	900
Sec	D Holloway (0626) 774194
Pro	P Ward (0626) 772894
Holes	18 L 6227 yds SSS 70
Recs	Am–65 JH Laidler (1980)
	Pro–66 P Millhouse (1987)
V'trs	H (recognised club member)
	SOC–WD WE–M before 4pm
Fees	£19 (£22)
Loc	2 miles N of Teignmouth on
	B3192

Thurlestone (1897)

Thurlestone, nr Kingsbridge

Tel	(0548) 560405/ 560221
Mem	700
Sec	R Marston (0548) 560405
Pro	N Whitley (0548) 560715
Holes	18 L 6337 yds SSS 70
Recs	Am–66 RP Knott
	Pro–67 PJ Yeo
V'trs	I or H
Fees	£18 W–£70 (1990)
Loc	Kingsbridge 5 miles

Tiverton (1932)

Post Hill, Tiverton EX16 4NE

Tel	(0884) 252114 (Clubhouse)
Mem	475 130(L) 45(J) 250(5)
Sec	M Crouch (0884) 252187
Pro	RE Freeman (0884) 254836
Holes	18 L 6263 yds SSS 71
Recs	Am–65 SC Waddington
	Pro–70 A Moore
V'trs	I H
Fees	On application
Loc	5 miles W of M5 Junction 27.
	1½ miles E of Tiverton on
	B3391

Torquay (1910)

**Petitor Road, St Marychurch,
Torquay TQ1 4QF**

Tel	(0803) 314591
Mem	800
Sec	BG Long
Pro	M Ruth (0803) 329113
Holes	18 L 6198 yds SSS 69
Recs	Am–66 M Pougiouros (1990)
	Pro–66 R Lewis (1989)
V'trs	H SOC
Fees	£17 (£20)

Torrington (1932)

Weare Trees, Torrington EX38 7EZ

Tel	(0805) 22229
Mem	378
Sec	GSC Green (Hon)
Holes	9 L 4418 yds SSS 62
Recs	Am–65 P Wheeler, PR Sturman
	(1990)
V'trs	U Sun am–NA SOC
Fees	£8 (£10)
Loc	Torrington 1 mile on Weare
	Gifford road

Warren (1892)

Dawlish EX7 0NF

Tel	(0626) 862255
Mem	650
Sec	DM Beesley
Pro	G Wicks (0626) 864002
Holes	18 L 5968 yds SSS 69
Recs	Am–65 J Langmead (1987)
V'trs	H SOC
Fees	£17 (£20) W–£60
Loc	1½ miles E of Dawlish

Wrangaton (1895)

Wrangaton, South Brent TQ10 9HJ

Tel	(0364) 73229
Mem	600
Sec	RR Hine
Pro	M Keitch (0367) 72162
Holes	18 L 5900 yds SSS 69
Recs	Am–66 SR Bryant
	Pro–67 FG Robins
V'trs	H SOC
Fees	£15 (£18)
Loc	Dartmoor, 10 miles SW of
	Ashburton

Yelverton (1904)

Golf Links Road, Yelverton PL20 6BN

Tel	(0822) 853618
Mem	700
Sec	Maj (Retd) DR Bettany (0822)
	852824
Pro	I Parker (0822) 853593
Holes	18 L 6293 yds SSS 70
Recs	Am–65 DNJ Wright (1990)
V'trs	H SOC
Fees	£14 (£18)
Loc	6 miles N of Plymouth on A386

Dorset

The Ashley Wood (1896)

**Tarrant Rawston, Blandford Forum
DT11 9HN**

Tel	(0258) 452253
Mem	520
Sec	P Fry
Pro	S Taylor
Holes	9 L 6274 yds SSS 70
Recs	Am–68 D Thorn, S Ricketts,
	N Rodgers
	Pro–67 S Taylor (1988)
V'trs	WD–U WE–NA before noon
	SOC
Fees	£12 (£14)
Loc	1½ miles SE of Blandford

Boscombe (1938)

Queen's Park, Bournemouth

Mem	337
Sec	JHH Burdett (0202) 483017
Holes	Play over Queen's Park

Bournemouth & Meyrick Park (1890)

**Meyrick Park, Bournemouth
BH2 6LH**

Tel	(0202) 290307
Mem	600
Sec	Ms J Bennett
Holes	Play over Meyrick Park

Bridport & West Dorset (1891)

East Cliff, West Bay, Bridport
DT6 4EP
Tel   (0308) 22597
Mem   700
Sec   PJ Ridler (0308) 421095
Pro   JE Parish (0308) 421491
Holes   18 L 5246 yds SSS 66
Recs   Am–61 M Rees (1990)
        Pro–66 S Bishop (1980),
        R Crockford (1983)
V'trs   WD/ Sat-U after 9.30am Sun–U
        after noon SOC
Fees   £12 (£18)
Loc   1½ miles S of Bridport at West
        Bay

Broadstone (1898)

Wentworth Drive, Broadstone
BH18 8DQ
Tel   (0202) 693363
Mem   750
Sec   JM Cowan (0202) 692595
Pro   N Tokely (0202) 692835
Holes   18 L 6183 yds SSS 70
Recs   Am–65 JH Nash (1988)
        Pro–64 S Hamill (1988)
V'trs   WD–H after 9.30am WE/
        BH–NA SOC–WD
Fees   £20 D–£25
Loc   4 miles N of Poole

Came Down (1896)

Came Down, Dorchester DT2 8NR
Tel   (0305) 812531
Mem   700
Sec   DE Matthews (Mgr) (0305)
        813494
Pro   (0305) 812670
Holes   18 L 6244 yds SSS 71
Recs   Am–67 M Foster (1989)
        Pro–68 M McKenna (1975)
V'trs   H Sun am–NA SOC
Fees   £16 (£20)
Loc   2 miles S of Dorchester

Canford School

Canford School, Wimborne
BH21 3AD
Tel   (0202) 841254
Mem   200
Sec   HA Jarvis
Holes   9 L 5918 yds SSS 68
V'trs   M SOC
Fees   £5
Loc   2 miles SE of Wimborne, off
        A341

Christchurch (1977)

Public
Iford Bridge, Barrack Road,
Christchurch
Tel   (0202) 473817
Pro   P Troth
Holes   9 L 4824 yds SSS 64
Recs   Am–65 D Pearcey
V'trs   U
Fees   £3.80 (£4.30)

Loc   Boundary of Bournemouth on
        Christchurch Road
Mis   Driving range

East Dorset (1978)

Hyde, Wareham BH20 7NT
Tel   (0929) 472244
Mem   900
Sec   JI Mullins
Pro   G Packer (0929) 472272
Holes   18 L 6146 yds SSS 69
V'trs   U H SOC–WD
Fees   £12 (£15)
Loc   Hyde, 5 miles W of Wareham,
        off Puddletown road
Mis   Driving range

Ferndown (1923)

119 Golf Links Road, Ferndown
BH22 8BU
Tel   (0202) 872022
Mem   700
Sec   E Robertson (0202) 874602
Pro   DN Sewell (0202) 873825
Holes   18 L 6442 yds SSS 71
        9 L 5604 yds SSS 68
Recs   Old Am–66 JHA Leggett
        Pro–68 DN Sewell New Am–67
        G Howell Pro–68 DN Sewell
V'trs   WD–I H after 9.30am
        SOC–Tues & Fri
Fees   Old £25 (£30) New £15 (£20)
Loc   6 miles N of Bournemouth

Halstock (1988)

Common Lane, Halstock
Tel   (0935) 89689
Mem   200
Sec   R Clifton
Pro   RF & RG Clifton
Holes   9 L 2083 yds SSS
Recs   Am–32 H Stallard
        Pro–32 RG Clifton
V'trs   U SOC
Fees   9 holes–£4.50
Loc   6 miles S of Yeovil, off A37
Mis   Driving range

Highcliffe Castle (1913)

107 Lymington Road, Highcliffe-on-
Sea, Christchurch BH23 4LA
Tel   (0425) 272953
Mem   350 100(L) 50(J)
Sec   DW Blakeman (0425) 272210
Pro   R Crockford (0425) 276640
Holes   18 L 4655 yds SSS 63
Recs   Am–58 S Jenkins
        Pro–60 D Sewell
V'trs   I H SOC
Fees   £14 (£20)
Loc   Bournemouth 8 miles

Isle of Purbeck (1892)

Studland BH19 3AB
Tel   (092 944) 361
Mem   600
Sec   J Robinson
Pro   P Sowerby (092 944) 354
Holes   18 L 6283 yds SSS 71

        9 L 2022 yds SSS 30
Recs   Am–67 N Holman
        Pro–72 K Sparkes
V'trs   U H SOC
Fees   Purbeck £19.50 (£24.50)
        Dene £8.50 (£10)
Loc   Swanage 2 miles

Knighton Heath (1976)

Francis Avenue, West Howe,
Bournemouth BH11 8NX
Tel   (0202) 572633
Mem   700
Sec   R Bestwick
Pro   M Torrens (0202) 578275
Holes   18 L 6120 yds SSS 69
Recs   Am–65 P Holbert (1988)
        Pro–64 A Beal (1990)
V'trs   WD–H after 9.30am WE–H
        after 10.30am
Fees   On request
Loc   3 miles N of Poole, nr junction
        of A348/ A3049

Lyme Regis (1893)

Timber Hill, Lyme Regis
Tel   (029 74) 2963
        (029 74) 2043 (Steward)
Mem   650
Sec   RG Fry
Pro   A Black (029 74) 3822
Holes   18 L 6262 yds SSS 70
Recs   Am–68 L Thompson (1988)
        Pro–66 MD Dack (1987)
V'trs   H WD–U after 9.15am (1pm
        Thurs) Sun-U after noon SOC
Fees   £16 (£18)
Loc   Between Lyme Regis and
        Charmouth off A3502/ A35

Meyrick Park (1894)

Public
Bournemouth BH2 6LH
Tel   (0202) 290871
Pro   J Sharkey
Holes   18 L 5878 yds SSS 69
V'trs   U
Fees   Summer £8.25 Winter £7.20
Mis   Closed Sun pm. Bournemouth
        and Meyrick Park clubs play
        here

Mid Dorset (1990)

Belchalwell, Blandford Forum
DT11 0EG
Tel   (0258) 861386
Sec   D Astill (Mgr)
Pro   A Pakes (0258) 861184
Holes   18 L 6500 yds SSS 71
V'trs   U
Fees   £15 (£20)

Parkstone (1910)

Links Road, Parkstone, Poole
BH14 9JU
Tel   (0202) 708025
Mem   500 160(L) 50(J)
Sec   AS Kinnear (0202) 707138
Pro   N Blenkarne (0202) 708092

For list of abbreviations see page 487.

Holes	18 L 6250 yds SSS 70
Recs	Am–65 RA Latham, T Spence
	Pro–63 P Alliss
V'trs	H WD–NA before 9.30am and
	12.30-2.10pm WE–NA before
	9.45am and 12.30-2.30pm
Fees	£24 D–£30 (£30 D–£36)
Loc	3 miles W of Bournemouth, off
	A35

Queen's Park (1905)

Public
**Queen's Park, South Drive,
Bournemouth**

Tel	(0202) 396198
Sec	D Pritchard
Pro	R Hill
Holes	18 L 6505 yds SSS 72
Recs	Am–69 M Butcher
	Pro–66 A Caygill, H Boyle
V'trs	U SOC
Fees	Oct-Apr £8 May-Sept £10
Loc	2 miles NE of Bournemouth
Mis	Closed Sun pm. Boscombe
	and Boscombe Ladies Clubs
	play here

Riversmeet (1983)

Public
**Stoney Lane South, Christchurch
BH23 1HW**

Tel	(0202) 473912/ 477987
Fax	(0202) 482200
Sec	W Holderness (Mgr)
Holes	18 hole approach course
V'trs	U
Fees	£3
Loc	2 miles W of Bournemouth

Sherborne (1895)

Clatcombe, Sherborne DT9 4RN

Tel	(0935) 812475
Sec	Mrs JMC Guy (0935) 814431
Pro	S Wright (0935) 812274
Holes	18 L 5949 yds SSS 68
Recs	Am–66 S Edgeley (1987)
	Pro–63 M Thomas
V'trs	H
Fees	£15 (£18)
Loc	1 mile N of Sherborne

Wareham (1922)

Sandford Road, Wareham BH20 4DH

Tel	(0929) 554147
Mem	550
Sec	Maj JL Holloway
Holes	18 L 5332 yds SSS 66
Recs	Am–67 K Knott (1989)
V'trs	WD–U 9.30am-5pm WE–M
	SOC
Fees	£12 D–£15
Loc	1 mile NE of Wareham, on
	A351

Weymouth (1909)

Weymouth DT4 0PF

Tel	(0305) 784994
Mem	700
Sec	C Robinson (0305) 773981

Pro	D Lochrie (0305) 773997
Holes	18 L 5980 yds SSS 69
Recs	Am–63 MJ Watson
	Pro–65 D Bennett
V'trs	WD/ WE–H SOC
Fees	£15 (£20)
Loc	A354, off Manor roundabout
	(Town Centre exit)

Durham

Aycliffe (1977)

Public
**School Lane, Newton Aycliffe
DL5 6QZ**

Tel	(0325) 300700
Pro	R Lister (0325) 310820
Holes	9 L 6054 yds SSS 69
V'trs	U
Fees	£2.20 (£3.30)
Loc	Sports complex on A6072,
	from A68. 1 mile W of Aycliffe
Mis	Floodlit driving range

Barnard Castle (1898)

Harmire Road, Barnard Castle

Tel	(0833) 37237
Mem	600
Sec	AW Lavender (0833) 38355
Pro	J Harrison (0833) 31980
Holes	18 L 5838 yds SSS 68
Recs	Am–65 M Porter (1984),
	J Egglestone, R Beadle (1990)
	Pro–63 P Harrison (1990)
V'trs	U SOC
Fees	£12 (£16) 5D–£30
Loc	N boundary of Barnard Castle
	on B6278

Beamish Park (1950)

Beamish, Stanley DH9 0RH

Tel	(091) 370 1133
Mem	520
Sec	L Gilbert (091) 370 1382
Pro	C Cole (091) 370 1984
Holes	18 L 6205 yds SSS 70
Recs	Am–67 A Stewart
V'trs	WD/ Sat-U before 4pm
	Sun–NA SOC
Fees	£11
Loc	Beamish, nr Stanley

Bishop Auckland (1894)

High Plains, Bishop Auckland

Tel	(0388) 602198
Mem	730
Sec	G Thatcher (0388) 663648
Pro	D Skiffington (0388) 661618
Holes	18 L 6420 yds SSS 71
Recs	Am–67 RJ Aisbitt
	Pro–65 P Harrison
V'trs	H (closed Good Friday and
	Christmas Day)
Fees	£12 (£15) (1990)
Loc	1/2 mile NE of Bishop Auckland

Blackwell Grange (1930)

**Briar Close, Blackwell, Darlington
DL3 8QX**

Tel	(0325) 464464
Mem	650
Sec	F Hewitson (Hon) (0325)
	464458
Pro	R Givens (0325) 462088
Holes	18 L 5621 yds SSS 67
Recs	Am–64 HP Jolly, S Santon,
	MW Rogers
	Pro–63 M Gregson
V'trs	U exc Wed 11am-2.30pm–NA
	Sat–booking only. Sun–comps
	in progress SOC
Fees	£12 (£14)
Loc	1 mile S of Darlington on A66

Brancepeth Castle (1924)

Brancepeth Village, Durham DH7 8EA

Tel	(091) 378 0075
Mem	768 118(L) 74(J) 114(5)
Sec	JT Ross
Pro	D Howdon (091) 378 0183
Holes	18 L 6415 yds SSS 71
Recs	Am–67 D Curry, P Page
	Pro–64 B Rumney (1990)
V'trs	SOC–WD WE–NA
Fees	£22 (£28)
Loc	4 1/2 miles W of Durham on A690

Chester-Le-Street (1909)

**Lumley Park, Chester-Le-Street
DH3 4NS**

Tel	(091) 388 3218
Mem	400 130(L) 90(J)
Sec	WB Dodds
Pro	A Hartley (091) 389 0157
Holes	18 L 6054 yds SSS 69
Recs	Am–67 SJ Watson
V'trs	WD–H WE–NA before 10.30am
	or 12-2pm or by arrangement
Fees	£12 (£18)
Loc	E of Chester-Le-Street

Consett & District (1911)

Elmfield Road, Consett DH8 5NN

Tel	(0207) 502186
Mem	650
Sec	J Horrill (0207) 562261
Pro	S Corbally (0207) 580210
Holes	18 L 6001 yds SSS 69
Recs	Am–65 H Ashby
V'trs	WD–U SOC–exc Sat
Fees	£10 (£15)
Loc	12 miles NW of Durham on
	A691. Gateshead 12 miles on
	A692

Crook (1919)

Low Job's Hill, Crook

Tel	(0388) 762429
Mem	450
Sec	R King
Holes	18 L 6075 yds SSS 69
Recs	Am–66 N Tweddle
V'trs	U SOC
Fees	£8 (£12)
Loc	1/2 mile E of Crook (A689)

For list of abbreviations see page 487.

Darlington (1908)

**Haughton Grange, Darlington
DL1 3JD**
Tel   (0325) 463936
Mem   410 87(L) 110(J) 70(5)
Sec   J Welsh (0325) 355324
Pro   I Todd (0325) 462955
Holes   18 L 6272 yds SSS 70
Recs   Am–64 H Teschner
Pro–67 M Gallacher
V'trs   WD–U 9.30–12 & 1.30–430pm
WE–M SOC
Fees   £15 D–£20
Loc   Off Salters Lane, NE of
Darlington

Dinsdale Spa (1910)

**Middleton St George, Darlington
DL2 1DW**
Tel   (0325) 332222
Mem   850
Sec   PJ Wright (0325) 332297
Pro   D Dodds (0325) 332515
Holes   18 L 6078 yds SSS 69
Recs   Am–64 IS Liddle (1990)
Pro–69 DM Edwards (1980)
V'trs   WD–U exc Tues–NA WE–M
Fees   £12.50 D–£15
Loc   5 miles SE of Darlington

Durham City (1887)

Littleburn, Langley Moor DH7 8HL
Tel   (091) 378 0069
Mem   750
Sec   LTI Wilson (091) 386 0200
Pro   S Corbally (091) 378 0029
Holes   18 L 6211 yds SSS 70
Recs   Am–66 A Ramshaw,
K Cheseldine
V'trs   WD–U WE–NA SOC
Fees   £12 (£16)
Loc   1½ miles W of Durham

Hobson Municipal (1978)

Public
**Hobson, nr Burnopfield, Newcastle-
upon-Tyne**
Tel   (0207) 70941
Pro   J Ord (0207) 71605
Holes   18 L 6502 yds SSS 71
Recs   Am–67 S Ord, J Hutton (1990)
V'trs   U SOC
Fees   £5 (£6.50)
Loc   Between Gateshead and
Consett on A692

Mount Oswald

South Road, Durham City DH1 3TQ
Tel   (091) 386 7527
Mem   120
Sec   SE Reeve
Holes   18 L 6009 yds SSS 69
Recs   Am–64 J Mee (1986)
Pro–66 J Mathews (1984)
V'trs   U SOC
Fees   £6.50 D–£11 (£7.50 D–£13)
Loc   SW of Durham on A1050

Roseberry Grange

Public
**Grange Villa, Chester-Le-Street
DH2 3NF**
Tel   (091) 370 0670
Pro   A Hartley (091) 370 0660
Holes   18 L 5628 yds SSS 68
Recs   Am–66 D Brolls (1989)
Pro–65 B Rumney (1988)
V'trs   U SOC
Fees   £4 (£5)
Loc   3 miles W of Chester-Le-Street
on A693

Seaham (1911)

Dawdon, Seaham SR7 7RD
Tel   (091) 581 2354
Mem   550
Sec   V Smith (091) 581 5413
Holes   18 L 5972 yds SSS 69
Recs   Am–64 J Sanderson Jr (1984)
V'trs   U SOC
Fees   £6 (£12) (1990)
Loc   Dawdon, 2 miles NE of A19

South Moor (1925)

**The Middles, Craghead, Stanley
DH9 6AG**
Tel   (0207) 232848
Mem   550
Sec   R Harrison (091) 370 0515
Holes   18 L 6445 yds SSS 71
Recs   Am–67 JE Handy
Pro–65 A Webster
V'trs   U
Fees   On application
Loc   8 miles NW of Durham

Stressholme (1976)

Public
Snipe Lane, Darlington
Tel   (0325) 353073
Pro   FC Thorpe (0325) 461002
Holes   18 L 6511 yds SSS 71
Recs   Am–69 S Aitken
Pro–64 N Coles
V'trs   U
Fees   £5 (£6)
Loc   2 miles S of Darlington on
A167

Woodham G & CC (1983)

**Burnhill Way, Newton Aycliffe
DH5 4PM**
Tel   (0325) 320574
Mem   400
Sec   GE Golightly
Pro   J Graham
Holes   18 L 6727 yds SSS 72
Recs   Am–74 S Raby
Pro–71 D Stirling
V'trs   U SOC WE–booking
Fees   £7 (£10)
Loc   1 mile N of Newton Aycliffe

Essex

Abridge G & CC (1964)

**Epping Lane, Stapleford Tawney
RM4 1ST**
Tel   (04028) 388
Mem   560
Sec   PG Pelling (04028) 396/7
Pro   B Cooke (04028) 333
Holes   18 L 6703 yds SSS 72
Recs   Am–68 NK Burch
Pro–68 D Feherty
V'trs   WD–H WE/ BH–NA
Fees   £30
Loc   Theydon Bois/ Epping Stations
3 miles

Ballards Gore (1980)

Gore Road, Canewdon, Rochford
Tel   (0702) 258917
Mem   700
Sec   NG Patient
Pro   M Pierce (0702) 258924
Holes   18 L 7062 yds SSS 74
V'trs   WD–U WE–M after 12.30pm
(summer) 11.30am (winter)
SOC
Fees   £18
Loc   1½ miles NE of Rochford

Basildon (1967)

Public
**Clayhill Lane, Sparrow's Hearn,
Kingswood, Basildon**
Tel   (0268) 533297
Pro   W Paterson (0268) 533532
Holes   18 L 6120 yds SSS 69
Recs   Am–67 R Reeve
Pro–63 W Longmuir
V'trs   U SOC
Fees   £5.25 (£10)
Loc   1 mile S of Basildon, off A176 at
Kingswood roundabout

Belfairs (1926)

Public
**Eastwood Road North, Leigh-on-Sea
SS9 4LR**
Tel   (0702) 526911
Pro   R Foreman (0702) 520202
Holes   18 L 5871 yds SSS 68
V'trs   WD–U exc Thurs am WE/
BH–booking
Fees   £7 (£11)
Mis   Southend GC and Belfairs GC
play here

Belhus Park Municipal (1972)

Public
**Belhus Park, South Ockendon
RM15 4QR**
Tel   (0708) 854260
Sec   L Bourne (Mgr) (0708) 852248
Pro   S Wimbleton
Holes   18 L 5450 yds SSS 66

Recs	Am–67 M Jennings, J Bearman Pro–63 R Joyce
V'trs	U
Fees	£3.95 (£6)
Loc	1 mile N of A13/ M25 Dartford Tunnel
Mis	Floodlit driving range

Bentley G & CC (1972)

Ongar Road, Brentwood CM15 9SS

Tel	(0277) 73179
Mem	525
Sec	JA Vivers
Pro	K Bridges (0277) 72933
Holes	18 L 6709 yds SSS 72
Recs	Am–71 J Moody (1987) Pro–69 S Cipa (1988), B Smith (1988)
V'trs	WD–UH WE–M after noon BH–after 11am SOC–WD
Fees	£15 D–£20
Loc	18 miles E of London. M25 Junction 28 3 miles

Birch Grove (1970)

Layer Road, Colchester CO2 0HS

Tel	(0206) 34276
Mem	250
Sec	Mrs M Marston
Holes	9 L 4108 yds SSS 60
Recs	Am–61 A Brown (1990)
V'trs	WD/ BH–U Sat-XL before 1pm Sun-U after 1pm SOC
Fees	£8 (£10)
Loc	3 miles S of Colchester on B1026

Boyce Hill (1921)

Vicarage Hill, Benfleet SS7 1PD

Tel	(0268) 793625
Mem	600
Sec	JE Atkins
Pro	G Burroughs (0268) 752565
Holes	18 L 5882 yds SSS 68
Recs	Am–65 RCD Gilbert Pro–61 G Burroughs
V'trs	WD–UH WE/ BH–MH SOC–Thurs only
Fees	D–£18
Loc	4 miles W of Southend

Braintree (1891)

Kings Lane, Stisted, Braintree CM7 8DA

Tel	(0376) 24117
Mem	600
Sec	HW Hardy (0376) 46079
Pro	T Parcell (0376) 43465
Holes	18 L 6026 yds SSS 69
Recs	Am–65 M Hawes, M Davis Pro–65 P Golding
V'trs	WD–U WE/ BH–H SOC
Fees	£20
Loc	1 mile W of Braintree, off A120 towards Stisted

Bunsay Downs (1982)

Public

Little Baddow Road, Woodham Walter, nr Maldon CM9 6RW

Tel	(024 541) 2648/ 2369
Holes	9 L 2913 yds SSS 68 9 hole Par 3
V'trs	WD–U WE/ BH–tee booking up to 1 week in advance
Fees	18 holes £8 (£8.50) 9 holes £6 (£6.50)
Loc	7 miles E of Chelmsford, off A414
Mis	Indoor driving range

Burnham-on-Crouch (1923)

Ferry Road, Creeksea, Burnham-on-Crouch CM0 8PQ

Tel	(0621) 782282
Mem	410
Sec	AS Hill
Holes	9 L 5918 yds SSS 68
Recs	Am–66 D Clarke Pro–64 FJ Winser
V'trs	WD–H WE/ BH–M
Fees	£16
Loc	1½ miles W of Burnham

Canons Brook (1962)

Elizabeth Way, Harlow CM19 5BE

Tel	(0279) 421482
Mem	650
Sec	GE Chambers
Pro	R Yates (0279) 418357
Holes	18 L 6745 yds SSS 73
Recs	Am–68 H Cornick Pro–65 G Burroughs
V'trs	WD–U WE/ BH–NA
Fees	D–£20
Loc	25 miles N of London

Castle Point (1988)

Public

Somnes Avenue, Canvey Island SS8 9FG

Tel	(0268) 510830
Sec	VW Russell (0268) 698909
Pro	J Hudson
Holes	18 L 5627 yds SSS 69
V'trs	U SOC
Fees	£6 (£10)
Loc	Waterside Farm, Canvey Island
Mis	Driving range

Channels (1983)

Belsteads Farm Lane, Little Waltham, Chelmsford

Tel	(0245) 440005
Mem	650
Sec	RJ Stubbings
Pro	IB Sinclair (0245) 441056
Holes	18 L 6033 yds SSS 69
V'trs	WD–U WE–M SOC–WD
Fees	£19
Loc	3 miles N of Chelmsford
Mis	Pitch & putt course

Chelmsford (1893)

Widford, Chelmsford

Tel	(0245) 250555
Mem	650
Sec	Wg Cdr BA Templeman-Rooke (0245) 256483
Pro	GD Bailey (0245) 257079
Holes	18 L 5912 yds SSS 68
Recs	Am–67 G Turner Pro–65 C Platts
V'trs	WD–I WE/ BH–M
Fees	On application
Loc	Off A1016 at Widford roundabout

Chigwell (1925)

High Road, Chigwell IG7 5BH

Tel	(081) 500 2059
Mem	700
Sec	MMcL Farnsworth
Pro	R Beard (081) 500 2384
Holes	18 L 6279 yds SSS 70
Recs	Am–66 AM Ronald Pro–66 H Flatman
V'trs	WD–I WE/ BH–M
Fees	£20 D–£25 (1990)
Loc	13½ miles NE of London (A113)

Clacton (1892)

West Road, Clacton-on-Sea CO15 1AJ

Tel	(0255) 424331
Mem	650
Sec	H Lucas (0255) 421919
Pro	SJ Levermore (0255) 426304
Holes	18 L 6243 yds SSS 70
Recs	Am–67 A Hull Pro–65 S Bryan
V'trs	H WE/ BH–H after 11am SOC
Fees	£15 (£23)
Loc	On sea front

Colchester (1909)

Braiswick, Colchester CO4 5AU

Tel	(0206) 852946
Mem	330 90(L) 70(J) 160(5)
Sec	Mrs J Boorman (0206) 853396
Pro	P Hodgson (0206) 853920
Holes	18 L 6319 yds SSS 70
Recs	Am–63 B Booth Pro–68 A Parcell
V'trs	WD–H WE/ BH–NA SOC
Fees	D–£20
Loc	¾ mile NW of Colchester North Station, towards West Bergholt

Fairlop Waters (1987)

Public

Forest Road, Barkingside, Ilford IG6 3JA

Tel	(081) 500 9911
Pro	A Bowers (081) 501 1881
Holes	18 L 6288 yds SSS 72
V'trs	U
Fees	£3.75 (£6)
Loc	2 miles from S end of M11, by Fairlop underground station
Mis	Driving range. 9 hole Par 3

Forrester Park (1975)

Beckingham Road, Great Totham,
Maldon CM9 8EA
Tel   (0621) 891406
Mem   850
Sec   T Forrester–Muir
Holes 18 L 6073 yds SSS 69
Recs   Am–73 A Barrel (1990)
V'trs WD–U WE–NA before 1pm
       SOC–WD
Fees   £12 (£15)
Loc   3 miles NE of Maldon on
       Tiptree road (B1022)

Frinton (1896)

1 The Esplanade, Frinton-on-Sea
CO13 9EP
Tel   (0255) 764618
Mem   800
Sec   PB Stokes
Pro   P Taggart (0255) 671618
Holes 18 L 6259 yds SS 70
       9 L 2508 yds SSS 33
Recs   Am–67 IA Quick
       Pro–66 CS Denny
V'trs H WE/ BH–NA before 11.30am
       SOC
Fees   D–£20 9 holes–£7.50
Loc   18 miles E of Colchester

Gosfield Lakes (1986)

The Manor House, Gosfield,
Halstead CO9 1SE
Tel   (0787) 474747
Mem   814
Sec   A O'Shea (Sec/ Mgr)
Pro   R Wheeler (0787) 474488
Holes Lakes 18 L 6512 yds SSS 71
       Meadows 9 L 1354 yds Par 56
V'trs Lakes WD–H WE–M
       Meadows–U SOC
Fees   Lakes D–£18 Meadows D–£6
Loc   7 miles N of Braintree (A1017)

Hainault Forest (1912)

Public
Chigwell Row, Hainault Forest
Tel   (081) 500 2097
Sec   HG Richards (Sec/ Mgr)
       (081) 500 0385
Pro   AE Frost (081) 500 2131
Holes No 1 18 L 5754 yds SSS 67
       No 2 18 L 6600 yds SSS 71
Recs   No 1 Am–65 TG Patmore
       Pro–65 A Frost
       No 2 Am–68 S Middleton
       Pro–68 AE Frost Jr
V'trs U
Fees   £6 (£8)
Loc   Hog Hill, Redbridge

Hartswood (1967)

Public
King George's Playing Fields,
Brentwood CM14 5AE
Tel   (0277) 218714
Sec   J Turner (0277) 218850
Pro   J Stanion
Holes 18 L 6238 yds SSS 70
Recs   Am–70 A Cornell

       Pro–70 W Longmuir
V'trs U SOC
Fees   £5 (£7.50)
Loc   E of Brentwood on Ingrave
       road (A128)
Mis   Hartswood Club plays here

Harwich & Dovercourt (1906)

Parkeston Road, Harwich
Tel   (0255) 3616
Mem   400
Sec   BQ Dunham
Holes 9 L 2950 yds SSS 69
V'trs WD–U SOC
Fees   On application
Loc   A120 to roundabout to
       Parkeston Quay, course
       entrance 20 yds on left

Havering

Public
Risebridge Chase, Lower Bedfords
Road, Romford
Tel   (0708) 41429
Sec   P Jennings
Pro   P Jennings
Holes 18 L 6252 yds SSS 70 9 hole
       Par 3
V'trs WD–U WE–restricted
Fees   £2.95 (£4.50)
Loc   2 miles from Brentwood
       Junction of M25, off A12
Mis   Risebridge Club plays here

Ilford (1907)

Wanstead Park Road, Ilford
Tel   (081) 554 5174
Mem   618
Sec   (081) 554 2930
Pro   K Ashdown (081) 554 0094
Holes 18 L 5702 yds SSS 68
Recs   Am–60 P Happe (1990)
       Pro–64 B Huggett, A Campbell
V'trs WD–U WE–telephone Pro
Fees   £10 (£20)

Maldon (1891)

Beeleigh Langford, Maldon CM9 6LL
Tel   (0621) 853212
Mem   480
Sec   GR Bezant
Holes 9 L 6197 yds SSS 69
Recs   Am–71 R Byford
       Pro–67 S Levermore
V'trs WD–U H WE–M SOC
Fees   £10 D–£12
Loc   3 miles NW of Maldon on
       B1019

Maylands (1936)

Harold Park, Romford
Tel   (040 23) 42055
Mem   600
Sec   (040 23) 73080
Pro   JS Hopkin (040 23) 46466
Holes 18 L 6351 yds SSS 70
Recs   Am–67 G Johnson
       Pro–67 H Flatman

V'trs WD–I WE/ BH–M SOC
Fees   £20 (£30)
Loc   2 miles E of Romford on A12.
       1 mile from M25 Junction 28
Mis   Buggies for hire

Orsett (1898)

Brentwood Road, Orsett RM16 3DS
Tel   (0375) 891352
Mem   900
Sec   PM Pritchard
Pro   R Newberry (0375) 891797
Holes 18 L 6614 yds SSS 72
Recs   Am–68 A Pollock, I Quick
       Pro–69 H Flatman,
       G Burroughs
V'trs WD–H SOC–Mon-Wed only
Fees   £25
Loc   4 miles NE of Grays on A128.
       M25 Junction 30/ 31

Pipps Hill CC

Aquatels Recreation Centre, Cranes
Farm Road, Basildon
Tel   (0268) 23456
Holes 9 L 2829 yds SSS 67
V'trs U SOC
Fees   On application
Loc   Nr Southend road (A127)

Quietwaters (1974)

Colchester Road, Tolleshunt
Knights, nr Maldon CM9 8HX
Tel   (0621) 860410
Mem   585
Sec   PD Keeble (Mgr)
Pro   D Pugh (0621) 819540
Holes 18 L 6194 yds SSS 70
Recs   Am–71 M Keeble (1988)
       Pro–68 K Ashdown (1988)
V'trs U BH–U after 1pm SOC
Fees   On application
Loc   8 miles S of Colchester, off
       B1026
Mis   Further 18 holes open 1991:
       18 L 6765 yds SSS 72

Rochford Hundred (1893)

Rochford
Tel   (0702) 544302
Mem   340 150(L) 60(J) 210(5)
Sec   To be appointed
Pro   GN Shipley
Holes 18 L 6256 yds SSS 70
Recs   Am–65 DK Wood
       Pro–65 C Tucker
V'trs WD–U H WE–M
Fees   On application
Loc   4 miles N of Southend-on-Sea

Romford (1894)

Heath Drive, Gidea Park, Romford
RM2 5QB
Tel   (0708) 740007 (Members)
Mem   690
Sec   BE Fox (0708) 740986
Pro   H Flatman (0708) 749393
Holes 18 L 6377 yds SSS 70
Recs   Am–68 D Girdlestone

For list of abbreviations see page 487.

V'trs WD–I WE–NA SOC
Fees £15 D–£25
Loc 1 mile E of Romford. 3 miles W of M25 Junction 29

Saffron Walden (1919)

Windmill Hill, Saffron Walden
CB10 1BX
Tel (0799) 22689 (Members)
Mem 900
Sec KW Reddall (Mgr) (0799) 22786
Pro P Davis (0799) 27728
Holes 18 L 6608 yds SSS 72
Recs Am–67 AD Emery (1988)
Pro–68 S Jackson (1983)
V'trs WD–UH WE/ BH–M SOC
Fees £25
Loc Saffron Walden, on B184

Stapleford Abbotts (1989)

Horseman's Side, Tysea Hill, Stapleford Abbotts RM4 1JU
Tel (04023) 81108
Fax (04023) 81108
Mem 800
Sec K Fletcher
Pro S Cranfield (04023) 81278
Holes Abbotts 18 L 6487 yds SSS Friars 9 L 1140 yds
V'trs U H exc WE/ BH–NA before noon SOC
Fees D–£25 (D–£30)
Loc Romford 2 miles. M25 Junction 28
Mis Further 18 holes open Sept 1991

Stoke by Nayland (1972)

Keepers Lane, Leavenheath, Colchester CO6 4PZ
Tel (0206) 262836
Mem 1250
Sec J Loshak
Pro K Lovelock (0206) 262769
Holes Gainsborough 18 L 6516 yds SSS 71; Constable 18 L 6544 yds SSS 71
Recs Gainsborough Am–66 RW Mann Pro–69 PL Cowan
V'trs WD–U WE/ BH–H after 10am SOC
Fees £18 (£20)
Loc Off A134 Colchester-Sudbury road on to B1036

Theydon Bois (1897)

Theydon Bois, Epping CM16 4EH
Tel (0992) 812279
Mem 600
Sec I McDonald (0992) 813054
Pro R Joyce (0992) 812460
Holes 18 L 5472 yds SSS 68
Recs Am–66 S Allen (1986), T Moncur (1988), N Moncur (1990) Pro–64 R Joyce (1989)
V'trs Thurs am-restricted WE–M
Fees £20 (£30)
Loc 1 mile S of Epping

Thorndon Park (1920)

Ingrave, Brentwood CM13 3RH
Tel (0277) 811666
Mem 300 140(L) 60(J) 130(5)
Sec JE Leggitt (0277) 810345
Pro BV White (0277) 810736
Holes 18 L 6455 yds SSS 71
Recs Am–66 MES Davis Pro–65 BJ Hunt, B Waites
V'trs WD–I WE/ BH–M
Fees £25 D–£35
Loc 2 miles SE of Brentwood on A128

Thorpe Hall (1907)

Thorpe Hall Avenue, Thorpe Bay SS1 3AT
Tel (0702) 582205
Mem 750
Sec RCP Hunter
Pro G Harvey (0702) 588195
Holes 18 L 6286 yds SSS 71
Recs Am–68 B Hillsden Pro–67 L Platts
V'trs WD–H WE/ BH–M
Fees On application
Loc E of Southend-on-Sea

Three Rivers (1973)

Stow Road, Purleigh, nr Chelmsford CM3 6RR
Tel (0621) 828631
Mem 600
Sec G Stafford
Pro L Platts
Holes 18 L 6609 yds SSS 72 9 L 1071 yds Par 3 course
V'trs WD–U WE/ BH–M SOC–Tues & Thurs
Fees D–£12
Loc 5 miles S of Maldon

Towerlands (1985)

Panfield Road, Braintree CM7 5BJ
Tel (0376) 26802
Fax (0376) 552487
Mem 325
Sec K Cooper
Holes 9 L 2703 yds SSS 66
V'trs WD–U WE–U after 2pm SOC–WD
Fees 18 holes–£10 (£12) 9 holes–£8
Loc 1 mile NW of Braintree
Mis Driving range

Upminster (1928)

114 Hall Lane, Upminster
Tel (040 22) 20249
Mem 900
Sec Mrs J Wylie (040 22) 22788
Pro N Carr (040 22) 20000
Holes 18 L 5951 yds SSS 68
Recs Am–64 AT Bird
V'trs WD–U WE/ BH–NA
Fees £18
Loc Station 3/4 mile

Warley Park (1975)

Magpie Lane, Little Warley, Brentwood
Tel (0277) 231352
Mem 600
Sec SP Greene (0277) 224891
Pro P O'Conner (0277) 212552
Holes 18 L 6261 yds SSS 70 9 L 3166 yds SSS 35
Recs Am–69 B Preston
V'trs WD–U WE–M
Fees £18
Loc 2 miles S of Brentwood. M25 Junction 29

Warren (1932)

Woodham Walter, Maldon CM9 6RW
Tel (024 541) 3258/ 3198
Mem 800
Pro M Walker (024 541) 4662
Holes 18 L 6211 yds SSS 69
Recs Am–65 M Robarts (1990) Pro–66 H Flatman
V'trs WD–I H WE–M
Fees £22 D–£26
Loc 7 miles E of Chelmsford, off A414

Woodford (1890)

2, Sunset Avenue, Woodford Green IG8 0ST
Tel (081) 504 0553/ 4254
Mem 397
Sec GJ Cousins (081) 504 3330
Pro A Johns (081) 504 4254
Holes 9 L 5806 yds SSS 68
Recs Am–69 M Everitt Pro–68 P Golding
V'trs WD–U before 3pm exc Tues & Thurs am–NA WE–M SOC
Fees £12
Loc 11 miles NE of London

Gloucestershire

Broadway (1896)

Willersey Hill, Broadway, Worcs WR12 7LG
Tel (0386) 858997
Mem 400 120(L) 70(J) 140(5)
Sec B Carnie (Sec/ Mgr) (0386) 853683
Pro J Freeman (0386) 853275
Holes 18 L 6211 yds SSS 70
Recs Am–66 DM Fletcher Pro–66 D Steele, R Adams
V'trs H Sat–M
Fees £17 (£21)
Loc 1 1/2 miles E of Broadway (A44)

Cirencester (1893)

Cheltenham Road, Cirencester GL7 7BH
Tel (0285) 653939
Mem 700
Sec ND Jones (0285) 652465

Pro	G Robbins (0285) 656124
Holes	18 L 6021 yds SSS 69
Recs	Am–64 D Rollo
	Pro–67 DJ Rees
V'trs	BH–H SOC–WD
Fees	£20 (£25)
Loc	1½ miles N of Cirencester on A435

Cleeve Hill (1976)

Public

Cleeve Hill, nr Cheltenham

Tel	(024 267) 2025
Pro	D Finch (024 267) 2592
Holes	18 L 6444 yds SSS 71
V'trs	U exc Sun am–NA SOC
Fees	£5.50 (£6.50)
Loc	3 miles N of Cheltenham on A46 to Winchcombe

Cotswold Edge (1980)

Upper Rushmire, Wotton-under-Edge GL12 7PT

Tel	(0453) 844167
Mem	800
Sec	NJ Newman
Pro	DJ Gosling (0453) 844398
Holes	18 L 6170 yds SSS 69
Recs	Am–N Barlow (1986)
	Pro–K Spurgeon (1985)
V'trs	WD–U WE–M SOC
Fees	£15
Loc	2 miles NE of Wotton-under-Edge on B4058 Tetbury road

Cotswold Hills (1902)

Ullenwood, nr Cheltenham
GL53 9QT

Tel	(0242) 522421
Mem	750
Sec	A O'Reilly (0242) 515264
Pro	N Boland (0242) 515263
Holes	18 L 6716 yds SSS 72
Recs	Am–68 R Day
	Pro–68 SD Brown (1987)
V'trs	I (recognised club members)
Fees	£20
Loc	3 miles S of Cheltenham

Forest of Dean (1974)

Lords Hill, Coleford GL16 8BD

Tel	(0594) 32583
Mem	450
Sec	R Sanzen-Baker
Pro	J Nicol (0594) 33689
Holes	18 L 5519 yds SSS 67
V'trs	U SOC
Fees	£10 (£15)
Loc	½ mile from Coleford on Parkend road

Gloucestershire Hotel (1976)

Matson Lane, Gloucester

Tel	(0452) 25653
Mem	500
Sec	R Jewell
Pro	R Jewell, P Darnell (0452) 411331

Holes	18 L 6127 yds SSS 69
	9 L 1980 yds SSS 27
Recs	Am–69 J Northam
	Pro–65 P Darnell
V'trs	U
Fees	£15 (£19)
Loc	2 miles S of Gloucester, off Painswick road

Lilley Brook (1922)

Cirencester Road, Charlton Kings,
Cheltenham GL53 8EG

Tel	(0242) 526785
Mem	700
Sec	K Skeen
Pro	F Hadden (0242) 525201
Holes	18 L 6226 yds SSS 70
Recs	Am–64 B Mitten (1987)
	Pro–63 I Sparkes (1990)
V'trs	H or I (recognised club members) SOC–WD
Fees	D–£18 (£25)
Loc	3 miles SE of Cheltenham on A435

Lydney (1909)

Lydney

Tel	(0594) 842614
Mem	300
Sec	DA Barnard (0594) 843940
Holes	9 L 5382 yds SSS 66
Recs	Am–63 MA Barnard (1988)
	Pro–68 F Goulding
V'trs	WD–U WE/ BH–M SOC
Fees	£12 W–£30
Loc	Off Lakeside Avenue

Minchinhampton (1889)

Minchinhampton, Stroud GL6 8BE

Tel	(045 383) 2642 (Old course)
	(045 383) 3866 (New course)
Mem	1721
Sec	DR Vickers (045 383) 3866
Pro	C Steele (045 383) 3860
Holes	Old 18 L 6295 yds SSS 70
	New 18 L 6675 yds SSS 72
Recs	Old Am–67 PH Fisher, L Scott
	Pro–67 RA Brown New Am–68
	RD Broad (1988)
	Pro–67 GH Marks, G Ryall
V'trs	H–restricted SOC
Fees	Old–£9 (£12) New–£20 (£25)
Loc	Old–3 miles E of Stroud. New–5 miles E of Stroud

Painswick (1891)

Painswick, nr Stroud GL6 6TL

Tel	(0452) 812180
Mem	350
Sec	RJ May
Pro	None
Holes	18 L 4780 yds SSS 64
Recs	Am–61 J Woolley
V'trs	WD/ Sat–U Sun–M SOC
Fees	£7.50 Sat–£10
Loc	½ mile N of Painswick on A46
Mis	Sun–course closes at 2pm Apr–Oct

Stinchcombe Hill (1889)

Stinchcombe Hill, Dursley
GL11 6AQ

Tel	(0453) 542015
Mem	500
Sec	JR Clarke (Hon)
Pro	A Valentine (0453) 543878
Holes	18 L 5723 yds SSS 68
Recs	Am–64 PC French (1979)
	Pro–64 I Bolt (1984)
V'trs	WD–U WE/ BH–NA before 10.30am SOC
Fees	£18 (£20) W–£45 F–£80
Loc	Dursley 1 mile

Tewkesbury Park Hotel (1976)

Lincoln Green Lane, Tewkesbury
GL20 7DN

Tel	(0684) 295405
Mem	550
Pro	P Cane (0684) 294892
Holes	18 L 6533 yds SSS 72
Recs	Am–69 B Wilson
	Pro–68 N Job
V'trs	WD–U H SOC–WD WE–residential SOC only
Fees	£18 (£22)
Loc	½ mile S of Tewkesbury on A38. 2 miles from M5 Junction 9
Mis	6 hole Par 3–£2. 4 bay practice range

Westonbirt (1971)

Westonbirt, Tetbury GL8 8QG

Tel	(066 88) 242
Mem	200
Sec	Bursar, Westonbirt School
Pro	C Steele (045 383) 3860
Holes	9 L 4504 yds SSS 61
Recs	Am–62 S Dunlop
V'trs	U SOC–WD
Fees	D–£5 (£5)
Loc	3 miles S of Tetbury off A433

Hampshire

Alresford (1890)

Cheriton Road, Alresford SO24 0PN

Mem	570
Sec	P Kingston (0962) 733746
Pro	M Scott (0962) 733998
Holes	12 L 6038 yds SSS 69
Recs	Am–68 T Chandler
	Pro–67 J Hay
V'trs	U H WE–after noon SOC
Fees	£13 D–£20 (£25)
Loc	1 mile S of Alresford on B3046

Alton (1908)

Old Odiham Road, Alton GU34 4BU

Tel	(0420) 82042
Mem	340
Sec	Mrs MJ Woodhead (0420) 84064
Pro	A Lamb (0420) 86518
Holes	9 L 5744 yds SSS 68

Recs Am–65 I McInally (1987)
Pro–65 A Stevens (1988)
V'trs WD/ Sat–U exc comp days
Sun/ BH–M or H(max 18)
SOC–WD
Fees £10 D–£15 (£15 D–£20)
Loc 2 miles N of Alton. 6 miles S of
Odiham off A32

Ampfield Par Three (1963)

Winchester Road, Ampfield, nr
Romsey SO51 9BQ
Tel (0794) 68480
Mem 500
Sec Mrs S Baker
Pro R Benfield (0794) 68750
Holes 18 L 2478 yds SSS 53
Recs Am–49 R Bailey
Pro–49 A Timms
V'trs WD–U WE/ BH–H (phone first)
SOC
Fees £8 (£15)
Loc On A31 Winchester to Romsey

Andover (1907)

51 Winchester Road, Andover
SP10 2EF
Tel (0264) 323980
Mem 415 60(L) 40(J)
Sec Maj BF Gerhard MBE (0264)
358040
Pro A Timms (0264) 324151
Holes 9 L 5933 yds SSS 68
Recs Am–68 I Stewart (1990)
Pro–66 I Young (1990)
V'trs WD–U WE/ BH–NA before
noon SOC
Fees £10 (£20)
Loc ¹/₂ mile S of Andover on A3057

Army Golf Club (1883)

Laffan's Road, Aldershot GU11 2HF
Tel (0252) 541104
Fax (0252) 376562
Mem 800
Sec RT Crabb(Sec/ Mgr) (0252)
540638
Pro P Thompson (0252) 547232
Holes 18 L 6579 yds SSS 71
Recs Am–69 G Young
Pro–69 I Young
V'trs M
Fees Special rates for Forces
Loc Between Aldershot and
Farnborough

Barton-on-Sea (1897)

Marine Drive, Barton-on-Sea
BH25 7DY
Tel (0425) 615308
Mem 392 117(L) 50(J)
Sec CJ Wingfield
Pro P Coombs (0425) 611210
Holes 18 L 5565 yds SSS 67
Recs Am–63 RM Tuddenham
Pro–66 P Alliss
V'trs H WD–U WE/ BH–NA before
11.15am SOC–Wed & Fri
Fees D–£21 (D–£24)
Loc 1¹/₂ miles from New Milton, off
A337. M27 Junction 1

Basingstoke (1928)

Kempshott Park, Basingstoke
RG23 7LL
Tel (0256) 465990
Mem 725
Sec I Osborough
Pro I Hayes (0256) 51332
Holes 18 L 6309 yds SSS 70
Recs Am–67 C Tuck (1989)
Pro–65 G Stubbington (1989)
V'trs WD–H WE–M SOC–Wed &
Thurs
Fees £14
Loc 3 miles W of Basingstoke on
A30. M3 Junction 7
Mis Buggy hire £10 per round

Basingstoke Hospitals

Aldermaston Road, Basingstoke
Tel (0256) 20347
Mem 275
Sec EEL Rowlands
Holes 9 L 5480 yds SSS 67
V'trs WD–U WE–contact Mgr SOC
Fees £6.50 (£9)
Loc 1¹/₂ miles N of Basingstoke

Bishopswood (1978)

Bishopswood Lane, Tadley,
Basingstoke RG26 6AT
Tel (0734) 815213
Mem 400
Sec MW Phillips (Mgr) (0734)
812200
Pro S Ward
Holes 9 L 6474 yds SSS 71
Recs Am–69 C Wilkins (1987)
Pro–68 R Boxall (1983)
V'trs Tues/ Thurs/ Fri–U Mon &
Wed–M WE–M
Fees £9
Loc 6 miles N of Basingstoke, off
A340
Mis Floodlit driving range

Blackmoor (1913)

Whitehill Bordon GU35 9EH
Tel (0420) 472775
Mem 680 85(L) 60(J)
Sec Maj HRG Spiller
Pro A Hall (0420) 472345
Holes 18 L 6213 yds SSS 70
V'trs H WE–NA
Fees £20 D–£30
Loc ¹/₂ mile W of Whitehill on A325

Botley Park (1989)

Winchester Road, Boorley Green,
Botley SO3 2UA
Tel (0489) 780888 (Ext 444)
Fax (0489) 789242
Mem 550
Sec S Benton
Pro T Barter
Holes 18 L 6026 yds SSS 71
V'trs M H SOC
Fees On application
Loc 6 miles E of Southampton on
B3354, nr Botley. M27 Junction 7
Mis Driving range

Bramshaw (1880)

Brook, Lyndhurst SO43 7HE
Tel (0703) 813433
Mem 1400
Sec RD Tingey
Pro A Egford (0703) 813434
Holes Forest 18 L 5774 yds SSS 68
Manor 18 L 6257 yds SSS 70
Recs Forest Am–67 G Hill
Pro–66 W Wiltshire Manor
Am–67 G Lovelady
Pro–66 G Stubbington
V'trs WD–U H WE–M
Fees £25
Loc 10 miles SW of Southampton.
M27 Junction 1

Brokenhurst Manor (1919)

Sway Road, Brockenhurst
Tel (0590) 23332
Mem 800
Sec RE Stallard
Pro C Bonner (0590) 23092
Holes 18 L 6222 yds SSS 70
Recs Am–64 K Weeks
Pro–66 D Haslam
V'trs WD–after 9.30am H SOC
NA–Tues–Ladies' Day
Fees D–£25 (D–£30)
Loc Brockenhurst 1 mile on B3055
to Sway

Burley (1905)

Burley, Ringwood BH24 4BB
Tel (04253) 2431
Mem 520
Sec GR Kendall
Pro R Watkins
Holes 9 L 3135 yds SSS 69
Recs Am–70 N Carpenter (1970),
W Medd (1984), A Locke (1990)
V'trs H
Fees £10 (£12.50) W–£40
Loc 4 miles SE of Ringwood

Corhampton (1891)

Sheeps Pond Lane, Droxford,
Southampton SO3 1QZ
Tel (0489) 877279
Mem 650
Sec P Taylor
Pro J Harris (0489) 877638
Holes 18 L 6088 yds SSS 69
Recs Am–66 R Edwards (1988)
Pro–65 P Dawson (1987)
V'trs WD–U H WE/ BH–M
SOC–Mons & Thurs
Fees £18 D–£28
Loc 9 miles S of Winchester

Dibden (1974)

Public
Main Road, Dibden, Southampton
SO4 5TB
Tel (0703) 845596
Pro A Bridge
Holes 18 L 6206 yds SSS 70
Recs Pro–63 I Young (1988)
V'trs U
Fees £4.30 (£6.30)

Loc	10 miles W of Southampton. 1/2 mile from Dibden round-about on A326 Fawley road
Mis	Further 9 holes + driving range open 1991

Dunwood Manor (1969)

Shootash Hill, Romsey SO5 10GF

Tel	(0794) 40549
Mem	700
Sec	Mrs H Johnson, P Dawson (Golf Mgr)
Pro	G Stubbington (0794) 40663
Holes	18 L 5865 yds SSS 69
Recs	Am–69 D Harris
	Pro–61 G Stubbington
V'trs	WE/ BH–restricted SOC–WD
Fees	£15 (£20)
Loc	Romsey 4 miles, off A27

Fleetlands (1961)

Fareham Road, Gosport PO13 0AW

Tel	(0705) 822351
Mem	120
Sec	A Eade (Ext 44384)
Holes	9 L 4775 yds SSS 63
Recs	Am–65 M Squibb
V'trs	M at all times
Loc	2 miles S of Fareham on A32 Gosport road. M27 Junction 12

Fleming Park (1973)

Public

Fleming Park, Eastleigh

Tel	(0703) 612797
Pro	D Miller
Holes	18 L 4436 yds SSS 62
Recs	Am–62 D Cox Pro–61 J Hay
V'trs	U SOC–WD
Fees	£3.85 (£5.95) (1990)
Loc	6 miles N of Southampton

Gosport & Stokes Bay (1885)

Military Road, Fort Road, Haslar, Gosport PO12 2AT

Tel	(0705) 581625
Mem	170
Sec	T Jopling (0705) 527941
Holes	9 L 5668 yds SSS 69
Recs	Am–69 M Stubley (1986)
	Pro–65 P Dawson (1985)
V'trs	U Sun–NA
Fees	D–£8 (May–Oct) D–£6 (Nov–Apr)
Loc	S boundary of Gosport

Great Salterns (1914)

Public

Portsmouth Golf Centre, Eastern Road, Portsmouth PO3 6QB

Tel	(0705) 664549
Pro	T Healey
Holes	18 L 5970 yds SSS 68
V'trs	U
Fees	£5
Loc	1 mile off M27 on A2030
Mis	Southsea Club plays here. Driving range

Hartley Wintney (1891)

London Road, Hartley Wintney, nr Basingstoke

Tel	(025 126) 2214
Mem	410
Sec	BD Powell (025 126) 4211
Pro	M Smith (025 126) 3779
Holes	9 L 6096 yds SSS 69
Recs	Am–70 M Wild
	Pro–63 R Lewington
V'trs	Wed–Ladies' Day SOC–Tues & Thurs WE/ BH–restricted
Fees	£10 (£18)
Loc	A30 between Camberley and Basingstoke

Hayling (1883)

Ferry Road, Hayling Island PO11 0BX

Tel	(0705) 463712/ 463777
Mem	900
Sec	RCW Stokes (0705) 464446
Pro	R Gadd (0705) 464491
Holes	18 L 6489 yds SSS 71
Recs	Pro–66 F Gilbride Am–66 D Harrison, K Weeks
V'trs	H WE/ BH–after 11.30am SOC
Loc	5 miles S of Havant on A3023

Hockley (1915)

Twyford, nr Winchester SO21 1PL

Tel	(0962) 713165
Mem	750
Sec	Wg Cdr JR Digby
Pro	T Lane (0962) 713678
Holes	18 L 6279 yds SSS 70
Recs	Am–67 PE Anthony, CJ Hyde, GP Cole
	Pro–65 T Underwood
V'trs	WD–U WE/ BH–M
Fees	£22
Loc	Winchester Station 2 miles on A3335

Leckford & Longstock (1929)

Leckford, Stockbridge SO20 6JS

Tel	(0264) 810320
Mem	200
Sec	J Wood
Pro	LG Lucas
Holes	9 L 3251 yds SSS 71
V'trs	M
Loc	5 miles W of Andover

Lee-on-the-Solent (1905)

Brune Lane, Lee-on-the-Solent

Tel	(0705) 550207
Mem	700
Sec	PA Challis (0705) 551170
Pro	John Richardson (0705) 551181
Holes	18 L 5793 yds SSS 69
Recs	Am–65 S Richardson
	Pro–66 M Faulkner
V'trs	WD–UH WE–MH SOC–Thurs
Fees	D–£18
Loc	3 miles S of Fareham

Liphook (1922)

Liphook GU30 7EH

Tel	(0428) 723271
Mem	800
Sec	Maj JB Morgan MBE (0428) 723785
Pro	I Large
Holes	18 L 6207 yds SSS 70
Recs	Am–70 R Tuddenham, M Wiggett
	Pro–66 TR Pinner
V'trs	I H (max 24) Sun–NA before 1pm
Fees	£20 D–£30 (£30 D–£40)
Loc	18 miles SW of Guildford on A3
Mis	Bohunt Manor Club plays here

Meon Valley Hotel G & CC (1977)

Sandy Lane, Shedfield, Southampton SO3 2HQ

Tel	(0329) 833455
Mem	700
Sec	T Hussey (Gen Mgr) CM Terry (Sec)
Pro	J Stirling
Holes	18 L 6519 yds SSS 71
Recs	Am–69 S Vear (1988)
	Pro–67 J Garner (1987)
V'trs	H SOC
Fees	£20 (£25)
Loc	2 miles NW of Wickham. N off A334
Mis	Further 9 holes open 1991

Moors Valley (1989)

Public

Horton Road, Ringwood

Tel	(0425) 479776
Holes	9 L 2750 yds Par 35
V'trs	U
Fees	£6 (£8)
Loc	4 miles SW of Ringwood, off A31

New Forest (1888)

Southampton Road, Lyndhurst SO43 7BU

Tel	(0703) 282450/ 282752
Mem	900
Sec	Mrs W Swann (0703) 282752
Pro	K Gilhespy (0703) 282450
Holes	18 L 5742 yds SS 68
Recs	Am–65 C White
	Pro–67 S Clay, R Brown
V'trs	U exc Sun am
Fees	£12 (£15)
Loc	On A35 Bournemouth to Southampton road

North Hants (1904)

Minley Road, Fleet GU13 8RE

Tel	(0252) 616443
Fax	(0252) 811627
Mem	700
Sec	IR Goodliffe
Pro	S Porter (0252) 616655
Holes	18 L 6257 yds SSS 70

Recs Am–66 MC Hughesdon (1976),
JS Cheetham, J Dodds (1988),
G Evans (1990)
Pro–67 B Hunt
V'trs WD–H by prior arrangement
WE/ BH–MH SOC–Tues &
Wed
Fees On application
Loc 3 miles W of Farnborough on
B3013. M3 Junction 4

Old Thorns (1982)

Longmoor Road, Liphook
GU30 7PE
Tel (0428) 724555
Fax (0428) 725322
Sec GM Jones
Pro P Loxley
Holes 18 L 6447 yds SSS 71
Recs Pro–69 I Aoki (1982)
V'trs U SOC
Fees £18 (£28) SOC–£45
Loc 1 mile off A3 from Liphook, on
B2131
Mis Driving range

Petersfield (1892)

Heath Road, Petersfield GU31 4EJ
Tel (0730) 63725
Mem 572(M) 97(L) 66(J)
Sec P Heraud (0730) 62386
Pro S Clay (0730) 67732
Holes 18 L 5710 yds SSS 68
Recs Am–69 P Flux
Pro–66 J Hay
V'trs WD–U WE/ BH–NA before
noon
Fees £12 D–£18 (£18 D–£24)
Loc ½ mile E of Petersfield

Portsmouth (1926)

Public
Crookhorn Lane, Widley,
Portsmouth PO7 5QL
Tel (0705) 372210
Pro R Brown
Holes 18 L 6259 yds SSS 70
V'trs U SOC (arrange with Pro)
Fees £6.40
Loc 1 mile N of Portsmouth, on
B2177

Romsey (1925)

Nursling, Southampton SO1 9XW
Tel (0703) 732218
Mem 825
Sec P Hargraves (0703) 734637
Pro M Desmond (0703) 736673
Holes 18 L 5752 yds SSS 68
Recs Am–65 J Archer (1990)
Pro–64 J Slade (1985)
V'trs WD–H WE/ BH–M H
Fees £16 (1990)
Loc 2 miles SE of Romsey on
Southampton road (A3057).
Nr M27/ M271 Junction 3

Rowlands Castle (1902)

Links Lane, Rowlands Castle
PO9 6AE
Tel (0705) 412216
Mem 500 150(L) 60(J)
Sec Capt. AW Aird (0705) 412784
Pro P Klepacz (0705) 412785
Holes 18 L 6627 yds SSS 72
Recs Am–70 N Cole, C Anderson
Pro–66 M Gregson
V'trs WD–UH WE–phone first Sat–M
SOC–Tues & Thurs
Fees D–£18 (D–£22) (1990)
Loc 9 miles S of Petersfield off
A3(M). 3 miles N of Havant

Royal Winchester (1888)

Sarum Road, Winchester SO22 5QE
Tel (0962) 852462
(0962) 865048 (Members)
Mem 700
Sec DP Williams (Mgr)
Pro DP Williams (0962) 862473
Holes 18 L 6218 yds SSS 70
Recs Am–67 J Curren
Pro–67 B Lane, D Feherty
V'trs WD–UH WE/ BH–M SOC–WD
Fees On application
Loc W of Winchester off A31

Sandford Springs (1989)

Wolverton, Basingstoke RG26 5RT
Tel (0635) 297881
Fax (0635) 298065
Mem 400
Sec G Tipple
Pro K Brake, A Dillon (0635)
297883
Holes 18 L 6064 yds SSS 70
V'trs WD–prior booking WE–M
SOC
Fees £20 D–£30
Loc Between Basingstoke and
Newbury on A339

Southampton Municipal (1935)

Public
Golf Course Road, Bassett,
Southampton
Tel (0703) 768407
Pro J Cave
Holes 18 L 6218 yds SSS 70
9 L 2391 yds SSS 33
Recs Am–64 P Dedman
Pro–62 SW Murray
V'trs U
Fees 18 hole:£4.20 (£6)
9 hole:£2.10 (£3)
Loc 2 miles N of Southampton
Mis Ordnance Survey Club plays
here

Southwick Park (1977)

Pinsley Drive, Southwick PO17 6EL
Tel (0705) 380131
Mem 600 60(L)
Sec NW Price
Pro J Green (0705) 380442

Holes 18 L 5855 yds SSS 68
Recs Am–67 R Edwards, R Berry
Pro–64 G Hughes
V'trs WD–U before 11am only
SOC–Tues
Fees On application. Servicemen
reduced rate
Loc Southwick village ½ mile

Southwood (1977)

Public
Ively Road, Farnborough GU14 0LJ
Tel (0252) 548700
Sec RE Smith (Hon)
Pro R Hammond
Holes 18 L 5553 yds SSS 67
Recs Am–69 (1988)
Pro–64 M Fagan (1988)
V'trs U
Fees £8
Loc 1 mile W of Farnborough off
A325

Stoneham (1908)

Bassett Green Road, Bassett,
Southampton SO2 3NE
Tel (0703) 768151
Mem 800
Sec Mrs AM Wilkinson (0703)
769272
Pro I Young (0703) 768397
Holes 18 L 6310 yds SSS 70
Recs Am–65 R Park
Pro–63 J Martin
V'trs WD–U WE–NA SOC–Mon/
Thurs/ Fri
Fees £25
Loc 2 miles N of Southampton

Tidworth Garrison (1908)

Tidworth
Tel (0980) 42321 (Steward)
Mem 700
Sec Lt Col DFT Tucker (0980)
42301
Pro T Godsen (0980) 42393
Holes 18 L 6075 yds SSS 69
Recs Am–65 JN Flemming, A Litton
Pro–65 I Young
V'trs SOC–Tues/ Thurs/ Fri
WE/ BH–NA before 3pm
Fees £15 (£20)
Loc Tidworth 1 mile on Bulford
road

Tylney Park (1973)

Rotherwick, Basingstoke
Tel (0256) 762079
Mem 700
Sec AD Bewley
Pro C de Bruin (Mgr)
Holes 18 L 6108 yds SSS 69
Recs Am–70 D Curd
Pro–68 S Watson (1988)
V'trs WD–U WE–M or H SOC
Fees £13 (£20)
Loc 2 miles NW of Hook. M3
Junction 5

For list of abbreviations see page 487.

Waterlooville (1907)

Cherry Tree Ave, Cowplain, Waterlooville PO8 8AP
Mem	800
Sec	C Chamberlain (0705) 263388
Pro	J Hay (0705) 256911
Holes	18 L 6647 yds SSS 72
Recs	Am–68 D Hickman (1987)
	Pro–66 H Stott (1988)
V'trs	WD/ WE–MH (Sun am–XL)
	SOC
Fees	£17 D–£20
Loc	10 miles N of Portsmouth on A3

Hereford & Worcester

Abbey Park G & CC

Dagnell End Road, Redditch, Worcs
Tel	(0527) 63918
Fax	(0527) 65872
Mem	1200
Sec	ME Bradley
Pro	RK Cameron
Holes	18 L 6398 yds SSS 71
V'trs	WD–U
Fees	£5.50 (£10)
Loc	B4101, off A441 Redditch–Birmingham road
Mis	Driving range

Belmont House (1983)

Belmont, Hereford HR2 9SA
Tel	(0432) 352666
Fax	(0432) 58090
Mem	500
Pro	M Welsh (0432) 352717
Holes	18 L 6480 yds SSS 71
Recs	Am–74 R Hemmings
	Pro–70 A Griffiths, J Lomas, S Marr
V'trs	U SOC
Fees	On application
Loc	1½ miles S of Hereford on A465

Blackwell (1893)

Blackwell, nr Bromsgrove B60 1PY
Tel	(021) 445 1781
Mem	300 100(L) 20(J)
Sec	S Allen (021) 445 1994
Pro	H MacDonald (021) 445 3113
Holes	18 L 6202 yds SSS 71
Recs	Am–68 AJ Thomson
	Pro–68 J Higgins (1990)
V'trs	WD–U WE/ BH–M
Fees	£28
Loc	3 miles E of Bromsgrove

Churchill & Blakedown (1926)

Churchill Lane, Blakedown, nr Kidderminster DY10 3NB
Tel	(0562) 700200
Mem	350
Sec	JH Lidstone
Pro	G Mercer

Holes	9 L 6472 yds SSS 71
V'trs	WD–U WE–M
Fees	D–£15
Loc	3 miles N of Kidderminster on A453

Droitwich (1897)

Ford Lane, Droitwich WR9 0BQ
Tel	(0905) 770129
Mem	768
Sec	MJ Taylor (0905) 774344
Pro	CS Thompson (0905) 770207
Holes	18 L 6040 yds SSS 69
Recs	Am–63 J Bickerton
V'trs	WD–U WE/ BH–M SOC–Wed & Fri
Fees	£18
Loc	1 mile N of Droitwich off A38. M5 Junction 5

Evesham (1894)

Craycombe Links, Fladbury, Pershore, Worcs WR10 2QS
Tel	(0386) 860395
Mem	340
Sec	FG Vincent (0386) 552373
Pro	JR Gray
Holes	9 L 6415 yds SSS 71
Recs	Am–71 JI Payne
V'trs	WD–M H NA on comp/ match days SOC
Fees	£15
Loc	4 miles W of Evesham (B4084)

Fulford Heath (1934)

Tanners Green Lane, Wythall, Birmingham B47 6BH
Tel	(0564) 822806 (Clubhouse)
	(0564) 824758 (Office)
Mem	675
Sec	RG Bowen (021) 705 5480
Pro	KA Hayward (0564) 822930
Holes	18 L 6256 yds SSS 70
Recs	Am–66 KJ Miller
	Pro–67 M James
V'trs	WD–H WE/ BH–M SOC
Fees	£25
Loc	8 miles S of Birmingham

Habberley (1924)

Trimpley Road, Kidderminster DY11 5RG
Tel	(0562) 745756
Mem	400
Sec	DB Lloyd (0562) 823509
Holes	9 L 5440 yds SSS 67
Recs	Am–62 D Kwei
V'trs	WD–U WE–M SOC
Fees	£10
Loc	3 miles NW of Kidderminster

Hereford Municipal

Public
Holmer Road, Hereford
Tel	(0432) 271639
Pro	J McLeod
Holes	9 L 3060 yds SSS 69
V'trs	U
Fees	£4 (£5.50)
Loc	Holmer Road (A49)

Herefordshire (1909)

Raven's Causeway, Wormsley, nr Hereford HR4 8LY
Tel	(0432) 71219
Mem	500 75(L) 85(J)
Sec	C Jones (0432) 760662
Pro	D Hemming (0432) 71465
Holes	18 L 6069 yds SSS 69
Recs	Am–65 D Park, M Welch (1990)
	Pro–61 B Barnes
V'trs	U
Fees	£11 (£15)
Loc	6 miles NW of Hereford
Mis	Buggy for hire

Kidderminster (1909)

Russell Road, Kidderminster
Tel	(0562) 822303
Mem	800
Sec	W Wiltshire (Mgr)
Pro	NP Underwood (0562) 740090
Holes	18 L 6223 yds SSS 70
V'trs	WD only
Fees	£18
Loc	Kidderminster Station 1 mile

King's Norton (1892)

Brockhill Lane, Weatheroak
Tel	(0564) 826789
Mem	950
Sec	LNW Prince (Sec/ Mgr)
Pro	C Haycock (0564) 822822
Holes	18 L 6754 yds SSS 72
	9 L 3290 yds SSS 36
Recs	Am–67 PR Swinburne (1989)
	Pro–65 G Farr (1988)
V'trs	WD–U WE–NA SOC
Fees	£20
Loc	8 miles S of Birmingham. M42 Junction 3, 2 miles

Kington (1926)

Bradnor Hill, Kington
Tel	(0544) 230340
Mem	500
Sec	GE Long, GR Wictome
Pro	R Bott (0544) 231320
Holes	18 L 5840 yds SSS 68
Recs	Am–65 K Alexander
V'trs	SOC WE–NA before 10.15am–restricted 1.30–2.45pm
Fees	£11 (£16)
Loc	1 mile N of Kington

Leominster (1967)

Ford Bridge, Leominster, Herefordshire HR6 0LE
Tel	(0568) 2863
Mem	600
Sec	JA Ashcroft (043 272) 493
Pro	R Price
Holes	18 L 6084 yds SSS 69
V'trs	I or H
Fees	£14 (£17)
Loc	3 miles S of Leominster on A49 (Leominster By-pass)

Little Lakes (1975)

Lye Head, Bewdley, Worcester DY12 2UZ
Tel (0299) 266385
Mem 400 50(L)
Sec T Norris (0562) 67495
Pro M Laing
Holes 9 L 6247 yds SSS 72
Recs Am–70 R Dean (1990)
　　　Pro–70 R Lane (1986)
V'trs WD–U WE–NA SOC
Fees £10
Loc 2½ miles W of Bewdley off A456

Pitcheroak (1973)

Public
Plymouth Road, Redditch B97 4PB
Tel (0527) 541054
Pro D Stewart
Holes 9 L 4584 yds SSS 62
V'trs U
Fees 18 holes £4 (£4.50) 9 holes £2.30 (£2.80)
Loc Redditch
Mis Redditch Kingfisher plays here

Redditch (1913)

Lower Grinsty, Green Lane, Callow Hill, Redditch B97 5PJ
Tel (0527) 543309
Mem 814
Sec C Holman
Pro F Powell (0527) 546372
Holes 18 L 6671 yds SSS 72
V'trs WD–U SOC
Fees £20
Loc 3 miles SW of Redditch. Heathfield Road, off A441

Ross-on-Wye (1903)

Two Park, Gorsley, Ross-on-Wye HR9 7UT
Tel (098 982) 267
Mem 760
Sec GH Cason
Pro A Clifford (098 982) 439
Holes 18 L 6500 yds SSS 73
Recs Am–69 J Stordy
　　　Pro–71 G Brand Jr
V'trs U SOC Wed-Fri (3 per week for 20+ players)
Fees £25 (£30) SOC–£21
Loc 5 miles N of Ross-on-Wye. M50 Junction 3

Tolladine (1895)

The Fairway, Tolladine Road, Worcester WR4 9BA
Tel (0905) 21074
Mem 350
Sec AJ Wardle (0905) 54841
Holes 9 L 5174 yds SSS 67
V'trs WD–U before 4pm –M after 4pm WE/ BH–M SOC
Fees £10
Loc M5 Junction 6 Warndon 1 mile

Worcester G & CC (1898)

Boughton Park, Worcester
Tel (0905) 422555
Mem 1100
Sec JM Kennedy
Pro C Colenso (0905) 422044
Holes 18 L 5946 yds SSS 68
Recs Am–67 M Jeffs
　　　Pro–67 C Haynes
V'trs WD–H WE–M SOC
Fees £18
Loc 1 mile W of Worcester

Worcestershire (1879)

Wood Farm, Malvern Wells WR14 4PP
Tel (0684) 573905
Mem 770
Sec GR Scott (0684) 575992
Pro GM Harris (0684) 564428
Holes 18 L 6449 yds SSS 71
Recs Am–67 PM Guest, MC Reynard, S Braithwaite
　　　Pro–66 R Larratt
V'trs WD–H WE–H after 10am
Fees £12 (£15) W–£45 1989 prices
Loc 2 miles S of Gt Malvern, off A449/ B4209

Hertfordshire

Aldenham G & CC (1975)

Church Lane, Aldenham, nr Watford
Tel (0923) 85 3929
Mem 560
Sec DW Phillips
Pro A McKay (0923) 85 7889
Holes 18 L 6500 yds SSS 71
Recs Am–67 P Wharton (1987)
　　　Pro–69 B Charles (1982)
V'trs U
Fees £15 D–£20
Loc M1 Junction 5-A41-B462

Arkley (1909)

Rowley Green Road, Barnet EN5 3HL
Tel (081) 449 0394
Mem 350
Sec GD Taylor
Pro M Squire (081) 440 8473
Holes 9 L 6045 yds SSS 69
Recs Am–67 SN McWilliams
　　　Pro–63 LV Baker
V'trs WD–U WE–M SOC-Wed-Fri
Fees £15 D–£20
Loc NW of Barnet, off A1(M)

Ashridge (1932)

Little Gaddesden, Berkhamsted HP4 1LY
Tel (044 284) 2244
Mem 750
Sec Mrs MA West
Pro G Pook (Golf Mgr) (044 284) 2307
Holes 18 L 6508 yds SSS 71
Recs Am–64 C Slattery
　　　Pro–66 JRM Jacobs

V'trs Ring Sec for bookings
Fees On application
Loc 5 miles NW of Berkhamsted on B4506

Batchwood Golf Centre (1935)

Public
Batchwood Drive, St Albans
Tel (0727) 52101
Pro J Thomson
Holes 18 L 6465 yds SSS 71
Recs Am–67 M Cassidy
　　　Pro–62 PP Wynne
V'trs U
Fees £5 (£6)
Loc NW of St Albans on A5081. 5 miles S of M1 Junction 9

Berkhamsted (1890)

The Common, Berkhamsted HP4 2QB
Tel (0442) 863730
Mem 280 113(L) 119(J) 150(5)
Sec ID Wheater (0442) 865832
Pro BJ Proudfoot (0442) 865851
Holes 18 L 6605 yds SSS 72
Recs Am–69 J Payne (1989)
　　　Pro–69 S Proudfoot (1987)
V'trs U H WE–M before 11.30am SOC-Wed & Fri
Fees On application
Loc 1 mile NE of Berkhamsted

Bishop's Stortford (1910)

Dunmow Road, Bishop's Stortford CM23 5HP
Tel (0279) 654027 (Clubhouse)
Mem 700
Sec Maj C Rolls (0279) 654715
Pro V Duncan (0279) 651324
Holes 18 L 6440 yds SSS 71
Recs Am–69 M Whitlock
　　　Pro–66 J Bennett
V'trs WD–U WE–M SOC
Fees £18
Loc E of B Stortford on A120. M11 Junction 8
Mis Buggies for hire

Boxmoor (1890)

18 Box Lane, Hemel Hempstead
Tel (0442) 242434
Mem 225
Sec NS James (0442) 259726
Holes 9 L 4854 yds SSS 64
Recs Am–62 D Boyd
V'trs U Sun–NA
Fees £10 Sat–£8
Loc 1 mile W of Hemel on B4505 to Chesham

Brickendon Grange (1964)

Brickendon, nr Hertford
Tel (099 286) 228
Mem 650
Sec N Martin (099 286) 258
Pro J Hamilton (099 286) 218
Holes 18 L 6325 yds SSS 70

For list of abbreviations see page 487.

Recs Am–70 J Paterson,
M Passingham
Pro–67 S James, K Robson
V'trs WD–U H WE/ BH–M SOC
Fees On application
Loc Bayford, 3 miles S of Hertford

Brookmans Park (1930)

Brookmans Park, Hatfield AL9 7AT
Tel (0707) 52487
Sec PA Gill
Pro MMR Plumbridge, I Jelley
(0707) 52468
Holes 18 L 6454 yds SSS 71
Recs Am–66 P Embleton
Pro–66 I Jelley
V'trs WD–UH WE/ BH–M SOC
Fees D–£20
Loc 3 miles S of Hatfield, off A1000

Bushey G & CC (1980)

High Street, Bushey WD2 1BJ
Tel (081) 950 2283
Mem 600
Pro G Atkinson (081) 950 2215
Holes 9 L 3000 yds SSS 69
Recs Pro–67
V'trs WD–before 6pm WE/ BH–after
2pm Wed–closed
Fees 18 holes £8 (£10) 9 holes £5
(£6)
Loc 2 miles S of Watford on A4008
Mis Driving range

Bushey Hall (1896)

Bushey Hall Drive, Bushey WD2 2EP
Tel (0923) 225802
Mem 600
Sec CA Brown
Pro D Fitzsimmons (0923) 222253
Holes 18 L 6099 yds SSS 69
Recs Am–66 M Bowen (1990)
Pro–67 M Squire (1990)
V'trs WD–H WE/ BH–M SOC–WD
Fees £18
Loc 1 mile SE of Watford

Chadwell Springs (1974)

Hertford Road, Ware SG12 9LE
Tel (0920) 463647
Mem 350
Sec K Horner (0920) 461447
Pro AN Shearn (0920) 462075
Holes 9 L 3021 yds SSS 69
V'trs WD–U WE–M
Fees WD–£12
Loc Between Ware and Hertford
on A119

Cheshunt Park (1976)

Public
Park Lane, Cheshunt EN7 6QD
Tel (0992) 24009
Pro AC Newton (0992) 24009
Holes 18 L 6608 yds SSS 71
V'trs U
Fees £4.50 (£6)
Loc A10 London–Cambridge; turn
off at College Road junction.
Proceed along Churchgate

Chorleywood (1890)

Common Road, Chorleywood
WD3 5LN
Tel (092 78) 2009
Mem 200 55(L) 40(J)
Sec RM Lennard
Holes 9 L 2838 yds SSS 67
Recs Am–65 N Leconte (1990)
Pro–61 M Squires (1990)
V'trs WD–U exc Tues & Thurs am
WE–Sat pm only SOC
Fees £10 (£12)
Loc 3 miles W of Rickmansworth
off A404. M25 Junction 18

Dyrham Park CC (1963)

Galley Lane, Barnet EN5 4RA
Tel (081) 440 3361
Mem 300
Sec DU Prentice
Pro W Large (081) 440 3904
Holes 18 L 6369 yds SSS 70
V'trs M SOC–Wed
Loc 10 miles N of London, W off A1
Mis Guests must be accompanied
by a member

East Herts (1898)

Hamels Park, Buntingford SG9 9NA
Tel (0920) 821923
Mem 700
Sec JA Harper (0920) 821978
Pro J Hamilton (0920) 821922
Holes 18 L 6449 yds SSS 71
Recs Am–68 JA Watts
Pro–64 R Joyce
V'trs WD–H exc Wed–NA WE–M
Fees On application
Loc ¼ mile N of Puckeridge on
A10

Elstree (1984)

Watling Street, Elstree WD6 3AA
Tel (081) 953 6115
Mem 600
Sec C Brown
Pro M Warwick
Holes 18 L 6100 yds SSS 69
Recs Am–68 C Woodcock (1987)
V'trs U
Fees On application
Loc A5183, 1 mile N of Elstree.
8 miles N of London. M1
Junction 4, 2 miles
Mis Floodlit driving range

Hadley Wood (1922)

Beech Hill, Hadley Wood, Barnet
EN4 0JJ
Tel (081) 449 4486
Mem 600
Sec JE Linaker (Sec/ Mgr) (081)
449 4328
Pro A McGinn (081) 449 3285
Holes 18 L 6473 yds SSS 71
Recs Am–67 CC Holton (1983),
N Leconte (1989)
Pro–67 PP Elson (1980)
V'trs WD–H or I WE/ BH–M
Fees On application

Loc 10 miles N of London, off A111
between Potters Bar and
Cockfosters. 2 miles S of M25
Junction 24

Hanbury Manor (1990)

Thundridge, Ware SG12 0SD
Tel (0920) 487722
Fax (0920) 487692
Mem 240
Sec Ms M Riches
Pro P Blaze
Holes 9 L 3461 yds SSS 73
V'trs H or M
Fees £40
Loc 22 miles N of London on A10.
8 miles N of M25 Junction 25

Harpenden (1894)

Hammonds End, Harpenden
AL5 2AX
Tel (0582) 712580
Mem 800
Sec RA Mortimer
Pro DH Smith (0582) 767124
Holes 18 L 6363 yds SSS 70
Recs Am–67 B Bulmer (1987)
V'trs WD–U WE/ BH–M SOC–WD
exc Thurs (Ladies Day)
Fees £15 D–£22
Loc 6 miles N of St Albans on B487

Harpenden Common (1931)

East Common, Harpenden AL5 1BL
Tel (0582) 712856
Mem 700
Sec D Gardner (0582) 715959
Pro N Lawrence (0582) 460655
Holes 18 L 5651 yds SSS 67
Recs Pro–63 N Brown, M Squires
(1989)
V'trs WD–U WE–M SOC H
Fees £14 (1990)
Loc 5 miles N of St Albans, on
A1081

Hartsbourne CC (1946)

Hartsbourne Avenue, Bushey Heath
WD2 1JW
Tel (081) 950 1133
Mem 400
Sec DJ Woodman
Pro G Hunt (081) 950 2836
Holes 18 L 6305 yds SSS 70
9 L 5432 yds SSS 70
Recs Am–67 E Silver
Pro–62 P Oosterhuis
V'trs NA
Loc 5 miles SE of Watford, off A4008

Hatfield London (1976)

Bedwell Park, Essendon, Hatfield
AL9 6JA
Tel (0707) 42624
Mem 100
Sec T Takizawa
Pro N Greer (0707) 50431
Holes 18 L 6878 yds SSS 72

V'trs U
Fees £11 (£24)
Loc B158

Knebworth (1908)

Deards End Lane, Knebworth SG3 6NL
Tel (0438) 814681 (Clubhouse)
Mem 900
Sec JC Wright (0438) 812752
Pro RY Mitchell (0438) 812757
Holes 18 L 6428 yds SSS 71
Recs Am–64 PR Robinson
        Pro–65 W Henry
V'trs WD–U H WE–M SOC–WD
Fees On application
Loc 1 mile S of Stevenage on B197

Letchworth (1905)

Letchworth SG6 3NQ
Tel (0462) 683203
Mem 900
Sec BM Barber
Pro SJ Mutimer (0462) 682713
Holes 18 L 6181 yds SSS 69
Recs Am–67 J Dickens
        Pro–66 NC Coles
V'trs WD–U WE–M SOC-Wed-Fri
Fees £22
Loc Letchworth, S off A505

Little Hay Golf Complex (1977)

Public
Box Lane, Bovingdon, Hemel Hempstead HP3 0DQ
Tel (0442) 833798
Pro D Johnson (Golf Dir)
Holes 18 L 6610 yds SSS 72
Recs Pro–69
V'trs U
Fees £5.10 (£7.50)
Loc 2 miles W of Hemel, on B4505 to Chesham
Mis Driving range

Mid Herts (1893)

Gustard Wood, Wheathampstead AL4 8RS
Tel (058 283) 2242
Mem 500(M) 125(L)
Sec RJH Jourdan
Pro N Brown (058 283) 2788
Holes 18 L 6060 yds SSS 69
Recs Am–68 P Mayles (1987)
        Pro–66 H Baiocchi, R Morris, J Pinsent (1987)
V'trs WD–UH exc Tues & Wed pm
        WE/ BH–M SOC
Fees On application
Loc 6 miles N of St Albans on B651

Moor Park (1923)

Rickmansworth WD3 1QN
Tel (0923) 773146
Fax (0923) 777109
Mem 1800
Sec JA Davies
Pro ER Whitehead

Holes High 18 L 6903 yds SSS 73
        West 18 L 5823 yds SSS 68
Recs High Am–69 RY Mitchell
        Pro–67 M King
        West Am– 63 AJ Eisner
        Pro–63 AD Locke, A Lees,
        EE Whitcombe
V'trs WD–H WE/ BH–M
Fees On request
Loc 1 mile SE of Rickmansworth,
        off Batchworth roundabout
        (A4145). M25 Junction 18,
        2 miles

Old Fold Manor (1910)

Hadley Green, Barnet EN5 4QN
Tel (081) 440 9185
Mem 520
Sec DV Dalingwater
Pro P Jones (081) 440 7488
Holes 18 L 6473 yds SSS 71
Recs Am–66 A Clark
        Pro–68 SL King
V'trs WD–I/ H WE–M
Fees £20 D–£25
Loc 1 mile N of Barnet on A1000

Panshanger (1976)

Public
Old Herns Lane, Welwyn Garden City
Tel (0707) 339507
Mem 352
Pro B Lewis, M Corlass
Holes 18 L 6626 metres SSS 72
Recs Am–71 S Walton (1987)
        Pro–70 R Green
V'trs U
Fees £5.50 (£6)
Loc 2 miles off A1, via B1000 to
        Hertford

Porters Park (1899)

Shenley Hill, Radlett WD7 7AZ
Tel (0923) 854127
Mem 650
Sec JH Roberts (Mgr)
Pro D Gleeson (0923) 854366
Holes 18 L 6313 yds SSS 70
Recs Am–65 CC Boal (1990)
        Pro–64 P Townsend
V'trs WD–H (phone first) WE/ BH–M
        SOC-Wed & Thurs
Fees £28–£40
Loc ½ mile E of Radlett on Shenley
        road

Potters Bar (1923)

Darkes Lane, Potters Bar EN6 1DE
Tel (0707) 52020
Fax (0707) 52987
Mem 550
Sec A Williams (Mgr)
Pro K Hughes (0707) 52987
Holes 18 L 6273 yds SSS 70
Recs Am–66 RR Davis
        Pro–65 D McClelland
V'trs WD–H WE/ BH–M SOC–Mon &
        Fri
Loc 1 mile N of M25 Junction 24, off
        A1000

Redbourn (1970)

Kinsbourne Green Lane, Redbourn, nr St Albans AL3 7QA
Tel (0582) 793493
Sec WM Dunn (0582) 792150
Pro S Baldwin
Holes 18 L 6407 yds SSS 71
        9 L 1361 yds SSS 27
Recs Am–67 P Wilkins, T Stafford
        (1990)
V'trs 18 hole:WD–U exc 4.30–6.15pm
        WE/ BH–NA before 3pm SOC
        9 hole:U
Fees 18 hole:£10 (£12) 9 hole:£3.50
Loc 4 miles N of St Albans. 4 miles
        S of Luton. 1 mile S of M1
        Junction 9, off A5
Mis Driving range

Rickmansworth (1937)

Public
Moor Lane, Rickmansworth WD3 1QL
Tel (0923) 773163
Pro I Duncan (0923) 775278
Holes 18 L 4412 yds SSS 62
Recs Am–62 L Silver
V'trs U
Fees £4.40 (£6.30)
Loc ½ mile SE of Rickmansworth off
        Batchworth roundabout
        (A4145). M25 Junction 18, 1 mile
Mis 9 hole pitch & putt

Royston (1892)

Baldock Road, Royston SG8 5BG
Tel (0763) 242177 (Members)
Mem 700
Sec Mrs S Morris (0763) 242696
Pro M Hatcher (0763) 243476
Holes 18 L 6032 yds SSS 69
Recs Am–65 T Moss
        Pro–63 B Waites
V'trs WD–U WE/ BH–M SOC
Fees £15
Loc SW of Royston on A505

Sandy Lodge (1910)

Sandy Lodge Lane, Northwood, Middx HA6 2JD
Tel (09274) 25429
Mem 700
Sec JN Blair
Pro A Fox (09274) 25321
Holes 18 L 6340 yds SSS 70
Recs Am–66 DS Scammell (1990)
        Pro–64 A Jacklin (1977)
V'trs WD/ WE/ BH–M or H SOC
Fees £22
Loc Adjacent Moor Park Station

Shendish (1988)

Shendish House, Apsley, Hemel Hempstead
Tel (0442) 232220
Sec R Morgan (Mgr)
Holes 9 L 5900 yds SSS 69
V'trs U
Fees £5 (£12)
Loc Off A41, M25 Junction 20

For list of abbreviations see page 487.

Stevenage (1980)

Public

Aston Lane, Stevenage SG2 7EL
Tel　(043 888) 424
Pro　K Bond
Holes　18 L 6451 yds SSS 71
Recs　Am–70 A Archer (1988)
　　　Pro–65 R Green (1989)
V'trs　U
Fees　£5.50 (£7)
Loc　Off A602 to Hertford. A1(M)
　　　Junction 7
Mis　Driving range. 9 hole Par 3

Verulam (1905)

London Road, St Albans AL1 1JG
Tel　(0727) 53327
Mem　600
Sec　GD Eastwood
Pro　P Anderson (0727) 861401
Holes　18 L 6457 yds SSS 71
Recs　Am–70
　　　Pro–65 R Mitchell
V'trs　WD–U WE/ BH–NA
Fees　£15 (Mon–£10)
Loc　1 miles SE of St Albans on
　　　A1081

Welwyn Garden City (1922)

Mannicotts, High Oaks Road,
Welwyn Garden City AL8 7BP
Tel　(0707) 322722
Mem　700
Sec　JL Carragher (0707) 325243
Pro　S Bishop (0707) 325525
Holes　18 L 6100 yds SSS 69
Recs　Am–65 J Bickerton (1989)
　　　Pro–63 N Faldo (1988)
V'trs　WD–H WE/ BH–NA
Fees　£20
Loc　1 mile N of Hatfield. A1(M)
　　　Junction 4 – B197 to Valley
　　　Road

West Herts (1890)

Cassiobury Park, Watford WD1 7SL
Tel　(0923) 224264
Mem　650
Sec　RAS Gordon (0923) 36484
Pro　CS Gough (0923) 220352
Holes　18 L 6488 yds SSS 71
Recs　Am–68 SA Masson
　　　Pro–67 R Whitehead
V'trs　WD–I WE/ BH–M SOC–Wed &
　　　Fri
Fees　£16
Loc　Off A412 between Watford and
　　　Rickmansworth

Whipsnade Park (1974)

Studham Lane, Dagnall HP4 1RH
Tel　(044 284) 2330
Mem　400
Sec　D Whalley
Pro　M Lewendon
Holes　18 L 6812 yds SSS 72
Recs　Am–71 A Calder
V'trs　WD–U WE–M SOC–WD

Fees　£15 D–£20
Loc　10 miles N of Hemel
　　　Hempstead off A4146,
　　　between Dagnall and Studham

Whitehill (1990)

Dane End, Ware SG12 0JS
Tel　(0920) 438495
Sec　Mrs S Smith (Prop)
Pro　S James, R Green
Holes　9 L 6820 yds SSS 72
V'trs　H (pre-booking necessary)
Fees　£6 (£7)
Loc　6 miles N of Ware
Mis　Extension to 18 holes May
　　　1991. Driving range

Humberside

Beverley & East Riding (1889)

The Westwood, Beverley HU17 8RG
Tel　(0482) 867190
Mem　460
Sec　A Walker (0482) 868757
Pro　I Mackie (0482) 869519
Holes　18 L 5949 yds SSS 68
Recs　Am–62 N Burnley
V'trs　U SOC–WD
Fees　£10 (£12.50)
Loc　Beverley–Walkington road

Boothferry (1981)

Public

Spaldington Lane, Spaldington,
Howden, Goole
Tel　(0430) 430364
Pro　S Wilkinson
Holes　18 L 6593 yds SSS 72
Recs　Am–70 R Giles (1988)
　　　Pro–70 M Ingham (1984)
　　　S Rolley (1987)
Fees　£4 (£7)
Loc　3 miles N of Howden on B1288.
　　　M62 Junction 37

Bridlington (1905)

Belvedere Road, Bridlington
YO15 3NA
Tel　(0262) 672092
Mem　663
Sec　C Wilson (0262) 674679
Pro　D Rands (0262) 674721
Holes　18 L 6491 yds SSS 71
Recs　Am–N Burnley
V'trs　U Sun-after 11.15am
Fees　£10 (£15) (1990)
Loc　Bridlington Station 1 1/2 miles

Brough (1891)

Brough HU15 1HB
Tel　(0482) 667374
Mem　650
Sec　HJ Oldroyd (0482) 667291
Pro　G Townhill (0482) 667483
Holes　18 L 6183 yds SSS 69

Recs　Am–64 PWJ Greenhough,
　　　MJ Kelley
　　　Pro–63 A Thompson
V'trs　WD–U exc Wed–NA before
　　　2pm
Fees　£15
Loc　10 miles W of Hull on A63

Cave Castle Golf Hotel (1989)

South Cave, N Humberside HU15 2EU
Tel　(0403) 421286/ 422245
　　　(Hotel)
Sec　JR Bean
Holes　18 L 6903 yds SSS 73
V'trs　U
Fees　£10 (£15)
Loc　South Cave, 10 miles W of Hull

Cleethorpes (1894)

Kings Road, Cleethorpes DN35 0PN
Tel　(0472) 814060
Mem　750
Sec　GB Standaloft
Pro　E Sharp
Holes　18 L 6015 yds SSS 69
Recs　Am–64 A Hare
　　　Pro–64 D Ramsey
V'trs　Wed pm–NA Sat pm/
　　　Sun am–XL
Fees　£12 (£15)
Loc　Cleethorpes 1 mile

Driffield (1934)

Sunderlandwick, Driffield
Tel　(0377) 43116
Mem　450
Sec　J Finch (0377) 46121
Holes　18 L 6177 yds SSS 70
V'trs　H
Fees　£10 (£15)
Loc　10 miles W of Bridlington

Elsham (1900)

Barton Road, Elsham, nr Brigg
DN20 0LS
Tel　(0652) 688382
Mem　650
Sec　BP Nazer (Mgr) (0652) 680291
Pro　S Brewer (0652) 680432
Holes　18 L 6411 yds SSS 71
Recs　Am–72 A Shepherd
　　　Pro–69 MT Hoyle
V'trs　WE–M SOC–WD
Fees　£15
Loc　Off M180 nr Brigg

Flamborough Head (1932)

Lighthouse Road, Flamborough,
Bridlington YO15 1AR
Tel　(0262) 850333
Mem　400
Sec　WR Scarle (0262) 676494
Holes　18 L 5438 yds SSS 66
Recs　Am–63 GR Allen
　　　Pro–63 P Dawson
V'trs　U
Fees　£10 (£13) W–£40
Loc　5 miles NE of Bridlington

Ganstead Park (1976)

Longdales Lane, Coniston, Hull
HU11 4LB
Tel	(0482) 811280 (Steward)
Mem	700
Sec	J Kirby (0482) 874754
Pro	M Smee (0482) 811121
Holes	18 L 6801 yds SSS 73
Recs	Am–67 M Smee (1987)
	Pro–67 H Clark (1976)
V'trs	U H WE–NA before noon SOC
Fees	£15 (£20)
Loc	5 miles E of Hull on A165

Grimsby (1923)

Littlecoates Road, Grimsby
DN34 4LU
Tel	(0472) 342823
Mem	550 150(L) 70(J)
Sec	AD Houlihan (0472) 342630
Pro	S Houltby (0472) 356981
Holes	18 L 6068 yds SSS 69
Recs	Am–66 M James
	Pro–66 BJ Hunt
V'trs	WD–U Sat pm/ Sun am–XL
Fees	£13 (£16) W–£45
Loc	1 mile W of Grimsby

Hainsworth Park (1983)

Brandesburton, Driffield YO25
Tel	(0964) 542362
Mem	400
Sec	BW Atkin (Prop)
Holes	9 L 5360 yds SSS 66
V'trs	WD–U WE–U after 4pm
	SOC–WD
Fees	£5 (£7.50)
Loc	8 miles N of Beverley (A165).
	Bridlington 15 miles

Hessle (1906)

Westfield Road, Cottingham
Tel	(0482) 650171
Mem	772
Sec	RL Dorsey
Pro	G Fieldsend (0482) 650190
Holes	18 L 6638 yds SSS 72
Recs	Am–66 A Wright (1984),
	MR Lamb (1990)
	Pro–69 B Thompson (1980)
V'trs	WD–U exc Tues 9.15am–1pm
	WE–NA before 11am
Fees	£15 (£25)
Loc	3 miles SW of Cottingham

Holme Hall (1908)

Holme Lane, Bottesford, Scunthorpe
DN16 3RF
Tel	(0724) 282053 (Caterer)
Mem	490 110(L) 75(J) 3(5)
Sec	AHF Holtby (0724) 862078
Pro	R McKiernan (0724) 851816
Holes	18 L 6475 yds SSS 71
Recs	Am–67 S Steele, A Thain,
	K Blow, FW Wood
	Pro–66 B Thompson
V'trs	WD–U WE–M H SOC–WD
Fees	D–£15
Loc	4 miles SE of Scunthorpe.
	M180 Junction 4

Hornsea (1898)

Rolston Road, Hornsea HU18 1XG
Tel	(0964) 532020
Mem	600
Sec	BW Kirton
Pro	B Thompson (0964) 534989
Holes	18 L 6461 yds SSS 71
Recs	Am–65 P Binnington (1986)
	Pro–67 B Thompson (1985)
V'trs	WD–U WE–restricted SOC
Fees	£15 D–£18 (£25))
Loc	300 yds past Hornsea Pottery

Hull (1921)

The Hall, 27 Packman Lane, Kirk
Ella, Hull HU10 7JT
Tel	(0482) 653026
Mem	756
Sec	R Toothill (Gen Mgr) (0482)
	658919
Pro	D Jagger (0482) 653074
Holes	18 L 6242 yds SSS 70
Recs	Am–64 JD Dockar, R Roper
	Pro–66 D Dunk, N Hunt,
	S Smith, D Jagger
V'trs	WD–U WE–NA
Fees	D–£20
Loc	5 miles W of Hull

Immingham (1975)

Church Lane, Immingham, Grimsby
DN40 2EU
Tel	(0469) 575298
Mem	600
Sec	E Cowton
Pro	N Harding (0469) 575493
Holes	18 L 5809 yds SSS 68
Recs	Am–66 J Payne
V'trs	WE–M Sun–NA before noon
Fees	£8 D–£12 (£12)
Loc	N of St Andrew's Church,
	Immingham

Kingsway

Public
Kingsway, Scunthorpe DN15 7ER
Tel	(0724) 840945
Sec	C Mann
Pro	C Mann
Holes	9 L 1915 yds SSS 59
V'trs	U
Fees	£2 (£2.40)
Loc	3/4 mile W of Scunthorpe

Normanby Hall (1978)

Public
Normanby Park, Scunthorpe
Tel	(0724) 720226
Pro	C Mann
Holes	18 L 6548 yds SSS 71
Recs	Am–68
	Pro–68 N Bundy
V'trs	U SOC–WD
Fees	£5.50 (£7)
Loc	5 miles N of Scunthorpe

Scunthorpe (1936)

Ashby Decoy, Burringham Road,
Scunthorpe DN17 2AB
Tel	(0724) 842913
Mem	490 130(L) 65(J)
Sec	EA Willsmore (0724) 866561
Pro	G Bailey (0724) 868972
Holes	18 L 6281 yds SSS 71
Recs	Am–67 J Payne
	Pro–67 K Waters
V'trs	U exc Sun–NA SOC–WD
Fees	£14 Sat–£17
Loc	2 miles SW of Scunthorpe

Springhead Park (1903)

Public
Willerby Road, Hull HU5 5JE
Tel	(0482) 656309
Sec	F Coggrave (Hon)
Pro	B Herrington
Holes	18 L 6439 yds SSS 71
Recs	Am–69 AD Hill, A Wright
	Pro–65 S Rolley
V'trs	U
Fees	£2.85 (£4)
Loc	4 miles W of Hull on Willerby rd

Sutton Park (1935)

Public
Salthouse Road, Hull
Tel	(0482) 74242
Sec	CD Smith (Hon)
Pro	P Rushworth (0482) 711450
Holes	18 L 6251 yds SSS 70
Recs	Am–67 A Wright
	Pro–64 L Herrington
V'trs	U
Fees	£2.85 (£4)
Loc	3 miles E of Hull

Withernsea (1909)

Chestnut Ave, Withernsea HU19 2PG
Tel	(0964) 612258
Mem	329 55(L) 40(J)
Sec	F Buckley (0964) 612214
Pro	G Harrison (0482) 492720
Holes	9 L 5112 yds SSS 64
Recs	Am–62 SH Kellet
	Pro–63 G Townhill
V'trs	WD–U WE–M SOC
Fees	£8
Loc	17 miles E of Hull on B1033.
	S side of Withernsea

Isle of Man

Castletown Golf Hotel (1892)

Fort Island, Derbyhaven
Tel	(0624) 822201 (Hotel)
Mem	300
Sec	JM Fowlds
Pro	M Crowe (0624) 822211
Holes	18 L 6716 yds SSS 72
Recs	Am–68 WR Ennett
V'trs	U SOC (arrange with Pro)
Fees	D–£20
Loc	1 1/4 miles E of Castletown

For list of abbreviations see page 487.

Douglas Municipal (1927)

Public

Pulrose Park, Douglas
Tel	**(0624) 661558**
Pro	K Parry
Holes	18 L 5922 yds SSS 68
Recs	Am–63
V'trs	U
Fees	£6
Loc	Douglas Pier 2 miles
Mis	Douglas Club plays here

Howstrake (1914)

Groudle Road, Onchan
Tel	**(0624) 620430**
Mem	400
Sec	MJ Betteridge
Holes	18 L 5367 yds SSS 66
Recs	Am–62 TP Kniveton
	Pro–69
V'trs	U SOC
Fees	£5 (£7)
Loc	1 mile N of Douglas

Peel (1896)

Rheast Lane, Peel
Tel	**(062 484) 2227**
Mem	500
Sec	DR Forth (062 484) 3456(am)
Holes	18 L 5914 yds SSS 68
Recs	Am–64 J Sutton
V'trs	WD–U WE/ BH–NA before 10.30am SOC
Fees	£10 (£12)
Loc	10 miles W of Douglas

Port St Mary

Public

Kallow Road, Port St Mary
Tel	**(0624) 834932**
Holes	9 L 2711 yds SSS 66
Recs	Am–66 A Horne (1989)
V'trs	U
Fees	£4 (£6)
Loc	Port St Mary, nr sea shore

Ramsey (1891)

Brookfield, Ramsey
Tel	**(0624) 813365/ 812244**
Mem	920
Sec	Mrs SJ Birchall (0624) 812244
Pro	P Lowrey (0624) 814736
Holes	18 L 6019 yds SSS 69
Recs	Am–65 S Boyd Pro–65 S Lyle
V'trs	WD–U after 10.30am WE–M SOC
Fees	£15
Loc	W boundary of Ramsey

Rowany (1895)

Port Erin
Tel	**(0624) 834108**
Mem	600
Sec	RG Jackson (Mgr) (0624) 73284
Holes	18 L 5840 yds SSS 69
Recs	Am–68 A Cain
V'trs	U H (for open comps) SOC
Fees	£8 (£12)
Loc	6 miles W of Castletown

Isle of Wight

Cowes (1908)

Crossfield Avenue, Cowes
PO31 8HN
Tel	**(0983) 292303**
Mem	250
Sec	D Weaver (0983) 292426
Holes	9 L 5880 yds SSS 68
Recs	Am–67 I Graham
V'trs	H Thurs–NA before 4pm (Ladies Day) Fri–NA after 5pm Sun am–NA
Fees	£12 (£15) W–£45
Loc	Crossfield Avenue (private road), nr Cowes High School

Freshwater Bay

Afton Down, Freshwater
Tel	**(0983) 752955**
Mem	500
Sec	HGV Gordon
Holes	18 L 5662 yds SSS 68
Recs	Am–64 J Greenhill (1990)
	Pro–66 T Underwood (1981)
V'trs	H SOC
Fees	£15 (£20) W–£75
Loc	400 yds off Military Road

Newport IW (1896)

St George's Down, nr Shide,
Newport PO30 3BA
Tel	**(0983) 525076**
Mem	350
Sec	J Ambrose
Holes	9 L 5704 yds SSS 68
Recs	Am–65 J Burton (1987)
V'trs	WD–U Sat–NA before 3.30pm Sun–NA before noon
Fees	£10 (£12)
Loc	1 mile SE of Newport

Osborne (1903)

Club House, East Cowes
Tel	**(0983) 295421**
Mem	260 90(L)
Sec	ARJ Goodall
Pro	I Taylor (0983) 295649
Holes	9 L 6286 yds SSS 70
Recs	Am–66 (1990)
V'trs	WD–U exc Ladies Day (Tues) 9am-1pm–NA WE–NA before noon SOC
Fees	£15 5D–£45
Loc	S of East Cowes in grounds of Osborne House

Ryde (1921)

Ryde House Park, Ryde
Tel	**(0983) 614809**
Mem	450
Sec	F Cockayne (0983) 64388
Holes	9 L 5220 yds SSS 66
Recs	Am–64 M Groves
	Pro–64 T Underwood, D Allen
V'trs	U exc Sun–NA before noon
Fees	£12.50 (£15)
Loc	On main Ryde/ Newport road

Shanklin & Sandown (1900)

Fairway Lake, Sandown PO36 9PR
Tel	**(0983) 403217**
Mem	700
Sec	GA Wormald
Pro	P Hammond (0983) 404424
Holes	18 L 6058 yds SSS 69
Recs	Am–65 D McToldridge
	Pro–65 R Wynn
V'trs	WD–U WE–NA before 3pm(summer) noon (winter) SOC–WD
Fees	£16 (£18) 5D–£65 (1990)
Loc	Sandown

Ventnor (1892)

Steephill Down Road, Ventnor
Tel	**(0983) 853326**
Mem	200
Sec	R Hose (0983) 853198
Holes	9 L 5752 yds SSS 68
Recs	Am–73 IH Guy
V'trs	WD–U Sun–NA before 2pm
Fees	£10
Loc	NW boundary of Ventnor

Kent

Ashford (1904)

Sandyhurst Lane, Ashford TN25 4NT
Tel	**(0233) 620180**
Mem	650
Sec	AH Story (0233) 622655
Pro	H Sherman (0233) 629644
Holes	18 L 6246 yds SSS 70
Recs	Am–66 SM Green
	Pro–63 RS Fidler
V'trs	WD–H WE/ BH–H SOC
Fees	D–£16 (D–£20)
Loc	Ashford 1½ miles (A20)

Barnehurst (1903)

Mayplace Road, East Barnehurst
DA7 6JU
Tel	**(0322) 523746**
Mem	250
Sec	J Thomson (0322) 54612
Pro	T Cullen (0322) 51205
Holes	9 L 5320 yds SSS 66
Recs	Am–64
	Pro–64
V'trs	Mon/ Wed/ Fri–U (Other days restricted)
Fees	£4.45 (£7)
Loc	Between Crayford and Bexley Heath

Bearsted (1898)

Ware Street, Bearsted, nr Maidstone
Tel	**(0622) 38389**
Mem	648
Sec	(0622) 38198
Pro	T Simpson (0622) 38024
Holes	18 L 6253 yds SSS 70
Recs	Am–68 D Jenner (1987)
	Pro–69 G Norton (1982)

V'trs	WD–I H WE–H M (recognised GC members) SOC
Fees	£18 D–£25
Loc	Maidstone 2¹⁄₂ miles

Bexley Heath (1907)

Mount Road, Bexley Heath BR8 7RJ
Tel	(081) 303 6951
Mem	350
Sec	SE Squires
Holes	9 L 5239 yds SSS 66
Recs	Am–65 HE Harding, KW Miles
V'trs	WD–H before 4pm
Fees	£12
Loc	Station 1 mile

Bromley (1948)

Public
Magpie Hall Lane, Bromley
Tel	(081) 462 7014
Pro	A Hodgson
Holes	9 L 5538 yds SSS 66
Recs	Am–66 HE Harding, KW Miles
V'trs	U
Fees	On application
Loc	Off Bromley Common (A21)

Broome Park (1981)

Barham, nr Canterbury CT4 6QX
Tel	(0227) 831701
Sec	D Lees (Hon)
Pro	T Britz (Ext 264)
Holes	18 L 6610 yds SSS 72
Recs	Am–64 A Roberts Pro–66 B Impett (1984)
V'trs	H WE–NA before noon SOC
Fees	£20 (£22)
Loc	M2/ A2-A260 Folkestone road, 1¹⁄₂ miles on RH side

Canterbury (1927)

Scotland Hills, Canterbury CT1 1TW
Tel	(0227) 463586
Mem	720
Sec	G Good (0227) 453532
Pro	P Everard (0227) 462865
Holes	18 L 6245 yds SSS 70
Recs	Am–66 RJ Davies Pro–64 K Redford
V'trs	WD–UH WE–NA before 3pm SOC–Tues & Thurs
Fees	£18 D–£24 (£25)
Loc	1 mile E of Canterbury on A257

Cherry Lodge (1969)

Jail Lane, Biggin Hill, nr Westerham TN16 3AX
Tel	(0959) 72250
Mem	840
Sec	JR Macarthur (Mgr)
Pro	N Child (0959) 72989
Holes	18 L 6652 yds SSS 72
Recs	Am–70 N Lancaster (1984) Pro–69 B Cameron (1986)
V'trs	WD–U WE–M
Fees	£20 D–£30
Loc	15 miles SE of London
Mis	Buggies available

Chestfield (Whitstable) (1925)

103 Chestfield Road, Whitstable CT5 3LU
Tel	(022 779) 4411
Sec	RW Leaver
Pro	J Brotherton (022 779) 3563
Holes	18 L 6181 yds SSS 70
Recs	Am–68 R Punyer Pro–64 B Cameron
V'trs	WD–H WE–M
Fees	On application
Loc	1 mile S of A229 and Chestfield Station

Chislehurst (1894)

Camden Place, Chislehurst BR7 5HJ
Tel	(081) 467 3055
Mem	740
Sec	NE Pearson (081) 467 2782
Pro	AS Costorphine (081) 467 6798
Holes	18 L 5128 yds SSS 65
Recs	Am–62 DC Theobald (1987) Pro–61 J Bennett
V'trs	WD–H WE–M
Fees	D–£20
Loc	M25 Junction 3-A20-A222

Cobtree Manor Park

Public
Chatham Road, Boxley, Maidstone
Tel	(0622) 53276
Pro	M Drew
Holes	18 L 5716 yds SSS 68
V'trs	WD–U WE/ BH–(book 1 wk in advance) SOC–WD
Fees	£5 (£7.50)
Loc	Maidstone 3 miles on A229 to Chatham

Corinthian (1987)

Gay Dawn Farm, Fawkham, nr Dartford, DA3 8LZ
Tel	(04747) 7559
Mem	400
Sec	SJ Billings
Holes	9 L 3118 yds SSS 36
V'trs	WD–U H WE/ BH–M SOC
Fees	£7.50
Loc	4 miles S of Dartford Tunnel. E of Brands Hatch along Fawkham Valley road
Mis	Artificial greens

Cranbrook (1969)

Benenden Road, Cranbrook TN17 4AL
Tel	(0580) 712833/ 712934
Mem	700
Sec	HM Borissow (0580) 712833
Pro	G Potter (0580) 712934
Holes	18 L 6128 yds SSS 70
Recs	Am–67 S Coulter Pro–70 S Barr
V'trs	WD–U WE/ BH–U exc comp days SOC
Fees	£8 (£11)
Loc	15 miles S of Maidstone. Sissinghurst 1¹⁄₄ miles
Mis	Buggies for hire Apr–Oct

Cray Valley (1972)

Sandy Lane, St Paul's Cray, Orpington
Tel	(0689) 31927
Mem	700
Sec	R Hill (0689) 39677
Pro	T Morgan (0689) 37909
Holes	18 L 5624 yds SSS 67 9 L 2100 yds SSS 60
V'trs	WD–U WE–H
Fees	£8 (£13)
Loc	15 miles SW of London

Darenth Valley (1973)

Public
Station Road, Shoreham, nr Sevenoaks TN14 7SA
Tel	(09592) 2944 (Clubhouse)
Pro	P Edwards (09592) 2922
Holes	18 L 6356 yds SSS 71
Recs	Am–69 W Leo Pro–68 B Owens, P Edwards
V'trs	WD–U SOC
Fees	£6.50 (£9)
Loc	3 miles N of Sevenoaks off A225

Dartford (1897)

Dartford Heath, Dartford
Tel	(0322) 223616
Mem	600
Sec	PJH Smith (0322) 226455
Pro	A Blackburn (0322) 226409
Holes	18 L 5914 yds SSS 68
Recs	Am–69 G Wright Pro–66 C Tucker
V'trs	WD–I WE–M H
Fees	£25
Loc	Dartford 2 miles

Deangate Ridge (1972)

Public
Hoo, Rochester ME3 8RZ
Tel	(0634) 251180
Pro	B Aram
Holes	18 L 6300 yds SSS 70
Recs	Am–67 AJ Rossiter (1985) Pro–65 N Allen (1990)
V'trs	U
Fees	£4.50 (£6)
Loc	Nr Isle of Grain

Edenbridge G & CC (1973)

Crouch House Road, Edenbridge TN8 5LQ
Tel	(0732) 865097
Mem	800
Sec	Mrs J Scully
Pro	(0732) 865202
Holes	18 L 6604 yds SSS 72 9 hole course
Recs	Am–72 I Hardy
V'trs	WD/ WE–booking necessary
Fees	£12 (£15)
Loc	2 miles W of Edenbridge. M25 Junction 6
Mis	16 bay floodlit driving range

Faversham (1910)

Belmont Park, Faversham
Tel   (079 589) 251
Mem   700
Sec   DB Christie (079 589) 561
Pro   GG Nixon (079 589) 275
Holes   18 L 6021 yds SSS 69
Recs   Am–65 R Chapman
         Pro–67 D Place
V'trs   WD–I or H WE–M SOC
Fees   £18 (£25)
Loc   Faversham and M2, 2 miles

Gillingham (1908)

Woodlands Road, Gillingham
Tel   (0634) 50999
Mem   450 100(L) 50(J) 120(5)
Sec   LP O'Grady (0634) 53017
Pro   B Impett (0634) 55862
Holes   18 L 5911 yds SSS 68
Recs   Am–65 T Williamson
         Pro–64 P Clark
V'trs   WD–I H WE/ BH–M
Fees   £18
Loc   A2/ M2, 2 miles

Hawkhurst (1968)

High Street, Hawkhurst TN18 4JS
Tel   (0580) 752396
Mem   450
Sec   AW Shipley
Pro   T Collins (0580) 753600
Holes   9 L 5769 yds SSS 68
Recs   Am–70 B Betts
         Pro–68 R Cameron
V'trs   WD–U
Fees   £10 (£14)
Loc   14 miles S of Tunbridge Wells
         on A268

Herne Bay (1902)

Eddington, Herne Bay CT6 7PG
Tel   (0227) 374097
Mem   480
Sec   B Warren (0227) 373964
Pro   D Lambert (0227) 374727
Holes   18 L 5466 yds SSS 67
Recs   Am–60 SJ Wood
         Pro–65 C Clark
V'trs   WD–U WE/ BH–H after 11am
         SOC–WD
Fees   £13 D–£18 (£18)
Loc   Herne Bay/ Canterbury road

High Elms (1969)

Public
High Elms Road, Downe, Orpington
Tel   (0689) 58175
Sec   C Poulter (Hon)
Pro   A Hodgson
Holes   18 L 6210 yds SSS 70
Recs   Am–68 I Farman
         Pro–A Hodgson
V'trs   U
Fees   £4.50 (£6.80)
Loc   Off A21 via Shire Lane

Holtye (1893)

Holtye, Cowden TN8 7ED
Tel   (034 286) 635
Mem   480
Sec   JP Holmes (034 286) 576
Pro   M Scarles
Holes   9 L 5259 yds SSS 66
Recs   Am–65 PD Scarles, JA Couling
         Pro–64 S Frost
V'trs   WD–U WE–NA before noon
         SOC–Tues only
Fees   On application
Loc   4 miles E of E Grinstead on
         A264. 6 miles W of Tunbridge
         Wells

Hythe Imperial (1950)

Prince's Parade, Hythe CT21 5RN
Tel   (0303) 67441
Mem   400
Sec   R Barrett (0303) 67554
Pro   G Ritchie
Holes   9 L 5533 yds SSS 67
Recs   Am–63 PI Kaye
         Pro–63 G Ritchie
V'trs   U H SOC
Fees   £10 (£15)
Loc   On coast, 4 miles W of
         Folkestone

Knole Park (1924)

**Seal Hollow Road, Sevenoaks
TN15 0HJ**
Tel   (0732) 452709
Mem   700
Sec   DJL Hoppe (0732) 452150
Pro   PE Gill (0732) 451740
Holes   18 L 6249 yds SSS 70
Recs   Am–64 RW Seamer
V'trs   WD–restricted WE/ BH–M H
         SOC
Fees   £20 D–£30 (1990)
Loc   Seal Hollow Road
Mis   Sevenoaks Town GC plays
         here

Lamberhurst (1890)

Church Road, Lamberhurst TN3 8DT
Tel   (0892) 890241
Mem   700
Sec   P Gleeson (0892) 890591
Pro   M Travers (0892) 890552
Holes   18 L 6232 yds SSS 70
Recs   Am–70 L Ferris
         Pro–67 J Hoskison
V'trs   WD–UH WE–NA before noon
Fees   £20 (£25)
Loc   5 miles SE of Tunbridge Wells,
         off A21

Langley Park (1910)

**Barnfield Wood Road, Beckenham
BR3 2SZ**
Tel   (081) 650 2090
Mem   650
Sec   JL Smart (081) 658 6849
Pro   GT Ritchie (081) 650 1663
Holes   18 L 6488 yds SSS 71
Recs   Am–66 T Trodd
         Pro–65 P Mitchell (1987)

V'trs   WD–I WE–M SOC–WD
Fees   £20
Loc   Bromley South Station 1 mile

Leeds Castle (1928)

**Leeds Castle, nr Maidstone
ME17 1PL**
Tel   (0622) 880467
Pro   C Miller
Holes   9 L 2880 yds Par 34
Recs   Pro–32 A Jacklin
V'trs   U SOC–WD
Fees   £7.50 (9 holes)
Loc   A20, 1 mile from M20
Mis   6-day advance booking

Littlestone (1888)

Littlestone, New Romney TN28 8RB
Tel   (0679) 62310
Mem   500
Sec   JD Lewis (0679) 63355
Pro   S Watkins (0679) 62231
Holes   18 L 6417 yds SSS 71
         9 L 3996 yds Par 64
Recs   Am–67 G Godmon (1984),
         S Wood (1988)
         Pro–67 T Gale (1985)
V'trs   WD–H WE–by arrangement
         SOC
Fees   On application
Loc   2 miles E of New Romney. 15
         miles SE of Ashford

Lullingstone Park (1967)

Public
**Parkgate Road, Chelsfield, nr
Orpington**
Tel   (0959) 34542
Pro   G Lloyd
Holes   18 and 9 hole courses
Fees   18 holes–£7.50. 9 holes–£4.25
Loc   Off Orpington by-pass (A224)

Mid Kent (1909)

**Singlewell Road, Gravesend
DA11 7RB**
Tel   (0474) 568035
Mem   1050
Sec   AF Reid
Pro   R Lee (0474) 332810
Holes   18 L 6206 yds SSS 70
V'trs   WD–H WE–M
Fees   On application
Loc   25 miles SE of London

North Foreland (1903)

Kingsgate, Broadstairs, Thanet
Tel   (0843) 62140
Mem   800
Sec   BJ Preston
Pro   M Lee (0843) 69628
Holes   18 L 6374 yds SSS 71 18 hole
         Approach & Putt
Recs   Am–66 P Walton
         Pro–65 M Lawrence
V'trs   WD–H WE–NA am -H pm
Fees   £15 (£20) Approach & Putt
         D–£5
Loc   Broadstairs Station 1 1/2 miles

Poult Wood (1974)

Poult Wood, Higham Lane, Tonbridge
Tel (0732) 364039
Mem 500
Sec A Hope (Prop) (0732) 366180
S Taylor (Hon)
Pro K Adwick
Holes 18 L 5569 yds SSS 67
V'trs U SOC–WD
Fees £4.75 (£7)
Loc 2 miles N of Tonbridge off A227

Prince's (1904)

Sandwich Bay, Sandwich
Tel (0304) 611118
Mem 550
Sec G Rowlands (0304) 612000
Pro P Sparks (0304) 613797
Holes 27 hole course (3x 9 holes):
Dunes/ Himalayas/ Shore.
Length 6238-6947 yds.
Par 71–72 SSS 70-73
Recs Himalayas/ Shore Am–67
M Goodin Pro–69 M Mannelli
Dunes/ Himalayas Am–69 S
Wood
V'trs U SOC–WD/ WE (book with
G Ramm)
Fees £29 D–£31 (£36 D–£38)
Loc Sandwich Bay
Mis Driving range

Rochester & Cobham Park (1891)

Park Pale, by Rochester ME2 3UL
Tel (047 482) 3411
Mem 720
Sec Maj JW Irvine (Mgr)
Pro M Henderson (047 482) 3658
Holes 18 L 6467 yds SSS 71
Recs Am–66 A Aram (1990)
Pro–67 R Cameron (1989)
V'trs WD–UH WE–M before 5pm
SOC-Tues & Thurs
Fees £20 (£20)
Loc 3 miles E of Gravesend exit on
A2

Royal Cinque Ports (1892)

Golf Road, Deal
Tel (0304) 374328
Mem 1015
Sec NS Phillips (0304) 374007
Pro A Reynolds (0304) 374170
Holes 18 L 6407 yds SSS 71
Recs Am–65 MF Bonallack (1964)
Pro–63 GD Manson (1981)
V'trs I
Fees On application
Loc Deal

Royal St George's (1887)

Sandwich CT13 9PB
Tel (0304) 613090
Mem 675
Sec GE Watts
Pro N Cameron (0304) 615236
Holes 18 L 6534 yds SSS 72
Recs Am–67 H Berwick
Pro–64 C O'Connor Jr
V'trs WD–I H WE–M SOC–WD
Fees £28 D–£40 (1990)
Loc Sandwich 1 mile

Ruxley Park (1975)

Sandy Lane, St Paul's Cray, Orpington
Tel (0689) 71490
Mem 250
Sec D Simpson (Prop)
Pro R Cornwell
Holes 18 L 5017 yds SSS 65
Recs Am–63 D Curtis
Pro–63 L Turner
V'trs WD–U WE/ BH–before
11.30am
Fees £8 (£10)
Loc Off A20 Ruxley roundabout at
Sidcup
Mis Driving range

St Augustines (1907)

Cottington Road, Cliffsend, Ramsgate
Tel (0843) 590333
Mem 300 80(L) 55(J) 120(5)
Sec R James
Pro DB Scott (0843) 590222
Holes 18 L 5138 yds SS 65
Recs Am–59 Dr S Hutton
Pro–61 P Mitchell
V'trs H SOC–WD
Fees £18 (£20) W–£60 M–£180
Loc 2 miles S of Ramsgate. Follow
signs to St Augustines Cross

Sene Valley (1888)

Sene, Folkestone CT18 8BL
Mem 650
Sec GL Hills (0303) 68513
Pro T Dungate (0303) 68514
Holes 18 L 6287 yds SSS 70
Recs Am–65 J Hamilton
Pro–69 G Will
V'trs WD–H or I SOC
Fees £16 (£20)
Loc 2 miles N of Hythe on B2065

Sheerness (1906)

Power Station Road, Sheerness ME12 3AE
Tel (0795) 662585
Mem 550
Sec JW Gavins
Holes 18 L 6500 yds SSS 71
Recs Am–68 JD Simmance
V'trs WD–U WE–M SOC
Fees £10 (£12)
Loc Sittingbourne 9 miles. M20, M2
or A2 to A249

Shortlands (1894)

Meadow Road, Shortlands, Bromley BR2 0PB
Tel (081) 460 2471
Mem 525

Sidcup (1891)

Hurst Road, Sidcup DA15 9AE
Tel (081) 300 2864
Mem 350
Sec A Watt (081) 300 2150
Pro R Taylor (081) 309 0679
Holes 9 L 5692 yds SSS 67
Recs Am–65 R Harris
Pro–64 D Webb
V'trs WD–H WE/ BH–M
Fees £15
Loc On A222. A2/ A20, 2 miles

Sittingbourne & Milton Regis (1929)

Wormdale, Newington, Sittingbourne ME9 7PX
Tel (0795) 842261
Mem 325 100(L) 72(J) 175(5)
Sec HDG Wylie
Pro JR Hearn (0795) 842775
Holes 18 L 6121 yds SSS 69
Recs Am–66
Pro–62
V'trs WD–H Sat–NA Sun–M SOC–
Tues & Thurs
Fees £16
Loc 1 mile N of M2 Junction 5
(A249)

Sundridge Park (1902)

Garden Lane, Bromley BR1 3NE
Tel (081) 460 1822
Mem 1200
Sec (081) 460 0278
Pro B Cameron (081) 460 5540
Holes East 18 L 6410 yds SSS 71
West 18 L 6027 yds SSS 69
Recs East Am–65 W Hodkin (1988)
Pro–64 R Cameron
West Am–67 P Lyons (1987)
Pro–65 R Fidler
V'trs H SOC–WD
Fees £30
Loc 1 mile N of Bromley, by
Sundridge Park Station. M25
Junction 3(South) or Junction
4(North)

Tenterden (1905)

Woodchurch Road, Tenterden
Tel (058 06) 3987
Mem 450
Sec DF Hunt (058 06) 4612
Pro G Pottern
Holes 9 L 5141 yds SSS 65
V'trs WD–U WE/ BH–M Sun–NA
before noon
Fees On application
Loc Tenterden 1 mile

Sec Mrs L Burrows
Pro J Bates
Holes 9 L 5261 yds SSS 66
Recs Am–64 B Kent
Pro–61 D Pratt
V'trs M
Loc Bromley, Kent

For list of abbreviations see page 487.

Tudor Park (1989)

Ashford Road, Bearsted, Maidstone
ME14 4NQ
Tel   (0622) 34334
Mem   740
Sec   T Davidson
Pro   M Boggia (0622) 39412
Holes 18 L 6000yds SSS 69
Recs   Am–68 J Miller (1990)
       Pro–67 P Lyons (1990)
V'trs H SOC–Tues–Thurs
Fees   £25 (£30)
Loc   3 miles E of Maidstone on A20.
       M20 Junction 8

Tunbridge Wells (1889)

Langton Road, Tunbridge Wells
TN4 8XH
Tel   (0892) 23034
Mem   360 86(L) 45(J)
Sec   EM Goulden (0892) 36918
Pro   K Smithson (0892) 41386
Holes 9 L 4684 yds SSS 62
Recs   Am–59 EC Chapman
       Pro–59 J Humphrey
V'trs WD–U WE/ BH–M
Fees   £18 D–£24
Loc   Tunbridge Wells, by Spa Hotel

Walmer & Kingsdown (1909)

The Leas, Kingsdown, Deal CT14 8EP
Tel   (0304) 373256
Mem   620
Sec   BW Cockerill
Pro   T Hunt (0304) 363017
Holes 18 L 6451 yds SSS 71
Recs   Am–69 A Randall
       Pro–70 M Lee
V'trs WD–U WE–after noon SOC
Fees   D–£20 (£22) W–£87
Loc   2½ miles S of Deal on clifftop

West Kent (1916)

West Hill, Downe, Orpington BR6 7JJ
Tel   (0689) 53737
Mem   385 100(L) 140(5)
Sec   AJ Messing (0689) 51323
Pro   RS Fidler (0689) 56863
Holes 18 L 6369 yds SSS 70
Recs   Am–62 DC Smith
       Pro–65 H Baiocchi
V'trs WD–H or I WE/ BH–M
Fees   £20
Loc   Orpington 5 miles

West Malling (1974)

Addington, nr Maidstone
Tel   (0732) 844785
Mem   550
Sec   MR Ellis
Pro   P Foston
Holes Spitfire 18 L 6142 yds Par 70
       Hurricane 18 L 6240 yds Par 70
Recs   Spitfire Am–70 R Parkhouse
       Pro–71 P Way
V'trs WD–U WE–UH after noon
Fees   £16 (£25)
Loc   A20 London Road

Westgate & Birchington (1893)

176, Canterbury Road, Westgate-on-
Sea CT8 8LT
Tel   (0843) 31115
Mem   325
Sec   JM Wood
Pro   R Game
Holes 18 L 4926 yds SSS 64
Recs   Am–60 Miss W Morgan
       Pro–60 J Hickman
V'trs H or I WD–NA before 10am
       WE–NA before noon
Fees   £12 (£15)
Loc   Westgate Station ¼ mile

Whitstable & Seasalter (1910)

Collingwood Rd, Whitstable CT5 1EB
Tel   (0227) 272020
Mem   250
Sec   D Spratt (0227) 273589
Holes 9 L 5284 yds SSS 63
V'trs WD–U WE–M
Fees   £10
Loc   Whitstable Station 1 mile

Wildernesse (1890)

Seal, Sevenoaks
Tel   (0732) 61526
Mem   800
Sec   KL Monk (0732) 61199
Pro   W Dawson (0732) 61527
Holes 18 L 6478 yds SSS 72
Recs   Am–66 P Benka, M Pinner
       Pro–65 I Grant
V'trs WD–I H SOC–Thurs
Fees   £22 D–£32
Loc   2 miles E of Sevenoaks (A25)

Woodlands Manor (1928)

Woodlands, Sevenoaks TN15 6AB
Tel   (095 92) 3805
Mem   650
Sec   EF Newman, J Mills (095 92)
       3806
Pro   N Allen (095 92) 4161
Holes 18 L 5858 yds SSS 68
Recs   Pro–65 N Coles
V'trs WD–U WE–H NA before noon
       SOC–WD
Fees   £9 (£15)
Loc   4 miles S of M25 Junction 3. Off
       A20 between W Kingsdown
       and Otford

Wrotham Heath (1906)

Seven Mile Lane Comp, Sevenoaks
TN15 8QZ
Tel   (0732) 884800
Mem   200 70(L) 55(J) 50(5)
Sec   JD Majendie (0732) 883099
Pro   H Dearden (0732) 883854
Holes 9 L 5823 yds SSS 68
Recs   Am–66 R Sloman (1983)
V'trs WD–H WE/ BH–M SOC–Fri
Fees   £12 D–£15
Loc   8 miles W of Maidstone on
       B2106. M26/ A20 Junction 1 mile

Lancashire

Accrington & District (1893)

West End, Oswaldtwistle,
Accrington
Tel   (0254) 32734
Mem   350
Sec   JE Pilkington (0254) 35070
Pro   W Harling (0254) 31091
Holes 18 L 5954 yds SSS 69
Recs   Am–64 J Pothwell
V'trs WD/ WE–U SOC
Fees   £15 (£18)
Loc   3 miles SW of Accrington

Ashton & Lea (1913)

Tudor Ave, Blackpool Rd, Lea, nr
Preston PR4 0XA
Tel   (0772) 726480
Mem   900
Sec   MG Gibbs (0772) 735282
Pro   P Laugher (0772) 720374
Holes 18 L 6289 yds SSS 70
Recs   Am–65 K Wallbank (1989)
       Pro–66 J Hawksworth (1988)
V'trs U SOC
Fees   £12.50 (£17) (1990)
Loc   3 miles W of Preston, off A583

Bacup (1912)

Maden Road, Bacup OL13 8HY
Tel   (0706) 873170
Mem   395
Sec   J Garvey (0706) 874485
Holes 9 L 5656 yds SSS 67
Recs   Am–65 M Butcher
       Pro–67 H Higgins
V'trs U
Fees   £8 (£9)
Loc   Bankside Lane

Baxenden & District (1913)

Top o' th' Meadow, Baxenden,
Accrington BB5 2EA
Tel   (0254) 234555
Mem   325
Sec   L Howard (0706) 213394
Holes 9 L 5740 yds SSS 68
Recs   Am–68 W Horvath
       Pro–66 C Tobin
V'trs WD–U WE/ BH–M
Fees   £7
Loc   2 miles SE of Accrington

Blackburn (1894)

Beardwood Brow, Blackburn
BB2 7AX
Tel   (0254) 51122
Mem   440 95(L) 110(J)
Sec   PD Haydock
Pro   A Rodwell (0254) 55942
Holes 18 L 6140 yds SSS 70
Recs   Am–66 MC Hartley (1989)
       Pro–66 M Foster
V'trs U SOC–WD WE/ BH–restricted
Fees   £14 (£18)
Loc   1 mile NW of Blackburn. M6
       Junction 31

Blackpool North Shore (1904)

Devonshire Road, Blackpool FY2 0RD
Tel	(0253) 51017
Mem	820
Sec	DS Walker (0253) 52054
Pro	B Ward (0253) 54640
Holes	18 L 6443 yds SSS 71
Recs	Am–67 T Foster (1988)
	Pro–63 C O'Connor
V'trs	U SOC WE–restricted
Fees	£18 (£20)
Loc	1/2 mile behind North prom

Blackpool Park (1925)

Public

North Park Drive, Blackpool FY3 8LS
Tel	(0253) 33960
Pro	B Purdie (0253) 31004
Holes	18 L 6192 yds SSS 69
Recs	Am–65 AV Moss
	Pro–68 D Lewis
V'trs	U
Fees	£5.50 (£7)
Loc	11/2 miles E of Blackpool, nr Stanley Park

Burnley (1905)

Glen View, Burnley BB11 3RW
Tel	(0282) 21045
Mem	600
Sec	G Dean (0282) 24328
Pro	RM Cade (0282) 55266
Holes	18 L 5891 yds SSS 69
Recs	Am–65 ID Gradwell, L Samuels, DA Brown, GD Haworth, P Preston Pro–66 JS Steer
V'trs	U SOC
Fees	£10 (£15)
Loc	Via Manchester Road to Glenview Road

Chorley (1898)

Hall o' th' Hill Heath, Charnock, nr Chorley PR6 9HX
Tel	(0257) 480263
Mem	400
Sec	GA Birtill (025 72) 63024
Pro	P Wesselingh (0257) 481245
Holes	18 L 6277 yds SSS 70
Recs	Am–65 WG Bromilow Pro–66 M Hughes
V'trs	WD–I WE–by arrangement SOC
Fees	On application
Loc	1 mile S of Chorley

Clitheroe (1891)

Whalley Road, Clitheroe BB7 1PP
Tel	(0200) 22618 (Clubhouse)
	(0200) 24242 (Proshop)
Mem	750 122(L) 68(J)
Sec	JB Kay (0200) 22292
Holes	18 L 6045 yds SSS 71
Recs	Am–68 P Marlow, M Gray
V'trs	U
Fees	£17 (£21)
Loc	2 miles S of Clitheroe

Colne (1901)

Law Farm, Skipton Old Road, Colne
Tel	(0282) 863391
Mem	300
Holes	9 L 5961 yds SSS 69
Recs	Am–69 J Gallagher
V'trs	U exc comp days SOC
Fees	£10 (£12)
Loc	11/2 miles N of Colne. From end of M65, signs to Keighley and Lothersdale

Darwen (1893)

Winter Hill, Darwen
Tel	(0254) 701287
Mem	360 70(L) 100(J) 40(5)
Sec	J Kenyon (0254) 581983
Pro	W Lennon (0254) 776370
Holes	18 L 5752 yds SSS 68
Recs	Am–66 Pro–65
V'trs	U
Fees	£10 (£15)
Loc	Darwen 11/2 miles

Dean Wood (1922)

Lafford Lane, Upholland, Skelmersdale WN8 0QZ
Tel	(0695) 622980
Mem	850
Sec	J Walls (0695) 622219
Pro	AB Coop
Holes	18 L 6129 yds SSS 70
Recs	Am–66 J Dawber, D Parkin, JB Dickinson Pro–66 RA Morris
V'trs	WD–U WE/ BH–M SOC
Fees	£20 (£25)
Loc	4 miles W of Wigan (A577)

Duxbury Park (1975)

Public

Duxbury Hall Road, Duxbury Park, Chorley PR7 4AS
Tel	(025 72) 41634 (Clubhouse)
Pro	D Clarke (025 72) 65380
Holes	18 L 6270 yds SSS 70
Recs	Am–74 A Jones Pro–66 J Anglada
V'trs	U
Fees	£3 (£4)
Loc	11/2 miles S of Chorley, off Wigan Lane

Fairhaven (1895)

Lytham Hall Park, Ansdell, Lytham St Annes FY8 4JU
Mem	900
Sec	B Hartley (0253) 736741
Pro	(0253) 736976
Holes	18 L 6883 yds SSS 73
Recs	Am–65 SG Birtwell Pro–65 R Commans
V'trs	WD–U WE–NA before 9.30am SOC–WD
Fees	£23 (£30)
Loc	Lytham 2 miles. St Annes 2 miles. M55 Junction 4

Fishwick Hall (1912)

Glenluce Drive, Farringdon Park, Preston PR1 5TD
Tel	(0772) 798300
Mem	600
Sec	RR Gearing (0772) 796866
Pro	S Bence (0772) 795870
Holes	18 L 6028 yds SSS 69
Recs	Am–66 C Cross
V'trs	Apply to Sec SOC
Fees	£15 (£20)
Loc	1 mile E of Preston, nr junction of A59 and M6 Junction 31

Fleetwood (1932)

Golf House, Princes Way, Fleetwood FY7 8AF
Tel	(039 17) 3114
Mem	548
Sec	K Volter (039 17) 3661
Pro	CT Burgess (039 17) 3661
Holes	L 18 L 6723 yds SSS 72
Recs	Am–69 JC Roberts Pro–70 S Bennett
V'trs	U SOC
Fees	£14 (£16)
Loc	1 mile W of Fleetwood

Great Harwood (1895)

Harwood Bar, Great Harwood
Tel	(0254) 884391
Mem	162 60(L) 30(J)
Sec	A Garraway (0254) 886802
Pro	K Caven (0254) 886728
Holes	9 L 6413 yds SSS 71
Recs	Am–68 J Aspinall Pro–64 AH Padgham
V'trs	U
Fees	£7 (£8)
Loc	Nr Blackburn

Green Haworth (1914)

Green Haworth, Accrington BB5 3SL
Tel	(0254) 37580
Mem	200
Sec	K Lynch
Holes	9 L 5470 yds SSS 67
Recs	Am–66 R Peters
V'trs	WD–U exc Wed–Ladies only after 5pm WE/ BH–M SOC
Fees	£5 (£6)
Loc	Willows Lane

Heysham (1910)

Trumacar Park, Middleton Road, Heysham, Morecambe LA3 3JH
Tel	(0524) 51011
Mem	900
Sec	A Hesketh
Pro	R Williamson (0524) 52000
Holes	18 L 6224 yds SSS 70
Recs	Am–66 PW Coyle (1984), B Bielby, S Swinton (1988) Pro–64 P Walker (1990)
V'trs	U
Fees	£13 D–£16 (Sat–£16 Sun–£20)
Loc	Morecambe 2 miles. 5 miles from M6

Ingol (1983)

Tanterton Hall Road, Ingol, Preston
PR2 7BY
Tel   (0772) 734556
Mem   700
Sec   H Parker
Holes   18 L 6225 yds SSS 70
Recs   Am–68 Pro–67
V'trs   U SOC
Fees   £15 (£18)
Loc   1½ miles NW of Preston (A6).
         M6 Junction 32

Knott End (1911)

Wyreside, Knott End on Sea,
Blackpool FY6 0AA
Tel   (0253) 810254
Mem   660
Sec   C Desmond (0253) 810576
Pro   K Short (0253) 811365
Holes   18 L 5351 metres SSS 68
Recs   Am–66 DJ Martel
V'trs   WD–U WE/ BH–by
         arrangement SOC–WD
Fees   £14 (£18)
Loc   Over Wyre, Knott End on Sea

Lancaster G & CC (1932)

Ashton Hall, Ashton-with-Stodday,
nr Lancaster LA2 0AJ
Tel   (0524) 752090
Mem   525 165(L) 125(J) 50(5)
Sec   Mrs J Hayhurst (0524) 751247
Pro   R Head (0524) 751802
Holes   18 L 6465 yds SSS 71
Recs   Am–66 M Brooks
V'trs   H (arrange with Sec or Pro)
Fees   £20
Loc   2½ miles S of Lancaster (A588)

Lansil (1947)

Caton Road, Lancaster LA1 3PD
Tel   (0524) 39269
Mem   450
Sec   D Crutchley (0524) 41800
Holes   9 L 5608 yds SSS 67
Recs   Am–68 DC Whiteway
V'trs   WD–U WE–U after 1pm
Fees   £5 (£10)
Loc   A683, 2 miles E of Lancaster

Leyland (1924)

Wigan Road, Leyland
Tel   (0772) 421359
Mem   750
Sec   GD Copeman (0772) 436457
Pro   C Burgess (0772) 423425
Holes   18 L 6123 yds SSS 69
Recs   Am–66 G Norris
         Pro–67 L Edwards (1990)
V'trs   WD–U WE–M SOC
Fees   £15
Loc   M6 Junction 28, 1 mile

Lobden (1888)

Whitworth, nr Rochdale
Tel   (0706) 343228
Mem   220
Sec   C Buchanan (0706) 343197

Holes   9 L 5770 yds SSS 68
Recs   Am–67 C Turner
V'trs   U
Fees   £6 (£8)
Loc   4 miles N of Rochdale

Longridge (1877)

Fell Barn, Jeffrey Hill, Longridge,
nr Preston PR3 2TU
Tel   (0772) 783291   782765
Mem   500
Sec   AW Southworth (0772) 782955
Pro   NS James
Holes   18 L 5726 yds SSS 68
Recs   Am–66 A Taylor (1990)
V'trs   U
Fees   Mon–Thurs–£12 Fri/ WE–£15
Loc   8 miles NE of Preston, off B6243

Lytham (Green Drive) (1922)

Ballam Road, Lytham FY8 4LE
Tel   (0253) 734782
Mem   700
Sec   R Kershaw (0253) 737390
Pro   FW Accleton (0253) 737379
Holes   18 L 6175 yds SSS 69
Recs   Am–64 C Rymer (1988)
         Pro–64 E Romero (1988)
V'trs   WD–U H WE–NA SOC–WD
Fees   £21

Marsden Park (1969)

Public
Townhouse Road, Nelson BB9 8DG
Tel   (0282) 67525
Pro   N Brown
Holes   18 L 5806 yds SSS 68
Recs   Am–66 MN Davies
         Pro–74 T Gillett
V'trs   U
Fees   D–£3.85 (D–£4.95)
Loc   Signposted Walton Lane,
         Nelson

Morecambe (1904)

Bare, Morecambe LA4 6AJ
Tel   (0524) 418050
Mem   1200
Sec   Maj. BC Hodgson (0524)
         412841
Pro   D Helmn (0524) 415596
Holes   18 L 5766 yds SSS 68
Recs   Am–64 J Swallow, DP Carney
         Pro–63 B Gallacher,
         P Oosterhuis
V'trs   U H SOC
Fees   £11 (£15)
Loc   On sea front

Nelson (1902)

Kings Causeway, Brierfield, Nelson
BB9 0EU
Tel   (0282) 64583
Mem   550
Sec   RW Baldwin
Pro   R Geddes (0282) 67000
Holes   18 L 5967 yds SSS 69
Recs   Am–65 S Duerden (1987),
         N Uttley (1989)

         Pro–68 H Shoesmith
V'trs   WD–U H exc Thurs pm–NA
         WE–U exc Sat before 4pm SOC
Fees   £13 (£15)
Loc   2 miles N of Burnley

Ormskirk (1899)

Cranes Lane, Lathom, Ormskirk
L40 5UJ
Tel   (0695) 572112
Mem   300
Sec   PD Dromgoole (0695) 572227
Pro   J Hammond (0695) 572074
Holes   18 L 6350 yds SSS 70
Recs   Am–63 DJ Eccleston
         Pro–67 MJ Slater
V'trs   I exc Sat–NA SOC
Fees   £20 (£25) Wed–£25
Loc   2 miles E of Ormskirk

Penwortham (1908)

Blundell Lane, Penwortham, Preston
PR1 0AX
Tel   (0772) 743207
Mem   700
Sec   J Parkinson (0772) 744630
Pro   J Wright (0772) 742345
Holes   18 L 5915 yds SSS 69
Recs   Am–62 A Gillespie
         Pro–66 W Fletcher
V'trs   WD–U WE–no parties
Fees   £16 (£22)
Loc   1½ miles W of Preston

Pleasington (1891)

Nr Blackburn BB2 5JF
Tel   (0254) 202177
Mem   520
Sec   L Ingham
Pro   GJ Furey (0254) 201630
Holes   18 L 6445 yds SSS 71
Recs   Am–64 SG Birtwell (1983)
         Pro–66 S Holden (1988)
V'trs   H
Fees   £22 (£27.50)
Loc   3 miles W of Blackburn

Poulton-le-Fylde (1982)

Public
Myrtle Farm, Breck Road, Poulton,
nr Blackpool
Tel   (0253) 892444
Mem   250
Sec   (0253) 893150
Holes   9 L 2979 yds SSS 69
Recs   Am–74 D Barker (1986)
         Pro–70 J Wraith (1985)
V'trs   U
Fees   £3.20 (£4.50)
Loc   3 miles E of Blackpool

Preston (1892)

Fulwood Hall Lane, Fulwood,
Preston PR2 4DD
Tel   (0772) 794234 (Clubhouse)
         (0772) 700436 (Steward)
Mem   800
Sec   JB Dickinson (0772) 700011
Pro   PA Wells (0772) 700022
Holes   18 L 6249 yds SSS 70

For list of abbreviations see page 487.

Recs Am–65 MA Holmes, J Wright
       Pro–66 JM Hulme
V'trs U H SOC–WD
Fees £17 D–£20 (£22)
Loc 1½ miles W of M6 Junction 32

Rishton (1927)

**Eachill Links, Hawthorn Drive,
Rishton BB1 4HG**
Tel (0254) 884442
Mem 250
Sec G Haworth (0254) 60226 (after
       6pm)
Holes 9 L 6199 yds SSS 69
Recs Am–66 G Walmsley
       Pro–69 M Jones
V'trs WD–U WE–M
Fees £8
Loc 3 miles E of Blackburn

Rossendale (1903)

**Ewood Lane, Head Haslingden,
Rossendale BB4 6LH**
Tel (0706) 213056
Mem 710
Sec WP Whittaker (0706) 831339/
       216234
Pro SJ Nicholls (0706) 213616
Holes 18 L 6262 yds SSS 70
Recs Am–67 A Siddle
       Pro–68 S Holden
V'trs WD/ Sun–U Sat–M
Fees £17 (£20)
Loc 7 miles N of Bury, nr end of
       M66

Royal Lytham & St Annes (1886)

**Links Gate, Lytham St Annes
FY8 3LQ**
Tel (0253) 724206
Mem 600
Sec Maj AS Craven (Retd)
Pro E Birchenough (0253) 720094
Holes 18 L 6673 yds SSS 73
Recs Am–66 R Foster, T Craddock
       Pro–65 C O'Connor,
       BGC Huggett, W Longmuir,
       S Ballesteros
V'trs WD–I H
Fees £36 D–£50
Loc St Annes 1 mile

St Annes Old Links (1901)

**Highbury Road, Lytham St Annes
FY8 2LD**
Tel (0253) 723597
Mem 975
Sec DJM Hemsted
Pro GG Hardiman (0253) 722432
Holes 18 L 6647 yds SSS 72
Recs Am–66 RD Squire, AC Nash
       Pro–66 AD Sowa, T Webber,
       GL Parslow
V'trs WD–NA before 9.15am and
       12–2pm WE/ BH–arrange with
       Sec SOC
Fees £25 (£30)
Loc Between St Annes and
       Blackpool, off A584

Shaw Hill Hotel

**Preston Road, Whittle-le-Woods,
Chorley PR6 7PP**
Tel (02572) 69221
Mem 500
Sec A Lawless (Gen Mgr)
Pro I Evans (02572) 79222
Holes 18 L 6467 yds SSS 71
Recs Am–68 A Squires
       Pro–69 I Evans
V'trs WD–U
Fees £20 (£30)
Loc A6, 1½ miles N of Chorley.
       M61 Junction 8. M6 Junction 28

Silverdale (1906)

**Red Bridge Lane, Silverdale,
Carnforth LA5 0SP**
Tel (0524) 701300
Mem 513
Sec EF Wright (05395) 63782
Holes 9 L 5288 yds SSS 67
Recs Am–66
V'trs U exc Sun (Summer)–M
Fees £8 (£12)
Loc 3 miles NW of Carnforth, by
       Silverdale Station

Stonyhurst Park (1980)

**Stonyhurst, Hurst Green, Blackburn
BB6 9QB**
Tel (0254) 86478
Mem 315
Sec AN Wilkinson
Holes 9 L 5529 yds SSS 66
V'trs WD–U (telephone first) WE–M
Fees £10
Loc B6243 Longridge–Clitheroe rd.
Mis Green fees payable at Bayley
       Arms, Hurst Green

Towneley (1932)

Public
**Towneley Park, Todmorden Road,
Burnley**
Tel (0282) 51636
Pro (0282) 38473
Holes 18 L 5862 yds SSS 68 9 hole
       course
Recs Am–67 T Foster (1990)
       Pro–65 D Whittaker (1985)
V'trs U
Fees £3.75 (£4.50)
Loc 1½ miles E of Burnley

Whalley (1912)

**Long Leese Barn, Clerkhill, Whalley,
nr Blackburn BB6 9DR**
Tel (025 482) 2236
Mem 475
Sec PC Burt (025 482) 2367
Pro H Smith
Holes 9 L 5953 yds SSS 69
Recs Am–67 G Richards
V'trs U exc Sat (Apr–Oct) SOC–WD
Fees £9 (£12)
Loc 7 miles E of Blackburn

Wilpshire (1890)

**72 Whalley Road, Wilpshire,
Blackburn BB1 9LF**
Tel (0254) 248260/ 249691
Mem 650
Pro W Slaven (0254) 249558
Holes 18 L 5911 yds SSS 68
Recs Am–64 H Green (1975),
       MJ Savage (1978), PC Livesey
       (1990)
       Pro–61 J Hawkesworth (1989)
V'trs WD–U WE/ BH–on request
Fees £13 (£21)
Loc 3 miles NE of Blackburn, off
       A666

Leicestershire

Birstall (1901)

Station Road, Birstall, Leicester
Tel (0533) 674450
Mem 350 86(L) 57(J)
Sec Ms S Wells (0533) 674322
Pro R Ball (0533) 675245
Holes 18 L 6203 yds SSS 70
Recs Am–68 K Wells, NH Abel,
       D Hunter Walker
       Pro–67 L Platts
V'trs Mon/ Wed/ Fri–I Other days–M
Fees £15
Loc 3 miles N of Leicester

Breedon Priory (1990)

Wilson, nr Derby
Tel (0332) 863081
Pro T Coxon
Holes 18 L 5500 yds Par 68
V'trs WD–U WE–NA before 2pm
Fees £12 (£15)
Loc Nr East Midlands Airport. M1
       Junction 24

Charnwood Forest (1890)

**Breakback Road, Woodhouse
Eaves, Loughborough LE12 8TA**
Tel (0509) 890259
Mem 267
Sec AG Stanley (0509) 890588
Pro M Lawrence (0509) 890509
Holes 9 L 5960 yds SSS 69
Recs Am–65 T Allen (1990)
V'trs WD–H WE/ BH–NA SOC
Fees £15
Loc M1 Junction 23, 3 miles

Cosby (1895)

**Chapel Lane, off Broughton Road,
Cosby, nr Leicester**
Tel (0533) 864759
Mem 650
Sec MD Riddle (0533) 861049
Pro D Bowring (0533) 848275
Holes 18 L 6277 yds SSS 70
V'trs WD–U before 4pm WE/ BH–M
       SOC–WD–H
Fees £18 D–£20
Loc 7 miles S of Leicester. ¼ mile
       S of Cosby

Enderby (1986)

Public
Mill Lane, Enderby, Leicester
Tel	**(0533) 849388**
Sec	LJ Speake (0533) 841133
Pro	C D'Araujo
Holes	9 L 4356 yds SSS 61
V'trs	U
Fees	18 holes–£2.25 (£2.75)
Loc	Enderby 2 miles. M1 Junction 21/ M69 Junction 1

Glen Gorse (1933)

Glen Road, Oadby, Leicester LE2 4RF
Tel	**(0533) 712226/ 714159**
Mem	360 110(L) 60(J)
Sec	K McKay (0533) 714159
Pro	R Larratt (0533) 713748
Holes	18 L 6641 yds SSS 72
Recs	Am–65 A Hare Pro–66 DT Steele
V'trs	WD–U WE/ BH–M SOC–WD
Fees	£17
Loc	3 miles S of Leicester on A6

Hinckley (1983)

Leicester Road, Hinckley LE10 3DR
Tel	**(0455) 615124**
Mem	500
Sec	J Toon
Pro	R Jones (0455) 615014
Holes	18 L 6462 yds SSS 71
Recs	Pro–67 K Dickens (1987)
V'trs	WD–U WE–NA Sun after noon SOC
Fees	£15
Loc	NE of Hinckley on A47

Humberstone Heights (1978)

Public
Gipsy Lane, Leicester
Tel	**(0533) 761905**
Sec	S Day (0533) 674835
Pro	P Highfield (0533) 764674
Holes	18 L 6444 yds SSS 71
Recs	Am–69 D Butler (1987) Pro–67 R Adams (1985)
V'trs	U
Fees	£4.50 (£5.50)
Loc	3 miles E of Leicester off A47

Kibworth (1905)

Weir Road, Kibworth Beauchamp, Leicester LE8 0LP
Tel	**(053 753) 792301**
Mem	550
Sec	Mrs W Potter
Pro	A Strange (053 753) 792283
Holes	18 L 6282 yds SSS 70
Recs	Am–67 EE Feasey Pro–67 J Briars
V'trs	WD–U WE–M SOC
Fees	£16
Loc	9 miles SE of Leicester on A6

Kirby Muxloe (1910)

Station Road, Kirby Muxloe, nr Leicester LE9 9EN
Tel	**(0533) 393107**
Mem	425
Sec	SF Aldwinckle (0533) 393457
Pro	RT Stephenson (0533) 392813
Holes	18 L 6303 yds SSS 70
Recs	Am–69 M Reay Pro–65 P Thomson
V'trs	WD–U before 3.45pm exc Tues–NA SOC-H
Fees	£12.50 D–£15 (£12.50 with Captain's permission only)
Loc	3 miles W of Leicester

Leicestershire (1890)

Evington Lane, Leicester LE5 6DJ
Tel	**(0533) 736035**
Mem	750
Sec	JL Adams (0533) 738825
Pro	JR Turnbull (0533) 736730
Holes	18 L 6330 yds SSS 70
Recs	Am–65 A Martinez, G Wolstenholme Pro–63 H Henning, I Mosey, S Sherratt
V'trs	U H SOC
Fees	£22 (£25)
Loc	2 miles E of Leicester

Lingdale (1967)

Joe Moore's Lane, Woodhouse Eaves, Loughborough
Tel	**(0509) 890703**
Mem	450
Sec	M Green
Pro	P Sellears (0509) 890684
Holes	9 L 6684 yds SSS 72
Recs	Am–68 R Walker
V'trs	U SOC
Fees	D–£12 (£20)
Loc	Loughborough 6 miles. 4 miles from M1 Junction 23

Longcliffe (1905)

Nanpantan, Loughborough
Tel	**(0509) 216321**
Mem	550
Sec	G Harle (0509) 239129
Pro	I Bailey (0509) 231450
Holes	18 L 6551 yds SSS 71
Recs	Am–69 M Wilson Pro–68 M Reay
V'trs	WD–H WE–M
Fees	£25
Loc	Loughborough 2¹/₂ miles. M1 Junction 23

Luffenham Heath (1911)

Ketton, Stamford, Lincs PE9 3UU
Tel	**(0780) 720205**
Mem	555
Sec	IF Davenport
Pro	JA Lawrence (0780) 720298
Holes	18 L 6254 yds SSS 70
Recs	Am–64 M Welch Pro–67 PJ Butler, RL Moffitt
V'trs	U SOC–WD
Fees	£25 (£30)
Loc	5 miles W of Stamford on A6121

Lutterworth (1904)

Lutterworth, Leicester
Tel	**(04555) 2532**
Mem	500
Sec	JC Bonfield
Pro	N Melvin
Holes	18 L 5570 yds SSS 67
Recs	Am–67 M Moore Pro–71 M Faulkner
V'trs	WD–U WE–M SOC
Fees	£14 D–£18
Loc	By M1 Junction 20

Market Harborough (1898)

Oxendon Road, Market Harborough
Tel	**(0858) 463684**
Mem	360
Sec	JNT Lord (0536) 771771
Pro	FJ Baxter
Holes	9 L 6080 yds SSS 69
Recs	Am–68 RC Gadd, W Sneath Pro–67 B Morris, D Mee
V'trs	WD–U SOC
Fees	£18
Loc	1 mile S of M Harborough

Melton Mowbray (1925)

Waltham Rd, Thorpe Arnold, Melton Mowbray
Tel	**(0664) 62118**
Mem	420
Sec	Mrs EA Sallis
Holes	9 L 6200 yds SSS 70
Recs	Am–64 N Street (1990) Pro–66 W Hill
V'trs	U H before 3pm –M after 3pm SOC
Fees	£10 (£15)
Loc	2 miles NE of Melton Mowbray on A607
Mis	Extension to 18 holes in 1991

Oadby (1974)

Public
Leicester Road Racecourse, Oadby, Leicester LE2 4AB
Tel	**(0533) 709052/ 700215**
Pro	S Ward (0533) 709052
Holes	18 L 6286 yds SSS 69
Recs	Am–65 S Davis (1988) Pro–73 C O'Connor Jr
V'trs	WD–U WE/ BH–book with Pro SOC–WD
Fees	£4 (£6)
Loc	2 miles S of Leicester

RAF Cottesmore (1982)

Oakham, Leicester LE15 7BL
Tel	**(0572) 812241 (Ext 429)**
Mem	195
Sec	JR Hall
Holes	9 L 5448 yds SSS 66
Recs	Am–72 Pro–70
V'trs	M
Loc	RAF Cottesmore

RAF North Luffenham (1975)

RAF North Luffenham, Oakham
LE15 8RL
Tel (0780) 720041 (Ext 273/ 240)
Mem 350 62(L) 25(J)
Sec JA Anderson (Ext 273)
Holes 9 L 6006 yds SSS 69
Recs Am–71 KP Hickman
V'trs M
Loc RAF N Luffenham, 1/2 mile from S shore of Rutland Water

Rothley Park (1911)

Westfield Lane, Rothley, Leicester
LE7 7LH
Tel (0533) 302019
Sec BS Durham (0533) 302809
Pro PJ Dolan (0533) 303023
Holes 18 L 6487 yds SSS 71
Recs Am–67 EE Feasey
Pro–68 PJ Dolan
V'trs WD–U exc Tues–NA WE/ BH–NA
Fees £20 (£25)
Loc 6 miles N of Leicester, W of A6

Scraptoft (1928)

Beeby Road, Scraptoft, Leicester
LE7 9SJ
Tel (0533) 419000
Mem 500
Sec AM Robertson (0533) 418863
Pro S Sherratt (0533) 419138
Holes 18 L 6166 yds SSS 69
Recs Am–66 D Gibson, CM Harries
Pro–A Bownes
V'trs WD–U WE–M SOC–WD
Fees £14 (£16)
Loc 3 miles E of Leicester

Ullesthorpe Court (1976)

Frolesworth Road, Ullesthorpe, Lutterworth
Tel (0455) 209023
Mem 600
Sec PE Woolley
Pro N Brown (0455) 209150
Holes 18 L 6650 yds SSS 72
Recs Am–72 R Espley
Pro–68
V'trs U SOC–WD
Fees £12.50
Loc 3 miles NW of Lutterworth

Western Park (1920)

Public
Scudamore Road, Leicester LE3 1UQ
Tel (0533) 872339/ 876158
Pro BN Whipham (0533) 872339
Holes 18 L 6532 yds SSS 71
Recs Am–68 DE Gibson
V'trs U
Fees £4.50 (£5.50)
Loc 4 miles W of Leicester. M1 Junction 21, 3 miles

Whetstone (1965)

Cambridge Road, Cosby, Leicester
LE9 5SH
Tel (0533) 861424
Mem 600
Sec B Dalby
Pro N Leatherland, D Raitt
Holes 18 L 5700 yds SSS 68
Recs Am–71 B Richmond, C Wells (1990) Pro–64 D Raitt (1989)
V'trs U SOC
Fees £7 (£9)
Loc S boundary of Leicester
Mis Driving range

Willesley Park (1921)

Measham Road, Ashby-de-la-Zouch
LE6 5PF
Tel (0530) 411532
Mem 600 99(L) 38(J)
Sec NH Jones (0530) 414596
Pro C Hancock (0530) 414820
Holes 18 L 6310 yds SSS 70
Recs Am–66 G Wolstenholme
Pro–65 L Jones
V'trs WD–H WE/ BH–H after 9.30am SOC
Fees £20 (£25)
Loc 2 miles S of Ashby on B5006. M1 Junctions 22/ 23/ 24. A42(M) Junction 10

Lincolnshire

Belton Park (1890)

Belton Lane, Londonthorpe Road, Grantham NG31 9SH
Tel (0476) 67399
Mem 950
Sec T Measures (Mgr)
Pro B McKee (0476) 63911
Holes 27 Brownlow L 6412 yds SSS 71; Ancaster L 6109 yds SSS 69; Belmont L 5857 yds SSS 68
Recs Am–69 DF Price
Pro–65 S Bennett
V'trs U SOC–WD exc Tues
Fees 18 holes–£15 (£20) 27/ 36 holes –£20 (£25)
Loc Grantham 2 miles

Blankney (1903)

Blankney, Lincoln
Tel (0526) 20263
Mem 400 100(L) 60(J) 100(5)
Sec IG McIntosh
Pro G Bradley (0526) 20202
Holes 18 L 6402 yds SSS 71
Recs Am–68 Pro–69
V'trs WD–U WE–M SOC
Fees £12 D–£16 (£20)
Loc 10 miles SE of Lincoln on B1188

Boston (1962)

Cowbridge, Horncastle Road, Boston PE22 7EL
Tel (0205) 362306
Mem 650 115(L) 46(J)
Sec DE Smith (0205) 350589

Pro TR Squires
Holes 18 L 5825 yds SSS 68
Recs Am–67 SG Wood
Pro–64 S Edwards (1989)
V'trs WD–U WE/ BH–H
Fees £12 (£18)
Loc 2 miles N of Boston on B1183

Burghley Park (1890)

St Martin's, Stamford PE9 3JX
Tel (0780) 53789
Mem 500 80(L) 80(J)
Sec PH Mulligan
Pro G Davies (0780) 62100
Holes 18 L 6133 yds SSS 69
Recs Am–65 PG Barker
Pro–70 B Thomson
V'trs WD–I or H WE/ BH–M SOC
Fees £18
Loc 1 mile S of Stamford, off A1 at roundabout

Canwick Park (1893)

Canwick Park, Washingborough Road, Lincoln
Tel (0522) 522166
Mem 576
Sec AC Hodgkinson (0526) 398978
Pro S Williamson (0522) 536870
Holes 18 L 6257 yds SSS 70
Recs Am–66 J Shelton
V'trs WD–U WE–M
Fees £8 (£12)

Carholme (1906)

Lincoln
Tel (0522) 523725
Mem 770
Sec G Robertshaw (0522) 525830
Pro G Leslie (0522) 536811
Holes 18 L 6114 yds SSS 69
Recs Am–69 R Taylor
V'trs U (exc Sun)
Fees On application
Loc Lincoln 1 mile

Gainsborough (1900)

Thonock, Gainsborough DN21 1PZ
Tel (0427) 613088
Mem 470
Sec DJ Garrison (Mgr)
Pro S Cooper
Holes 18 L 6551 yds SSS 71
Recs Am–66
V'trs U H WE/ BH–M SOC–WD
Fees £15 D–£20
Loc N of Gainsborough
Mis Floodlit driving range

Horncastle (1990)

West Ashby, Horncastle LN9 5PP
Tel (0507) 526800
Mem 125
Sec A Norton
Pro EC Wright
Holes 18 L 5772 yds SSS 68
V'trs U SOC
Fees £7.50 D–£12.50
Loc 1 mile from Horncastle, off A158
Mis Floodlit driving range

Lincoln (1891)

Lincoln
Tel	(042 771) 210
Mem	600
Sec	D Boag (042 771) 721
Pro	A Carter (042 771) 273
Holes	18 L 6438 yds SSS 71
Recs	Am–66 A Thain, P Taylor
	Pro–65 M James
V'trs	H WE–by appointment
Fees	£16 D–£20
Loc	12 miles W of Lincoln

Louth (1965)

Crowtree Lane, Louth LN11 9LJ
Tel	(0507) 602554
Mem	900
Sec	PC Bell (0507) 603681
Pro	AJ Blundell (0507) 604648
Holes	18 L 6477 yds SSS 71
Recs	Am–70 A Murray (1985),
	L Johnson (1986)
	Pro–69 C Hall (1989)
V'trs	U SOC–WD
Fees	£10 D–£12 (£12 D–£14) (1990)
Loc	Louth 1/2 mile

Market Rasen (1922)

Legsby Road, Market Rasen LN8 3DZ
Tel	(0673) 842319
Mem	550
Sec	E Hill
Pro	AM Chester (0673) 842416
Holes	18 L 6043 yds SSS 69
Recs	Am–66 C Osbourne (1990)
	Pro–65 S Bennett (1989)
V'trs	WD–I WE/ BH–M SOC
Fees	£12 D–£18
Loc	1 mile E of Market Rasen

Millfield (1985)

Laughterton, Lincoln LN1 2LB
Tel	(042 771) 255
Sec	P Guthrie
Holes	18 L 5973 yds SSS 69 9 hole
	Par 3 course
V'trs	U
Fees	£4 D–£6
Loc	12 miles W of Lincoln
Mis	Driving range

North Shore (1910)

North Shore Road, Skegness
PE25 1DN
Tel	(0754) 3298
Mem	525
Sec	RC Sykes (0754) 67280
Pro	J Cornelius (0754) 4822
Holes	18 L 6134 yds SSS 69
Recs	Am–71 G Hunter (1989)
V'trs	H SOC–WD
Fees	£17 (£22) (1990)
Loc	1 mile N of Skegness

RAF Waddington

Waddington, Lincoln LN5 9NB
Tel	(0522) 720271
Mem	70
Sec	Sgt A Rana (Ext 955)

Holes	18 L 5223 yds SSS 66
Recs	Am–68 T Graham (1987)
V'trs	By prior arrangement
Fees	£2
Loc	A607 Lincoln–Grantham road

Sandilands (1900)

Sandilands, Sutton-on-Sea LN12 2RJ
Tel	(0507) 41432
Mem	400
Sec	D Mumby (0507) 41617
Pro	D Vernon (0507) 41600
Holes	18 L 5995 yds SSS 69
Recs	Am–66 JR Payne
	Pro–63 FG Allott
V'trs	U SOC
Fees	£10 D–£15 (£15)
Loc	1 mile S of Sutton-on-Sea, off A52

Seacroft (1895)

Seacroft, Skegness PE25 3AU
Tel	(0754) 3020
Mem	340 190(L) 90(J)
Sec	HK Brader
Pro	R Lawie (0754) 69624
Holes	18 L 6478 yds SSS 71
Recs	Am–64 TH Bowman
	Pro–67 J Heib (1988)
V'trs	WD–U WE–XL before 11am
Fees	£18 (£25)
Loc	S boundary of Skegness

Sleaford (1905)

South Rauceby, Sleaford NG34 8PL
Tel	(052 98) 273
Mem	650
Sec	DBR Harris (0529) 303535
Pro	SD Harrison (052 98) 644
Holes	18 L 6443 yds SSS 71
Recs	Am–65 A Hare (1988)
V'trs	U H SOC–WD
Fees	£15 (£23)
Loc	1 mile W of Sleaford on A153

Spalding (1922)

Surfleet, Spalding PE11 4DG
Tel	(077 585) 234
Sec	WE Codling (077 585) 386
Pro	J Spencer (077 585) 474
Holes	18 L 5807 yds SSS 68
Recs	Am–65 G Palmer
	Pro–65 J Spencer
V'trs	U H SOC–Thurs
Fees	On application
Loc	4 miles N of Spalding, off A16

Stoke Rochford (1924)

Great North Rd, nr Grantham
Tel	(047 683) 275
Mem	515
Sec	JM Butler
Pro	A Dow (047 683) 218
Holes	18 L 6251 yds SSS 70
Recs	Am–65 A Hare, J Payne,
	M Wilson Pro–65 A Dow
V'trs	WE–U after 10.30am
Fees	On application
Loc	6 miles S of Grantham, at service station on A1

Sutton Bridge (1914)

New Road, Sutton Bridge
Tel	(0406) 350323 (Clubhouse)
Mem	340
Sec	KC Buckle (0945) 870455
Pro	R Wood (0406) 351080
Holes	9 L 5804 yds SSS 68
Recs	Pro–62 CJ Norton
V'trs	WD–H WE–NA
Fees	£15
Loc	Wisbech 8 miles

Woodhall Spa (1905)

Woodhall Spa LN10 6PU
Tel	(0526) 52511
Mem	450
Sec	SR Sharp
Pro	P Fixter (0526) 53229
Holes	18 L 6907 yds SSS 73
Recs	Am–68 FW Wood
	Pro–68 EB Williamson
V'trs	U-booking essential SOC
Fees	£18 (£25)
Loc	19 miles SE of Lincoln

Woodthorpe Hall (1986)

Woodthorpe, Alford LN13 0DD
Tel	(0507) 450294
Mem	210
Sec	PC Bell (Hon)
Holes	9 L 1990 yds SSS 59
V'trs	U
Fees	D–£4.50
Loc	3 1/2 miles from Alford, off B1371

London

Aquarius (1913)

Marmora Rd, Honor Oak,
London SE22
Tel	(081) 693 1626
Mem	400
Sec	PA Mutton
Pro	F Private
Holes	9 L 5034 yds SSS 65
Recs	Am–62 R Hare
	Pro–63 F Private
V'trs	M

Beckenham Place Park (1907)

Public
Beckenham Hill Road,
Beckenham SE6
Tel	(081) 650 2292
Pro	B Woodman (081) 658 5374
Holes	18 L 5722 yds SSS 68
Recs	Am–62 S Champion
	Pro–65 T Cotton
V'trs	WD–U WE–U after 2pm
Fees	£6.50 (£11) WE–booking fee
Mis	Braeside, Foxgrove and Beckenham Place Park Clubs play here

Brent Valley (1938)

Public
Church Road, Hanwell, London W7
Tel (081) 567 1287 (Bookings)
Sec P Bryant
Pro P Bryant
Holes 18 L 5426 yds SSS 66
Recs Am–65 S Harper (1985)
        Pro–61 R Green (1988)
V'trs U SOC
Fees £4 D–£6 (£5.50)

Bush Hill Park (1895)

Bush Hill, Winchmore Hill, London N21 2BU
Tel (081) 360 5738
Mem 665
Sec DJ Clark
Pro GW Low (081) 360 4103
Holes 18 L 5809 yds SSS 68
Recs Am–63 T Sheaff
        Pro–64 L Farmer
V'trs WD–U WE–M SOC
Fees £14

Chingford (1923)

Public
158 Station Road, Chingford, London E4
Tel (081) 529 2107
Pro R Gowers (081) 529 5708
Holes 18 L 6136 yds SS 70
Recs Am–65 P Barnes
        Pro–65 R Gowers
V'trs U
Fees £8
Mis Red coats must be worn

Dulwich & Sydenham Hill (1893)

Grange Lane, College Road, London SE21 7LH
Tel (081) 693 3961
Mem 850
Sec B Harmer
Pro D Baillie (081) 693 8491
Holes 18 L 6051 yds SSS 69
Recs Am–62 T Bridle
        Pro–63 LF Rowe
V'trs WD–I WE/ BH–M SOC
Fees £16

Eltham Warren (1890)

Bexley Road, Eltham, London SE9 2PE
Tel (081) 850 1166
Mem 400
Sec DJ Clare (081) 850 4477
Pro IA Coleman (081) 859 7909
Holes 9 L 5840 yds SSS 68
Recs Am–66 G Janes
        Pro–68 R Taylor
V'trs WD–I WE/ BH–M SOC
Fees £20

Finchley (1929)

Nether Court, Frith Lane, London NW7 1PU
Tel (081) 346 2436
Mem 500
Sec JR Pearce
Pro D Brown (081) 346 5086
Holes 18 L 6411 yds SSS 71
Recs Am–65 D Chatterton
        Pro–67 T Moore
V'trs WD–U WE–pm only SOC
Fees £26 (£36)

Hampstead (1893)

Winnington Road, London N2 0TU
Tel (081) 455 0203
Mem 533
Sec KF Young
Pro PJ Brown (081) 455 7089
Holes 9 L 5812 yds SSS 68
Recs Am–66 RDA Smith
        Pro–65 D Stevenson
V'trs WD/ WE–H
Fees £20 D–£25 (£28)

Hendon (1900)

Sanders Lane, Devonshire Road, London NW7 1DG
Tel (081) 346 6023
Mem 525
Sec DE Cooper
Pro S Murray (081) 346 8990
Holes 18 L 6253 yds SSS 70
Recs Am–68 AL MacLeod
        Pro–66 SWT Murray
V'trs WD–U WE/ BH–bookings SOC
Fees £22 D–£30 (£33)

Highgate (1904)

Denewood Road, Highgate, London N6 4AH
Tel (081) 340 1906
Fax (081) 348 9152
Mem 700
Sec J Zuill (081) 340 3745
Pro R Turner (081) 340 5467
Holes 18 L 5964 yds SSS 69
Recs Am–66 D Kingsman, P Bax
        Pro–66 I Martin (1987)
V'trs WD–U exc Wed–NA WE/ BH–M SOC
Fees £27

London Scottish (1865)

Windmill Enclosure, Wimbledon Common, London SW19 5NQ
Tel (081) 788 0135
Mem 250
Sec J Johnson (081) 789 7517
Holes Plays over Wimbledon Common course

Mill Hill (1925)

100 Barnet Way, Mill Hill, London NW7 3AL
Tel (081) 959 2282
Mem 450
Sec FH Scott (081) 959 2339
Pro A Daniel (081) 959 7261

Holes 18 L 6309 yds SSS 70
Recs Am–65 H Aarons
        Pro–67 J Hudson
V'trs WD–U H WE/ BH–U H after 11.30am SOC
Fees £16 (£25)

Muswell Hill (1893)

Rhodes Avenue, Wood Green, London N22 4UT
Tel (081) 888 2044
Mem 500
Sec JAB Connors (081) 888 1764
Pro IB Roberts (081) 888 8046
Holes 18 L 6474 yds SSS 71
Recs Am–67 PJ Montague
        Pro–65 H Weetman
V'trs WD–U WE–book with Pro SOC
Fees With h'cap–£20 (£30) Without h'cap–£25

North Middlesex (1928)

The Manor House, Friern Barnet Lane, London N20 0NL
Tel (081) 445 1732
Mem 560
Sec MC Reding (Mgr) (081) 445 1604
Pro ASR Roberts (081) 445 3060
Holes 18 L 5611 yds SSS 67
Recs Am–65 M Cohen
        Pro–64 S Levermore
V'trs WD–I WE/ BH–restricted
Fees £15 (£22)

Picketts Lock (1973)

Public
Picketts Lock Lane, Edmonton, London N9 0AS
Tel (081) 803 3611
Pro RG Gerken
Holes 9 L 2496 yds SSS 64
Recs Am–31 M Yates
        Pro–30 JTB Rayner
V'trs WD–U WE–booking advisable
Fees £3.50 (£4.50)
Mis Floodlit driving range

Richmond Park (1923)

Public
Roehampton Gate, Richmond Park, London SW15 5JR
Tel (081) 876 3205/ 1795
Pro J Slinger
Holes Dukes 18 L 5940 yds SSS 68
        Princes 18 L 5969 yds SSS 68
V'trs U SOC
Fees £5.50 (£8)
Mis Centurion and White Lodge clubs play here

Roehampton (1901)

Roehampton Lane, London SW15 5LR
Tel (081) 876 1621
Fax (081) 392 2386
Mem 900
Sec M Yates (081) 876 5505
Pro AL Scott (081) 876 3858

For list of abbreviations see page 487.

Holes　18 L 6046 yds SSS 69
Recs　Am–67 AL Scott Pro–62 H Stott
V'trs　WD–Introduced by member
　　　　WE–M

Royal Blackheath (1608)

Court Road, Eltham, London SE9 5AF
Tel　　(081) 850 1795
Mem　700
Sec　　Wg Cdr R Barriball RAF (Rtd)
Pro　　I McGregor (081) 850 1763
Holes　18 L 6209 yds SSS 70
Recs　Am–66 DM Woolmer
　　　　Pro–66 WC Thomas
V'trs　WD–I WE/ BH–M SOC
Fees　£25

Royal Epping Forest (1888)

Public
Forest Approach, Station Road,
Chingford, London E4 7AZ
Tel　　(081) 529 6407
Mem　296 50(L) 25(J)
Sec　　T Flack (081) 529 2195
Pro　　R Gowers (081) 529 5708
Holes　18 L 6220 yds SSS 70
Recs　Am–68 A Johns
　　　　Pro–65 R Gowers
V'trs　WE–booked times
Fees　£5.50 (£8)
Mis　　Red coats or trousers
　　　　compulsory

Royal Wimbledon (1865)

29 Camp Road, Wimbledon, London
SW19 4UW
Tel　　(081) 946 2125
Mem　800
Sec　　Maj. GE Jones
Pro　　H Boyle (081) 946 4606
Holes　18 L 6343 yds SSS 70
Recs　Am–66 JFM Connolly
　　　　Pro–71 R Burton
V'trs　NA

Shooter's Hill (1903)

Lowood, Eaglesfield Road, London
SE18 3DA
Tel　　(081) 854 1216
Mem　310 60(L) 31(J) 265(5)
Sec　　BR Adams (081) 854 6368
Pro　　M Ridge (081) 854 0073
Holes　18 L 5736 yds SSS 68
Recs　Am–63 M Holland
　　　　Pro–62 M Parker
V'trs　WD–I WE/ BH–M SOC–Tues &
　　　　Thurs only
Fees　£20

South Herts (1899)

Totteridge Lane, London N20 8QU
Tel　　(081) 445 0117
Mem　800
Sec　　AA Dogan (081) 445 2035
Pro　　RS Livingston (081) 445 4633
Holes　18 L 6470 yds SSS 71
　　　　9 L 1581 yds
Recs　Am–67 R Neil (1964)
　　　　Pro–66 D Thomas (1966)
V'trs　WD–IH WE/ BH–M
Fees　On application

Trent Park (1973)

Public
Bramley Road, Southgate, London N14
Tel　　(081) 366 7432
Pro　　C Easton
Holes　18 L 6008 yds SSS 69
Recs　Am–65 M Skinner (1989)
　　　　Pro–64 V Law (1979)
V'trs　WD–U SOC WE–NA before
　　　　11am
Fees　£4.50 (£6)

Wanstead (1893)

Wanstead, London E11 2LW
Tel　　(081) 989 0604
Mem　650
Sec　　K Jones (081) 989 3938
Pro　　G Jacom (081) 989 9876
Holes　18 L 6262 yds SSS 69
Recs　Am–62 P Sullivan
　　　　Pro–64 N Coles, P Brown
V'trs　WD–I WE/ BH–M
Fees　£20

West Essex (1900)

Bury Road, Stewardstonebury,
Chingford, London E4 7QL
Tel　　(081) 529 0928
Mem　645
Sec　　PH Galley MBE (081) 529 7558
Pro　　C Cox (081) 529 4367
Holes　18 L 6317 yds SSS 70
Recs　Am–66 KG Budd
　　　　Pro–EE Whitcombe
V'trs　WD–UH WE/ BH–MH
　　　　SOC–Mon/ Wed/ Fri
Fees　£15 D–£18

Wimbledon Common (1908)

19 Camp Road, Wimbledon
Common, London SW19 4UW
Tel　　(081) 946 0294
Mem　250
Sec　　BK Cox (081) 946 7571
Pro　　JS Jukes
Holes　18 L 5438 yds SSS 66
Recs　Am–65 T Mahon, MC Ball
　　　　Pro–64 JS Jukes
V'trs　WD–U WE–M Sun pm BH–NA
Fees　£12.50
Mis　　Pillarbox red outer garment
　　　　must be worn. London Scottish
　　　　play here

Wimbledon Park (1898)

Home Park Road, London SW19
Tel　　(081) 946 1002
Mem　580
Sec　　MK Hale (081) 946 1250
Pro　　D Wingrove (081) 946 4053
Holes　18 L 5465 yds SSS 66
Recs　Am–61 SJ Bennett, B King
　　　　Pro–60 M Gerrard
V'trs　WD–H I WE/ BH–after 3pm
　　　　SOC
Fees　D–£25 (£25)

Manchester (Greater)

Altrincham Municipal

Public
Stockport Road, Timperley,
Altrincham
Tel　　(061) 928 0761
Pro　　R West
Holes　18 L 6204 yds SSS 69
Recs　Am–67
　　　　Pro–67
V'trs　U
Fees　£3 (£4.50)
Loc　　9 miles SW of Manchester

Ashton-on–Mersey (1898)

Church Lane, Sale, Cheshire
M33 5QQ
Tel　　(061) 973 3220
Mem　180 70(L) 40(J) 60(5)
Sec　　AO Williams
Pro　　P Wagstaff (061) 962 3727
Holes　9 L 3073 yds SSS 69
Recs　Am–68 B Armitage, M Gleave
　　　　Pro–67 R Williamson, D Cooper
V'trs　WD–U H exc Tues–NA before
　　　　3pm WE–M
Fees　£12
Loc　　5 miles W of Manchester

Ashton-under-Lyne (1913)

Gorsey Way, Hurst, Ashton-under-
Lyne
Tel　　(061) 330 1537
Mem　450
Sec　　G Musgrave (061) 339 8655
Pro　　C Boyle (061) 308 2095
Holes　18 L 6209 yds SSS 70
Recs　Am–68
V'trs　WD–U WE/ BH–M SOC
Fees　£15
Loc　　8 miles E of Manchester

Avro (1980)

British Aerospace, Woodford
Tel　　(061) 439 5050
Mem　400
Sec　　AP Johnson (0625) 874402
Holes　9 L 5735 yds SSS 68
Recs　Am–72 R Wheeler (1989)
V'trs　M
Fees　£4 (£6)

Beacon Park (1982)

Public
Beacon Lane, Dalton, Up Holland,
Wigan WN8 7RU
Tel　　(0695) 622700
Sec　　JC McIlroy (Hon)
Pro　　R Peters
Holes　18 L 5927 yds SSS 69
Recs　Am–68 D Parkin, I Donaldson
V'trs　U
Fees　£2.95 (£3.95)
Loc　　Nr Ashurst Beacon and M58/
　　　　M6
Mis　　Beacon Club plays here

Blackley (1907)

Victoria Avenue, Manchester
M9 2HW
Tel	(061) 643 2980
Mem	500
Sec	CB Leggott (061) 643 4116
Pro	M Barton (061) 643 3912
Holes	18 L 6235 yds SSS 70
Recs	Am–65 D Royle
	Pro–66 J Nixon
V'trs	WD–U WE–M
Fees	£12
Loc	N Manchester area

Bolton (1891)

Lostock Park, Bolton BL6 4AJ
Tel	(0204) 43278
Mem	600
Sec	H Cook (0204) 43067
Pro	R Longworth (0204) 43073
Holes	18 L 6215 yds SSS 70
Recs	Am–66 JB Hope, DE Roocroft
	Pro–67 WSM Rooke
V'trs	U SOC
Fees	WD exc Wed–£22 Wed/ WE/ BH–£26
Loc	3½ miles W of Bolton. M61 Horwich exit 1½ miles

Bolton Municipal (1931)

Public
Links Road, Chorley New Road,
Bolton BL6 4AF
Tel	(0204) 42336
Pro	AK Holland
Holes	18 L 6012 yds SSS 69
Recs	Am–67 PK Abbott
	Pro–68 L Alamby
V'trs	U SOC–WD
Fees	£3.50 (£4.50)
Loc	A673, 3 miles W of Bolton. M61 Junction 6
Mis	Regent Park Club plays here

Bolton Old Links (1891)

Chorley Old Road, Montserrat,
Bolton BL1 5SU
Tel	(0204) 40050
Mem	750
Sec	E Monaghan (0204) 42307
Pro	P Horridge (0204) 43089
Holes	18 L 6406 yds SSS 72
Recs	Am–66 L Mooney (1981)
	Pro–64 J Cheetham (1990)
V'trs	U H exc comp Sats SOC
Fees	£20 (£25)
Loc	3 miles NW of Bolton on B6226

Brackley Municipal (1977)

Public
Bullows Road, Little Hulton
Tel	(061) 790 6076
Pro	S Lomax (Mgr)
Holes	9 L 3003 yds SSS 69
V'trs	U
Fees	£2.30 (£3) 9 holes
Loc	2 miles from Walkden, off A6

Bramall Park (1894)

20 Manor Road, Bramhall, Stockport
SK7 6NW
Tel	(061) 485 3119
Mem	715
Sec	JC O'Shea
Pro	M Proffit (061) 485 2205
Holes	18 L 6214 yds SSS 70
Recs	Am–68 B Steele
V'trs	I
Fees	£15 (£20)
Loc	8 miles S of Manchester. A6 to Bramhall Lane A5102. Turn right at Carrwood Road

Bramhall (1905)

Ladythorn Road, Bramhall, Stockport
SK7 2EY
Tel	(061) 439 4057
Mem	300 155(L) 85(J) 100(5)
Sec	F Chadfield (061) 439 4393
Pro	B Nield (061) 439 1171
Holes	18 L 6300 yds SSS 70
Recs	Am–64 AE Hill (1987)
	Pro–66 I Higby (1987)
V'trs	U exc Thurs SOC
Fees	D–£20 (D–£30)
Loc	Stockport

Breightmet (1911)

Red Bridge, Ainsworth, nr Bolton
Tel	(0204) 27381
Mem	200
Sec	R Weir
Holes	9 L 6416 yds SSS 71
Recs	Am–69 G Stanley (1982)
	Pro–68 P Alliss (1971)
V'trs	WE–NA SOC–WD
Fees	£8 (£10)
Loc	3 miles on Bury side

Brookdale (1905)

Woodhouses, Failsworth
Tel	(061) 681 4534
Mem	650
Sec	G Glass (061) 681 8996
Pro	P Devalle (061) 681 2655
Holes	18 L 6040 yds SSS 68
Recs	Am–65 G Lever
V'trs	U SOC–WD
Fees	£8 (£12)
Loc	5 miles N of Manchester

Bury (1890)

Unsworth Hall, Blackford Bridge,
Bury BL9 9TJ
Tel	(061) 766 4897
Mem	600
Sec	JP Meikle
Pro	M Peel
Holes	18 L 5961 yds SSS 69
Recs	Am–66 PD Hilton
	Pro–PWT Evans
V'trs	U SOC
Fees	£15 (£20)
Loc	A56, 5 miles N of Manchester. 3 miles N of M62 Junction 17

Castle Hawk (1975)

Heywood Road, Castleton, Rochdale
OL11 3BY
Tel	(0706) 40841
Fax	(0706) 860587
Mem	200
Sec	A Kershaw
Pro	M Vipond
Holes	27 L 5160 yds SSS 65
Recs	Am–57 R Baker
	Pro–56 G Bond
V'trs	U SOC
Fees	£4 (£5)
Loc	Castleton Station 1 mile. M62 Junction 20

Cheadle (1885)

Shiers Drive, Cheadle SK8 1HW
Tel	(061) 428 2160
Mem	350
Sec	PP Webster
Pro	M Redrup (061) 428 9878
Holes	9 L 5006 yds SSS 65
Recs	Am–66 BR Woodhouse (1990)
V'trs	H or I exc Tues & Sat–NA SOC
Fees	D–£10 (£12)
Loc	1 mile S of Cheadle. M63 Junction 11, 2 miles

Chorlton-cum-Hardy (1903)

Barlow Hall, Manchester M21 2JJ
Tel	(061) 881 3139
Mem	750
Sec	Mrs HM Stuart (061) 881 5830
Pro	D Screeton (061) 881 9911
Holes	18 L 6003 metres SSS 69
Recs	Am–63 JR Berry
	Pro–65 FS Boobyer
V'trs	U H SOC–Thurs
Fees	£15 (£17)
Loc	4 miles S of Manchester (A5103/ A5145)

Crompton & Royton (1913)

High Barn, Royton, Oldham OL2 6RW
Tel	(061) 624 2154
Mem	620
Sec	T Donovan (061) 624 0986
Pro	DA Melling
Holes	18 L 6212 yds SSS 70
Recs	Am–65 JA Osbaldeston
	Pro–65 D Durnian
V'trs	U SOC–WD
Fees	£14 (£18)
Loc	Oldham 3 miles

Davenport (1913)

Middlewood Road, Poynton,
Stockport
Tel	(0625) 877321
Mem	600
Sec	TD Swindells (0625) 876951
Pro	W Harris (0625) 877319
Holes	18 L 6066 yds SSS 69
Recs	Am–68 C Banfield
	Pro–67 B Evans
V'trs	U exc Sat–NA
Fees	£12 (£18)
Loc	5 miles S of Stockport

Davyhulme Park (1910)

Gleneagles Road, Davyhulme,
Manchester M31 2SA
Tel   (061) 748 2856
Mem   600
Sec   HA Langworthy (061) 748 2260
Pro   H Lewis (061) 748 3931
Holes   18 L 6237 yds SSS 70
Recs   Am–67 TF Sharp, B Connor
            Pro–68 KG Geddes, D Rees
V'trs   WD–H exc Wed–NA Sat–NA
            Sun–M SOC
Fees   £16 (£20) SOC–£17-20
Loc   7 miles SW of Manchester

Deane (1906)

Off Junction Road, Deane, Bolton
BL3 4NB
Tel   (0204) 61944
Mem   300
Sec   P Flaxman (0204) 651808
Pro   D Martindale
Holes   18 L 5583 yds SSS 67
Recs   Am–62 N Hazzleton
V'trs   WD–U WE–Restricted
Fees   £10 (£15)
Loc   2 miles W of Bolton. 1mile from
            M61 Junction 5

Denton (1909)

Manchester Road, Denton,
Manchester M34 2NU
Tel   (061) 336 3218
Mem   520
Sec   R Wickham
Pro   R Vere (061) 336 2070
Holes   18 L 6290 yds SSS 70
Recs   Pro–68 D Cooper, S Scanlon,
            D Durnian
V'trs   WD–U WE/ BH–NA before
            3pm SOC
Fees   £15 (£18)
Loc   5 miles SE of Manchester

Didsbury (1891)

Ford Lane, Northenden, Manchester
M22 4NQ
Tel   (061) 998 9278
Mem   760
Sec   B Turnbull (Sec/ Mgr)
Pro   P Barber (061) 998 2811
Holes   18 L 6273 yds SSS 70
Recs   Am–65 RI Walker
V'trs   WD–U H exc 12-2pm–NA
            WE–M
Fees   £13 (£15)
Loc   6 miles S of Manchester

Disley (1889)

Stanley Hall Lane, Disley, Stockport
Tel   (0663) 62071
Mem   600
Sec   JA Lomas (Hon)
Pro   AG Esplin (0663) 62884
Holes   18 L 6015 yds SSS 69
Recs   Am–68 A Peck
            Pro–63 B Charles
V'trs   Wed-Fri/ BH–NA
Fees   £10 (£12)
Loc   6 miles S of Stockport

Dukinfield (1913)

Yew Tree Lane, Dukinfield
Tel   (061) 338 2340
Mem   225 50(L) 45(J)
Sec   KP Parker (061) 338 2669
Holes   16 L 5544 yds SSS 67
Recs   Am–69 S Woolley
V'trs   WD–U exc Wed WE–M
Fees   £10.50
Loc   6 miles E of Manchester

Dunham Forest G & CC (1961)

Oldfield Lane, Altrincham WA14 4TY
Tel   (061) 928 2605
Mem   600
Sec   Mrs S Klaus
Pro   I Wrigley (061) 928 2727
Holes   18 L 6636 yds SSS 72
V'trs   WD–U WE/ BH–M SOC exc
            12.45–1.45pm
Fees   £20 (£25)
Loc   1 mile SW of Altrincham

Dunscar (1908)

Longworth Lane, Bromley Cross,
Bolton BL7 9QY
Tel   (0204) 53321
Mem   600
Sec   TM Yates (0204) 51090
Pro   G Treadgold (0204) 592992
Holes   18 L 5968 yds SSS 69
Recs   Am–64 JW Smethurst
            Pro–66 W Slater
V'trs   WD–U WE–restricted
Fees   £15 (£20)
Loc   3 miles N of Bolton, off A666

Ellesmere (1913)

Old Clough Lane, Worsley, nr
Manchester M28 5HZ
Tel   (061) 790 2122
Mem   330 80(L) 75(J) 50(5)
Sec   AC Kay
Pro   E McDonald (061) 790 8591
Holes   18 L 5957 yds SSS 69
Recs   Am–67 JA Pugh Pro–66 G Weir
V'trs   U exc comp days (recognised
            club members, check first with
            Pro) SOC–WD
Fees   £12 (£16)
Loc   6 miles W of Manchester, nr
            junction of M62/ A580

Fairfield Golf & Sailing Club (1892)

Booth Road, Audenshaw,
Manchester M34 5GA
Tel   (061) 370 1641
Mem   550
Sec   J Humphries (061) 336 3950
Pro   DM Butler (061) 370 2292
Holes   18 L 5664 yds SSS 68
Recs   Am–65 PW Wrigley,
            ARS Pownell
V'trs   WD–U WE–NA before noon
            SOC–WD
Fees   £12 (£15)
Loc   East boundary (A635)

Flixton (1893)

Church Road, Flixton, Manchester
Tel   (061) 748 2116 (Clubhouse)
            748 7545 (Catering/ SOC)
Mem   400
Sec   JG Frankland (061) 747 0296
Pro   R Ling (061) 746 7160
Holes   9 L 6410 yds SSS 71
Recs   Am–63 MJ Wallwork (1988)
            Pro–65 P Reeves (1985)
V'trs   WD–U WE/ BH–M
Fees   £15
Loc   6 miles SW of Manchester on
            B5213

Gathurst (1913)

Miles Lane, Shevington, nr Wigan
WN6 8EW
Tel   (025 75) 2861
Mem   300
Sec   J Clarke (025 75) 2432
Pro   D Clarke (025 75) 4909
Holes   9 L 6308 yds SSS 70
Recs   Am–67 S Ainscough
            Pro–66 D Clarke
V'trs   WD–U before 5pm WE/ BH/
            Wed–M SOC–WD
Fees   £10
Loc   4 miles W of Wigan. 1 mile S of
            M6 Junction 27

Gatley (1911)

Waterfall Farm, Styal Road, Heald
Green, Cheadle SK8 3TW
Tel   (061) 437 2091
Mem   400
Sec   P Hannam
Pro   S Crake (061) 436 2830
Holes   9 L 5934 yds SSS 68
Recs   Am–67 M Hoyland
            Pro–63 C Timperley
V'trs   WE/ Tues–NA Other days-by
            prior arrangement with Sec
Fees   £10
Loc   7 miles S of Manchester.
            Manchester Airport 2 miles

Great Lever & Farnworth

Lever Edge Lane, Bolton
Tel   (0204) 62582
Mem   470
Sec   PJ Holt (0204) 72550
Holes   18 L 5859 yds SSS 69
Recs   Am–67 D Barr
            Pro–65 SC Evans
V'trs   U
Fees   £9 (£12.50)
Loc   Bolton 1 1/2 miles

Greenmount (1920)

Greenmount, nr Bury
Tel   (020 488) 3712
Mem   180
Sec   HJ Billingham (020 488) 3401
Holes   9 L 4920 yds SSS 64
Recs   Am–62 G Dalziel
V'trs   WD–U exc Tues WE–M
Fees   £8
Loc   3 miles N of Bury

For list of abbreviations see page 487.

Haigh Hall (1972)

Public
**Haigh Hall Country Park, Haigh,
Wigan WN2 1PE**
Tel   (0942) 833337 (Clubhouse)
Pro   I Lee (0942) 831107
Holes 18 L 6423 yds SSS 71
Recs Am–67 J Silcock (1987)
        Pro–66 K Waters (1988)
V'trs U
Fees £4 (£6)
Loc 2 miles NW of Wigan. M6
        Junction 27. M61 Junction 6

Hale (1903)

Rappax Road, Hale WA15 0NU
Tel   (061) 980 4225
Mem 300
Sec   RV Murphy
Pro   J Jackson (061) 904 0835
Holes 9 L 5780 yds SSS 68
Recs Pro–65 D Durnian
V'trs WD–U exc Thurs–NA before
        5pm WE/ BH–M SOC
Fees £14
Loc 2 miles SE of Altrincham

Harwood (1926)

**'Springfield', Roading Brook Road,
Bolton BL2 5HT**
Tel   (0204) 22878
Mem 360
Sec   JS Fairhurst (0204) 28028
Pro   MW Evans (0204) 398472
Holes 9 L 5960 yds SSS 69
Recs Am–67 PM Lay, N Stirling
V'trs WD–U WE–M SOC
Fees £10
Loc Harwood, 4 miles NE of Bolton

Hazel Grove (1912)

**Club House, Hazel Grove, nr
Stockport SK7 6LU**
Tel   (061) 483 3217
Mem 550
Sec   HAG Carlisle (061) 483 3978
Pro   ME Hill (061) 483 7272
Holes 18 L 6300 yds SSS 70
Recs Am–65 D Parkin
        Pro–67 M Slater
V'trs U
Fees £22.50 (£27.50)
Loc 3 miles S of Stockport

Heaton Moor (1892)

Heaton Mersey, Stockport
Tel   (061) 432 2134
Mem 350
Sec   AA Gibbon (061) 432 6458
Pro   CR Loydall (061) 432 0846
Holes 18 L 5876 yds SSS 68
Recs Am–66 D Howorth
        Pro–66 D Cooper
V'trs U
Fees £10 (£14)
Loc Greater Manchester

Heaton Park (1912)

Public
**Heaton Park, Prestwich, Manchester
M25 5SW**
Tel   (061) 798 0295
Pro   J Pennington
Holes 18 L 5849 yds SSS 68
Recs Am–66 J Griffiths (1986),
        S Pilling (1988)
        Pro–65 AP Thomson, B Evans,
        I Collins, M Gray
V'trs U
Fees £4 (£6)
Loc N Manchester via M62 and
        M66 to Middleton Road

Hindley Hall (1905)

**Hall Lane, Hindley, Wigan
WN2 2SQ**
Tel   (0942) 55131
Mem 430
Sec   R Bell (0942) 58356
Pro   S Yates (0942) 55991
Holes 18 L 5840 yds SSS 68
Recs Am–63 JB Dickinson
        Pro–65
V'trs I SOC
Fees £18 (£20)
Loc 2¹/₂ miles S of Wigan. M61
        Junction 6

Horwich (1895)

Victoria Road, Horwich BL6 5PH
Tel   (0204) 696980
Mem 200
Sec   GR Sharp (0204) 696298
Holes 9 L 5404 yds SSS 67
Recs Am–64 J Farrimond
V'trs M SOC–WD
Loc 5 miles W of Bolton

Houldsworth (1910)

**Longford Road West, Higher
Levenshulme, Manchester
M19 3JW**
Tel   (061) 224 5055
Mem 300
Sec   JB Hogg (061) 336 5044
Pro   David Naylor (061) 224 4571
Holes 18 L 6078 yds SSS 69
Recs Am–67 R Arnold
        Pro–63 D Vaughan
V'trs U SOC
Fees £9 (£12)
Loc 4 miles S of Manchester

Leigh (1906)

**Kenyon Hall, Culcheth, Warrington
WA3 4BG**
Tel   (0925) 763130
Mem 700
Sec   GD Riley (0925) 762943
Pro   A Baguley (0925) 762013
Holes 18 L 5892 yds SSS 68
Recs Am–64 J Critchley
        Pro–65 P Allan (1990)
V'trs U H SOC
Fees £17 (£22)
Loc At Culcheth

Lowes Park (1914)

Hill Top, Walmersley, Bury BL9 6SU
Tel   (061) 764 1231
Mem 250
Sec   E Brierley (0706) 67331
Holes 9 L 6043 yds SSS 69
Recs Am–69 MJ Bailey (1984)
V'trs WD–U exc Wed–NA Sat comp
        days–NA Sun-by appointment
Fees WD–£7 Sun–£10
Loc 2 miles NE of Bury, off A56

Manchester (1882)

**Hopwood Cottage, Rochdale Road,
Middleton, Manchester M24 2QP**
Tel   (061) 643 2718
Fax   (061) 643 2472
Mem 600
Sec   KG Flett (061) 643 3202
Pro   B Connor (061) 643 2638
Holes 18 L 6450 yds SSS 72
Recs Am–66 RE Tattersall, M Russell
        Pro–65 I Mosey, D Cooper
V'trs WD–H WE–NA
Fees D–£23 (£30)
Loc 7 miles N of Manchester. M62
        Junction 20

Marland (1928)

Public
Springfield Park, Rochdale
Tel   (0706) 49801
Pro   D Wills
Holes 18 L 5209 yds SSS 66
Recs Am–68 B Walsh
        Pro–67 ME Hill
V'trs U
Fees £3.50 (£4.50)
Loc W boundary of Rochdale
        (A58). M62 Junctions 19/ 20,
        2 miles

Marple (1892)

**Hawk Green, Marple, Stockport
SK6 7EL**
Tel   (061) 427 2311
Mem 300 70(L) 60(J) 30(5)
Sec   M Gilbert (061) 427 6364
Pro   I Scott (061) 449 0690
Holes 18 L 5506 yds SSS 67
Recs Am–66 T Christie (1984)
V'trs WD–U exc Thurs–NA WE/
        BH–M SOC
Fees £11 (£13)
Loc 2 miles from High Lane North,
        off A6

Mellor & Townscliffe (1894)

**Tarden, Gibb Lane, Mellor,
nr Stockport SK6 5NA**
Tel   (061) 427 2208
Mem 470
Sec   K Bounds
Pro   MJ Williams (061) 427 5759
Holes 18 L 5939 yds SSS 69
Recs Am–67 CW Axon, MG Senior,
        GD Williams. Pro–64 MJ Slater
V'trs WD–U WE–M SOC
Fees £10 (£15)
Loc 7 miles SE of Stockport

North Manchester (1894)

Rhodes House, Manchester Old Road,
Middleton, Manchester M24 4PE
Tel   (061) 643 2941
Mem   300 60(L) 38(J) 80(5)
Sec   J Fallon (061) 643 9033
Pro   PJ Lunt (061) 643 7094
Holes 18 L 6542 yds SSS 72
Recs   Am–66 J Cheetham
        Pro–66 G Furey
V'trs   U
Fees   £16 (£25)
Loc   5 miles N of Manchester. M62
        Junction 18

Northenden (1913)

Palatine Road, Manchester M22 4FR
Tel   (061) 998 4738
Mem   700
Sec   JM Fleet (Mgr) CR Rankin
        (Hon)
Pro   WJ McColl (061) 945 3386
Holes 18 L 6435 yds SSS 71
Recs   Am–67 JEB Waddell
        Pro–64 D Durnian
V'trs   U SOC
Fees   £15 (£20)
Loc   5 miles S of Manchester

Old Manchester (1818)

Tel   (061) 766 4157
Mem   60
Sec   PT Goodall
Holes Club without a course

Oldham (1892)

Lees New Road, Oldham
Tel   (061) 624 4986
Mem   300 45(L) 35(J)
Sec   BC Heginbotham (0457)
        876326
Pro   A Laverty (061) 626 8346
Holes 18 L 5045 yds SSS 65
Recs   Am–66 D Maloney (1987)
        Pro–65 E Smith
V'trs   U SOC–WD
Fees   £8 (£10)
Loc   Off Oldham-Stalybridge road

Pike Fold (1909)

Cooper Lane, Victoria Avenue,
Blackley, Manchester M9 2QQ
Tel   (061) 740 1136
Mem   200
Sec   GVW Kendell
Holes 9 L 5789 yds SSS 68
Recs   Am–66 P Bradley (1989)
        Pro–66 JE Wiggett
V'trs   WD–U WE/ BH–M SOC
Fees   D–£6
Loc   5 miles N of Manchester. M62
        Junction 18, 2 miles

Prestwich (1908)

Hilton Lane, Prestwich
Tel   (061) 773 2544
Mem   470
Sec   WV Trees (061) 773 4578
Pro   GP Coope

Holes 18 L 4522 yds SSS 63
Recs   Am–60 J Lunosz
V'trs   WD–H WE–NA before 3pm
        SOC
Fees   £10 (£12)
Loc   2½ miles N of Manchester

Reddish Vale (1912)

Southcliffe, Reddish, Stockport
SK5 7EE
Tel   (061) 480 2359
Mem   550
Sec   JL Blakey (061) 432 6544
Pro   RA Brown (061) 480 3824
Holes 18 L 6086 yds SSS 69
Recs   Am–64 KR Gorton, D Young
        Pro–67 R Williamson
V'trs   WD–U exc 12.30-1.30pm–M
        WE–M SOC
Fees   £15
Loc   1 mile NNE of Stockport

Ringway (1909)

Hale Mount, Hale Barns, Altrincham
WA15 8SW
Tel   (061) 904 9609
Mem   345 165(L) 41(J) 25(5)
Sec   D Wright (061) 980 2630
Pro   N Ryan (061) 980 8432
Holes 18 L 6494 yds SSS 71
Recs   Am–67 RE Preston
V'trs   Tues–NA before 3pm Fri–M
        Sun–NA before 11am SOC
Fees   £20 (£25)
Loc   8 miles S of Manchester off
        M56 Junction 6 (A538)

Rochdale (1888)

Edenfield Road, Bagslate, Rochdale
OL11 5YR
Tel   (0706) 46024 (Clubhouse)
Mem   625
Sec   S Cockcroft (0706) 43818
Pro   A Laverty (0706) 522104
Holes 18 L 6002 yds SSS 69
Recs   Am–66 J Hawkard, R Kershaw,
        B Crabtree
        Pro–65 G Hammond
V'trs   U
Fees   £16 (£20)
Loc   M62 Junction 20, 3 miles on
        A680

Romiley (1897)

Goosehouse Green, Romiley,
Stockport SK6 4LJ
Tel   (061) 430 2392
Mem   750
Sec   F Beard (061) 430 7257
Pro   G Butler (061) 430 7122
Holes 18 L 6335 yds SSS 70
Recs   Am–64 N Ryan
        Pro–67 D Roberts
V'trs   U SOC
Fees   £16 (£20)
Loc   Station ¾ mile

Saddleworth (1904)

Mountain Ash, Uppermill,
nr Oldham, Lancs
Tel   (0457) 873653
Mem   660
Sec   HA Morgan
Pro   ET Shard
Holes 18 L 5976 yds SSS 69
Recs   Am–64 RC Hughes
        Pro–69 M Melling, A Gillies
V'trs   U
Fees   £12.50 (£16)
Loc   5 miles E of Oldham
Mis   Buggy for hire

Sale (1913)

Sale Lodge, Golf Road, Sale M33 2LU
Tel   (061) 973 3404
Mem   580
Sec   J Blair (061) 973 1638
Pro   M Lake (061) 973 1730
Holes 18 L 6351 yds SSS 70
Recs   Am–67 JR Barlow
V'trs   U SOC–WD
Fees   £13 (£20)

Stamford (1900)

Oakfield House, Huddersfield Road,
Stalybridge SK15 3PY
Tel   (04575) 2126
Mem   500
Sec   FE Rowles
Pro   B Badger (04575) 4829
Holes 18 L 5524 yds SSS 67
Recs   Am–66 H Fletcher
V'trs   WD–U WE comp days–after
        2.30pm SOC–WD
Fees   £8 (£12.50)
Loc   NE boundary of Stalybridge on
        B6175

Stand (1904)

The Dales, Ashbourne Grove,
Whitefield, Manchester M25 7NL
Tel   (061) 766 2388
Mem   700
Sec   EB Taylor (061) 766 3197
Pro   M Dance (061) 766 2214
Holes 18 L 6411 yds SSS 71
Recs   Am–67 J Seddon (1990)
        Pro–67 PM Eales
V'trs   U SOC–WD
Fees   £18 (£20)
Loc   5 miles N of Manchester. M62
        Junction 17

Stockport (1906)

Offerton Road, Offerton, Stockport
SK2 5HL
Tel   (061) 427 2001
Mem   495
Sec   HE Bagshaw (061) 427 4425
Pro   R Tattersall (061) 427 2421
Holes 18 L 6319 yds SSS 71
Recs   Am–65 KR Gorton
        Pro–66 E Lester
V'trs   U SOC
Fees   £15 (£20)
Loc   1 mile from Stockport on A627
        Hazel Grove to Marple road

Swinton Park (1926)

East Lancashire Road, Swinton,
Manchester M27 1LX
Tel	**(061) 794 1785**
Mem	425 100(L) 50(J)
Sec	F Slater (061) 794 0861
Pro	J Wilson (061) 793 8077
Holes	18 L 6712 yds SSS 72
Recs	Am–66 J Thornley (1984)
V'trs	WD–U WE–M SOC–Tues
Fees	£16 D–£20
Loc	On A580, 5 miles NW of Manchester

Tunshill (1901)

Kiln Lane, Milnrow, nr Rochdale
Tel	(0706) 342095
Mem	180
Sec	I Catlow
Holes	9 L 5812 yds SSS 68
Recs	Am–66 D Williams (1981), KM Hardy, R Hopley (1989)
V'trs	WD–U WE–M SOC
Fees	£7 (£8) (1990)
Loc	2 miles E of Rochdale. M62 Junction 21

Turton (1907)

Woodend Farm, Bromley Cross, nr Bolton
Tel	(0204) 852235
Mem	210 60(L) 35(J)
Sec	D Jackson (0204) 594171
Holes	9 L 5805 yds SSS 68
Recs	Am–67 TD Bullough
V'trs	WD–U exc Mon–M & Wed–NA 12.30–4pm WE/ BH–M
Fees	£10
Loc	3½ miles N of Bolton

Walmersley (1906)

Garrett's Close, Walmersley, Bury
Tel	(061) 764 1429
Mem	350
Sec	C Stock (061) 764 5057
Holes	9 L 5588 metres SSS 70
Recs	Am–67 I Bamborough
V'trs	WD–U exc Tues–NA Sat–NA Sun–M SOC–Wed–Fri
Fees	£10
Loc	2 miles N of Bury (A56). M66 Junction 1

Werneth (1909)

Green Lane Garden Suburb, Oldham OL8 3AZ
Tel	(061) 624 1190
Mem	350
Sec	JH Barlow
Pro	T Morley
Holes	18 L 5363 yds SSS 66
Recs	Am–62 LA Lawton Pro–63 S Holden
V'trs	WD–U WE–M SOC
Fees	£12
Loc	2 miles S of Oldham

Werneth Low (1912)

Gee Cross, Hyde, Tameside
Tel	**(061) 368 2503**
Mem	245 50(L) 60(J)
Sec	R Watson (061) 368 7388
Pro	A Bacchus (061) 336 6908
Holes	9 L 5734 yds SSS 68
Recs	Am–67 ST Madden Pro–57 D Cooper
V'trs	U exc Sun–NA BH–M
Fees	£9.50 Sat–£14.50
Loc	Werneth Low, 2 miles from Hyde

Westhoughton (1929)

Long Island, Westhoughton, Bolton BL5 2BR
Tel	**(0942) 811085**
Mem	200
Sec	DJ Kinsella
Pro	S Brian
Holes	9 L 5834 yds SSS 68
Recs	Am–64 T Woodward
V'trs	WD–U WE/ BH–M
Fees	£8
Loc	4 miles SW of Bolton

Whitefield (1932)

Higher Lane, Whitefield, Manchester M25 7EZ
Tel	**(061) 766 2728**
Mem	500
Sec	Mrs RL Vidler (061) 766 2904
Pro	P Reeves (061) 766 3096
Holes	18 L 6041 yds SSS 69 18 L 5714 yds SSS 68
V'trs	U SOC–WD
Fees	£18 (£25)
Loc	4 miles N of Manchester. M62 Junction 17

Whittaker (1906)

Littleborough OL15 0LH
Tel	**(0706) 78310**
Mem	120
Sec	GA Smith (0484) 428546
Holes	9 L 5576 yds SSS 67
Recs	Am–61 D Kernick Pro–65 MT Hoyle
V'trs	WD/ Sat–U Sun–NA
Fees	£6 (£8)
Loc	1½ miles N of Littleborough, off A58

Wigan (1898)

Arley Hall, Haigh, Wigan WN1 2UH
Tel	**(0257) 421360**
Mem	250
Sec	J Crompton (0257) 41051
Holes	9 L 6058 yds SSS 69
Recs	Am–68 RM Hodson
V'trs	U exc Tues & Sat
Fees	£13 (£18)
Loc	4 miles N of Wigan off A5106/ B5239. M6 Junction 27

William Wroe (1973)

Public
Pennybridge Lane, Flixton, Manchester
Tel	**(061) 748 8680**
Pro	B Parkinson
Holes	18 L 4395 yds SSS 61
Recs	Am–60 C Meadows, D Dunwoodie
V'trs	U-booking necessary
Fees	£3.30 (£5)
Loc	6 miles SW of Manchester, by M63
Mis	Acre Gate Club plays here

Withington (1892)

243 Palatine Road, West Didsbury, Manchester M20 8UD
Tel	**(061) 445 3912**
Mem	340 97(L) 38(J) 30(5)
Sec	A Larsen (061) 445 9544
Pro	RJ Ling (061) 445 4861
Holes	18 L 6410 yds SSS 71
Recs	Am–68 C Webb (1989) Pro–67 D Scholes
V'trs	WD–H exc Thurs SOC
Fees	£17 (£20)
Loc	6 miles S of Manchester on B5166

Worsley (1894)

Stableford Avenue, Monton Green, Eccles, Manchester
Tel	**(061) 789 4202**
Mem	625
Sec	B Dean
Pro	C Cousins
Holes	18 L 6217 yds SSS 70
Recs	Am–66 B Dean Pro–68 FS Boobyer
V'trs	I NA-9-9.45am & 12.15-1.30pm
Fees	£16
Loc	5 miles W of Manchester

Merseyside

Allerton Park (1934)

Public
Allerton Road, Liverpool
Tel	**(051) 428 1046**
Pro	B Large
Holes	18 L 5084 yds SSS 64
V'trs	U
Fees	£2.90
Loc	5 miles S of Liverpool

Alt (1975)

Public
Park Road, West Southport
Tel	**(0704) 30435**
Pro	W Fletcher (0704) 35268
Holes	18 L 5939 yds SSS 69
V'trs	U-phone booking
Fees	£2.40 (£3)
Loc	N of Marine Lake

Arrowe Park (1931)

Public
Arrowe Park, Woodchurch,
Birkenhead, Wirral
Tel	(051) 677 1527
Pro	C Scanlon
Holes	18 L 6377 yds SSS 70
V'trs	U
Fees	£3.25
Loc	3 miles from Birkenhead on A552. M53 Junction 3, 1 mile

Ashton-in-Makerfield (1902)

Garswood Park, Liverpool Road,
Ashton-in-Makerfield
Tel	(0942) 727267
Mem	500
Sec	F Moran (0942) 725617
Pro	P Allan (0942) 724229
Holes	18 L 6120 yds SSS 69
Recs	Am–66 GS Lacy
V'trs	WD–U exc Wed WE/ BH–M SOC
Fees	£18
Loc	Ashton 1 mile

Bidston (1913)

Scoresby Road, Leasowe, Moreton
L46 1QQ
Tel	(051) 638 3412
Mem	500
Sec	LA Kendrick (051) 638 8685
Pro	M Adams (051) 630 6650
Holes	18 L 6207 yds SSS 70
Recs	Am–67 P Whitehouse Pro–68 JM Hume
V'trs	WD–U WE–M SOC
Fees	£10 (£15)
Loc	Off Leasowe road

Bootle (1934)

Dunnings Bridge Road, Litherland
L30 2PP
Tel	(051) 928 6196
Mem	300
Sec	J Morgan (Hon)
Pro	G Brown (051) 928 1371
Holes	18 L 6362 yds SSS 70
Recs	Am–64 S Ashcroft Pro–69 R Boobyer
V'trs	U–book by phone SOC
Fees	£2.75 (£4)
Loc	5 miles N of Liverpool

Bowring (1913)

Public
Bowring Park, Roby Road, Huyton
Tel	(051) 489 1901
Pro	D Weston
Holes	9 L 5592 yds SSS 66
Recs	Am–67 G Spurrier
V'trs	U
Fees	£2.70
Loc	M62 motorway

Brackenwood

Public
Brackenwood Lane, Bebington,
Wirral L63 2LY
Tel	(051) 608 3093
Pro	C Disbury
Holes	18 L 6131 yds SSS 69
Recs	Am–67 D Charlton Pro–64 C Disbury
V'trs	U
Fees	£3.45
Loc	Nr M53 Junction 4

Bromborough (1904)

Raby Hall Road, Bromborough
Tel	(051) 334 2155
Mem	600
Sec	LB Silvester (051) 334 2978
Pro	P Andrew (051) 334 4499
Holes	18 L 6650 yds SSS 73
Recs	Am–67 J Berry
V'trs	U–contact Pro in advance
Fees	£18 (£25)
Loc	Mid Wirral, M53 Junction 4

Caldy (1908)

Links Hey Road, Caldy, Wirral
L48 1NB
Tel	(051) 625 5660
Mem	800
Sec	TDM Bacon
Pro	K Jones (051) 625 1818
Holes	18 L 6675 yds SSS 73
Recs	Am–68 RN Hughes
V'trs	WD–M until 9.30am –U from 9.30am–1pm –M from 1–2pm –U after 2pm. Booking required
Fees	D–£25 After 2pm–£20
Loc	1½ miles S of West Kirby
Mis	Buggies for hire

Childwall (1913)

Naylor's Road, Gateacre, Liverpool
L27 2YB
Tel	(051) 487 0654
Mem	650
Sec	L Upton
Pro	N Parr (051) 487 9871
Holes	18 L 6425 yds SSS 71
Recs	Am–66 M Gamble
V'trs	WE/ BH/ Tues-restricted
Fees	£10.50 (£16)
Loc	7 miles E of Liverpool. M62, 2 miles

Eastham Lodge (1973)

117 Ferry Road, Eastham, Wirral
L62 0AP
Tel	(051) 327 1483 (Clubhouse)
Mem	520
Sec	CS Camden (051) 327 3003
Pro	I Jones (051) 327 3008
Holes	15 L 5826 yds SSS 68
Recs	Am–64 EI Bradshaw Pro–66 I Jones
V'trs	WD–U WE/ BH–M SOC–Tues
Fees	£11
Loc	6 miles S of Birkenhead, off A41. M53 Junction 5. Signs to Eastham Country Park

Formby (1884)

Golf Road, Formby, Liverpool
L37 1LQ
Tel	(070 48) 74273
Mem	600
Sec	A Thirlwell (070 48) 72164
Pro	C Harrison (070 48) 73090
Holes	18 L 6695 yds SSS 73
Recs	Am–67 DJ Eccleston Pro–65 NC Coles
V'trs	WD–I H exc Wed–NA WE/ BH–NA
Fees	£35
Loc	By Freshfield Station

Formby Ladies' (1896)

Formby, Liverpool L37 1YL
Tel	(070 48) 74127
Sec	Mrs V Bailey (070 48) 73493
Pro	C Harrison (070 48) 73090
Holes	18 L 5426 yds SSS 71
Recs	Am–60 CD Lee
V'trs	U
Fees	£20 (£25)
Loc	Nr Southport

Grange Park (1891)

Toll Bar, Prescot Road, St Helens
WA10 3AD
Tel	(0744) 22980 (Members)
Mem	700
Sec	DA Wood (0744) 26318
Pro	PG Evans (0744) 28785
Holes	18 L 6480 yds SSS 71
Recs	Am–65 G Boardman (1989) Pro–66 R Ellis (1986)
V'trs	I
Fees	£18 (£25)
Loc	1½ miles W of St Helens on A58

Haydock Park (1877)

Golborne Park, Rob Lane, Newton-
le-Willows WA12 0HX
Tel	(0925) 224389
Mem	390 120(L)
Sec	G Tait (0925) 228525
Pro	PE Kenwright (0925) 226944
Holes	18 L 6014 yds SSS 69
Recs	Am–65 D Pilkington, P Boydell, K Sargent
V'trs	H or I SOC–WD exc Tues
Fees	£15
Loc	M6 Junction 23

Hesketh (1885)

Cockle Dick's Lane, off Cambridge
Road, Southport PR9 9QQ
Tel	(0704) 530226
Fax	(0704) 539250
Mem	580
Sec	PB Seal (0704) 536897
Pro	J Donoghue (0704) 530050
Holes	18 L 6478 yds SSS 72
Recs	Am–68 G Brand Pro–64 D Hayes
V'trs	WD–U WE/ BH–restricted SOC
Fees	£17 D–£22 (£25)
Loc	1 mile N of Southport

Heswall (1901)

**Cottage Lane, Gayton Heswall,
Wirral L60 8PB**
Tel   (051) 342 2193
Mem   902
Sec   CPR Calvert (051) 342 1237
Pro   AE Thompson (051) 342 7431
Holes 18 L 6472 yds SSS 72
Recs   Am–67 J Butterworth (1986)
          Pro–64 K Jones (1986)
V'trs U H BH–NA SOC–Wed & Fri
Fees   D–£20 (D–£25) SOC–£20 (Min
          24)
Loc   8 miles NW of Chester

Hillside (1909)

Hastings Road, Southport
Tel   (0704) 69902
Mem   800
Sec   PW Ray (0704) 67169
Pro   B Seddon (0704) 68360
Holes 18 L 6850 yds SSS 74
Recs   Am–67 S Struver
          Pro–66 M O'Grady, R Craig
V'trs By arrangement with Sec
Fees   D–£30 (£35)

Hoylake Municipal

Public
Carr Lane, Hoylake, Wirral L47 4BQ
Tel   (051) 632 2956
Pro   R Boobyer
Holes 18 L 6330 yds SSS 70
Recs   Am–67 S Roberts (1983)
          Pro–64 T Bennett (1982)
V'trs U SOC WE–phone booking
          one week in advance
Fees   £3.20
Loc   Liverpool 10 miles
Mis   West Hoyle Club plays here

Huyton & Prescot (1905)

Hurst Park, Huyton
Tel   (051) 489 1138
Mem   700
Sec   Mrs E Holmes (051) 489 3948
Pro   R Pottage (051) 489 2022
Holes 18 L 5738 yds SSS 68
Recs   Am–67
V'trs WD–U WE–M
Fees   £12 (£15)
Loc   7 miles E of Liverpool. 1 mile
          from Prescot (A57)

Leasowe (1891)

**Leasowe Road, Moreton, Wirral
L46 3RD**
Tel   (051) 677 5852
Mem   450
Sec   R Kerr
Pro   M Adams (051) 678 5460
Holes 18 L 6204 yds SSS 70
Recs   Am–63 J Maddocks
V'trs U Sun–M
Fees   £15 (£17.50)

Lee Park (1954)

**Childwall Valley Road, Gateacre,
Liverpool L27 3YA**
Tel   (051) 487 9861 (Clubhouse)
Mem   550
Sec   Mrs D Barr (051) 487 3882
Holes 18 L 6024 yds SSS 69
V'trs U SOC
Fees   On application
Loc   Liverpool 7 miles

Liverpool Municipal (1967)

Public
**Ingoe Lane, Kirkby, nr Liverpool
L32 4SS**
Tel   (051) 546 5435
Pro   D Weston
Holes 18 L 6571 yds SSS 71
Recs   Am–70 J Paton (1986)
          Pro–70
V'trs U WE–booking required
Fees   £2.20 (£2.20)
Loc   M57 exit to B5192
Mis   Kirkby Club plays here

Prenton (1905)

**Golf Links Road, Prenton,
Birkenhead L42 8LW**
Tel   (051) 608 1461
Mem   360 100(L) 69(J) 70(5)
Sec   GW Robinson (051) 608 1053
Pro   R Thompson (051) 608 1636
Holes 18 L 6411 yds SSS 71
Recs   Am–68 CJ Farey, AJ Rainford,
          WJ Beattie
V'trs U SOC–Wed & Fri
Fees   £18 (£20)
Loc   Outskirts of Birkenhead. M53
          Junction 3

RLGC Village Play (1895)

Hoylake, Wirral
Mem   40
Sec   J Chapman (051) 625 7013
Holes Play over Royal Liverpool

Royal Birkdale (1889)

**Waterloo Road, Birkdale, Southport
PR8 2LX**
Tel   (0704) 69903
Fax   (0704) 62327
Sec   NT Crewe (0704) 67920
Pro   R Bradbeer (0704) 68857
Holes 18 L 6703 yds SSS 73
Recs   Am–68 C Cassells (1989)
          Pro–64 M O'Meara (1987)
V'trs I H SOC
Fees   £32 D–£48 (£50)
Loc   1½ miles S of Southport

Royal Liverpool (1869)

Meols Drive, Hoylake L47 4AL
Tel   (051) 632 3101/ 3102
Fax   (051) 632 6737
Mem   650
Pro   J Heggarty (051) 632 5868
Holes 18 L 6821 yds SSS 74
Recs   Am–69 R Hayes
          Pro–64 B Waites

V'trs I SOC
Fees   £30 (£35)
Loc   10 miles W of Liverpool

St Helens (1985)

Public
Sherdley Park, St Helens
Tel   (0744) 813149
Sec   MH Devenish (0744) 31955
Pro   PR Parkinson
Holes 18 L 5941 yds SSS 69
Recs   Am–71 M Welsh (1990)
          Pro–69 PR Parkinson (1990)
V'trs U
Fees   £3.50 (£3.50)
Loc   2 miles E of St Helens A570.
          M62 Junction 2, 2 miles
Mis   Sherdley Park Club plays here

Southport & Ainsdale (1907)

**Bradshaws Lane, Ainsdale,
Southport PR8 3LG**
Tel   (0704) 78092
Mem   340 100(L) 60(J) 130(5)
Sec   IF Sproule (0704) 78000
Pro   M Houghton (0704) 77316
Holes 18 L 6612 yds SSS 73
Recs   Am–68 PJ Green, AK Sandwell
          (1990) Pro–67 DJ Russell,
          DI Vaughan (1983)
          Pro (L)–69 B New, M Walker,
          K Ehrnlund (1984)
V'trs WD–I H before 4pm –M after
          4pm WE/ BH–M
Fees   £20
Loc   3 miles S of Southport on A565

Southport Municipal

Public
Park Road, Southport
Tel   (0704) 535286
Pro   W Fletcher
Holes 18 L 6253 yds SSS 69
Recs   Pro–67 W Fletcher (1986)
V'trs U
Fees   £3.50 (£5)
Loc   N end of Southport promenade
Mis   Park Club plays here

Southport Old Links (1926)

Moss Lane, Southport
Tel   (0704) 24294/ 28207
Mem   390
Sec   JW Hodson
Holes 9 L 6486 yds SSS 71
Recs   Am–68 J Robinson
V'trs U exc WE comp days/ BH–NA
          SOC–WD
Fees   £15 (£20) W–£40
Loc   Churchtown, 3 miles NE of
          Southport centre

Wallasey (1891)

Bayswater Road, Wallasey L45 8LA
Tel   (051) 639 3630
Mem   350 90(L) 50(J) 45(5)
Sec   JA Sword (Sec/ Mgr) (051) 691
          1024

For list of abbreviations see page 487.

Pro	M Adams (051) 638 3888
Holes	18 L 6607 yds SSS 73
Recs	Am–68 P Morgan
	Pro–66 P Barber
V'trs	U
Fees	£20 (£24)
Loc	M53-signs to New Brighton

Warren (1911)

Public
Grove Road, Wallasey, Wirral
Tel	(051) 639 8223 (Clubhouse)
Pro	K Lamb (051) 639 5730
Holes	9 L 5914 yds SSS 68
Recs	Am–66 J Hayes
	Pro–66 JA MacLachlan
V'trs	U
Fees	£3

West Derby (1896)

**Yew Tree Lane, Liverpool
L12 9HQ**
Tel	(051) 228 1540
Mem	556
Sec	S Young (051) 254 1034
Pro	N Brace (051) 220 5478
Holes	18 L 6322 yds SSS 70
Recs	Am–66 M Gamble
	Pro–67 AC Coop
V'trs	SOC–WD after 9.30am
Fees	£18 (£25)
Loc	2 miles E of Liverpool, off A580-West Derby Junction

West Lancashire (1873)

**Blundellsands, Crosby, Liverpool
L23 8SZ**
Tel	(051) 924 4115
Mem	700
Sec	DE Bell (051) 924 1076
Pro	D Lloyd (051) 924 5662
Holes	18 L 6767 yds SSS 73
Recs	Am–69 G Boardman
	Pro–66 C Mason
V'trs	H SOC
Fees	£25 (£30) After 4pm–£15
Loc	Between Liverpool and Southport, off A565
Mis	Traditional links

Wirral Ladies (1894)

**93 Bidston Road, Birkenhead, Wirral
L43 6TS**
Tel	(051) 652 5797
Mem	550
Sec	Mrs DP Cranston–Miller (051) 652 1255
Pro	P Chandler (051) 652 2468
Holes	18 L 4966 yds SSS 70 (Ladies)
	18 L 5170 yds SSS 66 (Men)
Recs	Am–71 Miss H Lyall
V'trs	U H SOC
Fees	£12 (1990)
Loc	Birkenhead ¹/₂ mile. M53, 2 miles

Woolton (1901)

Doe Park, Speke Road, Woolton, Liverpool L25 7TZ
Tel	(051) 486 1601
Mem	750
Sec	KG Jennions (051) 486 2298
Pro	(051) 486 1298 (Shop)
Holes	18 L 5706 yds SSS 68
Recs	Am–63 J Edwards
	Pro–66 DJ Rees
V'trs	U exc comp days
Fees	£16 (£25)
Loc	South Liverpool
Mis	Buggy hire–£10

Middlesex

Airlinks (1984)

Public
Southall Lane, Hounslow TW5 9PE
Tel	(081) 561 1418
Sec	J Shortland (Mgr)
Pro	S Smith
Holes	18 L 5883 yds SSS 69
Recs	Am–60 K Dempster
V'trs	WD–U Sat am–NA
Fees	£6.50 (£8.50)
Loc	Just off M4

Ashford Manor (1898)

Fordbridge Road, Ashford TW15 3RT
Tel	(0784) 252049
Mem	800
Sec	BJ Duffy (0784) 257687
Pro	M Finney (0784) 255940
Holes	18 L 6372 yds SSS 70
Recs	Am–65 GA Homewood (1989)
	Pro–64 D Talbot
V'trs	H
Fees	£25 (£30)
Loc	Ashford, off A308

Crews Hill (1920)

Cattlegate Road, Crews Hill, Enfield EN2 8AZ
Tel	(081) 363 0787
Mem	600
Sec	EJ Hunt (081) 363 6674
Pro	J Reynolds (081) 366 7422
Holes	18 L 6208 yds SSS 70
Recs	Am–68 S Bishop
	Pro–65 H Flatman
V'trs	WD–I H WE/ BH–M SOC
Fees	On application
Loc	2¹/₂ miles N of Enfield. M25 Junction 24

Ealing (1923)

Perivale Lane, Greenford UB6 8SS
Tel	(081) 997 2595
Mem	600
Sec	CFS Ryder (081) 997 0937
Pro	A Stickley (081) 997 3959
Holes	18 L 6216 yds SSS 70
Recs	Am–65 A Rogers
	Pro–64 R Verwey
V'trs	WD–U WE–M
Fees	On application
Loc	Marble Arch 6 miles on A40

Enfield (1893)

Old Park Road South, Enfield EN2 7DA
Tel	(081) 363 3970
Fax	(081) 342 0381
Mem	625
Sec	NA Challis (081) 342 0313
Pro	L Fickling (081) 366 4492
Holes	18 L 6137 yds SSS 70
Recs	Am–66 A Rogers, S Whiffin
	Pro–66 L Fickling
V'trs	WD–H WE/ BH–M SOC–WD
Fees	£20 D–£30
Loc	1 mile NE of Enfield. M25 Junction 24

Fulwell (1904)

Hampton Hill TW12 1JY
Tel	(081) 977 3188
Mem	750
Sec	DC Evans (081) 977 2733
Pro	D Haslam (081) 977 3844
Holes	18 L 6490 yds SSS 71
Recs	Am–68 KD Corcoran, SR Warin
	Pro–63 P Buchan
V'trs	WD–I WE–M
Fees	£22 (£28)
Loc	Opposite Fulwell Station

Grim's Dyke (1910)

Oxhey Lane, Hatch End, Pinner HA5 4AL
Tel	(081) 428 4093
Mem	575
Sec	PH Payne (081) 428 4539
Pro	C Williams (081) 428 7484
Holes	18 L 5600 yds SSS 67
Recs	Am–65 J Thornton (1988)
	Pro–64 BJ Hunt (1978)
V'trs	WD–U H WE–M SOC
Fees	D–£25
Loc	2 miles W of Harrow (A4008)

Harefield Place (1947)

Public
The Drive, Harefield Place, Uxbridge UB10 8PA
Tel	(0895) 31169
Pro	P Howard (0895) 37287
Holes	18 L 5711 yds SSS 68
Recs	Am–65 A Schyns
	Pro–66 S Bottomley
V'trs	U
Fees	£6.50 (£10)
Loc	2 miles N of Uxbridge

Harrow School (1978)

Harrow-on-the-Hill
Mem	440 100(L) 40(J)
Sec	DA Fothergill (081) 869 1214
Holes	9 L 1845 yds SSS 30
V'trs	M
Loc	Harrow School

Haste Hill (1933)

Public
The Drive, Northwood
Tel	(092 74) 22877
Sec	T Le Brocq (Mgr)

Pro	T Le Brocq
Holes	18 L 5794 yds SSS 68
Recs	Am–68 J Joyce
V'trs	U
Fees	£5.70 (£8.70)
Loc	Northwood-Hillingdon

Hillingdon (1892)

18 Dorset Way, Hillingdon, Uxbridge UB10 0JR

Tel	(0895) 39810
Mem	375
Sec	LAN Holland (0895) 33956
Pro	DJ McFadden (0895) 51980
Holes	9 L 5459 yds SSS 67
Recs	Am–65 J Hall
	Pro–69 P Cheyney
V'trs	WD–U exc Thurs 12–4pm WE pm–M H SOC–Mon/ Tues/ Fri
Fees	18 holes D–£15
Loc	1 mile E of Uxbridge, by RAF Station, Uxbridge

Holiday Inn (1975)

Stockley Road, West Drayton

Mem	180
Sec	J O'Loughlin (0895) 444232
Pro	NC Coles
Holes	9 L 3800 yds SSS 62
V'trs	U SOC
Fees	18 holes–£4 (£4.50)
Loc	In grounds of Holiday Inn

Horsenden Hill (1935)

Public

Woodland Rise, Greenford

Tel	(081) 902 4555
Pro	T Martin
Holes	9 L 3264 yds SSS 56
V'trs	U
Fees	£2.30 (£3.50)
Loc	Greenford

Hounslow Heath (1979)

Public

Staines Road, Hounslow TW4 5DS

Tel	(081) 570 5271
Pro	P Cheyney
Holes	18 L 5820 yds SSS 68
V'trs	WD–U WE–booking essential
Fees	£4 (£5)
Loc	Opposite Green Lane, Staines Road

Lime Trees Park (1984)

Public

Ruislip Road, Northolt UB5 6QZ

Tel	(081) 845 3180
Fax	(081) 842 2097
Sec	N Sturgess
Pro	B Mylward
Holes	9 L 5815 yds SSS 69
Recs	Am–71 D Clark (1990)
	Pro–67 J Livesley (1990)
V'trs	U SOC
Fees	9 holes–£3.25 (£4.20)
Loc	Off A40, nr Polish war memorial
Mis	Driving range

Northwood (1891)

Rickmansworth Road, Northwood HA6 2QW

Tel	(092 74) 25329
Mem	420 240 (L)50(J) 111(5)
Sec	RA Bond (092 74) 21384
Pro	CJ Holdsworth (092 74) 20112
Holes	18 L 6493 yds SSS 71
Recs	Am–68 BE Marsden(1987)
	Pro–67 J Bland (1977)
V'trs	WD–H WE/ BH–NA SOC
Fees	£28
Loc	3 miles E of Rickmansworth

Perivale Park (1932)

Public

Ruislip Road, Greenford UB6 8EN

Tel	(081) 575 8655
Pro	J Hamlyn
Holes	9 L 5296 yds SSS 65
Recs	Am–64
V'trs	U
Fees	£2.80 (£4.20)
Loc	1 mile E of Greenford, off A40

Pinner Hill (1927)

Southview Road, Pinner Hill HA5 3YA

Tel	(081) 866 0963
Mem	750
Sec	JP Devitt
Pro	M Grieve (081) 866 2109
Holes	18 L 6293 yds SSS 70
Recs	Am–63 SR Warrin
	Pro–67 TH Cotton, G Player, T Wilkes, G Low, J Warren
V'trs	WD–H exc Wed & Thurs–U Sun/ BH–M SOC
Fees	£22 exc Wed & Thurs–£9.50
Loc	1 mile from West Pinner Green

Ruislip (1936)

Public

Ickenham Road, Ruislip HA4 7DQ

Tel	(0895) 632004
Fax	(0895) 635780
Pro	D Nash (0895) 638835
Holes	18 L 5702 yds SSS 68
Recs	Am–65 W Bennet
	Pro–65 A George
V'trs	U SOC
Fees	£5.60 (£8.60)
Loc	W Ruislip BR/ LTE Station
Mis	Driving range

Stanmore (1893)

Gordon Avenue, Stanmore HA7 2RL

Tel	(081) 954 4661
Mem	500
Sec	PF Wise (081) 954 2599
Pro	VR Law (081) 954 2646
Holes	18 L 5881 yds SSS 68
Recs	Am–66 H Preston
	Pro–66 G Low
V'trs	WD–H WE/ BH–M SOC
Fees	On application
Loc	E boundary of Harrow

Strawberry Hill (1900)

Wellesley Road, Twickenham

Tel	(081) 894 1246
Mem	350
Sec	RC Meer (081) 894 0165
Pro	P Buchan (081) 892 2082
Holes	9 L 2381 yds SSS 62
Recs	Am–61 RE Heryet
	Pro–59 H Fullicks, K Bousfield, R Gerken
V'trs	WD–U WE–M XL
Fees	£8
Loc	Strawberry Hill Station

Sudbury (1920)

Bridgewater Road, Wembley HA0 1AL

Tel	(081) 902 0218
Mem	640
Sec	WG Kirkwood (081) 902 3713
Pro	N Jordan (081) 902 7910
Holes	18 L 6282 yds SSS 70
Recs	Am–63 T Greenwood
	Pro–65 J Gill
V'trs	WD–H WE–M
Fees	£20
Loc	Junction of A4005/ A4090

Twickenham Park (1977)

Public

Staines Road, Twickenham TW2 5JD

Tel	(081) 783 1698
Pro	T Morgan (081) 783 1698
Holes	9 L 6014 yds SSS 69
V'trs	U
Fees	£3 (£4)
Loc	2 miles NW of Hampton Court, nr end of M3

West Middlesex (1891)

Greenford Road, Southall

Tel	(081) 574 3450
Mem	700
Sec	PJ Furness
Pro	L Farmer (081) 574 1800
Holes	18 L 6242 yds SSS 70
Recs	Am–65 J Walsh
	Pro–64 L Farmer
V'trs	WD–U WE–NA
Fees	Tues/ Thurs/ Fri–£15 (£27.50) Mon & Wed–£7.50
Loc	Junction of Uxbridge Road and Greenford Road

Whitewebbs (1932)

Public

Beggars Hollow, Clay Hill, Enfield EN2 9JN

Tel	(081) 363 2951
Pro	D Lewis (081) 363 4454
Holes	18 L 5755 yds SSS 68
Recs	Am–61 C Smith
	Pro–68 D Lewis
V'trs	U
Fees	£4.10 (£5.60)
Loc	1 mile N of Enfield

For list of abbreviations see page 487.

Wyke Green (1928)

Syon Lane, Isleworth
Tel   (081) 560 8777
Mem   618
Sec   TH Glover
Pro   A Fisher (081) 847 0685
Holes 18 L 6242 yds SSS 70
Recs   Am–65 MR Johnson
          Pro–64 C DeFoy
V'trs WD–U WE/ BH–NA before
          3pm SOC
Fees   £22 (£33)
Loc   ¹/₂ mile from Gillettes Corner
          (A4)

Norfolk

Barnham Broom Hotel (1977)

Barnham Broom, Norwich NR9 4DD
Tel   (060 545) 393
Fax   (060 545) 8224
Mem   560
Sec   A Long (Man Dir) P Ballingall
          (Golf Dir)
Pro   S Beckham
Holes Valley 18 L 6470 yds SSS 71;
          Hill 18 L 6628 yds SSS 72
V'trs I or H WE/ BH–NA (exc hotel
          residents) SOC
Fees   £20 £17.50-residents
Loc   8 miles SW of Norwich off A47.
          4 miles NW of Wymondham,
          off A11

Bawburgh

Long Lane, Bawburgh, Norwich
Tel   (0603) 746390
Mem   400
Sec   RJ Mapes
Pro   R Waugh
Holes 9 L 5278 yds SSS 66
Recs   Am–67 S Manser
          Pro–69 R Waugh
V'trs Sun-restricted before 11am
          SOC–WD
Fees   18 holes £10 (£12.50) 9 holes
          £6
Loc   S of A47, 1 mile from Norwich
          ring road. Turn left at Round
          Well PH. Rear of Royal Norfolk
          Showground
Mis   Driving range

Costessey Park (1983)

Costessey Park, Costessey, Norwich
NR8 5AL
Tel   (0603) 746333
Mem   500
Sec   BA Howson
Pro   D Johnson (0603) 747085
Holes 18 L 5853 yds SSS 68
V'trs U SOC–WD
Fees   £12 (£15)
Loc   3 miles W of Norwich, off A47
          at Round Well PH

Dereham (1934)

Quebec Road, Dereham NR19 2DS
Tel   (0362) 693122
Mem   520
Sec   G Dalrymple (0362) 695900
Pro   S Fox (0362) 695631
Holes 9 L 6225 yds SSS 70
Recs   Am–63 L Varney
          Pro–65 M Elsworthy
V'trs H WE–M
Fees   £14
Loc   Dereham ¹/₂ mile

Eaton (1910)

Newmarket Road, Norwich NR4 6SF
Tel   (0603) 52881
Mem   440 135(L) 70(J) 205(5)
Sec   (0603) 51686
Pro   F Hill (0603) 52478
Holes 18 L 6135 yds SSS 69
Recs   Am–64 AK Nichols (1990)
          Pro–65 M Spooner (1988)
V'trs I H WE–NA before noon
Fees   £20 (£24)
Loc   S Norwich

Fakenham (1973)

Fakenham
Tel   (0328) 2867
Mem   450
Sec   G Cocker (0328) 55665
Pro   J Westwood (0328) 3534
Holes 9 hole course
Recs   Am–70 D Hood
          Pro–70 M Leeder
V'trs WD–U WE–starting times
          alternate Sun am SOC
Fees   £8 (£11)
Loc   Fakenham racecourse

Feltwell (1976)

Thor Ave, off Wilton Road, Feltwell
Tel   (0842) 827644
Mem   400
Sec   Mrs C Sharp
Pro   M Snazell (0842) 827762
Holes 9 L 6260 yds SSS 70
V'trs U
Fees   £10 (£15)
Loc   1 mile S of Feltwell on B1112
Mis   Course laid out on former
          Feltwell aerodrome.

Gorleston (1906)

Warren Road, Gorleston,
Gt Yarmouth NR31 6JT
Tel   (0493) 661802
Mem   800
Sec   CB Court (0493) 661911
Pro   RL Moffit (0493) 662103
Holes 18 L 6400 yds SSS 71
Recs   Am–68 J Maddock (1981)
V'trs U H SOC
Fees   £15 (£20) W–£40
Loc   S of Gorleston, off A12

Granary Hotel G & CC

Little Dunham, King's Lynn PE32 2DF
Tel   (0328) 701310
Sec   J Harris (Prop)
Pro   C Denny (0362) 694383
Holes 9 L 2023 yds SSS 60
V'trs U
Loc   4 miles NE of Swaffham

Great Yarmouth & Caister (1882)

Beach House, Caister-on-Sea,
Gt Yarmouth
Tel   (0493) 720421
Mem   700
Sec   AA Hunton (0493) 728699
Pro   N Catchpole
Holes 18 L 6284 yds SSS 70
Recs   Am–67 M Sperrin
          Pro–66 E Murray
V'trs WE–NA before noon SOC
Fees   £8 (£10)
Loc   Caister-on-Sea

Hunstanton (1891)

Hunstanton
Tel   (0485) 532811
Mem   650 150(L) 60(J)
Sec   RH Cotton
Pro   J Carter (0485) 532751
Holes 18 L 6670 yds SSS 72
Recs   Am–65 S Robertson (1989)
          Pro–65 ME Gregson (1967)
V'trs WD–U after 9.30am WE/ BH–U
          after 10.30am SOC
Fees   £28 (£34)
Loc   ¹/₂ mile NE of Hunstanton

King's Lynn (1923)

Castle Rising, King's Lynn PE31 6BD
Tel   (0553) 631656
Mem   980
Sec   GJ Higgins (0553) 631654
Pro   C Hanlon (0553) 631655
Holes 18 L 6646 yds SSS 72
Recs   Am–71 A Brydon (1990)
          Pro–68 M Davis (1988)
V'trs WD–U H WE/ BH–NA SOC
Fees   £22 (£30)
Loc   4 miles NE of King's Lynn

Links Country Park Hotel (1979)

West Runton, Cromer
Tel   (026 375) 691
Mem   300
Sec   SG Mansfield (Hon)
Pro   M Jubb
Holes 9 L 4814 yds Par 66 SSS 64
Recs   Am–64 CJ Lamb (1988)
          Pro–65 R Mann, GR Harvey
          (1987)
V'trs U
Fees   D–£15 (D–£20)
Loc   Between Cromer and
          Sheringham

Mundesley (1903)

Links Road, Mundesley NR11 8ES
Tel (0263) 720279
Mem 400
Sec BD Baxter (0263) 720095
Pro TG Symmons (0831) 455461
Holes 9 L 5410 yds SSS 66
V'trs WD–U exc Wed 12-3pm
WE–NA before 11.30am
Fees £12 (£20)
Loc 7 miles S of Cromer

RAF Marham (1974)

RAF Marham, Kings Lynn PE33 9NP
Mem 200
Sec W/O RF Daniel (0760) 337261
(Ext 261)
Holes 9 L 5244 yds SSS 66
Recs Am–71
V'trs By prior arrangement–U exc
Sun am
Fees £5 (£7)
Loc Near Narborough, 11 miles SE
of Kings Lynn
Mis Course situated on MOD land,
and may be closed without
prior notice

Royal Cromer (1888)

Overstrand Road, Cromer NR27 0JH
Tel (0263) 512884
Mem 700
Sec Flt Lt E Robertson
Pro RJ Page (0263) 512267
Holes 18 L 6508 yds SSS 71
Recs Am–68 M Williamson (1989)
Pro–70 M Few (1988)
V'trs H SOC–WD
Fees £20 (£25)
Loc 1 mile E of Cromer

Royal Norwich (1893)

**Drayton High Road, Hellesdon,
Norwich NR6 5AH**
Tel (0603) 425712
Mem 780
Sec DF Cottier (0603) 429928
Pro B Lockwood (0603) 408459
Holes 18 L 6603 yds SSS 72
Recs Am–67 A Barker
Pro–66 HJ Boyle
V'trs WE/ BH–restricted SOC
Fees D–£22
Loc ½ mile W of Norwich ring
road, on Fakenham road

Royal West Norfolk (1892)

Brancaster, King's Lynn PE31 8AX
Tel (0485) 210223
Mem 760
Sec Maj. NA Carrington Smith
(0485) 210087
Pro RE Kimber (0485) 210616
Holes 18 L 6428 yds SSS 71
Recs Am–67 AH Perowne
Pro–66 M Elsworthy
V'trs No four balls allowed Mid
July–mid Sept–M WE–NA
before 10am SOC

Fees £22 (£27)
Loc 7 miles E of Hunstanton on
A419

Ryston Park (1932)

**Ely Road, Denver, Downham Market
PE38 0HH**
Tel (0366) 382133
Mem 320
Sec AJ Wilson (0366) 383834
Holes 9 L 6292 yds SSS 70
Recs Am–66 JP Alflatt (1975)
V'trs WE–M
Fees £15
Loc 1 mile S of Downham Market
on A10

Sheringham (1891)

Sheringham
Tel (0263) 822038
Mem 750
Sec MJ Garrett (0263) 823488
Pro MT Leeder (0263) 822980
Holes 18 L 6464 yds SSS 71
Recs Am–69 SD Miller
Pro–69 M Few
V'trs WD–U H after 9.15am SOC
Fees £23 (£28)
Loc ½ mile W of Sheringham

Sprowston Park (1980)

**Wroxham Road, Sprowston,
Norwich NR7 8RP**
Tel (0603) 410657
Fax (0603) 788884
Mem 650
Sec G Porter
Pro C Potter (0603) 415557
Holes 18 L 5985 yds SSS 69
Recs Am–69 S Terrington
Pro–65 N Catchpole
V'trs U SOC
Fees On application
Loc 2 miles NE of Norwich on
A1151
Mis Floodlit driving range

Swaffham (1922)

Cley Road, Swaffham
Tel (0760) 721611
Mem 450
Sec R Joslin (0760) 22487
Pro CJ Norton (036 621) 284
Holes 9 L 6252 yds SSS 70
Recs Am–68 G Head
Pro–64 CJ Norton
V'trs WD–U WE–M Sun am–NA
Fees £12
Loc Swaffham 1½ miles

Thetford (1912)

Brandon Road, Thetford IP24 3NE
Tel (0842) 752258
Mem 650
Sec RJ Ferguson (0842) 752169
Pro N Arthur (0842) 752662
Holes 18 L 6879 yds SSS 73
Recs Am–68 R Claydon
Pro–72 N Arthur

V'trs H SOC
Fees £25
Loc Brandon Road (B1107), off A11

Wensum Valley (1990)

**Beech Avenue, Taverham, Norwich
NR8 6HP**
Tel (0603) 261062
Mem 450
Sec Miss B Todd (0603) 261012
Pro M Spooner (0603) 261012
Holes 9 L 5987 yds SSS 68
Recs Pro–67 M Spooner (1990)
V'trs WD–U H WE–NA before noon
SOC
Fees £12 (£15)
Loc 4 miles NW of Norwich on
A1067
Mis Driving range

Northamptonshire

Cold Ashby (1974)

**Cold Ashby, nr Northampton
NN6 7EP**
Tel (0604) 740548
Fax (0604) 740548
Mem 600 40(L) 40(J)
Sec D Croxton
Pro A Skingle (0604) 740099
Holes 18 L 5957 yds SSS 69
Recs Am–68 S Crowson (1989)
Pro–61 D Dunk (1985)
V'trs WD–U WE–U after 2pm (if
booked) SOC
Fees £11 (£14)
Loc 5 miles E of M1 Junction 18,
between Leicester and
Northampton on A50

Collingtree Park (1989)

**Windingbrook Lane, Northampton
NN4 0XM**
Tel (0604) 700000
Fax (0604) 702600
Mem 600
Sec J Cook (Golf Dir)
Pro J Cook
Holes 18 L 6821 yds SSS 73
Recs Pro–68 P Harrison (1990)
V'trs H SOC
Fees £45 (incl buggy)
Loc ½ mile E of M1 Junction 15

Daventry & District
(1922)

Norton Road, Daventry
Tel (0327) 702829
Mem 300
Sec F Higham (0327) 703204
Pro M Higgins
Holes 9 L 2871 yds SSS 67
V'trs WD–U Sun–NA before 11am
SOC
Fees £8 (£10)

Delapre (1976)

Public

Eagle Drive, Nene Valley Way,
Northampton NN4 0DV
Tel	(0604) 764036/ 763957
Pro	J Corby (0604) 764036
Holes	18 L 6293 yds SSS 70 2 x 9 hole Par 3 courses
Recs	Am–66 M McNally
V'trs	U SOC
Fees	£5.20 (£6.50)
Loc	3 miles from M1 Junction 15, on A508
Mis	Pitch & putt. Driving range

Farthingstone Hotel (1974)

Farthingstone, nr Towcester
Tel	(0327) 36291
Fax	(0327) 36645
Mem	650
Sec	DC Donaldson (Prop/ Mgr)
Pro	M Gallagher (0327) 36533
Holes	18 L 6248 yds SSS 71
Recs	Am–68 K Leason (1989) Pro–66 D Thorp (1984), M Gallagher (1985), K Dickens (1989)
V'trs	U SOC
Fees	£15 D–£25 (£20 D–£30)
Loc	6 miles W of M1 Junction 16. 3 miles W of A5 at Weedon, on Farthingstone-Everdon road
Mis	Buggies for hire

Kettering (1891)

Headlands, Kettering
Tel	(0536) 512074
Mem	380 100(L) 45(J) 65(5)
Sec	JPB Galt (0536) 511104
Pro	K Theobald (0536) 81014
Holes	18 L 6035 yds SSS 69
Recs	Am–67 J Campbell Pro–67 J Gallagher
V'trs	WD–U WE/ BH–M SOC
Fees	£18
Loc	S boundary of Kettering

Kingsthorpe (1908)

Kingsley Road, Northampton
NN2 7BU
Tel	(0604) 711173
Mem	450
Sec	NC Liddington (0604) 710610
Pro	P Smith (0604) 719602
Holes	18 L 6006 yds SSS 69
Recs	Am–63 S McDonald Pro–64 B Larratt
V'trs	WD–U WE/ BH–MH SOC–WD
Fees	D–£16

Northampton (1893)

Harlestone, Northampton NN7 4NU
Tel	(0604) 845102
Mem	500 100(L) 70(J)
Sec	IMC Kirkwood (0604) 845155
Pro	M Chamberlain (0604) 845167
Holes	18 L 6534 yds SSS 71
V'trs	WD–U H WE–M SOC
Fees	£25
Loc	4 miles NW of Northampton, on A428 beyond Harlestone

Northamptonshire County (1909)

Church Brampton, Northampton
Tel	(0604) 842170
Mem	600
Sec	GG Morley (0604) 843025
Pro	SD Brown (0604) 842226
Holes	18 L 6503 yds SSS 71
Recs	Am–67 C Poxon (1986) Pro–64 J Higgins (1990)
V'trs	WD–H WE–H XL before 3.30pm Sat/ 11.15am Sun
Fees	£16 (£25)
Loc	5 miles NW of Northampton, off A50

Oundle (1894)

Oundle
Tel	(0832) 273267
Mem	600
Sec	R Davis
Pro	CM Cunningham (0832) 272273
Holes	18 L 5507 yds SSS 67
Recs	Am–68 Pro–67
V'trs	WD–U WE–M before 10.30am –U after 10.30am
Fees	£12 (£15)
Loc	1¹/₂ miles from Oundle on A427 Corby road

Priors Hall (1965)

Public

Stamford Road, Weldon, nr Corby
Tel	(0536) 60756
Pro	M Summers
Holes	18 L 6677 yds SSS 72
Recs	Am–75 R Beekie, M Scott, WF Kearney Pro–70 RH Kemp
V'trs	U
Fees	£2.80 (£4.30)
Loc	A43

Rushden (1919)

Kimbolton Road, Chelveston,
Wellingborough
Tel	(0933) 312581
Mem	350
Sec	R Tomlin (0933) 312197
Holes	9 L 6381 yds SSS 70
Recs	Am–67
V'trs	WD–U exc Wed pm WE–M Sat pm/ Sun am–XL BH–U SOC
Fees	£15
Loc	On A45, 2 miles E of Higham Ferrers

Staverton Park (1977)

Staverton, nr Daventry NN11 6JJ
Tel	(0327) 705911
Sec	AL McLundie
Pro	B Mudge (0327) 705506
Holes	18 L 6634 yds SSS 72
Recs	Am–67 Pro–64
V'trs	H SOC
Fees	£12.50 (£19.50)
Loc	1 mile S of Daventry, off A425. M1 Junctions 16/ 18, 15 mins

Wellingborough (1893)

Harrowden Hall, Great Harrowden,
Wellingborough NN9 5AD
Tel	(0933) 677234/ 673022
Mem	850
Sec	B North (0933) 677234
Pro	D Clifford (0933) 678752
Holes	18 L 6620 yds SSS 72
Recs	Am–69 AI Marshall (1988) Pro–69 D Clifford (1986)
V'trs	WD–U H exc Tues WE–M SOC–Wed-Fri
Fees	£20 D–£25
Loc	2 miles N of Wellingborough on A509 to Kettering

Northumberland

Allendale (1923)

Thornley Gate, Allendale, Hexham
NE47 9LG
Mem	90 20(L) 9(J)
Sec	JC Hall (091) 267 5875
Holes	9 L 4488 yds SSS 63
V'trs	U SOC
Fees	£4 (£5) W–£18
Loc	10 miles SW of Hexham

Alnmouth (1869)

Foxton Hall, Alnmouth
Tel	(0665) 830231
Mem	600
Sec	FK Marshall (0665) 830368
Holes	18 L 6414 yds SSS 71
Recs	Am–65 P Deeble
V'trs	U SOC–Mon–Thurs
Fees	£11 (£14) (1989)
Loc	5 miles SE of Alnwick
Mis	Dormy House accommodation

Alnmouth Village (1869)

Marine Road, Alnmouth
Tel	(0665) 830370
Mem	340
Sec	W Maclean (0665) 602096
Holes	9 L 6020 yds SSS 70
Recs	Am–63 D Weddell
V'trs	U
Fees	£6 (£10) W–£25

Alnwick (1907)

Swansfield Park, Alnwick
Tel	(0665) 602632
Mem	400
Sec	LE Stewart (0665) 602499
Holes	9 L 5387 yds SSS 66
Recs	Am–62 P Deeble
V'trs	U
Fees	D–£8
Loc	Swansfield Park, Alnwick, off A1

Arcot Hall (1909)

Dudley, Cramlington NE23 7QP
Mem	660
Sec	AG Bell (091) 236 2794
Pro	GM Cant (091) 236 2147
Holes	18 L 6389 yds SSS 70

Recs	Am–65 G Pickup (1990)
	Pro–65 P Walker (1990)
V'trs	WD–H WE/ BH–M SOC
Fees	£18
Loc	7 miles N of Newcastle, off A1

Bamburgh Castle (1904)

Bamburgh NE69 7DE
Tel	(066 84) 378
Mem	650
Sec	TC Osborne (066 84) 321
Holes	18 L 5465 yds SSS 67
Recs	Am–63 RS Rutter (1984)
V'trs	U H BH–NA SOC
Fees	D–£12 (£12 D–£16) W–£45
Loc	Bamburgh, 7 miles E of A1, via B1341 or B1342
Mis	Buggy for hire (summer)

Bedlingtonshire (1972)

Public
Acorn Bank, Bedlington
Tel	(0670) 822457
Sec	R Partis (Hon)
Pro	M Webb (0670) 822087
Holes	18 L 6224 metres SSS 73
Recs	Am–68 D Gray
	Pro–65 K Waters
V'trs	U
Fees	£4.50 D–£6 (£6 D–£8)
Loc	12 miles N of Newcastle

Bellingham (1893)

Bellingham NE48 2DT
Tel	(0434) 220530
Mem	250
Sec	TH Thompson (0434) 220281
Holes	9 L 5245 yds SSS 66
Recs	Am–63 I Wilson
V'trs	U exc comp days SOC
Fees	£6 (£7.50)
Loc	15 miles N of Hexham

Berwick-upon-Tweed (1890)

Goswick Beal, Berwick-upon-Tweed TD15 2RW
Tel	(0289) 87256
Mem	450
Sec	RC Oliver
Pro	M Leighton (0289) 87380
Holes	18 L 6425 yds SSS 71
Recs	Am–64 J Cotton
V'trs	WD–U WE–U 10am-2.30pm (1st tee) SOC
Fees	£9 D–£12 (£12 D–£18) W–£30
Loc	5 miles S of Berwick, off A1

Blyth (1905)

New Delaval, Blyth
Tel	(0670) 367728
Mem	580 120(L) 120(J)
Sec	WJF Lightley
Pro	K Phillips (0670) 356514
Holes	18 L 6498 yds SSS 71
Recs	Am–66 P Simpson (1989)
V'trs	WD–U WE–M BH–NA SOC–WD
Fees	£8 D–£10
Loc	W end of Plessey Road, Blyth

Close House (1968)

Close House, Heddon-on-the-Wall, Newcastle-upon-Tyne NE15 0HT
Tel	(0661) 852953
Mem	850
Sec	Mrs L Steel (0661) 852303
Holes	18 L 5511 yds SSS 67
Recs	Am–66 W Parker (1984), R Ingham (1986)
V'trs	M SOC–WD
Loc	9 miles W of Newcastle on A69

Dunstanburgh Castle (1907)

Embleton NE66 3XQ
Tel	(066 576) 562
Mem	350
Sec	PFC Gilbert
Holes	18 L 6298 yds SSS 70
Recs	Am–69
V'trs	U
Fees	£8.50 (£10.50)
Loc	7 miles NE of Alnwick on B1339

Haltwhistle

Greenhead, Nr Haltwhistle
Tel	(06977) 47367
Mem	300
Sec	WE Barnes (Hon)
Pro	J Metcalf
Holes	12 5968 yds SSS 69
V'trs	U SOC
Fees	£5 (£5)
Loc	Greenhead, 3 miles W of Haltwhistle

Hexham (1906)

Spital Park, Hexham NE46 3RZ
Tel	(0434) 602057
Mem	700
Sec	JC Oates (0434) 603072
Pro	I Waugh (0434) 604904
Holes	18 L 6272 yds SSS 70
Recs	Am–66 A Hinds
	Pro–67 I Waugh
V'trs	U
Fees	£8 (£11) W–£32 M–£70
Loc	21 miles W of Newcastle

Magdalene Fields (1903)

Public
Magdalene Fields, Berwick-upon-Tweed
Tel	(0289) 306384
Sec	R Patterson (0289) 305758
Holes	18 L 6551 yds SSS 71
Recs	Am–70 J Patterson
V'trs	U
Fees	£6.25 (1989)
Loc	Berwick centre 5 mins

Morpeth (1907)

The Common, Morpeth
Tel	(0670) 519980
Mem	660
Sec	G Hogg
Pro	MR Jackson (0670) 512065

Holes	18 L 5671 metres SSS 70
Recs	Am–67 K Brown (1983)
	Pro–68 T Horton (1976)
V'trs	H
Fees	£10 (£15)
Loc	1 mile S of Morpeth on A197

Newbiggin-by-the-Sea (1884)

Newbiggin-by-the-Sea
Tel	(0670) 817344 (Clubhouse)
Mem	500
Sec	D Lyall
Pro	D Fletcher (0670) 817833
Holes	18 L 6452 yds SSS 71
Recs	Am–67 B Bennett
	Pro–68 K Saint
V'trs	U after 10am SOC
Fees	£6 (£9) W–£25
Loc	Newbiggin, near Church Point

Ponteland (1927)

53 Bell Villas, Ponteland, Newcastle-upon-Tyne NE20 9BD
Tel	(0661) 72844/ 71872
Mem	460 150(L) 80(J) 30(5)
Sec	G Weetman (0661) 22689
Pro	A Crosby (0661) 22689
Holes	18 L 6512 yds SSS 71
Recs	Am–66 J Hayes, WMM Jenkins, DG Potter (1987)
	Pro–66 G Burrows
V'trs	WD–U WE/ BH–M
Fees	£10 D–£12
Loc	6 miles NW of Newcastle on A696, nr Airport

Prudhoe (1930)

Eastwood Park, Prudhoe-on-Tyne NE42 5DX
Tel	(0661) 32466
Mem	400
Sec	GB Garratt (0661) 34134
Pro	J Crawford (0661) 36188
Holes	18 L 5812 yds SSS 68
Recs	Am–65 DH Curry
	Pro–65 A Crosby
V'trs	WD–U WE–M SOC
Fees	£7 (£8)
Loc	15 miles W of Newcastle

Rothbury (1891)

Old Race Course, Rothbury, Morpeth
Tel	(0669) 21271 (Clubhouse)
Mem	370
Sec	WT Bathgate (0669) 20718
Holes	9 L 5560 yds SSS 67
Recs	Am–64 S Twynholm
V'trs	WD–U WE–U before noon NA–after noon
Fees	£8 (£13.50)
Loc	15 miles N of Morpeth on A697. W side of Rothbury

Seahouses (1913)

Beadnell Road, Seahouses NE68 7XT
| Tel | (0665) 720794 |
| Mem | 400 |

Sec JA Stevens (0665) 720809
Holes 18 L 5374 yds SSS 66
Recs Am–65 RS Rutter (1989)
V'trs U SOC
Fees £9 (£11.50)
Loc 14 miles N of Alnwick. 9 miles off A1

Slaley Hall G & CC (1988)

Slaley, Hexham
Tel (0434) 673350
Mem 200
Sec Mrs C Patterson
Pro B Patterson (Golf Dir)
Holes 18 L 6995 yds SSS 74
V'trs U H SOC
Fees On application
Loc 16 miles W of Newcastle. 7 miles S of Corbridge, off A68

Stocksfield (1913)

New Ridley NE43 7RE
Tel (0661) 843041
Mem 341 79(L) 70(J)
Sec DB Moon
Pro K Driver
Holes 18 L 5594 yds SSS 68
Recs Am–61 GED Bradley
Pro–66 P Harrison
V'trs U SOC
Fees £10 (£15)
Loc 3 miles E of A68. 1 mile S of A686

Tynedale (1908)

Public
Tyne Green, Hexham
Holes 9 L 5706 yds SSS 68
Recs Am–64 A Varty
V'trs U exc Sun-booking req
Fees £3 (£5) (1989)
Loc S side of Hexham

Warkworth (1891)

The Links, Warkworth, Morpeth
Tel (0665) 711596
Mem 400
Sec JW Anderson (0665) 75608
Holes 9 L 5817 yds SSS 68
Recs Am–67 AB Barrett
V'trs U
Fees £6 (£10)
Loc 15 miles NE of Morpeth

Wooler (1975)

Doddington, Wooler
Mem 250
Sec JH Curry (0668) 81956
Holes 9 L 6353 yds SSS 70
Recs Am–72 N Graham
V'trs U SOC
Fees D–£5 (D–£7)
Loc 3 miles N of Wooler on B6525

Nottinghamshire

Beeston Fields (1923)

Beeston, Nottingham NG9 3DD
Tel (0602) 257062
Mem 400 150(L) 52(J)
Sec JEL Grove
Pro A Wardle (0602) 220872
Holes 18 L 6404 yds SSS 71
Recs Am–66 P Benson
V'trs U SOC
Fees £18 (£25)
Loc 4 miles W of Nottingham. M1 Junction 25

Bulwell Forest (1902)

Public
Hucknall Road, Bulwell, Nottingham NG6 9LQ
Tel (0602) 770576
Fax (0602) 771229
Sec D Stubbs (Hon)
Pro CD Hall (0602) 763172/278008
Holes 18 L 5746 yds SSS 68
Recs Am–65 DN Smedley, JP Smith, D Newham   Pro–62 CD Hall
V'trs U
Fees £4 (£5)
Loc 4 miles N of Nottingham. M1 Junction 26

Chilwell Manor (1906)

Meadow Lane, Chilwell, Nottingham NG9 5AE
Tel (0602) 257050
Mem 620
Sec GA Spindley (0602) 258958
Pro E McCausland (0602) 258993
Holes 18 L 6379 yds SSS 69 18 L 5438 yds SSS 67
Recs Am–67 C Gray
Pro–66 B Waites
V'trs WD–U WE–NA SOC
Fees £12 D–£20
Loc 4 miles W of Nottingham

Coxmoor (1913)

Coxmoor Road, Sutton-in-Ashfield NG17 5LF
Tel (0623) 557359
Mem 650
Sec JW Tyler
Pro DJ Ridley (0623) 559906
Holes 18 L 6501 yds SSS 72
Recs Am–67 M Nunn
Pro–65 B Waites
V'trs H exc Ladies Day-Tues WE–NA SOC
Fees £22
Loc 1½ miles S of Mansfield. 3 miles from M1 Junction 27 on A611

Edwalton (1982)

Public
Edwalton, Nottingham
Tel (0602) 234775
Sec JF Shepperson (Hon)
Pro J Staples

Holes 9 L 3336 yds SSS 36 9 hole Par 3 course
V'trs U
Fees £3 Par 3 course–£1.90
Loc 2 miles S of Nottingham
Mis Driving range

Kilton Forest (1978)

Public
Blyth Road, Worksop S81 0TL
Tel (0909) 472488
Sec EL James (Hon)
Pro PW Foster (0909) 486563
Holes 18 L 6569 yds SSS 72
Recs Am–69 SJ Thorpe (1988)
Pro–72 DJ Ridley (1988)
V'trs WD–U WE–booking necessary SOC
Fees £4.40 (£6.50)
Loc 1 mile NE of Worksop on B6045

Mansfield Woodhouse (1973)

Public
Mansfield Woodhouse NG19 9EU
Tel (0623) 23521
Holes 9 L 2411 yds SSS 65
Recs Am–67 S Fisher
Pro–L Highfield Jr
V'trs U
Fees £2
Loc 2 miles N of Mansfield

Mapperley (1913)

Central Avenue, Plains Road, Mapperley, Nottingham NG3 5RH
Tel (0602) 265611
Mem 600
Sec SJD Kinghan
Pro R Daibell (0602) 202227
Holes 18 L 6224 yds SSS 70
Recs Am–68 B Tones (1986)
Pro–68 R Daibell (1986)
V'trs U SOC
Fees £9 (£11)
Loc 3 miles NE of Nottingham, off B684

Newark (1901)

Kelwick, Coddington, Newark NG24 2QX
Tel (0636) 626241
Mem 600
Sec AW Morgans (0636) 626282
Pro HA Bennett (0636) 626492
Holes 18 L 6486 yds SSS 71
Recs Am–70 C Bentley
Pro–69 CW Gray, DJ Britten
V'trs I H SOC
Fees £16 (£20)
Loc 4 miles E of Newark on A17

Nottingham City (1910)

Public
Lawton Drive, Bulwell, Nottingham NG6 8BL
Tel (0602) 278021
Sec DA Griffiths (Hon)
Pro CR Jepson (0602) 272767

Holes	18 L 6218 yds SSS 70
Recs	Am–66 T Payne (1987)
	Pro–66 T Smart
V'trs	WD–U WE–NA before noon
	SOC
Fees	£3.75 (£4)
Loc	M1 Junction 28, 3 miles

Notts (1887)

Hollinwell, Kirby-in-Ashfield NG17 7QR

Tel	(0623) 752042/ 753225
Mem	500
Sec	JR Walker (0623) 753225
Pro	BJ Waites (0623) 753087
Holes	18 L 7020 yds SSS 74
Recs	Am–67 IT Simpson,
	I MacKenzie
	Pro–64 J Bland
V'trs	WD–H WE/ BH–M
Fees	On application
Loc	4 miles S of Mansfield. M1
	Junction 27

Oxton (1974)

Oaks Lane, Oxton NG25 0RH

Tel	(0602) 653545
Mem	550
Sec	GC Norton (Golf Dir)
Pro	GC Norton
Holes	18 L 6600 yds SSS 72 9 L 3300
	yds SSS 37
Recs	Am–70 J Vaughan
	Pro–65 J Mellor
V'trs	WD–U WE/ BH–arrange times
	with Mgr SOC
Fees	£10 (£15)
Loc	9 miles N of Nottingham on
	A614
Mis	Floodlit driving range

Radcliffe-on-Trent (1909)

Dewberry Lane, Cropwell Road, Radcliffe-on-Trent NG12 2JH

Tel	(0602) 333000
Mem	650
Sec	WJ Stewart
Pro	P Hinton (0602) 332396
Holes	18 L 6423 yds SSS 71
V'trs	H SOC
Fees	£20 (£25)
Loc	6 miles E of Nottingham, off
	A52

Retford (1921)

Brecks Road, Ordsall, Retford DN22 7UA

Tel	(0777) 703733
Mem	360
Sec	A Harrison (0777) 860682
Pro	S Betteridge
Holes	18 L 6301 yds SSS 70
Recs	Am–72 PM Edwards (1990)
V'trs	WD–U WE–M SOC–WD
Fees	£15 D–£20
Loc	2 miles SW of Retford, off A638
	or A620. M1 Junction 30

Ruddington Grange

Wilford Road, Ruddington, Nottingham NG11 6NB

Tel	(0602) 846141
Mem	600
Sec	J Aston, DJT Johnson (Mgr)
Pro	RJ Ellis (0602) 211951
Holes	18 L 6490 yds SSS 71
Recs	Am–71 DJT Johnson (1988)
	Pro–68 C Hall (1990)
V'trs	U H BH–U exc comp days SOC
Fees	£18 D–£20 (£22 D–£26)
Loc	3 miles S of Nottingham

Rushcliffe (1910)

East Leake, nr Nottingham

Tel	(050 982) 2209
Mem	500
Sec	MG Booth (050 982) 2959
Pro	T Smart (050 982) 2701
Holes	18 L 6090 yds SSS 69
V'trs	NA
Loc	9 miles S of Nottingham

Sherwood Forest (1904)

Eakring Road, Mansfield NG18 3EW

Tel	(0623) 23327
Mem	600
Sec	K Hall (0623) 26689
Pro	K Hall (0623) 27403
Holes	18 L 6710 yds SSS 73
Recs	Am–65 PM Baxter
	Pro–68 C Gray, G Stafford
V'trs	U H SOC
Fees	£15 D–£20 (£20)
Loc	2 miles E of Mansfield

Stanton-on-the-Wolds (1906)

Stanton Lane, Keyworth NG12 5BH

Tel	(06077) 2044
Mem	500 167(L) 100(J)
Sec	HG Gray (06077) 2006
Pro	N Hernon ((06077) 2390
Holes	18 L 6437 yds SSS 71
Recs	Am–67 CA Banks, PJ Whitt
	Pro–69 C Jepson
V'trs	WD–U exc comp days WE–M
	SOC
Fees	£16 D–£18
Loc	9 miles S of Nottingham

Wollaton Park (1927)

Nottingham NG8 1BT

Tel	(0602) 787574
Mem	700
Sec	OB Kirk
Pro	R Hastings (0602) 784834
Holes	18 L 6494 yds SSS 71
Recs	Am–65 L White
V'trs	U SOC
Fees	£12 (£18.50)
Loc	Nottingham 2 miles

Worksop (1914)

Windmill Lane, Worksop S80 2SQ

Tel	(0909) 472696
Mem	500
Sec	PG Jordan (0909) 477731
Pro	JR King (0909) 477732
Holes	18 L 6651 yds SSS 72
Recs	Am–67 L Westwood (1989)
	Pro–69 A Carter (1987)
V'trs	WD–U H (phone first)
	WE/BH–M SOC
Fees	£16.50 D–£22(£22)
Loc	1 mile SE of Worksop, off
	A6009 via by-pass (A57). M1
	junction 30, 9 miles

Oxfordshire

Badgemore Park (1972)

Henley-on-Thames

Tel	(0491) 573667 (Clubhouse)
Fax	(0491) 576899
Mem	850
Sec	R Park (Mgr) (0491) 572206
Pro	M Wright (0491) 574175
Holes	18 L 6112 yds SSS 69
Recs	Am–67 SJ Mann
	Pro–65 M Howell
V'trs	WD–U WE–H SOC–WD
Fees	£22 SOC–£22
Loc	3/4 mile W of Henley on B290

Burford (1936)

Burford OX8 4JG

Tel	(099 382) 2149
Mem	680
Sec	R Cane (099 382) 2583
Pro	N Allen (099 382) 2344
Holes	18 L 6405 yds SSS 71
Recs	Am–67 DE Giles
	Pro–67 H Weetman
V'trs	WD–H SOC
Fees	On application
Loc	19 miles W of Oxford on A40

Cherwell Edge (1980)

Public

Chacombe, Banbury OX17 2EN

Tel	(0295) 711591
Sec	R Davies
Pro	R Davies
Holes	18 L 5925 yds SSS 69
Recs	Am–71
V'trs	U SOC–WD
Fees	£4.20 D–£7.50 (£5.50)
Loc	3 miles E of Banbury on B4525
	(A422)

Chesterton (1973)

Chesterton, nr Bicester OX6 8TE

Tel	(0869) 241204
Mem	650
Sec	BT Carter
Pro	JW Wilkshire (0869) 242023
Holes	18 L 6224 yds SSS 70
Recs	Am–68
	Pro–68
V'trs	WD–U WE/ BH–H SOC–WD
Fees	£12 (£18)
Loc	2 miles SW of Bicester

Chipping Norton (1890)

Southcombe, Chipping Norton
OX7 5QH
Tel   (0608) 642383
Mem   850
Sec   AJB Norman
Pro   R Gould (0608) 643356
Holes   18 L 6280 yds SSS 70
Recs   Am–67 A Perrie, J Morewood
V'trs   WD–U WE–M
Fees   £18
Loc   1 mile E of Chipping Norton

Frilford Heath (1908)

Frilford Heath, Abingdon OX13 5NW
Tel   (0865) 390864
Mem   750
Sec   JW Kleynhans
Pro   DC Craik (0865) 390887
Holes   Red 18 L 6768 yds SSS 73
        Green 18 L 6006 yds SSS 69
Recs   Red Am–68 S Walker Green
        Am–65 G Wolstenholme
V'trs   WD–I H WE/BH–M SOC
Fees   £28 (£40)
Loc   3 miles W of Abingdon on
        A338 Oxford/ Wantage road

Henley (1908)

Harpsden, Henley-on-Thames
RG9 4HG
Tel   (0491) 573304
Mem   750
Sec   J Hex (0491) 575742
Pro   M Howell (0491) 575710
Holes   18 L 6329 yds SSS 70
Recs   Am–65 D Griffin (1989)
        Pro–64 P Harrison (1989)
V'trs   WD–H WE–M
Fees   D–£28
Loc   Henley Station 1 mile

Huntercombe (1901)

Nuffield, Henley-on-Thames RG9 5SL
Tel   (0491) 641207
Mem   700
Sec   Lt Col TJ Hutchison
Pro   JB Draycott (0491) 641241
Holes   18 L 6261 yds SSS 70
Recs   Am–65 A Jackson
        Pro–63 J Morris
V'trs   WD–H after 10am WE/BH–NA
        SOC
Fees   £27.50
Loc   6 miles W of Henley on A423
Mis   Foursomes and singles only

North Oxford (1908)

Banbury Road, Oxford OX2 8EZ
Tel   (0865) 54415
Mem   701
Sec   W Forster (0865) 54924
Pro   R Harris (0865) 53977
Holes   18 L 5805 yds SSS 67
Recs   Am–64 S Donaghey
        Pro–M Faulkner
V'trs   U SOC
Fees   £18 (£25)
Loc   Between Oxford and
        Kidlington

RAF Benson (1975)

Royal Air Force, Benson
Tel   (0491) 37766
Mem   175
Sec   Sqn Ldr WB Sowerby MVO
        RAF (Ret'd) (0235) 848472
Holes   9 L 4395 yds SSS 61
V'trs   M
Loc   3½ miles NE of Wallingford

Southfield (1875)

Hill Top Road, Oxford OX4 1PF
Tel   (0865) 242158
Mem   500
Sec   AG Hopcraft
Pro   A Rees (0865) 244258
Holes   18 L 6230 yds SSS 70
Recs   Am–66 CM Barrett, GL Morley
        Pro–61 A Rees
V'trs   WD–U WE/ BH–M H SOC
Fees   £20
Loc   2 miles E of Oxford

Tadmarton Heath (1922)

Wigginton, Banbury OX15 5HL
Tel   (0608) 737649
Mem   600
Sec   RE Wackrill (0608) 737278
Pro   Les Bond (0608) 730047
Holes   18 L 5917 yds SSS 69
Recs   Am–66 R Welsh, M Steel
        Pro–63 G Smith
V'trs   WD–H by appointment WE–M
        SOC
Fees   £20 (1990)
Loc   5 miles W of Banbury, off
        B4035

Shropshire

Bridgnorth (1889)

Stanley Lane, Bridgnorth WV16 4SF
Tel   (0746) 763315
Mem   435
Sec   EH Thomas (0746) 762400
Pro   P Hinton (0746) 762045
Holes   18 L 6638 yds SSS 72
Recs   Am–67 C Banks (1985)
        Pro–66 P Hinton (1989)
V'trs   U SOC
Fees   £15 (£20)
Loc   1 mile N of Bridgnorth

Church Stretton (1898)

Trevor Hill, Church Stretton
Tel   (0694) 722281
Mem   470
Sec   R Broughton (0694) 722633
Holes   18 L 5008 yds SSS 66
Recs   Am–63 J Griffiths (1987)
V'trs   H WE–NA before 10.30am
        SOC
Fees   £10 (£15)
Loc   ½ mile W of Church Stretton,
        off A49

Hawkstone Park (1921)

Weston-under-Redcastle, nr
Shrewsbury SY4 5UY
Tel   (093924) 611   01939 200 611
Mem   400
Sec   KL Brazier (Mgr) AWB Lyle
        (Golf Dir)
Pro   K Williams (093924) 209
Holes   Hawkstone 18 L 6465 yds SSS 71
        Weston 18 L 5368 yds SSS 66
Recs   Am–67 AWB Lyle, MA Smith
        Pro–65 A Jacklin
V'trs   U after 10.35am SOC
Fees   Hawkestone £13 (£16) Weston
        £8.50 (£9.50)
Loc   7 miles S of Whitchurch.
        14 miles N of Shrewbury on A49
Mis   Buggies for hire. Golf hotel

Hill Valley G & CC (1975)

Terrick Road, Whitchurch
Tel   (0948) 3584
Mem   500
Sec   RB Walker
Pro   AR Minshall (0948) 3032
Holes   18 L 6050 yds SSS 69
        9 L 5106 yds SSS 65 9 hole Par
        3 course
Recs   Am–69 K Valentine
        Pro–64 W Milne
V'trs   U
Fees   £16 (£21) 9 holes–£9 Par 3
        course–£3
Loc   1 mile N of Whitchurch, off
        A41/ A49
Mis   John Garner golf school

Lilleshall Hall (1937)

Abbey Road, Lilleshall, nr Newport
TF10 9AS
Tel   (0952) 603840
Mem   600
Sec   DR Higgs (0952) 604776
Pro   NW Bramall (0952) 604104
Holes   18 L 5861 yds SSS 68
Recs   Am–65 P Baker
        Pro–70 J Anderson
V'trs   WD–U WE–M SOC
Fees   £15 (BH+day after–£25)
Loc   Between Lilleshall and
        Sheriffhales

Llanymynech (1933)

Pant, nr Oswestry SY10 8LB
Tel   (0691) 830542
Mem   760
Sec   NE Clews (0691) 830983
Pro   A Griffiths (0691) 830879
Holes   18 L 6114 yds SSS 69
Recs   Am–66 M Evans
        Pro–65 I Woosnam
V'trs   U before 4.30pm –M after
        4.30pm SOC
Fees   £11 (£16.50)
Loc   5 miles S of Oswestry on A483

Ludlow (1889)

Bromfield, Ludlow SY8 2BT
Tel   (058 477) 285
Mem   550

Sec M Cropper (Admin) RPJ Jones (058 477) 334
Pro G Farr (058 477) 366
Holes 18 L 6240 yds SSS 70
Recs Am–67 T Clare
Pro–65 PA Brookes
V'trs U
Fees £12 (£16) (1990)
Loc A49, 2 miles N of Ludlow

Market Drayton (1925)

Sutton, Market Drayton TF9 1LX
Tel (0630) 652266
Mem 450
Sec JJ Moseley (0630) 653661 (day)
Pro R Clewes
Holes 18 L 6225 yds SSS 70
V'trs WD–U WE–NA
Fees £15
Loc 1 mile S of Market Drayton

Meole Brace (1976)

Public
Meole Brace, Shrewsbury SY2 6QQ
Tel (0743) 64050
Pro I Doran
Holes 9 L 2915 yds SSS 68
Recs Am–66 J Mansell
Pro–68 R Cockcroft
V'trs U
Fees £2.55 (£3.20) 18 holes
Loc Junction A5/ A49 Meole Brace

Oswestry (1930)

Aston Park, Oswestry SY11 4JJ
Tel (069 188) 221
Mem 700
Sec Mrs PM Lindner (069 188) 535
Pro D Skelton (069 188) 448
Holes 18 L 6038 yds SSS 69
Recs Am–62 AL Strange
Pro–68 JW Walker
V'trs M or H SOC–WD
Fees £12 (£16)
Loc 3¼ miles E of Oswestry on A5

Shifnal (1929)

Decker Hill, Shifnal
Tel (0952) 460467/ 460330
Mem 500
Sec J Bell (0952) 460330
Pro J Flanaghan (0952) 460457
Holes 18 L 6422 yds SSS 71
Recs Am–66 R Howells
Pro–67 IN Doran
V'trs WD–phone first WE/ BH–M
Loc M54 Junction 4, 2 miles. 1 mile NE of Shifnal

Shrewsbury (1891)

Condover, Shrewsbury
Tel (074 372) 2976
Mem 450 160(L) 75(J)
Sec JA Morrison (074 372) 2977
Pro P Seal (074 372) 3751
Holes 18 L 6212 yds SSS 70
Recs Am–60 JR Burn
V'trs H SOC
Fees £12 (£18)
Loc 4 miles SW of Shrewsbury

Telford Hotel G & CC (1981)

Great Hay, Sutton Hill, Telford TF7 4DT
Tel (0952) 585642
Fax (0952) 586602
Mem 500
Sec Cdr JG Brigham (Ext 274)
Pro S Marr (0952) 586052
Holes 18 L 6766 yds SSS 72
9 hole Par 3 course
Recs Am–66 C Bufton (1986)
Pro–62 D Thorpe
V'trs H SOC
Fees £20 (£25)
Loc 1 mile SE of Telford, off A442
Mis Driving range

Wrekin (1905)

Wellington, Telford
Tel (0952) 244032
Mem 500 85(L) 90(J) 30(5)
Sec S Leys
Pro K Housden
Holes 18 L 5657 yds SSS 67
Recs Am–65 GC Clayton,R Jones, P Baker, F Tart
Pro–67 C Holmes
V'trs WD–U before 5pm –M after 5pm SOC
Fees £10 (£12)
Loc Wellington, off B5061

Somerset

Brean (1973)

Coast Road, Brean, Burnham-on-Sea TA8 2RT
Tel (0278) 751595
Mem 600
Sec WS Martin (Hon)
Pro G Coombes (0278) 751570
Holes 18 L 5200 yds SSS 67
Recs Am–67 C Clarke (1987)
V'trs WD–U H WE–pm only SOC–WD
Fees £8 (£12)
Loc 4 miles N of Burnham-on-Sea

Burnham & Berrow (1890)

St Christopher's Way, Burnham-on-Sea TA8 2PE
Tel (0278) 783137
Mem 800
Sec Mrs EL Sloman (0278) 785760
Pro NP Blake (0278) 784545
Holes 18 L 6547 yds SSS 73
9 L 6550 yds SSS 72
Recs Medal Am–68 G Thomas
C'ship Am–66 P Baker
V'trs I SOC
Fees £20 (£28) W–£100 9 hole–£7
Loc 1 mile N of Burnham-on-Sea

Enmore Park (1932)

Enmore, Bridgwater
Tel (027 867) 244
Mem 780

Sec DH Smith (027 867) 481
Pro N Wixon (027 867) 519
Holes 18 L 6443 yds SSS 71
Recs Am–66 T Lawrence
Pro–65 G Carter
V'trs U SOC–WD
Fees £18 (£25)
Loc 3 miles W of Bridgwater, off Durleigh road. M5 Junction 23

Kingweston (1983)

Somerton
Tel (0458) 43921
Mem 200
Sec JG Willetts
Holes 9 L 4516 yds SSS 62
V'trs M exc Wed & Sat 2-5pm–NA
Fees NA
Loc 1 mile SE of Butleigh, nr Glastonbury

Mendip (1908)

Gurney Slade, Bath BA3 4UT
Tel (0749) 840570
Mem 598
Sec Mrs JP Howe
Pro RF Lee (0749) 840793
Holes 18 L 5982 yds SSS 69
Recs Am–65 RH Flower
Pro–64 N Blenkarne
V'trs H SOC–WD
Fees £15 (£30)
Loc 3 miles N of Shepton Mallet (A37)

Minehead & West Somerset (1882)

Warren Road, Minehead
Tel (0643) 702057
Mem 492
Sec DR Pettit
Pro I Read (0643) 704378
Holes 18 L 6228 yds SSS 71
Recs Am–68 R Barrett
Pro–66 BJ Hunt
V'trs U after 9.15am SOC
Fees £17 (£20) W–£60
Loc E end of sea front

Taunton & Pickeridge (1892)

Corfe, Taunton TA3 7BY
Tel (082 342) 240
Mem 600
Sec GW Sayers (082 342) 537
Pro G Glew (082 342) 790
Holes 18 L 5927 yds SSS 68
Recs Am–66 CS Edwards (1989)
Pro–65 G Emerson (1984)
V'trs H SOC
Fees On application
Loc 5 miles S of Taunton on B3170

Vivary Park

Public
Taunton
Tel (0823) 289274 (Clubhouse)
Pro J Wright (0823) 333875
Holes 18 L 4620 yds SSS 63

For list of abbreviations see page 487.

V'trs   U exc Wed evenings-M
Booking necessary through
Pro
Fees   £5.25
Loc   Taunton
Mis   Vivary Club plays here

Wells (Somerset) (1893)

East Horrington Road, Wells BA5 3DS
Tel   (0749) 72868
Mem   780
Sec   GE Ellis (0749) 75005
Pro   A England (0749) 679059
Holes   18 L 5354 yds SSS 66
Recs   Am–64 RW Davis (1985),
J Goymer (1990)
Pro–65 R Clifton (1986)
V'trs   WD–U WE–H SOC–WD
Fees   £13.50 (£17.50) Mon-Fri £50
Loc   1 1/2 miles from Wells, off
Radstock road

Windwhistle G & CC (1932)

Cricket St Thomas, Chard TA20 4DG
Tel   (0460) 30231
Mem   450
Sec   I Neville Dodd (Sec/ Mgr)
Pro   I Yard
Holes   18 L 6442 yds SSS 71 9 hole
Course
V'trs   U-phone first SOC
Fees   On application
Loc   On A30, between Chard and
Crewkerne (signs to Wildlife
Park). M5 Junction 25

Yeovil (1919)

Sherborne Road, Yeovil BA21 5BW
Tel   (0935) 75949
Mem   695 150(L) 70(J)
Sec   J Riley (0935) 22965
Pro   G Kite (0935) 73763
Holes   18 L 6144 yds SSS 69
Recs   Am–66 J Pounder (1986)
Pro–65 G Laing (1987),
R Troake (1989)
V'trs   WD–U WE/ BH–H (phone Pro
for starting time) SOC
Fees   £18 (£20)
Loc   1 mile from Yeovil on A30 to
Sherborne

Staffordshire

Alsager G & CC (1977)

Audley Road, Alsager, Stoke-on-
Trent
Tel   (0270) 875700
Mem   640
Sec   Mrs EE Wynne
Pro   D Clare (0270) 877432
Holes   18 L 6192 yds SSS 70
V'trs   WD–U before 5pm -M after
5pm WE/ BH–M SOC
Fees   £10
Loc   2 miles E of M6 Junction 16.
Crewe 5 miles. Stoke 7 miles

Barlaston

Meaford Road, Barlaston, Stone
Tel   (078 139) 2795
Mem   450
Sec   M Degg
Holes   18 L 5800 yds SSS 68
Recs   Am–69 S Ashcroft (1983)
V'trs   U
Fees   £9 (£12)
Loc   1/4 mile S of Barlaston. 3/4 mile
N of Stone

Beau Desert (1921)

Hazel Slade, Cannock WS12 5PJ
Tel   (0543) 422626/ 422773
Mem   500
Sec   AJR Fairfield (0543) 422626
Pro   B Stevens (0543) 422492
Holes   18 L 6279 yds SSS 71
Recs   Am–67 P Broadhurst (1986)
Pro–64 T Minshall
V'trs   WD–U WE–phone in advance
BH–NA SOC
Fees   £25
Loc   4 miles NE of Cannock

Branston (1975)

Burton Road, Branston, Burton-on-
Trent
Tel   (0283) 43207
Fax   (0283) 66984
Mem   450 50(L) 60(J)
Sec   KL George
Pro   S Warner
Holes   18 L 6480 yds SSS 71
Recs   Am–69 T Bailey (1987)
Pro–67 P Kent
V'trs   WD–U WE–M before noon
SOC
Fees   £15 (£18)
Loc   1/2 mile from A38/ A5121
junction, towards Burton

Brocton Hall (1923)

Brocton, Stafford ST17 0TH
Tel   (0785) 662627
Mem   500
Sec   WR Lanyon (0785) 661901
Pro   R Johnson (0785) 661485
Holes   18 L 6095 yds SSS 69
Recs   Am–67 WB Taylor
V'trs   I H SOC
Fees   £18 (£20)
Loc   4 miles SE of Stafford, off A34

Burslem (1907)

Wood Farm, High Lane, Stoke-on-
Trent ST6 7JT
Tel   (0782) 837006
Mem   250
Sec   RJ Sutton (0782) 837704
Holes   9 L 5354 yds SSS 66
Recs   Am–64 M Keeling (1988)
Pro–66 T Williamson
V'trs   WD–U WE–NA
Fees   £10
Loc   Burslem 2 miles

Burton-on-Trent (1893)

43 Ashby Road, East Burton-on-Trent
DE15 0PS
Tel   (0283) 68708
Mem   600
Sec   A Maddock (0283) 44551
Pro   JM Lower (0283) 62240
Holes   18 L 6555 yds SSS 71
Recs   Am–69 JE Roberts
Pro–67 DA Stewart
V'trs   I or M
Fees   £9 (£13)
Loc   Burton 3 miles

Cannock Park Municipal

Public
Stafford Road, Cannock WS11 2AL
Tel   (0543) 578850
Sec   D Dunk
Pro   D Dunk
Holes   18 L 5229 yds SSS 65
V'trs   U
Fees   £3.50 (£5)
Loc   1/4 mile N of Cannock on A34.
2 miles from M6 Junction 11

Craythorne Golf Centre (1972)

Craythorne Road, Stretton, Burton-
on-Trent DE13 0AZ
Tel   (0283) 64329
Fax   (0283) 511908
Sec   J Bissell (Gen Mgr) (0283)
37992
Pro   S Hadfield (0283) 33745
Holes   18 L 5230 yds SSS 66 9 hole
course
Recs   Am–62 PCR Smith (1987)
V'trs   WD–U SOC
Fees   £11 (£12)
Loc   Stretton, 1 1/2 miles N of Burton-
A38/ A5121 Junction
Mis   Driving range

Drayton Park (1897)

Drayton Park, Tamworth B78 3TN
Tel   (0827) 251139
Mem   450
Sec   AO Rammell JP
Pro   MW Passmore (0827) 251478
Holes   18 L 6414 yds SSS 74
Recs   Am–66 M Biddle (1984)
Pro–65 DJ Russell (1987)
V'trs   WD–H WE/ BH–NA SOC–Tues
& Thurs
Fees   D–£21
Loc   2 miles S of Tamworth (A4091)

Goldenhill (1983)

Public
Mobberley Road, Goldenhill, Stoke-
on-Trent ST6 5SS
Pro   A Clingan (0782) 784715
Holes   18 L 5957 yds SSS 68
V'trs   U WE/ BH–book with Pro
Fees   £3.60 (£4.20)
Loc   Between Tunstall and
Kidsgrove, off A50

Greenway Hall (1908)

Stockton Brook, Stoke-on-Trent
Tel (0782) 503158
Mem 390
Sec EH Jones (Mgr) (0782) 503095
Holes 18 L 5676 yds SSS 67
Recs Am–65 A Bailey, A Dathan
V'trs Mon/ Wed/ Fri-H Tues &
Thurs-U WE–U Sun pm SOC
Fees On application
Loc 5 miles N of Stoke

Ingestre Park (1977)

nr Stafford
Tel (0889) 270061
Mem 650
Sec DD Humphries (Mgr) (0889) 270845
Pro D Scullion (0889) 270304
Holes 18 L 6334 yds SSS 70
Recs Am–67 D Hughes
Pro–68 D Scullion
V'trs WD–U WE/ BH–M
Fees £20
Loc 6 miles E of Stafford

Lakeside (1969)

Rugeley Power Station, Rugeley WS15 1PR
Tel (0889) 583181
Fax (0889) 576412
Mem 300
Sec EG Jones
Holes 9 L 4768 yds SSS 63
Recs Am–63 D Glenn (1990)
V'trs M
Loc Rugeley Power Station. 2 miles SE of Rugeley on A513
Mis Extension to 18 holes in 1991

Leek (1892)

Big Birchall, Leek ST13 5RE
Tel (0538) 385889
Mem 400 90(L) 45(J) 100(5)
Sec F Cutts (0538) 384779
Pro P Stubbs (0538) 384767
Holes 18 L 6240 yds SSS 70
Recs Am–63 D Evans
Pro–65 P Baker
V'trs U H before 3pm -M after 3pm
SOC–Wed only
Fees £20 (£25)
Loc 1/2 mile from Leek on Stone road (A520)

Newcastle Municipal (1973)

Public
Keele Road, Newcastle-under-Lyme
Tel (0782) 627596
Pro C Smith
Holes 18 L 5822 metres SSS 70
Recs Am–70 P Rowe
Pro–68 P Rowe
V'trs U
Fees £3.85 (£4.50)
Loc 2 miles NW of Newcastle on A525, opposite Keele University

Newcastle-under-Lyme (1908)

Whitmore Road, Newcastle-under-Lyme
Tel (0782) 616583
Mem 575
Sec RB Irving (0782) 617006
Pro P Symonds (0782) 618526
Holes 18 L 6450 yds SSS 71
Recs Am–64 MC Keates (1989)
Pro–68 A Pauly (1988)
V'trs WD–U H WE/ BH–M SOC
Fees £20

Onneley (1968)

Onneley, nr Crewe, Cheshire
Tel (0782) 750577
Mem 375
Sec LAC Kennedy (0270) 661842
Holes 9 L 5584 yds SSS 67
Recs Am–68 D Gilford
V'trs WD–U Sat/ BH–M Sun–NA
Fees £10
Loc Nr Woore, 1 mile off A51 to Newcastle

Park Hall (1989)

Public
Hulme Road, Weston Coyney, Stoke-on-Trent ST3 5BH
Pro A Clingan (0782) 599584
Holes 18 L 2335 yds Par 54
V'trs WD–U WE/ BH–book with Pro
Fees £2.70. (£3.20)
Loc 1 mile from Longton

Stafford Castle (1907)

Newport Road, Stafford ST16 1BP
Tel (0785) 223821
Mem 400
Sec MH Fisher
Holes 9 L 6462 yds SSS 71
Recs Am–70 S Sturgess
V'trs WD–U WE–after 1pm
Fees £10 (£14)
Loc 1/2 mile W of Stafford

Stone (1896)

Filleybrooks, Stone ST15 0NB
Tel (0785) 813103
Mem 181 53(L) 20(J) 30(5)
Sec MG Pharaoh (088 97) 224
Holes 9 L 6299 yds SSS 70
Recs Am–69 A Hurst (1988)
V'trs WD–U WE/ BH–M SOC–WD
Fees £10
Loc 1/2 mile W of Stone on A34

Tamworth (1978)

Public
Eagle Drive, Amington, Tamworth B77 4EG
Tel (0827) 53850
Sec BN Jones (0827)53858
Pro BN Jones
Holes 18 L 6695 yds SSS 72
Recs Am–67 CJ Christison
Pro–65 BN Jones

V'trs U SOC–WD
Fees £3.35
Loc 2 1/2 miles E of Tamworth on B5000. M42, 3 miles

Trentham (1895)

14 Barlaston Old Road, Trentham, Stoke-on-Trent ST4 8HB
Tel (0782) 642347
Mem 680
Sec Lt Cdr JR Smith RN(Retd) (0782) 658109
Pro D MacDonald (0782) 657309
Holes 18 L 6644 yds SSS 72
Recs Am–66 DJ Boughey (1987)
V'trs WD–U H WE/ BH–M (or enquire Sec) SOC–WD
Fees £15 (£18) 1989 prices
Loc 3 miles S of Newcastle, off A34. M6 Junction 15

Trentham Park (1936)

Trentham Park, Stoke-on-Trent ST4 8AE
Tel (0782) 642245
Mem 300 70(L) 60(J) 100(5)
Sec CH Lindop (0782) 658800
Pro R Clarke (0782) 642125
Holes 18 L 6403 yds SSS 71
Recs Am–67 PG Nuthall
V'trs U SOC–Wed & Fri
Fees £20 (£25)
Loc 4 miles S of Newcastle on A34. M6 Junction 15, 1 mile

Uttoxeter (1975)

Wood Lane, Uttoxeter ST14 7LZ
Tel (0889) 565108
Mem 650
Sec Mrs G Davies
Pro J Pearsall (0889) 564884
Holes 18 L 5695 yds SSS 69
Recs Am–69
V'trs WD–U WE–by arrangement SOC
Fees £10 (£15)
Loc Uttoxeter racecourse 1/2 mile

Westwood (1923)

Newcastle Road, Walbridge, Leek
Tel (0538) 383060
Mem 300
Sec AJ Lawton (0782) 503780
Holes 13 L 4766 yds SSS 68
Recs Am–68 SD Spooner
V'trs WD–U Sat-M BH–H SOC
Fees WD–£8
Loc W boundary of Leek on A53

Whittington Barracks (1886)

Tamworth Road, Lichfield WS14 9PW
Tel (0543) 432212
Mem 670
Sec (0543) 432317
Pro AR Sadler (0543) 432261
Holes 18 L 6457 yds SSS 74
Recs Am–65 CG Marks, CG Poxon
Pro–67 AR Sadler

V'trs   WD–H I WE/ BH + day after-M
        SOC–Wed & Thurs
Fees   D–£22
Loc   2¹/₂ miles from Lichfield on
        Tamworth road

Wolstanton (1904)

Dimsdale Old Hall, Newcastle
ST5 9DR
Tel   (0782) 616995
Mem   550
Sec   D Shelley (0782) 622413
Pro   (0782) 622718
Holes   18 L 5807 yds SSS 68
Recs   Am–65 P Sweetsur, M Hassall,
        R Maxfield
        Pro–66 CH Ward
V'trs   WD–I WE–M
Fees   £14
Loc   1¹/₂ miles NW of Newcastle

Suffolk

Aldeburgh (1884)

Aldeburgh IP15 5PE
Tel   (0728) 452408
Mem   750
Sec   RC Van de Velde (0728)
        452890
Pro   K Preston (0728) 453309
Holes   18 L 6330 yds SSS 71
        9 L 2114 yds SSS 64
Recs   Am–65 J Lloyd
        Pro–67 JM Johnson
V'trs   I
Fees   On application
Loc   6 miles E of A12, between
        Ipswich and Lowestoft

Bungay & Waveney Valley (1889)

Bungay
Tel   (0986) 892337
Mem   709
Sec   WJ Stevens
Pro   N Whyte
Holes   18 L 5950 yds SSS 68
Recs   Am–67 N Kidd
        Pro–64 T Spurgeon
V'trs   WD–U WE–M SOC
Fees   D–£15 (1990)
Loc   Bungay ¹/₂ mile

Bury St Edmunds (1922)

Tut Hill, Bury St Edmunds
Tel   (0284) 755979
Mem   830 130 (L) 34(J) 100(5)
Sec   CD Preece
Pro   M Jillings (0284) 755978
Holes   18 L 6615 yds SSS 72
Recs   Am–69 S Goodman, A Currie
        Pro–67 K Golding
V'trs   WD–U WE–M BH–U SOC
Fees   £20
Loc   2 miles W of Bury St Edmunds
        on B1106

Cretingham (1983)

Public
Grove Farm, Cretingham,
Woodbridge IP13 7BA
Tel   (072882) 275
Sec   J Austin (Prop)
Holes   9 L 1955 yds Par 30
Recs   Am–29 R Watts (1986)
        Pro–28 J Philpot (1990)
V'trs   U
Fees   £7 (£10) 18 holes
Loc   2 miles SE of Earl Soham

Diss (1903)

Stuston Common, Diss
Tel   (0379) 642847
Mem   500
Sec   J Bell (0379) 642679
Pro   N Taylor (0379) 644399
Holes   9 L 5900 yds SSS 68
Recs   Am–68 JE Doe Pro–T Pennock
V'trs   WD–NA after 4pm WE–NA
Fees   £10

Felixstowe Ferry (1880)

Ferry Road, Felixstowe IP4 9RY
Tel   (0394) 286834
Mem   750
Pro   I Macpherson (0394) 283975
Holes   18 L 6308 yds SSS 70
Recs   Am–68 I Whinney
        Pro–65 I Richardson
V'trs   U H WE–M before 10.30am
        SOC
Fees   £18 (£21)
Loc   2 miles NE of Felixstowe,
        towards Felixstowe Ferry

Flempton (1895)

Bury St Edmunds
Tel   (028 484) 291
Mem   250
Sec   PH Nunn (0638) 750100
Pro   M Jillings
Holes   9 L 6704 yds SSS 69
Recs   Am–67 Lt J Reynolds
        Pro–69 J Arbon
V'trs   WD–H WE/ BH–M H
Fees   £15 D–£20
Loc   5 miles NW of Bury St Edmunds
        on A1101

Fornham Park G & CC (1974)

St John's Hill Plantation, The Street,
Fornham All Saints, Bury St Edmunds
IP28 6JQ
Tel   (0284) 706777
Fax   (0284) 706721
Mem   700
Sec   S Clark
Pro   S Clark
Holes   18 L 6229 yds SSS 70
Recs   Am–68 S Blanshard (1987)
        Pro–65 S Wright (1986)
V'trs   WD–U WE–NA before
        10.30am SOC
Fees   £15 (£20)

Loc   From Cambridge, 1st exit on
        A45; from Ipswich, 3rd exit on
        A45

Haverhill (1974)

Coupals Road, Haverhill CB9 7UW
Tel   (0440) 61951
Mem   350
Sec   Mrs J Webster
Pro   S Mayfield (0440) 712628
Holes   9 L 5707 yds SSS 68
Recs   Am–67 P Brierley
        Pro–66 C Cook
V'trs   U SOC
Fees   £12 (£17)
Loc   Haverhill, 1 mile off A604.
        Signs to Calford Green

Ipswich (Purdis Heath) (1895)

Purdis Heath, Ipswich
Tel   (0473) 728941
        (0473) 727474 (Steward)
Mem   800
Sec   AE Howell
Pro   SJ Whymark (0473) 724017
Holes   18 L 6405 yds SSS 71
        9 L 1950 yds Par 31
Recs   Am–64 JVT Marks
        Pro–67 RA Knight
V'trs   18 hole-H or I 9 hole-U SOC
Fees   18 hole: £14 (£16)
        9 hole: £7 (£8)
Loc   3 miles E of Ipswich

Links (Newmarket) (1902)

Cambridge Road, Newmarket
CB8 0TG
Tel   (0638) 662708
Mem   685
Sec   Mrs T MacGregor (0638)
        663000
Pro   DP Thomson (0638) 662395
Holes   18 L 6424 yds SSS 71
Recs   Am–68 M Hartley
        Pro–70 S Barlow
V'trs   WD–H WE/ BH–H exc Sun-MH
        before 11.30am SOC
Fees   £18 (£25)
Loc   1 mile S of Newmarket

Newton Green (1907)

Newton Green, Sudbury
Tel   (0787) 77501/ 77216
Mem   400
Sec   G Bright (0787) 71119
Pro   K Lovelock
Holes   9 L 5488 yds SSS 67
Recs   Am–60 R Rowland
        Pro–29 A Davey (9 holes)
V'trs   WD–U WE–M
Fees   £10
Loc   4 miles E of Sudbury

Rookery Park (1891)

Carlton Colville, Lowestoft NR33 8HJ
Tel   (0502) 560380
Mem   750
Sec   To be appointed

Pro   M Elsworthy (0502) 515103
Holes 18 L 6649 yds SSS 72
       Par 3 course
Recs   Am–71 G Long (1985)
       Pro–69 P Kent (1985)
V'trs WD–U Sat/ BH–after 11am
       Sun–NA SOC
Fees   £16 (£20)
Loc   W of Lowestoft (A146)

Royal Worlington & Newmarket (1893)

Worlington, Bury St Edmunds
IP28 8SD
Tel   (0638) 712216
Mem   328
Sec   CP Simpson
Pro   M Hawkins (0638) 715224
Holes 9 L 6218 yds SSS 70
Recs   Am–67 DJ Millensted
       Pro–66 EE Beverley
V'trs I or H-phone first WE–NA
Fees   £25
Loc   6 miles NE of Newmarket, off
       A11

Rushmere (1895)

Rushmere Heath, Ipswich
Tel   (0473) 727109
Mem   750
Sec   RW Whiting (0473) 725648
Pro   NTJ McNeill (0473) 728076
Holes 18 L 6287 yds SSS 70
Recs   Am–66 F Knights (1989),
       M Turner (1990)
       Pro–67 NTJ McNeil (1984),
       S Beckham (1985)
V'trs WD–U WE/ BH–after 2.30pm
Fees   On application
Loc   Ipswich, off Woodbridge road
       (A12)

St Helena (1990)

Halesworth IP19 9XA
Tel   (0986) 875567
Fax   (0986) 874565
Mem   600
Sec   J Johnson
Pro   J Johnson
Holes 27 L 6580 yds SSS 72/ 36
V'trs H SOC
Fees   £12 D–£15 (£18) 9 holes–£6
Loc   1 mile from Halesworth, off
       A144 Bramfield road
Mis   Floodlit driving range

Southwold (1884)

The Common, Southwold
Tel   (0502) 723234
Mem   450
Sec   IG Guy (0502) 723248
Pro   B Allen (0502) 723790
Holes 9 L 6001 yds SSS 69
Recs   Am–67 S Fitzgerald
       Pro–65 R Mann
V'trs U (subject to fixtures)
Fees   On application
Loc   35 miles N of Ipswich

Stowmarket (1962)

Lower Road, Onehouse, Stowmarket
IP14 3DA
Tel   (0449) 736392
Mem   600
Sec   PW Rumball (0449) 736473
Pro   C Aldred
Holes 18 L 6119 yds SSS 69
Recs   Am–67 I Oakes
       Pro–66 H Flatman
V'trs H SOC–Thurs & Fri
Fees   £15 (£25)
Loc   2¹/₂ miles SW of Stowmarket

Thorpeness Hotel

Thorpeness
Tel   (0728) 452176
Mem   400
Sec   NW Griffin
Pro   T Pennock (0728) 452524
Holes 18 L 6208 yds SSS 71
Recs   Am–66 J Marks
       Pro–67 K McDonald
V'trs U
Fees   On application
Loc   2 miles N of Aldeburgh

Waldringfield Heath (1983)

Newbourne Road, Waldringfield,
Woodbridge IP12 4PT
Tel   (0473) 36768/ 36426
Mem   600
Sec   LJ McWade (0473) 36768
Pro   A Dobson (0473) 36417
Holes 18 L 5837 yds SSS 68
Recs   Pro–64 A Dobson (1990)
V'trs WD–U WE/ BH–M before noon
       SOC–WD
Fees   On application
Loc   3 miles N of Ipswich, off A12

Wood Valley (Beccles) (1899)

The Common, Beccles
Tel   (0502) 712244
Mem   200
Sec   Mrs LW Allen (0502) 712479
Pro   K Allen
Holes 9 L 2696 yds SSS 67
Recs   Pro–64 K Allen
V'trs WD–U Sun–M SOC
Fees   £7 (£8)
Loc   Lowestoft 10 miles. Norwich 18
       miles

Woodbridge (1893)

Bromeswell Heath, nr Woodbridge
Tel   (039 43) 2038
Mem   930
Sec   Capt LA Harpum RN
Pro   LA Jones (039 43) 3213
Holes 18 L 6314 yds SSS 70 9 L 2243
       yds SSS 31
Recs   Am–64 JVT Marks (1983)
       Pro–65 F Sunderland (1970)
V'trs H WE/ BH–M SOC
Fees   £15 D–£20 1989 prices
Loc   2 miles E of Woodbridge, off
       A12 Woodbridge by-pass
       towards Orford (B1084)

Surrey

The Addington (1913)

Shirley Church Road, Croydon
CR50 5AB
Tel   (081) 777 1055
Sec   (081) 777 6057
Pro   E Campbell (081) 777 1701
Holes 18 L 6242 yds SSS 71
Recs   Am–66 P Benka
       Pro–68 F Robson
V'trs H SOC–WD
Fees   On application
Loc   E Croydon 2¹/₂ miles

Addington Court (1931)

Public
Featherbed Lane, Addington,
Croydon CR0 9AA
Tel   (081) 657 0281/ 2/ 3
Sec   G Cotton
Pro   G Cotton
Holes Old 18 L 5577 yds SSS 67
       New 18 L 5513 yds SSS 66
       Lower 9 L 1812 yds SSS 62 18
       hole Pitch and Putt course
Recs   Pro–63 C Phillips
V'trs U
Fees   Old:£8.90 New:£7.50 9 hole:£5
Loc   3 miles E of Croydon

Addington Palace (1923)

Gravel Hill, Addington, Croydon
CR0 5BB
Tel   (081) 654 3061
Mem   700
Sec   J Robinson
Pro   M Pilkington (081) 654 1786
Holes 18 L 6410 yds SSS 71
Recs   Am–63 R Glading
       Pro–65 AD Locke
V'trs WD–H WE/ BH–M
Fees   £25
Loc   2 miles E of Croydon Station

Banstead Downs (1890)

Burdon Lane, Belmont, Sutton
SM2 7DD
Tel   (081) 642 2284
Mem   650
Sec   AW Schooling
Pro   I Marr (081) 642 6884
Holes 18 L 6169 yds SSS 69
Recs   Pro–MLA Perry
V'trs WD–H WE/ BH–M
Fees   £25
Loc   1 mile S of Sutton

Barrow Hills (1970)

Longcross, Chertsey KT16 0DS
Mem   250
Sec   RW Routley (0932) 848117
Holes 18 L 3090 yds SSS 53
Recs   Am–58 EJ Sewell (1979)
V'trs M
Fees   On application
Loc   4 miles W of Chertsey

Betchworth Park (1913)

Reigate Road, Dorking RH4 1NZ
Tel   (0306) 882052
Mem   725
Sec   DAS Bradney
Pro   A King (0306) 884334
Holes   18 L 6266 yds SSS 70
Recs   Am–66 J Robson
    Pro–65 NC Coles
V'trs   WD–by arrangement exc Tues
    & Wed am–NA WE–NA exc
    Sun pm
Fees   £20 (£27)
Loc   1 mile E of Dorking on A25

Bramley (1913)

Bramley, nr Guildford GU5 0AL
Tel   (0483) 893042
Mem   700
Sec   Mrs M Lambert (0483) 892696
Pro   G Peddie (0483) 893685
Holes   18 L 5966 yds SSS 68
Recs   Am–66 MI Farmer
    Pro–63 PR Gill
V'trs   WD–U WE–M SOC–WD
Fees   £17.50 D–£22
Loc   3 miles S of Guildford on A281
Mis   Driving range. Buggies for hire

Burhill (1907)

Walton-on-Thames KT12 4BL
Tel   (0932) 227345
Mem   1100
Sec   AJ Acres
Pro   L Johnson (0932) 221729
Holes   18 L 6224 yds SSS 70
Recs   Am–66 RJ Pollitt (1987)
    Pro–65 G Orr (1988)
V'trs   WD–H WE/ BH–M
Fees   On application
Loc   Between Walton-on-Thames
    and Cobham, off Burwood road

Camberley Heath (1913)

Golf Drive, Camberley GU15 1JG
Tel   (0276) 23258
Fax   (0276) 692505
Mem   725
Sec   A Heron
Pro   G Smith (0276) 27905
Holes   18 L 6461 yds SSS 70
Recs   Am–66 C Laurence
    Pro–67 A Perry
V'trs   WD–I WE–M SOC H
Fees   £17 D–£25
Loc   1¹/₄ miles S of Camberley on
    A325

Chessington Golf Centre (1983)

Public
Garrison Lane, Chessington KT9 2LW
Tel   (081) 391 0948
Sec   A Maxted (Mgr) (081) 974 1705
Pro   B Cuff, J Fitzpatrick, J Rodger
Holes   9 L 1400 yds SSS 54
Recs   Am–60 N Murphy
    Pro–54 R Hunter

V'trs   WD–U WE–NA before noon
Fees   9 holes–£2.50 (£3)
Loc   Off A243, opposite
    Chessington South Station.
    M25 Junction 9
Mis   Driving range

Chipstead (1906)

How Lane, Chipstead, Coulsdon CR3 3PR
Tel   (0737) 551053
Mem   600
Sec   SLD Spencer-Skeen (0737)
    555781
Pro   (0737) 554939
Holes   18 L 5450 yds SSS 67
Recs   Am–63 A Davey (1986)
    Pro–63 N Child (1980)
V'trs   WD–U WE/ BH–M
Fees   £20 After 2pm–£15
Loc   Chipstead Station 200 yds

Coombe Hill (1911)

Kingston
Tel   (081) 942 2284
Fax   (081) 949 5815
Mem   437
Sec   AL Foster
Pro   C De Foy (081) 949 3713
Holes   18 L 6286 yds SSS 71
Recs   Am–67 L Freedman,
    RL Glading
    Pro–64 BJ Hunt
V'trs   I or H SOC
Fees   By arrangement
Loc   Off Coombe Lane West. 1 mile
    from New Malden on A238

Coombe Wood (1904)

George Road, Kingston Hill, Kingston-upon-Thames KT2 7NS
Tel   (081) 942 3828 (Steward/
    Members)
Mem   620
Sec   T Duncan (081) 942 0388
Pro   D Butler (081) 942 6764
Holes   18 L 5210 yds SSS 66
Recs   Am–62 FJ Cocker
    Pro–60 D Butler (1987)
V'trs   WD–U H after 9am WE/ BH–M
    SOC–WD
Fees   £25
Loc   1 mile N of Kingston-upon-
    Thames, off A3 at Robin Hood
    roundabout

Coulsdon Court (1937)

Public
Coulsdon Road, Croydon CR3 2LL
Tel   (081) 660 0468
Pro   C Staff (081) 660 6083
Holes   18 L 6030 yds SSS 70
Recs   Am–66 K Smale
    Pro–66 G Ralph
V'trs   U
Fees   £10 (£12.50)
Loc   5 miles S of Croydon on B2030
Mis   Public course, now privately
    operated

Croham Hurst (1911)

Croham Road, South Croydon CR2 7HJ
Tel   (081) 657 5581
Mem   314 110(L) 80(J) 175(5)
Sec   R Passingham (Mgr)
Pro   E Stillwell (081) 657 7705
Holes   18 L 6274 yds SSS 70
Recs   Am–64 SF Robson
    Pro–66 B Firkins
V'trs   WD–I WE/ BH–M
Fees   £25
Loc   1 mile from S Croydon. M25
    Junction 6-A22-B270-B269

Crondall (1984)

Oak Park, Heath Lane, Crondall, nr Farnham GU10 5PB
Tel   (0252) 850880
Mem   400
Sec   Mrs R Smythe (Prop)
Pro   P Rees (0252) 850066
Holes   18 L 6278 yds SSS 70
V'trs   U SOC
Fees   £14 (£18)
Loc   Off A287 Farnham-Odiham
    road. M3 Junction 5, 4 miles
Mis   Covered driving range

Cuddington (1929)

Banstead Road, Banstead SM7 1RD
Tel   (081) 393 0952
Mem   795
Sec   DM Scott
Pro   R Gardner (081) 393 5850
Holes   18 L 6352 yds SSS 70
Recs   Am–69 PJ Gibbons
    Pro–63 W Grant
V'trs   WD–I WE–M (by appointment)
Fees   £30 (£35)
Loc   Banstead Station 200 yds

Dorking (1897)

Chart Park, Dorking
Tel   (0306) 889786
Mem   380
Sec   RM Payne (0306) 886917
Pro   P Napier
Holes   9 L 5106 yds SSS 65
Recs   Am–65 J Houston
    Pro–62 A King
V'trs   WD–U WE/ BH–M SOC–WD
Fees   £10
Loc   1 mile S of Dorking on A24

Drift (1976)

The Drift, East Horsley KT24 5HD
Tel   (048 65) 4641
Mem   700
Sec   C Rose
Pro   J Hagen (048 65) 4772
Holes   18 L 6414 yds SSS 71
Recs   Am–72 J Scarfe
    Pro–72 TM Powell
V'trs   WD–U SOC
Fees   £25 before 1pm £16 after 1pm
Loc   2 miles off A3. London 20
    miles. 2 miles off M25

Effingham (1927)

Effingham Crossroads, Effingham KT24 5PZ
Tel (0372) 52203/ 52204
Mem 980
Sec Col SC Manning
Pro S Hoatson (Mgr) (0372) 52606
Holes 18 L 6488 yds SSS 71
Recs Am–67 I Hawson (1986)
Pro–63 AD Locke
V'trs WD–H WE/ BH–M
Fees £27.50 before 2pm £22.50
after 2pm
Loc 8 miles N of Guildford

Epsom (1889)

Longdown Lane South, Epsom KT17 4JR
Tel (037 27) 23363
Mem 600
Sec KH Watson (037 27) 21666
Pro R Wynn (037 27) 41867
Holes 18 L 5607 yds SSS 67
Recs Am–65 G Stone (1990)
Pro–66 D Butler (1990)
V'trs WD–U WE/ BH–after noon
SOC–Wed & Fri
Fees £10 (£15)
Loc S of Epsom Downs Rail Station

Farnham (1896)

The Sands, Farnham GU10 1PX
Tel (025 18) 3163
Mem 700
Sec (025 18) 2109
Pro G Cowlishaw (025 18) 2198
Holes 18 L 6313 yds SSS 70
Recs Am–67 G Walmsley (1988)
Pro–67 J Bennett (1990)
V'trs WD–H WE–M SOC–Wed &
Thurs
Fees £20 D–£24
Loc Signposted off A31, about
1 mile E of Farnham

Farnham Park (1966)

Public
Farnham Park, Farnham GU9 0AU
Tel (0252) 715216
Sec P Chapman
Pro P Chapman
Holes 9 L 1163 yds Par 54
Recs Am–61 JA Pike (1966)
Pro–56 G Wheeler (1966)
V'trs U
Fees £2.40 (£3)
Loc By Farnham Castle
Mis Public course privately
operated

Fernfell G & CC (1985)

Barhatch Lane, Cranleigh GU6 7NG
Tel (0483) 276626
Mem 1000
Sec Miss GL Petersen (Mgr)
Pro T Longmuir (0483) 277188
Holes 18 L 5258 yds SSS 66
Recs Am–59 RJ Martin (1988)
V'trs WD–U WE/ BH–NA am
SOC–WD

Fees £12 (£15)
Loc 1 mile from Cranleigh, off A281.
A3, 8 miles. M25, 11 miles

Foxhills (1975)

Stonehill Road, Ottershaw KT16 0EL
Tel (093 287) 2050
Mem 900
Sec A Dupuy
Pro B Hunt (093 287) 3961
Holes 18 L 6880 yds SSS 73 18 L
6747 yds SSS 72
Recs Pro–65 P Dawson
V'trs WD–U
Fees £40 D–£50
Loc London 20 miles. Heathrow
10 miles
Mis Driving range. Buggies for hire

Gatton Manor Hotel G & CC (1969)

Ockley, nr Dorking RH5 5PQ
Tel (030 679) 555
Mem 250
Sec DG Heath
Pro R Sargent (030 679) 557
Holes 18 L 6903 yds SSS 72
Recs Am–72 J McLaren (1985)
Pro–73 R Sargent (1985)
V'trs U exc Sun before noon–M
SOC–WD
Fees £14 (£20)
Loc 1¹/₂ miles SW of Ockley, off
A29. M25 Junction 9, S on A24
Mis Driving range. Buggies D–£20

Goal Farm (1977)

Public
Goal Road, Pirbright GU24 0P2
Tel (048 67) 3183/ 3205
Holes 9 hole 1273 yds Par 3 course
Recs Am–27
V'trs Sat–reserved for club comps
SOC–WD
Fees 18 holes £3.80 (£4.20) 9 holes
£2 (£2.20)

Guildford (1886)

High Path Road, Merrow, Guildford GU1 2HL
Tel (0483) 575243
Mem 600
Sec HJ Warburton (0483) 63941
Pro PG Hollington (0483) 66765
Holes 18 L 6080 yds SSS 70
Recs Am–64 DG Lintott (1989)
Pro–67 PG Hollington (1987)
V'trs WD–U WE–M SOC–WD
Fees £25
Loc 2 miles E of Guildford

Hankley Common (1895)

Tilford, Farnham GU10 2DD
Tel (025 125) 2493
Mem 700
Sec JKA O'Brien
Pro P Stow (025 125) 3761
Holes 18 L 6418 yds SSS 71

Recs Am–66 J Lee (1987)
Pro–62 H Stott (1988)
V'trs WD–I WE–discretion of Sec
Fees £25 D–£30
Loc 3 miles SE of Farnham on
Tilford road

Hindhead (1904)

Churt Road, Hindhead GU26 6HX
Tel (0428) 604614
Mem 300 50(L) 100(J) 100(5)
Sec ML Brown
Pro N Ogilvy (0428) 604458
Holes 18 L 6357 yds SSS 70
Recs Am–65 W Rowland
Pro–65 DJ Rees
V'trs WD–U H WE/ BH–NA before
noon SOC–Wed & Thurs
Fees £30 (£34)
Loc 1¹/₂ miles N of Hindhead on
A287

Hoebridge Golf Centre (1982)

Public
The Club House, Old Woking Road, Old Woking GU22 8JH
Tel (04837) 22611
Sec TD Powell
Pro TD Powell
Holes 18 L 6587 yds SSS 71
Intermediate 9 L 2294 yds
Par 3 18 L 2298 yds
V'trs U
Fees 18 hole–£8.50 Inter–£5
Par 3–£4.50
Loc Between Old Woking and
West Byfleet. 2 miles off A3 on
A247
Mis Floodlit driving range

Home Park (1895)

Hampton Wick, Kingston-upon-Thames KT1 4AD
Tel (081) 977 6645
Mem 500
Sec ARW White (081) 977 2423
Pro L Roberts (081) 977 2658
Holes 18 L 6598 yds SSS 71
V'trs U
Fees £15 (£26)
Loc 1 mile W of Kingston

Kingswood (1928)

Sandy Lane, Kingswood, Tadworth KT20 6NE
Tel (0737) 832188
Mem 640
Sec M Fletcher (Admin)
Pro R Blackie (0737) 832334
Holes 18 L 6855 yds SSS 72
Recs Am–70 P Stanford
Pro–67 R Blackie
V'trs H SOC
Fees £28 (£40)
Loc 5 miles S of Sutton on A217.
M25 Junction 8, 2 miles

For list of abbreviations see page 487.

Laleham (1907)

Laleham Reach, Chertsey KT16 8RP
Tel	(0932) 564211
Mem	600
Sec	MA Ford
Pro	T Whitton
Holes	18 L 6203 yds SSS 70
Recs	Am–68 C Poulton
	Pro–66 R Mandeville,
	J Hitchcock
V'trs	WD–U 9.30-4.30pm WE–M
	SOC–Mon-Wed
Fees	£20
Loc	2 miles S of Staines

Leatherhead (1904)

Kingston Road, Leatherhead KT22 0DP
Mem	600
Sec	W Betts (037 284) 3966
Pro	R Hurst (037 284) 3956
Holes	18 L 6107 yds SSS 69
Recs	Am–67 T Paterson (1990)
	Pro–70 P Butler (1990)
V'trs	U SOC
Fees	£27.50 (£32.50)
Loc	½ mile from M25 Junction 9, on A243 to Chessington

Limpsfield Chart (1889)

Limpsfield RH8 0SL
Tel	(0883) 723405
Mem	395
Sec	WG Bannochie (0883) 713097
Holes	9 L 5718 yds SSS 68
Recs	Am–67 N Simmons
	Pro–64 B Huggett
V'trs	WD–Tues/ Fri/ Wed pm
	Sun–NA after 1pm (Apr–Oct)
Fees	On application
Loc	2 miles E of Oxted

Lingfield Park (1987)

Racecourse Road, Lingfield RH7 6PQ
Tel	(0342) 834602
Mem	600
Sec	C Manktelow
Pro	T Collingwood (0342) 832659
Holes	18 L 6500 yds SSS 72
Recs	Pro–67 E Stillwell (1987)
V'trs	WD–U WE/ BH–M SOC
Fees	£15 (£20)
Loc	Next to Lingfield racecourse. M25 Junction 6
Mis	Driving range

Malden (1926)

Traps Lane, New Malden KT3 4RS
Tel	(081) 942 0654
Mem	680
Sec	M Blanford
Pro	R Hunter (081) 942 6009
Holes	18 L 6201 yds SSS 70
Recs	Am–65 G Lashford
	Pro–67 A Waters
V'trs	WD–U WE–restricted (apply Sec) SOC–Wed-Fri
Fees	£21 (£35)
Loc	Nr A3, between Wimbledon and Kingston

Mitcham (1897)

Carshalton Road, Mitcham Junction CR4 4HN
Tel	(081) 648 1508
Mem	450
Sec	CA McGahan (081) 648 4197
Pro	JA Godfrey (081) 640 4280
Holes	18 L 5931 yds SSS 68
Recs	Am–D Wilde
V'trs	WD–U WE–NA before 2pm SOC
Fees	£8 (£8)
Loc	Mitcham Junction Station
Mis	Mitcham Village Club plays here

Moore Place

Public

Portsmouth Road, Esher KT10 9LN
Tel	(0372) 63533
Sec	KJ Sargeant (Hon)
Pro	D Allen
Holes	9 L 3512 yds SSS 58
Recs	Am–29 W Cavanagh
	Pro–25 P Loxley
V'trs	U
Fees	£4 (£5)
Loc	Centre of Esher on Portsmouth road

New Zealand (1895)

Woodham Lane, Woodham, Weybridge KT15 3QD
Tel	(0932) 345049
Mem	300
Sec	MJ Wood (0932) 342891
Pro	VR Elvidge (0932) 349619
Holes	18 L 6012 yds SSS 69
Recs	Am–66 P Cannings
	Pro–72 A Herd
V'trs	WD–H WE/ BH–NA
Fees	On application
Loc	Woking 3 miles. West Byfleet 1 mile. Weybridge 5 miles

North Downs (1899)

Northdown Road, Woldingham
Tel	(0883) 653298
Mem	650
Sec	JAL Smith (Mgr) (0883) 652057
Pro	P Ellis (0883) 653004
Holes	18 L 5787 yds SSS 68
Recs	Am–66 M Smallcorn (1989)
	Pro–65 W Humphreys (1987)
V'trs	WD–U WE–M SOC–Tues/ Wed/ Fri
Fees	£20 (1990)
Loc	3 miles E of Caterham

Oaks Sports Centre (1973)

Public

Woodmansterne Road, Carshalton SM5 4AN
Tel	(081) 643 8363
Pro	G Horley
Holes	18 L 5975 yds SSS 69
	9 L 1590 yds SSS 29
Recs	18 hole
	Pro–66 G Horley
	9 hole Pro–27 J Woodroffe

V'trs

V'trs	U
Fees	18 hole:£6 (£8) 9 hole:£3 (£4)
Loc	2 miles from Sutton on B278
Mis	Floodlit driving range

Purley Downs (1894)

106 Purley Downs Road, Purley CR2 0RB
Tel	(081) 657 8347
Mem	600
Sec	Miss KNR Pudner
Pro	G Wilson (081) 651 0819
Holes	18 L 6243 yds SSS 70
Recs	Am–66 M Hayes
	Pro–69 M Gregson
V'trs	WD–I WE–M
Fees	On application
Loc	3 miles S of Croydon

Puttenham (1894)

Puttenham, nr Guildford
Tel	(0483) 810498
Mem	500
Sec	G Simmons
Pro	G Simmons (0483) 810277
Holes	18 L 6200 yds SSS 70
V'trs	WD–H WE/ BH–M SOC–Wed & Thurs
Fees	On application
Loc	Midway between Guildford and Farnham on Hog's Back

RAC Country Club (1913)

Woodcote Park, Epsom KT18 7EW
Tel	(0372) 276311
Sec	K Symons
Pro	P Butler
Holes	18 L 6702 yds SSS 72 18 L 5474 yds SSS 67
V'trs	M SOC
Loc	Epsom Station 1¾ miles

Redhill & Reigate (1887)

Clarence Lodge, Pendleton Road, Redhill RH1 6LB
Tel	(0737) 244626/ 244433
Mem	500
Sec	FR Cole (0737) 240777
Pro	B Davies (0737) 244433
Holes	18 L 5238 yds SSS 66
V'trs	WD–U WE–NA before 11am Sun–NA (June-Sept)
Fees	£12 (£15)
Loc	Redhill 1 mile on A23

Reigate Heath (1895)

Reigate Heath RH2 8QR
Tel	(0737) 242610
Mem	300 90(L) 50(J)
Sec	Mrs DM Howard (0737) 245530
Pro	WH Carter
Holes	9 L 5554 yds SSS 67
Recs	Am–65 D Mahaney
	Pro–65 P Loxley
V'trs	WD–U Sun/ BH–M SOC–Wed & Thurs
Fees	On application
Loc	W boundary

Richmond (1891)

Sudbrook Park, Richmond
TW10 7AS
Tel   (081) 940 1463
Mem   500
Sec   JF Stocker (081) 940 4351
Pro   N Job (081) 940 7792
Holes   18 L 5965 yds SSS 69
Recs   Am–63 J Lawson
        Pro–61 J Bennett
V'trs   WD–H
Fees   £30
Loc   Between Richmond and
        Kingston-upon-Thames

Royal Mid-Surrey (1892)

Old Deer Park, Richmond TW9 2SB
Tel   (081) 940 1894
Mem   1200
Sec   MSR Lunt
Pro   D Talbot (081) 940 0459
Holes   Outer 18 L 6337 yds SSS 70
        Inner 18 L 5446 yds SSS 71
Recs   Outer Am–66 GH Micklem,
        JC Davies, D Gilford
        Pro–64 R Charles, B Gallacher
V'trs   WD–H or M WE/ BH–M SOC
Fees   £30
Loc   Off A316

St George's Hill (1912)

Weybridge KT13 0NL
Tel   (0932) 842406
Mem   600
Sec   MR Tapsell (0932) 847758
Pro   AC Rattue (0932) 843523
Holes   18 L 6492 yds SSS 71
        9 L 2360 yds SSS 35
Recs   Am–65 D Swanston
        Pro–65 M Faulkner
V'trs   WD–I H WE/ BH–NA 9 hole-U
Fees   D–£35 –£24 after 1.45pm 9
        hole £8 –£7 after 1.45pm –£6
        after 4pm
Loc   ¹/₂ mile N of M25/ A3 Junction
        on A245 to Woking

Sandown Park (1970)

Public
More Lane, Esher KT10 8AN
Tel   (0372) 63340
Sec   P Barriball (Mgr)
Pro   N Bedward
Holes   9 L 5658 yds SSS 67
        9 hole Par 3
Recs   Am–69 P O'Halloran
V'trs   U (Closed on race day until 30
        mins after last race)
Fees   £2.80 (£3.75)
Loc   Sandown Park Racecourse
Mis   Floodlit driving range.
        Sandown Park Club plays here

Selsdon Park Hotel (1929)

Addington Road, Sanderstead,
S Croydon CR2 8YA
Tel   (081) 657 8811
Fax   (081) 651 6171
Pro   T O'Keefe, I Naylor (081) 657
        4129

Holes   18 L 6402 yds SSS 71
Recs   Am–68 M Welch
V'trs   U SOC (min 12 golfers)
Fees   £20 Sat–£25 Sun/ BH–£30
Loc   3 miles S of Croydon on A2022
        Purley-Addington road

Shillinglee Park (1980)

Chiddingfold, Godalming GU8 4TA
Tel   (0428) 53237
Fax   (0428) 4391
Sec   R Mace (Prop)
Pro   R Mace
Holes   9 L 2400 yds Par 32
V'trs   U SOC
Fees   £12.50 D–£15 (£15 D–£17.50)
        9 holes–£7 (£8)
Loc   2¹/₂ miles SE of Chiddingfold
Mis   Pitch & putt course–£3

Shirley Park (1914)

194 Addiscombe Road, Croydon
CR0 7LB
Tel   (081) 654 1143
Mem   900
Sec   A Baird
Pro   H Stott (081) 654 8767
Holes   18 L 6210 yds SSS 70
Recs   Am–66 J Good
        Pro–65 J Bennett
V'trs   WD–U WE/ BH–M SOC
Fees   £25
Loc   On A232, 1 mile E of Croydon
        Station

Silvermere (1976)

Redhill Road, Cobham KT11 1EF
Tel   (0932) 67275
Mem   600
Sec   Mrs P Devereux (Hon)
Pro   D McClelland
Holes   18 L 6333 yds SSS 71
Recs   Pro–65 S Rolley (1986)
V'trs   WD–U WE–NA before 1pm
        SOC
Fees   £10 (£14)
Loc   Between Cobham and
        Byfleet.¹/₂ mile from M25
        Junction 10 on B366 to Byfleet
Mis   Floodlit driving range

Sunningdale (1901)

Sunningdale SL5 9RW
Tel   (0344) 21681
Mem   800
Sec   K Almond
Pro   K Maxwell (0344) 20128
Holes   Old 18 L 6586 yds SSS 71
        New 18 L 6676 yds SSS 71
Recs   Old Am–66 MC Hughesdon
        Pro–62 N Faldo
        New Am–65 M Lunt
        Pro–64 GJ Player
V'trs   WD–I WE–M
Fees   £58
Loc   Sunningdale Station ¹/₄ mile on
        A30

Sunningdale Ladies (1902)

Cross Road, Sunningdale
Tel   (0344) 20507
Mem   400
Sec   BWJ Ford
Holes   18 L 3622 yds SSS 60
Recs   WD/ WE–by appointment. No
        3 or 4 balls before 11am
Fees   D-Ladies £14 (£16) Men £18
        (£20)
Loc   Sunningdale Station ¹/₄ mile

Surbiton (1895)

Woodstock Lane, Chessington
Tel   (081) 398 3101
Mem   750
Sec   GA Keith MBE
Pro   P Milton (081) 398 6619
Holes   18 L 6211 yds SSS 70
Recs   Am–64 C Cowper
        Pro–65 C de Foy, H Stott
V'trs   WD–H WE/ BH–M
Fees   £24 D–£36
Loc   2 miles E of Esher

Tandridge (1925)

Oxted
Tel   (0883) 712273/ 4
Mem   650
Sec   To be appointed
Pro   A Farquhar (0883) 713701
Holes   18 L 6250 yds SSS 70
Recs   Am–68 JC Robson
        Pro–69 BGC Huggett
V'trs   Mon/ Wed/ Thurs only-H
        SOC–Mon/ Wed/ Thurs
Fees   £35
Loc   5 miles E of Redhill, off A25.
        M25 Junction 6

Thames Ditton & Esher (1892)

Portsmouth Road, Esher KT10 9AL
Tel   (081) 398 1551
Mem   300
Sec   BAJ Chandler
Pro   R Hutton
Holes   9 L 5415 yds SSS 65
Recs   Am–61 T Petitt
        Pro–61 D Regan
V'trs   WD–U WE–by arrangement
Fees   £6 (£8)

Tyrrells Wood (1924)

Leatherhead KT22 8QP
Tel   (0372) 376025 (2 lines)
Mem   744
Sec   Mrs P Humphries
Pro   P Taylor (0372) 375200
Holes   18 L 6219 yds SSS 70
Recs   Am–67 P Earl (1988)
        Pro–65 P Hoad (1988)
V'trs   WD–I BH/ Sat–NA Sun–NA
        before noon SOC
Fees   £30 (£36)
Loc   2 miles from Leatherhead, off
        A24 nr Headley. M25 Junction
        9, 1 mile

For list of abbreviations see page 487.

Walton Heath (1904)

Tadworth KT20 7TP
Tel   (0737) 812060
Mem   900
Sec   NG Dampney (0737) 812380
Pro   K Macpherson (0737) 812152
Holes   Old 18 L 6883 yds SSS 73
        New 18 L 6659 yds SSS 72
Recs   Old Am–68 R Revell
        Pro–65 P Townsend
        New Am–67 JK Tate
        Pro–64 C Clark
V'trs   WD–I H WE/ BH–M SOC
Fees   £45
Loc   3 miles S of Epsom. M25
        Junction 8, 2 miles

Wentworth (1924)

Virginia Water GU25 4LS
Tel   (0344) 842201
Fax   (0344) 842804
Mem   2335
Sec   JAR Doyle-Davidson
Pro   B Gallacher (0344) 843353
Holes   West 18 L 6945 yds SSS 74 East
        18 L 6176 yds SSS 70
        Edinburgh 18 L 6979 yds SSS
        73
        Executive 9 L 1902 yds Par 54
Recs   West Am–72 P McEvoy
        Pro–64 H Clarke East Am–65
        GB Wolstenholme
        Pro–62 DN Sewell, G Will
V'trs   WD–H by prior arrangement
        WE–M SOC–WD (limited)
Fees   On application
Loc   21 miles SW of London at A30/
        A39 junction

West Byfleet (1922)

Sheerwater Road, West Byfleet
KT14 6AA
Tel   (0932) 345230
Mem   550
Sec   DG Smith (0932) 343433
Pro   D Regan (0932) 346584
Holes   18 L 6211 yds SSS 70
Recs   Am–66 W Calderwood
        Pro–67 P Thomson
V'trs   WD–I WE/ BH–NA
Fees   £27
Loc   West Byfleet 1/2 mile on A245.
        M25 Junction 10

West Hill (1909)

Bagshot Road, Brookwood
GU24 0BH
Tel   (04867) 4365/ 2110
Mem   550
Sec   WD Leighton MBE
Pro   JA Clements (04867) 3172
Holes   18 L 6368 yds SSS 70
Recs   Am–66 WA Murray
        Pro–66 N Coles
V'trs   WD–H WE–M SOC
Fees   £25
Loc   5 miles W of Woking on A322

West Surrey (1909)

Enton Green, nr Godalming
GU8 5AF
Tel   (0483) 421275
Mem   750
Sec   RS Fanshawe
Pro   J Hoskison (0483) 417278
Holes   18 L 6259 yds SSS 70
Recs   Am–66 SD Cook
        Pro–67 B Lane
V'trs   H SOC–WD
Fees   £20 (£35)
Loc   1/2 mile SE of Milford Station

Windlemere (1978)

Public
Windlesham Road, West End,
Woking GU24 9QL
Tel   (0276) 858727
Sec   CD Smith
Pro   D Thomas
Holes   9 L 5346 yds SSS 66
V'trs   U
Fees   £4 (£4.80)
Loc   A319 at Lightwater
Mis   Floodlit driving range

Woking (1893)

Pond Road, Hook Heath, Woking
GU22 0JZ
Tel   (0483) 760053
Mem   500
Sec   AW Riley
Pro   J Thorne (0483) 769582
Holes   18 L 6322 yds SSS 70
Recs   Am–65 PJ Benka (1968)
V'trs   WD–I WE–M
Fees   £25
Loc   2 1/2 miles W of Woking, off
        Hollybank Road

Woodcote Park (1912)

Bridle Way, Meadow Hill, Coulsdon
CR3 2QQ
Tel   (081) 660 0176 (Clubhouse)
Mem   750
Sec   (081) 668 2788
Pro   I Martin (081) 668 1843
Holes   18 L 6624 yds SSS 71
Recs   Am–66 S Keppler
        Pro–66 C Bonner
V'trs   WD–U WE–M
Fees   £20 D–£25
Loc   Purley 2 miles

Worplesdon (1908)

Heath House Road, Woking
GU22 0RA
Tel   (04867) 89876 (Steward)
Mem   560
Sec   Maj REE Jones (04867) 2277
Pro   J Christine (04867) 3287
Holes   18 L 6440 yds SSS 71
Recs   Am–64 KG Jones (1988)
        Pro–62
V'trs   WD–H WE–M
Fees   On application
Loc   E of Woking off A322. 5 miles S
        of M3 Junction 3

Sussex (East)

Ashdown Forest Hotel
(Royal Ashdown Forest New
Course)

Chapel Lane, Forest Row RH18 5BB
Tel   (0342 82) 4866 (Hotel)
Fax   (0342 82) 4869
Mem   150 (Anderida GC)
Sec   AJ Riddick (Hotel Mgr)
Pro   M Landsborough (0342 82)
        2247
Holes   18 L 5510 yds SSS 67
V'trs   U SOC
Fees   £12.50 (£17.50) (1990)
Loc   4 miles S of E Grinstead, off A22.
        12 miles W of Tunbridge Wells
Mis   Hotel specialises in golf breaks

Brighton & Hove (1887)

Dyke Road, Brighton BN1 8YJ
Tel   (0273) 556482
Mem   270
Sec   SC Cawkwell
Holes   9 L 5722 yds SSS 68
Recs   Am–67
V'trs   U SOC Sun–NA before noon
Fees   £12 (£20)
Loc   15 mins N of Brighton

Cooden Beach (1912)

Cooden Beach, nr Bexhill-on-Sea
Tel   (042 43) 2040
Mem   700
Sec   RL Wilkins
Pro   K Robson (042 43) 3938
Holes   18 L 6450 yds SSS 71
Recs   Am–67 G Burton, CM Skinner,
        Sir H Birkmyre
        Pro–65 AG Harrison
V'trs   H SOC
Fees   £20 (£25)
Loc   W boundary of Bexhill

Crowborough Beacon
(1895)

Beacon Road, Crowborough TN6 1UJ
Tel   (0892) 661511
Mem   700
Sec   M Swatton (0892) 661511
Pro   D Newnham (0892) 653877
Holes   18 L 6279 yds SSS 70
Recs   Am–67 GCD Carter,
        SF Robson Pro–67 K Ashdown,
        K MacDonald
V'trs   I H WE/ BH–NA
Fees   £20
Loc   7 miles S of Tunbridge Wells on
        A26

Dale Hill (1973)

Ticehurst, nr Wadhurst TN5 7DQ
Tel   (0580) 200112
Mem   600
Sec   I Connelly (Golf Dir)
Pro   A Malcolm (0580) 201090
Holes   18 L 6055 yds SSS 69

Recs	Pro–68 K MacDonald
V'trs	WD–U WE/ BH–H after
	10.30am SOC
Fees	£12.50 (£16.50)
Loc	B2087, off A21 at Flimwell

The Dyke (1908)

Dyke Road, Brighton BN1 8YJ

Tel	(0273) 857296
Mem	750
Sec	B Gazzard
Pro	P Longmore (0273) 857260
Holes	18 L 6577 yds SSS 71
Recs	Am–68 N O'Byrne
	Pro–65 C Jones
V'trs	U exc Sun–NA
Fees	£16 D–£18 (£25)
Loc	4 miles N of Brighton

East Brighton (1893)

Roedean Road, Brighton BN2 5RA

Tel	(0273) 604838
Mem	700
Sec	KR Head
Pro	WH Street
Holes	18 L 6337 yds SSS 70
Recs	Am–68 A Turner
	Pro–63 S King
V'trs	WD–U H after 9am WE–NA
	before 11am SOC
Fees	£17 (£25)
Loc	N from Marina, Black Rock

East Sussex National (1989)

Little Horsted, Uckfield TN22 5TS

Tel	(0825) 86217
Mem	1000
Sec	J McLaughlin (Golf Dir)
Pro	G Dukart
Holes	East 18 L 7112 yds SSS West
	18 L 7072 yds SSS
Fees	D–£100 Hotel guests–£57.50
Loc	2 miles S of Uckfield, off A22
Mis	Driving range. Golf academy

Eastbourne Downs (1907)

East Dean Road, Eastbourne BN20 8ES

Tel	(0323) 20827
Mem	700
Sec	DJ Eldrett
Pro	T Marshall (0323) 32264
Holes	18 L 6635 yds SSS 72
Recs	Am–67 J Collison (1988)
	Pro–70 B Gallacher
V'trs	U exc Sun–NA before 1pm
Fees	£18 (£20)
Loc	1 mile W of Eastbourne on A259

Hastings (1973)

Public

Beauport Park, Battle Road, St Leonards-on-Sea TN38 0TA

Tel	(0424) 852977
Sec	R Thomson
Pro	M Barton (0424) 852981
Holes	18 L 6248 yds SSS 71
Recs	Am–69 V Massarella (1981)
	Pro–72 S Hall (1987)

V'trs	U-booking necessary SOC
Fees	£7 (£8.50)
Loc	3 miles N of Hastings, off
	A2100 Battle to St Leonards
	road
Mis	Beauport Park Club plays here.

Highwoods (Bexhill) (1925)

Ellerslie Lane, Bexhill-on-Sea TN39 4LJ

Tel	(0424) 212625
Mem	800
Sec	P Robins
Pro	MJ Andrews (0424) 212770
Holes	18 L 6218 yds SSS 70
Recs	Am–65 S Graham (1990)
	Pro–68 C Clark (1976)
V'trs	WD/Sat-H Sun am–M Sun pm–H
Fees	£18 (£22)
Loc	2 miles N of Bexhill

Hollingbury Park (1911)

Public

Ditching Road, Brighton BN1 7HS

Tel	(0273) 552010
Pro	P Brown (0273) 500086
Holes	18 L 6415 yds SSS 71
Recs	Am–68 G Derkson (1988)
	Pro–65 J Spence (1989)
V'trs	U SOC
Fees	£9.20 D–£13.80 (£11.50)
Loc	1 mile NE of Brighton

Horam Park (1985)

Public

Chiddingly Road, Horam TN21 0JJ

Tel	(04353) 3477
Pro	R Foster
Holes	9 L 5688 yds SSS 66
Recs	Pro–64 J Pinsent (1988)
V'trs	U SOC Sat-M before 4pm
Fees	£12.50 D–£18 (£14 D–£19)
	9 holes £6.50 (£7)
Loc	1/2 mile S of Horam towards
	Chiddingley. 12 miles N of
	Eastbourne on A267
Mis	Floodlit driving range

Lewes (1896)

Chapel Hill, Lewes

Tel	(0273) 473245
Mem	545
Sec	RBM Moore (0273) 483474
Pro	P Dobson (0273) 483823
Holes	18 L 5951 yds SSS 69
Recs	Am–67 N Duc (1990)
	Pro–67 CA Burgess (1988)
V'trs	WD–U WE–NA before 2pm
	SOC
Fees	£12 (£20)
Loc	1/2 mile from Lewes at E end of
	Cliffe High Street

Nevill (1914)

Benhall Mill Road, Tunbridge Wells TN2 5JW

Tel	(0892) 27820
Mem	400 200(L) 120(J) 150(5)
Sec	RA White (0892) 25818

Pro	P Huggett (0892) 32941
Holes	18 L 6336 yds SSS 70
Recs	Am–66 A Sykes (1975)
	Pro–66 M Warner (1988)
V'trs	WD–H WE/ BH–M
Fees	£24
Loc	Tunbridge Wells 1 mile

Peacehaven (1896)

Brighton Road, Newhaven BN9 9UH

Tel	(0273) 514049
Mem	280
Sec	DT Jenkins (0273) 512571
Pro	G Williams (0273) 512602
Holes	9 L 5235 yds SSS 66
Recs	Am–67 A Browning (1985)
V'trs	WD–U WE/ BH–after 11am
	SOC
Fees	On application
Loc	8 miles E of Brighton on A259

Piltdown (1904)

Uckfield TN22 3XB

Tel	(082 572) 2033
Mem	380
Sec	JC Duncan (Hon)
Pro	J Amos (082 572) 2389
Holes	18 L 6059 yds SSS 69
Recs	Am–67 A Smith (1988)
	Pro–69 S Frost, P Lovesey
V'trs	I or H exc BH/ Tues am/ Thurs
	am/ Sun am
Fees	£30 (£30)
Loc	1 mile W of Maresfield, off
	A272 towards Isfield

Royal Ashdown Forest (1888)

Chapel Lane, Forest Row, E Grinstead RH18 5LR

Tel	(034 282) 2018/ 3014 (034 282) 4866 (New Course)
Mem	450
Sec	KPA Mathews
Pro	M Landsborough
Holes	Old 18 L 6477 yds SSS 71
	New 18 L 5549 yds SSS 69
Recs	Am–67 RA Darlington
	Pro–62 HA Padgham
V'trs	On application (phone first)
Fees	£20 (£25) (1989)
Loc	4 miles S of E Grinstead on B2100 Hartfield road. M25 Junction 6

Royal Eastbourne (1887)

Paradise Drive, Eastbourne BN20 8BP

Tel	(0323) 30412
Mem	900
Sec	AJ Poole (0323) 29738
Pro	R Wooller (0323) 36986
Holes	18 L 6109 yds SSS 69
	9 L 2147 yds SSS 32
Recs	Am–65 J Beland (1980)
	Pro–62 J Pinsent (1987)
V'trs	U H SOC
Fees	18 hole:£18 (£24) 9 hole:£10 (£12)
Loc	1/2 mile from Town Hall

For list of abbreviations see page 487.

Rye (1894)

Camber, Rye TN31 7QS
Tel	(0797) 225241
Mem	800 105(L) 110(J)
Sec	JM Bradley
Pro	P Marsh (0797) 225218
Holes	18 L 6301 yds SSS 71 9 L 6625 yds SSS 72
Recs	Am–64 P Hurring (1988) Pro–67 C Ledger (1988)
V'trs	M
Loc	3 miles E of Rye

Seaford (1887)

East Blatchington, Seaford BN25 2JD
Tel	(0323) 892442
Mem	420 110(L) 37(J) 88(5)
Sec	MB Hichisson
Pro	P Stevens (0323) 894160
Holes	18 L 6233 yds SSS 70
Recs	Am–66 EA Snow, A Flygt Pro–67 H Weetman
V'trs	WD–U WE–M
Fees	£20, £15 after 12 noon £10 after 3pm
Loc	1 mile N of Seaford
Mis	Dormy House accommodation

Seaford Head (1907)

Public
Southdown Road, Seaford BN25 4JS
Tel	(0323) 890139
Pro	AJ Lowles
Holes	18 L 5812 yds SSS 68
Recs	Am–66 J Crawford Pro–66 M Andrews
V'trs	U
Fees	£6 D–£8.50 (£7.50 D–£9)
Loc	8 miles W of Eastbourne. 3/4 mile S of A259

Waterhall (1921)

Public
Devils Dyke Road, Brighton
BN1 8YN
Tel	(0273) 508658
Sec	D Birch (Hon)
Pro	P Charman
Holes	18 L 5775 yds SSS 68
Recs	Am–68 S Maplesden
V'trs	WD–U WE–U after 10.30am
Fees	£9.20 (£11.50)
Loc	3 miles N of Brighton between A23 and A27. 1 mile N of A2308

West Hove (1910)

369 Old Shoreham Road, Hove
BN3 7GD
Tel	(0273) 413411
Sec	R Charman (0273) 419738
Pro	C White (0273) 413494
Holes	18 L 6038 yds SSS 69
Recs	Am–66 N O'Byrne Pro–62 C Moody
V'trs	WD–U WE–M
Fees	£20 (£25)
Loc	300 yds N of Postslade & West Hove Station on A27

Willingdon (1898)

Southdown Road, Eastbourne
BN20 9AA
Tel	(0323) 410983
Mem	550
Sec	B Kirby (0323) 410981
Pro	CJ Patey (0323) 410984
Holes	18 L 6049 yds SSS 69
Recs	Am–64 DM Sewell (1986) Pro–62 J Sewell (1990)
V'trs	WD–U H WE–MH exc Sun am–NA SOC–H
Fees	D–£18 (£24)
Loc	1/2 mile N of Eastbourne, off A22 to London

Sussex (West)

Bognor Regis (1892)

Downview Road, Felpham, Bognor
Regis PO22 8JD
Tel	(0243) 865867
Mem	570 173(L)
Sec	BD Poston (0243) 821929
Pro	R Day (0243) 865209
Holes	18 L 6238 yds SSS 70
Recs	Am–65 G Evans (1989) Pro–66 R Wynn
V'trs	WD–H after 10am WE–M (Apr–Sept)
Fees	£18 (£24)
Loc	2 miles E of Bognor Regis

Copthorne (1892)

Borers Arm Road, Copthorne
RH10 3LL
Tel	(0342) 712508
Fax	(0342) 717682
Mem	565
Sec	J Appleton
Pro	J Burrell (0342) 712405
Holes	18 L 6505 yds SSS 71
Recs	Am–68 D Arnold, M Logan Pro–68 C Mason, R Boxall
V'trs	WD–U WE/ BH–after 1pm SOC
Fees	£20 (£35)
Loc	1 mile E of M23 Junction 10 on A264

Cottesmore (1974)

Buchan Hill, Crawley RH11 9AT
Tel	(0293) 528256
Fax	(0293) 522819
Mem	1600
Sec	MF Rogerson
Pro	P Webster (0293) 535399
Holes	18 L 6097 yds SSS 70 18 L 5321 yds SSS 68
Recs	Old Am–69 I Geddes Pro–70 D Russell
V'trs	WD–U WE–NA before 11am
Fees	£18 (£22)
Loc	4 miles S of Crawley

Cowdray Park (1949)

Midhurst GU29 0BB
Tel	(0730) 812088
Mem	700
Sec	Mrs JD Huggett (0730) 813599
Pro	S Hall (0730) 812091
Holes	18 L 6212 yds SSS 70
Recs	Am–69 D Fay Pro–68 G Ralph
V'trs	I or H WD–NA before 9am Sat–NA before 11am Sun/ BH–NA before 3pm SOC
Fees	£20 (£30)
Loc	1 mile E of Midhurst on A272

Effingham Park (1980)

nr Copthorne
Tel	(0342) 716528
Mem	400
Sec	J O'Donovan (Mgr) (0342) 712138
Pro	I Dryden
Holes	9 L 1749 yds Par 30
Recs	Am–29 Pro–26
V'trs	WD–U WE–M before noon -U after noon
Fees	£6 D–£8.50 (£7 D–£10)
Loc	B2028/ B2039

Gatwick Manor (1975)

Crawley
Tel	(0293) 24470
Sec	C Hemsley
Pro	BC Hemsley
Holes	9 L 1109 yds SSS 27
V'trs	U
Loc	A23 to Crawley, 1 mile past Gatwick Airport

Goodwood (1892)

Goodwood, nr Chichester
PO18 0PN
Tel	(0243) 785012 (Members)
Mem	900
Sec	M Hughes–N Arborough (0243) 774968
Pro	K MacDonald (0243) 774994
Holes	18 L 6383 yds SSS 70
Recs	Am–68 SB Ursell (1989) Pro–66 K MacDonald (1988)
V'trs	WD–U H after 9.30am WE–H after 10am SOC
Fees	£20 (£30)
Loc	3 miles NE of Chichester, on road to racecourse

Goodwood Park G & CC (1989)

Goodwood, Chichester PO18 0QB
Tel	(0243) 775987
Sec	B Geoghegan
Pro	R Beach
Holes	18 L 6530 yds SSS 72
V'trs	U SOC
Fees	£14 (£20)
Loc	4 miles N of Chichester

Ham Manor (1936)

West Drive, Angmering, nr
Littlehampton BN16 4JE
Tel   (0903) 783288
Mem   860
Sec   PH Sauberque
Pro   S Buckley (0903) 783732
Holes   18 L 6216 yds SSS 70
Recs   Am–64 F Wieland (1987)
         Pro–62 TA Horton
V'trs   WD/ WE–H
Fees   On application
Loc   Between Worthing and
         Littlehampton

Haywards Heath (1922)

High Beech Lane, Haywards Heath
RH16 1SL
Tel   (0444) 414310
Mem   625
Sec   J Duncan (0444) 414457
Pro   M Henning (0444) 414866
Holes   18 L 6202 yds SSS 70
Recs   Am–69 G Batt-Rawden,
         R Arnold
V'trs   WD/ WE–H-restricted
         SOC–Wed & Thurs
Fees   £15 (£25)
Loc   2 miles N of Haywards Heath

Hill Barn (1935)

Public
Hill Barn Lane, Worthing
Tel   (0903) 37301
Pro   P Higgins
Holes   18 L 6224 yds SSS 70
Recs   Am–66 H Francis, B Roberts
         Pro–63 J Kinsella
V'trs   U
Fees   £7 (£8)
Loc   NE of A27 at Warren Road
         roundabout

Ifield (1927)

Rusper Road, Ifield, Crawley
RH11 0LN
Tel   (0293) 20222
Fax   (0293) 612973
Mem   875
Sec   DT Howe
Pro   C Jenkins (0293) 23088
Holes   18 L 6314 yds SSS 70
Recs   Am–67 M Groombridge,
         CW Jones
         Pro–65 G Cowlishaw,
         P Mitchell
V'trs   WD–H WE–M SOC
Fees   £23
Loc   Nr Crawley

Littlehampton (1889)

170 Rope Walk, Littlehampton
BN17 5DL
Tel   (0903) 717170
Mem   650
Sec   KR Palmer (Sec/ Mgr)
Pro   CA Burgess (0903) 716369
Holes   18 L 6244 yds SSS 70
Recs   Am–68 S Graham
         Pro–66 C Giddings

V'trs   WD–U after 9.30am WE/
         BH–NA before noon SOC
Fees   £22 (£30)
Loc   W bank of River Arun,
         Littlehampton

Mannings Heath (1908)

Mannings Heath, Horsham
Tel   (0403) 210168
Mem   800
Sec   JD Coutts (0403) 210228
Pro   M Denny (0403) 210332
Holes   18 L 6402 yds SSS 71
Recs   Am–66 JM Dodds
         Pro–64 G Ralph
V'trs   WD–H–M after 5pm WE–NA
         SOC
Fees   £18
Loc   3 miles SE of Horsham (A281)

Paxhill Park (1990)

Lindfield
Tel   (0444) 484467
Sec   B Beauchamp (Gen Mgr)
Pro   D Melville
Holes   18 L 6196 yds SSS 68
V'trs   WD–U WE–pm only
Fees   £15 (£20)
Loc   1 mile N of Lindfield, off B2028

Pease Pottage (1986)

Horsham Road, Pease Pottage,
Crawley
Tel   (0293) 21706
Mem   40
Sec   M Cooper (0403) 50301
Pro   C Morley, N Lee
Holes   9 L 3511 yds SSS 57
Recs   Am–64 M Roberts (1988)
V'trs   U
Fees   £5 (£7)
Loc   S of Crawley, off A23
Mis   Floodlit driving range

Pyecombe (1894)

Pyecombe, Brighton BN4 7FF
Tel   (079 18) 4176
Mem   650
Sec   WM Wise MA (079 18) 5372
Pro   CR White (079 18) 5398
Holes   18 L 6234 yds SSS 70
Recs   Am–67 C Morris
         Pro–67 J Debenham
V'trs   WD–U exc Tues after 9.15am
         Sat–U after 2pm Sun–U after
         3pm SOC–WD exc Tues
Fees   £20 (£25)
Loc   5 miles N of Brighton on A272

Selsey (1906)

Golf Links Lane, Selsey PO20 9DR
Tel   (0243) 602203
Mem   400
Sec   EC Rackstraw (0243) 602029

Pro   P Grindley
Holes   9 L 5932 yds SSS 68
Recs   Am–66 A Kelly
V'trs   U
Fees   £9 (£12)
Loc   7 miles S of Chichester

Tilgate (1982)

Public
Titmus Drive, Tilgate, Crawley
Tel   (0293) 30103
Pro   H Spencer, D McClelland
         (0293) 545411
Holes   18 L 6359 yds SSS 70
Recs   Am–74 M Hearn (1988)
         Pro–68 J Hodgkinson (1986)
V'trs   U SOC–Mon-Thurs
Fees   £6.50 D–£12.50 (£9.50)
Loc   1½ miles SE of Crawley, off
         M23 Junction 11

West Chiltington (1988)

Public
Broadford Bridge Road, West
Chiltington RH20 2YA
Tel   (0798) 813574
Sec   SE Coulson
Pro   BW Barnes (0798) 812115
Holes   18 L 5969 yds SSS 69 9 hole
         Par 3
V'trs   U SOC
Fees   £10 (£15)
Loc   2 miles E of Pulborough
Mis   Driving range

West Sussex (1930)

Hurston Lane, Pulborough
RH20 2EN
Tel   (079 82) 2563
Mem   800
Sec   GR Martindale
Pro   T Packham (079 82) 2426
Holes   18 L 6221 yds SSS 70
Recs   Am–61 G Evans
V'trs   WD–I H after 9.30am exc
         Tues-M SOC–Wed & Thurs
Fees   On application
Loc   1½ miles E of Pulborough on
         A283

Worthing (1905)

Links Road, Worthing BN14 9QZ
Tel   (0903) 60801
Mem   1150
Sec   Maj RB Carroll
Pro   S Rolley (0903) 60718
Holes   Lower 18 L 6477 yds SSS 72
         Upper 18 L 5243 yds SSS 66
Recs   Lower Am–67 G Evans (1988)
         Pro–66 J Bennett (1989)
V'trs   WD–U WE–confirm in advance
         with Sec
Fees   £24 (£30)
Loc   Central Station 1½ miles
         (A27). ¼ mile from A24
         Junction

For list of abbreviations see page 487.

Tyne & Wear

Backworth (1937)

The Hall, Backworth, Shiremoor,
Newcastle-upon-Tyne ME27 0AH
Tel   (091) 268 1048
Mem   400
Holes   9 L 5930 yds SSS 69
Recs   Am–66
V'trs   Mon & Fri–U Tues–Thurs–M
        after 5pm WE–after 12.30pm
        exc comp Sats–after 6pm
Fees   £5 (£6.25)
Loc   Off Tyne Tunnel link road,
        Holystone roundabout

Birtley (Portobello) (1922)

Portobello Road, Birtley DH3 2LR
Tel   (091) 410 2207
Mem   220
Sec   GK Blain (091) 410 0710
Holes   9 L 5660 yds SSS 67
Recs   Am–64 G Hammond
V'trs   WD–U exc Fri–NA after 3pm
        WE/ BH–M SOC
Fees   £6 W–£20
Loc   3 miles from Birtley service
        area on A1(M)

Boldon (1912)

Dipe Lane, East Boldon
Tel   (091) 536 4182
Mem   600
Sec   RE Jobes (091) 536 5360
Pro   Phipps Golf (091) 536 5835
Holes   18 L 6348 yds SSS 70
Recs   Am–67 GR Simpson (1987)
        Pro–66 P Tupling (1980)
V'trs   U
Fees   £12 (£15)

City of Newcastle (1892)

Three Mile Bridge, Great North Road,
Gosforth, Newcastle-upon-Tyne
NE3 2DR
Tel   (091) 285 1775
Mem   400 110(L) 60(J)
Sec   AJ Matthew
Pro   AJ Matthew (091) 285 5481
Holes   18 L 6508 yds SSS 71
Recs   Am–67 M Blackburn (1989)
        Pro–67 W Tyrie (1988)
V'trs   U
Fees   £11 (£15)
Loc   A1, 3 miles N of Newcastle

Garesfield (1922)

Chopwell NE17 7AP
Tel   (0207) 561278/ 561309
Mem   440
Sec   JR Peart
Holes   18 L 6196 yds SSS 70
Recs   Am–69 A McClure (1986)
        Pro–70 D Dunk(1978)
V'trs   WD–U WE/ BH–NA before
        4.30pm SOC
Fees   £11 (£15)
Loc   7 miles SW of Newcastle,
        between High Spen and
        Chopwell

Gosforth (1906)

Broadway East, Gosforth,
Newcastle-upon-Tyne NE3 5ER
Tel   (091) 285 6710
Mem   370 90(L) 40(J) 40(5)
Sec   A Sutherland (091) 285 3495
Pro   D Race (091) 285 0553
Holes   18 L 6030 yds SSS 69
Recs   Am–67 J Hattrick (1987)
V'trs   WD–U WE–M before 4pm –U
        after 4pm SOC
Fees   £12 (£15)
Loc   3 miles N of Newcastle, off
        A6125

Gosforth Park Golfing Complex (1971)

High Gosforth Park, Newcastle-
upon-Tyne 3
Tel   (091) 236 4480/ 4867
Mem   450
Sec   A Mair (Dir)
Pro   G Garland
Holes   18 L 5807 yds SSS 68
Recs   Am–68 M Simpkin
        Pro–65 B Rumney
V'trs   U
Fees   £7.50
Loc   5 miles N of Newcastle
Mis   9 hole pitch & putt course

Heworth (1912)

Gingling Gate, Heworth,
Gateshead
Tel   (091) 469 2137
Mem   600
Sec   G Holbrow (091) 469 9832
Holes   18 L 6462 yds SSS 71
Recs   Am–65 D Moralee
        Pro–69 P Highmoor
V'trs   WD–U WE–after noon
Fees   £5 (£7.50)
Loc   SE boundary of Gateshead

Houghton-le-Spring (1912)

Copt Hill Links, Houghton-le-Spring
Tel   (091) 584 1198
Mem   500
Sec   N Wales
Pro   (0783) 584 7421
Holes   18 L 6416 yds SSS 71
Recs   Am–69 J Hogg
V'trs   U SOC
Fees   £8 (£12)
Loc   6 miles SW of Sunderland

Newcastle United (1892)

60 Ponteland Road, Newcastle-upon-
Tyne NE5 3JW
Tel   (091) 286 4693 (Clubhouse)
        (091) 286 9998 (Shop)
Mem   500
Sec   J Simpson
Pro   (091) 286 9998
Holes   18 L 6528 yds SSS 71
Recs   Am–64 N Graham
V'trs   WD–U WE–M SOC
Fees   £8 (£10)
Loc   Nuns Moor, Cowgate

Northumberland (1898)

High Gosforth Park, Newcastle-
upon-Tyne NE3 5HT
Tel   (091) 236 2009
Mem   500
Sec   D Lamb (091) 236 2498
Holes   18 L 6629 yds SSS 72
Recs   Am–68 DP Davidson, PWS
        Bent, DM Moffat
        Pro–65 A Jacklin, T Horton
V'trs   WD–I WE/ BH–M
Fees   £20
Loc   4 miles N of Newcastle

Ravensworth (1906)

Moss Heaps, Wrekenton, Gateshead
NE9 7UU
Tel   (091) 487 6014/ 2843
        (091) 482 5715 (Shop)
Mem   480
Sec   L Winter (091) 488 7549
Holes   18 L 5872 yds SSS 68
Recs   Am–63 K Kelly
        Pro–64 T Horton
V'trs   U SOC
Fees   £12 (£20)
Loc   3 miles S of Newcastle on
        B1296

Ryton (1891)

Doctor Stanners, Clara Vale, Ryton
NE40 3TD
Tel   (091) 413 3737
Mem   460
Sec   TV Wakeford (091) 267 9720
Holes   18 L 6300 yds SSS 69
Recs   Am–69 PR Brougham
V'trs   WD–U WE–U exc 8-9.30am
        and 12-1.30pm SOC
Fees   £10 (£12)
Loc   7 miles W of Newcastle, off
        A69

South Shields (1893)

Cleadon Hills, South Shields
NE34 8EG
Tel   (091) 456 0475
Mem   700
Sec   WH Loades (091) 456 8942
Pro   G Parsons (091) 456 0110
Holes   18 L 6264 yds SSS 70
Recs   Am–65 J Ellwood (1988)
        Pro–64 M Gregson
V'trs   U SOC–WD
Fees   £14 (£19)
Loc   Cleadon Hills, South Shields

Tynemouth (1913)

Spital Dene, Tynemouth, North
Shields NE30 2ER
Tel   (091) 257 4578
Mem   813
Sec   W Storey (091) 257 3381
Pro   J McKenna (091) 258 0728
Holes   18 L 6403 yds SSS 71
Recs   Am–65 CS Hill
        Pro–64 J Ord
V'trs   WD–U Sat/ Sun am–NA SOC
Fees   £12 (£14)
Loc   E of Newcastle-upon-Tyne

For list of abbreviations see page 487.

Tyneside (1879)

Westfield Lane, Ryton NE40 3QE
Tel   **(091) 413 2177**
Mem   660
Sec   JR Watkin (091) 413 2742
Pro   M Gunn
Holes   18 L 6042 yds SSS 69
Recs   Am–66 J Surtees, M Dunn, PS
    Highmoor, J Kennedy
    Pro–65 JR Harrison
V'trs   WD–U (exc 11.30-1.30pm)
    WE–NA before 3pm SOC
Fees   £12 (£16)
Loc   7 miles W of Newcastle. S of
    river, off A695

Wallsend (1973)

Public
Bigges Main, Wallsend NE28 8XF
Tel   **(091) 262 1973**
Pro   P Eaton (091) 262 2431
Holes   18 L 6608 yds SSS 72
V'trs   U
Fees   £6.50 (£8)
Loc   Between Newcastle and
    Wallsend on coast road

Washington Moat House (1980)

Stone Cellar Road, Usworth,
Washington NE37 1PH
Tel   **(091) 417 8346**
Mem   650
Sec   DV Duffy (Hon)
Pro   D Howden
Holes   18 L 6604 yds SSS 72
Recs   Am–71 D Armstrong (1984)
    Pro–66 N Briggs (1987)
V'trs   U SOC
Fees   £8.50 (£12.50)
Loc   By A1(M)-North turning to
    Washington on A195
Mis   Driving range. 9 hole pitch &
    putt

Wearside (1892)

Coxgreen, Sunderland SR4 9JT
Tel   **(091) 534 2518**
Mem   650
Sec   KD Wheldon (091) 534 1193
Pro   S Wynn (091) 534 4269
Holes   18 L 6315 yds SSS 70
Recs   Am–67 L Naisby, D Curry,
    D Wood Pro–68 A Bickerdike
V'trs   WD–H WE–M H SOC
Fees   D–£12 (£18)
Loc   2 miles W of Sunderland, off
    A183. 2 miles W of A19

Westerhope

Whorlton Grange, Westerhope,
Newcastle-upon-Tyne NE5 1PP
Tel   **(091) 286 9125**
Mem   700
Sec   GS Bazley (091) 286 7636
Pro   N Brown (091) 286 0594
Holes   18 L 6407 yds SSS 71
Recs   Am–66 A Morrison, R Roper
    Pro–67 D Russell

V'trs   WD–U WE/ BH–M
Fees   £10
Loc   5 miles W of Newcastle

Whickham (1911)

Hollinside Park, Whickham,
Newcastle-upon-Tyne NE16 5BA
Tel   **(091) 488 7309**
Mem   500
Sec   N Weightman (091) 488 1576
Pro   GN Towne (091) 488 8591
Holes   18 L 6129 yds SSS 69
Recs   Am–68
V'trs   U
Fees   £10 D–£12 (D–£15)
Loc   5 miles SW of Newcastle

Whitburn (1931)

Lizard Lane, South Shields NE34 7AF
Tel   **(091) 529 2144**
Mem   380 73(L) 61(J) 79(5)
Pro   D Stephenson (091) 529 4210
Holes   18 L 6046 yds SSS 69
Recs   Am–65 KW Fleming (1988)
    Pro–70 M Gunn
V'trs   U SOC
Fees   £10 (£15) (1990)
Loc   2 miles N of Sunderland on
    coast

Whitley Bay (1890)

Claremont Road, Whitley Bay
NE26 3UF
Tel   **(091) 252 0180**
Mem   700
Sec   B Dockar
Pro   WJ Light (091) 252 5688
Holes   18 L 6614 yds SSS 72
Recs   Am–68 GJ Clark
    Pro–66 J Fourie
V'trs   WD–U WE–M
Fees   £14
Loc   10 miles E of Newcastle

Warwickshire

Atherstone (1894)

The Outwoods, Coleshill Road,
Atherstone
Tel   **(0827) 713110**
Mem   265 40(L) 40(J)
Sec   VA Walton (0827) 892568
Holes   18 L 6239 yds SSS 70
Recs   Am–66 M Reay
    Pro–65
V'trs   WD–H WE–M SOC–WD
Fees   D–£15 BH–£20
Loc   ¼ mile from Atherstone on
    Coleshill road

City of Coventry (Brandon Wood) (1977)

Public
Brandon Lane, Coventry CV8 3GQ
Tel   **(0203) 543141**
Pro   C Gledhill
Holes   18 L 6530 yds SSS 71

Recs   Pro–68 AR Sadler
V'trs   U SOC
Fees   £5.40 (£6.90)
Loc   6 miles SE of Coventry, off A45
    Southbound
Mis   Floodlit driving range

Kenilworth (1889)

Crew Lane, Kenilworth
Tel   **(0926) 54296**
Mem   1003
Sec   BV Edwards (0926) 58517
Pro   S Mouland (0926) 512732
Holes   18 L 6408 yds SSS 71
Recs   Am–69 P Broadbent
V'trs   U H BH–M
Fees   £17 (£25)
Loc   1½ miles from Kenilworth.
    5 miles S of Coventry

Ladbrook Park (1908)

Poolhead Lane, Tanworth-in-Arden,
Solihull B94 5ED
Tel   **(05644) 2220 (Members)**
Mem   740
Sec   Mrs GP Taylor (05644) 2264
Pro   GR Taylor (05644) 2581
Holes   18 L 6418 yds SSS 71
Recs   Am–67 PJ Sant
    Pro–65 RDS Livingston
V'trs   WD–U H WE/ BH–M H
Fees   On application
Loc   12 miles S of Birmingham.
    M42 Redditch/ Evesham
    Junction

Leamington & County (1908)

Golf Lane, Whitnash, Leamington
Spa CV31 2QA
Tel   **(0926) 420298**
Mem   600
Sec   SM Cooknell (0926) 425961
Pro   I Grant (0926) 428014
Holes   18 L 6430 yds SSS 71
Recs   Am–65 RG Hiatt
    Pro–66 D Thomas
V'trs   U SOC
Fees   £23 (£30)
Loc   1½ miles S of Leamington Spa

Maxstoke Park (1896)

Castle Lane, Coleshill, Birmingham
B46 2RD
Tel   **(0675) 462158**
Mem   450
Sec   JC Evans (Hon)
Pro   RA Young (0675) 464915
Holes   18 L 6460 yds SSS 71
Recs   Am–66 AM Allen
    Pro–71 PJ Butler
V'trs   WD–U WE–M
Fees   £20
Loc   3 miles S of Coleshill

Newbold Comyn (1973)

Public
Newbold Terrace East, Leamington Spa
Tel   **(0926) 421157**
Pro   D Knight
Holes 18 L 6221 yds SSS 70
Recs   Am–70 G Knight
       Pro–S Hutchinson (1987)
V'trs WD–U WE–booking 1 week in advance
Fees   £3.40 (£4.40)
Loc   Off Willes Road (B4099)

Nuneaton (1906)

Golf Drive, Whitestone, Nuneaton
Tel   **(0203) 347810**
       (0203) 344268 (Steward)
Mem   650
Sec   G Pinder
Pro   N Gilks (0203) 340201
Holes 18 L 6412 yds SSS 71
Recs   Am–67 P Broadhurst
       Pro–67 C Holmes
V'trs WD–U H WE–M SOC
Fees   £14
Loc   2 miles S of Nuneaton

Purley Chase (1980)

Pipers Lane, Ridge Lane, Nr Nuneaton CV10 0RB
Tel   **(0203) 393118**
Mem   600
Sec   RG Place
Pro   D Llewelyn (0203) 395348
Holes 18 L 6604 yds SSS 72
Recs   Am–72 P Broadhurst
       Pro–64 P Elson
V'trs WD/ BH–U WE–U after 2.30pm SOC
Fees   £10 D–£12 (£15 D–£16)
Loc   4 miles WNW of Nuneaton on B4114 (A47). 1¹/₂ miles SW of A5 Mancetter Island
Mis   13 bay driving range

Rugby (1891)

Clifton Road, Rugby CV21 3RD
Tel   **(0788) 542306**
Mem   550
Sec   B Poxon (0788) 810066
Pro   D Sutherland (0788) 75134
Holes 18 L 5457 yds SSS 67
Recs   Am–65 R Clynick
       Pro–68 D Sutherland
V'trs WD–U WE/ BH–M SOC
Fees   D–£12
Loc   1 mile N of Rugby on B5414

Stratford-on-Avon (1894)

Tiddington Road, Stratford-on-Avon
Tel   **(0789) 414546**
Mem   770
Sec   JH Standbridge (0789) 205749
Pro   ND Powell (0789) 205677
Holes 18 L 6309 yds SSS 70
Recs   Am–67 PB Rodgers,
       NCF Dainton
       Pro–65 J Whitehead
V'trs U

Fees   On application
Loc   ¹/₂ mile E of Stratford on B4086

Warwick (1971)

Public
Warwick Racecourse, Warwick CV34 6HW
Tel   **(0926) 494316**
Sec   Mrs R Dunkley
Pro   P Sharp (0926) 491284
Holes 9 L 2682 yds SSS 66
Recs   Am–67 R Buckingham
       Pro–70 P Sharp
V'trs U exc while racing in progress
Fees   £3 (£4)
Loc   Centre of racecourse
Mis   Driving range

Welcombe Hotel

Warwick Road, Stratford-on-Avon CV37 0NR
Tel   **(0789) 299012 (Clubhouse)**
Sec   PJ Day (Golf Mgr) BAK Miller (Hotel Mgr) (0789) 295252
Holes 18 L 6202 yds SSS 70
Recs   Am–67 R Fletcher
V'trs WD–U H WE/ BH–U H after noon
Fees   £25 (£30)
Loc   Stratford 1¹/₂ miles on A439 towards Warwick

West Midlands

The Belfry (1977)

Public
Wishaw B76 9PR
Tel   **(0675) 70301**
Sec   SD Butler (Ext 280)
Pro   P McGovern (Ext 267)
Holes Brabazon 18 L 6975 yds SSS 73 Derby 18 L 6127 yds SSS 70
Recs   Brabazon Pro–63 E Darcy
       Derby Pro–69 J Brown
V'trs U
Fees   Brabazon £20 (£22) Derby £9 (£11)
Loc   4 miles N of M6 Junction 4

Bloxwich (1924)

Stafford Road, Bloxwich WS3 3PQ
Tel   **(0922) 405724**
Mem   500
Sec   AD Perry (0922) 476593
Pro   B Janes (0922) 476889
Holes 18 L 6277 yds SSS 70
Recs   Am–67 JPG Windsor
       Pro–65 J Rhodes
V'trs WD–U WE–M SOC
Fees   D–£17
Loc   On A34 N of Walsall

Boldmere

Public
Monmouth Drive, Sutton Coldfield, Birmingham BJ3 6JR
Tel   **(021) 354 3379**
Sec   D Dufty
Pro   T Short

Holes 18 L 4463 yds SSS 62
Recs   Am–57 G Marston (1987)
       Pro–57 P Weaver (1987)
V'trs U
Fees   £4.50 (£4.90)
Loc   By Sutton Park, 1 mile from Sutton Coldfield

Brand Hall (1946)

Public
Heron Road, Oldbury, Warley
Tel   **(021) 552 7475**
Pro   (021) 552 2195
Holes 18 L 5813 yds SSS 68
Recs   Am–64 B Burlison
V'trs U exc first 2 hrs Sat/ Sun
Fees   £3
Loc   6 miles NW of Birmingham. M5 Junction 2, 1¹/₂ miles

Calderfields

Aldridge Road, Walsall WS4 2JS
Tel   **(0922) 640540 (Clubhouse)**
Mem   550
Sec   K Goode
Pro   R Griffin (0922) 32243
Holes 18 L 6636 yds SSS 72
V'trs U
Fees   £8 (£15)
Loc   1 mile N of Walsall

Cocks Moor Woods (1926)

Public
Alcester Road, South King's Heath, Birmingham BK1 6ER
Tel   **(021) 444 3584**
Pro   S Ellis
Holes 18 L 5742 yds SSS 67
Recs   Am–65 V Pailing
       Pro–71 B Jones, K Dodsworth
V'trs U
Fees   £3.90 (£4.60)
Loc   6¹/₂ miles S of Birmingham

Copt Heath (1910)

1220 Warwick Road, Knowle, Solihull B93 9LN
Tel   **(0564) 772650**
Mem   700
Sec   W Lenton
Pro   BJ Barton
Holes 18 L 6504 yds SSS 71
Recs   Am–66 P McEvoy
       Pro–65 BJ Barton
V'trs WD–H WE/ BH–M SOC
Fees   £30
Loc   2 miles S of Solihull on A4141

Coventry (1887)

Finham Park, Coventry CV3 6PJ
Tel   **(0203) 411123**
Mem   750
Sec   JE Jarman (0203) 414152
Pro   P Weaver (0203) 411298
Holes 18 L 6613 yds SSS 72
Recs   Am–66 P Downes
       Pro–66 P Weaver
V'trs WD–H
Fees   £30
Loc   2 miles S of Coventry on A444

Coventry Hearsall (1896)

Beechwood Avenue, Coventry
CV5 6DF
Tel   (0203) 713470
Mem   450
Sec   WG Doughty
Pro   M Jennings (0203) 713156
Holes   18 L 5963 yds SSS 69
Recs   Am–70 J Marley (1987)
      Pro–66 B Morris (1987)
V'trs   WD–U WE–M
Fees   D–£19
Loc   1¹/₂ miles S of Coventry

Dartmouth (1910)

Vale Street, West Bromwich B71 4DW
Tel   (021) 588 2131
Mem   250
Sec   RH Smith
Holes   18 L 6060 yds SSS 69
Recs   Am–68 P Griffiths
      Pro–70 P Lester
V'trs   WD–U WE–restricted
Fees   £9
Loc   1 mile from W Bromwich,
      behind Churchfields High
      School. Nr Junction M5/ M6

Druids Heath (1974)

Stonnall Road, Aldridge WS9 8JZ
Tel   (0922) 55595
Mem   500 55(L) 35(J)
Sec   PM Halldron
Pro   M Daubney (0922) 59523
Holes   18 L 6914 yds SSS 73
Recs   Am–69 M Pearce
V'trs   WD–U WE–M
Fees   £12 (£17)
Loc   6 miles NW of Sutton Coldfield

Dudley (1894)

Turners Hill, Rowley Regis, Warley
Tel   (0384) 253719
Mem   320
Sec   RP Fortune (0384) 233877
Pro   L Bashford (0384) 254020
Holes   18 L 5715 yds SSS 67
Recs   Am–66 AA Davies
      Pro–63 R Livingstone
V'trs   WD–U WE–M
Fees   £16
Loc   2 miles S of Dudley

Edgbaston (1896)

Church Road, Birmingham B15 3TB
Tel   (021) 454 1736
Mem   830
Sec   To be appointed
Pro   AH Bownes (021) 454 3226
Holes   18 L 6118 yds SSS 69
Recs   Am–66 J Cook (1990)
      Pro–65 J Rhodes
V'trs   U
Fees   £22 (£28)
Loc   1 mile S of Birmingham

Enville (1935)

Highgate Common, Enville, nr
Stourbridge DY7 5BN
Tel   (0384) 872551
Mem   900
Sec   RJ Bannister (Sec/ Mgr) (0384)
      872074
Pro   S Power (0384) 872585
Holes   Highgate 18 L 6451 yds SSS 72
      Lodge 18 L 6207 yds SSS 70
Recs   Highgate Am–68 A Stubbs,
      NA Paul
      Pro–66 PH Hinton Lodge
      Am–65 C Elston (1989)
V'trs   WD–U WE/ BH–M H SOC
Fees   £20 D–£30
Loc   6 miles W of Stourbridge
Mis   Buggies for hire

Forest of Arden Hotel G & CC

Maxstoke Lane, Meriden, Coventry
CV7 7HR
Tel   (0676) 23721
Mem   700
Sec   G Sharpe (Mgr)
Pro   M Tarn (0676) 22118
Holes   Arden 18 L 6900 yds SSS 71
      Aylesford 18 L 6500 yds SSS 69
V'trs   WD–U WE–NA before 1pm
      SOC
Fees   Arden £18 (£22) Aylesford £16
      (£18)
Loc   Off A45 Birmingham-Coventry
      road. M42 Junction 6. M6
      Junction 4. NEC 3 miles

Gay Hill (1913)

Hollywood Lane, Birmingham B47 5PP
Tel   (021) 430 6523/ 7077
Mem   700
Sec   Mrs EK Devitt (021) 430 8544
Pro   A Hill (021) 474 6001
Holes   18 L 6532 yds SSS 71
Recs   Am–67 P Adams
      Pro–66 R Livingston
V'trs   WD–U WE–M SOC
Fees   £20 (1990)
Loc   7 miles S of Birmingham on
      A435. M42 Junction 3, 3 miles

Grange (1924)

Copsewood, Coventry CV3 1HS
Tel   (0203) 451465
Mem   350
Sec   E Soutar (0203) 446324
Holes   9 L 6002 yds SSS 69
V'trs   WD–U before 2.30pm Sat–NA
      Sun–NA before noon
Fees   £7 D–£10 Sun–£10

Great Barr (1961)

Chapel Lane, Birmingham B43 7BA
Tel   (021) 357 1232
Mem   600
Sec   K Pembridge (021) 358 4376
Pro   SM Doe (021) 357 5270

Holes   18 L 6545 yds SSS 72
Recs   Am–67 CM Lambert
      Pro–71 J Higgins
V'trs   WD–U WE–I (h'cap max 18)
      SOC
Fees   £20 (£25)
Loc   6 miles NW of Birmingham. M6
      Junction 7

Hagley (1980)

Wassell Grove, Hagley, nr
Stourbridge
Tel   (0562) 883701
Mem   600
Sec   VC Lewis
Holes   18 L 6353 SSS 72
Recs   Am–73 S Hull (1989)
V'trs   WD–U exc Wed before
      1.30pm WE–M after 1pm
      SOC–WD
Fees   £12 D–£14

Halesowen (1909)

The Leasowes, Halesowen B62 8QF
Tel   (021) 550 1041
Mem   600
Sec   Mrs M Bateman (021) 501 3606
Pro   M Crowther-Smith (021) 503
      0593
Holes   18 L 5754 yds SSS 68
Recs   Am–65 D Henn
      Pro–66
V'trs   WD–U WE–M SOC–WD exc
      Wed
Fees   £12 D–£15
Loc   M5 Junction 3, 2 miles

Handsworth (1895)

Sunningdale Close, Handsworth
Wood, Birmingham B20 1NP
Tel   (021) 554 0599
Mem   850
Sec   RL Neale (Hon)
Pro   M Hicks (021) 523 3594
Holes   18 L 6297 yds SSS 70
Recs   Am–65 DJ Russell
      Pro–71 HF Boyce
V'trs   WD–U WE/ BH–M SOC
Fees   £20 (£20)
Loc   3 miles NW of Birmingham. M5
      Junction 1. M6 Junction 7

Harborne (1893)

40 Tennal Road, Harborne,
Birmingham B32 2JE
Tel   (021) 427 1728
Mem   500
Sec   RA Eddy (021) 427 3058
      (mornings)
Pro   A Quarterman (021) 427 3512
Holes   18 L 6240 yds SSS 70
Recs   Am–65 JA Fisher, R Ellis
      Pro–65 E Cogle
V'trs   WD–U WE/ BH–M SOC
Fees   D–£15
Loc   3 miles SW of Birmingham. M5
      Junction 3

Harborne Church Farm
Public
Vicarage Road, Harborne,
Birmingham B17 0SN
Tel   (021) 427 1204
Pro   M Hampton
Holes   9 L 4514 yds SSS 62
Recs   Am–63 J Sankey
         Pro–60 PR Rudge
V'trs   U
Fees   18 holes–£3.20 (£4)
         9 holes–£1.70 (£2.10)
Loc   5 miles SW of Birmingham

Hatchford Brook (1969)
Public
Coventry Road, Sheldon,
Birmingham B26 3PY
Tel   (021) 743 9821
Pro   P Smith
Holes   18 L 6164 yds SSS 69
Recs   Am–69 A Allen (1987)
         Pro–68 P Smith (1988)
V'trs   U SOC–WD
Fees   £3.90 (£4.60)
Loc   City boundary close to airport.
         A45/ M42 Junction

Hilltop (1979)
Public
Park Lane, Handsworth, Birmingham
B21 8LJ
Pro   K Highfield (021) 554 4463
Holes   18 L 6114 yds SSS 69
Recs   Am–66 H Ali Pro–65 BN Jones
V'trs   U
Fees   £4.40 (£4.90)
Loc   M5 West Brom, opposite
         Hawthorns Football Ground

Himley Hall (1980)
Public
Himley Hall Park, Dudley
Tel   (0902) 895207
Holes   9 L 3145 yds SSS 36
V'trs   WD–U WE/ BH–restricted
Fees   18 holes–£4 (£4.50)
         9 holes–£2.50 (£3)
Loc   Grounds of Himley Hall Park.
         B4176, off Wolverhampton–
         Dudley road A449

Lickey Hills
Public
Rednal, Birmingham B45 8RR
Tel   (021) 453 3159
Pro   MS March
Holes   18 L 6010 yds SSS 69
Recs   Am–66 S Green
         Pro–72 R Livingston
V'trs   U
Fees   £4.40 (£4.90)
Loc   10 miles SW of Birmingham
Mis   Rose Hill Club plays here

Little Aston (1908)
Streetly, Sutton Coldfield B74 3AN
Tel   (021) 353 2066
Mem   250
Sec   NH Russell (021) 353 2942
Pro   J Anderson (021) 353 2942

Holes   18 L 6724 yds SSS 73
Recs   Am–66 Pro–68
V'trs   By prior arrangement WE–XL
Fees   On application
Loc   4 miles NW of Sutton Coldfield

Moor Hall (1932)
Four Oaks, Sutton Coldfield
Tel   (021) 308 6130
Mem   525
Sec   WC Brodie
Pro   A Partridge (021) 308 5106
Holes   18 L 6249 yds SSS 70
Recs   Am–65 J Cook
         Pro–67 NR McDonald
V'trs   WD–U H exc Thurs–U after
         12.30pm WE/ BH–M
Fees   £20 D–£26
Loc   1 mile E of Sutton

Moseley (1892)
Springfield Road, King's Heath,
Birmingham B14 7DX
Tel   (021) 444 2115
Mem   600
Sec   PT Muddiman (021) 444 4957
         (10am–1pm)
Pro   G Edge (021) 444 2063
Holes   18 L 6227 yds SSS 70
Recs   Am–64 A Forrester
         Pro–64 FE Miller
V'trs   I H or M
Fees   £25
Loc   S Birmingham

North Warwickshire (1894)
Hampton Lane, Meriden, Coventry
CV7 7LL
Tel   (0676) 22259
Mem   400
Sec   EG Barnes (Hon)
Pro   D Bradley
Holes   9 L 6362 yds SSS 70
Recs   Am–67 P Broadhurst, M Biddle
V'trs   WD–U WE/ BH–M SOC
Fees   £12 (£16)
Loc   Coventry 6 miles. Birmingham
         13 miles

North Worcestershire (1907)
Frankley Beeches Road, Northfield,
Birmingham B31 5LP
Tel   (021) 475 1047
Mem   550
Sec   BF Hudson
Pro   K Jones (021) 475 5721
Holes   18 L 5907 yds SSS 69
Recs   Am–64 DJ Russell
         Pro–63 K Dickens (1988)
V'trs   WD–U WE/ BH–NA
Fees   £10
Loc   7 miles SW of Birmingham

Olton (1893)
Mirfield Road, Solihull B91 1JH
Tel   (021) 705 1083
Mem   600
Sec   MA Perry (0564) 777953

Pro   D Playdon (021) 705 7296
Holes   18 L 6229 yds SSS 71
Recs   Am–63 J Berry
         Pro–66 D Llewellyn
V'trs   WD–U exc Wed am WE–M
Fees   £23
Loc   7 miles S of Birmingham

Oxley Park (1914)
Stafford Road, Bushbury,
Wolverhampton WV10 6DE
Tel   (0902) 20506
Mem   400
Sec   Mrs K Mann (0902) 25892
         (mornings)
Pro   LA Burlison (0902) 25445
Holes   18 L 6168 yds SSS 69
Recs   Am–64 CS White
         Pro–65 D Thorp, P Weaver
V'trs   U SOC
Fees   £16 (£18)
Loc   1 1/2 miles N of Wolverhampton

Patshull Park (1980)
Pattingham, Wolverhampton WV6
7HR
Tel   (0902) 700342 (Golf Admin)
Mem   375
Pro   DJ McDowall (Golf Dir)
Holes   18 L 6412 yds SSS 71
Recs   Pro–66 P Elson
V'trs   U SOC
Fees   £20 D–£30 (£25 D–£35)
Loc   7 miles W of Wolverhampton.
         M54 Junction 3, 5 miles

Penn (1908)
Penn Common, Wolverhampton
Tel   (0902) 341142
Mem   500
Sec   PW Thorrington
Pro   A Briscoe (0902) 330472
Holes   18 L 6465 yds SSS 71
Recs   Am–68 RJ Green
         Pro–70 J Rhodes, R Cameron
V'trs   WD–U WE–M SOC
Fees   £16
Loc   2 miles SW of Wolverhampton

Perton Park (1990)
Wrottesley Park Road, Perton,
Wolverhampton WV6 7HL
Tel   (0902) 380103/ 380073
Sec   E Greenway
Pro   R Franklyn
Holes   18 L 7076 yds SSS
V'trs   U SOC
Fees   £5 (£5)
Loc   Wolverhampton 6 miles, off
         A454
Mis   Driving range

Pype Hayes (1932)
Public
Eachelhurst Road, Walmley, Sutton
Coldfield B76 8EP
Tel   (021) 351 1014
Pro   JF Bayliss
Holes   18 L 5811 yds SSS 68
Recs   Am–62 L Jacks (1985)
         Pro–59 J Cawsey (1954)

V'trs   U
Fees   £4
Loc   5 miles NE of Birmingham

Robin Hood (1893)

St Bernards Road, Solihull B92 7DJ
Tel   (021) 706 0159
Mem   650
Sec   (021) 706 0061
Pro   RS Thompson (021) 706 0806
Holes   18 L 6609 yds SSS 72
Recs   Am–68 J Draper (1988)
V'trs   WD–U WE/ BH–M SOC–WD
Fees   £25 D–£30
Loc   7 miles S of Birmingham

Sandwell Park (1895)

Birmingham Road, West Bromwich B71 4JJ
Tel   (021) 553 0260 (Members)
Mem   600
Sec   JB Mawby (021) 553 4637
Pro   AW Mutton (021) 553 4384
Holes   18 L 6470 yds SSS 72
Recs   Am–67 B Charlton (1983)
         Pro–67 J Annable
V'trs   WD–U WE–MH SOC–WD
Fees   D–£25
Loc   West Bromwich/ Birmingham boundary. By M5 Junction 1

Shirley (1956)

Stratford Road, Monkspath, Shirley, Solihull B90 4EW
Tel   (021) 744 6001
Mem   450
Sec   AJ Phillips
Pro   C Wicketts (021) 745 4979
Holes   18 L 6510 yds SSS 71
Recs   Am–68 M Payne
         Pro–68
V'trs   WD–U WE–M
Fees   £20 D–£30
Loc   8 miles S of B'ham. 400 yds city side of M42 Junction 4

South Staffordshire (1892)

Danescourt Road, Tettenhall, Wolverhampton WV6 9BQ
Tel   (0902) 751065
Mem   600
Sec   H Williams
Pro   J Rhodes (0902) 754816
Holes   18 L 6621 yds SSS 72
Recs   Am–67 D Gifford
         Pro–66 A Sadler
V'trs   WD–U WE/ BH–M SOC
Fees   £14 D–£18 (1989)
Loc   3 miles W of Wolverhampton, off A41

Sphinx (1948)

Siddeley Avenue, Stoke, Coventry CV3 1FZ
Tel   (0203) 451361
Mem   300
Sec   GE Brownbridge (0203) 597731
Holes   9 L 4104 yds SSS 60

Recs   Am–62 PR Thorpe
V'trs   U exc Sun am
Fees   £3.50
Loc   Nr Binley Road, Coventry

Stourbridge (1892)

Worcester Lane, Pedmore, Stourbridge
Tel   (0384) 393062
Mem   720
Sec   FR McLachlan (0384) 395566
Pro   WH Firkins (0384) 393129
Holes   18 L 6178 yds SSS 69
Recs   Am–65 J Fisher
         Pro–63 WH Firkins
V'trs   WD–U exc Wed before 4pm–M WE/ BH–M
Fees   £20
Loc   1 mile S of Stourbridge on Worcester road

Sutton Coldfield (1889)

110 Thornhill Road, Sutton Coldfield B74 3ER
Tel   (021) 353 2014
Mem   517
Sec   AJ Bishop, M McClean (Admin) (021) 353 9633
Pro   JK Hayes (021) 353 9633
Holes   18 L 6541 yds SSS 71
Recs   Am–65 L Jacks (1986)
         Pro–64 PA Elson (1978)
V'trs   U H SOC
Fees   £25 (£25)
Loc   9 miles N of Birmingham

Swindon (1986)

Bridgnorth Road, Swindon, Dudley DY3 4PU
Tel   (0902) 897031
Mem   500
Sec   E Greenway (Mgr)
Pro   P Lester (0902) 896191
Holes   18 L 6042 yds SSS 69 9 hole Par 3 1135 yds
Recs   Am–68 N Bennett (1990)
         Pro–68 K Bayliss
V'trs   U SOC–WD
Fees   £12 (£18)
Loc   5 miles from Wolverhampton, Dudley and Stourbridge on B4176
Mis   Driving range

Walmley (Wylde Green) (1902)

Brooks Road, Wylde Green, Sutton Coldfield B72 1HR
Tel   (021) 373 0029
Mem   700
Sec   JPG Windsor
Pro   MJ Skerritt (021) 373 7103
Holes   18 L 6537 yds SSS 72
Recs   Am–69 ARJ Lowe
         Pro–72 B Waites
V'trs   WD–U WE–M
Fees   £18 D–£25
Loc   N boundary of Birmingham

Walsall (1907)

Broadway, Walsall
Tel   (0922) 22710
Mem   700
Sec   E Murray (0922) 613512
Pro   R Lambert (0922) 26766
Holes   18 L 6232 yds SSS 70
Recs   Am–66 RG Hiatt, D Blakeman
         Pro–66 N Brunyard
V'trs   WD–U WE–M SOC
Fees   £20 (£25)
Loc   1 mile S of Walsall

Warley (1921)

Public
Lightwoods Hill, Warley B67 5EO
Tel   (021) 429 2440
Pro   D Owen
Holes   9 L 2606 yds SSS 64
Recs   Am–62 M Daw
         Pro–58 B Fereday
V'trs   U
Fees   £3.60 (£4.20)
Loc   5 miles W of Birmingham

Windmill Village (1990)

Birmingham Road, Allesley, Coventry CU5 9AL
Tel   (0203) 407241
Pro   A Hunter
Holes   18 L 4759 yds Par 68
V'trs   U
Fees   £9.50
Loc   3 miles W of Coventry, off A45

Wiltshire

Bremhill Park (1967)

Shrivenham, Swindon
Tel   (0793) 782946
Sec   R Bentley (0793) 783846
Pro   P Borham
Holes   18 L 5889 yds SSS 70
Recs   Am–68
         Pro–66 M Howell (1988)
V'trs   U
Fees   £8 (£10)
Loc   4 miles E of Swindon

Brinkworth (1984)

Longmans Farm, Brinkworth, Chippenham SN15 5DG
Tel   (066 641) 277
Mem   250
Sec   D Fortune
Pro   P Boreham
Holes   18 L 5900 yds SSS 69
V'trs   U SOC
Fees   £4 (£5) (1990)
Loc   Brinkworth 2 miles on Wootton Bassett-Malmesbury road

Broome Manor (1976)

Public
Pipers Way, Swindon SN3 1RG
Tel   (0793) 532403
Sec   T Watt (Mgr)(0793) 495761

Pro	B Sandry (0793) 532403
Holes	18 L 6359 yds SSS 70
	9 L 2745 yds SSS 67
Recs	Am–69 A Norman-Thorpe,
	S Robertson
	Pro–66 M Bevan
V'trs	U
Fees	18 hole: £4.75 (£5.25)
	9 hole: £2.85 (£3.15)
Loc	Swindon 2 miles
Mis	25 bay floodlit driving range

Chippenham (1896)

Malmesbury Road, Chippenham

Tel	(0249) 652040
Mem	650
Sec	V J Carlisle
Pro	W Creamer (0249) 655519
Holes	18 L 5540 yds SSS 67
Recs	Am–62 M Darbyshire
	Pro–64 B Sandry
V'trs	H WE–M SOC
Fees	£18 (£24)
Loc	Chippenham 1 mile. M4
	Junction 17

High Post (1922)

Great Durnford, Salisbury SP4 6AT

Tel	(0722) 73231
Mem	600
Sec	WWR Goodwin (0722) 73356
Pro	AJ Harman (0722) 73219
Holes	18 L 6297 yds SSS 70
Recs	Am–64 K Weeks, RJ Searle
	Pro–65 P Alliss, N Sutton
V'trs	WD–U WE/ BH–H SOC
Fees	£15 D–£20 (£24) SOC–£24
Loc	4 miles N of Salisbury on A345

Kingsdown (1880)

Kingsdown, Corsham SN14 9BS

Tel	(0225) 742530
Mem	475 100(L) 45(J)
Sec	SH Phipps (0225) 743472
Pro	R Emery (0225) 742634
Holes	18 L 6445 yds SSS 71
Recs	Am–67 R Vinall (1989)
	Pro–68 G Clough (1989)
V'trs	WD–H WE–M
Fees	£20
Loc	5 miles E of Bath

Marlborough (1888)

The Common, Marlborough
SN8 1DU

Tel	(0672) 512147
Mem	710
Sec	L Ross (Mgr), S Lynch (Admin)
Pro	W McAdams (0672) 512493
Holes	18 L 6526 yds SSS 71
Recs	Am–64 D Rigby
	Pro–66 A Beale
V'trs	WD/ WE–H SOC
Fees	£15 D–£20 (£30)
Loc	1 mile N of Marlborough
	(A345)

North Wilts (1890)

Bishops' Cannings, Devizes SN10 2LP

Tel	(038 086) 257
Mem	600 96(L) 65(J)
Sec	Lt Cdr JBW McKelvie (038 086)
	627
Pro	GJ Laing (038 086) 330
Holes	18 L 5898 metres SSS 71
Recs	Am–66 EAJ Pulleyblank
	Pro–67 GJ Laing
V'trs	WE–NA before 10am
	(–M Xmas Day–Mar 31)
Fees	£12 (£18)
Loc	1 mile from A4 at Calne

RAF Upavon (1918)

York Road, Upavon, Pewsey SN9 6BQ

Tel	(0980) 630787
Mem	300
Sec	Sqn Ldr RG Pegrum (0980)
	630351 (Ext 4169)
Holes	9 L 5597 yds SSS 67
Recs	Am–66 Wg Cdr RB Duckett
V'trs	WD–U Sat am/ Sun am–M SOC
Fees	£12 (£15)
Loc	Upavon 3 miles on A342 to
	Andover

RMCS Shrivenham (1953)

RMCS Shrivenham, Swindon SN6 8LA

Tel	(0793) 782551 (Ext 2355)
Mem	350
Sec	GM Moss
Holes	9 L 5206 yds SSS 66
V'trs	M SOC
Loc	In grounds of Royal Military
	College of Science,
	Shrivenham. Entry must be
	arranged with Sec

Salisbury & South Wilts (1888)

Netherhampton, Salisbury

Tel	(0722) 742131
Mem	810
Sec	Wg Cdr AW Pawson (0722)
	742645
Pro	G Emerson (0722) 742929
Holes	18 L 6130 yds SSS 70
Recs	Am–61 RS Blake
	Pro–62 N Blenkarne
V'trs	WD–U WE–H SOC
Fees	£15 (£22)
Loc	Wilton 2 miles on A3094.
	Salisbury 2 miles

Swindon (1907)

Ogbourne St George, nr
Marlborough SN8 1TB

Tel	(067 284) 217
Mem	700
Sec	PV Dixon (067 284) 327
Pro	C Harraway (067 284) 287
Holes	18 L 6226 yds SSS 70
Recs	Am–66 RJ Binsted, S Robertson
	Pro–65 I Bolt
V'trs	WD–H WE–M SOC–WD
Fees	On application
Loc	5 miles S of M4 Junction 15 on
	A345

West Wilts (1891)

Elm Hill, Warminster BA12 0AU

Tel	(0985) 212702
Mem	420 70(L) 70(J) 40(5)
Sec	Maj LR Weaver (0985) 213133
Pro	A Harvey (0985) 212110
Holes	18 L 5701 yds SSS 68
Recs	Am–62 CG Burton (1989)
	Pro–64 R Emery (1985)
V'trs	WD–U H WE–U H after noon
	–NA before noon
Fees	£17 (£27)
Loc	Off A350, on Westbury road

Yorkshire (North)

Aldwark Manor (1978)

Aldwark Manor, Aldwark Alne, York
YO6 2NF

Tel	(03473) 353
Sec	GF Platt (Golf Dir)
Holes	9 L 2569 yds SSS 66
Recs	Pro–67 S Deller (1988),
	B Hessay (1989)
V'trs	SOC
Fees	£10 (£15)
Loc	5 miles SE of Boroughbridge,
	off A1. 13 miles NW of York, off
	A19

Ampleforth College (1962)

56 High Street, Helmsley, York
YO6 5AE

Mem	130
Sec	JE Atkinson (0439) 70678
Holes	10 L 4018 yds SSS 63
V'trs	U exc WD 2-4pm SOC–WD
Fees	£4 (£6)
Loc	Driveway of Gilling Castle.
	18 miles N of York (B1363)
Mis	Green fees payable at Fairfax
	Arms, Gilling East

Bedale (1896)

Leyburn Road, Bedale DL8 1EZ

Tel	(0677) 22568
Mem	450 100(L) 60(J)
Sec	GA Shepherdson (0677) 22451
Pro	AD Johnson (0677) 22443
Holes	18 L 5737 yds SSS 68
Recs	Am–66 J Swain
	Pro–64 J Hughes
V'trs	U SOC
Fees	£12 (£18)
Loc	N boundary of Bedale

Bentham (1922)

Robin Lane, Bentham, Lancaster

Tel	(05242) 61018
Mem	450
Sec	JM Philipson (05242) 62455
Holes	9 L 5752 yds SSS 69
Recs	Am–69 J Carter (1989)
V'trs	U
Fees	£8 (£10) W–£30
Loc	NE of Lancaster on B6480
	towards Settle. 13 miles E of
	M6 Junction 34

Catterick Garrison (1930)

Leyburn Road, Catterick Garrison
DL9 3QE
Tel	(0748) 833268
Mem	670
Sec	JK Mayberry
Pro	S Bradley (0748) 833671
Holes	18 L 6336 yds SSS 70
Recs	Am–65 CS Carveth
	Pro–69 D Edwards
V'trs	U H SOC
Fees	£12 (£16)
Loc	6 miles SW of Scotch Corner, off A1 at Catterick Garrison junction

Crimple Valley (1976)

Hookstone Wood Road, Harrogate
HG2 8PN
Tel	(0423) 883485
Mem	200
Sec	R Lumb
Pro	R Lumb
Holes	9 L 2500 yds SSS 33
V'trs	U
Fees	£3.50
Loc	Next to Yorkshire Fairground, Harrogate

Easingwold (1930)

Stillington Road, Easingwold, York
YO6 3ET
Tel	(0347) 21486
Mem	575
Sec	KC Hudson
Pro	J Hughes (0347) 21964
Holes	18 L 6262 yds SSS 70
Recs	Am–67 GW Mutch
	Pro–65 G Brown
V'trs	U
Fees	D–£14 (£18)
Loc	12 miles N of York on A19. S end of Easingwold

Filey (1897)

West Ave, Filey YO14 9BQ
Tel	(0723) 513293
Mem	937
Sec	TM Thompson
Pro	D England (0723) 513134
Holes	18 L 6030 yds SSS 69
Recs	Am–67 AS Roberts
	Pro–64 AS Murray
V'trs	U H BH–no visiting parties SOC
Fees	Summer £13 (£16) Winter £10 (£12.50)
Loc	1 mile from Filey centre

Fulford (York) (1909)

Heslington Lane, York YO1 5DY
Tel	(0904) 413579
Mem	580
Sec	JCA Gledhill
Pro	B Hessay (0904) 412882
Holes	18 L 6779 yds SSS 72
Recs	Am–66 G Harland (1989)
	Pro–62 I Woosnam
V'trs	By arrangement with Sec
Fees	£25 (£28)
Loc	2 miles S of York

Ganton (1891)

Station Road, Ganton, Scarborough
YO12 4PA
Tel	(0944) 70329
Mem	600
Sec	Air Vice Marshal RG Price
Pro	G Brown (0944) 70260
Holes	18 L 6693 yds SSS 73
Recs	Am–67 G Boardman
	Pro–65 N Coles
V'trs	By prior arrangement
Fees	On application
Loc	Scarborough 11 miles on A64

Ghyll (1907)

Ghyll Brow, Barnoldswick, Colne
BB8 6JQ
Tel	(0282) 842466
Mem	310
Sec	JL Gill (0282) 813205
Holes	9 L 5708 yds SSS 68
Recs	Am–64 M Boardman (1989)
V'trs	U exc Sun–NA
Fees	£6 (£8)
Loc	Barnoldswick 1 mile

Harrogate (1892)

Forest Lane Head, Harrogate
HG2 7TF
Tel	(0423) 863158
Mem	620
Sec	J McDougall (0423) 862999
Pro	P Johnson (0423) 862547
Holes	18 L 6241 yds SSS 70
Recs	Am–65 P Hall
	Pro–64 D Durnian
V'trs	WD–U WE/ BH–enquire first SOC–Tues & Fri
Fees	£21 (£30)
Loc	2 miles from Harrogate on Knaresborough road (A59)

Heworth (1912)

Muncaster House, Muncastergate,
York YO3 9JX
Tel	(0904) 424618
Mem	245 80(L) 50(J) 70(5)
Sec	JR Richards
Pro	SI Robinson (0904) 422389
Holes	11 L 6141 yds SSS 69
V'trs	U
Fees	£12 (£14)
Loc	NE boundary of York (A1036)

Kirkbymoorside (1951)

Manor Vale, Kirkbymoorside, York
YO6 6EG
Tel	(0904) 31525
Mem	650
Sec	DG Saunders
Holes	18 L 6017 yds SSS 69
Recs	Am–S Dunn, C Fletcher (1989)
V'trs	U
Fees	£12 (£18)
Loc	A170 between Helmsley and Pickering

Knaresborough (1919)

Boroughbridge Road,
Knaresborough HG5 0QQ
Tel	(0423) 863219
Mem	765
Sec	Gp Capt JI Barrow (0423) 862690
Pro	KI Johnstone (0423) 864865
Holes	18 L 6232 yds SSS 70
Recs	Am–65 JR McVicar
V'trs	U
Fees	£12 (£20)
Loc	1 1/2 miles N of Knaresborough

Loftus Hill (1989)

Boroughbridge Road, Ferrensby,
Knaresbrough HG5 9JT
Tel	(0423) 340731
Sec	J Townsend
Holes	9 L 5106 yds SSS 65
V'trs	WD–U WE–pm only
Fees	£8 D–£10 (£10 D–£12)
Loc	3 miles N of Knaresbrough

Malton & Norton (1910)

Welham Park, Norton, Malton
YO17 9QE
Tel	(0653) 692959
Mem	700
Sec	WG Wade (0653) 697912
Pro	ML Henderson (0653) 693882
Holes	18 L 6401 yds SSS 71
V'trs	WD–U WE–restricted on match days H SOC
Fees	£15.50 (£20) W–£65
Loc	Between York and Scarborough, off Welham Road, Norton

Masham (1900)

Burnholme, Swinton Road, Masham,
Ripon HG4 4HT
Tel	(0765) 89379
Mem	305
Sec	Mrs MA Willis (0765) 89491
Holes	9 L 5244 yds SSS 66
Recs	Am–69 G Furby (1987)
V'trs	WD–U before 5pm WE–M BH–NA
Fees	£10
Loc	10 miles N of Ripon

Oakdale (1914)

Oakdale, Harrogate HG1 2LN
Tel	(0423) 567162
Mem	775
Sec	FR Hindmarsh
Pro	R Jessop (0423) 560510
Holes	18 L 6456 yds SSS 71
Recs	Am–66 G Cuthbert (1989)
	Pro–66 P Hall (1989)
V'trs	WD–U 9.30–12.30 and after 2pm SOC
Fees	£16 (£21)
Loc	1/2 mile NE of Royal Hall, Harrogate

For list of abbreviations see page 487.

Pannal (1906)

Follifoot Road, Pannal, Harrogate
HG3 1ES
Tel   (0423) 871641
Mem   815
Sec   WK Davies (0423) 872628
Pro   M Burgess (0423) 872620
Holes   18 L 6659 yds SSS 72
Recs   Am–64 L Walker (1990)
        Pro–67 N Coles (1985)
V'trs   WD–H 9.30-12 and after
        1.30pm WE–H 10-12 and after
        2.30pm SOC
Fees   £20 D–£25 (£22)
Loc   2½ miles S of Harrogate, on
        A61

Pike Hills (1920)

Tadcaster Road, Askham Bryan,
York YO2 3UW
Tel   (0904) 706566
Mem   800
Sec   G Rawlings
Pro   I Gradwell (0904) 708756
Holes   18 L 6048 yds SSS 69
Recs   Am–65 AM Burton (1986)
V'trs   WD–U H before 4.30pm -M
        after 4.30pm WE/ BH–M SOC
Fees   Summer–£14 Winter–£10
Loc   3 miles W of York on Leeds
        road

Richmond (1892)

Bend Hagg, Richmond
Tel   (0748) 2457
Mem   454
Sec   BD Aston (0748) 4775
Pro   P Jackson
Holes   18 L 5704 yds SSS 68
Recs   Am–64 G Catt
        Pro–64 P Tupling
V'trs   U
Fees   £8 (£12)
Loc   3 miles S of Scotch Corner

Ripon City (1905)

Palace Road, Ripon HG4 3HH
Tel   (0765) 3640
Mem   280 50(L) 30(J) 70(5)
Sec   G Crompton (0765) 2997
Pro   T Davis (0765) 700411
Holes   9 L 5752 yds SSS 68
Recs   Am–65 M Grant
        Pro–65 A Dyson, P Hall
V'trs   U
Fees   £10 (£15)
Loc   1 mile N of Ripon, on A6108

Scarborough North Cliff (1927)

North Cliff Avenue, Burniston Road,
Scarborough YO12 6PP
Tel   (0723) 360786
Mem   835
Sec   JR Freeman
Pro   SN Deller (0723) 365920
Holes   18 L 6425 yds SSS 71
Recs   Am–66 MJ Kelly, R Newton
V'trs   U exc Sun before 10am and
        comp days H SOC

Fees   £16 (£20)
Loc   2 miles N of Scarborough on
        coast road

Scarborough South Cliff (1903)

Deepdale Avenue, off Filey Road,
Scarborough YO11 2UE
Tel   (0723) 360522
Mem   500
Sec   JA Sword (0723) 374737
Pro   DM Edwards (0723) 365150
Holes   18 L 6085 yds SSS 69
Recs   Am–68 SJ Thorpe (1987)
        Pro–66 MJ Slater (1987)
V'trs   U H
Fees   £16 (£21.50)
Loc   1 mile S of Scarborough

Selby (1907)

Mill Lane, Brayton, Selby YO8 9LD
Tel   (075 782) 622
Mem   749
Sec   BLC Moore
Pro   A Smith (075 782) 785
Holes   18 L 6246 yds SSS 70
Recs   Am–65 L Walker
        Pro–64 D Matthew
V'trs   WD–H WE–NA SOC–Wed-Fri
Fees   £15 D–£18
Loc   3 miles SW of Selby, off A19.
        5 miles N of M62 Junction 34

Settle (1895)

Giggleswick, Settle
Tel   (07292) 3593
Mem   250
Sec   JD Lassey
Holes   9 L 2276 yds SSS 31
Recs   Am–62 P Robinson
V'trs   U exc Sun-restricted SOC
Fees   D–£5
Loc   1 mile N of Settle on A65

Skipton (1905)

Off NW Bypass, Skipton BD23 1LL
Tel   (0756) 3922
Mem   605
Sec   JC Varley (Mgr) (0756) 2128
Pro   J Hammond (0756) 3257
Holes   18 L 6087 yds SSS 70
Recs   Am–69 RR Taylor (1989)
V'trs   U
Fees   £10 (£15)
Loc   Skipton 1 mile, off NW Bypass

Thirsk & Northallerton (1914)

Thornton-le-Street, Thirsk YO7 4AB
Tel   (0845) 22170
Mem   300
Sec   HD Swarbrick (0845) 587350
Pro   A Marshall, D Llewellyn
        (Touring Pro)
Holes   9 L 6257 yds SSS 70
Recs   Am–69 R Cable
        Pro–69 P Blaze
V'trs   WD–U Sun-M SOC
Fees   £10 D–£15 Sat/ BH–£15

Loc   2 miles N of Thirsk nr A19 and
        A168 roundabout

Whitby (1892)

Low Straggleton, Whitby YO21 3SR
Tel   (0947) 602768
Mem   800
Sec   A Dyson (0947) 600660
Pro   A Brook (0947) 602719
Holes   18 L 5710 yds SSS 67
Recs   Am–67
        Pro–68
V'trs   U SOC
Fees   £11 (£16.50) W–£45
Loc   2 miles N of Whitby on A174

York (1890)

Lords Moor Lane, Strensall, York
YO3 5XF
Tel   (0904) 491840
Mem   350 120(L) 120(J)
Sec   F Appleyard
Pro   A Mason (0904) 490304
Holes   18 L 6285 yds SSS 70
Recs   Am–66 D Oxley (1990)
        Pro–66 P Fowler
V'trs   U (phone Sec) SOC–WD/ Sun
Fees   £17 (£21)
Loc   3 miles N of York ring road
        (A1237)

Yorkshire (South)

Abbeydale (1895)

Twentywell Lane, Dore, nr Sheffield
S17 4QA
Tel   (0742) 360763
Mem   700
Sec   Mrs KM Johnston
Pro   N Perry (0742) 365633
Holes   18 L 6419 yds SSS 71
V'trs   U SOC–Tues & Fri
Fees   £20 (£25)
Loc   5 miles S of Sheffield

Austerfield Park (1974)

Cross Lane, Austerfield, nr Bawtry,
Doncaster DN10 6RF
Tel   (0302) 710841
Mem   425 45(L) 40(J) 100(5)
Sec   A Bradley (0709) 540928
Pro   J Taylor (0302) 719461
Holes   18 L 6824 yds SSS 73
Recs   Am–71 M Hayward (1990)
        Pro–67 J Brennand (1988)
V'trs   U
Fees   £11.50 (£14)
Loc   2 miles NE of Bawtry, off A614
Mis   Driving range

Barnsley (1925)

Public
Wakefield Road, Staincross,
Barnsley S75 6JZ
Tel   (0226) 382856
Pro   M Melling (0226) 382954
Holes   18 L 6048 yds SSS 69

Recs Am–64 RI Shaw (1988)
Pro–62 M Melling
V'trs U
Fees £3.25 (£4.40)
Loc 4 miles N of Barnsley on A61

Beauchief Municipal (1925)

Public
Abbey Lane, Sheffield S8 0DB
Tel (0742) 367274/ 620040
Pro B English
Holes 18 L 5428 yds SSS 66
Recs Am–65 PW Hickinson
Pro–63 P Tupling
V'trs U
Fees £5 (£5)
Loc A621 Sheffield

Birley Wood (1974)

Public
Birley Lane, Sheffield S12 3BP
Tel (0742) 647262
Pro S Sherratt
Holes 18 L 6275 yds SSS 70
V'trs U
Fees £3.50 (£5)
Loc 4 miles S of Sheffield on A616 to M1

Concord Park (1952)

Public
Shiregreen Lane, Sheffield S5 6AE
Tel (0742) 570274/ 570053
Holes 18 L 4321 yds SSS 62
Recs Am–61 J Fowler (1989)
V'trs U
Fees £5
Loc M1 Junction 34, 1 mile

Crookhill Park (1973)

Public
Conisborough, nr Doncaster DN12 2AH
Tel (0709) 862979
Pro R Swaine
Holes 18 L 5846 yds SSS 68
Recs Am–67 R Jones
Pro–70
V'trs U
Fees £4
Loc 3 miles W of Doncaster (A630)

Doncaster (1895)

Bawtry Road, Bessacarr, nr Doncaster DN4 7PD
Tel (0302) 868316
Mem 375
Sec AE Shaw (0302) 865632
Pro S Fox (0302) 868404
Holes 18 L 6230 yds SSS 70
Recs Am–66 H Green
Pro–66 H Clark
V'trs U H WE/ BH–after 11.30am
SOC–WD
Fees £15 (£20)
Loc 4½ miles S of Doncaster on A638

Doncaster Town Moor (1900)

The Belle Vue Club, Bellevue, Doncaster DN4 5HV
Tel (0302) 535286
Mem 500
Sec JC Padley (0302) 535458
Pro S Poole
Holes 18 L 6314 yds SSS 69
Recs Am–64 AJ Miller (1989)
Pro–69 D Snell
V'trs U exc Sun before 11.30am SOC
Fees £10 (£12)
Loc Inside racecourse

Dore & Totley (1913)

Bradway Road, Bradway, nr Sheffield S17 4QR
Tel (0742) 360492
Mem 580
Sec Mrs C Milner (0742) 369872
Pro M Pearson (0742) 366844
Holes 18 L 6265 yds SSS 70
Recs Am–S Field
Pro–P Cowen
V'trs WD–U WE/ BH–M
Fees £17
Loc 5 miles SW of Sheffield

Grange Park (1972)

Public
Upper Wortley Road, Kimberworth, Rotherham S61 2SJ
Tel (0709) 558884
Pro E Clark (0709) 559497
Holes 18 L 6461 yds SSS 71
Recs Am–68 J Beckitt
Pro–68 G Tickell
V'trs U
Fees £2.75 (£3.60)
Loc 2 miles W of Rotherham on A629

Hallamshire (1897)

Sandygate, Sheffield S10 4LA
Tel (0742) 302153
Mem 600
Sec R Burns
Pro G Tickell (0742) 305222
Holes 18 L 6396 yds SSS 71
Recs Am–66 W Bremner
Pro–63 JW Wilkinson
V'trs I
Fees £17 (£25)
Loc W boundary of Sheffield

Hallowes (1892)

Dronfield, Sheffield S18 6UA
Tel (0246) 413734
Mem 514
Sec KH Dowswell
Pro M Heggie (0246) 411196
Holes 18 L 6342 yds SSS 70
Recs Am–66 S Priest (1989)
Pro–67 R Ellis (1982)
V'trs WD–U WE/ BH–M (phone first)
Fees £18 D–£22
Loc Dronfield, 6 miles S of Sheffield on B6057

Hickleton (1909)

Hickleton, nr Doncaster
Tel (0709) 892496
Mem 485
Sec R Jowett (0709) 893506
Pro P Shepherd (0709) 895170
Holes 18 L 6403 yds SSS 71
Recs Am–69 P Goodwin (1988)
V'trs WD/ Sat am/ Sun pm–U SOC
Fees £10 (£15)
Loc 6 miles W of Doncaster, on A635 between Doncaster and Barnsley

Hillsborough (1920)

Worrall Road, Sheffield S6 4BE
Tel (0742) 343608
Mem 710
Sec AW Platts (0742) 349151
Pro G Walker (0742) 332666
Holes 18 L 5672 metres SSS 70
V'trs U
Fees £16 (£23)
Loc Wadsley, Sheffield

Lees Hall (1907)

Hemsworth Road, Norton, Sheffield S8 8LL
Tel (0742) 554402
Mem 700
Sec NE Westworth (0742) 552900
Pro JR Wilkinson
Holes 18 L 6137 yds SSS 69
Recs Am–65 AR Gellsthorpe
Pro–63 B Hutchinson
V'trs U SOC
Fees £16 (£25)
Loc 3 miles S of Sheffield. E of A61

Lindrick (1891)

Lindrick Common, nr Worksop, Notts S81 8BH
Tel (0909) 485802
Mem 500
Sec G Bywater (0909) 475282
Pro P Cowen (0909) 475820
Holes 18 L 6615 yds SSS 72
Recs Am–65 DF Livingston
Pro–65 G Bond, J Morgan
V'trs U by prior arrangement exc Tues am–NA SOC–WD
Fees £30 (£40) Winter–£20
Loc 4 miles W of Worksop on A57. M1 Junction 31

Phoenix (1932)

Brinsworth, Rotherham
Tel (0709) 382624
Mem 700
Sec J Burrows (0709) 370759
Pro A Limb
Holes 18 L 6170 yds SSS 69
V'trs U
Fees £12 (£16)
Loc Rotherham 2 miles. Bawtry road off M1 Tinsley roundabout

Renishaw Park (1911)

Golf House, Renishaw, Sheffield
S31 9UZ
Tel	(0246) 432044
Mem	400
Sec	T Bradley
Pro	S Elliott (0246) 435484
Holes	18 L 6253 yds SSS 70
Recs	Am–64 CS Bright
	Pro–66 D Dunk, R Emery,
	J Rhodes
V'trs	H SOC
Fees	£16 (£25)
Loc	7 miles from Sheffield. 2 miles
	from M1 Junction 30

Rotherham (1903)

Thrybergh Park, Rotherham
S65 4NU
Tel	(0709) 850466
Mem	400
Sec	F Green (0709) 850812
Pro	S Thornhill (0709) 850480
Holes	18 L 6324 yds SSS 70
Recs	Am–66 MJ Kelly
	Pro–66 B Hutchison
V'trs	WD–U SOC
Fees	£17 (£20)
Loc	4 miles E of Rotherham on
	A630

Roundwood (1976)

Green Lane, Rawmarsh, Rotherham
S62 6LA
Tel	(0709) 523471
Mem	400
Sec	T Barnfield (0709) 541792
Holes	9 L 5646 yds SSS 67
V'trs	WE–NA before 2.30pm on
	comp days
Fees	£5 (£7)
Loc	2 miles N of Rotherham on
	A633

Serlby Park (1905)

Serlby, Doncaster DN10 6BA
Tel	(0777) 818268
Mem	250
Sec	R Wilkinson (0302) 536336
Holes	9 L 5370 yds SSS 66
Recs	Am–63 A Pugsley (1988)
	Pro–65 M Bembridge (1965)
V'trs	M
Loc	12 miles S of Doncaster,
	between A614 and A638

Sheffield Transport Dept (1923)

Meadow Head, Sheffield
Tel	(0742) 373216
Mem	100
Sec	AE Mason
Holes	18 L 3966 yds SSS 62
Recs	Am–62 VR Hutton
V'trs	M
Loc	S of Sheffield on A61

Silkstone (1893)

Field Head, Silkstone, nr Barnsley
Tel	(0226) 790328
Mem	450
Sec	L Depledge (0226) 287053
Pro	K Guy (0226) 790128
Holes	18 L 6045 yds SSS 70
Recs	Am–67 TG Garner
V'trs	WD–U WE–M SOC–WD
Fees	£16
Loc	1 mile from M1 Junction 37

Sitwell Park (1913)

Shrogs Wood Road, Rotherham
Tel	(0709) 541046
Mem	500
Sec	J Straffen (0709) 365830
Pro	N Taylor (0709) 540961
Holes	18 L 6250 yds SSS 70
Recs	Am–67 RN Portas
V'trs	WD–U Sat–M Sun–NA before
	11.30am SOC
Fees	£14 (£16)
Loc	2¹/₂ miles E of Rotherham

Stocksbridge & District (1925)

30 Royd Lane, Townend, Deepcar,
nr Sheffield S30 5RZ
Tel	(0742) 882003
Mem	300
Sec	S Lee (0742) 882408
Holes	18 L 5200 yds SSS 65
Recs	Am–61 CR Dale (1977)
	Pro–61 TJ Brookes (1986)
V'trs	U SOC
Fees	£10 (£15)
Loc	9 miles W of Sheffield

Tankersley Park (1907)

High Green, Sheffield S30 4LG
Tel	(0742) 468247
Mem	574
Sec	S Jessop
Pro	I Kirk (0742) 455583
Holes	18 L 6241 yds SSS 70
Recs	Am–66 N Grice
	Pro–69 W Atkinson
V'trs	WD–U WE–M SOC–WD
Fees	£12 D–£15 (£15)
Loc	Chapeltown, 7 miles N of
	Sheffield. M1 Junction 35A
	(northbound)

Thorne (1980)

Kirton Lane, Thorne, Doncaster
DN8 5RJ
Tel	(0405) 812054
Sec	P Kitteridge (0302) 813827
Pro	RD Highfield
Holes	18 L 5146 yds SSS 65
V'trs	U
Fees	£5 (£6)
Loc	M18 Junction 5/6

Tinsley Park (1920)

Public
Darnall, Sheffield
Tel	(0742) 560237
Sec	S Conroy (Hon)
Pro	AP Highfield
Holes	18 L 6045 yds SSS 69
Recs	Am–70 D Robbins
	Pro–66 D Snell
V'trs	U
Fees	£4.50
Loc	M1 Junction 32, 1 mile

Wath-upon-Dearne (1904)

Abdy Rawmarsh, Rotherham
Tel	(0709) 872149
Mem	600
Sec	J Pepper (0709) 873153
Pro	C Bassett (0709) 878677
Holes	18 L 5857 yds SSS 68
V'trs	WD–U WE/ BH–M SOC
Fees	£12
Loc	Abdy Farm, 1¹/₂ miles S of
	Wath-upon-Dearne

Wheatley (1913)

Armthorpe Road, Doncaster
DN2 5QB
Tel	(0302) 831655
Mem	385 100(L) 50(J) 5(5)
Sec	KW Percival
Pro	T Parkinson (0302) 834085
Holes	18 L 6345 yds SSS 70
Recs	Am–65 B Bremner
	Pro–63 G Walker
V'trs	U SOC
Fees	£12 (£16)
Loc	3 miles E of Doncaster

Wombwell Hillies (1989)

Public
Wentworth View, Wombwell,
Barnsley S73 0LA
Tel	(0226) 754433
Sec	R Burkinshaw (Mgr)
Holes	9 L 2019 yds SSS 60
V'trs	U
Fees	18 holes–£3.50 (£5.80)
	9 holes–£2.20 (£2.90)
Loc	4 miles SE of Barnsley

Wortley (1894)

Hermit Hill Lane, Wortley, nr
Sheffield S30 4DF
Tel	(0742) 885294
Mem	300
Sec	JL Dalby
Pro	J Tilson (0742) 886490
Holes	18 L 5983 yds SSS 69
Recs	Am–65
	Pro–66
V'trs	WD–U WE–NA before 10am
	SOC
Fees	£14 (£20)
Loc	2 miles W of M1 Junction 36, off
	A629

Yorkshire (West)

Alwoodley (1908)

Wigton Lane, Alwoodley, Leeds
LS17 8SA
Tel   (0532) 681680
Mem   450
Sec   TG Turnbull
Pro   J Foss
Holes   18 L 6686 yds SSS 72
Recs   Am–68 F Haughton
        Pro–68 D Fitton
V'trs   WE–M SOC
Fees   £30
Loc   5 miles N of Leeds on A61

Baildon (1898)

Moorgate, Baildon, Shipley
BD17 5PP
Tel   (0274) 584266
Mem   700
Sec   D Farnsworth (0274) 584684
Pro   R Masters (0274) 595162
Holes   18 L 6085 yds SSS 70
Recs   Am–66 D Farnsworth
        Pro–64 G Brand, D Durnian
V'trs   WD–U before 5pm (restricted
        Tues) WE/ BH–restricted
Fees   £10 (£15)
Loc   5 miles NW of Bradford

Ben Rhydding (1948)

High Wood, Ben Rhydding, Ilkley
Tel   (0943) 608759
Mem   185 60(L) 36(J)
Sec   JDB Watts
Holes   9 L 4711 yds SSS 64
Recs   Am–64 H Barker
        Pro–64 GJ Brand
V'trs   WD–U WE–M
Fees   £7.50
Loc   Ilkley

Bingley (St Ives) (1931)

St Ives Estate, Bingley BD16 1AT
Tel   (0274) 562506
Sec   J Crolla (Hon)
Pro   R Firth
Holes   18 L 6466 yds SSS 71
Recs   Am–70 WM Hopkinson
        Pro–62 N Faldo
V'trs   WD–U before 4pm
Fees   £12 D–£16 (£20)
Loc   6 miles W of Bradford

Bradford (1891)

Hawksworth Lane, Guiseley, Leeds
LS20 8NP
Tel   (0943) 75570
Mem   500
Sec   P Atkinson
Pro   S Weldon (0943) 73719
Holes   18 L 6259 yds SSS 70
Recs   Am–67 R Foster, N Ludwell
V'trs   WD–U WE–NA before noon
        SOC–WD
Loc   8 miles N of Bradford

Bradford Moor (1907)

Scarr Hall, Pollard Lane, Bradford
Tel   (0274) 638313
Mem   375
Sec   D Armitage
Pro   R Hughes (0274) 631163
Holes   9 L 5854 yds SSS 68
Recs   Am–68 I Helliwell
        Pro–69 H Waller
V'trs   U
Fees   £7.50 (£8)

Bradley Park (1978)

Public
Bradley Road, Huddersfield
HD2 1PZ
Tel   (0484) 539988
Pro   PE Reilly
Holes   18 L 6202 yds SSS 70 9 hole
        Par 3
Recs   Am–69 R Hall
        Pro–64 P Carman
V'trs   U SOC
Fees   £5.75 (£6.75)
Loc   M62 Junction 25, 1 1/2 miles
Mis   Floodlit driving range

Branshaw (1912)

Branshaw Moor, Oakworth, nr
Keighley BD22 7ES
Tel   (0535) 643235
Mem   460
Sec   DA Town (0535) 605003
Holes   18 L 5858 yds SSS 69
Recs   Am–65 D Eeles (1990)
V'trs   WD–U SOC
Fees   £10 (£15)
Loc   2 miles SW of Keighley on
        B6143

Calverley (1984)

Woodhall Lane, Pudsey LS28 5JX
Tel   (0532) 569244
Mem   425
Sec   WW Gardner
Holes   18 L 5348 yds SSS 66 9 hole
        course
Recs   Am–66 M Woodhall
V'trs   WD–U WE–pm only
Fees   18 hole:£10 9 hole:£4
Loc   4 miles NE of Bradford
Mis   Driving range

Castle Fields (1900)

Rastrick Common, Brighouse
Mem   140
Sec   P Bentley (0484) 712108
Holes   6 L 2406 yds SSS 50
V'trs   M
Fees   £3
Loc   1 mile S of Brighouse

City of Wakefield (1936)

Public
Lupset Park, Horbury Road,
Wakefield WF2 8QS
Tel   (0924) 374316
Pro   R Holland (0924) 360282
Holes   18 L 6405 yds SSS 71

Clayton (1906)

Thornton View Road, Clayton,
Bradford
Tel   (0274) 880047
Mem   180 35(L) 35(J) 40(5)
Sec   FV Wood (0274) 574203
Holes   9 L 5515 yds SSS 67
Recs   Am–65 ND Hawkins
V'trs   WD–U Sat–U Sun–after 4pm
Fees   £8 D–£10 (£10)
Loc   3 miles W of Bradford

Recs (Bradford Moor header column, right)
Recs   Am–66 PE Monaghan,
        DA Ware
        Pro–67 P Cowen
V'trs   WD–U WE/ BH–NA SOC–WD
Fees   £4.10 (£6.20)
Loc   A642, 2 miles W of Wakefield.
        2 miles E of M1 Junction 39/ 40

Cleckheaton & District (1900)

483 Bradford Road, Cleckheaton
BD19 6BU
Tel   (0274) 874118
Mem   550
Sec   H Thornton (0274) 851266
Pro   M Ingham (0274) 851267
Holes   18 L 5994 yds SSS 69
Recs   Am–62 CA Bloice
        Pro–63 GA Caygill
V'trs   U SOC
Fees   £11 (£17.50)
Loc   Nr M62 Junction 26-A638

Crosland Heath (1914)

Crosland Heath, Huddersfield
Tel   (0484) 653216
Mem   320
Sec   D Walker (0484) 653262
Pro   J Andrew (0484) 653877
Holes   18 L 5972 yds SSS 70
Recs   Am–66 S Ellis
        Pro–65 SW Dellar
V'trs   U SOC
Fees   On application
Loc   3 miles W of Huddersfield

Dewsbury District (1891)

The Pinnacle, Mirfield
Tel   (0924) 492399
Mem   500
Sec   P Croft
Pro   N Hirst (0924) 496030
Holes   18 L 6256 yds SSS 71
Recs   Am–68 M Colcombe
        Pro–68 R Masters
V'trs   U SOC
Fees   £11
Loc   W boundary of Dewsbury

East Bierley (1928)

South View Road, Bradford
Tel   (0274) 681023
Mem   156 47(L) 30(J)
Sec   Mrs M Welch
Holes   9 L 4692 yds SSS 63
Recs   Am–59 R Watts
        Pro–62 B Hill

For list of abbreviations see page 487.

V'trs U exc Mon–NA after 4pm
       Sun–NA
Fees £6 (£8)
Loc 4 miles SE of Bradford

Elland (1910)

Hullen Edge, Elland
Tel (0422) 372505
Mem 250
Sec WH Pearson (0422) 373276
Pro J Tindall (0422) 374886
Holes 9 L 2763 yds SSS 66
Recs Am–64 C Hartland
V'trs U
Fees £8 (£12)
Loc Elland ¹/₂ mile. M62 Junction 24
       (Blackley)

Ferrybridge 'C' (1976)

PO Box 39, Stranglands Lane,
Knottingley WF11 8SQ
Tel (0977) 674188 (Ext 2656)
Mem 274
Sec NE Pugh (0977) 793884
Holes 9 L 5138 yds SSS 65
Recs Am–67 R MacDonald (1989)
V'trs M
Loc Ferrybridge "C" Power
       Station. ¹/₂ mile off A1, on
       B6136

Fulneck (1892)

Pudsey
Tel (0532) 565191
Mem 265
Sec J Brogden (0532) 574049
Holes 9 L 5564 yds SSS 67
Recs Am–64 I Holdsworth
V'trs WD–U WE/ BH–M SOC
Fees £8
Loc 5 miles W of Leeds

Garforth (1913)

Long Lane, Garforth, Leeds
LS25 2DS
Tel (0532) 862021
Mem 550
Sec FA Readman (0532) 863308
Pro K Findlater (0532) 862063
Holes 18 L 6327 yds SSS 70
Recs Am–63 AR Gelsthorpe
V'trs WD–U H WE/ BH–M SOC
Fees £14 D–£17 WE–M
Loc 9 miles E of Leeds, between
       Garforth and Barwick-in-Elmet

Gotts Park (1934)

Public
Armley Ridge Road, Armley, Leeds
LS12 2QX
Tel (0532) 636600
Pro JK Simpson
Holes 18 L 4960 yds SSS 64
V'trs U
Fees £3.75 (£4.10)
Loc 2 miles W of Leeds

Halifax (1895)

Union Lane, Ogden, Halifax HX2 8XR
Tel (0422) 244171
Mem 450
Sec JP Clark
Pro SA Foster (0422) 240047
Holes 18 L 6038 yds SSS 70
Recs Am–66 J Robinson, AMA
       Bagot, J Rushworth
       Pro–65 PW Good
V'trs U WE–parties welcome SOC
Fees £10 (£15)
Loc 4 miles N of Halifax on A629

Halifax Bradley Hall (1907)

Holywell Green, Halifax HX4 9AN
Tel (0422) 374108
Mem 608
Sec PM Pitchforth (0422) 376626
Pro P Wood (0422) 370231
Holes 18 L 6213 yds SSS 70
Recs Am–65 AR Whitworth
V'trs U SOC
Fees £13 (£20)
Loc S of Halifax on A6112

Halifax West End (1913)

Highroad Well, Halifax HX2 0NT
Tel (0422) 353608
Mem 300 100(L) 70(J)
Sec BR Thomas (0422) 367145
Pro D Rishworth (0422) 363293
Holes 18 L 6003 yds SSS 69
Recs Am–65 JR Crawshaw, JR Smith
       Pro–64 AJ Bickerdike
V'trs U SOC
Fees £9 (£12) (1990)
Loc 2 miles NW of Halifax

Hanging Heaton (1922)

Whitecross Road, Dewsbury
WF12 7DT
Tel (0924) 461606
Mem 550
Sec SM Simpson (0924) 461729
Pro G Hutchinson (0924) 467077
Holes 9 L 2868 yds SSS 67
Recs Am–66 P Cockburn
       Pro–AJ Bickerdyke
V'trs WD–U WE–M
Fees £10
Loc Dewsbury ³/₄ mile (A653)

Headingley (1892)

Back Church Lane, Adel, Leeds
LS16 8DW
Tel (0532) 673052
Mem 640
Sec RW Hellawell (0532) 679573
Pro (0532) 675100
Holes 18 L 6298 yds SSS 70
Recs Am–67 S Pullan
       Pro–64 S Field
V'trs U SOC
Fees £20 D–£25 (£30)
Loc 5 miles NW of Leeds, off A660
       Leeds-Skipton road

Headley (1906)

Headley Lane, Thornton, nr Bradford
BD13 3LX
Tel (0274) 833481
Mem 200
Sec JP Clark (0274) 832571
Holes 9 L 4914 yds SSS 64
Recs Am–61 A Cording (1985)
       Pro–66 M Ingham
V'trs U exc Sun
Fees £5 (£10)
Loc 5 miles W of Bradford

Hebden Bridge

Wadsworth, Hebden Bridge
Tel (0422) 842896
Mem 260
Sec Dr RG Pogson (0422) 843733
Holes 9 L 5114 yds SSS 66
Recs Am–63 IS Marsland
       Pro–63 M Ingham
V'trs U
Fees £7.50 (£10)
Loc 1 mile N of Hebden Bridge

Horsforth (1907)

Layton Rise, Layton Road, Horsforth,
Leeds LS18 5EX
Tel (0532) 586819
Mem 365 90(L) 85(J) 80(5)
Sec CB Carrington
Pro (0532) 585200
Holes 18 L 6293 yds SSS 70
Recs Am–67 S Lax
       Pro–67 HW Muscroft
V'trs U SOC
Fees D–£18 (£22)
Loc 6 miles NW of Leeds

Howley Hall (1900)

Scotchman Lane, Morley, Leeds
LS27 0NX
Tel (0924) 472432
Mem 465
Sec Mrs A Pepper (0924) 478417
Pro SA Spinks (0924) 473852
Holes 18 L 6029 yds SSS 69
Recs Am–66 S Hamer (1984)
V'trs U
Fees £15 D–£18 (D–£22)
Loc 4 miles SW of Leeds on B6123

Huddersfield (1891)

Fixby Hall, Lightridge Road, Fixby,
Huddersfield HD2 2EP
Tel (0484) 420110545
       (0484) 424623
Mem 700
Sec Miss D Rose (0484) 426203
Pro P Carman (0484) 426463
Holes 18 L 6402 yds SSS 71
Recs Am–67 S Pullan (1990)
       Pro–66 G Thornhill(1985)
V'trs U SOC
Fees £20.50 D–£26.50 (£22.50
       D–£29)
Loc 2 miles N of Huddersfield, off
       A6170. M62 Junction 24

Ilkley (1890)

Myddleton, Ilkley LS29 0BE
Tel	(0943) 607277
Mem	530
Sec	G Hirst (0943) 600214
Pro	JL Hammond (0943) 607463
Holes	18 L 6260 yds SSS 70
Recs	Am–65 AC Flather (1984)
	Pro–64 B Hutchinson (1972)
V'trs	U
Fees	£20 (£28)
Loc	Ilkley

Keighley (1904)

Howden Park, Utley, Keighley
Tel	(0535) 603179
Mem	600
Sec	DF Coyle (0535) 604778
Pro	S Dixon (0535) 665370
Holes	18 L 6134 yds SSS 70
Recs	Am–66 RS Mitchell, G Smith (1987)
	Pro–65 J Holchaks
V'trs	WD–U Sat–NA Sun/ BH–NA before 2pm -U after 2pm
Fees	£17 (£20)
Loc	1 mile W of Keighley

Leeds (1896)

Elmete Road, Roundhay, Leeds LS8 2LJ
Tel	(0532) 658775
Mem	480
Sec	GW Backhouse (0532) 659203
Pro	S Longster (0532) 658786
Holes	18 L 6097 yds SSS 69
Recs	Am–64 J Whiteley
	Pro–63 P Hall
V'trs	WD–U WE–M
Fees	£15 D–£20
Loc	4 miles NE of Leeds, off A58

Lightcliffe (1907)

Knowle Top Road, Lightcliffe
Tel	(0422) 202459
Mem	145 92(L) 87(J)
Sec	TH Gooder (0422) 201051
Pro	R Parry
Holes	9 L 5368 metres SSS 68
Recs	Am–66 NRA Denham, PH Wolfe
V'trs	U-exc comp days Sun am-M
Fees	£10 (£12)
Loc	3 miles E of Halifax

Longley Park (1911)

Maple Street, Somerset Road, Huddersfield HD5 9AX
Tel	(0484) 422304
Mem	400
Sec	KLW Ireland (0484) 429826
Pro	N Suckling
Holes	9 L 5324 yds SSS 66
Recs	Am–64 JD Oxley
	Pro–65 PW Booth
V'trs	WD–U exc Thurs WE–Restricted
Fees	£8 (£10)
Loc	Huddersfield ½ mile

Low Laithes (1925)

Parkmill Lane, Flushdyke, Ossett
Tel	(0924) 273275
Mem	450
Sec	D Walker (0924) 376553
Pro	P Browning (0924) 274667
Holes	18 L 6468 yds SSS 71
Recs	Am–67
	Pro–68
V'trs	U WE–no parties
Fees	D–£12 (D–£18)
Loc	2 miles N of Wakefield. M1 Junction 40

Marsden (1921)

Hemplow, Marsden, Huddersfield
Tel	(0484) 844253
Mem	184 48(L) 40(J)
Sec	S Shaw (0484) 845869
Pro	D Chapman
Holes	9 L 5702 yds SSS 68
Recs	Am–63 AJ Bickerdike
	Pro–A Bickerdike
V'trs	WD–U Sat–NA before 4pm Sun-M
Fees	£6
Loc	8 miles S of Huddersfield

Meltham (1908)

Thick Hollins Hall, Meltham, Huddersfield HD7 3DQ
Tel	(0484) 850227
Mem	450
Sec	BF Precious (0484) 682106
Pro	PF Davies (0484) 851521
Holes	18 L 6145 yds SSS 70
Recs	Am–68 AT Garner
	Pro–69 W Casper
V'trs	U
Fees	£12 (£15)
Loc	5 miles W of Huddersfield

Middleton Park (1934)

Public
Ring Road, Beeston Park, Middleton, Leeds 10
Tel	(0532) 709506
Pro	D Bulmer
Holes	18 L 5233 yds SSS 66
V'trs	U
Fees	£3.70
Loc	3 miles S of Leeds

Moor Allerton (1923)

Coal Road, Leeds LS17 9NH
Tel	(0532) 661154
Mem	1200
Sec	B Jackson
Pro	R Lane (0532) 665209
	H Clark (Tournament Pro)
Holes	18 L 6542 yds SSS 9 L 3541 yds SSS
Recs	Am–68
	Pro–65
V'trs	WD–U WE–NA SOC
Fees	£30 D–£36
Loc	5½ miles N of Leeds

Moortown (1909)

Harrogate Road, Leeds LS17 7DB
Tel	(0532) 686521
Mem	500
Sec	RH Brown
Pro	B Hutchinson (0532) 683636
Holes	18 L 6544 yds SSS 72
Recs	Am–69 C Turner
V'trs	WD–H WE/ BH–M I
Fees	£25 D–£32 (£32 D–£37)
Loc	5½ miles N of Leeds on A61

Normanton (1903)

Snydale Road, Normanton, Wakefield WF6 1PA
Tel	(0924) 892943
Mem	250
Sec	J McElhinney (0977) 702273
Pro	M Evans (0924) 220134
Holes	9 L 5284 yds SSS 66
Recs	Am–68 S Turner (1988)
	Pro–67 A Dyson (1988)
V'trs	U exc Sun–NA
Fees	£4.50 Sat/ BH –£8.50
Loc	1 mile from M62 Junction 31. A655 towards Wakefield

Northcliffe (1921)

High Bank Lane, Shipley, Bradford BD18 4LJ
Tel	(0274) 584085
Mem	660
Sec	R Anderson (0532) 567845
Pro	S Poot (0274) 587193
Holes	18 L 6065 yds SSS 69
Recs	Am–67 R Bell
	Pro–67 M James
V'trs	U SOC
Fees	£14 (£22)
Loc	3 miles NW of Bradford, off A650 Keighley road

Otley (1906)

West Busk Lane, Otley LS21 3NG
Tel	(0943) 461015
Mem	600
Sec	AF Flowers (0943) 465329
Pro	S McNally (0943) 463403
Holes	18 L 6235 yds SSS 70
Recs	Am–66 J Blears (1989)
	Pro–62 GJ Brand (1988)
V'trs	U SOC
Fees	£20 (£25)
Loc	Off Bradford road, Otley

Outlane (1906)

Slack Lane, Outlane, Huddersfield HD3 3YL
Tel	(0422) 374762
Mem	500
Sec	P Sykes
Pro	D Chapman
Holes	18 L 5735 yds SSS 69
Recs	Am–62 G Crosland
	Pro–62 W Garside
V'trs	U SOC
Fees	£10 (£15)
Loc	4 miles W of Huddersfield, nr M62

Painthorpe House (1961)

Painthorpe Lane, Crigglestone, nr Wakefield
Tel	(0924) 255083
Mem	120
Sec	H Kershaw (0924) 274527
Holes	9 L 4520 yds SSS 62
Recs	Am–64 J Turner, J Whitehouse
V'trs	U exc Sun–NA
Fees	£3 Sat–£5
Loc	1 mile from M1 Junction 39

Phoenix Park (1922)

Phoenix Park, Thornbury, Bradford 3
Tel	(0274) 667573
Mem	180
Sec	B Mitchell (0274) 667669
Pro	B Ferguson
Holes	9 L 4982 yds SSS 64
Recs	Am–66 C Lally
V'trs	WD/ BH–U WE–NA
Fees	£5
Loc	Thornbury Roundabout

Pontefract & District (1900)

Park Lane, Pontefract WF8 4QS
Tel	(0977) 792241
Mem	800
Sec	WT Smith (0977) 792115
Pro	J Coleman (0977) 706806
Holes	18 L 6227 yds SSS 70
Recs	Am–63 DC Rooke
	Pro–67 GW Townhill
V'trs	I SOC–Tues/ Thurs/ Fri
Fees	£20 (£25)
Loc	Pontefract 1 mile on B6134. M62 Junction 32

Pontefract Park (1973)

Public
Park Road, Pontefract
Tel	(0977) 702799
Holes	18 L 4068 yds SSS 62
V'trs	U
Fees	£2.90 (£4.10)
Loc	Between Pontefract and M62 roundabout

Queensbury (1923)

Queensbury, nr Bradford BD13 1QF
Tel	(0274) 882155
Mem	220 45(L) 20(J) 25(5)
Sec	A Robinson
Pro	S Yearsley (0274) 816864
Holes	9 L 5102 yds SSS 65
Recs	Am–64 S Rogers, H Wilkerson
	Pro–63 P Cowan
V'trs	U
Fees	£8 (£15)
Loc	Bradford 4 miles

Rawdon (1896)

Buckstone Drive, Micklefield Lane, Rawdon LS19 6BD
Tel	(0532) 506040
Mem	200 50(L) 50(J) 100(5)
Sec	RA Adams (0532) 506064
Pro	(0532) 505017
Holes	9 L 5982 yds SSS 69
Recs	Am–64 A Coverdale

V'trs	WD–H WE/ BH–M SOC
Fees	£15
Loc	6 miles NW of Leeds on A65 Leeds–Skipton road. A65/ A658 Junction

Riddlesden (1927)

Howden Rough, Riddlesden, Keighley
Tel	(0535) 602148
Mem	250
Sec	Mrs KM Brooksbank (0535) 607646
Holes	18 L 4185 yds SSS 61
Recs	Am–60 M Mitchell (1987)
	Pro–59 P Cowan (1983)
V'trs	U exc Sun–NA before 2pm
Fees	£5 (£10)
Loc	Keighley 3 miles

Roundhay (1923)

Public
Park Lane, Leeds LS8 2EJ
Tel	(0532) 662695
Pro	(0532) 661686
Holes	9 L 5322 yds SSS 65
Recs	Am–62 AR White
	Pro–62 M Bembridge
V'trs	U
Fees	£4.20 (£4.50)
Loc	4 miles N of Leeds on A58

Ryburn (1910)

Norland, Sowerby Bridge, Halifax
Tel	(0422) 831355
Mem	200
Sec	J Hoyle (0422) 843070
Holes	9 L 5002 yds SSS 65
Recs	Am–64 DS Lumb (1987)
	Pro–61 M Pearson (1987)
V'trs	U
Fees	£8 (£11)
Loc	3 miles S of Halifax

Sand Moor (1926)

Alwoodley Lane, Leeds LS17 7DJ
Tel	(0532) 681685
Mem	551
Sec	D Warboys (0532) 685180
Pro	J Foss (0532) 683925
Holes	18 L 6423 yds SSS 71
Recs	Am–65 A Culloden (1989)
	Pro–65 M Ure (1990)
V'trs	WD–U H by arrangement WE–NA
Fees	£25
Loc	5 miles N of Leeds, off A61

Scarcroft (1937)

Syke Lane, Leeds LS14 3BQ
Tel	(0532) 892263
Mem	500
Sec	RD Barwell (0532) 892311
Pro	M Ross (0532) 892780
Holes	18 L 6426 yds SSS 71
Recs	Am–67 E Shaw
	Pro–65 D Padgett
V'trs	WD–U WE/ BH–M or by arrangement SOC–WD exc Fri
Fees	£22 (£32)
Loc	7 miles N of Leeds, off A58

Shipley (1896)

Beckfoot Lane, Cottingley Bridge, Bingley BD16 1LX
Tel	(0274) 563212
Mem	600
Sec	SL Holman (0274) 568652
Pro	D Sutcliffe (0274) 563674
Holes	18 L 6218 yds SSS 70
Recs	Am–66 GM Shaw
	Pro–64 M Ingham (1987)
V'trs	WD–U exc Tues–NA before 2pm Sat–NA before 4pm
Fees	£18 (£24)
Loc	6 miles N of Bradford on A650

Silsden (1913)

Brunthwaite, Silsden, nr Keighley
Tel	(0535) 52998
Mem	300
Sec	G Davey (0943) 601490
Holes	14 L 4870 yds SSS 64
Recs	Am–61
V'trs	Sat-restricted Sun–U after 1pm
Fees	£5 (£8)
Loc	5 miles N of Keighley

South Bradford (1906)

Pearson Road, Odsal, Bradford BD6 1BH
Tel	(0274) 679195
Mem	220
Pro	M Hillas (0274) 673346
Holes	9 L 6004 yds SSS 69
Recs	Am–65 GM Yarnold
	Pro–67 S Miguel, A Caygill
V'trs	WD–U WE–M
Fees	On application
Loc	Bradford 2 miles, nr Odsal Stadium

South Leeds (1914)

Gipsy Lane, Ring Road, Beeston, Leeds LS11 5TV
Tel	(0532) 700479
Mem	560
Sec	J McBride (0532) 771676
Pro	M Lewis (0532) 702598
Holes	18 L 5835 yds SSS 68
Recs	Am–66 M Guy
	Pro–68 B Waites
V'trs	WD–U WE–M SOC
Fees	£14 (£20)
Loc	4 miles S of Leeds. 2 miles from M62 and M1

Temple Newsam (1923)

Public
Temple Newsam Road, Halton, Leeds 15
Tel	(0532) 645624
Sec	G Gower
Pro	D Bulmer (0532) 647362
Holes	Lord Irwin 18 L 6448 yds SSS 71 Lady Dorothy Wood 18 L 6029 yds SSS 70
V'trs	U SOC
Fees	£4.50 (£5)
Loc	5 miles NE of Leeds, off Selby road

Todmorden (1895)

Rive Rocks, Cross Stone,
Todmorden, Lancs 0L14 8RD

Tel	(070 681) 2986
Mem	125 40(L) 30(J)
Sec	T Priestley
Holes	9 L 5818 yds SSS 68
Recs	Am–67 G Morgan, J May
	Pro–68 B Hunt
V'trs	WD/ BH–U WE–M SOC
Fees	£10 (£12)
Loc	2 miles N of Todmorden

Wakefield (1891)

Woodthorpe, Wakefield WF2 6JH

Tel	(0924) 255104
Mem	500
Sec	DT Hall (0924) 250287
Pro	IM Wright (0924) 255380
Holes	18 L 6626 yds SSS 72
Recs	Am–67 T Margison (1982)
	Pro–66 HW Muscroft (1982)
V'trs	U SOC
Fees	£18 (£20)
Loc	3 miles S of Wakefield

West Bowling (1898)

Newall Hall, Rooley Lane, West
Bowling, Bradford BD5 8LB

Tel	(0274) 724449
Mem	400
Sec	MEL Lynn (0274) 393207
Pro	AP Swaine (0274) 728036
Holes	18 L 5657 yds SSS 67
Recs	Am–66 TJ Wade
	Pro–66 G Brand
V'trs	WD–U H WE–U after 1.30pm
	SOC

Fees	£15 (£25)
Loc	Junction of M606 and Bradford
	Ring Road East

West Bradford (1900)

Chellow Grange, Haworth Road,
Bradford BD9 6NP

Tel	(0274) 542767
Mem	450
Pro	NM Barber (0274) 542102
Holes	18 L 5705 yds SSS 68
Recs	Am–63 RJ Ellis (1984)
	Pro–66
V'trs	U
Fees	£12 (£18)
Loc	3 miles W of Bradford (B6269)

Wetherby (1910)

Linton Lane, Wetherby LS22 4JF

Tel	(0937) 63375
Mem	550
Sec	WF Gibb
Pro	D Padgett
Holes	18 L 6235 yds SSS 70
Recs	Am–68 N Robinson (1990)
	Pro–66 MB Ingham (1985)
V'trs	WE–U after 10am
	SOC–Wed–Fri
Fees	£15 (£20)
Loc	Wetherby 3/4 mile. Leave A1 at
	Wetherby roundabout

Whitwood (1987)

Public

Altofts Lane, Whitwood, Castleford
WF10 5PZ

Tel	(0977) 512835
Sec	S Hicks (Hon)

Pro	R Holland
Holes	9 L 6176 yds SSS 69
V'trs	WD–U WE–booking necessary
Loc	M62 Junction 31/ A655 towards
	Castleford, 1 mile

Woodhall Hills (1906)

Calverley, Pudsey LS28 5QY

Tel	(0532) 564771/ 554594
Mem	315
Sec	D Harkness
Pro	D Tear (0532) 562857
Holes	18 L 6102 yds SSS 69
Recs	Am–66 PA Crosby
	Pro–66 M Ingham
V'trs	WD–U Sat–U after 4.30pm Sun–
	U after 10.30am
Fees	£15 (£20)
Loc	4 miles W of Bradford, off A647

Woodsome Hall (1922)

Woodsome Hall, Fenay Bridge,
Huddersfield HD8 0LQ

Tel	(0484) 602971
Mem	394 194(L) 103(J) 65(5)
Sec	Mrs P Bates (0484) 602739
Pro	KB Scarr (0484) 602034
Holes	18 L 6080 yds SSS 69
Recs	Am–66 J Hanson
	Pro–65 D Jagger
V'trs	U exc Tues–NA before 4pm
	SOC
Fees	£18 (£22)
Loc	6 miles SE of Huddersfield on
	Sheffield/ Penistone road A629

Ireland

Co Antrim

Ballycastle (1890)

Cushendall Road, Ballycastle
BT64 6QP

Tel	(02657) 62536
Mem	754
Sec	TJ Sheehan, ME Page (Hon)
Pro	T Stewart (02657) 62506
Holes	18 L 5882 yds SSS 69
Recs	Am–66 J McAleese, RJ McCoy,
	E Hughes
	Pro–64 F Daly
V'trs	U H SOC
Fees	£10 (£14) W–£35 M–£85
Loc	N Antrim coast between
	Portrush and Cushendall (A2)

Ballyclare (1923)

25 Springvale Road, Ballyclare

Tel	(09603) 42352
Mem	400
Sec	H McConnell (09603) 22696
Holes	18 L 5840 yds SSS 71
Recs	Am–69 J Foster
	Pro–69 S Hamill
V'trs	WD–U WE–NA before 4pm

Fees	£10 (£15)
Loc	1 1/2 miles N of Ballyclare.
	14 miles N of Belfast

Ballymena (1903)

128 Raceview Road, Ballymena
BT42 4HY

Tel	(0266) 861207/ 861487
Mem	975
Sec	WRG Pogue (Mgr)
Pro	J Gallaher (0266) 861652
Holes	18 L 5168 yds SSS 67
Recs	Am–62 D Cunning
V'trs	WD/ Sun–U SOC
Fees	£7 (£9)
Loc	2 miles E of Ballymena on A42

Bushfoot (1890)

Portballintrae, Bushmills

Tel	(02657) 31317
Mem	603
Sec	P Ritchie
Holes	9 L 5572 yds SSS 67
Recs	Am–63 D Kyle (1990)
V'trs	U Sat–NA after noon SOC
Fees	£8 (£10) W–£20 M–£50
Loc	1 mile N of Bushmills

Cairndhu (1928)

192 Coast Road, Ballygally, Larne
BT40 2QC

Tel	(0574) 83248
Mem	800
Sec	Mrs J Robinson (0574) 83324
Pro	R Walker (0574) 83417
Holes	18 L 6112 yds SSS 69
Recs	Am–64 B McMillen, R Houston
	Pro–64 D Jones, P Townsend
V'trs	U
Fees	£9 (£12.50)
Loc	4 miles N of Larne

Carrickfergus (1926)

35 North Road, Carrickfergus
BT38 8LP

Tel	(09603) 63713
Mem	800
Sec	ID Jardine
Pro	R Stevenson (09603) 51803
Holes	18 L 5752 yds SSS 68
Recs	Am–63 D Baker Pro–64 N Drew
V'trs	U
Fees	£8.50 (£12)
Loc	Carrickfergus 1/2 mile via
	Albert Road
Mis	Buggies for hire

For list of abbreviations see page 487.

Cushendall (1937)

21 Shore Road, Cushendall
Tel (026 67) 71318
Mem 715
Sec S McLaughlin (0266) 73366
Holes 9 L 4678 yds SSS 63
Recs Am–62 S McKillop
V'trs WE–restricted SOC
Fees £8 (£10) M–£60
Loc Cushendall, 25 miles N of Larne

Dunmurry (1905)

91 Dunmurry Lane, Dunmurry, Belfast BT17 9JS
Tel (0232) 610834
Mem 380 120(L) 75(J)
Sec Mrs MB Scott
Pro G Bleakley (0232) 301179
Holes 18 L 5333 metres SSS 68
Recs Am–68 A Young
Pro–70 V Bruce
V'trs Tues & Thurs–NA after 5pm
Sat–NA before 5pm SOC
Fees £9 (£12) SOC–£6 (£10)
Loc Dunmurry 1/2 mile. Belfast 5 miles

Greenisland (1894)

156 Upper Road, Greenisland, Carrickfergus BT38 8RW
Tel (0232) 862236
Mem 510
Sec J Wyness (0232) 864583
Holes 9 L 5536 metres SSS 68
Recs Am–65
V'trs WD–U Sat–NA before 5pm
SOC–exc Sat
Fees £7 (£10)
Loc 9 miles NE of Belfast

Larne (1894)

54 Ferris Bay Road, Island Magee, Larne BT40 3RT
Tel (0574) 82228
Mem 375
Sec JB Stewart (09603) 72043
Holes 9 L 6114 yds SSS 69
Recs Am–66 IA Nesbitt
Pro–68 N Drew
V'trs WD–U WE–M after 5pm
SOC–WD/ Sun
Fees £6 (£10)
Loc 6 miles N of Whitehead on Browns Bay road

Lisburn (1891)

68 Eglantine Road, Lisburn BT27 5RQ
Tel (0846) 662186
Mem 977
Sec TC McCullough (0846) 677216
Pro BR Campbell (0846) 677217
Holes 18 L 5708 metres SSS 72
Recs Am–68 J Boyd
Pro–64 D Feherty (1989)
V'trs WD–U WE–M SOC–Mon & Thurs
Fees £10 (£15)
Loc 3 miles S of Lisburn on A3

Massereene (1895)

51 Lough Road, Antrim BT41 4DQ
Tel (08494) 29293
Mem 850
Sec Mrs M Agnew (08494) 28096
Pro J Smyth (08494) 64074
Holes 18 L 6614 yds SSS 72
V'trs U SOC
Fees £11 (£13)
Loc Antrim 1/2 mile

Royal Portrush (1888)

Dunluce Road, Portrush BT56 8JQ
Tel (0265) 822311
Mem 864 255(L)
Sec Miss W Erskine
Pro DA Stevenson (0265) 823335
Holes Dunluce 18 L 6772 yds SSS 73
Valley 18 L 6273 yds SSS 70
9 holes L 1187 yds
Recs Dunluce Am–67 G McGimpsey
Pro–66 J Hargreaves Valley
Am–65 MJC Hoey
V'trs WD–U Sat–NA before 2.30pm
Sun–NA before 10am SOC
Fees Dunluce £20 (£25) Valley £12 (£16)
Loc Portrush Coastal Rd 1/2 mile

Whitehead (1904)

McCrae's Brae, Whitehead, Carrickfergus BT38 9NZ
Tel (09603) 53792
Mem 700
Sec J Niblock, J Sheriff (09603) 53631
Holes 18 L 6426 yds SSS 71
Recs Am–68 A Hope
V'trs U exc Sat SOC–exc Sat
Fees £7.50 (£10)
Loc 1/2 mile from Whitehead, off road to Island Magee

Co Armagh

County Armagh (1893)

Newry Road, Armagh
Tel (0861) 522501
Mem 1000
Sec MF Joyce
Pro A Rankin (0861) 525864
Holes 18 L 6184 yds SSS 69
Recs Am–68 PG Toner
Pro–65 W Todd
V'trs U SOC–WD
Fees £8 (£14)
Loc 40 miles SW of Belfast by M1

Craigavon

Public

Golf/ Ski Centre, Turmoyra Lane, Silverwood, Lurgan, Craigavon
Tel (0762) 6606
Sec MM Shanks (0762) 42413
Holes 18 L 6496 yds SSS 71
Loc Lurgan 1 1/2 miles
Mis 12 hole pitch & putt course. Floodlit driving range

Lurgan (1893)

The Demesne, Lurgan BT67 9BN
Tel (0762) 322087
Mem 858
Sec Mrs G Turkington
Pro D Paul
Holes 18 L 5836 metres SSS 70
Recs Am–65 T Cummins
Pro–65 B Todd
V'trs U SOC
Fees £11 (£13.50)
Loc Lurgan 1/4 mile

Portadown (1906)

Carrickblacker, Portadown
Tel (0762) 355356
Mem 761
Sec Mrs ME Holloway
Pro P Stevenson
Holes 18 L 6119 yds SSS 70
Recs Am–68
Pro–63
V'trs WD–U WE–NA
Fees £6 (£10)
Loc 3 miles S of Portadown towards Gilford

Tandragee (1922)

Markethill Road, Tandragee, Craigavon BT62 2ER
Tel (0762) 840727
Mem 850
Sec A Best (0762) 841272
Pro J Black (0762) 841761
Holes 18 L 6084 yds SSS 69
Recs Am–62 P Topley
V'trs U SOC
Fees £7 (£10)
Loc Armagh 10 miles. Craigavon 8 miles

Belfast

Ballyearl Golf Centre

Public

585 Doagh Road, Newtownabbey BT36 8RZ
Tel (0232) 848287
Sec A Bevan
Holes 9 L 2362 yds Par 3 course
V'trs U
Fees £2.50 (£3)
Loc N of Mossley on B59
Mis Driving range

Balmoral (1914)

518 Lisburn Road, Belfast BT9 6EX
Tel (0232) 381514
Mem 850
Sec B Jenkins OBE (Mgr)
Pro G Bleakley (0232) 667747
Holes 18 L 5679 metres SSS 70
Recs Am–66 M Wilson
Pro–64 D Jones
V'trs U
Fees £10 (£15)
Loc 2 miles S of Belfast at Balmoral–Kings Hall

For list of abbreviations see page 487.

Belvoir Park (1927)

Newtownbreda, Belfast BT8 4AN
Tel	(0232) 641159/ 692817
Mem	1100
Sec	WI Davidson (0232) 491693/ 646113
Pro	GM Kelly (0232) 646714
Holes	18 L 6476 yds SSS 71
Recs	Am–66 TS Anderson Pro–66 P Alliss, EC Brown
V'trs	U Sat–NA
Fees	£15 (£18)
Loc	Belfast 3 miles

Cliftonville (1911)

Westland Road, Belfast
Tel	(0232) 744158
Mem	429
Sec	JM Henderson
Holes	9 L 4678 yds SSS 70
Recs	Am–66 WRA Tennant Pro–67 S Hamill
V'trs	U exc Sat
Fees	On application

Fortwilliam (1891)

Downview Avenue, Belfast
Tel	(0232) 370770
Mem	976
Pro	P Hanna (0232) 770980
Holes	18 L 5642 yds SSS 67
Recs	Am–63 G Glover Pro–65 P Leonard
V'trs	U SOC
Fees	£12 (£17)
Loc	2 miles N of Belfast

Gilnahirk (1983)

Public
Upper Bramel Road, Belfast
Tel	(0232) 448477
Mem	200
Sec	K Gray (Mgr)
Pro	K Gray
Holes	9 L 2699 metres SSS
V'trs	U
Fees	£2 (£2.50)
Loc	3 miles SE of Belfast

The Knock Golf Club (1895)

Summerfield, Dundonald, Belfast BT16 0QX
Tel	(0232) 482249
Mem	870
Sec	SG Managh (0232) 483251
Pro	G Fairweather (0232) 483825
Holes	18 L 5845 metres SSS 71
Recs	Am–67 KH Graham Pro–69 PR McGuirk
V'trs	U SOC–Mon & Thurs
Fees	D–£12 (£16)
Loc	4 miles E of Belfast on the upper Newtownards road

Knockbracken G & CC

Ballymaconaghy Road, Knockbracken, Belfast BT8 4SB
Tel	(0232) 792108
Mem	300
Sec	P Laverty (Hon)
Pro	D Patterson (0232) 401811
Holes	18 L 5312 yds SSS 68
Recs	Am–66
V'trs	WD–U WE–U after 11am SOC
Fees	£8 (£10)
Loc	2 miles SW of Belfast, nr Four Winds
Mis	Floodlit driving range

Malone (1895)

240 Upper Malone Road, Dunmurry, Belfast BT17 9LB
Tel	(0232) 612695
Mem	759 379(L) 211(J) 29(5)
Sec	JE Osborough (0232) 612758
Pro	PM O'Hagan (0232) 614917
Holes	18 L 6499 yds SSS 71 9 L 2895 yds SSS 34
Recs	Pro–68 E Jones
V'trs	Wed–NA after 2pm Sat–NA before 5pm SOC–Mon & Thurs
Fees	£10 (£13)
Loc	6 miles S of Belfast

Ormeau (1893)

Ravenhill Road, Belfast BT6 0BN
Tel	(0232) 641069
Mem	250 70(L) 30(J) 28(5)
Sec	R Burnett (0232) 459808
Holes	9 L 5308 yds SSS 65
V'trs	U
Fees	£5 (£7.50)
Loc	South Belfast

Shandon Park (1926)

73 Shandon Park, Belfast BT5 6NY
Tel	(0232) 793730
Mem	1048
Sec	H Wallace (Mgr) (0232) 401856
Pro	B Wilson (0232) 797859
Holes	18 L 6261 yds SSS 70
Recs	Am–64 N Anderson Pro–68 CP Posnett
V'trs	WD–U Sat–NA before 5pm SOC
Fees	£14 (£18)
Loc	Belfast 3 miles

Co Carlow

Borris (1908)

Deerpark, Borris
Tel	(0503) 73143
Mem	970
Sec	EC Lennon
Holes	9 L 6026 yds SSS 69
Recs	Am–67
V'trs	WD–U Sun–M SOC–WD/ Sat (Apr–Sept)
Fees	£6 (£7)

Carlow (1899)

Oak Park, Carlow
Tel	(0503) 31695
Mem	970
Sec	Mrs Meaney
Pro	A Gilbert
Holes	18 L 5844 metres SSS 70
Recs	Am–65 P Mulcare, RD Carr Pro–68 C O'Connor
V'trs	U
Fees	£12 (£15)
Loc	Carlow

Co Cavan

Belturbet (1950)

Erne Hill, Belturbet
Tel	(049) 22287
Mem	150
Sec	JC Enright
Holes	9 L 5180 yds SSS 64
Recs	Am–64 J Costello (1982)
V'trs	U
Fees	£5
Loc	Belturbet 1/2 mile

Blacklion (1962)

Toam, Blacklion, via Sligo
Tel	(072) 53024
Mem	120
Sec	R Thompson
Holes	9 L 5544 metres SSS 69
V'trs	U SOC
Fees	£5 (£10) W–£20
Loc	12 miles SW of Enniskillen on A4. 10 miles E of Manorhamilton on N16

Cabra Castle (1978)

Kingscourt
Mem	130
Sec	J Foley (042) 67904
Holes	9 L 5308 metres SSS 68
V'trs	U
Fees	£5
Loc	2 miles E of Kingscourt

County Cavan (1894)

Arnmore House, Drumelis
Tel	(049) 31283
Mem	300 150(L) 51(J)
Sec	T O'Reilly (049) 31292
Holes	18 L 5519 metres SSS 69
Recs	Am–66 A Cafferty Pro–65 J Purcell (1987)
V'trs	U
Fees	IR£8
Loc	2 miles W of Cavan

Virginia (1946)

Virginia
Mem	280
Sec	S Sheridan (042) 65766
Holes	9 L 4139 metres SSS 62
Recs	Am–64 P Gallagher
V'trs	U
Loc	50 miles NW of Dublin

Co Clare

Drumoland Castle

Public
Newmarket–on–Fergus
Tel   (061) 71144
Mem   230
Sec   J Healy
Holes   18 L 6098 yds SSS 71
Recs   Am–74 Dr C Hackett (1986)
V'trs   U SOC
Fees   D–£15
Loc   18 miles NW of Limerick

Ennis (1907)

Drumbiggle Road, Ennis
Tel   (065) 24074
Mem   482
Sec   J Cooney
Pro   M Ward (065) 20690
Holes   18 L 5358 metres SSS 68
Recs   Am–64 G Roche
          Pro–66 P Skerritt
V'trs   U exc Sun SOC
Fees   £12 SOC–£10
Loc   ½ mile NW of Ennis

Kilkee (1908)

East End, Kilkee
Tel   (065) 56048
Mem   343 160(L)
Sec   TM Lillis
Holes   9 L 6185 yds SSS 69
Recs   Am–66 D Nagle, N Cotter
V'trs   U SOC (exc July/ Aug)
Fees   £8 W–£50
Loc   E end of Kilkee

Kilrush (1934)

Public
Parknamoney, Kilrush
Tel   (065) 51138
Mem   150
Sec   N O'Regan
Holes   9 L 2739 yds SSS 67
Recs   Am–64 DF Nagle
V'trs   U SOC
Fees   £5
Loc   Kerry–Clare route

Lahinch (1892)

Lahinch
Tel   (065) 81003
Mem   1200
Pro   R McCavery (065) 81408
Holes   Old 18 L 6699 yds SSS 73
          Castle 18 L 5265 yds SSS 67
V'trs   WD–U WE–NA 9–10.30am and
          1–2pm SOC
Fees   £15 (£18) Castle £10
Loc   Ennistymon 2 miles on T69

Shannon (1966)

Shannon Airport
Tel   (061) 61020
Mem   403
Sec   JJ Quigley (061) 61849
Pro   A Pyke (061) 61551

Holes   18 L 6854 yds SSS 73
Recs   Am–63 J Purcell
          Pro–65 D Durnian
V'trs   WD–U SOC
Fees   £12
Loc   Shannon Airport

Spanish Point (1915)

Miltown Malbay
Tel   (065) 84198
Mem   100
Sec   G O'Loughlin
Holes   9 L 3820 yds SSS 54
Recs   Am–27 D Twomey
          Pro–23 P Skerritt
V'trs   U
Fees   £5 W–£24
Loc   Miltown Malbay 2 miles

Co Cork

Bandon (1910)

Castlebernard, Bandon
Tel   (023) 41111
Mem   520
Sec   B O'Neill (023) 41998
Pro   P O'Boyle (023) 42224
Holes   18 L 5663 metres SSS 69
Recs   Am–67 MB Stafford
V'trs   U
Fees   £10 (£12)
Loc   Bandon 1½ miles

Bantry Park (1975)

Donemark, Bantry
Tel   (027) 50579
Mem   250
Sec   B Harrington (027) 50665
Holes   9 L 6436 yds SSS 70
Recs   Pro–66 C O'Connor Jr
V'trs   U
Fees   D–£8 (1990)
Loc   Bantry 1 mile on Glengarriff
          road

Berehaven

Millcove, Castletownbere
Tel   (027) 70469
Mem   200
Sec   P Lyne (027) 70299
Holes   9 L 2605 yds SSS 66
Recs   Am–65 T Harrington (1990)
V'trs   U SOC
Fees   £6
Loc   2 miles E of Castletownbere on
          Glengarriff road

Charleville (1909)

Smiths Road, Charleville
Tel   (011) 81257
Mem   250
Sec   T Murphy
Holes   18 L 6380 yds SSS 69
Recs   Am–68 J Murphy
V'trs   U
Fees   £10
Loc   On Cork–Limerick road

Cobh (1986)

Ballywilliam, Cobh
Tel   (021) 812399
Mem   200
Sec   M Hennessy (021) 811372
Holes   9 L 4338 metres SSS 63
Recs   Am–65 G Mellerick
          Pro–64 C O'Connor Sr
V'trs   WD–U WE/ BH–NA before noon
Fees   £4 (£5)
Loc   16 miles E of Cork. 1 mile N of
          Cobh

Cork (1888)

Little Island, Cork
Tel   (021) 353263
Mem   350 160 (L)
Sec   M Sands (021) 353451
Pro   D Higgins (021) 353037
Holes   18 L 6065 metres SSS 72
Recs   Am–66 P Murphy
V'trs   WD–U exc 1–2pm & Thurs
          before 4.30pm WE–U from
          10.30am–12 and after 2.30pm
          SOC
Fees   £15 (£17)
Loc   5 miles E of Cork. ½ mile off
          Cork–Cobh road

Doneraile (1927)

Doneraile
Tel   (022) 24137
Mem   200
Sec   R Callaghan
Holes   9 L 5528 yds SSS 67
V'trs   U
Fees   £8
Loc   Doneraile ½ mile

Douglas (1909)

Douglas, Cork
Tel   (021) 891086
Mem   839
Sec   B Barrett (021) 895297
Pro   GS Nicholson (021) 362055
Holes   18 L 5664 metres SSS 69
Recs   Am–66 D O'Herlihy
          Pro–64 E Darcy
V'trs   WD–U exc Tues WE–NA
          before 11.30am SOC–WD
Fees   IR£13 (IR£14)
Loc   Cork 3 miles

Dunmore (1967)

Dunmore, Clonakilty
Tel   (023) 33352
Mem   127
Sec   M Minihan (023) 33858
Holes   9 L 4464 yds SSS 61
Recs   Am–65
          Pro–62
V'trs   U SOC
Fees   £5
Loc   3½ miles S of Clonakilty

East Cork (1971)

Gortacue, Midleton
Tel   (021) 631687/ 631273
Mem   400

For list of abbreviations see page 487.

Sec	M Moloney
Holes	18 L 5207 metres SSS 69
Recs	Am–66 B O'Regan (1983)
V'trs	WD–U WE–NA before noon BH–U
Fees	£10
Loc	2 miles N of Midleton on L35

Fermoy (1893)

Corin, Fermoy

Tel	(025) 31472
Mem	520
Sec	P McCarthy
Holes	18 L 5825 metres SSS 70
V'trs	U SOC
Fees	£10
Loc	Fermoy 2 miles

Glengarriff (1936)

Glengarriff

Tel	(027) 63150
Mem	31
Holes	9 L 4328 yds SSS 61
V'trs	U
Loc	Glengarriff 1 mile

Kanturk (1974)

Fairy Hill, Kanturk

Tel	(029) 50534
Mem	135
Sec	D O'Connell (029) 50696
Holes	9 L 5527 yds SSS 69
Recs	Am–72 D O'Riordan, M Arsdeacon (1987) J O'Connor (1989)
V'trs	U
Fees	£5
Loc	1½ miles SW of Kanturk

Kinsale (1912)

Ringenane, Belgooly, Kinsale

Tel	(021) 772197
Mem	310
Sec	PB Jones
Holes	9 L 5332 metres SSS 68
Recs	Am–66 C Coughlan
V'trs	U WE–NA SOC
Fees	£8
Loc	Kinsale 2 miles. Cork 16 miles

Macroom (1924)

Lackaduve, Macroom

Tel	(026) 41072
Mem	273
Sec	J O'Brien
Holes	9 L 5439 metres SSS 68
Recs	Am–66 J Mills
V'trs	U SOC
Fees	D–IR£5
Loc	Macroom ½ mile

Mallow (1948)

Balleyellis, Mallow

Tel	(022) 21145
Mem	1500
Sec	BG Wall (022) 21972
Pro	S Conway
Holes	18 L 6559 yds SSS 71

Recs	Am–66 J Murphy (1982)
V'trs	WD–U before 5pm SOC
Fees	D–£10
Loc	1½ miles SE of Mallow Bridge

Mitchelstown (1908)

Mitchelstown

Tel	(025) 24072
Mem	200
Sec	PA Brennan (025) 84115
Holes	9 L 5057 metres SSS 67
Recs	Am–64 A Pierce
V'trs	U SOC
Fees	£6
Loc	30 miles N of Cork

Monkstown (1908)

Parkgarriffe, Monkstown

Tel	(021) 841225
Mem	600
Sec	JP Curtin (021) 841376
Pro	B Murphy (021) 841686
Holes	18 L 5534 metres SSS 68
Recs	Am–66
V'trs	U
Fees	£11 (£12)
Loc	7 miles S of Cork

Muskerry (1897)

Carrigrohane

Tel	(021) 385297
Mem	713
Sec	JJ Moynihan
Pro	WM Lehane (021) 385104
Holes	18 L 5786 metres SSS 70
Recs	Am–66 J McHenry Pro–66 J Hegerty
V'trs	Mon/ Tues–U Wed–Fri/ WE –restricted (phone in advance) SOC
Fees	£17
Loc	7 miles NW of Cork

Skibbereen (1931)

Skibbereen

Tel	(028) 21227
Mem	300
Sec	J Hamilton (028) 21673
Holes	9 L 5774 yds SSS 68
Recs	Am–65 B McDaid
V'trs	U
Fees	£8 W–£48
Loc	1 mile W of Skibbereen

Youghal (1898)

Knockaverry, Youghal

Tel	(024) 92787
Mem	400
Sec	K Quill
Pro	D Higgins
Holes	18 L 6223 yds SSS 69
Recs	Am–65 F Wright
V'trs	U
Fees	IR£10
Loc	30 miles E of Cork on N25 from Rosslare

Co Donegal

Ballybofey & Stranorlar (1958)

Ballybofey

Tel	(074) 31093
Mem	206 75(L) 30(J)
Sec	I Kee (074) 31050
Holes	18 L 5922 yds SSS 69
Recs	Am–65 D Cleary
V'trs	U SOC
Fees	£6
Loc	Stranorlar 1/4 mile

Ballyliffin (1947)

Ballyliffin, Clonmany

Tel	(077) 76119
Mem	350
Sec	KJ O'Doherty (077) 74417
Holes	18 L 6611 yds SSS 72
Recs	Am–67 G Doherty
V'trs	U SOC–arrange with Sec
Fees	IR£6 (IR£8)
Loc	8 miles N of Buncrana. 15 miles N of Londonderry

Buncrana (1951)

Public
Buncrana

Mem	92
Pro	NS Doherty
Holes	9 L 2020 yds
V'trs	U

Bundoran (1894)

Great Northern Hotel, Bundoran

Tel	(072) 41302
Mem	400
Sec	JC Roarty (072) 41360
Pro	SL Robinson, D Robinson
Holes	18 L 6328 yds
Recs	Am–67 J Murray Pro–66 E Darcy
V'trs	WD–U WE–restricted SOC
Fees	£9 (£10)
Loc	East boundary of Bundoran

Donegal (1960)

Murvagh

Tel	(073) 34054
Mem	420
Sec	J Nixon (073) 22166
Holes	18 L 7271 yds SSS 73
Recs	Am–68 M Gannon
V'trs	U SOC exc Sun
Fees	£10 (£15)
Loc	7 miles S of Donegal on N18

Dunfanaghy (1903)

Public
Dunfanaghy

Tel	(074) 36335
Mem	70
Sec	D Arnold (074) 36142
Holes	18 L 5066 metres SSS 66
Recs	Am–64 J Brogan Pro–66 L Wallace

V'trs U SOC
Fees IR£5.50 (IR£6.50)
Loc ¼ mile from Dunfanaghy on N56

Greencastle (1892)

Via Lifford, Greencastle
Tel (077) 81013
Mem 300
Sec HM Morris (077) 82042
Holes 9 L 5426 yds SSS 65
Recs Am–62 C McCarroll
Pro–67 D Jones
V'trs WD–U WE–restricted SOC
Fees £7 (£10)
Loc Nr Moville

Gweedore (1923)

Derrybeg, Letterkenny
Tel (075) 31140
Mem 170
Sec C Campbell (075) 31545
Holes 18 L 6230 yds SSS 69
Recs Am–64 S Murphy
V'trs U
Fees £5 (£7) W–£28 M–£95
Loc West Donegal

Letterkenny (1913)

Barnhill, Letterkenny
Tel (074) 21150
Mem 500
Sec H O'Kane
Holes 18 L 6299 yds SSS 71
Recs Am–67 P Shiels
V'trs U SOC
Fees £8 SOC–£6
Loc 1 mile NE of Letterkenny

Narin & Portnoo (1931)

Narin, Portnoo
Tel (075) 45107
Mem 400
Sec DT McBride
Holes 18 L 5950 yds SSS 68
Recs Am–64 B McBride
Pro–62 R Browne
V'trs WD–U Sat–restricted
1–2.30pm Sun–restricted H SOC
Fees £9 (£10) SOC–£6
Loc 6 miles N of Ardara

North West (1891)

Lisfannon, Fahan
Tel (077) 61027
Mem 400
Sec D Coyle (077) 61843
Pro S McBriarty
Holes 18 L 6203 yds SSS 69
Recs Am–65 F Friel
Pro–64 M Doherty
V'trs U
Fees IR£5 (IR£10) W–IR£30 M–IR£45
Loc 12 miles N of Londonderry. Buncrana 2 miles
Mis Links course

Otway (1893)

Saltpans, Rathmullen, Letterkenny
Tel (074) 58319
Mem 110
Sec H Gallagher (074) 58210
Holes 9 L 4134 yds SSS 60
Recs Am–29 F Friel
V'trs U
Fees D–£3
Loc By Lough Swilly

Portsalon (1891)

Portsalon, Letterkenny
Tel (074) 59108
Mem 120
Sec M Kerr
Holes 18 L 5844 yds SSS 68
Recs Am–66 JG McBride
Pro–71 J Henderson
V'trs U
Fees £6
Loc 20 miles N of Letterkenny

Rosapenna (1898)

Golf Hotel, Rosapenna
Tel (074) 55301
Mem 89
Sec JJ McBride
Pro S Byrne
Holes 18 L 6254 yds SSS 71
Recs Am–M McGinley, D Boyce
Pro–68 F Daly
V'trs U
Fees IR£10 (IR£12)
Loc Via Letterkenny

Co Down

Ardglass (1896)

Castle Place, Ardglass
Tel (0396) 841219
Mem 676
Sec Mrs P Rooney
Holes 18 L 5462 metres SSS 69
Recs Am–66 J Milligan
Pro–69 H Jackson
V'trs U
Fees £7 (£10)
Loc Downpatrick 7 miles

Banbridge (1913)

Huntly Road, Banbridge BT32 3UR
Tel (08206) 22342
Mem 440
Sec TF Fee (08206) 23831
Holes 12 L 5879 yds SSS 68
Recs Am–65 K Stevenson, R Burns
V'trs U SOC
Fees £7 (£10)
Loc Banbridge 1 mile

Bangor (1903)

Broadway, Bangor BT20 4RH
Tel (0247) 270922
Mem 1100
Sec DB Wilson
Pro N Drew (0247) 462164
Holes 18 L 6322 yds SSS 70

Recs Am–64 P Barry
Pro–66 C O'Connor
V'trs WD–U before 5pm –M after 5pm WE–NA before 3pm SOC
Fees £13 (£18)
Loc 1 mile E of Bangor

Bright Castle (1979)

14 Coniamstown Road, Bright, Downpatrick BT30 8LU
Tel (0396) 841319
Mem 40
Sec R Reid
Holes 18 L 6730 yds SSS
Recs Am–70 A Ennis
V'trs U SOC
Fees £4 (£6)
Loc 5 miles from Downpatrick on Killough road

Carnalea (1927)

Station Road, Bangor BT19 1EZ
Tel (0247) 465004
Mem 800
Sec JH Crozier (0247) 270368
Pro M McGee (0247) 270122
Holes 18 L 5584 yds SSS 67
Recs Am–65 P McEvoy (1990)
V'trs U SOC–WD
Fees £8 (£11)
Loc By Carnalea Station

Clandeboye (1933)

Conlig, Newtownards BT23 3PN
Tel (0247) 271767/ 473706
Mem 1123
Sec TI Marks (0247) 271767
Pro P Gregory (0247) 271750
Holes Dufferin 18 L 5915 metres SSS 72;
Ava 18 L 5172 metres SSS 67
Recs Am–65 S King
Pro–68 J Heggarty, D Jones, D Feherty
V'trs WD–U Sat–M Sun–M before 10am and 12.30–1.30pm
Fees Dufferin £12 (£15) Ava £10 (£12)
Loc Conlig, off A21 Bangor–Newtownards road

Donaghadee (1899)

Warren Road, Donaghadee BT21 0PQ
Tel (0237) 883624
Mem 1250
Sec CD McCutcheon
Pro G Drew (0237) 882392
Holes 18 L 5576 metres Par 71
Recs Am–65 J Nelson
Pro–69 E Clarke
V'trs U exc Sat–M
Fees £8 (£10)
Loc Belfast 18 miles

Downpatrick (1932)

Saul Road, Downpatrick BT30 6PA
Tel (0396) 2152
Mem 713
Sec A Cannon

Holes	18 L 5702 metres SSS 69
V'trs	U
Fees	£8 (£10)

Helen's Bay (1896)

Golf Road, Helen's Bay, Bangor
BT19 1TL

Tel	(0247) 852601
Mem	735
Sec	JH Ward (0247) 852815
Pro	T Loughran (0247) 853313
Holes	9 L 5176 metres SSS 67
Recs	Am–67 JR Longmore
	Pro–67 L Esdale
V'trs	WD–U Sat/ BH–M Sun–U
Fees	On application
Loc	Belfast 12 miles

Holywood (1904)

Nuns Walk, Demesne Road,
Holywood

Tel	(02317) 2138
Mem	800
Sec	GR Magennis (02317) 3135
Pro	M Bannon (02317) 5503
Holes	18 L 5885 yds SSS 68
Recs	Am–61 J Watts
	Pro–64 M Bannon
V'trs	WD–1.30–2.15pm Sat–after 5pm
Fees	£12 (£17)

Kilkeel (1948)

Public

Mourne Park, Ballyardle, Kilkeel

Tel	(06937) 62296
Mem	400
Sec	SW Rutherford (06937) 73660
Holes	9 L 5623 metres SSS 69
Recs	Am–65 F Reilly
V'trs	U
Fees	£8 (£10)
Loc	3 miles W of Kilkeel on Newry road

Kirkistown Castle (1902)

142 Main Road, Cloughey,
Newtownards

Tel	(024 77) 71233/ 71353
Mem	800
Sec	RC Vine BEM
Pro	J Peden
Holes	18 L 5628 metres SSS 70
Recs	Am–68 Jas Brown
	Pro–71 RJ Polley, C O'Connor
V'trs	WD–U WE/ BH–NA 1st tee 9.30–10.30am and 12–1.30pm SOC
Fees	£9 (£15)
Loc	25 miles SE of Belfast

Mahee Island (1930)

Comber, Belfast

Tel	(0238) 541234
Mem	400
Sec	T Reid (Hon)
Holes	9 L 2790 yds SSS 67
Recs	Am–65 C Boyd
	Pro–65 N Drew
V'trs	U exc Sat–NA before 4.30pm SOC–WD exc Mon

Fees	£6 (£10)
Loc	Strangford Lough, 14 miles S of Belfast

Mourne (1946)

36 Golf Links Road, Newcastle
BT33 0AN

Tel	(039 67) 23218
Mem	275
Sec	PJ Rodgers (Sec/ Mgr)
	S Keenan (Hon)
Holes	Play over Royal Co Down

Royal Belfast (1881)

Holywood, Craigavad

Tel	(0232) 428165
Mem	1200
Sec	IM Piggot
Pro	D Carson
Holes	18 L 6184 yds SSS 70
Recs	Am–65 RAD McMillan
	Pro–67 C O'Connor
V'trs	I Sat–NA before 4.30pm
Fees	£16 (£20) (1990)
Loc	E of Belfast on A2

Royal County Down (1889)

Newcastle BT33 0AN

Tel	(03967) 23314
Mem	450
Sec	PE Rolph
Pro	ET Jones (03967) 22419
Holes	C'ship 18 L 6968 yds SSS 73
	No 2 18 L 4100 yds SSS 60
Recs	C'ship Am–66 J Bruen, JM Jamison
	Pro–67 A Compston, B Gadd
V'trs	Contact Sec for information
Fees	Summer D–£25 (D–£30)
	Winter D–£22 (D–£25)
Loc	Belfast 30 miles

Scrabo (1907)

233 Scrabo Road, Newtownards
BT23 4SL

Tel	(0247) 812355
Mem	750
Pro	W Todd
Holes	18 L 5699 metres SSS 71
Recs	Am–69 W Caughey (1987)
	Pro–67 N Drew (1987)
V'trs	WD–U WE–after 5pm SOC
Fees	£7 (£9.50)
Loc	2 miles W of Newtownards

The Spa (1907)

20 Grove Road, Ballynahinch
BT24 8BR

Tel	(0238) 562365
Mem	500
Sec	J McC Glass (0232) 812340
Holes	18 L 5938 metres SSS 72
Recs	Am–67 R Wallace
V'trs	U exc Wed–NA after 3pm Sat–NA
Fees	£7.50 (£12.50)
Loc	½ mile from Ballynahinch centre, off Dromore Street

Warrenpoint (1893)

Lr Dromore Rd, Warrenpoint

Tel	(069 37) 72219
Mem	1066
Sec	J McMahon (069 37) 73695
Pro	N Shaw (069 37) 72371
Holes	18 L 5628 metres SSS 70
Recs	Am–65 J Carvill
	Pro–68 D Feherty
V'trs	U SOC
Fees	£10 (£12)
Loc	5 miles S of Newry

Dublin City

Carrickmines (1900)

Carrickmines

Tel	(0001) 955972
Mem	371
Sec	GW McConnell (0001) 863020
Holes	18 L 6044 yds SSS 69
Recs	Am–68
	Pro–68
V'trs	M
Fees	£8 Sun–£10 Sat–NA
Loc	6 miles S of Dublin

Castle (1913)

Woodside Drive, Rathfarnham,
Dublin 14

Tel	(0001) 904207
Mem	800
Sec	LF Blackburne
Pro	D Kinsella (0001) 933444
Holes	18 L 6168 metres SSS 69
Recs	Am–69 J Bourke
	Pro–65 B Browne
V'trs	Mon/ Thurs/ Fri–U Wed–U before 12.30pm WE/ BH–M SOC
Fees	£13
Loc	5 miles S of Dublin

Clontarf (1912)

Donnycarney House, Malahide
Road, Dublin 3

Tel	(0001) 331520
Mem	1035
Sec	MG O'Brien (0001) 331892
Pro	J Craddock (0001) 331877
Holes	18 L 5447 metres SSS 68
Recs	Am–65 M O'Shea
	Pro–64 H Bradshaw
V'trs	WD–U WE–M SOC
Fees	£13
Loc	Dublin 2 miles

Edmondstown (1944)

Rathfarnham, Dublin 16

Tel	(0001) 932461
Mem	420
Sec	S Davies (0001) 931082
Pro	A Crofton (0001) 941049
Holes	18 L 5663 metres SSS 69
Recs	Am–68 A Bernstein
V'trs	WD–U SOC
Fees	£14 (£16)
Loc	5 miles S of Dublin

Elm Park G & SC (1927)

Nutley House, Donnybrook, Dublin 4
Tel   (0001) 693438/ 693014
Fax   (0001) 694505
Mem   1725
Sec   H Montag (0001) 693014
Pro   S Green (0001) 692650
Holes   18 L 5353 metres SSS 68
Recs   Am–63 PF Hogan
         Pro–63 P Townsend
V'trs   U–phone Pro
Fees   £22 (£25)
Loc   3 miles S of Dublin

Foxrock (1893)

Foxrock, Torquay Road, Dublin 18
Tel   (0001) 895668
Mem   550
Sec   WM Daly (0001) 893992
Pro   T O'Connor (0001) 893992
Holes   9 L 5699 metres SSS 69
Recs   Am–68 D Campbell
         Pro–66 M Murphy
V'trs   WD/ BH/ Sun–M Tues &
         Sat–NA
Fees   £15
Loc   5 miles S of Dublin

Grange (1911)

Whitechurch, Rathfarnham, Dublin 16
Tel   (0001) 932832
Mem   1050 235(L) 210(J) 12(5)
Sec   JA O'Donoghue (0001) 932889
Pro   WD Sullivan (0001) 932299
Holes   18 L 5517 metres SSS 69
Recs   Am–64 WB Buckley
         Pro–62 C O'Connor Jr
V'trs   WD–U exc Tues/ Wed pm–NA
         WE–M
Fees   £18 (£21)
Loc   Rathfarnham, 5 miles from
         centre of Dublin

Howth (1916)

Carrickbrack Road, Sutton, Dublin 13
Tel   (0001) 323055
Mem   1200
Sec   Ms A MacNeice
Pro   JF McGuirk (0001) 393895
Holes   18 L 5573 metres SSS 69
Recs   Am–66 M Roe
         Pro–71
V'trs   WD–U exc Wed WE–M
Fees   £12
Loc   9 miles NE of Dublin, nr Sutton
         Cross

Milltown (1907)

Lower Churchtown Road, Milltown, Dublin 14
Tel   (0001) 977060
Mem   1490
Sec   JB Cassidy (0001) 973199
Pro   C Greene (0001) 977072
Holes   18 L 5638 metres SSS 69
Recs   Am–67 J O'Brien
         Pro–64 C Greene
V'trs   WD–U exc Tues
Fees   £20 (£28)
Loc   4 miles S of Dublin

Rathfarnham (1896)

Newtown, Dublin 16
Tel   (0001) 931201/ 931561
Mem   561
Sec   VJ Coyle (0001) 931201
Pro   B O'Hara
Holes   9 L 5787 metres SSS 70
Recs   Am–70 C O'Carrol, N Hynes,
         T O'Donnell
V'trs   WD–U exc Tues WE–NA
Fees   £9
Loc   6 miles S of Dublin

Royal Dublin (1885)

Bull Island, Dollymount, Dublin 3
Tel   (0001) 336346
Fax   (0001) 336504
Mem   875
Sec   JA Lambe
Pro   L Owens (0001) 336477
         (Touring Pro C O'Connor Sr)
Holes   18 L 6858 yds SSS 73
Recs   Am–67 G O'Donovan (1984)
         Pro–63 B Langer, G Cullen
         (1985)
V'trs   U H exc Sat
Fees   £30 (£40)
Loc   3¼ miles NE of Dublin, on
         coast road to Howth

St Anne's (1921)

North Bull Island, Dollymount, Dublin 5
Tel   (0001) 332797
Mem   413
Sec   J Carberry (0001) 336471
Pro   P Skerritt
Holes   18 L 5660 metres SSS 69
Recs   Am–67 S Rodgers
         Pro–64 P Skerritt
V'trs   WE–BH–NA SOC
Fees   £15
Loc   Dublin 5 miles

Stackstown (1975)

Kellystown Road, Rathfarnham, Dublin 16
Tel   (0001) 942338/ 941993
Mem   840
Sec   L McCormack
Holes   18 L 5952 metres SSS 72
Recs   Am–70 P Harrington
V'trs   WD–U SOC
Fees   £8 (£10)
Loc   7 miles SE of Dublin

Sutton (1890)

Cush Point, Burrow Road, Sutton, Dublin 13
Tel   (0001) 323013
Mem   198 162(L) 95(J) 53(5)
Sec   JJ Geary
Pro   N Lynch
Holes   9 L 5522 yds SSS 67
Recs   Am–64 M Hanway
         Pro–64 L Owens (1987)
V'trs   Tues–NA Sat–NA before
         5.30pm
Fees   £12 (£15)
Loc   7 miles E of Dublin

Co Dublin

Balbriggan (1945)

Blackhall, Balbriggan
Tel   (0001) 412173
Mem   500
Sec   L Cashell (0001) 412229
Holes   18 L 5717 metres SSS 70
Recs   Am–68 R Nugent (1987)
         Pro–71 J Burns, J Kinsella
         (1988)
V'trs   WD–U WE–M SOC
Fees   £11 (£15)
Loc   ¼ mile S of Balbriggan.
         18 miles N of Dublin on N1

Ballinascorney (1971)

Ballinascorney, Tallaght
Tel   (0001) 512516
Mem   420
Sec   G Murphy
Holes   18 L 5464 yds SSS 67
V'trs   WD–U
Fees   £10 (£12)
Loc   8 miles SW of Dublin

Beaverstown (1985)

Beaverstown, Donabate
Tel   (01) 436439
Mem   600
Sec   E Smyth
Holes   18 L 5662 metres SSS 71
Recs   Am–72 M Perry (1987)
V'trs   WD–U WE/ BH–M SOC
Fees   £8 (£10)
Loc   4 miles N of Dublin Airport

Beech Park (1983)

Johnstown, Rathcoole
Tel   (0001) 580522/ 580100
Mem   500
Sec   M O'Halloran (Sec/ Mgr)
Holes   18 5730 metres SSS 70
Recs   Am–71 P Stapleton (1990)
         Pro–67 B Todd (1989)
V'trs   WD–U exc Tues/ Wed–M
         WE–M BH–NA
Fees   £12
Loc   Rathcoole 1 mile on Kilteel
         road

Corballis (1971)

Public
Donabate
Tel   (0001) 436346
Sec   PJ Boylan (0001) 436583
Holes   18 L 4971 yds SSS 64
V'trs   WD–U Sat–NA before 10am
         Sun–NA SOC
Fees   £5 (£6)
Loc   18 miles N of Dublin. Donabate
         2 miles

Deer Park (1974)

Public
Howth
Tel   (0001) 322624
Mem   250

For list of abbreviations see page 487.

Sec	J Brady
Holes	18 L 6647 yds SSS 73
	9 hole course
Recs	Am–72 N Hussey
V'trs	U
Fees	£7
Loc	8 miles NE of Dublin
Mis	Par 3 course. Pitch & putt

Donabate (1925)

	Balcarrick, Donabate
Tel	(0001) 436059
Mem	501
Sec	Mrs C Campion (0001) 436346
Pro	H Jackson
Holes	18 L 6187 yds SSS 69
Recs	Am–67 AJ Coughlan
	Pro–65 M Murphy
V'trs	WE/ BH–NA
Loc	Dublin Airport 8 miles

Dun Laoghaire (1910)

	Dun Laoghaire, Eglinton Park, Dublin
Tel	(0001) 801055
Mem	972
Sec	T Stewart (0001) 803916
Pro	O Mulhall (0001) 801694
Holes	18 L 5463 metres SSS 69
Recs	Am–66 P McCormack Jr
	Pro–65 P Skerritt
V'trs	WD–U exc 1–2pm WE–M after 5 pm SOC
Fees	IR£20
Loc	7 miles S of Dublin

Forrest Little (1972)

	Cloghran
Tel	(0001) 401183/ 401763
Mem	900
Sec	V Maslin
Pro	T Judd Jr
Holes	18 L 5865 metres SSS 70
Recs	Am–67 T Judd (1984)
	Pro–65 C O'Connor Jr (1984)
V'trs	WD–U
Fees	IR£11
Loc	Nr Dublin Airport

Hermitage (1905)

	Lucan
Tel	(0001) 265396
Mem	1153
Sec	Miss K Russell
Pro	D Daly (0001) 268491
Holes	18 L 6034 metres SSS 71
Recs	Am–65 T Moraw
	Pro–65 R Davis
V'trs	U SOC
Fees	£16 (£25)
Loc	Dublin 8 miles. Lucan 1 mile

The Island (1890)

	Corballis, Donabate
Tel	(0001) 436104
Mem	600
Sec	LA O'Connor (0001) 436205
Pro	None
Holes	18 L 6053 metres SSS 72

Recs	Am–B Moore, B Byrne
V'trs	WD–U WE–NA
Fees	£18
Loc	14 miles N of Dublin

Killiney (1903)

	Killiney
Tel	(0001) 851983
Mem	528
Sec	H Keegan (Sec/ Mgr)
Pro	P O'Boyle
Holes	9 L 6201 yds SSS 69
Recs	Am–72 N Duke
	Pro–65 H Bradshaw
V'trs	U
Fees	D–£12
Loc	8 miles S of Dublin

Kilternan Hotel (1977)

Public

	Kilternan
Tel	(0001) 955559
Mem	350
Sec	T Bradley
Pro	B Malone
Holes	18 L 5413 yds SSS 66
V'trs	M SOC–WD
Fees	£9 (£11)
Loc	5 miles S of Dublin

Lucan (1897)

	Celbridge Road, Lucan
Tel	(0001) 280246
Mem	740
Sec	M O'Halloran
Pro	G Long
Holes	18 L 5958 metres SSS 71
Recs	Am–73 T Gough
	Pro–67 H Bradshaw
V'trs	WD–U WE/ BH–M SOC–WD exc Thurs
Fees	£12
Loc	14 miles W of Dublin, nr Lucan

Malahide (1892)

	Beechwood, The Grange, Malahide
Tel	(0001) 461611
Mem	850
Sec	J O'Donovan (Sec/ Mgr)
Pro	D Barton
Holes	27 holes Blue/ Red 6619 yds SSS 71; Red/ Yellow 6331 yds SSS 70; Yellow/ Blue 6257 yds SSS 70
V'trs	WD–U WE–by arrangement
Fees	£16 (£25)
Loc	10 miles N of Dublin. Malahide 1½ mile

Newlands (1926)

	Clondalkin, Dublin 22
Tel	(0001) 592903
Mem	959
Sec	A O'Neill (0001) 593157
Pro	P Heeney (0001) 593538
Holes	18 L 6184 yds SSS 69
Recs	Am–66 R Burdon, P Hanley Jr
	Pro–68 C O'Connor

V'trs	Tues/ Wed pm–NA WD–NA 1.30–2.30pm WE/ BH–NA SOC
Fees	IR£14
Loc	6 miles SW of Dublin

Portmarnock (1894)

	Portmarnock
Tel	(0001) 323082
Fax	(0001) 393738
Mem	971
Sec	W Bornemann
Pro	P Townsend (0001) 325157
Holes	27 'A' L 7097 yds SSS 75 'B' L 7047 yds SSS 75 'C' L 6596 yds SSS 74
Recs	Am–68 JB Carr
	Pro–64 S Lyle (1989)
V'trs	I WE–XL
Fees	£35 (£45) Ladies–£15 WD only
Loc	8 miles NE of Dublin

Rush (1943)

	Rush
Tel	(0001) 437548
Mem	350
Sec	BJ Clear
Holes	9 L 5598 metres SSS 69
Recs	Am–68 PJ Dolan
V'trs	WD–U WE–M
Fees	£10
Loc	16 miles N of Dublin

Skerries (1906)

	Skerries
Tel	(0001) 491204
Mem	748
Sec	AJB Taylor (0001) 491567
Pro	J Kinsella (0001) 490925
Holes	18 L 5852 metres SSS 70
V'trs	U
Fees	IR£12 (IR£15)
Loc	20 miles N of Dublin

Slade Valley (1970)

	Lynch Park, Brittas
Tel	(0001) 582207
Mem	800
Sec	P Maguire (0001) 582183
Pro	G Egan
Holes	18 L 5337 metres SSS 68
Recs	Am–65
	Pro–64
V'trs	WD–U am WE–M
Fees	£12
Loc	8 miles W of Dublin, off N4

Woodbrook (1921)

	nr Bray
Tel	(0001) 824799
Fax	(0001) 821950
Mem	950
Sec	D Smyth
Pro	W Kinsella
Holes	18 L 6007 metres SSS 71
V'trs	WD–U WE–phone Sec SOC
Fees	£22 (£30)
Loc	Dublin 11 miles

Co Fermanagh

Enniskillen (1896)

Castlecoole, Enniskillen BT74 6HZ
Tel   (0365) 25250
Mem   600
Sec   CJ Greaves (0365) 24444
Holes   18 L 5574 metres SSS 70
Recs   Am–67 K Prenter
V'trs   U SOC
Fees   D–£7.50
Loc   1 mile SE of Enniskillen, on
        Castlecoole Estate

Co Galway

Athenry (1957)

Derrydonnel, Oranmore
Tel   (091) 94466
Mem   180
Sec   G Doherty (091) 44730
Holes   9 L 5448 yds SSS 67
Recs   Am–69 L Gardner
V'trs   WD–U Sun–M
Fees   £5 Sun–NA
Loc   10 miles E of Galway on
        Athenry road

Ballinasloe (1894)

Ballinasloe
Tel   (0905) 42126
Mem   700
Sec   W O'Rourke (0905) 42435
Holes   18 L 5830 yds SSS 67
Recs   Am–66 D Madden
        Pro–66 C O'Connor
V'trs   U SOC
Fees   £8
Loc   Ballinasloe 2 miles

Connemara (1973)

Aillebrack, Ballyconnelly, nr Clifden
Tel   (095) 23502
Mem   800
Sec   S Birmingham (Hon)
Holes   18 L 6186 metres SSS 73
V'trs   U H SOC–exc Sun & Open
        weeks
Fees   £10 (£16)
Loc   8 miles SW of Clifden

Galway (1895)

Blackrock, Salthill, Galway
Tel   (091) 23038
Mem   1020
Sec   WC Caulfield (091) 22169
Pro   D Wallace
Holes   18 L 5828 metres SSS 70
Recs   Am–64 S Keenan (1987)
        Pro–67 C Greene
V'trs   Restricted Tues & Sun
Fees   £15
Loc   Galway 3 miles

Gort (1924)

Laughtyshaughnessy, Gort
Tel   (091) 31336
Mem   120
Sec   P Grealish (091) 31375
Pro   E O'Connor
Holes   9 L 4976 metres SSS 66
Recs   Am–64 G Cooney
        Pro–66 C O'Connor
V'trs   U
Fees   D–£5
Loc   Gort 1 mile on Tubber road

Loughrea (1924)

Graigue, Loughrea
Tel   (091) 41049
Mem   185
Holes   9 L 5578 yds SSS 67
Recs   Am–67 S Glynn
V'trs   U SOC
Fees   IR£4 (IR£5)
Loc   1 mile N of Loughrea, off
        Dublin–Galway road. 20 miles
        E of Galway

Mount Bellew (1929)

Mount Bellew, Ballinasloe
Tel   (0905) 79259
Mem   200
Sec   J Clarke
Holes   9 L 5564 yds SSS 66
Recs   Am–68 I Hayden
V'trs   U SOC
Fees   £5 W–£25 M–£40
Loc   50km NE of Galway city on N63

Oughterard (1973)

Oughterard
Tel   (091) 82131
Mem   500
Sec   J Waters (091) 82381
Pro   M Ryan
Holes   18 L 6150 yds SSS 69
Recs   Am–71 N Finnegan (1989)
V'trs   U
Fees   £10 (£15)
Loc   15 miles W of Galway

Portumna (1907)

Portumna
Tel   (0509) 41059
Mem   160
Sec   G Ryan (0509) 41442
Holes   9 L 5776 yds SSS 68
Recs   Am–66 M Harney (1982)
        Pro–63 H Bradshaw
V'trs   U
Fees   £5
Loc   Portumna, on road to Ennis

Tuam (1907)

Barnacurragh, Tuam
Tel   (093) 24354
Mem   340
Sec   P King
Holes   18 L 6321 yds SSS 70
Recs   Am–69 DJ McGrath
        Pro–68 R Rafferty (1983)
V'trs   Sun–NA SOC–WD

Fees   £10
Loc   20 miles N of Galway

Co Kerry

Ballybunion (1896)

Ballybunion
Tel   (068) 27146
Mem   800
Sec   S Walsh
Pro   E Higgins (068) 27209
Holes   Old 18 L 6542 yds SSS
        New 18 L 6477 yds SSS
Recs   Am–67 P Mulcare
V'trs   U SOC
Fees   Old–£30 New–£20 D–£40
Loc   50 miles S of Limerick

Ceann Sibeal (1924)

Ballyferriter, Tralee
Tel   (066) 56255
Mem   158
Sec   G Partington (066) 51657
Pro   D O'Connor
Holes   18 L 6600 yds SSS 71
V'trs   U SOC
Fees   D–£12 W–£60 SOC–£8
Loc   Dingle Peninsula, nr
        Ballyferriter

Dooks (1889)

Glenbeigh
Tel   (066) 68205/68200 (Members)
Mem   440
Sec   M Shanahan (066) 67370
Holes   18 L 5346 metres SSS 68
Recs   Am–67 G Sullivan
V'trs   WD–UH before 5.30pm WE/
        BH–check first SOC
Fees   £15 (£15)
Loc   3 miles N of Glenbeigh, on
        Ring of Kerry

Kenmare (1903)

Kenmare
Tel   (064) 41291
Mem   150
Sec   SW Rowe
Holes   9 L 4400 metres SSS 64
Recs   Am–64 B Mulcahy
V'trs   U
Fees   £6

Killarney (1893)

O'Mahoney's Point, Killarney
Tel   (064) 31034
Mem   1214
Sec   T Prendergast
Pro   T Coveney (064) 31615
Holes   Mahoney's Point 18 L 6152
        metres SSS 72; Killeen 18 L
        6369 metres SSS 73
Recs   Mahoney's Point: Am–68 S
        Coyne(1968) Killeen: Am–73
        DF O'Sullivan
V'trs   U H SOC
Fees   £20
Loc   3 miles W of Killarney

Parknasilla (1974)

Parknasilla
Tel (064) 45122
Mem 30
Sec M Walsh (064) 45233
Pro C McCarthy (064) 45172
Holes 9 L 4834 yds SSS 65
V'trs U
Fees £7
Loc Great Southern Hotel, 2 miles
E of Sneem

Tralee (1904)

West Barrow, Ardfert
Tel (066) 36379 **Fax** (066) 36008
Mem 900
Sec PA Colleran
Holes 18 L 6252 metres SSS 72
Recs Am–66 G O'Sullivan
V'trs WD–U before 4.30pm exc
Wed–restricted WE/ BH–NA
exc 11–12.30 SOC–WD
Fees £22 (£30)
Loc 8 miles W of Tralee

Waterville (1889)

Ring of Kerry, Waterville
Tel (0667) 4102
Mem 252
Sec LA Morrissey
Pro L Higgins (0667) 4237
Holes 18 L 7184 yds SSS 74
Recs Pro–65 L Higgins
V'trs U H SOC
Fees £18

Co Kildare

Athy (1906)

Geraldine, Athy
Tel (0507) 31729
Mem 250
Sec M Stanley (0507) 26118
Holes 9 L 6158 yds SSS 69
V'trs WD–U Sat–M SOC–WD
Fees £5 (£8)
Loc 1 mile N of Athy on Kildare rd

Bodenstown (1983)

Bodenstown, Sallins
Tel (045) 97096
Mem 650
Sec P Cunningham
Holes Old 18 L 6132 metres SSS 71
Ladyhill 18 L 5278 metres SSS
68
V'trs WD–U exc WE–NA (Old course)
Fees Old–£8 Ladyhill–£7
Loc 4 miles from Naas on Clane rd.
18 miles from Dublin on N7

Cill Dara (1920)

Little Curragh, Kildare Town
Tel (045) 21433/ 21295
Mem 300
Sec S Mulqueeney (Hon)
Pro G Burke
Holes 9 L 5738 metres SSS 70

Recs ... (continued)

Recs Am–67 T Royce, P Doyle
(1989)
V'trs WD–U before 2pm Sat–NA
after noon Sun/ BH–NA SOC
Fees £7 Sat am–£10
Loc 1 mile W of Kildare town

Clongowes (1966)

Clongowes Wood College, Naas
Tel Clongowes Wood 68202
Mem 100
Sec A Pierce
Holes 9 L 5374 yds SSS 65
Recs Am–65 V Murray (1987)
V'trs NA
Loc Clane 2 miles. Naas 6 miles

Curragh (1883)

Curragh
Tel (045) 41238/ 41714
Mem 500 160(L)
Sec PJ Coffey (Hon)
Pro P Lawlor
Holes 18 L 6003 metres SSS 71
Recs Am–68 L Walker (1990)
Pro–69 A Whiston
V'trs WD–check with Sec
Fees IR£10 (IR£12)
Loc 3 miles S of Newbridge
Mis Golf played here since 1852.
Oldest club in the Republic

Knockanally (1985)

Donadea, North Kildare
Tel (045) 69322
Mem 165
Sec N Lyons
Pro P Hickey
Holes 18 L 6484 yds SSS 72
Recs Pro–66 K O'Donnell, D James
(1988)
V'trs U
Fees £10 (£13)
Loc Maynooth 7 miles. Kilcock
5 miles. Enfield 3 miles on
Dublin–Galway road

Naas (1896)

Kerdiffstown, Naas
Tel (045) 97509
Mem 514
Holes 9 L 6233 yds SSS 70
V'trs U SOC
Loc 2 miles N of Naas

Co Kilkenny

Callan (1930)

Geraldine, Callan
Tel (056) 25136
Mem 150
Sec M Duggan (052) 54362
Holes 9 L 5844 yds SSS 68
Recs Am–70 J Madden
Pro–71 M Kavanagh
V'trs U SOC
Fees £4 (£5)
Loc 1 mile SE of Callan. Kilkenny
10 miles

Castlecomer (1935)

Castlecomer
Tel (056) 41139
Mem 250
Sec S Farrell (056) 41258
Holes 9 L 6985 yds SSS 71
Recs Am–70 M Curry (1986)
V'trs U
Fees £6 (£8)
Loc 11 miles N of Kilkenny

Kilkenny (1896)

Glendine, Kilkenny
Tel (056) 22125
Mem 900
Sec S O'Neill
Pro M Kavanagh (056) 61730
Holes 18 L 6374 yds SSS 70
Recs Am–65 J White
Pro–68 B Todd
V'trs U
Fees £10 (£12)
Loc 1 mile N of Kilkenny

Co Laois

Abbey Leix (1895)

Abbey Leix, Portlaoise
Tel (0502) 31450
Mem 207
Holes 9 L 5680 yds SSS 67
V'trs WD–U WE–NA
Fees £4 (£5)
Loc 60 miles SW of Dublin on Cork
road

Heath (Portlaoise) (1930)

The Heath, Portlaoise
Tel (0502) 46533
Mem 520
Sec F Conway (0502) 21655
Pro E Doyle (0502) 46622
Holes 18 L 6247 yds SSS 70
Recs Am–67 T Tyrrell (1983)
V'trs U
Fees £8 (£12)
Loc 4 miles E of Portlaoise
Mis Floodlit driving range

Mountrath (1929)

Knockanina, Mountrath
Mem 150
Sec S Reynolds (0502) 32558
Holes 9 L 5300 yds SSS 66
Recs Am–67 S Carter
V'trs U
Fees £4
Loc Mountrath 2 miles

Portarlington (1909)

Garryhinch, Portarlington
Tel (0502) 23115
Mem 400
Sec JG Cannon (Hon)
Holes 9 L 5354 metres SSS 68
Recs Am–65

V'trs   U
Fees   £6 (£7) (1990)
Loc   Between Portarlington and
    Mountmellick on L116

Rathdowney (1931)

Rathdowney, Portlaoise
Tel   (0505) 46170
Mem   119
Sec   KF McDermott
Holes   9 L 6086 yds SSS 69
Recs   Am–71 J O'Malley
V'trs   U SOC
Fees   D–£5
Loc   1 mile S of Rathdowney

Co Leitrim

Ballinamore (1941)

Ballinamore
Tel   (078) 44346
Mem   86
Sec   P Duignan (078) 44163
Holes   9 L 5680 yds SSS 67
Recs   Am–69 P Duigan
V'trs   U SOC
Fees   £5 W–£25
Loc   1½ miles N of Ballinamore

Carrick–on–Shannon (1910)

Woodbrook, Carrick–on–Shannon
Tel   (078) 67015
Mem   169
Holes   9 L 5584 yds SSS 68
V'trs   U
Fees   IR£5
Loc   4 miles W of Carrick–on–
    Shannon on N4

Co Limerick

Adare Manor (1900)

Adare
Tel   (061) 396204
Mem   350
Sec   T Healy
Holes   9 L 5145 metres SSS 67
V'trs   WD–U WE–M
Fees   D–£10
Loc   10 miles S of Limerick

Castletroy (1937)

Castletroy, Limerick
Tel   (061) 335261
Mem   1066
Sec   L Hayes (061) 335753
Pro   N Cassidy (061) 338283
Holes   18 L 5793 metres SSS 71
V'trs   WD–U Sat am–U Sat pm/
    Sun–M SOC–Mon/ Wed/ Fri
Fees   £14 (£16)
Loc   2½ miles N of Limerick on
    Dublin road

Limerick (1891)

Ballyclough, Limerick
Tel   (061) 44083
Mem   1070
Sec   D McDonogh (061) 45146
Pro   J Cassidy (061) 42492
Holes   18 L 6479 yds SSS 71
Recs   Am–72 J Duggan (1990)
    Pro–69 N Hanson (1990)
V'trs   WD–U before 5pm exc Tues
    WE–M SOC–WD
Fees   £15
Loc   3 miles S of Limerick

Newcastle West (1938)

Newcastle West
Tel   (069) 62105
Mem   400
Holes   9 L 5482 yds SSS 67
V'trs   WD–U before 4pm Sun–U after
    4pm SOC
Fees   D–£6 (1990)
Loc   ½ mile S of Newcastle West

Co Londonderry

Brown Trout

209 Agivey Road, Aghadovey,
Coleraine
Tel   (0265) 868209
Mem   80
Sec   W O'Hara
Holes   9 L 2800 yds SSS 68
V'trs   U SOC
Fees   £5 (£7)
Loc   8 miles S of Coleraine

Castlerock (1901)

Circular Road, Castlerock
Tel   (0265) 848314
Mem   920
Sec   RG McBride
Pro   R Kelly
Holes   18 L 6121 metres SSS 72
    9 L 2457 metres SSS 34
Recs   Am–68 TBC Hoey
V'trs   WD–U exc Tues & Fri (Ladies
    preference) SOC
Fees   £11 (£22) 9 hole–£4 (£7)
Loc   5 miles W of Coleraine on A2

City of Derry (1912)

49 Victoria Road, Londonderry
Tel   (0504) 311610/ 46369
Mem   692
Sec   PJ Doherty
Pro   M Doherty (0504) 311496
Holes   Prehen 18 L 6406 yds SSS 71;
    Dunhugh 9 L 4708 yds SSS 63
Recs   Am–68 D Ballentine
V'trs   WD–U before 4pm –M after
    4pm WE–U H SOC
Fees   Prehen £9 (£12) Dunhugh £4
Loc   3 miles from E end of Craigavon
    Bridge towards Strabane

Kilrea (1920)

Drumagarner Road, Kilrea (All
correspondence to Sec:
125 Tamlaght Road, Rasharkin)
Tel   (02665) 71397
Mem   240
Sec   WR McIlmoyle
Holes   9 L 4326 yds SSS 62
Recs   Am–61 R Rees (1982)
V'trs   Tues & Wed–NA after 6pm
    (Apr–Aug) Sat–NA after
    12.30pm
Fees   £5 (£5)
Loc   ½ mile from Kilrea on
    Maghera road

Moyola Park (1976)

Shanemullagh, Castledawson,
Magherafelt BT45 8DG
Tel   (0648) 68468
Mem   800
Sec   M A Steele
Pro   V Teague (0648) 68830
Holes   18 L 6517 yds SSS 71
Recs   Am–71 T McNeill
    Pro–70 D Smyth
V'trs   U SOC
Fees   £9 (£12)
Loc   40 miles N of Belfast by M2

Portstewart (1894)

117 Strand Road, Portstewart
BT55 7PG
Tel   (026 583) 2015
Mem   1408
Sec   M Moss BA (026 583) 3839
Pro   A Hunter (026 583) 2601
Holes   Strand 18 L 6714 yds SSS 72
    Blue 9 L 2662 yds Par 32
    Town 18 L 4733 yds SSS 62
Recs   Strand Am–69 TBC Hoey,
    D Ballentine
    Pro–66 E Polland
V'trs   SOC–by arrangement
Fees   Strand £15 (£20) W–£60
    Town £5 (£7) W–£20
Loc   W boundary of Portstewart

Co Longford

Co Longford (1894)

Glack, Dublin Road, Longford
Tel   (043) 46310
Mem   327
Sec   A Mitchell (043) 41541
Holes   18 L 6008 yds SSS 69
V'trs   U SOC
Fees   £8 (£10)
Loc   Longford ½ mile on Dublin
    road

Co Louth

Ardee (1911)

Townparks, Ardee
Tel   (041) 53227
Mem   390
Sec   S Kelly (Sec/ Mgr)
Holes   18 L 5833 yds SSS 69
Recs   Am–67 J Carroll
   Pro–70 C O'Connor
V'trs   U SOC
Fees   £10
Loc   1/2 mile N of Ardee

County Louth (1892)

Baltray, Drogheda
Tel   (041) 22327
Mem   350
Sec   M Delany (041) 22329
Pro   P McGuirk (041) 22444
Holes   18 L 6978 yds SSS 72
Recs   Am–66 F Gannon
   Pro–65 J Heggarty
V'trs   By prior arrangement
Fees   On request
Loc   3 miles NE of Drogheda

Dundalk (1905)

Blackrock, Dundalk
Tel   (042) 21379
Mem   850
Sec   P Moriarty (042) 21731
Pro   J Cassidy (042) 22102
Holes   18 L 6115 metres SSS 72
V'trs   U SOC
Fees   £10 (£12)
Loc   3 miles S of Dundalk
Mis   Driving range

Greenore (1896)

Greenore
Tel   (042) 73212
Fax   (042) 73433
Mem   500
Sec   B Rafferty (Sec/ Mgr)
Holes   18 L 6140 yds SSS 69
Recs   Am–67 S McParland
   Pro–67 C O'Connor Sr
V'trs   WD–U before 5pm WE/ BH–by
   arrangement SOC
Fees   £8 (£12)
Loc   15 miles N of Dundalk on
   Carlingford Lough

Co Mayo

Achill Island (1951)

Public
Keel, Achill Island
Tel   (098) 43202
Mem   40
Sec   P Lavelle
Holes   9 L 2723 yds SSS 66
Recs   Am–58 P Lavelle (1989)
V'trs   U H SOC
Fees   £3
Loc   Keel

Ballina (1910)

Mosgrove, Shanaghy, Ballina
Tel   (096) 21050
Mem   222
Sec   V Frawley (096) 21795
Holes   9 L 5702 yds SSS 66
Recs   Am–64 J Corcoran (1984)
   Pro–66 C O'Connor
V'trs   U
Fees   £7 (£7) W–£20
Loc   1 mile E of Ballina

Ballinrobe (1895)

Public
Ballinrobe, Claremorris
Tel   (092) 41448
Mem   200
Sec   P Holian (092) 41659
Holes   9 L 5790 yds SSS 68
Recs   Am–67 B Finlay
V'trs   U Sun–NA SOC
Fees   £5 W–£15 M–£40
Loc   1 1/2 miles NW of Ballinrobe on
   Castlebar road

Ballyhaunis (1929)

Coolnaha, Ballyhaunis
Tel   (0907) 30014
Mem   185
Sec   JG Forde (0907) 30013
Holes   9 L 5393 metres SSS 68
Recs   Am–70 D Charlton Jr (1990)
V'trs   U exc Thurs (Ladies Day)–M
   SOC–WD
Fees   £5
Loc   2 miles N of Ballyhaunis. Horan
   Airport 7 miles

Belmullet (1925)

Belmullet, Ballina
Tel   (097) 85713
Mem   70
Sec   K Donnelly (Hon)
Holes   9 L 2829 yds SSS 67
V'trs   U
Fees   £3 W–£14
Loc   3 miles W of Belmullet

Castlebar (1910)

Rocklands, Castlebar
Tel   (094) 21649
Mem   350
Sec   B MacDonald
Holes   18 L 6109 yds SSS 69
Recs   Am–67 J Langan
V'trs   U exc Sun
Fees   £10
Loc   Castlebar 1 mile, towards
   Galway

Claremorris (1918)

Claremorris
Tel   (094) 71527
Mem   140
Sec   TJ Farragher (094) 71082
Holes   9 L 6454 yds SSS 69
Recs   Am–68 P Killeen
   Pro–63 C O'Connor
V'trs   U

Fees   £4 W–£15
Loc   2 miles S of Claremorris

Mulrany (1887)

Public
Mulrany, Westport
Tel   (098) 36185
Mem   120
Sec   Fr M Kenny (098) 36107
Holes   9 L 6380 yds SSS 70
V'trs   U
Fees   D–£3 W–£15
Loc   Castlebar 20 miles. Westport
   18 miles

Swinford (1922)

Brabazon Park, Swinford
Tel   (094) 51378
Mem   108
Holes   9 L 5901 yds SSS 68
V'trs   U
Fees   D–£5 (£12) W–£25
Loc   Off Dublin–Kiltimagh road

Westport (1908)

Carowholly, Westport
Tel   (098) 25113
Mem   393
Pro   K Mongan
Holes   18 L 6667 yds SSS 73
V'trs   U
Fees   £12 (£15)
Loc   Westport 2 miles

Co Meath

Blackbush (1987)

Thomastown, Dunshaughlin
Tel   (01) 250021
Mem   650
Holes   18 L 7000 yds SSS73
   9 L 2800 yds
V'trs   WD–U WE–NA before 4pm
   SOC; 9 hole course–U
Loc   1/2 mile E of Dunshaughlin off
   N4. Dublin 20 miles
Mis   Driving range

Gormanston College (1961)

Franciscan College, Gormanston
Tel   (01) 412203
Mem   160
Sec   Br Laurence Brady
Pro   B Browne
Holes   9 L 1973 metres
V'trs   NA
Loc   22 miles N of Dublin

Headfort (1928)

Kells
Tel   (046) 40857
Mem   882
Pro   J Purcell (046) 40639
Holes   18 L 6480 yds SSS 70
Recs   Am–67 D McGrane (1990)

	Pro–64 D Smyth (1973)
V'trs	U SOC
Fees	£10 (£15)

Laytown & Bettystown (1909)

Bettystown	
Tel	(041) 27170
Mem	850
Pro	S Garvey
Holes	18 L 6254 yds SSS 68
V'trs	U SOC–WD
Fees	£13 (£18)
Loc	25 miles N of Dublin

Royal Tara (1923)

Bellinter, Navan	
Tel	(046) 25244/ 25584
Mem	900
Sec	D Foley
Pro	A Whiston
Holes	18 L 5757 metres SSS 70
Recs	Am–66 M McQuaid
V'trs	U
Fees	£10 (£12)
Loc	25 miles N of Dublin off N3

Trim (1970)

Newtownmoynagh, Trim	
Tel	(046) 31463
Mem	350
Sec	PJ Darby (046) 31438
Holes	9 L 6266 yds SSS 70
Recs	Am–64 P Rayfus
V'trs	WD–U exc Ladies day
	WE–restricted SOC–exc Sun
Fees	£8
Loc	2¹/₂ miles SW of Trim

Co Monaghan

Castleblayney (1985)

Castleblayney	
Mem	140
Sec	D McGlynn (042) 40197
Holes	9 L 2678 yds SSS 66
Recs	Am–70 J McCarthy (1987)
V'trs	U SOC
Fees	£3 (£4)

Clones (1913)

Hilton Park, Clones	
Tel	(049) 56017
Mem	245
Holes	9 L 5790 yds SSS 68
Recs	Am–64 D McGuigan
V'trs	WD–U Sun–NA before noon
Fees	£6 (£6)
Loc	2¹/₂ miles from Clones

Nuremore (1964)

Nuremore, Carrickmacross	
Tel	(042) 61438
Mem	138
Holes	9 L 6032 yds SSS 69
Recs	Am–67 O O'Neill
V'trs	U

Fees	£5 (£8)
Loc	1 mile S of Carrickmacross on Dublin road

Rossmore (1916)

Rossmore Park, Monaghan	
Tel	Monaghan 81316
Mem	325
Sec	P Hunt
Holes	9 L 5859 yds SSS 68
Recs	Am–64 R Berry
V'trs	WD–U WE/ BH–U exc comp days SOC
Fees	£4 (£5)
Loc	2 miles on Cootehill road

Co Offaly

Birr (1893)

The Glenns, Birr	
Tel	(0509) 20082
Mem	320
Sec	P O'Gorman (0509) 20271
Holes	18 L 6216 yds SSS 70
Recs	Am–66 JB Carr Pro–68 RJ Browne
V'trs	U SOC–exc Sun
Fees	D–£6
Loc	Birr 2 miles

Edenderry (1910)

Kishavanna, Edenderry	
Tel	(0405) 31072
Mem	300
Holes	9 L 5791 yds SSS 69
V'trs	U exc Thurs (Ladies Day)
Fees	£5 (£6)
Loc	1 mile E of Edenderry

Tullamore (1896)

Brookfield, Tullamore	
Tel	(0506) 21439
Mem	755
Sec	WM Rossiter (0506) 21310
Pro	JE Kelly
Holes	18 L 6314 yds SSS 71
Recs	Am–64 D White
	Pro–68 H Boyle, J Martin, D Jones
V'trs	WD–U exc Tues (Ladies Day) Sat–M 12.30–3pm Sun–NA SOC
Fees	£9 D–£12
Loc	2¹/2 miles S of Tullamore
Mis	Buggies for hire

Co Roscommon

Athlone (1892)

Hodson Bay, Athlone	
Tel	(0902) 92073/ 92235
Mem	750
Sec	D Clarke
Pro	M Quinn
Holes	18 L 6500 yds SSS 70
Recs	Am–63 P Egan Pro–70 M Quinn
V'trs	U SOC–WD
Fees	£10
Loc	Shores of Lough Ree

Ballaghaderreen (1937)

Ballaghaderreen	
Mem	112
Sec	Rev L Henry
Holes	9 L 5663 yds SSS 65
Recs	Am–68 F McGovern (1989)
Fees	£5
Loc	Ballaghaderreen 3 miles

Boyle (1911)

Roscommon Road, Boyle	
Tel	(079) 62594
Mem	169
Sec	D Conlon (Hon)
Holes	9 L 4957 metres SSS 66
Recs	Am–65 A Wynne (1987)
V'trs	U SOC
Fees	£5
Loc	Boyle 11/2miles

Castlerea (1905)

Clonalis, Castlerea	
Tel	(0907) 20068
Mem	145
Sec	B Stenson (0907) 20279
Holes	9 L 5466 yds SSS 66
Recs	Am–63 R de Lacy Staunton
V'trs	U
Fees	£3 (£5)
Loc	Knock Road, Castlerea

Roscommon (1904)

Mote Park, Roscommon	
Tel	(0903) 6382
Mem	158
Holes	9 L 5657 yds SSS 69
V'trs	U
Fees	£3
Loc	1 mile E of Roscommon

Co Sligo

Ballymote (1940)

Ballymote	
Tel	(071) 83460
Mem	42
Sec	P Mullen
Holes	9 L 5152 yds SSS 63
Recs	Am–67 P Mullen
V'trs	U
Fees	£3
Loc	Carrigans

County Sligo (1894)

Rosses Point	
Tel	(071) 77186
Mem	762
Sec	GA Eakins (071) 77134
Pro	J McGonigle (071) 77171
Holes	18 L 6003 metres SSS 72
Recs	Am–65 MD O'Brien
	Pro–67 C O'Connor Sr
V'trs	WD–U WE/ BH–M 9–10.30am and 1.30–2.45pm SOC
Fees	£15 (£15)
Loc	5 miles NW of Sligo

Enniscrone (1931)

Enniscrone
Tel   (096) 36297
Mem   420
Sec   JM Fleming
Holes 18 L 6570 yds SSS 72
Recs   Am–69 D Basquil
       Pro–71 C O'Connor Sr,
       J O'Leary
V'trs WD–U WE/ BH–telephone first
       SOC
Fees   D–£10–£14
Loc   Ballina road, S of Enniscrone
Mis   SOC–(096) 36335

Strandhill (1932)

Strandhill
Tel   (071) 68188
Mem   316
Sec   R Johnston
Holes 18 L 5937 yds SSS 68
V'trs WD–U WE–restricted SOC
Fees   IR£8 (IR£10)
Loc   6 miles W of Sligo

Co Tipperary

Cahir Park (1968)

Kilcommon, Cahir
Tel   (052) 41474
Mem   187
Sec   K Murphy
Holes 9 L 6262 yds SSS 69
Recs   Am–68
V'trs U SOC–WD/ Sat
Fees   £6 (£6)
Loc   1 mile S of Cahir

Carrick–on–Suir (1939)

Garravone, Carrick–on–Suir
Tel   (051) 40047
Mem   180
Sec   MG Kelly
Holes 9 L 5948 yds SSS 68
Recs   Am–67 C Carleton (1987)
V'trs U SOC–WD/ Sat
Fees   £5
Loc   2 miles on Dungarvan road

Clonmel (1911)

Lyreanearla, Mountain Road,
Clonmel
Tel   (052) 21138
Mem   544
Sec   W O'Sullivan (052) 24050
Pro   R Hayes
Holes 18 L 6330 yds SSS 69
Recs   Am–63 M O'Neill
V'trs WD–U WE–SOC
Fees   £8 (£10)
Loc   3 miles SW of Clonmel

Nenagh (1929)

Beechwood, Nenagh
Tel   (067) 31476
Mem   600
Sec   B O'Brien (Hon)
Pro   J Coyle (067) 33242
Holes 18 L 5483 metres SSS 68
Recs   Am–64 P Lyons (1984)
V'trs U SOC
Fees   £7 Sat–£9 Sun–£12
Loc   3 miles NE of Nenagh on
       Limerick–Dublin road

Rockwell College (1964)

Rockwell College, Cashel
Mem   88
Sec   Rev P Downes (062) 61444
Holes 9 L 4136 yds SSS 60
V'trs NA
Loc   3 miles S of Cashel on main
       Cork–Dublin road

Roscrea (1893)

Roscrea
Tel   (0505) 21130
Mem   337
Sec   SM Deeley (0505) 21225
Holes 9 L 6059 yds SSS 69
Recs   Am–65 D Corcoran
V'trs U
Fees   £5
Loc   2 miles on Dublin road

Templemore (1970)

Manna South, Templemore
Tel   (0504) 31522
Mem   210
Sec   JK Moloughney (0504) 31720
Holes 9 L 5442 yds SSS 66
Recs   Am–68
V'trs U exc Sun SOC
Fees   £5 (£6)
Loc   ½ mile S of Templemore

Thurles (1909)

Turtulla, Thurles
Tel   (0504) 21983/ 22466
Mem   555
Sec   T Ryan (0504) 23787
Pro   S Hunt
Holes 18 L 5904 metres SSS 71
Recs   Am–66 DF O'Sullivan
       Pro–70 H Bradshaw
V'trs WD–U Sun–NA
Fees   £9 Sat–£10
Loc   1 mile S of Thurles on the
       Horse & Jockey road

Tipperary (1896)

Rathanny, Tipperary
Tel   (062) 51119
Mem   321
Sec   J Considine
Holes 9 L 5805 metres SSS 70
V'trs U
Fees   D–£8
Loc   Tipperary 1 mile

Co Tyrone

Dungannon (1890)

Mullaghmore, Dungannon
Tel   (08687) 22098
Mem   425
Sec   J McCausland (08687) 22095
Holes 18 L 5914 yds SSS 68
Recs   Am–62 D Clarke (1989)
V'trs U
Fees   £7 (£9)
Loc   1 mile W of Dungannon

Fintona (1896)

Ecclesville Demesne, Fintona
Tel   (0662) 841480
Mem   250
Sec   G McNulty (0662) 841514
Holes 9 L 5716 yds SSS 70
Recs   Am–68 E Donnell
       Pro–69 L Higgins, J Kinsilla,
       L Robinson
V'trs U exc comp days SOC–WD
Fees   D–£5 (£10)
Loc   8 miles S of Omagh

Killymoon (1889)

200 Killymoon Road, Cookstown
BT80 8TW
Tel   (064 87) 63762/ 62254
Mem   700
Sec   L Hodgett
Pro   BJ Hamill
Holes 18 L 5498 metres SSS 69
Recs   Am–64 A O'Neill
       Pro–65 D Smyth
V'trs U SOC
Fees   £10 (£14)
Loc   1 mile S of Cookstown, off A29

Newtownstewart (1914)

38 Golf Course Road,
Newtownstewart BT78 4HU
Tel   (06626) 61466
Mem   500
Sec   JE Mackin (06626) 71487
Holes 18 L 5468 metres SSS 69
Recs   Am–66 G Forbes (1989)
       Pro–66 J Fisher
V'trs U SOC
Fees   £6 (£8) W–£25 M–£50
Loc   2 miles SW of Newtownstewart
       on B84

Omagh (1910)

83A Dublin Road, Omagh
BT78 1HQ
Tel   (0662) 243160/ 241442
Mem   654
Sec   JA McElholm (0662) 243749
Holes 18 L 5208 metres SSS 68
Recs   Am–63 H Johnston (1985)
V'trs U SOC
Fees   £6 (£8)
Loc   Omagh ½ mile

For list of abbreviations see page 487.

Strabane (1908)

Ballycolman, Strabane
Tel (0504) 382271
Mem 600
Sec JJ Harron (0504) 883093
Pro None
Holes 18 L 5458 metres SSS 69
Recs Am–64 C Patton
　　　　Pro–69
V'trs WD–U SOC
Fees £6 (£10)
Loc ¹/₂ mile from Strabane, nr Fir
　　　　Trees Hotel

Co Waterford

Dungarvan (1924)

Ballinacourty, Dungarvan
Tel (058) 41605/ 43310
Mem 340
Sec N Hayes
Holes 9 L 5721 metres SSS 69
Recs Am–66 J McHenry (1984)
V'trs U SOC–WD (Apr–Sept)
　　　　SOC–WE (Oct–Mar)
Fees D–£7 SOC–£7
Loc 3 miles E of Dungarvan.
　　　　30 miles W of Waterford

Lismore (1965)

Lismore, Ballyin
Tel (058) 54026
Mem 200
Sec M O'Shea (058) 54184
Pro T Maher
Holes 9 L 5127 metres SSS 67
Recs Am–65 T Murphy (1987)
　　　　Pro–65 L Higgins (1978)
V'trs U SOC–exc Sun
Fees £5 W–£20
Loc 1 mile N of Lismore

Tramore (1894)

Tramore
Tel (051) 86170
Mem 550
Sec J Cox
Pro P McDaid
Holes 18 L 5999 metres SSS 71
Recs Am–66 E Power
　　　　Pro–66 H Boyle
V'trs U
Fees £16 (£20)
Loc 7 miles S of Waterford

Waterford (1912)

Newrath, Waterford
Tel (051) 76748
Mem 641
Sec J Condon
Holes 18 L 6232 metres SSS 70
V'trs U

Co Westmeath

Moate (1940)

Moate
Tel (0902) 81271
Mem 252
Sec A Power
Holes 9 L 5348 yds SSS 66
V'trs U
Fees £4 (£5)
Loc 1 mile N of Moate

Mullingar (1894)

Belvedere, Mullingar
Tel (044) 48366
Mem 586
Pro J Burns
Holes 18 L 6370 yds SSS 71
Recs Am–63 P Walton
　　　　Pro–64
V'trs U SOC
Fees £10 (£15)
Loc 3 miles S of Mullingar

Co Wexford

Courtown (1936)

Courtown Harbour, Gorey
Tel (055) 25166
Mem 480
Sec J Sheehan (055) 21533
Pro J Coone
Holes 18 L 6398 yds SSS 70
Recs Am–67 J McGill (1987)
　　　　Pro–68 M Murphy (1976)
V'trs U SOC
Fees £10 (£13)
Loc 2¹/₂ miles SE of Gorey

Enniscorthy (1908)

Knockmarshal, Enniscorthy
Tel (054) 33191
Mem 300
Sec J Winters
Holes 18 L 5332 metres SSS 68
Recs Am–69 C Morris (1990)
V'trs U SOC–exc Sun
Fees £7 (£9)
Loc 1¹/₂ mile SW of Enniscorthy

New Ross (1917)

Tinneranny, New Ross
Tel (051) 21433
Mem 250
Sec (051) 21451
Holes 9 L 5578 metres SSS 69
Recs Am–66 M O'Brien
　　　　Pro–65 C O'Connor
V'trs U exc Sun SOC
Fees £5 (£7)
Loc 1 mile W of New Ross

Rosslare (1908)

Strand, Rosslare
Tel (053) 32113
Mem 400
Sec Miss A O'Keefe (053) 32203

Pro A Skerritt (053) 32238
Holes 18 L 6502 yds SSS 71
Recs Am–65 D Noonan (1978)
V'trs U SOC
Fees £12 (£15)
Loc 10 miles S of Wexford

Wexford (1966)

Mulgannon, Wexford
Tel (053) 42238
Mem 300
Sec A Doyle (053) 44720
Holes 18 L 6109 yds SSS 69
V'trs U SOC
Fees £6 (£7)
Loc Wexford ¹/₂ mile

Co Wicklow

Arklow (1927)

Abbeylands, Arklow
Tel (0402) 32492
Mem 400
Holes 18 L 5770 yds SSS 68
V'trs WD–U Sat–U after 5pm
　　　　Sun–NA SOC–Mon–Sat
Fees £10 (£12)
Loc Arklow

Baltinglass (1928)

Baltinglass
Tel (0508) 81530
Mem 350
Sec D Lord
Pro M Murphy
Holes 9 L 6070 yds SSS 68
Recs Am–66 D Kilcoyne,
　　　　Rev McDonnell
　　　　Pro–70 S Hunt
V'trs U SOC
Fees £4 (£6)
Loc 38 miles S of Dublin

Blainroe (1978)

Blainroe
Tel (0404) 68168
Mem 600
Sec W O'Sullivan
Pro J McDonald
Holes 18 L 6681 yds SSS 72
V'trs U
Fees £7 (£12) W–£35
Loc 3¹/₂ miles S of Wicklow on
　　　　coast

Bray (1897)

Ravenswell Road, Bray
Tel (0001) 862484
Mem 272
Sec JM McStravick
Pro M Walby
Holes 9 L 5230 metres SSS 70
V'trs U before 6pm SOC–WD
Fees £8
Loc 12 miles S of Dublin

For list of abbreviations see page 487.

Coollattin (1950)

Coollattin, Shillelagh
Tel   (055) 29125
Mem   350
Sec   R McCrea (055) 26302
Holes   9 L 6070 yds SSS 69
Fees   £4 (£7)
Loc   50 miles S of Dublin

Delgany (1908)

Delgany
Tel   (0404) 874645/ 874833
Mem   800
Sec   J Deally (0404) 874536
Pro   E Darcy (0404) 874536
Holes   18 L 5249 yds SSS 69
Recs   Am–63
V'trs   U exc comp days SOC–Mon/
    Thurs/ Fri
Fees   £11 (£14)
Loc   Greystones 2 miles

Greystones (1895)

Greystones
Tel   (0001) 876624
Mem   850
Sec   O Walsh (0001) 874136
Pro   K Daly
Holes   18 L 5387 metres SSS 68
Recs   Am–67 Pro–66
V'trs   Mid–week
Fees   £12 (£15)
Loc   Greystones, 18 miles S of
    Dublin

Old Conna (1987)

Ferndale Road, Bray
Tel   (0001) 826055
Mem   550
Sec   K Gleeson (Hon)
Pro   N Murphy (0001) 820842
Holes   18 L 6600 yds SSS 72
V'trs   WD–U before 4pm SOC
Fees   £12
Loc   2 miles N of Bray

Wicklow (1904)

Dunbur Road, Wicklow
Tel   (0404) 67379
Mem   408
Sec   J Kelly
Holes   9 L 5556 yds SSS 66
Recs   Am–65 W Mitchell, LJ Mooney
    Pro–65 K Daly, M Bannon
V'trs   SOC–WD
Fees   £10 (£15)

Woodenbridge (1884)

Arklow
Tel   (0402) 35202
Mem   250
Sec   TH Crummy
Holes   9 L 6104 yds SSS 68
Recs   Am–67 M Holden,
    J Kavanagh
V'trs   U exc Sat & Thurs
Fees   £12 (£15)
Loc   45 miles S of Dublin. 4 miles
    W of Arklow

Scotland

Border Region

Berwickshire

Duns (1894)

Hardens Road, Duns
Mem   200
Sec   A Campbell (0361) 82717
Holes   9 L 5826 yds SSS 68
Recs   Am–66 WV Paton, G Clark,
    G Wood
V'trs   U SOC
Fees   £6 (£6)
Loc   1 mile W of Duns off A6105

Eyemouth (1880)

Gunsgreen House, Eyemouth
Tel   (08907) 50551
Mem   240
Sec   C Jeffries
Pro   C Maltman
Holes   9 L 4608 metres SSS 65
Recs   Am–62 J Patterson
V'trs   U exc Sun am–NA
Fees   D–£7
Loc   4 miles N of border, off A1

The Hirsel (1948)

Kelso Road, Coldstream
Tel   (0890) 2678
Mem   270
Sec   GH Toyne (0890) 2568
Holes   9 L 5680 yds SSS 68
Recs   Am–64 M Ledgerwood (1990)
V'trs   U SOC
Fees   £6 (£8)
Loc   ½ mile W of Coldstream (A697)

Lauder (1896)

Public
Lauder
Tel   (05782) 409
Mem   95
Sec   G Bryson
Holes   9 L 6002 yds SSS 70
Recs   Am–70 JFC Jeffries
    Pro–70 W Park Jr (1905)
V'trs   U
Fees   WD–£3.50 Sun–£4
Loc   ½ mile W of Lauder

Peeblesshire

Innerleithen (1886)

Leithen Water, Leithen Road,
Innerleithen
Tel   (0896) 830951
Mem   175
Sec   S Wyse (0896) 830071
Holes   9 L 5820 yds SSS 68

Recs   Am–66 WN Smith
V'trs   U
Fees   £5 (£5) W–£20
Loc   Innerleithen 1½ miles on
    Heriot road

Peebles (1892)

Public
Kirkland Street, Peebles
Tel   (0721) 20197
Mem   600
Sec   G Garvie
Holes   18 L 6137 yds SSS 69
Recs   Am–64 D Campbell,
    JK Wells
    Pro–70 RDBM Shade
V'trs   H
Fees   £7.50 D–£11 (£12 D–£15)
    W–£45
Loc   23 miles S of Edinburgh

West Linton (1890)

West Linton EH46 7HN
Tel   (0968) 60463
Mem   615
Sec   G Scott (0968) 75843
Pro   D Stewart (0968) 60256
Holes   18 L 6132 yds SSS 69
Recs   Am–67 S MacKenzie (1989)
    Pro–71 B Gallacher
V'trs   U WE–no parties
Fees   £10 D–£13 (£12 D–£16)
Loc   NW of Peebles on A702

Roxburghshire

Hawick (1877)

Vertish Hill, Hawick
Tel   (0450) 72293
Mem   510
Sec   GA Rennie (Hon)
Holes   18 L 5929 yds SSS 69
Recs   Am–63 AJ Ballantyne
    Pro–64 N Faldo
V'trs   U
Fees   £5 D–£8 (£8)
Loc   ½ mile S of Hawick
Mis   Golfing package D–£15

Jedburgh (1892)

Dunion Road, Jedburgh
Tel   (0835) 63587
Mem   200
Sec   R Strachan
Holes   9 L 5492 yds SSS 67
Recs   Am–63 E Redpath (1987)
V'trs   U
Fees   £5 (£6)
Loc   Jedburgh 1 mile

Kelso (1887)

Berrymoss Racecourse Road, Kelso
Tel (0573) 23009
Mem 350
Sec JP Payne (0573) 23259
Holes 18 L 6066 yds SSS 69
Recs Am–64 JF Thomas
V'trs U SOC
Fees £7 D–£11 (£8 D–£12) (1990)
Loc Inside Kelso racecourse. Kelso 1 mile

Melrose (1880)

Dingleton, Melrose
Tel (089 682) 2855
Mem 300
Sec W Macrae (089 682) 2391
Holes 9 L 5579 yds SSS 68
Recs Am–62 G Matthew (1989)
V'trs U
Fees £5 (£6)
Loc S boundary of Melrose

Minto (1926)

Denholm, Hawick
Tel (0450) 87220
Mem 400
Sec Mrs E Mitchell (0450) 72180
Holes 18 L 5460 yds SSS 68
Recs Am–66 I Oliver
V'trs U SOC
Fees £7 (£10)
Loc Denholm, 6 miles E of Hawick

St Boswells (1899)

St Boswells
Tel (0835) 22359
Mem 300
Sec GB Ovens
Holes 9 L 5250 yds SSS 65
Recs Am–62 CI Ovens (1989)
V'trs U SOC
Fees £5 (£6)
Loc Off A68 at St Boswells Green, by River Tweed

Selkirkshire

Galashiels (1884)

Public
Ladhope Recreation Ground, Galashiels
Tel (0896) 3724
Mem 250 60(J)
Sec WD Millar (0750) 21669
Holes 18 L 5309 yds SSS 67
Recs Am–62 KW Simpson
Pro–70 J Braid
V'trs U SOC
Fees £4.20 (£4.70)
Loc ¼ mile NE of Galashiels

Selkirk (1883)

Selkirk
Tel (0750) 20621
Mem 303
Sec R Davies (0750) 20427

Holes 9 L 5560 yds SSS 67
Recs Am–60 MD Cleghorn
V'trs U SOC
Fees D–£8
Loc 1 mile S of Selkirk on A7

Torwoodlee (1895)

Galashiels
Tel (0896) 2260
Mem 280
Sec A Wilson
Holes 9 L 5800 yds SSS 68
Recs Am–64 RV Rutherford
Pro–64 A Wilson
V'trs WD–U exc Thurs–NA after 4pm Sat–NA SOC
Fees £10 (£12)
Loc 1 mile N of Galashiels on A7

Central Region

Clackmannanshire

Alloa (1891)

Schawpark, Sauchie, Alloa
Tel (0259) 722745
Mem 535 80(L) 130(J)
Sec AM Frame (0259) 50100
Pro W Bennett (0259) 724476
Holes 18 L 6240 yds SSS 70
Recs Am–63 AJ Liddle
Pro–66 R Weir, G Harvey
V'trs U WE–no parties
Fees £8 D–£13 (£14)
Loc Sauchie

Alva

Beauclerc Street, Alva FK12 5LE
Tel (0259) 60431
Mem 200
Sec A McGuire (0259) 60455
Holes 9 L 2423 yds SSS 64
Recs Am–63 R Lyon, G Kennedy, N Chalmers (1990)
V'trs U
Fees £3.50 (£4.50)
Loc Back Road, Alva, on A91 Stirling–St Andrews road

Braehead (1891)

Cambus, Alloa
Tel (0259) 722078
Mem 700
Sec JA Harrison (0259) 215135
Holes 18 L 6013 yds SSS 69 Par 70
Recs Am–64 D Mackison
V'trs U–booking necessary
Fees £10 D–£15 (£15 D–£20)
Loc 2 miles W of Alloa (A907)

Dollar (1890)

Brewlands House, Dollar
Tel (0259) 42400
Mem 350
Sec MB Shea

Holes 18 L 5144 yds SSS 66
V'trs U SOC
Fees £6 D–£8 (£10)
Loc Dollar

Muckhart (1908)

Muckhart, by Dollar FK14 7JH
Tel (025 981) 423
Mem 450 100(L) 100(J)
Sec J Muston (Mgr)
Pro K Salmoni (025 981) 493
Holes 18 L 6192 yds SSS 70
Recs Am–66 E Carnegie (1983)
V'trs U SOC
Fees £10 (£13)
Loc A91, 3 miles E of Dollar. Turn right for Rumbling Bridge

Tillicoultry (1899)

Alva Road, Tillicoultry FK13 6BL
Tel (0259) 50124
Mem 400
Sec R Whitehead
Holes 9 L 2528 yds SSS 66
Recs Am–63 I McCaig
V'trs WD/ WE–U SOC
Fees £3.50 D–£5 (£5.50 D–£7)
Loc 9 miles E of Stirling

Tulliallan (1902)

Kincardine, by Alloa
Tel (0259) 30396
Mem 525 53(L) 100(J) 19(5)
Sec JS McDowall (0324) 485420
Pro S Kelly (0259) 30798
Holes 18 L 5982 yds SSS 69
Recs Am–65 A Pickles, D Johnson
Pro–70 D Huish, S Walker, G Gray
V'trs U exc comp days
Fees £7 (£9)
Loc 5 miles E of Alloa

Perthshire

Callander (1890)

Aveland Road, Callander FK17 8EN
Tel (0877) 30090
Mem 540
Sec FV Wood
Pro W Kelly (0877) 30975
Holes 18 L 5125 yds SSS 66
Recs Am–62 GK MacDonald
Pro–59 D Matthew
V'trs U SOC
Fees On application
Loc Off A84, E end of Callander

Dunblane New (1923)

Dunblane
Tel (0786) 823711
Mem 600
Sec AG Duncan (Match sec)
Pro RM Jamieson
Holes 18 L 5878 yds SSS 68
Recs Am–64 GK McDonald
Pro–64 RM Jamieson

V'trs WD–Mon/ Tues/ Thurs/ Fri am
WE–M SOC
Fees £16 (£20)
Loc 6 miles N of Stirling

Killin (1913)

Killin
Tel (05672) 312
Mem 298
Sec A Chisholm
Holes 9 L 2410 yds SSS 65
Recs Am–61 G Smith
V'trs U SOC–Apr–Jun/ Sept
Fees £8 (£10)
Loc Killin, W end of Loch Tay

Stirlingshire

Balmore (1906)

Balmore, by Torrance
Tel (0360) 2120240
Mem 700
Sec GP Woolard (041) 332 0392
Holes 18 L 5735 yds SSS 67
Recs Am–63 A Brodie
V'trs M SOC
Fees £15 R/ D
Loc 2 miles N of Glasgow

Bonnybridge (1924)

Larbert Road, Bonnybridge
Tel (0324) 812822
Mem 425
Sec JJ Keilt
Holes 9 L 6058 yds SSS 69
Recs Am–66 D Riddell
Pro–66 J McTear
V'trs I
Fees By arrangement
Loc 3 miles W of Falkirk

Bridge of Allan (1895)

Sunnylaw, Bridge of Allan
Tel (0786) 832332
Mem 300
Sec JC Whaley (0786) 833914
Holes 9 L 4932 yds SSS 65
Recs Am–62 ID McFarlane
V'trs U exc Sat
Fees £7 (£10)

Buchanan Castle (1936)

nr Drymen
Tel (0360) 60369
Mem 830
Sec JI Hay (0360) 60307
Pro C Dernie (0360) 60330
Holes 18 L 6015 yds SSS 69
Recs Am–68 N Macrae
Pro–66 D Huish, W Milne
V'trs M or by arrangement with Sec
Loc 18 miles NW of Glasgow

Campsie (1895)

Crow Road, Lennoxtown
Tel (0360) 310244
Mem 400

Sec JM Donaldson (0360) 312249
Holes 18 L 5517 yds SSS 67
Recs Am–70 J Hope
Pro–73 K Stevely
V'trs WD–U before 4.30pm
Fees £6
Loc B822 Fintry road

Falkirk (1922)

Stirling Road, Camelon, Falkirk
Tel (0324) 611061/ 612219
Mem 500
Sec A Bennie
Holes 18 L 6257 yds SSS 70
Recs Am–66
V'trs WD–U until 4pm WE–NA SOC
exc Wed & Sat
Fees On application
Loc 1½ miles W of Falkirk on A9

Falkirk Tryst (1885)

86 Burnhead Road, Larbert
Tel (0324) 562415
Mem 450
Sec JA Stevenson (0324) 562054
Pro D Slicer (0324) 562091
Holes 18 L 6053 yds SSS 69
Recs Am–64 J Rankin
Pro–65 J Chillas
V'trs WD–U exc Wed–NA WE–M
SOC
Fees £9 D–£13
Loc 3 miles N of Falkirk

Glenbervie

Stirling Road, Larbert FK5 4SJ
Tel (0324) 562605
Mem 600
Sec Mrs M Purves
Pro G McKay (0324) 562725
Holes 18 L 6469 yds SSS 71
Recs Am–64 KW Goodwin (1989)
Pro–63 C Innes
V'trs WD–I WE–M SOC–Tues &
Thurs
Fees £15 D–£20
Loc 1 mile N of Larbert on Stirling
road

Grangemouth (1973)

Public
Polmonthill, Grangemouth FK2 0YA
Tel (0324) 711500
Mem 700
Sec DG Walls
Pro SJ Campbell (0324) 714355
Holes 18 L 6527 yds SSS 71
Recs Am–67 N Scaife (1990)
V'trs U
Fees £5 (£8)
Loc 3 miles E of Falkirk

Polmont (1901)

Manuelrigg, Maddiston, Falkirk
Tel (0324) 711277
Mem 200
Sec P Lees (0324) 713811
Holes 9 L 3044 yds SSS 69
Recs Am–71 W Shanks

V'trs U Sat NA–before 1pm
Fees £5 (£7) £3 after 6pm
Loc 4 miles S of Falkirk

Stirling (1869)

Queen's Road, Stirling FK8 2QY
Tel (0786) 73801
Mem 1000
Sec WC McArthur (0786) 64098
Pro J Chillas (0786) 71490
Holes 18 L 6409 yds SSS 71
Recs Am–64 R Gregan (1983)
Pro–64 W Milne (1988)
V'trs WD–U WE–NA SOC
Fees On application
Loc King's Park, Stirling

Strathendrick (1901)

Drymen
Mem 360
Sec R Smith (0360) 40582
Holes 9 L 4962 yds SSS 65
Recs Am–62 P Haggarty
Pro–64 C Dernie
V'trs M
Loc Drymen

Dumfries & Galloway

Dumfriesshire

Crichton Royal (1884)

Dumfries
Mem 400
Sec JP Cairns
Holes 9 L 3084 yds SSS 69
Recs Am–67 RB Shearman
Pro–67 D Gemmell
V'trs M
Loc 1 mile from Dumfries on
Bankend road

Dumfries & County (1912)

Nunfield, Edinburgh Road, Dumfries
DG1 1JX
Tel (0387) 53585
Mem 600 150(L) 100(J)
Sec JK Wells
Pro GD Gray (0387) 68918
Holes 18 L 5928 yds SSS 68
Recs Am–64 D James, IR
Brotherston, W Blayney
Pro–63 A Thomson, F Mann
J McAlister
V'trs WD–U exc 12.30–2pm–NA
Sat–NA Sun–NA before 10am
Fees £12 (£15) W–£40
Loc 1 mile NE of Dumfries, on
A701

Dumfries & Galloway (1880)

Laurieston Avenue, Maxwelltown, Dumfries
Tel	(0387) 53582
Mem	450
Sec	J Donnachie (0387) 63848
Pro	J Fergusson (0387) 56902
Holes	18 L 5782 yds SSS 68
Recs	Am–63 I Reid
	Pro–63 K Baxter
V'trs	U
Fees	£12 (£15)
Loc	Dumfries

Langholm (1892)

Langholm
Tel	(03873) 80559
Mem	150
Sec	A Edgar (03873) 80878
Holes	9 L 2872 yds SSS 68
Recs	Am–67 G Davidson
V'trs	U
Fees	£5 (£5)
Loc	1/4 mile E of Langholm

Lochmaben (1926)

Castlehill Gate, Lochmaben DG11 1NT
Tel	(03887) 810552
Mem	350
Sec	JK Purves
Holes	9 L 5304 yds SSS 66
Recs	Am–62 D Hutchison
	Pro–64 G Gray
V'trs	WD–U before 5pm WE–U exc comp days
Fees	D–£5
Loc	4 miles W of Lockerbie on A709. Dumfries 8 miles

Lockerbie (1889)

Corrie Road, Lockerbie
Tel	(057 62) 3363
Mem	360
Sec	JA Carruthers (0387) 810352
Holes	18 L 5418 yds SSS 66
Recs	Am–65 R Nairn (1988)
V'trs	U
Fees	£6 W–£25
Loc	1/2 mile from Lockerbie, on Corrie road

Moffat (1884)

Coatshill, Moffat DG10 9SB
Tel	(0683) 20020
Mem	400
Sec	TA Rankin
Holes	18 L 5218 yds SSS 66
Recs	Am–60 GJ Rodaks (1979)
V'trs	WD–restricted Wed after 12 noon
Fees	D–£9 (D–£13.50)
Loc	Signposted on A701 from Beattock (A74)

Powfoot (1903)

Cummertrees, Annan
Tel	(04617) 227
Mem	820
Sec	RG Anderson (04612) 2866
Pro	G Dick (04617) 327
Holes	18 L 6266 yds SSS 70
Recs	Am–65 C Wright
	Pro–67 J Stevens
V'trs	WD–U WE–Limited
Fees	Winter £8 (£9) 5D–£32
	Summer £13 (£15) 5D–£52
Loc	4 miles W of Annan

Sanquhar (1894)

Blackaddie Road, Sanquhar
Tel	(0659) 50577
Mem	180
Sec	Mrs J Murray (0659) 58181
Holes	9 L 5630 yds SSS 68
Recs	Am–66 I Brotherston (1982)
	J Copeland
V'trs	U SOC
Fees	£8 (£10)
Loc	1/2 mile W of Sanquhar by A76. Dumfries 30 miles. Prestwick Airport 30 miles

Southerness (1947)

Southerness, Dumfries DG2 8AZ
Tel	(0387) 88677
Mem	700
Sec	Major (Ret'd) DDJ Palmer
Holes	18 L 6554 yds SSS 72
Recs	Am–65 M Gronberg (1990)
V'trs	H (telephone first) SOC
Fees	On application
Loc	16 miles SW of Dumfries, off A710

Thornhill (1892)

Black Nest, Thornhill DG3
Tel	(0848) 30546
Mem	570
Sec	RL Kerr (0848) 30218
Holes	18 L 6011 yds SSS 69
Recs	Am–66 BR Kerr
V'trs	U
Fees	£8 (£10)
Loc	14 miles N of Dumfries

Kirkcudbrightshire

Castle Douglas (1905)

Abercromby Road, Castle Douglas
Tel	(0556) 2801
Mem	450
Sec	AJ Guy
Holes	9 L 5400 yds SSS 66
Recs	Am–62 W Blayney, J Shepherd (1989)
V'trs	U
Fees	£8 W–£25
Loc	Castle Douglas

Colvend (1908)

Sandyhills, nr Dalbeattie DG5 4PY
Tel	(055 663) 398
Mem	400
Sec	JB Henderson
Holes	9 L 2322 yds SSS 63
Recs	Am–63 W Blayney (1990)
V'trs	U exc Tues after 2pm & Thurs after 5.30pm (Apr–Sept) SOC
Fees	£7 (£7)
Loc	6 miles S of Dalbeattie on A710 Solway Coast road

Dalbeattie (1897)

Dalbeattie
Tel	(0556) 611421
Mem	230
Sec	T Moffat
Holes	9 L 4200 yds SSS 60
V'trs	U
Fees	£6 (£6)

Gatehouse (1922)

Gatehouse of Fleet
Mem	250
Sec	W McMillan (055) 814252
Holes	9 L 2398 yds SSS 63
Recs	Am–60 S Martin
V'trs	U
Fees	£6 W–£30
Loc	3/4 mile N of Gatehouse

Kirkcudbright (1893)

Stirling Crescent, Kirkcudbright
Mem	400
Sec	A Gordon (0557) 30542
Holes	18 L 5681 yds SSS 67
Recs	Am–62 S Calladine
V'trs	U
Fees	£8 W–£30
Loc	Kirkcudbright

New Galloway (1902)

New Galloway
Mem	216
Sec	JT Watson (0556) 2794
Holes	9 L 2509 yds SSS 65
Recs	Am–66 N Porteous (1990)
V'trs	U
Fees	£7.50 Sun–£10
Loc	S end of New Galloway on A762

Wigtownshire

Newton Stewart

Kirroughtree Avenue, Minnigaff, Newton Stewart
Tel	(0671) 2172
Mem	300
Sec	DC Matthewson
Holes	9 L 5512 yds SSS 67
Recs	Am–64 IS Thomson (1990)
V'trs	U H
Fees	£7 (£9) W–£35
Loc	Newton Stewart, on A75

Portpatrick Dunskey (1903)

Golf Course Road, Portpatrick
DG9 8TB
Tel   (0776) 81273
Mem   400
Sec   JA Horberry (0776) 81231
Holes 18 L 5644 yds SSS 67
       9 L 1442 yds
Recs   Am–64 R Russell (1990)
       Pro–64 A Hunter, C Innes
       (1990)
V'trs U H SOC
Fees   £10 D–£15 (£12 D–£20) W–£50
       9 hole course D–£5
Loc   8 miles SW of Stranraer

St Medan (1905)

Monreith, Newton Stewart DG8 8NJ
Tel   (098 87) 358
Mem   300
Sec   D O'Neill (098 85) 555
Holes 9 L 2277 yds SSS 62
Recs   Am–60 J Grundy (1990)
V'trs U SOC
Fees   £7 W–£35
Loc   3 miles S of Port William on
       A747

Stranraer (1906)

Creachmore, Leswalt, Stranraer
Tel   (0776) 87245
Mem   450
Sec   WI Wilson CA (0776) 3539
Holes 18 L 6300 yds SSS 71
Recs   Am–66 CG Findlay
       Pro–72 J Panton
V'trs WE–NA before 9.30am and
       11.45am–1.30pm
Fees   £10 (£12.50) W–£40
Loc   2 miles from Stranraer on A718

Wigtown & Bladnoch (1960)

Wigtown
Tel   (098 84) 3354
Mem   130
Sec   J Bateman
Holes 9 L 2731 yds SSS 67
Recs   Am–64 R McGinn, DT McRae
V'trs U
Fees   £6 (£8)
Loc   Wigtown

Wigtownshire County (1894)

Mains of Park, Glenluce, Newton
Stewart DG8 0NN
Tel   (058 13) 420
Mem   250
Sec   R McCubbin (058 13) 277
Holes 18 L 5715 yds SSS 68
Recs   Am–66 K Hardie
V'trs U exc Wed–NA after 6pm
Fees   £10 D–£14 (£12 D–£15)
Loc   8 miles E of Stranraer on A75

Fife Region

Fife

Aberdour (1904)

Seaside Place, Aberdour KY3 0TX
Tel   (0383) 860688
Mem   420 160(L)
Sec   BP Drever (0383) 860353
Pro   A Hope (0383) 860256
Holes 18 L 5469 yds SSS 67
Recs   Am–63 S Meiklejohn
V'trs Sun/ comp Sat–NA
Fees   £10 D–£14
Loc   Aberdour
Mis   Visitors may make reservations
       1 day in advance with Pro

Anstruther (1890)

Marsfield Shore Road, Anstruther
Tel   (0333) 310956
Mem   500
Sec   M Yuill (0333) 312055
Holes 9 L 4504 yds SSS 63
Recs   Am–63 R Wallace, T Anderson,
       A Forrester
V'trs U SOC
Fees   £6 (£8) (1990)
Loc   9 miles S of St Andrews

Auchterderran (1904)

Woodend Road, Cardenden
Tel   (0592) 721579
Mem   100
Sec   W Nicolson
Holes 9 L 5400 yds SSS 66
Recs   Am–66 C McRae
V'trs U
Fees   £2.70 (£4.20)
Loc   1 mile N of Cardenden

Balbirnie Park (1983)

Balbirnie Park, Markinch,
Glenrothes
Tel   (0592) 752006
Mem   500
Sec   A Grant
Holes 18 L 6210 yds SSS 70
Recs   Am–70 G Birnie
V'trs U
Fees   £12 D–£15 (£15 D–£20)
Loc   2 miles E of Glenrothes

Ballingry (1908)

Public
Lochore Meadows Country Park,
Crosshill, Lochgelly
Tel   (0592) 860086
Mem   150
Sec   W Glencross (0592) 861316
Holes 9 L 6482 yds SSS 71
Recs   Am–68 S Meiklejohn (1990)
V'trs U
Fees   £3.80 (£5)

Burntisland (1797)

Tel   (0592) 873229
Mem   120
Sec   AD McPherson
Holes Play over Dodhead Course,
       Burntisland

Burntisland Golf House Club (1898)

Dodhead, Burntisland
Tel   (0592) 873247
Mem   750
Sec   I McLean (0592) 874093
Pro   S Walker
Holes 18 L 5897 yds SSS 69
Recs   Am–65 DA Paton
V'trs U
Fees   £10 D–£14 (£13 D–£19)
Loc   1 mile E of Burntisland on B923

Canmore (1898)

Venturefair, Dunfermline
Tel   (0383) 724969
Mem   480 60(L) 80(J)
Sec   JC Duncan (0383) 726098
Pro   S Craig (0383) 728416
Holes 18 L 5437 yds SSS 66
Recs   Am–61 R Wallace
V'trs WD–U
Fees   £8 D–£15
Loc   1 mile N of Dunfermline on A823

Crail Golfing Society (1786)

Balcomie Clubhouse, Fifeness, Crail
KY10 3XN
Tel   (0333) 50278
Mem   750 200(L)
Sec   Mrs C Penhale (0333) 50686
Pro   G Lennie (0333) 50960
Holes 18 L 5720 yds SSS 68
Recs   Am–64 RW Malcolm
       Pro–66 B Gallacher
V'trs U
Fees   On application
Loc   11 miles SE of St Andrews

Cupar (1855)

Hillarvitt, Cupar
Tel   (0334) 53549
Mem   475
Sec   IR Wilson (0334) 53254
Holes 9 L 5074 yds SSS 65
Recs   Am–62 J Fairfield, C Wilson
V'trs Sat–NA SOC–WD/ Sun
Fees   £4 (£5)
Loc   10 miles W of St Andrews

Dunfermline (1887)

Pitfirrane, Crossford, Dunfermline
KY12 8QV
Tel   (0383) 723534
Mem   500
Sec   H Matheson
Pro   J Montgomery
Holes 18 L 6217 yds SSS 70
Recs   Am–65 AD Martin
       Pro–65 A Brooks

V'trs WD–I 9.30–4pm SOC–WD
Fees £12 D–£20
Loc 2 miles W of Dunfermline on A994

Dunnikier Park (1963)

Public
Dunnikier Way, Kirkcaldy KY1 3LP
Tel (0592) 261599
Mem 600 35(L) 75(J)
Sec RA Waddell (0592) 200627
Holes 18 L 6601 yds SSS 72
Recs Am–65 S Duthie (1988)
Pro–65 A Hunter (1988)
V'trs U SOC
Fees £3.20 (£4.40)
Loc N boundary of Kirkcaldy
Mis Dunnikier Park Club plays here

Earlsferry Thistle (1875)

Melon Park, Elie
Tel (0333) 310053
Mem 60
Sec J Fyall
Holes Play over Elie Golf House Club Course

Falkland (1976)

Public
The Myre, Falkland KY7 7AA
Tel (0337) 57404
Mem 240
Sec Mrs CR Forsythe (0337) 57356
Holes 9 L 2384 metres SSS 66
Recs Am–67 W Garland (1987)
V'trs U SOC
Fees D–£5 (D–£7) W–£17.50
Loc On A912 Kirkcaldy–Perth road

Glenrothes (1958)

Public
Golf Course Road, Glenrothes KY6 2LA
Tel (0592) 758686/ 758678
Mem 600 35(L) 120(J)
Sec LD Dalrymple (0592) 754561
Holes 18 L 6444 yds SSS 71
Recs Am–65 C Birrell
Pro–69 R Craig, B Lawson
V'trs U
Fees £3.20 (£4.40)
Loc Glenrothes West

Golf House Club (1875)

Elie, Leven KY9 1AS
Tel (0333) 330327
Mem 500
Sec A Sneddon (0333) 330301
Pro R Wilson (0333) 330955
Holes 18 L 6241 yds SSS 70 9 L 2277 yds SSS 32
Recs Am–63 AW Mathers
Pro–62 K Nagle
V'trs July–Sept ballot. WE–no party bookings. WE–NA before 3pm (May–Sept)
Fees £16 D–£24 (£22 D–£30)
Loc St Andrews 12 miles

Kinghorn (1887)

Public
Macduff Cres, Kinghorn KY3 9RE
Tel (0592) 890345
Holes 18 L 5246 SS 67
Recs Am–62 AJ McIntyre
V'trs U
Fees £2.80 (£3.95)
Loc 3 miles W of Kirkcaldy (A921)
Mis Kinghorn and Kinghorn Thistle Clubs play here

Kinghorn Ladies (1905)

Kinghorn
Tel (0592) 890345
Mem 47
Sec Miss E Douglas (0592) 890512
Holes Play over Kinghorn Municipal

Kirkcaldy (1904)

Balwearie Road, Kirkcaldy KY2 5LT
Tel (0592) 260370
Mem 450 100(L)
Sec JI Brodley (0592) 263316
Pro B Lawson (0592) 203258
Holes 18 L 6007 yds SSS 70
Recs Am–67 B Glancy, C Devine, S McKay
V'trs U
Fees £10 D–£15 (£12 D–£18)
Loc SW end of Kirkcaldy

Ladybank (1879)

Annsmuir, Ladybank KY7 7RA
Tel (0337) 30320
Mem 770
Sec AM Dick (0337) 30814
Pro MJ Gray (0337) 30725
Holes 18 L 6641 yds SSS 72
Recs Am–67 S Syme (1987)
Pro–66 W Reilly, P Stewart (1984), K Knox (1990)
V'trs WD–U 9.15am–5pm M–after 5pm WE–NA 10.15am–5pm SOC
Fees £15 (£18) W–£50
Loc 6 miles SW of Cupar

Leslie (Fife) (1898)

Balsillie Laws, Leslie, Glenrothes KY6 3EZ
Mem 300
Sec M Burns (0592) 741449
Holes 9 L 4940 yds SSS 64
Recs Am–63 J Spital
Pro–64 J Chillas
V'trs U
Fees £4 (£5)
Loc M90 Junction 5/ 7, 11 miles

Leven Golfing Society (1820)

Links Road, Leven KY8 4HS
Tel (0333) 26096
(0333) 21390 (Starter)
Mem 350
Sec J Bennett (0333) 23898
Holes Play over Leven Links

Leven Links (1846)

Leven
Tel (0333) 21390 (Starter)
Sec M Innes (0333) 23509 (Links Joint Committee)
Pro G Finlayson
Holes 18 L 6434 yds SSS 71
Recs Am–64 J Hawkesworth (1984), K Goodwin (1986)
Pro–63 P Hoad (1984)
V'trs WD–U before 5pm Sat–no parties Sun–NA before 10.30am SOC
Fees £13 (£18)
Loc ½ mile E of Leven, on promenade

Leven Municipal

Public
North Links, Leven KY8 1DH
Tel (0333) 27057
Sec K Davidson
Holes 18 L 5600 yds SSS 66
Recs Am–63 P Lamont
V'trs U
Fees £3.20 (£4.40)
Loc Adjoins Leven Links
Mis Scoonie Club plays here

Leven Thistle (1867)

3 Balfour Street, Leven
Tel (0333) 26397
Mem 400
Sec J Scott (0333) 23798
Holes Play over Leven Links

Lochgelly (1910)

Cartmore Road, Lochgelly
Tel (0592) 780174
Mem 400
Sec RF Stuart (0383) 512238
Holes 18 L 5491 yds SSS 67
Recs Am–64 D Walker (1988)
V'trs U
Fees £5 (£7)
Loc NW edge of Lochgelly

Lundin (1869)

Golf Road, Lundin Links KY8 6BA
Tel (0333) 320202
Mem 700
Sec AC McBride
Pro DK Webster (0333) 320051
Holes 18 L 6377 yds SSS 71
Recs Am–65 KWS Gray, S Machin
Pro–63 AD Hare
V'trs WD–U H Sat–NA before 2.30pm Sun–M H
Fees £15 D–£22.50 Sat–£18
Loc 3 miles E of Leven

Lundin Ladies (1891)

Woodielea Road, Lundin Links KY8 6AR
Tel (0333) 320022/ 320832
Mem 220
Sec Mrs H Melville (0333) 320553

For list of abbreviations see page 487.

Holes 9 L 4730 yds SSS 67
Recs Am–67 Miss L Bennett
V'trs U
Fees £3.50 (£4.50)
Loc 3 miles E of Leven

Methil (1892)

Links House, Links Road, Leven
Tel (0333) 25535
Mem 50
Sec ATJ Traill
Holes Play over Leven Links

Pitreavie (1922)

Queensferry Road, Dunfermline
KY11 5PR
Tel (0383) 722591
Mem 700
Sec D Carter
Pro J Forrester (0383) 723151
Holes 18 L 6086 yds SSS 69
Recs Am–65 D Manson (1990)
V'trs U (phone Pro first) SOC
(Parties–max 36–must be
booked in advance)
Fees £9 (£12) (1990)
Loc 2 miles off M90, between
Rosyth and Dunfermline

St Michael's (1903)

Leuchars
Tel (033483) 9365
Mem 455
Sec AJR MacKenzie
Holes 9 L 5578 yds SSS 68
Recs Am–66 N Manzie (1988)
V'trs Sun am–NA (Mar–Oct) SOC
Fees D–£10 (D–£10)
Loc 5 miles N of St Andrews on
Dundee road

Saline (1912)

Kinneddar Hill, Saline
Tel (0383) 852591
Mem 340
Sec R Hutchison (0383) 852344
Holes 9 L 5302 yds SSS 66
Recs Am–A Brown
V'trs U exc medal Sat
Fees £5 (£7)
Loc 5 miles NW of Dunfermline

Scotscraig (1817)

Golf Road, Tayport DD6 9DZ
Tel (0382) 552515
Mem 600
Sec K Gourlay
Holes 18 L 6496 yds SSS 71
Recs Am–65 M Milne Jr
Pro–61 M Mouland
V'trs WD–U WE–by prior
arrangement SOC
Fees On application
Loc 10 miles N of St Andrews

Thornton (1921)

Station Road, Thornton
Tel (0592) 771111
Mem 630
Sec N Robertson
Holes 18 L 6175 yds SSS 69
Recs Am–65 R Malcolm
V'trs U
Fees £8 D–£12 (£12 D–£18)
Loc Thornton, 1 mile E of A92

St Andrews Clubs

Royal & Ancient (1754)

St Andrews
Tel (0334) 72112
Fax (0334) 77580
Mem 1800
Sec MF Bonallack OBE
Pro J Panton (Hon)
Holes Play over St Andrews courses

New Golf Club (1902)

3–6 Gibson Place, St Andrews
KY16 9JE
Tel (0334) 73426
Mem 1700
Sec JW Bell (Sec/ Mgr)
Holes Play over St Andrews courses

St Andrews (1843)

Links House, The Links, St Andrews
KY16 9JB
Tel (0334) 74637
Mem 1500
Sec WS Simpson (0334) 73017
Holes Play over St Andrews courses
V'trs Rules in accordance with Links
Management Committee, Golf
Place, St Andrews

St Regulus Ladies'

9 Pilmour Links, St Andrews
KY16 9JG
Tel (0334) 74699
Mem 170
Sec Mrs M Irvine
Holes Play over St Andrews courses

St Rule Ladies' (1898)

12 The Links, St Andrews KY16 9JB
Tel (0334) 72988
Mem 490
Sec Mrs R Hair
Holes Play over St Andrews Courses

St Andrews Thistle (1817)

St Andrews
Mem 176
Sec DL Joy (0334) 73749
Holes Play over St Andrews courses

St Andrews Courses

Old Course (15th Century)

Public
St Andrews
Tel (0334) 75757 (Tee reservations)
(0334) 73393 (Starter)
Fax (0334) 77036
Holes 18 L 6566 yds SSS 72
Recs Am–66 C McLachlan
Pro–62 C Strange (1987)
V'trs H I No Sun play SOC
Fees £30
Loc St Andrews Links

Balgove (1972)

Public
St Andrews
Tel (0334) 75757
Fax (0334) 77036
Holes 9 (Beginners course)
V'trs U
Fees £2
Loc St Andrews Links

Eden Course (1913)

Public
St Andrews
Tel (0334) 75757 (Tee reservations)
(0334) 73938 (Starter)
Fax (0334) 77036
Holes 18 L 6400 yds SSS 70
Recs Am–72 RW Guy, A Clark
V'trs U SOC
Fees £11 W–£70 3D–£35 (unlimited
play on Eden, Jubilee and New
Courses)
Loc St Andrews Links

Jubilee Course (1897)

Public
St Andrews
Tel (0334) 75757 (Tee reservations)
(0334) 73938 (Starter)
Fax (0334) 77036
Holes 18 L 6805 yds SSS 72
V'trs U SOC
Fees £13 W–£70 3D–£35 (unlimited
play over Jubilee, Eden and
New Courses)
Loc St Andrews Links

New Course (1896)

Public
St Andrews
Tel (0334) 75757 (Tee reservations)
(0334) 73393 (Starter)
Fax (0334) 77036
Holes 18 L 6604 yds SSS 72
Recs Am–67 GM Mitchell
Pro–63 F Jowie
V'trs U
Fees £13 W–£70 3D–£30 (unlimited
play over Jubilee, Eden and
New courses)
Loc St Andrews Links

For list of abbreviations see page 487.

Grampian Region

Aberdeenshire

Aboyne (1883)

Formaston Park, Aboyne
Tel   (03398) 86328
Mem   725 180(J)
Sec   Mrs M MacLean (03398) 87078
Pro   I Wright (03398) 86469
Holes   18 L 5304 yds SSS 66
Recs   Am–62 G Forbes, C Forbes
        Pro–63 S Walker
V'trs   U
Fees   £9 (£13) W–£35
Loc   E end of Aboyne

Auchmill (1975)

Public
Provost Rust Drive, Aberdeen
Tel   (0224) 714577
Holes   18 L 5439 metres SSS 69
V'trs   U
Fees   Summer £4.95 Winter £3.50
Loc   3 miles NW of Aberdeen

Ballater (1892)

Victoria Road, Ballater AB3 5QX
Tel   (03397) 55567
Mem   600
Sec   A Ingram
Pro   F Mann (03397) 55658
Holes   18 L 6106 yds SSS 69
Recs   Am–65 S Henderson
        Pro–66 G Collison, F Coutts
V'trs   U
Fees   £10 (£12) W–£36 F–£60
Loc   42 miles W of Aberdeen on
        A93

Balnagask

Public
St Fitticks Road, Aberdeen
Tel   (0224) 876407
Pro   I Smith
Holes   18 L 5472 metres SSS 69
V'trs   U
Fees   Summer £4.95 Winter £3.50
Loc   1½ miles SE of Aberdeen
Mis   Nigg Bay Club plays here

Bon Accord (1872)

19 Golf Road, Aberdeen AB2 1QB
Tel   (0224) 633464
Mem   950
Sec   JT Burnett
Holes   Play over King's Links

Braemar (1902)

Cluniebank Road, Braemar AB3 5XX
Tel   (03397) 41618
Mem   287
Sec   GA McIntosh (0224) 733836
Holes   18 L 4916 yds SSS 64
Recs   Am–61 W Main
        Pro–64 L Vannet (1988)
V'trs   U SOC
Fees   £6 D–£9 (£9 D–£11)
Loc   Braemar ½ mile

Caledonian (1899)

20 Golf Road, Aberdeen AB2 1QB
Tel   (0224) 632443
Mem   960
Sec   WA Adams
Holes   Play over King's Links

Cruden Bay (1791)

Cruden Bay AB4 7NN
Tel   (0779) 812285
Mem   588
Sec   IAD McPherson
Pro   D Symington (0779) 812414
Holes   18 L 6370 yds SSS 71 9 L 4710
        yds SSS 62 (St Olaf Course)
Recs   Am–66 PJ Macleod (1987),
        D Jamieson (1989)
        Pro–63 D Thomson (1989)
V'trs   WD–U WE–H exc comp days
        SOC–WD
Fees   £16 (£22)
Loc   22½ miles NE of Aberdeen

Deeside (1903)

Bieldside, Aberdeen
Tel   (0224) 869457
Mem   500
Sec   NM Scott (0224) 869457
Pro   FJ Coutts (0224) 861041
Holes   18 L 5972 yds SSS 69
        9 L 6632 yds SSS 72
Recs   Am–64 AK Pirie, RH Willox
        Pro–64 S Torrance
V'trs   I
Fees   £12 (£15)
Loc   4 miles W of Aberdeen

Dunecht House (1925)

Dunecht, Skene AB3 7AX
Mem   360
Sec   GD Duguid (0224) 487178
Holes   9 L 3135 yds SSS 70
Recs   Am–72 A Angus (1987)
V'trs   M
Loc   12 miles W of Aberdeen on
        B944

Fraserburgh (1881)

Philorth, Fraserburgh AB4 5TL
Tel   (0346) 28287
Mem   420 72(L) 130(J)
Sec   JW Love (0346) 27464
Holes   18 L 6217 yds SSS 70
Recs   Am–66 A Ritchie, C McDonald,
        A Ironside
        Pro–67 I Smith
V'trs   U SOC
Fees   £7 (£9)
Loc   1 mile E of Fraserburgh

Hazlehead (1927)

Public
Hazlehead, Aberdeen
Tel   (0224) 321830
Sec   J Murchie (0224) 315747
Pro   I Smith
Holes   18 L 5673 metres SSS 70
        18 L 5303 metres SSS 68
        9 L 2531 metres SSS 34
Recs   Am–65 D Jamieson
        Pro–67 P Oosterhuis
V'trs   U
Fees   Summer £4.95 Winter £3.50
Loc   3 miles W of Aberdeen

Huntly (1900)

Huntly
Tel   (0466) 2643
Mem   600
Sec   G Angus
Holes   18 L 5399 yds SSS 66
Recs   Am–61 N Mason
V'trs   U
Fees   £8 (£10) W–£20
Loc   38 miles NE of Aberdeen

Insch

Golf Terrace, Insch
Tel   (0464) 20363
Mem   200
Sec   G Miller (0464) 20252/ 20243
Holes   9 L 5488 yds SSS 67
Recs   Am–67 H McKenzie (1982)
        G Bruce (1988)
V'trs   U
Fees   £4 (£5) W–£10
Loc   28 miles NW of Aberdeen off
        A96 Inverness road

Inverallochy

Public
Inverallochy, nr Fraserburgh
Mem   200
Sec   GM Young (034 65) 2324
Holes   18 L 5137 yds SSS 65
Recs   Am–60
V'trs   U
Fees   D–£5
Loc   3½ miles off A92, nr
        Fraserburgh

Inverurie (1923)

Blackhall Road, Inverurie
Tel   (0467) 20207
Mem   450 110(L)
Sec   J Ramage (0467) 24080
Holes   18 L 5096 yds SSS 65
Recs   Am–63 M Percival
V'trs   U SOC–WD
Fees   D–£8 (£10)
Loc   16 miles N of Aberdeen. 1 mile
        W of Inverurie

Kemnay (1908)

Kemnay
Mem   300
Sec   Dr G Young (0467) 42681
Holes   9 L 2751 yds SSS 67
Recs   Am–66

For list of abbreviations see page 487.

V'trs	WD/ WE–U exc Mon & Thurs–NA after 5.30
Fees	£5 (£6)
Loc	Aberdeen 15 miles

King's Links

Public

Golf Road, Aberdeen AB2 1QB

Tel	(0224) 632269
Pro	B Davidson (0224) 641577
Holes	18 L 5838 metres SSS 71
V'trs	U
Fees	Summer £4.95 Winter £3.50
Loc	1 mile E of Aberdeen
Mis	Bon Accord, Caledonian and Northern Clubs play here

Kintore (1911)

Kintore

Tel	(0467) 32631
Mem	350 38(L) 60(J)
Sec	J Black
Holes	18 L 5985 yds SSS 69
V'trs	WD–U before 4pm WE–U
Fees	£7 (£8)
Loc	12 miles NE of Aberdeen on A96

McDonald (1927)

Ellon

Tel	(0358) 20576
Mem	650
Sec	F Chadwick (0358) 21397
Pro	R Urquhart (0358) 22891
Holes	18 L 5986 yds SSS 69
Recs	Am–65
	Pro–67
V'trs	U
Fees	On application
Loc	15 miles N of Aberdeen

Murcar (1909)

Bridge of Don, Aberdeen AB2 8BD

Tel	(0224) 704345
Mem	830
Sec	R Matthews (0224) 704354
Pro	A White (0224) 704370
Holes	18 L 6226 yds SSS 70 9 hole course
Recs	Am–65 R Grant, J Savege, E Morrison
	Pro–65 PA Smith
V'trs	U before noon
Fees	£10 D–£16 (D–£18)
Loc	5 miles NE of Aberdeen
Mis	9 hole course at Strabathie

Newburgh–on–Ythan (1888)

Newburgh

Mem	200 35(L) 50(J)
Sec	AC Stevenson (03586) 89438
Holes	9 L 3202 yds SSS 71
Recs	Am–70
	Pro–69 F Coutts
V'trs	U exc Tues after 3pm
Fees	£7 (£9)
Loc	12 miles N of Aberdeen

Newmacher (1989)

Newmacher, Aberdeen AB5 0NU

Tel	(06517) 2127
Sec	ME Stubbings
Pro	G Taylor
Holes	18 L 6605 yds SSS 73
V'trs	H
Fees	£10 (£16)
Loc	12 miles N of Aberdeen on A947

Oldmeldrum (1885)

Oldmeldrum

Tel	(06512) 2648
Mem	450
Sec	JN Duncan (06512) 2626
Holes	18 L 5988 yds SSS
Recs	Am–71 G Presly (1990)
V'trs	WD–U before 5pm
	WE–telephone first
Fees	£8 (£10)
Loc	17 miles NW of Aberdeen

Peterhead (1841)

Craigewan Links, Peterhead AB42 6LT

Tel	(0779) 72149
Mem	525
Sec	A Brandie (0779) 73350
Holes	18 L 6173 yds SSS 70 9 L 2237 yds SSS 62
Recs	Am–64 K Buchan (1988)
	Pro–64 J Farmer (1980)
V'trs	U
Fees	£7 (£11)
Loc	34 miles N of Aberdeen, on coast

Portlethen (1983)

Badentoy Road, Portlethen, Aberdeen AB1 1RP

Tel	(0224) 782575
Mem	1250
Sec	IJ Thompson
Pro	Muriel Thomson (0224) 782571
Holes	18 L 6735 yds SSS 72
Recs	Am–78 S Rennie (1990)
	Pro–66 P Smith (1990)
V'trs	WD–U WE–NA before 11am SOC
Fees	£8 (£10)
Loc	6 miles S of Aberdeen on A92

Royal Aberdeen (1780)

Balgownie, Links Road, Bridge of Don, Aberdeen AB2 8AT

Tel	(0224) 702571
Mem	350 117(J)
Sec	GF Webster
Pro	R MacAskill (Gen Mgr) (0224) 702221
Holes	18 L 6372 yds SSS 71 18 L 4066 yds SSS 60
Recs	Am–64 J Fought
	Pro–65 S McAllister
V'trs	I H SOC
Fees	£20 D–£25 (£22)
Loc	2 miles from Aberdeen, off A92 Ellon road

Tarland (1908)

Tarland AB3 4YN

Tel	(0339) 81413
Mem	240
Sec	JH Honeyman
Holes	9 L 5812 yds SSS 68
Recs	Am–69 A Paterson
V'trs	WD–U WE–Enquiry advisable SOC–WD only
Fees	£6 (£8) (1990)
Loc	Aberdeen 30 miles. Aboyne 5 miles

Torphins (1894)

Torphins

Tel	(033 982) 493
Mem	350
Sec	H Shepherd
Holes	9 L 2330 yds SSS 63
Recs	Am–64 K Leslie
V'trs	U SOC
Fees	£4 (£5)
Loc	Banchory 6 miles. 1/2 mile W of Torphins via Wester Beltie

Turriff (1899)

Rosehall, Turriff

Tel	(0888) 62745
Mem	750
Sec	JD Stott (0888) 62982
Pro	A Hemsley (0888) 63025
Holes	18 L 6145 yds SSS 69
Recs	Am–63 G Wallace (1990)
	Pro–64 S Aird,
	P Lawrie (1989)
V'trs	H WE–NA before 10am SOC
Fees	£9 D–£10 (£10 D–£12)
Loc	Turriff
Mis	Buggies for hire

Westhill (1977)

Westhill, Skene

Tel	(0224) 740159 (Bookings)
	(0224) 743361 (Clubhouse)
Mem	500
Sec	JL Webster
Pro	N Hamilton
Holes	18 L 5866 yds SSS 69
Recs	Am–66 LR Fowler
V'trs	WD–U before 4.30pm and after 7pm –M 4.30–7pm Sat–U after 3.30pm Sun–U after 10am
Fees	£7 D–£9 (£8 D–£11)
Loc	Aberdeen 6 miles on A944

Banffshire

Buckpool (1933)

Barhill Road, Buckie AB56 1DU

Tel	(0542) 32236
Mem	500
Sec	Mrs IE Jagger (0542) 34322
Holes	18 L 6257 yds SSS 70
V'trs	U
Fees	D–£7 (D–£10) W–£25
Loc	W end of Buckpool, 1/2 mile off A98

Cullen (1879)

The Links, Cullen, Buckie
Tel	(0542) 40685
Mem	512
Sec	LIG Findlay (0542) 40174
Holes	18 L 4610 yds SSS 62
Recs	Am–58 B Main (1979)
V'trs	WD–U WE–restricted Jul/ Aug SOC
Fees	D–£5 (£5.50) W–£26
Loc	Off A98 midway between Aberdeen and Inverness

Duff House Royal (1909)

The Barnyards, Banff AB4 3SX
Tel	(026 12) 2062
Mem	547 152(L) 132(J)
Sec	M Pierog (026 12) 2461
Pro	RS Strachan (026 12) 2075
Holes	18 L 6161 yds SSS 69
Recs	Am–63 DC Clarke
V'trs	WD–U WE–NA 8.30–10am and 12–2pm; Jul/Aug–NA 5–6.30pm
Fees	£6.50 (£9)
Loc	Moray Firth coast

Dufftown (1896)

Dufftown
Tel	(0340) 20325
Mem	210
Holes	18 L 5308 yds SSS 66
Recs	Am–68 S Milne (1989) Pro–68 A Aird (1990)
V'trs	U
Fees	D–£5 (D–£6) (1990)
Loc	1 mile from Dufftown on Tomintoul road

Keith (1963)

Fife Park, Keith
Tel	(05422) 2649
Mem	400
Sec	GD Morrison (05422) 2696
Holes	18 L 5811 yds SSS 68
Recs	Am–65
V'trs	U
Fees	£5 (£6)
Loc	Fife Park

Royal Tarlair (1926)

Buchan Street, Macduff AB4 1TA
Tel	(0261) 32548/ 32897
Mem	556
Sec	Mrs E Black
Holes	18 L 5866 yds SSS 68
Recs	Am–66 W Sim
V'trs	U
Fees	£5 D–£6 (£6 D–£8)

Strathlene (1877)

Buckie AB5 2DJ
Tel	(0542) 31798
Mem	300
Sec	JF Weir
Holes	18 L 5957 yds SSS 69
Recs	Am–65 AG Ross
V'trs	U SOC
Fees	£4 (£6) W–£20
Loc	½ mile E of Buckie

Kincardineshire

Auchenblae (1894)

Public
Auchenblae
Mem	60
Sec	Al Robertson (056 12) 407
Holes	9 L 2174 yds SSS 30
Recs	Am–60 Al Robertson
V'trs	U exc Wed & Fri 5.30–9pm
Fees	D–£4 (D–£6)
Loc	11 miles S of Stonehaven. 5 miles N of Laurencekirk

Banchory (1905)

Kinneskie, Banchory
Tel	(033 02) 2365
Mem	700
Sec	E Girvan
Pro	DW Smart (033 02) 2447
Holes	18 L 5246 yds SSS 66
Recs	Am–60 D Reith (1990) Pro–61 A Thomson, D Matthew
V'trs	U
Fees	£14 (£16)
Loc	SW of Banchory centre

Stonehaven (1888)

Cowie, Stonehaven
Tel	(0569) 62124
Mem	500
Sec	RO Blair
Holes	18 L 5128 yds SSS 65
Recs	Am–61 RG Forbes (1987)
V'trs	Sat– NA before 3.45pm Sun–NA before 10.45am
Fees	£10 £12.50 (1990)
Loc	1 mile N of Stonehaven

Morayshire

Elgin (1906)

Hardhillock, Birnie Road, Elgin
IV30 3SX
Tel	(0343) 542338
Mem	490 150(L) 150(J)
Sec	DJ Chambers
Pro	I Rodger (0343) 542884
Holes	18 L 6401 yds SSS 71
Recs	Am–64 NS Grant (1972) Pro–66 H Bannerman (1973)
V'trs	WD–U after 9.30am WE–U after 10am SOC
Fees	£12 D–£18 (£17.50 D–£25)
Loc	1 mile S of Elgin

Forres (1889)

Muiryshade, Forres IV36 0RD
Tel	(0309) 72949
Mem	716 130(J)
Sec	DF Black (0309) 72013
Pro	S Aird (0309) 72250
Holes	18 L 6141 yds SSS 69
Recs	Am–64 A Moir
V'trs	U SOC
Fees	£10 (£15)
Loc	1 mile S of Forres

Garmouth & Kingston (1932)

Garmouth, Fochabers
Tel	(034 387) 388
Mem	300
Sec	A Robertson
Holes	18 L 5637 yds SSS 67
Recs	Am–66 Pro–70
V'trs	U SOC
Fees	£4 D–£6
Loc	NE of Elgin

Grantown (1890)

Grantown-on-Spey
Tel	(0479) 2079
Mem	420
Sec	D Elms (0479) 2715
Pro	W Mitchell (0479) 2398
Holes	18 L 5672 yds SSS 67
Recs	Am–60 G Bain Pro–62 D Webster
V'trs	WD–U WE–U after 10am SOC
Fees	£9 (£11)
Loc	E side of Grantown

Hopeman (1923)

Hopeman
Tel	(0343) 830578
Mem	300
Sec	J Blyth (0343) 830336
Holes	18 L 5500 yds SSS 67
V'trs	U Sun–U after 9.30am SOC
Fees	£5 (£7) (1989)
Loc	7 miles N of Elgin on B9012

Moray (1889)

Stotfield Road, Lossiemouth
IV31 6QS
Tel	(034 381) 2018
Mem	1136
Sec	J Hamilton
Pro	A Thomson (034 381) 3330
Holes	Old 18 L 6643 yds SSS 72 New 18 L 6005 yds SSS 69
Recs	Old Am–68 MM MacLeman, NS Grant, N Robson Pro–66 T Minshall, D Huish New Am–67 K Thomson Pro–67 AT MacKenzie, DW Armor
V'trs	U H SOC
Fees	On application
Loc	6 miles N of Elgin

Spey Bay (1907)

Spey Bay Hotel, Spey Bay,
Fochabers IV32 7PJ
Tel	(0343) 820424
Mem	150
Holes	18 L 6059 yds SSS 69
Recs	Am–66 M Cameron
V'trs	U
Fees	£5.50 D–£6 (£7 D–£8)
Loc	5 miles off A96 at Fochabers
Mis	Seaside Links

For list of abbreviations see page 487.

Highland Region

Caithness

Lybster (1926)

Main Street, Lybster
Mem 86
Sec M Bowman
Holes 9 L 1896 yds SSS 62
Recs Am–60 E Larnach (1982)
V'trs U
Fees D–£3 W–£15
Loc 13 miles S of Wick on A9

Reay (1893)

Reay, by Thurso
Tel **(084 781) 288**
Mem 364 42(L) 37(J)
Sec NH McDonald (084 787) 222
Holes 18 L 5865 yds SSS 68
Recs Am–65 RS Taylor
V'trs U exc comp days
Fees D–£5 W–£18 F–£25
Loc Thurso 11 miles
Mis Most northerly seaside links on British mainland

Thurso (1964)

Public
Newlands of Geise, Thurso
Tel **(0847) 63807**
Mem 310
Sec J Owens (0847) 64030
Holes 18 L 5818 yds SSS 69
Recs Am–63 G Dunnett (1989)
V'trs U
Fees £6 (£6)
Loc Railway station 2 miles

Wick (1870)

Reiss, Wick KW1 5LJ
Tel **(0955) 2726**
Mem 265
Sec Mrs MSW Abernethy (0955) 2702
Holes 18 L 5976 yds SSS 69
Recs Am–63 R Taylor (1988)
Pro–68 Dai Rees
V'trs U
Fees £5 (£6) W–£20 (1990)
Loc 3 miles N of Wick (signposted on A9)

Inverness-shire

Abernethy (1893)

Nethy Bridge
Tel **(047 982) 305**
Mem 200
Sec WG Templeton (047 982) 214
Holes 9 L 2484 yds SSS 66
Recs Am–61 I Murray
V'trs U SOC
Fees D–£7
Loc Aviemore 10 miles. Grantown 5 miles

Boat-of-Garten (1898)

Boat-of-Garten PH24 3BQ
Tel **(047 983) 282 (Shop)**
(047 983) 351 (Clubhouse)
Mem 396
Sec JR Ingram
Holes 18 L 5720 yds SSS 68
Recs Am–65 AP Thomson
Pro–70 GW McIntosh
V'trs U
Fees £10 (£12) (1990)
Loc 27 miles S of Inverness
Mis Starting sheet at WE

Carrbridge (1980)

Carrbridge
Tel **(047 984) 674**
Mem 460
Sec EG Drayson
Holes 9 L 2623 yds SSS 66
Recs Am–67
V'trs U exc comp days–NA
Fees D–£5.50 (D–£6)

Fort Augustus (1930)

Markethill, Fort Augustus
Mem 110
Sec ID Aitchison (0320) 6460
Holes 9 L 5454 yds SSS 68 (18 tees)
Recs Am–69 F Boyd (1985)
V'trs U
Fees £5 (£5) Mon–Fri £15
Loc W end of Fort Augustus

Fort William (1974)

North Road, Fort William
Tel **(0397) 4464**
Mem 300
Sec J Allan
Holes 18 L 5686 metres SSS 71
V'trs U
Fees £8
Loc 3 miles N of Fort William, on A82

Inverness (1883)

Culcabock Road, Inverness IV2 3XQ
Tel **(0463) 239882**
Mem 1100
Sec J Fraser
Pro AP Thomson (0463) 231989
Holes 18 L 6226 yds SSS 70
Recs Am–
Pro–63 J Farmer
V'trs WE/ BH–restricted SOC
Fees £10 D–£14 (£12 D–£16) (1990)
Loc 1 mile S of Inverness

Kingussie (1891)

Gynack Road, Kingussie PH21 1LR
Tel **(0540) 661374 (Clubhouse)**
Mem 620
Sec WM Cook (0540) 661600
Holes 18 L 5555 yds SSS 67
Recs Am–64 N Robertson (1989)
Pro–68 AG Havers
V'trs U
Fees £8 D–£11
Loc 1/2 mile from Kingussie, off A9

Newtonmore (1893)

Newtonmore PH20 1AT
Tel **(05403) 328**
Mem 420
Sec RJ Cheyne
Holes 18 L 5880 yds SSS 68
Recs Am–64 I Barclay
V'trs U SOC
Fees D–£9 (£12) W–£36
Loc 46 miles S of Inverness

Sconser (1964)

Between Broadford and Sligachan, Isle of Skye
Mem 120
Sec I Stephen (0478) 2000
Holes 9 L 4796 yds SSS 63
Recs Am–62 M Whatley
V'trs U
Fees £4 D–£6 W–£12
Loc Between Broadford and Portree

Skeabost (1982)

Public
Skeabost Bridge, Isle of Skye IV5 19NP
Mem 150
Sec S MacNab Stuart (047 032) 202 (Skeabost House Hotel)
Holes 9 L 3224 yds SSS 62
V'trs U
Fees £3
Loc 6 miles from Portree on Dunvegan road

Torvean (1962)

Public
Glenurquhart Road, Inverness
Tel **(0463) 237543 (Starter)**
(0463) 236648 (Clubhouse)
Mem 403
Sec AS Menzies (0463) 225651
Holes 18 L 5784 yds SSS 68
Recs Am–67 DC Walker
Pro–70 R Weir
V'trs U
Fees £6.60 (£7.70)
Loc W side of Inverness on A82

Traigh

5, Back of Keppoch, Arisaig
Tel **(06875) 262**
Mem 20
Sec T McEachen
Holes 9 L 2100 yds SSS 68
V'trs U
Fees £2 (£5)
Loc 3 miles W of Arisaig on A830 Fort William–Mallaig road

For list of abbreviations see page 487.

Nairnshire

Nairn (1887)

Seabank Road, Nairn IV12 4HB
Tel   (0667) 52103
Mem   830
Sec   D Patrick (0667) 53208
Pro   R Fyfe (0667) 52787
Holes 18 L 6556 yds SSS 71
       9 L 1918 yds
Recs   Am–66 S Tomisson
       Pro–65 D Small
V'trs U SOC
Fees   £18 (£22) W–£50
Loc   Nairn West Shore

Nairn Dunbar (1899)

Lochloy Road, Nairn
Tel   (0667) 52741
Mem   500
Sec   Mrs SJ McLennan
Pro   BR Mason (0667) 53964
Holes 18 L 6431 yds SSS 71
Recs   Am–68 W Barron
       Pro–63 RM Collinson
V'trs U
Fees   £12 (£15) W–£65
Loc   In Nairn

Ross & Cromarty

Alness (1904)

Ardross Rd, Alness
Tel   (0349) 883877
Mem   300
Sec   JG Miller
Holes 9 L 2436 yds SSS 63
Recs   Am–62 C MacIver (1983)
       C Taylor (1989)
V'trs U exc Mon–NA 5–7pm SOC
Fees   £3 (£4)
Loc   ¼ mile N of Alness

Fortrose & Rosemarkie (1888)

Ness Road East, Fortrose
Tel   (0381) 20529
Mem   725
Sec   Mrs M Collier
Pro   GA Hampton (0381) 20733
Holes 18 L 5973 yds SSS 69
Recs   Am–64 G Paterson
V'trs U SOC
Fees   £9 D–£12.50 (£12) 5D–£33
Loc   Black Isle. Inverness 12 miles

Gairloch (1898)

Gairloch IV21 2BQ
Tel   (0445) 2407
Mem   285
Sec   JM Dingwall
Holes 9 L 2093 yds SSS 63
V'trs U
Fees   D–£6 W–£20
Loc   60 miles W of Dingwall

Invergordon (1954)

King George Street, Invergordon
Tel   (0349) 852116
Mem   140 50(L) 60(J)
Sec   I Hosie
Holes 9 L 6028 yds SSS 69
Recs   Am–65 D Ross
V'trs U SOC
Fees   £3 (£4)
Loc   Invergordon

Lochcarron (1911)

Lochcarron, Strathcarron
Mem   124
Sec   GB Jones (05202) 259
Holes 9 L 3470 yds SSS 62
V'trs U
Fees   £3
Loc   ½ mile E of Lochcarron

Muir of Ord (1875)

Great North Road, Muir of Ord
IV6 7SX
Tel   (0463) 870825
Mem   687
Sec   Mrs C Moir
Pro   JT Hamilton (0463) 870601
Holes 18 L 5202 yds SSS 65
Recs   Am–62 S McIntosh (1989)
V'trs U SOC
Fees   D–£8 (£9) W–£35
Loc   15 miles N of Inverness on
       A862 or A9/ A832

Strathpeffer Spa (1888)

Strathpeffer IV14 9AS
Tel   (0997) 21219
Mem   300 60(L) 80(J)
Sec   N Roxburgh (0997) 21396
Holes 18 L 4792 yds SSS 65
Recs   Am–60 D Krzyzanowski
       Pro–66 A Herd
V'trs U SOC
Fees   £8 D–£10 5D–£30
Loc   ¼ mile N of Strathpeffer

Tain (1890)

Tain
Tel   (0862) 2314
Mem   450
Sec   WW Russell
Pro   None
Holes 18 L 6222 yds SSS 70
Recs   Am–66 J Miller, S Shaw,
       K Berry
V'trs U
Fees   £8 D–£12 (£9 D–£14)
Loc   35 miles N of Inverness

Tarbat (1908)

Portmahomack
Tel   (0862 87) 236
Mem   160
Sec   D Wilson
Holes 9 L 2328 yds SSS 63
Recs   Am–63 D Mackay
V'trs UH Sun–NA SOC
Fees   D–£4 (D–£5)
Loc   6 miles SE of Tain

Sutherland

Bonar-Bridge & Ardgay (1904)

Bonar–Bridge, Ardgay
Mem   100
Sec   A Turner (054 982) 248
       H Sutherland
Holes 9 L 4626 yds SSS 63
Recs   Am–66 D Mackenzie (1989)
V'trs U
Fees   D–£4
Loc   ½ mile N of Bonar-Bridge on A9

Brora (1891)

Golf Road, Brora KW9 6QS
Tel   (0408) 21417
Mem   390
Sec   H Baillie (0408) 21436
Holes 18 L 6110 yds SSS 69
Recs   Am–61 J Miller
       Pro–67 D Huish
V'trs U exc comp days –H for open
       comps SOC
Fees   D–£10 W–£45 M–£75
Loc   68 miles N of Inverness (A9)

Durness (1988)

Public
Balnakeil, Durness
Mem   80
Sec   Mrs L Mackay (097 181) 364
Holes 9 L 5468 yds SSS 68
Recs   Am–73 J Miller, C Pritchard,
       RR Macdonald (1988)
V'trs U
Fees   £5 W–£20 F–£30
Loc   57 miles NW of Lairg on A838

Golspie (1889)

Ferry Road, Golspie
Tel   (04083) 3266
Mem   420
Sec   JL Catchpole
Holes 18 L 5836 yds SSS 68
Recs   Am–65 J Miller
       Pro–65 D Huish
V'trs U SOC
Fees   D–£10 W–£50
Loc   11 miles N of Dornoch

Helmsdale

Helmsdale
Tel   (043) 12240
Sec   J Mackay, Ivybank, Dunrobin
       Street
Holes 9
V'trs U
Fees   £3 (£3)

Royal Dornoch (1877)

Golf Road, Dornoch IV25 3LW
Tel   (0862) 810219
Mem   650 180(L) 25(J)
Sec   ICR Walker
Pro   WE Skinner (0862) 810902
Holes C'ship 18 L 6581 yds SSS 72
       Struie 18 L 5242 yds SSS 66

For list of abbreviations see page 487.

Recs	Am–66 DWR Chalmers
	Pro–66 A Webster
V'trs	U
Fees	On application
Loc	51 miles N of Inverness
Mis	Helipad by clubhouse. Airstrip nearby

Lothian Region

East Lothian

Aberlady (1912)

Aberlady
Mem	35
Sec	K Hope (0875) 7374
Holes	Play over Kilspindie course

Bass Rock (1873)

29 Marmion Road, North Berwick
EH39 4NZ
Mem	104
Sec	SH Butterworth (0620) 2038
Holes	Play over North Berwick

Burgh Links (1894)

Public
East Links, North Berwick
Tel	(0620) 2726
Mem	400
Sec	DR Montgomery (0620) 2340
Holes	18 L 6079 yds SSS 69
Recs	Am–65 D Drummond
V'trs	U
Fees	On application
Loc	Edinburgh 23 miles
Mis	Glen Club plays here

Dirleton Castle (1854)

Gullane
Tel	(0620) 843496
Mem	100
Sec	RH Atkinson
Holes	Play over Gullane courses

Dunbar (1794)

East Links, Dunbar EH42 1LP
Tel	(0368) 62317
Mem	650
Sec	AJR Poole
Pro	D Small (0368) 62086
Holes	18 L 6426 yds SSS 71
Recs	Am–66 J Grant (1989)
	Pro–64 R Weir (1989)
V'trs	U SOC
Fees	D–£15 (D–£25) (1990)
Loc	1/2 mile E of Dunbar

Gifford (1904)

Gifford
| Mem | 450 |
| Sec | DA Fantom (062 081) 267 |

Holes	9 L 6138 yds SSS 69
V'trs	Tues & Wed–NA after 4pm
	WE–NA after noon
Fees	D–£5
Loc	4 1/2 miles S of Haddington

Glen (1906)

East Links, North Berwick EH39 4LE
Mem	400
Sec	DR Montgomery (0620) 2340
Holes	Play over Burgh Links

Gullane (1882)

Gullane EH31 2BB
Tel	(0620) 843115 (Starter)
Fax	(0620) 842327
Mem	711 300(L) 50(J) 125(5)
Sec	AJB Taylor (0620) 842255
Pro	J Hume (0620) 843111
Holes	No 1 18 L 6466 yds SSS 71
	No 2 18 L 6219 yds SSS 70
	No 3 18 L 5128 yds SSS 65
	9 hole course for children
Recs	No 1 Am–65 ME Lewis
	Pro–64 RDBM Shade
	No 2 Am–64 RCH Robertson
	Pro–66 H Bannerman
V'trs	U
Fees	No 1 £26 D–£39 (£35)
	No 2 £12 D–£18 (£15 D–£23)
	No 3 £8 D–£12 (£10 D–£15)
	Children's course free
Loc	18 miles E of Edinburgh on A198

Haddington (1865)

Public
Amisfield Park, Haddington
Tel	(062 082) 3627
Mem	320
Sec	T Shaw (062 082) 2584/ 3627
Pro	J Muir (062 082) 2727
Holes	18 L 6280 yds SSS 70
Recs	Am–65 S Stephens
V'trs	WD–U WE–U exc 10–12 and 2–4pm
Fees	£6.25 D–£9 (£8 D–£11.50) (1989)
Loc	17 miles E of Edinburgh on A1. 3/4 mile E of Haddington

The Honourable Company of Edinburgh Golfers (1744)

Muirfield, Gullane EH31 2EG
Tel	(0620) 842123
Mem	695
Sec	Gp Capt JR Prideaux
Holes	18 L 6601 yds SSS 73 (Championship 6963 yds)
Recs	Am–71 DED Neave
	Pro–63 R Davis (1987)
V'trs	WD–Tues/ Thurs/ Fri am only WE/ BH–NA I H SOC
Fees	£45 D–£60
Loc	NE outskirts of Gullane, opposite sign for Greywalls Hotel on A198 Edinburgh– N Berwick road

Kilspindie (1867)

Aberlady, Longniddry
EH32 0QD
Tel	(08757) 216/ 358
Mem	460 150(L) 60(J)
Sec	HF Brown (08757) 358
Pro	GJ Sked (08757) 695
Holes	18 L 4957 metres SSS 66
Recs	Am–62 RJ Humble (1990)
	Pro–60 L Vannet (1988)
V'trs	U–advisable to phone Sec. Play subject to members' demands SOC–WD
Fees	On application
Loc	Aberlady

Longniddry (1921)

Links Road, Longniddry EH32 0NL
Tel	(0875) 52141
Mem	980
Sec	GC Dempster CA
Pro	WJ Gray (0875) 52228
Holes	18 L 6219 yds SSS 70
Recs	Am–63 C Hardin (1987)
	Pro–63 P Harrison (1987)
V'trs	U H SOC–Mon–Thurs after 9.18am and 2pm
Fees	£18 D–£27
Loc	13 miles E of Edinburgh, off A1

Luffness New (1894)

Aberlady EH32 0QA
Tel	(0620) 843114
Mem	650
Sec	Lt Col JG Tedford (0620) 843336
Holes	18 L 6122 yds SSS 69
Recs	Am–63 R Winchester
	Pro–62 C O'Connor
V'trs	H or I WE/ BH–NA SOC
Fees	On application
Loc	Gullane 1 mile (A198). Longniddry 4 miles

Musselburgh (1938)

Monktonhall, Musselburgh
Tel	(031) 665 2005
Mem	500
Sec	JR Brown
Pro	T Stangoe (031) 665 7055
Holes	18 L 6623 yds SSS 72
Recs	Am–65 JM Noon
	Pro–67 EC Brown, B Devlin G Cunningham, A Jacklin
V'trs	U
Loc	1 mile S of Musselburgh

Musselburgh Old Course

Silver Ring Clubhouse, Millhill, Musselburgh
Mem	70
Sec	W Finnigan
Holes	9 L 5380 yds SSS 67
Recs	Am–67 P Hosie
V'trs	WD/ BH–U WE–U after 10am
Fees	18 holes–£2.40
Loc	7 miles E of Edinburgh on A1

North Berwick (1832)

West Links, Beach Road, North Berwick
Tel	(0620) 2135
Mem	300
Sec	R Russell
Pro	D Huish (0620) 3233
Holes	18 L 6315 yds SSS 70
Recs	Am–65 E O'Connell
	Pro–63 G Laing
V'trs	U H
Fees	£15 D–£22 (£22 D–£31.50)
Loc	24 miles E of Edinburgh

Royal Musselburgh (1774)

Prestongrange House, Prestonpans
Tel	(0875) 810276
Mem	700
Sec	RS Gordon
Pro	A Minto (0875) 810139
Holes	18 L 6237 yds SSS 70
V'trs	WD–U WE–M
Fees	£12 D–£20 (£20)
Loc	8 miles SE of Edinburgh on A198 North Berwick road
Mis	Electric buggies for hire

Tantallon (1853)

32 Westgate, North Berwick EH39 4AH
Tel	(0620) 2114
Mem	300
Sec	GA Milne
Holes	Play over North Berwick West Links

Thorntree (1856)

Prestongrange House, Prestonpans
Mem	100
Sec	J Hanratty
Holes	Play over Royal Musselburgh course

Winterfield

Public
Back Road, Dunbar
Tel	(0368) 62280
Mem	300
Sec	M O'Donnell (0368) 62564
Pro	J Sandilands (0368) 63562
Holes	18 L 5053 yds SSS 65
Recs	Am–61 R Walkinshaw, J Huggan Pro–65 SWT Murray
V'trs	U
Fees	On application–phone Pro
Loc	W side of Dunbar

Midlothian

Baberton (1893)

Juniper Green, Edinburgh EH14 5DU
Tel	(031) 453 3361
Mem	800
Sec	DM McBain (031) 453 4911
Pro	K Kelly
Holes	18 L 6098 yds SSS 69
Recs	Am–64 RW Bradly Pro–62 B Barnes
V'trs	M SOC–WD
Loc	5 miles W of Edinburgh

Braidhills No 1 (1893)

Public
Edinburgh
Tel	(031) 447 6666 (Starter) (031) 661 5351 (Ext 209)
Pro	J Boath (031) 447 8205
Holes	18 L 5239 yds SSS 68
Recs	Am–65
V'trs	U–phone bookings not accepted
Loc	3 miles S of Edinburgh

Braidhills No 2 (1894)

Public
Edinburgh
Tel	(031) 447 6666 (Starter) (031) 661 5351 (Ext 209)
Pro	J Boath (031) 447 8205
Holes	18 L 4832 yds SSS 63
Recs	Am–65
V'trs	U–phone bookings not accepted
Loc	3 miles S of Edinburgh
Mis	Open Apr–Oct only

Braids United (1897)

Braid Hills Approach, Edinburgh 10
Tel	(031) 447 3327
Mem	100
Sec	G Hind (031) 445 2044
Holes	Play over Braids 1 and 2

Broomieknowe (1906)

36 Golf Course Road, Bonnyrigg EH19 2HZ
Tel	(031) 663 9317
Mem	500
Sec	JL Carson
Pro	M Patchett (031) 660 2035
Holes	18 L 5754 yds SSS 68
Recs	Am–64 P Gallagher Pro–64 J Hamilton, A Horne, J Hume, WB Murray
V'trs	WD–U WE/ BH–NA
Fees	£12 (£15)
Loc	7 miles S of Edinburgh

Bruntsfield Links Golfing Society (1761)

32 Barnton Avenue, Davidson's Mains, Edinburgh EH4 6JH
Tel	(031) 336 2006
Mem	1000
Sec	MW Walton (031) 336 1479
Pro	B Mackenzie (031) 336 4050
Holes	18 L 6407 yds SSS 71
Recs	Am–69 AGG Miller
V'trs	WD–M before 5pm –H after 5pm SOC
Fees	On application
Loc	3 miles W of Edinburgh

Carrick Knowe (1930)

Public
Glendevon Park, Edinburgh 12
Tel	(031) 337 1096 (Starter) (031) 661 5351 (Ext 209)
Holes	18 L 6299 yds SSS 70

Recs	Am–64 R Bradley
V'trs	U–phone bookings not accepted
Fees	£5 (1990)
Loc	5 miles W of Edinburgh
Mis	Carrickvale Club plays here

Craigentinny (1891)

Public
Edinburgh
Tel	(031) 554 7501 (Starter) (031) 661 5351 (Ext 209)
Holes	18 L 5418 yds SSS 66
Recs	Am–64
V'trs	U–phone bookings not accepted
Fees	On application
Loc	2½ miles E of Edinburgh
Mis	Lochend Club plays here

Craigmillar Park (1895)

1 Observatory Road, Edinburgh EH9 3HG
Tel	(031) 667 2837
Mem	460 100(L) 70(J) 38(5)
Sec	Mrs JH Smith (031) 667 0047
Pro	B McGhee (031) 667 0047
Holes	18 L 5846 yds SSS 68
V'trs	WD–I or H before 3.30pm WE/ BH–NA
Fees	On application
Loc	Blackford, Edinburgh

Dalmahoy

Dalmahoy, Kirknewton EH27 8EB
Tel	(031) 333 4105
Sec	Ms J Wilson
Pro	S Maxwell
Holes	East 18 L 6664 yds SSS 72 West 18 L 5386 yds SSS 66
Recs	East Am–68 S Smith Pro–62 B Barnes
Fees	On application
Loc	7 miles W of Edinburgh on A71

Duddingston (1895)

Duddingston, Edinburgh EH15 3QD
Tel	(031) 661 1005
Mem	580
Sec	JC Small (031) 661 7688
Pro	A McLean (031) 661 4301
Holes	18 L 6647 yds SSS 72
Recs	Am–64 G Macgregor Pro–65 S Torrance
V'trs	WD–I H SOC–Tues & Thurs
Fees	£16 Soc–£13.50
Loc	Duddingston Road West

Glencorse (1890)

Milton Bridge, Penicuik EH26 0RD
Tel	(0968) 77177
Mem	400
Sec	DA McNiven (0968) 77189
Pro	C Jones (0968) 76481
Holes	18 L 5205 yds SSS 66
Recs	Am–61 G Jack (1990) Pro–61 A Brooks (1990)
V'trs	WD before 4pm SOC–WD
Fees	£10 (£15)
Loc	8 miles S of Edinburgh

Kingsknowe (1908)

326 Lanark Road, Edinburgh EH14 2JD
Tel	**(031) 441 1144**
Mem	728
Sec	S McMichael (031) 441 1145
Pro	W Bauld (031) 441 4030
Holes	18 L 5966 yds SSS 69
Recs	Am–63 JJ Little
	Pro–64 WB Murray
V'trs	WD–U before 4.30pm WE–M
Fees	£10 D–£15
Loc	SW Edinburgh

Liberton (1920)

297 Gilmerton Road, Edinburgh
EH16 5UJ
Tel	**(031) 664 8580**
Mem	815
Sec	JM Jackson (031) 664 3009
Pro	To be appointed
Holes	18 L 5299 yds SSS 66
Recs	Am–61 RMF Jack, D Rennie
	Pro–63 JL Brash
V'trs	Tues–Thurs–NA after 5pm WE/
	BH–No visiting clubs
Fees	£11 (£18)
Loc	3 miles S of Edinburgh

Lothianburn (1893)

Biggar Road, Edinburgh
Tel	**(031) 445 2206**
Mem	430 75(L) 75(J) 50(5)
Sec	EW Horberry (031) 445 5067
Pro	P Morton (031) 445 2288
Holes	18 L 5750 yds SSS 69
Recs	Am–63 PW Lamb (1983)
V'trs	WD–U before 5pm –M after
	5pm WE–NA SOC
Fees	£7.50 D–£10 (£10 D–£13.50)
Loc	Nr city boundary, on A702.
	Lothianburn exit from
	Edinburgh by–pass

Merchants of Edinburgh (1907)

Craighill Gardens, Morningside,
Edinburgh EH10 5PY
Tel	**(031) 447 1219**
Mem	730
Sec	AM Montgomery (031) 447 7093
Pro	CA Imlah (031) 447 8709
Holes	18 L 4889 yds SSS 64
Recs	Am–61 WJ Jeffrey Jr
V'trs	M or I SOC
Fees	£6 D–£8
Loc	SW of Edinburgh

Mortonhall (1892)

231 Braid Road, Edinburgh EH10 6PB
Tel	**(031) 447 2411**
Mem	500
Sec	PT Ricketts (031) 447 6974
Pro	DB Horn (031) 447 5185
Holes	18 L 6557 yds SSS 71
Recs	Am–66 C Cassells
	Pro–68 G Cunningham
V'trs	I
Fees	£15 (£20)

Murrayfield (1896)

43 Murrayfield Road, Edinburgh
EH12 6EU
Tel	**(031) 337 1009**
Mem	775
Sec	JP Bullen (031) 337 3478
Pro	J Fisher (031) 337 3479
Holes	18 L 5727 yds SSS 68
Recs	Am–64 DED Neave
	Pro–63 WB Murray
V'trs	WD–I WE–M
Fees	£15 D–£21
Loc	2 miles W of Edinburgh

Newbattle (1934)

Abbey Road, Eskbank, Dalkeith
EH22 3AD
Tel	**(031) 663 2123**
Mem	600
Pro	J Henderson (031) 660 1631
Holes	18 L 6012 yds SSS 69
Recs	Am–64 P Hardwick
V'trs	WD–U before 4pm WE–M
Fees	£9 D–£15
Loc	6 miles S of Edinburgh on A7
	and A68

Portobello (1853)

Public
Stanley Street, Portobello,
Edinburgh
Tel	**(031) 669 4361 (Starter)**
	(031) 661 5351 (Ext 209)
Mem	60
Holes	9 L 2419 yds SSS 32
Recs	Am–27
V'trs	U–phone bookings not
	accepted
Fees	On application
Loc	4 miles E of Edinburgh on A1

Prestonfield (1920)

6 Priestfield Road North, Edinburgh
EH16 5HS
Tel	**(031) 667 1273**
Mem	700
Sec	MDAG Dillon
Pro	B Commins (031) 667 8597
Holes	18 L 6216 yds SSS 70
Recs	Am–62 AM Dun (1976)
V'trs	Sat–NA 8–10.30am and
	12–1.30pm Sun–NA before
	11.30am SOC
Fees	£11 D–£14 (£15 D–£20) (1990)
Loc	2 miles SE of Edinburgh, off
	A68 Dalkeith road

Ratho Park (1928)

Ratho, Newbridge, Midlothian
EH28 8NX
Tel	**(031) 333 1252/ 1752**
Mem	550 98(L) 65(J)
Sec	JC McLafferty (031) 333 1752
Pro	A Pate (031) 333 1406
Holes	18 L 5900 yds SSS 68
Recs	Am–63 C Macphail (1989)
	Pro–64 WG Stowe
V'trs	U SOC–Tues/ Wed/ Thurs
Fees	£15 D–£20 (£27)
Loc	8 miles W of Edinburgh (A71)

Ravelston (1912)

24 Ravelston Dykes Road,
Edinburgh EH4 5NZ
Tel	**(031) 315 2486**
Mem	610
Sec	F Philip (031) 312 6850
Holes	9 L 5332 yds SSS 66
Recs	Am–67 DE Doig (1987)
	Pro–66 W Murray (1987)
V'trs	WD–I
Loc	Off Queensferry Road (A90),
	Forth Road Bridge road

Royal Burgess Golfing Society of Edinburgh (1735)

181 Whitehouse Road, Barnton,
Edinburgh EH4 6BY
Tel	**(031) 339 2012**
Mem	620 50(J)
Sec	JP Audis (031) 339 2075
Pro	G Yuille (031) 339 6474
Holes	18 L 6494 yds SSS 71
Recs	Am–64
	Pro–63
V'trs	I SOC
Fees	On request
Loc	Queensferry road

Silverknowes (1947)

Public
Silverknowes, Parkway, Edinburgh
EH4 5ET
Tel	**(031) 336 3843 (Starter)**
	(031) 661 5351 (Ext 209)
Holes	18 L 6210 yds SSS 70
Recs	Am–66
V'trs	U–phone bookings not
	accepted
Fees	On application
Loc	4 miles W of Edinburgh

Swanston (1927)

111 Swanston Road, Fairmilehead,
Edinburgh EH10 7DS
Tel	**(031) 445 2239**
Mem	500
Sec	J Allan
Pro	I Seith (031) 445 4002
Holes	18 L 5024 yds SSS 65
Recs	Am–63 G Millar
V'trs	U exc comp days–NA WE–NA
	after 1pm
Fees	£6 D–£8 (£8 D–£12)
Loc	W of Edinburgh, on Biggar
	road (A702)

Torphin Hill (1895)

Torphin Road, Edinburgh
EH13 0PG
Tel	**(031) 441 1100**
Mem	450
Sec	DO Campbell
Holes	18 L 5025 yds SSS 66
Recs	Am–62 G Wilkie, AL Turner
V'trs	WD–U WE–U exc comp days
	SOC
Fees	£8 (£12)
Loc	SW boundary of Edinburgh

For list of abbreviations see page 487.

Turnhouse (1909)

154 Turnhouse Road, Corstorphine,
Edinburgh EH12 0AD
Tel   (031) 339 1014
Mem   500
Sec   AB Hay (031) 655 6119
Pro   K Whitson (031) 339 7701
Holes 18 L 6171 yds SSS 69
Recs   Am–65 E McIntosh (1990)
       Pro–64 D Huish
V'trs M or by arrangement
Fees   On application
Loc   Turnhouse Road (A9080)

West Lothian

Bathgate (1892)

Edinburgh Road, Bathgate EH48 1BA
Tel   (0506) 52232
Mem   492
Sec   HG Smith (0506) 630505
Pro   S Strachan (0506) 630553
Holes 18 L 6326 yds SSS 70
Recs   Am–64 J McLean
V'trs U
Fees   £10 (£15)
Loc   Bathgate

Deer Park CC (1978)

Carmondean, Livingston EH54 9PG
Tel   (0506) 38843 (Steward)
       (0506) 37800
Mem   400
Sec   W Yule
Pro   W Yule
Holes 18 L 6636 yds SSS 72
Recs   Am–72
V'trs U
Fees   £5 (£8.50)
Loc   Knightsridge, N of Livingston
       New Town, nr M8

Dundas Park (1957)

3 Loch Place, South Queensferry
EH30 9NG
Tel   (031) 331 1601
Mem   450
Sec   RH Crowe
Holes 9 L 5510 metres SSS 69
Recs   Am–66 J McLaren
V'trs M I SOC
Loc   Dundas Estate (Private), S of
       Queensferry on A8000

Greenburn (1953)

6 Greenburn Road, Fauldhouse
EH47 9HG
Tel   (0501) 70292
Mem   500
Sec   D Watson (0501) 71154
Pro   H Ferguson (0501) 71187
Holes 18 L 6210 yds SSS 71
Recs   Am–66 B McGlinchey,
       B Watson
V'trs U
Fees   £7 (£8)
Loc   4 miles S of M8 Junction 4
       (East) or Junction 5 (West)

Harburn (1921)

West Calder EH55 8RS
Tel   (0506) 871256
Mem   486 51(L) 97(J)
Sec   F Vinter (0506) 871131
Pro   R Redpath (0506) 871582
Holes 18 L 5853 yds SSS 68
Recs   Am–62 M Kirk
V'trs U
Fees   £9 (£12.50)
Loc   2 miles S of West Calder

Linlithgow (1913)

Braehead, Linlithgow
Tel   (0506) 842585
Mem   400
Pro   D Smith (0506) 844356
Holes 18 L 5858 yds SSS 68
Recs   Am–64 J Cuddihy (1975)
       Pro–65 J White (1988)
V'trs U
Fees   £9 D–£12 (£12 D–£15)
Loc   SW of Linlithgow

Niddry Castle (1983)

Winchburgh
Sec   AM Lamont (0506) 890185
Holes 9 L 5476 yds SSS 67
V'trs U
Fees   £4 (£6) (1989)
Loc   Winchburgh

Polkemmet (1981)

Public
Whitburn, Bathgate EH47 0AD
Tel   (0501) 43905
Holes 9 L 2967 metres SSS 37
V'trs U
Fees   £1.70 (£2.20)
Loc   Between Whitburn and Harthill
       on B7066
Mis   15–bay driving range

Pumpherston (1895)

Drumshoreland Road, Pumpherston
Tel   (0506) 32869
Mem   265 4(L) 78(J)
Sec   AH Docharty (0506) 854652
Holes 9 L 5154 yds SSS 65
Recs   Am–61 I Loch Jr (1987)
V'trs M
Loc   14 miles W of Edinburgh

Uphall

Uphall
Tel   (0506) 856404
Mem   500
Sec   A Dobie
Holes 18 L 5567 yds SSS 67
V'trs U
Fees   £9 D–£15 (£12 D–£20)
Loc   Livingston 2 miles

West Lothian (1892)

Airngath Hill, by Linlithgow EH49 7RH
Tel   (0506) 826030
Mem   500
Sec   TB Fraser (0506) 825476

Holes 18 L 6578 yds SSS 71
Recs   Am–64 AG O'Neill (1990)
       Pro–68 J Farmer (1980)
V'trs U
Fees   £9 D–£12 (£11 D–£18)
Loc   1 mile S of Linlithgow, towards
       Bo'ness

Orkney & Shetland Region

Orkney (1889)

Grainbank, Kirkwall, Orkney
Tel   (0856) 2457
Mem   214
Sec   JR Sim (0856) 2435
Holes 18 L 5406 yds SSS 68
Recs   Am–65 KD Peace
       Pro–71 I Smith
V'trs U
Fees   £8 W–£30 F–£40
Loc   1 mile W of Kirkwall

Shetland (1894)

PO Box 18, Lerwick, Shetland
Tel   (059 584) 369
Mem   324
Sec   LE Groat (Mgr) (059) 3065
Holes 18 L 5776 yds SSS 70
V'trs U
Fees   £5
Loc   3½ miles N of Lerwick

Stromness (1890)

Ness, Orkney
Tel   (0856) 850772
Mem   120
Sec   FJ Groundwater (0856) 850622
Holes 18 L 4665 yds SSS 64
Recs   Am–62 CH Poke
       Pro–66 R Macaskill
V'trs U
Fees   £6

Strathclyde Region

Argyll

Blairmore & Strone (1896)

Strone–by–Dunoon
Tel   (036984) 676
Mem   160
Sec   AB Horton (036984) 217
Holes 9 L 2122 yds SSS 62
Recs   Am–63 JA Kirby (1987)
V'trs Mon–Fri after 6pm Sat–NA
       12–4pm
Fees   £5 (£5) W–£20
Loc   High Road at Strone, N of
       Dunoon

Carradale (1900)

Carradale PA28 6QT
Tel (05833) 387
Mem 172
Sec Dr JA Duncan
Holes 9 L 2387 yds SSS 63
Recs Am–62 S Campbell
V'trs U
Fees D–£4
Loc Carradale, 15 miles N of Campbeltown

Colonsay

Public
Isle of Colonsay PA61 7YP
Tel (09512) 316
Mem 100
Sec K Byrne
Holes 18 L 4775 yds Par 72
V'trs U
Fees Full membership £5 per family per annum
Loc W coast of Colonsay, at Machrins

Cowal (1891)

Ardenslate Road, Dunoon
Tel (0369) 2216
Mem 509
Sec J Bruce (0369) 5673
Pro RD Weir (0369) 2395
Holes 18 L 6251 yds SSS 70
Recs Am–64 A Brodie
V'trs WD–U H WE–restricted SOC
Fees On application
Loc NE boundary of Dunoon

Craignure (1981)

Isle of Mull Hotel, Isle of Mull
Tel (068 02) 370/ 351
Mem 57
Sec Mrs S Campbell
Holes 9 L 4436 metres SSS 64
V'trs U
Fees D–£5
Loc Craignure 1 mile

Dalmally (1989)

Dalmally
Tel (08382) 216
Mem 78
Sec GD Kay (08382) 291
Holes 9 L 2277 yds SSS 62
Recs Am–66 K MacIntyre (1990)
V'trs U
Fees £3 (£3)
Loc 1 mile W of Dalmally on A85

Dunaverty (1889)

Southend
Mem 350
Sec J Galbraith
Pro W McMillan
Holes 18 L 4799 yds SSS 64
Recs Am–63 D Taylor, D Watson
Pro–65 EC Brown
V'trs U
Fees £5
Loc 10 miles S of Campbeltown

Glencruitten (1905)

Oban
Tel (0631) 62868/ 64115
Mem 350 105(L) 115(J)
Sec CM Jarvie (0631) 62308
Holes 18 L 4452 yds SSS 63
Recs Am–55 JM Wilson
Pro–60 H Bannerman, G Cunningham
V'trs U
Fees £8 (£9)
Loc Oban 1 mile

Innellan (1891)

Innellan
Tel (0369) 3546
Mem 200
Sec JG Arden
Holes 9 L 4878 yds SSS 63
Recs Am–63
V'trs U SOC
Fees £4 (£5)
Loc 4 miles S of Dunoon

Kyles of Bute (1907)

Tighnabruaich
Tel (0700) 811355
Mem 160
Sec JA Carruthers
Holes 9 L 2389 yds SSS 32
Recs Am–64 T Whyte (1985)
V'trs U
Fees D–£4 W–£16
Loc 26 miles W of Dunoon

Lochgilphead (1963)

Blarbuie Road, Lochgilphead
Tel (0546) 2340
Mem 210
Sec PW Tait (0546) 2149
Holes 9 L 4484 yds SSS 63
Recs Am–63 T Armour
V'trs U SOC
Fees £4 (£6)
Loc Lochgilphead ¹/₂ mile

Machrie Hotel (1891)

Port Ellen, Isle of Islay
Tel (0496) 2310 Fax (0496) 2404
Sec M Macpherson
Holes 18 L 6226 yds SSS 70
Recs Am–66 I Middleton
Pro–67 M Seymour
V'trs U
Fees £17.50 D–£30
Mis Play over Machrie course

Machrihanish (1876)

Campbeltown, Machrihanish
Tel (0586) 81213
Mem 516 158(L) 125(J)
Sec Mrs A Anderson
Pro K Campbell (0586) 81277
Holes 18 L 6228 yds SSS 70
9 hole course
Recs Am–66 SJ Campbell
Pro–65 R Walker

V'trs U
Fees £10 D–£13 (£15)
Loc 5 miles W of Campbeltown

Tarbert (1910)

Kilberry Road, Tarbert
Tel (0880) 820565
Mem 101
Sec J Reid (0880) 820389
Holes 9 L 4460 yds SSS 64
Recs Am–62 D Lamont (1990)
Pro–63
V'trs U
Fees £4 D–£5 W–£20
Loc 1 mile W of Tarbert on B8024

Tobermory (1896)

Tobermory, Isle of Mull
Mem 150
Sec Dr WH Clegg (0688) 2020
Holes 9 L 2460 yds SSS 64
Recs Am–70 D Brown (1988)
Pro–70 B Walpole (1990)
V'trs U
Fees D–£5 W–£16
Loc Tobermory, Isle of Mull
Mis Tickets from Western Isles Hotel

Vaul

Scarinish, Isle of Tiree
Mem 50
Sec N McArthur (08792) 339
Holes 9 L 3123 yds SSS 70
V'trs U exc Sun–NA
Fees £3
Loc E coast of Tiree

Ayrshire

Annanhill (1957)

Public
Irvine Road, Kilmarnock
Tel (0563) 21644
Mem 350
Sec RM Davidson (0563) 29502
Holes 18 L 6270 yds SSS 70
Recs Am–65 I McKenzie
Pro–65 J Farmer
V'trs WD/ Sun–U Sat–NA SOC–exc Sat
Fees D–£3.75 (D–£8.75)
Loc 1 mile W of Kilmarnock

Ardeer (1880)

Greenhead, Stevenston
Tel (0294) 64542
Mem 500
Sec P Watson (0294) 63630
Holes 18 L 6630 yds SSS 72
Recs Am–67 NG Walker
Pro–68 A Brooks, I Stanley, R Walker
V'trs U exc Sat–NA
Fees D–£14 (Sun £18)
Loc ¹/₂ mile off A78 N of Stevenston

Auchenharvie (1981)

Public
Moor Park Road, West Brewery Park, Saltcoats
Mem 100
Sec WJ Thomson
Pro R Rodgers (0292) 603103
Holes 9 L 5300 yds SSS 66
Recs Am–67 R Galloway, J Murphy, P Rodgers, A Wylie
V'trs WD–U WE–U after 9.30am
Fees £2.40 (£3.60)
Loc Low road between Saltcoats and Stevenston

Ballochmyle (1937)

Ballochmyle, Mauchline KA5 6LE
Tel (0290) 50469
Mem 860
Sec DG Munro
Holes 18 L 5952 yds SSS 69
Recs Am–66 NC Brown, I Guthrie, D Wallace
Pro–65 A Hunter (1987)
V'trs WD/ WE–U BH–M SOC exc Wed/ Sat/ BH
Fees D–£12.50 (£19)
Loc 1 mile S of Mauchline on B705, off A76
Mis Buggies available

Beith (1896)

Bigholm Road, Beith
Tel (050 55) 3166
Mem 380
Sec M Rattray (050 55) 2011
Holes 9 L 5580 yds SSS 67
Recs Am–64 K Ross
V'trs U exc Sat & Sun pm
Fees D–£5
Loc 1 mile E of Beith

Belleisle (1927)

Public
Ayr
Tel (0292) 41258
Sec H Diamond
Pro JS Easey (0292) 41314
Holes 18 L 6545 yds SSS 71
Recs Am–63 K Gimson
Pro–64 J Farmer
V'trs WD–U WE–H
Fees £6.40 D–£10 (£7.80 D–£12.20)
Loc S of Ayr in Belleisle Park
Mis Belleisle Club plays here

Dalmilling (1960)

Public
Westwood Avenue, Whitletts, Ayr
Tel (0292) 63893
Pro D Gemmell
Holes 18 L 5401 yds SSS 66
Recs Am–61 G McKay
V'trs U
Fees £5 D–£8 (£6.60 D–£10) (1990)
Loc NE boundary of Ayr
Mis Dalmilling Club plays here

Girvan (1900)

Public
Golf Course Road, Girvan
Tel (0465) 4272
Mem 180
Sec WB Tait (0465) 2011
Holes 18 L 5095 SSS 65
Recs Am–61 J Cannon
Pro–61 K Stevely
V'trs U
Fees £4.40 (£5.60)

Glasgow Gailes (1787)

Gailes, Irvine KA11 5AE
Tel (0294) 311347
Mem 1100
Sec DW Deas (041) 942 2011
Pro J Steven (041) 942 8507
Holes 18 L 6493 yds SSS 71
Recs Am–62 CW Green
Pro–67 R Brownlie
V'trs WD–I WE/ BH–M SOC
Fees £25 D–£30
Loc 1 mile S of Irvine

Irvine (1887)

Bogside, Irvine
Tel (0294) 78139
Mem 450
Sec A MacPherson (0294) 75979
Pro K Erskine (0294) 75626
Holes 18 L 6408 yds SSS 71
Recs Am–65 DA Roxburgh (1981)
Pro–66 R Weir (1987)
V'trs U SOC–WD
Fees £15 D–£20
Loc 1 mile N of Irvine towards Kilwinning

Irvine Ravenspark (1907)

Public
Irvine
Tel (0294) 79550
Mem 400
Sec RC Palmer (0294) 76983
Pro P Bond (0294) 76467
Holes 18 L 6496 yds SSS 71
Recs Am–66 F Moore
V'trs U
Fees £1.60 (£3.70)

Kilbirnie Place (1922)

Largs Road, Kilbirnie
Tel (0505) 683398
Mem 300
Sec A Rice
Holes 18 L 5411 yds SSS 67
Recs Am–64 G McLean
V'trs U exc Sat
Fees £3.50 Sun–£8
Loc ½ mile W of Kilbirnie

Kilmarnock (Barassie) (1887)

29 Hillhouse Road, Barassie, Troon KA10 6SY
Tel (0292) 311077
Mem 430
Sec RL Bryce (0292) 313920
Pro WR Lockie (0292) 311322
Holes 18 L 6473 yds SSS 71
Recs Am–66 JW Milligan (1988)
Pro–63 GP Emmerson, C Van der Velde (1989)
V'trs WE/ Wed–NA SOC–Tues & Thurs
Fees D–£27
Loc Opposite Barassie Station

Kilmarnock Municipal

Public
Ayr Road, Kilmarnock
Tel (0563) 21915
Mem 400
Sec F McCulloch
Holes 18 L 5460 yds SSS 69
9 hole course
Recs Am–63 S Fraser
Pro–66 E Brown
V'trs U

Largs (1891)

Irvine Road, Largs KA30 8EU
Tel (0475) 673594
Mem 800
Sec F Gilmour (0475) 672497
Pro R Stewart (0475) 686192
Holes 18 L 6257 yds SSS 70
Recs Am–C White
V'trs U
Fees £14 D–£20
Loc 1 mile S of Largs

Loudoun Gowf (1909)

Galston
Tel (0563) 820551
Mem 475
Sec TR Richmond (0563) 821993
Holes 18 L 5854 yds SSS 68
Recs Am–64 G Davidson
V'trs WD–U WE–M SOC
Fees £10 D–£15
Loc 5 miles E of Kilmarnock

Maybole

Public
Memorial Park, Maybole
Mem 100
Sec H McKay
Holes 9 L 2635 yds SSS 65 (for 18)
Recs Am–64 WW McCulloch
V'trs U
Fees £2 (£2.80) (1989)
Loc S of Maybole, off (A77) Glasgow–Stranraer road

New Cumnock (1901)

New Cumnock
Mem 250
Sec P Pollock
Holes 9 L 2365 yds SSS 63
Recs Am–65 R Hodge
V'trs U
Loc Cumnock road

Prestwick (1851)

2 Links Road, Prestwick KA9 1QG
Tel   (0292) 77404
Fax   (0292) 77255
Mem   580
Sec   DE Donaldson
Pro   FC Rennie (0292) 79483
Holes   18 L 6631 yds SSS 72
Recs   Am–68 PM Mayo, P Deeble,
          B Andrade (1987)
          Pro–67 EC Brown, C O'Connor
V'trs   WD–I on application only
Fees   On application
Loc   Prestwick Airport 1 mile, nr
          Railway Station

Prestwick St Cuthbert (1899)

East Road, Prestwick KA9 2SX
Tel   (0292) 77101
Mem   698
Sec   R Morton
Holes   18 L 6470 yds SSS 71
Recs   Am–66 G Hogg (1984)
V'trs   WD/ BH–U WE–M SOC–WD
Fees   £10 D–£15
Loc   1/2 mile E of Prestwick

Prestwick St Nicholas (1851)

Grangemuir Road, Prestwick KA9 1SN
Tel   (0292) 77608
Mem   600 125(L) 62(J)
Sec   JR Leishman
Pro   S Smith (0292) 79755
Holes   18 L 5926 yds SSS 68
Recs   Am–63 P Girvan
          Pro–63 A Johnstone
V'trs   WD–I WE/ BH–NA
Fees   On application
Loc   Prestwick

Routenburn (1914)

Largs
Tel   (0475) 673230
Mem   400
Sec   JE Smeaton (0475) 674171
Pro   R Torrance (0475) 674289
Holes   18 L 5650 yds SSS 67
Recs   Am–65 AO Harrington
          Pro–65 S Torrance
V'trs   U SOC–WD
Fees   £2.60 D–£3.70 (£6.30) W–£19

Royal Troon (1878)

Craigend Road, Troon KA10 6EP
Tel   (0292) 311555
Mem   800
Sec   JD Montgomerie
Pro   RB Anderson (0292) 313281
Holes   Old (C'ship) 18 L 7097 yds SSS
          74;
          Portland 18 L 6274 yds SSS 71
Recs   Old Am–70 CW Green,
          J Harkis
          Pro–64 G Norman Portland
          Am–65 GS Reynolds
V'trs   WD–I H Mon–Thurs only
          (H'cap limit–18) XL WE–NA

Seafield (1930)

Public
Ayr
Tel   (0292) 41258
Sec   H Diamond
Pro   JS Easey (0292) 41314
Holes   18 L 5457 yds SSS 67
Recs   Am–65 R Gibson
V'trs   U
Fees   £4.60 D–£7.10 (£5.40 D–£8.50)
Loc   S of Ayr in Belleisle Park
Mis   Belleisle Club plays here

Skelmorlie (1891)

Skelmorlie PA17 5ES
Tel   (0475) 520152
Mem   305
Sec   J Morrison
Holes   13 L 5056 yds SSS 65
Recs   Am–62 J McCreadie (1990)
          Pro–69 J Braid, G Duncan
V'trs   U exc Sat (Apr–Oct)
Fees   D–£7.50 Sun–£12
Loc   Wemyss Bay Station 1 1/2 miles

Troon Municipal

Public
Harling Drive, Troon
Tel   (0292) 312464
Pro   G Cunningham
Holes   Lochgreen 18 L 6687 yds SSS 72
          Darley 18 L 6327 yds SSS 70
          Fullarton 18 L 4784 yds SSS 63
Recs   Lochgreen Am–66 R Milligan
          Pro–65 J Chillas Darley
          Am–66 M Rossi
          Pro–66 J White Fullarton
          Am–58 A McQueen
V'trs   U SOC–exc Sat
Fees   Lochgreen/ Darley £4.80
          D–£7.60 (£5.80 D–£8.60)
          Fullarton £3 D–£3.90 (£3.60
          D–£6)
Loc   4 miles N of Prestwick at
          Station Brae

Troon Portland (1894)

1 Crosbie Road, Troon
Tel   (0292) 311555
Mem   120
Sec   J Currie (0292) 311863
Holes   Play over Portland at Royal
          Troon

Troon St Meddans (1907)

Harling Drive, Troon KA10 6NF
Mem   200
Sec   DG Baxter (0292) 313291
Holes   Play over Troon Municipal
          courses Lochgreen and Darley

Turnberry Hotel (1906)

Turnberry KA26 9LT
Tel   (0655) 31000
Sec   CJ Rouse (Gen Mgr)
Pro   RS Jamieson
Holes   Ailsa 18 L 6950 yds SSS 70
          Arran 18 L 6276 yds SSS 69
Recs   Ailsa Am–70 GK MacDonald
          Pro–63 M Hayes, G Norman
          Arran Am–66 AP Parkin
          Pro–66 J McTear
V'trs   U H after noon
Fees   On application
Loc   5 miles N of Girvan on A77
Mis   Turnberry Club plays here

West Kilbride (1893)

West Kilbride KA23 9HT
Tel   (0294) 823128
Mem   1000
Sec   ED Jefferies (0294) 823911
Pro   G Howie (0294) 823042
Holes   18 L 6452 yds SSS 71
Recs   Am–67 G Shaw (1987)
          Pro–67 J Panton
V'trs   WD–U WE–M BH–NA SOC
Fees   On application
Loc   West Kilbride

Western Gailes (1897)

Gailes, Irvine KA11 5AE
Tel   (0294) 311649
Mem   450
Sec   AK McBean
Holes   18 L 6614 yds SSS 72
Recs   Am–67 RA Muscroft (1986)
          Pro–65 B Gallacher (1986)
V'trs   WD–H exc Thurs (booking
          necessary)
Fees   £30 D–£35 (pre–booked)
Loc   3 miles N of Troon

Bute

Brodick (1897)

Brodick, Isle of Arran
Tel   (0770) 2349
Mem   525
Sec   HM Macrae
Pro   PS McCalla (0770) 2513
Holes   18 L 4404 yds SSS 62
Recs   Am–61 D Bell, A Neilson
V'trs   U SOC
Fees   D–£8
Loc   Brodick Pier 1 mile

Bute (1888)

Kingarth, Isle of Bute
Mem   115
Sec   J Burnside (070083) 648
Holes   9 L 2497 yds SSS 64
Recs   Am–65 G McArthur (1990)
V'trs   U
Fees   D–£3 W–£10
Loc   Stravanan Bay, off A845
          Rothesay–Kilchattan Bay road

For list of abbreviations see page 487.

Corrie (1892)

Corrie, Isle of Arran
Tel	(077 081) 223
Mem	220
Sec	R Craigie Aitchison
Holes	9 L 1948 yds SSS 61
Recs	Am–62 JC Reid
V'trs	U exc Sat pm
Fees	D–£3 W–£12 M–£20 (1990)
Loc	6 miles N of Brodick

Lamlash (1889)

Lamlash, Isle of Arran
Tel	(07706) 296
Mem	435
Sec	J Henderson (07706) 272
Holes	18 L 4681 yds SSS 63
Recs	Am–62 B Morrison
	Pro–64 R Burke
V'trs	U
Fees	D–£6 After 4pm–£4 W–£35
Loc	3½ miles S from Brodick Pier on A841

Lochranza

Lochranza, Isle of Arran
Tel	(077 083) 273
Mem	20
Sec	EG Riley
Holes	9 L 1700 yds SSS
Recs	Am–26 GM Anderson
V'trs	U–novices welcome

Machrie Bay (1891)

Machrie Bay, Brodick, Isle of Arran KA27 8DZ
Tel	(077 084) 267
Mem	160
Sec	Mrs M Tunnell
Holes	9 L 2082 yds SSS 61
Recs	Am–62 A Kelso
	Pro–59 W Hagen
V'trs	U
Fees	D–£3 W–£9 F–£12
Loc	W coast, 9 miles from Brodick

Millport (1888)

Millport, Isle of Cumbrae KA28
Tel	(0475) 530311
Mem	231 96(L) 98(J)
Sec	WD Patrick (0475) 530308
Holes	18 L 5831 yds SSS 68
Recs	Am–64 AD Harrington
V'trs	U
Fees	£6.50 D–£9.50 (£7.50 D–£10.50) W–£30 F–£41 M–£112
Loc	Isle of Cumbrae. Car ferry from Largs

Port Bannatyne

Port Bannatyne, Isle of Bute
Mem	210
Sec	IL MacLeod (0700) 2009
Holes	13 L 4730 yds SSS 63
Recs	Am–61 J Ewing
	Pro–64 W Watson
V'trs	U
Fees	£5.50 (£5.50)
Loc	2 miles N of Rothesay

Rothesay (1892)

Canada Hill, Rothesay, Isle of Bute
Tel	(0700) 2244
Mem	300
Sec	J Barker (0700) 3744
Pro	J Dougal (0700) 3554
Holes	18 L 5358 yds SSS 67
Recs	Am–63 G Murray (1984)
	Pro–72 RDBM Shade (1968)
V'trs	U (Parties welcome)
Fees	£8.50 (£11.50) W–£40

Shiskine (1896)

Blackwaterfoot, Isle of Arran
Tel	(077086) 226
Mem	244 76(L) 22(J)
Sec	JR Liddell (Match Sec) (077086) 313
Holes	12 L 2990 yds SSS 42
Recs	Am–39 J Melvin, J Brown
	Pro–36 DH McGillivray
V'trs	U SOC
Fees	£4 (£4.50) W–£25 (1989)
Loc	11 miles from Brodick
Mis	Links course

Whiting Bay (1895)

Whiting Bay, Isle of Arran
Tel	(07707) 487
Mem	290
Holes	18 L 4405 yds SSS 63
Recs	Am–63 JD Simpson, D Burn
V'trs	U
Fees	D–£4 W–£17 F–£25 M–£40

Dunbartonshire

Bearsden (1891)

Thorn Road, Bearsden G61 4BE
Tel	(041) 942 2351
Mem	600
Sec	WS Chalmers
Holes	9 L 6014 yds SSS 69
Recs	Am–64 D MacLeod
V'trs	M
Loc	7 miles NW of Glasgow

Cardross (1895)

Cardross, Dumbarton G82 5LB
Tel	(0389) 841213
Mem	800
Sec	R Evans CA (0389) 841754
Pro	R Craig (0389) 841350
Holes	18 L 6466 yds SSS 71
Recs	Am–65 JLS Kinloch (1981)
	Pro–65 J White (1990)
V'trs	WD–U WE–M SOC
Fees	£13 D–£20
Loc	4 miles W of Dumbarton

Clober (1951)

Craigton Road, Milngavie, Glasgow G62 7HP
Tel	(041) 956 1685
Mem	575
Holes	18 L 5068 yds SSS 65
Recs	Am–61 PW Smith, J Graham

V'trs	WD–U before 4pm WE–M BH–NA SOC
Fees	£7
Loc	7 miles NW of Glasgow

Clydebank & District (1905)

Hardgate, Clydebank
Tel	(0389) 73289
Mem	780
Sec	W Manson (0389) 72832
Pro	C Elliott
Holes	18 L 5815 yds SSS 68
Recs	Am–64 D Galbraith
V'trs	WD–I
Fees	D–£12 W–£40 M–£75
Loc	2 miles N of Clydebank

Clydebank Municipal

Public

Overtoun Road, Dalmuir, Clydebank
Tel	(041) 952 6372
Sec	Clydebank District Council (041) 941 1331
Pro	R Bowman (041) 952 6372
Holes	18 L 5349 yds SSS 66
Recs	Am–63 J Semple
	Pro–64 R Bowman
V'trs	U exc Sat 11am–2.30pm
Fees	Mon–Sat £3 Sun–£3.45
Loc	8 miles W of Glasgow
Mis	Clydebank Overtoun Club plays here

Cumbernauld (1977)

Public

Palacerigg Country Park, Cumbernauld G67 3HU
Tel	(0236) 734969
Mem	250
Sec	JH Dunsmore
Holes	18 L 6412 yds SSS 71
Recs	Am–67 G Wilson
	Pro–66 J Farmer
V'trs	U SOC–WD only
Fees	£6 (£7)
Mis	Palacerigg GC plays here

Dougalston (1977)

Milngavie, Glasgow
Tel	(041) 956 5750
Sec	W McInnes
Holes	18 L 6269 yds SSS 71
Recs	Am–71 J Carnegie, J McLaren (1987) Pro–73 B Barnes
V'trs	U SOC
Fees	£6 (£7)
Loc	7 miles N of Glasgow on A81
Mis	Craigmaddie Club plays here

Douglas Park (1897)

Hillfoot, Bearsden
Tel	(041) 942 2220
Mem	400 250(L) 100(J)
Sec	DN Nicholson
Pro	D Scott (041) 942 1482
Holes	18 L 5957 yds SSS 69
Recs	Am–64 F Giovannetti
	Pro–66 A Hunter, S McAllister
V'trs	M SOC
Loc	Bearsden, at Hillfoot Station

For list of abbreviations see page 487.

Dullatur (1896)

Dullatur, Glasgow G68 0AR
Tel   (0236) 723230
Mem   420 60(L)
Sec   W Laing (0236) 27847
Pro   D Sinclair
Holes   18 L 6253 yds SSS 70
Recs   Am–62 D Kane Jr (1989)
           Pro–68 J Farmer
V'trs   WD–U WE–M SOC
Fees   £14 After 1.30pm–£8
Loc   3 miles N of Cumbernauld

Dumbarton (1888)

Broadmeadow, Dumbarton
Tel   (0389) 32830
Mem   500
Sec   R Turnbull
Holes   18 L 5981 yds SSS 69
Recs   Am–64 CW Green
V'trs   WD–U WE/ BH–M
Fees   D–£10
Loc   3/4 mile N of Dumbarton

Glasgow (1787)

Killermont, Bearsden, Glasgow
G61 2TW
Tel   (041) 942 2340
Mem   800
Sec   DW Deas (041) 942 2011
Pro   J Steven (041) 942 8507
Holes   18 L 5968 yds SSS 69
Recs   Am–63 JS Cochran
           Pro–65 H Weetman
V'trs   M
Loc   4 miles NW of Glasgow

Hayston (1926)

Campsie Road, Kirkintilloch,
Glasgow G66 1RN
Tel   (041) 776 1244
Mem   445 70(L) 60(J)
Sec   R McCambley (041) 776 4688
Pro   S Barnett (041) 775 0882
Holes   18 L 6042 yds SSS 69
Recs   Am–62 LS Mann
           Pro–69 K Stables
V'trs   WD–I before 4.30pm –M after
           4.30pm WE–M SOC
Fees   £12
Loc   1 mile N of Kirkintilloch
Mis   Buggies for hire

Helensburgh (1893)

25 East Abercromby Street,
Helensburgh G84 9JD
Tel   (0436) 74173
Mem   825
Sec   Mrs AC McEwan
Pro   J Farrell (0436) 75505
Holes   18 L 6058 yds SSS 69
Recs   Am–64 A Scott
           Pro–65 RT Drummond,
           D Chillas, B Marchbank
V'trs   WD–U WE–NA
Fees   £8 D–£12
Loc   25 miles W of Glasgow

Hilton Park (1927)

Auldmarroch Estate, Stockiemuir
Road, Milngavie G62 7HB
Tel   (041) 956 5124/ 1215
Mem   1200
Sec   Mrs JA Dawson (041) 956 4657
Pro   W McCondichie (041) 956
           5125
Holes   Hilton 18 L 6043 yds SSS 70
           Allander 18 L 5374 yds SSS 67
Recs   Hilton Am–65 ND Kelly
           Pro–64 AF Anderson Allander
           Am–66 I Weir
           Pro–63 F Morris, N Wood
V'trs   WD–U before 5pm WE–M
Fees   On application
Loc   8 miles N of Glasgow

Kirkintilloch (1894)

Todhill, Campsie Road, Kirkintilloch
G66 1RN
Tel   (041) 776 1256
Mem   420 92(L) 104(J) 35(5)
Sec   IM Gray (041) 775 2387
Holes   18 L 5269 yds SSS 66
Recs   Am–61 S Shaw
           Pro–68 R Weir
V'trs   M
Fees   SOC–£7 D–£12
Loc   7 miles N of Glasgow

Milngavie (1895)

Laighpark, Milngavie G62 8EP
Tel   (041) 956 1619
Mem   390
Sec   Mrs S Ness
Holes   18 L 5818 yds SSS 68
Recs   Am–64 RGB McCallum, R Blair
V'trs   M SOC
Fees   On application
Loc   NW of Glasgow

Vale of Leven (1907)

Northfield Road, Bonhill, Alexandria
Tel   (0389) 52351
Mem   450
Sec   W McKinlay (0389) 52508
Holes   18 L 5156 yds SSS 66
Recs   Am–60 G Brown (1988)
           Pro–63 EC Brown (1959)
V'trs   U exc Sat (Apr–Sept) SOC
           (max 36 members)
Fees   D–£6 (D–£10)
Loc   Off A82 at Bonhill

Windyhill (1908)

Windyhill, Bearsden
Tel   (041) 942 2349
Mem   650
Sec   AJ Miller
Pro   R Collinson (041) 942 7157
Holes   18 L 6254 yds SSS 70
Recs   Am–66 DJ Shaw
V'trs   WD–I Sun–M SOC–WD
Fees   £10
Loc   8 miles NW of Glasgow

Lanarkshire

Airdrie (1877)

Rochsoles, Airdrie
Tel   (0236) 62195
Mem   425
Pro   A McCloskey (0236) 54360
Holes   18 L 6004 yds SSS 69
Recs   Am–64 G Russo, R Marshall
V'trs   M I WE/ BH–NA SOC
Fees   D–£15
Loc   Airdrie 1 mile

Alexandra Park (1880)

Public
Sannox Gardens, Alexandra Parade,
Glasgow
Tel   (041) 556 3711
Mem   250
Sec   G McArthur
Holes   9 L 1968 yds SSS 30
V'trs   U
Fees   £1.10 (£1.40)
Loc   1/2 mile E of Glasgow

Bellshill (1905)

Orbiston, Bellshill ML4 2RZ
Tel   (0698) 745124
Mem   600
Sec   A Currie
Holes   18 L 6607 yds SSS 72
Recs   Am–68 J Simpson, A Megan,
           M Brown
           Pro–70 J McCallum
V'trs   U exc WD 5–6.30pm
Fees   £11 (£15)
Loc   10 miles S of Glasgow
           between Bellshill and
           Motherwell

Biggar (1895)

Public
Public Park, Broughton Road, Biggar
ML12
Tel   (0899) 20618 (Clubhouse)
           (0899) 20319 (Reservations)
Mem   250
Sec   WS Turnbull (0899) 20566
Holes   18 L 5416 yds SSS 66
Recs   Am–62 B Kerr (1987)
           Pro–65 W Murray (1981)
V'trs   U
Fees   £5 (£7.50)
Loc   Biggar 1/2 mile

Bishopbriggs (1906)

Brackenbrae Road, Bishopbriggs,
Glasgow G64 2DU
Tel   (041) 772 1810
Mem   400
Sec   J Magin (041) 772 8938
Holes   18 L 6041 yds SSS 69
Recs   Am–64 I Gillan, AF Dunsmore,
           S Finlayson
           Pro–63 M Miller
V'trs   M or I
Fees   £14
Loc   6 miles N of Glasgow

Blairbeth (1910)

Burnside, Rutherglen
Tel	(041) 634 3355
Mem	400
Sec	FT Henderson (041) 632 0604
Holes	18 L 5448 yds SSS 67
Recs	Am–60 DB Howard
	Pro–69 WG Cunningham
V'trs	M
Loc	1 mile S of Rutherglen

Bothwell Castle (1922)

Blantyre Road, Bothwell G71
Tel	(0698) 853177
Mem	1137
Sec	ADC Watson (0698) 852395
Pro	WA Walker (0698) 852052
Holes	18 L 6240 yds SSS 70
Recs	Am–64 F Jardine (1977)
	Pro–65 L Johnson (1986)
V'trs	WD–U 8.30am–3.30pm
Fees	£10 D–£18
Loc	3 miles N of Hamilton

Calderbraes (1893)

57 Roundknowe Road, Uddingston
Tel	(0698) 813425
Mem	300
Sec	S McGuigan (041) 773 2287
Holes	9 L 5046 yds SSS 67
Recs	Am–65 D Gilchrist (1986)
V'trs	M
Loc	Start of M74

Cambuslang (1891)

Westburn Drive, Cambuslang
G72 8ET
Tel	(041) 641 3130
Mem	200 100(L) 75(J)
Sec	W Lilly
Holes	9 L 6072 yds SSS 69
Recs	Am–65 AM Grant
V'trs	I
Loc	Cambuslang Station 3/4 mile

Carluke (1894)

Hallcraig, Carluke
Tel	(0555) 71070
Mem	460 100(L)
Sec	JH Muir (0555) 70620
Pro	A Brooks (0555) 51053
Holes	18 L 5805 yds SSS 68
Recs	Am–64 K Harrison
	Pro–64 G Cunningham,
	R Davis, W Milne
V'trs	WD–U before 4pm WE/BH–NA
Fees	£8 D–£12
Loc	Glasgow 20 miles

Carnwath (1907)

Main Street, Carnwath
Tel	(0555) 840251
Mem	380
Sec	GP Pollock (0555) 4359
Holes	18 L 5955 yds SSS 69
Recs	Am–65 B Holbrook
V'trs	U exc Sat–NA
Fees	£11 Sun–£13
Loc	Lanark 7 miles

Cathkin Braes (1888)

Cathkin Road, Rutherglen, Glasgow
G73 4SE
Tel	(041) 634 6605
Mem	880
Sec	GL Stevenson
Pro	S Bree (041) 634 0650
Holes	18 L 6266 yds SSS 71
Recs	Am–65 J Graham (1984)
	Pro–66 W Milne (1988)
V'trs	WD–I
Fees	£14
Loc	5 miles S of Glasgow
	on B759

Cawder (1933)

Cadder Road, Bishopbriggs,
Glasgow
Tel	(041) 772 7101
Mem	1200
Sec	GT Stoddart (041) 772 5167
Pro	K Stevely (041) 772 7102
Holes	Cawder 18 L 6295 yds SSS 71;
	Keir 18 L 5877 yds SSS 68
Recs	Cawder Am–68 CW Green
	Pro–65 R Weir Keir Am–63
	G Rodaks, GH Murray
V'trs	WD–U WE–NA SOC–WD
Fees	£18
Loc	Bishopbriggs Station 1 1/4 miles

Coatbridge (1971)

Public
Townhead Road, Coatbridge
Tel	(0236) 28975
Mem	300
Sec	O Dolan (0236) 26811
Pro	G Weir (0236) 21492
Holes	18 L 6020 yds SSS 69
Recs	Am–69 A Webster (1989)
V'trs	U
Fees	£1.75
Loc	Townhead

Colville Park (1922)

Jerviston Estate, Motherwell
ML1 4UG
Tel	(0698) 63017
Mem	540 64(L) 140(J)
Sec	S Connacher (0698) 65378
Pro	Golf Shop (0698) 65779
Holes	18 L 6265 yds SSS 70
Recs	Am–65 G King
	Pro–66 SD Brown
V'trs	M SOC–WD only
Fees	£12
Loc	1 mile NE of Motherwell on
	A723

Cowglen (1906)

301 Barrhead Road, Glasgow
Tel	(041) 632 0556
Mem	450
Sec	RJG Jamieson (0292) 266600
Pro	J McTear (041) 649 9401
Holes	18 L 6006 yds SSS 69
Recs	Am–63 D Barclay Howard
	Pro–63 S Torrance
V'trs	M
Loc	S side of Glasgow

Crow Wood (1925)

Muirhead, Chryston, Glasgow
Tel	(041) 799 2011
Mem	558
Sec	RD Britton (041) 248 7495
Pro	(041) 779 1943
Holes	18 L 6249 yds SSS 70
Recs	Am–64 D Chalmers
	Pro–66 J McTear
V'trs	M
Loc	5 miles NE of Glasgow

Deaconsbank (1922)

Public
Glasgow
Tel	(041) 638 7044
Sec	C Cosh
Holes	18 L 4800 yds SSS 63
V'trs	U
Fees	£3.75 (£5.50)
Loc	5 miles S of Glasgow nr
	Thornliebank

Douglas Water (1922)

Douglas Water, Lanark
Tel	(055 588) 361
Mem	150
Sec	R McMillan
Holes	9 L 2916 yds SSS 69
Recs	Am–66 H Gold
V'trs	U
Fees	£3 (£5)
Loc	7 miles SW of Lanark

Drumpellier (1894)

Drumpellier Ave, Coatbridge
ML5 1RX
Tel	(0236) 24139/ 28723
Mem	450
Sec	W Brownlie (0236) 23065/
	28538
Pro	I Collins (0236) 32971
Holes	18 L 6227 yds SSS 70
Recs	Am–65 AD Ferguson,
	G Shanks, ISS Russell
	Pro–63 R Weir
V'trs	I
Fees	£14 D–£20
Loc	8 miles E of Glasgow

East Kilbride (1900)

Chapelside Road, Nerston, East
Kilbride G74 4PF
Tel	(035 52) 20913
Mem	700
Sec	JH King (041) 641 3446
Pro	A Taylor (035 52) 22192
Holes	18 L 6419 yds SSS 71
Recs	Am–65 WF Bryce
	Pro–64 D Ingram
V'trs	M SOC
Fees	£10 D–£15
Loc	8 miles S of Glasgow

Easter Moffat (1922)

Plains, by Airdrie ML6 8NP
Tel	(0236) 842289/ 842878
Mem	450
Sec	JG Timmons

Pro	B Dunbar (0236) 843015
Holes	18 L 6221 yds SSS 70
Recs	Am–67
	Pro–66 R Shade
V'trs	WD only
Fees	£8 D–£10
Loc	3 miles E of Airdrie

Haggs Castle (1910)

70 Dumbreck Road, Dumbreck, Glasgow G41 4SN	
Tel	**(041) 427 0480**
Mem	970
Sec	I Harvey (041) 427 1157
Pro	J McAlister (041) 427 3355
Holes	18 L 6464 yds SSS 71
Recs	Am–66 J Semple (1987)
	Pro–62 S Torrance (1984)
V'trs	M SOC–Weds only
Fees	SOC–£16 D–£24
Loc	SW Glasgow

Hamilton (1892)

Riccarton, Ferniegair, by Hamilton	
Tel	**(0698) 282872**
Mem	480
Sec	PE Soutter (0698) 286131
Pro	MJ Moir (0698) 282324
Holes	18 L 6255 yds SSS 70
Recs	Am–62 G Hogg
V'trs	M or by arrangement
Fees	£12 D–£20
Loc	1½ miles S of Hamilton

Hollandbush (1954)

Public

Acre Tophead, Lesmahagow, Coalburn	
Tel	**(0555) 893484**
Mem	500
Sec	J Hamilton
Pro	I Rae (0555) 893646
Holes	18 L 6110 yds SSS 70
Recs	Am–63 G Brown
V'trs	U
Fees	£4.50 (£6.50)
Loc	Between Coalburn and Lesmahagow

King's Park (1934)

Public

150A Croftpark Avenue, Croftfoot, Glasgow G54	
Holes	9 L 2010 yds SSS 30
Recs	Am–27 I Simpson
V'trs	U
Fees	D–£1.50 (£1.20)
Loc	3½ miles S of Glasgow

Kirkhill (1910)

Greenlees Road, Cambuslang, Glasgow	
Tel	**(041) 641 3083 (Clubhouse)**
	(041) 641 8499 (Office)
Mem	570
Sec	CC Stanfield (041) 634 4276
Holes	18 L 5889 yds SSS 69
Recs	Am–63 D Martin
	Pro–68 R Weir

V'trs	WD–by prior arrangement
	WE/ BH–NA SOC
Fees	£10 D–£15
Loc	Cambuslang

Knightswood (1929)

Public

Lincoln Avenue, Glasgow G13	
Tel	**(041) 959 2131**
Mem	76
Sec	M Kelly (041) 636 1225
Holes	9 L 2736 yds SSS 33
V'trs	U
Fees	D–£1.50 (£1.20)
Loc	4 miles W of Glasgow

Lanark (1851)

The Moor, Lanark	
Tel	**(0555) 3219**
Mem	500 130(L) 200(J)
Sec	GH Cuthill
Pro	R Wallace (0555) 61456
Holes	18 L 6426 yds SSS 71 9 L 1562 yds SSS 28
Recs	Am–64 CV McInally
	Pro–64 AS Oldcorn
V'trs	WD–U until 4pm WE–M 9 hole course–U
Fees	£14 D–£20 9 hole course £2
Loc	30 miles S of Glasgow, off A74

Larkhall

Public

Burnhead Road, Larkhall	
Tel	**(0698) 881113**
Mem	400
Sec	I Gilmour
Holes	9 L 6754 yds SSS 72
Recs	Am–69 S Crolla, G Russell
V'trs	U exc Tues 5–8pm & Sat 7am–5pm
Loc	SW of Larkhall on B7109

Leadhills (1935)

Leadhills, Biggar	
Tel	**(0659) 74222**
Mem	100
Sec	H Shaw
Holes	9 L 2031 yds SSS 62
V'trs	U
Fees	£3 (£4)
Loc	6 miles off A74 at Abington
Mis	Highest golf course in Great Britain; 1500 ft above sea level

Lenzie (1889)

19 Crosshill Road, Lenzie G66 5DA	
Tel	**(041) 776 1535**
Mem	483 125(L) 125(J)
Sec	AW Jones (041) 776 4377
Pro	J McCallum (041) 777 7748
Holes	18 L 5982 yds SSS 69
Recs	Am–64 S Lindsay
	Pro–66 G Weir (1989)
V'trs	M SOC
Loc	Glasgow 6 miles

Lethamhill (1933)

Public

Cumbernauld Road, Glasgow G3	
Tel	**(041) 770 6220**
Holes	18 L 5946 yds SSS 68
Recs	Am–70 R Harker
V'trs	U
Fees	£2.50 (£3)
Loc	3 miles E of Glasgow

Linn Park (1924)

Public

Simshill Road, Glasgow G44	
Tel	**(041) 637 5871**
Mem	90
Sec	R Flanagan
Holes	18 L 4592 yds SSS 65
Recs	Am–62 J Cassidy (1989)
V'trs	U
Fees	£2.70 (£3)
Loc	4 miles S of Glasgow

Littlehill (1926)

Public

Auchinairn Road, Bishopbriggs, Glasgow	
Tel	**(041) 772 1916**
Holes	18 L 6228 yds SSS 70
Recs	Am–69
V'trs	U
Fees	£1.80 D–£3 (£2.40)
Loc	3 miles N of Glasgow

Mount Ellen (1905)

Gartcosh, Glasgow G69 9EY	
Tel	**(0236) 872277**
Mem	480
Sec	WJ Dickson
Pro	G Reilly
Holes	18 L 5525 yds SSS 68
V'trs	WD–U from 9am–4pm WE–NA
Fees	£8
Loc	8 miles NE of Glasgow

Pollok (1892)

90 Barrhead Road, Pollokshaws, Glasgow G43 1BG	
Tel	**(041) 632 1080**
Mem	500
Sec	A Mathison Boyd (041) 632 4351
Holes	18 L 6257 yds SSS 70
Recs	Am–62 G Shaw
	Pro–62 G Cunningham
V'trs	I XL WE–NA SOC–WD
Fees	£18 D–£22
Loc	3 miles SW of Glasgow on B462

Ruchill (1928)

Public

Brassey Street, Maryhill, Glasgow G20	
Mem	60
Sec	DF Campbell (041) 946 7676
Holes	9 L 2240 yds SSS 31
V'trs	U
Fees	D–£1.50 (£1.20)
Loc	2½ miles NW of Glasgow

Sandyhills (1905)

223 Sandyhills Road, Glasgow
G32 9NA
Tel   (041) 778 1179
Mem   460
Sec   G Muir CA (0698) 812203
Holes 18 L 6253 yds SSS 70
Recs   Am–65 J Hay
V'trs M SOC
Loc   4 miles E of Glasgow

Shotts (1895)

Blairhead, Benhar Road, Shotts
Tel   (0501) 20431
Mem   700
Sec   J McDermott
Pro   G Graham (0501) 22658
Holes 18 L 6290 yds SSS 70
Recs   Am–65 AJ Ferguson
       Pro–65 B Gunson
V'trs WD–U Sat–NA before 4.30pm
Fees   D–£12 (D–£15)
Loc   Between Glasgow &
       Edinburgh on B7057. M8, 1½
       miles

Strathaven (1908)

Strathaven ML10 6NL
Tel   (0357) 20539
Mem   950
Sec   AW Wallace (0357) 20421
Pro   M McCrorie (0357) 21812
Holes 18 L 6226 yds SSS 70
Recs   Am–66 RJC Milton, S Kirkland,
       AW Wallace, IA Ferguson,
       E McEwan
       Pro–63 D Huish
V'trs WD–I before 4pm WE–NA
Fees   On request
Loc   Outskirts of Strathaven, off
       Glasgow road

Strathclyde Park

Public
Mote Hill, Hamilton
Mem   110
Sec   AJ Duncan (0698) 459201
Pro   K Davidson
Holes 9 L 6294 yds SSS 70
Recs   Am–67 A Brown
V'trs U exc medal days (phone to
       book (0698) 60155)
Fees   £1.20
Loc   Hamilton
Mis   Driving range

Torrance House (1969)

Public
Strathaven Road, East Kilbride
Tel   (03552) 48638
Mem   650
Sec   D McIver (03552) 49720
Pro   J Dunlop (03552) 33451
Holes 18 L 6415 yds SSS 71
Recs   Am–67 A Pitt
       Pro–66 I Collins
V'trs U
Fees   £7
Loc   E Kilbride, on Strathaven road

Wishaw (1897)

55 Cleland Road, Wishaw
Tel   (0698) 372869
Mem   475 100(L) 50(J)
Sec   JW Douglas
Pro   JG Campbell (0698) 358247
Holes 18 L 6134 yds SSS 69
Recs   Am–64 W Denholm, A Brown
       Pro–63 A Hunter
V'trs WD after 4pm–NA Sat–NA
Fees   £8 D–£10.50 Sun–£15.50

Renfrewshire

Barshaw Municipal

Public
Barshaw Park, Paisley
Tel   (041) 889 2908
Mem   68
Sec   W Collins (041) 884 2533
Holes 18 L 5703 yds SSS 67
V'trs U
Fees   £3
Loc   1 mile E of Paisley Cross, off
       A737

Bonnyton (1957)

Eaglesham, Glasgow G76 0QA
Tel   (035 53) 2781
Mem   950
Sec   H Beach
Pro   To be appointed
Holes 18 L 6252 yds SSS 71
Recs   Am–67 F Black
       Pro–68 J Wilson
V'trs I SOC–WD
Fees   £14
Loc   SW of Eaglesham

Caldwell (1903)

Caldwell, Uplawmoor
Tel   (050 585) 329
Mem   450
Sec   DP MacLean (041) 333 9770
Pro   K Baxter (050 585) 616
Holes 18 L 6046 yds SSS 69
Recs   Am–64 JM Sharp (1974)
       Pro–63 C Innes (1987),
       G Collinson (1988), C Gilles
       (1989)
V'trs WD–Contact in advance
       before 4pm–M after 4pm
       WE–M
Fees   £12 D–£17
Loc   5 miles SW of Barrhead on
       A736 Glasgow–Irvine road

Cathcart Castle (1895)

Mearns Road, Clarkston
Tel   (041) 638 0082
Mem   700
Sec   WG Buchan (041) 638 9449
Pro   D Naylor (041) 638 3436
Holes 18 L 5832 yds SSS 68
Recs   Am–62 S Black
       Pro–64 A White
V'trs M
Loc   7 miles SW of Glasgow

Cochrane Castle (1895)

Craigston, Johnstone PA5 0HF
Tel   (0505) 20146
Mem   400
Sec   JC Cowan
Pro   S Campbell (0505) 28465
Holes 18 L 6226 yds SSS 70
Recs   Am–66 D Abercrombie
       Pro–71 S Kelly
V'trs WD–U WE–M
Fees   £8 D–£13
Loc   ½ mile S of A737. 1 mile from
       Johnstone

East Renfrewshire (1922)

Pilmuir, Newton Mearns G77 6RT
Tel   (03555) 258
Mem   450
Sec   AL Gillespie CA (041) 226
       4311
Pro   GD Clarke (03555) 206
Holes 18 L 6097 yds SSS 70
Recs   Am–64 A Dow
       Pro–65 WR Lockie
V'trs By arrangement
Loc   2 miles SW of Newton Mearns

Eastwood (1893)

Muirshield, Loganswell, Newton
Mearns, Glasgow G77 6RX
Tel   (03555) 261
Mem   650
Sec   CB Scouler (03555) 280
Pro   K McWade (03555) 285
Holes 18 L 5864 yds SSS 68
Recs   Am–62 IA Carslaw
       Pro–67 P Mills
V'trs M SOC
Loc   9 miles SW of Glasgow

Elderslie (1908)

Elderslie
Tel   (0505) 23956
Mem   400
Sec   W Muirhead
Holes 18 L 6037 yds SSS 69
Recs   Am–65 D Burns (1990)
       Pro–68 G Weir (1990)
V'trs M
Loc   Paisley 2 miles

Erskine (1904)

Bishopton PA7 5PH
Tel   (0505) 862302
Mem   400 200(L)
Sec   TA McKillop
Pro   P Thomson (0505) 862108
Holes 18 L 6287 yds SSS 70
Recs   Am–66 IG Riddell
       Pro–64 MC Douglas
V'trs WD–I WE–M
Fees   £11
Loc   5 miles NW of Paisley

Fereneze (1904)

Barrhead G78 1HJ
Tel   (041) 881 1519
Mem   700
Sec   AD Gourley (041) 221 6394

Pro A Armstrong (041) 880 7058
Holes 18 L 5821 yds SSS 68
Recs Am–64 EH McMillan
Pro–67 R Drummond, D Huish,
J McTear, R Weir
V'trs M SOC–WD
Fees SOC–£11
Loc 9 miles SW of Glasgow

Gleddoch (1974)

Langbank PA14 6YE
Tel (047 554) 304
Mem 500
Pro K Campbell (047 554) 704
Holes 18 L 6375 yds SSS 71
Recs Am–69 DJ McDougall,
D Sinclair
Pro–67 J Chillas, C Gillies
V'trs WD–U before 3.30pm SOC
Fees £20
Loc 16 miles W of Glasgow by M8/
A8

Gourock (1896)

Cowal View, Gourock PA19 6HD
Tel (0475) 31001
Mem 660 106(L) 112(J)
Sec CM Campbell (0475) 38242
Pro RM Collinson (0475) 36834
Holes 18 L 6492 yds SSS 71
Recs Am–64 N Skinner
Pro–69 D Graham
V'trs WD–I SOC
Fees On application
Loc 3 miles SW of Gourock Station

Greenock (1890)

Forsyth Street, Greenock PA16 8RE
Tel (0475) 20793
Mem 483 129(L) 128(J)
Sec EJ Black (0475) 26819
Pro G Ross (0475) 87236
Holes 18 L 5888 yds SSS 68 9 L 2149
yds SSS 32
Recs Am–64 MC Mazzoni
Pro–66 H Thomson, J Panton,
H Boyle
V'trs WD–U WE/ BH–M
Fees D–£12 (D–£15)
Loc 1 mile SW of Greenock on A8

Kilmacolm (1891)

Kilmacolm
Tel (050 587) 2139
Mem 623
Sec RF McDonald
Pro D Stewart (050 587) 2695
Holes 18 L 5890 yds SSS 68
Recs Am–64 M Stevenson
Pro–66 EC Brown
V'trs WD–U WE–M
Loc 10 miles W of Paisley

Lochwinnoch (1897)

Burnfoot Road, Lochwinnoch
Tel (0505) 842153
Mem 500
Sec Mrs E McBride
Pro G Reilly (0505) 843029

Holes 18 L 6223 yds SSS 70
Recs Am–67 IJ Gilmour, A
Hutchieson
Pro–63 M Miller (1987)
V'trs WD–U before 4.30pm WE–M
SOC
Fees £8 (£10)
Loc 9 miles S of Paisley

Old Ranfurly (1905)

Bridge of Weir
Tel (0505) 613612
Mem 375
Sec R Mitchell
Holes 18 L 6089 yds SSS 69
Recs Am–62 A Hunter (1983)
V'trs WD–I WE–M SOC
Loc Bridge of Weir

Paisley (1895)

Braehead, Paisley PA2 8TZ
Tel (041) 884 2292
Mem 750
Sec WJ Cunningham (041) 884
3903
Pro G Gilmour (041) 884 4114
Holes 18 L 6424 yds SSS 71
Recs Am–64 DW Perrie
V'trs WD–I SOC
Fees £10 D–£14
Loc Braehead, Paisley

Port Glasgow (1895)

Port Glasgow PA14 5XE
Tel (0475) 704181
Mem 375
Sec NL Mitchell (0475) 706273
Holes 18 L 5712 yds SSS 68
Recs Am–63 JW McKechnie
V'trs WD–U before 5pm –M after
5pm WE–NA SOC
Fees £8 D–£12
Loc 1 mile S of Port Glasgow

Ralston (1904)

Ralston, Paisley
Tel (041) 882 1349
Mem 440 165(L) 100(J)
Sec JW Horne (041) 883 7045
Pro D Barbour (041) 810 4925
Holes 18 L 6100 yds SSS 69
Recs Am–63 J Armstrong
V'trs M
Loc 2 miles E of Paisley

Ranfurly Castle (1889)

Golf Road, Bridge of Weir
Tel (0505) 612609
Mem 360 160(L) 100(J)
Sec J Walker
Pro A Forrow (0505) 614795
Holes 18 L 6284 yds SSS 70
Recs Am–65 WMB Brown
Pro–65 W Lockie (1989)
V'trs WD–I WE–M SOC–WD
Loc 7 miles W of Paisley

Renfrew (1894)

Blythswood Estate, Inchinnan Road,
Renfrew PA4 9EG
Tel (041) 886 6692
Mem 450 110(L) 80(J)
Sec A Kerr
Holes 18 L 6818 yds SSS 73
Recs Am–68 M Smith (1988)
Pro–70 J Chillas, WB Milne
V'trs M SOC
Fees On application
Loc Glasgow Airport 2 miles

Whinhill (1911)

Beith Road, Greenock
Tel (0475) 24694
Mem 350
Sec A Polonis
Holes 18 L 5454 yds SSS 67
Recs Am–66 W Brewster
V'trs U
Loc 2 miles S of Greenock

Whitecraigs (1905)

72 Ayr Road, Giffnock, Glasgow
G46 6SW
Tel (041) 639 1681
Mem 1150
Sec RW Miller (041) 639 4530
Pro W Watson (041) 639 2140
Holes 18 L 6230 yds SSS 70
V'trs WD–I WE–M SOC–WD
Fees £18 D–£22
Loc Whitecraigs Station 5 mins

Williamwood (1906)

Clarkston Road, Glasgow G44
Tel (041) 637 1783
Mem 680
Sec RG Cuthbert (041) 226 4311
Pro J Gardner (041) 637 2715
Holes 18 L 5878 yds SSS 68
Recs Am–61 H Kemp (1990)
Pro–61 BJ Gallacher (1974)
V'trs M
Loc 5 miles S of Glasgow

Stirlingshire

Aberfoyle (1890)

Aberfoyle
Tel (087 72) 493
Mem 300
Sec A Macdonald (087 72) 441
Holes 18 L 5204 yds SSS 66
Recs Am–64 EJ Barnard
V'trs U
Fees D–£10
Loc Braeval, Aberfoyle

Kilsyth Lennox (1900)

Tak–Ma–Doon Road, Kilsyth
Tel (0236) 822190
Mem 250
Sec AG Stevenson (0236) 823213
Holes 9 L 5930 yds SSS 69

Recs	Am–66 R Irvine (1986), W Erskine (1987)
V'trs	WD–U until 5pm –M after 5pm Sat–NA before 4pm Sun–NA before 2pm SOC–WD
Fees	£8
Loc	Glasgow 12 miles

Tayside Region

Angus

Arbroath (1903)

Public
Elliot, by Arbroath

Tel	(0241) 72069
Mem	550
Sec	J Thomson
Pro	L Ewart (0241) 75837
Holes	18 L 6078 yds SSS 69
Recs	Am–65 R Cargill
V'trs	U
Fees	£6 (£10)
Loc	1 mile S of Arbroath

Brechin (1893)

Trinity, Brechin DD9 7PD

Tel	(03562) 2383
Mem	650
Sec	AB May (03562) 2326
Pro	B Mason (03562) 5270
Holes	18 L 5267 yds SSS 66
Recs	Am–61 A Helmsley
V'trs	U ex Wed SOC
Fees	£7 D–£10.50 (£8 D–£11.50) Mon–Fri £25
Loc	1 mile N of Brechin on Aberdeen road (B966)

Buddon Links (1981)

Public
Carnoustie Golf Links, Links Parade, Carnoustie DD7 7JE

Tel	(0241) 53249 (Starter)
Sec	EJC Smith (0241) 53789
Holes	18 L 5732 yds SSS 68
V'trs	U
Fees	£5
Loc	12 miles E of Dundee by A92 or A930

Burnside

Public
Carnoustie Golf Links, Links Parade, Carnoustie DD7 7JE

Tel	(0241) 53249 (Starter)
Sec	EJC Smith (0241) 53789
Holes	18 L 6020 yds SSS 69
V'trs	WD–U WE–U after 10.30am
Fees	£13
Loc	12 miles E of Dundee, by A92 or A930

Caird Park (1926)

Public
Dundee

Tel	(0382) 453606
Mem	413
Sec	D Farquhar Jr (0382) 457217
Pro	J Black (0382) 459438
Holes	18 L 6303 yds SSS 70
Recs	Am–66 W Thompson (1987)
V'trs	U
Loc	Mains Loan, off Kingsway by–pass

Caird Park (1982)

Public
Caird Park, Dundee

Tel	(0382) 23141 (Ext 414) (Bookings Ext 295)
Pro	K Todd
Holes	Yellow 9 L 1692 yds SSS 29 Red 9 L 1983 yds SSS 29
V'trs	U
Loc	Caird Park, Dundee

Camperdown (1960)

Public
Camperdown Park, Dundee

Tel	(0382) 623398
Mem	600
Sec	R Gordon (0382) 814445
Pro	R Brown
Holes	18 L 6561 yds SSS 72
Recs	Am–68 A Morgan
V'trs	U
Fees	£6.50 (£7.50)
Loc	2 miles NW of Dundee

Carnoustie (1842)

3 Links Parade, Carnoustie DD7 7JE

Tel	(0241) 52480
Mem	900
Sec	DW Curtis
Holes	Play over Carnoustie courses

Carnoustie Caledonia (1887)

Links Parade, Carnoustie DD7 7JF

Tel	(0241) 52115
Mem	390
Sec	DC Thomson
Holes	Play over Carnoustie courses

Carnoustie Championship

Public
Links Parade, Carnoustie DD7 7JE

Tel	(0241) 53249 (Starter)
Sec	EJC Smith (0241) 53789
Holes	18 L 6936 yds SSS 74
Recs	Am– Pro–65 J Newton
V'trs	WD–H Sat–H after 1.30pm Sun–H after 11am
Fees	£30
Loc	12 miles E of Dundee, by A92 or A930

Carnoustie Ladies (1873)

Links Parade, Carnoustie

Tel	(0241) 55252
Mem	106
Sec	Mrs S Macdonald (0241) 52073
Holes	Play over Carnoustie Championship, Burnside and Buddon Links

Carnoustie Mercantile (1896)

Links Parade, Carnoustie

Tel	(0241) 52525
Mem	500
Sec	R Campbell (0241) 52020
Holes	Play over Carnoustie courses

Dalhousie (1868)

Links Parade, Carnoustie

Tel	(0241) 53208
Mem	262
Sec	GW Ellis
Holes	Play over Carnoustie courses

Downfield (1932)

Turnberry Ave, Dundee DD2 3QP

Tel	(0382) 825595
Mem	784
Sec	BF Mole
Pro	C Waddell (0382) 89246
Holes	18 L 6804 yds SSS 73
Recs	Am–67 A Lionella (1967) Pro–67 R Weir (1982)
V'trs	WD–U 9.30–noon and 2.18–4pm WE–M
Fees	£16 D–£24 (1990)
Loc	N of Dundee, off A923

Edzell (1895)

High St, Edzell, by Brechin DD9 7TF

Tel	(03564) 235
Mem	650
Sec	JM Hutchison (03564) 7283
Pro	JB Webster (03564) 462
Holes	18 L 6299 yds SSS 70
Recs	Am–65 JKA Bruce (1985) Pro–66 AJ Webster (1975)
V'trs	WD–NA 5–6.15pm WE–NA 8–10am & 12.30–2.30pm SOC
Fees	£9 D–£13.50 (£11 D–£16.50) W–£45 M–£90
Loc	6 miles NW of Brechin

Forfar (1871)

Cunninghill, Forfar DD8 2RL

Tel	(0307) 62120
Mem	475 150(L) 150(J)
Sec	PH Wallace (0307) 63773
Pro	P McNiven (0307) 65683
Holes	18 L 5497 metres SSS 69
Recs	Am–66 DM Chapman, CC Sinclair Pro–65 E Brown
V'trs	U exc Sat SOC
Fees	£13 (£20)
Loc	1½ miles E of Forfar

Kirriemuir (1908)

Kirriemuir
Tel	(0575) 72144
Mem	600
Pro	A Caira (0575) 73317
Holes	18 L 5541 yds SSS 67
Recs	Am–62 JL Adamson
V'trs	WD–U WE–M SOC
Fees	D–£12.50 After 4pm–£7
Loc	NE outskirts of Kirriemuir

Letham Grange (1987)

Colliston, Arbroath DD11 4RL
Tel	(024) 189373
Fax	(024) 189414
Mem	620
Sec	Mrs H MacDougall
Pro	D Scott (024) 189377
Holes	18 L 6789 yds SSS 73
Recs	Am–73 W Taylor (1987)
	Pro–72 J Farmer (1988)
V'trs	WD–U H exc Tues before
	10am WE–M before 10.30am
	& 1–2pm BH–U SOC
Fees	£15 D–£22.50 (£18)
Loc	4 miles N of Arbroath on A993

Monifieth Golf Links

Princes Street, Monifieth, Dundee
Tel	(0382) 532767
Mem	1500
Sec	JAR Fraser (0382) 78117
Pro	I McLeod (0382) 532945
Holes	Medal 18 L 6650 yds SSS 72
	Ashludie 18 L 5123 SSS 66
Recs	Am–63 JL Adamson
	Pro–64 S Sewgolum
V'trs	WD–U Sat–NA before 2pm
	Sun–restricted SOC
Fees	Medal £15 D–£22.50 Sun–£16
	D–£23; Ashludie £9 D–£12
	Sun–£10 D–£14
Loc	6 miles E of Dundee
Mis	Abertay, Broughty, Grange/
	Dundee and Monifieth clubs
	have playing rights over both
	courses

Montrose

Public
Traill Drive, Montrose DD10 8SW
Tel	(0674) 72932
Fax	(0674) 72634
Sec	Mrs M Stewart
Pro	K Stables (0674) 72634
Holes	Medal 18 L 6451 yds SSS 71
	Broomfield 18 L 4815 yds
	SSS 63
Recs	Pro–Medal 63 G Cunningham,
	D Huish
V'trs	WD–U Sat–no 4 ball
	(Apr–Sept) WE–NA before
	2pm & 10am Sun
Fees	Medal £10 (£12.50) Broomfield
	£7 (£9.50)
Loc	1 mile from Montrose, off A92
Mis	Royal Montrose, Caledonia
	and Mercantile clubs play here

Montrose Caledonia (1896)

Dorward Road, Montrose
Tel	(0674) 72313
Sec	J Adamson (0674) 83438
Holes	Play over Montrose courses

Montrose Mercantile (1879)

East Links, Montrose DD10 8SW
Tel	(0674) 72408
Mem	750
Sec	G Foulkes (0674) 73187
Holes	Play over Montrose courses

Panmure (1845)

Barry, by Carnoustie
Tel	(0241) 53120
Mem	480
Sec	Capt JC Ray
Pro	T Shiel
Holes	18 L 6317 yds SSS 70
Recs	Am–68 S Macdonald, DMA
	Steel, RDBM Shade
	Pro–65 R de Vicenzo, R Cole,
	D Webster
V'trs	WD/ Sun–U Sat–NA
Fees	£9 D–£14
Loc	2 miles W of Carnoustie

Royal Montrose (1810)

Dorward Road, Montrose DD10 8SW
Tel	(0674) 72376
Mem	650
Sec	JD Sykes (0674) 73528
Holes	Play over Montrose courses

Kinross-shire

Bishopshire (1903)

Kinnesswood
Mem	170
Sec	AB Moffat (0592) 860379
Holes	9 L 2180 yds SSS 63
Recs	Am–63 J Morris
V'trs	U
Fees	£2 (£3)
Loc	3 miles E of Kinross, off M90

Green Hotel (1900)

2 The Muirs, Kinross
Tel	(0577) 63467
Fax	(0577) 63180
Mem	450
Sec	Mrs M Stewart
Holes	Red 18 L 6223 yds SSS
	Blue 18 L 6392 yds SSS
V'trs	U
Fees	£11 (£15)
Loc	17 miles S of Perth
Mis	Kinross GC plays here

Milnathort (1910)

South Street, Milnathort
Tel	(0577) 64069
Mem	400
Holes	9 L 5969 yds SSS 69
Recs	Am–66 I Reid
V'trs	U SOC
Fees	D–£6 (£10)
Loc	1 mile N of Kinross. M90
	Junction 6 (North) or Junction 7
	(South)

Perthshire

Aberfeldy (1895)

Taybridge Road, Aberfeldy
PH15 2BH
Tel	(0887) 20535
Mem	260
Sec	AM Stewart (0887) 20117
Holes	9 L 2733 yds SSS 67
Recs	Am–66 A McNeill (1987) JM
	Munro (1988)
V'trs	U
Fees	£7 D–£10 W–£25 F–£35
Loc	10 miles from Aberfeldy, off A9

Alyth (1894)

Pitcrocknie, Alyth
Tel	(082 83) 2268
Mem	850
Sec	W Sullivan
Pro	T Melville (082 83) 2411
Holes	18 L 6226 yds SSS 70
Recs	Am–67 E Lindsay, JL Adamson
	Pro–64 I Young
V'trs	U
Fees	£6 D–£9 (£9 D–£13)
Loc	Dundee 16 miles

Auchterarder (1892)

Ochil Road, Auchterarder PH3 1LS
Tel	(0764) 62804
Mem	650
Sec	JI Stewart (0764) 63840
Pro	K Salmoni (0764) 63711
Holes	18 L 5757 yds SSS 68
Recs	Am–66 K Gillon (1989)
	Pro–65 W Guy (1988)
V'trs	U SOC
Fees	£8.50 D–£11 (£12 D–£17)
	(1990)
Loc	1 mile SW of Auchterarder

Blair Atholl (1892)

Blair Atholl
Tel	(079 681) 407
Mem	390
Sec	JA McGregor (079 681) 274
Holes	9 L 2855 yds SSS 69
Recs	Am–66
V'trs	U
Fees	D–£6 (D–£7) W–£22
Loc	35 miles N of Perth, off A9
Mis	Buggies for hire

Blairgowrie (1889)

Rosemount, Blairgowrie PH10 6LG
Tel   (0250) 2594
Mem   1200
Sec   JN Simpson (Sec/ Mgr) (0250) 2622
Pro   GW Kinnoch (0250) 3116
Holes   Rosemount 18 L 6588 yds SSS 72; Lansdowne 18 L 6895 yds SSS 73; Wee 9 L 4614 yds SSS 63
Recs   Rosemount Am–64 E Giraud Pro–66 G Norman Lansdowne Am–68 BRN Grieve Pro–69 J McAlister
V'trs   Mon/ Tues/ Thurs–U H 8.30am– 12 & 2–3.30pm Wed/ Fri/ WE–restricted
Fees   £20 (£30)
Loc   15 miles NE of Perth, off A93. 16 miles NW of Dundee, off A923

Comrie (1891)

Comrie
Mem   270
Sec   DG McGlashan (0764) 70544
Pro   H Donaldson
Holes   9 L 2983 yds SSS 69
Recs   Am–65 A Philp
V'trs   U
Fees   £6 (£7)
Loc   7 miles W of Crieff

Craigie Hill (1982)

Cherrybank, Perth PH2 0NE
Tel   (0738) 24377 (Clubhouse)
Mem   700
Sec   WA Miller (0738) 20829
Pro   F Smith (0738) 22644
Holes   18 L 5379 yds SSS 66
Recs   Am–60 G Still (1988) Pro–63 W Murray (1986)
V'trs   U exc Sat
Fees   £10 (£12)
Loc   W boundary of Perth

Crieff (1891)

Perth Road, Crieff PH7 3LR
Tel   (0764) 2909 (Bookings)
Mem   670
Sec   LJ Rundle (0764) 2397
Pro   DJW Murchie, JM Stark
Holes   Ferntower 18 L 6402 yds SSS 71; Dornock 9 L 4772 yds SSS 63
Recs   Ferntower Am–67 Pro–66
V'trs   U H NA–12–2pm or after 5pm SOC
Fees   Ferntower £14 (£16) Dornock £9 (£10) 18 holes
Loc   17 miles W of Perth (A85). Crieff 1 mile

Dalmunzie (1948)

Public
Glenshee, Blairgowrie
Tel   (025 085) 226
Mem   52
Sec   S Winton
Holes   9 L 2035 yds SSS 60

V'trs   U
Fees   9 holes £5 D–£7
Loc   22 miles N of Blairgowrie on A93. (Dalmunzie Hotel sign)

Dunkeld & Birnam (1910)

Fungarth, Dunkeld
Tel   (03502) 524
Mem   300
Sec   Mrs W Sinclair
Holes   9 L 4945 yds SSS 66
Recs   Am–64 I Sinclair
V'trs   WD–U WE–telephone first
Fees   £7 (£12) (1990)
Loc   Dunkeld 1 mile, off A923

Dunning (1953)

Rollo Park, Dunning
Sec   Miss C Westwood
Holes   9 L 4836 yds SSS 64
V'trs   WD–U before 5pm –M after 5pm Sat–NA before 4pm Sun–NA before 1pm
Fees   D–£5
Loc   9 miles SW of Perth, off A9
Mis   Party bookings in writing to Sec

Glenalmond

Trinity College, Glenalmond
Sec   J Stewart (073 888) 270
Holes   9 L 5812 yds SSS 68
Recs   Am–70 CMW Robertson Pro–72 M Dennis
V'trs   M
Loc   10 miles NW of Perth

The Gleneagles Hotel

Gleneagles
Tel   (0764) 63543
Sec   Ms S Mackie
Pro   I Marchbank (0764) 62231
Holes   King's 18 L 6471 yds SSS 71 Queen's 18 L 5965 yds SSS 69 Wee 9 L 1481 yds Par 27
Recs   King's Am–65 GM Rutherford Queen's Pro–62 I Woosnam Queen's Pro–63 C Stadler
V'trs   Visitors must book in advance
Fees   On application
Loc   16 miles SW of Perth on A9
Mis   Driving range. Pitch & putt. Dun Ochil, Dun Whinny and Glenearn clubs play here

King James VI (1858)

Moncrieffe Island, Perth
Tel   (0738) 25170 (0738) 32460 (Starter)
Mem   600
Pro   A Coles (0738) 32460
Holes   18 L 6026 yds SSS 69
Recs   Am–63 G Clark Pro–63 W Guy
V'trs   U exc Sat Sun–by reservation
Fees   £9 D–£13.50 (D–£18)
Loc   Island in River Tay, Perth

Murrayshall (1981)

Murrayshall, New Scone, Perth PH2 7PH
Tel   (0738) 51171
Fax   (0738) 52595
Mem   400
Sec   A Euan Rodger
Pro   N Mackintosh (0738) 52784
Holes   18 L 5877 metres SSS 71
Recs   Am–67 G Redford Pro–67 J Farmer
V'trs   U SOC–WD/ WE
Fees   £20 (£25)
Loc   3 miles E of Perth, off A94
Mis   Driving range

Muthill (1935)

Peat Road, Muthill PH5 2AD
Tel   (076 481) 523
Mem   400
Sec   WH Gordon (0764) 3319
Holes   9 L 2371 yds SSS 63
Recs   Am–64 C MacGregor Pro–68 RM Jamieson, W Milne
V'trs   U
Fees   D–£5
Loc   3 miles S of Crieff on A822

North Inch

Public
c/o Perth & Kinross District Council, 3 High Street, Perth PH1 5JU
Tel   (0738) 36481 (Starter)
Sec   R Smith (Mgr) (0738) 39911
Holes   18 L 4340 metres SSS 65
V'trs   U SOC
Fees   £3 (£5.40)
Loc   Nr Perth and A9, by River Tay. Follow signs to Bell's Sports Centre

Pitlochry (1909)

Golf Course Road, Pitlochry
Tel   (0796) 2792 (Starter)
Mem   350
Sec   DCM McKenzie JP (0796) 2114
Pro   J Wilson
Holes   18 L 5811 yds SSS 68
Recs   Am–63 CP Christy, MM Niven Pro–64
V'trs   U
Fees   D–£10 D–£13 (£9)
Loc   ½ mile from W end of Main Street, via Larchwood Road

Royal Perth Golfing Society (1834)

1/2 Atholl Crescent, Perth PH1 5NG
Tel   (0738) 22265
Mem   250
Sec   RPJ Blake (0738) 33171
Holes   Play over North Inch course

St Fillans (1903)

South Lochearn Rd, St Fillans
PH6 2NG
Tel	(076 485) 312
Mem	400
Sec	AJN Abercrombie (0764) 3643
Holes	9 L 5668 yds SSS 68
Recs	Am–66 W Gemmell (1989)
V'trs	U SOC (max 16)
Fees	D–£6 (D–£7) 5D–£20
Loc	12 miles W of Crieff, on A85 to Crianlarich

Strathtay (1909)

Tighanoisinn, Grandtully PH15 2QT
Mem	120
Sec	J Armstrong–Payne (08874) 367
Holes	9 L 4082 yds SSS 63
Recs	Am–61 AM Deboys
V'trs	U exc Mon & Wed–NA after 5pm SOC
Fees	D–£4 (£5) (1990)
Loc	4 miles W of Ballinluig (A827), towards Aberfeldy

Taymouth Castle (1923)

Kenmore PH15 2NT
Tel	(08873) 228
Mem	200
Sec	MJ Mulcahey (Golf Dir)
Pro	A Marshall
Holes	18 L 6066 yds SSS 69
Recs	Am–63 MM Niven
V'trs	U WE–booking essential SOC
Fees	£11 D–£17 (£15 D–£22) Mon–Fri £50
Loc	6 miles W of Aberfeldy
Mis	Buggies for hire

Western Isles Region

Askernish (1891)

Lochboisdale, South Uist
Mem	30
Holes	9 (18 tees) L 5114 yds SSS 67
Recs	Am–66 K Robertson
V'trs	U
Fees	£2 (£2) W–£10
Loc	5 miles NW of Lochboisdale

Stornoway (1890)

Lady Lever Park, Stornoway, Outer Hebrides
Tel	(0851) 2240
Mem	250
Sec	P Dickie (0851) 3602
Holes	18 L 5119 yds SSS 66
Recs	Am–62 KW Galloway Pro–65 JC Farmer
V'trs	U Sun–NA
Fees	£5 D–£8 W–£25 F–£35
Loc	In grounds of Lews Castle, Isle of Lewis

Wales

Clwyd

Abergele & Pensarn (1910)

Tan-y-Goppa Road, Abergele
LL22 8DS
Tel	(0745) 824034
Mem	1250
Sec	HE Richards
Pro	I Runcie (0745) 823813
Holes	18 L 6086 yds SSS 69
Recs	Am–J Buckley (1980) Pro–65 D Vaughan (1987)
V'trs	U SOC
Fees	£12 (£14)

Bryn Morfydd (1982)

The Princess Course, Llanrhaeadr, nr Denbigh LL16 4NP
Tel	(074 578) 280
Mem	50
Sec	ED Muirhead
Holes	9 L 1190 yds SSS 27
V'trs	U SOC
Fees	£4
Loc	2½ miles E of Denbigh on A525

Denbigh (1922)

Henllan Road, Denbigh LL16
Tel	(0745) 814159
Mem	550
Sec	GC Parry
Pro	M Jones
Holes	18 L 5582 yds SSS 67
Recs	Am–64 H Parry (1989) Pro–69 C Defoy (1986)
V'trs	U SOC
Fees	£10 (£15)
Loc	2 miles NW of Denbigh (B5382)

Flint (1966)

Cornist Park, Flint CH6 5HJ
Tel	(035 26) 2327
Mem	348
Sec	H Griffith (035 26) 2186
Pro	M Staton
Holes	9 L 5829 yds SSS 68
Recs	Am–67 JP Snead, G Houston
V'trs	WD–U before 5pm WE–M SOC–WD/ Sat
Fees	D–£6
Loc	Station 1½ miles. Flint 1 mile. M56 8 miles

Hawarden (1911)

Groomsdale Lane, Hawarden, Deeside CH5 3EH
Tel	(0244) 531447
Mem	320
Sec	T Hinks-Edwards (0352) 57955
Pro	M Carty
Holes	9 L 5620 yds SSS 67
Recs	Am–65 SR Neale
V'trs	M SOC
Loc	6 miles W of Chester off A55

Holywell (1906)

Brynford, Holywell
Tel	(0352) 710040
Mem	330
Sec	EK Carney (0352) 710539
Pro	M Carty
Holes	10 L 3117 yds SSS 71
Recs	Am–70 G Houston Pro–N Jones
V'trs	WD–U WE–M
Fees	£6 (£8)
Loc	2 miles S of Holywell

Mold (1909)

Pantmywyn, nr Mold
Tel	(0352) 740318
Mem	350 55(L) 110(J)
Sec	A Newall
Pro	M Carty
Holes	18 L 5521 yds SSS 67
Recs	Am–65 P Jones Pro–64 D Wills
V'trs	U SOC
Fees	£12 (£15)
Loc	Mold 4 miles

Old Colwyn (1907)

Woodland Avenue, Old Colwyn
LL29 9NL
Tel	(0492) 515581
Mem	350
Sec	GI Jones
Holes	9 L 5268 yds SSS 66
Recs	Am–63 C Oldham, JD Jones Roberts Pro–67 DJ Rees
V'trs	WD–U WE–by arrangement SOC
Fees	£5 (£6)
Loc	2 miles E of Colwyn Bay

Old Padeswood (1978)

Station Road, Padeswood, nr Mold
Tel	(0244) 547401
Mem	500
Sec	BV Hellen (0352) 770506
Pro	A Davies
Holes	18 L 6728 yds SSS 72
Recs	Am–69 L Lockett (1987) Pro–65 I Higsby
V'trs	U exc comp days SOC–WD
Fees	£10 D–£15 (£15)
Loc	2 miles from Mold on A5118

Padeswood & Buckley (1933)

The Caia, Station Lane, Padeswood, nr Mold CH7 4JD
Tel	(0244) 550537
Mem	592
Sec	R McLauchlan
Pro	D Ashton (0244) 543636
Holes	18 L 5823 yds SSS 68
Recs	Am–66 S Hurstfield
V'trs	WD–U 9am–4pm –M after 4pm Sat–U Sun–NA SOC–WD Ladies Day–Wed

Fees £13 (£15)
Loc 8 miles W of Chester off
A5118. 2nd golf club on right

Prestatyn (1905)

Marine Road East, Prestatyn
LL19 7HS
Tel (0745) 854320/ 888353
Mem 650
Sec R Woodruff (Mgr)
Pro M Staton
Holes 18 L 6792 yds SSS 73
Recs Am–68 J Bamford
V'trs H SOC
Fees £12 (£16)
Loc 1 mile E of Prestatyn

Rhuddlan (1930)

Rhuddlan, Rhyl LL18 6LB
Tel (0745) 590217
Mem 466 144(L) 80(J)
Sec D Morris
Pro G Cox (0745) 590898
Holes 18 L 6473 yds SSS 71
Recs Am–68 G Marsden (1990)
V'trs H or I Sun–M SOC–WD
Fees £16 (£20)
Loc 3 miles S of Rhyl

Rhyl (1890)

Coast Road, Rhyl
Tel (0745) 353171
Mem 380
Sec W Wilson (0745) 855912
Holes 9 L 6153 yds SSS 70
Recs Am–66 M Ellis Pro–67 H
Cotton, N von Nida, C Ward
V'trs U SOC
Fees £8 (£10)
Loc Coast road between Rhyl and
Prestatyn

Ruthin–Pwllglas (1920)

Pwllglas, Ruthin
Tel (082 42) 2296
Mem 360
Sec RD Roberts (082 42) 4658
Holes 10 L 5362 yds SSS 66
Recs Am–64 MG Hughes
V'trs U SOC
Fees £8 (£12)
Loc Pwllglas, 2¹/2 miles S of Ruthin

St Melyd (1922)

The Paddock, Meliden Road,
Prestatyn LL19 9NB
Tel (0745) 854405
Mem 530
Sec CS McKechnie
Pro NH Lloyd (0745) 888858
Holes 9 L 5857 yds SSS 68
Recs Am–65 AR Grace (1990)
Pro–68 N Hill
V'trs U SOC
Fees £8 (£12)
Loc On A547 between Prestatyn
and Meliden

Vale of Llangollen (1908)

Holyhead Road, Llangollen LL20 7PR
Tel (0978) 860040
Mem 600
Sec TF Ellis
Pro DI Vaughan
Holes 18 L 6661 yds SSS 72
Recs Am–69 Pro–68
V'trs U
Fees £15 (£18)
Loc 1¹/2 miles E of Llangollen on A5

Wrexham (1906)

Holt Road, Wrexham
Tel (0978) 261033
Mem 650
Sec KB Fisher (0978) 364268
Pro DA Larvin (0978) 351476
Holes 18 L 6078 yds SSS 69
Recs Am–66 S Edwards, N Chidley
Pro–67 JE Davies
V'trs H SOC–WD
Fees On application
Loc 2 miles NE of Wrexham on A534

Dyfed

Aberystwyth (1911)

Bryn-y-Mor, Aberystwyth SY23 2HY
Tel (0970) 615104
Mem 390
Sec W Hughes (0970) 623826
Pro G Brownlie (0970) 625103
Holes 18 L 5868 yds SSS 68
Recs Am–63 W Pugh, MA Owen
Pro–64 A Hodson
V'trs U SOC
Fees £8 D–£10 (£10 D–£12)
Loc Aberystwyth ¹/2 mile

Ashburnham (1894)

Cliffe Terrace, Burry Port SA16 0HN
Tel (05546) 2466
Mem 730
Sec DE Gravelle (05546) 2269
Pro RJ Playe (05546) 3846
Holes 18 L 6916 yds SSS 72
Recs Am–70 CI Morgan Pro–67
M Cahill, S Torrance,
P Townsend
V'trs H
Fees £15 D–£20 (£20 D–£25)
Loc 5 miles W of Llanelli

Borth & Ynyslas (1885)

Borth SY24 5JS
Tel (0970) 871202
Mem 445
Sec RB Mair
Pro JG Lewis (0970) 871557
Holes 18 L 6100 yds SSS 70
Recs Am–65 M Stimson
Pro–68 JG Lewis
V'trs WD–U WE/ BH–by prior
arrangement SOC
Fees £12 (£15)
Loc N of Borth, off A487 between
Aberystwyth and Machynlleth

Cardigan (1928)

Gwbert-on-Sea SA43 1PR
Tel (0239) 612035
Mem 300
Sec J Rhapps
Pro C Parsons
Holes 18 L 6641 yds SSS 72
Recs Am–66 A Evans
V'trs U
Fees D–£12 (£15) W–£45
Loc 2¹/2 miles NW of Cardigan

Carmarthen (1907)

Blaenycoed Road, Carmarthen
Tel (0267) 87214
Mem 700
Sec WR Nicholl (0267) 87588
Pro P Gillis
Holes 18 L 6212 yds SSS 71
Recs Am–68 M Thomas (1987)
Pro–69 B Barnes
V'trs U SOC
Fees £12 (£15)
Loc 4 miles NW of Carmarthen

Cilgwyn (1977)

Llangybi, Lampeter SA48 8NN
Tel (0570 45) 286
Mem 150
Sec LB Evans
Holes 9 L 5318 yds SSS 67
Recs Am–66 DG Evans Pro–69
D Creamer
V'trs U SOC
Fees £5 (£6.50) W–£20
Loc 5 miles NE of Lampeter, off
A485 at Llangybi

Glynhir (1909)

Glynhir Road, Llandybie, nr
Ammanford SA18 2TF
Tel (0269) 850472
Mem 340
Sec JT Thomas (0269) 850571
EP Rees
Pro S Rastall (0269) 851010
Holes 18 L 6090 yds SSS 70
Recs Am–66 R Collins
V'trs SOC–WD only
Fees Winter £5 (£6) W–£30 Summer
£10 (£15) 5D–£35 W–£50
Loc 3¹/2 miles N of Ammanford

Haverfordwest (1904)

Arnolds Down, Haverfordwest
SA61 2XQ
Tel (0437) 763565
Mem 700
Sec MA Harding (0437) 764523
Pro A Pile (0437) 768409
Holes 18 L 5945 yds SSS 70
Recs Am– Pro–67 AJ Pile
V'trs U SOC
Fees £12 (£16) Mon–Fri £40
Loc 1 mile E of Haverfordwest on
A40 Carmarthen road
Mis Buggy for hire

Milford Haven (1913)

Hubbertson, Milford Haven
Tel	(0646) 692368
Mem	259 54(L) 50(J)
Sec	D Britton (0646) 697660
Pro	A Pile
Holes	18 L 6071 yds SSS 71
Recs	Am–68 L Rees
	Pro–71 B Huggett
V'trs	U SOC
Fees	£10 (£12)
Loc	W boundary of Milford Haven

Newport (Pembs) (1925)

Newport
Tel	(0239) 820244
Mem	350
Sec	R Dietrich
Pro	C Parsons
Holes	9 L 3089 yds SSS 69
Recs	Am–67 A Evans
V'trs	U SOC
Fees	£8.50 (£8.50)
Loc	2¹/₂ miles NW of Newport, towards Newport Beach

St Davids City (1902)

Whitesands Bay, St Davids
Tel	(03483) 607
Mem	200
Sec	GB Lewis
Holes	9 L 5911 yds SSS 70
Recs	Am–67 KB Walsh (1989), JC Evans (1990)
V'trs	U SOC–WD
Fees	D–£9
Loc	2 miles W of St Davids, nr Whitesands Bay

South Pembrokeshire (1970)

Defensible Barracks, Pembroke Dock
Tel	(0646) 683817
Mem	250
Sec	GW Thomas (0646) 682035
Holes	9 L 5804 yds SSS 69
Recs	Am–66 S Toy, A Jones
V'trs	U before 4.30pm SOC
Fees	D–£6 Mon–Fri–£15
Loc	Pembroke Dock

Tenby (1888)

The Burrows, Tenby
Tel	(0834) 2787
Mem	600
Sec	TR Arnold (0834) 2978
Pro	T Mountford (0834) 4447
Holes	18 L 6450 yds SSS 71
Recs	Am–65 G Clement
V'trs	U SOC
Fees	£15 (£20) W–£75
Loc	Tenby

Gwent

Blackwood (1914)

Cwmgelli, Blackwood
Tel	(0495) 223152
Mem	300
Sec	AM Reed-Gibbs
Holes	9 L 5304 yds SSS 66
Recs	Am–65 DL Stevens, NR Phillips, R Collett
	Pro–64 F Hill
V'trs	I SOC
Fees	£8 (£10)
Loc	¹/₄ mile N of Blackwood

Caerleon (1974)

Public
Broadway, Caerleon
Tel	(0633) 420342
Sec	A Campbell
Pro	A Campbell
Holes	9 L 3092 yds SSS
Recs	Am–71 C French (1988)
V'trs	U
Fees	18 holes–£2.90 (£4.20) 9 holes–£1.90 (£2.50)
Loc	M4 Junction 25, 3 miles
Mis	Driving range

Greenmeadow (1980)

Treherbert Road, Croesyceiliog, Cwmbran NP44 2BZ
Tel	(06333) 69321
Mem	430
Sec	PJ Richardson
Pro	C Coombs (06333) 62626
Holes	15 L 5593 yds SSS 68
Recs	Am–66 M Challinger (1989)
	Pro–66 C Jenkins (1987)
V'trs	U SOC
Fees	£9 (£11)
Loc	4 miles from Newport on B4042. M4 Junction 26

Llanwern (1928)

Golf House, Tennyson Ave, Llanwern NP6 2DY
Tel	(0633) 412380
Mem	625
Sec	DJ Peak (0633) 412029
Pro	S Price (0633) 415233
Holes	18 L 6139 yds SSS 69 9 L 5686 yds SSS 69
Recs	Am–65 K Fitzgerald
	Pro–67 G Davies, R Richards (1987)
V'trs	WD–U WE–restricted I H SOC
Fees	WD–£20
Loc	1 mile from M4 Junction 24

Monmouth (1921)

Leasebrook Lane, Monmouth
Tel	(0600) 2212
Mem	350
Sec	KA Prichard (0594) 33394
Holes	9 L 5454 yds SSS 66
Recs	Am–65 DJ Wills (1979)
	Pro–68 DR Hemming (1978)
V'trs	U SOC
Fees	£10 (£15) Mon–Fri £35
Loc	Signposted 1 mile along A40 Monmouth–Ross road

Monmouthshire (1892)

Llanfoist, Abergavenny
Tel	(0873) 3171
Mem	480 106(L) 90(J)
Sec	GJ Swayne (0873) 2606
Pro	P Worthing (0873) 2532
Holes	18 L 6045 yds SSS 69
Recs	Am–66 PS Lewis
	Pro–62 D Thomas
V'trs	U H SOC
Fees	£16 (£22)
Loc	Abergavenny Station 2 miles

Newport (1903)

Great Oak, Rogerstone, Newport NP1 9FX
Tel	(0633) 892683/ 894496 (0633) 892643/ 896794
Mem	700
Sec	AD Jones
Pro	R Skuse (0633) 893271
Holes	18 L 6370 yds SSS 71
Recs	Am–65 CJ Dinsdale
	Pro–67 M Hughes
V'trs	WD–U exc Tues Sat–M 1–4pm SOC–WD exc Tues
Fees	£15 (£20)
Loc	Newport 3 miles on B4591. M4 Junction 27, 1 mile

Pontnewydd (1875)

Maesgwyn Farm, West Pontnewydd, Cwmbran NP44 1AB
Tel	(06333) 2170
Mem	250
Sec	HR Gabe (06333) 67185
Holes	10 L 5340 yds SSS 67
Recs	Am–63 M Hayward
V'trs	WD–U WE–M SOC
Fees	£10
Loc	W outskirts of Cwmbran

Pontypool (1903)

Lasgarn Lane, Trevethin, Pontypool
Tel	(0495) 763655
Mem	566 65(L) 72(J)
Sec	Mrs E Wilce (0495) 764794
Pro	J Howard (0495) 755544
Holes	18 L 6015 yds SSS 69
Recs	Am–64 M Hayward (1982) NR Davies (1985)
	Pro–A Sherborne
V'trs	U H SOC
Fees	£13 (£17.50)
Loc	1 mile N of Pontypool (A4042)

Rolls of Monmouth (1982)

The Hendre, Monmouth NP5 4HG
Tel	(0600) 5353
Mem	250
Sec	JD Ross
Holes	18 L 6723 yds SSS 72
Recs	Am–71 D Wills
	Pro–68 M Thomas
V'trs	U SOC

Fees   £20 (£24)
Loc   3¹/₂ miles W of Monmouth on
B4233

St Mellons (1937)

St Mellons, Cardiff CF3 8XS
Tel   (0633) 680401
Mem   500 93(L) 70(J) 27(5)
Sec   Mrs K Newling (0633) 680408
Pro   B Thomas (0633) 680101
Holes   18 L 6225 yds SSS 70
Recs   Am–67 S Hopkins
Pro–66 E Foster
V'trs   WD–U WE–M
Fees   £20
Loc   4 miles E of Cardiff on A48

St Pierre (1962)

Chepstow NP6 6YA
Tel   (0291) 625261
Fax   (02912) 79975
Sec   M Knox-Johnston, TJ Cleary
Pro   R Doig
Holes   18 L 6748 yds SSS 73 18 L
5762 yds SSS 68
Recs   Old Am–69 AM Williams
Pro–63 H Henning
New Am–63 M Bearcroft
V'trs   H SOC–WD
Fees   On application
Loc   2 miles W of Chepstow (A48)

Tredegar & Rhymney (1921)

Tredegar, Rhymney
Tel   (0685) 840743
Mem   182
Sec   V Davies
Holes   9 L 5564 yds SSS 67
Recs   Am–64 CL Jones
Pro–33 WS Phillips
V'trs   U
Fees   £5
Loc   1¹/₂ miles W of Tredegar

Tredegar Park (1923)

Bassaleg Road, Newport NP9 3PX
Tel   (0633) 895219
Mem   800
Sec   AA Skinner DFM (0633)
894433
Pro   ML Morgan (0633) 894517
Holes   18 L 6097 yds SSS 70
Recs   Am–67 A Wesson
V'trs   I
Fees   £15 (£20)
Loc   Off M4 Junction 27

West Monmouthshire (1906)

Pond Road, Nantyglo NP3 4JX
Tel   (0495) 310233
Mem   500
Sec   AL Offers (0495) 303663
Holes   18 L 6118 yds SSS 69
Recs   Am–65 R Phillips (1981)
V'trs   U
Fees   On application

Loc   Nr Dunlop Semtex, off
Brynmawr Bypass, towards
Winchestown
Mis   Highest tee in Wales (14th),
1450 ft above sea level

Gwynedd

Aberdovey (1892)

Aberdovey LL35 0RT
Tel   (065 472) 210
Mem   800
Sec   JM Griffiths (065 472) 493
Pro   J Davies (065 472) 602
Holes   18 L 6445 yds SSS 71
Recs   Am–67 B Macfarlane
Pro–67 J Smith
V'trs   NA–8.30–9.30am & 1–2pm
Fees   On application
Loc   W end of Aberdovey

Abersoch (1907)

Abersoch
Tel   (075 881) 2622
Mem   600
Sec   P Jones
Holes   9 L 5800 yds SSS 68
V'trs   U SOC
Fees   On application
Loc   ¹/₂ mile S of Abersoch

Bala (1973)

Penlan, Bala LL23 7SW
Tel   (0678) 520359
Mem   250
Sec   MJ Wright
Holes   10 L 4934 yds SSS 64
Recs   Am–64 DB Aykroyd
V'trs   WD–U WE–NA pm SOC
Fees   £8 (£10) W–£25
Loc   ¹/₂ mile SW of Bala

Bala Lake Hotel

Bala LL23 7YF
Tel   (0678) 520344
Fax   (0678) 521193
Mem   50
Sec   D Pickering
Holes   9 hole course
V'trs   U
Fees   £7 (£8)
Loc   1¹/₂ miles from Bala on B4403

Betws-y-Coed (1977)

Clubhouse, Betws-y-Coed LL24
Tel   (069 02) 556
Mem   350
Sec   GB Archer
Holes   9 L 2515 yds SSS 32
Recs   Am–63 DWP Hughes (1990)
V'trs   U SOC
Fees   £10 (£12)
Loc   ¹/₂ mile off A5, in Betws-y-
Coed

Caernarfon (1907)

Llanfaglan, Caernarfon LL54 5RP
Tel   (0286) 3783
Mem   600
Sec   JI Jones
Holes   18 L 5870 yds SSS 69
Recs   Am–69 Pro–66
V'trs   U SOC
Fees   £10
Loc   2¹/₂ miles W of Caernarfon

Conwy (Caernarvonshire) (1890)

Conway
Tel   (0492) 593400
Mem   700
Sec   EC Roberts (0492) 592423
Pro   JP Lees (0492) 593225
Holes   18 L 6901 yds SSS 73
V'trs   H WE–restricted SOC
Fees   £15 (£20)
Loc   ¹/₂ mile W of Conway, off A55

Criccieth (1905)

Ednyfed Hill, Criccieth
Tel   (0766) 522154
Mem   200
Sec   MG Hamilton (0766) 522697
Holes   18 L 5755 yds SSS 68
V'trs   U
Fees   £7 W–£20
Loc   18 miles S of Caernarfon.
4 miles W of Portmadoc

Dolgellau (1911)

Pencefn Road, Dolgellau
Tel   (0341) 422603
Mem   300
Sec   DW Jones (0341) 422593
Holes   9 L 4671 yds SSS 63
Recs   Am–65 E Owen (1987),
EW Owen (1989)
Pro–61 L James (1937)
V'trs   U SOC
Fees   £6 (£7.50)
Loc   Dolgellau ¹/₂ mile

Ffestiniog (1896)

Y, Cefn, Ffestiniog
Tel   (0766) 762637 (Clubhouse)
Mem   138
Sec   A Roberts (0766) 831829
Holes   9 L 5032 metres SSS 66
Recs   Am–
V'trs   U
Fees   £5 W–£15
Loc   1 mile from Ffestiniog on Bala
road

Llandudno (Maesdu) (1915)

Hospital Road, Llandudno LL30 1HU
Tel   (0492) 76450
Mem   950
Sec   J Hallam
Pro   S Boulden (0492) 75195
Holes   18 L 6513 yds SSS 72

Recs Am–67 G Jones, CT Brown
Pro–66 PJ Butler
V'trs U H–recognised GC members
SOC
Fees £15 (£20)
Loc 1 mile S of Llandudno Station,
nr Hospital

Llandudno (North Wales) (1894)

72 Bryniau Road, West Shore,
Llandudno LL30 2DZ
Tel (0492) 75325
Mem 680
Sec GD Harwood
Pro RA Bradbury (0492) 76878
Holes 18 L 6132 yds SSS 69
Recs Am–66 JHM Williams,
S Goldspink
Pro–63 WS Collins
V'trs U SOC–phone Sec
Fees £15 (£20) Mon–Fri £50
Loc ³/4 mile from Llandudno on
West Shore

Llanfairfechan (1971)

Llannerch Road, Llanfairfechan
LL33 0EB
Tel (0248) 680144
Mem 330
Sec MJ Charlesworth (0248)
680524
Holes 9 L 3119 yds SSS 57
Recs Am–53 MJ Charlesworth
(1983)
V'trs U
Fees £5 (£6)
Loc 7 miles E of Bangor on A55

Nefyn & District (1907)

Nefyn
Tel (0758) 720218
Mem 750
Sec Lt Col RW Parry (0758) 720966
Pro JR Pilkington
Holes 18 L 6294 yds SSS 71
Recs Am–68 TG Gruffydd
Pro–67 I Woosnam
V'trs H SOC
Fees £15 (£20)
Loc 1¹/2 miles W of Nefyn

Penmaenmawr (1910)

Conway Old Road, Penmaenmawr
LL34 6RD
Tel (0492) 623330
Mem 500
Sec Mrs JE Jones
Holes 9 L 5143 yds SSS 66
Recs Am–65 M Bellis
V'trs U SOC
Fees £10 (£12)
Loc 4 miles W of Conway

Portmadoc (1900)

Morfa Bychan, Porthmadog LL49 9UC
Tel (0766) 512037
Mem 500
Sec GW Jones

Pro P Bright (0766) 513828
Holes 18 L 6380 yds SSS 70
Recs Am–63 J Morrow
V'trs U SOC
Fees D–£12 (D–£15)
Loc 2 miles W of Porthmadog
towards Black Rock Sands

Pwllheli (1900)

Pwllheli
Tel (0758) 612520
Mem 630
Sec RE Williams
Pro GD Verity
Holes 18 L 6105 yds SSS 69
Recs Am–66 MG Hughes (1988)
Pro–67 D Screeton
V'trs U
Fees On application
Loc ¹/2 mile SW of Pwllheli

Rhos-on-Sea Residential (1899)

Pernrhyn Bay, Llandudno
Tel (0492) 49641
Mem 500
Sec T Frame
Pro M Greenough
Holes 18 L 6064 yds SSS 69
Recs Am–64 JR Jones
V'trs U
Fees On application
Loc On coast at Rhos-on-Sea

Royal St David's (1894)

Harlech LL46 2UB
Tel (0766) 780203 (0766) 780857
(Bookings)
Mem 700
Sec RI Jones (0766) 780361
Pro J Barnett
Holes 18 L 6427 yds SSS 71
Recs Am–66 JL Morgan (1951),
TJ Melia (1976)
Pro–64 K Stables (1988)
V'trs U H SOC
Fees £16 (£20)
Loc W of Harlech
Mis Buggies £10 per round

St Deiniol (1905)

Penbryn, Bangor LL57 1PX
Tel (0248) 353098
Mem 500
Sec DL Davies
Pro P Lovell
Holes 18 L 5048 metres SSS 67
Recs Am–63 GA Roberts (1979)
V'trs U
Fees £6 (£6)
Loc Off A5/ A55 Junction, 1 mile E
of Bangor on A5022

Isle of Anglesey

Anglesey (1914)

Rhosneigr
Tel (0407) 810219
Mem 350
Sec RD Jones (0407) 810930
Pro P Lovell (0407) 811202
Holes 18 L 6204 yds SSS 70
Recs Am–66 M Robinson (1990)
V'trs U SOC
Fees £8 (£10)
Loc 8 miles SE of Holyhead, off
A4080

Baron Hill (1895)

Beaumaris LL58 8YW
Tel (0248) 810231
Mem 360
Sec ED Thomas
Pro P Maton
Holes 9 L 5062 metres SSS 67
Recs Am–65 AW Jones
V'trs U exc comp days SOC–WD &
Sat (apply Sec)
Fees £6 (£7) W–£25
Loc 1 mile NW of Beaumaris

Bull Bay (1913)

Amlwch LL68 9RY
Tel (0407) 830960
Mem 650
Sec JR Tickle
Pro N Dunroe (0407) 831188
Holes 18 L 6160 yds SSS 70
Recs Am–66 D McLean, A Llyr
Pro–65 M Barton
V'trs H SOC
Fees £10.50 (£15)
Loc Amlwch ¹/2 mile on A5025

Holyhead (1912)

Trearddur Bay, Holyhead
LL65 2YG
Tel (0407) 763276/ 762119
Mem 484 225(L) 109(J)
Sec L Toth
Pro P Capper (0407) 762022
Holes 18 L 5540 metres SSS 70
Recs Am–64 D McLean
Pro–69 H Gould
V'trs H SOC
Fees On application
Loc Holyhead Station 1 mile

Llangefni (1983)

Public
Llangefni
Tel (0248) 722193
Pro P Lovell
Holes 9 L 1467 yds
V'trs U
Fees £1.25 (£1.85)
Loc Llangefni ¹/2 mile on B5111

For list of abbreviations see page 487.

Mid Glamorgan

Aberdare (1921)

Abernant, Aberdare
Tel	(0685) 871188
Mem	500
Sec	L Adler
Pro	AW Palmer (0685) 878735
Holes	18 L 5875 yds SSS 69
Recs	Am–63 S Dodd (1988)
	Pro–67 AW Palmer
V'trs	I or H Sat–M SOC
Fees	£11 (£14)
Loc	Aberdare 1/2 mile

Bargoed (1912)

Heolddu, Bargoed
Tel	(0443) 830143
Mem	400
Sec	WR Coleman (0443) 822377
Holes	18 L 6233 yds SSS 69
Recs	Am–65 B Dredge
V'trs	WD–U WE–M SOC–WD
Fees	£12
Loc	NW boundary of Bargoed

Bryn Meadows Hotel G & CC (1973)

The Bryn, nr Hengoed CF8 7SM
Tel	(0495) 225590/ 224103
Mem	500
Sec	B Mayo
Pro	P Worthing (0495) 221905
Holes	18 L 6200 yds SSS 69
Recs	Am–66 G Davies
	Pro–68 S Price
V'trs	U
Fees	£12.50 (£15)
Loc	Newport, Gwent 12 miles

Caerphilly (1905)

Mountain Road, Caerphilly CF8 1HJ
Tel	(0222) 883481
Mem	780
Sec	(0222) 863441
Pro	G Brownlee (0222) 869104
Holes	14 L 6063 yds SSS 71
Recs	Am–65 L Absolom
	Pro–68 B Huggett
V'trs	WD–U WE–M
Fees	£14 W–£30 M–£70
Loc	7 miles N of Cardiff, off A469. Rail/ bus stations 1/4 mile

Castell Heights (1987)

Blaengwynlais, Caerphilly CF8 1NG
Tel	(0222) 886666 (Bookings)
	(0222) 886686 (Clubhouse)
Mem	1000
Sec	J Talbot
Pro	R Sandow
Holes	9 L 2688 yds SSS 66
V'trs	U
Fees	9 holes–£3
Loc	4 miles from M4 Junction 32, on Tongwynlais to Caerphilly road. By Mountain Lakes GC

Creigiau (1921)

Creigiau, Cardiff CF4 8NN
Tel	(0222) 890263
Mem	700
Sec	DB Jones
Pro	C Thomas (0222) 891909
Holes	18 L 5980 yds SSS 69
Recs	Am–67 D Samuel
V'trs	WD–U WE/ BH–M SOC–WD
Fees	£18
Loc	5 miles NW of Cardiff

Llantrisant & Pontyclun (1927)

Talbot Green, Llantrisant
Tel	(0443) 222148
Mem	500
Sec	JM Williams (0443) 224601
Pro	N Watson (0443) 228169
Holes	12 L 5712 yds SSS 69
Recs	Am–65 TJ Lewis (1974)
	Pro–65 JJ Hastings (1982)
V'trs	WD–U WE/ BH–M
Fees	£15
Loc	10 miles N of Cardiff. 2 miles N of M4 Junction 34

Maesteg (1912)

Mount Pleasant, Maesteg
Tel	(0656) 732037
Mem	600
Sec	WH Hanford (0656) 734106
Pro	G Hopkins (0656) 735742
Holes	18 L 5845 yds SSS 69
Recs	Am–69 J James,
	W Hodgson,
	R Lewis
	Pro–64 G Ryall (1989)
V'trs	WD–H SOC
Fees	£12 (£15)
Loc	1 mile W of Maesteg on B4282 Port Talbot road. M4 Junction 36(East), Junction 40(West)

Merthyr Tydfil (1908)

Cilsanws Mountain, Cefn Coed, nr Merthyr Tydfil CF48 2HW
Tel	(0685) 723308
Mem	100
Sec	V Price
Holes	11 L 5794 yds SSS 68
Recs	Am–66 N Evans
	Pro–70 J Howard
V'trs	U
Fees	£8 (£10)
Loc	Off A470

Morlais Castle (1900)

Pant, Dowlais, Merthyr Tydfil
Tel	(0685) 722822
Mem	400
Sec	N Powell
Holes	18 L 6320 yds SSS 71
Recs	Am–
V'trs	U exc Sat 12–4pm/ Sun 8am–12–NA SOC–WD (small)
Fees	£10 (£10)
Loc	3 miles N of Merthyr Tydfil, nr Mountain Railway

Mountain Ash (1907)

Cefnpennar
Tel	(0443) 472265
Mem	555
Sec	G Matthews (0443) 474022
Pro	J Sim (0443) 478770
Holes	18 L 5535 yds SSS 68
Recs	Am–63 SJ Lewis
	Pro–66 R Evans
V'trs	WD–U WE–M
Fees	£12
Loc	9 miles NW of Pontypridd

Mountain Lakes (1988)

Blaengwynlais, Caerphilly CF8 1NG
Tel	(0222) 861128
Mem	400
Sec	RS Smith (Hon)
Pro	R Sandow (0222) 886666
Holes	18 L 6851 yds SSS 73
V'trs	H SOC (book with Pro)
Fees	£12 (£15)
Loc	4 miles from M4 Junction 32, on Tongwynlais to Caerphilly road. By Castell Heights GC

Pontypridd (1905)

Ty Gwyn Road, Pontypridd CF37 4DJ
Tel	(0443) 402359
Mem	730
Sec	JG Graham (0443) 409904
Pro	K Gittins (0443) 491210
Holes	18 L 5650 yds SSS 68
Recs	Am–66 MC Sallam, PL Jenkins (1989)
V'trs	WD–U H WE/ BH–M H SOC–WD H
Fees	On application
Loc	E of Pontypridd off A470. 12 miles NW of Cardiff

Pyle & Kenfig (1922)

Waun-y-Mer, Kenfig CF33 4PU
Tel	(065 671) 3093
Mem	860
Sec	RC Thomas
Pro	R Evans (0656) 772446
Holes	18 L 6655 yds SSS 73
Recs	Am–70 S Cox, S Curiel, N Evans
	Pro–68 D Matthew, C Gray, M Steadman
V'trs	WD–U WE–M
Fees	£20 D–£25
Loc	Porthcawl 2 miles

Rhondda (1910)

Penrhys, Pontygwaith, Rhondda
Tel	(0443) 433204
Mem	400
Sec	K Jones
Pro	None
Holes	18 L 6428 yds SSS 71
Recs	Am–69 P Derham (1988)
	Pro–68 K Dabson (1989)
V'trs	U H SOC
Fees	£10
Loc	6 miles W of Pontypridd

Royal Porthcawl (1891)

Porthcawl
Tel	(065 671) 2251
Mem	800
Sec	AW Woolcott
Pro	G Poor (065 671) 6984
Holes	18 L 6691 yds SSS 74
Recs	Am–68 S Dodds
	Pro–65 B Barnes
V'trs	I WE/ BH–M SOC–H
Fees	On application
Loc	22 miles W of Cardiff. M4 Junction 37

Southerndown (1905)

Ewenny, Bridgend CF35 5BT
Tel	(0656) 880326
Mem	650
Sec	R Brickell (0656) 880476
Pro	DG McMonagle
Holes	18 L 6705 yds SSS 73
Recs	Am–66 H Stott
	Pro–64 G Hunt
V'trs	WD–U WE/ BH–M SOC–Tues & Thurs–H
Fees	£22 (£28)
Loc	Ewenny, Ogmore–by–Sea, nr Ogmore Castle ruins

Whitehall (1922)

The Pavilion, Nelson, Treharris
Tel	(0443) 740245
Mem	320
Sec	VE Davies
Holes	9 L 5750 yds SSS 68
Recs	Am–66 M Heames
	Pro–62 I Woosnam
V'trs	WD–U WE–M
Fees	£6
Loc	15 miles NW of Cardiff

Powys

Brecon (1902)

Llanfaes, Brecon
Tel	(0874) 2004
Mem	210
Sec	DHE Roderick (0874) 5547
Holes	9 L 5218 yds SSS 66
Recs	Am–61 R Dixon
	Pro–66 WO Moses
V'trs	U
Fees	£8
Loc	1/2 mile from Brecon on A40

Builth Wells (1923)

Golf Club Road, Builth Wells
LD2 3NN
Tel	(0982) 553296
Mem	425
Sec	MA Sanders
Pro	W Evans (0982) 553293
Holes	18 L 5376 yds SSS 67
V'trs	UH SOC
Fees	£12 (£15)
Loc	Llandovery road

Cradoc (1967)

Penoyre Park, Cradoc, Brecon
LD3 9LP
Tel	(0874) 3658
Mem	710
Sec	GSW Davies
Pro	D Beattie (0874) 5524
Holes	18 L 6234 yds SSS 71
Recs	Am–65 DK Wood (1982)
V'trs	Sun–M SOC
Fees	£13 (£16)
Loc	2 miles NW of Brecon, off B4520

Knighton (1913)

Little Ffrydd Wood, Knighton
Tel	(0547) 528646
Mem	124
Sec	EJP Bright (Hon)
Holes	9 L 5320 yds SSS 66
Recs	Am–66 M Caine
	Pro–71 H Vardon
V'trs	U SOC
Fees	£4 (£6)
Loc	1/2 mile SW of Knighton

Llandrindod (1905)

Llandrindod Wells
Tel	(0597) 823873/ 822010
Mem	550
Sec	FT James (Sec/ Mgr)
Holes	18 L 5759 yds SSS 68
Recs	Am–65 CJ Davies (1988)
V'trs	U SOC
Fees	£10 (£15)
Loc	1 mile E of Llandrindod Wells

Llanidloes (St Idloes)

Penrhalt, Llanidloes
Tel	(055 12) 2559
Mem	120
Sec	A Wynn Edwards (055 12) 2205
Holes	9 L 5210 yds SSS 66
Recs	Am–63 J Davies
V'trs	U
Fees	£3 (£4) W–£12
Loc	1/2 mile on Trefeglwys Road

Machynlleth (1905)

Ffordd Drenewydd, Machynlleth
SY20 8UH
Tel	(0654) 702000
Mem	233
Sec	G Holdsworth (0654) 703264
Holes	9 L 5726 yds SSS 67
Recs	Am–65 Pro–65
V'trs	U Sun–NA before 11.30am SOC
Fees	£10
Loc	1 mile E of Machynlleth, off A489

Old Rectory Hotel (1968)

Llangattock, Crickhowell NP8 1PH
Tel	(0873) 810373
Mem	200
Sec	D Best
Holes	9 L 1409 yds SSS 54
V'trs	U
Fees	£6
Loc	8 miles W of Abergavenny

St Giles Newtown (1919)

Pool Road, Newtown
Tel	(0686) 625844
Mem	290
Sec	KG Williams
Pro	DP Owen
Holes	9 L 5864 yds SSS 68
Recs	Am–64 A Jones
	Pro–64 AP Parkin
V'trs	WD/ BH–I WE–restricted
Fees	£6 (£7) SOC–£7
Loc	3/4 mile E of Newtown

Welshpool (1929)

Golfa Hill, Welshpool
Tel	(093 883) 249
Mem	300
Sec	RGD Jones (0938) 3377
Holes	18 L 5708 yds SSS 69
Recs	Am–65 DH Ryan
	Pro–69 S Bowen
V'trs	U
Fees	£8 (£15)
Loc	4 1/2 miles from Welshpool, on Dolgellau road

South Glamorgan

Brynhill (1921)

Port Road, Colcot, Barry
Tel	(0446) 735061
Mem	700
Sec	DP Lloyd (0446) 720277
Pro	P Fountain (0446) 733660
Holes	18 L 6021 yds SSS 69
Recs	Am–67 P Cooper
V'trs	WD/ Sat–U SOC–WD
Fees	£15 Sat–£15 SOC–£12
Loc	A4050, 8 miles W of Cardiff

Cardiff (1921)

Sherborne Avenue, Cyncoed,
Cardiff CF2 6SJ
Tel	(0222) 753067
Mem	930
Sec	K Lloyd (0222) 753320
Pro	T Hanson (0222) 754772
Holes	18 L 6015 yds SSS 70
Recs	Am–65 J Lee (1988)
	Pro–63 L Farmer (1987)
V'trs	WD–H WE–M SOC–Thurs
Fees	£25
Loc	3 miles N of Cardiff. 2 miles from Pentwyn exit of A48(M). M4 Junction 29

Dinas Powis (1914)

Dinas Powis
Tel	(0222) 512727
Mem	650
Sec	JD Hughes
Pro	G Bennett
Holes	18 L 5377 yds SSS 66
Recs	Am–65 P Davidson
	Pro–67 P Fountain
V'trs	U
Fees	£15 (£20)
Loc	3 miles W of Cardiff

Glamorganshire (1890)

Lavernock Road, Penarth CF6 2UP
Tel	**(0222) 707048**
Sec	GC Crimp (0222) 701185
Pro	A Kerr-Smith (0222) 707401
Holes	18 L 6150 yds SSS 70
Recs	Am–65 MG Mouland (1979), N Grimmitt (1989) Pro–65 A Jacklin (1969)
V'trs	WD/ WE–H SOC
Fees	£15 (£20)
Loc	5 miles SW of Cardiff

Llanishen (1905)

Cwm, Lisvane, nr Cardiff
CF4 5UD
Tel	**(0222) 752205**
Mem	900
Sec	ET Davies (0222) 755078
Pro	RA Jones (0222) 755076
Holes	18 L 5296 yds SSS 66
Recs	Am–64 MJG Strange Pro–63 JT Taylor
V'trs	WD–U WE–M H SOC
Fees	£20
Loc	5 miles N of Cardiff

RAF St Athan (1977)

Barry CF6 9WA
Tel	**(0446) 751043**
Mem	415
Sec	DM Llewellyn (0446) 742142
Holes	9 L 5957 yds SSS 69
V'trs	U Sun am–NA
Fees	£8 (£10)
Loc	2 miles E of Llantwit Major

Radyr (1902)

Radyr, nr Cardiff CF4 8BS
Tel	**(0222) 842442**
Mem	880
Sec	Maj MB Richards (0222) 842408
Pro	S Gough (0222) 842476
Holes	18 L 6031 yds SSS 70
Recs	Am–64 P Price Pro–63 PW Evans
V'trs	WD–H WE–M SOC–Wed & Fri
Fees	£10
Loc	5 miles NW of Cardiff

Wenvoe Castle (1936)

Wenvoe, nr Cardiff
Tel	**(0222) 591094**
Mem	525 100(L) 50(J)
Sec	EJ Dew (0222) 594371
Pro	MA Pycroft (0222) 593649
Holes	18 L 6422 yds SSS 71
Recs	Am–68 N Jones (1989) Pro–66 PW Evans (1990)
V'trs	WD–H WE/ BH–M SOC
Fees	£17
Loc	4 miles W of Cardiff

Whitchurch (Cardiff) (1915)

Pantmawr Road, Whitchurch, Cardiff
CF4 6XD
Tel	**(0222) 620125**
Mem	438 111(L) 90(J)
Sec	DO Bartlett (0222) 620985
Pro	E Clark (0222) 614660
Holes	18 L 6319 yds SSS 70
Recs	Am–62 J Povall Pro–62 I Woosnam
V'trs	WD–U WE/ BH–M H SOC–WD
Fees	£20 (£25)
Loc	3 miles NW of Cardiff on A470. M4 Junction 32, 2 miles

West Glamorgan

Clyne (1920)

120 Owls Lodge Lane, Mayals,
Swansea
Tel	**(0792) 401989**
Mem	650
Sec	BR Player
Pro	M Bevan (0792) 402094
Holes	18 L 6312 yds SSS 71
Recs	Am–66 C Dickens(1982) Pro–64 M Bevan (1990)
V'trs	U H SOC
Fees	£13 (£17)
Loc	Swansea

Fairwood Park (1969)

Blackhills Lane, Upper Killay,
Swansea SA2 7JN
Tel	**(0792) 203648**
Mem	725
Sec	J Beer, J Pettifer (Mgr)
Pro	M Evans (0792) 299194
Holes	18 L 6606 yds SSS 72
Recs	Am–69 R Maliphant, I Roberts (1989) Pro–67 J Lomas (1989), A Griffiths, M Wooton (1990)
V'trs	U SOC
Fees	£17 (£22)
Loc	Swansea Airport 1/4 mile

Glynneath (1931)

Penycraig, Pontneathvaughan,
Glynneath SA11 5UG
Tel	**(0639) 720452**
Mem	350
Sec	RM Ellis (0639) 720679
Holes	18 L 5425 yds SSS 67
Recs	Am–66 JL Davies Pro–66 P Mayo
V'trs	U
Fees	£10 (£20)
Loc	2 miles N of Glynneath on B4242

Inco (1965)

Clydach, Swansea
Tel	**(0792) 844216**
Mem	260
Sec	DGS Murdoch (0792) 843336
Holes	12 L 6273 yds SSS 70
Recs	Am–68 V Smith, N O'Sullivan
V'trs	U
Fees	£8 (£9)
Loc	Swansea Valley

Langland Bay (1904)

Langland, Swansea SA3 4QR
Tel	**(0792) 366023**
Mem	620
Sec	TJ Jenkins (0792) 361721
Pro	TJ Lynch (0792) 366186
Holes	18 L 5830 yds SSS 69
Recs	Am–63 K Jones, S Dodd (1989) Pro–69 D Ridley
V'trs	U SOC
Fees	£15 (£17)
Loc	6 miles W of Swansea

Morriston (1919)

160 Clasemont Road, Morriston,
Swansea SA6 6AJ
Tel	**(0792) 771079**
Mem	400
Sec	LT Lewis (0792) 796528
Pro	DA Rees (0792) 772335
Holes	18 L 5773 yds SSS 68
Recs	Am–68 MJ Thomas Pro–64 DA Rees
V'trs	U H SOC–WD
Fees	£11.50 (£18.50)
Loc	4 miles NW of Swansea on A48. M4 Junction 46, 1 mile

Neath (1934)

Cadoxton, Neath
Tel	**(0639) 643615**
Mem	450
Sec	JR Evans (0639) 632759
Pro	EM Bennett
Holes	18 L 6500 yds SSS 72
Recs	Am–69 BOS Vanstone Pro–66 F Hill
V'trs	U
Fees	£8 (£12)
Loc	Neath 2 miles

Palleg (1930)

Palleg Road, Lower Cwmtwrch,
Swansea Valley SA9 1QT
Tel	**(0639) 842193**
Mem	200
Sec	AW Stanley (0639) 730772
Holes	9 L 3209 yds SSS 72
Recs	Am–71 C Williams, N Turner (1990)
V'trs	WD–U WE–NA
Fees	£8
Loc	Ystalyfera 1 mile. Ystradgynlais 1 mile

For list of abbreviations see page 487.

Pennard (1896)

2 Southgate Road, Southgate, nr
Swansea SA3 2BT
Tel   (044 128) 3131
Mem 775
Sec   JD Eccles (044 128) 3131/ 3170
Pro   MV Bennett (044 128) 3451
Holes 18 L 6275 yds SSS 71
Recs Am–69 H Guest
      Pro–66 G Ryall (1987)
V'trs U H SOC
Fees £13 (£17) W–£55
Loc   8 miles W of Swansea, by
      A4067 and B4436

Pontardawe (1924)

Cefn Llan, Pontardawe, Swansea
Tel   (0792) 863118
Mem 700
Sec   L Jones
Pro   RA Ryder (0792) 830977
Holes 18 L 6061 yds SSS 70
Recs Am–66 B Fisher
      Pro–71 D Thomas, R Brook
V'trs H SOC
Fees £12.50
Loc   5 miles N of M4 Junction 45
      (A4067)

Swansea Bay (1894)

Jersey Marine, Neath SA10 6JP
Tel   (0792) 812198/ 814153
Mem 400
Sec   Mrs D Goatcher
Pro   M Day
Holes 18 L 6302 yds SSS 70
Recs Am–67 A Evans
V'trs U
Fees £13 (£18)
Loc   1/2 mile from Jersey Marine, off
      A483 between Swansea and
      Neath.

Driving Ranges

England

Bedfordshire

Mowsbury Driving Range

Kimbolton Road, Bedford MK41 8DQ
Tel   (0234) 216374
Hrs   Open 9am–9pm.
Pro   Tuition available.
Bays 14 covered floodlit.
Fees £1.60 for 60 balls.
Loc   3 miles N of Bedford on B660.

Stockwood Park Golf Range

Stockwood Park, London Road,
Luton LU7 4LX
Tel   (0582) 413704
Hrs   Open 8am–9.30pm (exc
      winter WE–8am–6pm). Tuition
      available.
Bays 20 covered floodlit
Fees £1.35 for 50 balls.
Loc   1 mile S of Luton on A6.

Tilsworth Golf Centre

Dunstable Road, Tilsworth, Leighton
Buzzard
Tel   (0525) 210721/2
Hrs   Open 10am–9.30pm. Tuition
      available–£7 per 1/2 hour.
Bays 30 floodlit.
Fees £1.35 for 50 balls.
Loc   2 miles N of Dunstable, off A5.
Mis   9 hole course. Golf shop.

Berkshire

Downshire Golf Range

Easthampstead Park, Wokingham
Tel   (0344) 424066
Hrs   Open 8am–dusk WD, 7am–
      dusk WE. Tuition available.
Bays 22
Fees £1 for 30 balls.
Loc   Off Nine Mile Ride, between
      Bracknell and Wokingham.
Mis   18 hole course. 9 hole pitch &
      putt.

Hawthorn Hill Golf Range

Drift Road, Hawthorn Hill, nr
Maidenhead SL6 3ST
Tel   (0628) 771030/ 75588/ 26035
Hrs   Open 8am–10pm. Tuition
      available.
Bays 36 covered floodlit.
Fees £2 for 55 balls.
Loc   4 miles S of Maidenhead on
      A330.
Mis   18 hole course.

Lavender Park Golf Centre

Swinley Road, Ascot
Tel   (0344) 884074
Hrs   Open 10am–10pm WD,
      10am–9pm WE.
Bays 24 floodlit.
Fees £1.60 for 45 balls.
Loc   W of Ascot on B3017.
Mis   9 hole course.

Sindlesham Driving Range

Mole Road, Wokingham RG11 5DB
Tel   (0734) 788494
Hrs   Open 7am–10pm. Tuition
      available.
Bays 30 floodlit.
Fees £1 for 25 balls.
Loc   W of Wokingham, off A329.

Buckinghamshire

Colnbrook Golf Driving Range

Galleymead Road, Colnbrook,
Slough SL3 0EN
Tel   (0753) 682670/ 685127
Hrs   Open 9.30am–10.30pm.
      Tuition available.
Bays 27 floodlit.
Fees 50p for 20 balls.
Loc   5 miles from M4 Junction 5, or
      M25 Junction 14.

Wavendon Golf Centre

Lower End Road, Wavendon, Milton
Keynes MK17 8DA
Tel   (0908) 281811
Hrs   Open 8am–10pm WD,
      6am–10pm WE. Tuition
      available.
Bays 26 covered floodlit.
Fees Bucket of balls £1.50.
Loc   1 1/2 miles from M1 Junction 13.
Mis   18 hole course. 9 hole Par 3
      course. Golf shop.

Windmill Hill Golf Complex

Tattenhoe Lane, Bletchley, Milton
Keynes
Tel   (0908) 378623
Hrs   Open 9am–9pm WD,
      9am–8pm WE. Tuition
      available.
Bays 5 open and 23 covered floodlit.
Fees £1.30 for 45 balls.
Loc   4 miles from M1 Junction 14,
      on A421.
Mis   18 hole course. Practice
      bunker. Golf shop.

Cambridgeshire

Abbotsley Golf Range

Eynesbury Hardwicke, St Neots
PE19 4XN
Tel   (0480) 215153
Hrs   Open 8.30am–10.30pm. Tuition
         available: Vivien Saunders.
Bays   14 covered floodlit.
Fees   £2 for 70 balls.
Loc   2 miles S of St Neots (B1046).
         M11 Junction 13, on to A45.
Mis   27 hole course. Practice
         bunkers. Golf shop.

Hemingford Golf Centre

Rideaway, Hemingford Abbots,
Huntingdon PE18 9HQ
Hrs   Open 10am–10pm. Tuition
         available.
Bays   30 floodlit.
Fees   £1.60 for 45 balls.
Loc   10 miles W of Cambridge on
         A604.
Mis   9 hole course. Golf shop.

Channel Islands

Les Mielles

St Ouens Bay, Jersey
Tel   (0534) 82787
Hrs   Open 10am–dusk. Tuition
         available.
Bays   30.
Fees   50p for 20 balls.
Loc   Five Mile Road.
Mis   9 hole Par 3 course.

Cleveland

Middlesbrough Driving Range

Ladgate Lane, Middlesbrough TS5 7YZ
Tel   (0642) 315533
Hrs   Open 10am–9pm WD,
         10am–5pm WE. Tuition
         available–(0642) 315361.
Bays   20 covered floodlit.
Fees   Bucket of balls £1.70.
Loc   2 miles S of Middlesbrough, nr
         A174.
Mis   18 hole course.

Devon

Ilfracombe & Woolacombe Driving Range

Woolacombe Road, Ilfracombe
EX34 7HF
Tel   (0271) 866222
Hrs   Open 8am–6pm (Summer),
         10am–4pm (Winter–WE only).
         Tuition available.

Bays   18 bays, 12 covered.
Fees   £1.85 for 50 balls.
Loc   1 mile from Mullacott Cross on
         B3343.
Mis   18 hole putting course.
         Practice bunkers.

Dorset

East Dorset Driving Range

Hyde, Wareham BH20 7NT
Tel   (0929) 472272
Hrs   Open 10am–10pm WD, 10am–
         6pm WE. Tuition available.
Bays   22 bays, 12 covered.
Fees   Bucket of balls £2
Loc   5 miles from Wareham.
Mis   18 hole course. Golf shop.

Halstock Driving Range

Common Lane, Halstock, nr Yeovil
Tel   (0935) 89689
Hrs   Open 10am–7.30pm. Tuition
         available.
Bays   12 covered floodlit.
Fees   Bucket of balls £1.70.
Loc   6 miles S of Yeovil, off A37.
Mis   9 hole course. Practice
         bunker. Putting.

Iford Bridge Golf Range

Barrack Road, Christchurch
Tel   (0202) 473817
Hrs   Open 8am–dusk. Tuition
         available.
Bays   14 open.
Fees   £1.50 for 50 balls.
Loc   Bournemouth/ Christchurch
         boundary.
Mis   Practice bunker. Putting.

Durham

Aycliffe Golf Driving Range

School Lane, Newton Aycliffe DL5 6QZ
Tel   (0325) 300700
Hrs   Open 10am–9pm WD, 10am–
         7pm WE. Tuition available.
Bays   18 covered floodlit.
Fees   Bucket of balls £1.25/ £1.50.
Loc   1 mile W of Newton Aycliffe on
         A6072.
Mis   9 hole course.

Essex

Belhus Park Leisure Complex

South Ockenden, Thurrock RM15 4PX
Tel   (0708) 852248
Hrs   Open 10am–10pm WD,
         9am–6pm (Sat), 9am–8pm

         (Sun). Tuition available.
Bays   11.
Fees   £1.55 for 50 balls.
Loc   1 mile N of A13/ M25 (Dartford
         Tunnel).

Brentwood Park Golf Range

Brentwood Park, Warley Gap,
Brentwood CM13 3LE
Tel   (0277) 211994
Hrs   Open 9am–10pm. Tuition
         available.
Bays   22 covered floodlit.
Fees   Bucket of balls £2–£3.
Loc   1 mile S of Brentwood on
         Warley road. M25 Junction 28,
         2 miles.

Bunsay Downs Indoor Driving Range

Little Baddow Road, Woodham
Walter CM9 6RW
Tel   (024541) 2648/ 2369
Hrs   Open 7am–11pm WD,
         6am–11pm WE. Tuition
         available.
Bays   4.
Fees   £1 for 50 balls.
Loc   1¹/₂ miles N of Danbury, off
         A414 towards Woodham
         Walter.
Mis   9 hole course. Golf shop.

Colchester Golf Range

Old Ipswich Road, Ardleigh,
Colchester
Tel   (0206) 230974
Hrs   Open 10am–9pm WD,
         10am–5pm WE. Tuition
         available.
Bays   12 floodlit.
Fees   £1.25 for 30 balls.
Loc   1 mile NE of Colchester, off
         A12.
Mis   Practice bunkers. Putting.

Fairlop Waters Golf Range

Forest Road, Barkingside, Ilford
Tel   (081) 500 9911
Hrs   Open 10am–9.30pm. Tuition
         available.
Bays   36 covered floodlit.
Fees   £1.20 for 40 balls.
Loc   2 miles from S end of M11, by
         Fairlop Tube Station.
Mis   18 and 9 hole courses. Golf
         shop.

Towerlands Golf Range

Panfield Road, Braintree CM7 5BJ
Tel   (0376) 26802
Hrs   Open 8.30am–dusk.
Bays   6.
Fees   £1.25 for 50 balls.
Loc   1 mile NW of Braintree.
Mis   9 hole course.

Warren Park Golf Centre

Whalebone Lane North, Chadwell
Heath RM6 6SB
Tel   (081) 597 1120
Hrs   Open 10am–10pm WD/ Sun,
     10am–9pm Sat. Tuition and
     video lessons available.
Bays 30 covered floodlit.
Fees £1.50 for 35 balls.
Loc   A12 between Gants Hill and
     Romford.
Mis   Golf discount store.

Gloucestershire

Gloucester Hotel & CC

Robinswood Hill, Gloucester
Tel   (0452) 25653
Hrs   Open 10am–10pm. Tuition
     available.
Bays 12 floodlit.
Fees £1 for 30 balls.
Loc   2 miles S of Gloucester.
Mis   18 hole course. 9 hole Par 3
     course.

Hampshire

Basingstoke Golf Centre

Worting Road, West Ham, Basingstoke
Tel   (0256) 50054
Hrs   Open 9.30am–9.30pm. Tuition
     available–M Reeves.
Bays 24 floodlit.
Fees £1 for 30 balls.
Loc   Basingstoke Leisure Park.
Mis   9 hole Par 3 course. Golf shop.

Old Thorns Driving Range

Longmoor Road, Liphook GU30 7PE
Tel   (0428) 72455 Tuition available.
Bays 4 covered.
Fees Bucket of balls £2.
Loc   1 mile from Liphook on B2131.
Mis   18 hole course. Putting.

Portsmouth Golf Centre

Eastern Road, Portsmouth
Tel   (0705) 664549
Hrs   Open 8am–9pm. Tuition
     available.
Bays 30 covered floodlit.
Fees £1.60 for 50 balls.
Mis   Golf shop.

Tadley Driving Range

Bishopswood Lane, Tadley,
Basingstoke RG26 6AT
Tel   (0734) 815213
Hrs   Open 8am–9pm. Tuition
     available.
Bays 12 covered floodlit.
Fees Bucket of balls £1.70.
Loc   6 miles N of Basingstoke, off
     A340.
Mis   9 hole course. Golf shop.

Hereford & Worcester

Abbey Park Driving Range

Dagnell End Road, Redditch
Tel   (0527) 63918
Hrs   Open dawn–dusk. Tuition
     available.
Bays 12 covered.
Fees Bucket of balls £1.
Loc   On B4101, off A441 Redditch–
     Birmingham road. M42
     Junction 2.
Mis   18 hole course. Golf shop.

Hertfordshire

Bushey Golf Range

High Street, Bushey WD2 1BJ
Tel   (081) 950 2283
Hrs   Open 9am–10pm. Tuition
     available.
Bays 27 covered floodlit.
Fees £1 for 40 balls.
Loc   1½ miles S of Watford. 3 miles
     W of M1.
Mis   9 hole course.

Elstree Golf Range

Watling Street, Elstree WD6 3AA
Tel   (081) 953 6115
Hrs   Open 10am–10pm. Individual
     and group tuition available.
Bays 44 covered floodlit.
Fees £2 for 65 balls.
Loc   8 miles N of London. 2 miles
     from A41 along A5183.
Mis   18 hole course.

Little Hay Golf Range

Box Lane, Bovingdon, Hemel
Hempstead HP3 0DQ
Tel   (0442) 833798
Hrs   Open 10am–10pm. Tuition
     available.
Bays 23 covered floodlit.
Fees Basket of balls £1.
Loc   2 miles W of Hemel on B4505.
     1 mile from A41.
Mis   18 hole course.

Stevenage Golf Range

Aston Lane, Stevenage SG2 7EL
Tel   (043 888) 424
Hrs   Open 7.30am–9.30pm. Tuition
     available.
Bays 24 covered floodlit.
Fees £1.50 for 50 balls.
Loc   Off A602 Hertford road.
Mis   18 and 9 hole courses.

Watford Driving Range

Sheepcot Lane, Garston, Watford
Tel   (0923) 675560
Hrs   Open 10am–10pm. Tuition
     available.
Bays 18 covered floodlit.
Fees £1 for 35 balls.
Loc   N Watford.

Welwyn Hatfield Sports Centre

Stanborough Road, Welwyn Garden
City
Tel   (0707) 331056
Hrs   Open 10am–10pm.
Bays 24 floodlit.
Fees £1.50 for 48 balls.
Loc   S of Welwyn Garden City, nr
     A1(M).

Whaddon Golf Centre

Whaddon, Royston
Tel   (0223) 207325
Hrs   Open 9am–9pm WD,
     9am–dusk WE. Tuition
     available.
Bays 14 covered floodlit.
Fees £1 for 50 balls.
Loc   4 miles N of Royston, off
     A1198.
Mis   9 hole Par 3 course.

Whitehill Golf Centre

Dane End, Ware SG12 0JS
Tel   (0920) 438495
Hrs   Open 7am–10pm WD,
     7am–dusk WE.
     Tuition: S James, R Green.
Bays 25 open and 25 covered
     floodlit.
Fees Bucket of balls £2.
Loc   6 miles N of Ware, off A10.
Mis   18 hole course. Practice
     bunker.

Humberside

Hull Golf Centre

National Avenue, Hull HU5 4JB
Tel   (0482) 492720
Hrs   Open 9.30am–9pm WD,
     9.30am–7.30pm WE. Tuition
     available.
Bays 24 covered floodlit.
Fees Bucket of balls £1.
Mis   Pitch & putt.

Kent

Chatham Golf Centre

Street–End Road, Chatham
Tel   (0634) 848925
Hrs   Open 10am–10pm. Tuition
     available.
Bays 36 floodlit.
Fees £1.70 for 50 balls.

Edenbridge G & CC

Crouch House Road, Edenbridge TN8 5LQ
Tel   (0732) 865202
Hrs   Open 8am–10pm. Tuition available.
Bays   16 floodlit.
Fees   Basket of balls £1.95.
Loc   15 mins from Sevenoaks, Tonbridge and M25.
Mis   18 hole course. 9 hole Par 3 course. Golf shop. Putting.

Princes Golf Range

Princes Golf Club, Sandwich Bay
Tel   (0304) 613797
Hrs   Open 8am–dusk. Tuition available.
Bays   Open practice area.
Fees   Bucket of balls £2–£3.
Loc   Sandwich Bay.

Ruxley Park Golf Centre

Sandy Lane, St Pauls Cray, Orpington BR5 3HY
Tel   (0689) 871490
Hrs   Open 8am–10pm Tuition available.
Bays   28 covered floodlit bays
Fees   £2.30 for 50 balls
Loc   Nr Ruxley roundabout (A20)
Mis   18 hole course. Shop

Lancashire

Kearsley Golf Range

Moss Lane, Kearsley, Bolton BL4 8SF
Tel   (0204) 75726
Hrs   Open 11am–10pm WD, 11am–5pm WE. Tuition available.
Bays   10 covered floodlit.
Fees   £1.10 for 25 balls.
Loc   4 miles S of Bolton on A666.
Mis   9 hole pitch & putt.

Phoenix Golf Driving Range

Fleetwood Road, Norbreck, Blackpool
Tel   (0253) 854846
Hrs   Open 9am–dusk. Tuition available.
Bays   23 open and covered floodlit.
Fees   Basket of balls £1.40.
Loc   N Blackpool.
Mis   9 hole Par 3 course. Practice bunkers.

Preston Golf Driving Range

Lightfoot Lane, Fulwood, Preston
Tel   (0772) 861827
Hrs   Open 9.30am–9pm WD, 9am–12.00 WE. Individual and group tuition available.
Bays   23 covered floodlit.

Fees   £1.50 for 50 balls.
Loc   1 mile W of M6 Junction 32, nr Rugby Club.
Mis   Practice bunker.

Leicestershire

Range Inn Golf Range

Melton Road, Leicester
Tel   (0533) 664400
Hrs   Open 10am–10pm. Tuition available.
Bays   25 covered floodlit.
Fees   £1.20 for 60 balls.
Loc   N Leicester.
Mis   9 hole pitch & putt.

Whetstone Golf Range

Cambridge Road, Cosby, Leicester
Tel   (0533) 861424
Hrs   Open 8am–dusk. Tuition available.
Bays   20.
Fees   £1.50 for 70 balls.
Loc   S of Leicester.
Mis   18 hole course.

Lincolnshire

Horncastle Golf Range

Horncastle Golf Club, West Ashby, Horncastle LN9 5PP
Tel   (0507) 526800
Hrs   Open 8am–11pm. Tuition available.
Bays   25 covered floodlit.
Fees   £2.50 for 100 balls.
Loc   Horncastle 1 mile, off A158.
Mis   18 hole course. Golf shop.

Lincoln Golf Range

Washingborough Road, Washingborough, Lincoln
Hrs   Open 10.30am–9pm. Tuition available.
Bays   20 floodlit.
Fees   Basket of balls £1.30.
Loc   Washingborough, SW of Lincoln.
Mis   9 hole Par 3 course.

Thonock Driving Range

Thonock, Gainsborough DN21 1PZ
Tel   (0427) 613088
Hrs   Open 8am–9pm. Tuition available.
Bays   20 covered floodlit.
Fees   £1 for 48 balls.
Loc   N of Gainsborough.
Mis   18 hole course.

London

Chingford Golf Range

Waltham Way, Chingford, London E4 8AQ
Tel   (081) 529 2409
Hrs   Open 9.30am–10pm. Tuition and video lessons available.
Bays   18 covered floodlit
Fees   £1.30 for 40 balls.
Loc   1 mile N of North Circular Road, at Chingford. 3 miles S of M25 Junction 26.
Mis   2-tier range. Putting green. Practice bunker. Golf shop. Club repair.

Fairways Golf Range

Walthamstowe Avenue, Chingford, London E4 2BP
Tel   (081) 531 5126
Hrs   Open 10am–10pm WD, 9.30am–9.30pm WE.
Bays   24 floodlit.
Fees   £1 for 40 balls.

Finchley Golf Driving Range

444 High Road, Finchley, London N12
Tel   (081) 445 9697
Hrs   Open 9am–10pm. Tuition available.
Bays   24 floodlit.
Fees   Bucket of balls from £1.50.
Loc   Off North Circular Road.
Mis   Putting.

Picketts Lock Golf Driving Range

Picketts Lock Lane, Edmonton, London N9 0AS
Tel   (081) 803 4756
Hrs   Open 10am–9.30pm WD, 9am–8.30pm WE. Tuition available.
Bays   20 covered.
Fees   £1.50 for 70 balls.
Loc   Picketts Lock Leisure Centre.

Manchester (Greater)

Beacon Park Driving Range

Dalton, Up Holland, Wigan WN8 7RU
Tel   (0695) 622700
Hrs   Open 8.30am–9.30pm WD, 7am–9.30pm WE. Tuition available—£6.50–£8.95 per ¹/₂ hour.
Bays   24 covered floodlit.
Fees   £1.25 for 48 balls.
Loc   Nr Up Holland. M6 Junction 26.
Mis   Golf shop.

Castle Hawk Driving Range

Chadwick Lane, Castleton, Rochdale
OL11 3BY
Tel   (0706) 59995
Hrs   Open 9.30am–8pm WD,
       9.30am–6pm WE. Tuition
       available.
Bays   10 covered floodlit.
Fees   £1.50 for 50 balls.
Loc   Castleton Station 1 mile. M62
       Junction 20.

Merseyside

Formby Golf Driving Range

Moss Side, Formby L37 0AF
Tel   (07048) 75952
Hrs   Open 9.30am–9.30pm. Tuition
       available.
Bays   20 covered floodlit.
Fees   £1.30 for 45 balls.
Loc   Formby By–pass A565.
Mis   Putting. Golf shop.

Middlesex

Ealing Golf Range

Rowdell Road, Northolt
Tel   (081) 845 4967
Hrs   Open 10am–10pm. Tuition
       available.
Bays   36 covered floodlit.
Fees   £1 for 30 balls.
Loc   A40 Target roundabout.
Mis   Putting.

Lime Trees Park Golf Range

Ruislip Road, Northolt UB5 6QZ
Tel   (081) 845 3180
Hrs   Open 10am–10pm. Tuition
       available.
Bays   21 floodlit.
Fees   Bucket of balls £1.
Loc   Off A40, nr Polish war
       memorial.
Mis   9 hole course.

Ruislip Driving Range

Ickenham Road, Ruislip HA4 7DQ
Tel   (0895) 638081
Hrs   Open 10am–10pm. Tuition
       available.
Bays   40 floodlit.
Fees   Bucket of balls £1.
Loc   W Ruislip.
Mis   18 hole course.

Norfolk

Norwich Golf Centre

Long Lane, Bawburgh, Norwich
Tel   (0603) 410657
Hrs   Open 8am–dusk. Tuition
       available.
Bays   10.
Fees   Bucket of balls £1.50.
Loc   S of A47, at rear of Royal
       Norfolk Showground.
Mis   9 hole course. Golf shop.

Sprowston Park Driving Range

Wroxham Road, Sprowston,
Norwich NR7 8RP
Tel   (0603) 410657
Hrs   Open 10am–9pm WD,
       10am–5pm WE. Tuition
       available.
Bays   20 covered floodlit.
Fees   Bucket of balls £1–£2.
Loc   2 miles NE of Norwich on
       A1151.
Mis   18 hole course. Golf shop.

Northamptonshire

Delapre Golf Complex

Eagle Drive, Nene Valley Way,
Northampton NN4 0DV
Tel   (0604) 764036/ 763957
Hrs   Open 9am–10pm Tuition
       available.
Bays   36 open and 25 covered
       floodlit bays
Fees   Bucket of balls £1.10–£2.60
Loc   3 miles from M1 Junction 15,
       on A508
Mis   18 hole course. 2 Par 3 courses.
       Pitch & putt. Golf shop.

Nottinghamshire

Carlton Forum Golf Range

Foxhill Road, Carlton, Nottingham
Tel   (0602) 612949
Hrs   Open 10am–10pm WD,
       10am–5pm WE. Tuition
       available.
Bays   28 covered floodlit.
Fees   Bucket of balls 70p.
Loc   N side of Nottingham.

Oxton Driving Range

Oaks Lane, Oxton NG25 0RH
Tel   (0602) 653545
Hrs   Open 8am–9.30pm. Tuition
       available.
Bays   30 covered floodlit.
Fees   Bucket of balls £2.
Loc   9 miles N of Nottingham on
       A614.
Mis   18 and 9 hole courses.

Staffordshire

Craythorne Golf Centre

Craythorne Road, Stretton,
Burton–on–Trent DE13 0AZ
Tel   (0283) 64329
Hrs   Open 9am–9pm WD/ Sat,
       9am–dusk Sun. Tuition
       available.
Bays   14 covered floodlit.
Fees   Bucket of balls £1.
Loc   Stretton, 1½ miles N of
       Burton–A5121/ A38 Junction.
Mis   18 and 9 hole courses.

Suffolk

Ipswich Golf Centre

Bucklesham Road, Ipswich IP3 8TZ
Tel   (0473) 726821
Hrs   Open 8.30am–dusk. Tuition
       available.
Bays   12 open and covered.
Fees   £1 for 45 balls.
Loc   2 miles E of Ipswich.
Mis   Golf shop.

Surrey

Beverley Park Golf Range

Kingston By–Pass, New Malden
KT3 4PH
Tel   (081) 949 9200
Hrs   Open 10am–10pm.
Bays   60 floodlit.
Fees   Bucket of balls £1.50 .
Loc   Off A3, Kingston By–Pass.

Chessington Golf Centre

Garrison Lane, Chessington
KT9 2LW
Tel   (081) 391 0948
Hrs   Open 8am–10pm. Tuition and
       video lessons available.
Bays   18 covered floodlit.
Fees   £1 for 45 balls
Loc   Off A243, opposite
       Chessington South Station.
       M25 Junction 9
Mis   9 hole course. Club repair

Croydon Golf Centre

175 Long Lane, Addiscombe
Tel   (081) 656 1690
Hrs   Open 10am–10pm WD,
       10am–9pm WE. Tuition
       available.
Bays   24 covered floodlit.
Fees   £1.40 for 40 balls.
Loc   3 miles E of Croydon.

Fairmile Golf Range

Portsmouth Road, Cobham
Tel	(0932) 64419
Hrs	Open 10am–10pm WD, 9am–9pm WE Tuition available.
Bays	24 covered floodlit bays
Fees	Bucket of balls £1.50–£2.40
Loc	12 miles SW of London, on A307 between Esher and Cobham
Mis	Practice bunkers. Putting.

Hoebridge Golf Centre

Old Woking GU22 8JH
Tel	(04837) 22611
Hrs	Open 8am–10pm. Tuition available.
Bays	25 covered floodlit.
Fees	£1.70 for 50 balls.
Loc	2 miles off A3 on A247, between Old Woking and West Byfleet
Mis	18 hole course. Par 3 Course. 9 hole intermediate course. Golf shop

Oak Park Golfing Complex

Oak Park, Heath Lane, Crondall, Farnham GU10 5PB
Tel	(0252) 850880
Hrs	Open 9am–9pm. Tuition available.
Bays	16 covered floodlit.
Fees	Bucket of balls £1–£2.
Loc	Off A287, Farnham–Odiham road. M3 Junction 5, 4 miles.
Mis	18 hole course. Practice bunker. Putting.

Oaks Sports Centre

Woodmansterne Road, Carshalton SM5 4AN
Tel	(081) 643 8363
Hrs	Open 9am–10pm. Tuition available.
Bays	14 covered floodlit.
Fees	£1 for 40 balls.
Loc	2 miles from Sutton on B278.
Mis	18 and 9 hole courses.

Richmond Driving Range

Twickenham Road, Richmond TW9 2SS
Tel	(081) 940 5570
Hrs	Open 9am–8.30pm WD, 9am–5.30pm WE (Sept–Apr close at 1pm Sat) Tuition available–S Simpson
Bays	25 covered floodlit bays
Fees	£2 for 75 balls
Loc	By Royal Mid–Surrey GC, off A316 Chertsey Road

Sandown Golf Centre

More Lane, Esher KT10 8AN
Tel	(0372) 63340
Hrs	Open 10am–10pm.
Bays	33 floodlit.
Fees	£2 for 70 balls.
Loc	Sandown Park racecourse.
Mis	9 hole course. 9 hole Par 3 course. Range closed during race meetings.

Silvermere Driving Range

Silvermere Golf Club, Redhill Road, Cobham KT11 1EF
Tel	(0932) 67275
Hrs	Open 10am–9.30pm Tuition available.
Bays	32 floodlit.
Fees	£2 for 70 balls.
Loc	Between Cobham and Byfleet. 1/2 mile from M25 Junction 10, on B366 to Byfleet.
Mis	18 hole course. Chipping targets.

Windlemere Driving Range

Windlesham Road, West End, Woking GU24 9QL
Tel	(0276) 858727
Hrs	Open 8am–10pm. Tuition available.
Bays	12 covered floodlit.
Fees	£2 for 50 balls.
Loc	A319 at Lightwater, nr Bagshot.
Mis	9 hole course. Golf shop. Club repair.

Sussex (East)

Horam Park Driving Range

Chiddingly Road, Horam TN21 0JJ
Tel	(04353) 3477
Hrs	Open 9am–10pm. Tuition and video lessons available.
Bays	18 covered floodlit.
Fees	Bucket of balls £2.
Loc	1/2 mile S of Horam on Chiddingly road.
Mis	9 hole course. Golf shop. Club repair.

Sussex (West)

Fairway Golf Driving Range

Horsham Road, Pease Pottage, Crawley
Tel	(0293) 521706
Hrs	Open 9am–10pm. Tuition available.
Bays	27 floodlit.
Fees	£2 for 70 balls.
Loc	S of Crawley, off A23.
Mis	9 hole course.

Tyne & Wear

Gosforth Park Golfing Complex

High Gosforth Park, Newcastle–upon–Tyne
Tel	(091) 236 4480
Hrs	Open 8am–10pm. Tuition available.
Bays	30 covered floodlit.
Fees	£1.50 for 70 balls.
Loc	5 miles N of Newcastle.
Mis	9 hole pitch & putt. Putting.

Washington Golf Range

Stone Cellar Road, Washington
Tel	(091) 417 2626
Hrs	Open 10am–10pm. Tuition available.
Bays	21 floodlit.
Fees	£1.20 for 50 balls.
Loc	A1(M)–North turning to Washington.
Mis	18 hole course. Pitch & putt.

Warwickshire

Brandon Wood Golf Range

Brandon Lane, Wolston, nr Coventry CV8 3GQ
Tel	(0203) 543141
Hrs	Phone for details. Tuition available.
Bays	4 open and 11 covered floodlit.
Fees	Bucket of balls £1–£2.
Loc	6 miles SE of Coventry, off A45 Southbound.
Mis	18 hole course.

Purley Chase Golf Range

Ridge Lane, Nuneaton CV10 0RB
Tel	(0203) 393118/ 395348
Hrs	Open 8am–8pm. Tuition available.
Bays	13 covered floodlit.
Fees	Bucket of balls £1.
Loc	2 miles S of Mancetter (A5).
Mis	18 hole course.

Stratford Oaks Golf Range

Bearley Road, Snitterfield, Stratford–on–Avon CV37 0EZ
Tel	(0789) 731571
Hrs	Open 10am–9pm WD, 10am–6pm WE. Tuition available.
Bays	26 covered floodlit.
Fees	£2.60 for 100 balls.
Loc	4 miles NE of Stratford.
Mis	18 hole course opening 1991.

Warwick Golf Centre

Racecourse, Warwick CV34 5RX
Tel	(0926) 494316
Hrs	Open 10am–9pm WD, 9am–4.30pm WE. Tuition available.
Bays	28 covered floodlit.
Fees	£1 for 30 balls.
Loc	Inside Warwick racecourse.
Mis	9 hole course. Golf shop. Putting. Range closed during race meetings.

West Midlands

Four Ashes Golf Centre

Four Ashes Road, Dorridge, Solihull
B93 8NQ
Tel	(0564) 779055
Hrs	Open 10am–10pm WD, 10am–6pm WE. Tuition available.
Bays	28 covered floodlit.
Fees	£1.20 for 45 balls.
Loc	3 miles S of Solihull. M42 Junction 4.
Mis	Golf shop.

Swindon Ridge Golf Range

Blackhill Wood, Bridgenorth Road,
Swindon, nr Dudley DY3 4PU
Tel	(0902) 896191
Hrs	Open 9am–9.30pm WD, 9am–6pm WE. Tuition available.
Bays	27 floodlit.
Fees	£1.20 for 40 balls.
Loc	5 miles S of Wolverhampton.
Mis	18 hole course. 9 hole Par 3 course. Practice bunker. Putting.

Three Hammers Golf Complex

Old Stafford Road, Coven, nr
Wolverhampton WV10 7PP
Tel	(0902) 790428
Hrs	Open 9.30am–10pm WD, 9am–7pm WE. Tuition available.
Bays	23 covered floodlit.
Fees	Bucket of balls £1.
Loc	5 miles N of Wolverhampton. M6 Junction 10.
Mis	18 hole short course. Golf shop.

Wiltshire

Broome Manor Driving Range

Pipers Way, Swindon SN3 1RG
Tel	(0793) 532403
Hrs	Open 9.30am–9pm. Tuition available.
Bays	20 floodlit.
Fees	Bucket of balls £1.40.
Loc	Swindon 2 miles.
Mis	18 and 9 hole courses.

Yorkshire (South)

Austerfield Park Driving Range

Austerfield, Bawtry, Doncaster
DN10 6RF
Tel	(0302) 710841
Hrs	Open 8am–9pm. Tuition available.
Bays	10 floodlit.
Fees	£1.20 for 60 balls.
Loc	2 miles from Bawtry on A614.
Mis	18 hole course.

Yorkshire (West)

Bradley Park Driving Range

Bradley Road, Huddersfield
Tel	(0484) 539988
Hrs	Open 9am–10pm. Tuition available–£10 for 40 mins.
Bays	14 covered floodlit.
Fees	£2 for 80 balls.
Loc	1½ miles from M62 Junction 25.
Mis	18 hole course. 9 hole Par 3 course.

Ireland

Ballyearl Golf Centre

585 Doagh Road, Newtownabbey,
Belfast BT36 8RZ
Tel	(0232) 848287
Hrs	Open 9am–10pm. Tuition available.
Bays	27 covered floodlit –two tier.
Fees	£1.50 for 50 balls.
Loc	1 mile N of Mossley, off B59.
Mis	9 hole Par 3 course.

The Black Bush Driving Range

Thomastown, Dunshaughlin,
Co Meath
Tel	(1) 250021
Hrs	Open 9am–11pm No tuition available.
Bays	6 covered floodlit.
Fees	Bucket of balls £1.
Loc	½ mile E of Dunshaughlin on Ratoath road.
Mis	18 and 9 hole courses.

Craigavon Golf Centre

Turmoyra Lane, Silverwood, Lurgan,
Craigavon, Co Armagh
Tel	(0762) 326606
Hrs	Open 9am–9.30pm WD, 9am–5pm WE. Tuition available.
Bays	20 covered floodlit.
Fees	£1.30 for 50 balls.
Loc	1½ miles from Lurgan.
Mis	18 hole course. Pitch & putt. Putting.

Downpatrick Golf Range

86 Ardglass Road, Downpatrick,
Co Down BT30 7DX
Tel	(0396) 613558
Hrs	Open 9am–9pm. Tuition available.
Bays	24 covered floodlit.
Fees	£1.25 for 50 balls.
Loc	½ mile SE of Downpatrick on B1.
Mis	Practice bunker. Putting. Golf shop.

Heath Driving Range

The Heath, Portlaoise, Co Laois
Tel	(502) 46533
Hrs	Open 10am–10pm. Tuition available.
Bays	10 covered floodlit.
Fees	£1.50 for 75 balls.
Loc	4 miles NE of Portlaoise.
Mis	18 hole course.

Knockbracken Golf Centre

Ballymaconaghy Road,
Knockbracken, Belfast
Tel	(0232) 792108
Hrs	Open 9am–11pm.
Bays	30 floodlit.
Fees	£1 for 50 balls.
Loc	2 miles SW of Belfast.
Mis	18 hole course. Putting.

Leopardstown Golf Centre

Foxrock, Dublin 18
Tel	(1) 895341/ 895671
Hrs	Open 10am–10pm WD, 9am–6pm WE Tuition available.
Bays	50 open and 36 covered floodlit.
Fees	Bucket of balls £1.50–£2.
Loc	5 miles S of Dublin.
Mis	9 hole course. 18 hole pitch & putt.

Lochgeorge Driving Range

Lochgeorge, Claregalway, Co Galway
Tel	(91) 98202
Hrs	Open 11am–9pm WD/ Sat, 12–7pm Sun.
Bays	7 open and 8 covered floodlit.
Loc	7 miles N of Galway on Tuam road.

Scotland

Auchenharvie Driving Range

Moorpark Road West, Stevenston
KA20 3HU
Tel	(0294) 603103
Hrs	Open 9am–9pm WD, 9am–4pm WE. Tuition available.
Bays	18 floodlit.
Fees	£1.10 for 50 balls.

For list of abbreviations see page 487.

Loc 1 mile W of Stevenston.
Mis 9 hole course.

Clydeway Golf Centre

Blantyre Farm Road, Uddingston, Lanarkshire
Tel (041) 641 8899
Hrs Open 10am–9pm WD, 10am–6pm WE. Tuition available.
Bays 25 floodlit.
Fees £1.40 for 50 balls.
Loc 1½ miles from Glasgow Zoo.
Mis Golf shop.

Glenrothes Golf Range

Stenton Road, Glenrothes, Fife
Tel (0592) 775374
Hrs Open 10am–9pm WD, 10am–6pm WE. Tuition available.
Bays 20 covered floodlit.
Fees £1.25 for 50 balls.
Loc SW of Glenrothes, by Technical College.

Normandy Golf Range

Inchinnan Road, Renfrew PA4 9ES
Tel (041) 886 7477
Hrs Open 9.30am–8.30pm WD, 9.30am–5.30pm WE. Tuition and video lessons available.
Bays 5 open and 20 covered floodlit.
Fees £1.30 for 50 balls.
Loc 1 mile W of Glasgow Airport. M8, 1 mile.

Polkemmet Driving Range

Whitburn, Bathgate, W Lothian EH47 0AD
Tel (0501) 43905
Hrs Open 10am–9pm WD, 9am–9pm WE (Summer); 12–8.30pm WD, 10am–4.30pm WE (Winter).
Bays 15 covered floodlit.
Fees £1.10 for 50 balls.
Loc Between Whitburn and Harthill on B7066.
Mis 9 hole course.

Port Royal Golf Range

Ingliston, Edinburgh, Midlothian
Tel (031) 333 4377
Hrs Open 10am–11pm. Tuition available.
Bays 24 floodlit.
Fees £1.25 for 50 balls.
Loc Nr Edinburgh Airport.
Mis 9 hole Par 3 course. Putting. Golf shop. Club repair.

St Andrews Links Driving Range

St Andrews Links, St Andrews, Fife KY16
Hrs Open daily. Tuition available.
Bays 20 covered floodlit.
Fees Bucket of balls £1–£2.
Loc ½ mile from St Andrews, off A91.
Mis Putting, pitching and bunker facilities.

Strathclyde Park Golf Range

Mote Hill, Hamilton, Lanarkshire
Hrs Open 9.30am–9.30pm. Tuition available.
Bays 24 floodlit.
Fees Bucket of balls £2–£2.50.
Loc A723, just off M74.
Mis 9 hole course.

Tayside Golf Driving Range

The Downs, Barry, nr Carnoustie DD7 7SA
Tel (0382) 534226
Hrs Open 9am–11pm. Tuition available–G Harvey.
Bays 15 floodlit.
Fees £1.50 for 50 balls.
Loc 7 miles from Dundee on Carnoustie road.

Wales

South Wales Golf Range

Port Road East, Barry
Tel (0446) 742434
Hrs Open 9am–8pm WD, 9am–5pm WE. Tuition available.
Bays 16 covered floodlit.
Fees Bucket of balls £1.70.
Loc 8 miles from Cardiff on A4050.
Mis 9 hole Par 3 course. Putting.

Tregroes Driving Range

Fishguard, Dyfed SA65 9QF
Tel (0348) 872316
Hrs Open 10am–8pm. Tuition available.
Bays 6 covered floodlit.
Fees £1 for 50 balls.
Loc 1 mile S of Fishguard on A40.

Something Old, Something New

Michael Gedye

Ask a golfer about places to play in Europe, particularly on holiday, and he will most likely propose the Algarve, the Costa del Sol or the whole sweep of the Mediterranean coast that covers eastern Spain and southern France. The burgeoning market for vacation resorts with golf has become an important factor in the development of new golf courses and has changed not only the appearance of the land but the value of golfing tourism to these regions. Had one, however, asked the golfer's grandfather the same question, he would undoubtedly have chosen differently. He would have considered a series of elegant resorts along the Atlantic coastline stretching from Bordeaux in France south to Lisbon in Portugal, resorts where golf was an important element in the social round.

At the turn of the century and in the golden age before the First World War, those who were sufficiently well-heeled or well-connected took their holidays on the Atlantic seaboard of southwestern France and the northern coast of the Iberian peninsula. The cream of international society met to take the waters, play the casinos and generally create sophisticated retreats for a privileged few. Trade to Britain, particularly in wine, had long established a British presence in both Bordeaux and Oporto. Where the British played or worked, golf was sure to follow and the earliest courses built on the continent were sited near these western coasts. In fact, three of the four oldest golf courses in Continental Europe are to be found here – Golf de Pau (1856), Golf de Biarritz (1888) and Oporto Golf Club (1890).

These were joined by further courses as the fame and popularity of the holiday coasts continued; no less than 13 still survive from the days of the hickory shaft, historic testimony to an elegant era that ended with the Second World War. The rise of package holidays and charter flights to Mediterranean shores during the last 25 years has attracted a new breed of golfer to new areas in the south; the pioneers on the Atlantic coasts were overlooked.

However, the domestic game also grew, nowhere more dramatically than in France, with the result that a number of excellent new courses grace the northern and western coasts, providing golf for local enthusiasts as well as visitors. The new layouts provide an interesting contrast with the old, the latter part of a golfing timewarp and heritage from a noble past. Together they are links in a colourful golfing chain that is gaining renewed interest and respect among travelling golfers.

The trail commences on the outskirts of Lisbon, where the Lisbon Sports Club provided 14 holes for the expatriate community from 1922 while nearby Estoril, in its time considered the most fashionable resort in Europe, formed a club in 1928. The present Estoril course, designed in 1945 by Mackenzie Ross of Turnberry fame, is relatively short but a golfing gem. From the comfortable old clubhouse, strategic and well-manicured holes wind through a forest of pine and eucalyptus – a continuing delight.

These older clubs have been joined more recently by Quinta da Marinha, a Robert Trent Jones design, above the cliffs west of Estoril and the short but highly attractive compact nine holes of Estoril Sol by Ronald Fream. Just south of the River Tagus, Frank Pennink's pine-forest masterpiece at Aroeira is currently being restored to its former splendour under new ownership. A further very demanding 18-hole championship course by Trent Jones lies on a pine-speckled seaside sandbar at Tróia near Setúbal. Additional golf is both planned and under construction in the Lisbon area which is set to become a significant golfing region in the future.

Further up the coast, near the famous battleground of Torres Vedras, the Vimeiro course offers nine Pennink-designed holes next to a seaside hotel. Even further north, in the region of Oporto, golf found one of its earliest European footholds in the Oporto Golf Club, formed by a group of golf-starved port wine shippers in 1890. The course is very level and still essentially British. Just south of the town, Miramar, has nine holes of picturesque golf built in 1934 among the dunes beside the sea. In contrast, the new Estela 18-hole course, to the north near Povoa de Varzim, brings a touch of modern class to traditional golfing linksland. Laid out in narrow, winding green ribbons along the seashore between punishing grassy dunes and with a prevailing

cross-wind, the well-kept course can test players of all levels, as the 1990 Volvo Tour Atlantic Open proved.

The Atlantic coast of Spain stretches from Galicia in the west to Navarra and the Pyrenees in the east. Thirteen courses, seven of which have 18 holes, have been built over the past century and are mostly members' clubs, hardly affected by international tourism. They provide an interesting example of domestic golf over the years and their claim to fame lies not so much in their quality as in the fact that two of them have spawned the most successful pair of professional players in Spanish history – Severiano Ballesteros in Santander and José Maria Olazabal from Fuenterrabia, near San Sebastián.

In the west, two aero clubs (Vigo and Santiago) have 9 holes on or near their respective airports while Club de Golf de la Coruña was opened in 1962 with a 6000-yard 18-hole layout. Of chief interest is Golf La Toja, on a resort island by Pontevedra, with the course winding through pines and bordering the sea on both sides. Although only nine holes, two circuits cover 6877 yards from the back tees. Moving east, Asturias boasts two 18-hole courses – the short parkland of Club de Golf de Castielo (1958) and the comparatively new Club de Deportivo La Barganiza, opened in 1982. On a peninsula in the middle of Santander Bay, Real Golf de Pedreña overlooks the sea and offers interesting holes with a wealth of mature trees. Designed by Englishman Harry Colt in 1928, the course not only nurtured Ballesteros but was the venue for the Spanish Open in 1988.

For a touch of golfing history, however, one needs to venture further east into Basque country, where the 18 holes of the Real Sociedad de Neguri date from 1911. For contrast, Club de Campo La Bilbaina, (constructed in 1976) offers a further 18 holes in the Bilbao area. On the border with France, Real Club de Golf de San Sebastián dates from 1910 and is one of Spain's oldest. Its gently rolling fairways undulate through well-established trees and at 6622 yards form an absorbing test of the game. Completing the link with the past, Real Golf de Zauruz has nine holes near San Sebastián which were opened in 1916.

Turning north into France is a further connection with golf of a former era, the golden years of Biarritz. Its attractive climate drew European royalty and the wealthy which in turn encouraged golf. After all, the first club in Continental Europe was only an hour inland at Pau, formed by the British in 1856. The Biarritz course followed, designed along the cliff-top by Scot, Willie Dunn, in 1888. Next came Golf de Nivelle at St Jean de Luz, laid out in 1907 over sloping wooded land by the redoubtable JH Taylor and then, to meet the demand for the game after the war, three more courses were added – Golf de Chiberta

(Simpson 1926), Chantaco (Colt 1928) and Golf d'Hossegor (Morrison 1929). Of these, probably the best and most popular is Chiberta, which combines links and undulating forest holes of considerable charm. It is interesting to note that this group of established courses on the Atlantic coast of south-west France has, along with the northern coast of Spain, a tradition for producing champions. The Basque Arnaud Massy, first foreign winner of the Open in 1907, has been followed by Catherine Lacoste (US Ladies' Open champion in 1967) and leading lady professional Marie Laure de Lorenzi.

In complete contrast, two new courses a little up the coast represent the latest in modern American golfing design. The first, Golf de Siegnosse by Robert Von Hagge, is carved through a vast pine forest with narrow undulating fairways and numerous grassy mounds and hollows; not too much water but a highly strategic challenge only two years old. The other is Golf de la Côte d'Argent at Moliets (opened in 1988) which bears all the hallmarks of architect Robert Trent Jones. It is unique in that part of the course is open links country by the sea, part rugged heathland and part files through avenues of tall pines. Plenty of room from the tee at most holes but at 7100 yards it is no pushover.

Moving up into the Gironde and true wine country around Bordeaux, one finds the brand new 18 holes of Golf du Gujan Mestras, where heather, fern and gorse complement the gently undulating fairways through the pines, with water in play on eight holes. By the sea, the John Harris-designed course at Lacanau has attracted visitors since 1980 while around Bordeaux itself, there are five courses of quite varied character, the oldest being Golf Bordelais (1900). Golf de Pessac, just opened, offers three separate nines on the edge of the Landes forest. The well-manicured, very playable course had an unusual driving range where floating balls are aimed into a large circular water hazard. Probably the best test in the area is Golf de Médoc, an inland links-style course of just under 7000 yards, where the breeze can play a significant part over its exposed holes, each individually sponsored by Grand Cru châteaux. Finally one must include Golf de Royan on the Côte de Beauté at the northern entrance to the Gironde estuary, for its spectacular holes which plunge past tall stands of pine with ocean views present a golfing challenge for all.

The Atlantic coastline of Iberia and France was the preferred locale for a former generation of golfers who no doubt recognised opportunities to recreate courses in the Scottish style. New developments along these same shores form an intriguing comparison and a fine strand of golfing opportunity.

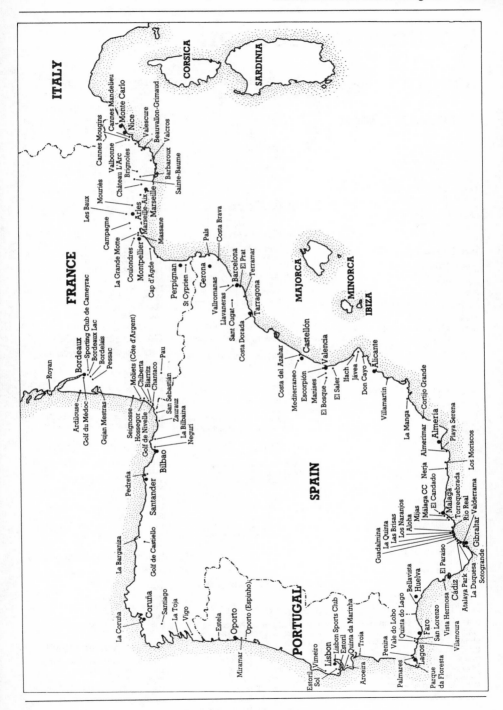

Continental section

Austria

Innsbruck & West

Achensee (1934)

A-6213 Pertisau/Tyrol
Tel   (05243) 5377
Mem   430
Pro   D Posch, I Schaffer
Holes   9 L 3920 m SSS 62
Fees   200s (300s)
Loc   Pertisau, 50km NE of
        Innsbruck

Innsbruck-Igls (1956)

A-6074 Rinn, Oberdorf 11
Tel   (05223) 8177
Mem   650
Pro   I Shaw
Holes   18 L 5935 m SSS 71
        9 L 4657 m SSS 66
Fees   400s (500s)
Loc   18 hole course at Rinn, 10km E
        of Innsbruck. 9 hole course at
        Lans, 8km from Innsbruck
Mis   Handicap certificate required.
        Booking necessary

Kaiserwinkl GC Kössen

A-6345 Kössen, Muhlau 1
Tel   (05375) 2122
Fax   (05375) 2122-13
Mem   250
Pro   C de Castro, K Conboy
Holes   18 L 5920 m SSS 71
Fees   350s (450s)
Loc   40km N of Kitzbühel, nr
        German border

Kitzbühel (1955)

A-6370 Kitzbühel
Tel   (05356) 3007
Mem   400
Pro   S Brown, P Wagstaff
Holes   9 L 6085 m SSS 72
Fees   250s (350s)
Loc   Kitzbühel

Schwarzsee-Kitzbühel (1988)

A-6370 Kitzbühel, Hinterstadt 18
Tel   (05356) 71645
Mem   380
Pro   J Lamberg
Holes   18 L 6247 m SSS 72
Fees   500s (600s)
Loc   5km from Kitzbühel
Mis   Booking necessary

Seefeld-Wildmoos (1987)

A-6100 Seefeld, Postfach 22
Tel   (05212) 2313/2316
Mem   238
Pro   M Mawdsley
Holes   18 L 6046m SSS 72
Fees   280s (400s)
Loc   4km W of Seefeld. 24km W of
        Innsbruck
Mis   Tee booking necessary
        Jul–Sept

Linz & North

Linz-St Florian (1960)

A-4490 St Florian, Tillysburg 28
Tel   (07223) 2873
Mem   652
Pro   J Crisp
Holes   18 L 6091 m SSS 72
Fees   450s (580s)
Loc   St Florian, 15km SE of Linz

Schloss Ernegg (1973)

A-3261 Steinakirchen, Schlosshotel
Ernegg
Tel   (07488) 214 (May-Oct)
Fax   (07488) 6771
Mem   130
Pro   P Kreier
Holes   18 L 5699 m SSS 70
        9 L 2076 m SSS 62
Fees   350s (450s)
Loc   Steinakirchen, 60km SE of Linz
Mis   Driving range, pitch & putt

Wels (1981)

A-4512 Weisskirchen/Wels,
Weyerbach 37
Tel   (07243) 6038
Mem   420
Pro   J Wraith
Holes   18 L 6100 m SSS 72
Fees   300s (400s)
Loc   5km from Salzburg-Vienna
        highway. 8km SE of Wels
Mis   Driving range, pitch & putt.
        Handicap certificate required

Salzburg Region

Badgastein (1962)

A-5640 Badgastein, Postfach 59
Tel   (06434) 2775/2516
Mem   330
Pro   S Wildman
Holes   9 L 5804m SSS 71
Fees   250s (300s) W-1600s
Loc   Badgastein 2km
Mis   Open May-Oct

Europa Sport Region (1983)

A-5700 Zell am See, Golfstr 25
Tel   (06542) 6161
Fax   (06542) 6035
Mem   580
Pro   D Shaw
Holes   18 L 6218 m SSS 72
        9 L 5650 m SSS 69
Fees   18 hole: 420s (530s) 9 hole:
        370s (420s)
Loc   Zell am See, 95km SW of
        Salzburg
Mis   Driving range D-100s. Open
        May-Oct

Goldegg

A-5622 Goldegg, Postfach 6
Tel   (06415) 8585
Fax   (06415) 8580
Mem   250
Pro   R Richards
Holes   9 L 4456 m SSS 64
Fees   280s (330s)
Loc   75km SW of Salzburg

Gut Altentann (1989)

A-5302 Henndorf am Wallersee,
Salzburg
Tel   (06214) 6026
Mem   310
Pro   J Mannie
Holes   18 L 6180 m SSS 72
Fees   800s
Loc   Henndorf, 16km N of Salzburg
Mis   Driving range. Open Apr-Oct

Gut Brandlhof (1983)

A-5760 Saalfelden, Sporthotel Gut
Brandlhof
Tel   (06582) 2176/555
Mem   195
Pro   N Rayne
Holes   18 L 6300 m SSS 73
Fees   350s (400s)
Loc   Saalfelden, 60km SW of
        Salzburg towards Zell am See

Salzburg Klesheim (1955)

A-5071 Wals, bei Salzburg
Tel   (0662) 850851
Mem   420
Pro   D Howard
Holes   9 L 5700m SSS 70
Fees   300s (350s)
Loc   5km N of Salzburg

Salzkammergut (1932)

A-4820 Bad Ischl, Postfach 145
Tel   (06132) 6340
Mem   450
Pro   I Hay, F Laimer, Ch Schuster

Holes	9 L 5900 m SSS 71
Fees	350–400s
Loc	6km W of Bad Ischl, nr Strobl.
	50km E of Salzburg

Schloss Fuschl (1964)

A-5322 Hof/Salzburg	
Tel	(06229) 390
Mem	200
Pro	F Torrano
Holes	9 L 3054 m SSS 61
Fees	150–200s (200s)
Loc	Hof, 12km E of Salzburg
Mis	Driving range

South East

Austria-Wörther See

A-9062 Moosburg, Golfstr 2	
Tel	(04272) 83486
Fax	(04272) 82055
Mem	267
Pro	M Sullivan, J Wraith
Holes	18 L 6216 m SSS 72
Fees	450s (450s)
Loc	6km N of Wörther See
Mis	Driving range

Bad Kleinkirchheim-Reichenau (1984)

A-9546 Bad Kleinkirchheim, Postfach 9	
Tel	(04275) 594
Fax	(04240) 8282-18
Mem	350
Pro	G Manson
Holes	18 L 6084 m SSS 72
Fees	450s
Loc	Kleinkirchheim, 50km NW of Klagenfurt, via Route 95

Gut Murstätten (1989)

A-8403 Lebring, Oedt 4	
Tel	(03182) 3555
Fax	(03182) 3688
Mem	300
Pro	D Eddy
Holes	18 L 6398 m SSS 74
	9 L 3034 m SSS 72
Fees	350s (450s)
Loc	25km S of Graz
Mis	Driving range, pitch & putt

Kärntner (1927)

A-9082 Dellach, 16 Maria Wörth	
Tel	(04273) 2515
Mem	250
Pro	C Prasthofer, D Marsh
Holes	18 L 5700 m SSS 70
Fees	D-400s
Loc	Dellach, S side of Wörther See. 15km W of Klagenfurt

Klopeiner See-Turnersee

A-9122 St Kanzian, Klopeinerstr 5	
Tel	(04239) 3800
Fax	(04239) 3800-18
Mem	151
Holes	18 L 6109 m SSS 72
Fees	450s (450s)
Loc	25km E of Klagenfurt
Mis	Driving range

Murhof (1963)

A-8130 Frohnleiten, Adriach 53	
Tel	(03127) 2101
Mem	380
Pro	GJ Mackintosh
Holes	18 L 6371 m SSS 73
Fees	350s
Loc	Frohnleiten, 25km N of Graz. 150km S of Vienna
Mis	Golf hotel guests–220s

Schloss Frauenthal (1988)

A-8523 Deutschlandberg, Ulrichsberg 3	
Tel	(03462) 5717
Mem	240
Pro	M Thompson
Holes	9 L 5736 m SSS 70
Fees	250s (350s)
Loc	45km SW of Graz
Mis	Driving range

Wörther See/Velden (1988)

A-9231 Köstenberg, Oberdorf 70	
Tel	(04274) 7045/7087
Fax	(04274) 708715
Mem	199
Pro	K Cunningham
Holes	18 L 6152 m SSS 72
Fees	450s (450s)
Loc	30km W of Klagenfurt. 12km from Velden
Mis	Driving range-100s

Steiermark

Dachstein Tauern (1990)

A-8967 Haus/Ennstal, Oberhaus 59	
Tel	(03686) 2630
Fax	(03686) 2630-15
Mem	170
Pro	R Andrews
Holes	18 L 5777 m SSS 71
Fees	500s (600s)
Loc	2km from Schladming. 100km SE of Salzburg

Ennstal-Weissenbach G & LC (1978)

A-8940 Liezen, Postfach 28	
Tel	(03612) 24774
Fax	(03612) 24555
Pro	T Robinson

Holes	9 L 5630m SSS 70
Fees	300s
Loc	5km SW of Liezen, off Salzburg-Graz road

Schloss Pichlarn (1972)

A-8952 Irdning, Ennstal Steiermark	
Tel	(03682) 24393
Fax	(03682) 22841–6
Mem	530
Pro	A Mitchell, M Caines, J Mackie
Holes	18 L 6123m SSS 72
Fees	400s (450s)
Loc	2km E of Irdning, off Salzburg–Graz road. 120km SE of Salzburg

Vienna & East

Brunn (1988)

A-2345 Brunn, Rennweg	
Tel	(02236) 31572/33711
Fax	(02236) 33863
Mem	290
Pro	R Jerman, W Barnett
Holes	18 L 6076 m SSS 72
Fees	D-600s
Loc	15km S of Vienna
Mis	Driving range-200s

Colony Club Gutenhof (1988)

A-2325 Himberg, Gutenhof	
Tel	(02235) 88055
Fax	(0222) 5124571-18
Mem	1000
Pro	A Cox, G Felton
Holes	East 18 L 6335 m SSS 73
	West 18 L 6397 m SSS 73
Fees	500s (600s)
Loc	22km SE of Vienna

Donnerskirchen (1988)

A-7082 Donnerskirchen	
Tel	(02683) 8110/8171
Fax	(02683) 817231
Mem	200
Pro	N Conrad
Holes	18 L 5937 m SSS 71
Fees	390s (480s)
Loc	45km SE of Vienna
Mis	Driving range-100s (130s). Pitch & putt

Enzesfeld (1970)

A-2551 Enzesfeld	
Tel	(02256) 81272
Mem	480
Pro	R Morris
Holes	18 L 6176 m SSS 72
Fees	450s (600s)
Loc	32km S of Vienna towards Vienna Neustadt
Mis	Handicap certificate required

Föhrenwald (1968)

A-2700 Wiener Neustadt,
Postfach 105
Tel   (02622) 29171
Mem   450
Pro   A Andrews, S Page
Holes   18 L 6043 m SSS 72
Fees   300s (400s)
Loc   5km S of Wiener Neustadt on
        Route B54

Hainburg/Donau (1977)

A-2410 Hainburg, Auf der
Heide 762
Tel   (02165) 2628
Mem   195
Pro   R Jerman
Holes   9 L 5950m SSS 71
Fees   250s (350s)
Mis   Open Mar-Nov

St Pölten Schloss Goldegg (1989)

A-3100 St Pölten Schloss Goldegg
Tel   (02741) 7360
Mem   200
Pro   JC Dockray
Holes   18 L 6249 m SSS 73
Fees   400s (500s)
Loc   8km NW of St Pölten. 60km W
        of Vienna
Mis   18 hole Target Golf

Semmering (1926)

A-2680 Semmering, Hochstr 108
Tel   (02664) 8154
Pro   H Blaschek
Holes   9 L 3786 m SSS 60
Fees   200s (300s)
Loc   30km SW of Vienna Neustadt
Mis   Open May–Oct. Driving range

Wien (1901)

A-1020 Wien, Freudenau 65a
Tel   (0222) 2189564 (Clubhouse)
        (0222) 2189667
        (Caddymaster)
Mem   670
Pro   W Walters, T Rogerson
Holes   18 L 5861 m SSS 71
Fees   D-600s
Loc   10 mins SE of Vienna

Wienerwald (1981)

A-3053 Laaben, Forsthof 21
Tel   (0222) 823111
Mem   50
Holes   9 L 4652 m SSS 65
Fees   300s (500s)
Loc   Laaben, 35km W of Vienna

Belgium

Antwerp Region

Bossenstein (1989)

Bossenstein Kasteel, 2250 Broechem
Tel   (03) 485 64 46
Fax   (03) 485 78 41
Pro   J Blair, A Christiaens
Holes   18 L 6203 m SSS 72
        9 L 1500 m
Fees   1000fr (1500fr)
Loc   15km E of Antwerp. 5km N of
        Lier
Mis   Driving range

Cleydael (1988)

Kasteel Cleydael, 2630 Aartselaar
Tel   (03) 887 00 79/887 18 74
Fax   (03) 887 00 15
Mem   450
Pro   R Loveday
Holes   18 L 6059 m SSS 72
Fees   1500fr (2000fr-only after 2pm)
Loc   8km S of Antwerp. 40km N of
        Brussels
Mis   Driving range

Inter-Mol (1984)

Begijnhoefstraat 11, 2360 Oud-
Turnhout
Tel   Fax   (014) 584273
Mem   180
Pro   A Jones
Holes   9 L 1411 m SSS 56
Fees   300fr (400fr)
Loc   Mol-Achterlos, 50km E of
        Antwerp

Lilse (1988)

Haarlebeek 3, 2418 Lille
Tel   (014) 55 19 30
Mem   350
Pro   A Van Damme, F Van Damme
Holes   9 L 4582 m SSS 65
Fees   400fr (600fr)
Loc   Lille, 10km SW of Turnhout, nr
        E7. 25km E of Antwerp

Rinkven G & CC (1980)

St Jobsteenweg 120, 2970 Schilde
Tel   (03) 384 0784
Mem   1000
Pro   M Waldron, F Dhondt
Holes   27 L 6128 m SSS 73
Fees   1250fr (2500fr)
Loc   17km NE of Antwerp, off E19
Mis   Handicap certificate required

Royal Antwerp (1888)

Georges Capiaulei 2, 2950 Kapellen
Tel   (03) 666 8456
Mem   990
Pro   J Halliwell

Holes   18 L 6140 m SSS 73
        9 L 2264 m SSS 33
Fees   1300fr (1400fr)
Loc   Kapellen, 20km N of Antwerp

Steenhoven (1985)

Eerselseweg 40, 2400 Postel-Mol
Tel   (014) 37 72 50
Mem   100
Pro   J Wilkinson
Holes   18 L 5950 m SSS 71
Fees   1500fr (2500fr)
Loc   30 mins W of Antwerp
Mis   Handicap certificate required.
        Tee booking necessary

Ternesse G & CC (1976)

Uilenbaan 15, 2160 Wommelgem
Tel   (03) 353 0292
Fax   (03) 354 02 30
Mem   700
Pro   S Bouillon, V Waters
Holes   18 L 5876 m SSS 72
Fees   1250fr (2500fr)
Loc   E of Antwerp on E313

Ardennes & South

Château Royal d'Ardenne

5560 Houyet Dinant
Tel   (082) 66 62 28
Mem   350
Pro   P Delmas
Holes   18 L 5363 m SSS 71
Fees   1000fr (1500fr)
Loc   9km SE of Dinant on Rochefort
        road

Falnuée (1987)

Rue E Pirson 55, 5830 Mazy
Tel   (081) 63 30 90
Fax   (081) 63 37 64
Mem   450
Pro   M Duhamel
Holes   18 L 5700 m SSS 69
Fees   600fr (800fr)
Loc   18km NW of Namur. Mons–
        Liège highway Junction 13

Golf d'Andenne (1988)

Ferme du Moulin 52, Stud,
5220 Andenne
Tel   (085) 84 34 04
Mem   150
Pro   F Vercruyce, C Bertier
Holes   9 L 2447 m SSS 66
Fees   500fr (700fr)
Loc   Andenne, 20km E of Namur

Mont Garni (1989)

Rue du Mont Garni 3, 7331 Saint
Ghislain
Tel   (065) 62 27 19
Fax   (065) 62 34 10
Mem   300
Pro   F Gabias
Holes   18 L 6353 m SSS 73
Fees   800fr (1200fr)
Loc   St Ghislain, 15km W of Mons.
        65km SW of Brussels

Rougemont

Chemin du Beau Vallon 45,
5170 Profondeville
Tel   (081) 41 14 18
Mem   260
Pro   R Braems
Holes   9 L 2356 m SSS 34
Fees   600fr (800fr)
Loc   10km S of Namur

Royal GC du Hainault (1933)

Rue de la Verrerie 2, 7050 Erbisoeul
Tel   (065) 22 96 10/22 94 74 (Sec)
Fax   (065) 22 51 54
Mem   650
Pro   F Lefever
Holes   18 L 6108 m SSS 72 9 L 3233 m
Fees   1000fr (1500fr)
Loc   6km NW of Mons towards Ath

Brussels & Brabant

Bercuit (1982)

Les Gottes 3, 1390 Grez-Doiceau
Tel   (010) 841501
Mem   500
Pro   P Toussaint
Holes   18 L 5986 m SSS 72
Fees   D-800fr (2500fr)
Loc   27km SE of Brussels. Brussels –
        Namur highway exit 8.

Brabantse (1982)

Steenwagenstraat 11, 1820
Melsbroek
Tel   (02) 752 82 05
Mem   500
Pro   E Rovzar, P Vanderstricht
Holes   18 L 4618 m SSS 65
Fees   800fr (1500fr)
Loc   10km NE of Brussels, nr
        airport

Château de la Bawette (1988)

Chaussée de la Bawette 5, 1300
Wavre
Tel   (010) 22 33 32
Fax   (010) 22 90 04
Mem   600

Pro   D Aime, K Murray
Holes   18 L 6049 m SSS 72
        9 L 2130 m SSS 33
Fees   1500fr (2000fr)
Loc   1km N of Wavre. 20km S of
        Brussels

Duisberg Militaire

Hertswegenstraat 39,
1982 Duisburg
Tel   767 9752/3890 (Ext 388)
Holes   9 L 3630 m SSS 60
Fees   D-200fr (300fr)
Loc   Brussels 13km

Keerbergen (1979)

50 Vlieghavenlaan, 3140
Keerbergen
Tel   (015) 23 49 61
Mem   820
Pro   W Vanbegin, D Ruduck,
        W Mann (015) 23 49 63
Holes   18 L 5530 m SSS 69
Fees   1200fr (1800fr)
Loc   29km NE of Brussels

Rigenée (1981)

Rue de Châtelet 62, 6321 Villers-la-
Ville
Tel   (071) 87 77 65
Mem   550
Pro   Ch Ditlefsen, H Ladmirant
        F Descampe (Touring)
Holes   18 L 6150 m SSS 72
Fees   850fr (1350fr)
Loc   35km S of Brussels towards
        Charleroi

Royal Amicale Anderlecht (1987)

Dreve Olympique 1, 1070 Bruxelles
Tel   (02) 521 16 87
Mem   320
Pro   P Michielsen, J-P Michielsen
Holes   9 L 2660 m SSS 69
Fees   500fr (800fr)
Loc   Brussels

Royal Golf Club de Belgique (1906)

Château de Ravenstein, 3080
Tervueren
Tel   (02) 767 5801
Fax   (02) 767 28 41
Mem   1280
Pro   J Williams, C Ledbury
Holes   18 L 6075 m SSS 72
        9 L 1960 m Par 32
Fees   1550fr (2550fr)
Loc   Tervueren, 15km E of Brussels
Mis   18 hole course limited to h'cap
        (men–20 ladies–24). Phone
        before visit. Handicap
        certificate required.

Royal Waterloo (1923)

Vieux Chemin de Wavre, 1380
Ohain
Tel   (02) 633 18 50/15 97
Fax   (02) 633 28 66
Mem   1900
Pro   G Will, J Blair
Holes   18 L 6276 m SSS 73
        18 L 6269 m SSS 72
        9 L 2143 m SSS 33
Fees   D-1500fr (D-2500fr)
Loc   22km SE of Brussels
Mis   Handicap certificate required

Sept Fontaines (1987)

1021, Chaussée d'Alsemberg,
1420 Braine l'Alleud
Tel   (02) 353 02 46/353 03 46
Fax   (02) 354 68 75
Mem   1000
Pro   A Watts, T Goossens
Holes   18 L 6047 m SSS
        18 L 4500 m SSS
        9 hole short course
Fees   1000fr (1500fr)
Loc   Braine, 15km S of Brussels.
        Motorway exit Huizingen

Winge G & CC (1988)

Wingerstraat 6, 3390 Sint Joris
Winge
Tel   (016) 63 40 53
Fax   (016) 63 21 40
Mem   350
Pro   F Van Donck, P Townsend,
        M Vanmeerbeek
Holes   18 L 6149 m SSS 72
Fees   1250–1750fr
Loc   35km E of Brussels via Leuven

East

Flanders-Nippon (1988)

Vissenbroekstraat 15, 3500 Hasselt
Tel   (011) 22 37 93/22 79 55
Mem   300
Pro   J Gulesserian
Holes   18 L 5922 m SSS 72
        9 L 1726 m SSS 32
Fees   1000fr (1500fr)
Loc   Hasselt, 85km E of Brussels

Henri-Chapelle (1988)

Rue du Vivier 3, 4841 Henri-Chapelle
Tel   (087) 88 19 91
Fax   (087) 88 36 55
Mem   300
Pro   H Timmer, H Rijnders
Holes   18 L 6045 m SSS 72
        9 L 2255 m SSS 34
        9 hole Par 3 course
Fees   18 hole:1000fr (1500fr)
        9 hole:750fr (1000fr) Par 3:300fr
Loc   15km NE of Verviers. 30km E
        of Liège
Mis   Driving range-100fr

For list of abbreviations see page 487.

International Gomze (1986)

4140 Gomze-Andoumont
Tel (041) 60 92 07 **Fax** 60 92 06
Mem 180
Pro LJ Cain
Holes 18 L 6034 m SSS 72
Fees 1000fr (1250fr)
Loc 15km S of Liège. Spa 20km

Limburg G & CC (1966)

Golfstraat 1, 3530 Houthalen
Tel (011) 38 35 43 **Fax** 84 12 08
Mem 650
Pro J Renders
Holes 18 L 6101 m SSS 72
Fees 1000fr (1500fr)
Loc Houthalen, 15km N of Hasselt

Royal GC des Fagnes (1930)

Balmoral, 4900 Spa
Tel (087) 77 16 13
Mem 350
Pro WYS Robertson
Holes 18 L 5948 m SSS 71
Fees D-800–1000fr (D-1500fr)
Loc Spa 5km. 35km SE of Liège

Royal GC du Sart Tilman (1930)

541 Route du Condroz, 4200 Ougrée
Tel (041) 36 20 21
Mem 700
Pro B Janjic, A Verlegh
Holes 18 L 6002 m SSS 71
Fees D-1000–1500fr (D-1500fr)
Loc 10km S of Liège on Route 620
towards Marche

Spiegelven GC Genk (1988)

Wiemesmeerstraat, 3600 Genk
Tel (011) 35 35 16
Fax (011) 36 41 84
Mem 550
Pro A van Pixten
Holes 18 L 6198 m SSS 72
Fees 900fr (1300fr)
Loc Genk, 18km E of Hasselt.
20km N of Maastricht

West & Oost Vlanderen

Damme G & CC (1987)

Doornstraat 16, 8340 Damme-Sijsele
Tel (050) 35 35 72
Mem 400
Pro G Pearce
Holes 18 L 6046 m SSS 72
Fees 1000fr (1300fr)
Loc 10km E of Bruges

Oudenaarde G & CC (1975)

Kasteel Petegem, Kortrykstraat 52
9790 Wortegem-Petegem
Tel (055) 31 54 81 **Fax** 31 98 49
Mem 850
Pro C Morton, T Welsh
Holes 18 L 6039 m SSS 73
Fees 800fr (1400fr)
Loc 3km SW of Oudenaarde
Mis Handicap certificate required

Royal Latem (1909)

9830 St Martens-Latem
Tel (091) 82 54 11 **Fax** 82 90 19
Mem 820
Pro J Verplancke
Holes 18 L 5767 m SSS 70
Fees 1000fr (1500fr)
Loc 10km SW of Ghent on route
N43 Ghent-Deinze

Royal Ostend (1903)

Koninklijke Baan 2, 8420 De Haan
Tel (059) 23 32 83
Fax (059) 23 37 49
Mem 500
Pro G Maxwell
Holes 18 L 5265 m SSS 68
Fees 1150fr (1800fr)
Loc 8km N of Ostend towards
De Haan

Royal Zoute

Caddiespad 14 8300 Knokke-Heist
Tel (050) 60 12 27 (Sec)
60 72 11 (Caddymaster)
60 37 81 (Starter)
Mem 1500
Holes 18 L 6172 m SSS 73
18 L 3607 m SSS 60
Fees 1500-1700fr (1900-2500fr)
Loc Knokke 1km

Czechoslovakia

Bohemia Poděbrady (1964)

R.Armády 623, 290 01 Poděbrady
Tel (0324) 4383
Mem 60
Holes 9 L 6240 m SSS 72
Fees 200kcs (400kcs)
Loc E side of Poděbrady
Mis Open May–Oct

Karlovy Vary (1960)

PO Box 60, 360 21 Karlovy Vary
Tel (017) 25740
Mem 250
Pro K Skopovy

Holes 18 L 6063 m SSS 72
Fees 400kcs (500kcs)
Loc 8km from Karlovy Vary (Road
No 6)
Mis Open Apr-Oct

Lokomotiva-Brno (1967)

Antonínská 5, 602 00 Brno
Tel (05) 757523
Mem 90
Holes 9 L 4641 m SSS 66
Fees 80kcs (120kcs)
Loc Svratka, 80km NW of Brno.
100km SE of Prague
Mis Open May–Oct

Mariánské Lázně (1905)

**PO Box 49/C, 353 01 Mariánské
Lázně**
Tel (0165) 5195
Mem 330
Pro N Němec (0165) 4300
Holes 18 L 6080 m SSS 72
Fees 400kcs (500kcs)
Loc 2km NE of Mariánské Lázně,
opposite Golf Hotel
Mis Open May–Oct. Driving range

Nová Ostrava (1968)

Cingrova 10, 702 00 Ostrava 1
Tel (069) 234780
Mem 220
Holes 18 L 5702 m SSS 71
Fees 300kcs (400kcs)
Loc Silherovice, 15km from
Ostrava
Mis Open Apr–Oct

Praha (1969)

Na Morani 4, 128 00 Praha 2
Tel (0229) 2828
Mem 300
Holes 9 L 5960 m SSS 72
Fees 200kcs (400kcs)
Loc Prague–Motol, towards Plzeň

Semily (1971)

Nádražní 203, 513 01 Semily
Tel (0431) 2705
Mem 70
Holes 8 L 4037 m SSS 64
Fees 100kcs
Loc 2km from Semily. 100km NW
of Prague
Mis Open Apr–Oct

Slavoj Praha (1928)

Kolodějská 4, 100 00 Praha 10
Tel (02) 770481
Mem 70
Holes 9 L 4400 m SSS 66
Fees Mainly for diplomats
Loc 30km from Prague towards
Dobříš
Mis Open Apr–Oct

Denmark

Bornholm Island

Bornholm (1971)

Plantegevej 3B, 3700 Rønne
Tel (53) 95 68 54
Mem 455
Holes 18 L 4789 m SSS 68
Fees 130kr (130kr)
Loc 4km E of Rønne

Nordbornholm (1987)

Spellingevej 3, Rø, 3760 Gudhjem
Tel (56) 48 40 50
Mem 150
Holes 18 L 5512 m SSS 71
Fees 130kr (130kr)
Loc Rø, 8km W of Gudhjem.
22km NE of Rønne
Mis Tee booking necessary

Funen

Odense (1927)

Hestehaven 201, 5220 Odense
Tel (65) 95 90 00
Fax (65) 95 90 88
Mem 1200
Pro P Dixon
Holes 18 L 6156 m SSS 71
9 L 4154 m SSS 60
Fees 120kr
Loc SE outskirts of Odense

SCT Knuds (1954)

Slipshavnsvej 16, 5800 Nyborg
Tel (65) 31 12 12
Mem 717
Pro H Hansen
Holes 18 L 6027 m SSS 71
Fees 130kr D-160kr (300kr)
Loc 3km SE of Nyborg

Svendborg (1970)

Tordensgaardevej 5, Sørup, 5700
Svendborg
Tel (62) 22 40 77
Mem 570
Pro S Jensen (62) 22 87 88
Holes 18 L 5692 m SSS 70
Fees 150kr W-800kr
Loc 4km NW of Svendborg

Vestfyns (1974)

Rønnemosegård, Krengerupvej 27,
5620 Glamsbjerg
Tel (64) 72 15 77
Mem 525
Pro S Tinning
Holes 9 L 5680 m SSS 71
Fees 100kr
Loc Glamsbjerg, 40km SW of
Odense
Mis 7 extra holes open 1991

Jutland

Aalborg (1908)

Jargersprisvej, Restup Enge, 9000
Aalborg
Tel (08) 34 14 76
Mem 900
Pro M Thuen
Holes 18 L 5800 m SSS 70
Fees D-140kr (180 kr)
Loc 7km SW of Aalborg

Aarhus (1931)

Ny Moesgaardvej 50, 8270 Hojbjerg
Tel (06) 27 63 22
Mem 1600
Pro P Greve
Holes 18 L 5796 m SSS 70
9 L 6093 m SSS 72
Fees 18 hole:140kr (180kr)
9 hole: 80kr (120kr)
Loc 6km S of Aarhus. 18 hole:
Route 451 South. 9 hole: Route
E3 North

Brønderslev (1971)

PO Box 94, 9700 Brønderslev
Tel (98) 82 32 81
Mem 630
Pro LM Jacobsen
Holes 18 L 5710 m SSS 71
Fees 150kr
Loc 3km W of Brønderslev

Dejbjerg (1966)

Letagervej 1, Dejbjerg, 6900 Skjern
Tel (97) 35 09 59
Mem 320
Holes 9 L 5066m SSS 67
Fees D-100kr (D-120kr)
Loc 25km from W coast on Skjern-
Rinkøbing road (Route 28).
6km N of Skjern

Ebeltoft (1966)

Strandgårdshøj, 8400 Ebeltoft
Tel (86) 34 47 87
Mem 400
Holes 18 L 5150 m SSS 67
Fees D-100kr W-350kr
Loc 1/2 km N of Ebeltoft

Esbjerg (1921)

Sønderhedevej, Marbaek,
6710 Esbjerg
Tel (75) 26 92 19
Mem 1100
Pro A Tinning
Holes 18 L 6434 m SSS 74
Fees 160kr
Loc 15km N of Esbjerg

Fanø Island (1900)

6720 Nordby
Tel (05) 16 32 82
Mem 239
Pro N Aafeldt
Holes 18 L 4642 m SSS 65
Fees D-80kr W-400 kr
Loc Take Fanø Island Ferry from
Esbjerg

Gyttegård (1978)

Billundvej 43, 7250 Hejnsvig
Tel (75) 33 56 49
Mem 350
Pro A Thygesen
Holes 9 L 5442 m SSS 69
Fees 100kr
Loc 2km NE of Hejnsvig. 10km S of
Grindsted

Haderslev (1971)

Egevej 22, 6100 Haderslev
Tel (74) 52 83 01
Mem 450
Holes 18 L 5137 m SSS 67
Fees D-100kr
Loc 1 1/2 km NW of Haderslev

Hans Herreds

Starkaervej, 9690 Fjerritslev
Tel (98) 21 14 44
Mem 200
Holes 9 L 2024 m SSS 62
Fees 70kr (90kr)
Loc 1km N of Fjerritslev. 40km W
of Aalborg

Herning

Golfvej 2, 7400 Herning
Tel (97) 21 18 81
Mem 850
Pro M Stendorf
Holes 18 L 5571 m SSS 70
Fees D-100kr
Loc 2km E of Herning on Route 15

Himmerlands G & CC

Centervej 1, Gatten, 9670 Løgstør
Tel (98) 66 16 00
Fax (98) 66 14 56
Mem 620
Pro R Kristensen, S Rolner
Holes Old 18 L 5269 m SSS 68
New 18 L 6102 m SSS 74
9-hole Par 3 course
Fees 180kr W-1000kr
Loc Gatten, 35km NW of Hobro
towards Løgstør (Route 29).
Signposted W from Gatten

Hjorring (1985)

Vinstrupvej, PO Box 215, 9800
Hjorring
Tel (98) 90 03 99
Mem 450
Pro A Routledge
Holes 18 holes SSS 71
Fees 120kr
Loc N of Hjorring. 50km N of
Aalborg

For list of abbreviations see page 487.

Holstebro (1970)

Råsted, 7570 Vemb
Tel   (07) 48 51 55
Mem   750
Pro   R Howett
Holes 18 L 6073 m SSS 72
Fees   D-150kr (180kr)
Loc   13km W of Holstebro

Horsens (1972)

Silkeborgvej, 8700 Horsens
Tel   (05) 61 51 51
Mem   400
Pro   G Oakley
Holes 18 L 5905 m SSS 72
       6 hole course
Fees   100kr
Loc   1km W of Horsens towards
       Silkeborg

Hvide Klit

Hvideklitvej 28, 9982 Aalbaek
Tel   (98) 48 90 21/48 84 26
Mem   510
Pro   O Smidt (98) 48 80 08
Holes 18 L 5875 m SSS 72
Fees   160kr
Loc   3km N of Aalbaek. 24km N of
       Frederikshavn

Juelsminde (1973)

Bobroholtvej 11a, 7130 Juelsminde
Tel   (75) 69 34 92
Mem   405
Pro   P Mason (75) 69 46 11
Holes 9 L 6050 m SSS 72
Fees   100kr
Loc   20km S of Horsens on coast.
       2km N of Juelsminde
Mis   6 hole Par 3 course

Kaj Lykke

Porsholtsvej 13, 6740 Bramming
Tel   (75) 10 22 46
Mem   500
Pro   J Elkins
Holes 18 L 6050 m SSS 72
Fees   100kr (120kr)
Loc   18km E of Esbjerg

Kolding (1933)

Emerholtsvej, 6000 Kolding
Tel   (75) 52 37 93
Mem   610
Pro   F Atkinson (75) 53 37 93
Holes 18 L 5376 m SSS 69
Fees   120kr (200kr)
Loc   3km N of Kolding

Lemvig (1986)

Soegaardevejen 6, 7620 Lemvig
Mem   400
Pro   C Maas (97) 48 52 93
Holes 9 L 2822 m SSS 70
Fees   80kr (100kr)
Loc   35km NE of Holstebro

Nordvestjysk (1971)

Nystrupvej 19, 7700 Thisted
Tel   (97) 97 41 41
Mem   400
Pro   K Maas
Holes 9 L 5713 m SSS 70
Fees   D-100kr (120kr)
Loc   17km NW of Thisted

Randers (1958)

Himmelbovej, Fladbro, 8900
Randers
Tel   (86) 42 88 69
Mem   750
Pro   G Townhill
Holes 18 L 5453 m SSS 69
Fees   120kr (140kr)
Loc   5km W of Randers towards
       Silkeborg

Ribe (1981)

Rønnehave, Snepsgårdevej 14,
Postboks 37, 6760 Ribe
Tel   (05) 44 12 30
Mem   265
Pro   P Thomson
Holes 9 L 5222 m SSS 67
Fees   80kr (100kr)
Loc   8km SE of Ribe on Haderslev
       road

Silkeborg (1966)

Sensommervej 15C, 8600 Silkeborg
Tel   (86) 85 33 99
Mem   1020
Pro   M Kelly
Holes 18 L 5949 m SSS 72
Fees   160kr (200kr)
Loc   5km E of Silkeborg

Skive

Resen, 7800 Skive
Tel   (97) 52 44 09
Mem   200
Holes 9 holes SSS 70
Fees   D-60kr
Loc   3km NW of Skive. 32km NW of
       Viborg

Sønderjyllands (1970)

Uge Hedegård, 6360 Tinglev
Tel   (04) 68 75 25
Mem   420
Pro   T Mitchell (04) 68 81 98
Holes 18 L 5666 m SSS 69
Fees   D-100kr
Loc   3km NE of Tinglev. 15km S of
       Abenraa

Vejle (1970)

Faellessletgård, Ibaekvej, 7100
Vejle
Tel   (75) 85 81 85
Mem   1050
Pro   D Chad, J Smith
Holes 18 L 6042 yds SSS 71
Fees   140kr (160kr) W-800kr

Loc   5km SE of Vejle
Mis   Driving range. Par 3 course.

Viborg (1973)

Møllevej 26, Overlund, Viborg 8800
Tel   (86) 67 30 10
Mem   550
Pro   A Martin
Holes 18 L 5902 m SSS 71
Fees   150kr
Loc   2km E of Viborg

Zealand

Asserbo (1946)

Bødkergaardsvej, 3300
Frederiksvaerk
Tel   (42) 12 03 29
Mem   450
Pro   J Nielsen
Holes 9 L 5447 m SSS 69
Fees   140kr (200kr) W-800kr
Loc   3km from Frederiksvaerk
       towards Liseleje

Copenhagen (1898)

Dyrehaven 2, 2800 Lyngby
Tel   (01) 63 04 83
Mem   1050
Pro   D Poke, D Hille, H Aafeldt
Holes 18 L 5701 m SSS 70
Fees   150kr (200kr)
Loc   13km N of Copenhagen, in
       deer park

Furesø (1974)

Hestkøbvaenge 4, 3460 Birkerød
Tel   (42) 81 74 44
Mem   1000
Pro   C Smith
Holes 18 L 5679 m SSS 71
Fees   160kr (240kr)
Loc   25km N of Copenhagen
Mis   WE-NA before 10am

Gilleleje (1970)

Ferlevej 52, 3250 Gilleleje
Tel   (49) 71 80 56/71 95 16
Mem   1000
Pro   P Dangerfield
Holes 18 L 6641 yds SSS 72
Fees   D-170kr (210kr)
Loc   62km N of Copenhagen

Hedeland (1980)

Staerkendevej 232, 2640
Hedehusene
Tel   (42) 13 61 69
Mem   600
Pro   A Palsby-Kristensen
Holes 18 L 6050 m SSS 72
Fees   120kr (150kr)
Loc   7km SE of Roskilde.
       20km SW of Copenhagen

For list of abbreviations see page 487.

Helsingør

G1 Hellebaekvej, 3000 Helsingør
Tel (49) 21 29 70
Mem 1086
Pro R Taylor
Holes 18 L 5705 m SSS 71
Fees 160kr (240kr)
Loc 2km N of Helsingør

Hillerød (1966)

Nysogård, Ny Hammersholt,
3400 Hillerød
Tel (42) 26 50 46
Mem 950
Pro M Tulloch (42) 25 40 30
Holes 18 L 5452 m SSS 70
Fees 150kr (220kr)
Loc 3km S of Hillerød
Mis WE-NA before noon.
Handicap certificate required

Holbaek (1964)

Dragerupvej 50, 4300 Holbaek
Tel (53) 43 45 79
Mem 450
Pro M Irving, M Davies
Holes 9 L 5960 m SSS 70
Fees 80kr (100kr)
Loc Kirsebaerholmen, 2km E of
Holbaek

Kalundborg (1974)

Kildekaergård, Rosnaesvej 225,
4400 Kalundborg
Tel (03) 50 13 85
Mem 370
Sec P Jacobsen
Pro M Irving
Holes 9 L 5064 m SSS 68
Fees 60kr (90kr)
Loc Rosnaes, 8km W of
Kalundborg

Køge (1970)

Gl.Hastrupvej 12, 4600 Køge
Tel (53) 65 10 00
Mem 750
Pro P Taylor
Holes 18 L 6042 m SSS 72
Fees 120kr (180kr)
Loc 3km S of Køge. Copenhagen
38km

Kokkedal (1971)

Kokkedal Allee 9, 2980 Kokkedal
Tel (42) 86 99 59
Mem 1130
Pro N Willett
Holes 18 L 5958 m SSS 72
Fees 140kr (200kr)
Loc Hørsholm, 30km N of
Copenhagen
Mis WE-Visitors pm only.
Handicap certificate required

Korsør (1964)

Tårnborgparken, Ørnumvej 8, 4220
Korsør
Tel (53) 57 18 36
Mem 600
Pro M Irving
Holes 18 L 5998 m SSS 72
Fees D-120 (D-150kr)
Loc 1km E of Korsør, on Korsør Bay
Mis 6 hole Par 3 course

Midtsjaellands

Rødtjørnevej 19, 4180 Sorø
Tel (53) 63 27 74
Mem 225
Pro T Card
Holes 9 L 3670 m Par 60
Fees D-60kr (D-80kr)
Loc Sorø, 10km W of Ringsted

Mølleåens (1970)

Stenbaekgård, Bastrup,
3450 Lynge
Tel (42) 18 86 31/18 86 79
Fax (42) 18 86 43
Mem 1131
Pro R Jackson
Holes 18 L 5730 m SSS 70
Fees 130kr (180kr)
Loc 32km NW of Copenhagen
Mis Driving range

Odsherred (1967)

4573 Hojby
Tel (59) 30 20 76
Mem 600
Pro S Jensen
Holes 18 L 5710 m SSS 70
Fees 120kr (140kr)
Loc 5km SW of Nykøbing

Roskilde (1973)

Kongemarken 34, 4000 Roskilde
Tel (42) 37 01 80
Mem 643
Pro S Kaas (42) 35 13 08
Holes 12 L 4853 m SSS 69
Fees 100kr (140kr)
Loc 5km W of Roskilde

Rungsted (1937)

2960 Rungsted Kyst
Tel (42) 86 34 44
Mem 1100
Pro R Beattie
Holes 18 L 5900 m SSS 72
Fees 200kr (250kr)
Loc Rungsted, 30km N of
Copenhagen

Skovlunde (1980)

c/o Hasselvej 35, 2740 Skovlunde
Tel (42) 91 76 28
Mem 850

Holes 9 L 5018 m SSS 67
9 hole Par 3 course
Fees 100kr (140kr) Par 3:40kr
Loc Ballerup, 15km NW of
Copenhagen

Søllerød

Øverødvej 239, 2840 Holte
Tel (42) 80 17 84
Mem 1100
Pro J Korfitsen (42) 80 18 77
Holes 18 L 5872 m SSS 72
Fees 160kr (220kr)
Loc 19km N of Copenhagen

Storstrømmen (1969)

Virketvej 44, 4863 Eskilstrup
Tel (53) 83 80 80
Mem 488
Pro A Mackay (53) 83 82 02
Holes 18 L 6195 m SSS 73
Fees D-125kr (D-175kr 3D-310kr)
Loc 15km N of Nykøbing Falster

Sydsjaellands (1974)

Borupgården, Mogenstrup,
4700 Naestved
Tel (03) 76 15 03
Mem 600
Pro K Atkinson
Holes 18 L 5675 m SSS 70
Fees 125kr (150kr)
Loc 10km SE of Naestved towards
Praestø
Mis Driving range

Finland

Alands

PB111, 22101 Mariehamn
Tel (928) 43883
Holes 18 L 5350 m SSS 68
Loc Mariehamn, Aland (off SW
coast of Finland)

Aulangon (1959)

13600 Hämeenlinna
Tel (917) 537740
Mem 548
Holes 9 L 2450 m SSS 67
Fees D-100fmk
Loc Hämeenlinna 5km

Aura Golf (1958)

Ruissalo 85, 20100 Turku
Tel (921) 589201
Fax (921) 589121
Mem 1200
Pro A Mäki
Holes 18 L 5873 m SSS 71
Fees 150fmk (150fmk)
Loc Ruissalo Island, 9km SW of
Turku

Espoon Golfseura (1982)

Box 26, 02781 Espoo
Tel   (90) 811 212
Mem   1100
Pro   D Bird
Holes   18 L 6183 m SSS 74
Fees   120fmk
Loc   Espoo, 24km W of Helsinki

Helsingin Golfklubi (1932)

Talin Kartano, 00350 Helsinki 35
Tel   550235/557899
Mem   1170
Pro   S Nyström, J Hämäläinen
Holes   18 L 5900 m SSS 71
Fees   140fmk (160fmk)
Loc   7km W of Helsinki

Karelia Golf (1988)

80510 Onttola
Tel   (973) 854711/732411
Mem   450
Pro   J Ngigi
Holes   18 L 6223 m SSS 74
Fees   140fmk (170fmk)
Loc   18km from Joensuu. 480km NE
        of Helsinki
Mis   Open May-Sept

Kartano Golf (1988)

Karhulahti, 79600 Joroinen
Tel   (972) 72257
Mem   200
Holes   18 hole course
Fees   120fmk (120fmk)
Loc   20km S of Varkaus. 330km NE
        of Helsinki

Keimola Golf Oy (1990)

Kirkantie 32, 01750 Vantaa
Tel   (90) 896991
Fax   (90) 896790
Mem   700
Pro   J Utter
Holes   27 L 5870-5924 m SSS 71-74
Fees   120fmk (120fmk)
Loc   15km N of Helsinki

Kerigolf (1989)

Hotel Kerimaa, 58200 Kerimäki
Tel   (957) 575 1261/2
Fax   (957) 575 1300
Mem   190
Holes   18 L 6208 m SSS 75
Fees   150fmk
Loc   18km E of Savonlinna. 380km
        NE of Helsinki

Kokkolan (1957)

POB 164, 67101 Kokkola
Tel   (968) 21636
Mem   535
Pro   R Linna
Holes   9 L 5618 m SSS 71
Fees   100fmk
Loc   Kokkola 2km

Kurk (1985)

02550 Evitskog
Tel   (90) 263456
Fax   (90) 263829
Mem   750
Pro   D Brumpton, N Miller,
        L Elstone
Holes   18 L 5860 m Par 73
        Par 3 course
Fees   120fmk (160fmk)
Loc   40km W of Helsinki

Kymen Golf (1964)

Mussalo Golfcourse, 48310 Kotka
Tel   (952) 604555
Fax   (952) 604706
Mem   1150
Pro   M Suolanen
Holes   18 L 6004 m SSS 72
Fees   100fmk (120fmk)
Loc   Kotka, Mussalo Island.
        120km E of Helsinki

Lahden Golf (1959)

15230 Lahti Takkula
Tel   (918) 841311
Mem   342
Pro   V Kankkoner
Holes   9 L 6102 m SSS 73
Fees   D-60fmk W-300fmk
Loc   Lahti 6km

Master Golf Oy (1988)

Puotistentie 4, 02940 Espoo
Tel   (90) 853 7002
Fax   (90) 853 7027
Mem   775
Pro   K Tellqvist
Holes   18 L 6219 m SSS 72
        9 hole course
Fees   150fmk (200fmk)
Loc   25km NW of Helsinki

Meri-Teijo (1990)

**Mathildedalin Kartano, 25660
Mathildedal**
Tel   (924) 363801
Fax   (924) 363890
Mem   200
Holes   18 hole course
Loc   20km S of Salo. 70km E of
        Turku. 130km W of Helsinki

Mikkelin Golf (1967)

Kalervonkatu 5, 50130 Mikkeli
Tel   (955) 151759
Holes   9 L 2540 m SSS 68
Fees   50fmk (200fmk)
Loc   384km N of Helsinki.
        2km from Mikkeli

Oulu (1964)

Hallituskatu 25, 90100 Oulu
Tel   (981) 571192
Fax   (981) 229728
Mem   750

Pro   J Alatalo
Holes   9 L 5218 m SSS 68
Fees   100fmk
Loc   Kaukovainio, 3km from Oulu

Pickala Golf (1988)

Pickala Village, 02580 Siuntio
Tel   (90) 296 6251
Pro   Mrs A Sipronen (90) 296 6253
Holes   27 L 6199-6328 m Par 72
Loc   Southern Finland
Mis   Driving range. Further 9 holes
        open 1991

Porin Golfkerho (1939)

PL 25, 28601 Pori
Tel   (939) 415559
Mem   450
Pro   P Makela
Holes   9 L 5654 m SSS 71
Fees   D-80fmk
Loc   5km NW of Pori, at
        Kalafornia

St Laurence Golf (1989)

Kaivurinkatu, 08200 Lohja
Tel   (912) 86603
Fax   (912) 86666
Mem   600
Pro   D Brumpton
Holes   18 L 6335 m SSS 75
        Par 3 Practice course
Fees   100fmk (150fmk)
Loc   50km W of Helsinki
Mis   Driving range

Sarfvik Golf

Pl 27, 02321 Espoo
Tel   (90) 297 7122
Fax   (90) 297 7134
Pro   V Kalliala
Holes   18 L 5885 m SSS 72
        18 L 6000 m SSS 73
Fees   250fmk
Loc   20km W of Helsinki

Suur-Helsingin (1965)

Franzeninkatu 3B, 81 0050 Helsinki
Tel   855 8687
Mem   800
Pro   M Louhio
Holes   2 x 18 hole courses
Fees   100fmk
Loc   25km W of Helsinki
Mis   Driving range

Tammer Golf (1965)

Box 269, 33101 Tampere 10
Tel   (931) 611316
Mem   1250
Pro   J Pentikäinen
Holes   18 L 5870 m SSS 71
Fees   D-120fmk
Loc   Ruotula, 5km from Tampere
Mis   Open May-Oct

Tawast G & CC (1988)

Paavola, 13270 Hämeenlinna
Tel   (917) 197502 Fax (917) 197509
Mem   400
Pro   H Kuussaari
Holes 18 L 6063 m SSS 73
Loc   5km E of Hämeenlinna

Tuusula (1984)

PL 178, 4301 Hyrylä
Tel   (90) 259466 Fax (90) 254660
Mem   900
Pro   G Thompson
Holes 18 L 5900 m SSS 72
Fees   120fmk (150fmk)
Loc   30km N of Helsinki, nr airport

Vaasan-Vaasa (1969)

Sandog 3, 65100 Vaasa 10
Tel   (961) 121742/269989
Mem   206
Holes 9 L 2570 m SSS 70
Fees   50fmk
Loc   Kraklund, 6km SE of Vaasa on
        Route 717
Mis   Driving range

Viipurin Golf (1938)

54530 Luumäki
Tel   (953) 16840 (Summer)
Mem   610
Pro   P Ahokas
Holes 9 L 2450 m SSS 65
Fees   D-80fmk
Loc   2km from Lappeenranta,
        behind Etelä-Saimaa hospital

Yyteri Golf (1990)

Pl 36, 28101 Pori
Tel   (939) 340340 Fax (090) 340345
Pro   CJ Mitchell
Holes 18 L 5738 m SSS 72
Fees   150fmk
Loc   20km from Pori
Mis   Driving range

France

Bordeaux & Dordogne

Arcachon (1955)

35 Bd d'Arcachon, 33260 La Teste
De Buch
Tel   56 54 44 00
Mem   750
Pro   J Cantagrel, J Artola, F du Reau
Holes 18 L 5930 m SSS 71
Fees   D-160-250fr
Loc   60km SW of Bordeaux

L'Ardilouse (1980)

Domaine de l'Ardilouse,
33680 Lacanau-Océan
Tel   56 03 25 60
Mem   300
Pro   J-L Pega
Holes 18 L 6000 m SSS 72
Fees   140-160fr (160-210fr)
Loc   45km NW of Bordeaux

Aubazine

19190 Beynat
Tel   55 27 25 66
Mem   550
Pro   JF Encuentra
Holes 18 L 5420 m SSS 70
Fees   130fr (170fr)
Loc   15km E of Brive
Mis   Public course

Bordeaux Lac (1977)

Avenue de Pernon, 33300 Bordeaux
Tel   56 50 92 72
Mem   1300
Pro   J Delgado, J Purgato,
        V Fructuoso, JM Duhalde
Holes 18 L 6083 m SSS 72
        18 L 6150 m SSS 72
Fees   160fr
Loc   6km N of Bordeaux
Mis   Public course. Closed Tues

Bordelais (1900)

Domaine de Kater, Ave d'Eysines,
33200 Bordeaux-Caudéran
Tel   56 28 56 04
Mem   492
Pro   M Saubaber
Holes 18 L 4833 m SSS 67
Fees   160fr (200fr)
Loc   3km NW of Bordeaux
Mis   Course closed Mon

Domaine de Rochebois (1989)

24200 Vitrac
Tel   53 28 18 01
Mem   90
Pro   C Campbell
Holes 9 L 2990 m SSS 36
Fees   D-120–180fr (D-150–200fr)
Loc   6km S of Sarlat (Perigord).
        180km E of Bordeaux

Graves et Sauternais (1989)

St Pardon de Conques, 33210
Langon
Tel   56 62 25 43
Mem   180
Pro   V Trojani
Holes 18 L 5810 m SSS 71
Fees   140fr (180fr)
Loc   5km from Langon. 45km SW of
        Bordeaux via A62
Mis   Driving range

Gujan (1990)

Route de Souguinet, 33470 Gujan
Mestras
Tel   56 66 86 36
Holes 18 L 6300 m SSS 72
        9 L 2520 m SSS 35
Fees   18 holes:180-280fr (250-280fr)
        9 holes:115-170fr (135fr)
Loc   12km E of Arcachon on RN
        250. 40km W of Bordeaux

Lolivarie (1984)

La Croix Sagelat, 24170 Belvès
Tel   53 30 22 69
Mem   60
Pro   F Mayes
Holes 9 L 2200 m SSS 35
Fees   100fr (120fr)
Loc   60km NW of Cahors.
        60km E of Bergerac

Marmande (1989)

Carpette, 47200 Marmande
Tel   53 20 87 60
Mem   151
Pro   E Bouquier
Holes 9 L 6106 m SSS 72
Fees   D-100fr
Loc   Marmande, 75km SE of
        Bordeaux
Mis   Pitch & putt

Mas del Teil

La Chapelle Auzac, 46200 Souillac
Tel   65 37 01 48
Mem   120
Pro   P Dugény
Holes 9 L 2040 m SSS 33
Fees   100fr (120fr)
Loc   25km S of Brive

Périgueux (1980)

Domaine de Saltgourde,
24430 Marsac
Tel   53 53 02 35
Mem   412
Pro   E Smith
Holes 18 L 6120 m SSS 71
Fees   D-150fr
Loc   3km W of Périgueux, via
        Angoulême–Riberac road
Mis   Public course

Sporting Club de Cameyrac (1972)

Cameyrac, 33450 Saint-Loubes
Tel   56 72 96 79
Mem   450
Pro   V Bouneau, R Mas
Holes 18 L 6057 m SSS 72
        9 L 1600 m SSS 28
Fees   120fr (200fr)
Loc   15km E of Bordeaux

For list of abbreviations see page 487.

Brittany

Ajoncs d'Or (1976)

Kergrain Lantic, 22410 Saint-Quay
Portrieux
Tel   96 71 90 74
Mem   510
Pro   P Rault-Maisonneuve,
          A Pouette
Holes 18 L 6125 m SSS 72
Fees   170–180fr
Loc   17km N of Saint-Brieuc.
          6km W of Etables
Mis   Public course

Baden

Kernic, 56870 Baden
Tel   97 57 18 96
Pro   J Piron
Holes 18 L 6145 m Par 72
Fees   140–220fr
Loc   12km SW of Vannes

Boisgelin

Pléhédel, 22290 Lanvollon
Tel   96 22 31 24
Holes 9 L 2356 m Par 34
Fees   70fr (100fr)
Loc   10km S of Paimpol on D7.

Brest-Iroise (1976)

Lann-Rohou, Saint-Urbain, 29800
Landerneau
Tel   98 85 16 17
Mem   650
Pro   V Schwechlen, P Le Verche
Holes 18 L 5885 m Par 72
          9 hole short course
Fees   190fr
Loc   25km E of Brest
Mis   Public course

Dinard (1887)

35800 St-Briac-sur-Mer
Tel   99 88 32 07
Mem   360
Pro   A Rosinski
Holes 18 L 5010 m Par 69
Fees   180fr
Loc   8km W of Dinard

La Freslonnière (1989)

Le Bois Briand, 35650 Le Rheu
Tel   99 60 84 09
Fax   99 60 94 98
Mem   280
Pro   D Wakeford
Holes 18 L 5671 m SSS 71
Fees   180fr (220fr)
Loc   4km SW of Rennes, off N24

Kerver (1988)

Domaine de Kerver, 56730 Saint-
Gildas-de-Rhuys
Tel   97 45 30 09
Mem   200
Pro   JL Leroux, C Olivard, P Leroux
Holes 18 L 6147 m SSS 73
Fees   140–220fr
Loc   30km S of Vannes

L'Odet Golf (1986)

Clohars-Fouesnant, 29118 Benodet
Tel   98 54 87 88
Mem   420
Pro   K Strachan
Holes 18 L 6235 m SSS 73
          9 hole Par 3 course
Fees   140–220fr
Loc   4km S of Benodet. 15km SE of
          Quimper
Mis   Public course

Les Ormes (1988)

Château des Ormes, 35120 Dol-de-
Bretagne
Tel   99 48 40 27
Fax   99 48 21 28
Mem   180
Pro   C Hoube
Holes 18 L 6070m SSS 72
Fees   180fr (200fr)
Loc   8km S of Dol, off D795

Pen Guen

22380 Saint-Cast-le-Guildo
Tel   96 41 91 20
Pro   J Bourel, J-M Loustalen
Holes 9 L 2580 m SSS 70
Fees   100-150fr
Loc   25km W of Dinard

Quimper-Cornouaille (1959)

Manoir du Mesmeur, 29133
La Forêt-Fouesnant
Tel   98 56 97 09
Mem   250
Pro   L Salgado
Holes 9 L 5641 m SSS 69
Fees   D-120fr W-545fr
Loc   15km SE of Quimper

Rennes (1957)

BP 1117, 35014 Rennes Cedex
Tel   99 64 24 18
Mem   400
Pro   P Le Fur, L Lecoq
Holes 18 L 5845 m SSS 70
Fees   D-120fr (150fr)
Loc   7km S of Rennes via N177
          towards Chavagne

Rennes Saint Jacques

35136 Saint-Jacques-de-la-Lande
Tel   99 64 24 18
Pro   P Le Fur, L Le Coq
Holes 18 L 6100 m Par 72
          9 L 2100 m Par 32
          9 hole short course
Fees   140–220fr
Loc   5km SW of Rennes

Sables-d'Or-les-Pins (1925)

22240 Fréhel
Tel   96 41 42 57
Mem   200
Pro   L Le Coq
Holes 9 L 5253 m SSS 70
Fees   D-135-160fr
Loc   6km SW of Fréhel. 30km W of
          Dinard
Mis   Extension to 18 holes June
          1991

Saint Laurent (1975)

Ploemel, 56400 Auray
Tel   97 56 85 18
Mem   450
Pro   D Jouan, P Brown
Holes 18 L 6112 m SSS 72
          9 L 3020 m SSS 35
Fees   140–220fr
Loc   Ploemel, 16km SW of Auray
Mis   Public course

St Malo-Le Tronchet (1986)

Le Tronchet, 35540 Miniac Morvan
Tel   99 58 96 69
Mem   250
Pro   C Bourakhowitch
Holes 18 L 6049 m SSS 72
          9 L 2684 m SSS 36
Fees   180fr (1990)
Loc   23km S of St Malo, off RN 137

Saint-Samson (1964)

Route de Kérénoc,
22560 Pleumeur-Bodou
Tel   96 23 87 34
Mem   250
Pro   D Fournet
Holes 18 L 5682 m SSS 72
Fees   D-150fr (D-180fr)
Loc   7km N of Lannion on Tregastel
          road

Sauzon (1985)

Sauzon, 56360 Belle-Ile-en-Mer
Tel   97 31 64 65
Mem   280
Holes 18 L 5820 m SSS 72
Fees   150-200fr
Loc   Island off S coast of Brittany,
          near Quiberon
Mis   Public course

Val Queven (1989)

Kerrousseau, 56530 Queven
Tel   97 05 17 96
Mem   300
Pro   L Miriel
Holes   18 L 6127 m SSS 72
Fees   130–200fr
Loc   10km W of Lorient

Central East

Aix-les-Bains (1936)

Ave du Golf, 73100 Aix-les-Bains
Tel   79 61 23 35
Mem   460
Pro   IS Lambie
Holes   18 L 5597 m SSS 71
Fees   180fr (250fr)
Loc   3km S of Aix

Albon (1989)

Domaine de Senaud, Albon,
26140 St Rambert d'Albon
Tel   75 03 18 76/75 03 03 90
Mem   350
Pro   J Visseaux
Holes   18 L 6211 m Par 72
Fees   160–180fr (220–240fr)
Loc   60km S of Lyon, motorway
        exit Chanas

Annecy (1953)

Echarvines, 74290 Talloires
Tel   50 60 12 89
Mem   400
Pro   J Noailly, D Bonnaz
Holes   18 L 5017 m SSS 68
Fees   175fr (200fr)
Loc   13km E of Annecy

Les Arcs

Arc 1800, 73700 Bourg-St-Maurice
Tel   79 07 48 00
Mem   396
Pro   A Leclerq, R Gollias
Holes   18 L 4853 m SSS 67
Fees   D-180fr
Loc   Les Arcs, 90km E of
        Chambery on N90
Mis   4 holes pitch & putt

Les Baumes (1986)

Les Baumes, 26420 La Chapelle-en-
Vercors
Tel   75 48 11 62/75 48 21 45
Mem   35
Holes   9 L 2300 m Par 32
Fees   75fr (90fr)
Loc   45km SW of Grenoble
Mis   Open May-Oct

Besançon (1968)

La Chevillote, 25620 Mamirolle
Tel   81 55 73 54
Mem   450

Pro   G Stewart
Holes   18 L 6090 m SSS 72
Fees   150fr (200fr)
Loc   12km E of Besançon

Bossey G & CC (1985)

Château de Crevin, 74160 St-Julien-
en-Genevois
Tel   50 43 75 25
Mem   900
Pro   M Cobley, D Damevin,
        F Dissat
Holes   18 L 6022 m Par 71
Fees   WD-300fr
Loc   6km S of Geneva
Mis   Driving range

Chamonix (1934)

BP 31, 74402 Chamonix Cedex
Tel   50 53 06 28
Mem   400
Pro   JC Bonnaz, D Damiano
Holes   18 L 6087 m SSS 72
Fees   150–180fr 5D-850fr
Loc   3km N of Chamonix (RN 506).
        Geneva 80km
Mis   Public course

Château de Chailly

21320 Chailly-sur-Armançon
Tel   80 90 30 40
Fax   80 90 30 00
Pro   GL Popp
Holes   18 L 6146 m SSS 72
Fees   190fr (250fr)
Loc   45km NW of Dijon

Le Clou

01330 Villars-les-Dombes
Tel   74 98 19 65
Mem   450
Pro   JP Sellier, S Sametzky
Holes   18 L 5000 m SSS 67
Fees   D-130fr (D-180fr)
Loc   30km NE of Lyon

Dijon-Bourgogne (1972)

Bois des Norges, 21490 Norges
La Ville
Tel   80 35 71 10
Mem   450
Pro   B Radcliffe
Holes   18 L 6164 m SSS 72
        9 hole pitch & putt
Fees   140fr (200fr)
Loc   10km N of Dijon towards
        Langres

Divonne (1931)

01220 Divonne-les-Bains
Tel   50 20 07 19
Mem   600
Pro   M Alsurguren, M Suhas
Holes   18 L 6055 m SSS 72
Fees   250fr (450fr)
Loc   Divonne 1/2 km. 18km N of
        Geneva

Esery (1990)

Esery, 74930 Reignier
Tel   50 36 58 70
Fax   50 36 57 62
Mem   800
Pro   J Noailly, A Malcolm, A Cazes,
        P Damiano
Holes   18 L 6350 m SSS 75
Fees   250fr (1990)
Loc   10km E of Geneva
Mis   Handicap certificate required

Flaine-les-Carroz (1984)

74300 Flaine
Tel   50 90 85 44
Mem   80
Pro   P Lacroix
Holes   18 L 4180 m Par 63
Fees   130–180fr (D-170fr)
Loc   4km N of Flaine. 60km SE of
        Geneva Airport

Lyon (1964)

38280 Villette-d'Anthon
Tel   78 31 11 33
Mem   750
Pro   L Capoccia
Holes   27 L 6415 m SSS 72
Fees   130fr (250fr)
Loc   25km E of Lyon

Lyon-Verger (1977)

69360 Saint-Symphorien D'Ozon
Tel   78 02 84 20
Mem   590
Pro   H Sauzet, P Malartre
Holes   18 L 5800 m SSS 69
Fees   170fr (250fr)
Loc   14km S of Lyon on A7 exit
        Solaize, or RN7 2km S of
        Feyzin
Mis   Closed Fri

Méribel (1973)

BP 24, 73550 Méribel
Tel   79 00 52 67
Mem   230
Pro   G Watine
Holes   18 L 5200 m SSS 70
Fees   200fr (250fr)
Loc   15km S of Moutiers.
        35km S of Albertville
Mis   Open June-Oct

Mont-d'Arbois (1964)

74120 Megève
Tel   50 21 29 79
Fax   50 93 02 63
Mem   400
Pro   JB Alsuguren, G Parodi,
        P Provençal
Holes   18 L 6130 m SSS 72
Fees   180-280fr
Loc   3km SE of Megève
Mis   Comps every WE

Montgenèvre

05100 Montgenèvre
Tel   92 21 94 23
Holes 9 L 3000 m Par 36
Fees   150fr (170fr)
Loc   10km NE of Briançon.
       145km E of Grenoble

Royal Golf Evian (1905)

Rive Sud du lac de Genève,
74500 Evian
Tel   50 26 85 00
Fax   50 75 38 40
Mem   250
Pro   J-M Bochaton, A Pery
Holes 18 L 6006 m SSS 72
Fees   D-160–260fr (D-260-290fr)
Loc   2km W of Evian. 40km NE of
       Geneva Airport

Tignes (1968)

Le Val Claret, 73320 Tignes
Tel   79 06 37 42
Mem   250
Pro   B Kvot
Holes 9 L 1830 m SSS 31
Fees   120fr (120fr)
Loc   30km S of Bourg-Saint-
       Maurice
Mis   Open June-Sept

Central West

Angers (1963)

49320 St Jean des Mauvrets
Tel   41 91 96 56
Mem   350
Pro   J Bourel
Holes 18 L 5460 m Par 70
Fees   140fr (180fr)
Loc   14km SE of Angers.
       Right bank of Loire.

Anjou G & CC (1990)

Route de Cheffes, 49330 Champigné
Tel   41 42 01 01
Fax   41 42 04 37
Mem   150
Pro   D Dalies
Holes 18 L 6150 m SSS 72
       6 hole short course
Fees   150fr (200fr)
Loc   23km N of Angers

Ardrée (1988)

BP 1, 37360 Saint-Antoine-du-
Rocher
Tel   47 56 77 38
Mem   150
Pro   B Sparks
Holes 18 L 5804 m SSS 71
Fees   180–250fr (250-280fr)
Loc   10km N of Tours

Avrillé La Perrière (1988)

Château de la Perrière, 49240
Avrillé
Tel   41 69 22 50
Mem   450
Pro   E Rider
Holes 18 L 6120 m SSS 71
       9 hole Par 3 course
Fees   170fr (220fr)
Loc   5km N of Angers

La Baule (1976)

Domaine de Saint-Denac,
44117 Saint-André-des-Eaux
Tel   40 60 46 18
Mem   500
Pro   E Mauger
Holes 18 L 6200 m Par 72
Fees   160-300fr
Loc   Avrillac, 3km NE of La Baule
Mis   Driving range

La Bretesche (1968)

Domaine de la Bretesche
44780 Missillac
Tel   40 88 30 03
Fax   40 88 36 28
Mem   300
Pro   T Mathon
Holes 18 L 6080 m SSS 72
Fees   140–260fr
Loc   8km NW of Pontchâteau. 50km
       NW of Nantes

Châtellerault (1987)

Parc Thermal, 86270 La Roche Posay
Tel   49 86 20 21
Pro   E Rider
Holes 18 L 5813 m SSS 71
Fees   140fr (185fr)
Loc   La Roche-Posay, 20km E of
       Châtellerault. 40km NE of
       Poitiers

Cholet (1989)

Allée du Chêne Landry, 49300
Cholet
Tel   41 71 05 01
Mem   220
Pro   O Canhapé
Holes 18 L 6083 m SSS 72
Fees   180fr (220fr)
Loc   2km N of Cholet. Nantes 70km

Cognac (1987)

Saint-Brice, 16100 Cognac
Tel   45 32 18 17
Mem   700
Pro   M Vickery
Holes 18 L 6255 m SSS 72
Fees   150fr (200fr)
Loc   5km E of Cognac

Fontenelles

Saint-Gilles-Croix-de-Vie,
85220 Aiguillon-sur-Vie
Tel   51 54 13 94

Pro   L Bernis
Holes 18 L 6185 m Par 72
Fees   140–220fr
Loc   6km E of St-Gilles-Croix-de-
       Vie. 75km SW of Nantes

Haut-Poitou

8630 Saint-Cyr
Tel   49 62 53 62
Mem   450
Pro   D Maxwell
Holes 18 L 6500 m SSS 75
       9 L 1800 m Par 31
Fees   150fr (180fr)
Loc   20km N of Poitiers.
       70km S of Tours

L'Hirondelle

Chamfleuri 16000 Angoulême
Tel   45 61 16 94
Mem   350
Pro   G Peña
Holes 9 L 2285 m SSS 34
Fees   90fr (120fr)
Loc   1km S of Angoulême

Laval (1972)

Le Jariel, 53000 Changé-Les-Laval
Tel   43 53 16 03
Holes 9 L 2839 m SSS 35
Fees   D-90fr (100fr 2D-150fr)
Loc   7km N of Laval

Loudun Saint-Hilaire

Roiffe, 86120 Les Trois-Moutiers
Tel   49 98 78 06
Mem   320
Pro   T Abbas
Holes 18 L 6325 m Par 72
Fees   110fr (160fr)
Loc   15km NW of Loudun
Mis   Public course

Le Mans Mulsanne (1961)

72230 Mulsanne
Tel   43 42 00 36
Mem   440
Pro   M Dugue
Holes 18 L 5821 m SSS 71
Fees   150–225fr (220-330fr)
Loc   Mulsanne, 12km S of Le Mans
Mis   Handicap certificate required

Mazières (1987)

Le Petit Chêne, 79310 Mazières-en-
Gâtine
Tel   49 63 28 33
Mem   150
Pro   P Grassin
Holes 18 L 6015 m SSS 72
Fees   120fr (150fr)
Loc   15km SW of Parthenay.
       25km NE of Niort
Mis   Public course

Nantes

44360 Vigneux de Bretagne
Tel 40 63 25 82
Mem 480
Pro H Prot, P Bonhome
Holes 18 L 5940 m SSS 72
Fees 150fr (240fr)
Loc Nantes 15km

Oleron

La Vieille Perrotine, 17310 St Pierre
d'Oleron
Tel 46 47 11 59
Fax 46 47 49 59
Pro D Richalot
Holes 9 L 3000 m SSS 36
6 hole short course
Fees D-100fr (D-120fr)
Loc Island S of La Rochelle.
A10 Junction 25 (Saintes)
Mis Driving range

Pessac (1989)

Rue de la Princesse, 33600 Pessac
Tel 56 36 24 47
Pro G de Maugras, JM Richard
Holes 9 L 3100 m SSS 36; 9 L 3142 m
SSS 36; 9 L 3023 m SSS 36;
9 hole Par 3
Fees 180-250fr (250-280fr)
Loc 4km W of Bordeaux

Poitevin

Terrain des Chalons, 86000 Poitiers
Tel 49 61 23 13
Mem 100
Pro P Signeux
Holes 9 L 2660 m SSS 35
Fees 85fr (100fr)
Loc 3km E of Poitiers

Pornic (1912)

49 bis, Boulevard de l'Océan,
Sainte-Marie/Mer, 44210 Pornic
Tel 40 82 06 69
Mem 280
Pro G Romain
Holes 9 L 5120 m SSS 68
Fees D-100-180fr
Loc 1km E of Pornic. 35km S of La
Baule

Port Bourgenay

Port Bourgenay, 85440 Talmont-
Saint-Hilaire
Tel 51 22 29 87
Pro L Bernis
Holes 18 holes Par 72
Fees 140-220fr
Loc 15km SE of Sables d'Olonne.
100km S of Nantes

La Rochelle

La Prée, 17137 Marsilly
Tel 46 01 24 42
Mem 350
Pro L Landoas

Holes 18 L 6012 m SSS 72
Fees 130-180fr (180-210fr)
Loc 6km N of La Rochelle

Royan (1977)

Maine-Gaudin, 17420 Saint-Palais
Tel 46 23 16 24
Mem 415
Pro J-P Prieur
Holes 18 L 6033 m SSS 71
Fees 150fr (180fr)
Loc Saint-Palais, 7km W of Royan
Mis Public course. Closed Tues

Saintes

Fontcouverte, 17100 Saintes
Tel 46 74 27 61
Mem 350
Pro R Burguet
Holes 9 L 2435 m SSS 68
Fees 80fr (100fr)
Loc 3km NE of Saintes
Mis Public course

Savenay

44260 Savenay
Tel 40 24 36 03
Pro P Bonhomme
Holes 18 L 6335 m Par 73
9 hole short course
Fees 140-220fr
Loc 35km NW of Nantes

Touraine (1971)

Château de la Touche, 37510
Ballan-Miré
Tel 47 53 20 28
Mem 520
Pro M Vol, D Astruc, T Vandooren
Holes 18 L 5671 m SSS 71
Fees 160-200fr (230-250fr)
Loc Villandry, 8km SW of Tours

Centre

Les Bordes (1987)

La Ferté St Cyr, 41220 Saint-Laurent-
Nouant
Tel 54 87 72 13
Pro C Young
Holes 18 L 6436 m Par 72
Fees 330fr (360fr)
Loc 30km SW of Orléans

Chalon-sur-Saône (1976)

Parc de Saint Nicholas, 71380
Chatenoy-en-Bresse
Tel 85 48 61 64/85 93 49 65
Mem 700
Pro J Vezin 85 48 62 42
Holes 18 L 5844 m SSS 71
Fees 100fr (100fr)
Loc 2km NE of Chalon
Mis Public course. Pitch & putt

Charade (1985)

Royat, 63130 Charade
Tel 73 35 73 09
Mem 250
Pro R Picabea
Holes 9 L 2300 m SSS 32
Fees D-70fr (90fr)
Loc 8km W of Clermont-Ferrand.
Royat 3km

Château de Cheverny

La Rousselière, 41700 Cheverny
Tel 54 79 24 70
Fax 54 79 25 52
Mem 200
Pro P Rault
Holes 18 L 6276 m SSS 73
Fees 180fr (250fr)
Loc 15km S of Blois. 200km SW of
Paris, via A10

Clairis (1974)

Domaine de Clairis, 89150 Savigny-
sur-Clairis
Tel 86 86 33 90
Mem 180
Pro P Schilling
Holes 9 hole course
Fees 90fr (160fr)
Loc St Valérien, 12km W of Sens

La Commanderie Mâcon (1964)

L'Aumusse, Crottet, 01290 Pont-de-
Veyle
Tel 85 30 44 12/85 30 40 24
Mem 350
Pro C Soules, P Wakeford
Holes 18 L 5550 m SSS 69
Fees 160fr (200fr)
Loc 7km E of Mâcon on RN 79

La Dombes (1986)

Mionnay, 01390 St-André-de-Corcy
Tel 78 91 84 84
Mem 220
Pro F Dietsch
Holes 9 L 2484 m SSS 70
Fees 100fr Sat-160fr Sun-200fr
Loc 20km N of Lyon towards Bourg

La Jonchère

Montgrenier, 23230 Gouzon
Tel 55 62 23 05
Mem 202
Pro P Isambert
Holes 18 L 5858 m SSS 71
Fees 140fr (180fr)
Loc 30km SW of Montluçon.
100km NE of Limoges

Limoges (1976)

Avenue du Golf, 87000 Limoges
Tel 55 30 21 02
Mem 550

Pro   Y Saubaber, R Larretche
Holes 18 L 6218 m SSS 72
Fees   66fr
Loc   2km S of Limoges on N20

Marcilly (1986)

Domaine de la Plaine, 45240
Marcilly-en-Villette
Tel   38 76 11 73
Mem   520
Pro   G Raison, P Guichard
Holes 18 L 6324 m SSS 73
       9 hole course
Fees   110fr (170fr)
Loc   20km SE of Orléans

Mezeyrac (1988)

Soulages Bonneval, 12210 Laguiole
Tel   65 44 41 41
Mem   130
Pro   P Vincent
Holes 9 L 2564 m SSS 68
Fees   100fr (150fr)
Loc   Mezeyrac, 50km NE of Rodez.
       150km NW of Montpellier

Le Nivernais

58470 Magny Cours
Tel   86 58 18 30
Mem   400
Pro   P Raguet
Holes 18 L 5665 m Par 71
Fees   80fr (150fr)
Loc   12km S of Nevers on N7
Mis   Public course

Rigolet (1928)

63240 Le Mont-Dore
Tel   73 65 00 79
Pro   L Mencagli
Holes 9 L 2115 m SSS 34
Fees   D-100fr W-500fr
Loc   2½ km E of Mont-Dore.
       35km SW of Clermont-
       Ferrand
Mis   Open May-Oct

Roncemay (1989)

89110 Aillant-sur-Tholon
Tel   86 73 69 87
Mem   340
Pro   JC Iturrioz, P Iturrioz
Holes 18 L 6401 m SSS 73
Fees   WD-200fr
Loc   25km NW of Auxerre
Mis   WE-only with member

Sologne (1955)

Route de Jouy-le-Potier, 45240
Ardon
Tel   38 76 57 33/38 76 50 01
Holes 18 L 7200 yds Par 72
Fees   130fr (220fr)
Loc   25km S of Orléans on RN20

Sporting-Club de Vichy (1907)

Allée Baugnies, 03700
Bellerive/Allier
Tel   70 32 39 11
Mem   450
Pro   Ch Roumaud
Holes 18 L 5427 m SSS 70
Fees   220fr (300fr)
Loc   In Vichy

Sully-sur-Loire

L'Ousseau, 45600 Viglain
Tel   38 36 52 08
Mem   220
Pro   P Antoine
Holes 18 L 5863 m SSS 72
Fees   180fr (350fr)
Loc   3km SW of Sully-sur-Loire

Val de Loire

45450 Donnery
Tel   38 59 20 48/38 59 25 15
Mem   280
Pro   JM Duboc
Holes 18 L 5840 m SSS 71
Fees   D-180fr (250fr 2D-420fr)
Loc   16km E of Orléans

Val de l'Indre

Villedieu-sur-Indre, 36320
Tregonce
Tel   54 26 59 44
Mem   190
Pro   A Gautier
Holes 18 L 6250 m SSS 72
Fees   140-200fr
Loc   10km NW of Chateauroux.
       80km SE of Tours on
       RN 143

Val-de-Cher

Nassigny, 03190 Vallon-en-Sully
Tel   70 06 71 15
Mem   200
Pro   JC Gassiat
Holes 18 L 5200 m
Fees   140fr (Sun-200fr 2D-350fr)
Loc   Nassigny, 20km N of
       Montluçon on N144
Mis   Closed Tues

Vaugouard (1987)

Chemin des Bois, Fontenay-sur-
Loing, 45210 Ferrières
Tel   38 95 81 52
Fax   38 95 79 78
Mem   350
Pro   V Loustaud
Holes 18 L 5914 m SSS 72
Fees   200fr (330fr)
Loc   10km N of Montargis.
       Paris 100km

Villerest (1985)

Domaine de Champlong, 42300
Roanne
Tel   77 69 70 60
Mem   180
Pro   B Le Tanter
Holes 9 L 2008 m Par 31
Fees   70-90fr (90-120fr)
Loc   5km SW of Roanne towards
       Clermont-Ferrand
Mis   Public course

Les Volcans (1984)

La Bruyère des Moines, 63870
Orcines
Tel   73 62 15 51
Mem   600
Pro   L Roux, G Roux,
       O Roux
Holes 18 L 6242 m SSS 72
       9 L 1815 m SSS 29
Fees   180fr (250fr)
Loc   12km W of Clermont-Ferrand
       on RN 141

Corsica

Spérone (1990)

Domaine de Spérone, 20169
Bonifacio
Tel   95 73 13 69 Fax-95 73 06 97
Holes 18 L 6200m Par 72
Loc   S point of Corsica, SE of
       Bonifacio

Languedoc-Roussillon

Bombequiols (1986)

Mas de Bombequiols, Saint-André-
de-Buèges, 34190 Ganges
Tel   67 73 72 67
Holes 9 L 2800 m SSS 35
Fees   130 (160fr)
Loc   45km NW of Montpellier
       towards Ganges

Cap d'Agde (1989)

4 Ave des Alizés,
34300 Cap d'Agde
Tel   67 26 54 40
Mem   360
Holes 18 L 6160 m SSS 72
Fees   210fr (260fr)
Loc   25km E of Béziers.
       65km W of Montpellier
Mis   Public course

Coulondres (1984)

4, Rue des Erables,
34980 Saint-Gely-du-Fesc
Tel 67 84 13 75
Mem 230
Pro V Schwechlen
Holes 18 L 6175 m SSS 72
Fees 160fr (180fr)
Loc 10km N of Montpellier towards
Ganges

La Grande-Motte

34280 La Grande-Motte
Tel 67 56 05 00
Fax 67 29 18 84
Mem 300
Pro P Porquier
Holes 18 L 6200 m SSS 72
18 L 4000 m Par 58
6 hole course
Fees 200fr (280fr 2D-500fr)
Loc 18km E of Montpellier

Massane

Domaine de Massane, 34670
Baillargues
Tel 67 87 23 23
Pro N Armand
Holes 18 L 6375 m SSS 74
9 hole course
Fees 180fr (250fr)
Loc Baillargues, 9km E of
Montpellier

Nîmes Campagne
(1968)

Route de Saint Gilles,
30900 Nîmes
Tel 66 70 17 37
Mem 640
Pro T Lassale,
A Brioland
Holes 18 L 6200 m SSS 72
Fees 180fr Sat-250fr Sun-350fr
Loc 2km from Nîmes, by Airport

St Cyprien (1974)

Le Mas D'Huston,
66750 St Cyprien Plage
Tel 68 21 01 71
Mem 700
Pro P Lacroix,
J-P Harrismendy,
E Bocau,
M Malafosse
Holes 18 L 6480 m SSS 73
9 L 2724 m SSS 35
Fees Hotel guests-170fr (370fr)
Others-195fr (420fr)
Loc 15km SE of Perpignan

Lille & Channel Coast

AA-Saint-Omer

Chemin des Bois, Acquin-
Westbecourt, 62380 Lumbres
Tel 21 38 59 90   Fax 21 38 59 90
Mem 627
Pro Y Raout, S Raout
Holes 18 L 6313 m SSS 73
9 L 2003 m SSS 31
Fees 210fr (250fr)
Loc 10km W of Saint-Omer.
40km S of Calais
Mis Handicap certificate required
(18 hole course)

Amiens (1951)

80115 Querrieu
Tel 22 91 02 04
Mem 530
Pro B Dachicourt
Holes 18 L 6124 m SSS 72
Fees 150fr (250fr)
Loc 7km NE of Amiens on Route
D929

Bondues (1968)

Château de la Vigne, BP 54, 59910
Bondues
Tel 20 23 20 62
Mem 1050
Pro P Iturrioz, A Vandamme,
A White
Holes 18 L 6223 m SSS 73
18 L 6000 m SSS 72
Fees D-200fr (D-300fr) (1990)
Loc 10km NE of Lille
Mis Handicap certificate required

Brigode (1970)

36 Avenue de Golf, 59650
Villeneuve D'Ascq
Tel 20 91 17 86
Mem 600
Pro J Bulmer
Holes 18 L 6182 m SSS 72
Fees 200fr (300fr)
Loc 8km NE of Lille

Dunkerque (1983)

Fort Vallières, Coudekerque-
Village, 59380 Bergues
Tel 28 61 07 43
Pro M Youngs, R Iturrioz
Holes 18 L 6300 m SSS 71
Fees 100-130fr (130-165fr) (1990)
Loc 5km E of Dunkerque
Mis Public course

Les Flandres (1957)

137, Bd Clemenceau, 59700 Marcq-
en-Baroeul
Tel 20 72 20 74
Mem 425
Pro R Loth

Holes 9 L 4549 m SSS 64
Fees 175fr
Loc 4km N of Lille, on Croise
Laroche racecourse

Hardelot

Ave du Golf, 62152 Neufchâtel-
Hardelot
Tel 21 83 73 10
Mem 650
Pro L Maisonnave
Holes 18 L 5870 m SSS 72
Fees D-230fr (D-290fr)
Loc Hardelot, 15km S of Boulogne

Mesnil-Saint-Laurent

02720 Homblières
Tel 23 68 19 48
Mem 160
Pro B Dachicourt
Holes 9 L 6110 m SSS 72
Fees 130fr (160fr)
Loc 5km SE of Saint-Quentin.
100km NE of Paris

Nampont-St-Martin (1978)

Maison Forte, 80120 Nampont-
St-Martin
Tel 22 29 92 90/22 29 89 87
Mem 600
Pro H Courtessi
Holes 18 L 5786 m SSS 72
Fees 130-150fr (150-180fr)
Loc 12km S of Montreuil-sur-Mer
on route N1. 30km SE of
Le Touquet
Mis Driving range. Further 9 holes
open 1991

Le Sart (1910)

5 Rue Jean Jaures,
59650 Villeneuve D'Ascq
Tel 20 72 02 51
Mem 500
Pro R Wattinne
Holes 18 L 5721 m SSS 71
Fees 200fr (300fr 2D-480fr)
Loc 5km E of Lille. Motorway Lille-
Ghent Junction 9 (Breucq-
Le Sart)

Thumeries (1932)

Bois Lenglart, 59239 Thumeries
Tel 20 86 58 98
Mem 330
Pro B Tiradon
Holes 9 L 2923 m SSS 35
Fees 140fr (210fr)
Loc 15km S of Lille

Le Touquet (1904)

Ave du Golf, 62520 Le Touquet
Tel 21 05 20 22
Mem 660
Pro P Philippon

Holes 18 L 5895 m SSS 71
18 L 6140 m SSS 72
9 hole course
Fees 18 holes 200fr (260fr)
9 holes 100fr (140fr)
Loc 2km S of Le Touquet

Valenciennes

Chemin Vert, 59770 Marly-les-
Valenciennes
Tel 27 46 30 10
Mem 215
Pro J Roux
Holes 9 L 2380 m SSS 33
Fees 80fr (120fr)
Loc 2km SE of Valenciennes

Wimereux (1906)

Route d'Ambleteuse, 62930
Wimereux
Tel 21 32 43 20
Mem 600
Pro H Marconi
Holes 18 L 6361 m Par 62
Fees 150–185fr (160–220fr)
Loc 6km N of Boulogne on D940.
30km S of Calais

Normandy

Bagnoles-de-l'Orne (1925)

Route de Domfront,
61140 Bagnoles-de-l'Orne
Tel 33 37 81 42
Pro H Dauge
Holes 9 L 2200 m SSS 70
Fees D-40fr (60fr) W-180fr
Loc Bagnoles, 80km S of Caen
Mis Public course

Bellême-Saint-Martin (1988)

Les Sablons, 61130 Bellême
Tel 33 73 15 35
Fax 33 83 65 51
Mem 352
Pro R Austin
Holes 18 L 6055 m SSS 72
Fees 140fr (200fr)
Loc 40km NE of Le Mans.
160km SW of Paris

Beuzeval

Gonville-sur-Mer, 14510 Houlgate
Tel 31 91 06 97
Pro A Forrester
Holes 18 L 5830 m SSS 72
Fees 180-200fr (200-220fr)
Loc 3km S of Houlgate towards
Gonneville

Bréhal (1964)

50290 Bréhal
Tel 33 51 58 88
Mem 320

Holes 9 L 2055 m Par 31
Fees 100-120fr
Loc 10km N of Granville
along St Martin beach
Mis Public course

Cabourg-Le Home (1955)

38 Av Président Réné Coty, Le
Home Varaville, 14390 Cabourg
Tel 31 91 25 56
Mem 300
Pro L Allain
Holes 18 L 5122 m SSS 68
Fees On application
Loc 4km W of Cabourg

Cherbourg (1973)

Domaine des Roches,
50470 La Glacerie
Tel 33 44 45 48
Mem 270
Pro J-F Lenoir
Holes 9 L 2842 m SSS 36
Fees 90fr (100fr)
Loc 6km S of Cherbourg

Clécy

Manoir de Cantelou, 14570 Clécy
Tel 31 69 72 72
Holes 18 L 5975 m SSS 72
Fees 150fr (200fr)
Loc 30km S of Caen, via D562

Coutainville (1925)

Ave du Golf, 50230 Agon-
Coutainville
Tel 33 47 03 31
Mem 330
Pro I Folliot
Holes 9 L 5360 m SSS 69
Fees 120–180fr
Loc 12km W of Coutances.
75km S of Cherbourg

Dieppe (1897)

76200 Dieppe
Tel 35 84 25 05
Mem 520
Pro S Ortiz
Holes 18 L 5763 m SSS 70
Fees 170fr (200fr)
Loc 2km W of Dieppe

Étretat (1908)

BP No 7, 76790 Étretat
Tel 35 27 04 89/27 04 56
(Clubhouse)
Mem 320
Pro J Morea
Holes 18 L 5840 m SSS 72
Fees 130–175fr (190–265fr)
Loc 28km N of Le Havre.
Étretat ¹/₂ km

Fontenay-en-Cotentin (1975)

Fontenay-sur-Mer, 50310
Montebourg
Tel 33 21 44 27
Mem 90
Pro A Quibeuf (summer)
Holes 9 L 2954 m Par 36
Fees 110fr (130fr)
Loc 32km SE of Cherbourg, via
RN13/D42

Granville (1912)

Bréville, 50290 Bréhal
Tel 33 50 23 06
Mem 400
Pro E Alvarez
Holes 18 L 5854 m Par 72
9 L 2323 m Par 33
Fees 18 hole:110fr (160fr)
9 hole:80fr (110fr)
Loc 5km N of Granville

Le Havre (1933)

Hameau Saint-Supplix
76930 Octeville-sur-Mer
Tel 35 46 36 50/35 46 36 11
Mem 450
Pro R Truman
Holes 18 L 5830 m SSS 70
Fees 150fr (300fr)
Loc 10km N of Le Havre

New Golf Deauville (1929)

14 Saint Arnoult, 14800 Deauville
Tel 31 88 20 53
Mem 650
Pro C Hausseguy
Holes 18 L 5933 m SSS 71
9 L 3033 m SSS 72
Fees 170–220fr (240-330fr)
Loc 3km S of Deauville

Omaha Beach (1986)

Ferme St Sauveur, 14520 Port-en-
Bessin
Tel 31 21 72 94
Mem 450
Pro S Lesné
Holes 18 L 6214 m SSS 72
9 L 2937m
Fees 180-220fr (220-250fr)
Loc 8km N of Bayeux

Rouen

Rue Boucicaut,
76130 Mt St Aignan
Tel 35 76 38 65
Mem 600
Pro J-P Quibeuf
Holes 18 L 5522 m SSS 70
Fees D-160fr
Loc 4km N of Rouen

Saint-Gatien Deauville (1987)

14130 Saint-Gatien-des-Bois
Tel   31 65 19 99
Mem   230
Pro   JP Turin
Holes   18 L 6200 m SSS 72
        9 L 3000 m SSS 36
Fees   160–200fr (240-300fr)
Loc   8km E of Deauville.
        Honfleur 8km

Saint-Julien

Saint-Julien-sur-Calonne, 14130
Pont-l'Evêque
Tel   31 64 19 15
Pro   A Quibeuf
Holes   18 L 6210 m SSS 72
        9 2133 m SSS 33
Fees   250fr
Loc   3km SE of Pont l'Evêque

Saint-Saëns (1987)

76680 Saint-Saëns
Tel   35 34 25 24
Mem   250
Pro   P Vedrinelle
Holes   18 L 6004 m SSS 71
Fees   D–125fr (D-250fr)
Loc   30km NE of Rouen

Le Vaudreuil (1962)

27100 Le Vaudreuil
Tel   32 59 02 60
Mem   350
Pro   J Lecuellet
Holes   18 L 6411 m SSS 73
Fees   150fr (250fr)
Loc   6km NE of Louviers.
        25km SE of Rouen

North East

Ammerschwihr

BP 19, Route des Trois Epis, 68770
Ammerschwihr
Tel   89 47 17 30
Pro   D Racine
Holes   18 L 6235 m Par 72
        9 hole short course
Fees   140fr (180fr)
Loc   8km W of Colmar.
        60km N of Mulhouse
Mis   Driving range

Ardennes

Les Poursaudes, 08430 Villers-le-
Tilleul
Tel   24 35 64 65
Mem   180
Pro   B Favre-Victoire
Holes   9 L 2816 m SSS 36
Fees   150fr
Loc   20km SE of Charleville

Bâle (1926)

68220 Hagenthal-le-Bas, Ht Rhin
Tel   89 68 50 91
Mem   630
Pro   A Perrone, C Bisel
Holes   18 L 6255 m SSS 74
Fees   150fr (220fr)
Loc   15km SW of Basle
Mis   Open Apr-Oct

Bitche (1988)

Rue des Prés, 57230 Bitche
Tel   87 96 15 30
Mem   700
Pro   D Taylor, G Copp
Holes   18 L 6082 m SSS 72
        9 L 2293 m SSS 34
Fees   18 hole:110fr (180fr)
        9 hole:70fr (110fr)
Loc   75km NW of Strasbourg.
        55km SE of Saarbrücken
Mis   Public course

Combles

55000 Combles-en-Barrois
Tel   29 45 16 03
Mem   226
Pro   M Vian
Holes   9 L 2241 m SSS 33
Fees   120fr (150fr)
Loc   Bar-le-Duc, 70km W of
        Nancy

Épinal (1985)

Rue du Merle-Blanc, 88001 Épinal
Tel   29 31 45 45
Pro   R Golias, D Mory
Holes   18 L 5700 m SSS 70
Fees   D–60fr
Loc   Épinal, 70km S of Nancy
Mis   Public course

La Largue

Chemin du Largweg, 68580
Mooslargue
Tel   89 25 71 11
Mem   150
Pro   K Marriott
Holes   18 L 6150 m SSS 72
Fees   180fr (240fr)
Loc   25km W of Basle

Madine

Nonsard, 55210 Vigneulles
Tel   29 89 56 00/29 89 32 50
Mem   30
Pro   M Brasset
Holes   9 L 2930 m Par 36
Fees   50fr (80fr)
Loc   40km SE of Verdun.
        45km SW of Metz
Mis   Public course

Metz-Cherisey (1963)

Château de Cherisey, 57420 Verny
Tel   87 52 70 18
Mem   480
Pro   J Gould, P Schwartzberg
Holes   18 L 6075 m Par 72
Fees   150fr (200fr)
Loc   15km SE of Metz. Nancy 35km

Nancy-Aingeray

Aingeray, 54460 Liverdun
Tel   83 24 53 87/83 24 58 99
Mem   250
Pro   A Gass
Holes   18 L 5525 m SSS 69
Fees   140fr (220fr)
Loc   17km NW of Nancy

Prunevelle (1930)

Ferme des Petits-Bans, 25420
Dampierre-sur-le-Doubs
Tel   81 98 11 77/33 03 04
Mem   300
Pro   R Lesouder
Holes   18 L 6281 m SSS 73
Fees   130fr (140fr)
Loc   10km S of Montbéliard. A36
        Motorway exit Montbéliard
        Sud via Besançon on D126 to
        Dampierre-sur-le-Doubs
Mis   Open 15 Mar-10 Oct

Reims-Champagne (1928)

Château des Dames de France,
51390 Gueux
Tel   26 03 60 14 (Clubhouse)
Mem   620
Pro   P Harrison, E Censier
Holes   18 L 6026 m SSS 72
Fees   200fr (300fr)
Loc   10km W of Reims

Rhin Mulhouse (1969)

BP1152, 68053 Mulhouse Cedex
Tel   89 26 07 86
Mem   532
Pro   A Price
Holes   18 L 5991 m SSS 72
Fees   150fr (250fr)
Loc   Ile du Rhin-Chalampe.
        20km E of Mulhouse

Strasbourg (1934)

Route du Rhin, 67400 Illkirch
Tel   88 66 17 22
Mem   600
Pro   JP Tairraz, N Madeuf
Holes   18 L 6047 m SSS 72
Fees   WD only-200fr
Loc   10km S of Strasbourg

Troyes-Cordelière

10210 Chaource
Tel   25 40 11 05
Mem   380
Pro   M Vian
Holes   18 L 6154 m SSS 72

Fees 180fr (250fr)
Loc NE of Chaource on N443.
      30km SE of Troyes

Vittel

BP 122, 88800 Vittel
Tel 29 08 18 80 (1 May-30 Sept)
Mem 400
Pro D Mory, M Lachaux
Holes 18 L 6271 m SSS 72
      18 L 6100 m SSS 72
      9 hole course
Fees 150fr Sat-250fr Sun-200fr
Loc Vittel, 70km S of Nancy.
      Épinal 45km

Paris Region

Belesbat

91820 Boutigny-sur-Essonne
Tel 64 57 85 46
Fax 64 57 86 95
Pro D Mercier
Holes 18 L 6047 m SSS 72
Fees 200fr (400fr)
Loc 40km S of Paris, between
      Etampes and Fontainebleau

La Boulie

La Boulie, 78000 Versailles
Tel 39 50 59 41
Mem 1500
Pro F Castel, M Garaialde,
J P Quillo, G Watine
Holes 18 L 6055 m SSS 71
      18 L 6206 m SSS 72
      9 hole course
Fees WD-400fr-by invitation
Loc 15km SW of Paris

Cély-en-Bière (1990)

**Le Château, Route de Saint-
Germain, 77930 Cély-en-Bière**
Tel 64 38 03 07
Holes 18 hole course

Chantilly (1909)

Vineuil Saint Firmin, 60500 Chantilly
Tel 44 57 04 43
Mem 500
Pro A Chardonnet, P Léglise,
      G Lamy
Holes Vineuil 18 L 6597 m SSS 71
      Longères 9 L 2625 m SSS 35
Fees WD-300fr
Loc 45km N of Paris
Mis WE-only with member

Chaumont-en-Vexin (1963)

60240 Chaumont-en-Vexin
Tel 44 49 00 81/44 49 14 76
Mem 350
Holes 18 L 6195 m SSS 72
Fees 200fr (400fr)
Loc 65km NW of Paris

Chevry (1976)

91190 Gif-sur-Yvette
Tel 60 12 40 33
Pro D Maxwell, P Maréchal
Holes 9 L 2693 m SSS 34
Fees 95–160fr
Loc 25km SW of Paris
Mis Public course. Pitch & putt

Compiègne (1895)

Ave Royale, 60200 Compiègne
Tel 44 40 15 73
Mem 900
Pro M Amat
Holes 18 L 5873 m SSS 71
Fees 200fr (350fr)
Loc Compiègne, 70km NE of Paris

Coudray (1960)

**Ave du Coudray, 91830 Le Coudray-
Montceaux**
Tel 64 93 81 76
Mem 850
Pro JL Schneider, M Lebrun,
      C Langlois
Holes 18 L 5384 m SSS 70
      9 hole course
Fees 210fr (475fr)
Loc 35km S of Paris on A6

Crecy-la-Chapelle (1987)

**Ferme de Monpichet,
77580 Crécy-la-Chapelle**
Tel 64 04 70 75
Mem 150
Pro M Wallace, W Cunliffe
Holes 18 L 6211 m SSS 72
Fees 150fr (300fr)
Loc 20km E of Paris by A4

Domont-Montmorency

**Route de Montmorency, 95330
Domont**
Tel 39 91 07 50
Mem 350
Pro R Changart, Ch Gassiat,
      Ch Chabriel
Holes 18 L 5775 m SSS 71
Fees 240fr (450fr)
Loc 18km N of Paris
Mis Pitch & putt

Fontainebleau (1908)

Route d'Orleans, 77300 Fontainebleau
Tel 64 22 22 95
Mem 450
Pro JP Hirigoyen, Th Vallin
Holes 18 L 6022 m SSS 72
Fees 350fr (630fr)
Loc 1km SW of Fontainebleau. SE
      of Paris

Fourqueux (1963)

Rue St Nom 36, 78112 Fourqueux
Tel 34 51 41 47
Mem 520

Pro H Gioux, G Loth
Holes 27 holes-9 L 3135 m Par 37
      9 L 2890 m Par 36;
      9 L 2725 m Par 37
Fees 300fr (370fr)
Loc 4km SW of Saint-Germain-en-
      Laye. W of Paris

La Grenouillère

**Île de la Grenouillère,
78290 Croissy-sur-Seine**
Tel 39 18 43 81
Mem 400
Pro P Lefebvre, A Alsuguren,
      JP Kevorkian, C Paillet
Holes 9 L 2120 m SSS 27
Fees 120fr (240fr)
Loc 25km W of Paris

International Club du Lys

**Rond-Point du Grand Cerf,
60260 Lamorlaye**
Tel 44 21 26 00
Pro F Saubaber
Holes 18 L 5986 m SSS 71
      18 L 4798 m SSS 66
Fees 200fr (400fr)
Loc 5km S of Chantilly

Isabella (1969)

**RN12, Sainte-Appoline,
78370 Plaisir**
Tel 30 54 10 62
Mem 280
Holes 9 L 2454 m SSS 34
Fees 170fr (280fr) (1988)
Loc 28km W of Paris, RN12 to
      Dreux

Lac de Germigny

**Germigny l'Evêque, 77910
Varredes**
Tel 64 35 02 87
Pro J Sepchat, S Sametzky
Holes 9 L 2484 m SSS 68
Fees 120fr (250fr)
Loc 50km E of Paris, nr Meaux

Marolles-en-Brie

**Mail de la Justice, 94440 Marolles-
en-Brie**
Tel 45 95 18 18
Pro P Mendiburu
Holes 9 L 2300 m Par 33
Fees 140fr (195fr)
Loc 15km SE of Paris, via RN 19

Meaux-Boutigny (1985)

**Le Bordet, Rue de Barrois,
77470 Trilport**
Tel 60 25 63 98
Mem 450
Pro A Delannoy
Holes 18 L 6100 m SSS 71
      9 hole course
Fees 180fr (300fr)
Loc 45km E of Paris-Highway 4

Morfontaine (1926)

Mortefontaine, 60128 Plailly
Tel   44 54 68 27
Mem   450
Pro   S De Galard, M Philippon
Holes 18 L 6063 m SSS 72
          9 L 2550 m SSS 36
Fees   NA
Loc   10km S of Senlis. N of Paris
Mis   Members' guests only

Ormesson (1969)

Chemin du Belvedere, 94490
Ormesson-sur-Marne
Tel   45 76 20 71
Mem   475
Pro   F Leclercq
Holes 18 L 6129 m SSS 72
Fees   220fr (380fr)
Loc   21km SE of Paris

National Golf Club (1990)

BP 16, 78041 Guyancourt Cédex
Tel   30 43 36 00
Holes Albatros 18 hole course
          Oiselet 9 hole course
Fees   80–190fr (80–290fr)
Loc   SW of Paris, nr Versailles

Ozoir-la-Ferrière (1926)

Château des Agneaux,
77330 Ozoir-la-Ferrière
Tel   60 02 60 79
Mem   580
Pro   G Henichard, T Murphy
Holes 18 L 6105 m SSS 72
          9 L 2700 m Par 35
Fees   18 hole:250fr (400fr)
          9 hole:130fr (250fr)
Loc   25km SE of Paris via A4 (Sortie
          Val Maubuée)

Le Prieuré (1965)

Sailly, 78440 Gargenville
Tel   34 76 70 12
Mem   1453
Pro   J Alsuguren, M Lachaux,
          G Bourdy
Holes Ouest 18 L 6274 m SSS 72
          Est 18 L 6157 m SSS 72
Fees   225fr (375fr)
Loc   10km W of Meulan. 45km NW
          of Paris

Rebetz

Route de Noailles, 60240 Chaumont-
en-Vexin
Tel   44 49 15 54
Mem   350
Pro   M Meyrat
Holes 18 L 6434 m SSS 73
Fees   200fr (400fr)
Loc   65km NW of Paris, via D43

Rochefort

78730 Rochefort-en-Yvelines
Tel   30 41 31 81
Pro   M Berthouloux

Holes 18 L 5735 m SSS 71
Fees   220fr (420fr)
Loc   35km SW of Paris

Saint-Aubin (1976)

91190 Saint-Aubin
Tel   69 41 25 19
Pro   C Chabrier, Q Dubart
Holes 18 L 5617 m SSS 70
Loc   30km SW of Paris

Saint-Cloud (1911)

60 Rue du 19 Janvier, Garches 92380
Tel   47 01 01 85
Mem   2000
Pro   JP Tairraz, R Giraud, A Leclerc,
          JC Bard, P Galitzine
Holes 18 L 5980 m SSS 71
          18 L 4857 m SSS 67
Fees   290fr Sat-400fr Sun-550fr
Loc   Porte Dauphine, 9km W of Paris
Mis   Handicap certificate required

Saint-Germain (1922)

Route de Poissy,
78100 St-Germain-en-Laye
Tel   34 51 75 90
Mem   800
Pro   M Dallemagne, E Lafitte
          O St-Hilaire, D Hausseguy
Holes 18 L 6024 m SSS 72
          9 L 2030 m SSS 33
Fees   400fr
Loc   20km NW of Paris
Mis   WE-only with member

Saint-Nom-La-Bretêche (1959)

78860 Saint-Nom-La-Bretêche
Tel   34 62 54 00
Mem   1600
Sec   P Galitzine
Pro   A Cadet, R Golias, A Ferran,
          P Rouquet, G Leven
Holes 18 L 6685 yds SSS 72
          18 L 6712 yds SSS 72
Fees   WD only-400fr
Loc   24km W of Paris on A-13
Mis   Handicap certificate required

Saint-Pierre du Perray (1974)

Saint-Pierre du Perray, 91100
Corbeil
Tel   60 75 17 47
Pro   E Hemberger
Holes 18 L 6169 m SSS 72
Loc   30km SE of Paris, off N6
Mis   Public course

Saint-Quentin-en-Yvelines

Base de Loisirs RN12, 78190 Trappes
Tel   30 50 86 40
Pro   JP Chardonnet
Holes 18 L 5900 m SSS 71
          9 L 3063 m SSS 36
Loc   20km SW of Paris
Mis   Public course

Seraincourt (1964)

Gaillonnet-Seraincourt, 95450 Vigny
Tel   34 75 47 28
Fax   34 75 75 47
Mem   380
Pro   J-P Gachet, L Salgado
Holes 18 L 5699 m SSS 70
Fees   200fr (420fr)
Loc   35km NW of Paris

Vaucouleurs

78910 Civry-la-Forêt
Tel   34 87 62 29
Mem   400
Pro   D Chaumillon, O Daavet
Holes 18 L 6298 m SSS 72
          18 L 5700 m SSS 68
Fees   200fr (400fr)
Loc   50km W of Paris, between
          Mantes and Houdan

Villarceaux (1971)

Chaussy, 95710 Bray-et-Lu
Tel   34 67 73 83
Mem   600
Pro   R Alsuguren, D Mercier
Holes 18 L 6101 m Par 72
Fees   170fr (375fr)
Loc   40km NW of Paris

Villennes (1985)

Route d'Orgeval, 78670 Villennes-
sur-Seine
Tel   39 75 30 00
Mem   3000
Pro   P Guy, O Jaret
Holes 9 L 2575 m SSS 34
Fees   95-160fr
Loc   25km W of Paris, off N13
Mis   Driving range. Public course.

Provence & Côte d'Azur

Aix Marseille (1935)

13290 Les Milles
Tel   42 24 40 41/ 42 24 23 01
Mem   550
Pro   R Cotton, B Cotton,
          P Cotton
Holes 18L 6291 m SSS 73
Fees   170fr (320fr)
Loc   7km SW of Aix-en-Provence.
          15km N of Marseille

Barbaroux

Route de Cabasse, 83170 Brignoles
Tel   94 59 07 43
Pro   N von Nida
Holes 18 L 6367 m SSS 72
Fees   300fr
Loc   Brignoles, 50km E of Aix.
          35km N of Toulon

Les Baux (1987)

Domaine de Manville, 13520 Les
Baux-de-Provence
Tel   90 54 37 02
Mem   250
Pro   W Murray
Holes   9 L 2790 m SSS 36
Fees   90fr (120fr)
Loc   15km NE of Arles

Beauvallon-Grimaud

Boulevard des Collines, 83120
Sainte Maxime
Tel   94 96 16 98
Mem   320
Pro   P Delaville
Holes   9 L 2503 m SSS 34
Fees   180-220fr (200-300fr)
Loc   3km SW of Sainte Maxime

Biot

06410 Biot
Tel   93 65 08 48
Pro   H Giraud, L Casella,
       R Pettavino
Holes   18 L 5064 m SSS 70
Fees   190fr (220fr)
Loc   Antibes 5km. Nice 15km

Le Bourget

Montmeyran, 26120 Chabeuil
Tel   75 59 41 71
Mem   250
Pro   H Ranieri
Holes   13 L 3070m Par 46
Fees   70fr (100fr)
Loc   12km SE of Valence.
       100km N of Avignon

Cannes-Mandelieu (1891)

06210 Mandelieu-La Napoule
Tel   93 49 55 39
Mem   300
Pro   A Monge, R Gorgerino,
       R Damiano, C Nunez
Holes   18 L 5871 m SSS 71
       9 L 2852 m SSS 34
Fees   250fr (280fr)
Loc   Mandelieu, 7km W of Cannes

Cannes-Mougins (1978)

175 Route d'Antibes, 06250 Mougins
Tel   93 75 79 13
Mem   330 170(L) 50(J)
Pro   M Damiano, P Lemaire,
       R Sorrel
Holes   18 L 6300 m SSS 72
Fees   270fr (300fr)
Loc   8km N of Cannes

Château L'Arc (1985)

Domaine de Château L'Arc, 13710
Fuveau
Tel   42 53 28 38
Mem   400
Pro   R Pujol, R Guidetti, J Pickford
Holes   18 L 6300 m SSS 73

Fees   230fr (330fr) (1989)
Loc   15km SE of Aix-en-Provence

Châteaublanc

Les Plans, 84310 Morières-les-
Avignon
Tel   90 33 39 08 Fax 90 33 43 24
Mem   350
Pro   J-L Walter Martin
Holes   18 L 6275 m SSS 73
       9 hole Par 3 course
Fees   160fr (250fr) Par 3-100fr
Loc   5km SE of Avignon, nr Airport

Digne-les-Bains (1990)

Saint-Pierre de Gaubert, 0400 Digne
Tel   92 32 38 38 Fax 92 32 09 04
Mem   200
Pro   P Pee
Holes   18 L 5910 m SSS 73
       6 hole short course
Fees   140-220fr
Loc   Digne, 100km NE of Aix-en-
       Provence

Estérel (1989)

Latitudes Valescure, Ave du Golf,
83700 Saint-Raphaël
Tel   94 82 46 60
Fax   94 82 46 77
Holes   18 L 5921 m SSS 71
Fees   220fr (240fr)
Loc   2km N of Saint-Raphaël

Gap-Bayard (1988)

Centre d'Oxygénation, 05000 Gap
Tel   92 50 16 83
Mem   200
Pro   O Rougeot
Holes   18 L 6023 m SSS 72
Fees   140fr (170fr)
Loc   7km N of Gap. 80km S of
       Grenoble
Mis   Open May-Oct

Grand Avignon (1988)

BP 121, Les Chênes Verts, 84270
Vedene
Tel   90 31 49 94
Fax   90 31 01 21
Mem   132
Pro   S Lanfranchi
Holes   18 L 6027 m SSS 71
       9 hole short course
Fees   180fr (250fr)
Loc   Vedene, 5km NE of Avignon

Monte Carlo (1910)

06320 La Turbie
Tel   93 41 09 11
Mem   500
Pro   C Houtart, F Ruffier-Meray,
       R Halsall
Holes   18 L 5667 m SSS 71
Fees   250fr (350fr)
Loc   Mont Agel, La Turbie, 3km N
       of Monte Carlo
Mis   Handicap certificate required

Opio-Valbonne (1966)

Château de la Begude, 06560
Valbonne
Tel   93 42 00 08
Pro   J Norsworthy
Holes   18 L 6200 m SSS 72
Fees   270fr (300fr)
Loc   10km N of Cannes

Pierrevert (1986)

Domaine de la Grande-Gardette,
04860 Pierrevert
Tel   92 72 17 19
Mem   450
Pro   L Dubouexic 92 72 05 69
Holes   18 L 6040 m SSS 72
Fees   180fr (230fr)
Loc   4km NW of Manosque.
       45km NE of Aix

Roquebrune (1989)

CD 7, 83520 Roquebrune-sur-
Argens
Tel   94 82 92 91   Fax 94 82 94 74
Mem   200
Pro   B Ducoulombier, CA Ghizzone
Holes   18 L 6031 m SSS 72
Fees   200fr (200fr)
Loc   35km N of Saint-Tropez.
       40km SW of Cannes

La Sainte-Baume (1988)

83860 Nans-les-Pins
Tel   94 78 60 12 Fax 94 78 63 30
Pro   B Diagne, B Lacroix
Holes   18 L 6134 m SSS 72
Fees   160fr (240fr)
Loc   35km NE of Marseilles via
       RN 560

Servanes (1989)

Domaine de Servanes, 13890
Mouriès
Tel   90 47 59 95 Fax 90 47 52 58
Mem   200
Pro   J-M Kazmierczak
Holes   18 L 6047 m SSS 72
Fees   180fr (250fr)
Loc   25km SE of Arles

Valcros (1964)

83250 La Londe-les-Maures
Tel   94 66 81 02
Pro   P Hurfin
Holes   18 L 5184 m SSS 68
Fees   180fr (250fr)
Loc   10km W of Le Lavandou

Valescure (1896)

BP 451, 83704 St-Raphaël Cedex
Tel   94 82 40 46   Fax 94 82 41 42
Mem   620
Pro   E Cougourdan, M Bromet,
       M Semo
Holes   18 L 5065 m Par 68
Fees   220fr (250fr)
Loc   5km E of St-Raphaël

For list of abbreviations see page 487.

Vievola (1978)

06430 Tende
Tel   93 04 61 02
Mem   60
Pro   N Giordano
Holes   9 L 2024 m SSS 64
Fees   110fr (180fr)
Loc   4km from Italian border on RN
        204. 40km N of Monte Carlo
Mis   Open May-Oct

Pyrenees & South West

Agen Bon-Encontre (1982)

Route de Saint-Ferréol, 47240 Bon-
Encontre
Tel   53 96 95 78
Holes   9 L 5760 m SSS 70
Fees   80–150fr (100–200fr)
Loc   5km SE of Agen on N113

Albret (1986)

Le Pusocq, 47230 Barbaste
Tel   53 65 53 69
Mem   250
Pro   J Navas
Holes   18 L 5911 m SSS 71
Fees   120fr (150fr)
Loc   Barbaste, 30km W of Agen

Ariège (1986)

09240 La Bastide-de-Serou
Tel   61 64 56 78
Mem   340
Holes   18 L 6000 m SSS 71
Fees   120fr (150fr)
Loc   Unjat, 17km NW of Foix

La Barouge (1956)

81660 Pont de l'Arn
Tel   63 61 08 00/63 67 06 72
Mem   350
Pro   D Charria
Holes   18 L 5623 m SSS 70
Fees   160fr (200fr)
Loc   2km N of Mazamet.
        82km E of Toulouse

Biarritz (1888)

Ave Edith Cavell, 64200 Biarritz
Tel   59 03 71 80
Mem   750
Pro   R Simpson, O Leglise,
        Mlle S Fourment
Holes   18 L 5379 m SSS 69
Fees   200-300fr

Casteljaloux (1989)

Route de Mont-de-Marsan, 47700
Casteljaloux
Tel   53 93 51 60
Mem   150
Pro   F Thollon-Pommerol

Holes   18 L 5916 m SSS 72
Fees   150-190fr (180-220fr)
Loc   60km NW of Agen

Castelnaud (1987)

'La Menuisière', 47290 Castelnaud
de Gratecambe
Tel   53 01 74 64
Fax   53 01 78 99
Mem   250
Pro   C Arsac
Holes   18 L 6322 m SSS 73
        9 L 2184 m SSS 27
Fees   120–160fr (140–200fr)
Loc   10km N of Villeneuve on N21.
        40km N of Agen
Mis   Driving range

Chantaco (1928)

Route d'Ascain, 64500 St Jean-de-
Luz
Tel   59 26 14 22/59 26 19 22
Mem   500
Pro   JC Harismendy
Holes   18 L 5722 m SSS 70
Fees   200fr (250fr)
Loc   2km S of St Jean-de-Luz, on
        Route d'Ascain

Chiberta (1926)

Boulevard des Plages, 64600 Anglet
Tel   59 63 83 20
Mem   800
Pro   P Dufourg, H Brousson
Holes   18 L 5650 m SSS 70
Fees   180–280fr
Loc   3km N of Biarritz. Airport 5km
Mis   WE/High season-starting
        time necessary

Côte d'Argent

40660 Moliets
Tel   58 48 54 65
Pro   F Ducousso
Holes   18 L 6500 m SSS 72
        9 hole course
Fees   180-250fr (250fr)
Loc   Moliets, 30km N of Bayonne

Espalais (1987)

L'Ilot, 82400 Valence d'Agen
Tel   63 29 04 56
Mem   150
Holes   9 L 5434 m Par 35
Fees   100fr (150fr)
Loc   25km SE of Agen

Étangs de Fiac (1989)

Brazis, Fiac, 81500 Lavaur
Tel   63 70 64 70
Mem   350
Pro   M Wallace 63 70 70 85
Holes   9 L 2837 m SSS 35
Fees   120fr (175fr) W-500fr
Loc   40km NE of Toulouse

Fleurance (1989)

Lassalle, 32500 Fleurance
Tel   62 06 26 26/62 06 25 27
Mem   140
Pro   G Camlong
Holes   9 L 2878 m Par 35
Fees   100fr (120fr)
Loc   20km N of Auch. 50km S of
        Agen

Hossegor (1929)

40150 Hossegor
Tel   58 43 56 99
Mem   470
Pro   Y Hausseguy, M Hausseguy
Holes   18 L 6004 m SSS 71
Fees   230fr
Loc   15km N of Bayonne, on coast

Laloubère

Hippodrome, 65310 Laloubère
Tel   62 96 11 14
Mem   300
Pro   J Ayala
Holes   9 L 5960 m SSS 72
Fees   120fr
Loc   3km S of Tarbes

Lannemezan

La Demi-Lune, 65300 Lannemezan
Tel   62 98 01 01
Mem   280
Pro   R Lasserre
Holes   18 L 5872 m Par 70
Fees   130fr (160fr)
Loc   38km SE of Tarbes

Luchon (1908)

BP 40, 31110 Bagnères de Luchon
Tel   61 79 03 27
Mem   240
Pro   R Picabea
Holes   9 L 2375 m SSS 66
Fees   110fr (140fr)
Loc   Luchon, 90km SE of Tarbes

Mont-de-Marsan

Pessourdat, 40090 Saint-Avit
Tel   58 75 63 05 (Sec)
Mem   150
Pro   O Beaufranc
Holes   9 L 2503 m SSS 34
Fees   100fr
Loc   8km NE of Mont-de-Marsan.
        70km N of Pau
Mis   Covered practice range

La Nivelle (1907)

Place William Sharp, 64500 Ciboure
Tel   59 47 18 99/59 47 19 72
Mem   480
Pro   J Palli, S Lecuona
Holes   18 L 5570 m SSS 69
Fees   220–320fr
Loc   1½ km S of St Jean-de-Luz

Pau (1856)

Rue de Golf, 64140 Pau-Billère
Tel	59 32 02 33
Mem	530
Pro	A Harismendy, D Loustalet
Holes	18 L 5389 m SSS 69
Fees	200fr (220fr)
Loc	2km S of Pau. Bordeaux 200km

Les Roucous (1987)

82110 Sauveterre
Tel	63 95 83 70
Fax	63 95 82 47
Mem	200
Holes	9 L 2622 m SSS 68
Fees	130fr (150fr)
Loc	26km S of Cahors. 38km N of Montauban

Royal Artiguelouve (1986)

Domaine St Michel, 64230 Artiguelouve
Tel	59 83 09 29
Mem	400
Pro	A Lopez
Holes	18 L 6063 m Par 71
Fees	160fr (180fr)
Loc	8km NW of Pau, off Bayonne road

Salies-de-Béarn (1988)

Route d'Orthez, 64270 Salies-de-Béarn
Tel	59 38 37 59
Mem	80
Holes	9 L 2300 m SSS 62
Fees	80-100fr (100-120fr)
Loc	60km E of Biarritz

Scottish Golf d'Aubertin (1987)

64290 Aubertin
Tel	59 82 73 73
Mem	100
Holes	18 L 4806 m Par 66
Fees	100fr (120fr)
Loc	20km S of Pau

Seignosse (1989)

Carrefour Boucau, 40510 Seignosse
Tel	58 43 17 32 Fax-58 43 16 67
Holes	18 L 6124 m Par 72
Fees	180-260fr (200-260fr)
Loc	30km N of Biarritz, nr Airport

Toulouse (1951)

31000 Vieille-Toulouse
Tel	61 73 45 48
Mem	380
Pro	R Olalainty
Holes	18 L 5602 m SSS 69
Fees	170fr (220fr)
Loc	8km S of Toulouse

Toulouse-Palmola (1973)

31680 Buzet-Sur-Tarn
Tel	61 84 20 50
Mem	750
Pro	D Barquez
Holes	18 L 6166 m SSS 72
Fees	200fr (350fr 2D-600fr)
Loc	20km NE of Toulouse

Toulouse-Seilh

Route de Grenade, Seilh, 31840 Aussonne
Tel	61 42 59 30
Mem	300
Pro	J Garaïalde, J-P Hontas
Holes	Red 18 L 6164 m SSS 72
	Yellow 18 L 4146 m SSS 61
Fees	Red 200fr (250fr) Yellow 180fr (230fr)
Loc	15km N of Toulouse. Airport 5km

Germany

Aachen & Saar

Aachen (1927)

Schürzelter Str 300, 5100 Aachen
Tel	(0241) 12501
Mem	575
Pro	W Van Mook
Holes	18 L 5903 m Par 71
Fees	D-40DM (D-50DM)
Loc	Aachen-Seffent, 5km NW of Aachen

Düren (1975)

Rurstr 45, 5166 Kreuzau
Tel	(02422) 560
Mem	330
Pro	H Gross, R Hamann
Holes	9 L 5706 m SSS 70
Fees	40DM (50DM)
Loc	Trierbachweg, N of Düren

Eifel (1977)

Kölner Str, 5533 Hillesheim
Tel	(06593) 1241 Fax 9421
Mem	470
Pro	C Gess (06593) 8537
	G Dornan (06593) 9391
Holes	9 L 6180 m Par 72
Fees	35DM (50DM)
Loc	70km S of Cologne

Nahetal (1970)

Postfach 1518, 6550 Bad Kreuznach
Tel	(06708) 2145/3755
Mem	730
Pro	H Goerke, F Schmaderer, G Pietruschka
Holes	18 L 6065 m SSS 72
Fees	40DM (60DM)
Loc	6km S of Bad Kreuznach. 70km SW of Frankfurt

Pfalz (1971)

Weinstr, 6730 Neustadt
Tel	(06327) 2973
Mem	750
Pro	G Hopp, A Suchet
Holes	18 L 6180 m SSS 72
Fees	50DM (60DM)
Loc	Geinsheim, 15km SE of Neustadt towards Speyer

Saar-Pfalz Katharinenhof (1982)

c/o Am Staden 18, 6600 Saarbrücken
Tel	(06843) 8797 (Clubhouse)
Mem	425
Pro	J Morris (06843) 8878
Holes	9 L 6161 m SSS 72
Fees	30DM D-50DM (80DM)
Loc	15km S of Saarbrücken towards Blieskastel
Mis	WE-only with member

Saarbrücken (1961)

Oberlimbergerweg, 6634 Wallerfangen-Gisingen
Tel	(06837) 401
Mem	800
Pro	W Rappenecker, C Coughlan, R Heymanns
Holes	18 L 6231 m SSS 73
Fees	45DM (65DM)
Loc	B406 towards Wallerfangen. 8km N of Saarlouis

Trier-Mosel (1977)

Postfach 1905, 5500 Trier
Tel	(06507) 4374
Mem	460
Pro	H Goerke
Holes	9 L 6100 m SSS 72
Fees	30DM (50DM)
Loc	20km NE of Trier
Mis	Driving range, pitch & putt

Woodlawn

6792 Ramstein Flugplatz
Tel	(06371) 476240 Fax 42158
Mem	Military GC-Visitors limited
Pro	E Sudy
Holes	18 L 6225 yds Par 70
Fees	$10 ($12)
Loc	Ramstein 3km

Berlin

Berlin G & CC

Golfweg 22, 1000 Berlin 39, US Forces Europe
Tel	8196533
Mem	800
Pro	R Wise
Holes	18 L 6350 yds Par 70
Fees	$25 ($30)
Loc	Wannsee District (Berlin)

Berlin-Wannsee (1895)

Am Stoepchenweg, 1000 Berlin
Tel 8055075
Mem 575
Pro U Tapperthofen, J Galbraith
Holes 9 L 5690 m SSS 70
Fees 30DM (40DM)
Loc 17km SW of Berlin

British GC Gatow (1969)

BFPO 45, RAF Gatow
Tel 3092670/3657660
Mem 400
Holes 9 L 5687 m SSS 70
Fees 10DM (20DM)
Loc 16km from Berlin
Mis British Forces & British Passport holders only

Central

Aschaffenburg (1977)

Kirchnerstr 13, 8750 Aschaffenburg
Tel (06021) 91840/(06024) 7222
Mem 560
Pro M Richardson
Holes 9 L 5000 m SSS 67
Fees 40DM (50DM)
Loc Hösbach/Feldkahl, 7km E of Aschaffenburg

Bad Kissingen (1911)

Euerdorferstr 11, 8730 Bad Kissingen
Tel (0971) 3608
Mem 640
Pro J Dibb, T Pearman
Holes 18 L 5675 m SSS 70
Fees 40DM (50DM)
Loc Bad Kissingen 2km. 50km N of Würzburg

Bad Mergentheim (1971)

Postfach 1304, 6990 Bad Mergentheim
Tel (07931) 7579
Pro H Laird
Holes 9 L 4230 m Par 64
Fees 35DM (45DM)
Loc 40km S of Würzburg

Bad Nauheim

Postfach 1524, 6350 Bad Nauheim
Tel (06032) 2153
Mem 370
Pro B Raschke (06032) 33797
Holes 9 L 5440 m SSS 68
Fees 35DM (50DM)
Loc 40km N of Frankfurt

Bad Wildungen (1930)

3590 Bad Wildungen
Tel (05621) 4877/2260
Mem 100
Pro A Stein
Holes 9 L 5670 m Par 70
Fees D-35DM (45DM)
Loc Bad Wildungen 1½ km. 30km SW of Kassel

Darmstadt-Traisa (1973)

Dippelshof, 6109 Mühltal-Traisa
Tel (06151) 146543
Mem 330
Pro M Rose
Holes 9 L 5150 m SSS 67
Fees 50DM (65DM)
Loc Traisa, nr Darmstadt

Frankfurter (1913)

Golfstr 41, 6000 Frankfurt 71
Tel (069) 666 2318
Fax (069) 666 7018
Mem 900
Pro H Strüver, T Gowdy, G Winckler
Holes 18 L 6455 yds SSS 71
Fees D-65DM (85DM)
Loc 6km SW of Frankfurt, nr Airport

Hanau-Wilhelmsbad (1959)

Wilhelmsbader Allee 32, 6450 Hanau
Tel (06181) 82071
Fax (06181) 86967
Mem 880
Pro M Day
Holes 18 L 6192 m Par 72
Fees 60DM (80DM)
Loc 4km NW of Hanau on B8-40/AB66. Frankfurt 15km

Heidelberg (US Army) (1957)

An der Bundestr 291, 6836 Oftersheim
Tel (06202) 53767
Mem 800
Pro G Puckett (Mgr)
Holes 18 L 6650 m SSS 72
Fees $20 ($30)
Loc 10km SW of Heidelberg

Heidelberg-Lobenfeld (1968)

Biddersbacherhof, 6921 Lobbach-Lobenfeld
Tel (06226) 40490/41615
Fax (06226) 42464
Mem 800
Pro (06226) 41955
Holes 18 L 6215 m SSS 72
Fees 50DM (70DM) (1990)
Loc 30km E of Heidelberg

Homburg (1899)

Saalburgchaussee 2, 6380 Bad Homburg
Tel (06172) 38808
Mem 630
Pro F Tauber, JH Cairns

Holes 10 holes SSS 69
Fees 30DM (50DM)
Loc On B456 to Usingen

Kronberg G & LC (1954)

Schloss Friedrichshof, Hainstr 25, 6242 Kronberg/Taunus
Tel (06173) 1426
Mem 506
Pro A Schilling, J Harder, J Thompson, J Harris
Holes 18 L 5365 m SSS 68
Fees 50DM (70DM)
Loc 16km NW of Frankfurt

Main-Taunus (1979)

Lange Seegewann 2, 6200 Wiesbaden-Delkenheim
Tel (06122) 52550/52208(Sec)
Mem 888
Pro D Howard, S Bailey
Holes 18 L 6045 m SSS 72
Fees 70DM (90DM)
Loc 15km NW of Frankfurt Airport
Mis Handicap certificate required

Mannheim-Viernheim (1930)

Alte Mannheimerstr 3, 6806 Viernheim
Tel (06204) 71313 (Clubhouse) (06204) 78737 (Sec)
Mem 500
Pro C Jenkins, M Kagel, Th Gutmann (06204) 71307
Holes 9 L 6060 m SSS 72
Fees 50DM (60DM)
Loc 10km NE of Mannheim
Mis WE-only with member

Mittelrheinischer (1938)

Denzerheide, 5427 Bad Ems
Tel (02603) 6541
Pro J Nixon
Holes 18 L 6050 m SSS 72
Fees 50DM (75DM)
Loc 13km E of Koblenz, nr Bad Ems (6km)

Oberhessischer Marburg (1973)

Postfach 1828, 3550 Marburg/Lahn
Tel (06427) 8558
Mem 400
Pro T Rigby
Holes 9 L 6098 m SSS 72
Fees 30DM (40DM)
Loc 8km N of Marburg, off B3 towards Reddehausen

Paderborner Land (1983)

Wilseder Weg 25, 4790 Paderborn
Tel (05251) 4377
Pro A van der Donck
Holes 9 L 5670 m SSS 70
Fees 20DM (30DM)
Loc Salzkotten/Thule, between B-1 and B-64

For list of abbreviations see page 487.

Rhein-Main (1977)

Steubenstrasse 9, 6200 Wiesbaden
Tel   (06121) 373014
Pro   T Cary
Holes   18 L 5966 m SSS 71
Fees $20
Loc   Wiesbaden 6km
Mis   Members and guests only

Rheinblick

6200 Wiesbaden-Marchenland
Tel   Military 3889
Mem   US Forces
Pro   P Greenfield
Holes   18 L 6604 yds SSS 70
Fees $5 ($10)
Loc   Wiesbaden 2km
Mis   Guests limited

Rheintal (1971)

c/o Karl-Valentinstr 10, 6800
Mannheim 51
Tel   (0621) 797679
Mem   120
Pro   A Winkler
Holes   18 L 5840 m SSS 71
Fees $20 ($35)
Loc   Oftersheim, SE of Mannheim

Rhoen (1971)

Am Golfplatz, 6417 Hofbieber 1
Tel   (06657) 7077/1334
Mem   650
Pro   N Staples
Holes   18 L 5676 m SSS 70
Fees   30DM (40DM)
Loc   Hofbieber, 11km E of Fulda

Schloss-Braunfels (1970)

Homburger Hof, 6333 Braunfels
Tel   (06442) 4530 Fax (06444) 8275
Mem   850
Pro   D McLellan, C Monk,
        M Crosthwaite (06442) 5752
Holes   18 L 6288 m SSS 73
Fees   50DM (80DM)
Loc   70km N of Frankfurt

Schotten (1974)

Lindenstr 5, 6479 Schotten/
Eschenrod
Tel   (06044) 1375
Mem   260
Pro   G Kleffel, HA Sclapp
Holes   9 L 4330 m SSS 64
Fees   20DM (50DM)
Loc   Frankfurt 64km
Mis   Driving range, pitch & putt

Sennelager (British Army) (1963)

Bad Lippspringe, BFPO 16
Tel   (82) 2515
Mem   850
Holes   Old 18 L 5835 m SSS 72
        New 9 L 5214 m SSS 68

Fees   (Forces) 25DM (35DM)
        (Civilians) 35DM (45DM)
Loc   9km E of Paderborn off Route 1
Mis   WE-only with member before
        2pm

Spessart (1972)

Golfplatz Alsberg, 6483 Bad Soden-
Salmünster
Tel   (06056) 3594
Mem   700
Pro   S Walker
Holes   18 L 6039 m SSS 72
Fees   50DM (70DM) W-175DM
Loc   70km NE of Frankfurt, via A66
Mis   Handicap certificate required

Taunus G & LC (1979)

Merzhauser Landstr, 6395 Weilrod-
Altweilnau
Tel   (06083) 865
Pro   M Bonn, J Wilson
Holes   18 holes SSS 72
Fees   35DM (50DM)
Loc   15km NW of Bad Homburg

Wiesbaden (1893)

Chauseehaus, 6200 Wiesbaden
Tel   (0611) 460238
Mem   475
Pro   G Cox, R Kelland
        (0611) 468316
Holes   9 L 5320 m Par 68
Fees   45DM (70DM)
Loc   8km NW of Wiesbaden,
        towards Schlangenbad

Wiesloch-Hohenhardter Hof G & LC (1983)

Hohenhardter Hof, 6908 Wiesloch-
Baiertal
Tel   (06222) 72081
Pro   H Rübmann
Holes   18 L 6080 m SSS 72
Fees   30DM (40DM)
Loc   17km S of Heidelberg

Winterberg (1962)

Postfach 1053, 5788 Winterberg
Tel   (02981) 1770
Mem   240
Pro   I Clegg, D Hollmann
Holes   9 L 5680 m SSS 70
Fees   30DM (40DM)
Loc   2km N of Winterberg, nr
        Silbach

Würzburg-Kitzingen (1980)

Schustergasse 3, 8700 Würzburg
Tel   (0931) 571152
Mem   210
Pro   F Dzwilewski, B Salter
Holes   9 L 6666 yds SSS 72
Fees $15 ($20)
Loc   15km SE of Würzburg

Hamburg & North

Altenhof (1971)

Eckernförde, 2330 Altenhof
Tel   (04351) 41227
Mem   650
Pro   N Robinson
Holes   18 L 6071 m SSS 72
Fees   45DM (60DM)
Loc   3km S of Eckernförde. 20km
        NW of Kiel

Am Sachsenwald (1985)

Am Riesenbett, 2055 Dassendorf
Tel   (04104) 6120
Mem   833
Pro   M Grogan, A Roberts,
        A Smid
Holes   18 L 6118 m SSS 72
Fees   40DM (50DM)
Loc   20km SE of Hamburg

An der Goehrde (1968)

3139 Zernien-Braasche
Tel   (05863) 556
Mem   250
Pro   G Gilligan
Holes   9 L 6107 m SSS 72
Fees   30DM (40DM)
Loc   40km E of Lüneburg. 30km E
        of Uelzen

An der Pinnau (1982)

Jebbenberg 32, 2084 Rellingen
Tel   (04106) 81800
Mem   590
Pro   S Arrowsmith, B Griffiths,
        A Arrowsmith
Holes   18 L 6129 m SSS 72
Fees   35DM (45DM)
Loc   40km NW of Hamburg,
        nr Renzel
Mis   Course address:
        Pinnebergerstr 81,
        2085 Quickborn

Auf der Wendlohe

Oldesloerstr 251, 2000 Hamburg 61
Tel   (040) 550 5014/5
Mem   850
Pro   G Jones, M Bradley, J Gibbons
Holes   18 L 6060 m SSS 72
Fees   40DM
Loc   15km N of Hamburg
Mis   WE-only with member

Bad Bramstedt (1975)

2357 Bad Bramstedt, PO Box 1305,
Ochsenweg 38
Tel   (04192) 6376
Fax   (04192) 7707
Mem   180
Holes   9 L 5724 m SSS 70
Fees   35DM (45DM)
Loc   S of Bad Bramstedt, by B4.
        48km N of Hamburg on A7

Buxtehude (1982)

Zum Lehmfeld 1, 2150 Buxtehude
Tel   (04161) 81333
Mem   550
Pro   M Fitton, S Bates
Holes 18 L 6505 m SSS 74
Fees   40-50DM (50-60DM)
Loc   30km SW of Hamburg on
       Route 73 from Harburg

Club Zur Vahr (1905)

Bgm-Spitta-Allee 34, 2800 Bremen
Tel   Bremen-(0421) 230041
        Garlstedt-(04795) 417
Mem   1200
Pro   H Weber, M Grantham,
        D Britten
Holes Garlstedt 18 L 6430 m SSS 75
        Bremen 9 L 5862 m SSS 71
Fees   Garlstedt-60DM (90DM)
        Bremen-50DM (70DM)
Loc   Garlstedt-15km N of Bremen.

Dithmarschen

Dorfstr 11, 2242 Warwerort
Tel   (04834) 6300
Mem   180
Pro   PH Clark
Holes 9 L 5284 m SSS 68
Fees   25DM (35DM)
Loc   Warwerort, 14km W of Heide

Föhr (1966)

2270 Nieblum auf Föhr
Tel   (04681) 3277
Mem   414
Pro   A Assmus
Holes 9 L 6045 m SSS 72
Fees   45DM (55DM)
Loc   3km SW of Wyk, by Airport

Förde Glücksburg

2392 Glücksburg-Bockholm
Tel   (04631) 2547
Mem   290
Pro   D Ohle
Holes 9 holes SSS 72
Fees   30DM (40DM)
Loc   10km NE of Flensburg

Grossensee (1975)

Hamburgerstr 17, 2077 Grossensee
Tel   (04154) 6473
Mem   300
Pro   G Schurr
Holes 9 L 6154 m SSS 72
Fees   30DM (40DM)
Loc   30km NE of Hamburg, off
        Lübeck road

Grossflottbeker (1901)

Otto-Ernst Str 32, 2000 Hamburg
Tel   (040) 827208
Mem   300
Pro   K Storrier
Holes 9 L 4945 m SSS 66
Fees   D-30DM (D-40DM)
Loc   10km W of Hamburg

Gut Grambek (1981)

Schlosstr 21, 2411 Grambek
Tel   (04542) 4627
Mem   520
Pro   C Smailes
Holes 18 L 6029 m SSS 71
Fees   40DM (60DM)
Loc   30km S of Lübeck.
        50km E of Hamburg

Gut Kaden (1984)

Kadenerstrasse 9, 2081 Alveslohe
Tel   (04193) 92021/2/3
Mem   420
Pro   W Mych
Holes 18 L 6076 m SSS 72
Fees   50DM
Loc   Alveslohe, 30km N of
        Hamburg
Mis   WE-only with member

Gut Waldhof (1969)

Am Waldhof, 2359 Kisdorferwohld
Tel   (04194) 383
Mem   750
Pro   HJ Jersombeck, T Parker
Holes 18 L 6073 m Par 72
Fees   40DM (50DM)
Loc   34km N of Hamburg via
        Autobahn A7 to Kaltenkirchen,
        or via route B432
Mis   WE-only with member

Hamburg (1906)

In de Bargen 59, 2000 Hamburg
Tel   (040) 812177
Mem   1030
Pro   A Mazza, S Blume
Holes 18 L 5925 m SSS 71
Fees   45DM (60DM)
Loc   Blankenese, 14km W of
        Hamburg
Mis   WE-only with member

Hamburg-Ahrensburg (1964)

Am Haidschlag 39-45, 2070
Ahrensburg
Tel   (04102) 51309 Fax 51300
Mem   849
Pro   H Heiser, C Kirchner, P Nitra
Holes 18 L 5782 m SSS 70
Fees   50DM (60DM)
Loc   20km NE of Hamburg.
        Motorway exit Ahrensburg
Mis   WE-only with member

Hamburg-Waldorfer (1960)

Schevenbarg, 2075 Ammersbek
Tel   (040) 605 1337
Mem   850
Pro   G Bennett, S Parker
Holes 18 L 6154 m SSS 73
Fees   50DM (60DM)
Loc   20km N of Hamburg
Mis   Driving range, pitch & putt

Hamburger GC In der Lüneburger Heide (1957)

Am Golfplatz 24, 2105 Seevetal 1
Tel   (04105) 2331
Fax   (04105) 52571
Mem   730
Pro   S Wächter
Holes 18 L 5735 m SSS 70
Fees   50DM (60DM)
Loc   25km S of Hamburg

Hoisdorf (1977)

Hof Bornbek/Hoisdorf,
2073 Lütjensee
Tel   (04107) 7831
Mem   800
Pro   M Stewart
Holes 18 L 6010 m Par 71
Fees   50DM (60DM)
Loc   25km NE of Hamburg

Husumer Bucht (1987)

Husum/Nordsee, Hohlacker,
2251 Schwesing
Tel   (04841) 72238
Fax   (04841) 72541
Mem   154
Pro   R Kebbel (04841) 74721
Holes 9 L 6118 m SSS 72
Fees   35DM (50DM)
Loc   5km E of Husum. 40km SW of
        Flensburg

Kitzeberg (1902)

Sophienblatt 46, 2300 Kiel 1
Tel   (0431) 63048/23404
Mem   360
Pro   N Sumner
Holes 9 L 5700 m Par 70
Fees   30DM (40DM)
Loc   10km NE of Kiel

Küsten GC Hohe Klint (1978)

Rosenhof 25, 2190 Cuxhaven
Tel   (04721) 48057
Mem   496
Pro   E Kranz, N Deus
Holes 18 L 6150 m SSS 72
Fees   40DM (50DM)
Loc   12km SW of Cuxhaven on
        Route 6, nr Oxstedt

Lohersand (1958)

Golfplatz, 2371 Lohe-Föhrden
Tel   (04336) 3333
Mem   340
Pro   K Waldon (04336) 606
Holes 9 L 6040 m Par 72
Fees   30DM (40DM)
Loc   8km NW of Rendsburg, off
        Route 77
Mis   Driving range

Lübeck-Travemünder (1921)

Kowitzberg 41, 2400
Lübeck-Travemünde
Tel   (04502) 74018
Pro   A Varley
Holes 9 L 6086 m SSS 72
Fees   30DM (50DM)
Loc   NE of Lübeck

Marine Westerland (1980)

Marinefliegerhorst, 2280 Westerland
Tel   (04651) 7037
Mem   450
Pro   A Pemöller
Holes 9 L 5234 m SSS 68
Fees   30DM (35DM)
Loc   Sylt Island, 75km W of
       Flensburg by Danish border

Maritim Timmendorfer Strand (1973)

Am Golfplatz, 2408 Timmendorfer
Strand
Tel   (04503) 5152
Mem   785
Pro   R Hinz
Holes 18 L 6095 m SSS 72
       18 L 3755 m SSS 60
Fees   D-40DM (D-70DM)
Loc   15km N of Lübeck

Mittelholsteinischer Aukrug (1969)

2356 Aukrug-Bargfeld
Tel   (04873) 595
Pro   R Denton
Holes 18 L 6140 m SSS 72
Fees   35DM (50DM)
Loc   10km W of Neumunster.
       Mitte exit on Route 430

Norderney (1956)

Box 1233, 2982 Norderney
Tel   (04932) 680
Mem   225
Pro   R Bremer
Holes 9 L 4890 m SSS 66
Fees   25DM (30DM)
Loc   70km W of Wilhelmshaven

Oldenburgischer (1964)

2900 Oldenburg, Postbox 2928
Tel   (04402) 7240
Mem   582
Pro   J Walter
Holes 18 L 6087 m SSS 72
Fees   30DM (40DM)
Loc   10km N of Oldenburg, nr Rastede

Ostfriesland (1980)

Postbox 1220, 2964 Wiesmoor
Tel   (04944) 3040 Fax 30477
Mem   480
Pro   S Parry (04944) 2228
Holes 18 L 6256 m SSS 73
Fees   40DM (50DM)
Loc   25km SW of Wilhelmshaven

St Dionys (1972)

Widukindweg, 2123 St Dionys
Tel   (04133) 6277
Mem   565
Pro   KH Mahl, G Hillson
Holes 18 L 6225 m SSS 73
Fees   60DM (80DM)
Loc   10km N of Lüneburg

St Peter-Ording (1971)

Hauke Haien-Weg 1, 2252 St Peter-
Ording
Tel   (04863) 1545/746
Mem   150
Pro   T Holroyd
Holes 9 L 5730 m SSS 70
Fees   30DM (35DM)
Loc   80km SW of Flensburg

Schloss Lüdersburg (1985)

2127 Lüdersburg bei Lüneburg
Tel   (04153) 6112   Fax 6255
Mem   450
Pro   G Birch, S Cope, J Froom
Holes 18 L 6180 m SSS 73
       6 hole Par 3 course
Fees   40DM (60DM)
Loc   18km E of Lüneburg.
       55km SE of Hamburg

Soltau (1982)

Golfplatz Hof Loh, 3040 Soltau
Tel   (05191) 14077
Mem   420
Holes 18 L 6224 m SSS 73
       9 L 2340 m SSS 54
Fees   30DM (40DM)
Loc   Tetendorf, 3km S of Soltau

Tietlingen (1979)

Tietlingen 6c, 3032 Fallingbostel
Tel   (05162) 3889
Mem   420
Pro   W McVey
Holes 9 L 6042 m SSS 72
Fees   25DM (40DM)
Loc   65km N of Hanover, between
       Walsrode and Fallingbostel

Wentorf-Reinbeker (1901)

Golfstrasse 2, 2057 Wentorf
Tel   (040) 7202610/7202141
Mem   380
Pro   W Lloyd
Holes 9 L 5768 m SSS 70
Fees   30DM (45DM)
Loc   20km SE of Hamburg
Mis   Co-Founder of German Golf
       Union 1907

Wildeshausen (1978)

Glauerstr, 2878 Wildeshausen
Tel   (04431) 1232
Mem   350
Pro   R Foster
Holes 9 L 6080 m SSS 72
Fees   20DM (30DM)
Loc   3km NW of Wildeshausen

Wilhelmshaven (1979)

Parkstr 19, 2940 Wilhelmshaven
Tel   (04425) 1721
Mem   635
Pro   P Allen
Holes 9 L 6058 m SSS 72
Fees   30DM (40DM)
Loc   8km N of Wilhelmshaven

Worpswede (1974)

Grüner Weg 3, 2822 Schwanewede 1
Tel   (0421) 621425/(04673) 7313
Mem   314
Pro   R Prössel
Holes 9 L 6200 m SSS 72
Fees   40DM (50DM)
Loc   Giehlermuhlen, 20km N of
       Bremen, off B74

Wümme (1984)

Hof Emmen, Westerholz, 2723
Scheessel
Tel   (04263) 3352
Mem   380
Pro   K Wright
Holes 9 L 3071 m SSS 36
Fees   30DM (40DM)
Loc   10km N of Rotenberg, between
       Bremen and Hamburg

Hanover & Weserbergland

Bad Driburg (1976)

Am Kurpark, 3490 Bad Driburg
Tel   (05253) 842500
Fax   (05253) 842539
Mem   290
Pro   R Issitt
Holes 9 L 6106 m SSS 72
Fees   30DM (35DM) W-160DM
Loc   22km E of Paderborn

Bad Salzdetfurth-Hildesheim (1972)

Postfach 1445, 3200 Hildesheim
Tel   (05063) 1516
Pro   W Müller
Holes 9 L 6210 m SSS 72
Fees   25DM (30DM)
Loc   10km SE of Hildesheim

Bad Salzuflen G & LC

Am Schwaghof, 4902 Bad Salzuflen
Tel   (05222) 10773
Mem   550
Pro   J Paterson
Holes 18 L 6163 m Par 72
Fees   40DM (50DM)
Loc   3km NE of Bad Salzuflen

Braunschweig (1926)

Schwartzkopffstr 10,
3300 Braunschweig
Tel (0531) 691369
Mem 570
Pro R Wiseman
Holes 18 L 5893 m SSS 71
Fees 40DM (50DM)
Loc Braunschweig 5km

British Army (Hohne) (1962)

Hohne BFPO 30
Tel (05051) 4549
Mem 250
Holes 9 L 5682 m SSS 71
Fees 20DM (25DM)
Loc 6km S of Bergen Celle

Burgdorf (1970)

Waldstr 27, 3167 Burgdorf-
Ehlershausen
Tel (05085) 7628/7144
Mem 400
Pro L Theeuwen
Holes 18 L 6460 m SSS 74
Fees 30DM (40DM)
Loc Burgdorf-Ehlershausen, 20km
NE of Hanover

Gifhorn (1982)

Postfach 1341, 3170 Gifhorn
Tel (05371) 16737
Mem 310
Pro N Coombs
Holes 9 L 6160 m SSS 72
Fees 30DM (40DM)
Loc 15km N of Braunschweig
Mis Further 9 holes open 1991

Göttingen (1969)

Levershausen, 3410 Northeim 1
Tel (05551) 61915/7952
Mem 660
Pro W Kreuzer, R Odell
Holes 18 L 6050 m SSS 72
Fees 40DM (50DM)
Loc 12km N of Göttingen, towards
Northeim

Hannover (1923)

Am Blauen See, 3008 Garbsen 1
Tel (05137) 73235
Mem 600
Pro H Koch, B Schul
Holes 18 L 5855 m SSS 71
Fees 35DM (50DM)
Loc 15km NW of Hanover

Harz (1969)

Am Breitenberg 107, 3388 Bad
Harzburg 1
Tel (05322) 6737/1096
Mem 350

Pro M Spence
Holes 9 L 5562 m SSS 70
Fees 30DM (40DM)
Loc Centre of Bad Harzburg.
50km S of Braunschweig

Herford (1984)

Heideholz 8, 4973 Vlotho-Exter
Tel (05228) 7434
Mem 210
Pro G Pilkington
Holes 9 L 6184 m SSS 72
Fees 30DM (40DM)
Loc 30km NE of Bielefeld.
80km W of Hanover
Mis Handicap certificate required

Herzogstadt Celle (1985)

Beukenbusch 1, 3100 Celle
Tel (05086) 395
Mem 230
Pro W Knowles
Holes 18 L 5915 m SSS 71
Fees 30DM (40DM)
Loc 6km NE of Celle, towards
Lüneburg. 40km NE of
Hanover

Isernhagen (1983)

Auf Gut Lohne, 3004 Isernhagen
Tel (05139) 2998
Fax (05139) 27033
Mem 550
Pro U Bruns, J Bruns
Holes 18 L 6379 m SSS 73
Fees 30DM (40DM)
Loc Gut Lohne, 12km NE of
Hanover

Kassel-Wilhelmshöhe

Wolfsschlucht 27, 3500 Kassel
Tel (0561) 33509
Pro P Smith, U Wagener
Holes 18 L 5675 m SSS 70
Fees 40DM (50DM)
Loc 5km W of Kassel

Lippischer (1980)

Huxollweg, 4933 Blomberg-Cappel
Tel (05231) 459
Mem 490
Pro R Newsome, D Krause
Holes 18 L 6110 m SSS 72
Fees 40DM (50DM)
Loc 12km E of Detmold

Pyrmonter (1972)

Postfach 100 828, 3250 Hameln
Tel (05281) 8196
Mem 400
Pro W Murray
Holes 18 L 5720 m SSS 71
Fees 30DM (35DM)
Loc 4km S of Bad Pyrmont.
20km S of Hameln
Mis Extension to 18 holes in 1991

St Lorenz

Klostergut, 3338 Schöningen
Tel (05352) 1697 Fax 53120
Mem 162
Holes 9 L 6578 SSS 74
Fees 20DM (30DM)
Loc 30km SE of Braunschweig.
100km E of Hanover

Salzgitter Liebenburg (1985)

Sportpark Mahner Berg, Postfach
511329, 3320 Salzgitter-Bad
Tel (05341) 37376
Mem 233
Pro G Dyck
Holes 9 L 6062 m SSS 72
Fees 25DM (35DM)
Loc 27km SW of Braunschweig

Schloss Schwöbber (1985)

Schloss Schwöbber, 3258 Aerzen 16
Tel (05154) 2004
Mem 1044
Pro R Lewington, E Runcie
Holes 18 L 6222 m SSS 73
18 hole short course
Fees 45DM D-65DM (50DM
D-75DM)
Short course-30DM (40DM)
Loc 10km SW of Hameln.
60km SW of Hanover
Mis Driving range-20DM

Sieben-Berge (1965)

Schlosstr 1, 3211 Rheden/Gronau
Tel (05182) 2680
Mem 250
Pro J Dunford
Holes 9 L 6126 m SSS 72
Fees 30DM (40DM)
Loc 35km S of Hanover
Mis Driving range

Weserbergland (1982)

Sparenbergstr 9, 3450 Holzminden
Tel (15531) 10033
Pro S Fisher
Holes 18 holes SSS 72
Fees 20DM (30DM)
Loc 35km S of Hameln

Munich & South Bavaria

Altötting-Burghausen Schloss Piesing (1986)

Piesing 2, 8261 Haiming
Tel (08678) 7001/3
Fax (08677) 2021
Mem 383
Pro HW Rosenkranz (08678) 7002
Holes 18 L 5105 m SSS 67
Fees 40DM (50DM)
Loc 4km N of Burghausen towards
Haiming

Augsburg (1959)

Engelshofer Str 2, 8903 Bobingen-
Burgwalden
Tel   (08234) 5621
Mem   700
Pro   P Ries
Holes 18 L 5833 m SSS 71
Fees   50DM (80DM)
Loc   18km SW of Augsburg.
       Munich 50km

Bad Tölz (1973)

8170 Wackersberg
Tel   (08041) 9994
Mem   336
Pro   S Rohrsetzer
Holes 9 L 2942 m SSS 71
Fees   40DM (50DM)
Loc   5km W of Bad Tölz.
       55km S of Munich

Bad Wörishofen

Schlingenerstr 27, 8951 Rieden
Tel   (08346) 777
Mem   520
Pro   M Seidel, H Hoerenz,
       A Cawdron
Holes 18 L 6318 m SSS 71
Fees   50DM (70DM)
Loc   10km S of Bad Wörishofen

Berchtesgaden (1955)

Postfach 3460, 8240 Berchtesgaden
Tel   (08652) 2100/3787
Mem   230
Holes 9 L 5135 m SSS 67
Fees   20DM (30DM)
Loc   Obersalzburg, 3km from
       Berchtesgaden. 25km S of
       Salzburg

Beuerberg (1982)

Gut Sterz, 8196 Beuerberg
Tel   (08179) 671/728
Mem   570
Pro   A Hahn, JP Koriath, J Bray
Holes 18 L 6518 m SSS 74
Fees   60DM (85DM)
Loc   Beuerberg, 45km SW of
       Munich

Chiemsee

8210 Prien-Bauernberg
Tel   (08051)4820
Mem   365
Pro   R Krause
Holes 9 L 5960 m SSS 71
Fees   40DM (50DM-on request)
Loc   70km SE of Munich, nr Prien
       (3km)

Dachau (1947)

An der Flosslände 1, 8060 Dachau
Tel   (08131) 10879
Mem   250
Pro   C De Castro
Holes 9 L 2960 m SSS 71

Fees   35DM (40DM)
Loc   2km E of Dachau. 17km NW of
       Munich

Erding-Grunbach (1973)

Aribostr 2, 8058 Erding
Tel   (08122) 6465
Mem   500
Pro   G Warner
Holes 18 L 6140 m SSS 72
Fees   40DM (50DM)
Loc   30km NE of Munich

Eschenried (1983)

Kurfurstenweg 7, 8066 Eschenried
Tel   (08131) 3238/79655
Mem   450
Pro   G Stewart
Holes 9 L 6194 m SSS 72
Fees   35DM (50DM)
Loc   8km NW of Munich

Falkenhof G & LC (1983)

PO Box 1560, 8263 Burghausen
Tel   (08677) 2394
Mem   160
Pro   S Tasker
Holes 9 L 3030 m SSS 72
Fees   30DM (40DM)
Loc   Falkenhof-Marktl, 48km N of
       Salzburg
Mis   Driving range

Feldafing (1926)

Tutzingerstr 15, 8133 Feldafing
Tel   (08157) 7005
Mem   800
Pro   T Flossman, A Steinfurth,
       I Myskow
Holes 18 L 5708 m SSS 70
Fees   60DM (85DM)
Loc   32km S of Munich
Mis   Driving range, pitch & putt.
       WE-only with member

Garmisch-Partenkirchen
(1928)

Postfach 1345 Garmisch-
Partenkirchen
Tel   (08824) 8344/1632
Mem   540
Pro   A Hagl
Holes 18 L 6200 m SSS 72
Fees   65DM (80DM)
Loc   Garmisch 6km

Grafing-Oberelkofen

Postfach 1120, Hochreiterhof 7, 8018
Grafing
Tel   (08092) 7494
Mem   350
Pro   K Sparkes
Holes 9 L 5874 m SSS 71
Fees   45DM (60DM)
Loc   Grafing, 30km SE of Munich

Hohenpähl (1988)

Gut Hochschloss, 8121 Pähl
Tel   (08808) 1330
Fax   (08808) 775
Mem   410
Pro   R Barry, N Kanert,
       A Stöcklein
Holes 18 L 6057 m SSS 72
Fees   D-50DM (D-80DM)
Loc   40km S of Munich on B2

Höslwang im Chiemgau
(1977)

Chiemseestr 18, 8200 Rosenheim
Tel   (08031) 12198
Pro   F Carli
Holes 9 L 6210 m SSS
Fees   25DM (40DM)
Loc   Chiemsee

Im Chiemgau (1982)

Kötzing 1, 8224 Chieming
Tel   (08669) 7557
Fax   (08669) 38153
Mem   530
Pro   G Thomson
Holes 18 L 6200 m SSS 73
       9 holes Par 3
Fees   45DM (70DM)
Loc   60km W of Salzburg

Isarwinkel

Postfach 95, 8183 Rottach Egern
Tel   (08022) 6430
Mem   170
Holes 9 L 4226 m SSS 63
Fees   20DM (30DM)
Loc   Bad Tölz, 55km S of Munich
Mis   Handicap certificate required.
       Open Apr-Oct

Leitershofen (1980)

Deuringerstr, 8902 Stadtbergen
Tel   (0821) 434919
Mem   125
Pro   P Garnier-Bradley
Holes 9 L 3090 m SSS 72
Fees   25DM (30DM)
Loc   5km SW of Augsburg

Margarethenhof am
Tegernsee (1982)

8184 Gmund am Tegernsee
Tel   (08022) 7366
Pro   F Bernardi
Holes 18 L 6056 m SSS 72
Fees   40DM (60DM)
Loc   Tegernsee, 45km S of Munich

München Nord-
Eichenried (1989)

Münchenstr 57, 8059 Eichenried
Tel   (08123) 1004
Mem   815

Pro	E Dimmit, T Paterson,
	T Holroyd, M Kaussler
Holes	18 L 6318 m Par 72
Fees	60DM (85DM)
Loc	19km NE of Munich
Mis	Driving range, pitch & putt

Münchener (1910)

Tölzerstr, 8021 Strasslach

Tel	(08170) 450
Fax	(08170) 611
Mem	1130
Pro	A Castillo-Fernandez,
	H Fluss
Holes	Strasslach 18 L 6177 m SSS 72
	Thalkirchen 9 L 2528 m SSS 69
Fees	70DM
Loc	Strasslach: 10km from Munich.
	Thalkirchen: Munich
Mis	WE-only with member

Olching (1981)

Feurstr 89, 8037 Olching

Tel	(08142) 15963
Mem	550
Pro	C Knauss, D Cabus,
	A Steinfurth
Holes	18 L 6021 m SSS 72
Fees	40DM (60DM)
Loc	15km W of Munich

Reit im Winkl (1985)

Birnbacherstr 34,
8216 Reit im Winkl

Tel	(08640) 8216
Mem	280
Pro	S Mühlbauer
Holes	9 L 5900 m SSS 70
Fees	30DM (40DM)
Loc	100km SE of Munich, nr
	Austrian border

St Eurach G & LC (1973)

Eurach 8, 8127 Iffeldorf

Tel	(08801) 1332
Mem	489
Pro	W John, D Praun
Holes	18 L 6509 m SSS 74
Fees	WD-80DM
Loc	40km S of Munich
Mis	WE-no guests allowed

Schloss Igling (1989)

8939 Igling

Tel	(08248) 1003
Mem	60
Pro	J Wilkinson
Holes	9 L 5364 m SSS 68
Fees	35DM (45DM)
Loc	3km NW of Landsberg. 50km
	W of Munich
Mis	Course open June 1991

Schloss Klingenburg-Günzburg (1979)

Schloss Klingenburg, 8876
Jettingen-Scheppach

Tel	(08225) 3030
Mem	500
Pro	H Bessner
Holes	18 L 6065 m SSS 72
Fees	50DM (75DM)
Loc	40km W of Augsburg.
	5km from Stuttgart-Munich
	motorway, exit Burgau

Starnberg (1986)

Uneringerstr, 8130 Starnberg/
Hadorf

Tel	(08151) 12157
Mem	700
Pro	C Kilian, R Postiglione,
	S Rohrsetzer
Holes	18 L 6344 m SSS 73
Fees	60DM (80DM)
Loc	30km S of Munich
Mis	WE-booking necessary

Tegernseer GC Bad Wiessee (1958)

Robognerhof 1, 8182 Bad Wiessee

Tel	(08022) 8769
Mem	545
Pro	B Pringle, R Buschert
Holes	18 L 5501 m SSS 69
Fees	70DM (90DM)
Loc	Tegernsee, 50km S of Munich
Mis	Driving range-10DM

Tutzing (1983)

8132 Tutzing-Deixlfurt

Tel	(08158) 3600
Mem	600
Pro	D Hennings
Holes	18 L 6159 m SSS 72
Fees	60DM (80DM)
Loc	Starnberger See, 30km SW of
	Munich

Werdenfels (1973)

Postfach 1345, 8100 Garmisch-
Partenkirchen

Tel	(08821) 2473
Mem	200
Pro	B Davidson
Holes	9 L 5896 m SSS 71
Fees	35DM (45DM)
Loc	2km S of Garmisch on B23,
	towards Farchant

Wörthsee (1982)

Gut Schluifeld, 8031 Wörthsee

Tel	(08153) 2425
Mem	740
Pro	J Mills, J Gay
Holes	18 L 6270 m SSS 73
Fees	50DM (75DM)
Loc	Wörthsee, 60km W of Munich
Mis	Pitch & putt

Nuremberg & North Bavaria

Am Reichswald

Postfach 140101, 8500 Nürnberg 14

Tel	(0911) 305730
Pro	J Gornert (0911) 305959
Holes	18 L 6345 m SSS 73
Fees	50DM (75DM)
Loc	10km N of Nuremberg

Ansbach Schloss Colmberg (1960)

Postfach 1340, 8800 Ansbach

Tel	(0981) 88711
Fax	(0981) 88544
Mem	230
Pro	M Woodhouse
Holes	9 L 4200 m Par 66
Fees	40DM
Loc	Colmberg, 15km NW of
	Ansbach

Bamberg (1973)

Postfach 1525, 8600 Bamberg

Tel	(09547) 7212/7109
Mem	490
Pro	I Donnelly (0951) 43973
Holes	18 L 6175 m SSS 72
Fees	50DM (60DM)
Loc	Gut Leimerhof, 16km N of
	Bamberg

Bayerwald G & LC (1970)

Frauenwaldstr 2, 8392 Waldkirchen

Tel	(08581) 1040
Mem	420
Pro	S Case
Holes	9 L 6080 m SSS 72
Fees	35DM (45DM)
Loc	Waldkirchen, 30km NW of
	Passau

Coburg Schloss Tambach (1981)

8636 Weitramsdorf

Tel	(09567) 1212
Mem	320
Pro	DA Entwhistle
Holes	9 L 6150 m SSS 72
Fees	30DM (40DM)
Loc	Tambach, 9km W of Coburg,
	opposite Animal Park

Donau Rassbach (1986)

Rassbach 8, 8391 Thyrnau-Passau

Tel	(08501) 1313
Mem	200
Pro	PG Leech
Holes	18 L 6400 m SSS 73
Fees	D-35DM (D-45DM)
Loc	10km E of Passau
Mis	Driving range-5DM

Erlangen (1977)

Postfach 1767, 8520 Erlangen
Tel   (09126) 5040
Mem   180
Pro   W Hachey
Holes 9 holes Par 63
Fees   25DM
Loc   Am Schlienhof, 15km E of
          Erlangen. 15km N of
          Nuremberg
Mis   Members and guests only

Fränkische Schweiz (1974)

Kanndorf 8, 8553 Ebermannstadt
Tel   (09194) 4827
Mem   470
Pro   K Messingschlager,
          D Blakeman
Holes 18 L 6050 m SSS 72
Fees   40DM (50DM)
Loc   5km E of Ebermannstadt.
          40km N of Nuremberg

Furth im Wald (1982)

Voithenberg 1, 8492 Furth im Wald
Tel   (09973) 1240
Mem   180
Pro   J Edgar
Holes 9 L 5903 m SSS 71
Fees   30DM (40DM)
Loc   70km NE of Regensburg

Herzogenaurach (1967)

Altenbergerstr 36, 8500 Nürnberg
Tel   (0911) 616183
Mem   210
Holes 9 L 6090 m SSS 72
Fees   10DM
Loc   Next to Herzo base
Mis   Guests with members only

Hof (1985)

Poststr 2, 8670 Hof
Tel   (09281) 43749
Mem   258
Pro   N Fourie
Holes 9 L 3105 m SSS 72
Fees   35DM (45DM)
Loc   5km NE of Hof

Ingolstadt (1977)

Spitzelmühle, Gerolfingerstr,
8070 Ingolstadt
Tel   (0841) 85778
Mem   350
Pro   J Pugh, M Mayers
Holes 9 L 5500 m SSS 69
Fees   50DM (70DM)
Loc   3km from Ingolstadt towards
          Gerolfing

Lichtenau-Weickershof (1980)

Weickershof 1, 8814 Lichtenau
Tel   (09827) 6907 Fax 7242
Mem   548
Pro   F Piater, J Speed (09827) 7288

Holes 18 L 6070 m SSS 72
Fees   50DM (70DM)
Loc   10km E of Ansbach

Oberfranken (1966)

Postfach 1349, 8650 Kulmbach
Tel   (09221) 319
Mem   490
Pro   D Entwhistle, A Parker
          (09221) 1022
Holes 18 L 6152 m SSS 72
Fees   40DM (60DM)
Loc   Thurnau, 18km NW of
          Bayreuth. 14km SW of
          Kulmbach

Oberpfälzer Wald G & LC (1977)

8462 Kemnath/Ödengrub
Tel   (09439) 466
Mem   450
Pro   D Holloway
Holes 18 L 5769 m SSS 70
Fees   40DM (50DM)
Loc   Kemnath bei Fuhrn.
          10km E of Schwarzenfeld,
          towards Neunburg

Regensburg G & LC (1966)

8411 Altenthann
Tel   (09403) 505
Fax   (09403) 4391
Mem   580
Pro   R Maw, D McGuinness
Holes 18 L 5785 m SSS 71
Fees   50DM (75DM)
Loc   14km E of Regensburg,
          nr Walhalla

Rottaler (1972)

Bergstr 17, 8333 Linden
Tel   (08561) 2861
Mem   450
Pro   R Porter
Holes 18 L 6100 m SSS 72
Fees   40DM (50DM)
Loc   5km W of Pfarrkirchen on
          B388. 120km E of München

Rusel G & LC (1981)

Postfach 1321, Werftstr 17, 8360
Deggendorf
Tel   (09920) 911
Mem   338
Pro   JA Taylor (09920) 1279
Holes 9 L 6070 m SSS 72
Fees   40DM (50DM)
Loc   10km NE of Deggendorf,
          towards Regen. 60km NW of
          Passau
Mis   Driving range, pitch & putt

Sagmühle (1984)

Postfach 1124, 8394 Bad Griesbach
Tel   (08532) 2038
Mem   475
Pro   J O'Flynn, M Knauss, A Kraus,
          G Bundschuh

Holes 18 L 6217 m SSS 72
Fees   40DM (50DM)
Loc   25km SW of Passau

Schlossberg (1985)

Grünbach 4, 8386 Reisbach
Tel   (08734) 7035
Mem   470
Pro   P Haworth
Holes 18 L 6070 m SSS 72
Fees   35DM (45DM)
Loc   Somershausen, 15km from
          Dingolfing. 100km NE of
          Munich, off Route 11

Schmidmühlen G & CC (1970)

Lange Gasse 2, 8450 Amberg
Tel   (09621) 1846
Mem   105
Pro   B Rowe
Holes 9 L 5328 m SSS 68
Fees   20DM (25DM)
Loc   35km NW of Regensburg

Stiftland (1982)

Ernestgrün 35, 8591 Neualbenreuth
Tel   (09638) 1271/(09632) 1066
Mem   160
Pro   P Dunn
Holes 9 L 6122 m SSS 72
Fees   30DM (40DM)
Loc   30km E of Marktredwitz.
          50km N of Weiden

Wittelsbacher GC Rohrenfeld

8858 Neuburg
Tel   (08431) 44118
Mem   260
Pro   G Koenig
Holes 18 L 6317 m SSS 73
Fees   50DM (70DM)
Loc   20km W of Ingolstadt. 85km N
          of Munich
Mis   Driving range

Rhineland

Bad Neuenahr G & LC (1979)

Remagener Weg, 5483 Bad
Neuenahr-Ahrweiler
Tel   (02641) 2325
Mem   590
Pro   M Nickel
Holes 18 L 6060 m SSS 72
Fees   50DM (75DM)
Loc   Bad Neuenahr, 40km S of Bonn

Bergisch-Land

Siebeneickerst 386, 5600 Wuppertal 1
Tel   (02053) 7177
Pro   J Bauerdick, W Kothe
Holes 18 L 5920 m SSS 71

Fees   55DM (70DM)
Loc   Elberfeld, 8km W of Wuppertal
Mis   WE/BH-only with member.
    Driving range

Bielefeld (1977)

Dornbergerstrasse 375,
4800 Bielefeld-Hoberge 1
Tel   (0521) 105103
Mem   438
Pro   HW Kahre (0521) 104450
Holes   13 holes SSS 72
Fees   30DM
Mis   WE-only with member

Bochum (1982)

Im Mailand 127, 4630 Bochum 1
Tel   (0234) 799832
Mem   700
Pro   E Newgas, R Pütter
Holes   18 L 5300 m SSS 68
Fees   30DM (40DM)
Loc   Bochum-Stiepel, 7km S of
    Bochum

Bonn-Godesberg (1960)

Dechant-Heimbachstr 16,
5300 Bonn 2
Tel   (0228) 344003 (Clubhouse)
    (0228) 317494 (Sec)
Mem   800
Pro   K Riechart
Holes   18 L 5900 m Par 71
Fees   50DM (70DM)
Loc   Oberbachem, 4km from Bad
    Godesberg

Burg Konradsheim (1988)

Frenzenstr 148A, 5042 Konradsheim
Tel   (02235) 76094
Mem   250
Pro   H Ranft, R Hickinbotham
Holes   9 L 6147 m SSS 72
Fees   50DM (60DM)
Loc   15km SW of Cologne

Burg Overbach (1984)

Postfach 1213, 5203 Much
Tel   (02245) 5550
Mem   700
Pro   R Hauser, T Menne,
    N Remmel
Holes   18 L 6056 m SSS 72
Fees   40DM (60DM)
Loc   Much, 45km E of Cologne,
    off A4

Dortmund (1956)

Reichmarkstr 12, 4600 Dortmund-
Reichsmark
Tel   (0231) 774133/774609
Mem   650
Pro   V Knörnschild, F Schneider,
    M Menchen
Holes   18 L 6174 m SSS 72
Fees   40DM (60DM)
Loc   8km S of Dortmund
Mis   WE-only with member

Düsseldorf (1961)

Rommerljansweg 12, 4030 Ratingen
Tel   (02102) 81092
Fax   (02102) 81782
Mem   900
Pro   J Kupitz, D Hollbach, A Piater
Holes   18 L 5905 m SSS 71
Fees   WD-60DM
Loc   11km N of Düsseldorf
Mis   WE-only with member

Düsseldorf/Hösel

Grunerstr 13, 4000 Düsseldorf 1
Tel   (0211) 631171/(02102) 68629
Mem   550
Pro   F Eckl, M Pyatt
Holes   18 L 6160 m SSS 72
Fees   25DM (35DM)
Loc   Hösel, 15km NE of Düsseldorf

Emstal (1977)

Gut Beversundern, Postfach 1431,
4450 Lingen
Tel   (0591) 63837
Mem   280
Pro   D Bryan
Holes   9 L 5320 m SSS 68
Fees   30DM (40DM)
Loc   3km N of Lingen, Route B70 to
    Meppen

Essen Haus Oefte (1959)

Laupendahler Landstr, 4300 Essen
Tel   (02054) 83911
Mem   650
Pro   R Sommer (02054) 84722
Holes   18 L 6100 m SSS 72
Fees   50DM (60DM)
Loc   14km SW of Essen

Essen-Heidhausen (1970)

Preutenborbeckstr 36, 4300 Essen 16
Tel   (0201) 404111
Mem   780
Pro   G Kothe, J McGarva
Holes   18 L 5937 m SSS 71
Fees   35DM (50DM)
Loc   10km S of Essen on B224, nr
    Werden

Etuf-Essen (1962)

Freiherr-vom-Steinstr 92a, 4300
Essen 1
Tel   (0201) 441426
Mem   390
Pro   U Knappmann
Holes   9 L 4580 m SSS 64
Fees   35DM (45DM)
Loc   6km S of Essen

Gelstern

Gelstern 2, 5885 Schalksmühle
Tel   (02351) 56460
Mem   300
Pro   PR Byrom
Holes   9 L 5842 m SSS 70
Fees   25DM (35DM)
Loc   5km W of Lüdenscheid

Hubbelrath (1961)

Bergische Landstr 700, 4000
Düsseldorf 12
Tel   (02104) 72178/71848
Mem   1417
Pro   G Danz, HP Ranft, M Brock,
    S Eckrodt, R Noëlle,
    F Willemsen, R Beattie
Holes   East 18 L 6066 m SSS 72
    West 18 L 4325 m SSS 62
Fees   60DM (90DM)
Loc   Hubbelrath, 13km E of
    Düsseldorf, on Route B7

Issum-Niederrhein (1973)

Pauenweg 68, 4174 Issum 1
Tel   (02835) 3626
Mem   685
Pro   S Tomkinson,
    P Grunwell
Holes   18 L 5862 m SSS 71
Fees   50DM (60DM)
Loc   10km E of Geldern

Juliana (1979)

Frielinghausen 1,
4322 Sprockhövel
Tel   (0202) 647070
Fax   (0202) 649891
Mem   500
Pro   G Hillier, M Neumann,
    D Proplesch, F Scheffer
Holes   18 L 6100 m SSS 71
Fees   40DM (50DM)
Loc   30km E of Düsseldorf

Köln G & LC

Golfplatz 2, 5060 Bergisch
Gladbach 1
Tel   (02204) 63114/63138
Mem   630
Pro   K Marx, A Stein
Holes   18 L 6045 m Par 72
Fees   50DM (75DM)
Loc   15km E of Cologne

Köln-Marienburger (1949)

Schillingsrotter Weg, 5000 Köln 51
Tel   (0221) 384053
Mem   300
Pro   H Becker
Holes   9 L 3075 m SSS 72
Fees   40DM (50DM)
Loc   In Cologne

Krefeld (1930)

Eltweg 2, 4150 Krefeld 12
Tel   (02151) 570071/72
Mem   640
Pro   N Brunyard, G Schader
Holes   18 L 6060 m SSS 72
Fees   70DM (80DM)
Loc   7km SE of Krefeld.
    Düsseldorf 16km

Laarbruch GC (RAF) (1962)

Laarbruch, BFPO 43
Tel   Weeze 895441
Mem   200
Holes   9 L 4471 yds SSS 62
Fees   20DM
Loc   Laarbruch 9 British Forces
Mis   Access to course may be
        restricted

Märkischer Hagen (1964)

Tiefendorferstr 48, 5800 Hagen
Tel   (02334) 51778
Mem   400
Pro   D Giese, R Stehmans
Holes   9 L 6114 m SSS 72
Fees   25DM (40DM)
Loc   Berchum, 5km NE of Hagen

Münster-Wilkinghege (1963)

Steinfurterstr 448, 4400 Münster
Tel   (0251) 211201
Mem   700
Pro   CB Westerman
Holes   18 L 5955 m SSS 71
Fees   30DM (50DM)
Loc   2km N of Münster

Münsterland (1950)

Bagno, 4430 Steinfurt
Tel   (02551) 5178
Mem   275
Pro   C Leader
Holes   9 L 4834 m Par 66
Fees   30DM (40DM)
Loc   Burgsteinfurt, 25km NW of
        Münster

Niederrheinischer (1956)

Grossenbaumer Allee 240, 4100
Duisburg 28
Tel   (0203) 721469
Mem   402
Pro   J Dennison
Holes   9 L 6090 m SSS 72
Fees   40DM (60DM)
Loc   8km S of Duisburg

Nordkirchen

Golfplatz 6, 4717 Nordkirchen
Tel   (02596) 2495
Mem   340
Pro   A Rössler
Holes   9 L 6200 m SSS 72
Fees   30DM (40DM)
Loc   30km S of Münster

Osnabrück (1955)

Karmannstr 1, 4500 Osnabrück
Tel   (05402) 636
Mem   300
Pro   H Theeuwen, B Krüger
Holes   18 L 5881 m Par 71
Fees   40DM (60DM)
Loc   13km SE of Osnabrück

RAF Germany (1956)

RAF Brüggen, BFPO 25
Tel   (02163) 88463/5207
Mem   800
Pro   G Cowley
Holes   18 L 6522 yds SSS 71
Fees   30DM
Loc   On B230, 1km from Dutch/
        German border. 25km W of
        Mönchengladbach

RAF Gütersloh

RAF Gütersloh, BFPO 47
Tel   (05241) 842409
Mem   425
Holes   9 L 5761 yds SSS 68
Fees   12DM
Loc   5km W of Gütersloh

RAF Wildenrath

BFPO 42
Tel   (02432) 18 5440
Mem   300 Service personnel
Holes   9 L 4335 yds SSS 61
Fees   10DM
Loc   RAF Wildenrath

Rhein Sieg (1971)

Postfach 1216, 5202 Hennef
Tel   (02242) 6501
Mem   280
Pro   H Knopp, D MacLauchlan,
        Von Rumohr
Holes   18 L 6070 m Par 72
Fees   50DM (60DM)
Loc   Hennef, 30km SE of Cologne

Royal Artillery & Dortmund Garrison (1969)

Napier Barracks, BFPO 20
Tel   Dortmund 202551
Mem   420
Holes   18 L 5338 m SSS 70
Fees   15DM (20DM)
Loc   Dortmund Brackel
Mis   Not open to public; visitors
        by prior arrangement only

Sauerland (1958)

Falkenhorst 15, 5760 Arnsberg 1
Tel   (02932) 4314
Mem   320
Pro   T Croft
Holes   9 L 5874 m SSS 71
Fees   30DM (35DM)
Loc   35km E of Dortmund, nr
        Arnsberg
Mis   Driving range

Schloss Georghausen (1962)

Georghausen 8, 5253 Lindlar-
Hommerich
Tel   (02207) 4938
Mem   730
Pro   G Kessler, G Baum, J Kaynig
Holes   18 L 6045 m SSS 72

Fees   45DM (60DM)
Loc   30km E of Cologne

Schloss Myllendonk (1964)

Myllendonkerstr 113, 4052
Korschenbroich 1
Tel   (02161) 641049
Mem   700
Pro   G Kerkman
Holes   18 L 6120 m SSS 72
Fees   60DM (80DM)
Loc   Korschenbroich, 5km E of
        Mönchengladbach

Schmitzhof (1975)

Arsbeckerstr 160, 5144 Wegberg
Tel   (02436) 479
Mem   650
Pro   E Theeuwen
Holes   18 L 6310 m SSS 73
Fees   30DM (50DM)
Loc   20km SW of
        Mönchengladbach,
        in Wegberg-Merbeck

Siegen-Olpe (1966)

PO Box 120 112, 5900 Siegen
Tel   (02762) 7589
Mem   390
Pro   K Hahn
Holes   9 L 5724 m SSS 70
Fees   30DM (35DM)
Loc   10km NW of Siegen.
        80km E of Cologne
Mis   WE-telephone first

Tecklenburger Land (1971)

Wallen-Lienen 1,
4542 Tecklenburg
Tel   (05455) 1035
Mem   302
Pro   JP Laarman
Holes   9 L 6160 m SSS 72
Fees   40DM (60DM)
Loc   15km SW of Osnabrück

Varmert (1977)

5883 Kierspe-Varmert
Tel   (02269) 7299
Mem   500
Pro   G Thomas, N Doidge,
        P Hinton
Holes   9 L 6048 m SSS 72
Fees   35DM (50DM)
Loc   22km S of Ludenscheid.
        50km NE of Cologne

Velper G & CC (1981)

Heinrich-Hensiekstr 1,
4535 Westerkappeln-Velpe
Tel   (05456) 820
Mem   300
Pro   SL Walker (05456) 287
Holes   9 L 5782 m SSS 70
Fees   20DM (30DM)
Loc   8km W of Osnabrück

Vestischer Recklinghausen (1974)

4350 Recklinghausen
Tel   (02361) 26520
Mem   650
Pro   U Lechtermann, E Schilling,
        W Bollert
Holes   18 L 6111 m SSS 72
Fees   35DM (50DM)
Loc   Nr Loemühle Airport, N of
        Recklinghausen
Mis   Driving range

Waldbrunnen (1983)

Brunnenstr 7, 5469 Windhagen
Tel   (02645) 15621
Mem   370
Pro   M Butzkies
Holes   9 L 4816 m SSS 66
Fees   30DM (45DM)
Loc   8km S of Bad Honnef.
        35km NW of Koblenz

Warendorf (1987)

Vohren 41, 4410 Warendorf
Tel   (02586) 1792
Pro   K Phillips
Holes   9 L 6160 m SSS 72
Fees   30DM (50DM)
Loc   35km E of Münster, nr Vohren
Mis   Driving range

Wasserburg Anholt (1972)

Am Schloss 3, 4294 Isselburg
Tel   (02874) 3444
Mem   400
Pro   F di Matteo
Holes   18 L 6141 m SSS 72
Fees   35DM D-50DM (45DM D-
        60DM)
Loc   Parkhotel, Wasserburg Anholt.
        15km W of Bocholt

Werl (1973)

Unnaerstr 23, 4760 Werl
Tel   (02377) 6307
Mem   300
Pro   A Grandison
Holes   9 L 4640 m SSS 66
Fees   25DM (30DM)
Loc   30km E of Dortmund

Westerwald (1979)

Postfach 1231, 5238 Hachenburg
Pro   H-J Labonte (02620) 2230
Holes   9 holes SSS 72
Fees   30DM (40DM)
Loc   Hachenburg, 60km E of Bonn

Westfälischer Gütersloh

4830 Gütersloh
Tel   (05244) 2340
Mem   600
Pro   M Schwichtenberg
Holes   18 L 6175 m SSS 72
Fees   30DM (60DM)
Loc   8km SE of Gütersloh, nr
        Neuenkirchen

Stuttgart & South West

Algäuer G & LC (1984)

Hofgut Boschach, 8942 Ottobeuren
Tel   (08332) 1310
Mem   620
Pro   M Chesters
Holes   18 L 6215 m SSS 72
Fees   50DM (70DM)
Loc   2km S of Ottobeuren. 20km N
        of Kempten

Bad Herrenalb-Bernbach

7506 Bad Herrenalb
Tel   (07083) 8898
Mem   450
Pro   P Congreve, M Adamson
Holes   9 L 5200 m SSS 68
Fees   40DM (50DM)
Loc   25km W of Baden-Baden

Baden-Baden (1901)

Fremersbergstr 127, 7570 Baden-
Baden
Tel   (07221) 23579
Mem   400
Pro   E Totzke (07221) 24526
Holes   18 L 4575 m Par 64
Fees   50DM (65DM) W-250DM
Loc   1km S of Baden-Baden

Baden-Hills (1982)

Postfach 1153, 7558 Bischweier
Tel   (07222) 42274
Pro   R Walker
Holes   18 L 5672 m Par 72
Fees   20DM (30DM)
Loc   20km S of Rastatt
Mis   Booking and handicap
        certificate required

Bodensee Weissensberg (1986)

Lampertsweiler 51,
8995 Weissensberg
Tel   (08389) 89190
Fax   (08389) 89191
Mem   150
Pro   C Potts, M Steinbeisser
Holes   18 L 6112 m SSS 71
Fees   70DM (90DM)
Loc   5km NE of Lindau
Mis   Handicap certificate
        required

Freiburg (1970)

Krüttweg 1, 7815 Kirchzarten
Tel   (07661) 5569
Mem   540
Pro   P Weggenmann
Holes   18 L 6068 m SSS 72
Fees   50DM (60DM)
Loc   Freiburg-Kappel/Kirchzarten

Freudenstadt (1929)

Postfach 322, 7290 Freudenstadt
Tel   (07441) 3060
Mem   450
Pro   S Ramsden
Holes   9 L 5857 m SSS 71
Fees   35DM (55DM)
Loc   Freudenstadt, 75km SW of
        Stuttgart
Mis   Open Mar-Nov

Gütermann Gutach (1924)

7809 Gutach/Breisgau
Tel   (07681) 21243
Mem   300
Pro   D Pugh
Holes   9 L 5280 m SSS 68
Fees   40DM (60DM)
Loc   20km NE of Freiburg

Haghof G & LC (1983)

Alfdorf 2, 7077 Haghof
Tel   (07182) 3040
Pro   B Reilly
Holes   9 L 2932 m SSS 71
Fees   30DM
Loc   Welzheim, 50km NE of
        Stuttgart
Mis   WE-no visitors

Hechingen-Hohenzollern (1955)

Golfplatz Hagelwasen, 7470
Hechingen
Tel   (07471) 2600
Mem   380
Pro   K Schieban, P Eisenhut
Holes   9 SSS 70
Fees   35DM
Loc   Hechingen, 50km S of
        Stuttgart
Mis   WE-only with member

Heilbronn-Hohenlohe (1964)

Postfach 1341, 7107 Neckarsulm
Tel   (07941) 7886
Mem   525
Pro   B Amara
Holes   18 L 6082 m SSS 72
Fees   50DM (70DM)
Loc   Friedrichsruhe–Öhringen.
        45km N of Stuttgart, nr
        Heilbronn

Hochstatt Härtsfeld-Ries (1981)

7086 Neresheim
Tel   (07326) 7979
Pro   P Smith
Holes   9 L 6170 m SSS 72
Fees   25DM (30DM)
Loc   30km E of Heidenheim.
        Munich 100km

For list of abbreviations see page 487.

Hohenstauffen (1959)

Im Holderbrett 9, 7311 Hochdorf
Tel   (07162) 27171/20050
Mem   160
Pro   R Miller
Holes 9 L 6540 yds SSS 72
Fees   35DM (45DM)
Loc   15km E of Goppingen.
           45km E of Stuttgart

Konstanz (1965)

Langenrain, Kargegg, 7753
Allensbach 3
Tel   (07533) 5124
Mem   617
Pro   M Bingger, D Geary
Holes 18 L 6058 m SSS 72
Fees   50DM (70DM)
Loc   15km NW of Konstanz, nr
           Langenrain
Mis   Members of recognised golf
           clubs only

Lindau-Bad Schachen
(1954)

Am Schönbühl 5, 8990
Lindau/Bodensee
Tel   (08382) 78090
Mem   750
Pro   R Richardson, H Kersting,
           B Wargel
Holes 18 L 5690 m SSS 70
Fees   50DM (70DM)
Loc   nr Lindau, Bodensee

Markgräflerland (1986)

Villa Umbach, 7842 Kandern
Tel   (07626) 6609
Fax   (07626) 6609/8690
Mem   515
Pro   I Martin
Holes 9 L 6100 m SSS 72
Fees   40DM (60DM)
Loc   Kandern, 10km N of Lörrach.
           14km NW of Basle

Oberschwaben-Bad
Waldsee (1968)

Hofgut Hopfenweiler, 7967 Bad
Waldsee
Tel   (07524) 5900
Mem   520
Pro   W Jersombeck,
           T Schinnenburg
Holes 18 L 6148 m SSS 72
Fees   45DM (60DM)
Loc   Bad Waldsee, 75km NE of
           Friedrichshafen, Bodensee

Oberstdorf

8980 Oberstdorf
Tel   (08322) 2895
Mem   304
Pro   B Rowe
Holes 9 L 2795 m Par 70
Fees   40DM (55DM)
Loc   Oberstdorf 3km. 10km S of
           Sonthofen, nr Austrian border

Oeschberghof L & GC
(1976)

Golfplatz 1, 7710 Donaueschingen
Tel   (0771) 84525
Mem   550
Pro   T Gerhardt, I McCrea,
           O Hevler
Holes 18 L 6580 m SSS 74
Fees   65DM (110DM)
Loc   Donaueschingen, 120km E of
           Freiburg
Mis   Handicap certificate required

Ortenau (1981)

Gereut 9, 7630 Lahr-Reichenbach
Tel   (07821) 77217/77227
Mem   420
Pro   A Hochgürtel
Holes 9 L 5450 m SSS 70
Fees   30DM (40DM)
Loc   35km SE of Strasbourg.
           50km N of Freiburg

Reischenhof

7959 Wain
Tel   (07353) 1732
Fax   (07353) 1050
Mem   150
Pro   H Francis
Holes 9 L 6288 m SSS 73
Fees   25DM (30DM)
Loc   3km S of Wain. 30km S of Ulm
Mis   Driving range

Rhein Badenweiler
(1971)

7847 Badenweiler
Tel   (07632) 5031
Mem   550
Pro   A Price
Holes 18 L 6134 m SSS 72
Fees   50DM (75DM)
Loc   16km W of Badenweiler.
           30km SW of Freiburg

Rickenbach (1980)

Postfach 1041, 7884 Rickenbach
Tel   (07765) 8880
Mem   350
Pro   CR Dew
Holes 9 L 2749 m Par 69
Fees   30DM (50DM)
Loc   Bad Sackingen, 30km E of
           Basle

Schloss Liebenstein
G & LC (1982)

Postfach 27, 7129 Neckarwestheim
Tel   (07133) 16019
Mem   950
Pro   W Kretschy, R Hartzheim ,
           A Wurdel
Holes 18 L 5847 m SSS 71
Fees   40DM (60DM)
Loc   35km N of Stuttgart

Schloss Weitenburg (1984)

Sommerhalde 11, 7245 Starzach-
Sulzau
Tel   (07472) 8061 Fax 8062
Mem   600
Pro   D Creamer, G Pottage
Holes 18 L 6069 m SSS 72
           9 hole course
Fees   18 hole:50DM (70DM)
           9 hole:30DM (40DM)
Loc   50km SW of Stuttgart in Neckar
           Valley
Mis   Driving range

Sonnenalp (1976)

Hotel Sonnenalp, 8972 Ofterschwang
Tel   (08321) 7276 (Sec)
           (08321) 720 (Hotel)
Mem   180
Pro   B Kennedy, A MacDonald,
           D Lamplough
Holes 18 L 5938 m SSS 71
Fees   70DM (85DM) Discount for
           hotel guests
Loc   4km W of Sonthofen

Stuttgarter Neckartal
(1974)

Aldingerstr, Gebaudt 975,
7140 Ludwigsburg-Pattonville
Tel   (07141) 871319
Mem   300
Pro   H Rübmann
Holes 18 L 6310 m SSS 73
Fees   50DM (80DM)
Loc   5km NE of Stuttgart, nr
           Kornwestheim
Mis   WE-only with member

Stuttgarter Solitude (1927)

7256 Monsheim
Tel   (07044) 6909
Mem   640
Pro   F Lengsfeld
Holes 18 L 6045 m SSS 72
Fees   50DM (70DM)
Loc   15km W of Stuttgart

Ulm (1963)

Wochenauer Hof 2, 7901 Illerrieden
Tel   (07306) 2102
Mem   370
Pro   MA Emery
Holes 18 L 6170 m Par 72
Fees   35DM (50DM)
Loc   15km S of Ulm, between
           Illerkirchberg and Illerrieden

Waldegg-Wiggensbach
(1988)

Hof Waldegg, 8961 Wiggensbach
Tel   (08370) 733
Mem   430
Pro   J Taylor
Holes 18 L 4757 m SSS 65
Fees   40DM (50DM)
Loc   10km W of Kempten, nr
           Swiss/Austrian border

Greece

Afantou (1973)

Afantou, Rhodes
Tel (0241) 51255/51256
Mem 96
Pro G Sotiropoulous,
V Anasstassiou
Holes 18 L 6060 m SSS 72
Fees 2000dra (10000dra)
Loc 20km S of Rhodes town

Corfu (1972)

PO Box 71, Corfu
Tel (0661) 94220/1
Mem 100
Pro D Crawley
Holes 18 L 6300 m SSS 72
Fees 7000dra (Jul/Aug-4200dra)
Loc Ermones Bay, 16km W of
Corfu town

Glyfada (1963)

PO Box 70116 Glyfada, Athens
Tel (894) 6820/(893) 1721
Mem 1300
Pro J Sotiropoulos
Holes 18 L 6189 m SSS 72
Fees 3000dra (5000dra)
Loc 12km S of Athens

Porto Carras G & CC (1979)

Porto Carras, Halkidiki
Tel (0375) 71381/71221
Pro Mrs P Andrade
Holes 18 L 6086 m SSS 72
Fees D-2000dra W-10000dra
Loc Sithonia Peninsula, 100km SE
of Thessaloniki

Iceland

Akureyri (1935)

PO Box 896, 602 Akureyri
Tel (96) 22974 Fax (96) 26476
Mem 380
Pro DG Barnwell (96) 623846
Holes 18 L 5857 m SSS 73
Fees £20 (£25)
Loc 1km from Akureyri (N coast)
Mis World's most northern 18-hole
course. Home of the Arctic
Open

Borgarness (1973)

PO Box 112, 310 Borgarnes
Tel (93) 71663 Fax (93) 71041
Mem 60
Pro P Chandler
Holes 18 L 5260 m SSS 70
9 L 2630 m SSS 70
Fees 1000 Ikr

Loc 5km from Borgarnes. 100km N
of Reykjavik (W coast)

Éskifjardar (1976)

735 Éskifirdi
Mem 50
Holes 9 L 4412 m SSS 66
Fees D-800 Ikr
Loc 3km W of Éskifjördur (E coast)

Hellu (1974)

Austurveg 1, Huolsvelli
Mem 74
Holes 9 L 3886 m SSS 61
Fees 100 Ikr
Loc Huolsvelli (S coast)

Hornafjardar

Hornafirdi
Tel (97) 8030
Mem 44
Holes 9 L 3610 m SSS 63
Fees 200 Ikr
Loc Hofn (SE coast)

Húsavíkur

PO Box 23, Kötlum, 640 Húsavík
Tel (96) 41000
Mem 90
Holes 9 L 2686 m SSS 70
Fees 800 Ikr
Loc 2km from Húsavík (N coast)
Mis Open June-Sept

Ísafjardar (1978)

PO Box 367, Ísafjördur
Tel (94) 3696 (Captain)
Mem 90
Holes 9 L 4860 m SSS 67
Fees £10 (£10)
Loc 3km W of Ísafjördur (NW coast)

Jökull (1973)

Brautarholt 26, 355 Ólafsvík
Tel (354) 93 61151/61666
Mem 45
Holes 9 L 4530 m SSS 65
Fees D-800 Ikr
Loc 5km SE of Ólafsvík (W coast)

Keilir (1967)

Hvaleyri, Hafnarfjördur
Tel (91) 53360
Mem 400
Pro T Asgeirsson
Holes 18 L 5117 m SSS 68
Fees 1000 Ikr
Loc 10km S of Reykjavik (SW coast)

Leynir (1965)

PO Box 9, Akranes
Tel (93) 12711
Mem 160
Holes 9 L 2640 m SSS 70
Fees 800 Ikr
Loc 2km from Akranes (SW coast)

Ness-Nesklubburinn (1964)

PO Box 66, 172 Seltjarnes
Tel 611930
Mem 181
Pro M Knipe
Holes 9 L 4986 m SSS 68
Fees 1400 Ikr
Loc 3km W of Reykjavík

Ólafsfjardar (1968)

Adalgata 12, 625 Ólafsfjördur
Tel (96) 62364
Mem 49
Holes 9 L 4652 m SSS 67
Fees £8
Loc Ólafsfjördur (N coast)

Reykjavíkur (1934)

Grafarholti, Box 4071,
124 Reykjavik
Tel (91) 84735
Mem 816
Pro J Drummond (91) 82815
Holes 18 L 5956 m SSS 70
Fees 1000 Ikr
Loc 8km E of Reykjavík

Saudárkróks (1970)

Saudárkrókur
Tel (95) 35075
Mem 60
Holes 9 L 5708 m SSS 71
Fees 1000 Ikr
Loc 1 1/2 km W of Saudárkrókur
(N coast)

Selfoss (1971)

Selfoss
Mem 48
Holes 9 L 5070 m SSS 69
Loc Selfoss (SW coast)

Sudurnesja (1964)

PO Box 112, 230 Keflavik
Tel (92) 14100
Mem 300
Pro P Hunter
Holes 18 L 5961 m SSS 73
Loc N of Keflavik (SW coast).
Airport 5km

Vestmannaeyja (1938)

Tel (98) 12363
Mem 221
Pro P Grünwell
Holes 9 L 2881 m SSS 69
Fees 1000 Ikr
Loc 2km W of town centre. Large
island off S coast. 20 min flight
from Reykjavík.

For list of abbreviations see page 487.

Italy

Como/Milan/Bergamo

Barlassina CC (1952)

Via Privata Golf 42,
20030 Birago di Camnago (MI)
Tel   (0362) 560621/2/3
Fax   (0362) 560934
Mem   300
Pro   N Rendina, S Betti
Holes   18 L 6073 m SSS 72
Fees   70000L (100.000L)
Loc   22km N of Milan

Bergamo L'Albenza (1960)

Via Longoni 12,
24030 Almenno San Bartolomeo
Tel   (035) 640028/640707
Mem   480
Pro   S Locatelli, M Rendina,
        F Ripamonti, C Rocca
Holes   18 L 6198 m SSS 72
        9 L 2962 m SSS 36
Fees   40.000L (60.000L)
Loc   Bergamo 13km. Milan 45km

Carimate (1962)

Via Airoldi, 22060 Carimate
Tel   (031) 790226
Mem   500
Pro   E Songia, M Frigerio, B Molteni
Holes   18 L 5982 m SSS 71
Fees   40.000L (60.000L)
Loc   15km S of Como.
        27km N of Milan

Franciacorta

Loc Castagnola, 25040 Corte Franca
Tel   (030) 984167
Pro   R Napoleoni
Holes   18 L 6060 m SSS 72
        9 L 1150 m Par 72
Loc   Nigoline, 25km E of Bergamo
        SE of Bergamo

Lanzo Intelvi (1962)

22024 Lanzo Intelvi (CO)
Tel   (031) 840169
Mem   188
Pro   G Frigerio
Holes   9 L 2438 m SSS 66
Fees   25.000L (50.000L)
Loc   32km NW of Como
Mis   Open May-Oct

Menaggio & Cadenabbia (1907)

Via Golf 12, 22010 Grandola
E Uniti (CO)
Tel   (0344) 32103/31564
Mem   260
Pro   G Delfino

Holes   18 L 5277 m SSS 69
Fees   50.000L (70.000L)
Loc   5km W of Menaggio.
        30km N of Como

Milano (1928)

20052 Parco di Monza (MI)
Tel   (039) 303081/303082
Mem   1050
Pro   G Grappasonni (039) 304561
Holes   18 L 6239 m SSS 73
        9 L 2976 m SSS 36
Fees   50.000L (60.000L)
Loc   6km N of Monza.
        18km NE of Milan

Molinetto CC (1982)

SS Padana Superiore 11,
20063 Cernusco sul Naviglio (MI)
Tel   (02) 9238500/9249373
Fax   (02) 9233460
Mem   600
Pro   F Perini, B Giordano,
        A Merletti
Holes   18 L 6010 m Par 72
Fees   60.000L (70.000L)
Loc   Cernusco, 10km E of Milan
Mis   Driving range

Monticello (1975)

Via Volta 4, 22070 Cassina Rizzardi
Tel   (031) 928055
Fax   (031) 880207
Mem   1200
Pro   A Croce, V Damonte,
        E Bianchi, A Schiroli,
        M Gavarini, L Frigerio
Holes   18 L 6413 m SSS 72
        18 L 6056 m SSS 72
Fees   50.000L (90.000L)
Loc   10km SE of Como

La Pinetina (1971)

Via al Golf 4, 22070 Appiano Gentile
Tel   (031) 933202
Mem   420
Pro   M Sabbatino
Holes   18 L 6001 m SSS 71
Fees   35.000L (50.000L)
Loc   12km SW of Como

La Rossera (1970)

Via Montebello 4, 24060 Chiuduno
Tel   (035) 838600
Mem   230
Pro   M de Zuniga, G Watson
Holes   9 L 2510 m SSS 68
Fees   40.000L (60.000L)
Loc   18km

Le Rovedine (1978)

Via C Marx, 20090 Noverasco di
Opera (MI)
Tel   (02) 5242730
Mem   450
Pro   R Benassi, L Marsala,
        L Ghirardo, G Veronelli

Holes   9 L 2890 m SSS 71
Fees   17.500L (21.500L)
Loc   4km S of Milan
Mis   Public course

Royal Sant'Anna (1978)

22040 Annone di Brianza (CO)
Tel   (0341) 577551
Holes   9 L 5370 m SSS 69
Fees   25.000L (30.000L)
Loc   15km SE of Como. Milano 40km

Santa Martretta (1974)

Via Chitola 49, 27029 Vigevano (PV)
Tel   (0381) 76872
Mem   208
Pro   S Camporini
Holes   9 L 5880 m Par 72
Fees   30.000L (50.000L)
Loc   25km SE of Novara. 35km SW
        of Milan

Villa D'Este (1926)

Via Cantù 13, 22030 Montorfano (CO)
Tel   (031) 200200
Fax   (031) 200786
Mem   400
Pro   GC Frigerio, P Molteni,
        G Ciprandi
Holes   18 L 5787 m SSS 71
Fees   70.000L (100.000L)
Loc   Montorfano, 7km SE of Como
Mis   Driving range

Zoate

20067 Zoate di Tribiano (MI)
Tel   (02) 90632183/90631861
Pro   L Grappasoni, S Zerega
Holes   18 L 6116 m Par 72
Loc   Zoate, 17km SE of Milan

Elba

Acquabona

57037 Portoferraio, Isola di Elba (LI)
Tel   (0565) 940066
Mem   350
Pro   G Ciprandi, G Crespi
Holes   9 L 5144 m SSS 67
Fees   30.000-50.000L
Loc   5km NW of Porto Azzurro.
        6km NW of Porto Ferraio

Emilia Romagna

Adriatic GC Cervia (1985)

Via Ielenia Gora, 48016 Milano
Marittima
Tel   (0544) 992786/992370 (Sec)
Mem   465
Pro   R Paris (0544) 992000
Holes   18 L 6275 m SSS 72
Fees   42.000L (55.000L)
Loc   20km SE of Ravenna

Bologna (1959)

Via Sabatini 69, 40050 Monte San
Pietro
Tel   (051) 969100
Mem   450
Pro   B Ghezzo, C Ferrari
Holes   18 L 6103 m SSS 72
Fees   45.000L (55.000L)
Loc   20km W of Bologna
Mis   Driving range

Croara (1977)

29010 Croara di Gazzola
Tel   (0523) 977105/977148
Fax   (0523) 977100
Mem   433
Pro   G Turrini, E Vergari,
        P de Ascentiis
Holes   18 L 6065 m SSS 72
Fees   30.000L (50.000L)
Loc   16km SW of Piacenza.
        84km SE of Milan

Marigola (1975)

Via Vallata 5, 19032 Lerici (SP)
Tel   (0187) 970193
Fax   (0187) 65622
Mem   60
Pro   CA Le Chevallier
Holes   9 L 2120 m Par 54
Fees   25.000L (35.000L)
Loc   6km SE of La Spezia

La Rocca (1985)

Via Campi 8, 43038 Sala Baganza
Tel   (0521) 834037
Mem   300
Pro   R Bolognesi
Holes   9 L 2891 m SSS 70
Fees   £10 (£14)
Loc   8km S of Parma

Gulf of Genoa

Degli Ulivi (1932)

Via Campo Golf 59, 18038 San Remo
Tel   (0184) 557093/505108
Mem   450
Pro   M Bianco, G Ammirati,
        G de Andreis
Holes   18 L 5230 m SSS 67
Fees   50.000L (70.000L)
Loc   5km N of San Remo

Garlenda (1965)

Via Golf 7, 17030 Garlenda
Tel   (0182) 580012
Fax   (0182) 580561
Mem   600 130(L) 85(J)
Pro   F Zanini, F Picco, G Girardi
Holes   18 L 5973 m SSS 71
Fees   60.000L (85.000L)
Loc   15km N of Alassio

Pineta di Arenzano

Piazza del Golf, 16011 Arenzano
(GE)
Tel   (010) 9111817
Mem   550
Pro   S Gori, A Mori, V Mori
Holes   9 L 5527 m SSS 70
Fees   40.000L (60.000L)
Loc   Arenzano Pineta, 20km W of
        Genoa

Rapallo (1930)

Via Mameli 377, 16035 Rapallo (GE)
Tel   (0185) 261777/8
Fax   (0185) 261779
Mem   778
Pro   M Canessa, M Erbisti, C Costa,
        A Brizzolari, M Avanzino,
        A Schiaffino
Holes   18 L 5694 m SSS 70
Fees   75.000L (Sat-100.000L)
Loc   25km SE of Genoa. Nr A12
        motorway exit Rapallo

Lake Garda & Dolomites

Asiago (1967)

Via Meltar 2,36012 Asiago
Tel   (0424) 462721
Mem   492
Pro   B Antonello
Holes   9 L 2948 m SSS 71
Fees   60.000L
Loc   3km N of Asiago.
        50km N of Vicenza
Mis   Open Jun-Oct

Bogliaco (1912)

Via Golf 11, 25088 Toscolano
Maderno
Tel   (0365) 643006
Mem   300
Pro   L Tavernini
Holes   9 L 2572 m SSS 67
Fees   35.000L (50.000L)
Loc   Lake Garda, 40km NE of
        Brescia
Mis   Driving range

Ca' degli Ulivi (1988)

Via Ghiandare 2, 37010 Marciaga di
Costermano (VR)
Tel   (045)
        7256497/7256877/7256592
Mem   400
Pro   G Kromichal, V Innocente
Holes   18 L 6000m SSS 72
        9 hole course
Fees   70.000L (90.000L)
Loc   Above village of Garda.
        Verona Airport 35km
Mis   Driving range

Campo Carlo Magno (1922)

c/o Golf Hotel, Madonna di
Campiglio
Tel   (0465) 41003
Fax   (0465) 40294
Mem   45
Pro   A Silva
Holes   9 L 4992 m SSS 68
Loc   Madonna di Campiglio 1km.
        74km NW of Trento
Mis   Open Jul-Sept

Gardagolf (1985)

Via Angelo Omodeo 2, 25080 Soiano
Del Lago (BS)
Tel   (0365) 674707 (Sec)
Mem   380
Pro   F Maestroni, F Ghezzo,
        B Maestroni
Holes   18 L 6505 m SSS 74
        9 L 2415 m Par 34
Fees   40.000L (50.000L)
Loc   Lake Garda, 30km NE of
        Brescia.
Mis   Driving range

Petersberg (1987)

Unterwinkel 5, 39040 Petersberg
(BO)
Tel   (0471) 615122
Fax   (0471) 615698
Mem   150
Pro   C Mawdsley
Holes   9 L 2500 m SSS 66
Fees   45.000L (55.000L)
Loc   35km SE of Bolzano

Verona (1963)

Ca' del Sale 15, 37066
Sommacampagna
Tel   (045) 510060
Fax   (045) 510242
Mem   500
Pro   E Ridolfi, M Bolognesi
Holes   18 L 6307 m SSS 72
Fees   60.000L
Loc   7km W of Verona

Naples & South

Circolo Golf Napoli (1983)

Via Campiglione 11,
80072 Arco Felice (NA)
Tel   (081) 8674296
Mem   58
Holes   9 L 4776 m SSS 68
Fees   30.000L (35.000L)
Loc   Pozzuoli, 10km W of Naples
Mis   Guests with members only.

Porto d'Orra (1977)

PB 102, 88063 Catanzaro Lido
Tel   (0961) 791045
Mem   141
Pro   L de Gori

Holes 9 L 2492 m SSS 70
Fees 25.000L
Loc 9km N of Catanzaro Lido

Riva Dei Tessali (1971)

74011 Castellaneta
Tel (099) 6439251
Mem 147
Pro B Cosenza
Holes 18 L 5960 m SSS 71
Fees 42.000L
Loc 34km SW of Taranto

San Michele

Loc Bosco 8/9, 87022 Cetraro (CS)
Tel (0982) 91012 Fax 91430
Mem 60
Pro L Gallardo
Holes 9 L 2037 m SSS 60
Fees 30.000L (35.000L)
Loc Cetraro, 50km N of Cosenza.
250km SE of Naples

Rome

Castelgandolfo (1987)

Via S Spirito 13, 00040
Castelgandolfo
Tel (06) 9312301/9313084
Mem 390
Pro A Venier, Z Martinez
Holes 18 L 6025 m SSS 71
Fees 80.000L
Loc 22km SE of Rome

Eucalyptus

Via Cogna 5, 04011 Aprilia (LT)
Tel (06) 926252/9268120
Fax (06) 8443314
Mem 250
Pro GV Canonica
Holes 9 L 6375 m SSS 72
Fees 125.000L (140.000L)
Loc 20km S of Rome on Aprilia-
Anzio road

Fioranello

CP 96, 00040 Santa Maria delle Mole
Tel (06) 608291/608058
Mem 250
Pro R Croce, A Pelliccioni
Holes 9 L 5276 m SSS 68
Fees 25.000L (30.000L)
Loc Santa Maria, 17km SE of Rome
Mis Driving range

Fiuggi (1928)

Superstrada Anticolana 1,
03015 Fiuggi
Tel (0775) 55250
Mem 210
Pro R Terrinoni
Holes 9 L 5697 m SSS 70
Fees 25.000L (30.000L)
Loc 60km SE of Rome
Mis Driving range

Marina Velca

01016 Marina Velca/Tarquinia
Tel (0766) 812109
Mem 150
Pro R Napoleoni
Holes 9 L 2604 m SSS 50
Fees D-5.000L
Loc 80km N of Rome on coast

Olgiata (1961)

Largo Olgiata 15, 00123 Roma
Tel (06) 3789141
Mem 800
Pro U Grappasonni
Holes 18 L 6396 m SSS 72
9 L 2968 m SSS 71
Fees 40.000L (50.000L)
Loc 19km NW of Rome, nr La
Storta
Mis Driving range

Parco de' Medici (1990)

Autostrada Roma-Fiumicino, 00148
Roma
Tel (06) 6553477
Fax (06) 6553344
Pro R Terrinoni, M Mannelli,
S Pietrobono, A Luzzi
Holes 18 L 6164 m SSS 72
Fees 50.000L (70.000L)
Loc SW of Rome, nr airport
Mis Further 9 holes open 1991

Roma (1903)

Via Appia Nuova 716, 00178 Roma
Tel (06) 783407/786129
Mem 1000
Pro P Manca, C Croce, M Peri,
M Sardella, R Bernardini
Holes 18 L 5825 m SSS 71
Fees 6.000L
Loc 7^{1}/2 km SE of Rome towards
Ciampino

Sardinia

Is Molas (1975)

CP 49, 09010 Pula
Tel (070) 9241011/2 Fax 9241022
Mem 396
Pro A Paolillo
Holes 18 L 6131 m SSS 72
Fees 70.000L
Loc Pula, 32km S of Cagliari.

Pevero GC Costa Smeralda (1972)

07020 Porto Cervo
Tel (0789) 96072/96210/96211
Fax (0789) 96572
Mem 450
Pro L Cau
Holes 18 L 6186 m SSS 72
Fees 65.000-90.000L
Loc Porto Cervo, 30km N of Olbia,
on Costa Smeralda

Stresa & Lake Maggiore

Alpino Di Stresa (1925)

28040 Vezzo (NO)
Tel (0323) 20101/20642
Mem 280
Pro P Giacono
Holes 9 L 5359 m SSS 67
Fees 30.000L (40.000L)
Loc 7km W of Stresa

Castelconturbia (1984)

Via Suno, 28010 Agrate Conturbia
Tel (0322) 832093 (Clubhouse)
Mem 540
Pro A Angelini, B Murdaca, A Zito
Holes Red 9 L 3330 m Par 36
Yellow 9 L 3070 m Par 36
Blue 9 L 3210 m Par 36
Fees 60.000L (80.000L) (1989)
Loc 23km N of Novara. Milan 60km
Mis Driving range

Iles Borromées

Via Bono Lamberti, 28049 Stresa (NO)
Tel (0323) 29285/30243 Fax 30243
Mem 385
Pro G Veronelli
Holes 9 L 3110 m SSS 72
Fees 40.000L (60.000L)
Loc 5km S of Stresa. 70km NW of
Milan

Piandisole (1964)

Via Pineta 1, 28057 Premeno (NO)
Tel (0323) 47100
Mem 180
Pro V Viero
Holes 9 L 2830 m SSS 67
Fees 30.000L (40.000L)
Loc Premeno, 30km N of Stresa

Varese (1934)

Via Vittorio Veneto 32, 21020
Luvinate (VA)
Tel (0332) 227394/229302
Mem 637
Pro S Abbiati, M Ballarin,
A Ballarin, V Viero
Holes 18 L 5936 m SSS 72
Fees 50.000L (70.000L)
Loc 5km NW of Varese

Turin & North West

Biella 'Le Betulle' (1958)

Valcarozza, 13050 Magnano (VC)
Tel 679151
Mem 300
Pro M Guersoli, A Reale
Holes 18 L 6100 m SSS 72
Fees 60.000L (90.000L)
Loc 17km SW of Biella

Cervino (1955)

11021 Cervinia-Breuil (AO)
Tel   (0166) 949131
Mem   350
Pro   L Cantarella, D Caputo,
        A Pittaluga
Holes   9 L 5046 m SSS 67
Fees   45.000L-60.000L
Loc   53km NE of Aosta

Le Chioccole CC (1983)

**Loc Fraschetta, Cascina Roma,
12062 Cherasco (CN)**
Tel   (0172) 48772/48759
Mem   380
Pro   V Pelle, M Moraldo
Holes   18 L 5863 m SSS 71
Fees   40.000L (60.000L)
Loc   Cherasco, 45km S of Turin

Claviere (1926)

**Strada Nazionale 45, 10050 Claviere
(TO)**
Tel   (0122) 878917 (Clubhouse)
        (011) 2398346 (Sec)
Mem   980
Pro   L Merlino, F Giacotto
Holes   9 L 4650 m SSS 64
Fees   70.000L
Loc   96km W of Turin
Mis   Open Jun-Oct

Courmayeur

11013 Courmayeur
Tel   (0165) 89103
Pro   F Venier
Holes   9 L 2650 m SSS 67
Fees   D-4.000L
Loc   5km NE of Courmayeur
Mis   Open Jul-Sept. Driving
        range

Le Fronde (1975)

**Via Sant-Agostino 68,
10051 Avigliana (TO)**
Tel   (011) 938053/930540
Mem   350
Pro   M Rolando, A Cali
Holes   18 L 6081 m SSS 72
Fees   50.000L (60.000L)
Loc   Avigliana, 20km W of Turin
Mis   Driving range

Margara (1975)

**Via Tenuta Margara 5, 15043 Fubine
(AL)**
Tel   (0131) 772377
Mem   170
Pro   G Sità
Holes   18 L 6218 m SSS 72
Fees   10.000L (15.000L)
Loc   15km NW of Alessandria

I Roveri (1971)

Rotta Cerbiatta 24, 10070 Fiano (TO)
Tel   (011) 923571
Pro   M Vinzi, G Colombatto,
        G Bertaina
Holes   18 L 6218 m SSS 72
        9 L 3107 m SSS 36
Fees   70.000L (90.000L)
Loc   16km NW of Turin

La Serra (1970)

**Via Astigliano 42, 15048 Valenza
(AL)**
Tel   (0131) 954778
Mem   320
Pro   A Caputo
Holes   9 L 2820 m SSS 70
Fees   25.000L (40.000L)
Loc   4km W of Valenza. 7km N of
        Alessandria
Mis   Open Mar-Nov. Driving range

Sestrieres (1932)

**Piazza Agnelli 4, 10058 Sestrieres
(TO)**
Tel   (0122) 76276/76243
Mem   400
Pro   M Vinzi, S Bertaina
Holes   18 L 4598 m SSS 65
Fees   35.000L (45.000L)
Loc   Sestrieres, 96km W of Turin
Mis   Highest course in Europe.
        Open Jun - Sept

Stupinigi (1972)

**Corso Unione Sovietica 506,
10135 Torino**
Tel   (011) 343975
Pro   D Canonica, F Luzi
Holes   9 L 1975 m SSS 63
Loc   Mirafiore, Turin
Mis   Closed Aug

Torino (1924)

**Via Grange 137, 10070 Fiano
Torinese**
Tel   (011) 9235440/9235670
Mem   800
Pro   O Bolognesi, L Merlino,
        S Bertaina
Holes   18 L 6216 m SSS 72
        18 L 6211 m SSS 72
Fees   60.000L (80.000L)
Loc   23km NW of Turin

Vinovo (1984)

Via Stupinigi 182, 10048 Vinovo
Tel   (011) 9653880
Mem   230
Pro   P Panero, S Fiammengo,
        R Valzorio
Holes   9 L 4164 m SSS 62
Fees   25.000L (35.000L)
Loc   3km SW of Turin

Tuscany & Umbria

Casentino (1985)

**Località Palazzo, 52014 Poppi
(Arezzo)**
Tel   (0575) 520167
Fax   (0575) 593206
Mem   350
Pro   A Pissilli
Holes   9 L 2810 m Par 36
Fees   25.000L (30.000L)
Loc   Poppi, 50km SE of Florence

Conero GC Sirolo (1987)

Via Betellico 6, 60020 Sirolo (AN)
Tel   (071) 7360613
Holes   18 L 6185 m Par 72
        9 hole short course
Fees   WD-35.000L
Loc   Sirolo, 20km SE of Ancona

Firenze Ugolino

**Strada Chiantigiana 3, 50015
Grassina**
Tel   (055) 205 1009
Mem   700
Pro   F Rosi, R Campagnoli, C Poletti
Holes   18 L 5785 m SSS 70
Fees   40.000L (60.000L)
Loc   Grassina, 9km S of Florence

Montecatini (1985)

**Via Dei Brogi 5, Loc. Pievaccia,
51015 Monsummano Terme**
Tel   (0572) 62218
Mem   184
Pro   M Ravinetto
Holes   18 L 6144 m SSS 71
Fees   50.000L
Loc   8km N of Montecatini Terme.
        50km NW of Florence (A11)
Mis   Driving range

Perugia (1960)

06074 Santa Sabina-Ellera
Tel   (075) 795204
Fax   (075) 795370
Mem   420
Pro   A Barlozzi, M Taricone
Holes   9 L 3067 m SSS 70
Fees   25.000L (30.000L)
Loc   6km NW of Perugia
Mis   Driving range

Punta Ala (1964)

Via del Golf 1, 58040 Punta Ala (GR)
Tel   (0564) 922121
Mem   330
Pro   J Hall, P Manca, F Rosi
Holes   18 L 6190 m SSS 72
Fees   35.000L-60.000L
Loc   40km NW of Grosseto.
        Siena 90km. Florence 150km

For list of abbreviations see page 487.

Tirrenia (1968)

56018 Tirrenia (PI)
Tel   (050) 37518
Fax   (050) 33286
Mem   390
Pro   M Mulas
Holes   9 L 3065 m SSS 72
Fees   40.000L (50.000L)
Loc   15km SW of Pisa on coast

Venice &
North East

Albarella (1988)

Isola de Albarella,
45010 Rosolino
Tel   (0426) 67124
Pro   L Paolillo
Holes   18 L 6065 m SSS 72
Fees   40.000L (50.000L)
Loc   64km S of Venice
Mis   Driving range

Ca' della Nave (1986)

Piazza Vittoria 14, 30030 Martellago
Tel   (041) 5401555
Mem   300
Pro   M Napeoleoni
Holes   18 L 6340 m SSS 72
   9 hole Par 3
Fees   60.000L
Loc   Martellago, 20km NW of
   Venice

Cansiglio (1956)

CP 152, 31029 Vittorio Veneto
Tel   (0438) 585398
Mem   245
Pro   U Scafa
Holes   9 L 5726 m SSS 70
Fees   40.000L (50.000L) (1990)
Loc   21km NE of Vittorio Veneto

Padova (1966)

35050 Valsanzibio di Galzigano
Tel   (049) 9130078
Mem   600
Pro   A Lionello, P Bernardini
Holes   18 L 6053 m SSS 72
Fees   50.000L (60.000L)
Loc   Valsanzibio, 20km S of Padua

San Floriano-Gorizia
(1987)

Via Oslavia 5, 34070 San Floriano
del Collio
Tel   (0481) 884131
Fax   (0481) 884214
Mem   100
Pro   E Pavan
Holes   9 L 2600 m SSS 55
Fees   20000L (25000L)
Loc   6km NW of Gorizia. 50km SE
   of Udine, nr Yugoslav border
Mis   Open Mar-Dec. Driving range

Trieste (1954)

Via Padriciano 80, 34012 Trieste
Tel   (040) 226159/227062
Mem   200
Pro   E Pavan
Holes   9 L 2725 m SSS 69
Fees   20.000L (22.000L)
Loc   Padriciano, 7km E of Trieste

Udine (1971)

33034 Fagagna-Villaverde (UD)
Tel   (0432) 800418
Mem   210
Pro   L Tavarini
Holes   9 L 2944 m SSS 71
Fees   30.000L
Loc   15km NW of Udine

Venezia (1928)

Via del Forte, 30011 Alberoni
Tel   (041) 731015/731333
Fax   (041) 731339
Mem   450
Pro   T Scarso, R Pavan, R Trentin
Holes   18 L 6126 m SSS 72
Fees   50.000L (60.000L) (1990)
Loc   Venice Lido

Villa Condulmer (1960)

Via della Croce 3, 31021 Zerman di
Mogliano Veneto
Tel   (041) 457062
Mem   480
Pro   U Scafa, M Ceolin
Holes   18 L 5995 m SSS 71
   9 hole short course
Fees   40.000L (Sun-50.000L)
Loc   17km N of Venice

Luxembourg

CC Grand-Ducal de
Luxembourg (1936)

1, Route de Treves, 2633
Senningerberg
Tel   Luxembourg 34090
Mem   1200
Pro   E Saquet, S Clough, A Bruce
Holes   18 L 5765 m SSS 71
Fees   1500fr (2000fr)
Loc   Luxembourg 7km

Malta

Royal Malta (1888)

Marsa, Malta
Tel   232842/233851
Mem   350
Pro   R Josie
Holes   18 L 5800 yds SSS 67
Fees   £M7 W-£M35
Loc   Marsa, 3 miles from Valetta

Netherlands

Amsterdam &
Noord Holland

Amsterdamse (1934)

Zwartelaantje 4, 1099 CE
Amsterdam-Duivendrecht
Tel   (020) 943650
Mem   460 80(J)
Pro   Mrs M de Boer, J Dale
Holes   9 L 5260 m SSS 68
Fees   50fl (70fl)
Loc   8km SE of Amsterdam

Haarlemmermeersche

Cruquiusdijk 122, 2141 EV
Vijfhuizen
Tel   (02508) 3124
Mem   700
Pro   V Kelly, W Voskamp
Holes   9 L 6087 m SSS 72
Fees   40fl
Loc   Haarlemmermeer, W of
   Amsterdam

Kennemer G & CC (1910)

PO Box 85, 2040 AB Zandvoort
Tel   (02507) 12836/18456
Mem   840
Pro   J Buchanan
Holes   27 holes SSS 72:
   Van Hengel 9 L 2951 m
   Pennink 9 L 2916 m
   Colt 9 L 2932 m
Fees   75fl (100fl)
Loc   Zandvoort, 6km W of Haarlem
Mis   Handicap certificate required

Marine Nieuwediep (1958)

PO Box 932, 1780AX Den Helder
Mem   340
Holes   9 L 4780 m SSS 66
Fees   10fl
Loc   Nieuwe Haven
Mis   Situated on naval base; entry
   by permit or introduction only

De Noordhollandse (1982)

Sluispolderweg 6, 1817 BM Alkmaar
Tel   (072) 156807 (Sec)
   (072) 156179 (Caddymaster)
Mem   495
Pro   P Horn (072) 156175
Holes   9 L 6118 m SSS 72
Fees   25fl (35fl)
Loc   2km N of Alkmaar
Mis   Public course. Driving range.

Olympus (1973)

Abcouderstraatweg 46, 1105 AA
Amsterdam Zuid-Oost
Tel   (02946) 5373
Mem   600
Pro   CJ Broekhuysen,
   GW Hutchison

Holes 9 L 2905 m SSS 70
Fees 30fl
Loc S of Amsterdam, nr E2 and AMC Hospital

Spaarnwoude (1977)

Het Hoge Land 3, 1981 LT Velsen
Tel (023) 382708
Fax (023) 387274
Mem 1500
Pro AC Wessels
Holes 18 L 5406 m SSS 68
Fees 22fl (22fl) (1990)
Loc Spaarnwoude, 14km W of Amsterdam. 10km NE of Haarlem

Breda & South West

Domburgsche (1914)

Schelpweg 26, 4357 BP Domburg
Tel (01188) 1573
Mem 600
Pro L Verberne
Holes 9 L 5139 m SSS 67
Fees 50fl (60fl)
Loc 15km NW of Middelburg

N-B Toxandria (1928)

Veenstraat 89, 5124 NC Molenschot
Tel (01611) 2347
Mem 800
Pro R Leach
Holes 18 L 5925 m SSS 71
Fees 50fl (70fl)
Loc 8km NE of Breda
Mis Introduction necessary. Please phone in advance

Wouwse Plantage (1981)

Zoomvlietweg 66, 4725 TD Wouwse Plantage
Tel (01657) 593
Mem 650
Pro P Helsby, A McLean
Holes 18 L 6016 m SSS 72
Fees 45fl
Loc Wouwse Plantage, 10km E of Bergen-op-Zoom, nr Roosendaal
Mis Handicap certificate required. WE-only with member

East Central

Edese (1979)

Nationaal Sportcentrum Papendal, Amsterdamseweg, Arnhem
Tel (08306) 21985
Mem 500
Pro C Borst
Holes 9 L 3050 m SSS 72
Fees 25fl (35fl)
Loc NW of Arnhem, towards Ede

Hattemse G & CC (1930)

Veenwal 11, 8051 AS Hattem
Tel (05206) 41909
Mem 400
Pro E Vaartjes
Holes 9 L 5808 yds SSS 68
Fees 50fl (60fl)
Loc Hattem, 5km S of Zwolle

Keppelse (1926)

Oude Zutphenseweg 15, Hoog-Keppel
Tel (08348) 1416
Mem 200
Pro C Butti
Holes 9 L 5402 m SSS 67
Fees 25fl (35fl)
Loc Laag-Keppel, 25km E of Arnhem

De Koepel (1983)

Postbox 88, 7640 AB Wierden
Tel (05496) 76150
Mem 450
Pro A Young
Holes 9 L 2863 m SSS 70
Fees 50fl (60fl)
Loc 7km W of Almelo

Nunspeetse G & CC (1985)

Plesmanlaan 30, Nunspeet
Tel (03412) 58034
Fax (03412) 60526
Mem 575
Pro W van Mook
Holes 27 holes L 6100 m SSS 72
Fees 60fl (80fl)
Loc Nunspeet, 25km SW of Zwolle

Rosendaelsche (1895)

Apeldoornseweg 450, 6816 SN Arnhem
Tel (085) 421438
Mem 800
Pro JGM Dorrestein, P Coleman (085) 437283
Holes 18 L 6057 m SSS 72
Fees 50fl (70fl)
Loc 5km N of Arnhem on Route N50

Sallandsche 'de Hoek' (1934)

PO Box 24, 7430 AA Diepenveen
Tel (05709) 1214 (Clubhouse)
(05709) 3269 (Sec)
Mem 525
Pro J Balvert (05709) 2774/2705
Holes 18 L 5894 m SSS 71
Fees 50fl (70fl)
Loc 6km N of Deventer

Twentsche (1930)

Enschedesestraat 381, 7552 CV Hengelo
Tel (074) 912773
Mem 400
Pro J Poppe

Holes 9 L 5444 m SSS 69
Fees 25fl (30fl)
Loc 3km SE of Hengelo

Veluwse (1957)

Nr 57, 7346 AC Hoog Soeren
Tel (05769) 1275
Mem 400
Pro S Gilmour
Holes 9 L 6264 yds SSS 70
Fees 60fl (70fl)
Loc 5km W of Apeldoorn

Eindhoven & South East

Berendonck (1987)

Panhuisweg 39, 6603 KH Wijchen
Tel (08894) 20039
Mem 350
Pro A Allen, M Kavanagh
Holes 9 L 5788 m SSS 70
Fees 18 holes-25fl (35fl)
Loc 5km SW of Nijmegen
Mis Public course. WE-comps

Best G & CC

Golflaan 1, 5683 RZ Best
Tel (04998) 96696
Fax (04998) 91443
Holes 18 L 6079 m SSS 72
Fees 50fl (70fl)
Loc Best, 15km NW of Eindhoven

Crossmoor G & CC (1986)

Laurabosweg 8, 6006 VR Weert
Tel (04950) 18438
Mem 600
Pro R Brown, J Loomans
Holes 18 L 6052 m SSS 72
9 hole Par 3 course
Fees 60fl (75fl)
Loc Weert/Altweertheide, 30km SE of Eindhoven

De Dommel (1928)

Zegenwerp 12, 5271 NC St Michielsgestel
Tel (04105) 12316
Mem 475
Pro M Groenendaal
Holes 12 L 5565 m SSS 69
Fees 50fl (70fl)
Loc 10km S of 's-Hertogenbosch

Eindhovensche (1930)

Eindhovenseweg 300, 5553 VB Valkenswaard
Tel (04902) 14816
Mem 700
Pro G Jeurissen, J Renders
Holes 18 L 5897 m SSS 71
Fees 60fl (90fl)
Loc 14km S of Eindhoven

Geysteren G & CC (1974)

Het Spekt 2, 5862 AZ Geysteren
Tel   (04784) 1809/2592
Mem   735
Pro   LG van Mook
Holes   18 L 6063 m SSS 72
Fees   60fl (75fl)
Loc   Off N271, nr Wanssum. 25km
        N of Venlo

Haviksoord (1976)

Maarheezerweg Nrd 11, 5595 XG
Leende (NB)
Tel   (04906) 1818
Mem   350
Holes   9 L 5856 m SSS 71
Fees   25fl (35fl)
Loc   10km S of Eindhoven
Mis   Handicap certificate required

Het Rijk van Nijmegen (1985)

Postweg 17, 6561 KJ Groesbeek
Tel   (08891) 76644
Fax   (08891) 76942
Mem   850
Pro   B Gee, P Hoogkarspel
Holes   18 L 6048 m SSS 72
        9 L 4824 m SSS 66
        9 L 4166 m SSS 62
Fees   50fl (75fl)
Loc   5km E of Nijmegen

De Schoot (1973)

Schootsedijk 18, 5491 TD Sint
Oedenrode
Tel   (04138) 73011
Mem   450
Pro   C Brown
Holes   9 L 2392 m SSS 66
Fees   25fl (30fl)
Loc   20km N of Eindhoven

Tongelreep G & CC (1984)

Velddoornweg 2, 5644 SZ Eindhoven
Tel   (040) 520962
Mem   450
Pro   J Stevens
Holes   9 L 5260 m SSS 68
Fees   25fl (35fl)
Loc   5km S of Eindhoven
Mis   WE-by introduction only.
        Handicap certificate required

Limburg Province

Hoenshuis G & CC (1987)

Hoensweg 17, 6367 GM Voerendaal
Tel   (045) 753300
Mem   600
Pro   R Salmon
Holes   18 L 6118 m SSS 72
Fees   40fl (50fl)
Loc   Limburg, 10km NE of
        Maastricht
Mis   Driving range

Wittem G & CC (1956)

Dalbissenweg 22, 6281 NC
Mechelen
Tel   (04455) 1397
Mem   550
Pro   A Horsman
Holes   9 L 5880 m SSS 71
Fees   35fl (50fl)
Loc   Mechelen, 23km N of
        Maastricht

North

Gelpenberg (1970)

Gebbeveenweg 1, 7854 TD Aalden
Tel   (05917) 1784
Fax   (05917) 2174
Mem   410
Pro   W Stevens (05917) 2174
Holes   9 L 5867 m SSS 71
Fees   50fl (60fl)
Loc   16km W of Emmen

Lauswolt G & CC (1964)

Harinxmaweg 8A,
9244 CH Beetsterzwaag
Tel   (05126) 2594
Mem   450
Pro   J Too
Holes   9 L 5993 m SSS 71
Fees   60fl (80fl)
Loc   Beetsterzwaag, 5km S of
        Drachten

Noord Nederlandse G & CC (1950)

Pollselaan 5, 9756 CJ Glimmen
Tel   (05906) 1275
Mem   750
Pro   KC Visser
Holes   18 L 5680 m SSS 70
Fees   60fl (90fl)
Loc   12km S of Groningen, off A28

Rotterdam & The Hague

Broekpolder (1981)

Watersportweg 100, 3138 HD
Vlaardingen
Tel   (010) 4750011/ 2748140/
        4748142
Mem   860
Pro   J Stoop, J Hage, M Maddison
Holes   18 L 6048 m SSS 72
Fees   35-60fl (50-80fl)
Loc   15km W of Rotterdam, off A20

Haagsche G & CC (1893)

Groot Haesebroekeseweg 22,
2242 EC Wassenaar
Tel   (01751) 79607
Mem   1400

Pro   A Loesberg
Holes   18 L 5674 m SSS 71
Fees   90fl
Loc   6km N of The Hague
Mis   Introduction required-phone

Kleiburg (1974)

c/o Vredenburchlaan 47,
2661 HE Bergenshenhoek
Tel   (01810) 14225
Pro   W Koudijs
Holes   18 L 5534 m SSS 69
Fees   25fl
Loc   25km W of Rotterdam
Mis   Public course

Kralingen (1933)

Kralingseweg 200, 3062 CG
Rotterdam
Tel   (010) 4527646 (Shop)
Mem   325
Pro   R van den Heijkant
Holes   9 L 5277 yds SSS 66
Fees   25fl (30fl)
Loc   5km from centre of Rotterdam

De Merwelanden (1955)

Golfbaan Crayestein, Baanhoekweg
50, 3313 LP Dordrecht
Tel   (078) 211221
Pro   H Kuijsters, C Kuijsters
Holes   9 holes SSS 68
Fees   40fl (47.50fl)
Loc   25km SE of Rotterdam
Mis   Driving range

Noordwijkse (1915)

Randweg 25, PO Box 70,
2200 AB Noordwijk
Tel   (02523) 73761
Mem   900
Pro   T O'Mahoney (02523) 76993
Holes   18 L 6286 m SSS 74
Fees   60fl (80fl)
Loc   5km N of Noordwyk.
        15km NW of Leiden
Mis   Links course

Oude Maas (1975)

Veerweg 2, 3161 EX Rhoon
Tel   (01890) 18058
Pro   R Goor
Holes   9 L 5876 m SSS 71
        9 hole Par 3
Fees   20fl (32fl)
Loc   10km S of Rotterdam
Mis   Public course

Wassenaarse Rozenstein (1984)

Hoge Klei 1, 2242 XZ Wassenaar
Tel   (01751) 17846
Pro   GTG Janmaat
Holes   9 L 6070 m SSS 72
Fees   30fl (60fl)
Loc   14km NE of The Hague
Mis   Driving range, pitch & putt

Zeegersloot (1984)

**Kromme Aarweg 5, PO Box 190,
2400 AD Alphen aan der Rijn**
Tel   (01720) 74567
Fax   (01720) 94660
Mem   1000
Pro   S Muts (01720) 73473
Holes 18 L 5063 m SSS 67
         9 hole Par 3 course
Fees   30fl (40fl) Par 3-15fl (25fl)
Loc   Zegerlake, Alphen. 15km N of
         Gouda. 20km S of Amsterdam

Utrecht & Hilversum

Almeerderhout (1986)

**Watersnipweg 19-21, 1341 AA
Almere**
Tel   (03240) 21818
Pro   G Davidson
Holes 18 L 5896 m SSS 71
         9 hole Par 3
Fees   50fl (70fl)
Loc   30km N of Hilversum
Mis   Driving range

De Haar (1974)

**PO Box 104, Parkweg 5,
3450 AC Vleuten**
Tel   (03407) 2860
Mem   450
Pro   A Saddington, J Saxton
Holes 9 L 6650 yds SSS 72
Fees   100fl (100fl)
Loc   10km NW of Utrecht

Hilversumsche (1910)

**Soestdijkerstraatweg 172,
1213 XJ Hilversum**
Tel   (035) 857060
Mem   730
Pro   M Morbey, R Cattell
Holes 18 L 5856 m SSS 71
Fees   60fl (90fl)
Loc   3km E of Hilversum, nr Baarn
Mis   Phone booking required

Leusdense De Hoge Kleij

Appelweg 4, 3832 Leusden
Tel   (033) 616944
Mem   800
Pro   TJ Giles
Holes 18 L 6053 m SSS 72
Fees   50fl (70fl)
Loc   10km SE of Amersfoort
         20km NE of Utrecht via A28
Mis   WE-max handicap 29

Nieuwegeinse (1985)

Postbus 486, 3430 AL Nieuwegein
Tel   (03402) 40769/42192
Mem   430
Pro   R Visser
Holes 9 L 2348 m SSS 66
Fees   25fl (37.50fl)

Loc   7km S of Utrecht
Mis   Driving range

Utrechtse "De Pan" (1894)

**Amersfoortseweg 1, 3735 LJ Bosch
en Duin**
Tel   (03404) 55223 (Sec)
         (03404) 56225 (Clubhouse)
Mem   800
Pro   C Dorrestein (03404) 56427
Holes 18 L 6073 m SSS 72
Fees   75fl (100fl)
Loc   10km E of Utrecht, off A28
Mis   Advisable to ring first

Zeewolde

Postbus 1461, 1200 BL Hilversum
Tel   (03242) 2103
Mem   900
Pro   P van Wijk, I Flegg
Holes 18 L 5954 m SSS 71
Fees   35-40fl (45-50fl)
Loc   20km N of Hilversum.
         60km NE of Amsterdam

Norway

Bergen (1937)

PO Box 470, 5001 Bergen
Tel   (05) 182077
Mem   300
Pro   S Norris
Holes 9 L 4461 m SSS 66
Fees   D-100kr
Loc   8km N of Bergen

Borregaard (1927)

PO Box 348, 1701 Sarpsborg
Tel   (09) 157401
Mem   500
Pro   F Mudie
Holes 9 L 4500 m SSS 64
Fees   D-100kr
Loc   Opsund, 1km N of Sarpsborg

Hedmark (1980)

PO Box 71, 2401 Elverum
Tel   (064) 13588
Mem   390
Pro   K Dudman
Holes 9 L 2842 m SSS 35
Fees   120kr (120kr)
Loc   Starmoen Fritidspark, 10km E
         of Elverum. 35km E of Hamar.
         150km N of Oslo
Mis   Further 9 holes open Aug 1991

Kjekstad (1976)

PO Box 201, 3440 Royken
Tel   (03) 285850/285353
Mem   1150
Pro   D Craig
Holes 18 L 5100 m SSS 68

Fees   130kr
Loc   40km SW of Oslo. 12km SE of
         Drammen on Route 282

Kristiansand (1973)

PO Box 31, 4601 Kristiansand
Tel   (042) 45863
Mem   350
Pro   D Brough
Holes 9 L 2485 m SSS 70
Fees   100kr
Loc   8km E of K'sand, off E18

Onsoy

Postboks 458, 1601 Fredrikstad
Tel   (09) 333590/333555
Mem   200
Pro   S Meistedt
Holes 18 L 5600 m SSS 72
Fees   D-150kr
Loc   10km W of Fredrikstad. Oslo
         80km

Oslo (1924)

Bogstad, 0757 Oslo 7
Tel   (02) 504402
Fax   (02) 730912
Mem   3200
Pro   S Newey
Holes 18 L 6719 yds SSS 72
Fees   220kr (275kr)
Loc   8km NW of Oslo centre. Follow
         signs to "Bogstad Camping".
Mis   Handicap certificate required
         (men-24 ladies-32). Restricted
         WD-before 2pm WE-after 2pm

Oustoen (1965)

PO Box 82-Ljan, 1113 Oslo
Tel   (472) 535295/486563 (Sec)
Mem   300
Holes 18 L 6200m SSS 71
Fees   200kr
Loc   Small island in Oslofjord,
         10km W of Oslo
Mis   Private club. V'trs must be
         accompanied by a member.

Skjeberg (1986)

**PO Box 149,
         1742 Klavestadhaugen**
Tel   (09) 166310
Mem   450
Pro   G Midtvòge
Holes 18 L 5500 m SSS 73
Fees   D-100kr
Loc   Hevingen, 2km N of Sarpsborg

Stavanger (1956)

Longebakke 45, 4042 Hafrsfjord
Tel   (04) 555431
Mem   850
Pro   R Lees
Holes 18 L 5090 m SSS 68
Fees   165kr (220kr)
Loc   6km SW of Stavanger

Trondheim (1950)

PO Box 169, 7001 Trondheim
Tel   (07) 531885
Mem   330
Pro   T Vollan
Holes   9 L 5632 m SSS 72
Fees   100kr
Loc   Trondheim 3km

Vestfold (1958)

PO Box 64, 3101 Tùnsberg
Tel   (033) 65655 (Sec)
Mem   1050
Pro   G Beal
Holes   18 L 5860 m SSS 72
Fees   D-120kr (180kr)
Loc   Tùnsberg 8km

Portugal

Algarve

Alto do Vale (1990)

Alvor, 8500 Portimão
Tel   (082) 459119
Fax   (082) 459558
Holes   18 L 6648 m SSS 72
Fees   £25
Loc   5km W of Portimão

Palmares

Palmares, Lagos
Tel   (082) 62961/62953
Fax   (082) 62534
Mem   300
Pro   L Espadinha
Holes   18 L 5961 m SSS 72
Fees   6000esc
Loc   Meia Praia, 5km E of Lagos

Parque da Floresta (1987)

Budens, 8650 Vila do Bispo
Tel   (082) 6533/4/5
Holes   18 L 6476 yds SSS 72
Fees   D-4000esc
Loc   16km W of Lagos, nr Salema

Penina (1966)

PO Box 146, Penina, 8502 Portimão
Tel   (082) 415415
Fax   (082) 415000
Mem   220
Pro   R Liddle, J Lourenço
Holes   Ch'ship 18 L 6889 yds SSS 73
    Monchique 9 L 3500 yds SSS
    35; Quinta 9 L 2278 yds SSS 31
Fees   Ch'ship-8500esc. Monchique-
    5000esc. Quinta-4000esc
Loc   5km W of Portimão.
    12km E of Lagos

Pine Cliffs G & CC

Pinhal do Concelho, 8200 Albufeira
Tel   (089) 50884/5
Pro   D Ingram, D Silva
Holes   9 L 2324 m SSS 67
Fees   NA
Loc   7km W of Vilamoura
Mis   Course reserved for property
    owners and Sheraton Hotel
    residents only

Quinta Do Lago (1974)

Quinta Do Lago, 8135 Almancil
Tel   (089) 394782/ 394529/
    396002/3
Fax   (089) 394013
Pro   D Gomes Silva, P Millhouse,
    S Gil, R Valente
Holes   4 x 9 holes:
    A-9 L 3137 m Par 36
    B-9 L 3225 m Par 36
    C-9 L 3263 m Par 36
    D-9 L 3068 m Par 36
Fees   18 holes-10.000esc
Loc   15km W of Faro. Airport 20km
Mis   Driving range

San Lorenzo (1988)

Quinta do Lago, Almancil, 8100
Loulé
Tel   (089) 396522
Pro   B Evans, A Rodrigues
Holes   18 L 6238 m SSS 73
Fees   10.000esc (Limited availability)
Loc   16km W of Faro
Mis   Handicap certificate required

Vale Do Lobo (1968)

Vale Do Lobo, Almancil
Tel   (089) 94444
Mem   500
Pro   D Harding
Holes   27 holes SSS 70-72
    Green 9 L 2813 m Par 35
    Orange 9 L 2975 m Par 36
    Yellow 9 L 3036 m Par 36
Fees   8000esc (Villa guests-50%)
Loc   19km W of Faro. Airport 19km
Mis   27 bay driving range

Vilamoura (1969)

Vilamoura, 8125 Quarteira
Tel   Vilamoura Um (089) 313652
    Vilamoura Dois (089) 315562
    Vilamoura Tres (089) 880722
Mem   300
Pro   J Catarino, C Santos, A Coelho
Holes   Vilamoura Um 18 L 6331 m
    SSS 72;
    Vilamoura Dois 18 L 6192 m
    SSS 71;
    Vilamoura Tres 18 L 5888 m
    SSS 71; 9 L 3146 m
Fees   6500esc (7000esc) (Discounts
    for Vilamoura guests)
Loc   Quarteira, 25km W of Faro

Azores

São Miguel (1961)

PO Box 55, 9501 Ponta Delgada
Tel   (096) 31925/54341
Fax   (096) 34951
Mem   250
Pro   L Indio
Holes   9 L 5910 m SSS 71
Fees   D-2500esc
Loc   São Miguel Island
Mis   Driving range

Terceira Island (1954)

9760 Praia da Vitória
Tel   (095) 25847
Mem   1000
Pro   E Mendes Correia
Holes   18 L 6332 yds SSS 70
Fees   D-US$ 30
Loc   13km from Angra do
    Heroismo, Praia da Vitória and
    Lajes international airport
Mis   Driving range

Lisbon & Central Portugal

Aroeira

Fonte da Telha, 2825 Monte da
Caparica
Tel   (01) 2263244/2261802
Fax   (01) 2261358
Pro   J Moura
Holes   18 L 6040 m SSS 72
Fees   4500esc
Loc   20km S of Lisbon, off Setúbal–
    Costa da Caparica road
Mis   Course reopened 1990 after
    total refurbishment

Estoril (1945)

Avenida República, 2765 Estoril
Tel   (01) 2680176/ 2681376
Mem   800
Pro   J Rodrigues, H Paulino,
    C Aleixo
Holes   18 L 5210 m SSS 68
    9 L 2350 m SSS 65
Fees   4240esc WD only
Loc   N of Estoril on Sintra road.
    30km W of Lisbon
Mis   WE-members only. Driving
    range

International Golf Academy Estoril-Sol (1976)

Quinta do Outeira, Linhó, 2710
Sintra
Tel   (01) 9232461
Mem   150
Pro   M Gallagher, A Dantas Jr
Holes   9 L 4228 m Par 62
Fees   3300esc

Loc   7km N of Estoril. Lisbon 35km
Mis   Extensive practice and training
       facilities

Lisbon Sports Club (1922)

Casal da Carragueira, Belas,
2475 Queluz
Tel   (01) 4310077
Mem   900
Pro   J Baltazar
Holes 18 L 5866 m SSS 68
Fees   D-3500esc (5000esc)
Loc   Belas-Queluz, 20km NW of
       Lisbon

Marinha G & CC (1984)

Quinta da Marinha, 2750 Cascais
Tel   (01) 289881/489901
Mem   500
Pro   A Dantas
Holes 18 L 5606 m SSS 71
Fees   4000esc
Loc   2km W of Cascais.
       32km W of Lisbon
Mis   Driving range

Tróia Golf

Torralta, Tróia, 2900 Setúbal
Tel   (065) 44151/44236
Mem   140
Pro   F Pina
Holes 18 L 6338 m SSS 74
Fees   D-4500esc
Loc   S of Setúbal on Tróia
       peninsula. 50km S of Lisbon

Vimeiro

Praia do Porto Novo, Vimeiro,
2560 Torres Vedras
Tel   (061) 98157
Holes 9 L 2466 m SSS 35
Fees   2000esc
Loc   Vimeiro, 20km N of Torres
       Vedras. 65km N of Lisbon

Madeira

Santo Da Serra (1967)

Sto Antonio da Serra, 9100
Santa Cruz
Tel   (091) 55139
Mem   130
Pro   J de Sousa
Holes 9 L 2622 yds SSS 67
Fees   1500esc
Loc   22km E of Funchal. Airport 6km

North

Estela (1989)

Rio Alto, Estela, 4490 Povoa de
Varzim
Tel   (052) 685567
Mem   400

Pro   CA Agostinho
Holes 18 L 6107 m SSS 73
Fees   4000esc
Loc   7km N of Povoa de Varzim.
       40km N of Oporto (Route 13)

Miramar (1934)

Praia de Miramar, 4405 Valadares
Tel   (02) 7622067
Fax   (02) 7625897
Mem   600
Pro   M Ribeiro, J Couto,
       G Hutchinson
Holes 9 L 2477 m SSS 66
Fees   5000esc
Loc   Miramar, 12km S of Oporto

Oporto (1890)

Sisto-Paramos, 4500 Espinho
Tel   (02) 722008
Fax   (02) 726895
Mem   600
Pro   E Maganinho, J Maganinho
Holes 18 L 5780 m SSS 70
Fees   5000esc
Loc   Espinho, 15km S of Oporto
Mis   Links course

Vidago (1970)

Pavilhão Golf, 5425 Vidago
Tel   (076) 97356
Mem   600
Pro   M Carneiro
Holes 9 L 2449m SSS 64
Fees   D-2500esc (1989)
Loc   50km N of Vila Real.
       130km NE of Oporto

Spain

Alicante & Murcia

Don Cayo (1974)

Conde de Altea 49, Altea
Tel   (96) 584 07 16/584 80 46
Pro   G Sanz
Holes 9 L 6044 m SSS 72
Fees   D-2800P
Loc   4km N of Altea

Ifach (1974)

Crta Moraira-Calpe Km 3,
Urb San Jaime, Benisa
Holes 9 L 3408 m SSS 59
Fees   2500P D-3000P
Loc   13km N of Calpe. 5km W of
       Moraira

Jávea (1981)

Ctra Benitachell Km4, Jávea
Tel   (96) 579 25 84/579 18 13
Mem   650

Pro   J-A Moyano, J-M Carriles
Holes 9 L 6070 m SSS 72
Fees   D-4000P
Loc   Lluca, Jávea. 80km NE of
       Alicante

La Manga (1971)

30385 Los Belones, Cartagena
Tel   (968) 56 45 11
Mem   2000
Pro   J Weir, J Mellado, V Ballesteros
Holes North 18 L 5873 m SSS 72
       South 18 L 6238 m SSS 73
       Atamaria 9 L 5118 m SSS 67
Fees   D-4600P (Residents)
Loc   30km NE of Cartagena, nr
       Murcia airport

Quesada (1989)

Avda de las Naciones 168, 03170
Rojales (Alicante)
Tel   (96) 572 21 79/572 21 81
Fax   (96) 572 21 74
Pro   G Sanz
Holes 18 L 6050 m Par 72
Loc   Rojales, 40km S of Alicante

Villa Martín (1972)

Apartado 35, Torrevieja
Tel   (965) 32 03 50 54 58
Pro   E Pareja
Holes 18 L 5899 m SSS 72
Fees   3500P
Loc   8km S of Torrevieja

Almería

Almerimar (1976)

Urb Almerimar, 04700 El Ejido
Tel   (951) 48 02 34
Fax   (951) 48 43 33
Pro   J Parrón
Holes 18 L 5928 m SSS 72
Fees   5500P W-27.500P
Loc   35km W of Almería

Cortijo Grande (1976)

Apdo 2, Cortijo Grande, 04630
Turre
Tel   (51) 47 91 64/47 91 76
Mem   72
Holes 9 holes open 1990
Fees   D-2000P
Loc   20km W of Turre. 85km N of
       Almería, nr Mojácar

Playa Serena (1979)

Urb Playa Serena, Roquetas de Mar
Tel   (951) 33 30 55
Mem   300
Pro   F Parrón
Holes 18 L 6301 m SSS 72
Fees   D-4800P
Loc   20km S of Almería

For list of abbreviations see page 487.

Balearic Islands

Canyamel

Urb Canyamel, Crta de Cuevas,
07580 Capdepera, Mallorca
Tel   (971) 56 44 57
Holes   18 L 6115 m SSS 72
Fees   4800P
Loc   70km NE of Palma, nr Cala
          Ratjada

Pollensa (1984)

Predio Son Porquer, Ctra Palma-
Pollensa Km 49, Apdo No 9,
Mallorca
Tel   (971) 53 32 16
Fax   (971) 53 32 65
Mem   231
Pro   C Insua
Holes   9 L 5304 m SSS 70
Fees   4600P
Loc   Pollensa, 50km N of Palma

Poniente (1978)

Costa de Calvia, Mallorca
Tel   (971) 68 10 48
Fax   (971) 68 01 48
Mem   100
Pro   B Salter, P Ruiz, P Rodriguez
Holes   18 L 6430 m SSS 72
Fees   5700P
Loc   12km SW of Palma towards
          Cala Figuera
Mis   Driving range

Real Golf Bendinat (1986)

C. Campoamor, 07184 Calvia,
Mallorca
Tel   (971) 40 52 00
Fax   (971) 70 07 86
Mem   400
Pro   R Galiano
Holes   9 L 2327 m SSS 66
Fees   D-4600P
Loc   7km W of Palma centre

Real Golf de Menorca (1976)

Apartado 97, Mahón, Menorca
Tel   (971) 36 39 00
Mem   350
Pro   J Tollegrosa
Holes   9 L 5724 m SSS 70
Loc   7km N of Mahón

Roca Llisa (1971)

Apartado 200, Ibiza
Tel   (971) 31 97 18
Mem   500
Pro   G Castillo
Holes   9 L 5902 m SSS 70
Fees   4000P
Loc   8km NE of Ibiza town, towards
          Cala Llonga

Santa Ponsa (1976)

Santa Ponsa, Mallorca
Tel   (971) 69 02 11/69 08 00
Mem   350
Pro   S Bruna
Holes   18 L 6520 m SSS 74
Fees   4800P
Loc   18km W of Palma
Mis   Hotel guests 50% discount

Son Parc (1977)

Apdo 634, Mahón, Menorca
Tel   (971) 36 88 06
Mem   300
Holes   9 L 2746 m SSS 69
Fees   D-3800P
Loc   Mercadel, 18km N of Mahón

Son Servera (1967)

07559 Costa de Los Pinos, Son
Servera, Mallorca
Tel   (971) 56 78 02
Fax   (971) 56 81 46
Mem   312
Pro   S Sota
Holes   9 L 5956 m SSS 72
Fees   D-3600P
Loc   Son Servera, 64km E of
          Palma

Son Vida (1964)

Son Vida, 07013 Palma de Mallorca
Tel   (971) 23 76 20
Mem   500
Pro   F Fuentes
Holes   18 L 5414 m SSS 68
Fees   4000P
Loc   5km NW of Palma

Vall D'Or (1986)

Apdo 23, 07660 Cala D'Or,
Mallorca
Tel   (971) 83 70 01/83 70 68
Fax   (971) 83 72 99
Mem   130
Pro   A González
Holes   9 L 5462 m SSS 70
Fees   4500P
Loc   60km E of Palma, between
          Cala D'Or and Porto Colón
Mis   Extension to 18 holes in 1991

Barcelona & Cataluña

Bonmont-Terres Noves (1990)

43300 Mont-Roig del Camp
(Tarragona)
Tel   (977) 837021
Fax   (977) 837077
Holes   18 L 6355 m Par 72
Loc   S of Tarragona

Costa Brava (1962)

Santa Cristina d'Aro, Girona
Tel   (972) 83 71 50
Fax   (972) 83 72 72
Mem   740
Pro   M Gil
Holes   18 L 5558 m SSS 71
Fees   Summer-6600P Winter-5000-
          6000P
Loc   Playa de Aro 5km. 30km SE of
          Girona

Costa Dorada (1983)

Apartado 600, Tarragona
Tel   (977) 65 33 61
Pro   F Jimenez
Holes   9 L 5944 m SSS 73
Loc   Tarragona

Llavaneras (1945)

Camino del Golf, 08392 Sant Andreu
Llavaneres
Tel   (93) 792 60 50
Mem   975
Pro   F González, J Bertrán, J Pérez,
          J González
Holes   9 L 4298 m SSS 63
Fees   4000P (6000P)
Loc   Sant Andreu, 4km N of Mataró.
          34km N of Barcelona
Mis   Extension to 18 holes in 1991

Mas Nou (1987)

Urb Mas Nou, 17250 Playa de Aro
Tel   (972) 82 60 84/82 61 18
Fax   (972) 82 61 17
Mem   130
Pro   I Torrado, P Martínez
Holes   18 L 6218 m SSS 72
          9 hole Par 3 course
Fees   5000P (6500P)
Loc   35km SE of Gerona on Costa
          Brava
Mis   Driving range

Pals

Pals, Gerona
Tel   (972) 63 60 06
Fax   (972) 63 70 09
Mem   750
Pro   J Anglada, J Riera, J Romero,
          J Portell
Holes   18 L 6222 m SSS 72
Fees   D-4500-8500P
Loc   40km E of Gerona.
          135km NE of Barcelona

Real Golf "El Prat" (1956)

8820 El Prat de Llobregat
Tel   (93) 379 02 78
Mem   2200
Pro   P Marin, M Rodriguez
Holes   3 x 9 holes 5944-6256 m SSS
          72-74
Fees   3640P (6048P)
Loc   El Prat, Airport 3km. 15km S of
          Barcelona

For list of abbreviations see page 487.

Real Golf de Cerdaña (1929)

Apdo 63, Puigcerdá (Gerona)
Tel   (972) 88 13 38/88 09 50
Mem   300
Pro   S Diaz
Holes   18 L 5735 m SSS 70
Loc   Cerdaña, 1km from Puigcerdá.

Reus Aiguesverds (1989)

Crta Cambrils, Mas Guardià, 43206 Reus
Tel   (977) 75 27 25
Mem   350
Pro   J Cruz
Holes   18 L 6905 yds SSS 74
Fees   4000P-5000P (5000P-6000P)
Loc   10km W of Tarragona

Sant Cugat (1914)

08190 Sant Cugat del Valles
Tel   (93) 674 39 08/674 39 58
Mem   1500
Pro   A Demelo
Holes   18 L 5209 m SSS 68
Fees   3500P (7000P)
Loc   20km NW of Barcelona

Terramar (1922)

Apdo 6, 08870 Sitges
Tel   (93) 894 05 80/894 20 43
Fax   (93) 894 70 51
Mem   990
Pro   S Perez, J Hernández, A Barra
Holes   18 L 5578 m SSS 70
Fees   3200-5400P
Loc   Sitges, 37km S of Barcelona.
    Tarragona 60km

Vallromanes (1969)

C/Afveras, 08188 Vallromanes
Tel   (93) 568 03 62
Mem   1200
Pro   J Gallardo
Holes   18 L 6038 m SSS 72
Fees   D-3500P (6700P)
Loc   23km N of Barcelona between
    Alella and Granollers.
    A7 Junction 13/A19 Junction 5

Canary Islands

Costa Teguise (1978)

Lanzarote
Tel   (928) 81 35 12
Fax   (928) 81 34 90
Pro   NG Perez
Holes   18 L 5853 m SSS 72
Fees   5000P
Loc   7km N of Arrecife
Mis   Driving range

Golf del Sur (1987)

San Miguel de Abona, Tenerife
Tel   (922) 70 45 55
Pro   J Golding, M Golding
Holes   North 9 L 2510 m SSS 36
    Links 9 L 2308 m SSS 35
    South course SSS 36
Fees   18 holes 4000P
    9 holes 2000P
Loc   Tenerife Sur airport 3km

Maspalomas (1968)

Av de Africa, Maspalomas, 35100 Las Palmas de Gran Canaria
Tel   (928) 76 25 81/76 73 43
Fax   (928) 76 82 45
Pro   A Gutierrez
Holes   18 L 6216 m SSS 72
Fees   6000P
Loc   S coast of Gran Canaria

Real Golf de Las Palmas (1891)

PO Box 183, 35000 Las Palmas de Gran Canaria
Tel   (928) 35 10 50/35 01 04
Fax   (928) 35 01 10
Mem   750
Pro   F Santana, E Perera, S Sanchez
    F Santana, F Fleitas
Holes   18 L 5690 m SSS 71
Fees   WD-4500P WE-NA
Loc   Bandama, 14km Las Palmas
Mis   Driving range, pitch & putt

Tenerife (1932)

El Peñón, Tacoronte, Tenerife
Tel   (922) 25 02 40/25 10 48
Mem   626
Pro   G Gonzalez
Holes   18 L 5397 m SSS 68
Fees   3500P WD only
Loc   N of island, 10 mins from Santa
    Cruz

Córdoba

Pozoblanco (1984)

San Gregorio 2, Pozoblanco, (Córdoba)
Tel   (957) 10 02 39/10 00 06
Holes   9 L 3660 m SSS 62
Loc   Pozoblanco 3km

Los Villares (1976)

Avda del Generalismo 1-2, PO Box 463, Córdoba
Tel   (957) 35 02 08
Mem   404
Pro   JM Carriles
Holes   18 L 6087 m SSS 72
Fees   2000P
Loc   9km N of Córdoba, towards
    Obejo

Galicia

Aero Club de Santiago (1976)

General Pardiñas 34, Santiago de Compostela (La Coruña)
Tel   (981) 59 24 00
Pro   J Ybarra
Holes   9 L 6151 m SSS 72
Fees   2500P
Loc   Santiago Airport

Aero Club de Vigo (1951)

Reconquista 7, Vigo
Tel   (986) 22 11 60/24 24 93
Pro   DS Roman
Holes   9 L 5734 m SSS 70
Loc   Peinador Airport, 8km from
    Vigo

La Coruña (1962)

Apartado 737, 15080 La Coruña
Tel   (981) 28 52 00
Mem   1500
Pro   J Santiago
Holes   18 L 5782 m SSS 72
Fees   2000P
Loc   Arteijo, 7km SW of La Coruña

La Toja (1970)

Isla de La Toja, El Grove, Pontevedra
Tel   (986) 73 07 26/73 08 18
Mem   450
Pro   P Medrano
Holes   9 L 6046 m SSS 72
Fees   4000-7000P
Loc   La Toja island. 30km W of
    Pontevedra

Málaga Region

Añoreta (1990)

Urb Añoreta Golf, 29730 Rincón de la Victoria
Tel   (952) 40 50 00
Fax   (952) 40 40 50
Pro   JA Gómez
Holes   18 holes Par 72
Loc   Málaga 12km

El Candado (1965)

Urb El Candado, El Palo, Málaga
Tel   (952) 29 46 66
Pro   M Lucas
Holes   9 L 4508 m SSS 65
Loc   El Palo, 5km E of Málaga on
    Route N340

Málaga Club de Campo (1925)

Apartado 324, Málaga
Tel   (952) 38 12 55
Fax   (952) 38 21 41
Mem   550
Pro   J Sanchez
Holes 18 L 6249 m SSS 72
Fees   4000P
Loc   Torremolinos 4km.
        12km S of Málaga, nr Airport
Mis   Parador guests 50% reduction

Mijas (1976)

Apartado 138, Fuengirola, Málaga
Tel   (957) 47 68 43
Pro   J Rosa
Holes Los Lagos 18 L 6348 m SSS 73
        Los Olivos 18 L 5896 m SSS 71
Fees   D-3500P
Loc   4km NW of Fuengirola
Mis   Handicap certificate required

Los Moriscos (1974)

C.Recogidas, 18005 Granada
Tel   (958) 60 04 12
Pro   V Carralero
Holes 9 L 5702 m SSS 71
Fees   D-1800P
Loc   8km W of Motril, nr Salobrena.
        80km E of Málaga

Nerja G & CC

PO Box 154, Nerja, Málaga
Tel   (952) 52 02 08
Pro   A Carsin
Holes 9 L 3000 m SSS 59
Loc   1km E of Nerja on motorway
        Málaga-Almería

La Siesta

Sitio de Calahonda, Mijas-Costa
(Málaga)
Tel   (952) 83 63 70
Pro   M Cabanillas
Holes 9 hole Par 3 course
Loc   20km E of Málaga
Mis   Driving range

Torrequebrada (1977)

Apdo 67, 29630 Benalmadena-Costa
Tel   (52) 44 27 42/56 11 02
Pro   J Jiménez
Holes 18 L 5860 m SSS 72
Fees   5500-6500P W-29000-34000P
Loc   18km S of Málaga

Madrid Region

Barberán (1967)

Apartado 150.239, Cuatro Vientos,
Madrid
Tel   (91) 218 85 05
Pro   V Hernandez
Holes 9 L 6127 m SSS 72
Loc   Madrid 10km

Las Encinas de Boadilla (1984)

Crta Boadilla-Pozuelo Km 1400,
Boadilla del Monte, Madrid
Tel   (91) 633 11 00
Mem   400
Pro   A Gomez
Holes 9 L 1464 m SSS 50
Fees   700P (2300P)
Loc   Pozuelo, 12km W of Madrid

Herreria (1966)

PO Box 28200, San Lorenzo del
Escorial, (Madrid)
Tel   (91) 890 51 11/890 52 44
Mem   3500
Pro   M Aparicio
Holes 18 L 6015 m SSS 72
Fees   3500P (5500P)
Loc   Escorial, 50km W of Madrid

Lomas-Bosque (1973)

Urb El Bosque, Villaviciosa de
Odón, (Madrid)
Tel   (91) 616 75 00
Mem   460
Pro   M Alvárez
Holes 27 L 6075 m SSS 72
Fees   4000P (8000P)
Loc   Madrid 20km

La Moraleja (1976)

La Moraleja, Alcobendas (Madrid)
Tel   (91) 650 07 00
Mem   600
Pro   V Barrios, M Montes
Holes 18 L 5617 m SSS 69
Fees   2500P (3000P)
Loc   9km N of Madrid on Burgos
        road

Nuevo De Madrid (1972)

Las Matas (Madrid)
Tel   (91) 630 08 20
Pro   J Marimon
Holes 18 L 6037 m SSS 72
Loc   18km NW of Madrid on La
        Coruña road

Puerta de Hierro (1904)

28305 Madrid
Tel   (91) 216 1745
Mem   1442
Pro   J Gallardo, J Benito
Holes 18 L 6347 m SSS 73
Fees   2000P (3000P)
Loc   4km N of Madrid on Route VI
Mis   V'trs must be accompanied by
        a member

Real Automovil Club de España (1967)

José Abascal 10, 28003 Madrid
Tel   (91) 657 00 01
Mem   3200
Pro   F Alvarez, J Alvarez,
        F Valera

Holes 18 L 6505 m SSS 72
        09 hole Par 3 course
Fees   3000P (7000P)
Loc   San Sebastián de los Reyes,
        28km N of Madrid on Burgos
        road

Somosaguas (1971)

Somosaguas, 28011 Madrid
Tel   (91) 212 16 47
Pro   M Cabrera, A Garrido
Holes 9 L 5621 m SSS 69
Fees   2000P (3000P)
Loc   Somosaguas

Valdelaguila (1975)

Apdo 9, Alcalá de Henares,
Madrid
Tel   (91) 885 96 59
Pro   A Puebla
Holes 9 L 5714 m SSS 70
Fees   D-1000P (1500P)
Loc   8km S of Alcalá

Villa de Madrid CC (1984)

Crta Castilla, 28040 Madrid
Tel   (91) 207 03 95
Mem   3500
Pro   M Morcillo
Holes 27 L 6118 m SSS 73
Fees   1800P (3600P)
Loc   4km NW of Madrid, in the
        Casa de Campo
Mis   Municipal club from 1984.
        Course built 1932.

Marbella & Estepona

Aloha (1975)

29660 Nueva Andalucía, Málaga
Tel   (952) 81 08 76/81 37 50
        81 23 88 (Caddymaster)
Fax   (952) 81 08 76
Mem   1500
Pro   JL Mangas (952) 81 47 55
Holes 18 L 6261 m SSS 72
        9 hole short course
Fees   10.000P
Loc   8km S of Marbella, nr Puerto
        Banus

Atalaya Park G & CC (1968)

Crta Benahavis, Estepona, Marbella
Tel   (952) 78 18 94
Mem   500
Pro   D Strachan
Holes 18 L 6212 m SSS 72
Fees   7000P
Loc   Between Marbella/Estepona.
        60km SW of Málaga
Mis   Hotel guests 50% discount.

Las Brisas (1968)

Apdo 147, Urb Nueva Andalucía,
Marbella
Tel   (952) 81 08 75/81 30 21
Fax   (952) 81 55 18
Mem   1250
Pro   S Miguel
Holes   18 L 6198 m SSS 73
Fees   9000P
Loc   8km S of Marbella, nr Puerto
        Banus

La Duquesa G & CC (1987)

Urb El Hacho, Manilva, Málaga
Tel   (952) 89 04 25/89 04 26
Mem   400
Pro   JM Canizares, S Ruiz
Holes   18 L 6142 m SSS 72
Fees   5000P
Loc   10km S of Estepona

Guadalmina (1959)

Guadalmina Alta, San Pedro de
Alcántara, Marbella
Tel   (952) 78 13 17
Mem   3000
Pro   A Hernandez, F Hernandez
Holes   18 L 6060 m SSS 72
        18 L 6200 m SSS 72
        9 L 1005 m Par 27
Fees   6000P
Loc   San Pedro, 12km S of Málaga
Mis   Driving range

Los Naranjos (1977)

Apdo 64, 29660 Nueva Andalucía,
Marbella
Tel   (952) 81 52 06/81 36 59
Fax   (952) 81 14 28
Pro   M Escudero
Holes   18 L 6484 m SSS 75
Fees   D-9000P
Loc   8km S of Marbella, nr Puerto
        Banus

El Paraiso (1974)

Ctra Cádiz-Málaga Km 167,
Estepona, Marbella
Tel   (952) 78 47 12/78 47 16
Mem   750
Pro   J Franco
Holes   18 L 6142 m SSS 73
Fees   D-7000P
Loc   14km S of Marbella

La Quinta (1989)

Crta de Ronda, Marbella
Tel   (952) 78 38 16/78 38 50
Mem   200
Pro   M Pinero, J Pinero, D Morito
Holes   18 L 5700 m SSS 71
Fees   8000P
Loc   4km N of San Pedro de
        Alcántara

Rio Real (1965)

Apdo 82, Marbella
Tel   (952) 77 17 00 (Ext 3086)
Fax   (952) 77 04 72
Pro   A Miguel
Holes   18 L 6130 m SSS 72
Fees   D-7500P
Loc   Marbella 5km

San Roque (1990)

PO Box 127, San Roque, 11360 Cádiz
Tel   (956) 61 06 49/61 04 27
Fax   (956) 78 04 30
Holes   18 L 6440 m SSS 74
Fees   6000-8000P
Loc   15km E of Gibraltar

Sotogrande (1964)

Paseo del Parque, Sotogrande,
Cádiz
Tel   (956) 79 20 50/79 20 51
Mem   1000
Pro   T Gonzalez, J Quiros
Holes   18 L 5885 m SSS 72
        18 L 6263 m SSS 72
        9 L 1299 m SSS 29
Fees   8000P (10000P)
Loc   30km N of Gibraltar, nr
        Guadiaro

Valderrama (1985)

Sotogrande, Cádiz
Tel   (956) 79 27 75
Mem   112
Pro   J Zumaquero
Holes   18 L 6326 m SSS 72
Fees   D-7000P
Loc   30km N of Gibraltar, nr
        Guadiaro

North Coast

Barganiza (1982)

Apartado 277, 33080 Oviedo,
Asturias
Tel   (985) 74 24 68
Mem   580
Pro   M Bellido
Holes   18 L 5298 m SSS 69
Fees   5000P
Loc   12km N of Oviedo on Gijon old
        road

Castiello (1958)

Apartado de Correos, 161 Gijón
Tel   (985) 36 63 13
Mem   450
Pro   A Sierra
Holes   18 L 4817 m SSS 67
Fees   2000P
Loc   5km S of Gijón on Oviedo old
        road
Mis   WE-comps during summer

Laukariz (1976)

Laukariz, Munguía, Vizcaya
Tel   (94) 674 08 58/674 04 62
Pro   F García, S Larrázabal,
        E Garaizar
Holes   18 L 6112 m SSS 72
Fees   D-4000P
Loc   15km N of Bilbao towards
        Mungía

Real Golf de Neguri (1911)

Apdo Correos 9, 49990 Algorta
Tel   (94) 469 02 00/04/08
Mem   2500
Pro   C Celles, L Losada, JM Fuente,
        R Larrazabal
Holes   18 L 6319 m SSS 72
        6 hole Par 3 course
Fees   4000P
Loc   La Galea, 20km N of Bilbao

Real Golf de Pedreña (1928)

Apartado 233, Santander
Tel   (942) 50 00 01/50 02 66
Mem   1050
Pro   R Sota
Holes   18 L 5721 m SSS 70
Fees   5000P
Loc   20km from Santander, on Bay
        of Santander

Real San Sebastián (1910)

PO Box 6, Fuenterrabia, Guipúzcoa
Tel   (943) 61 68 45/61 68 46
Mem   2500
Pro   Jesús Arruti, José Arruti,
        J Gorostegui
Holes   18 L 6020 m SSS 71
Fees   5000P
Loc   Jaizubia Valley, 14km NE of
        San Sebastián

Real Zarauz (1916)

Apartado 82, Zarauz, Guipúzcoa
Tel   (943) 83 01 45
Mem   1100
Pro   N Belartieta, B Celles
Holes   9 L 4882 m SSS 67
Fees   D-2000-4000P
Loc   Zarauz, 25km W of San
        Sebastián

Pamplona

Ulzama (1965)

Guerendiain (Navarra)
Tel   (948) 30 51 62
Pro   R Echeverría
Holes   9 L 5984 m SSS 71
Loc   21km N of Pamplona

Seville & Gulf of Cádiz

Bellavista (1976)

Crta Huelva-Punta Umbría, Apdo 335, Huelva
Tel   (955) 31 90 17
Fax   (955) 31 90 25
Mem   700
Pro   M Sanchez
Holes   9 L 6252 m SSS 72
Fees   3500-5000P
Loc   Aljaraque, 6km SW of Huelva, towards Punta Umbria

Pineda De Sevilla (1939)

Apartado 796, Sevilla
Tel   (954) 61 14 00/61 33 99
Pro   P Garrido, L González
Holes   9 L 5684 m SSS 71
Fees   1300P (2000P)
Loc   3km S of Seville on Cádiz road

Vista Hermosa (1975)

Apartado 77, Urb Vista Hermosa, Puerto de Santa María, Cádiz
Tel   (956) 85 00 11/85 66 26
Mem   1300
Pro   M Velasco
Holes   9 L 5492 m SSS 70
Fees   4000-8000P
Loc   25km W of Cádiz

Valencia & Castellón

El Bosque (1989)

Crta Godelleta, 46370 Chiva
Tel   (96) 251 10 11
Fax   (96) 251 10 09
Mem   400
Pro   A Pinto
Holes   18 L 6367 m SSS 74
Fees   4000P (4000P)
Loc   Nr Chiva, 24km W of Valencia, off Madrid road

Costa De Azahar (1960)

Ctra Grao-Benicasim, Castellón de la Plana
Tel   (964) 22 70 64
Mem   600
Pro   A Sanchez
Holes   9 L 2724 m SSS 70
Fees   D-2000P W-8000P
Loc   5km NE of Castellón, on coast

Escorpión (1975)

Apartado Correos 1, Betera (Valencia)
Tel   (96) 160 12 11
Mem   1400
Pro   A Sanchez, J Rodriguez, P Contreras
Holes   18 L 6345 m SSS 73
Fees   3000P (5000P)
Loc   Betera, 20km N of Valencia

Manises (1964)

Apartado 22.029, Manises (Valencia)
Tel   (96) 379 08 50
Mem   110
Pro   FE Pinto
Holes   9 L 2607 m Par 72
Loc   8km W of Valencia

Mediterraneo CC (1978)

Urb La Coma, Borriol, (Castellón)
Tel   (964) 32 12 27
Mem   1300
Pro   V Garcia, JR López
Holes   18 L 6038 m SSS 72
Fees   3500-4500P (4500-5000P)
Loc   Borriol, 5km NW of Castellón

El Saler (1968)

Parador Luis Vives, 46012 El Saler (Valencia)
Tel   (96) 161 11 86
Mem   700
Pro   JA Cabo
Holes   18 L 6485 m SSS 75
Fees   D-4500P W-21750P
Loc   Oliva, 18km S of Valencia, towards Cullera

Zaragoza

Aero Club de Zaragoza (1966)

Coso 34, Zaragoza
Tel   (976) 21 43 78
Holes   9 L 4953 m SSS 66
Fees   2000P (3000P)
Loc   12km SW of Zaragoza, by airbase

La Penaza (1973)

Apartado 3039, Zaragoza
Tel   (976) 34 28 00/34 22 48
Mem   850
Pro   F Pino, P García, MA Giménez
Holes   18 L 6161 m SSS 72
Fees   D-4480P (5600P)
Loc   15km SW of Zaragoza on Madrid road, nr airbase

Sweden

East Central

Ängsö (1979)

Skultunavägen 7, 722 17 Västerås
Tel   (0171) 41012
Mem   1075
Pro   P Gullberg
Holes   18 holes SSS 72
Fees   100kr (140kr)
Loc   15km E of Västerås

Ärila (1951)

Nicolai, 611 92 Nyköping
Tel   (0155) 14967
Mem   1400
Pro   O Jansson
Holes   18 L 5735 m SSS 72
Fees   140kr
Loc   5km SE of Nyköping

Askersund (1980)

69603 Ammeberg
Tel   (0583) 34440
Mem   980
Pro   L Johansson
Holes   18 L 5800 m SSS 72
Fees   150kr
Loc   10km SE of Askersund towards Ammeberg. 1km on road to Kärra

Enköping (1970)

Box 206, 199 02 Enköping
Tel   (0171) 20830
Mem   1200
Pro   P Karlsson
Holes   18 L 5660 m SSS 71
Fees   120kr (200kr)
Loc   3km E of Enköping, off E18

Eskilstuna (1951)

Strängnäsvägen, 633 49 Eskilstuna
Tel   (016) 142629
Mem   950
Pro   A Robinson
Holes   18 L 5610 m SSS 70
Fees   100kr (120kr)

Fagersta (1970)

Box 2051, 737 02 Fagersta
Tel   (0223) 54060
Mem   1000
Holes   9 L 5775 m SSS 72
Fees   70kr (1990)
Loc   7km W of Fagersta (Route 65). 70km N of Västerås

Katrineholm (1959)

Box 74, 641 21 Katrineholm
Tel   (0150) 39011/39012
Mem   950
Pro   S Eriksson
Holes   18 L 5850 m SSS 72
Fees   140kr
Loc   7km E of Katrineholm

Korslöt (1963)

Box 278, 731 26 Köping
Tel   (46221) 81090
Mem   950
Pro   B Malmquist
Holes   18 L 5636 m SSS 71
Fees   80kr (110kr)
Loc   5km N of Köping (Route 250)

Linde (1984)

Dalkarlshyttan, 711 31 Lindesberg
Tel   (0581) 13960
Mem   1040
Pro   J Blom
Holes   18 L 5539 m SSS 71
Fees   100kr (120kr)
Loc   42km N of Örebro on R60.
    Lindesberg 1½ km

Örebro (1939)

Lanna, 710 15 Vintrosa
Tel   (019) 91065
Mem   1160
Holes   18 L 5865 m SSS 72
Fees   200kr
Loc   20km W of Örebro on
    Route E18
Mis   6 hole pitch & putt

Roslagen

Box 110, 761 22 Norrtälje
Tel   (0176) 37194
Fax   (0176) 37103
Mem   1200
Pro   L Modin
Holes   18 L 5512 m SSS 71
    9 hole course
Fees   150kr (200kr)
Loc   7km N of Norrtälje

Sala (1970)

Box 16, 733 21 Sala
Tel   (0224) 53077/53055/53064
Mem   920
Pro   T Borgling
Holes   18 L 5570 m SSS 71
Fees   100kr
Loc   Fallet Sala, 8km E of Sala
    towards Uppsala, Route 67/72

Sigtunabygden (1961)

Box 89, 193 00 Sigtuna
Tel   (0760) 54012
Mem   1070
Pro   H Reis
Holes   18 L 5740 m SSS 72
Fees   130kr (200kr)
Loc   Arlanda, 50km N of Stockholm

Södertälje (1952)

Box 91, 151 21 Södertälje
Tel   (0755) 38240
Mem   1100
Pro   B Tomlinson (0755) 47674
Holes   18 L 5875 m SSS 72
Fees   150kr (200kr)
Loc   4km W of Södertälje

Stjernfors (1973)

c/o Hagabacksvej 4, 717 00 Storå
Tel   (0580) 41048
Mem   520
Holes   10 L 5548 m SSS 70
Fees   70kr
Loc   5km S of Kopparberg

Strängnäs (1968)

Box 21, 645 21 Strängnäs
Tel   (0152) 14731
Mem   1000
Pro   K Jansson (0152) 14702
Holes   18 L 5790 m SSS 72
Fees   120kr (170kr)
Loc   3km S of Strängnäs

Torshalla (1960)

PO Box 587, 631 08 Eskilstuna
Tel   (016) 358722/356782
Mem   625
Holes   9 L 5869 m SSS 72
Fees   100kr (150kr)
Loc   Torshälla 2km

Trosa-Vagnhärad (1972)

Box 80, 619 00 Trosa
Tel   (0156) 22211/17617
Mem   788
Pro   C Rose
Holes   9 L 5860 m SSS 72
Fees   90kr
Loc   5km W of Trosa, towards
    Uttervik
Mis   Extension to 18 holes 1991

Upsala (1937)

Box 12015, 750 12 Uppsala
Tel   (018) 462580
Mem   1790
Pro   (018) 461241
Holes   18 L 6176 m SSS 74
    9 L 1643 m SSS 56
Fees   150kr (220kr)
Loc   10km W of Uppsala
Mis   Driving range

Västerås (1931)

Bjärby, 724 81 Västerås
Tel   (021) 357543
Fax   (021) 357573
Mem   1400
Pro   T Ljungqvist
Holes   18 L 5380 m SSS 69
Fees   100kr (150kr)
Loc   2km N of Västerås

Far North

Boden (1946)

Box 107, 961 21 Boden
Tel   (0921) 61071
Mem   355
Pro   J Gidlund
Holes   9 L 5796 m SSS 73
Fees   50kr
Loc   17km SW of Boden

Gällivare-Malmberget (1973)

Box 52, 982 21 Gällivare
Tel   (0970) 10660
Mem   1965
Pro   P Mattsson
Holes   9 L 5270 m SSS 70
Fees   50kr
Loc   4km N of Gällivare, towards
    Malmberget

Härjedalsfjällen (1972)

Vintergatan 5, 820 95 Funäsdalen
Tel   (0684) 21240
Mem   520
Pro   V Agardh
Holes   18 L 5300 m SSS 72
Fees   100kr
Loc   Nr Norwegian border

Härnösand (1957)

Box 52, 871 22 Härnösand
Tel   (0611) 66169
Mem   1250
Pro   F Guedra
Holes   18 L 5265 m SSS 69
Fees   100kr
Loc   Vängnön, 12km N of
    Härnösand on E4

Luleå (1955)

Box 314, 95125 Luleå
Tel   (0920) 56091/56174
Mem   1100
Pro   L Stewart
Holes   18 L 5675 m SSS 72
Fees   100kr
Loc   Rutvik, 12km E of Luleå

Östersund-Frösö (1947)

Box 40, 83201 Frösön
Tel   (063) 43001
Mem   1300
Pro   G Knutsson
Holes   18 L 6000 m SSS 73
Fees   100kr
Loc   Island of Frösö
Mis   Open May-Sept

Öviks GC Puttom (1967)

Idrottens Hus, 891 32 Örnsköldsvik
Tel   (0660) 82488/64091
Mem   1400
Pro   T Mogren (0660) 64080
Holes   18 L 5795 m SSS 72
Fees   120kr
Loc   15km N of Örnsköldsvik on E4
Mis   Season Jun-Sept

Piteå (1960)

Nötön, 94190 Piteå
Tel   (0911) 14990
Mem   520
Pro   A Gillard
Holes   9 L 5905 m SSS 72
Fees   50kr
Loc   2km NE of Piteå
Mis   Midnight sun golf Jun/Jul

Skellefteå (1967)

Box 152, 931 22 Skellefteå
Tel   (0910) 79333/79866
Mem   1081
Pro   N Fosker, S Skinner
Holes   18 L 6135 m SSS 73
Fees   120kr
Loc   Skellefteå 5km

Sollefteå-Långsele (1970)

Box 213, 881 01 Sollefteå
Tel   (0620) 21477
Mem   712
Holes   18 L 5890 m SSS 72
Fees   80kr
Loc   Österforse, 15km SW of
        Sollefteå (Route 89)

Sundsvall (1952)

Roddvägen 31, 862 00 Kvissleby
Tel   (060) 561020
Mem   825
Pro   T Bjornsson
Holes   18 L 5885 m SSS 72
Fees   100kr
Loc   Skottsund, 15km S of Sundsvall

Timrå

Box 17, 860 32 Fagervik
Tel   (060) 570153
Mem   960
Pro   G Campbell (060) 579263
Holes   18 L 5715 m SSS 72
Fees   140kr (160kr)
Loc   1km S of Sundsvall Airport
Mis   Driving range

Umeå (1954)

Vintergatan 18, 902 54 Umeå
Tel   (090) 41071/23495
Mem   1167
Pro   J Anderson
Holes   18 L 5752 m SSS 72
Fees   120kr
Loc   16km SE of Umeå

Gothenburg

Albatross (1973)

Lillhagsvägen, 422 50 Hisings-Backa
Tel   (031) 551901/550500
Fax   (031) 555900
Mem   1200
Pro   P Johansson
Holes   18 L 6020 m SSS 72
Fees   150kr (200kr)
Loc   10km N of Gothenburg on
        Hising Island

Delsjö (1962)

Kallebäck, 412 76 Göteborg
Tel   (031) 406959
Mem   1020
Pro   E Cedervall
Holes   18 L 5785 m SSS 71
Fees   150kr

Loc   5km E of Gothenburg
        (Route 40)
Mis   Driving range

Forsegårdens (1982)

Gamla Forsv 1, 434 47 Kungsbacka
Tel   (0300) 13649
Mem   925
Pro   J Moreau
Holes   18 L 6110 m SSS 72
Fees   170kr (200kr)
Loc   5km SE of Kungsbacka.
        50km S of Gothenburg

Göteborg (1902)

Box 2056, 436 02 Hovås
Tel   (031) 282444
Fax   (031) 283129
Mem   950
Pro   E Öster
Holes   18 L 5935 yds SSS 69
Fees   200kr (250kr)
Loc   11km S of Gothenburg
        (RD 158)

Gullbringa (1967)

442 95 Kungälv
Tel   (0303) 27161
Fax   (0303) 27778
Mem   1200
Pro   P Johansson
Holes   18 L 5775 m Par 72
Fees   200kr
Loc   14km W of Kungälv, towards
        Marstrand

Kungsbacka (1971)

Hamra Gård 515, 43040 Särö
Tel   (031) 936277
Mem   1150
Pro   P Nellbeck
Holes   18 L 5855 m SSS 72
Fees   200kr (250kr)
Loc   7km N of Kungsbacka on
        Route 158

Lysegården (1966)

Box 82, 442 21 Kungälv
Tel   (0303) 23426
Fax   (0303) 23075
Mem   1418
Pro   G Crisp
Holes   18 L 5670 m SSS 71
        9 L 5444 m SSS 70
Fees   18 hole:180kr. 9 hole:120kr
Loc   10km N of Kungälv

Mölndals (1979)

Box 77, 437 21 Mölndal
Tel   (031) 993030
Mem   1200
Pro   D Robinson
Holes   18 L 5625 m SSS 73
Fees   120kr (150kr)
Loc   Lindome, 20km S of
        Gothenburg

Öijared (1958)

Pl 1082, 448 00 Floda
Tel   (0302) 30604
Mem   1542
Pro   E Dawson
Holes   18 L 5875 m SSS 71
        18 L 5655 m SSS 71
Fees   150kr (200kr)
Loc   35km NE of Gothenburg, nr
        Naas
Mis   WE-Members & guests only
        before 3pm

Partille (1971)

Box 234, 433 24 Partille
Tel   (031) 987004/987019 (Shop)
Mem   1100
Holes   18 L 5475 m SSS 71
Fees   130kr (160kr)
Loc   Öjersjö, 10km NE of
        Gothenburg
Mis   Driving range

Särö (1899)

Box 74, 43040 Särö
Tel   (031) 936317
Mem   850
Pro   J Hampf
Holes   9 holes Par 27
        9 holes Par 34
Fees   100kr (130kr)
Loc   10km W of Kungsbacka.
        Gothenburg 18km (Route 158)

Stora Lundby (1983)

Pl 4035, 440 06 Grabo
Tel   (0302) 44200
Fax   (0302) 44125
Mem   1400
Pro   L Svensson, P Houbrandt
Holes   18 L 6040 m Par 72
        9 hole Par 3 course
Fees   18 hole:180kr Par 3-60kr
Loc   25km NE of Gothenburg
Mis   Championship course

North

Avesta (1963)

Box 168, 774 00 Avesta
Tel   (0226) 10363/10866/12766
Mem   1210
Pro   G Long
Holes   18 L 5560 m SSS 71
Fees   120kr (120kr)
Loc   3km NE of Avesta

Bollnäs

Box 72, 82101 Bollnäs
Tel   (0278) 50540/51310 (Shop)
Mem   1800
Pro   N Forsberg
Holes   18 L 5870 m Par 72
Fees   100kr
Loc   15km S of Bollnäs on Route 83

Falun-Borlänge (1956)

Pl 8218, 791 93 Falun	
Tel	(023) 31015
Mem	1000
Pro	A Ryberg
Holes	18 L 6085 m SSS 72
Fees	120kr (150kr)
Loc	Aspeboda, 8km N of Borlänge

Gävle (1949)

Bönavägen 93, 805 95 Gävle	
Tel	(026) 113163
Mem	1350
Pro	W Youngman
Holes	18 L 5735 m SSS 73
	9 L 2910 m SSS 36
Fees	120kr (140kr)
Loc	3km N of Gävle

Hagge (1963)

Hagge, 771 00 Ludvika	
Tel	(0240) 28087
Mem	610
Pro	G Wallner
Holes	18 L 5519 m SSS 71
Fees	100kr
Loc	7km S of Ludvika

Hofors (1965)

Box 117, 813 00 Hofors	
Tel	(0290) 85125
Mem	1380
Pro	O Hedblom, T Arreman
Holes	18 L 5400 m SSS 70
Fees	100kr (120kr)
Loc	5km SE of Hofors

Högbo (1962)

Daniel Tilas Väg 4, 811 92 Sandviken	
Tel	(026) 45015
Mem	1550
Pro	G Sandegard
Holes	18 L 5680 m SSS 71
Fees	120kr (150kr)
Loc	6km N of Sandviken (Route 272)

Hudiksvall (1964)

Tjuvskär 52 08, 824 00 Hudiksvall	
Tel	(0650) 15930
Mem	760
Pro	MB Larsson
Holes	18 L 5750 m SSS 72
Fees	80kr (100kr)
Loc	4km SE of Hudiksvall

Leksand (1977)

Box 25, 793 21 Leksand	
Tel	(0247) 14640
Fax	(0247) 14157
Mem	1288
Pro	P Jönsson (0247) 10749
Holes	18 L 5640 m SSS 72
Fees	130kr (150kr)
Loc	2km N of Leksand

Ljusdal (1973)

Box 151, 827 00 Ljusdal	
Tel	(0651) 14366
Mem	1800
Holes	18 L 5920 m SSS 72
Fees	80kr
Loc	2km E of Ljusdal

Mora (1980)

Box 264, 792 01 Mora	
Tel	(0250) 10182
Mem	1100
Pro	P Michols
Holes	18 L 5600 m Par 72
Fees	110kr (130kr)
Loc	40km NW of Rättvik
Mis	Driving range

Rättvik (1954)

Box 29, 795 00 Rättvik	
Tel	(0248) 11030
Fax	(0248) 10281
Mem	1200
Pro	M Ahlgren, K Staffas
Holes	18 L 5321 m SSS 69
Fees	110kr (130kr) (1990)
Loc	2km N of Rättvik

Sälen

Box 20, 780 67 Sälen	
Tel	(0280) 20670/20671
Mem	900
Pro	P Hamblett
Holes	18 holes SSS 72
Fees	D-120kr
Loc	230km NW of Borlänge. 400km NW of Stockholm

Söderhamn (1961)

Oxtorget 1C, 826 00 Söderhamn	
Tel	(0270) 51000
Mem	582
Pro	M Andersson
Holes	18 L 5940 m SSS 72
Fees	D-70kr
Loc	8km N of Söderhamn

Skane & South

Ängelholm (1973)

Box 1117, 26222 Ängelholm	
Tel	(0431) 30260
Mem	1050
Pro	Y Mahmoud
Holes	18 L 5760 m SSS 72
Fees	100-170kr
Loc	10km E of Ängelholm on route 114

Båstad (1929)

Box 1037, 26901 Båstad	
Tel	(0431) 73136
Mem	1750
Pro	P Hansson
Holes	18 L 5760 m SSS 71
	18 L 6337 m SSS 72
Fees	250kr
Loc	4km W of Båstad (Route 115)
Mis	Handicap certificate required

Barsebäck (1969)

Box 214, 240 22 Löddeköpinge	
Tel	(046) 776230
Mem	1795
Pro	I Christersson
Holes	Old 18 L 5910 m SSS 72
	New 18 L 5855 m SSS 72
Fees	D-200kr
Loc	35km N of Malmö
Mis	WD-visitors welcome

Bedinge (1931)

Box 20, 230 21 Beddingestrand	
Tel	(0410) 25514
Mem	700
Pro	I Persson
Holes	18 L 4500 m SSS 66
Fees	D-100kr W-500kr
Loc	Beddingestrand, 20km E of Trelleborg

Bokskogen (1963)

Box 30, 230 40 Bara I	
Tel	(040) 481004
Mem	1200
Pro	J Larsson
Holes	18 L 6050 m SSS 73
	9 L 5490 m SSS 70
Fees	120kr (160kr)
Loc	15km SE of Malmö, off E14

Bosjökloster (1974)

243 95 Höör	
Tel	(0413) 25858
Mem	1000
Pro	O Asplund
Holes	18 L 5890 m SSS 72
Fees	150kr
Loc	7km S of Höör. 40km NE of Malmö

Eslöv (1966)

Box 150, 241 22 Eslöv	
Tel	(0413) 18610
Mem	1150
Pro	C Wikström (0413) 16213
Holes	18 L 5630 m SSS 71
Fees	150kr (190kr)
Loc	4km S of Eslöv (Route 113)

Falsterbo (1909)

PO Box 71, Fyrvägen, 230 11 Falsterbo	
Tel	(040) 470078/475078
Mem	1000
Pro	D Leet
Holes	18 L 6400 yds SSS 72
Fees	150-270kr (1990)
Loc	35km SW of Malmö
Mis	Summer WE-only with member

Flommens (1935)

230 11 Falsterbo
Tel   (040) 475016
Mem   1146
Pro   B Kristoffersson, G Mueller
Holes 18 L 5610 m SSS 72
Fees   170kr (200kr)
Loc   35km SW of Malmö

Hässleholm (1978)

Skyrup, 282 00 Tyringe
Tel   (0451) 53111
Mem   1000
Pro   J Kers
Holes 18 L 5830 m SSS 72
Fees   120kr (170kr)
Loc   15km NW of Hässleholm

Helsingborg (1924)

26040 Viken
Tel   (042) 236147
Mem   450
Holes 9 L 4578 m SSS 65
Fees   70kr (90kr)
Loc   15km NW of Helsingborg

Hylliekrokens (1983)

Limhamnsvägen 85, 216 18 Malmö
Tel   (040) 160262/160900
Mem   800
Pro   N Mårtensson
Holes 9 L 1040 m Par 54
Fees   55kr (75kr) (1990)
Loc   3km SW of Malmö

Kristianstad (1924)

Box 41, 296 00 Åhus
Tel   (044) 247656
Mem   1500
Pro   D Green
Holes 18 L 5810 m SSS 72
       9 L 2945 m SSS 36
Fees   D-150kr (D-180kr)
Loc   18km SE of Kristianstad.
       Airport 20km

Landskrona (1960)

Erikstorp, 261 61 Landskrona
Tel   (0418) 19528
Mem   1900
Pro   A Olsson
Holes Old 18 L 5700 m SSS 71
       New 18 L 4000 m SSS 62
Fees   130kr (160kr) (1990)
Loc   4km N of Landskrona, towards
       Borstahusen
Mis   Season Mar-Nov

Ljunghusens (1932)

Kinellsvag, Ljunghusen, 236 42
Höllviken
Tel   (040) 450384
Mem   1231
Pro   G Sandegard
Holes 3 x 9 holes:
       1-18 L 5895 m SSS 73
       10-27 L 5670 m SSS 71
       19-9 L 5455 m SSS 70

Fees   140-200kr
Loc   Falsterbo Peninsula.
       30km SW of Malmö

Lunds Akademiska (1936)

Kungsmarken, 225 90 Lund
Tel   (046) 99005
Mem   1300
Pro   V MacDougall
Holes 18 L 5780 m SSS 72
Fees   100kr (140kr)
Loc   5km E of Lund

Malmö

Box 21068, 20021 Malmö
Tel   (040) 292945
Mem   1100
Pro   H Bergdahl
Holes 18 L 5720 m SSS 71
Fees   100kr (120kr)
Loc   NE of Malmö, by motorway
       from Gothenburg
Mis   Driving range

Mölle (1943)

260 42 Mölle
Tel   (042) 347520
Fax   (042) 347523
Mem   1000
Pro   J Pyk-Jargård
Holes 18 L 5640 m SSS 70
Fees   170kr
Loc   Mölle, 35km NW of
       Helsingborg
Mis   WE-restrictions May-Aug

Österlen (1945)

Lilla Vik, 272 00 Simrishamn
Tel   (0414) 24230
Mem   725
Pro   G Mueller (0414) 24005
Holes 18 L 5855 m SSS 72
Fees   100kr
Loc   Vik, 8km N of Simrishamn

Östra Göinge (1981)

Box 114, 289 00 Knislinge
Tel   (044) 60060
Mem   800
Pro   J Kjellgren
Holes 18 L 5898 m Par 72
Fees   100kr
Loc   20km N of Kristianstad

Perstorp (1964)

PO Box 87, 284 00 Perstorp
Tel   (0435) 35411
Mem   800
Pro   J Kennedy
Holes 18 L 5675 m SSS 71
       6 hole short course
Fees   110kr (150kr)
Loc   1km S of Perstorp.
       45km E of Helsingborg

Romeleåsen (1969)

Kvarnbrodda, 240 14 Veberöd
Tel   (046) 82012/82014
Fax   (046) 82113
Mem   1100
Pro   J Byard
Holes 18 L 5783 m SSS 72
Fees   100kr (200kr)
Loc   6km S of Veberöd.
       25km E of Malmö

Rya (1934)

Rya 5500, 225 90 Helsingborg
Tel   (042) 221082
Mem   1200
Pro   J Grant
Holes 18 L 5761 m SSS 72
Fees   140kr (170kr)
Loc   10km S of Helsingborg

St Ibb (1972)

Ulf Ohrvik Victoriagatan 7c,
261 35 Landskrona
Tel   (0418) 72363
Fax   (046) 775898
Mem   525
Holes 9 L 5180 m SSS 68
Fees   120kr (150kr)
Loc   Island of Hven
Mis   Ferry from Landskrona

Skepparslov (1984)

Udarpssäteri, 291 69 Kristianstad
Tel   (044) 229508
Mem   1200
Holes 18 L 5900 m SSS 72
Fees   100kr (150kr)
Loc   7km W of Kristianstad

Söderåsen (1966)

Box 41, 260 50 Billesholm
Tel   (042) 73337
Mem   850
Pro   T Lidholm
Holes 18 L 5920 m SSS 73
Fees   100kr (120kr)
Loc   20km E of Helsingborg

Torekov (1924)

Box 81, 26093 Torekov
Tel   (0431) 63355
Mem   1250
Pro   G Hall
Holes 18 L 5701 m SSS 72
Fees   160-200kr
Loc   3km N of Torekov

Trelleborg (1963)

Maglarp, Pl 401, 231 93 Trelleborg
Tel   (0410) 30460
Mem   975
Pro   M Malmstrom
Holes 18 L 5080 m SSS 68
Fees   160kr (170kr)
Loc   5km W of Trelleborg

Vasatorp (1973)

Box 13035, 250 13 Helsingborg
Tel   **(042) 235058**
Mem   1800
Pro   K Davies (042) 235045
Holes   18 L 5875 m SSS 72
    9 L 2940 m SSS
Fees   150-180kr
Loc   8km E of Helsingborg

Wittsjö (1962)

Ubbaltsgården, 280 22 Vittsjö
Tel   **(0451) 22635**
Mem   950
Pro   G Dahl
Holes   18 L 5461 m SSS 71
Fees   110kr (150kr)
Loc   2km E of Vittsjö

Ystad (1930)

Box 162, 271 00 Ystad
Tel   **(0411) 50350**
Mem   900
Pro   J Grant
Holes   18 L 5800 m SSS 72
Fees   150kr
Loc   7km E of Ystad, towards
    Simrishamn

South East

Älmhult (1975)

Box 152, 343 00 Älmhult
Tel   **(0476) 14135**
Mem   790
Pro   B Mårtensson
Holes   9 L 5350 m SSS 70
Fees   D-80kr
Loc   2km E of Älmhult on Route 120

Åtvidaberg (1954)

Box 180, 597 24 Åtvidaberg
Tel   **(0120) 11425**
Mem   1000
Pro   B Nygren (0120) 12510
Holes   18 L 5856 m SSS 72
Fees   130kr (150kr)
Loc   30km SE of Linköping

Carlskrona (1949)

PO Almö, 370 24 Nättraby
Tel   **(0457) 35123**
Mem   1000
Pro   A Malmberg
Holes   18 L 5525 m Par 70
Fees   D-140kr
Loc   18km SW of Karlskrona

Eksjö (1938)

Skedhult, 575 91 Eksjö
Tel   **(0381) 13525**
Mem   1000
Pro   M Wissinger
Holes   18 L 5930 m SSS 72
Fees   120kr (120kr)
Loc   6km W of Eksjö on Nässjö road

Emmaboda (1976)

Kyrkogatan, 360 60 Vissefjärda
Tel   **(0471) 20505/20540**
Mem   612
Holes   9 L 5165 m SSS 68
Fees   60kr
Loc   12km S of Emmaboda

Finspång (1965)

Viberga Gård, 612 92 Finspång
Tel   **(0122) 13940**
Mem   1200
Pro   J Kjellvall
Holes   18 L 5800 m SSS 72
Fees   140kr
Loc   2km E of Finspång (Route 51).
    Norrköping 25km.

Hook (1942)

560 13 Hok
Tel   **(0393) 21420**
Mem   850
Pro   A Steen (0393) 21310
Holes   18 L 5758 m SSS 72
    9 hole Par 3
Fees   120kr (150kr)
Loc   Hok, 30km SE of Jönköping,
    towards Växjö
Mis   Further 9 holes open 1991

Isaberg (1968)

Box 40, 332 00 Gislaved
Tel   **(0370) 36330**
Mem   1500
Pro   S Carpenter
Holes   18 L 5800 m SSS 72
    9 L 2960 m SSS 36
Fees   D-150kr W-750kr
Loc   18km N of Gislaved, nr
    Nissafors. 60km S of Jönköping

Jönköping (1936)

Kettilstorp, 552 67 Jönköping
Tel   **(036) 76567**
Fax   **(036) 76511**
Mem   1230
Pro   A Turnbull
Holes   18 L 6370 m SSS 70
Fees   140kr (1990)
Loc   Kettilstorp, 3km S of Jönköping
Mis   Handicap certificate required.
    Telephone in advance

Kalmar (1947)

Box 278, 391 23 Kalmar 1
Tel   **(0480) 72111**
Mem   1100
Pro   H Weinhofer
Holes   18 L 5950 m SSS 72
Fees   150kr (180kr)
Loc   9km N of Kalmar

Karlshamn (1962)

292 00 Karlshamn
Tel   **(0454) 50085**
Mem   720
Pro   B Fredriksson

Holes   18 L 5861 m SSS 72
Fees   D-120kr
Loc   Morrum, 10km W of
    Karlshamn

Lagan (1966)

Box 63, 340 14 Lagan
Tel   **(0372) 30450**
Mem   1050
Holes   18 L 5600 m SSS 71
Fees   120kr (120kr)
Loc   Lagan, 10km N of Ljungby, on
    Route E4

Landeryd (1987)

Box 110 40, 580 11 Linköping
Tel   **(013) 162520**
Fax   **(013) 150493**
Mem   1200
Pro   K Kinell
Holes   18 L 5675 m SSS 72
Fees   120kr
Loc   10km SW of Linköping

Linköping (1945)

Box 10054, 580 10 Linköping
Tel   **(013) 120646**
Mem   1250
Pro   B Lemke, B Patterson
Holes   18 L 5675 m SSS 71
Fees   150kr
Loc   3km SW of Linköping

Mjölby (1983)

Box 171, 595 00 Mjölby
Tel   **(0142) 12570**
Mem   950
Pro   A Starkman
Holes   18 L 5485 m SSS 71
Fees   120kr
Loc   35km WSW of Linköping (E4)

Motala (1956)

PO Box 264, 591 23 Motala
Tel   **(0141) 50856/50840 (Sec)**
Mem   1100
Pro   S Johansson (0141) 50834
Holes   18 L 5905 m SSS 72
Fees   100kr (150kr)
Loc   3km S of Motala via Route 50
    or 32

Norrköping (1928)

Klinga, Box 2150, 600 02 Norrköping
Tel   **(011) 35235**
Mem   1400
Pro   P Karström (011) 35236
Holes   18 L 5860 m SSS 73
Fees   150kr (200kr)
Loc   Klinga, 2km S of Norrköping
    on E4

Nybro (1971)

Box 235, 382 00 Nybro
Tel   **(0480) 55044**
Mem   1000
Pro   J Evergren
Holes   18 L 5829 m SSS 72

Fees   80kr (100kr) W-450kr
Loc   10km E of Nybro, towards
       Kalmar

Öland (1983)

Box 112, 387 00 Borgholm
Tel   (0485) 73123
Mem   600
Holes 9 hole course
Fees   80kr (100kr)
Loc   Källatorp, 40km N of Borgholm

Oskarshamn (1972)

Box 148, 572 01 Oskarshamn
Tel   (0491) 94033
Mem   900
Pro   I Hult
Holes 18 L 5545 m SSS 72
Fees   100kr (120kr)
Loc   10km SW of Oskarshamn, nr
       Forshult

Ronneby (1964)

Box 26, 372 21 Ronneby
Tel   (0457) 10315
Mem   1116
Pro   F Johnsson
Holes 18 L 5323 m SSS 70
Fees   150kr
Loc   3km S of Ronneby

Söderköping (1983)

605 90 Norrköping
Tel   (011) 70579
Mem   910
Pro   L Cernold (011) 70039
Holes 18 L 5730 m SSS 72
Fees   120kr (150kr)
Loc   Västra Husby, 9km W of
       Söderköping

Tobo (1971)

Tobo Gård, 598 00 Vimmerby
Tel   (0492) 30028/30346
Pro   L Wiberg
Holes 18 L 5950 m SSS 73
Fees   80kr
Loc   10km S of Vimmerby, nr
       Storebro. 60km SW of
       Västervik

Tranås (1952)

N Storgatan 130, 573 00 Tranås
Tel   (0140) 11661
Mem   900
Pro   S Reese
Holes 18 L 5830 m SSS 72
Fees   100kr
Loc   2km N of Tranås

Vadstena (1957)

Hagalund, 592 00 Vadstena
Tel   (0143) 12440
Mem   900
Pro   C Bolgakoff
Holes 9 L 5486 m SSS 70
Fees   100kr

Loc   3km S of Vadstena, towards
       Vaderstad
Mis   Further 9 holes open 1991

Värnamo (1962)

Box 146, 331 01 Värnamo
Tel   (0370) 23123
Mem   625
Pro   A Marshall
Holes 18 L 6253 m SSS 72
Fees   100kr (120kr)
Loc   8km E of Värnamo on
       Route 127
Mis   Driving range

Västervik (1959)

Box 62, 593 22 Västervik
Tel   (0490) 32420
Mem   1050
Pro   P Johansson (0490) 31521
Holes 18 L 5760 m SSS 72
Fees   D-120kr
Loc   1km SE of Västervik

Växjö (1959)

Box 227, 351 05 Växjö
Tel   (0470) 21539
Mem   975
Pro   L Ibsonius (0470) 14004
Holes 18 L 5860 m SSS 72
Fees   100kr (120kr)
Loc   3km N of Växjö

Vetlanda (1983)

Box 249, 574 23 Vetlanda
Tel   (0383) 18310
Mem   1030
Pro   S Petersson
Holes 18 holes Par 72
Fees   120kr
Loc   Östanå, 3km W of Vetlanda.
       60km SE of Jönköping

Visby

Box 1038, 621 21 Visby
Tel   (0498) 45058
Mem   1200
Pro   F Bergqvist (0498) 45100
Holes 18 L 5855 m SSS 72
Fees   180kr
Loc   Kronholmen, 25km S of Visby,
       Gotland Island

South West

Alingsås (1985)

Hjälmared 4050, 441 95 Alingsås
Tel   (0322) 52421
Mem   1075
Pro   A Liljedahl
Holes 18 L 5600 m SSS 72
Fees   140kr (180kr)
Loc   5km SE of Alingsås towards
       Borås

Bäckavattnet (1977)

Box 288, 30107 Halmstad
Tel   (035) 44271
Mem   1000
Pro   S Grant
Holes 18 L 5735 m SSS 72
Fees   150kr
Loc   13km E of Halmstad (RD25)

Billingen (1949)

St Kulhult, 540 17 Lerdala
Tel   (0511) 80291
Mem   600
Pro   B Falk (0511) 80298
Holes 18 L 5605 m Par 71
Fees   80kr (100kr)
Loc   15km NE of Skara.
       35km E of Lidköping

Borås (1933)

Östra Vik, Kråkered, 505 95 Borås
Tel   (033) 50142
Fax   (033) 50176
Mem   1450
Pro   K Fasth
Holes North 18 L 5855 m SSS 72
       South 18 L 5100 m SSS 70
Fees   140kr (160kr)
Loc   6km S of Borås, on Route 41
       towards Varberg
Mis   Season Apr-Oct. Tee booking
       necessary. Driving range

Ekarnas (1970)

Balders Väg 12, 467 00 Grästorp
Tel   (0514) 11450
Mem   3900
Holes 9 L 4480 m SSS 64
Fees   60kr
Loc   25km E of Trollhättan.
       Lidköping 35km

Falkenberg (1949)

Golfvägen, 311 75 Falkenberg
Tel   (0346) 50287
Mem   1350
Pro   S-A Bolten
Holes 27 L 5650-5770 m SSS 72
Fees   110-220kr
Loc   5km S of Falkenberg

Falköping

Box 99, 521 02 Falköping
Tel   (0515) 31270
Mem   1000
Holes 18 L 5835 m SSS 73
Fees   D-100kr
Loc   7km E of Falköping on
       Route 46 towards Skovde

Halmstad (1930)

302 73 Halmstad
Tel   (035) 30077
Mem   2125
Pro   B Grafton, PO Johansson,
       M Sorling

Holes	18 L 6253 m SSS 74
	18 L 5755 m SSS 72
Fees	200-250kr
Loc	Tylosand, 9km W of Halmstad

Hökensås (1962)

	PO Box 116, 544 00 Hjo
Tel	(0503) 16059
Mem	1460
Pro	J Lindström
Holes	18 L 5540 m SSS 71
Fees	100kr (150kr)
Loc	8km S of Hjo on Route 195

Hulta (1972)

	Box 54, 517 01 Bollebygd
Tel	(033) 88180
Mem	1200
Pro	W Byard
Holes	18 L 6000 m SSS 73
Fees	150kr
Loc	Bollebygd, 25km W of Borås

Laholm (1964)

	Box 101, 312 22 Laholm
Tel	(0430) 30601
Mem	1200
Pro	T Lindwall
Holes	18 L 5430 m SSS 70
Fees	160kr (180kr)
Loc	5 miles E of Laholm on Route 24

Lidköping (1967)

	Box 2029, 531 02 Lidköping
Tel	(0510) 46122/46144
Mem	900
Pro	T Lundahl
Holes	18 L 5565 m SSS 70
Fees	100kr (120kr)
Loc	5km E of Lidköping

Mariestad (1975)

	PO Box 299, 542 23 Mariestad
Tel	(0501) 17383
Mem	1120
Pro	P Berggren
Holes	18 L 5890 m SSS 72
Fees	120kr
Loc	4km W of Mariestad, at Lake Vänern

Marks (1962)

	Brättingstorpsvägen 28, 511 58 Kinna
Tel	(0320) 14220
Mem	1200
Pro	G Nyberg
Holes	18 L 5530 m SSS 69
Fees	130kr (160kr)
Loc	Kinna, 30km S of Borås

Onsjö (1974)

	Box 100, 462 00 Vänersborg
Tel	(0521) 64149
Mem	750
Pro	N Goodison (0521) 62575

Holes	18 L 5730 m SSS 72
Fees	80kr (100kr)
Loc	4km S of Vänersborg. 8km N of Gothenburg.

Töreboda (1965)

	Box 18, 545 21 Töreboda
Tel	(0506) 16240
Mem	775
Pro	D McLean
Holes	18 L 5355 m SSS 70
Fees	120kr
Loc	7km E of Töreboda

Trollhättan (1963)

	Box 254, 461 26 Trollhättan
Tel	(0520) 41000
Mem	1184
Pro	G Clark (0520) 41010
Holes	18 L 6200 m SSS 73
Fees	130kr
Loc	Koberg, 20km SE of Trollhättan

Ulricehamn (1947)

	Box 179, 523 01 Ulricehamn
Tel	(0321) 10021
Mem	1000
Pro	A Halim
Holes	18 L 5538 m SSS 71
Fees	D-120kr
Loc	Backasen, 2km E of Ulricehamn

Varberg (1950)

	Box 39, 432 21 Varberg
Tel	(0340) 37470
Mem	1000
Pro	F Englund
Holes	18 L 5797 m SSS 73
Fees	120kr
Loc	15km E of Varberg

Stockholm

Ågesta (1958)

	Ågesta, 123 52 Farsta
Tel	(08) 604 5641
Mem	1367
Pro	R Tomlinson
Holes	18 L 5705 m SSS 72
	9 L 3660 m SSS 59
Fees	D-150kr (D-200kr)
Loc	Farsta, 15km S of Stockholm

Björkhagen (1973)

	Box 430, 121 04 Johanneshov
Tel	(08) 773 0431
Mem	608
Pro	K Johnson
Holes	9 L 4589 m SSS 66
Fees	100kr (130kr) (1990)
Loc	10km S of Stockholm

Bro-Balsta (1978)

	Box 96, 197 00 Bro
Tel	(0758) 48430
Mem	1100
Pro	A Sjöhagen
Holes	18 hole course
Fees	160kr (220kr)
Loc	Thoresta, 30km NW of Stockholm

Djursholm (1931)

	Hagbardsvägen 1, 182 63 Djursholm
Tel	(08) 755 1477
Mem	1603
Pro	G Deverell
Holes	18 L 5595 m SSS 71
	9 L 4400 m SSS 64
Fees	200kr (250kr)
Loc	12km N of Stockholm

Drottningholm (1956)

	PO Box 183, 170 11 Drottningholm
Tel	(08) 759 0085 Fax 759 0851
Mem	850
Pro	Ms C Montgomery
Holes	18 L 5825 m SSS 72
Fees	200kr (250kr)
Loc	16km W of Stockholm

Haninge (1983)

	Årsta Slott, 136 91 Haninge
Tel	(0750) 32240/32270
Fax	(0750) 32340
Mem	1550
Pro	B Deilert
Holes	18 L 5930 m SSS 73
Fees	200kr (230kr)
Loc	30km S of Stockholm towards Nynäsham

Ingarö (1962)

	Fogelvik, 130 35 Ingarö
Tel	(0766) 28244
Mem	800
Pro	RL Morin
Holes	18 L 5603 m SSS 71
Fees	200kr (230kr)
Loc	32km E of Stockholm via Route 222

Lidingö (1932)

	Box 1035, 181 21 Lidingö
Tel	(08) 765 7911
Fax	(08) 765 5479
Mem	1000
Pro	P Hansson, D Johnston
Holes	18 L 5770 m SSS 71
Fees	240kr
Loc	6km NE of Stockholm

Lindö (1978)

	Box 1043, 186 92 Vallentuna
Tel	(0762) 72260
Mem	500
Holes	18 L 2850 m SSS 71
Loc	20km N of Stockholm
Mis	Driving range

Nynäshamn (1977)

Box 4, 148 00 Ösmo
Tel   (0752) 27190
Mem   1200
Pro   S Ohlsson
Holes 18 L 5730 m SSS 72
Fees   180kr
Loc   Ösmo, 50km S of Stockholm
Mis   Visitors welcome after 1pm

Saltsjöbaden (1929)

Box 51, 133 21 Saltsjöbaden
Tel   (08) 717 0125
Fax   (08) 717 9713
Mem   1200
Pro   M Sheard (08) 717 1035
Holes 18 L 5685 m SSS 72
       9 L 3640 m SSS 60
Fees   18 hole:D-200kr (250kr)
       9 hole:D-140kr (160kr)
Loc   15km E of Stockholm via
       Route 228

Sollentuna (1967)

Skillingegården, 191 77 Sollentuna
Tel   (08) 754 3625
Mem   1100
Pro   K Ekberg
Holes 18 L 5910 m SSS 72
Fees   200kr (250kr)
Loc   19km N of Stockholm.
       1km W of E4 (Rotebro)
Mis   Handicap certificate required.
       Driving range

Stockholm (1904)

Kevingestrand 20, 182 31 Danderyd
Tel   (08) 755 0031
Mem   993
Pro   K Gow
Holes 18 L 5510 m SSS 71
Fees   200kr
Loc   7km NE of Stockholm via
       Route E3
Mis   WE-members' guests only

Täby (1968)

Skålhamra Gård, 183 43 Täby
Tel   (0762) 23261
Mem   1240
Pro   T Holmström
Holes 18 L 5776 m SSS 73
Fees   200-250kr
Loc   3km N of Stockholm

Ullna (1981)

Rosenkälla, 18400 Åkersberga
Tel   (0762) 26075
Fax   (0762) 26068
Mem   580
Pro   J Cockin
Holes 18 L 5710 m SSS 72
Fees   300kr
Loc   20km N of Stockholm via
       Route E3
Mis   Open Apr-Oct. Driving range

Viksjö (1969)

Fjällens Gård, 175 45 Järfälla
Tel   (0758) 16600/16708
Mem   1280
Pro   S Cherif
Holes 18 L 5930 m SSS 73
Fees   180kr (200kr)
Loc   18km NW of Stockholm

Wermdö G & CC (1966)

Torpa, 139 00 Värmdö
Tel   (0766) 20849
Mem   750
Pro   M Jansson
Holes 18 L 5630 m SSS 72
Fees   275kr (325kr)
Loc   25km E of Stockholm via
       Route 222

West Central

Arvika

Box 33, 671 01 Arvika 1
Tel   (0570) 54133
Pro   Å Söderqvist
Holes 9 L 5815 m SSS 71
Fees   D-70kr
Loc   11km E of Arvika on (Route 61)

Billerud (1961)

PO Box 192, 661 00 Säffle
Tel   (0555) 91313
Mem   925
Pro   R Bailey
Holes 18 L 5874 m SSS 72
Fees   120kr
Loc   Valnäs, 15km N of Säffle

Fjällbacka (1965)

450 71 Fjällbacka
Tel   (0525) 31150
Mem   900
Pro   M Ericsson
Holes 18 L 5850 m SSS 72
Fees   D-160kr
Loc   2km N of Fjällbacka (Route 163)
Mis   Handicap certificate required

Forsbacka (1969)

Box 136, 662 00 Åmål
Tel   (0532) 43055
Mem   550
Pro   M El Sayed
Holes 18 L 5860 m SSS 72
Fees   100kr
Loc   6km W of Åmål (Route 164)

Karlskoga (1975)

Bricketorp 647, 691 94 Karlskoga
Tel   (0586) 28597
Mem   975
Pro   P Glimaker (0586) 28663
Holes 18 L 5705 m Par 72
Fees   120kr
Loc   Valåsen, 5km E of Karlskoga
       via Route E18

Karlstad (1957)

PO Box 294, 651 07 Karlstad
Tel   (054) 36353
Mem   1300
Pro   H Reis
Holes 18 L 5900 m SSS 72
       9 L 2900 m SSS
Fees   150kr
Loc   12km E of Karlstad (Route 63)

Kristinehamn (1974)

Box 3037, 681 03 Kristinehamn
Tel   (0550) 82310
Mem   950
Pro   A Reumert
Holes 18 L 5800 m SSS 71
Fees   120kr
Loc   3km N of Kristinehamn

Lyckorna (1967)

Box 66, 459 00 Ljungskile
Tel   (0522) 20176
Mem   1100
Pro   U Ligner
Holes 18 L 5845 m SSS 72
Fees   150kr
Loc   20km S of Uddevalla

Orust (1981)

Pl 8290, 440 80 Ellös
Tel   (0304) 053170
Mem   1500
Pro   S Eriksson
Holes 18 L 5770 m SSS 72
Fees   110kr (130kr)
Loc   Ellös, 10km from Henån.
       80km N of Gothenburg

Saxå (1964)

Asphyttegatan 24, 682 00 Filipstad
Tel   (0590) 24071
Mem   980
Pro   F Speight
Holes 9 L 5860 m SSS 73
Fees   100kr
Loc   15km E of Filipstad (Route 63)

Skaftö (1963)

Röd 4476, 450 34 Fiskebäckskil
Tel   (0523) 22544
Mem   700
Pro   M Kinhult
Holes 12 L 5305 m SSS 67
Fees   150kr
Loc   15km SW of Uddevalla,
       towards Fiskebäckskil

Strömstad (1967)

Box 129, 452 00 Strömstad 1
Tel   (0526) 11788
Mem   1000
Pro   T Hunter (0526) 14244
Holes 18 L 5615 m SSS 71
Fees   120kr W-660kr
Loc   6km N of Strömstad
Mis   Driving range

Sunne (1970)

Box 108, 686 00 Sunne
Tel (0565) 60300
Mem 340
Pro A Olsson (0560) 10776
Holes 9 L 2845 m SSS 71
Fees 70kr
Loc 2km S of Sunne. 60km N of Karlstad on Route 234

Torreby (1961)

Torreby Slott, 455 00 Munkedal
Tel (0524) 21365/21109
Mem 1450
Pro J Grahn, K Grahn
Holes 18 L 5885 m SSS 72
Fees D-120-160kr
Loc Munkedal 8km. Uddevalla 30km.

Uddeholm (1965)

683 03 Rada
Tel (0563) 60564/60025
Fax (0563) 60460
Mem 1500
Pro T Palm
Holes 18 L 5833 m SSS 72
Fees D-130kr
Loc 80km N of Karlstad, via RD62

Switzerland

Bern

Blumisberg (1959)

3184 Wünnewil
Tel (037) 36 34 38   **Fax** 36 35 23
Mem 670
Pro F Schiroli, W Marx
Holes 18 L 6048 m SSS 73
Fees 60fr (80fr)
Loc Blumisberg, 16km SW of Bern

Neuchâtel (1928)

2072 Saint-Blaise
Tel (038) 33 55 50
Mem 400
Pro T Charpié
Holes 18 L 5840 m SSS 70
Fees 50fr (70fr)
Loc Voens/Saint-Blaise, 5km E of Neuchâtel. 30km W of Bern

Bernese Oberland

Gstaad- Saanenland (1962)

3780 Gstaad
Tel (030) 426 36
Mem 196
Pro B Herrmann
Holes 9 L 5580 m SSS 69
Fees 25fr (30fr)
Loc Saanenmöser, 15km N of Gstaad
Mis Open June-Oct

Interlaken-Unterseen (1964)

Postfach 110, 3800 Interlaken
Tel (036) 22 60 22
Mem 500
Pro B Chenaux
Holes 18 L 5980 m SSS 72
Fees 60fr (70fr)
Loc Interlaken 3km

Riederalp (1986)

3987 Riederalp
Tel (028) 27 29 32/27 14 63
Mem 250
Pro M Cole
Holes 9 L 3016 m SSS 54
Fees 25fr (30fr)
Loc 10km NE of Brig
Mis Season June-Oct

Lake Geneva & South West

Bonmont (1983)

Château de Bonmont, 1261 Chéserex
Tel (022) 69 23 45
Mem 600
Pro F Boillat, G Kaye, Y Radal
Holes 18 L 6160 m Par 71
Fees D-60fr
Loc 3km from Nyon. 30km NE of Geneva

Crans-sur-Sierre (1906)

3963 Crans-sur-Sierre-Montana
Tel (027) 41 21 68/41 27 03
Fax (027) 41 46 71
Mem 1510
Pro J Bonvin, RJ Barras, J-M Barras, B Cordonnier, B Mittaz, A Rey, M Bonvin, A Jeanquartier
Holes 18 L 6260 m SSS 72 9 L 2667 m SSS 35
Fees 18 hole:70-80fr W-420-500fr 9 hole:35-40fr
Loc 20km E of Sion. Geneva 2 hrs

Domaine Impérial (1987)

CP 84, 1196 Gland
Tel (0221) 64 45 45
Mem 1000
Pro R Guignet, A Jeanquartier, G Martin, M Scopetta
Holes 18 L 6254 m SSS 74
Fees WD-80fr
Loc Nyon, 20km N of Geneva
Mis Visitors-am only (max h'cap 30)

Geneva (1923)

70 Route de la Capite, 1223 Cologny
Tel (022) 735 75 40
Fax (022) 735 71 05
Mem 1000
Pro JM Larretche, H Muscroft, P Bagnoud, J Berthet
Holes 18 L 6250 m Par 72
Fees 60fr
Loc Geneva 4km
Mis WE-only with member.

Lausanne (1921)

Le Chalet à Gobet, 1000 Lausanne 25
Tel (021) 784 13 15
Mem 850
Pro A Gallardo, M Gallardo, M More, D Ingram
Holes 18 L 6165 m SSS 74
Fees 60fr (80fr)
Loc 7km N of Lausanne towards Le Mont

Montreux (1900)

Case Post 187, 1820 Montreux
Tel (025) 26 46 16 (Dir/Sec)
Fax (025) 27 10 47
Mem 500
Pro P Bagnoud, J Bagnoud, T Cordoba
Holes 18 L 6410 m SSS 72
Fees 60fr (80fr)
Loc Aigle, 15km S of Montreux
Mis Handicap certificate required-max 30

Verbier (1969)

1936 Verbier
Tel (026) 7 49 95
Mem 140
Pro C Torribio
Holes 18 hole Par 3 course
Fees D-15fr (20fr)
Loc Centre of Verbier
Mis Open June-Oct

Villars (1922)

Case Postale 152, 1884 Villars
Tel (025) 35 42 14
Mem 400
Pro JL Chable, G Chable
Holes 18 L 4093 m SSS 61
Fees 35fr (50fr)
Loc 7km E of Villars towards Les Diablerets
Mis Open June-Oct

Lugano & Ticino

Lugano (1923)

6983 Magliaso
Tel (091) 71 15 57
Fax (091) 71 65 58
Mem 900
Pro D Maina, G Parisi, I Tremolada
Holes 18 L 5740 m SSS 71
Fees 60fr (100fr)
Loc 8km W of Lugano towards Ponte Tresa
Mis Handicap certificate required

For list of abbreviations see page 487.

Patriziale Ascona (1928)

Via al Lido 81, 6612 Ascona
Tel	(093) 35 21 32
Fax	(093) 35 07 96
Mem	350 250(L) 100(J)
Pro	F Codiga, F Salmina, M Garcia
Holes	18 L 5893 m SSS 71
Fees	60fr (80fr)
Loc	Ascona, 5km W of Locarno
Mis	Handicap limit-30

St Moritz & Engadine

Arosa (1946)

7050 Arosa
Tel	(081) 31 22 15
Mem	258
Pro	M Buchter
Holes	9 L 4450 m SSS 64
Fees	35fr
Loc	Arosa, 30km S of Chur
Mis	Open June–mid Oct. Driving range

Bad Ragaz (1957)

Hans Albrechtstr, 7310 Bad Ragaz
Tel	(085) 9 15 56 Fax 9 49 57
Mem	550
Pro	C Gaud, M Caligari, T Smith
Holes	18 L 5750 m SSS 71
Fees	70fr (80fr)
Loc	20km N of Chur. 100km SE of Zürich
Mis	Handicap certificate required

Davos (1929)

Postfach, 7270 Davos Dorf
Tel	(083) 5 56 34
Mem	600
Pro	HJ Hörenz
Holes	18 L 5715 yds SSS 67
Fees	50fr (60fr)
Loc	1km outside Davos
Mis	Open May-Oct

Engadin (1893)

7503 Samedan
Tel	(082) 6 52 26 Fax 6 46 82
Mem	490
Pro	A Casera, A Chiogna, F Hurtado, I Tremolada, J Wallwork
Holes	18 L 6350 m SSS 72
Fees	60fr
Loc	Samedan, 6km NE of St Moritz

Lenzerheide Valbella (1950)

7078 Lenzerheide
Tel	(081) 34 13 16
Mem	400
Pro	H Schumacher, R Blaesi
Holes	18 L 5269 m Par 69
Fees	60fr

Loc	20km S of Chur towards St Moritz
Mis	Handicap certificate required

Vulpera (1923)

7552 Vulpera Spa
Tel	(084) 9 96 88
Mem	220
Pro	P Jones
Holes	9 L 2021 m SSS 62
Fees	40fr (50fr) W-230fr
Loc	Tarasp,60km NE of St Moritz

Zürich & North

Breitenloo (1964)

Bassersdorf, 8309 Oberwil
Tel	(01) 836 40 80/836 64 86
Mem	380
Pro	Th Villiger
Holes	18 L 6100 m SSS 72
Fees	60fr (80fr)
Loc	Zürich Airport 8km

Bürgenstock (1928)

6366 Bürgenstock
Tel	(041) 61 24 34
Pro	G Denny
Holes	9 L 1935 m Par 34
Fees	35fr
Loc	15km S of Lucerne
Mis	Open May-Sept

Dolder (1907)

Kuthausstrasse 66, 8032 Zürich
Tel	(01) 261 50 45
Pro	D Dieter, C Brazerol
Holes	9 L 1735 m SSS 58
Fees	WD-50fr
Loc	Zürich
Mis	Open Apr–Nov. Handicap certificate required. WE-only members/guests of Hotels Waldhaus, Dolder & Grand Dolder

Hittnau-Zürich G & CC (1964)

8335 Hittnau
Tel	(01) 950 24 42
Mem	485
Pro	E Bauer, D Parini
Holes	18 L 6020 m SSS 71
Fees	WD-60fr
Loc	Hittnau, 30km E of Zürich
Mis	WE-closed for non-members

Lucerne (1903)

6006 Dietschiberg
Tel	(041) 36 97 87 Fax 36 82 48
Mem	350
Pro	L Mudry, B Lagger
Holes	18 L 5700 m SSS 71
Fees	60fr
Loc	Lucerne 2km
Mis	Handicap certificate required

Ostschweizischer (1948)

9246 Niederbüren
Tel	(071) 81 18 56
Mem	360
Pro	CB Craig
Holes	18 L 5920 m SSS 71
Fees	D-50fr (60fr)
Loc	25km NW of St Gallen

Schinznach-Bad (1929)

5116 Schinznach-Bad
Tel	(056) 43 12 26
Mem	235
Pro	H Zimmerman, V Krajewski
Holes	9 L 6036 m Par 72
Fees	40fr (50fr)
Loc	6km S of Brugg. 35km W of Zürich

Schönenberg

8821 Schönenberg
Tel	(01) 788 16 24
Mem	400
Pro	T Charpié, J Wallwork, L Freeman
Holes	18 L 6340 m SSS 73
Fees	D-60fr
Loc	20km S of Zürich

Zürich-Zumikon (1931)

8126 Zumikon
Tel	(01) 918 00 50
Mem	700
Pro	G Denny, B Griss
Holes	18 L 6360 m SSS 74
Fees	WD-90fr
Loc	Zürich 10km
Mis	Visitors must be introduced. WE-closed for non-members

Yugoslavia

Bled (1974)

Cesta Svobode 13, 64260 Bled
Tel	(064) 78 282 Fax 78 282
Mem	350
Pro	D Jurman, M Lamberger
Holes	18 L 6320 m SSS 73
Fees	17Lstg W-102Lstg
Loc	3km W of Bled. Ljubljana Airport 30km
Mis	Further holes open 1991

Golf Lipica

66210 Sežana
Tel	(067) 73 781/73 541
Fax	(067) 72 818
Mem	30
Pro	D Kraljič
Holes	9 L 6240 m Par 72
Fees	D-35DM W-210DM
Loc	30km NE of Trieste. 100km SW of Ljubljana

Part V
Government of the Game

Introduction

The Editor and Publishers of the **Golfer's Hand-book** *are grateful to the General Committee of the Royal & Ancient Club for its agreement to reproduce the* Statement of Functions of the Club. *A brief history of how the Royal & Ancient came to be the Governing Body of the Game has been added, followed by a description of the important work of the Championship Committee, especially in its responsibility for The Open.*

The Royal & Ancient Golf Club

In Britain it is not unusual for the Governing Body of a Sport to have its origins in a private club, which later comes to be recognised as the authority through which the game is administered. The Royal & Ancient Golf Club of St Andrews is a prime example and enjoys a similar status to the Marylebone Cricket Club. With the world-wide spread of golf and cricket this century, both have emerged as the international body to which most other countries look for rulings and guidance.

The Royal & Ancient Club's records date back to 1754 when the Society of St Andrews Golfers adopted the rules which had been formulated in 1744 by the Gentlemen Golfers of Leith, later to become the Honourable Company of Edinburgh Golfers; the older club located across the Forth at Muirfield.

When in 1834 King William IV granted the St Andrews Gentlemen Golfers the right and privilege of using the title *Royal & Ancient*, the Honourable Company had temporarily lost cohesion and the R&A gradually acquired the status of the premier club. During the latter half of the Victorian age, in the 1880s and 1890s when, following the spread of the railway system, many new clubs were founded, they looked to the R&A for leadership and advice.

With the appointment of the first Rules of Golf Committee in 1897, the R&A became recognised as the Governing Authority in all countries except the United States and Mexico where the United States Golf Association controls the game. Golf federations of many countries are affiliated to the R&A. This is made clear in the *Statement of Functions* of the R&A, reproduced with the permission of the General Committee. The work of the Championship Committee is expanded in a note below, with particular reference to The Open Championship.

The success of The Open in recent years, both as a spectacle and financially, has meant that the R&A can now support fully the development of the game, while remaining the guardian of its traditions. Its encouragement of young players, especially through the Boys and Youths Championships and the Golf Foundation, has helped produce the higher standards of play and younger champions now so apparent to all followers of the game.

Statement of Functions of the Royal & Ancient Golf Club throughout the world

With the developing interest in golf and the increasing complexity of the administration of the game, the Royal & Ancient Golf Club feels that a statement of its activities in this field would be of interest.

The functions for which the Club is responsible fall into three clearly defined categories. First, functions of an international nature, secondly functions of a national nature, and finally, the running of a Club with wide national and international Membership.

International Functions

In 1897 the Royal & Ancient became the Governing Authority on the Rules of Golf at the suggestion of the leading Golf Clubs in the United Kingdom at the time. Since then an ever increasing number of countries have sought affiliation to it, until today they number over 60, including several other Unions or Associations (eg the Ladies' Golf Union, European Golf Association, South American Golf Federation and Asia-Pacific Golf Confederation).

The Club in its negotiations with the United States Golf Association on matters pertaining to the Rules of Golf is not merely representing Great Britain and Ireland, but these many countries as well.

In 1919, when it took over the running of the Open and Amateur Championships, the Royal & Ancient became responsible for the Rules of Amateur Status and in matters pertaining thereto likewise represents these many countries.

The Royal & Ancient also supplies one of the two Joint Chairmen and Joint Secretaries of the World Amateur Golf Council which is responsible for the organisation of all World Amateur Team Championships.

There is close liaison at all times with the Professional Golfers' Association and the PGA European Tour.

National Functions

Prior to the First World War, a group of Clubs had been responsible for the running of the Open and Amateur Championships. In 1919 a meeting of these Clubs confirmed that the Royal & Ancient should be the Governing Authority for the game and agreed it should assume responsibility for the two Championships.

The decision that the Royal & Ancient should be the Governing Authority was endorsed at a Meeting of the English, Scottish, Irish and Welsh Unions in 1924, at which Meeting what is now the Council of National Golf Unions was formed with the object amongst others of directing the system of Standard Scratch Scores and Handicaps.

In 1948 the Royal & Ancient took over the Boys and in 1963 the Youths Championship from the private interests which had previously run them; this was done at the request of the individuals concerned. In 1969 the Royal & Ancient itself inaugurated the British Seniors Amateur Championship.

In addition to the organisation of five Championships, the Royal & Ancient is also responsible for the selection of Teams to represent Great Britain & Ireland in the Walker Cup, the Eisenhower Trophy, the St Andrews Trophy, and other International Tournaments. It is responsible for the organisation of such events when they are held in Great Britain and Ireland.

Club Functions

The Membership of the Club is limited to a total of 1,800, of which 1,050 may be resident in Great Britain and Ireland and 750 elsewhere: this Overseas Membership is spread over countries throughout the world.

The Membership both at home and abroad is representative and includes many who have given and are giving great services to golf in this country and abroad to many different Unions and Associations. This permits broad and effective representation on all the Club Committees concerned with international and national functions.

Exercise of International Functions

1. Rules of Golf

(a) *Committee:*
The Rules of Golf Committee exists for the purpose of reviewing the Rules of Golf from time

to time and of making decisions on their interpretation and publishing these decisions where necessary.

The Committee consists of twelve Members elected by the Club, of whom three retire each year and are not eligible for re-election for one year, except in the case of the Chairman and Deputy Chairman, and of up to twelve additional persons invited annually to join the Committee from Golf Authorities at home and abroad.

At present the bodies represented are:

Council of National Golf Unions
United States Golf Association
European Golf Association
Australian Golf Union
New Zealand Golf Association
Royal Canadian Golf Association
South African Golf Union
Asia-Pacific Golf Confederation
South American Golf Federation
Japan Golf Association

(b) Revision of the Rules of Golf:

As the only other Governing Authority for the Rules of Golf is the USGA, the R&A works closely with this body when amendments to the Rules are under consideration for the purpose of maintaining uniformity in the Rules and their interpretation. Every four years a Conference takes place with the USGA for the purpose of deciding on the changes to be made. The quadrennial conference held in 1987 made numerous amendments to the 1984 Rules; these were mainly to clarify points of doubt which had emerged since 1984. The changes took effect on January 1st 1988. Although the Conference takes place quadrennially, the Rules are under constant review and investigations as to possible improvements start not long after a revision has taken place, so that ample time can be given to consult with interested parties.

Two years after a revision has taken place an important meeting is held with the USGA in the United States at the time of the Walker Cup to discuss progress and to start clearing the ground for the next Conference.

(c) Decisions:

The Rules of Golf Committee has a Decisions Sub-Committee which answers queries from Clubs and from all the Unions and Associations affiliated to the R&A. Those Decisions which seem to establish important or interesting points of interpretation are available in the form of a loose-leaf Decisions Service published jointly by the R&A and the USGA and issued world-wide. The number of subscribers to this Service is about 3,500 and is increasing steadily as golf expands.

2. Implements and Ball

The Committee consists of four Members elected by the Club, one Member of the Rules of Golf Committee and one Member of the Championship Committee, together with Consultant Members invited by the Committee to advise on technical matters. One of the elected Members retires each year but the Chairman may be re-elected immediately for the sake of continuity.

The Committee works in close co-operation with the USGA I & B Committee in interpreting the Rules and Appendices relating to the control of the form and make of golf clubs and the specifications of the golf ball to ensure that the game and established golf courses are not harmed by technical developments.

3. Rules of Amateur Status

(a) Committee:

The Committee consists of five members, of which four are elected by the Club and one provided by the Council of National Golf Unions. There are also Advisory Members to the Committee, representing the same Golfing Authorities as on the Rules of Golf Committee.

(b) Revision of Rules of Amateur Status:

A procedure, similar to that for the Rules of Golf, is adopted for revision of the Rules of Amateur Status and no policy changes are made without full consultation with all the affiliated Unions, the USGA and the PGA.

(c) Decisions:

The work of the Committee consists of (a) dealing with Applications for reinstatement to Amateur Status, (b) answering inquiries about the nature of prizes, conditions for Tournaments, etc, arising out of the increased impact of commercial sponsors on Amateur golf and the issue of guidelines and Decisions, (c) answering queries from individuals regarding their own position under the Rules and (d) controlling Scholarships and other Grants-in-aid.

Exercise of National Functions

The Championship Committee

The Championship Committee is responsible for the control of the five Championships and of the International Matches and Tournaments mentioned above.

The Committee consists of twelve elected Members elected by the Club, of whom three retire annually and are not eligible for re-election for one year. Two additional Members may also

be invited to join the Committee annually together with two Business Members co-opted for four years.

For the organisation of any particular event, others may be co-opted, if required.

The work of this Committee has greatly increased in recent years, as is clearly evident from the staging of the Open Championship, for which prizes in 1990 amounted to £827,700. At the same time, more substantial reserve funds have been built up to ensure the continuance of the Open Championship as a premier world event.

The Committee makes annual donations to a number of golfing bodies, especially those concerned with the training and development of junior golf and for research on greenkeeping matters.

Selection Committee

The Selection Committee consists of a Chairman, who is a Member of the Club, and other Members, who need not be Members of the Club, appointed by the General Committee. These other Members have for some years now been representative of each of the four Home Unions. Normally they hold their appointments for four years.

Exercise of Club Functions

The domestic affairs of the Club are run by Committees which it is not necessary to describe in this statement.

It is appropriate, however, to mention that the Club does not own a Golf Course. It is, nevertheless, much concerned with the maintenance and improvements of all four Golf Courses in St Andrews. These Courses are controlled by the St Andrews Links Trust and are run by the Links Management Committee. Three of the Trustees and four Members of the Management Committee are appointed by the Club and equal numbers are appointed by the North-East Fife District Council. The Chairman of the Trust is appointed by the Secretary of State for Scotland and the current MP is also a Trustee. The Club contributes an annually negotiated sum to the Trust in return for Members' playing privileges.

Finance

International Functions

After taking into account income derived from subscriptions to the Rules of Golf Decisions Service and the sale of official Rules publications, the net expenses of the Rules of Golf, Rules of Amateur Status and Rules for Implements and Ball are borne by External Activities.

National Functions

Income and expenditure of all Championships run by the R&A and the expenses of Teams representing Great Britain & Ireland are accounted for in separate divisions of one Account.

Surpluses of all income over expenditure in the External Activities Account are held in reserve to ensure the continuance of the running of the various events at a high standard.

The Royal & Ancient Golf Club as a private Members' Club does not in any way benefit from the External Activities Account.

General Committee

Responsibility for directing and co-ordinating the three functions of the R&A—as a private club, as a governing authority for golf and as the body responsible for organising and running the championships and international matches—rests with the Club's General Committee, which controls all matters of policy. The Committee consists of sixteen R&A Members, eight of whom are elected by the Club; the other eight *ex-officio* members are the Captain and Chairmen of the Finance, Membership, House, Green, Rules of Golf, Championship and Amateur Status Committees.

The execution of the decisions of the Club Committees and of the decisions taken by the Members at Business Meetings is in the hands of the Secretary of the R&A, who is assisted by several senior officers and the appropriate infrastructure of secretaries and clerical staff.

Contacts with Affiliated Golfing Authorities

The R&A endeavours to consult with all those Golfing Authorities concerned whenever an issue of importance arises. This covers, in particular, matters relating to Rules of Golf, Rules of Amateur Status, and the Championships.

Meetings are held when appropriate with representatives of Golfing Authorities in Great Britain & Ireland and the European Golf Association. Consultations with other Golfing Authorities abroad are regularly conducted by correspondence.

In January 1970, a Conference attended by Golfing Unions and Associations in this country and representatives of the European Golf Association was held under the auspices of the R&A to discuss all matters of mutual interest, and in particular to establish the best means of communication in the future between the Unions and Associations concerned. This was followed by a similar Conference at Chantilly, Paris in 1976.

In May 1980 the first ever International Golf Conference was held in St Andrews at which 33 countries affiliated to the R&A were represented and to which the USGA, PGA and other golfing bodies in this country sent observers. Owing to the great success of this Conference the R&A agreed to organise similar meetings every four years from 1985.

The R&A is represented at Meetings of the World Amateur Golf Council and the Council of National Golf Unions and on the CCPR.

January 1985 (revised)

MF Bonallack OBE
Secretary
Royal & Ancient Golf Club
of St Andrews
Fife KY16 9JD

The Championship Committee

Until 1919 the Open and Amateur Championships of Great Britain were organised by a group of leading Clubs in Scotland and England. The Club where the Championship was to be played was charged with running it for that year. In 1919, the Royal & Ancient, by then the recognised governing authority of the game, was invited to take over the responsibility for both Championships and ever since its Championship Committee has controlled both. Once the course on which a Championship is to be played has been decided, usually several years ahead, the Committee works closely with the Club concerned.

The Amateur, which is nearly as old as The Open, may have lost some of its public appeal with the growth of Professional golf and the defection of so many able young amateurs to its lucrative tour. However, the Amateur Championship is still considered the most prestigious event in the amateur game and is always played on one of the best courses.

The Championship Committee today controls several more events besides the two oldest Championships. The Boys, started privately in 1921, and the Youths, in 1954, both now come under its wing, as does the Seniors which was inaugurated by the R&A in 1969. In addition, the biennial amateur matches against the United States and the Rest of Europe for the Walker Cup and the St Andrews Trophies respectively, are run by the Committee when played in Great Britain, as also are Boys' and Youths' Internationals against the Rest of Europe. The R&A Selection Committee chooses the team for all these amateur matches, as well as the team which competes for the Eisenhower Trophy, the World Amateur Team Championship. This was first played at St Andrews in 1958 and has since been held every two years in different parts of the world.

The remarkable development of The Open to the great occasion it is today has meant heavily increased responsibilities for the Championship Committee. TV and the media have given it an audience in millions compared with the few thousand interested in the past. The R&A's determination to match the growing interest with a new attitude and astute promotion has given the event the kudos and following it now enjoys. The last 20 years has seen the winner's cheque grow from £1200 to £85,000, the total prize money from £15,000 to £827,700 in 1990, when the attendance was 208,680. The financial success of The Open has provided considerable sums of money for the development of junior golf, and other worthy causes connected to golf.

The R&A works closely with the Club of the course where the Championship is to be played, whose members take on many of the essential duties necessary if it is to run smoothly. These include spectator control where local Clubs take charge of a hole each, usually providing three-hour shifts of up to 16 members at a time. This can involve as many as 800 men daily. Local volunteer stewards also cover such diverse duties as course controllers, supervision of litter collection and spectator stand control. Security, courtesy transport, car park supervision and public catering, to name a few of the mass of services necessary, are provided under contract by companies expert in these fields. Close liaison with the area police authority is vital. Facilities for the Press, Television and the vast tented village, each involving several hundred people, occupy large areas and are a major limiting factor when considering possible venues for future championships.

Important for both competitors and spectators and appreciated by both is the radio network which provides up-to-the-minute scores and positions of the leading players which appear very quickly on the leader boards erected at strategic points round the course. The system developed over many years is as quick, informative and accurate as any in existence.

The Committee consists of thirteen Royal & Ancient members, who devote much time to their tasks. It has a full-time secretary who, together with the Secretary of the Club and some

of his staff, is involved in the planning of The Open and other events throughout the year. Members of the Committee work long hours during Open week. From first light at about 5am, when the Head Greenkeeper and a nominated member of the Committee tour the course deciding the pin positions on each green for the day, to dusk when the last competitor comes in, all are occupied, mostly out on the course at selected points, in two-way radio contact with the centre, ready to give a ruling when required. In the final rounds the leading players are accompanied by a member of the committee for the whole round.

The many stands erected around the course, providing seats for sometimes 18,000 spectators, often quite close to greens, make for special problems. A loose shot which ends under a stand will probably mean the ball may be dropped without penalty in an area nearby, which has been pre-designated by the committee; this shot should be of equal difficulty as it would have been if the stand had not been there. In these cases often an official decision is required.

At the end of every round each competitor's card must be immediately checked and recorded following which, in the case of a leader, he will meet the press in the interview room.

It is the Championship Committee too which decides if any round has to be halted, postponed or cancelled due to storm and tempest. Such decisions, so difficult with so many factors, consequent on a postponement, to be considered, have been eased a little with improved weather forecasting and continuous contact with the local weather bureau.

It will be seen that the work of the Committee is never ending with the myriad of tasks necessary to ensure the even flow to a Championship. The success of The Open is due to sound planning, moving with the times and the expertise of the R&A staff which is the executive arm of the Committee. The Open may be the Championship with which all are familiar; however, it must be remembered that the many other events under the R&A's control also require planning and organisation. The work for these events goes on largely unnoticed, but must not be forgotten.

Rules of Golf

As Approved by
The Royal & Ancient Golf Club
of St Andrews, Scotland
and the
United States Golf Association

25th EDITION
EFFECTIVE 1st JANUARY 1988

Rules of Golf Committee

The Rules of Golf Committee shall consist of twelve Members of the Club to be elected by the Club, and additional Members not exceeding ten in number (who need not be Members of the Club) from Golf Authorities at home and abroad invited annually to join the Committee by the twelve Members elected by the Club. Such Invited Members shall, irrespective of the date of their invitation to become Members of the Rules of Golf Committee, remain so only until the date of the first Autumn Business Meeting occurring after their being invited to become Members but may again be invited thereafter. During their term of office such Invited Members (if not Members of the Club) shall be admitted as Temporary Members of the Club.

The Rules of Golf are the subject of quadrennial review by the R&A and the USGA in order to maintain uniformity and keep abreast of changing conditions.

Queries on the Rules may only be referred to the Rules of Golf Committee through the Secretary of the Club or the Association responsible for the competition. Many queries have to be returned unanswered because they have been sent direct to the Committee by individuals.

CONTENTS

Foreword
to the 1988 Edition of the Rules of Golf

The Royal & Ancient Golf Club of St. Andrews and the United States Golf Association have carried out their customary quadrennial review of the Rules of Golf and have agreed upon certain amendments which they believe will improve the Rules.

The extensive changes in the Rules which were introduced in 1984 have received universal approval. Consequently, a minimal number of substantive changes were considered necessary. These are summarised on page 715.

The R.&A. and USGA would like to record their appreciation of the valuable assistance which they have received from a number of golfing bodies throughout the world. The new Rules will become effective on 1st January 1988.

The combining of the Decisions Services of the R.&A. and USGA into a single volume has proved to be an outstanding success and has done much to establish uniformity of interpretation of the Rules worldwide.

We would like to take this opportunity to express our sincere thanks to our respective Committees and all those who have in so many ways helped us in our endeavours.

W.J.F. Bryce
Chairman
Rules of Golf Committee
Royal & Ancient Golf Club of St. Andrews

C. Grant Spaeth
Chairman
Rules of Golf Committee
United States Golf Association

CHANGES

Principal Changes introduced in the 1988 Code

Rule 2.   Match Play
Expanded to state that a player may concede the next stroke, a hole or the match, and that a concession may not be declined or withdrawn.

Rule 3-3.   Stroke Play. Doubt as to Procedure
If a competitor fails to announce in advance his decision to invoke this Rule, the score with the original ball, rather than the higher score, will count.

Rule 4-4.   Maximum of Fourteen Clubs
Amended to state that a player may borrow a club from anyone on the course, but that the person from whom it was borrowed may not thereafter use the club.

Rule 5 and Appendix III
After 1st January 1990 it will no longer be permitted to use the small (1.620") ball.

Rule 5-3.   Ball Unfit for Play
A stricter definition is adopted stating that a ball is unfit for play if it is visibly cut, cracked or out of shape, but a ball is not unfit for play solely because mud or other materials adhere to it, its surface is scratched or scraped or its paint is damaged or discoloured.

Rule 18.   Ball at Rest Moved
If a ball at rest moves after address (other than as a result of a stroke) the ball shall be replaced rather than played as it lies. This procedure is now consistent with that prescribed in other subsections of this Rule.

Rule 19-5.   Ball in Motion Deflected or Stopped by Another Ball
Clarifies that when two balls in motion collide, each player shall play his ball as it lies.

Rule 25-1b (ii) and 1c (ii). Casual Water, Ground Under Repair and Certain Damage to Course. Relief. In a Hazard

Rule 26-1b.   Ball in Water Hazard

Rule 28c.   Ball Unplayable
Amended to state that the ball must be dropped keeping the point where the ball lay (or where it last crossed the margin of the hazard, as the case may be) between the spot on which the ball is dropped and the hole. It is no longer permitted to stand on that line and drop a ball an arm's length to the side.

The Rules of Golf

Section I   Etiquette

Courtesy on the Course

Safety

Prior to playing a stroke or making a practice swing, the player should ensure that no one is standing close by or in a position to be hit by the club, the ball or any stones, pebbles, twigs or the like which may be moved by the stroke or swing.

Consideration for Other Players

The player who has the honour should be allowed to play before his opponent or fellow-competitor tees his ball.

No one should move, talk or stand close to or directly behind the ball or the hole when a player is addressing the ball or making a stroke.

In the interest of all, players should play without delay.

No player should play until the players in front are out of range.

Players searching for a ball should signal the players behind them to pass as soon as it becomes apparent that the ball will not easily be found. They should not search for five minutes before doing so. They should not continue play until the players following them have passed and are out of range.

When the play of a hole has been completed, players should immediately leave the putting green.

Priority on the Course

In the absence of special rules, two-ball matches should have precedence over and be entitled to pass any three- or four-ball match.

A single player has no standing and should give way to a match of any kind.

Any match playing a whole round is entitled to pass a match playing a shorter round.

If a match fails to keep its place on the course and loses more than one clear hole on the players in front, it should invite the match following to pass.

Care of the Course

Holes in Bunkers

Before leaving a bunker, a player should carefully fill up and smooth over all holes and footprints made by him.

Replace Divots; Repair Ball-Marks and Damage by Spikes

Through the green, a player should ensure that any turf cut or displaced by him is replaced at once and pressed down and that any damage to the putting green made by a ball is carefully repaired. Damage to the putting green caused by golf shoe spikes should be repaired *on completion of the hole*.

Damage to Greens—Flagsticks, Bags, etc.

Players should ensure that, when putting down bags or the flagstick, no damage is done to the putting green and that neither they nor their caddies damage the hole by standing close to it, in handling the flagstick or in removing the ball from the hole. The flagstick should be properly replaced in the hole before the players leave the putting green. Players should not damage the putting green by leaning on their putters, particularly when removing the ball from the hole.

Golf Carts

Local notices regulating the movement of golf carts should be strictly observed.

Damage Through Practice Swings

In taking practice swings, players should avoid causing damage to the course, particularly the tees, by removing divots.

Section II   Definitions

Addressing the Ball

A player has "addressed the ball" when he has taken his stance and has also grounded his club, except that in a hazard a player has addressed the ball when he has taken his stance.

Advice

"Advice" is any counsel or suggestion which could influence a player in determining his play, the choice of a club or the method of making a stroke.

Information on the Rules or on matter of public information, such as the position of hazards or the flagstick on the putting green, is not advice.

Ball Deemed to Move

See "Move or Moved".

Ball Holed
See "Holed".

Ball Lost
See "Lost Ball".

Ball in Play
A ball is "in play" as soon as the player has made a stroke on the teeing ground. It remains in play until holed out, except when it is lost, out of bounds or lifted, or another ball has been substituted under an applicable Rule, whether or not such Rule permits substitution; a ball so substituted becomes the ball in play.

Bunker
A "bunker" is a hazard consisting of a prepared area of ground, often a hollow, from which turf or soil has been removed and replaced with sand or the like. Grass-covered ground bordering or within a bunker is not part of the bunker. The margin of a bunker extends vertically downwards, but not upwards.

Caddie
A "caddie" is one who carries or handles a player's clubs during play and otherwise assists him in accordance with the Rules.

When one caddie is employed by more than one player, he is always deemed to be the caddie of the player whose ball is involved, and equipment carried by him is deemed to be that player's equipment, except when the caddie acts upon specific directions of another player, in which case he is considered to be that other player's caddie.

Casual Water
"Casual water" is any temporary accumulation of water on the course which is visible before or after the player takes his stance and is not in a water hazard. Snow and ice are either casual water or loose impediments, at the option of the player, except that manufactured ice is an obstruction. Dew is not casual water.

Committee
The "Committee" is the committee in charge of the competition or, if the matter does not arise in a competition, the committee in charge of the course.

Competitor
A "competitor" is a player in a stroke competition. A "fellow-competitor" is any person with whom the competitor plays. Neither is partner of the other.

In stroke play foursome and four-ball competitions, where the context so admits, the word "competitor" or "fellow-competitor" includes his partner.

Course
The "course" is the whole area within which play is permitted (see Rule 33-2).

Equipment
"Equipment" is anything used, worn or carried by or for the player except any ball he has played at the hole being played and any small object, such as a coin or a tee, when used to mark the position of a ball or the extent of an area in which a ball is to be dropped. Equipment includes a golf cart, whether or not motorised. If such a cart is shared by more than one player, its status under the Rules is the same as that of a caddie employed by more than one player. See "Caddie".

Fellow Competitor
See "Competitor".

Flagstick
The "flagstick" is a movable straight indicator, with or without bunting or other material attached, centred in the hole to show its position. It shall be circular in cross-section.

Forecaddie
A "forecaddie" is one who is employed by the Committee to indicate to players the position of balls during play. He is an outside agency.

Ground Under Repair
"Ground under repair" is any portion of the course so marked by order of the Committee or so declared by its authorised representative. It includes material piled for removal and a hole made by a greenkeeper, even if not so marked. Stakes and lines defining ground under repair are in such ground. The margin of ground under repair extends vertically downwards, but not upwards.

Note 1: Grass cuttings and other material left on the course which have been abandoned and are not intended to be removed are not ground under repair unless so marked.

Note 2: The Committee may make a Local Rule prohibiting play from ground under repair.

Hazards
A "hazard" is any bunker or water hazard.

Hole
The "hole" shall be 4¼ inches (108mm) in diameter and at least 4 inches (100mm) deep. If a lining is used, it shall be sunk at least 1 inch (25mm) below the putting green surface unless the nature of the soil makes it impracticable to do so; its outer diameter shall not exceed 4¼ inches (108mm).

Holed

A ball is "holed" when it is at rest within the circumference of the hole and all of it is below the level of the lip of the hole.

Honour

The side entitled to play first from the teeing ground is said to have the "honour".

Lateral Water Hazard

A "lateral water hazard" is a water hazard or that part of a water hazard so situated that it is not possible or is deemed by the Committee to be impracticable to drop a ball behind the water hazard in accordance with Rule 26-1b.

That part of a water hazard to be played as a lateral water hazard should be distinctively marked.

Note: Lateral water hazards should be defined by red stakes or lines.

Loose Impediments

"Loose impediments" are natural objects such as stones, leaves, twigs, branches and the like, dung, worms and insects and casts or heaps made by them, provided they are not fixed or growing, are not solidly embedded and do not adhere to the ball.

Sand and loose soil are loose impediments on the putting green, but not elsewhere.

Snow and ice are either casual water or loose impediments, at the option of the player, except that manufactured ice is an obstruction.

Dew is not a loose impediment.

Lost Ball

A ball is "lost" if:

a. It is not found or identified as his by the player within five minutes after the player's side or his or their caddies have begun to search for it; or

b. The player has put another ball into play under the Rules, even though he may not have searched for the original ball; or

c. The player has played any stroke with a provisional ball from the place where the original ball is likely to be or from a point nearer the hole than that place, whereupon the provisional ball becomes the ball in play.

Time spent in playing a wrong ball is not counted in the five-minute period allowed for search.

Marker

A "marker" is one who is appointed by the Committee to record a competitor's score in stroke play. He may be a fellow-competitor. He is not a referee.

Matches

See "Sides and Matches".

Move or Moved

A ball is deemed to have "moved" if it leaves its position and comes to rest in any other place.

Observer

An "observer" is one who is appointed by the Committee to assist a referee to decide questions of fact and to report to him any breach of a Rule. An observer should not attend the flagstick, stand at or mark the position of the hole, or lift the ball or mark its position.

Obstructions

An "obstruction" is anything artificial, including the artificial surfaces and sides of roads and paths and manufactured ice, except:

a. Objects defining out of bounds, such as walls, fences, stakes and railings;

b. Any part of an immovable artificial object which is out of bounds; and

c. Any construction declared by the Committee to be an integral part of the course.

Out of Bounds

"Out of bounds" is ground on which play is prohibited.

When out of bounds is defined by reference to stakes or a fence or as being beyond stakes or a fence, the out of bounds line is determined by the nearest inside points of the stakes or fence posts at ground level excluding angled supports.

When out of bounds is defined by a line on the ground, the line itself is out of bounds.

The out of bounds line extends vertically upwards and downwards.

A ball is out of bounds when all of it lies out of bounds.

A player may stand out of bounds to play a ball lying within bounds.

Outside Agency

An "outside agency" is any agency not part of the match or, in stroke play, not part of a competitor's side, and includes a referee, a marker, an observer or a forecaddie. Neither wind nor water is an outside agency.

Partner

A "partner" is a player associated with another player on the same side.

In a threesome, foursome, best-ball or four-ball match, where the context so admits, the word "player" includes his partner or partners.

Penalty Stroke

A "penalty stroke" is one added to the score of a player or side under certain Rules. In a threesome or foursome, penalty strokes do not affect the order of play.

Provisional Ball
A "provisional ball" is a ball played under Rule 27-2 for a ball which may be lost outside a water hazard or may be out of bounds.

Putting Green
The "putting green" is all ground of the hole being played which is specially prepared for putting or otherwise defined as such by the Committee. A ball is on the puting green when any part of it touches the putting green.

Referee
A "referee" is one who is appointed by the Committee to accompany players to decide questions of fact and apply the Rules of Golf. He shall act on any breach of a Rule which he observes or is reported to him.

A referee should not attend the flagstick, stand at or mark the position of the hole, or lift the ball or mark its position.

Rub of the Green
A "rub of the green" occurs when a ball in motion is accidentally deflected or stopped by any outside agency (see Rule 19-1).

Rule
The term "Rule" includes Local Rules made by the Committee under Rule 33-8a.

Sides and Matches
Side: A player, or two or more players who are partners.

Single: A match in which one plays against another.

Threesome: A match in which one plays against two, and each side plays one ball.

Foursome: A match in which two play against two, and each side plays one ball.

Three-ball: A match-play competition in which three play against one another, each playing his own ball. Each player is playing two distinct matches.

Best ball: A match in which one plays against the better ball of two or the best ball of three players.

Four-ball: A match in which two play their better ball against the better ball of two other players.

Stance
Taking the "stance" consists in a player placing his feet in position for and preparatory to making a stroke.

Stipulated Round
The "stipulated round" consists of playing the holes of the course in their correct sequence unless otherwise authorised by the Committee. The number of holes in a stipulated round is 18 unless a smaller number is authorised by the Committee. As to extension of stipulated round in match play, see Rule 2-3.

Stroke
A "stroke" is the forward movement of the club made with the intention of fairly striking at and moving the ball, but if a player checks his downswing voluntarily before the clubhead reaches the ball he is not deemed to have made a stroke.

Teeing Ground
The "teeing ground" is the starting place for the hole to be played. It is a rectangular area two club-lengths in depth, the front and the sides of which are defined by the outside limits of two tee-markers. A ball is outside the teeing ground when all of it lies outside the teeing ground.

Through the Green
"Through the green" is the whole area of the course except

a. The teeing ground and putting green of the hole being played; and

b. All hazards on the course.

Water Hazard
A "water hazard" is any sea, lake, pond, river, ditch, surface drainage ditch or other open water course (whether or not containing water) and anything of a similar nature.

All ground or water within the margin of a water hazard is part of the water hazard. The margin of a water hazard extends vertically upwards and downwards. Stakes and lines defining the margins of water hazards are in the hazards.

Note: Water hazards (other than lateral water hazards) should be defined by yellow stakes or lines.

Wrong Ball
A "wrong ball" is any ball other than:

a. The ball in play,

b. A provisional ball or

c. In stroke play, a second ball played under Rule 3-3 or Rule 20-7b.

Note: Ball in play includes a ball substituted for the ball in play when the player is proceeding under an applicable Rule which does not permit substitution.

Section III
The Rules of Play

THE GAME

Rule 1. The Game

1-1. General

The Game of Golf consists in playing a ball from the <u>teeing ground</u> into the hole by a <u>stroke</u> or successive strokes in accordance with the Rules.

1-2. Exerting Influence on Ball

No player or caddie shall take any action to influence the position or the movement of a ball except in accordance with the rules.

PENALTY FOR BREACH OF RULE 1-2:
Match play—Loss of hole; Stroke play—Two strokes.

Note: In the case of a serious breach of Rule 1-2, the Committee may impose a penalty of disqualification.

1-3. Agreement to Waive Rules

Players shall not agree to exclude the operation of any Rule or to waive any penalty incurred.

PENALTY FOR BREACH OF RULE 1-3:
Match play—Disqualification of both sides;
Stroke play—Disqualification of competitors concerned.

(Agreeing to play out of turn in stroke play— see Rule 10-2c.)

1-4. Points Not Covered by Rules

If any point in dispute is not covered by the Rules, the decision shall be made in accordance with equity.

Rule 2. Match Play

2-1. Winner of Hole; Reckoning of Holes

In match play the game is played by holes.

Except as otherwise provided in the Rules, a hole is won by the side which holes its ball in the fewer strokes. In a handicap match the lower net score wins the hole.

The reckoning of holes is kept by the terms: so many "holes up" or "all square", and so many "to play".

A side is "dormie" when it is as many holes up as there are holes remaining to be played.

2-2. Halved Hole

A hole is halved if each side holes out in the same number of strokes.

When a player has holed out and his opponent has been left with a stroke for the half, if the player thereafter incurs a penalty, the hole is halved.

2-3. Winner of Match

A match (which consists of a <u>stipulated</u> <u>round</u>, unless otherwise decreed by the Committee) is won by the side which is leading by a number of holes greater than the number of holes remaining to be played.

The Committee may, for the purpose of settling a tie, extend the stipulated round to as many holes as are required for a match to be won.

2-4. Concession of Next Stroke, Hole or Match

When the opponent's ball is at rest or is deemed to be at rest under Rule 16-2, the player may concede the opponent to have holed out with his next stroke and the ball may be removed by either side with a club or otherwise.

A player may concede a hole or a match at any time prior to the conclusion of the hole or the match.

Concession of a stroke, hole or match may not be declined or withdrawn.

2-5. Claims

In match play, if a doubt or dispute arises between the players and no duly authorised representative of the Committee is available within a reasonable time, the players shall continue the match without delay. Any claim, if it is to be considered by the Committee, must be made before any player in the match plays from the next teeing ground or, in the case of the last hole of the match, before all players in the match leave the putting green.

No later claim shall be considered unless it is based on facts previously unknown to the player making the claim and the player making the claim had been given wrong information (Rules 6-2a and 9) by an opponent. In any case, no later claim shall be considered after the result of the match has been officially announced, unless the Committee is satisfied that the opponent knew he was giving wrong information.

2-6. General Penalty

The penalty for a breach of a Rule in match play is loss of hole except when otherwise provided.

Rule 3. Stroke Play

3-1. Winner

The competitor who plays the <u>stipulated</u> <u>round</u> or rounds in the fewest strokes is the winner.

3-2. Failure to Hole Out

If a competitor fails to hole out at any hole and

does not correct his mistake before he plays a stroke from the next teeing ground or, in the case of the last hole of the round, before he leaves the putting green, *he shall be disqualified.*

3-3. Doubt as to Procedure

a. Procedure

In stroke play only, when during play of a hole a competitor is doubtful of his rights or procedure, he may, without penalty, play a second ball. After the situation which has caused the doubt has arisen, the competitor should, before taking further action, announce to his marker or a fellow-competitor his decision to invoke this Rule and the ball with which he will score if the Rules permit.

The competitor shall report the facts to the Committee before returning his score card unless he scores the same with both balls; if he fails to do so, *he shall be disqualified.*

b. Determination of Score for Hole

If the Rules allow the procedure selected in advance by the competitor, the score with the ball selected shall be his score for the hole.

If the competitor fails to announce in advance his decision to invoke this Rule or his selection, the score with the original ball or, if the original ball is not one of the balls being played, the first ball put into play shall count if the Rules allow the procedure adopted for such ball.

Note: A second ball played under Rule 3-3 is not a provisional ball under Rule 27-2.

3-4. Refusal to Comply with a Rule

If a competitor refuses to comply with a Rule affecting the rights of another competitor, *he shall be disqualified.*

3-5. General Penalty

The penalty for a breach of a Rule in stroke play is two strokes except when otherwise provided.

CLUBS AND THE BALL

The Royal & Ancient Golf Club of St. Andrews and the United States Golf Association reserve the right to change the Rules and make and change the interpretations relating to clubs, balls and other implements at any time.

Rule 4. Clubs

If there may be any reasonable basis for doubt as to whether a club which is to be manufactured conforms with Rule 4 and Appendix II, the manufacturer should submit a sample to the Royal & Ancient Golf Club of St Andrews for a ruling, such

sample to become its property for reference purposes. If a manufacturer fails to do so, he assumes the risk of a ruling that the club does not conform with the Rules of Golf.

A player in doubt as to the conformity of a club should consult the Royal & Ancient Golf Club of St Andrews.

4-1. Form and Make of Clubs

A club is an implement designed to be used for striking the ball.

A putter is a club designed primarily for use on the putting green.

The player's clubs shall conform with the provisions of this Rule and with the specifications and interpretations set forth in Appendix II.

a. General

The club shall be composed of a shaft and a head. All parts of the club shall be fixed so that the club is one unit. The club shall not be designed to be adjustable except for weight. The club shall not be substantially different from the traditional and customary form and make.

b. Shaft

The shaft shall be generally straight, with the same bending and twisting properties in any direction, and shall be attached to the clubhead at the heel either directly or through a single plain neck or socket. A putter shaft may be attached to any point in the head.

c. Grip

The grip consists of that part of the shaft designed to be held by the player and any material added to it for the purpose of obtaining a firm hold. The grip shall be substantially straight and plain in form and shall not be moulded for any part of the hands.

d. Clubhead

The distance from the heel to the toe of the clubhead shall be greater than the distance from the face to the back. The clubhead shall be generally plain in shape.

The clubhead shall have only one face designed for striking the ball, except that a putter may have two such faces if their characteristics are the same, they are opposite each other and the loft of each is the same and does not exceed ten degrees.

e. Club Face

The face shall not have any degree of concavity and, in relation to the ball, shall be hard and rigid. It shall be generally smooth except for such markings as are permitted by Appendix II. If the basic structural material of the head and face of a club, other than a putter, is metal, no inset or attachment is permitted.

f. Wear

A club which conforms with Rule 4-1 when

new is deemed to conform after wear through normal use. Any part of a club which has been purposely altered is regarded as new and must conform, in the altered state, with the Rules.

g. Damage

If a player's club ceases to conform with Rule 4-1 because of damage sustained in the normal course of play, the player may:

(i) use the club in its damaged state, but only for the remainder of the stipulated round during which such damage was sustained; or

(ii) without unduly delaying play, repair it.

A club which ceases to conform because of damage sustained other than in the normal course of play shall not subsequently be used during the round.

(Damage changing playing characteristics of club—see Rule 4-2.)

4-2. Playing Characteristics Changed

During a stipulated round, the playing characteristics of a club shall not be purposely changed.

If the playing characteristics of a player's club are changed during a round because of damage sustained in the normal course of play, the player may:

(i) use the club in its altered state; or

(ii) without unduly delaying play, repair it.

If the playing characteristics of a player's club are changed because of damage sustained other than in the normal course of play, the club shall not subsequently be used during the round.

Damage to a club which occurred prior to a round may be repaired during the round, provided the playing characteristics are not changed and play is not unduly delayed.

4-3. Foreign Material

No foreign material shall be applied to the club face for the purpose of influencing the movement of the ball.

PENALTY FOR BREACH OF RULE 4-1, -2 or -3:
Disqualification

4-4. Maximum of Fourteen Clubs

a. Selection and Replacement of Clubs

The player shall start a stipulated round with not more than fourteen clubs. He is limited to the clubs thus selected for that round except that, without unduly delaying play, he may:

(i) if he started with fewer than fourteen, add as many as will bring his total to that number; and

(ii) replace, with any club, a club which becomes unfit for play in the normal course of play.

b. Borrowing or Sharing Clubs

The addition or replacement of a club or clubs may be made by borrowing from anyone; only the borrower may use such club or clubs for the remainder of the round.

The sharing of a club or clubs is prohibited except that partners may share clubs, provided that the total number of clubs carried by the partners so sharing does not exceed fourteen.

PENALTY FOR BREACH OF RULE 4-4a or b, REGARDLESS OF NUMBER OF EXCESS CLUBS CARRIED:

Match play—At the conclusion of the hole at which the breach is discovered, the state of the match shall be adjusted by deducting one hole for each hole at which a breach occurred. Maximum deduction per round: two holes.

Stroke play—Two strokes for each hole at which any breach occurred; maximum penalty per round: four strokes.

Bogey and par competitions—Penalties as in match play.

Stableford competitions—see Note to Rule 32-1b.

c. Excess Club Declared Out of Play

Any club carried or used in breach of this Rule shall be declared out of play by the player immediately upon discovery that a breach has occurred and thereafter shall not be used by the player during the round.

PENALTY FOR BREACH OF RULE 4-4c:
Disqualification

Rule 5. The Ball

5-1. General

The ball the player uses shall conform to specifications set forth in Appendix III on maximum weight, minimum size, spherical symmetry, initial velocity and overall distance when tested under specified conditions.

Note: In laying down the conditions under which a competition is to be played (Rule 33-1), the Committee may stipulate that the ball to be used shall be of certain specifications, provided these specifications are within the limits prescribed by Appendix III, and that it be of a size, brand and marking as detailed on the current List of Conforming Golf Balls issued by the Royal & Ancient Golf Club of St. Andrews.

5-2. Foreign Material

No foreign material shall be applied to a ball for the purpose of changing its playing characteristics.

PENALTY FOR BREACH OF RULES 5-1 or 5-2:
Disqualification.

5-3. Ball Unfit for Play

A ball is unfit for play if it is visibly cut, cracked or out of shape. A ball is not unfit for play solely because mud or other materials adhere to it, its surface is scratched or scraped or its paint is damaged or discoloured.

If a player has reason to believe his ball has become unfit for play during play of the hole being played, he may during the play of such hole lift his ball without penalty to determine whether it is unfit, provided he announces his intention in advance to his opponent in match play or his marker or a fellow-competitor in stroke play and gives his opponent, marker or fellow-competitor an opportunity to examine the ball. If he lifts the ball without announcing his intention in advance or giving his opponent, marker or fellow-competitor an opportunity to examine the ball, *he shall incur a penalty of one stroke.*

If it is determined that the ball has become unfit for play during play of the hole being played, the player may substitute another ball, placing it on the spot where the original ball lay. Otherwise, the original ball shall be replaced.

If a ball breaks into pieces as a result of a stroke, the stroke shall be replayed without penalty (see Rule 20-5).

> *PENALTY FOR BREACH OF RULE 5-3:
> Match play—Loss of hole; Stroke play—
> Two strokes.*

*If a player incurs the general penalty for breach of Rule 5-3, no additional penalty under the Rule shall be applied.

Note 1: The ball may not be cleaned to determine whether it is unfit for play — see Rule 21.

Note 2: If the opponent, marker or fellow-competitor wishes to dispute a claim of unfitness, he must do so before the player plays another ball.

PLAYER'S RESPONSIBILITIES

Rule 6. The player

Definition

A "marker" is one who is appointed by the Committee to record a competitor's score in stroke play. He may be a fellow-competitor. He is not a referee.

6-1. Conditions of Competition

The player is responsible for knowing the conditions under which the competition is to be played (Rule 33-1).

6-2. Handicap

a. Match Play

Before starting a match in a handicap competition, the players should determine from one another their respective handicaps. If a player begins the match having declared a higher handicap which would affect the number of strokes given or received, *he shall be disqualified;* otherwise, the player shall play off the declared handicap.

b. Stroke Play

In any round of a handicap competition, the competitor shall ensure that his handicap is recorded on his score card before it is returned to the Committee. If no handicap is recorded on his score card before it is returned, or if the recorded handicap is higher than that to which he is entitled and this affects the number of strokes received, *he shall be disqualified* from that round of the handicap competition; otherwise, the score shall stand.

Note: It is the player's responsibility to know the holes at which handicap strokes are to be given or received.

6-3. Time of Starting and Groups

a. Time of Starting

The player shall start at the time laid down by the Committee.

b. Groups

In stroke play, the competitor shall remain throughout the round in the group arranged by the Committee unless the Committee authorises or ratifies a change.

> PENALTY FOR BREACH OF RULE 6-3:
> *Disqualification.*
> (Best-ball and four-ball play—see Rules 30-3a and 31-2.)

Note: The Committee may provide in the conditions of a competition (Rule 33-1) that, if the player arrives at his starting point, ready to play, within five minutes after his starting time, in the absence of circumstances which warrant waiving the penalty of disqualification as provided in Rule 33-7, the penalty for failure to start on time is *loss of the first hole in match play or two strokes at the first hole in stroke play* instead of disqualification.

6-4. Caddie

The player may have only one caddie at any one time, *under penalty of disqualification.*

For any breach of a Rule by his caddie, the player incurs the applicable penalty.

6-5. Ball

The responsibility for playing the proper ball rests with the player. Each player should put an identification mark on his ball.

6-6. Scoring in Stroke Play

a. Recording Scores
After each hole the marker should check the score with the competitor and record it. On completion of the round the marker shall sign the card and hand it to the competitor. If more than one marker records the scores, each shall sign for the part for which he is responsible.

b. Signing and Returning Card
After completion of the round, the competitor should check his score for each hole and settle any doubtful points with the Committee. He shall ensure that the marker has signed the card, countersign the card himself and return it to the Committee as soon as possible.

PENALTY FOR BREACH OF RULE 6-6b:
Disqualification.

c. Alteration of Card
No alteration may be made on a card after the competitor has returned it to the Committee.

d. Wrong Score for Hole
The competitor is responsible for the correctness of the score recorded for each hole. If he returns a score for any hole lower than actually taken, *he shall be disqualified.* If he returns a score for any hole higher than actually taken, the score as returned shall stand.

Note 1: The Committee is responsible for the addition of scores and application of the handicap recorded on the card—see Rule 33-5.
Note 2: In four-ball stroke play, see also Rule 31-4 and -7a.

6-7. Undue Delay
The player shall play without undue delay. Between completion of a hole and playing from the next teeing ground, the player shall not unduly delay play.

PENALTY FOR BREACH OF RULE 6-7:
Match play—Loss of hole; Stroke play—
Two strokes.
For repeated offence—Disqualification.

If the player unduly delays play between holes, he is delaying the play of the next hole and the penalty applies to that hole.

6-8. Discontinuance of Play

a. When Permitted
The player shall not discontinue play unless:
(i) the Committee has suspended play;
(ii) he believes there is danger from lightning;
(iii) he is seeking a decision from the Committee on a doubtful or disputed point (see Rules 2-5 and 34-3); or
(iv) there is some other good reason such as sudden illness.

Bad weather is not of itself a good reason for discontinuing play.
If the player discontinues play without specific permission from the Committee, he shall report to the Committee as soon as practicable. If he does so and the Committee considers his reason satisfactory, the player incurs no penalty. Otherwise, *the player shall be disqualified.*

Exception in match play: Players discontinuing match play by agreement are not subject to disqualification unless by so doing the competition is delayed.

Note: Leaving the course does not of itself constitute discontinuance of play.

b. Procedure When Play Suspended by Committee
When play is suspended by the Committee, if the players in a match or group are between the play of two holes, they shall not resume play until the Committee has ordered a resumption of play. If they are in the process of playing a hole, they may continue provided they do so without delay. If they choose to continue, they shall discontinue either before or immediately after completing the hole, and shall not thereafter resume play until the Committee has ordered a resumption of play.

PENALTY FOR BREACH OF RULE 6-8b:
Disqualification

c. Lifting Ball When Play Discontinued
When during the play of a hole a player discontinues play under Rule 6-8a, he may lift his ball. A ball may be cleaned when so lifted. If a ball has been so lifted, the player shall, when play is resumed, place a ball on the spot from which the original ball was lifted.

PENALTY FOR BREACH OF RULE 6-8c:
Match Play—Loss of hole; Stroke play—
Two strokes.

Rule 7. Practice

7-1. Before or Between Rounds

a. Match Play
On any day of a match play competition, a player may practise on the competition course before a round.

b. Stroke Play
On any day of a stroke competition or play-off, a competitor shall not practise on the competition course or test the surface of any putting green on the course before a round or play-off. When two or more rounds of a stroke competition are to be played over consecutive days, practice between those rounds on any competition course remaining to be played is prohibited.

Exception: Practice putting or chipping on or near the first teeing ground before starting a round or play-off is permitted.

PENALTY FOR BREACH OF RULE 7-1b:
Disqualification.

Note: The Committee may in the conditions of a competition (Rule 33-1) prohibit practice on the competition course on any day of a match play competition or permit practice on the competition course or part of the course (Rule 33-2c) on any day of or between rounds of a stroke competition.

7-2. During Round

A player shall not play a practice stroke either during the play of a hole or between the play of two holes except that, between the play of two holes, the player may practise putting or chipping on or near the putting green of the hole last played, any practice putting green or the teeing ground of the next hole to be played in the round, provided such practice stroke is not played from a hazard and does not unduly delay play (Rule 6-7).

Exception: When play has been suspended by the Committee, a player may, prior to resumption of play, practise (a) as provided in this Rule, (b) anywhere other than on the competition course and (c) as otherwise permitted by the Committee.

PENALTY FOR BREACH OF RULE 7-2:
Match play—Loss of hole; Stroke play—
Two strokes.

In the event of a breach between the play of two holes, the penalty applies to the next hole.

Note 1: A practice swing is not a practice stroke and may be taken at any place, provided the player does not breach the Rules.
Note 2: The Committee may prohibit practice on or near the putting green of the hole last played.

Rule 8. Advice; Indicating Line of Play

Definition
"Advice" is any counsel or suggestion which could influence a player in determining his play, the choice of a club or the method of making a stroke.
Information on the Rules or on matters of public information, such as the position of hazards or the flagstick on the putting green, is not advice.

8-1. Advice

A player shall not give advice to anyone in the competition except his partner. A player may ask for advice from only his partner or either of their caddies.

8-2. Indicating Line of Play

a. Other Than on Putting Green
Except on the putting green, a player may have the line of play indicated to him by anyone, but no one shall stand on or close to the line while the stroke is being played. Any mark placed during the play of a hole by the player or with his knowledge to indicate the line shall be removed before the stroke is played.

Exception: Flagstick attended or held up — see Rule 17-1.

b. On the Putting Green
When the player's ball is on the putting green, the player, his partner or either of their caddies may, before but not during the stroke, point out a line for putting, but in so doing the putting green shall not be touched. No mark shall be placed anywhere to indicate a line for putting.

PENALTY FOR BREACH OF RULE:
Match play—Loss of hole; Stroke play—
Two strokes.

Note: In a team competition without concurrent individual competition, the Committee may in the conditions of the competition (Rule 33-1) permit each team to appoint one person, e.g., team captain or coach, who may give advice (including pointing out a line for putting) to members of that team. Such person shall be identified to the Committee prior to the start of the competition.

Rule 9. Information as to Strokes Taken

9-1. General
The number of strokes a player has taken shall include any penalty strokes incurred.

9.2 Match Play
A player who has incurred a penalty shall inform his opponent as soon as practicable. If he fails to do so, he shall be deemed to have given wrong information, even if he was not aware that he had incurred a penalty.

An opponent is entitled to ascertain from the player, during the play of a hole, the number of strokes he has taken and, after play of a hole, the number of strokes taken on the hole just completed.

If during the play of a hole the player gives or is deemed to give wrong information as to the number of strokes taken, he shall incur no penalty if he corrects the mistake before his opponent has played his next stroke. If the player fails so to correct the wrong information, *he shall lose the hole.*

If after play of a hole the player gives or is deemed to give wrong information as to the number of strokes taken on the hole just com-

pleted and this affects the opponent's understanding of the result of the hole, he shall incur no penalty if he corrects his mistake before any player plays from the next teeing ground or, in the case of the last hole of the match, before all players leave the putting green. If the player fails so to correct the wrong information, *he shall lose the hole.*

9-3. Stroke Play

A competitor who has incurred a penalty should inform his marker as soon as practicable.

ORDER OF PLAY

Rule 10. Order of Play

10-1. Match Play

a. Teeing Ground

The side entitled to play first from the teeing ground is said to have the "honour".

The side which shall have the honour at the first teeing ground shall be determined by the order of the draw. In the absence of a draw, the honour should be decided by lot.

The side which wins a hole shall take the honour at the next teeing ground. If a hole has been halved, the side which had the honour at the previous teeing ground shall retain it.

b. Other Than on Teeing Ground

When the balls are in play, the ball farther from the hole shall be played first. If the balls are equidistant from the hole, the ball to be played first should be decided by lot.

Exception: Rule 30-3c (best-ball and four-ball match play).

c. Playing Out of Turn

If a player plays when his opponent should have played, the opponent may immediately require the player to cancel the stroke so played and play a ball in correct order, without penalty (see Rule 20-5).

10-2. Stroke Play

a. Teeing Ground

The competitor entitled to play first from the teeing ground is said to have the "honour".

The competitor who shall have the honour at the first teeing ground shall be determined by the order of the draw. In the absence of a draw, the honour should be decided by lot.

The competitor with the lowest score at a hole shall take the honour at the next teeing ground. The competitor with the second lowest score shall play next and so on. If two or more competitors have the same score at a hole, they shall play from the next teeing ground in the same order as at the previous teeing ground.

b. Other Than on Teeing Ground

When the balls are in play, the ball farthest from the hole shall be played first. If two or more balls are equidistant from the hole, the ball to be played first should be decided by lot.

Exceptions: Rules 22 (ball interfering with or assisting play) and 31-5 (four-ball stroke play).

c. Playing Out of Turn

If a competitor plays out of turn, no penalty is incurred and the ball shall be played as it lies. If, however, the Committee determines that competitors have agreed to play in an order other than that set forth in Clauses 2a and 2b of this Rule to give one of them an advantage, *they shall be disqualified.*

(Incorrect order of play in threesomes and foursomes stroke play—see Rule 29-3).

10-3. Provisional Ball or Second Ball from Teeing Ground

If a player plays a provisional ball or a second ball from a teeing ground, he should do so after his opponent or fellow-competitor has played his first stroke. If a player plays a provisional ball or a second ball out of turn, Clauses 1c and 2c of this Rule shall apply.

10-4. Ball Moved in Measuring

If a ball is moved in measuring to determine which ball is farther from the hole, no penalty is incurred and the ball shall be replaced.

TEEING GROUND

Rule 11. Teeing Ground

Definition

The "teeing ground" is the starting place for the hole to be played. It is a rectangular area two club-lengths in depth, the front and the sides of which are defined by the outside limits of two tee-markers. A ball is outside the teeing ground when all of it lies outside the teeing ground.

11-1. Teeing

In teeing, the ball may be placed on the ground, on an irregularity of surface created by the player on the ground or on a tee, sand or other substance in order to raise it off the ground.

A player may stand outside the teeing ground to play a ball within it.

11-2. Tee-Markers

Before a player plays his first stroke with any ball from the teeing ground of the hole being played, the tee-markers are deemed to be fixed. In such circumstances, if the player moves or

allows to be moved a tee-marker for the purpose of avoiding interference with his stance, the area of his intended swing or his line of play, *he shall incur the penalty for a breach of Rule 13-2.*

11-3. Ball Falling Off Tee

If a ball, when not in play, falls off a tee or is knocked off a tee by the player in addressing it, it may be re-teed without penalty, but if a stroke is made at the ball in these circumstances, whether the ball is moving or not, the stroke counts but no penalty is incurred.

11-4. Playing Outside Teeing Ground

a. Match Play

If a player, when starting a hole, plays a ball from outside the teeing ground, the opponent may immediately require the player to cancel the stroke so played and play a ball from within the teeing ground, without penalty.

b. Stroke Play

If a competitor, when starting a hole, plays a ball from outside the teeing ground, *he shall incur a penalty of two strokes* and shall then play a ball from within the teeing ground.

If the competitor plays a stroke from the next teeing ground without first correcting his mistake or, in the case of the last hole of the round, leaves the putting green, without first declaring his intention to correct his mistake, *he shall be disqualified.*

Strokes played by a competitor from outside the teeing ground do not count in his score.

PLAYING THE BALL

Rule 12. Searching for and Identifying Ball

Definitions

A "hazard" is any bunker or water hazard.

A "bunker" is a hazard consisting of a prepared area of ground, often a hollow, from which turf or soil has been removed and replaced with sand or the like. Grass-covered ground bordering or within a bunker is not part of the bunker. The margin of a bunker extends vertically downwards, but not upwards.

A "water hazard" is any sea, lake, pond, river, ditch, surface drainage ditch or other open water course (whether or not containing water) and anything of a similar nature.

All ground or water within the margin of a water hazard is part of the water hazard. The margin of a water hazard extends vertically upwards and downwards. Stakes and lines defining the margins of water hazards are in the hazards.

12-1. Searching for Ball; Seeing Ball

In searching for his ball anywhere on the course, the player may touch or bend long grass, rushes, bushes, whins, heather or the like, but only to the extent necessary to find and identify it, provided that this does not improve the lie of the ball, the area of his intended swing or his line of play.

A player is not necessarily entitled to see his ball when playing a stroke.

In a hazard, if the ball is covered by loose impediments or sand, the player may remove by probing, raking or other means as much thereof as will enable him to see a part of the ball. If an excess is removed, no penalty is incurred and the ball shall be re-covered so that only a part of the ball is visible. If the ball is moved in such removal, no penalty is incurred; the ball shall be replaced and, if necessary, re-covered. As to removal of loose impediments outside a hazard, see Rule 23.

If a ball lying in casual water, ground under repair or a hole, cast or runway made by a burrowing animal, a reptile or a bird is accidentally moved during search, no penalty is incurred; the ball shall be replaced, unless the player elects to proceed under Rule 25-1b.

If a ball is believed to be lying in water in a water hazard, the player may probe for it with a club or otherwise. If the ball is moved in so doing, no penalty is incurred; the ball shall be replaced, unless the player elects to proceed under Rule 26-1.

PENALTY FOR BREACH OF RULE 12-1:
Match play—Loss of hole; Stroke play—Two strokes.

12-2. Identifying Ball

The responsibility for playing the proper ball rests with the player. Each player should put an identification mark on his ball.

Except in a hazard, the player may, without penalty, lift a ball he believes to be his own for the purpose of identification and clean it to the extent necessary for identification. If the ball is the player's ball, he shall replace it. Before the player lifts the ball, he shall announce his intention to his opponent in match play or his marker or a fellow-competitor in stroke play and give his opponent, marker or fellow-competitor an opportunity to observe the lifting and replacement. If he lifts his ball without announcing his intention in advance or giving his opponent, marker or fellow-competitor an opportunity to observe, or if he lifts his ball for identification in a hazard, *he shall incur a penalty of one stroke* and the ball shall be replaced.

If a player who is required to replace a ball fails to do so, *he shall incur the penalty* for a breach of Rule 20-3a, but no additional penalty under Rule 12-2 shall be applied.

Rule 13. Ball Played As It Lies; Lie, Area of Intended Swing and Line of Play; Stance

Definitions

A "hazard" is any bunker or water hazard.

A "bunker" is a hazard consisting of a prepared area of ground, often a hollow, from which turf or soil has been removed and replaced with sand or the like. Grass-covered ground bordering or within a bunker is not part of the bunker. The margin of a bunker extends vertically downwards, but not upwards.

A "water hazard" is any sea, lake, pond, river, ditch, surface drainage ditch or other open water course (whether or not containing water) and anything of a similar nature.

All ground or water within the margin of a water hazard is part of the water hazard. The margin of a water hazard extends vertically upwards and downwards. Stakes and lines defining the margins of water hazards are in the hazards.

13-1. Ball Played As It Lies

The ball shall be played as it lies, except as otherwise provided in the Rules. (Ball at rest moved – see Rule 18.)

13-2. Improving Lie, Area of Intended Swing or Line of Play

Except as provided in the Rules, a player shall not improve or allow to be improved:

the position or lie of his ball,
the area of his intended swing,
his line of play or
the area in which he is to drop or place a ball

by any of the following actions:

moving, bending or breaking anything growing or fixed (including immovable obstructions and objects defining out of bounds) or removing or pressing down sand, loose soil, replaced divots, other cut turf placed in position or other irregularities of surface

except as follows:

as may occur in fairly taking his stance,
in making a stroke or the backward movement of his club for a stroke,
on the teeing ground in creating or eliminating irregularities of surface or
on the putting green in removing sand and loose soil as provided in Rule 16-1a or in repairing damage as provided in Rule 16-1c.

The club may be grounded only lightly and shall not be pressed on the ground.

Exception: Ball lying in or touching hazard – see Rule 13-4.

13-3. Building Stance

A player is entitled to place his feet firmly in taking his stance, but he shall not build a stance.

13-4. Ball Lying in or Touching Hazard

Except as provided in the Rules, before making a stroke at a ball which lies in or touches a hazard (whether a bunker or a water hazard), the player shall not:

a. Test the condition of the hazard or any similar hazard,

b. Touch the ground in the hazard or water in the water hazard with a club or otherwise, or

c. Touch or move a loose impediment lying in or touching the hazard.

Exceptions:

1. At address or in the backward movement for the stroke, the club may touch any obstruction or any grass, bush, tree or other growing thing.

2. The player may place his clubs in a hazard, provided nothing is done which may constitute testing the soil or improving the lie of the ball.

3. The player after playing the stroke, or his caddie at any time without the authority of the player, may smooth sand or soil in the hazard, provided that, if the ball still lies in the hazard, nothing is done which improves the lie of the ball or assists the player in his subsequent play of the hole.

PENALTY FOR BREACH OF RULE:
Match play—Loss of hole; Stroke play— Two strokes.
(Searching for ball – see Rule 12-1.)

Rule 14. Striking the Ball

Definition

A "stroke" is the forward movement of the club made with the intention of fairly striking at and moving the ball, but if a player checks his downswing voluntarily before the clubhead reaches the ball he is deemed not to have made a stroke.

14-1. Ball to be Fairly Struck At

The ball shall be fairly struck at with the head of the club and must not be pushed, scraped or spooned.

14-2. Assistance

In making a stroke, a player shall not accept physical assistance or protection from the elements.

PENALTY FOR BREACH OF RULE 14-1 or -2;
Match play—Loss of hole; Stroke play— Two strokes.

14-3. Artificial Devices and Unusual Equipment

Except as provided in the Rules, during a stipulated round the player shall not use any artificial device or unusual equipment:

a. For the purpose of gauging or measuring distance or conditions which might affect his play; or

b. Which might assist him in gripping the club, in making a stroke or in his play, except that plain gloves may be worn, resin, tape or gauze may be applied to the grip (provided such application does not render the grip non-conforming under Rule 4-1c) and a towel or handkerchief may be wrapped around the grip.

PENALTY FOR BREACH OF RULE 14-3:
Disqualification.

14-4. Striking the Ball More than Once

If a player's club strikes the ball more than once in the course of a stroke, the player shall count the stroke and *add a penalty stroke*, making two strokes in all.

14-5. Playing Moving Ball

A player shall not play while his ball is moving.

Exceptions:
Ball falling off tee—Rule 11-3.
Striking the ball more than once— Rule 14-4.
Ball moving in water—Rule 14-6.

When the ball begins to move only after the player has begun the stroke or the backward movement of his club for the stroke, he shall incur no penalty under this Rule for playing a moving ball, but he is not exempt from any penalty incurred under the following Rules

Ball at rest moved by player—Rule 18-2a.
Ball at rest moving after address— Rule 18-2b.
Ball at rest moving after loose impediment touched—Rule 18-2c.

14-6. Ball Moving in Water

When a ball is moving in water in a water hazard, the player may, without penalty, make a stroke, but he must not delay making his stroke in order to allow the wind or current to improve the position of the ball. A ball moving in water in a water hazard may be lifted if the player elects to invoke Rule 26.

PENALTY FOR BREACH OF RULE 14-5 or -6:
Match play—Loss of hole; Stroke play—
Two strokes.

Rule 15. Playing a Wrong Ball

Definition

A "wrong ball" is any ball other than:
a. The ball in play,
b. A provisional ball or
c. In stroke play, a second ball played under Rule 3-3 or Rule 20-7b.

Note: Ball in play includes a ball substituted for the ball in play when the player is proceeding under an applicable Rule which does not permit substitution.

15-1. General

A player must hole out with the ball played from the teeing ground unless a Rule permits him to substitute another ball. If a player substitutes another ball when proceeding under an applicable Rule which does not permit substitution, that ball is not a wrong ball; it becomes the ball in play and, if the error is not corrected as provided in Rule 20-6, *the player shall incur a penalty of loss of hole in match play or two strokes in stroke play.*

15-2. Match Play

If a player plays a stroke with a wrong ball except in a hazard, *he shall lose the hole.*

If a player plays any strokes in a hazard with a wrong ball, there is no penalty. Strokes played in a hazard with a wrong ball do not count in the player's score. If the wrong ball belongs to another player, its owner shall place a ball on the spot from which the wrong ball was first played.

If the player and opponent exchange balls during the play of a hole, the first to play the wrong ball other than from a hazard shall lose the hole; when this cannot be determined, the hole shall be played out with the balls exchanged.

15-3. Stroke Play

If a competitor plays a stroke with a wrong ball, *he shall incur a penalty of two strokes,* unless the only stroke or strokes played with such ball were played when it was lying in a hazard, in which case no penalty is incurred.

The competitor must correct his mistake by playing the correct ball. If he fails to correct his mistake before he plays a stroke from the next teeing ground or, in the case of the last hole of the round, fails to declare his intention to correct his mistake before leaving the putting green, *he shall be disqualified.*

Strokes played by a competitor with a wrong ball do not count in his score.

If the wrong ball belongs to another competitor, its owner shall place a ball on the spot from which the wrong ball was first played.

(Lie of ball to be placed or replaced altered —see Rule 20-3b.)

THE PUTTING GREEN

Rule 16. The Putting Green

Definitions

The "putting green" is all ground of the hole being played which is specially prepared for putting or otherwise defined as such by the Committee. A ball is on the putting green when any part of it touches the putting green.

A ball is "holed" when it is at rest within the circumference of the hole and all of it is below the level of the lip of the hole.

16-1. General

a. Touching Line of Putt

The line of putt must not be touched except:
  (i)   the player may move sand and loose soil on the putting green and other loose impediments by picking them up or by brushing them aside with his hand or a club without pressing anything down;
  (ii) in addressing the ball, the player may place the club in front of the ball without pressing anything down;
  (iii) in measuring—Rule 10-4;
  (iv) in lifting the ball—Rule 16-1b;
  (v)   in pressing down a ball-marker;
  (vi) in repairing old hole plugs or ball marks on the putting green—Rule 16-1c; and
  (vii) in removing movable obstructions — Rule 24-1.

(Indicating line for putting on putting green —see Rule 8-2b.)

b. Lifting Ball

A ball on the putting green may be lifted and, if desired, cleaned. A ball so lifted shall be replaced on the spot from which it was lifted.

c. Repair of Hole Plugs and Ball Marks

The player may repair an old hole plug or damage to the putting green caused by the impact of a ball, whether or not the player's ball lies on the putting green. If the ball is moved in the process of such repair, it shall be replaced, without penalty.

d. Testing Surface

During the play of a hole, a player shall not test the surface of the putting green by rolling a ball or roughening or scraping the surface.

e. Standing Astride or on Line of Putt

The player shall not make a stroke on the putting green from a stance astride, or with either foot touching, the line of the putt or an extension of that line behind the ball. For the purpose of this Clause only, the line of putt does not extend beyond the hole.

f. Position of Caddie or Partner

While making the stroke, the player shall not allow his caddie, his partner or his partner's caddie to position himself on or close to an extension of the line of putt behind the ball.

g. Playing Stroke While Another Ball in Motion

A player shall not play a stroke while another ball is in motion after a stroke on the putting green.

(Lifting ball interfering with or assisting play while another ball in motion—see Rule 22.)

PENALTY FOR BREACH OF RULE 16-1:
Match play—Loss of hole; Stroke play— Two strokes.

16-2. Ball Overhanging Hole

When any part of the ball overhangs the lip of the hole, the player is allowed enough time to reach the hole without unreasonable delay and an additional ten seconds to determine whether the ball is at rest. If by then the ball has not fallen into the hole, it is deemed to be at rest. If the ball subsequently falls into the hole, the player is deemed to have holed out with his last stroke, and *he shall add a penalty stroke to his score* for the hole; otherwise there is no penalty under this Rule.

(Undue delay—see Rule 6-7.)

Rule 17. The Flagstick

17-1. Flagstick Attended, Removed or Held Up

Before and during the stroke, the player may have the flagstick attended, removed or held up to indicate the position of the hole. This may be done only on the authority of the player before he plays his stroke.

If the flagstick is attended, removed or held up by an opponent, a fellow-competitor or the caddie of either with the player's knowledge and no objection is made, the player shall be deemed to have authorised it. If a player or a caddie attends, removes or holds up the flagstick or stands near the hole while a stroke is being played, he shall be deemed to be attending the flagstick until the ball comes to rest.

If the flagstick is not attended before the stroke is played, it shall not be attended or removed while the ball is in motion.

17-2. Unauthorised Attendance

a. Match Play

In match play, an opponent or his caddie shall not attend, remove or hold up the flagstick without the player's knowledge or authority while the player is making a stroke or his ball is in motion.

b. Stroke Play

In stroke play, if a fellow-competitor or his caddie attends, removes or holds up the flagstick without the competitor's knowledge or authority while the competitor is making a stroke or his ball is in motion, *the fellow-competitor shall incur the penalty* for breach of this Rule. In such circumstances, if the competitor's ball strikes the flagstick or the person attending it, the competitor incurs no penalty and the ball shall be played as it lies, except that, if the stroke was played from the putting green, the stroke shall be replayed.

PENALTY FOR BREACH OF RULE 17-1 or -2:
Match play—Loss of hole; Stroke play—
Two strokes.

17-3. Ball Striking Flagstick or Attendant

The player's ball shall not strike:
a. The flagstick when attended, removed or held up by the player, his partner or either of their caddies, or by another person with the player's knowledge or authority; or
b. The player's caddie, his partner or his partner's caddie when attending the flagstick, or another person attending the flagstick with the player's knowledge or authority, or equipment carried by any such person; or
c. The flagstick in the hole, unattended, when the ball has been played from the putting green.

PENALTY FOR BREACH OF RULE 17-3;
Match play—Loss of hole; Stroke play—
Two strokes, and the ball shall be played
as it lies.

17-4. Ball Resting Against Flagstick

If the ball rests against the flagstick when it is in the hole, the player or another person authorised by him may move or remove the flagstick and if the ball falls into the hole, the player shall be deemed to have holed out at his last stroke; otherwise the ball, if moved, shall be placed on the lip of the hole, without penalty.

BALL MOVED, DEFLECTED OR STOPPED

Rule 18. Ball At Rest Moved

Definitions

A ball is deemed to have "moved" if it leaves its position and comes to rest in any other place.

An "outside agency" is any agency not part of the match or, in stroke play, not part of a competitor's side, and includes a referee, a marker, an observer or a forecaddie. Neither wind nor water is an outside agency.

"Equipment" is anything used, worn or carried by or for the player except any ball he has played at the hole being played and any small object, such as a coin or a tee, when used to mark the position of a ball or the extent of an area in which a ball is to be dropped. Equipment includes a golf cart, whether or not motorised. If such a cart is shared by more than one player, its status under the Rules is the same as that of a caddie employed by more than one player. See "Caddie".

A player has "addressed the ball" when he has taken his stance and has also grounded his club, except that in a hazard a player has addressed the ball when he has taken his stance.

Taking the "stance" consists in a player placing his feet in position for and preparatory to making a stroke.

18-1. By Outside Agency

If a ball at rest is moved by an outside agency, the player shall incur no penalty and the ball shall be replaced before the player plays another stroke.

(Player's ball at rest moved by another ball —see Rule 18-5.)

18-2. By Player, Partner, Caddie or Equipment

a. General

When a player's ball is in play, if:
(i) the player, his partner or either of their caddies lifts or moves it, touches it purposely (except with a club in the act of addressing it) or causes it to move except as permitted by a Rule, or
(ii) equipment of the player or his partner causes the ball to move,

the player shall incur a penalty stroke. The ball shall be replaced unless the movement of the ball occurs after the player has begun his swing and he does not discontinue his swing.

Under the Rules no penalty is incurred if a player accidentally causes his ball to move in the following circumstances:

In measuring to determine which ball farther from hole—Rule 10-4

In searching for covered ball in hazard or for ball in casual water, ground under repair, etc.—Rule 12-1

In the process of repairing hole plug or ball mark—Rule 16-1c

In the process of removing loose impediment on putting green—Rule 18-2c

In the process of lifting ball under a Rule —Rule 20-1

In the process of placing or replacing ball under a Rule—Rule 20-3a

In complying with Rule 22 relating to lifting ball interfering with or assisting play

In removal of movable obstruction—Rule 24-1.

b. Ball Moving After Address

If a player's ball in play moves after he has addressed it (other than as a result of a stroke), the player shall be deemed to have moved the ball and *shall incur a penalty stroke*. The player shall replace the ball unless the movement of the ball occurs after he has begun his swing and he does not discontinue his swing.

c. Ball Moving After Loose Impediment Touched

Through the green, if the ball moves after any loose impediment lying within a club-length of it has been touched by the player, his partner or either of their caddies and before the player has addressed it, the player shall be deemed to have moved the ball and *shall incur a penalty stroke*. The player shall replace the ball unless the movement of the ball occurs after he has begun his swing and he does not discontinue his swing. On the putting green, if the ball moves in the process of removing any loose impediment, it shall be replaced without penalty.

18-3. By Opponent, Caddie or Equipment in Match Play

a. During Search

If, during search for a player's ball, it is moved by an opponent, his caddie or his equipment, no penalty is incurred and the player shall replace the ball.

b. Other Than During Search

If, other than during search for a ball, the ball is touched or moved by an opponent, his caddie or his equipment, except as otherwise provided in the Rules, *the opponent shall incur a penalty stroke*. The player shall replace the ball.
(Ball moved in measuring to determine which ball farther from the hole—see Rule 10-4.)
(Playing a wrong ball—see Rule 15-2.)
(Ball moved in complying with Rule 22 relating to lifting ball interfering with or assisting play.)

18-4. By Fellow-Competitor, Caddie or Equipment in Stroke Play

If a competitor's ball is moved by a fellow-competitor, his caddie or his equipment, no penalty is incurred. The competitor shall replace his ball.
(Playing a wrong ball—see Rule 15-3.)

18-5. By Another Ball

If a ball in play and at rest is moved by another ball in motion after a stroke, the moved ball shall be replaced.

PENALTY FOR BREACH OF RULE:
Match play—Loss of hole. Stroke play—
Two strokes.

*If a player who is required to replace a ball fails to do so, he shall incur the general penalty for breach of Rule 18 but no additional penalty under Rule 18 shall be applied.

Note 1: If a ball to be replaced under this Rule is not immediately recoverable, another ball may be substituted.

Note 2: If it is impossible to determine the spot on which a ball is to be placed, see Rule 20-3c.

Rule 19. Ball in Motion Deflected or Stopped

Definitions

An "outside agency" is any agency not part of the match or, in stroke play, not part of a competitor's side, and includes a referee, a marker, an observer or a forecaddie. Neither wind nor water is an outside agency.

"Equipment" is anything used, worn or carried by or for the player except any ball he has played at the hole being played and any small object, such as a coin or a tee, when used to mark the position of a ball or the extent of an area in which a ball is to be dropped. Equipment includes a golf cart, whether or not motorised. If such a cart is shared by more than one player, its status under the Rules is the same as that of a caddie employed by more than one player. See "Caddie".

19-1. By Outside Agency

If a ball in motion is accidentally deflected or stopped by any outside agency, it is a rub of the green, no penalty is incurred and the ball shall be played as it lies except:
a. If a ball in motion after a stroke other than on the putting green comes to rest in or on any moving or animate outside agency, the player shall, through the green or in a hazard, drop the ball, or on the putting green place the ball, as near as possible to the spot where the outside agency was when the ball came to rest in or on it, and
b. If a ball in motion after a stroke on the putting green is deflected or stopped by, or comes to rest in or on any moving or animate outside agency except a worm or an insect, the stroke shall be cancelled and the ball shall be replaced.

If the ball is not immediately recoverable, another ball may be substituted.

(Player's ball deflected or stopped by another ball – see Rule 19-5.)

Note: If the referee or the Committee determines that a competitor's ball has been purposely deflected or stopped by an <u>outside</u> <u>agency</u>, Rule 1-4 applies to the competitor. If the outside agency is a fellow-competitor or his caddie, Rule 1-2 applies to the fellow-competitor.

19-2. By Player, Partner, Caddie or Equipment

a. Match Play
If a player's ball is accidentally deflected or stopped by himself, his partner or either of their caddies or <u>equipment</u>, *he shall lose the hole.*

b. Stroke Play
If a competitor's ball is accidentally deflected or stopped by himself, his partner or either of their caddies or <u>equipment</u>, *the competitor shall incur a penalty of two strokes.* The ball shall be played as it lies, except when it comes to rest in or on the competitor's, his partner's or either of their caddies' clothes or equipment, in which case the competitor shall, <u>through the green</u> or in a <u>hazard</u>, drop the ball, or on the <u>putting green</u> place the ball, as near as possible to where the article was when the ball came to rest in or on it.

Exception: Dropped Ball – see Rule 20-2a. (Ball purposely deflected or stopped by player, partner or caddie – see Rule 1-2.)

19-3. By Opponent, Caddie or Equipment in Match Play

If a player's ball is accidentally deflected or stopped by an opponent, his caddie or his <u>equipment</u>, no penalty is incurred. The player may play the ball as it lies or, before another stroke is played by either side, cancel the stroke and replay it (see Rule 20-5). If the player elects to replay the stroke and the original ball is not immediately recoverable, another ball may be substituted.

If the ball has come to rest in or on the opponent's or his caddie's clothes or equipment, the player may <u>through the green</u> or in a <u>hazard</u> drop the ball, or on the putting green place the ball, as near as possible to where the article was when the ball came to rest in or on it.

Exception: Ball striking person attending flagstick—see Rule 17-3b.

(Ball purposely deflected or stopped by opponent or caddie—see Rule 1-2.)

19-4. By Fellow-Competitor, Caddie or Equipment in Stroke Play

See Rule 19-1 regarding ball deflected by outside agency.

19-5. By Another Ball

If a player's ball in motion after a stroke is deflected or stopped by a ball at rest, the player shall play his ball as it lies. In stroke play, if both balls lay on the <u>putting green</u> prior to the stroke, *the player incurs a penalty of two strokes.* Otherwise, no penalty is incurred.

If a player's ball in motion after a stroke is deflected or stopped by another ball in motion, the player shall play his ball as it lies. There is no penalty unless the player was in breach of Rule 16-1g, in which case *he shall incur the penalty for breach of that Rule.*

Exception: Ball in motion after a stroke on the putting green deflected or stopped by moving or animate outside agency—see Rule 19-1b.

PENALTY FOR BREACH OF RULE:
*Match play—Loss of hole; Stroke play—
Two strokes.*

RELIEF SITUATIONS AND PROCEDURE

Rule 20. Lifting, Dropping and Placing: Playing from Wrong Place

20.1 Lifting
A ball to be lifted under the Rules may be lifted by the player, his partner or another person authorised by the player. In any such case, the player shall be responsible for any breach of the Rules.

The position of the ball shall be marked before it is lifted under a Rule which requires it to be replaced. If it is not marked, the player *shall incur a penalty of one stroke* and the ball shall be replaced. If it is not replaced, *the player shall incur the general penalty* for breach of this Rule but no additional penalty under Rule 20-1 shall be applied.

If a ball or a ball-marker is accidentally moved in the process of lifting the ball under a Rule or marking its position, no penalty is incurred and the ball or the ball-marker shall be replaced.

Note: The position of a ball to be lifted should be marked by placing a ball-marker, a small coin or other similar object immediately behind the ball. If the ball-marker interferes with the play, <u>stance</u> or <u>stroke</u> of another player, it should be placed one or more clubhead-lengths to one side.

20-2. Dropping and Re-dropping

a. By Whom and How

A ball to be dropped under the Rules shall be dropped by the player himself. He shall stand erect, hold the ball at shoulder height and arm's length and drop it. If a ball is dropped by any other person or in any other manner and the error is not corrected as provided in Rule 20-6, *the player shall incur a penalty stroke.*

If the ball touches the player, his partner, either of their caddies or their equipment before or after it strikes the ground, the ball shall be redropped, without penalty. There is no limit to the number of times a ball shall be re-dropped in such circumstances.

(Taking action to influence position or movement of ball—see Rule 1-2.)

b. Where to Drop

When a ball is to be dropped, it shall be dropped as near as possible to the spot where the ball lay, but not nearer the hole, except when a Rule permits or requires it to be dropped elsewhere. If a ball is to be dropped in a hazard, the ball shall be dropped in and come to rest in that hazard.

Note: A ball when dropped must first strike the ground where the applicable Rule requires it to be dropped. If it is not so dropped, Rules 20-6 and -7 apply.

c. When to Re-drop

A dropped ball shall be re-dropped without penalty if it:

(i)   rolls into a hazard;
(ii) rolls out of a hazard;
(iii) rolls onto a putting green;
(iv) rolls out of bounds;
(v)   rolls back into the condition from which relief was taken under Rule 24-2 (immovable obstruction) or Rule 25 (abnormal ground conditions and wrong putting green);
(vi) rolls and comes to rest more than two club-lengths from where it first struck the ground; or
(vii) rolls and comes to rest nearer the hole than its original position unless otherwise permitted by the Rules.

If the ball again rolls into such position, it shall be placed as near as possible to the spot where it first struck the ground when re-dropped.

If a ball to be re-dropped or placed under this Rule is not immediately recoverable, another ball may be substituted.

20-3. Placing and Replacing

a. By Whom and Where

A ball to be placed under the Rules shall be placed by the player or his partner. A ball to be replaced shall be replaced by the player, his partner or the person who lifted or moved it. In any such case, the player shall be responsible for any breach of the Rules.

If a ball or a ball-marker is accidentally moved in the process of placing or replacing the ball, no penalty is incurred and the ball or the ball-marker shall be replaced.

b. Lie of Ball to Be Placed or Replaced Altered

If the original lie of a ball to be placed or replaced has been altered:

(i)   except in a hazard, the ball shall be placed in the nearest lie most similar to the original lie which is not more than one club-length from the original lie, not nearer the hole and not in a hazard;
(ii) in a water hazard, the ball shall be placed in accordance with Clause (i) above, except that the ball must be placed in the water hazard;
(iii) in a bunker, the original lie shall be recreated as nearly as possible and the ball shall be placed in that lie.

c. Spot Not Determinable

If it is impossible to determine the spot where the ball is to be placed:

(i)   through the green, the ball shall be dropped as near as possible to the place where it lay but not nearer the hole or in a hazard;
(ii) in a hazard, the ball shall be dropped in the hazard as near as possible to the place where it lay but not nearer the hole;
(iii) on the putting green, the ball shall be placed as near as possible to the place where it lay but not nearer the hole or in a hazard.

d. Ball Fails to Remain on Spot

If a ball when placed fails to remain on the spot on which it was placed, it shall be replaced without penalty. If it still fails to remain on that spot:

(i)   except in a hazard, it shall be placed at the nearest spot not nearer the hole or in a hazard where it can be placed at rest;
(ii) in a hazard, it shall be placed in the hazard at the nearest spot not nearer the hole where it can be placed at rest.

PENALTY FOR BREACH OF RULE 20-1,-2 or -3;
*Match play—Loss of hole; Stroke play—
Two strokes.*

20-4. When Ball Dropped or Placed is in Play

If the player's ball in play has been lifted, it is again in play when dropped or placed.

A substituted ball becomes the ball in play if it is dropped or placed under an applicable Rule,

whether or not such Rule permits substitution. A ball substituted under an inapplicable Rule is a wrong ball.

20-5. Playing Next Stroke from Where Previous Stroke Played

When, under the Rules, a player elects or is required to play his next stroke from where a previous stroke was played, he shall proceed as follows: if the stroke is to be played from the teeing ground, the ball to be played shall be played from anywhere within the teeing ground and may be teed; if the stroke is to be played from through the green or a hazard, it shall be dropped; if the stroke is to be played on the putting green, it shall be placed.

PENALTY FOR BREACH OF RULE 20-5;
*Match play—Loss of hole; Stroke play—
Two strokes.*

20-6. Lifting Ball Wrongly Dropped or Placed

A ball dropped or placed in a wrong place or otherwise not in accordance with the Rules but not played may be lifted, without penalty, and the player shall then proceed correctly.

20-7. Playing from Wrong Place

For a ball played outside teeing ground, see Rule 11-4.

a. Match Play

If a player plays a stroke with a ball which has been dropped or placed in a wrong place, *he shall lose the hole.*

b. Stroke Play

If a competitor plays a stroke with (i) his original ball which has been dropped or placed in a wrong place, (ii) a substituted ball which has been dropped or placed under an applicable Rule but in a wrong place or (iii) his ball in play when it has been moved and not replaced in a case where the Rules require replacement, *he shall,* provided a serious breach has not occurred, *incur the penalty prescribed by the applicable Rule* and play out the hole with the ball.

If, after playing from a wrong place, a competitor becomes aware of that fact and believes that a serious breach may be involved, he may, provided he has not played a stroke from the next teeing ground or, in the case of the last hole of the round, left the putting green, declare that he will play out the hole with a second ball dropped or placed in accordance with the Rules. The competitor shall report the facts to the Committee before returning his score card; if he fails to do so, *he shall be disqualified.* The Committee shall determine whether a serious breach of the Rule occurred. If so, the score with the second ball shall count and *the competitor shall add two penalty strokes to his score with that ball.*

If a serious breach has occurred and the competitor has failed to correct it as prescribed above, *he shall be disqualified.*

Note: If a competitor plays a second ball, penalty strokes incurred by playing the ball ruled not to count and strokes subsequently taken with that ball shall be disregarded.

Rule 21. Cleaning Ball

A ball on the putting green may be cleaned when lifted under Rule 16-1b. Elsewhere, a ball may be cleaned when lifted except when it has been lifted

a.   To determine if it is unfit for play (Rule 5-3)
b.   For identification (Rule 12-2), in which case it may be cleaned only to the extent necessary for identification
c.   Because it is interfering with or assisting play (Rule 22).

If a player cleans his ball during play of a hole except as provided in this Rule, *he shall incur a penalty of one stroke* and the ball, if lifted, shall be replaced.

If a player who is required to replace a ball fails to do so, *he shall incur the penalty* for breach of Rule 20-3a, but no additional penalty under Rule 21 shall be applied.

Exception: If a player incurs a penalty for failing to act in accordance with Rule 5-3, 12-2 or 22, no additional penalty under Rule 21 shall be applied.

Rule 22. Ball Interfering with or Assisting Play

Any player may:
a. Lift his ball if he considers that it might assist any other player or
b. Have any other ball lifted if he considers that it might interfere with his play or assist the play of any other player, but this may not be done while another ball is in motion. In stroke play, a player required to lift his ball may play first rather than lift. A ball lifted under this Rule shall be replaced.

If a ball is accidentally moved in complying with this Rule, no penalty is incurred and the ball shall be replaced.

PENALTY FOR BREACH OF RULE:
*Match play—Loss of hole; Stroke play—
Two strokes.*

Rule 23. Loose Impediments

Definition

"Loose impediments" are natural objects such as stones, leaves, twigs, branches and the like, dung, worms and insects and casts or heaps made by them, provided they are not fixed or growing, are not solidly embedded and do not adhere to the ball.

Sand and loose soil are loose impediments on the putting green but not elsewhere.

Snow and ice are either casual water or loose impediments, at the option of the player, except that manufactured ice is an obstruction.

Dew is not a loose impediment.

23-1. Relief

Except when both the loose impediment and the ball lie in or touch a hazard, any loose impediment may be removed without penalty. If the ball moves, see Rule 18-2c.

When a player's ball is in motion, a loose impediment on his line of play shall not be removed.

> PENALTY FOR BREACH OF RULE:
> *Match play—Loss of hole; Stroke play—*
> *Two strokes.*

(Searching for ball in hazard—see Rule 12-1.)
(Touching line of putt—see Rule 16-1a.)

Rule 24. Obstructions

Definition

An "obstruction" is anything artificial, including the artificial surfaces and sides of roads and paths and manufactured ice, except:

a. Objects defining out of bounds, such as walls, fences, stakes and railings;

b. Any part of an immovable artificial object which is out of bounds; and

c. Any construction declared by the Committee to be an integral part of the course.

24-1. Movable Obstruction

A player may obtain relief from a movable obstruction as follows:

a. If the ball does not lie in or on the obstruction, the obstruction may be removed; if the ball moves, no penalty is incurred and the ball shall be replaced.

b. If the ball lies in or on the obstruction, the ball may be lifted, without penalty, and the obstruction removed. The ball shall through the green or in a hazard be dropped, or on the putting green be placed, as near as possible to the spot directly under the place where the ball lay in or on the obstruction, but not nearer the hole.

The ball may be cleaned when lifted under Rule 24-1.

When a ball is in motion, an obstruction on the player's line of play other than an attended flagstick and equipment of the players shall not be removed.

24-2. Immovable Obstruction

a. Interference

Interference by an immovable obstruction occurs when a ball lies in or on the obstruction, or so close to the obstruction that the obstruction interferes with the player's stance or the area of his intended swing. If the player's ball lies on the putting green, interference also occurs if an immovable obstruction on the putting green intervenes on his line of putt. Otherwise, intervention on the line of play is not, of itself, interference under this Rule.

b. Relief

Except when the ball lies in or touches a water hazard or a lateral water hazard, a player may obtain relief from interference by an immovable obstruction, without penalty, as follows:

(i) **Through the Green:** If the ball lies through the green, the point on the course nearest to where the ball lies shall be determined (without crossing over, through or under the obstruction) which (a) is not nearer the hole, (b) avoids interference (as defined) and (c) is not a hazard or on a putting green. The player shall lift the ball and drop it within one club-length of the point thus determined on ground which fulfils (a), (b) and (c) above.

Note: The prohibition against crossing over, through or under the obstruction does not apply to the artificial surfaces and sides of roads and paths or when the ball lies in or on the obstruction.

(ii) **In a Bunker:** If the ball lies in or touches a bunker, the player shall lift and drop the ball in accordance with Clause (i) above, except that the ball must be dropped in the bunker.

(iii) **On the Putting Green:** If the ball lies on the putting green, the player shall lift the ball and place it in the nearest position to where it lay which affords relief from interference, but not nearer the hole nor in a hazard.

The ball may be cleaned when lifted for relief under Rule 24-2b.
(Ball rolling back into condition from which relief taken—see Rule 20-2c(v).)

Exception: A player may not obtain relief under Rule 24-2b if (a) it is clearly unreasonable

for him to play a stroke because of interference by anything other than an immovable obstruction or (b) interference by an immovable obstruction would occur only through use of an unnecessarily abnormal stance, swing or direction of play.

Note: If a ball lies in or touches a <u>water hazard</u> (including a <u>lateral water hazard</u>), the player is not entitled to relief without penalty from interference by an immovable obstruction. The player shall play the ball as it lies or proceed under Rule 26-1.

PENALTY FOR BREACH OF RULE:
Match play—Loss of hole; Stroke play—Two strokes.

Rule 25. Abnormal Ground Conditions and Wrong Putting Green

Definitions
"Casual water" is any temporary accumulation of water on the <u>course</u> which is visible before or after the player takes his <u>stance</u> and is not in a water hazard. Snow and ice are either casual water or <u>loose impediments</u>, at the option of the player, except that manufactured ice is an obstruction. Dew is not casual water.

"Ground under repair" is any portion of the <u>course</u> so marked by order of the Committee or so declared by its authorised representative. It includes material piled for removal and a hole made by a greenkeeper, even if not so marked. Stakes and lines defining ground under repair are in such ground. The margin of ground under repair extends vertically downwards, but not upwards.

Note 1: Grass cuttings and other material left on the course which have been abandoned and are not intended to be removed are not ground under repair unless so marked.

Note 2: The Committee may make a Local Rule prohibiting play from ground under repair.

25-1. Casual Water, Ground Under Repair and Certain Damage to Course

a. Interference
Interference by <u>casual water, ground under repair</u> or a hole, cast or runway made by a burrowing animal, a reptile or a bird occurs when a ball lies in or touches any of these conditions or when the condition interferes with the player's <u>stance</u> or the area of his intended swing. If the player's ball lies on the <u>putting green</u>, interference also occurs if such condition on the putting green intervenes on his line of putt.

If interference exists, the player may either play the ball as it lies (unless prohibited by Local Rule) or take relief as provided in Clause b.

b. Relief
If the player elects to take relief, he shall proceed as follows:
(i) **Through the Green:** If the ball lies <u>through the green</u>, the point on the <u>course</u> nearest to where the ball lies shall be determined which (a) is not nearer the hole, (b) avoids interference by the condition, and (c) is not in a <u>hazard</u> or on a <u>putting green</u>. The player shall lift the ball and drop it without penalty within one club-length of the point thus determined on ground which fulfils (a), (b) and (c) above.
(ii) **In a Hazard:** If the ball lies in or touches a hazard, the player shall lift and drop the ball either:
(a) Without penalty, in the hazard, as near as possible to the spot where the ball lay, but not nearer the hole, on ground which affords maximum available relief from the condition;
or
(b) *Under penalty of one stroke*, outside the hazard, keeping the point where the ball lay directly between the hole and the spot on which the ball is dropped.

Exception: If a ball lies in or touches a <u>water hazard</u> (including a <u>lateral water hazard</u>), the player is not entitled to relief without penalty from a hole, cast or runway made by a burrowing animal, a reptile or a bird. The player shall play the ball as it lies or proceed under Rule 26-1.
(iii) **On the Putting Green:** If the ball lies on the <u>putting green</u>, the player shall lift the ball and place it without penalty in the nearest position to where it lay which affords maximum available relief from the condition, but not nearer the hole nor in a <u>hazard</u>.

The ball may be cleaned when lifted under Rule 25-1b.
(Ball rolling back into condition from which relief taken—see Rule 20-2c(v).)

Exception: A player may not obtain relief under Rule 25-1b if (a) it is clearly unreasonable for him to play a stroke because of interference by anything other than a condition covered by Rule 25-1a or (b) interference by such a condition would occur only through use of an unnecessarily abnormal stance, swing or direction of play.

c. Ball Lost Under Condition Covered by Rule 25-1
It is a question of fact whether a ball lost after having been struck toward a condition covered by Rule 25-1 is lost under such condition. In order to treat the ball as lost under such condition, there must be reasonable evidence to

that effect. In the absence of such evidence, the ball must be treated as a lost ball and Rule 27 applies.

(i) **Outside a Hazard**—If a ball is lost outside a hazard under a condition covered by Rule 25-1, the player may take relief as follows: the point on the course nearest to where the ball last crossed the margin of the area shall be determined which (a) is not nearer the hole than where the ball last crossed the margin, (b) avoids interference by the condition and (c) is not in a hazard or on a putting green. He shall drop a ball without penalty within one club-length of the point thus determined on ground which fulfils (a), (b) and (c) above.

(ii) **In a Hazard**—If a ball is lost in a hazard under a condition covered by Rule 25-1, the player may drop a ball either;
(a) Without penalty, in the hazard, as near as possible to the point at which the original ball last crossed the margin of the area, but not nearer the hole, on ground, which affords maximum available relief from the condition;
or
(b) *Under penalty of one stroke*, outside the hazard, keeping the point at which the original ball last crossed the margin of the hazard directly between the hole and the spot on which the ball is dropped.

Exception: If a ball lies in a water hazard (including a lateral water hazard), the player is not entitled to relief without penalty for a ball lost in a hole, cast or runway made by a burrowing animal, a reptile or a bird. The player shall proceed under Rule 26-1.

25-2. Embedded Ball

A ball embedded in its own pitch-mark in the ground in any closely mown area through the green may be lifted, cleaned and dropped, without penalty, as near as possible to the spot where it lay but not nearer the hole. "Closely mown area" means any area of the course, including paths through the rough, cut to fairway height or less.

25-3. Wrong Putting Green

If a ball lies on a putting green other than that of the hole being played, the point on the course nearest to where the ball lies shall be determined which (a) is not nearer the hole and (b) is not in a hazard or on a putting green. The player shall lift the ball and drop it without penalty within one club-length of the point thus determined on ground which fulfils (a) and (b) above. The ball may be cleaned when so lifted.

Note: Unless otherwise prescribed by the Committee, the term "a putting green other than that of the hole being played" includes a practice putting green or pitching green on the course.

PENALTY FOR BREACH OF RULE:
*Match play—Loss of hole; Stroke play—
Two strokes.*

Rule 26. Water Hazards
(Including Lateral Water Hazards)

Definitions

A "water hazard" is any sea, lake, pond, river, ditch, surface drainage ditch or other open water course (whether or not containing water) and anything of a similar nature.

All ground or water within the margin of a water hazard is part of the water hazard. The margin of a water hazard extends vertically upwards and downwards. Stakes and lines defining the margins of water hazards are in the hazards.

Note: Water hazards (other than lateral water hazards) should be defined by yellow stakes or lines.

A "lateral water hazard" is a water hazard or that part of a water hazard so situated that it is not possible or is deemed by the Committee to be impracticable to drop a ball behind the water hazard in accordance with Rule 26-1b.

That part of a water hazard to be played as a lateral water hazard should be distinctively marked.

Note: Lateral water hazards should be defined by red stakes or lines.

26-1. Ball in Water Hazard

It is a question of fact whether a ball lost after having been struck toward a water hazard is lost inside or outside the hazard. In order to treat the ball as lost in the hazard, there must be reasonable evidence that the ball lodged in it. In the absence of such evidence, the ball must be treated as a lost ball and Rule 27 applies.

If a ball lies in, touches or is lost in a water hazard (whether the ball lies in water or not), the player may *under penalty of one stroke:*

a. Play his next stroke as nearly as possible at the spot from which the original ball was last played (see Rule 20-5);
or
b. Drop a ball behind the water hazard, keeping the point at which the original ball last crossed the margin of the water hazard directly between the hole and the spot on which the ball

is dropped, with no limit to how far behind the water hazard the ball may be dropped;

or

c. *As additional options available only if the ball lies in, touches or is lost in a lateral water hazard,* drop a ball outside the water hazard within two club-lengths of (i) the point where the original ball last crossed the margin of the water hazard or (ii) a point on the opposite margin of the water hazard equidistant from the hole. The ball must be dropped and come to rest not nearer the hole than the point where the original ball last crossed the margin of the water hazard.

The ball may be cleaned when lifted under this Rule.

(Ball moving in water in a water hazard—see Rule 14-6.)

26-2. Ball Played within Water Hazard

a. Ball comes to rest in Hazard

If a ball played from within a water hazard comes to rest in the hazard after the stroke, the player may:

(i)   proceed under Rule 26-1; or

(ii) *under penalty of one stroke,* play his next stroke as nearly as possible at the spot from which the last stroke from outside the hazard was played (see Rule 20-5).

b. Ball Lost or Unplayable Outside Hazard or Out of Bounds

If a ball played from within a water hazard is lost or declared unplayable outside the hazard or is out of bounds, the player, after taking a *penalty of one stroke* under Rule 27-1 or 28a, may:

(i)   play a ball as nearly as possible at the spot from which the original ball was last played (see Rule 20-5);or

(ii) *under an additional penalty of one stroke,* proceed under Rule 26-1b or, if applicable, Rule 26-1c, using as the reference point the point where the original ball last crossed the margin of the hazard before it came to rest in the hazard; or

(iii) *under an additional penalty of one stroke,* play his next stroke as nearly as possible at the spot from which the last stroke from outside the hazard was played (see Rule 20-5).

Note: If a ball played from within a water hazard is declared unplayable outside the hazard, nothing in Rule 26-2b precludes the player from proceeding under Rule 28b or c.

PENALTY FOR BREACH OF RULE:
Match play—Loss of hole; Stroke play—
Two strokes.

Rule 27. Ball Lost or Out of Bounds; Provisional Ball

If the original ball is lost under a condition covered by Rule 25-1 (casual water, ground under repair and certain damage to the course), the player may proceed under that Rule. If the original ball is lost in a water hazard, the player shall proceed under Rule 26.

Such Rules may not be used unless there is reasonable evidence that the ball is lost under a condition covered by Rule 25-1 or in a water hazard.

Definitions

A ball is "lost" if:

a. It is not found or identified as his by the player within five minutes after the player's side or his or their caddies have begun to search for it; or

b. The player has put another ball into play under the Rules, even though he may not have searched for the original ball; or

c. The player has played any stroke with a <u>provisional ball</u> from the place where the original ball is likely to be or from a point nearer the hole than that place, whereupon the provisional ball becomes the <u>ball in play</u>.

Time spent in playing a <u>wrong ball</u> is not counted in the five-minute period allowed for search.

"Out of bounds" is ground on which play is prohibited.

When out of bounds is defined by reference to stakes or a fence, or as being beyond stakes or a fence, the out of bounds line is determined by the nearest inside points of the stakes or fence posts at ground level excluding angled supports.

When out of bounds is defined by a line on the ground, the line itself is out of bounds.

The out of bounds line extends vertically upwards and downwards.

A ball is out of bounds when all of it lies out of bounds.

A player may stand out of bounds to play a ball lying within bounds.

A "provisional ball" is a ball played under Rule 27-2 for a ball which may be lost outside a <u>water hazard</u> or may be <u>out of bounds</u>.

27-1. Ball Lost or Out of Bounds

If a ball is lost outside a <u>water hazard</u> or is <u>out of bounds</u>, the player shall play a ball, *under penalty of one stroke,* as nearly as possible at the spot from which the original ball was last played (see Rule 20-5).

PENALTY FOR BREACH OF RULE 27-1:
Match play—Loss of hole; Stroke play—
Two strokes

27-2. Provisional Ball

a. Procedure

If a ball may be lost outside a water hazard or may be out of bounds, to save time the player may play another ball provisionally as nearly as possible at the spot from which the original ball was played (see Rule 20-5). The player shall inform his opponent in match play or his marker or a fellow competitor in stroke play that he intends to play a provisional ball, and he shall play it before he or his partner goes forward to search for the original ball. If he fails to do so and plays another ball, such ball is not a provisional ball and becomes the ball in play *under penalty of he and distance* (Rule 27-1); the original ball is deemed to be lost.

b. When Provisional Ball Becomes Ball in Play

The player may play a provisional ball until he reaches the place where the original ball is likely to be. If he plays a stroke with the provisional ball from the place where the original ball is likely to be or from a point nearer the hole than that place, the original ball is deemed to be lost and the provisional ball becomes the ball in play

If the original ball is lost outside a water hazard or is out of bounds, the provisional ball becomes the ball in play, *under penalty of stroke and distance* (Rule 27-1).

c. When Provisional Ball to Be Abandoned

If the original ball is neither lost outside a water hazard nor out of bounds, the player shall abandon the provisional ball and continue play with the original ball. If he fails to do so, any further strokes played with the provisional ball shall constitute playing a wrong ball and the provisions of Rule 15 shall apply.

Note: If the original ball lies in a water hazard, the player shall play the ball as it lies or proceed under Rule 26. If it is lost in a water hazard or unplayable, the player shall proceed under Rule 26 or 28, whichever is applicable.

Rule 28. Ball Unplayable

The player may declare his ball unplayable at any place on the course except when the ball lies in or touches a water hazard. The player is the sole judge as to whether his ball is unplayable.

If the player deems his ball to be unplayable, he shall, *under penalty of one stroke*:

a. Play his next stroke as nearly as possible at the spot from which the original ball was last played (see Rule 20-5); or

b. Drop a ball within two club-lengths of the spot where the ball lay, but not nearer the hole; or

c. Drop a ball behind the point where the ball lay, keeping that point directly between the hole and the spot on which the ball is dropped, with no limit to how far behind that point the ball may be dropped.

If the unplayable ball lies in a bunker and the player elects to proceed under Clause b or c, a ball must be dropped in the bunker.

The ball may be cleaned when lifted under this Rule.

PENALTY FOR BREACH OF RULE:
*Match play—Loss of hole; Stroke play—
Two strokes.*

OTHER FORMS OF PLAY

Rule 29. Threesomes and Foursomes

Definitions

Threesome: A match in which one plays against two, and each side plays one ball.

Foursome: A match in which two play against two, and each side plays one ball.

29-1. General

In a threesome or a foursome, during any stipulated round the partners shall play alternately from the teeing grounds and alternately during the play of each hole. Penalty strokes do not affect the order of play.

29-2. Match Play

If a player plays when his partner should have played, *his side shall lose the hole.*

29-3. Stroke Play

If the partners play a stroke or strokes in incorrect order, such stroke or strokes shall be cancelled and *the side shall incur a penalty of two strokes.* The side shall correct the error by playing a ball in correct order at the spot from which it first played in incorrect order (see Rule 20-5). If the side plays a stroke from the next teeing ground without first correcting the error or, in the case of the last hole of the round, leaves the putting green without declaring its intention to correct the error, *the side shall be disqualified.*

Rule 30. Three-Ball, Best-Ball and Four-Ball Match Play

Definitions

Three-Ball: A match play competition in which three play against one another, each playing his own ball. Each player is playing two distinct matches.

Best-Ball: A match in which one plays against the better ball of two or the best ball of three players.

Four-Ball: A match in which two play their better ball against the better ball of two other players.

30-1. Rules of Golf Apply

The Rules of Golf, so far as they are not at variance with the following special Rules, shall apply to three-ball, best-ball and four-ball matches.

30-2. Three-Ball Match Play

a. Ball at Rest Moved by an Opponent

Except as otherwise provided in the Rules, if the player's ball is touched or moved by an opponent, his <u>caddie</u> or <u>equipment</u> other than during search, Rule 18-3b applies. *That opponent shall incur a penalty stroke in his match with the player,* but not in his match with the other opponent.

b. Ball Deflected or Stopped by an Opponent Accidentally

If a player's ball is accidentally deflected or stopped by an opponent, his <u>caddie</u> or <u>equipment</u>, no penalty shall be incurred. In his match with that opponent the player may play the ball as it lies or, before another stroke is played by either side, he may cancel the stroke and replay it (see Rule 20-5). In his match with the other opponent, the ball shall be played as it lies.

Exception: Ball striking person attending flagstick—see Rule 17-3b.

(Ball purposely deflected or stopped by opponent—see Rule 1-2.)

30-3. Best-Ball and Four-Ball Match Play

a. Representation of Side

A side may be represented by one partner for all or any part of a match; all partners need not be present. An absent partner may join a match between holes, but not during play of a hole.

b. Maximum of Fourteen Clubs

The side shall be penalised for a breach of Rule 4-4 by any partner.

c. Order of Play

Balls belonging to the same side may be played in the order the side considers best.

d. Wrong Ball

If a player plays a stroke with a <u>wrong ball</u> except in a <u>hazard</u>, *he shall be disqualified for that hole,* but his partner incurs no penalty even if the wrong ball belongs to him. The owner of

the ball shall replace it on the spot from which it was played, without penalty. If the ball is not immediately recoverable, another ball may be substituted.

e. Disqualification of Side

(i) *A side shall be disqualified* for a breach of any of the following by any partner:

Rule 1-3 – Agreement to Waive Rules.
Rule 4-1,
  -2 or -3 – Clubs.
Rule 5-1
  or -2 – The Ball
Rule 6-2a – Handicap (playing off higher handicap).
Rule 6-4 – Caddie.
Rule 6-7 – Undue Delay (repeated offence).
Rule 14-3 – Artificial Devices and Unusual Equipment.

(ii) *A side shall be disqualified* for a breach of any of the following by all partners:

Rule 6-3 – Time of Starting and Groups.
Rule 6-8 – Discontinuance of Play.

f. Effect of Other Penalties

If a player's breach of a Rule assists his partner's play or adversely affects an opponent's play, *the partner incurs the applicable penalty in addition to any penalty incurred by the player.*

In all other cases where a player incurs a penalty for breach of a Rule, the penalty shall not apply to his partner. Where the penalty is stated to be loss of hole, the effect shall be to disqualify the player for that hole.

g. Another Form of Match Played Concurrently

In a best-ball or four-ball match when another form of match is played concurrently, the above special Rules shall apply.

Rule 31. Four-Ball Stroke Play

In four-ball stroke play two competitors play as partners, each playing his own ball. The lower score of the partners is the score for the hole. If one partner fails to complete the play of a hole, there is no penalty.

31-1. Rules of Golf Apply

The Rules of Golf, so far as they are not at variance with the following special Rules, shall apply to four-ball stroke play.

31-2. Representation of Side

A side may be represented by either partner for all or any part of a <u>stipulated round</u>; both partners need not be present. An absent competitor

may join his partner between holes, but not during play of a hole.

31-3. Maximum of Fourteen Clubs
The side shall be penalised for, a breach of Rule 4-4 by either partner.

31-4. Scoring
The marker is required to record for each hole only the gross score of whichever partner's score is to count. The gross scores to count must be individually identifiable; otherwise *the side shall be disqualified.* Only one of the partners need be responsible for complying with Rule 6-6b.

(Wrong score—see Rule 31-7a.)

31-5. Order of Play
Balls belonging to the same side may be played in the order the side considers best.

31-6. Wrong Ball
If a competitor plays a stroke with a <u>wrong ball</u> except in a <u>hazard</u>, *he shall add two penalty strokes to his score for the hole* and shall then play the correct ball. His partner incurs no penalty even if the wrong ball belongs to him.

The owner of the ball shall replace it on the spot from which it was played, without penalty. If the ball is not immediately recoverable, another ball may be substituted.

31-7. Disqualification Penalties

a. Breach by One Partner
A side shall be disqualified from the competition for a breach of any of the following by either partner:

Rule 1-3 –	Agreement to Waive Rules.
Rule 3-4 –	Refusal to Comply with Rule.
Rule 4-1,	
-2 or -3 –	Clubs.
Rule 5-1	
-2 –	The Ball.
Rule 6-2b –	Handicap (playing off higher handicap; failure to record handicap).
Rule 6-4 –	Caddie.
Rule 6-6b –	Signing and Returning Card.
Rule 6-6d –	Wrong Score for Hole, i.e. when the recorded lower score of the partners is lower than actually taken. If the recorded lower score of the partners is higher than actually taken, it must stand as returned.

Rule 6-7 –	Undue Delay (repeated offence).
Rule 7-1 –	Practice Before or Between Rounds.
Rule 14-3 –	Artificial Devices and Unusual Equipment.
Rule 31-4 –	Gross Scores to count Not Individually Identifiable.

b. Breach by Both Partners
A side shall be disqualified:
(i) for a breach by both partners of Rule 6-3 (Time of Starting and Groups) or Rule 6-8 (Discontinuance of Play), or
(ii) if, at the same hole, each partner is in breach of a Rule the penalty for which is disqualification from the competition or for a hole.

c. For the Hole Only
In all other cases where a breach of a Rule would entail disqualification, *the competitor shall be disqualified only for the hole at which the breach occurred.*

31-8. Effect of Other Penalties
If a competitor's breach of a Rule assists his partner's play, *the partner incurs the applicable penalty in addition to any penalty incurred by the competitor.*

In all other cases where a competitor incurs a penalty for breach of a Rule, the penalty shall not apply to his partner.

Rule 32. Bogey, Par and Stableford Competitions

32-1. Conditions
Bogey, par and Stableford competitions are forms of stroke competition in which play is against a fixed score at each hole. The Rules for stroke play, so far as they are not at variance with the following special Rules, apply.

a. Bogey and Par Competitions
The reckoning for bogey and par competitions is made as in match play. Any hole for which a competitor makes no return shall be regarded as a loss. The winner is the competitor who is most successful in the aggregate of holes.

The marker is responsible for marking only the gross number of strokes for each hole where the competitor makes a net score equal to or less than the fixed score.

Note: Maximum of 14 Clubs—Penalties as in match play—see Rule 4-4.

b. Stableford Competitions
The reckoning in Stableford competitions is

made by points awarded in relation to a fixed score at each hole as follows

Hole Played in	Points
More than one over fixed score or no score returned	0
One over fixed score	1
Fixed score	2
One under fixed score	3
Two under fixed score	4
Three under fixed score	5

The winner is the competitor who scores the highest number of points.

The marker shall be responsible for marking only the gross number of strokes at each hole where the competitor's net score earns one or more points.

Note: Maximum of 14 Clubs (Rule 4-4) — Penalties applied as follows: From total points scored for the round, deduction of two points for each hole at which any breach occurred; maximum deduction per round: four points.

32-3. Disqualification Penalties

a. From the Competition
A competitor shall be disqualified from the competition for a breach of any of the following:

Rule 1-3 –	Agreement to Waive Rules.
Rule 3-4 –	Refusal to Comply with Rule.
Rule 4-1, -2 or -3 –	Clubs.
Rule 5-1 – or -2 –	The Ball.
Rule 6-2b –	Handicap (playing off higher handicap; failure to record handicap).
Rule 6-3 –	Time of Starting and Groups.
Rule 6-4 –	Caddie.
Rule 6-6b –	Signing and Returning Card.
Rule 6-6d –	Wrong Score for Hole, except that no penalty shall be incurred when a breach of this Rule does not affect the result of the hole.
Rule 6-7 –	Undue Delay (repeated offence).
Rule 6-8 –	Discontinuance of Play.
Rule 7-1 –	Practice Before or Between Rounds.
Rule 14-3 –	Artificial Devices and Unusual Equipment.

b. For a Hole
In all other cases where a breach of a Rule would entail disqualification, *the competitor shall be disqualified only for the hole at which the breach occurred.*

ADMINISTRATION

Rule 33. The Committee

33-1. Conditions; Waiving Rule
The Committee shall lay down the conditions under which a competition is to be played.

The Committee has no power to waive a Rule of Golf.

Certain special rules governing stroke play are so substantially different from those governing match play that combining the two forms of play is not practicable and is not permitted. The results of matches played and the scores returned in these circumstances shall not be accepted.

In stroke play the Committee may limit a referee's duties.

33-2. The Course

a. Defining Bounds and Margins
The Committee shall define accurately:
(i) the course and out of bounds,
(ii) the margins of water hazards and lateral water hazards,
(iii) ground under repair, and
(iv) obstructions and integral parts of the course.

b. New Holes
New holes should be made on the day on which a stroke competition begins and at such other times as the Committee considers necessary, provided all competitors in a single round play with each hole cut in the same position.

Exception: When it is impossible for a damaged hole to be repaired so that it conforms with the Definition, the Committee may make a new hole in a nearby similar position.

c. Practice Ground
Where there is no practice ground available outside the area of a competition course, the Committee should lay down the area on which players may practise on any day of a competition, if it is practicable to do so. On any day of a stroke competition, the Committee should not normally permit practice on or to a putting green or from a hazard of the competition course.

d. Course Unplayable
If the Committee or its authorised representative considers that for any reason the course is not in a playable condition or that there are circumstances which render the proper playing of the game impossible, it may, in match play or

stroke play, order a temporary suspension of play or, in stroke play, declare play null and void and cancel all scores for the round in question. When play has been temporarily suspended, it shall be resumed from where it was discontinued, even though resumption occurs on a subsequent day. When a round is cancelled, all penalties incurred in that round are cancelled.

(Procedure in discontinuing play—see Rule 6-8.)

33-3. Times of Starting and Groups

The Committee shall lay down the times of starting and, in stroke play, arrange the groups in which competitors shall play.

When a match play competition is played over an extended period, the Committee shall lay down the limit of time within which each round shall be completed. When players are allowed to arrange the date of their match within these limits, the Committee should announce that the match must be played at a stated time on the last day of the period unless the players agree to a prior date.

33-4. Handicap Stroke Table

The Committee shall publish a table indicating the order of holes at which handicap strokes are to be given or received.

33-5. Score Card

In stroke play, the Committee shall issue for each competitor a score card containing the date and the competitor's name, or in foursome, or four-ball stroke play, the competitors' names.

In stroke play, the Committee is responsible for the addition of scores and application of the handicap recorded on the card.

In four-ball stroke play, the Committee is responsible for recording the better-ball score for each hole and in the process applying the handicaps recorded on the card, and adding the better-ball scores.

In bogey, par and Stableford competitions, the Committee is responsible for applying the handicap recorded on the card and determining the result of each hole and the overall result or points total.

33-6. Decision of Ties

The Committee shall announce the manner, day and time for the decision of a halved match or of a tie, whether played on level terms or under handicap.

A halved match shall not be decided by stroke play. A tie in stroke play shall not be decided by a match.

33-7. Disqualification Penalty; Committee Discretion

A penalty of disqualification may in exceptional individual cases be waived, modified or imposed if the Committee considers such action warranted.

33-8. Local Rules

a. Policy

The Committee may make and publish Local Rules for abnormal conditions if they are consistent with the policy of the Governing Authority for the country concerned as set forth in Appendix I to these Rules.

b. Waiving Penalty

A penalty imposed by a Rule of Golf shall not be waived by a Local Rule.

Rule 34. Disputes and Decisions

34-1. Claims and Penalties

a. Match Play

In match play if a claim is lodged with the Committee under Rule 2-5, a decision should be given as soon as possible so that the state of the match may, if necessary, be adjusted.

If a claim is not made within the time limit provided by Rule 2-5, it shall not be considered unless it is based on facts previously unknown to the player making the claim and the player making the claim had been given wrong information (Rules 6-2a and 9) by an opponent. In any case, no later claim shall be considered after the result of the match has been officially announced, unless the Committee is satisfied that the opponent knew he was giving wrong information.

b. Stroke Play

Except as provided below, in stroke play no penalty shall be rescinded, modified or imposed after the competition is closed. A competition is deemed to have closed when the result has been officially announced or, in stroke play qualifying followed by match play, when the player has teed off in his first match.

A penalty of disqualification shall be imposed at any time if a competitor:

(i) returns a score for any hole lower than actually taken (Rule 6-6d) for any reason other than failure to include a penalty which he did not know he had incurred; or

(ii) returns a score card on which he has recorded a handicap which he knows is higher than that to which he is entitled, and this affects the number of strokes received (Rule 6-2b).

34-2. Referee's Decision

If a referee has been appointed by the Committee, his decision shall be final.

34-3. Committee's Decision

In the absence of a referee, the players shall refer any dispute to the Committee, whose decision shall be final.

If the Committee cannot come to a decision, it shall refer the dispute to the Rules of Golf Committee of the Royal & Ancient Golf Club of St. Andrews, whose decision shall be final.

If the point in doubt or dispute has not been referred to the Rules of Golf Committee, the player or players have the right to refer an agreed statement through the Secretary of the Club to the Rules of Golf Committee for an opinion as to the correctness of the decision given. The reply will be sent to the Secretary of the Club or Clubs concerned.

If play is conducted other than in accordance with the Rules of Golf, the Rules of Golf Committee will not give a decision on any question.

APPENDIX I

LOCAL RULES (RULE 33-8) AND CONDITIONS OF THE COMPETITION (RULE 33-1)
Part A Local Rules

The Committee may make and publish Local Rules (for Specimen Local Rules see Part B) for such abnormal conditions as:

1. Obstructions

a. General

Clarifying the status of objects which may be obstructions (Rule 24).

Declaring any construction to be an integral part of the course and, accordingly, not an obstruction, e.g. built-up sides of teeing grounds, putting greens and bunkers (Rules 24 and 33-2a).

b. Stones in Bunkers

Allowing the removal of stones in bunkers by declaring them to be "movable obstructions" (Rule 24).

c. Roads and Paths

(i)   Declaring artificial surfaces and sides of roads and paths to be integral parts of the course, or

(ii) Providing relief of the type afforded under Rule 24-2b from roads and paths not having artificial surfaces and sides if they could unfairly affect play.

d. Fixed Sprinkler Heads

Providing relief from intervention by fixed sprinkler heads within two club-lengths of the putting green when the ball lies within two club-lengths of the sprinkler head.

e. Temporary Immovable Obstructions

Specimen Local Rules for application in Tournament Play are available from the Royal & Ancient Golf Club of St Andrews.

2. Areas of the Course Requiring Preservation

Assisting preservation of the course by defining areas, including turf nurseries, young plantations and other parts of the course under cultivation, as "ground under repair" from which play is prohibited.

3. Unusual Damage to the Course or Accumulation of Leaves (or the like)

Declaring such areas to be "ground under repair" (Rule 25).

Note: For relief from aerification holes see Specimen Local Rule 7 in part B of this Appendix.

4. Extreme Wetness, Mud, Poor Conditions and Protection of Course

(a.) Lifting an Embedded Ball, Cleaning

Where the ground is unusually soft, the Committee may, by temporary Local Rule, allow the lifting of a ball which is embedded in its own pitch-mark in the ground in an area "through the green" which is not "closely mown" (Rule 25-2) if it is satisfied that the proper playing of the game would otherwise be prevented. The Local Rule shall be for that day only or for a short period, and if practicable shall be confined to specified areas. The Committee shall withdraw the Local Rule as soon as conditions warrant and should not print it on the score card. In similarly adverse conditions, the Committee may, by temporary Local Rule, permit the cleaning of a ball "through the green".

(b.) Preferred Lies" and "Winter Rules"

Adverse conditions, including the poor condition of the course or the existence of mud, are sometimes so general, particularly during winter months, that the Committee may decide to grant relief by Local Rule either to protect the course or to promote fair and pleasant play. Such Local Rule shall be withdrawn as soon as conditions warrant.

5. Other Local Conditions which Interfere with the Proper Playing of the Game

If this necessitates modification of a Rule of Golf the approval of the Governing Authority must be obtained.

Other matters which the Committee could cover by Local Rule include:

6. Water Hazards

a. Lateral Water Hazards

Clarifying the status of sections of water hazards which may be lateral water hazards (Rule 26).

b. Provisional Ball

Permitting the play of a provisional ball for a ball which may be in a water hazard of such character that it would be impracticable to determine whether the ball is in the hazard or to do so would unduly delay play. In such a case, if a provisional ball is played and the original ball is in a water hazard, the player may play the original ball as it lies or continue the provisional ball in play, but he may not proceed under Rule 26-1.

7. Defining Bounds and Margins

Specifying means used to define out of bounds, hazards, water hazards, lateral water hazards and ground under repair.

8. Dropping Zones
Establishing special areas in which balls may or shall be dropped when it is not feasible or practicable to proceed exactly in conformity with Rule 24-2b (Immovable Obstruction), Rule 25-1b or Rule 25-1c (Ground Under Repair), Rule 26-1 (Water Hazards and Lateral Water Hazards) or Rule 28 (Ball Unplayable).

9. Priority on the Course
The Committee may make regulations governing Priority on the Course (see Etiquette).

Part B Specimen Local Rules
Within the policy set out in Part A of this Appendix the Committee may adopt a Specimen Local Rule by referring, on a score card or notice board, to the examples given below. However Specimen Local Rules 4, 5 or 6 should not be printed or referred to on a score card as they are all of limited duration.

1. Fixed Sprinkler Heads
All fixed sprinkler heads are immovable obstructions and relief from interference by them may be obtained under Rule 24-2. In addition, if such an obstruction on or within two club-lengths of the putting green of the hole being played intervenes on the line of play between the ball and the hole, the player may obtain relief, without penalty, as follows:

If the ball lies off the putting green but not in a hazard and is within two club-lengths of the intervening obstruction, it may be lifted, cleaned and dropped at the nearest point to where the ball lay which (a) is not nearer the hole, (b) avoids such intervention and (c) is not in a hazard or on a putting green.

PENALTY FOR BREACH OF LOCAL RULE:
Match play—Loss of hole; Stroke play—
Two strokes.

2. Stones in Bunkers
Stones in bunkers are movable obstructions. Rule 24-1 applies.

3. Ground Under Repair: Play Prohibited
If a player's ball lies in an area of "ground under repair" from which play is prohibited, or if such an area of "ground under repair" interferes with the player's stance or the area of his intended swing the player must take relief under Rule 25-1.

PENALTY FOR BREACH OF LOCAL RULE:
Match play—Loss of hole; Stroke play—
Two strokes.

4. Lifting an Embedded Ball
(Specify the area if practical) . . . through the green, a ball embedded in its own pitch mark in ground other than sand may be lifted, cleaned and dropped, without penalty, as near as possible to the spot where it lay but not nearer the hole.

PENALTY FOR BREACH OF LOCAL RULE:
Match play—Loss of hole; Stroke play—
Two strokes.

5. Cleaning Ball
(Specify the area if practicable) . . . through the green a ball may be lifted, cleaned and replaced without penalty.

Note: The position of the ball shall be marked before it is lifted under this Local Rule—see Rule 20-1.

6. "Preferred Lies" and "Winter Rules"
A ball lying on any "closely mown area" through the green may, without penalty, be moved or may be lifted, cleaned and placed within six inches of where it originally lay, but not nearer the hole. After the ball has been so moved or placed, it is in play.

PENALTY FOR BREACH OF LOCAL RULE:
Match play—Loss of stoke; Stroke play—
Two strokes.

7. Aerification Holes
If a ball comes to rest in an aerification hole, the player may, without penalty, lift the ball and clean it. Through the green, the player shall drop the ball as near as possible to where it lay, but not nearer the hole. On the putting green, the player shall place the ball at the nearest spot not nearer the hole which avoids such situation.

PENALTY FOR BREACH OF LOCAL RULE:
Match play—Loss of hole; Stroke play—
Two strokes

Part C Conditions of the Competition
Rule 33-1 provides, "The Committee shall lay down the conditions under which a competition is to be played". Such conditions should include many matters such as method of entry, eligibility, number of rounds to be played, settling ties, etc. which is not appropriate to deal with in the Rules of Golf or this Appendix.

However there are four matters which might be covered in the Conditions of Competition to which the Commitee's attention is specifically drawn by way of a Note to the appropriate Rule. These are:

1. Specification of the Ball (Note to Rule 5-1)
Arising from the regulations for ball-testing under Rule 5-1, Lists of Conforming Golf Balls will be issued from time to time. It is recommended that the Lists should be applied to all National and

County (or equivalent) Championships and to all top class events when restricted to low handicap players. In order to apply the Lists to a particular competition the Committee must lay this down in the Conditions of the Competition This should be referred to in the Entry Form, and also a notice should be displayed on the Club notice board and at the 1st Tee along the following lines:

(Name of Event)

(Date and Club)

The ball the player uses shall be named on the current List of Conforming Golf Balls issued by the Royal & Ancient Golf Club of St. Andrews.

Note 1: A penalty statement will be required and must be either:

(a)"PENALTY FOR BREACH OF CONDITION: Disqualification"

or

b)"PENALTY FOR BREACH OF CONDITION: *Match play—Loss of each hole at which a breach occurred: Stroke play—Two strokes for each hole at which a breach occurred.*"

If option (b) is adopted this only applies to use of a ball which, whilst not on the List of Conforming Golf Balls, does conform to the specifications set forth in Rule 5 and Appendix III. The penalty for use of a ball which does not so conform is disqualification.

Note 2: In Club events it is recommended that no such condition be applied.

2. Time of Starting (Note to Rule 6-3a)

If the Committee wishes to act in accordance with the Note, the following wording is recommended:

"If, in the absence of circumstances which warrant waiving the penalty of disqualification as provided in Rule 33-7, the player arrives at his starting point, ready to play, within five minutes after his starting time, the penalty for failure to start on time is loss of the first hole in match play or two strokes at the first hole in stroke play."

3. Practice

The Committee may make regulations governing practice in accordance with the Note to Rule 7-1, Exception (c) to Rule 7-2, Note 2 to Rule 7 and Rule 33-2c.

4. Advice in Team Competitions

If the Committee wishes to act in accordance with the Note, the following wording is recommended:

"In accordance with the Note to Rule 8-1 of the Rules of Golf each team may appoint one person (in addition to the persons from whom advice may be asked under that Rule) who may give advice to members of that team. Such person [*if it is desired to insert any restriction on who may be nominated insert such restriction here]* shall be identified to the Committee prior to the start of the competition."

APPENDICES II AND III

Any design in a club or ball which is not covered by Rules 4 and 5 and Appendices II and III, or which might significantly change the nature of the game, will be ruled on by the Royal & Ancient Golf Club of St Andrews and the United States Golf Association.

Note: Equipment approved for use or marketed prior to January 1st, 1984 which conformed to the Rules in effect in 1983 but does not conform to the 1984 Rules may be used until December 31st, 1989; thereafter all equipment must conform to the current Rules.

APPENDIX II

Design of Clubs

Rule 4-1 prescribes general regulations for the design of clubs. The following paragraphs, which provide some detailed specifications and clarify how Rule 4-1 is interpreted, should be read in conjunction with this rule.

4-1b. Shaft

Generally Straight. The shaft shall be at least 18 inches (457mm) in length. It shall be straight from the top of the grip to a point not more than 5 inches (127mm) above the sole, measured along the axis of the shaft and the neck or socket.

Bending and Twisting Properties. The shaft must be so designed and manufactured that at any point along its length;

(i) it bends in such a way that the deflection is the same regardless of how the shaft is rotated about its longitudinal axis; and

(ii) it twists the same amount in both directions.

Attachment to Clubhead. The neck or socket must not be more than 5 inches (127mm) in length, measured from the top of the neck or

CLUBS

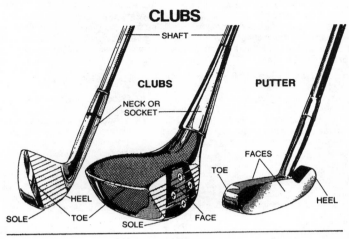

SHAFT

CLUBS   PUTTER

NECK OR
SOCKET

FACES

TOE

HEEL

HEEL

SOLE   TOE   FACE

SOLE

GRIPS

CLUB GRIP CIRCULAR

PUTTER GRIP FLAT SIDE (Permitted on Putters only)

GROOVES

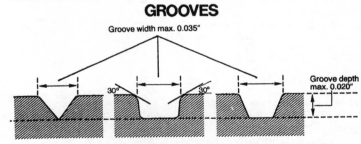

Groove width max. 0.035"

30°   30°

Groove depth
max. 0.020"

EXAMPLES OF PERMISSIBLE GROOVE CROSS-SECTIONS

socket to the sole along its axis. The shaft and the neck or socket must remain in line with the heel, or with a point to the right or left of the heel, when the club is viewed in the address position. The distance between the axis of the shaft or the neck or socket and the back of the heel must not exceed 0.625 inches (16mm).

Exception for Putters: The shaft or neck or socket of a putter may be fixed at any point in the head and need not remain in line with the heel. The axis of the shaft from the top to a point not more than 5 inches (127mm) above the sole must diverge from the vertical in the toe-heel plane by at least 10 degrees when the club is in its normal address position.

4-1c. Grip

(i) For clubs other than putters, the grip must be generally circular in cross-section, except that a continuous, straight, slightly raised rib may be incorporated along the full length of the grip.

(ii) A putter grip may have a non-circular cross-section, provided the cross-section has no concavity and remains generally similar throughout the length of the grip.

(iii) The grip may be tapered but must not have any bulge or waist.

(iv) For clubs other than putters the axis of the grip must coincide with the axis of the shaft.

4-1d. Clubhead

Dimensions. The dimensions of a clubhead (see diagram) are measured, with the clubhead in its normal address position, on horizontal lines between vertical projections of the outermost points of (i) the heel and the toe and (ii) the face and the back. If the outermost point of the heel is not clearly defined, it is deemed to be 0.625 inches (16mm) above the horizontal plane on which the club is resting in its normal address position.

Plain in Shape. The clubhead shall be generally plain in shape. All parts shall be rigid, structural in nature and functional.

Features such as holes through the head, windows or transparencies, or appendages to the main body of the head such as plates, rods or fins for the purpose of meeting dimensional specifications, for aiming or for any other purpose are not permitted. Exceptions may be made for putters.

Any furrows in or runners on the sole shall not extend into the face.

4-1e. Club Face

Hardness and Rigidity. The club face must not be designed and manufactured to have the effect at impact of a spring which would unduly influence the movement of the ball.

Markings. Except for specified markings, the surface roughness must not exceed that of decorative sandblasting. Markings must not have sharp edges or raised lips, as determined by a finger test. Markings within the area where impact is intended (the 'impact area') are governed by the following:

(i) **Grooves.** A series of straight grooves with diverging sides and a symmetrical cross-section may be used. (See diagram). The width and cross-section must be generally consistent across the face of the club and along the length of the grooves. Any rounding of groove edges shall be in the form of a radius which does not exceed 0.020 inches (0.5mm). The width of the grooves shall not exceed 0.035 inches (0.9mm), using the 30 degree method of measurement on file with the Royal & Ancient Golf Club of St Andrews. The distance between edges of adjacent grooves must not be less than three times the width of a groove, and not less than 0.075 inches (1.9mm). The depth of a groove must not exceed 0.020 inches (0.5mm).

(ii) **Punch Marks.** Punch marks may be used. The area of any such mark must not exceed 0.0044 square inches (2.8 sq mm). A mark must not be closer to an adjacent mark than 0.168 inches (4.3mm) measured from centre to centre. The depth of a punch mark must not exceed 0.040 inches (1.0mm). If punch marks are used in combination with grooves, a punch mark may not be closer to a groove than 0.168 inches (4.3mm), measured from centre to centre.

Decorative Markings. The centre of the impact area may be indicated by a design within the boundary of a square whose sides are 0.375 inches (9.5mm) in length. Such a design must not unduly influence the movement of the ball. Markings outside the impact area must not be greater than 0.040 inches (1.00mm) in depth and width

Non-metallic Club Face Markings. The above specifications for markings do not apply to non-metallic clubs with loft angles less than 24 degrees, but markings which could unduly influence the movement of the ball are prohibited. Non-metallic clubs with a loft or face angle exceeding 24 degrees may have grooves of maximum width 0.040 inches (1.0mm) and maximum depth of 1 1/2 times the groove width, but must otherwise conform to the markings specifications above.

APPENDIX III

The Ball

a. Weight

The weight of the ball shall not be greater than 1.620 ounces avoirdupois (45.93gm).

b. Size

The diameter of the ball shall not be less than 1.680 inches (42.67mm). This specification will be satisfied if, under its own weight, a ball falls through a 1.680 inches diameter ring gauge in fewer than 25 out of 100 randomly selected positions, the test being carried out at a temperature of 23±1°C.

c. Spherical Symmetry

The ball shall be designed and manufactured to perform in general as if it were spherically symmetrical.

As outlined in procedures on file at the Royal & Ancient Golf Club of St. Andrews and the United States Golf Association, differences in peak angle of trajectory, carry and time of flight will be measured when 40 balls of the same types are launched, spinning 20 about one axis and 20 about another axis.

These tests will be performed using apparatus approved by the Royal & Ancient Golf Club of St. Andrews and the United States Golf Association. If in two successive tests differences in the same two or more measurements are statistically significant at the 5% level of significance and exceed the limits set forth below, the ball type will not conform to the symmetry specification.

Measurement	Maximum Absolute Difference of the Means
Peak angle of trajectory	0.9 grid units (approx. 0.4 degrees)
Carry distance	2.5 yards
Flight time	0.16 seconds

Note: Methods of determining whether a ball performs as if it were generally spherically symmetrical may be subject to change as instrumentation becomes available to measure other properties accurately, such as the aerodynamic coefficient of lift, coefficient of drag and moment of inertia.

d. Initial Velocity

The velocity of the ball shall not be greater than 250 feet (76.2m) per second when measured on apparatus approved by the Royal & Ancient Golf Club of St. Andrews. A maximum tolerance of 2% will be allowed. The temperature of the ball when tested shall be 23±1°C.

e. Overall Distance Standard

A brand of golf ball, when tested on apparatus approved by the Royal & Ancient Golf Club of St. Andrews under the conditions set forth in the Overall Distance Standard for golf balls on file with the Royal & Ancient Golf Club of St. Andrews, shall not cover an average distance in carry and roll exceeding 280 yards (256 metres) plus a tolerance of 6%.

Note: The 6% tolerance will be reduced to a minimum of 4% as test techniques are improved.

Notes to Appendix III

1: The size specification in (b) above will take effect from 1st January, 1990. Until that date the previous size specification of a diameter not less than 1.620 inches (41.15mm) will apply.

2: The Overall Distance Standard will apply only to balls which meet the new size specification of a diameter not less than 1.680 inches (42.67mm).

3: In international team competitions, until 31st December, 1989, the previous size specification of a diameter not less than 1.620 inches (41.15mm) will apply.

HANDICAPS

The Rules of Golf do not legislate for the allocation and adjustment of handicaps or their playing differentials. Such matters are within the jurisdiction and control of the National Union concerned and queries should be directed accordingly.

RULES OF AMATEUR STATUS

As approved by the Royal & Ancient Golf Club of St. Andrews

(Effective from 1st January 1987)

Definitions of an Amateur Golfer
An Amateur Golfer is one who plays the game as a non-remunerative or non-profit-making sport.

The Governing Body
The Governing Body of golf for the Rules of Amateur Status in any country is the National Union of the country concerned except in Great Britain and Ireland where the Governing Body is the Royal & Ancient Golf Club of St. Andrews.

Any person who considers any action he is proposing to take might endanger his Amateur Status should submit particulars to the Committee for consideration.

RULE 1

Forfeiture of Amateur Status at any age

The following are examples of acts which are contrary to the Definition of an Amateur Golfer and cause forfeiture of Amateur Status:

1. Professionalism.
a. Receiving payment or compensation for serving as a Professional golfer or a teaching or playing assistant to a Professional golfer.
b. Taking any action for the purpose of becoming a Professional golfer except applying unsuccessfully for the position of a teaching or playing assistant of a Professional golfer.

Note 1. Such actions including filing application to a school or competition conducted to qualify persons to play as Professionals in tournaments; receiving services from or entering into an agreement, written or oral, with a sponsor or Professional agent; agreement to accept payment or compensation for allowing one's name or likeness as a skilled golfer to be used for any commercial purpose; and holding or retaining membership in any organisation of Professional golfers.

Note 2. Receiving payment or compensation as a shop assistant is not itself a breach of the Rules, provided duties do not include playing or giving instruction.

2. Playing for Prize Money.
Playing for prize money or its equivalent in a match, tournament or exhibition.

3. Instruction.
Receiving payment or compensation for giving instruction in playing golf, either orally, in writing, by pictures or by other demonstrations, to either individuals or groups.

Exceptions:
1. Golf instruction may be given by an employee of an educational institution or system to students of the institution or system and by camp counsellors to those in their charge, provided that the total time devoted to golf instruction during a year comprises less than 50 per cent of the time spent during the year in the performance of all duties as such employee or counsellor.

2. Payment or compensation may be accepted for instruction in writing, provided one's ability or reputation as a golfer was not a major factor in his employment or in the commission or sale of his work.

4. Prizes and Testimonials
(a) Acceptance of a prize or prize voucher of retail value exceeding as follows:

	In GB & I and rest of Europe	Elsewhere
For an event of more than 2 rounds	£300	$500 US or the equivalent
For an event of 2 rounds or less	£200	$350 US or the equivalent

or such lesser figure, if any, as may be decided by the Governing Body of golf in any country, or
(b) Acceptance of a testimonial in Great Britain and Ireland and the rest of Europe of retail value exceeding £300, elsewhere of retail value exceeding $500 US or the equivalent, or such lesser figure as may be decided by the Governing Body of golf in any country, or
(c) For a junior golfer, of such age as may be determined by the Governing Body of golf in any country, taking part in an event limited exclusively to juniors, acceptance of a prize or prize voucher in Great Britain and Ireland and the rest of Europe of retail value exceeding £100; elsewhere of retail value exceeding $200 US or the equivalent, or such lesser figure, if any, as may be decided by the Governing Body of golf in any country, or
(d) Conversion of a prize or prize voucher into money, or

(e) Accepting a gratuity in connection with a golfing event.

Exceptions:

1. Prizes of only symbolic value, provided that their symbolic nature is distinguished by distinctive permanent marking.

2. More than one testimonial award may be accepted from different donors even though their total retail value exceeds £300 or $500 US, provided they are not presented so as to evade such value limit for a single award.

Note 1: Events covered. The limits referred to in Clauses (a) or (c) above apply to total prize or prize vouchers received by any one person for any event or series of events in any one tournament or exhibition, including hole-in-one or other events in which golf skill is a factor.

Note 2: 'Retail value' is the price at which merchandise is available to anyone at a retail source, and the onus of proving the value of a particular prize rests with the donor.

Note 3: Purpose of prize vouchers. A prize voucher may be issued and redeemed only by the Committee in charge of a competition for the purchase of goods from a Professional's shop or other retail source, which may be specified by the Committee. It may not be used for such items as travel or hotel expenses, a bar bill, or a Club Subscription.

Note 4: Maximum Value of Prizes in any event for individuals. It is recommended that the total value of scratch or each division of handicap prizes should not exceed twice the maximum retail value of prize permitted in Rule 1-4(a) and (c) in an 18-hole competition, three times in a 36-hole competition, four times in a 54-hole competition and five times in a 72-hole competition.

Note 5: Testimonial Awards. Such awards relate to notable performances or contributions to golf as distinguished from tournament prizes.

5. Lending Name or Likeness.

Because of golf skill or golf reputation receiving or contracting to receive payment, compensation or personal benefit, directly or indirectly, for allowing one's name or likeness to be used in any way for the advertisement or sale of anything, whether or not used in or appertaining to golf except as a golf author or broadcaster as permitted by Rule 1-7.

Note: A player may accept equipment from anyone dealing in such equipment provided no advertising is involved.

6. Personal Appearance.

Because of golf skill or golf reputation, receiving payment or compensation, directly or indirectly, for a personal appearance.

Exception:
Actual expenses in connection with personal appearances may be paid or reimbursed provided no golf competition of exhibition is involved.

7. Broadcasting or Writing.

Because of golf skill or golf reputation, receiving payment or compensation, directly or indirectly, for broadcasting concerning golf, a golf event or golf events, writing golf articles or books, or allowing one's name to be advertised or published as the author of golf articles or books of which he is not actually the author.

Exceptions:
1. Broadcasting or writing as part of one's primary occupation or career, provided instruction in playing golf is not included (Rule 1-3).
2. Part-time broadcasting or writing, provided (a) the player is actually the author of the commentary, articles or books, (b) instruction in playing golf is not included and (c) the payment or compensation does not have the purpose or effect, directly or indirectly, of financing participation in a golf competition or golf competitions.

8. Expenses.

Accepting expenses, in money or otherwise, from any source to engage in a golf competition or exhibition.

Exceptions:
A player may receive expenses, not exceeding the actual expenses incurred, as follows: 1. From a member of the family or legal guardian;
   or
2. As a player in a golf competition or exhibition limited exclusively to players who have not reached their 18th birthday;
   or
3. As a representative of his Country, County, Club or similar body in team competitions or team training camps at home or abroad, or as a representative of his Country taking part in a National Championship abroad immediately preceding or following directly upon an international team competition, where such expenses are paid by the body he represents, or by the body controlling golf in the territory he is visiting; *or*
4. As an individual nominated by a National or County Union or Club to engage in an event at home or abroad provided that:

(a) The player nominated has not reached such age as may be determined by the Governing Body of Golf in the country from which the nomination is made.

(b) The expenses shall be paid only by the National Union or County Union responsible in the area from which the nomination is made and shall be limited to twenty competitive days in any one calendar year. The expenses are deemed in include reasonable travelling time and practice days in connection with the twenty competitive days.

(c) Where the event is to take place abroad, the approval of the National Union of the country in which the event is to be staged and, if the nominating body is not the National Union of the country from which the nomination is made, the approval of the National Union shall first be obtained by the nominating body.

(d) Where the event is to take place at home, and where the nomination is made by a County Union or Club, the approval of the National Union or the County Union in the area in which the event is to be staged shall first be obtained.

(*Note:* The Term 'County Union' covers any Province, State or equivalent Union or Association;)

or

5. As a player invited for reasons unrelated to golf skill, e.g. celebrities, business associates, etc., to take part in golfing events;

or

6. As a player in an exhibition in aid of a recognised Charity provided the exhibition is not run in connection with another golfing event.

or

7. As a player in a handicap individual or handicap team sponsored golfing event where expenses are paid by the sponsor on behalf of the player to take part in the event provided the event has been approved as follows:

(a) where the event is to take place at home the approval of the Governing Body (see Definition) shall first be obtained in advance by the sponsor, and

(b) where the event is to take place both at home and abroad the approval of the two or more Governing Bodies shall first be obtained in advance by the sponsor. The application for this approval should be sent to the Governing Body of golf in the country where the competition commences.

(c) where the event is to take place abroad the approval of two or more Governing Bodies shall first be obtained by the sponsor. The application for this approval should be sent to the Governing Body of golf in the country whose players shall be taking part in the event abroad

Note 1: Business Expenses. It is permissible to play in a golf competition while on a business trip with expenses paid provided that the golf part of the expenses is borne personally and is not charged to business. Further, the business involved must be actual and substantial, and not merely a subterfuge for legitimising expenses when the primary purpose is a golf competition.

Note 2: Private Transport. Acceptance of private transport furnished or arranged for by a tournament sponsor, directly or indirectly, as an inducement for a player to engage in a golf competition or exhibition shall be considered accepting expenses under Rule 1-8.

9. Scholarships.

Because of golf skill or golf reputation, accepting the benefits of a scholarship or grant-in-aid other than ones whose terms and conditions have been approved by the Amateur Status Committee of the Royal & Ancient Golf Club of St. Andrews.

10. Membership.

Because of golf skill accepting membership in a Golf Club without full payment for the class of membership for the purpose of playing for that Club.

11. Conduct Detrimental to Golf.

Any conduct, including activities in connection with golf gambling, which is considered detrimental to the best interests of the game.

Rule 2

Procedure for Enforcement and Reinstatement

1. Decision on a Breach. Whenever information of a possible breach of the Definition of an Amateur Golfer by a player claiming to be an Amateur shall come to the attention of the appropriate Committee of the Governing Body, the Committee, after such investigation as it may deem desirable, shall decide whether a breach has occurred. Each case shall be considered on its merits. The decision of the committee shall be final.

2. Enforcement. Upon a decision that a player has acted contrary to the Definition of an Amateur Golfer, the Committee may declare the Amateur Status of the player forfeited or require the player to refrain or desist from specified actions as a condition of retaining his Amateur Status.

The Committee shall use its best endeavours to ensure that the player is notified and may notify any interested Golf Association of any action taken under this paragraph.

3. Reinstatement. The Committee shall have sole power to reinstate a player to Amateur Status or to deny reinstatement. Each application for reinstatement shall be decided on its merits. In considering an application for reinstatement, the Committee shall normally be guided by the following principles:

a. Awaiting Reinstatement.

The professional holds an advantage over the amateur by reason of having devoted himself to the game as his profession; other persons infringing the Rules of Amateur Status also obtain advantages not available to the Amateur. They do not necessarily lose such advantage merely by deciding to cease infringing the Rules. Therefore, an applicant for reinstatement to Amateur Status shall undergo a period awaiting reinstatement as prescribed by the Committee.

The period awaiting reinstatement shall start from the date of the player's last breach of the Definition of an Amateur Golfer unless the Committee decides that it shall start from the date when the player's last breach became known to the Committee.

b. Period Awaiting Reinstatement.

The period awaiting reinstatement shall normally be related to the period the player was in breach. However, no applicant shall normally be eligible for reinstatement until he has conducted himself in accordance with the Definition of an Amateur Golfer for a period of at least two consecutive years. The Committee, however, reserves the right to extend or to shorten such a period. A longer period will normally be required of applicants who have been in breach for more than five years. Players of national prominence who have been in breach for more than five years shall not normally be eligible for reinstatement.

c. One Reinstatement

A player shall not normally be reinstated more than once.

d. Status While Awaiting Reinstatement.

During the period awaiting reinstatement an applicant for reinstatement shall conform with the Definition of an Amateur Golfer.

He shall not be eligible to enter competitions as an Amateur. He may, however, enter competitions, and win a prize, solely among members of a Club of which he is a member, subject to the approval of the Club; but he may not represent such Club against other Clubs.

Forms of Application for Countries under the jurisdiction of the Royal & Ancient Golf Club

(a) Each application for reinstatement shall be submitted on the approved form to the County Union where the applicant wishes to play as an Amateur. Such Union shall, after making all necessary enquiries, forward it through the National Union (and in the case of lady applicants, the Ladies Golf Union) and the appropriate Professional Golfers' Association, with comments endorsed thereon, to the Governing Body of golf in that country. Forms of application for reinstatement may be obtained from the Royal & Ancient Golf Club or from the National or County Unions. The application shall include such information as the Royal & Ancient Golf Club may require from time to time and it shall be signed and certified by the applicant.

(b) Any application made in countries under the jurisdiction of the Royal & Ancient Golf Club of St. Andrews which the Governing Body of golf in that country considers to be doubtful or not to be covered by the above regulations may be submitted to the Royal & Ancient Golf Club of St. Andrews whose decision shall be final.

R. & A. POLICY ON GAMBLING

The Definition of an Amateur Golfer provides that an Amateur golfer is one who plays the game as a non-remunerative or non-profit-making sport. When gambling motives are introduced evils can arise to threaten the integrity of both the game and the individual players.

The R&A does not object to participation in wagering among individual golfers or teams of golfers when participation in the wagering is limited to the players, the players may only wager on themselves or their teams, the sole source of all money won by players is advanced by the players and the primary purpose is the playing of the game for enjoyment.

The distinction between playing for prize money and gambling is essential to the validity of the Rules of Amateur Status. The following constitute golf wagering and not playing for prize money:

1. Participation in wagering among individual golfers.

2. Participation in wagering among teams.

Organised Amateur events open to the general golfing public and designed and promoted to create cash prizes are not approved by the R&A. Golfers participating in such events without irrevocably waiving their right to cash prizes are deemed by the R&A to be playing for prize money.

The R&A is opposed to and urges Unions and Clubs, and all other sponsors of golf competitions to prohibit types of gambling such as: Calcuttas, auction sweepstakes and any other forms of gambling organised for general participation or permitting participants to bet on someone other than themselves or their teams.

Attention is drawn to Rule 1-11 relating to conduct detrimental to the game, under which players can forfeit their Amateur Status. It is the Club which, by permitting competitions where excessive gambling is involved, or illegal prizes are offered, bears the responsibility for which the individual is penalised and Unions have the power to invoke severe sanctions against a Club or individual for consistently ignoring this policy.

The Standard Scratch Score and Handicapping Scheme 1983

Revised 1st April 1989

This scheme does not apply to ladies' clubs under the jurisdiction of the Ladies' Golf Union.

Published and administered by the Council of National Golf Unions and adopted by the Unions affiliated to the European Golf Association

Foreword

The Standard Scratch Score and Handicapping Scheme was prepared by the British Golf Unions' Joint Advisory Council in 1925 at the request of the Royal & Ancient Golf Club of St Andrews and has been in operation throughout Great Britain and Ireland since 1st March, 1926.

The Scheme incorporated in this book, known as the Standard Scratch Score and Handicapping Scheme 1983, introduced a new concept in handicapping based on the system presently in use by the Australian Golf Union. The Council of National Golf Unions acknowledges the assistance received from that Union and its officials in formulating the Scheme, which takes account of all scores returned by players under Medal Play conditions.

No change has been made in the present method of fixing the Standard Scratch Scores of courses but, on the principle that uniformity and equity in handicapping can be more effectively achieved if there is uniformity and equity in the fixing of Standard Scratch Scores, the Council of National Golf Unions has examined the Course Rating System of the United States Golf Association and has agreed that the Scratch Rating calculated by that procedure may be progressively adopted by National Unions as the Standard Scratch Score pursuant to clause 1.

An amended edition of the Scheme was published on the 1st January 1986 incorporating all amendments from the 1st January 1983 to that date. Further amendments made since the 1st January 1986 are incorporated in this revised edition of the Scheme.

The principal changes are:

(a) The introduction of a Competition Scratch Score (clause 20, Appendices E, F and G).

(b) The discontinuation of the Winter Period following the introduction of the Competition Scratch Score.

(c) For the purpose of calculating the Competition Scratch Score a requirement for players to enter their current Playing Handicaps on score cards when the Qualifying Competition is not a handicap event (clause 13.(9)).

(d) The giving of authority to Unions, at their discretion, to permit Home Clubs to increase handicaps of players in any of the Categories 2, 3 and 4 without reference to the Union or Area Authority (clause 9.(7)).

(e) The giving of authority to Unions, at their discretion, to direct that scores with a nett differential of zero and above returned by a player in Categories 3 and/or 4 at a club where he is not a member shall be disregarded for handicap increase (clause 9.(8)).

(f) Procedure for allotment of handicaps (clause 15.(3)).

(g) The introduction of flexibility into the fixing of Par for individual holes (clause 5).

Copyright 1989 © Council of National Golf Unions.

Part One
Definitions

Definition
A. UNION.
B. AREA AUTHORITY.
C. HOME CLUB.
D. AFFILIATED CLUB.
E. HANDICAPPING AUTHORITY.
F. HANDICAP COMMITTEE.
G. HANDICAPS.
H. CATEGORIES OF HANDICAP.
I. MEASURED COURSE.
J. DISTANCE POINT.

K. MEDAL TEE.
L. MEDAL PLAY CONDITIONS.
M. QUALIFYING COMPETITION.
N. QUALIFYING SCORE.
O. AGGREGATE FOURBALL
 COMPETITION.
P. STANDARD SCRATCH SCORE.
Q. COMPETITION SCRATCH SCORE.
R. NETT DIFFERENTIAL.
S. BUFFER ZONE

Part Two

The Golf Course and the Standard Scratch Score

Clause
1. The STANDARD SCRATCH SCORE.
2. Course measurement.
3. Alterations to courses.
4. Tees.
5. Par.
6. Preferred lies.
7. Permitted adjustments to a MEASURED COURSE.

Part Three

Handicapping

8. Introduction.
9. Rights and obligations of the UNION.
10. Rights and obligations of the AREA AUTHORITY.
11. Rights and obligations of the AFFILIATED CLUB.
12. Rights and obligations of the HANDICAP COMMITTEE.
13. Rights and obligations of the player.
14. QUALIFYING SCORES.
15. Allotment of handicaps.
16. Alteration of handicaps.
17. Suspension, lapsing and loss of handicaps.
18. Restoration of handicaps.
19. Powers of the HANDICAP COMMITTEE relating to general play.
20. COMPETITION SCRATCH SCORE.

Part One

Definitions

Throughout the scheme whenever a word or expression is used which is defined within the following definitions the word or expression is printed in capital letters.

A – Union

A UNION is any national organisation in control of amateur golf in any country.

B – Area Authority

An AREA AUTHORITY is any authority appointed by a UNION to act on behalf of that UNION for the purposes of the Scheme within a specified area.

C – Affiliated Club

An AFFILIATED CLUB is a club affiliated to a UNION or AREA AUTHORITY which pays to the UNION and AREA AUTHORITY a specified annual per capita fee in respect of each eligible member.

D – Home Club

A player's HOME CLUB is an AFFILIATED CLUB of which the player is a member. If the player is a member of more than one AFFILIATED CLUB he shall nominate one as his HOME CLUB.

E – Handicapping Authority

The HANDICAPPING AUTHORITY for a player is his HOME CLUB subject to the overall jurisdiction of the UNION.

F – Handicap Committee

The HANDICAP COMMITTEE is the body appointed by an AFFILIATED CLUB to administer the Scheme within the Club.

G – Handicaps

(1) EXACT HANDICAP – a player's EXACT HANDICAP is his handicap calculated in accordance with the provisions of the Scheme to one decimal place.
(2) PLAYING HANDICAP – a player's PLAYING HANDICAP is his EXACT HANDICAP calculated to the nearest whole number (0.5 is rounded upwards).

H – Categories of Handicap

Handicaps are divided into the following CATEGORIES:
CATEGORY 1: Handicaps of 5 or less.
CATEGORY 2: Handicaps of 6 to 12 inclusive.

CATEGORY 3: Handicaps of 13 to 20 inclusive.
CATEGORY 4: Handicaps of 21 to 28 inclusive.

I – Measured Course

Any course played over by an AFFILIATED CLUB the measured length of which has been certified in accordance with the requirements of clause 2.

J – Distance Point

The DISTANCE POINT is the position of a permanent marker indicating the point from which the length of a hole is measured.

K – Medal Tee

A MEDAL TEE is a rectangular area the front of which shall not be more than 10 yards (9 metres) in front of the relevant DISTANCE POINT and the rear of which shall not be less than 2 yards (2 metres) behind the DISTANCE POINT.
NOTE: Special rules apply when the length of a MEASURED COURSE has been temporarily reduced by more than 100 yards (91 metres) – see clause 7(b).

L – Medal Play Conditions

MEDAL PLAY CONDITIONS prevail during stroke, par and Stableford competitions played with full handicap allowance over 18 holes under the Rules of Golf from MEDAL TEES. MEDAL PLAY CONDITIONS shall not prevail when the length of the course played varies by more than 100 yards (91 metres) from the length of the MEASURED COURSE.
NOTE: Special rules apply when the length of a MEASURED COURSE has been temporarily reduced by more than 100 yards (91 metres) – see clause 7(b).

M – Qualifying Competition

A QUALIFYING COMPETITION is any competition in which MEDAL PLAY CONDITIONS prevail subject to restrictions and limitations contained in the Scheme or imposed by UNIONS.

N – Qualifying Score

A QUALIFYING SCORE is any score including a "no return" returned in a QUALIFYING COMPETITION.

O – Aggregate Fourball Competition

An AGGREGATE FOURBALL COMPETITION is a QUALIFYING COMPETITION in which the completed scores at each hole of a team of not more than two amateur players are aggregated.

P – Standard Scratch Score

The STANDARD SCRATCH SCORE is the score allotted to an 18 hole golf course after the application of clause 1.

Q – Competition Scratch Score

The COMPETITION SCRATCH SCORE is the score determined by clause 20.

R – Nett Differential

The NETT DIFFERENTIAL is the difference (+ or –) between the nett score returned by a player in a QUALIFYING COMPETITION and the COMPETITION SCRATCH SCORE.

S – Buffer Zone

The BUFFER ZONE is a zone which applies only to scores returned by players in QUALIFYING COMPETITIONS with NETT DIFFERENTIALS of +1 and +2 after application of the COMPETITION SCRATCH SCORE.

Part Two

The Golf Course and the Standard Scratch Score

1. The Standard Scratch Score

1.(1) The STANDARD SCRATCH SCORE is the score which a scratch player is expected to return over a MEASURED COURSE. In the case of a nine-hole course it represents two rounds.
1.(2) The allocation of STANDARD SCRATCH SCORES shall be the responsibility of the UNION.
1.(3) The Table on page 771 will provide a guide to officials in making their assessments.
1.(4) In assessing the STANDARD SCRATCH SCORE of a course, officials will take as the starting point the provisional Standard Scratch Score from the Table. They will then consider the following points:
(a) The terrain and general layout of the course.
(b) Normal ground conditions – Is run average, above average or below average?
(c) Sizes of greens and whether watered or unwatered.
(d) Hazards – Are greens well guarded or open?
(e) Width of fairways, the effect of trees and nature of rough.
(f)   Nearness of "out of bounds" to fairways and greens.

Table of Provisional Standard Scratch Scores

Standard length of Course	Lengths included in Standard Length		Provisional Standard Scratch Score
Yards	Yards	Metres	
7100	7001-7002	6402-6584	74
6900	6801-7000	6219-6401	73
6700	6601-6800	6036-6218	72
6500	6401-6600	5853-6035	71
6300	6201-6400	5670-5852	70
6100	5951-6200	5442-5669	69
5800	5701-5950	5213-5441	68
5500	5451-5700	4984-5212	67
5300	5201-5450	4756-4983	66
5100	5001-5200	4573-4755	65
4900	4801-5000	4390-4572	64
4700	4601-4800	4207-4389	63
4500	4401-4600	4024-4206	62
4300	4201-4400	3841-4023	61
4100	4001-4200	3659-3840	60

1 yard = 0.91440 metres
1 metre = 1.09361 yards

(g) Average weather conditions throughout the playing year. Is the course exposed and subject to high winds for most of the year? Is it sheltered from the full effects of adverse weather?

(h) The distance by which the length of the course varies from the standard length shown in column one of the Table.

1.(5) Having considered all these points, officials will fix the STANDARD SCRATCH SCORE of the course by: (a) Confirming the Provisional Standard Scratch Score as the STANDARD SCRATCH SCORE.

(b) Adding a stroke or strokes to the Provisional Standard Scratch Score.

(c) Deducting a stroke or strokes from the Provisional Standard Scratch Score.

1.(6) At the discretion of the UNION courses of less than 4001 yards may be allocated such STANDARD SCRATCH SCORES as the UNION shall determine.

2. Course Measurement

Measurement shall be by plan or projection along the horizontal plane from the DISTANCE POINT on the MEDAL TEE to the centre of the green of each hole.

In the case of a dog-leg hole, measurement shall be along the centre line of the fairway to the axis and then to the centre of the green.

Measurement shall be carried out by a qualified surveyor, or someone competent and experienced in the handling of surveying instruments, who shall grant a certificate showing details of the length of each hole and the total playing length of the course. Subsequent alterations to the length of the course will require a certificate only for the altered hole or holes which shall be measured in the manner prescribed above.

3. Alterations to Courses

When alterations have been carried out to a course increasing or decreasing its length, the club shall submit a "Form of Application" through its AREA AUTHORITY to the UNION. In the case of a new course, a "Form of Application" shall be submitted by the club through its AREA AUTHORITY to the UNION who will fix the STANDARD SCRATCH SCORE. The UNION is responsible for all STANDARD SCRATCH SCORES in the country over which it has jurisdiction.

4. Tees

All clubs with the necessary facilities should have back and forward MEDAL TEES with a yardage measurement from each tee and a separate STANDARD SCRATCH SCORE as measured from back and forward MEDAL TEES permanently marked.

To facilitate the use of the correct tees the Royal & Ancient Golf Club of St Andrews recommends that tee boxes or other objects in use to mark the teeing ground shall be painted as follows:

Ladies' Standard MEDAL TEES	Red
Men's Forward MEDAL TEES	Yellow
Men's Back MEDAL TEES	White

When a National Championship is being played over a course the tee markers may be coloured Blue.

5. Par

The STANDARD SCRATCH SCORE must not be allocated amongst the individual holes, but should be printed as a total on the card. The par figure for each hole should be printed alongside each hole on the card. Par for each hole shall be fixed by the club in relation to the length and playing difficulty of each hole and shall be fixed within the following ranges:

	Yards	Metres
Par 3	0–250	0–229
Par 4	220–500	201–457
Par 5	440+	402+

e.g. if a hole is 460 yards (421 metres) it may be allotted par 4 or 5 depending upon its average playing difficulty.

The total of the Par figures for each hole of a course will not necessarily coincide with the STANDARD SCRATCH SCORE of that course. Par should be used for Stableford and similar competitions.

6. Preferred Lies

When preferred lies are in operation the following points shall be taken into consideration: MEDAL PLAY CONDITIONS will apply notwithstanding the application of a Local Rule for preferred lies as a result of adverse conditions during the period from 1st November to 30th April. Preferred lies may be used during that period but are not mandatory upon clubs during any part thereof. The Local Rule may apply to specified holes only. Outside that period MEDAL PLAY CONDITIONS will not apply if preferred lies are in operation unless the consent of the UNION or AREA AUTHORITY has been first obtained.

It is emphasised that preferred lies shall apply only when a Local Rule has been made and published in accordance with Appendix 1 of the Rules of Golf as follows:

"A ball lying on any "closely mown area" through the green may, without penalty, be moved or may be lifted, cleaned and placed within six inches of where it originally lay, but not nearer the hole. After the ball has been so moved or placed, it is in play."

Penalty for breach of Local Rule: Match Play – Loss of hole; Stroke play – Two strokes.

NOTE: "closely mown area" means any area of the COURSE, including paths through the rough, cut to fair-way height or less. (Rule 25-2).

7. Permitted Adjustment to a Measured Course

Whilst each AFFILIATED CLUB must endeavour to maintain the length of its MEASURED COURSE at all times MEDAL PLAY CONDITIONS nevertheless prevail when the length of a course has been reduced in the following circumstances:

(a) When, to allow movement of the playing position on the MEDAL TEE or the use of a temporary green, the length of the course being played has been reduced by not more than 100 yards (91 metres) from the length of the MEASURED COURSE. The tee positions used must nevertheless be within the area defined by Definition K. NOTE: The maximum movement forward on any MEDAL TEE must not exceed 10 yards (9 metres) – See Definition K.

(b) When, to allow work to proceed on course alterations or for reasons other than weather conditions, it is necessary to reduce the playing length of the MEASURED COURSE by between 100 and 300 yards (91 and 274 metres). In these circumstances, the club shall reduce the

STANDARD SCRATCH SCORE of the MEASURED COURSE temporarily by 1 stroke and report to the UNION, or to such other body nominated by the UNION, the reduction in the STANDARD SCRATCH SCORE, and the reason for it. The club must also notify the UNION or other body when the course has been restored to its measured length and the official STANDARD SCRATCH SCORE reinstated.

Part Three Handicapping

8. Introduction

8.(1) The Council of National Golf Unions Standard Scratch Score and Handicapping Scheme has been revised to achieve a uniformity and equity in handicapping throughout Great Britain and Ireland and those member countries of the European Golf Association adopting the Scheme. The nature of the game of golf, with its varying playing conditions, makes handicapping a relatively inexact operation. Nevertheless, if the same principles are sensibly and universally applied by HANDICAP COMMITTEES, a high degree of uniformity in handicapping can be achieved. It is therefore of paramount importance that all parties to the Scheme fulfil their obligations to it and these are set out below.
8.(2) Handicapping within the Scheme is delegated to AFFILIATED CLUBS subject to the overall jurisdiction of the UNION.

9. Rights and Obligations of the Union

The UNION:
9.(1) Shall have overall jurisdiction for the administration of the Scheme.
9.(2) May delegate any part of that jurisdiction to an AREA AUTHORITY.
9.(3) Shall ratify all PLAYING HANDICAPS reduced to scratch or below immediately after the reduction.
9.(4) Shall have the right to obtain information upon handicaps from AFFILIATED CLUBS at any time.
9.(5) Shall establish within the UNION conditions, restrictions and limitations to be imposed in respect of competitions deemed to be QUALIFYING COMPETITIONS.
9.(6) Shall settle any dispute referred to it. Its decision shall be final.
9.(7) May at its discretion authorise HOME CLUBS to increase the handicaps of players in any of the CATEGORIES 2, 3, and 4 pursuant to clause 19. When such authority has been given the requirements of clause 19.(2) and (3) that the increase shall be effected by the UNION or AREA AUTHORITY

shall not apply. Notwithstanding the foregoing, the Union may, if it considers that handicaps have been unjustifiably increased by a HOME CLUB, require that club to comply with all of the provisions of clause 19.

9.(8) May at its discretion direct that scores returned by a player in CATEGORIES 3 and/or 4 at a club where he is not a member shall be disregarded for handicap increase pursuant to CLAUSE 16.(3).

10. Rights and Obligations of the Area Authority

The AREA AUTHORITY shall:

10.(1) Administer the responsibilities delegated to it by the UNION.

10.(2) Have the right to obtain information upon handicaps from AFFILIATED CLUBS at any time.

11. Rights and Obligations of the Affiliated Club

The AFFILIATED CLUB shall:

11.(1) Act as the HANDICAPPING AUTHORITY for all members for whom it is the HOME CLUB subject to the overall jurisdiction of the UNION.

11.(2) Ensure that the Scheme is properly applied in the club.

11.(3) Ensure that all handicaps are calculated in accordance with the Scheme.

11.(4) Appoint a HANDICAP COMMITTEE to perform the obligations set out in clause 12 below.

12. Rights and Obligations of the Handicap Committee

The HANDICAP COMMITTEE shall:

12.(1) Maintain a list in which the names of competitors must be entered prior to competing in a QUALIFYING COMPETITION at the club.

12.(2) Ensure, so far as possible, that all cards taken out in QUALIFYING COMPETITIONS are returned to the committee including incomplete cards.

12.(3) At the conclusion of each round of a QUALIFYING COMPETITION calculate the COMPETITION SCRATCH SCORE as required by clause 20.

12.(4) Post on the club's notice board all changes of members' PLAYING HANDICAPS immediately they are made.

12.(5) Ensure that a record of members' current PLAYING HANDICAPS is available in a prominent position in the club house.

12.(6) When the club is a player's HOME CLUB:

(a) Maintain on his behalf a handicap record sheet which shall include the information shown in Appendix A.

(b) Ensure his scores are recorded immediately after completion of each QUALIFYING COMPETITION at the HOME CLUB or the reporting of a QUALIFYING SCORE returned elsewhere.

(c) Keep his EXACT HANDICAP up to date at all times.

(d) Notify the UNION and AREA AUTHORITY immediately the committee reduces a member's PLAYING HANDICAP to scratch or below and obtain ratification from the UNION or, if so delegated, from the AREA AUTHORITY.

NOTE: The reduction is effective before ratification.

(e) Unless some other body has been appointed by the HOME CLUB for this purpose, exercise the power to suspend handicaps contained in clause 17.

(f) When a member changes his HOME CLUB send to the new HOME CLUB a copy of the player's current handicap record sheet.

(g) Specify the conditions which apply when a player wishes to obtain a handicap under the provisions of clause 15.

(h) Exercise the powers to adjust players' handicaps contained in clause 19.

(i) As required by sub clause 19.(5) advise players of changes made to their handicaps under the provisions of clause 19.

13. Rights and Obligations of the Player

The player shall:

13.(1) Have one handicap only which shall be allotted and adjusted by his HOME CLUB. That handicap shall apply elsewhere including other clubs of which the player is a member.

13.(2) If he is a member of more than one AFFILIATED CLUB select one as his HOME CLUB and notify that club and the others of his choice.

13.(3) Not change his HOME CLUB except by giving advance notice of the change which can take effect only at the end of a calendar year unless he has ceased to be a member of his HOME CLUB or both clubs agree to the change taking place at an earlier date.

13.(4) Report to his HOME CLUB the names of all other AFFILIATED CLUBS of which he is, becomes, or ceases to be, a member and report to all other AFFILIATED CLUBS of which he is a member:

(a) The name of his HOME CLUB and any changes of his HOME CLUB and

(b) Alterations to his PLAYING HANDICAP made by his HOME CLUB.

13.(5) Ensure that before competing in a QUALIFYING COMPETITION his entry has been inserted in the competition entry list.

13.(6) Ensure that all competition cards in QUALIFYING COMPETITIONS, whether or not complete, are returned to the organising committee.

13.(7) Subject to the provisions of clause 9.(8) report to his HOME CLUB immediately all QUALIFYING SCORES (including no returns) returned away from his HOME CLUB advising the HOME CLUB of the date of the QUALIFYING COMPETITION, the venue and the COMPETITION SCRATCH SCORE together with the following:

(a) After a stroke play QUALIFYING COMPETITION the gross score returned.

(b) After a Stableford QUALIFYING COMPETITION the par of the course and the number of points scored.

(c) After a par QUALIFYING COMPETITION the par of the course and the score versus par.

NOTE 1: Players are reminded that failure to report scores returned away from their HOME CLUBS (including no returns) is likely to lead to the suspension of offending players' handicaps under the provisions of clause 17.

NOTE 2: In the event of a QUALIFYING COMPETITION being declared abandoned or scores returned being deemed by clause 20 not to be QUALIFYING SCORES the player is required to report the above information only if he has returned a NETT DIFFERENTIAL of less than zero.

13.(8) Prior to playing in any competition at a club other than his HOME CLUB ensure that any appropriate reductions to his PLAYING HANDICAP have been made or alternatively comply with the obligations set out in clause 16.(11).

13.(9) Enter his current PLAYING HANDICAP on all cards returned in a QUALIFYING COMPETITION even though the event may not be a handicap competition.

14. Qualifying Scores

14.(1) The only scores to be recorded on a player's handicap record sheet are:

(a) QUALIFYING SCORES as defined.

(b) NETT DIFFERENTIALS of less than zero returned in any abandoned round of a QUALIFYING COMPETITION or in any round of a QUALIFYING COMPETITION when that round has been deemed under the provisions of clause 20 not to be a QUALIFYING SCORE.

(c) Correct scores in a QUALIFYING COMPETITION which are disqualified for any reason.

(d) Scores returned in a QUALIFYING COMPETITION played over 18 holes on a course reduced in length under the provisions of clause 7.

(e) Scores returned in a QUALIFYING COMPETITION played over a MEASURED COURSE when local rules are in operation for preferred lies (as permitted by clause 6) or for any other purpose provided the rules are authorised by Appendix 1 of the Rules of Golf or have been approved by the Rules of Golf Committee of the Royal & Ancient Golf Club of St Andrews.

(f) The individual scores and no returns returned by players in AGGREGATE FOURBALL COMPETITIONS.

NOTE: The competition must be a QUALIFYING COMPETITION.

NOTE: QUALIFYING SCORES returned in Stableford

and par competitions shall be converted into NETT DIFFERENTIALS by using the tables in Appendix C.

14.(2) The following returns shall not be accepted as QUALIFYING SCORES in any circumstances:

(a) Scores returned in any better ball fourball competition.

(b) Scores returned in competitions over less than 18 holes.

(c) Scores returned in any competition which is not played in accordance with the Rules of Golf and authorised Local Rules.

(d) Scores returned in "running medals". A running medal is an extended competition in which the player has the option of selecting the day or days on which he shall compete and/or how many returns he shall make. A competition extended over two or more days solely to accommodate the number of players entered is not a running medal.

(e) Subject to clause 14.(1)(b) scores returned in any round of a QUALIFYING COMPETITION deemed under the provisions of clause 20 not to be QUALIFYING SCORES.

(f) Any competition other than an AGGREGATE FOUR-BALL COMPETITION in which competitors play in partnership with another competitor.

(g) Stableford and par competitions played with less than full handicap allowance.

(h) Scores returned in events run by organisations which are not HANDICAPPING AUTHORITIES unless such events have been previously approved by a UNION as a QUALIFYING COMPETITION.

15. Allotment of Handicaps

15.(1) The maximum handicap is 28. (Maximum EXACT HANDICAP 28.0.)

15.(2) A handicap can be allotted only to an amateur member of an AFFILIATED CLUB.

15.(3) To obtain a handicap a player shall submit three cards preferably marked over a MEASURED COURSE which shall be adjusted by the HANDICAP COMMITTEE so that any score of more than 2 over par at any hole shall be amended to 2 over par. After these adjustments have been made an EXACT HANDICAP shall be allotted equivalent to the number of strokes by which the best of the three rounds differs from the STANDARD SCRATCH SCORE. The HANDICAP COMMITTEE may allot a player an initial whole number EXACT HANDICAP less than the best score if it has reason to consider that a lower handicap is more appropriate to the player's ability. In exceptional circumstances a higher handicap may be allotted than that indicated by the best score. When a player fails to return cards justifying an EXACT HANDICAP of 28.0 he may, at the discretion of the HANDICAP COMMITTEE, be given an EXACT HANDICAP of 28.0. The player's PLAYING HANDICAP shall equal the EXACT HANDICAP allotted.

15.(4) A player without a handicap shall not be allotted a CATEGORY 1 HANDICAP without the written authority of the UNION, or AREA AUTHORITY if so delegated.

16. Alteration of Handicaps

16.(1) Definition H divides handicaps into the following four CATEGORIES:
CATEGORY 1: Handicaps of 5 or less.
CATEGORY 2: Handicaps of 6 to 12 inclusive.
CATEGORY 3: Handicaps of 13 to 20 inclusive.
CATEGORY 4: Handicaps of 21 to 28 inclusive.
16.(2) If a player returns a NETT DIFFERENTIAL of zero or within the BUFFER ZONE his EXACT HANDICAP is not changed.
16.(3) Subject to the provisions of sub clauses 9.(8), 20.(3) and 20.(4), if a player returns a score with a NETT DIFFERENTIAL of +3 or more or records a "no return" his EXACT HANDICAP is increased by 0.1.
16.(4) If a player returns a NETT DIFFERENTIAL of less than zero his EXACT HANDICAP is reduced by an amount *per stroke that the* NETT DIFFERENTIAL *is below zero*, the amount per stroke being determined by his HANDICAP CATEGORY.
16.(5) The recording of scores shall be kept by NETT DIFFERENTIAL i.e. the difference (+ or −) between the player's nett score and the COMPETITION SCRATCH SCORE. The date, NETT DIFFERENTIAL, EXACT HANDICAP and PLAYING HANDICAP must be recorded on the player's handicap record sheet.
16.(6) EXACT HANDICAPS shall be adjusted as follows, with reference to the handicap adjustment table, Appendix B:

CATEGORY	PLAYING HANDICAP	If NETT DIFFERENTIAL is:	
		Above BUFFER ZONE. Add *only*	Below CSS. Subtract for *each* Stroke below
1	Up to 5	0.1	0.1
2	6 to 12	0.1	0.2
3	13 to 20	0.1	0.3
4	21 to 28	0.1	0.4

For example:
If a player on 11.2 returns a score with a NETT DIFFERENTIAL of 4 his EXACT HANDICAP becomes 11.3. If he then returns a score with a NETT DIFFERENTIAL of −7 his EXACT HANDICAP is reduced by 7 times 0.2 = 1.4, i.e. to an EXACT HANDICAP of 9.9 and his PLAYING HANDICAP is 10 which is immediately his new handicap. 16.(7) When a player's handicap is to be reduced so that it goes from a higher CATEGORY to a lower CATEGORY, it shall be reduced at the rate appropriate to the higher CATEGORY only so far as brings his PLAYING HANDICAP into the lower CATEGORY and the balance of the reduction

shall be at the rate appropriate to the lower CATEGORY.
For example:
If a player on 21.2 returns a score with a NETT DIFFERENTIAL of −6, i.e. 6 strokes below his PLAYING HANDICAP of 21, his handicap is reduced as follows:
21.2−(2 times 0.4) (i.e. −0.8)=20.4
20.4−(4 times 0.3) (i.e. −1.2)=19.2
16.(8) A player whose EXACT HANDICAP contains 0.5 or over shall be given the next higher handicap, e.g. 12.5 exact would be 13 PLAYING HANDICAP. This applies when handicaps are to be increased or reduced.
NOTE: EXACT HANDICAP −0.5 rounded upwards is PLAYING HANDICAP scratch and not plus one.
16.(9) Reductions shall be made on the day the score becomes known to the HOME CLUB.
16.(10) Increases shall be made at the end of each calendar month or at such shorter intervals as the HOME CLUB may decide.
16.(11) If, for any reason, a player is unable to report to his HOME CLUB a QUALIFYING SCORE or SCORES which may have a NETT DIFFERENTIAL of less than zero or has been unable to ascertain, after reporting such scores, whether or not his PLAYING HANDICAP has been reduced, he shall then, before competing in a further competition at a club other than his HOME CLUB, either:
(a) For that competition only, make such reduction to his PLAYING HANDICAP as shall be appropriate under the Scheme by applying the COMPETITION SCRATCH SCORE if known, otherwise the STANDARD SCRATCH SCORE to his gross score, or
(b) Report to the committee organising the competition any relevant score returned which after deduction of his PLAYING HANDICAP is two above the STANDARD SCRATCH SCORE or less. The committee may, for that competition only, reduce the player's PLAYING HANDICAP.
NOTE: Increases to PLAYING HANDICAPS may not be made under the provisions of this sub clause.
16.(12) The procedure for the restoration of handicaps which have been lost is contained in clause 18.

17. Suspension, Lapsing and Loss of Handicaps

17.(1) The HANDICAP COMMITTEE, or other body appointed by the HOME CLUB for the purposes of this clause, shall suspend the handicap of any player who in its opinion has constantly or blatantly failed to comply with his obligations under the Scheme. The player must be notified of the period of suspension and of any other conditions imposed. No player's handicap shall be suspended without first affording him the opportunity of appearing before the committee or other body.

17.(2) If a player is suspended from membership of his HOME CLUB his handicap shall lapse automatically until his membership is reinstated.

17.(3) A player's handicap is lost immediately he ceases to be a member of an AFFILIATED CLUB or loses his amateur status.

17.(4) Whilst a player's handicap is suspended, lapsed or has been lost he shall not enter or compete in any competition which requires a competitor to be the holder of a handicap for either entering or competing in the competition.

18. Restoration of Handicaps

18.(1) A player who has lost his handicap for any reason other than suspension or lapsing may obtain a new handicap by complying with the requirements of clause 15. When allotting him a handicap the HANDICAP COMMITTEE will give due consideration to the handicap he last held. A CATEGORY 1 HANDICAP shall not be allotted without the written approval of the UNION, or AREA AUTHORITY if so delegated. 18.(2) The lapsed handicap of a player suspended from membership of his HOME CLUB shall be reinstated when his membership is restored and shall be the same as the handicap he held when his membership was suspended.

19. Powers of the Handicap Committee Relating to General Play

19.(1) Whenever the HANDICAP COMMITTEE of a player's HOME CLUB considers that a player's EXACT HANDICAP is too high and does not reflect his current playing ability the HANDICAP COMMITTEE must, subject to the provisions of sub clause (3) of this clause, reduce his EXACT HANDICAP to the figure it considers appropriate.

19.(2) (a) Whenever the HANDICAP COMMITTEE of a player's HOME CLUB considers that a player's EXACT HANDICAP is too low and does not reflect his current playing ability the HANDICAP COMMITTEE must, subject to the provisions of sub clause (3) of this clause, recommend to the UNION, or AREA AUTHORITY if so delegated, that his EXACT HANDICAP should be increased to the figure it considers appropriate. (b) In the event of a UNION delegating to HOME CLUBS the unconditional authority to increase the handicaps of players in any of the CATEGORIES 2, 3 AND 4 HOME CLUBS need not submit to the UNION or AREA AUTHORITY proposals in respect of any changes of handicaps of players in the nominated CATEGORIES.

19.(3) When the HANDICAP COMMITTEE has decided that the EXACT HANDICAP of a player should be reduced to less than 5.5 or that the EXACT HANDICAP of a player should be increased the HANDICAP COMMITTEE must refer the matter to the UNION, or AREA AUTHORITY if so delegated, with its recommended adjustment. The UNION or AREA AUTHORITY shall then authorise the recommended variation, reject the recommendation or refer the matter back to the HANDICAP COMMITTEE for further consideration. The UNION or AREA AUTHORITY shall be supplied with all the information upon which the recommendation is based and with any further information required.

19.(4) When deciding whether to effect or recommend an adjustment of handicap the HANDICAP COMMITTEE of the player's HOME CLUB shall consider all available information regarding the player's golfing ability.

It shall consider in particular:

(a) The frequency of QUALIFYING SCORES recently returned by the player to and below his PLAYING HANDICAP.

(b) The player's achievements in match play, four-ball better-ball competitions and other non-qualifying events.

(c) QUALIFYING SCORES returned by the player in stroke play competitions which are adversely affected by one or more particularly bad holes. It may prove helpful to take into account the number of points the player would have scored if these QUALIFYING SCORES had been in Stableford competitions played with full handicap allowance.

19.(5) The HANDICAP COMMITTEE shall advise a player of any change of handicap under this clause and the change will become effective when the player becomes aware of the adjustment.

19.(6) The HANDICAP COMMITTEE or other body organising a competition at a club which is not the player's HOME CLUB may if it considers his handicap is too high because of scores reported pursuant to sub clause 16.(11)(b) or for any other reason reduce that handicap. Any reduction made under this sub clause shall apply only to the competition for which it is made.

19.(7) Decisions made by a HANDICAP COMMITTEE, UNION or AREA AUTHORITY under this clause shall be final.

NOTES:

1. In the interests of equitable handicapping it is essential that all HANDICAP COMMITTEES keep the handicaps of the members for whom they act as the HOME CLUB under review and that adjustments of handicaps are considered as soon as it comes to the committee's notice that a player's handicap may no longer correctly reflect his current general golfing ability.

2. The HANDICAP COMMITTEE should consider dealing more severely with a player whose general standard of play is known to be improving than it would with a player who it is believed has returned scores below his general ability but whose general playing ability is not considered to be improving.

20. Competition Scratch Score

20.(1) At the conclusion of each round of a QUALI-FYING COMPETITION the COMPETITION SCRATCH SCORE shall be calculated by following the procedure set out in Appendix E and applying the relevant Table in either Appendix F or G.

20.(2) In the event of one round of a QUALIFYING COMPETITION extending over more than one day the COMPETITION SCRATCH SCORE shall be calculated for each day.

20.(3) The relevant Table dictates any adjustment to be made to the STANDARD SCRATCH SCORE to provide the COMPETITION SCRATCH SCORE or to direct that the scores returned shall not count as QUALI-FYING SCORES (indicated by "N/C" in the Table column heading). When the COMPETITION SCRATCH SCORE has been established all NETT DIFFERENTIALS shall be calculated in relation thereto and handicap adjustments made and entered in the player's Handicap Record Sheets. (See Definition S – BUFFER ZONE.)

20.(4) If the Table indicates that the scores returned shall not count as QUALIFYING SCORES then the COMPETITION SCRATCH SCORE shall be deemed to be three strokes more than the STANDARD SCRATCH SCORE. All players who after the application of the COMPETITION SCRATCH SCORE to their scores have returned a NETT DIFFERENTIAL of less than zero shall have their EXACT HANDICAPS reduced to the extent dictated by the NETT DIFFER-ENTIAL so calculated. A NETT DIFFERENTIAL of zero or above shall not result in a handicap increase.

20.(5) If a QUALIFYING COMPETITION is abandoned for any reason the COMPETITION SCRATCH SCORE shall be regarded as equal to the STANDARD SCRATCH SCORE and players returning NETT DIFFER-ENTIALS of less than zero shall have their EXACT HANDICAPS reduced to the extent dictated by the NETT DIFFERENTIAL. A NETT DIFFERENTIAL of zero or above shall not result in a handicap increase.

NOTE: UNIONS, AREA AUTHORITIES and any organisations so authorised by a UNION shall establish the COMPETITION SCRATCH SCORES for any events they organise.

Appendix A

Handicap Record Sheet

NAME _____

HOME CLUB _____

OTHER CLUBS _____

Date	Nett dif-ferential	Handicap		Date	Nett dif-ferential	Handicap	
		Exact	Playing			Exact	Playing
May 1	B/F	21.0	21	June 30	B/F	19.4	19
6	2	21.0	21	July			
7	4	21.1	21	8	7	19.5	19
20	N/R	21.2	21	9	6	19.6	19
21	–6	19.2	19	29	8	19.7	19 Note 2
				30	3	19.8	20
June 4	1	19.2	19	Aug 6	2	19.8	20
5	4	19.3	19	7	–6	18.0	18
25	7	19.4	19	20	0	18.0	18
26	2	19.4	19	21	7	18.1	18

Notes to Appendix A

1 The sheet above shows the PLAYING HANDICAPS when increases are made on the last day of each calendar month.

2 If the increases had been made immediately the PLAYING HANDICAP would have been increased to 20 on the 8th July and the NETT DIFFEREN-TIALS of 6, 8 and 3 respectively on the 9th, 29th and 30th July would each have been reduced by 1. Thus, with the operation of the BUFFER ZONE, the EXACT HANDICAP would have remained at 19.7 on 31st July and been 0.1 less than those shown thereafter.

3 NETT DIFFERENTIAL is the difference (+ or –) between the Nett Score returned by a player in a QUALIFYING COMPETITION and the COMPETITION SCRATCH SCORE.

4 Scores returned on courses other than that of the player's HOME CLUB should be distinguished by marking the NETT DIFFERENTIAL thus: □

5 Reductions of handicaps are effected immediately.

6 Increases of handicaps shall be made at the end of each calendar month or at such shorter intervals as the HOME CLUB may decide.

Appendix B

Table of Handicap Adjustments

Nett Differentials	-1	-2	-3	-4	-5	-6	-7	-8	-9	-10	-11	-12	Over Buffer Zone
Exact Handicaps Up to 5.4	-0.1	-0.2	-0.3	-0.4	-0.5	-0.6	-0.7	-0.8	-0.9	-1.0	-1.1	-1.2	+0.1
5.5– 5.6	-0.2	-0.3	-0.4	-0.5	-0.6	-0.7	-0.8	-0.9	-1.0	-1.1	-1.2	-1.3	+0.1
5.7– 5.8	-0.2	-0.4	-0.5	-0.6	-0.7	-0.8	-0.9	-1.0	-1.1	-1.2	-1.3	-1.4	+0.1
5.9– 6.0	-0.2	-0.4	-0.6	-0.7	-0.8	-0.9	-1.0	-1.1	-1.2	-1.3	-1.4	-1.5	+0.1
6.1– 6.2	-0.2	-0.4	-0.6	-0.8	-0.9	-1.0	-1.1	-1.2	-1.3	-1.4	-1.5	-1.6	+0.1
6.3– 6.4	-0.2	-0.4	-0.6	-0.8	-1.0	-1.1	-1.2	-1.3	-1.4	-1.5	-1.6	-1.7	+0.1
6.5– 6.6	-0.2	-0.4	-0.6	-0.8	-1.0	-1.2	-1.3	-1.4	-1.5	-1.6	-1.7	-1.8	+0.1
6.7– 6.8	-0.2	-0.4	-0.6	-0.8	-1.0	-1.2	-1.4	-1.5	-1.6	-1.7	-1.8	-1.9	+0.1
6.9– 7.0	-0.2	-0.4	-0.6	-0.8	-1.0	-1.2	-1.4	-1.6	-1.7	-1.8	-1.9	-2.0	+0.1
7.1– 7.2	-0.2	-0.4	-0.6	-0.8	-1.0	-1.2	-1.4	-1.6	-1.8	-1.9	-2.0	-2.1	+0.1
7.3– 7.4	-0.2	-0.4	-0.6	-0.8	-1.0	-1.2	-1.4	-1.6	-1.8	-2.0	-2.1	-2.2	+0.1
7.5– 7.6	-0.2	-0.4	-0.6	-0.8	-1.0	-1.2	-1.4	-1.6	-1.8	-2.0	-2.2	-2.3	+0.1
7.7–12.4	-0.2	-0.4	-0.6	-0.8	-1.0	-1.2	-1.4	-1.6	-1.8	-2.0	-2.2	-2.4	+0.1
12.5–12.7	-0.3	-0.5	-0.7	-0.9	-1.1	-1.3	-1.5	-1.7	-1.9	-2.1	-2.3	-2.5	+0.1
12.8–13.0	-0.3	-0.6	-0.8	-1.0	-1.2	-1.4	-1.6	-1.8	-2.0	-2.2	-2.4	-2.6	+0.1
13.1–13.3	-0.3	-0.6	-0.9	-1.1	-1.3	-1.5	-1.7	-1.9	-2.1	-2.3	-2.5	-2.7	+0.1
13.4–13.6	-0.3	-0.6	-0.9	-1.2	-1.4	-1.6	-1.8	-2.0	-2.2	-2.4	-2.6	-2.8	+0.1
13.7–13.9	-0.3	-0.6	-0.9	-1.2	-1.5	-1.7	-1.9	-2.1	-2.3	-2.5	-2.7	-2.9	+0.1
14.0–14.2	-0.3	-0.6	-0.9	-1.2	-1.5	-1.8	-2.0	-2.2	-2.4	-2.6	-2.8	-3.0	+0.1
14.3–14.5	-0.3	-0.6	-0.9	-1.2	-1.5	-1.8	-2.1	-2.3	-2.5	-2.7	-2.9	-3.1	+0.1
14.6–14.8	-0.3	-0.6	-0.9	-1.2	-1.5	-1.8	-2.1	-2.4	-2.6	-2.8	-3.0	-3.2	+0.1
14.9–15.1	-0.3	-0.6	-0.9	-1.2	-1.5	-1.8	-2.1	-2.4	-2.7	-2.9	-3.1	-3.3	+0.1
15.2–15.4	-0.3	-0.6	-0.9	-1.2	-1.5	-1.8	-2.1	-2.4	-2.7	-3.0	-3.2	-3.4	+0.1
15.5–15.7	-0.3	-0.6	-0.9	-1.2	-1.5	-1.8	-2.1	-2.4	-2.7	-3.0	-3.3	-3.5	+0.1
15.8–20.4	-0.3	-0.6	-0.9	-1.2	-1.5	-1.8	-2.1	-2.4	-2.7	-3.0	-3.3	-3.6	+0.1
20.5–20.8	-0.4	-0.7	-1.0	-1.3	-1.6	-1.9	-2.2	-2.5	-2.8	-3.1	-3.4	-3.7	+0.1
20.9–21.2	-0.4	-0.8	-1.1	-1.4	-1.7	-2.0	-2.3	-2.6	-2.9	-3.2	-3.5	-3.8	+0.1
21.3–21.6	-0.4	-0.8	-1.2	-1.5	-1.8	-2.1	-2.4	-2.7	-3.0	-3.3	-3.6	-3.8	+0.1
21.7–22.0	-0.4	-0.8	-1.2	-1.6	-1.9	-2.2	-2.5	-2.8	-3.1	-3.4	-3.7	-4.0	+0.1
22.1–22.4	-0.4	-0.8	-1.2	-1.6	-2.0	-2.3	-2.6	-2.9	-3.2	-3.5	-3.8	-4.1	+0.1
22.5–22.8	-0.4	-0.8	-1.2	-1.6	-2.0	-2.4	-2.7	-3.0	-3.3	-3.6	-3.9	-4.2	+0.1
22.9–23.2	-0.4	-0.8	-1.2	-1.6	-2.0	-2.4	-2.8	-3.1	-3.4	-3.7	-4.0	-4.3	+0.1
23.3–23.6	-0.4	-0.8	-1.2	-1.6	-2.0	-2.4	-2.8	-3.2	-3.5	-3.8	-4.1	-4.4	+0.1
23.7–24.0	-0.4	-0.8	-1.2	-1.6	-2.0	-2.4	-2.8	-3.2	-3.6	-3.9	-4.2	-4.5	+0.1
24.1–24.4	-0.4	-0.8	-1.2	-1.6	-2.0	-2.4	-2.8	-3.2	-3.6	-4.0	-4.3	-4.6	+0.1
24.5–24.8	-0.4	-0.8	-1.2	-1.6	-2.0	-2.4	-2.8	-3.2	-3.6	-4.0	-4.4	-4.7	+0.1
24.9–28.0	-0.4	-0.8	-1.2	-1.6	-2.0	-2.4	-2.8	-3.2	-3.6	-4.0	-4.4	-4.8	+0.1

Appendix C

Table for converting Par and Stableford scores to nett differentials
(Note – the Table is based on full handicap allowance)

Scores versus PAR	7 down	6 down	5 down	4 down	3 down	2 down	1 down	All Square	1 up	2 up	3 up	4 up	5 up	6 up	7 up
STABLEFORD points scored	29	30	31	32	33	34	35	36	37	38	39	40	41	42	43
Par 7 less than CSS	0	-1	-2	-3	-4	-5	-6	-7	-8	-9	-10	-11	-12	-13	-14
Par 6 less than CSS	+1	0	-1	-2	-3	-4	-5	-6	-7	-8	-9	-10	-11	-12	-13
Par 5 less than CSS	+2	+1	0	-1	-2	-3	-4	-5	-6	-7	-8	-9	-10	-11	-12
Par 4 less than CSS	+3	+2	+1	0	-1	-2	-3	-4	-5	-6	-7	-8	-9	-10	-11
Par 3 less than CSS	+4	+3	+2	+1	0	-1	-2	-3	-4	-5	-6	-7	-8	-9	-10
Par 2 less than CSS	+5	+4	+3	+2	+1	0	-1	-2	-3	-4	-5	-6	-7	-8	-9
Par 1 less than CSS	+6	+5	+4	+3	+2	+1	0	-1	-2	-3	-4	-5	-6	-7	-8
Par equal to CSS	+7	+6	+5	+4	+3	+2	+1	0	-1	-2	-3	-4	-5	-6	-7
Par 1 more than CSS	+8	+7	+6	+5	+4	+3	+2	+1	0	-1	-2	-3	-4	-5	-6
Par 2 more than CSS	+9	+8	+7	+6	+5	+4	+3	+2	+1	0	-1	-2	-3	-4	-5
Par 3 more than CSS	+10	+9	+8	+7	+6	+5	+4	+3	+2	+1	0	-1	-2	-3	-4
Par 4 more than CSS	+11	+10	+9	+8	+7	+6	+5	+4	+3	+2	+1	0	-1	-2	-3
Par 5 more than CSS	+12	+11	+10	+9	+8	+7	+6	+5	+4	+3	+2	+1	0	-1	-2
Par 6 more than CSS	+13	+12	+11	+10	+9	+8	+7	+6	+5	+4	+3	+2	+1	0	-1

Example:-
(a) 3 up on a Par 72 course with an CSS of 70. Par is 2 more than CSS so Nett Differential = -1.
(b) 37 Stableford points on a course with Par 68 & CSS 69. Par is 1 less than CSS so Nett Differential = -2.

Appendix D

Decisions

1. Running Medals – Clause 14.(2)(d)

(a) Any competition which can be described as a "Running Medal" *is not a* QUALIFYING COMPETITION.

(b) The following are defined as "Running Medals":

(i) An 18-hole competition extended over two or more days for any reason other than to accommodate the number of players entered.

(ii) An 18-hole competition played on one day or over several days in which players are allowed to return more than one score.

NOTE: If from a series of any number of scores special prizes are awarded for the best eclectic score or the best nett or gross aggregate of a prescribed number of scores, the individual scores in the series would not be regarded as constituting a "running medal" provided each score is returned under MEDAL PLAY CONDITIONS in a QUALIFYING COMPETITION, as defined in the Scheme, and not returned solely for the purpose of the eclectic, nett or gross aggregate awards.

2. Qualifying Scores

(a) If a club with a large number of QUALIFYING COMPETITIONS in the calendar year wishes to deprive certain of the competitions of their status as QUALIFYING COMPETITIONS it may do so provided competitors are so advised before play commences.

(b) It would be outside the spirit of the Handicapping Scheme to declare that all Club Medal Competitions during a specified period would not be regarded as QUALIFYING COMPETITIONS, although played under full MEDAL PLAY CONDITIONS.

(c) In both (a) and (b) above it would be more appropriate to play unofficial MEDAL COMPETITIONS under conditions which would not give them the status of QUALIFYING COMPETITIONS.

NOTE: A declaration that a competition is not a QUALIFYING COMPETITION disqualifies all scores returned in that competition for handicapping purposes. Thus a player returning a score below his handicap will not have his handicap reduced.

(d) A competition will not lose the status of QUALIFYING COMPETITION when played under conditions when, because of work proceeding or ground conditions in the area, pegging-up has been made obligatory by the club on a restricted area of the course, provided the playing of QUALIFYING COMPETITIONS under such conditions has the prior approval of the UNION or AREA AUTHORITY.

3. Upwards adjustment of Handicaps

(a) Clubs may elect to adjust handicaps upwards at the end of each calendar month or at shorter intervals, including immediate adjustment after completion of each QUALIFYING COMPETITION at the club.

(b) There could be slight differences in EXACT HANDICAPS produced by each method when comparison is made at the end of a calendar month.

(c) The procedure for recording NETT DIFFERENTIALS set out in the Scheme should be adhered to whatever method is used.

(d) There is no objection to clubs electing to adjust handicaps upwards at the end of each calendar month, or at more frequent intervals, taking steps to adjust and record EXACT and PLAYING HANDICAPS so that at the end of each month they correspond with those derived by adjusting handicaps after the playing of each QUALIFYING COMPETITION.

4. Limitation of Handicaps

Clubs have inquired whether they may impose a limit of handicap to some of their competitions e.g. insist that a 24 handicap player competes from a handicap of 18. This is permitted by Rule of Golf 33-1. However, when recording the player's scores for handicapping purposes, adjustments must be made to ensure that the NETT DIFFERENTIAL is recorded from his current PLAYING HANDICAP i.e. in the example quoted 24 instead of 18.

This is comparatively simple for MEDAL COMPETITION, but is impractical for Stableford and Par competitions as it is unlikely for example that a player would record a score at a hole where a stroke allowance of one from an 18 handicap gave him no points, whereas from a handicap of 24 with a stroke allowance of two at that particular hole he might have registered one point.

5. Incomplete Cards and No Returns

(a) All cards must be returned, whether complete or not.

(b) It is expected that every player who enters for an 18-hole QUALIFYING COMPETITION intends to complete the round.

(c) Since an Incomplete Card and a No Return have the effect of increasing a player's handicap, the club would be justified in refusing to accept a card or record a 'N.R.' when the player has walked in after playing only a few holes.

(d) Cards should not be issued to players when there is obviously insufficient light for them to complete the round.

(e) Sympathetic consideration should be given to players who have had to discontinue play for any cause considered to be reasonable by the organising committee.

(f) Clauses 17 and 19 of the Scheme give clubs the discretion to deal with players who persistently submit Incomplete Cards or make No Returns if they consider they are attempting to 'build a handicap'.

6. Reduction of Handicaps during a Competition

Where the conditions of a competition do not provide otherwise the handicap of a player applying at the beginning of a competition shall apply throughout that competition. This provision shall apply to a competition in which supplementary prizes are awarded for the best scores returned in an individual round or in combinations of individual rounds of the competition. The provisions shall not apply in circumstances where the winner is the player returning the lowest aggregate score in two or more separate competitions.

Where a player's handicap has been reduced during the course of a competition in which the original handicap continues to apply the player shall play from his reduced handicap in all other competitions commencing after the handicap reduction.

7. Overseas Scores

Scores returned in tournaments organised by the European Golf Association are QUALIFYING SCORES for handicapping purposes and must be returned to the HOME CLUB pursuant to clause 13.(7). Other scores returned in overseas tournaments may be returned and used, if considered appropriate, under the terms of clause 19.

8. Clause 19

Applications have been made to CONGU for approval of formulae which reduce handicaps by more than the reductions required by clause 16. Clubs have asked for permission to effect reductions on this basis under the authority given by clause 19. The decision of CONGU is that reductions made in this way are not permitted.

Reductions pursuant to clause 19 can be made only when the HANDICAP COMMITTEE has reason to believe that the handicap of a player may be too high. The Committee must consider all available information regarding the player's ability. A low score in a single event is not sufficient evidence alone to justify a clause 19 reduction.

If the handicap of any player is reduced other than to the extent required by clause 16 or by the correct application of clause 19, the player's handicap will not be a CONGU handicap and cannot be used in any competition for which a CONGU handicap is required.

Appendix E

Standard Scratch Score and Handicapping Scheme The Competition Scratch Score

Procedure

1. Enter in Boxes A, B and C the number of competitors, **including no returns**, from each of the Categories 1, 2 and 3 & 4.
2. Enter the total number of competitors, **including no returns**, in Box D.
3. Enter in Box E the number of competitors who have returned nett scores two over SSS and better. For Par and Stableford competitions use the converted equivalent.
4. In Boxes F, G and H enter the percentages of the adjacent boxes in relation to Box D as indicated.
5. Round the number in Box F to the nearest 5% if the percentage is less than 30% otherwise to the nearest 10% and enter the result in Box I.
6. Round the number in Box G to the nearest 10% (nearest 5% when percentage exceeds 95%) and enter the result in Box J (see footnote).
7. Enter in Box K the total of Boxes I and J deducted from 100. (The percentage in Box K may not coincide with the rounded percentage Box C would give if calculated.)
8. Round the number in Box H to the nearest whole number (0.5 upwards) and enter the result in Box L.
9. Select the relevant Table – Table A when the total number of competitors exceeds 30, otherwise Table B. Select the row which contains the percentages shown in Boxes I, J and K.
10. In the row selected find the column which includes the number in Box L. The SSS adjustment is shown in the heading of that column and that number is added to or deducted from the SSS to provide the COMPETITION SCRATCH SCORE ("CSS"). For each QUALIFYING COMPETITION the CSS replaces the SSS for all handicapping purposes. The application of the BUFFER ZONE will relate to the CSS and not the SSS.
11. The heading N/C at the top of a column in the Tables indicates that scores returned shall not result in handicap increases. Reductions of handicap will be made on the basis that the CSS is three strokes higher than the SSS.
12. When a competition has been abandoned for any reason reductions of handicaps shall be on the basis that the CSS is equal to the SSS *but no handicaps shall be increased.*

13. HANDICAP COMMITTEES are reminded that they no longer have a discretion to determine that a QUALIFYING COMPETITION shall or shall not be "non-counting".

NOTE: Occasionally the rounding of Boxes F and G will produce a total of Boxes I and J in excess of 100. When this occurs round the number in Box G downwards and insert the amended number in Box J.

Number of Competitors Including No Returns

PERCENTAGES   ROUNDED %

Category 1	A	A x 100 / D	F	I
Category 2	B	B x 100 / D	G	J
Category 3 & 4	C	100 minus I & J		K
Total entry	D	Total:		100
Number of Nett Scores at 2 over SSS and better	E	E x 100 / D	H	L

Appendix F

Table A More than 30 competitors

Categories			Adjustments to SSS to determine the CSS					
1	2	3&4	N/C	+3	+2	+1	0	−1
0%	0%	100%	0-4	5-7	8-10	11-15	16-30	31+
0%	10%	90%	0-4	5-7	8-11	12-15	16-32	33+
0%	20%	80%	0-5	6-7	8-11	12-16	17-34	35+
0%	30%	70%	0-5	6-8	9-12	13-17	18-36	37+
0%	40%	60%	0-5	6-8	9-12	13-18	19-38	39+
0%	50%	50%	0-5	6-8	9-13	14-19	20-40	41+
0%	60%	40%	0-5	6-9	10-14	15-20	21-41	42+
0%	70%	30%	0-5	6-9	10-14	15-21	22-43	44+
0%	80%	20%	0-5	6-9	10-15	16-22	23-45	46+
0%	90%	10%	0-6	7-10	11-15	16-23	24-47	48+
0%	100%	0%	0-6	7-10	11-16	17-24	25-49	50+
5%	0%	95%	0-5	6-7	8-11	12-16	17-32	33+
5%	10%	85%	0-5	6-7	8-11	12-16	17-34	35+
5%	20%	75%	0-5	6-8	9-12	13-17	18-36	37+
5%	30%	65%	0-5	6-8	9-13	14-18	19-38	39+
5%	40%	55%	0-5	6-8	9-13	14-19	20-39	40+
5%	50%	45%	0-5	6-9	10-14	15-20	21-41	42+
5%	60%	35%	0-5	6-9	10-14	15-21	22-43	44+
5%	70%	25%	0-5	6-9	10-15	16-22	23-45	46+
5%	80%	15%	0-6	7-10	11-15	16-23	24-47	48+
5%	90%	5%	0-6	7-10	11-16	17-24	25-49	50+
5%	95%	0%	0-6	7-10	11-16	17-24	25-50	51+
10%	0%	90%	0-5	6-8	9-12	13-17	18-34	35+
10%	10%	80%	0-5	6-8	9-12	13-18	19-36	37+
10%	20%	70%	0-5	6-8	9-13	14-18	19-38	39+
10%	30%	60%	0-5	6-9	10-13	14-19	20-39	40+
10%	40%	50%	0-5	6-9	10-14	15-20	21-41	42+
10%	50%	40%	0-5	6-9	10-14	15-21	22-43	44+
10%	60%	30%	0-6	7-9	10-15	16-22	23-45	46+
10%	70%	20%	0-6	7-10	11-16	17-23	24-47	48+
10%	80%	10%	0-6	7-10	11-16	17-24	25-49	50+
10%	90%	0%	0-6	7-10	11-17	18-25	26-51	52+
I	J	K	VALUES OF L̇ (Percentages)					

Categories			Adjustments to SSS to determine the CSS					
1	2	3&4	N/C	+3	+2	+1	0	−1
15%	0%	85%	0-5	6-8	9-12	13-18	19-36	37+
15%	10%	75%	0-5	6-8	9-13	14-19	20-38	39+
15%	20%	65%	0-5	6-9	10-13	14-20	21-39	40+
15%	30%	55%	0-5	6-9	10-14	15-20	21-41	42+
15%	40%	45%	0-5	6-9	10-15	16-21	22-43	44+
15%	50%	35%	0-6	7-10	11-15	16-22	23-45	46+
15%	60%	25%	0-6	7-10	11-16	17-23	24-47	48+
15%	70%	15%	0-6	7-10	11-16	17-24	25-49	50+
15%	80%	5%	0-6	7-11	12-17	18-25	26-51	52+
15%	85%	0%	0-6	7-11	12-17	18-25	26-52	53+
20%	0%	80%	0-5	6-8	9-13	14-19	20-38	39+
20%	10%	70%	0-5	6-9	10-14	15-20	21-39	40+
20%	20%	60%	0-5	6-9	10-14	15-21	22-41	42+
20%	30%	50%	0-6	7-9	10-15	16-22	23-43	44+
20%	40%	40%	0-6	7-10	11-15	16-22	23-45	46+
20%	50%	30%	0-6	7-10	11-16	17-23	24-47	48+
20%	60%	20%	0-6	7-10	11-16	17-24	25-49	50+
20%	70%	10%	0-6	7-11	12-17	18-25	26-51	52+
20%	80%	0%	0-6	7-11	12-18	19-26	27-53	54+
25%	0%	75%	0-5	6-9	10-14	15-20	21-39	40+
25%	10%	65%	0-5	6-9	10-14	15-21	22-41	42+
25%	20%	55%	0-6	7-9	10-15	16-22	23-43	44+
25%	30%	45%	0-6	7-10	11-15	16-23	24-45	46+
25%	40%	35%	0-6	7-10	11-16	17-24	25-47	48+
25%	50%	25%	0-6	7-10	11-17	18-24	25-49	50+
25%	60%	15%	0-6	7-11	12-17	18-25	26-51	52+
25%	70%	5%	0-6	7-11	12-18	19-26	27-53	54+
25%	75%	0%	0-6	7-11	12-18	19-27	28-54	55+
30%	0%	70%	0-6	7-9	10-14	15-21	22-41	42+
30%	10%	60%	0-6	7-10	11-15	16-22	23-43	44+
30%	20%	50%	0-6	7-10	11-16	17-23	24-45	46+
I	J	K	VALUES OF L (Percentages)					

1	2	3&4	N/C	+3	+2	+1	0	−1
30%	30%	40%	0-6	7-10	11-16	17-24	25-47	48+
30%	40%	30%	0-6	7-11	12-17	18-25	26-49	50+
30%	50%	20%	0-6	7-11	12-17	18-26	27-51	52+
30%	60%	10%	0-6	7-11	12-18	19-26	27-53	54+
30%	70%	0%	0-7	8-11	12-18	19-27	28-55	56+
40%	0%	60%	0-6	7-10	11-16	17-23	24-45	46+
40%	10%	50%	0-6	7-10	11-16	17-24	25-47	48+
40%	20%	40%	0-6	7-11	12-17	18-25	26-49	50+
40%	30%	30%	0-6	7-11	12-18	19-26	27-51	52+
40%	40%	20%	0-7	8-11	12-18	19-27	28-53	54+
40%	50%	10%	0-7	8-12	13-19	20-28	29-55	56+
40%	60%	0%	0-7	8-12	13-19	20-29	30-57	58+
50%	0%	50%	0-6	7-11	12-17	18-25	26-49	50+
50%	10%	40%	0-7	8-11	12-18	19-26	27-51	52+
50%	20%	30%	0-7	8-12	13-18	19-27	28-53	54+
50%	30%	20%	0-7	8-12	13-19	20-28	29-55	56+
50%	40%	10%	0-7	8-12	13-20	21-29	30-57	58+
50%	50%	0%	0-7	8-13	14-20	21-30	31-59	60+
I	**J**	**K**	**VALUES OF L (Percentages)**					

1	2	3&4	N/C	+3	+2	+1	0	−1
60%	0%	40%	0-7	8-12	13-19	20-27	28-53	54+
60%	10%	30%	0-7	8-12	13-19	20-28	29-55	56+
60%	20%	20%	0-7	8-12	13-20	21-29	30-57	58+
60%	30%	10%	0-7	8-13	14-20	21-30	31-59	60+
60%	40%	0%	0-7	8-14	14-21	22-31	32-61	62+
70%	0%	30%	0-7	8-13	14-20	21-30	31-57	58+
70%	10%	20%	0-7	8-13	14-21	22-31	32-59	60+
70%	20%	10%	0-8	9-13	14-21	22-31	32-60	61+
70%	30%	0%	0-8	9-14	15-22	23-32	33-62	63+
80%	0%	20%	0-8	9-13	14-22	23-32	33-60	61+
80%	10%	10%	0-8	9-14	15-22	23-33	34-62	63+
80%	20%	0%	0-8	9-14	15-23	24-34	35-64	65+
90%	0%	10%	0-8	9-14	15-23	24-34	35-64	65+
90%	10%	0%	0-8	9-15	16-24	25-35	36-66	67+
100%	0%	0%	0-9	10-15	16-24	25-36	37-68	69+
I	**J**	**K**	**VALUES OF L (Percentages)**					

Appendix G

Table B Less than 31 competitors

1	2	3&4	N/C	+3	+2	+1	0	−1
0%	0%	100%	0-3	4-5	6-8	9-12	13-30	31+
0%	10%	90%	0-3	4-6	7-9	10-13	14-32	33+
0%	20%	80%	0-3	4-6	7-9	10-14	15-34	35+
0%	30%	70%	0-4	5-6	7-10	11-14	15-36	37+
0%	40%	60%	0-4	5-6	7-10	11-15	16-38	39+
0%	50%	50%	0-4	5-7	8-10	11-16	17-40	41+
0%	60%	40%	0-4	5-7	8-11	12-17	18-41	42+
0%	70%	30%	0-4	5-7	8-11	12-17	18-43	44+
0%	80%	20%	0-4	5-7	8-12	13-18	19-45	46+
0%	90%	10%	0-4	5-7	8-12	13-19	20-47	48+
0%	100%	0%	0-4	5-8	9-13	14-19	20-49	50+
5%	0%	95%	0-3	4-6	7-9	10-13	14-32	33+
5%	10%	85%	0-4	5-6	7-9	11-15	15-34	35+
5%	20%	75%	0-4	5-6	7-10	11-15	16-36	37+
5%	30%	65%	0-4	5-6	7-10	11-15	16-38	39+
5%	40%	55%	0-4	5-7	8-11	12-17	17-39	40+
5%	50%	45%	0-4	5-7	8-11	12-17	18-41	42+
5%	60%	35%	0-4	5-7	8-11	12-17	18-43	44+
5%	70%	25%	0-4	5-7	8-12	13-18	19-45	46+
5%	80%	15%	0-4	5-7	8-12	13-19	20-47	48+
5%	90%	5%	0-4	5-8	9-13	14-20	21-49	50+
5%	95%	0%	0-4	5-8	9-13	14-20	21-50	51+
10%	0%	90%	0-3	4-6	7-9	10-14	15-34	35+
10%	10%	80%	0-4	5-6	7-10	11-15	16-36	37+
10%	20%	70%	0-4	5-6	7-10	11-15	16-38	39+
10%	30%	60%	0-4	5-7	8-11	12-16	17-39	40+
10%	40%	50%	0-4	5-7	8-11	12-17	18-41	42+
10%	50%	40%	0-4	5-7	8-12	13-18	19-43	44+
I	**J**	**K**	**VALUES OF L (Percentages)**					

1	2	3&4	N/C	+3	+2	+1	0	−1
10%	60%	30%	0-4	5-7	8-12	13-18	19-45	46+
10%	70%	20%	0-4	5-8	9-12	13-19	20-47	48+
10%	80%	10%	0-4	5-8	9-13	14-20	21-49	50+
10%	90%	0%	0-4	5-8	9-13	14-20	21-51	52+
15%	0%	85%	0-4	5-6	7-10	11-15	16-36	37+
15%	10%	75%	0-4	5-7	8-10	11-16	17-38	39+
15%	20%	65%	0-4	5-7	8-11	12-16	19-39	40+
15%	30%	55%	0-4	5-7	8-11	12-17	18-41	42+
15%	40%	45%	0-4	5-7	8-12	13-18	19-43	44+
15%	50%	35%	0-4	5-7	8-12	13-18	19-45	46+
15%	60%	25%	0-4	5-8	9-13	14-19	20-47	48+
15%	70%	15%	0-4	5-8	9-13	14-20	21-49	50+
15%	80%	5%	0-4	5-8	9-13	14-21	22-51	52+
15%	85%	0%	0-4	5-8	9-14	15-21	22-52	53+
20%	0%	80%	0-4	5-7	8-11	12-16	17-38	39+
20%	10%	70%	0-4	5-7	8-11	12-16	17-39	40+
20%	20%	60%	0-4	5-7	8-11	12-17	18-41	42+
20%	30%	50%	0-4	5-7	8-12	13-18	19-43	44+
20%	40%	40%	0-4	5-7	8-12	13-19	20-45	46+
20%	50%	30%	0-4	5-8	9-13	14-19	20-47	48+
20%	60%	20%	0-4	5-8	9-13	14-20	21-49	50+
20%	70%	10%	0-4	5-8	9-13	14-21	22-51	52+
20%	80%	0%	0-5	6-8	9-14	15-22	23-53	54+
25%	0%	75%	0-4	5-7	8-11	12-17	18-39	40+
25%	10%	65%	0-4	5-7	8-11	12-17	18-41	42+
25%	20%	55%	0-4	5-7	8-12	13-18	19-43	44+
I	**J**	**K**	**VALUES OF L (Percentages)**					

1	2	3&4	N/C	+3	+2	+1	0	-1
Categories			Adjustments to SSS to determine the CSS					
25%	30%	45%	0-4	5-8	9-12	13-19	20-45	46+
25%	40%	35%	0-4	5-8	9-13	14-20	21-47	48+
25%	50%	25%	0-4	5-8	9-13	14-20	21-49	50+
25%	60%	15%	0-4	5-8	9-14	15-21	22-51	52+
25%	70%	5%	0-5	6-8	9-14	15-22	23-53	54+
25%	75%	0%	0-5	6-9	10-14	15-22	23-54	55+
30%	0%	70%	0-4	5-7	8-12	13-18	19-41	42+
30%	10%	60%	0-4	5-7	8-12	13-18	19-43	44+
30%	20%	50%	0-4	5-8	9-12	13-19	20-45	46+
30%	30%	40%	0-4	5-8	9-13	14-20	21-47	48+
30%	40%	30%	0-4	5-8	9-13	14-20	21-49	50+
30%	50%	20%	0-5	6-8	9-14	15-21	22-51	52+
30%	60%	10%	0-5	6-9	10-14	15-22	23-53	54+
30%	70%	0%	0-5	6-9	10-15	16-23	24-55	56+
40%	0%	60%	0-4	5-8	9-13	14-19	20-45	46+
40%	10%	50%	0-4	5-8	9-13	14-20	21-47	48+
40%	20%	40%	0-5	6-8	9-14	15-21	22-49	50+
40%	30%	30%	0-5	6-8	9-14	15-21	22-51	52+
40%	40%	20%	0-5	6-9	10-14	15-22	23-53	54+
40%	50%	10%	0-5	6-9	10-15	16-23	24-55	56+
40%	60%	0%	0-5	6-9	10-15	16-24	24-57	58+
50%	0%	50%	0-5	6-8	9-14	15-21	22-49	50+
50%	10%	40%	0-5	6-9	10-14	15-22	23-51	52+
50%	20%	30%	0-5	6-9	10-15	16-22	23-53	54+
50%	30%	20%	0-5	6-9	10-15	16-23	24-55	56+
50%	40%	10%	0-5	6-9	10-16	17-24	25-57	58+
50%	50%	0%	0-5	6-10	11-16	17-25	26-59	60+
60%	0%	40%	0-5	6-9	10-15	16-23	24-53	54+
60%	10%	30%	0-5	6-9	10-15	16-24	25-55	56+
60%	20%	20%	0-5	6-9	10-16	17-24	25-57	58+
60%	30%	10%	0-5	6-10	11-16	17-25	26-59	60+
60%	40%	0%	0-5	6-10	11-17	18-26	27-61	62+
70%	0%	30%	0-5	6-10	11-16	17-25	26-57	58+
70%	10%	20%	0-5	6-10	11-16	17-25	26-59	60+
70%	20%	10%	0-5	6-10	11-17	18-26	27-60	61+
70%	30%	0%	0-5	6-10	11-17	18-27	28-62	63+
80%	0%	20%	0-5	6-10	11-17	18-26	27-60	61+
80%	10%	10%	0-5	7-10	11-18	19-27	28-62	63+
80%	20%	0%	0-6	7-11	12-18	19-28	29-64	65+
90%	0%	10%	0-6	7-11	12-18	19-28	29-64	65+
90%	10%	0%	0-6	7-11	12-19	20-29	30-66	67+
100%	0%	0%	0-6	7-11	12-19	20-30	31-68	69+
I	J	K	VALUES OF L (Percentages)					

Stationery

Enquiries regarding storage binders and handicap record sheets suitable for use in connection with the Standard Scratch Score and Handicapping Scheme 1983 to be directed to Hon. Secretary of the Council of National Golf Unions: A. Thirlwell, Formby Golf Club, Formby, Liverpool L37 1LQ.

Forms of application for an alteration to the Basic Standard Scratch Score or an addition for course value to the Provisional Standard Scratch Score may be obtained from the Secretaries of:
(a) County Golf Unions or District Committees.

(b) Area Authorities.
(c) National Golf Unions.
(d) Council of National Golf Unions.

Application of Handicaps

Stroke Index

Each club should draw up a list, called the Stroke Index, giving the order of holes at which any handicap strokes awarded should be taken. This order should be printed on the club's score card. The general principle for fixing the order of the Stroke Index is that the hole at which it is most difficult to achieve par should be Stroke Index 1, the next most difficult, Stroke Index 2 and so on until the easiest which should be Stroke Index 18.

However, certain other factors should be taken into consideration. Stroke Index 1 should not be one of the very early or very late holes on the course. The reason is that if a game were to finish all square and go on to the 19th and subsequent holes to determine the winner, the person in receipt of only one stroke would have an unfair advantage if he were to receive it at the 19th or 20th. Similarly, if Stroke Index 1 were a hole at the very end of the round, then the person in receipt of only one stroke might never be able to use it as the game might well be over by then. In general, therefore, Stroke Index 1 should not be at holes 1, 2, 17 or 18.

The other important factor to be taken into account in fixing the order of Stroke Index is that the strokes should be fairly evenly spread out over the 18 holes. If Stroke Index 1 is in the first 9 holes, Stroke Index 2 should be in the second 9 holes and so on. For example, if a person were to receive, say, four strokes, it would not be fair if he received them all in the early holes or all in the late holes.

Competition Formats and Handicap Allowances

Note 1: *In all calculations of handicap allowances, fractions under 1/2 are ignored and those of 1/2 or over are rounded up to the next higher figure.*

Note 2: *Handicap allowances shown are recommendations only. They are not Rules of Golf. The allowance to be used is at the discretion of the committee who should stipulate that allowance in the conditions of the competition.*

Competitions take two basic forms – match play or stroke play. In match play two players or sides compete against each other on a hole by hole basis. In stroke play a player or side competes against the whole field on his score over the whole round or rounds.

Single

Format
One player competes directly against one other player. It applies only to match play.

Handicap Allowance
The player with the higher handicap of the two receives strokes amounting to $3/4$ of the difference between the two players' handicaps. These strokes are taken at the holes indicated by the Stroke Index.

Foursome

Format
Two players form a side and hit alternate shots with one ball. The two players drive alternately from successive tees. Can be used for both match play and stroke play.

Handicap Allowance
Match play: The two players on each side add their handicaps together. The couple with the higher combined handicaps receive strokes amounting to $3/8$ of the difference between the combined handicaps of the two sides. These strokes are taken at the holes indicated by the Stroke Index.
Stroke play: The two players forming a side add their handicaps together and divide by 2. This figure is deducted from the side's gross score.

Mixed Foursome

Format
Same as Foursome except that each side must consist of a man and a woman.

Handicap Allowance
Same as Foursome.

Four-Ball Better-Ball

Format
Two players form a side, each playing his own ball throughout. The better score of the partners is the score of the side. Can be used for both match play and stroke play.

Handicap Allowance
Match play: The three players with the highest handicaps of the four each receive strokes amounting to $3/4$ of the difference between their own handicaps and that of the lowest handicap of the four. These strokes are taken at the holes indicated by the Stroke Index.

Example: A–16; B–12; C–20; D–8. Player A would receive (16–8) x $3/4$ =6 strokes; B would receive (12–8) x $3/4$ =3 strokes; C would receive (20–8) x $3/4$ =9 strokes; D would receive 0 strokes.

Stroke play: $3/4$ of each player's full handicap is allocated at the holes according to the Stroke Index and the stroke or strokes deducted at these holes.

Four-Ball Aggregate

Format
Two players form a side, each playing his own ball throughout. The combined score of the two partners is the score for the side. Can be used for both match play and stroke play.

Handicap Allowance
Match play: Same as Four-ball Better-ball. *Stroke play:* Same as Four-ball Better-ball.

Greensome

Format
Two players form a side and both drive off each tee. Either ball may be selected to continue the hole and subsequent shots are played alternately until the hole is completed. *Example:* If player A's drive is selected at any hole, B must play the second shot at that hole, A the third shot and so on alternately until the ball is holed and vice versa if player B's drive is selected. Can be used for both match play and stroke play.

Handicap Allowance
Match play: Multiply the lower handicap of the two partners by .6 and the higher handicap by .4 and add the two figures together to give the full greensome handicap of the side. The couple with the higher greensome handicap receive strokes amounting to $3/4$ of the difference between the greensome handicaps of the two sides. These strokes are taken at the holes indicated by the Stroke Index. *Example:* A–2; B–10; C–8; D–12. AB *v* CD: Side AB full greensome handicap = (2 x .6)+(10 x .4)=5.2. Side CD full greensome handicap =(8 x .6)+(12 x .4)=9.6. Side CD receives strokes amounting to $3/4$ of the difference between the two couples, i.e. (9.6–5.2) x $3/4$=3 strokes.
Stroke play: The two players forming a side deduct their full greensome handicap (as calculated above) from their gross score.

Bogey/Par

Format

Each player or side plays against the bogey (or par) for each hole, counting a win if he holes out in less than the bogey (or par) for the hole, a half if he equals it and a loss if he holes out in more. The aggregate of wins, losses and halves is taken to give a final score of so many holes up (or down as the case may be) to bogey (or par). Suitable for stroke play only.

Handicap Allowance

Each player receives strokes amounting to 3/4 of his full handicap. In the case of foursomes, each side receives strokes amounting to 3/8 of the combined handicaps of the partners. In all cases these strokes are allocated at the holes according to the Stroke Index and the stroke or strokes deducted at these holes.

Stableford

Format

The Stableford system of scoring was invented in 1931 by Dr Frank Stableford of the Wallasey and Royal Liverpool Golf Clubs and the first competition was played on 16th May, 1932 at Wallasey GC. Each player or side plays against the par for each hole and receives points according to how he scores in relation to par. The scoring system is as follows: 2 or more over par–0 points; 1 over par–1 point; par–2 points; 1 under par–3 points; 2 under par–4 points; 3 under par–5 points and so on. The number of points gained at each of the 18 holes is added together to give a total points score. Suitable for stroke play only.

Handicap Allowance

7/8 of full handicap.

Eclectic

Format

Competitors play two or more rounds choosing their better or best score at each hole to make up their eclectic score. Suitable for stroke play only.

Handicap Allowance

If played over two rounds, each competitor deducts 5/6 of his full handicap from his eclectic score for the two rounds. If played over three rounds, deduct 4/5 of his handicap from his eclectic score. If played over four rounds deduct 3/4, five rounds, 2/3, and six or more rounds, 1/2.

Round Robin

Format

This is a form of league where each competitor or side plays every other competitor or side in the league. Suitable for match play only and can be used for singles, foursomes, four-ball betterball, four-ball aggregate or greensomes, with the appropriate handicap allowance applying according to the type of competition.

Mixed Events

In competitions where men and women compete on an equal footing, the women's handicaps should be increased by the difference between the men's and ladies' Standard Scratch Scores if the women play from the ladies' tees. If the women play from the men's tees, their handicaps should be increased by the difference between the two Standard Scratch Scores plus an equitable figure (somewhere between 2 and 6) to take account of the distance between the men's and ladies' tees, one stroke being added for every 200 yards of difference over the 18 holes.

This adjustment does not apply where each side must consist of a man and woman; it only applies where women are in direct competition with men or where a side may consist of any combination of men and women, i.e. two men, two women or one man and one woman.

Bisques

Instead of receiving strokes to be taken at holes according to the Stroke Index, in match play friendly games, a number of bisques can be agreed upon instead. A bisque is a stroke which may be used at any hole the recipient decides upon after the completion of the hole. Because bisques can be used more advantageously than strokes, which may be of no value at certain holes, a lesser number of bisques than handicap strokes allowance is usually agreed upon. A player may use any number of bisques from his quota at any hole but he must announce whether he is using any of them before any stroke is played from the next tee. The bisque form of handicapping is not used in official competitions. It is suitable only for singles or foursomes, not for four-ball games.

Draws for Match Play Competitions

Cold Draw

When the number of entries is not a whole power of 2, i.e. 4, 8, 16, 32, 64 etc, a number of first round byes are necessary. Subtract the number of entries from the nearest of these numbers above the number of entries to give the number of byes. *Example:* (a) 28 entries – subtracting from 32 gives 4 first round byes; (b) 33 entries – subtracting from 64 gives 31 first round byes.

All names (or numbers representing names) are put in a hat and the requisite number of byes drawn out singly and placed in pairs in the second round of the draw, alternately at the top and bottom, i.e. the first two names go at the top of the draw, the next two at the bottom and so on until all the byes have been drawn. If there is an odd number of byes, the last drawn is bracketed to play against the winner of either the first or last first round match. Having drawn all the byes, the remaining names are then drawn and placed in pairs in the first round in the order drawn in the middle of the draw.

Automatic Draw

When a stroke play qualifying round(s) is used to determine the qualifiers for the ensuing match play, the automatic draw is used, based on the qualifying position of each qualifier, i.e. the leading qualifier is number 1 in the draw, the second qualifier is number 2 and so on.

The following table gives the automatic draw for up to 64 qualifiers. Use the first column for 64 qualifiers, the second column for 32 qualifiers, and so on.

64	32	16	8	4	2
1	1				
64		1			
33	32				
32			1		
17	17				
48		16			
49	16				
16				1	
9	9				
56		9			
41	24				
24			8		
25	25				
40		8			
57	8				
8					1
5	5				
60		5			
37	28				
28			5		
21	21				
44		12			
53	12				
12				4	
13	13				
52		13			
45	20				
20			4		
29	29				
36		4			
61	4				
4					
3	3				
62		3			
35	30				
30			3		
19	19				
46		14			
51	14				
14				3	
11	11				
54		11			
43	22				
22			6		
27	27				
38		6			
59	6				
6					2
7	7				
58		7			
39	26				
26			7		
23	23				
42		10			
55	10				
10				2	
15	15				
50		15			
47	18				
18			2		
31	31				
34		2			
63	2				
2					

The LGU System of Handicapping

Effective from 1 February 1990

CONTENTS

Section I
Definitions

Throughout the text defined terms are printed as capitals when used for the first time.

Committee

The term **Committee** is deemed to refer to the Committee of the Ladies' Section. The term **Club Committee** refers to the Committee in charge of the course. Where the management of the club and/or course is entirely in the hands of the Ladies' Committee the term **Club Committee** shall be deemed to refer to such.

Completed Scores

A score is deemed completed for handicap purposes when a gross score has been entered on the card for each hole and the card has been checked and signed by both marker and player. The card should also show the player's name and the date.

Differential

The differential is the difference between the gross score and the SCRATCH SCORE of the course on which it is returned.

    The average differential is the sum of the differentials divided by their number.

Extra Day Scores

An Extra Day Score is one which is marked other than in competition.

Handicap Advisers

Handicap Advisers and their Deputies are persons appointed by the National Organisation to assist HANDICAP SECRETARIES in dealing with

problems and exceptional cases, and to keep records of all players with handicaps under 4.

Handicap Secretary

A player's Handicap Secretary is the Handicap Secretary of her HOME CLUB. The Handicap Secretary of an INDIVIDUAL MEMBER of the LGU or of a NATIONAL ORGANISATION is respectively, the Administrator of the LGU or the Secretary of the National Organisation. The Handicap Secretary of a visitor from overseas, unless she joins an affiliated club as an annual member, is the Administrator, LGU.

Home Club

The Home Club is the club which a member of more than one club has chosen to be that where her handicap records shall be maintained and of which the Handicap Secretary shall be her Handicap Secretary.

Home Course

A Home Course is any course situated at and associated with a player's Home Club.

Individual Members

a. of the LGU: Players temporarily resident overseas, for a period of not less than one year, are entitled to apply for individual membership of the LGU.

b. of the National Organisations: Players unable to become an annual playing member of an affiliated club may apply to their National Organisation for individual membership.

Lapsed Handicaps

A handicap has lapsed if four scores have not been returned in an LGU year by Category C, D and E players, six scores by Category B players (unless increasing to Category C) and ten scores by Category A players (unless increasing to Category B).

LGU Tees and Teeing Grounds

The LGU tees, indicated by a permanent mark on the right hand side of the tee, are those from which the Scratch Score has been fixed. The actual teeing ground in play (see Rules of Golf Definition) is indicated by **red** tee markers which, for the convenience of the greenkeeper, may be moved in any direction from the permanent mark provided the hole is not altered in length by more than ten yards.

NOTE: In the event of the teeing ground having been accidentally or otherwise moved beyond the permitted limit the score cannot count for handicap or for LGU Competitions unless a special Scratch Score has been allotted by the National Organisation.

Live Score

A live score is one which has been returned (in accordance with Regulation III.4) in the current LGU year (1 February to 31 January) or in the preceding LGU year.

National Organisation

The National Organisations are: the English Ladies' Golf Association, the Irish Ladies' Golf Union, the Scottish Ladies' Golfing Association and the Welsh Ladies' Golf Union. In the case of overseas affiliated clubs for **National Organisation** read **LGU**.

Scratch Score

The Scratch Score of a course is the score expected of a Scratch player in normal Spring and Autumn conditions of wind and weather.

Section II
Introduction

1. Basis of the System

The chief features of the LGU System of Handicapping are: that all handicaps shall be fixed on the basis of the LGU Scratch Score; that handicaps shall be assessed on actual scores returned and not on general form; and that the player's handicap shall be the same in every club.

2. Overseas Unions and Clubs

Overseas affiliated Unions and Clubs shall be permitted to make such adjustments to these regulations as may be deemed by their Executive Committee to be necessary on account of climatic or other conditions peculiar to the territory administered by them, so long as these adjustments do not depart from the fundamental principles of the LGU System of Handicapping as stated in the paragraph above or contravene the Rules of Golf as laid down by the Royal & Ancient Golf Club of St Andrews. The LGU must be informed as and when such adjustments are made.

3. Queries

Queries on LGU Regulations should be and on the Rules of Golf and may be submitted in accordance with the following procedures:

a. COMMITTEES of Affiliated Clubs should submit queries to their National Organisation.

b. Members of Affiliated Clubs may submit queries to their National Organisation and must have their statements signed as read on behalf of the Ladies' Committee. If there is any difference of opinion the Committee or opposing party should submit their own statement in writing.

c. Secretaries of Affiliated Clubs should refer queries on handicaps to their Handicap Secretary.

d. Handicap Secretaries of Affiliated Clubs should refer queries to their HANDICAP ADVISER or National Organisation, in that order.

e. Overseas Unions and Clubs. In the case of clubs affiliated to an affiliated Ladies' Golf Union outside Great Britain and Ireland or directly affiliated to the LGU, queries should be submitted to the LGU. Statements should be signed as read on behalf of such Union or Club Committee.

Correspondence of this nature sent to the LGU and the National Organisations is filed for reference and cannot be returned.

Section III

The Player's Responsibilities and Rights

1. General

Playing off the Correct Handicap. It is the player's responsibility to know and to apply the Handicapping Regulations and to play off the correct handicap at all times. She should be able to produce a current Handicap Certificate when required to do so. In case of doubt or disagreement between the player and her Handicap Secretary as to what is the player's correct handicap, she should play from the lower until an official decision can be obtained from the Handicap Adviser or the National Organisation.

Handicap Reduction. Any reduction in handicap is automatic and comes into force immediately, except

i. in the event of a tie in a competition, where this is resolved by a replay or a play-off; and

ii. in a 36-, 54- or 72-hole competition played within eight days.

Playing away from Home. A player must notify her Handicap Secretary of any score (which might affect her handicap) returned by her on any course other than at her Home Club.

2. Eligibility to Hold an LGU Handicap

An LGU handicap may be obtained and held by an amateur lady golfer who is either

a. an annual playing member, including a country, junior or life member (whether honorary or paying) of a club affiliated to the LGU either directly or through its National Organisation; or

b. an individual member of either the LGU or one of the four National Organisations; or

c. a temporary member of an affiliated club, provided her membership is to last for a period of not less than twelve months.

NOTE: Should membership cease or expire the player's LGU handicap is no longer valid, but her scores remain LIVE if returned before such cessation or expiry.

3. How to Gain an LGU Handicap

Four Extra Day Scores must be returned on the course or courses of an LGU affiliated club or clubs, the Scratch Score of which must be not less than 60. Play must be in twos (threes and fours are not acceptable), no more than one player per marker, and must be in accordance with Regulations III.4(a), (b), (c), (d) and (e).

4. Scores Acceptable for LGU Handicap

To be acceptable for handicap:

a. Scores must be returned in accordance with the Rules of Golf as approved by the Royal & Ancient Golf Club of St Andrews and with the Club's Local Rules and Bye-Laws, which must not contravene any R. & A. Rule or LGU Regulation. The gross score must be entered for every hole.

b. Scores must be returned on the course of an LGU affiliated club with an LGU Scratch Score of not less than 60. Play must be from LGU TEES. Extra Day Scores returned on a course of which a player is not a member must be countersigned by an official of the local ladies' committee, which should certify that the Scratch Score is correctly stated. Completed cards should either be returned in person by the player to her Handicap Secretary without delay or left in the card box of the club visited, with the name and address of the home club and the cost of postage. Competition scores returned on a course of which a player is not a member must be signed by an official of the competition committee who must have con-

firmed the Scratch Score of the day with the Secretary of the host club.

NOTE: Scores returned on non-affiliated courses overseas (see lists in the Lady Golfer's Handbook) **may** count for handicap at the discretion of the LGU. Such cards, duly countersigned by a local official as showing the correct Scratch Score and accompanied by relevant information about local conditions, type of soil, terrain, course difficulties, etc., should be forwarded to the Administrator, LGU, The Scores, St Andrews, Fife, KY16 9AT, with a stamped, addressed envelope to the Handicap Secretary of the player's Home Club.

c. Scores must be marked by an annual playing member of a recognised golf club or association, who has or has had a handicap. A marker should not mark the card of more than one player.

d. A score must be that of the first round of the day on any one course, except in the case of a competition consisting of 36 holes played on one day, when both scores shall count.

e. Scores may be returned when the following conditions apply:

    i. Winter Conditions. Where, for the preservation of the course, the Club Committee has made a Local Rule that the ball may be teed or placed without penalty through the green.

    ii. Summer Conditions.

    a. Where, for the preservation of the course, the Club Committee has made a Local Rule that the ball may be placed without penalty through the green;

    b. Where, for the preservation of the course, the Club Committee has made a Local Rule that tee pegs must be used through the green and a deduction from the Scratch Score of two strokes where more than nine holes are affected, and of one stroke where nine or fewer holes are affected, has been made by the Ladies' Committee (and notified to the area Scratch Score Committee member).

    iii. The Green. Where, for the preservation of the green, a temporary hole (see Rules of Golf Definitions) is off but adjacent to the green, provided this does not alter the length of the hole by more than ten yards.

NOTE: LGU TEES. Where, for the preservation of the course, the teeing ground has been moved beyond the permitted ten yards, scores may count for handicap only if a special Scratch Score has been allotted by the National Organisation.

f. Gross scores returned in a competition from which a player has been disqualified under Rule of Golf 6–2b on her nett score shall count for handicap.

g. ECLECTICS AND ALL RUNNING COMPETITIONS: Scores from these competitions do not count as competition scores for handicap purposes (except for the first round of an eclectic competition).

h. SOCIETY DAY COMPETITIONS; Handicap Secretaries should accept scores returned from Society Day competitions as competition scores if they are satisfied that the society is a *bona fide* one and the competition was played under LGU Rules and Regulations.

i. All scores returned in Stroke Competitions, even if declared null and void, count for LGU handicap purposes, subject to Regulations III.4(a) to (h) above and provided competitors play from **LGU Tees** (see Definition and Note) and the SS of the Course is not less than 60. Scores may be returned in twos, threes or fours, as arranged by the Committee.

NOTE: The exception to this is in a competition where the best-ball or better-ball score (see Rules of Golf Definitions) is to count, and in Pro-Am and Am-Am team events.

j. i EXTRA DAY SCORES must be returned in accordance with Regulations III.4(a) to (e) and should normally be marked in twos, but at the discretion of the Committee may be marked in threes, in which case a notice to this effect must be posted on the Notice Board (but see Regulation III.3 for gaining a first handicap). Extra Day Scores marked in fours are NOT acceptable.

ii Players may take out a maximum of 20 Extra Day cards in any LGU year. Those taken out to gain and re-gain a handicap do not count in the maximum of 20. Each club should keep an Extra Day Book which the player must sign before play commences. A player taking out an Extra Day card on an away course must include this in her 20 and must inform her home club of such a card.

5. Calculation of LGU Handicap

Handicaps are divided into five categories: Silver Division – A, B, C – and Bronze Division – D and E. Handicaps are calculated as follows, on the basis of live scores returned in accordance with Regulation III.4 above:

NOTE 1: For all handicaps, scores must be returned on courses with a Scratch Score of not less than 60.

NOTE 2: In all calculations above Scratch $1/2$, $2/3$ and $3/4$ count as 1 and $1/3$, $1/4$ count as 0. In all calculations below Scratch fractions of $1/2$ and less count as 0, fractions greater than $1/2$ count as 1.

a. **Bronze Division**
    (i) **Category E, 36*–30.** The handicap is the difference between the player's best live

score and the Scratch Score of the course on which it was played, i.e. the handicap is her best DIFFERENTIAL. If the differential is more than 36 the handicap is 36* (*Example E[1]*). If the differential is 36–30 then that is the handicap (*Example E[2]*). If the best differential is less than 30 the handicap is 30 until the average of the **two** best differentials is less than $29\frac{1}{2}$ (*Example E[3]*).

EXAMPLES:

E^1	Best gross score 118	SS 72	Differential	46
			Handicap 36*	
E^2	Best gross score 102	SS 69	Differential	33
			Handicap 33	
E^3	Best gross score 101	SS 74	Differential	27
	106	SS 70	Previous best differential	36
			Average differential	$31\frac{1}{2}$
			Handicap 30	

(ii) **Category D, 29–19.** The handicap is the average of the two best differentials (*Examples D[1], D[2]*), but if the average is less than $18\frac{1}{2}$ the handicap is 19 until the average of the **four** best differentials is less than $18\frac{1}{2}$ (*Example D[3]*).

EXAMPLES:

D^1	Gross score	99	SS 73	Best differential	26
	Gross score	104	SS 73	Previous best differential	31
				Average differential	$28\overline{\frac{1}{2}}$
				Handicap 29	
D^2	Gross score	95	SS 71	Best differential	24
	Gross score	98	SS 70	Previous best differential	28
				Average differential	$\overline{26}$
				Handicap 26	
D^3	Gross scores			Best differentials	
		87	SS 72		15
		92	SS 72		20
				Average differential	$17\overline{\frac{1}{2}}$
				but . . . **Handicap 19**	
		96	SS 73		23
		94	SS 71		23
				Average differential (of four)	$20\frac{1}{4}$
				Handicap 19	

b. **Silver Division**
(i) **Category C, 18–10.** The handicap is the average of the four best differentials (*Example C[1]*), but if this average is less than $9\frac{1}{2}$ the handicap is 10 until the conditions for Category B are fulfilled.

EXAMPLES:

C^1 Best differentials

10		
11		
13		
17	Average $12\frac{3}{4}$	**Handicap 13**

C^2 EDS = Extra Day Scores; CS = Competition Scores.
Best differentials

10 (EDS)			
9 (CS)			
7 (EDS)			
6 (CS)	Average 8	but . . .	**Handicap 10**
—			
11 (CS)			
13 (CS)			
12 (CS)			
14 (CS)			

Average differential of six Comp scores = $10\frac{5}{6}$

Handicap 10

(ii) **Category B, 9–4.** The handicap is the average of the six best differentials of scores returned in competition. (*Example B[1]*), but if this average is less than $3\frac{1}{2}$ the handicap is 4 until the conditions for Category A are fulfilled (*Example B[2]*).

EXAMPLES:

B^1 Best differentials from competition scores

7		
5		
5		
6		
4		
4	Average differential $5\frac{1}{6}$	**Handicap 5**

B^2 Best differentials from competition scores:
H1, H2 = HOME COURSES, A1, A2 etc = Away Courses

3 (H1)		
5 (H2)		
4 (H1)		
2 (H1)		
2 (H1)		
3 (A1)	Average differential $3\frac{1}{6}$ but . . .	**Handicap 4**
—		
6 (A1)		
7 (A2)		
6 (H2)		
8 (A1)	Average differential 4.6	**Handicap 4**

(iii) **Category A, 3 and under.** To obtain a handicap of 3 or under a player must return at least ten scores in competition. Only six of these scores may be from a Home Course, and the remaining four must be from at least two different Away courses. The handicap is the average of the ten best differentials so obtained (*Example A[1] and A[2]*).

EXAMPLES: (Abbreviations as in B2)

A^1 Best differentials from competition scores:

0	(H)
+1	(H)
+1	(H)
0	(H)
3	(H)
0	(H)
1	(A1)
0	(A1)
1	(A2)
3	(A2) Average differential 0.6 **Handicap 1**

A^2 Best differentials from competition scores:

+1	(H)
+1	(H)
+2	(H)
1	(A1)
+2	(H)
+1	(A2)
0	(H)
+1	(H)
2	(A3)
0	(A1) Average differential +0.5
	Handicap Scratch (+0.5 = 0)

6. Annual Revision of Handicaps and LAPSED HANDICAPS

a. General

On 31 January each year all handicaps shall be recalculated on the basis of scores returned during the preceding twelve months and in accordance with the Regulations in force during that period. Any increase in handicap resulting from such recalculation shall be limited by the Table of Permitted Increases (Table I) for Revised Handicaps set out below. At no other time during the year may a player's handicap be increased (except in accordance with Regulation III.7(b) or (c)).

TABLE I – TABLE OF PERMITTED INCREASES FOR REVISED HANDICAPS

Handicaps plus to 34 may go up 2 strokes.
Handicap 35 may go up 1 stroke.

A handicap limited by the Table of Permitted Increases for Revised Handicaps shall be marked with an asterisk until the calculation of live scores results in a handicap equal to or less than that held.

b. Minimum Number of Scores to be Returned

Handicap Categories E, D, C. To retain a handicap players with handicaps 36*–10 must have returned at least four scores.

Handicap Category B. To retain a handicap players with handicaps 9–4 must have returned at least six scores. If six scores have been returned but not all in competition, the handicap shall be increased by one stroke and shall be marked with a Ø until the appropriate scores have been returned and the calculation results in a handicap equal to or less than that held prior to Revision.

Exception: If players with handicap 9 prior to Revision have returned at least four scores (not necessarily all in competition) and the average of the best four is 9½ or more, the handicap shall not lapse and shall be calculated in accordance with Regulations governing handicaps 18–10 and the Table of Permitted Increases (Table I) for Revised Handicaps.

Handicap Category A. To retain a handicap players with handicaps 3 and under must have returned at least ten scores. If ten scores have been returned in competition, but the necessary 'away' scores have not been returned, the Revised handicap shall be marked with a Ø until the necessary "away" scores have been returned. If ten scores have been returned but not all in competition, the handicap shall be increased by one stroke and shall be marked with a Ø until all the necessary conditions have been fulfilled and the calculation results in a handicap equal to or less than that held prior to Revision.

Exception: If players with handicap 3 prior to Revision have returned at least six scores in competition and the average of the best six is 3½ or more, the handicap shall not lapse and shall be calculated in accordance with Regulations governing handicaps 9–4 and the Table of Permitted Increases (Table I) for Revised Handicaps.

c. Lapsed Handicaps

A handicap lapses if a player has not returned the minimum number of scores necessary to retain a handicap (see **b.** above). When a player's handicap has lapsed he does not have a valid handicap until the conditions have been fulfilled to regain it (see **d.** below) and is ineligible to enter competitions.

d. To Regain a Handicap which has Lapsed

Handicap Categories E, D, C. To regain a handicap which has lapsed players with handicaps 36*–10 must return the number of Extra Day scores necessary to increase the number of **live** scores to four. The handicap shall then be calculated in accordance with Regulations, but it shall be limited by the Table of Permitted Increases (Table II) for Lapsed Handicaps set out below and must be confirmed, before use, by the player's Handicap Secretary.

Handicap Category B. To regain a handicap which has lapsed players with handicaps 9–4 must return the necessary Extra Day scores to

increase the number of **live** scores to six. The handicap shall then be calculated in accordance with Regulations (except that the scores need not be returned in competition), but it shall be limited by the Table of Permitted Increases (Table II) for Lapsed Handicaps set out below and must be confirmed, before use, by the player's Handicap Secretary. Until scores returned fulfil all the conditions necessary for this Category of player, the handicap shall be marked with a Ø.

Handicap Category A. To regain a handicap which has lapsed players with handicaps under 4 must return the necessary Extra Day scores to increase the number of **live** scores to ten. The handicap shall then be calculated in accordance with Regulations (except that the scores need not be returned in competition), but it shall be limited by the table of Permitted Increases (Table II) for Lapsed Handicaps set out below and must be confirmed, before use, by the player's Handicap Secretary. Until scores returned fulfil all the conditions necessary for this Category of player, the handicap shall be marked with a Ø.

Transition to a Higher Category. The number of scores required to regain a handicap by players in Categories A or B should be determined after taking into account the scores returned and the Table (II) of Permitted Increases for Lapsed Handicaps. For instance, a player previously in Category A, after a lapse of several years may require only six scores, and similarly a player previously in Category B may require only four, if the former handicap category is not maintained or bettered by the scores returned.

TABLE II – TABLE OF PERMITTED INCREASES FOR LAPSED HANDICAPS

(i) If lapsed for less than one year the handicap shall be limited to two strokes higher than that last held.

(ii) For each year in excess of one the handicap may be increased by a further stroke.

EXAMPLES:

Handicap Lapsed	Necessary EDS Returned	Max Inc over Previous Handicap
i January 31 1982	1982–83 (LGU Year)	2 strokes (less than one year)
ii	1983–84 (LGU Year)	3 strokes (one–two years)
iii	1984–85 (LGU Year)	4 strokes (two+ two years)
iv	1985–86 (LGU Year)	5 strokes (two + three years)
v	1986–87 (LGU Year)	6 strokes (two + four years) and so on . . .

A handicap limited by the Table of Permitted Increases for Lapsed Handicaps shall be marked with an asterisk.

7. Special Categories of Handicap

a. Juniors. An LGU Junior handicap (limit 45) may be obtained and held by any girl who is a junior, i.e. who has not reached her twelfth birthday on 1 January, by returning two scores over nine specified holes. Any nine holes on the course may be chosen to make up the round, at the discretion of the club, and a special SS for those holes must be obtained from the National Organisation. Each score returned, and the special SS for the nine holes, shall be doubled in order to arrive at the number of strokes above SS. Handicaps will be reduced in accordance with Regulations (one card 45–30, etc.). Juniors may hold a standard LGU handicap but may not hold both.

To retain a Junior LGU handicap two scores over nine holes must be returned annually. An LGU Junior handicap shall be acceptable for all junior competitions, and these Regulations shall apply to all players with Junior handicaps. Handicap Certificates for LGU Junior handicaps will be issued by the Handicap Secretary and *the date and year when the player will attain her twelfth birthday must be entered on the Handicap Certificate.*

b. Former Professional Golfers. On reinstatement as an amateur a player who has been a professional golfer must apply for a handicap to the Administrator, LGU. The Executive Council shall, at their discretion, allot a handicap of not more than Scratch on the basis of live scores returned during the player's period of probation in accordance with the Regulations governing handicaps of 3 and under. For the first two years after reinstatement the player's Handicap Secretary must submit all scores returned twice yearly on 1 January and 1 July to the Administrator, LGU, The Scores, St. Andrews, Fife, KY16 9AT. Handicaps will be reviewed by the Executive Council and revised at their discretion.

c. After Serious Illness and Disablement. A person wishing to regain a handicap or have her handicap reassessed after serious illness or disablement may apply through her Club Committee to the National Organisation with all relevant details, including a minimum of four live scores returned, so that consideration may be given to the circumstances and the player may obtain a realistic handicap.

Handicaps shall be adjusted in accordance with Regulations.

d. Individual Members and Visitors from Overseas. The handicaps of individual members of the LGU or of the National Organisations shall be managed by the Administrator of the LGU or

the Secretary of the appropriate National Organisation. All scores returned must be countersigned by the Handicap Secretary of the club at which they were returned and forwarded to the appropriate Secretary, who will act as Handicap Secretary for these players.

Handicaps of visitors from overseas who are not annual playing members of an affiliated club in Great Britain or Ireland shall be managed by the Secretary of the LGU, to whom scores should be forwarded after countersignature as above.

e. Senior Veterans and Disabled Players. Where a club has members who do not normally play 18 holes but who wish to play competitive golf informally, it is suggested that special handicaps be allotted by the Committee on the basis of nine-hole scores doubled. The Committee should specify which nine holes are to be played and allot for those holes a 'scratch score', which should also be doubled to arrive at the handicap. *Handicaps so obtained are not LGU handicaps and are not valid for any purpose for which an LGU handicap is required.*

8. Membership of More than One Club

a. A member belonging to more than one affiliated club must inform the Ladies' Secretary and Handicap Secretary of each club of the other affiliated clubs to which she belongs and also of any scores (together with Scratch Score) which may affect her handicap.

b. Handicap Secretary. If a player is a member of more than one club she must decide which club she wishes to be her Home Club for handicap purposes and notify the Ladies' Secretary of that club accordingly. A player's Handicap Secretary shall be the Handicap Secretary of her Home Club.

c. A member changing her Home Club must ask for a copy of her Handicap Record Sheet and take it with her Handicap Certificate to the Handicap Secretary of her new Home Club.

d. A member joining an additional club must inform the Ladies' Secretary and the Handicap Secretary of such club of her existing or lapsed handicap, and of the scores, with relative dates, on which it was gained, and also the names of all clubs of which she is or has been a member.

e. A member shall play on the same handicap at all clubs.

For details of the following, please refer to the Lady Golfer's Handbook:

- Responsibilities of Affiliated Clubs and of the National Organisations in relation to Handicapping, Competitions and Other Matters
- Scratch Scores
- LGU Tees and Teeing Grounds in Play
- Starting Places
- Handicap Records and Certificates
- LGU Silver and Bronze Medal Competitions
- LGU Gold and Silver Medal Competitions
- LGU Challenge Bowl Competitions
- Coronation Foursomes Competition
- LGU Pendant Competition
- Australian Spoons Competitions

Governing Bodies

Home Unions

Golfing Union of Ireland

The Golfing Union of Ireland, founded in 1891, embraces 263 Clubs. Its objects are:
(1) Securing the federation of the various Clubs.
(2) Arranging Amateur Championships, Inter-Provincial and Inter-Club Competitions, and International Matches.
(3) Securing a uniform standard of handicapping.
(4) Providing for advice and assistance to affiliated Clubs in all matters appertaining to Golf, and generally to promote the game in every way, in which this can be better done by the Union than by individual Clubs.

Its functions include the holding of the *Close* Championship for Amateur Golfers and Tournaments for Team Matches.

Its organisation consists of Provincial Councils in each of the four Provinces elected by the Clubs in the Province – each province electing a limited number of delegates to the Central Council which meets annually.

Welsh Golfing Union

The Welsh Golfing Union was founded in 1895 and is the second oldest of the four National Unions. Unlike the other Unions it is an association of Golf Clubs and Golfing Organisations. The present membership is 121. For the purpose of electing the Executive Council, Wales is divided into ten districts which between them return 22 members.

The objects of the Union are:
(a) To take any steps which may be deemed necessary to further the interests of the game in Wales.
(b) To hold a Championship Meeting or Meetings each year.
(c) To encourage, financially and/or otherwise, Inter-Club, Inter-County, and International Matches, and such other events as may be authorised by the Council.
(d) To assist in setting up and maintaining a uniform system of Handicapping.

(e) To assist in the maintenance of the Sports Turf Research Institute.
(f) To co-operate with the Royal & Ancient Golf Club of St Andrews through the medium of the Council of National Golf Unions.

Note: The union recognises the Royal & Ancient Golf Club of St Andrews as the ruling authority.

The Scottish Golf Union

The Scottish Golf Union was founded in 1920 and embraces 660 clubs. Subject to the stipulation and declaration that the Union recognises the Royal & Ancient Golf Club of St Andrews as the Ruling Authority in the game of golf, the objects of the Union are:
(a) To foster and maintain a high standard of Amateur Golf in Scotland and to administer and organise and generally act as the governing body of amateur golf in Scotland.
(b) To institute and thereafter carry through annually a Scottish Amateur Championship, a Scottish Open Amateur Stroke Play Championship and other such competitions and matches as they consider appropriate.
(c) To administer and apply the rules of the Standard Scratch Score and Handicapping Scheme as approved by the Council of National Golf Unions from time to time.
(d) To deal with other matters of general or local interest to amateur golfers in Scotland.

The Union's organisation consists of Area Committees covering the whole of Scotland. There are 16 Areas, each having its own Association or Committee elected by the Clubs in that particular area and each Area Association or Committee elects one delegate to serve on the Executive of the Union.

The English Golf Union

The English Golf Union was founded in 1924 and embraces 34 County Unions with over 1,350 affiliated clubs, 22 clubs overseas, and over 130 Golfing Societies and Associations. Its objects are:

(1) To further the interests of Amateur Golf in England.

(2) To assist in maintaining a uniform system of handicapping.

(3) To arrange an English Championship; an English Stroke Play Championship; an English County Championship, International and other Matches and Competitions.

(4) To co-operate with the Royal & Ancient Golf Club of St Andrews and the Council of National Golf Unions.

(5) To co-operate with other National Golf Unions and Associations in such manner as may be decided.

The Council of National Golf Unions

At a meeting of Representatives of Golf Unions and Associations in Great Britain and Ireland, called at the special request of the Scottish Golf Union, and held in York, on 14th February, 1924, resolutions were adopted from which the Council of National Golf Unions was constituted.

The Council holds an Annual Meeting in March, and such other meetings as may be necessary. Two representatives are elected from each national Home Union – England, Scotland, Ireland and Wales – and hold office until the next Annual meeting when they are eligible for re-election.

The principal function of the Council, as laid down by the York Conference, was to formulate a system of Standard Scratch Scores and Handicapping, and to co-operate with the Royal & Ancient Championship Committee in matters coming under their jurisdiction. The responsibilities undertaken by the Council at the instance of the Royal & Ancient Golf Club or the National Unions are as follows:

1 The Standard Scratch Score and Handicapping Scheme, formulated in March, 1926, approved by the Royal & Ancient, and last revised in 1983.

2 The nomination of two members on the Board of Management of The Sports Turf Research Institute, with an experimental station at St Ives, Bingley, Yorkshire.

3 The management of the Annual Amateur International Matches between the four countries – England, Scotland, Ireland and Wales.

United States Golf Association

The USGA is the national governing body of golf. Its single most important goal is preserving the integrity and values of the game.

Formed on 22nd December, 1894, a year when two clubs proclaimed different US Amateur Champions, representatives of five clubs met at a dinner at the Calumet Club in New York City. They created a central governing body to establish uniform rules, to conduct national championships and to nurture the virtues of sportsmanship in golf.

The names of the standing committees give an idea of what the USGA does:

Rules of Golf, Championship, Amateur Status and Conduct, Implements and Ball, Handicap, Women's, Sectional Affairs, Green Section, Public Links, Women's Public Links, Junior Championship, Girls' Junior, Senior Championship, Senior Women's Championship, Bob Jones Award, Museum, Green Section Award, Finance, Public Information, Membership, Regional Association, Associates, Intercollegiate Relations, Mid-Amateur Championship, International Team Selection, Development, Turfgrass Research, Nominating.

The USGA, as the governing body of the game in the United States, makes and interprets the Rules of Golf in co-operation with the Royal & Ancient Golf Club of St Andrews, Scotland; developed and maintains the national system of handicapping; controls the standards of the ball and the implements of the game; works in turfgrass and turf management; and, generally speaking, preserves and promotes the game.

The Professional Golfers' Association

The Professional Golfers' Association was founded in 1901 to promote interest in the game of golf; to protect and advance the mutual and trade interests of its members; to arrange and hold meetings and tournaments periodically for the members; to institute and operate funds for the benefit of the members; to assist the members to obtain employment; and effect any other objects of a like nature as may be determined from time to time by the Association.

Classes of Membership

There shall be nine (9) classes of membership:

(i) Class A   Members engaged as the nominated professional on a full-time basis at a PGA Club, PGA Course or PGA Driving Range in one of the seven Regions; and members engaged as the nominated professional on a full-time basis, at an establishment in one of the seven Regions at which the public can play and/or practise which, in the opinion of the Executive Committee does not qualify as a PGA Club, Course or Driving Range but does warrant Class A status. NOTE: Class A(T) – Class A members currently engaged at an establishment which has been inspected and approved as a PGA Training Establishment and cur-

(ii) Class B   Members engaged by a Class A or D member to assist the nominated professional at any PGA Establishment in one of the seven Regions on a full-time basis.

(iii) Class C   Tournament playing members (men and women).

(iv) Class D   Members engaged as the nominated professional on a full-time basis at a PGA Establishment within the seven Regions which does not qualify as a 'Class A' establishment, or engaged on a full-time basis within the seven Regions by any other Company or any other individual designated by the Executive Committee for this purpose. (Former Class G.)

(v) Class E   Honorary Associate Members (HAM). Those who in the opinion of the Executive Committee through their past or continuing membership justify retaining the full privileges of membership as Honorary Associate Members (HAM).

(vi) Class F   Associate Members (AM).
(a) Those who have ceased to be eligible for other categories of membership who in the opinion of the Executive Committee through their past membership justify retaining limited privileges of membership as Associate Members; and (b) Members of the PGA European Tour or WPGET who do not qualify for Class C membership but who in the opinion of the Executive Committee justify limited privileges of membership as Associate Members.

(vii) Class G   Honorary Life Members (HLM) Those recommended by the Board to a Special General Meeting of the Association for election as Honorary Life Members. No form of application is needed nor need reference be made to the Regional Committee concerned.

(viii) Class H   Members who are qualified members of the Association, and ineligible for any other class of membership, engaged on a full-time basis at an establishment acceptable to the Association outside the jurisdiction of the seven Regions. (Overseas.)

(ix) Class O   Members who have not qualified at the official training centre of the Association, who are ineligible for any other class of membership, and who are current members of another PGA approved by the Association and have held such membership for not less than two years.

The Management of the Association is under the overall direction and control of a Board. The Association is divided into seven Regions each of which employs a full-time secretary and runs tournaments for the benefit of members within its Region.

The Association is responsible for arranging and obtaining sponsorship of the Ryder Cup, Club Professionals' Championship, PGA Cup matches, Seniors' Championship, PGA Assistants' Championship, Assistants' Match Play Championship and other National Championships.

Anyone who intends to become a club professional must serve a minimum of three years in registration and qualify at the PGA Training School before election as a full Member.

PGA European Tour

To be eligible to become a member of the PGA European Tour a player must possess certain minimum standards which shall be determined by the Tournament Committee. In 1976 a Qualifying School for potential new members was introduced to be held annually. The leading players are awarded cards allowing them to compete in all PGA European Tour tournaments.

In 1985 the PGA European Tour became ALL EXEMPT with no more Monday pre-qualifying. Full details can be obtained from the Wentworth Headquarters.

Women Professional Golfers' European Tour

The Women Professional Golfers' European Tour (WPG European Tour) was founded in 1988 to further the development of women's professional golf throughout Europe and its membership is open to all nationalities. An amateur wishing to join the Tour must be 18 years of age, have a handicap of 1 or less and is on probation for eight rounds in tournaments, during which she must attain certain playing standards as determined by the Tournament Committee.

Government of the Amateur and Open Golf Championship

In December 1919 on the invitation of the clubs who had hitherto controlled the amateur and Open Golf Championships, the Royal & Ancient

took over the government of those events. These two championships are controlled by a committee appointed by the Royal & Ancient Golf Club of St Andrews. The Committee shall be called the Royal and Ancient Golf Club Championship Committee and shall consist of twelve members (who shall be members of the Club) to be elected by the Club, and additional members not exceeding two (who shall not necessarily be members of the Club) from Golf Authorities both at home and abroad, who shall be invited annually to join the Committee by the twelve members elected by the Club. Such invited members shall, irrespective of the date of their invitation to become members of the Committee, remain members only until the date of the first Autumn Meeting occurring after the date of their invitation to become members. During their term of office, such invited members (who are not already members of the Club) shall be admitted as honorary temporary members of the Club. Two Business Members, who shall be members of the Club, shall be co-opted on the nomination of the Chairman of the Championship Committee after consultation with the Chairman of the General Committee.

LGU

The Ladies' Golf Union was founded in 1893 with the following objects:

(1) To promote the interests of the game of Golf.

(2) To obtain a uniformity of the rules of the game by establishing a representative legislative authority.

(3) To establish a uniform system of handicapping.

(4) To act as a tribunal and court of reference on points of uncertainty.

(5) To arrange the Annual Championship Competition and obtain the funds necessary for that purpose.

Ninety years on only the language has changed, the present Constitution defining the objects as:

(1) To uphold the rules of the game, to advance and safeguard the interests of women's golf and to decide all doubtful and disputed points in connection therewith.

(2) To maintain, regulate and enforce the LGU System of Handicapping.

(3) To employ the funds of The Union in such a manner as shall be deemed best for the interests of women's golf, with power to borrow or raise money to use for the same purpose.

(4) To maintain and regulate International events, Championships and Competitions

held under the LGU regulations and to promote the interests of Great Britain and Ireland in Ladies International Golf.

(5) To make, maintain and publish such regulations as may be considered necessary for the above purposes.

The constituents of the LGU are:

Home Countries. The English Ladies' Golf Association (founded 1952), the Irish Ladies' Golf Union (founded 1893), the Scottish Ladies' Golfing Association (founded 1904), the Welsh Ladies' Golf Union (founded 1904), plus ladies' societies, girls' schools and ladies' clubs affiliated to these organisations. *Overseas.* Affiliated ladies' golf unions and golf clubs in the Commonwealth and any other overseas ladies' golfing organisation affiliated to the LGU.

Individual lady members of clubs within the above categories are regarded as *members of the LGU.*

The Rules of the Game and of Amateur Status, which the LGU is bound to uphold, are those published by the Royal & Ancient Golf Club of St Andrews.

In endeavouring to fulfil its responsibilities towards advancing and safeguarding women's golf, the LGU maintains contact with other golfing organisations – the Royal & Ancient Golf Club of St Andrews, the Council of National Golf Unions, the Golf Foundation, the Central Council of Physical Recreation, the Sports Council, the Women Professional Golfers' European Tour and the Women's Committee of the United States Golf Association. This contact ensures that the LGU is informed of developments and projected developments and has an opportunity to comment upon and to influence the future of the game for women.

Either directly or through its constituent national organisations the LGU advises and is the ultimate authority on doubts or disputes which may arise in connection with the handicapping system and regulations governing competitions played under LGU conditions.

The handicapping system, together with the system for assessment of Scratch Scores, is formulated and published by the LGU. The handicapping system undergoes detailed revision and is republished every four years, in the year following the revision of the Rules of Golf. Handicap Certificates are provided by the LGU and distributed through the national organisations and appointed club officials to every member of every affiliated club which has fulfilled the requisite conditions for obtaining an LGU handicap. No other form of certificate is recognised as evidence of an LGU handicap.

The funds of the LGU are administered by the Hon. Treasurer on the authority of the Executive Council, and the accounts are submitted annually for adoption in General Meeting.

All ladies' British Open Championships and the Home International matches, at both senior and junior level, are organised annually by the LGU. International events involving a British or a combined British and Irish team are organised and controlled by the LGU when held in this country and the LGU acts as the co-ordinating body for the Commonwealth Tournament in whichever of the four participating countries it is held, four-yearly, by rotation. The LGU selects and trains the teams, provides the uniforms and pays all the expenses of participation, whether held in this country or overseas. The LGU also maintains and regulates certain competitions played under handicap, such as Medal Competitions, Coronation Foursomes, Challenge Bowls, Australian Spoons and the LGU Pendant Competition.

The day-to-day administration of certain of the LGU responsibilities in the home countries is undertaken by the national organisations, such as that concerned with handicapping regulations, Scratch Scores, and the organisation of Challenge Bowls and Australian Spoons Competitions.

Membership subscriptions to the LGU are assessed on a per capita basis of the club membership. To save unnecessary expense and duplication of administrative work in the home countries LGU subscriptions are collected by the national organisations along with their own, and transmitted in bulk to the LGU.

Policy is determined and control over all the LGU's activities is exercised by an Executive Council of eight members – two each elected by the English, Irish, Scottish and Welsh national organisations. The Chairman is elected annually by the Councillors and may hold office for one year only, during which term her place on the Council is taken by her Deputy and she has no vote other than a casting vote. The President and the Hon. Treasurer of the Union also attend and take part in Council meetings but with no vote. The Council meets five times a year.

The Annual General Meeting is held in January. The formal business includes presentation of the Report of the Executive Council for the previous year and of the Accounts for the last completed financial year, the election or re-election of President, Vice-Presidents, Hon. Treasurer and Auditors, and a report of the election of Councillors and their Deputies for the ensuing year and of the European Technical Committee representative. Voting is on the following basis: Executive Council, one each (8); members in the four home countries, one per national organisation (4) and in addition one per 100 affiliated clubs or part thereof (at present 22); one per overseas Commonwealth Union with a membership of 50 or more clubs (at present 3), and one per 100 individually affiliated clubs (1).

The Lady Golfer's Handbook is published annually by the LGU and is distributed free to all affiliated clubs and organisations and to appointed Handicap Advisers. It is also available for sale to anyone interested. It contains the regulations for handicapping and Scratch Score assessment, for British Championships and international matches (with results for the past twenty years) and for LGU competitions, and sets out the Rules of the Union. It also lists every affiliated organisation, with names and addresses of officials, and every affiliated club, with Scratch Score, county of affiliation, number of members, and other useful information.

Miscellaneous Rulings

Limitation of the Golf Ball

At the Autumn Business Meeting, 1920, of the Royal & Ancient Club the following resolution was adopted: *On and after 1st May, 1921, the weight of the ball shall not be greater than 1.62 ounces avoirdupois, and the size not less than 1.62 inches in diameter. The Rules of Golf Committee and the Executive Committee of the United States Golf Association will take whatever steps they think necessary to limit the powers of the ball with regard to distance, should any ball of greater power be introduced.* The United States Golf Association intimated, May, 1929, that they had resolved to adopt *an easier and pleasanter ball for the average golfer*, and from 1st January, 1931, to 31st December, 1932, the standards of specification of the ball in competitions under their jurisdiction was not less than 1.68 inches in diameter, and not greater than 1.55 ounces in weight. In January, 1932, another alteration was made in the specification of the ball, the weight being increased to 1.62 and the size remaining the same, viz, not less than 1.68.

The Royal Canadian Golf Association adopted the USGA specification as from 1st January, 1948. The effect of this difference between the legislation of the Royal & Ancient, the Royal Canadian Golf Association, and the USGA is that golfers competing in the United States and Canada must use a ball that is larger, but no heavier, than the ball which is legal in other parts of the world.

In May, 1951, a special committee was set up by the Royal & Ancient Golf Club and the United States Golf Association to discuss the desirability of uniformity in the Rules of Golf and the form and make of clubs and balls. The committee recommended that both sizes of ball (1.62 inches and 1.68 inches in diameter both having the same weight, 1.62 ounces) be legal in all countries. At their autumn meeting the United States Golfers' Association rejected this proposal but agreed that in international team competition in the United States, the size of the ball be not less than 1.62 inches in diameter.

The matter of a uniform ball worldwide was investigated by a special committee from the R&A and the USGA but was dropped in 1974 when the two bodies could not reach agreement.

In 1987, however, the Royal & Ancient Golf Club of St Andrews proposed and adopted an amendment which decreed that the diameter of the golf ball should be not less than 1.68 inches (42.67 mm) instead of 1.62 inches (41.15 mm). The change of rule was introduced on 1st January 1990. An official statement declared: 'With the steady and, in most countries, rapid decline in the use of the 1.62 inch ("small") ball, the R&A has been considering changing to the 1.68 inch ("large") ball for some time, but has held off from doing so mainly because of the large number of Japanese golfers still using the small ball. With the use of the small ball in Japan now dropping steadily and in most other countries now being at 10% or less, it seems an appropriate time to make this change." A maximum initial velocity standard of not greater than 250 feet per second on special apparatus was introduced by the R&A in 1976.

The R&A issues lists of conforming golf balls annually.

Limitation of Number of Clubs

At the Business Meeting of the Royal & Ancient Golf Club, May, 1937, the Rules of Golf Committee submitted a recommendation that on and after 1st January, 1938, the preamble to the Rules of Golf shall read: *The game of golf consists of a ball being played from a teeing ground to a hole by successive strokes with clubs (not exceeding fourteen in number) and balls made in conformity with the directions laid down in the clause on* 'Form and make of golf clubs and balls'. The recommendation was not approved by the members.

In September, 1938, at the Business Meeting of the Royal & Ancient, a similar recommendation was approved by the members, and the limitation of the number of clubs to fourteen became operative as from 1st May, 1939.

The United States Golf Association decided to limit the number of clubs to fourteen as from 1st January, 1938.

Steel-Shafted Clubs

The Royal & Ancient Golf Club authorised steel shafts, November, 1929, in the following announcement: *The Rules of Golf Committee have decided that steel shafts, as approved by the Rules of Golf Committee are declared to conform with the requirements of the clause in the Rules of Golf on the form and make of golf clubs.*

Laminated Shafts

The Rules of Golf Committee on 5th December, 1932, announced that clubs with laminated shafts built entirely of wood are permissible.

Recognised Golf Clubs

The Rules of Golf Committee, in answering a query, gave the opinion that a recognised Golf Club is one which has regularly appointed office-bearers.

The English Golf Union decided that a recognised Golf Club for the purpose of competitive golf in England is a golf club affiliated to the English Golf Union through its County Union, or where there is no County Union direct to the English Golf Union as an Associate Member.

Championship Conditions

Men

The Amateur Championship

The Championship, until 1982, was decided entirely by match play over 18 holes except for the final which was over 36 holes. Since 1983 the Championship has comprised two stroke-play rounds of 18 holes each from which the top 64 scores over the 36 holes qualify for the match-play stages. Matches are over 18 holes except for the final which is over 36 holes.

Full particulars of conditions of entry and method of play can be obtained from the Championship Entries Department, Royal & Ancient Golf Club, St Andrews, Fife KY16 9JD.

The Seniors' Open Amateur

The Championship consists of 18 holes on each of two days, the lowest 50 scores over the 36 holes and any tying for 50th place then playing a further 18 holes the following day.

Conditions for entry include:

Entrants must have attained the age of 55 years prior to the first day on which the Championship is played.

Entries are limited to 252 competitors.

Full particulars of conditions of entry and method of play can be obtained from Championship Entries Department, Royal & Ancient Golf Club, St Andrews, Fife KY16 9JD.

National Championships

The English, Scottish, Irish and Welsh Amateur Championships are played by holes, each match consisting of one round of 18 holes except the final which is contested over 36 holes.

Full particulars of conditions of entry and method of play can be obtained from the secretaries of the respective national Unions.

English Open Amateur Stroke Play Championship

The Championship consists of one round of 18 holes on each of two days after which the leading 45 and those tying for 45th place play a further two rounds. The remainder are eliminated.

Conditions for entry include:

Entrants must have a handicap not exceeding three.

Where the entries exceed 130, an 18-hole qualifying round is held the day before the Championship. Certain players are exempt from qualifying.

Full particulars of conditions of entry and method of play can be obtained from the Secretary, English Golf Union.

Youths

British Youths' Open Amateur Championship

The Championship consists of 18 holes on each of two days, the lowest 40 scores over the 36 holes and any tying for 40th place then playing a further 36 holes the following day.

Conditions of entry include:

Entrants must be under 21 years of age at 00.00 hours on 1st January in the year of the Championship.

Entries are limited to 150 competitors, the higher handicaps being balloted out if necessary.

Full particulars of conditions of entry and method of play can be obtained from the Championship Entries Department, Royal & Ancient Golf Club, St Andrews, Fife KY16 9JD.

Boys

Boys' Amateur Championship

The Championship is played by match play, each match consisting of one round of 18 holes except for the final which is over 36 holes.

Conditions of entry include:

Entrants must be under 18 years of age at 00.00 hours on 1st January in the year of the Championship.

Entries are limited to 192 competitors, the higher handicaps being balloted out if necessary.

Full particulars of conditions of entry and method of play can be obtained from the Championship Entries Department, Royal & Ancient Golf Club, St Andrews, Fife KY16 9JD.

Ladies

Ladies' British Open Amateur Championship

The Championship consists of one 18-hole qualifying round on each of two days. If entries exceed 110 there will be 64 qualifiers for matchplay. If entries number 110 or less, 32 will qualify for matchplay. Handicap limit is 4.

Ladies' British Open Amateur Stroke Play Championship

The Championship consists of 72 holes stroke play; 18 holes are played on each of two days after which the first 32 and all ties for 32nd place qualify for a further 36 holes on the third day. Handicap limit is 4.

Ladies' British Open Championship

The Championship consists of 72 holes stroke play. 18 holes are played on each of four days, the field being reduced after the first 36 holes.

Entries accepted from lady amateurs with a handicap not exceeding scratch and from lady professionals.

Full particulars of conditions of entry and method of play for all three Championships can be obtained from the Administrator, LGU, The Scores, St Andrews, Fife KY16 9AT.

National Championships

Conditions of entry and method of play for the English, Scottish, Welsh and Irish Ladies' Close Championships can be obtained from the Secretaries of the respective associations.

Other championships organised by the respective national associations, from whom full particulars can be obtained, include English Ladies', Intermediate, English Ladies' Stroke-Play, Scottish Girls' Open Amateur Stroke Play (under 21) and Welsh Ladies' Open Amateur Stroke Play.

Girls

Girls' British Open Amateur Championship

The Championship consists of two 18-hole qualifying rounds, followed by match play in two flights each of sixteen players.

Conditions of entry include:

Entrants must be under 18 years of age on the 1st January in the year of the Championship.

Competitors are required to hold a certified LGU international handicap not exceeding 15, or to be members of their National Junior Team for the current year.

Full particulars of conditions of entry and method of play can be obtained from the Administrator, LGU, The Scores, St Andrews, Fife KY16 9AT.

National Championships

The English, Scottish, Irish and Welsh Girls' Close Championships are open to all girls of relevant nationality and appropriate age which may vary from country to country. A handicap limit may be set by some countries.

Full particulars of conditions of entry and method of play can be obtained via the secretaries of the respective associations.

International Match Conditions

Men–Amateur

Walker Cup–Great Britain and Ireland *v United States*

Deed of Gift to United States Golf Association International Challenge Trophy

Mr GH Walker of the United States presented a Cup for international competition to be known as *The United States Golf Association International Challenge Trophy*, popularly described as *The Walker Cup*.

The Cup shall be played for by teams of amateur golfers selected from Clubs under the jurisdiction of the United States Golf Association on the one side and from England, Scotland, Wales, Northern Ireland and Eire on the other.

The International Walker Cup Match shall be held every two years in the United States of America and Great Britain and Ireland alternately.

The teams shall consist of not more than ten players and a captain.

The contest consists of four foursomes and eight singles matches over 18 holes on each of two days.

St Andrews Trophy

First staged in 1956, the St Andrews Trophy is a biennial match played between two teams of Amateur golfers representing Great Britain and Ireland and the Continent of Europe. The match is played over two consecutive days with four morning foursomes being followed each afternoon by eight singles.

Team selection for the Great Britain and Ireland team is carried out by the Selection Committee of the Royal & Ancient Golf Club; that for the Continent of Europe team, a much harder task in view of the geographical and multi-national problems, by a committee of the European Golf Association.

Eisenhower Trophy (formerly World Cup)

Founded in 1958 in recognition of the need for an official team championship for amateurs. Each country enters a team of four players who play stroke play over 72 holes, the total of the three best individual scores to be counted each day. (One score to be discarded.) The winner to be the team with the lowest aggregate for the 72 holes. The first event was played at St Andrews in 1958 and the trophy has been played for every second year.

European Team Championship

Founded in 1959 by the European Golf Association for competition among member countries of the Association. The Championship is held biennially and played in rotation round the countries which are grouped in four geographical zones.

Each team consists of six players who play two qualifying rounds of 18 holes, the five best scores of each round constituting the team aggregate. Flights for match play are then arranged according to qualifying round rankings. For the match play, teams consist of five players, playing two foursomes in the morning and five singles in the afternoon.

A similar championship is held every year for junior teams.

From 1990, the European Golf Association began organising the International European Championships – formally known as the European Individual Amateur Championships – on an annual basis.

Home Internationals (Raymond Trophy)

The first official International Match recorded was in 1903 at Muirfield between England and Scotland when singles only were played.

In 1932 International Week was inaugurated under the auspices of the British Golf Unions' Joint Advisory Council with the full approval of the four National Golf Unions. The Council of National Golf Unions is now responsible for running the matches.

Teams of 11 players from England, Scotland, Ireland and Wales engage in matches consisting of 5 foursomes and 10 singles over 18 holes, the

foursomes being in the morning and the singles in the afternoon. Each team plays every other team.

The eligibility of players to play for their country shall be their eligibility to play in the Amateur Championship of their country.

Men–Professional

Ryder Cup

This Cup was presented by Mr Samuel Ryder, St Albans, England (who died 2nd January, 1936), for competition between a team of British professionals and a team of American professionals. The trophy was first competed for in 1927. In 1929 the original conditions were varied to confine the British team to British-born professionals resident in Great Britain, and the American team to American-born professionals resident in the United States, in the year of the match. In 1977 the British team was extended to include European players. The matches are played biennially, in alternate continents, in accordance with the conditions as agreed between the respective PGAs.

World Cup
(formerly Canada Cup)

Founded in America in 1953 as an International Team event for professional golfers with the intention of spreading international goodwill.

Each country is represented by two players, the best team score over 72 holes being the winners of the World Cup and the best individual score the International Trophy. It is played annually, but not in 1986.

Ladies

Great Britain and Ireland v United States
(Curtis Cup)

For a trophy presented by the late Misses Margaret and Harriot Curtis of Boston, USA, for biennial competition between teams from the United States of America and Great Britain and Ireland.

The match is sponsored jointly by the United States Golf Association and the Ladies' Golf Union who may select teams of not more than 8 players.

The match consists of 3 foursomes and 6 singles of 18 holes on each of two days, the foursomes being played each morning.

Great Britain and Ireland
v Continent of Europe
(Vagliano Trophy)

For a trophy presented to the Comité des Dames de la Fédération Française de Golf and the Ladies' Golf Union by Monsieur AA Vagliano, originally for annual competition between teams of women amateur golfers from France and Great Britain and Ireland but, since 1959, by mutual agreement, for competition between teams from the Continent of Europe and Great Britain and Ireland.

The match is played biennially, alternately in Great Britain and Ireland and on the Continent of Europe, with teams of not more than 9 players plus a non-playing captain.

The match consists of 4 foursomes and 8 singles, of 18 holes on each of two days. The foursomes are played each morning.

Women's World Amateur Team Championship
(Espirito Santo Trophy)

For the Espirito Santo Trophy presented by Mrs Ricardo Santo of Portugal for biennial competition between teams of not more than three women amateur golfers who represent a national association affiliated to the World Amateur Golf Council. First competed for in 1964.

The tournament consists of 72 holes stroke play, 18 holes on each of four days, the two best scores in each round each day constituting the team aggregate.

Commonwealth Tournament
(Lady Astor Trophy)

For a trophy presented by the late Viscountess Astor CH, and the Ladies' Golf Union for competition once in every four years between teams of women amateur golfers from Commonwealth countries.

The inaugural Commonwealth Tournament was played at St Andrews in 1959 between teams from Australia, Canada, New Zealand, South Africa and Great Britain and was won by the British team. The tournament is played in rotation in the competing countries, for the present Great Britain, Australia, Canada, and New Zealand, each country being entitled to nominate 6 players including a playing or non-playing captain.

Each team plays every other team and each team match consists of 2 foursomes and 4 singles over 18 holes. The foursomes are played in the morning and the singles in the afternoon.

European Ladies' Amateur Team Championship

The Championship is held biennially between teams of amateur women golfers from the European countries. Each team consists of not more than 6 players who play two qualifying rounds, the five best scores in each round constituting the team aggregate. The match play draw is made in flights according to the position in the qualifying rounds. The match play consists of 2 foursomes and 5 singles on each of three days.

A similar championship is held in alternate years for junior ladies' teams, under 22 years of age.

Home Internationals

Teams from England, Scotland, Ireland and Wales compete annually for a trophy presented to the LGU by the late Mr TH Miller. The qualifications for a player being eligible to play for her country are the same as those laid down by each country for its Close Championship.

Each team plays each other team. The matches consist of 6 singles and 3 foursomes, each of 18 holes. Each country may nominate teams of not more than 8 players.

Youths

England v Scotland

The International Match between England and Scotland is played the day before the Youths' Championship begins. This match consists of 5 foursomes followed by 10 singles.

Great Britain and Ireland v Continent of Europe

The International Match between Great Britain and Ireland and the Continent of Europe for the EGA Trophy is played each year over two days. The venue of this match alternates between Great Britain and Ireland and the Continent of Europe. On each day there are 4 foursomes followed by 8 singles.

Boys

England v Scotland; Wales v Ireland

The International Matches between England and Scotland (10 players a side) and Wales and Ireland (10 players a side) are played on the Thursday preceding the Boys' Championship. The following day the winners of these two matches play against each other, as do the losers. To be eligible to play in these matches a boy must qualify by age to be eligible to play in the Boys' Championship.

Great Britain and Ireland v Continent of Europe

The International Match between Great Britain and Ireland and the Continent of Europe for the Jacques Leglise Trophy is played on the Saturday preceding the Boys' Championship. This match consists of 4 foursomes followed by 8 singles.

Girls

Home Internationals

Teams from England, Scotland, Ireland and Wales compete annually for the Stroyan Cup. The qualifications for a player for the Girls' International Matches shall be the same as those laid down by each country for its Girls' Close Championship except that a player shall be under 18 years on the 1st January in the year of the Championship.

Each team, consisting of not more than 8 players, plays each other team, a draw taking place to decide the order of play between the teams. The matches consist of 7 singles, each of 18 holes.

Golf Associations

The Golf Foundation

During the last decade, the growth of golf throughout Britain has scaled new heights with each passing year as more and more people become smitten with its addictive qualities. It was Tony Jacklin who initially sparked this explosion of interest with his victories in the Open Championship and the United States Open nearly 20 years ago and further fuel has been added by the emergence of Spain's Severiano Ballesteros as one of the most exciting players the game has ever seen. The exploits of the world's leading professionals are now regularly beamed into millions of homes via television and so people who would never have dreamed of taking an interest in the game have been fascinated and eventually drawn into finding out for themselves its magnetic qualities.

Many of these people are youngsters – girls and boys who witness the achievements of today's stars and feel that they too would like to experience the allure and charm of golf with dreams, perhaps, of emulating some of the modern day heroes and heroines. In a great many cases, these dreams are frustrated at the outset. If the parents of a child do not play golf then all the questions the child may have about starting golf can go unanswered. He or she may enquire about the game from school teachers but unless one of them is a golfer, it is unlikely that this approach will bear any fruit so the seeds of interest are soon stifled and the child turns to other games which are included in the school curriculum.

It is this gap in the education of young, potential golfers that The Golf Foundation fills. Founded in 1952, The Golf Foundation's original motives of promoting the development of junior golf throughout the country still hold good today and in the space of 37 years, thousands of junior golfers have benefited from its work. From this number have emerged some famous names such as Bernard Gallacher, Brian Barnes, Peter Oosterhuis, Michelle Walker and more recently Paul Way, Michael McLean and Ronan Rafferty, all of whom received instruction and assistance under The Golf Foundation Coaching Scheme for Schools and Junior Groups.

This scheme forms the basis of the Foundation's work whereby it subsidises instruction by qualified members of the Professional Golfer's Association (PGA) to students of schools, universities and other places of higher education and to junior members of golf clubs who are in full-time education. This enables schools who do not have golf as part of their sports programme to take advantage of giving their pupils an introduction to the game and a solid grounding in its techniques.

But the work of The Golf Foundation does not begin and end there; the Foundation realised that young people's initial interest in the game must be sustained. Thus, over the years it has expanded its field of operations to cover the development of a junior golfer right through to the adult ranks. This area includes the awarding of vouchers for individual tuition for promising girls and boys; the sponsoring of Open Coaching Centres during school holidays; the encouragement of school competitive golf and assisting the formation of National and County Schools' Golf Associations; the operation of a film and visual aids service; the organisation of the Team Championship for Schools and the Age Group Championships; the promotion of an Eclectic Competition for club juniors; the operation of a Merit Award Scheme whereby juniors can have their progress measured and rewarded. The Foundation has recently initiated the Coaching Award for Teachers in School whereby teachers who play golf themselves receive basic instruction from PGA professionals which they can then impart to pupils so that the pupils have some grounding when they receive further instruction under The Golf Foundation Coaching Scheme for Schools and Junior Groups.

The Foundation also makes an annual award to the boy or girl showing the most improvement as a result of Golf Foundation tuition and in 1983 this award was won by a 17-year-old boy who is deaf and has limited speech – proof, if any were needed, of the therapeutic powers of the game and evidence of the particular interest The Golf Foun-

dation takes in handicapped young people.

The implementation of these activities and the running of the coaching scheme costs a great deal of money and The Golf Foundation relies heavily on club golfers for a large part of its income. Organisations within the game and companies also assist in providing funds so that its work can continue and expand.

At present, the future of British golf looks bright, but in order to maintain that progress, more and more youngsters must be given the opportunity to learn about and play golf. As one old scribe once wrote, *it is a game at which you may exhaust yourself but never your subject,* and it is a game that teaches self-discipline, good manners, sportsmanship and an appreciation of other people's qualities. It is *the game of a lifetime* for it can be played by people of all ages. The Golf Foundation hopes that you too, once you have experienced the pleasures of golf, will find it a lasting source of enjoyment.

The National Association of Public Golf Courses

(Affiliated to English Golf Union)

1927 saw the foundation of the Association by the late FG Hawtree (Golf Course Architect) and the late JH Taylor (five times Open Champion). They were both farsighted enough to see the need for cohesion between *Private* golf, *Public* golf and the Local Councils. Up to the outbreak of World War II the Association struggled on, sustained by a small amount of very welcome financial support from the *News of the World.* This enabled the *unofficial* Championship to be staged.

After the War, the Association was revitalised and the Championship was recognised by the National Union, and so from a shaky start of 240 qualifiers, there are now some 3500 Public Course golfers trying to qualify, from a total estimated membership of 50,000. The success and importance of the *Public Courses Championship of England* prompted the commencement of the Championship for Ladies and then the Championship for Juniors – which share equal importance. Soon after the establishment of Individual Championships there came the introduction of various Club Team events, and these have now progressed to National Level with a vast following from Club members. Thus the Association now organises some 14 national events annually for the membership.

Some years ago it was realised that the Local Councils (Course Management Authorities) could not enjoy official recognition and membership of the County Unions or National Unions except through the Association. This has now been remedied and many CMA are full subscribing members of the Association, and many others permit the *Courtesy of the Course* for all our National and Zonal Tournaments. Advice is offered to CMA – when requested – on such matters as Course Construction, Club formation and integration, establishment of Standard Scratch Score and Par Values, and many other topics concerned with the management of the game of golf.

Some overseas organisations and Councils have already sought our advice and help in recent years, when forming their own Courses, Clubs and Associations.

The Constitutional aims have not changed over the years, and the Association is proud to have maintained these Aims through the activities provided by the National Executive of the Association. The aims are:

1. To unite the Clubs formed on Public Courses in England and Wales, and their Course Managements in the furtherance of the interests of Amateur Golf.
2. To promote Annual Public Courses Championships and such other matches, competitions and tournaments as shall be authorised by the executive of the Association.
3. To afford direct representation of Public Course Interests in the National Union.

The total organisation of the Association is wholly voluntary and honorary, from the President down through Vice-Presidents, Chairmen, Secretary, Treasurer and Zone Secretaries. It is quite fantastic for an unpaid Organisation to cover such an exacting field of work, but most gratifying to the National Executive who have secured the progress of recent years.

Association of Golf Club Secretaries

Membership is 1500, consisting of Secretaries and retired Secretaries of Clubs largely situated in Great Britain but also from Clubs in other parts of the World. The Association offers from the Headquarters at Weston-super-Mare, Avon advice on all aspects of Golf Club Management, and a training course for new and intending Secretaries. Apart from national events, including a Conference, the Association organises golfing and business meetings for its members at regional level. There are 11 regions within Great Britain.

Association of Golf Writers

Secretary: Renton Laidlaw, *Evening Standard,* 2 Derry Street, London W8 5EE.

The Sports Turf Research Institute
(Bingley, West Yorkshire)

The Institute is officially recognised as the national centre for sports and amenity turf. Non-com-

mercial and non-profit making, its affairs are administered by a Board, whose members are nominated by the sport controlling bodies in membership of the Institute. Golf is represented by nominees of the Royal & Ancient Golf Club of St Andrews, four individual National Golf Unions, and the Councils of National Golf Unions.

The institute's aim is to raise the standard of turf used for all sports. Valuable data is accumulated from research activities and is disseminated to subscribing clubs and organisations.

The British Association of Golf Course Architects

Objects of the Association: to encourage the highest standards of Golf Course Design and Construction; to have the fullest regard to the best interests of Members' Clients; to maintain a Register of Members fully qualified by training and experience in the design and construction of Golf Courses; to promote the interests of its members and the game of golf; to support research and development in golf course Design, Construction and Maintenance; to enable members to meet together, share knowledge and experience, and discuss matters affecting their work; to follow the best accepted principles of golf course architecture with the object of providing the maximum enjoyment of the game for all players.

The British Association of Golf Course Constructors

Objects: To promote the development of the golf course construction industry, to promote the adoption of policies to ensure a high quality of workmanship and working practices, to collect and disseminate information of value regarding the construction of golf courses to other members of the association, to members of the allied industries and to the public to promote the training and education of personnel within the industry and to maintain agreed standards of golf course construction by adherence to contractual procedures and codes of practice.

British and International Golf Greenkeepers' Association

The Association was formed in 1987 resulting from an amalgamation of the British, English and Scottish Associations. The Association has an official magazine, *Greenkeeping Management,* which is issued free to all members.

The objects are to promote and advance all aspects of greenkeeping; to assist and encourage the proficiency of members; to arrange an International Annual Conference, educational seminars, functions and competitions; to maintain

a Benevolent Fund; to act as an employment agency; to provide a magazine; to collaborate with any body or organisation which may benefit the Association or its members or with which there may be a common interest; to carry out and perform any other duties which shall be in the general interests of the Association or its members.

National Golf Clubs' Advisory Association

The National Golf Clubs' Advisory Association was founded in 1922. The objects are to protect the interests of Golf Clubs in general and to give legal advice and direction, under the opinion of Counsel, on the administrative and legal responsibilities of Golf Clubs. In cases taken to the Courts for decisions on any points which in the opinion of the Executive Committee involve principles affecting the general interests of affiliated clubs financial assistance may sometimes be given.

European Golf Association
Association Européenne de Golf

Formed at a meeting held at Luxembourg, 20th November, 1937, membership shall be restricted to European National Amateur Golf Associations or Unions. The Association shall concern itself solely with matters of an international character. The Association shall have as its prime objects:

(a) To encourage international development of golf and strengthen bonds of friendship between the national organisations and to encourage the formation of new ones.

(b) To co-ordinate dates of the Open and Amateur Championships of its members.

(c) To arrange when such have been decided upon, European Team Championships and Matches of international character.

(d) To decide and publish the Calendar dates of the Open and Amateur Championships and Matches.

Golf Club Stewards' Association

The Golf Club Stewards' Association was founded as early as 1912. Its members are Stewards in Golf Clubs throughout the UK and Eire. It has a National Committee and Regional Branches in the South, North-West, Midlands, East Anglia, Yorkshire, Wales and the West, North-East Scotland and Ireland. The objects of the Association are to promote the interests of members; to administer a Benevolent Fund for members in need and to arrange golf competitions and matches. It also serves as an Agency for the employment of Stewards in Golf Clubs.

Addresses of British and Overseas Golfing Organisations

United Kingdom

National

Amateur Golf Championship
Sec, MF Bonallack, OBE, Royal & Ancient Golf Club, St Andrews. *Tel* (0334) 72112 *Fax* (0334) 77580.

Artisan Golfers' Association
Hon Sec, A Everett, 51 Rose Hill, Park West, Sutton, Surrey. *Tel* 081-644 7037.

Association of Golf Club Secretaries
Sec, Ray Burniston, 7a Beaconsfield Road, Weston-super-Mare, BS23 1YE. *Tel* (0934) 641166.

Association of Public Golf Courses
Sec, AK Witte, 35 Sinclair Grove, Golders Green, London NW11 9JH. *Tel* 081-458 5433.

Boys' Amateur Golf Championship
Sec, MF Bonallack, OBE, Royal & Ancient Golf Club, St Andrews.

British Association of Golf Course Architects
Hon Sec & Treas, MG Hawtree, 5 Oxford Street, Woodstock, Oxford OX7 1TQ. *Tel* (0993) 811976.

British Association of Golf Course Constructors
Howard Swan, Telford Farm, Willingale, Ongar, Essex CM5 0QF. *Tel* (0277) 896229 *Fax* (0245) 491620.

British & International Golf Greenkeepers' Association
Exec Dir, Neil Thomas BA *Educ Officer*, David Golding, Aldwark Manor, Aldwark, Alne, York Y06 2NF. *Tel* (03473) 581/2 *Fax* (03473) 8864.

Regional Administrators
Scottish Region Mr C Kennedy, 82 Dumbreck Road, Glasgow, G41 9DW. *Tel* 041-427 4701 (*home*), 041-427 4242 (*office*).

Northern Region Mr D Hannam, 12 Moorfield Avenue, Menston, Nr Ilkley, W Yorks LS29 6HB. *Tel* (0943) 72008.

Midland & North Wales Mr A Phipps-Jones, 1 Devonshire Place, Priors Park, Tewkesbury, Glos GL20 5ES. *Tel* (0684) 295405 (*club*), (0684) 850129 (*home*).

South East Region Mr N Exley, 1 The Farmhouse, Hills Lane, Northwood, Middx HA6 2QL. *Tel* (09274) 25329 (*club*), (09274) 24737 (*home*).

South West & South Wales Region Mr G Child, Archways, Churston Road, Churston Ferrers, South Devon. *Tel* (0803) 845274, (0803) 844056 (*home*).

British Left-Handed Golfers' Society
Hon Sec, AC Kirkland, Squirrel Cottage, Mereheath Lane, Knutsford, Cheshire. *Tel* (0565) 4671.

Council of National Golf Unions
Hon Sec, Alan Thirlwell, Formby GC, Golf Road, Formby, Liverpool L37 1LQ. *Tel* (070 48) 72164.

Golf Club Stewards' Association
Sec, G Shaw, 50 The Park, St Albans, Herts. *Tel* (0727) 57334.

Chairman, Roger Gregory, Southwick Park Golf Club, Southwick Park, Fareham, Hants. *Tel* (0705) 380131.

Special Events, DJ Lithgow, Great Barr Golf Club, Chapel Lane, Great Barr, Birmingham B43 7BA. *Tel* 021-357 1232.

Regional Secretaries
South Roy Martin, Edward Court Hotel, Wokingham, Berks. *Tel* (0734) 775886.

Midlands Carol Reay, Robin Hood Golf Club. *Tel* 021-706 0159.

North East B Duncan, Whitburn Golf Club, Lizard Lane, Tyne & Wear. *Tel* (0783) 292144.

Yorkshire K Millington, Whitby Golf Club. *Tel* (0947) 601632/602768.

Wales & West C Hursey, Hockley Golf Club, Winchester, Hants. *Tel* (0962) 714572.

Golf Foundation
Dir Miss Lesley Attwood, 57 London Road, Enfield, Middx EN2 6DU. *Tel* 081-367 4404.

Golf Society of Great Britain
Mrs EJ Drummond, Southview, Warren Road, Thurlestone, Devon TQ7 3NT. *Tel* (0548) 560630.

Hill Samuel School Foursomes
Competition Hon Sec, GR Scott, Yew Tree Cottage, 93 Wells Road, Malvern, Worcs WR14 4PB. *Tel* (0684) 565605.

Hole in One Golf Society
Sec, EW Parker, 1 Vigilant Way, Gravesend, Kent. *Tel* (0474) 534298.

Ladies' Golf Union
Administrator, Mrs Alma Robertson, The Scores, St Andrews, Fife KY16 9AT. *Tel* (0334) 75811.

The Society of One-Armed Golfers
Hon Sec, Don Reid, 11 Coldwell Lane, Felling, Tyne & Wear NE10 9EX. *Tel* 091-469 4742.

The Professional Golfers' Association
Exec Dir, J Lindsey, National Headquarters, Apollo House, The Belfry, Sutton Coldfield, West Midlands, B76 9PT. *Tel* (0675) 70333 *Telex* 338481 (PGA G) *Fax* (0675) 70674.

Scottish Region *Sec,* Sandy Jones, Glenbervie Golf Club, Stirling Road, Larbert FK5 4SJ. *Tel* (0324) 562451.

Irish Region *Sec,* Michael McCumiskey, Dundalk Golf Club, Blackrock, Dundalk, Co Louth, Eire. *Tel* (010 353) 4221193/7 *Fax* (010 353) 4221899.

North Region Headquarters, *Sec,* Norman Fletcher, No 2 Cottage, Bolton Golf Club, Lostock Park, Chorley New Road, Bolton, Lancs BL6 4AJ. *Tel* (0204) 496137/8 *Fax* (0204) 47959.

West Region *Sec,* Bill Morton, Exeter Golf and Country Club, Topsham Road, Countess Wear, Exeter, Devon EX2 7AE. *Tel* (0392) 877657 *Fax* (0392) 876382.

Midland Region *Sec,* Ronald Smith, PGA National Headquarters, The Shirlaw Suite, King's Norton Golf Club, Brockhill Lane, Weatheroak, Nr Alvechurch, Worcs. *Tel* (0564) 824909. *Fax* (0564) 822805

South Region *Sec,* Jeremy Kilby, Merrist Wood House, Worplesdon, Guildford, Surrey GU3 3PE. *Tel* (0483) 233411. *Fax* (0483) 236584.

East Region *Sec,* David Wright, John O'Gaunt Golf Club, Sutton Park, Sandy, Biggleswade, Beds SG19 2LY. *Tel* (0767) 261888.

PGA European Tour
Executive Director, KD Schofield, PGA European Tour, The Wentworth Club, Wentworth Drive, Virginia Water, Surrey GU25 4LS. *Tel* (0344) 842881 *Fax* (0344) 842929.

Women Professional Golfers' European Tour
Exec Dir, Joe Flanagan, The Tytherington Club, Macclesfield, Cheshire SK10 2JP. *Tel* (0625) 611444.

Public Schools' Old Boys' Golf Association
Jt Secs, P de Pinna, Bruins, Wythwood, Haywards Heath, West Sussex. *Tel (home)* (0444) 454883 *(office)* 071-929 0811 and JBM Urry, Dormers, 232 Dickens Heath Road, Shirley, Solihull, West Midlands. *Tel (home)* (0564) 823114, *(office)* 021-328 5665.

Public Schools' Golfing Society
Hon Sec, JNS Lowe, Flushing House, Church Road, Great Bookham, Surrey KT23 3JT. *Tel* (0372) 58651.

Seniors' Championship
Sec, MF Bonallack, OBE, Royal & Ancient Golf Club, St Andrews.

Senior Golfers' Society
Sec, Brigadier D Ross, CBE, Milland Farmhouse, Liphook, Hants GU30 7JP. *Tel* (042 876) 200.

Sports Turf Research Institute
Bingley, West Yorks BD16 1AU. *Tel* (0274) 565131 *Fax* (0274) 561 891.

Youths' Amateur Golf Championship
Sec, MF Bonallack, OBE, Royal & Ancient Golf Club, St Andrews.

England

Bedfordshire County Golf Union
Hon Sec, CLE Spurr, 8 Gainsborough Avenue, St Albans, Herts AL1 4NL. *Tel* (0727) 57834.

Bedfordshire Ladies' County Golf Association
Hon Sec, Mrs M Clark, 3 Sherbourne Avenue, Luton, Beds LU2 7BB. *Tel* (0582) 575883.

Berks, Bucks and Oxon Union of Golf Clubs
Sec, R Stewart, Leyacre, Lodersfield, Lechlade, Glos GL7 3DJ. *Tel* (0637) 52926.

Berks, Bucks and Oxon Golfers Alliance
Hon Sec, Monica Green, Wayside, Aylesbury Road, Monks Risborough, Aylesbury, Bucks.

Berkshire Ladies' County Golf Association
Hon Sec, Mrs BE Baird, 11 Lynton Green, College Road, Maidenhead, Berks SL6 6AN. Tel (0628) 21462.

Buckinghamshire Ladies' County Golf Association
Hon Sec, Mrs S Tunstall, Springfield Bungalow, Butlers Cross, Aylesbury, Bucks. Tel (0296) 624375.

Cambridgeshire Area Golf Union
Sec, RAC Blows, 2a Dukes Meadow, Stapleford, Cambs CB2 5BH. Tel (0223) 842062.

Cambs and Hunts Ladies' County Golf Association
Hon Sec, Mrs A Guy, The Paddock, 14 Mingle Lane, Stapleford, Cambs. CB2 5BG. Tel (0223) 843267.

Channel Islands Ladies' GA
Hon Sec, Mrs JMT Willis, Oakenbirch, Park Estate, St Brelade, Jersey. Tel (0534) 42072.

Cheshire County Ladies' Golf Association
Hon Sec, Mrs B Walker, 12 Higher Downs, Knutsford, Cheshire WA16 8AW.

Cheshire PGA
Tournament Director, Keith Brain, The Virgate, Abbey Way, Hartford, Northwich, Cheshire CW8 1LY.

Cheshire Union of Golf Clubs
Hon Sec, BC Jones, 4 Curzon Mews, Wilmslow, Cheshire SK9 5JN. Tel (0625) 532866.

Cornwall Golf Union
Hon Sec, JG Rowe, 8 Lydcott Crescent, Widegates, Looe, Cornwall PL13 1QG. Tel (05034) 492.

Cornwall Ladies' County Golf Association
Hon Sec, Mrs A Eddy, Penmester, Hain Walk, St Ives, Cornwall. Tel (0736) 795392.

Cumbria Ladies' County Golf Association
Hon Sec, Mrs T Turner, Cawdor, Garth Heads Road, Appleby, Cumbria CA16 6UD. Tel (07683) 51672.

Cumbria Union of Golf Clubs
Hon Sec, T Edmondson, Thorn Lea, Lazonby, Penrith, Cumbria. Tel (0768) 83231.

Derbyshire Alliance
Hon Sec, R Reid, c/o Buxton & High Peak GC, Fairfield, Buxton, Derbyshire. Tel (0298) 3112.

Derbyshire Ladies' County Golf Association
Hon Sec, Mrs D Cartledge, 11 Pine Close, Smalley, Derbyshire DE7 6EH. Tel (0332) 880929.

Derbyshire PGA
Sec, Mr M Ronan, Erewash Valley Golf Club, Stanton-by-Dale, Nr Ilkeston, Derby. Tel (0602) 324667.

Derbyshire Union of Golf Clubs
Hon Sec, CF Ibbotson, 67 Portland Close, Mickleover, Derby DE3 5BR. Tel (0332) 512465.

Devon County Golf Union
Hon Sec, J Marshall, Appledowne, Keyberry Park, Newton Abbot, Devon TQ12 1DF. Tel (0626) 52999.

Devon County Ladies' Golf Association
Hon Sec, Lady M Beauchamp, The White House, Harpford, Nr Sidmouth, Devon EX10 0NJ.

Devon Professional Golfers' Alliance
Hon Sec, Michael J Dunk, Sunhaven, 2 Landscore Close, Crediton, Devon. Tel (036 32) 3145.

Dorset County Golf Union
Hon Sec, Lt Col MD Hutchins, 38 Carlton Road, Bournemouth BH1 3TG. Tel (0202) 290821.

Dorset Ladies' County Golf Association
Miss JM Rhodes, 4 Egdon Glen Crossways, Dorchester, Dorset DT2 8BQ. Tel (0305) 852547.

Durham County Golf Union
Hon Sec, WP Murray, Highnam Lodge, Park Mews, Hartlepool, Cleveland TS26 0DX. Tel (0429) 273185.

Durham County Ladies' Golf Association
Sec, Mrs CF Anderson, 107 Harlsey Road, Hartburn, Stockton-on-Tees.

English Golf Union
Sec, K Wright, 1–3 Upper King Street, Leicester LE1 6XF. Tel (0533) 553042 Fax (0533) 471322.

Midland Group Sec, RJW Baldwin, Chantry Cottage, Friar Street, Droitwich, Worcs WR9 8EQ. Tel (0905) 778560.

Northern Group Hon Sec, EG Bunting, 7 Northbrook Court, Hartlepool, Cleveland TS26 0DJ. Tel (0429) 274828.

South Eastern Group Hon Sec, MA Hobson, 22 Wye Court, Malvern Way, Ealing, London W13 8EA. Tel 081-997 7466.

South Western Group Sec, JT Lumley, Hartland, Potterne, Devizes, Wilts SN10 5PA. Tel (0380) 3935.

English Ladies' Golf Association
Sec, Mrs MJ Carr, Edgbaston Golf Club, Church Road, Birmingham B15 3TB. Tel 021-456 2088.

Northern Division Hon Sec, Mrs L Young, 10 Cleehill Drive, North Shields, Tyne & Weir NE29 9EW. Tel 091-257 6925.

Midlands Division Hon Sec, Mrs C Stevenson, 3 Leaholme Gardens, Pedmore, Stourbridge, West Midlands DY9 0XX. Tel (0562) 884582.

South-Eastern Division *Hon Sec,* Mrs E Block, 71 Parkanaur Avenue, Thorpe Bay, Essex SS1 3JA. *Tel* (0702) 588336.

South-Western Division *Hon Sec,* Mrs VJ Wilde, 19 Ferndown Close, Kingsweston, Bristol. *Tel* (0272) 683543.

English Schools' Golf Association
Hon Sec, R Snell, 20 Dykenook Close, Whickham, Newcastle-upon-Tyne. *Tel* 091-488 3538.

Essex County Amateur Golf Union
Hon Sec, EV Sadler, 9 Willow Walk, Hadleigh, Benfleet, Essex SS7 2RW. *Tel* (0702) 559871.

Essex Ladies' County Golf Association
Hon Sec, Mrs J Bourne, 1 The Paddocks, Stock, Essex. *Tel* (0277) 810466.

Gloucestershire and Somerset Professional Golfers' Association
Sec, Noel Boland, Cotswold Hills GC. *Tel* (0242) 515263.

Gloucestershire Golf Union
Hon Sec, RF Crisp, 2 Hartley Close, Sandy Lane, Charlton Kings, Cheltenham GL53 9DN. *Tel* (0242) 514024.

Gloucester Ladies' County Golf Association
Hon Sec, Mrs L Williams, 1 Avon Crescent, Cumberland Road, Bristol BS1 6XQ. *Tel* (0272) 264606.

Hampshire Ladies' County Golf Association
Hon Sec, Mrs E Buckley, 182 Bassett Green Road, Southampton, Hants SO2 3LW. *Tel* (0703) 789273.

Hampshire, Isle of Wight and Channel Islands Golf Union
Hon Sec/Treas, JLS McCracken, *Glyngarth,* Tower Road, Hindhead, Surrey GU26 6SL. *Tel* (042 873) 4090.

Hampshire Professional Golfers' Association
Sec, Chris Maltby, 3 Lily Close, Kempshott Down, Basingstoke, Hants RG22 5NT. *Tel* (0256) 466070.

Herts County Professional Golfers' Alliance
Hon Sec, RA Gurney, 1 Field Lane, Letchworth, Herts SG6 3LF. *Tel* (0462) 682256.

Hertfordshire County Ladies' Golf Association
Hon Sec, Mrs EM Copley, 22 The Avenue, Radlett, Herts WD7 7DW. *Tel* (0923) 857184.

Hertfordshire Golf Union
Hon Sec, WA de Podesta, 2 The Heath, Radlett, Herts WD7 7DF. *Tel* (0923) 857184.

Isle of Man Golf Union
Hon Sec, GR Hotchkiss, 22 Mount View Road, Onchan, Isle of Man. *Tel* (0624) 622991.

Isle of Wight Ladies' Golf Association
Hon Sec, Mrs J Kirkham, *Roskilling,* Solent View Road, Seaview, Isle of Wight PO34 5HY. *Tel* (0983) 613256.

Kent County Golf Union
Hon Sec, BM Evans, 52 Queens Road, Littlestone, New Romney, Kent TN28 8LY. *Tel* (0679) 63613.

Kent County Ladies' Golf Association
Hon Sec, Mrs D Hall-Thompson, Colleton House, North Road, Hythe, Kent CT21 4AS. *Tel* (0303) 66285.

Kent Professional Golfers' Union
Sec, E Impett, 20 The Grove, Barnham, Kent. *Tel* (0227) 831655.

Lancashire Ladies' County Golf Association
Hon Sec, Miss P Hurst, 25 Park Road, Golborne, Warrington, Cheshire WA3 3PU.

Lancashire PGA
Sec, George Hill, 32 Pembridge Road, Blackley, Manchester M9 2LE. *Tel* 061-795 8547.

Lancashire Union of Golf Clubs
Sec, N Hardman, 4 Cedarwood Close, Lytham Hall Park, Lytham, Lancs FY8 4PD. *Tel* (0253) 733323.

Leicestershire and Rutland Ladies' County Golf Association
Hon Sec, Mrs DL Sabey, 4 Bailey's Lane, Burton Overy, Leics LE8 ODD. *Tel* (053759) 2697.

Leicestershire and Rutland Golf Union
Hon Sec, GH Upward, 187 Leicester Road, Groby, Leicester. *Tel* (0533) 873675.

Leicestershire Professional Golfers' Association
Sec, Mr D Freeman, 218 Hamilton Lane, Scraptoft, Leics. *Tel* (0533) 414735.

Lincolnshire Ladies' County Association
Hon Sec, Mrs M Johns, 85 South Parade, Boston, Lincs PE21 7PN. *Tel* (0205) 69948.

Lincolnshire Professional Golfers' Association
Sec, Robin Lawie, Seacroft GC, Skegness, Lincs. *Tel* (0754) 3020.

Lincolnshire Union of Golf Clubs
Hon Sec, TJ Hale *Dapselah,* Allenby Cres., Fotherby, Nr Louth LN11 0UJ. *Tel* (0507) 604298.

Middlesex County Golf Union
Hon Sec, PSV Cooke, 36 Grants Close, Mill Hill, London NW7 1DD. *Tel* 081-349 0414.

Middlesex Ladies' County Golf Association
Hon Sec, Mrs C Hume, 62 Church Crescent, London N3 1BJ.

Middlesex Professional Golfers' Association
Chmn, L Fickling, Enfield Golf Club, Old Park Road, Southwindmill Hill, Enfield, Middx. *Tel* 081-366 4492.

Midland Golf Union
Hon Sec, RJW Baldwin, Chantry Cottage, Friar Street, Droitwich, Worcs WR9 8EQ. *Tel* (0905) 778560.

Norfolk County Golf Union
Hon Sec/Treas, RJ Trower, 12a Stanley Avenue, Thorpe, Norwich, Norfolk. *Tel* (0603) 31026.

Norfolk Ladies' County Association
Hon Sec, Mrs VM Munro, 17 Taylor Avenue, Cringleford, Norfolk NR4 6XY. *Tel* (0603) 56049.

Norfolk PGA
Hon Sec, M Garrett, Sheringham GC, Sheringham, Norfolk. *Tel* (0263) 823488.

North East and North West PGA
Sec Ray Sentance, 7 Larch Lea, Ponteland, Newcastle upon Tyne NE20 9LG. *Tel* (0661) 25151.

Northamptonshire Golf Union
Joint Hon Secs, RG Halliday and TCA Knight, c/o 12 Edge Hill Road, Duston, Northampton NN5 6BY. *Tel* (0604) 51031.

Northamptonshire Ladies' County Golf Association
Hon Sec, Mrs MML Coker, 534 Wellingborough Road, Northampton NN3 3HZ. *Tel* (0604) 409298.

Northamptonshire PGA
Hon Sec, G Mobbs, Ivycroft, Back Lane, Chapel Brampton, Northants. *Tel* (0605) 843305.

Northumberland Ladies' County Golf Association
Hon Sec, Mrs M Canning, 23 Mast Lane, Cullercoats, North Shields NE30 3DF. *Tel* 091-252 5382.

Northumberland Union of Golf Clubs
Hon Sec, WE Procter, 5 Oakhurst Drive, Kenton Park, Gosforth, Newcastle-upon-Tyne NE3 4JS. *Tel* 091-285 4981 *(home)*, 091-274 5310 *(office)*.

Nottinghamshire County Ladies' Golf Association
Hon Sec, Mrs B Jackson, Cranmer Lodge, Main Street, Kinoulton, Notts, NA12 3EL. *Tel* (0949) 81201.

Nottinghamshire PGA
Sec, RW Futer, 52 Barden Road, Mapperley, Nottingham NG3 5QD. *Tel* (0602) 269635.

Nottinghamshire Union of Golf Clubs
Hon Sec, E Peters, 48 Weaverthorpe Road, Woodthorp, Notts NG5 4NB. *Tel* (0602) 266560.

Oxfordshire Ladies' County Golf Association
Hon Sec, Miss BM Nicklin, 532 Banbury Road, Oxford OX2 8EG. *Tel* (0865) 58300.

Sheffield PGA
Sec, Graham Walker, Hillsborough GC, Worrall Road, Sheffield S6 4BE. *Tel* (0742) 332666.

Sheffield Union of Golf Clubs
Sec, JHV Wheeler, 8 Newfield Court, 586 Fulwood Road, Sheffield S10 3QE.

Shropshire and Herefordshire Union of Golf Clubs
Hon Sec, JR Davies, 23 Poplar Crescent, Bayston Hill, Shrewsbury SY3 0QB. *Tel* (0743) 722655.

Shropshire and Herefordshire PGA
Sec, Mr P Hinton, Bridgnorth Golf Club, Stanley Lane, Bridgnorth, Shropshire. *Tel* (07462) 2045.

Shropshire Ladies' County Golf Association
Hon Sec, Mrs O Higgs, 122 Fieldhouse Drive, Muxton, Telford, Shropshire TF8 8BB. *Tel* (0952) 604522.

Somerset Golf Union
Hon Sec, GC Bacon, Longwood, Grange Road, Saltford, Bristol BS18 3AG. *Tel* (0225) 872166.

Somerset Ladies' County Golf Association
Hon Sec, T Richards, *Tresawsen*, Mill Lane, Corfe, Taunton TA3 7AH.

South-Western Counties Golf Association
Hon Sec/Treas, JT Lumley, Hartland, Potterne, Devizes, Wilts SN10 5PA. *Tel* (0380) 3935.

Staffordshire Ladies' County Golf Association
Hon Sec, Mrs DB Banks, 11 Westhill, Finchfield Hill, Wolverhampton WV3 9HL. *Tel* (0902) 753279.

Staffordshire and Shropshire Union of Professional Golfers
Sec, E Griffiths, 22 Wynn Road, Penn, Wolverhampton. *Tel* (0902) 332180 *(home)*.

Staffordshire Union of Golf Clubs
Hon Sec, A Smith, 19 Broadway, Walsall, W Midlands WS1 3EX. *Tel* (0922) 24988.

Suffolk County Golf Union
Hon Sec, J Cook, 2 Barton Road, Felixstowe, Suffolk IPU 7JH. *Tel* (0394) 286429.

Suffolk Ladies' County Golf Association
Hon Sec, Miss A Seward, 20 Meadowside, Snowdon Hill, Wickham Market, Woodbridge, Suffolk. *Tel* (0728) 747609.

Suffolk PGA
Sec, Mark Jillings, Bury St Edmunds GC,
Fornham All Saints, Bury St Edmunds, Suffolk
IP28 2LG. *Tel* (0284) 755978.

Surrey County Golf Union
Hon Sec, MW Ashton, Rushmoor Cottage,
Rushmoor Close, Fleet, Hants GU13 9LD. *Tel*
(0252) 614078.

Surrey Ladies' County Golf Association
Hon Sec, Mrs DL Hall, *Chestnut Bend,* Grub
Street, Limpsfield, Surrey RH8 0SH. *Tel* (0883)
723163.

Surrey PGA
Sec, P Bowles, 27 Lower Wood Road,
Claygate, Surrey KT10 0EU.
Tel (0372) 63882.

Sussex County Golf Union
DG Pulford, 12 Rodmell Avenue, Saltdean,
Brighton, E Sussex BN2 8LT. *Tel* (0273) 304415.

Sussex County Ladies' Golf Association
Hon Sec, Mrs FR Milton, Flat 1, 22 Granville
Road, Eastbourne, East Sussex BN20 7HA. *Tel*
(0323) 28452.

Sussex Professional Golfers' Union
Sec, C Pluck, 96 Cranston Avenue, Bexhill-on-
Sea, Sussex. *Tel* (0424) 221298.

**Warwickshire Ladies' County Golf
Association**
Hon Sec, Mrs J Plant, 57 White House Green,
Solihull, W Midlands B91 1SP. *Tel* 021-705 8062.

**Warwickshire Professional Golfers'
Association**
Sec, J Tunnicliffe, 5 Church Lane, Stoneleigh,
Warwickshire. *Tel* (0203) 418113.

Warwickshire Union of Golf Clubs
Hon Sec, JBM Urry, Dormers, 232 Dickens Heath
Road, Shirley, Solihull B90 1QQ. *Tel* (0564)
823114 *(home);* 021-328 5665. *(office)*

Wiltshire County Golf Union
Hon Sec/Treas, RF Buthlay, 10 Priory Park,
Bradford-on-Avon, Wilts. BA15 1QU. *Tel* (022 16)
6401.

**Wiltshire Ladies' County Golf
Association**
Hon Sec, Mrs P Board, South Lodge, Northleigh,
Bradford-on Avon, Wilts. *Tel* (02216) 3387.

Wiltshire PGA
L Ross, Professional, Marlborough GC, The
Common, Marlborough, Wilts. *Tel* (0672) 512493.

**Worcestershire Association of
Professional Golfers**
Sec, Chris Thompson, Droitwich GC, Ford Lane,
Droitwich WR9 0BH, Worcs. *Tel* (0905) 770207.

**Worcestershire County Ladies' Golf
Association**
Hon Sec, S Smith, 12 Russell Road,
Kidderminster, Worcs. DY10 3HT.

Worcestershire Union of Golf Clubs
Hon Sec, WR Painter, 70 Cardinal Drive,
Kidderminster, Worcs DY10 4RY. *Tel* (0562)
823109.

**Yorkshire Ladies' County Golf
Association**
Hon Sec, Mrs M Elliott, Ingle Court, Lepton,
Huddersfield, Yorks. *Tel* (0484) 602011.

**Yorkshire Professional Golfers'
Association**
Sec, Jim Pape, 1 Summerhill Gardens, Leeds,
Yorks LS8 2EL. *Tel* (0532) 664746.

Yorkshire Union of Golf Clubs
Hon Sec, Alan Cowman, 50 Bingley Road,
Bradford, West Yorks BD9 6HH.
Tel (0274) 542661.

Ireland

Irish Golf Union
Sec, Ivan ER Dickson, Glencar House, 81
Eglington Road, Donnybrook, Dublin 4.
Tel (0001) 694111.

Ulster Branch *Sec,* Alfred Collis, MBE, 58a High
Street, Holywood, Co Down, BT18 9AE. *Tel*
Holywood 7427 *(home),* Holywood 3708 *(office).*

Leinster Branch *Sec,* Ken Haughton,
1 Clonskeagh Square, Clonskeagh Road,
Dublin 14. *Tel* (0001) 696977/696727.

Munster Branch *Hon Sec,* Richard Barry,
Sunville, Dromsligo, Mallow, Co Cork.
Tel (22) 21117/221123 *(office),* (22) 22760
(home).

Connacht Branch *Hon Sec,* Tom Greally,
Abbey Hotel, Roscommon.
Tel Roscommon 26240 *(home)* .

Irish Ladies' Golf Union
Sec, Miss MP Turvey, 1 Clonskeagh Square,
Clonskeagh Road, Dublin 14. *Tel* (0001) 696244.

Northern District *Hon Sec,* Mrs L Watson,
14D Adelaide Park, Belfast BT9 6FX.
Tel (0232) 682152.

Southern District *Hon Sec,* Mrs N Flynn,
11 Barnstead Drive, Church Road, Blackrock,
Cork. *Tel* Cork (21) 291698.

Eastern District *Hon Sec,* Mrs D O'Sullivan, 4
Castletown Court, Celbridge, Co. Kildare.

Western District *Hon Sec,* Mrs A Bradshaw, Dooney Rock, Cleveragh Drive, Sligo. *Tel* Sligo (71) 62351.

Midland District *Hon Sec,* Mrs B Jordan, 6 Glena Terrace, Spawell Road, Wexford. *Tel* Wexford (53) 22865.

Scotland

Aberdeen Ladies' County Golf Association
Hon Sec, Mrs SAH Bain, 9 Earlswell Place, Cults, Aberdeen AB1 9LG. *Tel* (0224) 861502.

Angus Ladies' County Golf Association
Hon Sec, Mrs DJ Gordon, The Hawthorns, 7 Grange Avenue, Monifieth, Dundee. *Tel* (0382) 532799.

Ayrshire Ladies' County Golf Association
Hon Sec, Mrs A McMillan, 8 Station Road, Prestwick KA9 1AQ. *Tel* (0292) 77330.

Border Counties' Ladies Golf Association
Hon Sec, Mrs E Wanless, Fullarton, Darnick, Melrose, Roxburghshire. *Tel* (089682) 2962.

Dumfriesshire Ladies' County Golf Association
Hon Sec, Miss MJ Greig, Strathdon, 10 Nelson Street, Dumfries. *Tel* (0387) 54429.

Dunbartonshire and Argyll Ladies' County Association
Hon Sec, Mrs M Gibson, 49 Ledi Drive, Bearsden, Glasgow G61 4JN. *Tel* 041-942 4328.

East Lothian Ladies' County Association
Hon Sec, Mrs IG Campbell, Glenlair, Main Street, Gullane. *Tel* (0620) 842534.

Fife County Ladies' Golf Association
Hon Sec, Mrs CH Matheson, Greyfriars, Greyfriars Garden, St Andrews. *Tel* (0334) 72639.

Galloway Ladies' County Golf Association
Hon Sec, Mrs Y Gordon, 3 Seggies, Kirkcudbright. *Tel* (0557) 30542.

Lanarkshire Ladies' County Golf Association
Hon Sec, Mrs GE Duncanson, 75 Kenmure Gardens, Bishopbriggs, Glasgow G64 2BZ. *Tel* 041-772 1720.

Midlothian County Ladies' Golf Association
Hon Sec, Mrs K MacKay, 37 Thomson Drive, Currie, Midlothian EH14 5EY. *Tel* 031-449 3441.

Northern Counties' Ladies Golf Association
Hon Sec, Miss R Cameron, Sounion, Sanquhar Terrace, Forres. *Tel* (0309) 72148.

Perth and Kinross Ladies' County Golf Association
Hon Sec, J Jones, Broom, Caledonian Crescent, Auchterarder, Perthshire. *Tel* (0764) 62254.

Renfrewshire Ladies' County Golf Association
Hon Sec, Miss MA Stewart, 21 Holmhead Road, Glasgow G44 3AS. *Tel* 041-637 1307.

Stirling and Clackmannan Ladies' Golf Association
Sec, Mrs JC Williamson, 7 Craighorn Drive, Falkirk FK1 5NX. *Tel* (0324) 29672.

Scottish Golf Union
Sec, JW Hume, The Cottage, 181a Whitehouse Road, Barnton, Edinburgh EH4 6BY. *Tel* 031-339 7546.

Area Associations:
Angus G Hardie, Conachan, 4 Cliffburn Road, Arbroath, Angus DD11 5BB. *Tel* (0241) 73018 *(home).*

Argyll and Bute *Hon Sec,* DG Smith, 120 Auchamore Road, Dunoon, Argyll PA23 7JJ.

Ayrshire RL Crawford, 14 Maxwell Gardens, Hurlford, Kilmarnock, Ayrshire KA1 5BY. *Tel* (0563) 31932 *(home),* (0563) 21190 *(office).*

Borders *Hon Sec,* RG Scott, *Buckholmburn House,* Edinburgh Road, Galashiels TD1 2EY. *Tel* (0896) 2697.

Clackmannanshire Tom Allan, 19 Duke Street, Alva, Clackmannanshire.

Dunbartonshire RW Jenkins, Dunedin, 14 Hawthorn Avenue, Lenzie G66 4RA. *Tel* 041-776 1148.

Fife BR Wright, 2 West Fergus Place, Kirkcaldy, Fife KY1 1UR. *Tel* (0592) 263304 *(home),* (0592) 206605 *(office).*

Glasgow GO McInnes, 4 Dalziel Court, 56 Dalziel Drive, Glasgow G41. *Tel* 041-427 3156 *(home),* 041-226 4471 *(office).*

Lanarkshire JT Durrant, 30 Woodlands Crescent, Bothwell, Glasgow G71 8PP. *Tel* (0698) 852331.

Lothians IR Graham, 29 Morningside Grove, Edinburgh EH10 5PX. *Tel* 031-447 3281.

North JP Ford, Timbertop, Croy, Inverness IV1 2PH. *Tel* (066 78) 363.

North-East IAD McPherson, Cruden Bay Golf Club, Cruden Bay, Peterhead, AB4 7NN. *Tel* (0779) 812395 *(home),* (0779) 812285 *(office).*

Perth and Kinross DY Rae, 18 Carlownie Place, Auchterarder PH3 1BT. *Tel* (0764) 62837.

Renfrewshire JI McCosh, *Muirfield*, 20 Williamson Place, Johnstone, Renfrewshire PA5 9DU. *Tel* (0505) 27974 *(home)*.

South JH Somerville, Cherry Cottage, Kirkcudbright. *Tel* (0557) 30445.

Stirlingshire RM McLaren, 2 Ochil Crescent, Auchterarder PH3 1NA. *Tel* (0764) 62167.

Scottish Golfer's Alliance
Sec/Treas, Mrs MA Caldwell, 5 Deveron Avenue, Giffnock, Glasgow G48 6NH.

Scottish Ladies' Golfing Association
Sec, Mrs ML Park, Chacewood, 49 Fullarton Drive, Troon KA10 6LF. *Tel* (0292) 313047.

Scottish Ladies' Golfing Association—County Golf
Hon Sec, Miss MJ Greig, Strathdon, Nelson Street, Dumfries. *Tel* (0387) 54429.

Scottish Schools' Golf Association
Hon Sec, Mr Edward Dixon, History Dept, Grangemouth High School, Grangemouth, Central Region.

West of Scotland Girls' Golfing Association
Hon Sec, Mrs PI McKay, 7 Gardenside Avenue, Uddingston, Glasgow G71 7BU.

Wales

Anglesey Golf Union
Hon Sec, GP Jones, 20 Gwelfor Estate, Cemaes Bay, Anglesey. *Tel* (0407) 710755.

Brecon and Radnor Golf Union
Hon Sec GL Williams, 10 Penpentre, Llanfaes, Brecon.

Caernarvonshire and Anglesey Ladies' County Golf Association
Hon Sec, Mrs BR Williams, Deunant, Llangefni, Anglesey LL7 7YP. *Tel* (0248) 722338.

Caernarvonshire and District Golfing Union
Hon Sec, R Eric Jones, 23 Bryn Rhos, Rhosbodrual, Caernarfon, Gwynedd LL55 2BT. *Tel* (0286) 3486.

Denbighshire Golfing Union
Hon Sec, J. Johnson, 15 Ffordd Elfed, Wrexham, Clwyd.

Denbighshire and Flintshire Ladies' County Golf Association
Sec, Mrs Nan Evans, *Gwendor,* 11 Berse Road, Wrexham, Clwyd LL11 2BH. *Tel* (0978) 755773.

Dyfed Golfing Union
Hon Sec, JR Jones, 55 Clover Park, Haverfordwest, Dyfed.

Flintshire Golfing Union
Hon Sec, H Griffith, Cornist Lodge, Cornist Park, Flint, Clwyd. *Tel* (03526) 2186.

Glamorgan County Golf Union
Hon Sec, John Banfill, 332 North Road, Cardiff. *Tel* (0222) 628493.

Glamorgan Ladies' County Golf Association
Mrs S Williams, 19 Trem-y-Don, Barry, South Glamorgan. *Tel* (0446) 734865.

Gwent Golf Union
Sec, CM Buckley, 3 Oak Court, Woodfield Park, Blackwood, Gwent. *Tel* (0495) 223520.

Mid Wales Ladies' County Golf Association
Sec, Miss A James, Ael-y-Bryn, Pontfaen Road, Lampeter, Dyfed. *Tel* (0570) 422463.

Monmouthshire Ladies' County Golf Association
Hon Sec, Mrs Ruth Morris, Flat 2, 405 Chepstow Road, Newport, Gwent. *Tel* (0633) 279638.

North Wales PGA
Sec, Peter Bright, Porthmadog Golf Club, Morfa Bycham, Porthmadog, Gwynedd. *Tel* (0766) 3828.

South Wales Professional Golfers' Association
Hon Sec, B Thomas, St Mellons Golf Club, Mid-Glam. *Tel* (0633) 680101.

Welsh Golfing Union
Sec, DG Lee, *Powys House,* Cwmbran, Gwent NP44 1PB.

Welsh Ladies' Golf Union
Hon Sec, Miss P Roberts, Ysgoldy Gynt, Llanhennock, Newport, Gwent NP6 1LT. *Tel* (0633) 420642.

Overseas

America: USA & Canada

Canadian Ladies' Golf Association
Exec Dir, Leonard Murphy, 1600 James Naismith Drive, Gloucester, Ontario K1B 5N4. *Tel* (613) 748 5642.

Canadian Professional Golfers' Association
General Manager, Robert H Noble, 59 Berkeley Street, Toronto M5A 2W5. *Tel* Toronto (416) 368 6104.

Canadian (Royal) Golf Association
Exec Dir, SD Ross, Golf House, RR no 2, Oakville, Ontario L6J 4Z3.

Provincial Golf Associations
British Columbia *Sec/Treas,* RE Maze, Room 322, 1675 West 8th Ave, Vancouver, BC V6J 1V2.

Alberta *Manager,* ER Wood, 200-H Haddon Road, Calgary, Alberta T2V 2Y6.

Saskatchewan *Exec Dir,* WF Macrae, 2205 Victoria Avenue, Regina, Saskatchewan S4P 0S4.

Manitoba *Exec Dir,* DI Macdonald, 1700 Ellice Ave, Winnipeg, Manitoba R3H 0B1.

Ontario *Exec Dir,* WJ Williams, 400 Esna Park Drive, Unit 11, Markham, Ontario L3R 1H5.

Quebec *Exec Director,* CH Gribbin, 3300 Cavendish Blvd, Suite 250, Montreal, Quebec H4B 2M8.

New Brunswick *Sec/Treas,* EA Trites, 3 Sunset Lane, St John, New Brunswick E2H 1C8.

Nova Scotia *Sec/Treas,* W MacDonald, 14 Limardo Drive, Dartmouth, Nova Scotia B3A 3X4.

Newfoundland–Labrador *Sec,* CR Cook, PO Box 5361, St Johns, Newfoundland.

Prince Edward Island *Sec/Treas,* David Kassner, PO Box 51, Charlottetown, PEI C1A 7K2.

Golf Course Association
111 East Wacker Drive, Chicago, Illinois 60601, USA. *Tel* Chicago (312) 644 6610.

International Golf Association
Exec Dir, Burch Riber, PO Box 176, Glenville Station, Greenwich, CT 06831-0876. *Tel* (203) 531 1113 *Fax* (203) 531 4373.

Ladies Professional Golf Association
Commissioner, Charles S Mechem Jr, 2570 Volusia Avenue, Suite B, Daytona Beach, Florida 32114. *Tel* (904) 254-8800 *Fax* (904) 254-4755.

TPA Tour
(USA), *Commissioner,* Deane R Beman, Sawgrass, Ponte Vedra, Florida 32082.

United States Golf Association
Exec Dir, David B Fay, USGA Golf House, Liberty Corner Road, Far Hills, New Jersey 07931. *Tel* Jersey City (201) 234 2300.

United States Professional Golfers' Association
Chief Executive Officer, John J Rossi, Box 12458, 100 Avenue of the Champions, Palm Beach Gardens, Florida 33418. *Tel* (407) 624 8400.

Central America

Bahamas Golf Federation
Sec, Milford Lockhart, PO Box N4568, Nassau.

Barbados Golf Association
Sec, TM Hanton, c/o Sandy Lane GC, St James.

Bermuda Golf Association
Sec-Treas, Mrs Eric N Parker, PO Box 433, Hamilton 5. *Tel* 809 298 1367.

Jamaica Golf Association
Constant Spring Golf Club, Constant Spring, Kingston 8.

Mexican Golf Association
Cincinnati, No. 40-104, Mexico 18, DF.

Trinidad and Tobago Golf Association
Texaco Trinidad Inc, Point-à-Pierre, Trinidad, West Indies.

South America

Asociación Argentina de Golf
Gen Manager, JT Salorio; *Hon Sec,* Ignacio JR Soba Rojo, Corrientes 538, Piso 11, 1043 Buenos Aires.

Argentine Professional Golfers' Association
Av. Corrientes 538, Piso 11, 1043 Buenos Aires.

Asunción Golf Union
Casilla de Correo 302, Asunciòn, Paraguay.

Bolivian Golf Federation (Federación Boliviana de Golf)
Sec, Raul Zabalaga, Casilla de Correo 6130, La Paz.

Brazilian Golf Confederation
(Confederacão Brasileira de Golf), *Exec Sec,* AE Nardy, Rua 7 de Abril, 282-8°, and - S/83-01044, São Paulo.

Chilean Golf Federation
Casilla 13307, Correo 21, Santiago.

Colombian Golf Union (Federación Colombiana de Golf)
Sec, Boris Sokoloff, Carrer 7A, 72-64 of Int 26 Apartado 90985, Bogotà.

Ecuador Golf Federation (Asociación Equatoriana de Golf)
Casilia 521, Guayaquil.

Guyana Golf Union
c/o Demerara Bauxite Co Limited, Mackenzie.

Paraguay Golf Association
Asunción Golf Union, Casilla de Correo 302, Asunción.

Peru Golf Federation (Federación Peruana de Golf)
Sec, HB Sanchez, Casilla 5637, Lima.

South American Golf Federation
Exec Sec, E Anchordoqui, Avda. Brasil 3025, Piso 50, Montevideo, Uruguay.

Uruguay Golf Association (Asociación Uruguaya de Golf)
Sec, Jorge Brignoni, Casilla de Correo 1484, Montevideo.

Venezuela Golf Federation
Unidad Comercial, *La Florida,* Local 5, Avenida Avila, La Florida, Caracas 1050.

Asia and Far East

Asia-Pacific Golf Confederation
Sec Gen, EJH Yong, 52, 1st Floor, Jalan Hang, Lekiu 50100, Kuala Lumpur.

Asia Professional Golf Circuit
Co-ordinator, John Benda, Asia Golf Circuit Agency, 230 East Foothill Drive, Phoenix, Arizona 85020. *Tel* (602) 395 9384 *Fax* (602) 395 9370.

China Golf Association
Sec Gen, Charles C Chang, 71 Lane 369, Tunhau S Road, Taipei, Taiwan (106).

Ceylon Golf Union
2 Gower Street, Colombo 5, Sri Lanka.

Professional Golfers' Association of the Republic of China
2nd Floor, No. 196 Pei Ling 5th Road, Taipei, Taiwan, R.O.C. *Tel* (02) 8220318/8229684.

Hong Kong Golf Association
Sec, Michael J Steele, Room 110, Yuto Sang Bldg 37, Queens Road, Central, Hong Kong.

Hong Kong Professional Golfers' Association
Hon Sec, AR Hamilton, PO Box 690, Hong Kong. *Tel* Hong Kong (5) 222111. *Telex* HX73751.

Indian Golf Union
Hon Sec, Raj Bir Singh, Tata Centre (3rd Floor), 43 Chowringhee Road, Calcutta 700071.

Indonesian Golf Association
Hon Sec, Soebroto Koesmardjo, c/o Bank Bumi Daya, Jln Imam Bonjol, 61-PO Box 106, Jakarta Pusat.

Japan Golf Association
Sec Gen, Ms A Kato, 606-6th Floor, Palace Building, Marunouchi, Chiyoda-ku, Tokyo, Japan. *Tel* Tokyo (3) 215 0003.

Japan Ladies' Professional Golfers' Association
Kuranae Kogyo Kaikan 7F, Shinbasi 2-19-10, Minato-ku, Tokyo. *Tel* Tokyo (3) 571 0928.

Japan Professional Golf Association
Sec Gen, Kikuo Minakata, Tomin-Ueno Building, 4F, 1-7-15, Higashi-Ueno, Taito-Ku, Tokyo 110.

Korean Golf Association
Sec General, Room 1B, 13th Floor, Manhattan Bldg, 36-2, Yeo-Eui-Do-Dowg, Yeong Deung Po-Ku, Seoul. *Tel* Seoul (2) 783 4748/2783 4749.

Malaysian Golf Association
Hon Sec, Tan Kok Ke, 12A Persiaran Ampang, 55000 Kuala Lumpur.

New Guinea Papua Territory Amateur Golf Association
Sec, Jack Page, PO Box 382, Lae, TPNG.

Pakistan Golf Federation
Hon Sec, Zafar Ahmed, PO Box No. 1295, Rawalpindi. *Telex* PGF/13-A-1V.

Papua New Guinea Ladies' Golf Association
Mrs Mavis Harvey, PO Box 1256, Port Moresby, TPNG. *Tel* 675 214745.

Papua New Guinea Golf Association
Sec, Jack Page, PO Box 382, Lae, Papua New Guinea.

Republic of the Philippines Golf Association
Sec Gen, Benigno M Gopez, 209 Administration Building, Rizal Memorial Sports Complex, Vito Cruz, Manila. *Tel* 632-588845 *Fax* 632-5211587.

Singapore Golf Association
Hon Sec, Gerald Loong, Singapore Golf Association, 4 Battery Rd, No 12-00 Bank of China Building, Singapore 0104. *Telegraphic address* Golfing Singapore; *Telex* RS 42354 Acapas.

Sri Lanka Ladies' Golf Union
c/o Royal Colombo Golf Club, PO Box 309, Colombo.

Sri Lanka Golf Union
2 Gower Street, Colombo 5, Sri Lanka.

Thailand Golf Association
Hon Sec, Likhit Sudarat, Railway Training Centre, Vibhavadee Rangsit Road, Bangkok 10900. *Tel* 51 34988/9 *Telex* 20806 SCCFOOD TH.

Australasia

Australian Golf Union
Exec Dir, CA Phillips, Golf Australia House, 155 Cecil Street, South Melbourne, Victoria 3205. *Tel* (03) 6997944 *Fax* (03) 6908510.

Members of the Union:

Victoria *Exec Dir*, D Fox, Victorian Golf Association, 15 Bardolph Street, Burwood, Victoria. *Tel* (03) 296731 *Fax* (03) 291077.

New South Wales *Exec Dir* B. Scott, New South Wales Golf Association, 17 Brisbane Street, Darlinghurst, New South Wales. *Tel* (02) 2648433 *Fax* (02) 2614750.

Tasmania *Exec Off*, B Eaton, Tasmanian Golf Council, 2 Queen Street, Bellerive, Tasmania 7018. *Tel* (002) 443600 *Fax* (002) 443201.

Queensland *Exec Dir*, AR Rollins, Queensland Golf Union, Cnr Wren Street & Walden Lane, Bowen Hills, Queensland 4006. *Tel* (07) 8541105 *Fax* (07) 2571520.

Western Australia *Exec Dir*, G Fitzhardinge, Western Australian Golf Association, Suite 1–4, 49 Melville Parade, South Perth 6151 Western Australia. *Tel* (09) 3672490 *Fax* (09) 3682255.

South Australia *Exec Dir*, P Howard, South Australian Golf Association, 249 Henley Beach Road, Torrensville 5031, South Australia. *Tel* (08) 3526899 *Fax* (08) 3523900.

Australian Ladies' Golf Union

Exec Dir, Mrs KD Brown, 22 McKay Road, Rowville 3178, Victoria. *Tel* (03) 7644019 *Fax* (03) 7645219.

Members of the Union

Victoria *Sec*, Miss K Mahlook, 598A Glenhuntly Road, Elsternwick 3185, Victoria. *Tel* (03) 5238511 *Fax* (03) 5281056.

New South Wales *Sec*, Miss Wendy V Weil, 17 Brisbane Street, Darlinghurst 2010, New South Wales. *Tel* (02) 2647327.

Queensland *Sec*, Mrs Helen Birchell, Unit 3, Cnr Wren Street & Walden Lane, Bowen Hills, Queensland 4006. *Tel* (07) 2528155.

Western Australia *Sec*, Mrs Rhonda Meloncelli, Unit 3, 66 Mill Point Road, South Perth 6151, Western Australia. *Tel* (09) 3682618.

South Australia *Sec*, Mrs JE Roberts, 2 Marshall Street, Glengowrie 5044, South Australia. *Tel* (08) 2947838.

Tasmania *Hon Sec/Treas*, Mrs R Toogood, 86 Roslyn Avenue, Kingston Beach 7050, Tasmania. *Tel* (002) 296622.

Australian Professional Golfers' Association – PGA Tour

Sec, Barbara Molesworth, 4/140 George Street, Hornsby 2077 New South Wales. *Tel* (02) 476333 *Fax* (02) 4777625.

New Zealand Golf Association (Inc)

Dominion Sports House, Mercer Street, Wellington, PO Box 11842. *Tel* Wellington (4) 845 408. *Telegrams* Enzedgolf.

New Zealand Professional Golfers' Association

PO Box 27337, Wellington. *Tel* (04) 722687 *Fax* (04) 712152.

New Zealand Ladies' Golf Union

Sec, Mrs PE Jessup, PO Box 13-029, Wellington 4. *Tel/Fax* 793 868.

Africa (south of Sahara)

Botswana Golf Union

Sec, RA Armstrong, PO Box 1033, Gaborone. *Tel* Gaborone (31) 53989 *(home)*.

Ghana Golf Association

Sec, MM Ezan, PO Box 8, Achimola.

Kenya Golf Union

PO Box 49609, Nairobi. *Tel* Nairobi (2) 720074.

Kenya Ladies' Golf Union

PO Box 45615, Nairobi.

Malawi Golf Union

PO Box 1198, Blantyre.

Malawi Ladies' Golf Union

PO Box 5319, Limbe.

Nigerian Golf Association

Sec Ms M Chinakwe, c/o National Sports Commission, Surulere, PO Box 145, Lagos.

Sierra Leone Golf Federation

The Captain, Freetown Golf Club, PO Box 237, Lumley Beach, Freetown.

South African Golf Union

Exec Dir, JM Kellie, PO Box 1537, Cape Town 8000. *Cablegram address:* Sagolfunion, Cape Town. *Tel* Cape Town (21) 467585 *(office)*, (21) 653617 *(home)*.

Provincial Unions:
Border Golf Union *Hon Sec*, Mrs J Davenport, Box 1773, East London 5200, CP. *Tel* (0431) 403899.

Eastern Province Golf Union *Hon Sec*, CAL Fowles, PO Box 146, Port Elizabeth 6000, CP. *Tel* (041) 21919.

Karoo Golf Association *Hon Sec*, Mrs CL Hobson, PO Box 71, Middleburg 5900, CP.

OFS & Northern Cape Golf Union *Hon Sec*, RF Davidson, PO Box 517, Bloemfontein 9300, OFS. *Tel* (051) 470511.

Natal Golf Union *Sec*, RT Runge, PO Box 1939, Durban 4000, Natal. *Tel* (031) 223877.

South-West Africa Golf Union *Hon Sec*, H Hanstein, PO Box 2989, Windhoek 9000. (061) 222786.

Transkei Golf Union *Sec,* Philip Geldehuys, PO Box 210, Umtata, Transkei.

Transvaal Golf Union *Sec,* RC Witte, PO Box 391661, Bramley 2018, Transvaal. *Tel* (011) 6403714/5.

Western Province Golf Union *Sec* BW Myles, Box 153, Howard Place, 7450, CP. *Tel* (021) 536728.

South African Ladies' Golf Union
Sec, Mrs E Cutler, PO Box 135, 1930 Vereeniging, Transvaal.

South African Professional Golfers' Association
Sec, Lee Wiltshire, PO Box 55253, Posbus Northlands, 2116 Johannesburg. *Tel* (011) 884 3404 *Fax* (011) 884 3436.

Swaziland Golf Union
S Mabuza, PO Box 1739, Mbabane.

Tanzania Golf Union
Hon Sec, Bashir Tejani, Tanzania Golf Union, PO Box 4879, Dar es Salaam.

Uganda Golf Union
Sec, Kitante Road, PO Box 2574, Kampala.

Zaire Golf Federation
Pres, Tshilombo Mwin Tshitol, BP 1648, Lubumbashi. *Tel* 2269.

Zambian Golf Union
Hon Sec, Amon T Chibiya, PO Box 37445, Lusaka. *Telex* ZA 40098.

Zambia Ladies' Golf Union
Sec, Mrs C Howell, PO Box 32150, Lusaka. *Tel* Lusaka (1) 251668, *Telex* ZA 40098.

Zimbabwe Golf Association
Sec, B de Kock, PO Box 3327, Harare.

Zimbabwe Ladies' Golf Union
PO Box 3814, Harare.

Europe

Austrian Golf Federation
Sec, G Jungk, Haus des Sports, Prinz-Eugen-Strasse 12, A-1040 Vienna. *Tel* Vienna (222) 505 32 45 *Fax* (222) 505 49 62.

Belgian Royal Federation of Golf
Sec, Eric Steghers, Siège Administratif et Secretariat, Chemin de Baudemont 23, 1400 Nivelles. *Tel* (067) 220440 *Fax* (067) 220444.

Czechoslovak Golf Federation
Sec, H Goldscheider, Na Porici, 12, 11530 Prague 1. *Tel* Prague (2) 2350065-84 *Telex* 122650.

Danish Golf Union (Dansk Golf Union)
Gen Sec, Leif Asbjorn, Toftevj 26, 2625 Vallensbaek. *Tel* Copenhagen (2) 64 06 66.

European Golf Association
Gen Sec, C Storjohann, En Ballègue, Case Postale CH-1066, Epalinges, Lausanne, Switzerland. *Tel* 010-41-21-7843532 *Telex* 450804 Golf *Fax* 41-21-7843536.

Amateur Technical Committee: *Hon Sec,* JL Dupont, 51 Av Victor Hugo, 93300 Aubervilliers. *Tel* Paris (1) 833 4949.

Finnish Golf Union (Finlands Golfforbund)
Hon Sec, J Huhtanen, Radiokatu 12, SF-00240 Helsinki. *Tel* Helsinki (90) 1581 *Telex* 121797.

French Golf Federation (Fédération Française de Golf)
Hon Sec, J Labatut, 69 Avenue Victor Hugo, 75783 Paris, Cedex 16. *Tel* Paris (1) 45021355 *Telex* 614 406 FF Golf *Fax* 33 (1) 45003068.

French Professional Golfers' Association
69 Avenue Victor Hugo, 75116 Paris 16. *Tel* Paris (1) 500 43 72.

German Golf Association (Deutscher Golf Verband)
Sec, Heinz Biemer, Postfach 2106, 6200 Wiesbaden. *Tel* 010 49 (6121) 526041 *Telex* 4 186 459 *Fax* 49 (6121) 599493.

German PGA (Deutscher Golflehrer Verband)
Sec, Mrs Suzanne Mühlbauer, Eberlestrasse 13, 89 Augsburg. *Tel* 010 49 (821) 528900.

Hellenic Golf Federation
Hon Sec, George Th Lusi, PO Box 70003, GR 16610, Glyfada, Athens, Greece. *Tel* Athens (1)894 6820 or Athens (1)894 1933 *Telex* 212493 MYLG GR or 224524 DIOR GR.

Hungarian Golf Association
President, Dr F Gati, c/o Hungarian Blue Danube Golf Club, 111 Milkos-ug 11, 12, H-1035 Budapest.

Iceland Golf Union (Golfsanband Islands)
Gen Sec, Frimann Gunlaugsson, Reykjavik 121, PO Box 1076. *Tel* Reykjavik (1) 686686 *Telex* 2314 1S1 1S.

International Greenkeepers' Assoc
Hon Sec, Mrs B Harradine, Via Golf, CH6987, Caslano, Switzerland.

Italian Golf Federation (Federazione Italiana Golf)
Sec Gen, Stefano Manca, 388 Via Flaminia I-00196 Rome. *Tel* Rome (6) 394 641 *Telex* 613192 Golfed I.

Luxembourg Golf Club Grand Ducal
Sec, Miss J Schwartz, 1 Route de Treve 2633,
Senningerberg. *Tel* (352) 34090.

Netherlands Golf Federation
Man Dir, Henk J Heyster, PO Box 221,
3454 ZL De Meern. *Tel* 010 31-3406-21888
Fax 31-3406-21177.

Netherlands Professional Golfers' Assoc
Sec, A Wessels, Karel De Grotelaan 190,
Deventer.

Norwegian Golf Union (Norges Golfforbund)
Gen Sec, Anna Donnestad, Hauger Skolevei 1,
1351 Rud. *Tel* Oslo (2) 51 88 00 *Telex* 18586
NIFN.

Portuguese Golf Federation (Federación Portuguesa de Golfe)
Sec, Eduardo Vieira, Rua Almeida Brandao 39,
1200 Lisbon. *Tel* Lisbon (1) 661126 *Telex* 43447
FISPOR P.

Slovenian Golf Association
Sec, M Bozio, Golf Association of Slovenia,
c/o Golf Club Bled, C. Svobode 13, 64260 Bled,
Yugoslavia.

Spanish Golf Association (Real Federación Espanola de Golf)
Gen Sec L Alvarez De Bohorquez, Capitan Haya
9-5 Dcha, Madrid 28020. *Tel* 010 34 455 26 82 /
455 27 57 *Fax* 91-456-3290.

Swedish Golf Federation (Svenska Golf Forbundet)
Sec Gen, Lars Granberg, PO Box 84,
S-182 11 Danderyd. *Tel* Stockholm (8) 753 04 55
Telex 16608 *Fax* 08-7558439.

Swedish PGA
Exec Dir, Christer Lindberg,
Chairman, John Cockin. PO Box 35, S-181 21
Lidingö. *Tel* Stockholm (8) 767 83 23.

Swiss Golf Association (Association Suisse de Golf)
Sec, JC Storjohann, En Ballègue, Case Postale
CH-1066, Epalinges, Lausanne. *Tel* Lausanne
(21) 32 7701 *Telex* 45450804.

Swiss Professional Golfers' Association
Hon Sec, Jakob Kressig, Perrelet 9, 2074 Marin.
Tel (038) 33 23 79.

Yugoslavia Golf Federation
Sec, Marko Bozic, Golf Association of Slovenia,
Golf Club Bled, C svobode 24, 64260 Bled.

Middle East

Cyprus Golf Union
Chairman, Major DB Hurren REME, c/o JSGC
Dhekelia, BFPO 58.

Israel Golf Union
Sec, Alon Ben-David, PO Box 1010, Caesarea
30660.

Libyan Golf Union
PO Box 879, Tripoli.

United Arab Emirates Golf Union and Egyptian Golf Federation
c/o Gezira Sporting Club, Gezira, Cairo, Egypt.
Tel Cairo (2) 80 6000.

Part VI
Golf History

The Origin of Golf

David Hamilton

Beginnings

The game of golf was not a sudden invention; it evolved and matured out of many other stick-and-ball games played in medieval Europe. France had its game of *chole* and England had a stick-and-ball game called 'cambuca'. Only two games, however, are serious contenders as the forerunner of the modern game of golf. The first was *colf* (or *koffe*), popular in the Low Countries, and the second was the game already known as 'golf' (or 'gouff' or 'gollfe' in the random, phonetic spelling of the day), which is persistently mentioned in Scottish records from medieval times onwards.

Dutch *colf*

The Dutch *colf* was popular and appears frequently in early Dutch records – of which many more have survived than the few scrappy Scottish documents of the same period – from 1300 onwards. A major study by Steven van Hengel, *Early Golf* (privately published in 1982), has at last described the game from original documents. A single iron-headed club, which had considerable loft, was used. It seems to have been mostly a town game, played towards a target such as a door, and may have been popular with children. The game became a nuisance in the towns, but only occasionally did regulations successfully move it out into the open fields nearby, where it may have been played into a hole in the ground. The Dutch towns where *colf* was popular were inland and, without adjacent coastal links, it could not be played very successfully outside the towns. When the canals were frozen, a form might be played using a post, or even a hole, in the ice as the target.

In Scotland, early records are less well preserved, and portrait and landscape painting did not exist. Nevertheless, sufficient is known about the early game of 'golf' to suggest that until about 1650 it may have resembled *colf*, as many records show that it was played in the churchyard or street. Scotland and the Low Countries were closely linked by trade, and hence there are good reasons why the games should have been similar.

Move to links

But by 1650 another version of the Scottish golf can be seen emerging as the dominant form, changing it to resemble the modern game. At this time it moved out of the towns on to the hard links – land beside the east-coast towns and ports, where in winter (and early golf was a winter game) a game of skill developed, combining lengthy shots with accuracy as the hole was neared. Wooden-headed clubs, which could be expensive, were now the kind most in use and even in the Low Countries were known as 'Scotch cleeks'. In Scotland an iron club was reserved for bunkers or ruts. The target in this long game was a hole in the ground.

The earliest description of the Scottish game of golf, taken from a Latin grammar for schools, Aberdeen 1632. It mentions bunkers, iron clubs, holes and sand used for teeing up. (Courtesy of Aberdeen University Library.)

Why should the game have been different in Scotland from that played elsewhere in Europe and why should it have changed in this way? Perhaps the interest of the aristocracy and the Stuart monarchs was important, since they took up golf seriously; they could afford to buy the expensive equipment. For this reason golf appeared in London after the Union of the Crowns, when James VI of Scotland ascended the throne of Great Britain

as James I. In Scotland too, the east-coast ports, notably Leith near Edinburgh, had links, whereas the Low Countries' *colf*-playing towns were inland, with wet, heavy land in winter.

There is no evidence that the Dutch game evolved along the same lines as its Scottish counterpart, and indeed *colf* disappeared about 1700, probably eliminated by the growth of the towns and the congestion of their streets. Ball-and-stick games in Holland developed in a different way to give *kolf*, an indoor game played over a short, formal court. It seems reasonable to conclude that, in the absence of other evidence, golf as we now know it evolved in Scotland, but perhaps later than was once supposed.

The first Clubs

In the late 1600s, golf was popular in Scotland along the east coast and two centres in particular were of interest. St Andrews had keen aristocratic student golfers, whose fathers were among those who played at Leith. Numerous diaries and local records show the popularity of Leith, and it was not surprising that here the world's first Golf Club was founded – the Honourable Company of Edinburgh Golfers. There were many golfing cliques in Leith and the club's foundation was probably a response to the fading fortunes of the town, in decline after the Union of the Parliaments. Already the Leith races were popular and a trophy had been given by the Town Council. The new Company of Golfers was also provided with a trophy – a silver club – and though this did not herald any sudden change in the game, it did mean that rules had to be drawn up for the new competition – the first rules of golf.

Other Clubs were founded in the seventeenth century, imitating the Leith golfers, and, as Scottish attitudes relaxed in an increasingly sociable century, these Clubs became known for their heavy drinking and hearty eating. They seem to have had little turnover of members, who were often bound together for reasons other than golf – often military or masonic. The Clubs played a valuable role in supporting the early club- and ballmakers, and were vigilant in protecting the rights of the townspeople to use the links for recreation. Many records show that golf was still popular with the tradespeople of the towns, who were not members of the Golf Clubs. Whether these poorer golfers played with the expensive equipment used by the rich or with a cheaper club and ball is not certain.

Temporary cessation

The early 1800s saw a crisis in the Scottish game. Industrialization brought rapid expansion to the towns without regard for amenities, and public links such as those at Leith, Aberdeen, Glasgow

The Trophy for the Gentlemen Golfers of Edinburgh (later the Honourable Company) on display.

and Leven were throttled. Some Clubs, like the Honourable Company of Edinburgh Golfers and the Glasgow Club, ceased to exist for a spell and others dispersed to new, quieter areas, such as Musselburgh. The game itself appeared to be less popular.

The game takes off

But in the year 1848 a revolution in the game occurred. The appearance of the new gutty ball, made out of malleable gutta-percha, produced a cheap, durable alternative to the short-lived featherie or the wooden ball of the common game. Less dramatic but of similar significance was the change from the brittle woods to tough hickory for club shafts. To the older men who earned their living by club- and ball-making, like Allan Robertson, it seemed that their trade was in danger, but others, like 'old' Tom Morris, realized that the new equipment might help spread the game. In this belief they were correct beyond any reasonable expectation. The new well-off middle class produced by the growth of industry flocked to Scotland for their holidays using the expanding rail network. St Andrews and North Berwick were favourite places and there the visitors imitated the games of the old leisured class. Their wives and families also learned the game on these Scottish holidays, and women's golf was born at St Andrews. Celebrities such as AJ Balfour, then Secretary of State for Ireland, were keen players and helped its popularity further.

Back home, in England and elsewhere, they drew up plans for courses for which they hired Scottish help. From Scotland poured a stream of designers and professionals, like Willie Dunn and, later, Donald Ross. The Carnoustie Club (drawn from the artisans of the town) produced a remarkable number of young emigrés who could be found playing golf and tending the courses all over North America.

English and US expansion

Blackheath claimed great antiquity, dating back to the Stuart kings. The first English Club of the modern era, however, was perhaps the Old Manchester Club (1818), though the first of the continuous modern era was the Royal North Devon (1864) at Westward Ho!, a Club which had the distinction of raising JH Taylor who became the first professional to beat the Scots at their own game. In Ireland, Royal Belfast (1881) was the first golf club to be formed, and in Europe, Pau (1856) led the way. Britain's expanding Empire spread golf around the world. In Britain, a new burst of Club foundation occurred, reaching its peak in the 1890s. The number of clubs rose from less than 100 in 1875 to 1300 in 1900. Golf had been played in a small way in America before the foundation of the St Andrews Golf Club of Yonkers in 1888, but the Club's pioneers had met with ridicule. This Club's course was primitive, but by 1895 came America's first open championship links, at Newport, Rhode Island – although as late as 1899 leading British professionals like Harry Vardon met little opposition on tours in America.

'Old' and 'young' Tom Morris.

Early competitive play

Competitive golf dates from the inter-Club matches of the early nineteenth century, the first of which was recorded in 1818 when two of the Edinburgh Clubs playing over Bruntsfield Links, the Burgess Golfing Society and the Bruntsfield Links Club, competed against each other. In 1857 the Prestwick Club organized a successful inter-club tournament, and in 1860 they arranged an event for professional golfers, which later became known as the Open Championship. They may have wished to show the skills of the invited professionals, particularly their own man, Tom Morris, whom they had hired as a ball- and club-maker, and who looked after the Prestwick links – the first such salaried post for a golfer. Sadly, Allan Robertson did not live to play in the competition, though the year previously he was the first to have broken 80 in a round over the Old Course. The Open was unusual in being a stroke-play competition, as the early inter-Club tournaments were match play.

New horizons

Golf prospered and by the time of Willie Park's success the small number of professional golfers could hope for larger stakes in challenge matches and the rewards of occasional tournaments. Park was perhaps the first to capitalize on his fame in the modern way as a golf consultant and by publicizing his own branded clubs, notably an infallible putter, and by using mass production, advertising and postal sales he was highly successful. At St Andrews the first golf club manufacturing firm that had not been set up by a professional golfer appeared – the Forgan's firm, which survived for almost a century.

Scottish professional dominance ended in 1894 when an English-born professional, JH Taylor, won the Open. The rise of American golf was signalled when WJ Travis won the British Amateur Championship in 1904.

Though a home-bred player, JJ McDermott, had won the US Open in 1911, it was Francis Ouimet's win in 1913 that caught the popular imagination. Another feature of the growing dominance of America was the appearance of the Haskell ball in 1902, quickly capturing the market. Club design changed to suit the new ball: heads became deeper and the scarehead design changed to the socket joint.

Improved status

Professionals' status remained low until the end of the century and they were usually called by their second names only. Even Open Champions had to tee the ball up for their amateur partners in exhibition matches, and even James Braid

From George M Colville Five Open Champions and the Musselburgh Golf Story, Musselburgh 1980.

never entered Walton Heath clubhouse by the front door. JH Taylor organized the professionals in Britain, promoting their image until they became national figures even outside the narrow world of sport. Their new-found popularity was marked by an increasing number of tournaments, notably the sponsorship by the *News of the World* of the first tournament of the modern era. The changing status of professionals in Britain was pioneered and continued by Henry Cotton, who, on being appointed to Ashridge GC in 1937, made the bold stipulation that he be made an honorary member of the Club. The modern professional had arrived.

Today golf is played world-wide, and is perhaps the most popular participant outdoor sport in the world. The government of the game still bears out its Scottish origins – the Royal & Ancient Golf Club of St Andrews shares with the United States Golf Association the regulation of all golf. And only in Scotland is it still universally the game of the ordinary people.

From George M Colville Five Open Champions and the Musselburgh Golf Story, Musselburgh 1980.

Evolution of the Rules of Golf

J Stewart Lawson

Authors note: Revised Rules of Golf came into force on 1 January 1988, but 1984 was a significant date in the evolution of the Rules.

The late Henry Longhurst always maintained that perfectly adequate rules for the game of golf could be written on the back of a score card. When challenged to show how this could be done, Henry produced a set of ten Rules, the key one reading: *The game shall be played in the traditional manner* . . . Sadly, Henry was never pressed to say to which of the many different traditions he was referring. Should we, for example, be following the Leith system (*At Holling, you are to play your Ball honestly for the Hole, and not to play upon your Adversary's Ball, not lying in your way to the Hole* – The Gentlemen Golfers, 1744) or the Brunonian system (*It shall be deemed fair to play a ball against the adversary's ball, provided the player does not touch the adversary's ball with his club* – Edinburgh Burgess Golfing Society, 1814)?

No doubt there are many traditionalists who will shake their heads mournfully over the 1984 version of the Rules of Golf. Not only are the playing rules presented in an entirely new and, it is hoped, more logical order, but several important changes of principle and procedure have also been made. What many people forget, however, is that from the very outset the rules of the game have been organic: they have grown and proliferated; they have changed their form and shape many times; and, by discarding provisions as they became outmoded, they have supported Darwin's theory of the survival of the fittest. Nevertheless, through all phases of this evolution, the organism's backbone has remained unaffected: the game of golf still *consists in playing a ball from the teeing ground into the hole by a stroke or successive strokes in accordance with the Rules* – Rule 1-1.

Early rules

Golf in Scotland had managed to survive three centuries without any apparent need for written rules when, in 1744, the Gentlemen Golfers at Leith drew up thirteen Articles & Laws in Playing at Golf, the occasion being the first competition for the City of Edinburgh's Silver Club and the Gentlemen Golfers apprehending that entrants from other parts of the country might not be familiar with the Leith tradition. As other golfing societies were formed in the ensuing years, each drew up its own rules of play, but the leadership of the Gentlemen Golfers, later to become The Honourable Company of Edinburgh Golfers, was generally acknowledged. From the 1830s onwards, however, due to a temporary eclipse of the Honourable Company, this leadership gradually passed to the Society of St Andrews Golfers, which in 1834 had been granted the title of Royal & Ancient Golf Club of St Andrews. This shift of influence to the Royal & Ancient is illustrated by the fact that, whereas in 1810 the first 15 Rules of the Glasgow Golf Club were, with one minor difference, word for word the same as those of the Honourable Company, in 1851 the newly formed Prestwick Golf Club decided to adopt the St Andrews Rules of Play.

The last quarter of the nineteenth century saw a tremendous expansion of golf both at home and overseas, and there was a growing demand for a uniform code of rules. Widespread interest was shown when the Royal & Ancient announced the publication of a new set of Rules in 1891, and great importance was attached to the revisions these contained. It was natural, in these circumstances, that the leading clubs should invite the Royal & Ancient to assume responsibility for producing a uniform code, and the first Rules of Golf Committee was appointed in 1897. The United States Golf Association had been organized in 1894, and these two bodies, the Royal & Ancient and the USGA, now became the game's two governing authorities, responsible for the formulation of rules and for their interpretation. During the first half of the present century, the Royal & Ancient and the USGA shared the same basic code of rules, but each body issued its own interpretative Decisions, and many differences arose, particularly in the area of the game's equipment: the Royal & Ancient's banning of the centre-shafted putter after WJ Travis had won the British Amateur with a Schenectady; the eventual disagreement (now at last resolved) over the

minimum size of the golf ball; and the legalization of steel shafts by the USGA some years before the Royal & Ancient followed suit. Interpretation of the playing rules also differed, and the USGA, without the same long tradition of match play, had no qualms about abolishing the stymie.

Royal & Ancient–USGA co-operation

By 1950 there was a grave danger of the Royal & Ancient and the USGA drifting farther apart, but conferences held in 1951, which representatives from Canada and Australia also attended, resulted in the formulation of a uniform code, the only initial difference being over the size of the ball; a couple of minor divergencies in the playing rules which arose later did not last long and uniformity has been maintained ever since. Arrangements were also made in 1951 for the Royal & Ancient and the USGA to meet periodically to review the Rules, and these meetings now take place every four years; on the Royal & Ancient's part, only after detailed consultation with the 65 Golfing Unions and Associations affiliated to it. It would have been anomalous, however, to have uniform rules if they were not being interpreted in the same way. A comprehensive analysis of Royal & Ancient and USGA Decisions carried out a few years ago revealed several important differences of interpretation, and a Joint Decisions Committee was therefore appointed to establish uniformity in this area as well as in the Rules themselves. So successful has this new venture been that in 1984 the Royal & Ancient and the USGA jointly published a book of uniform Decisions on the Rules of Golf, now revised annually and the two bodies have co-operated in the production of films about the Rules.

One alteration in the 1984 Rules may have startled more than traditionalists: the change in the manner in which a ball is to be dropped. In future, the player *shall stand erect, hold the ball at shoulder height and arm's length and drop it* (Rule 20-2a) and there is no requirement that he must face the hole when doing so. The chief reason for this change was that the spot where the ball first strikes the ground when dropped is important (see Rule 20-2c), but under the old Rule how was the player – standing erect, facing the hole and dropping the ball over his shoulder – to identify that spot with any certainty? The change is certainly a major one, and the traditionalists might claim that the old Rule embodied a procedure hallowed by nearly two and a half centuries of usage. But would they be right?

Ways of dropping the ball

Article 8 of the 1744 code at Leith required a player whose ball was lost to *drop another Ball*, but it did not say in what manner this should be done. In 1754 at St Andrews the player was at liberty to take his ball out of *water, or any watery filth, and throw it behind the hazard six yards at least.* The Edinburgh Burgess Golfing Society varied not only the manner of dropping but even the identity of the dropper: in 1773 the ball was to be dropped by *the opposite party*, i.e. the opponent; in 1776 it was to be thrown over his head by the player; in 1807 the player was to drop it over his shoulder; and in 1839 the *right* shoulder was specified. Facing the hole when dropping was first introduced by the Honourable Company of Golfers at Leith in 1809, but the method of dropping varied again: *the player shall ... fronting the hole to which he is playing, drop the ball over the back of his head.* Finally, in 1829 and 1834 the Musselburgh Golf Club required that the ball be dropped by *a cady.* Which of these several variations on the dropping theme would the traditionalists accept as Henry Longhurst's *traditional manner?*

The first written Rules of Golf were no more than 14 years old when it was thought necessary to amend them, but it was clear that the Gentlemen Golfers in 1758 believed that they had now got the wording absolutely right and that no further change would be required. Did not their Captain, Thomas Boswall, preface the amendment with these bold words, *That in all time Coming the Law shall be ...?* Successive generations of legislators have been equally sanguine in believing that they have produced a perfect set of rules, and the Royal & Ancient and the USGA doubtless hope that the 1984 code has closed all loopholes and provided for all eventualities. Is evolution now complete? Has the definitive tradition at last been established? Only time will tell.

The Championships of Great Britain

History of the Open Championship

The Open Championship was initiated by Prestwick Golf Club in 1860 and was played there until 1870. The Club presented the Championship Belt which was to be held for a year by the winner and which would become the absolute property of any player who won three years in succession. The competition consisted of three rounds of the 12 holes Prestwick then had, to be played on one day. The Open did not become a four round contest until 1892. There were few entrants in the early years and nearly all were professionals, who sometimes also were greenkeepers and clubmakers, with a few amateurs.

Young Tom Morris won the Belt outright in 1870. There was no contest the following year, but in 1872 Prestwick, the Royal and Ancient and the Honourable Company, who were still playing at Musselburgh, subscribed to provide the present trophy, which was not to be won outright. Since then only three winners would have so earned it: Jamie Anderson and Bob Ferguson during the following ten years and Peter Thomson since in 1954-56. The Championship was to be held on the courses of the three subscribing Clubs in turn. Young Tom won the first for the new cup in 1872 at St Andrews, but died tragically at the age of 24 in 1875.

The three courses continued to be used until 1892 when it was first played at Muirfield to where the Honourable Company had moved. That year was also the first in which the Championship became a 72-hole contest over two days. In 1890, at Prestwick, John Ball had become the first amateur to win. Only two others have followed his success, Harold Hilton in 1892 and 1897, and Bobby Jones in 1926, 1927 and 1930. Roger Wethered tied with Jock Hutchison at St Andrews in 1920, but lost the play-off; if he had not incurred a penalty stroke through treading on his ball in the third round, he may well have won.

The Triumvirate

The year 1894 saw the first occasion the Open was played in England at Sandwich and the first English professional to win, JH Taylor. He won again the next year and for the fifth time in 1913.

Harry Vardon and James Braid were the two others of the *great triumvirate* who together won sixteen Opens between 1894 and 1914. Taylor's five wins were spread over twenty years and Vardon's six over nineteen. Braid's wins were concentrated into ten years from 1901 to 1910, all of them in Scotland. Vardon won three times at Prestwick but never at St Andrews where Taylor and Braid both won twice. Only Taylor managed a win at Hoylake. No other player won more than once during their supremacy. The winning scores at the time were very high by today's standards, for although the courses were marginally shorter, the equipment and clothing were primitive compared with those in use now. At Sandwich Taylor's score was 326, or 38 over an average of 4s. His 304 at Hoylake in 1913 was played in appalling weather, wearing a tweed jacket, cap and boots, and using wooden shafts and leather grips. He had no protective clothing or umbrella and won by 8 strokes from Ted Ray. The last winning total over 300 was Hagen's 301 at Hoylake in 1924.

Better Standards

That improved equipment has helped combat the greater length and heavier rough of today's Championship courses is suggested by comparing the average winning scores for decades of this century.

Decade	Average winning score	Decade	Average winning score
1905-14	302	1956-65	280
1920-29	295	1966-75	280
1930-39	289	1976-85	277
1946-55	284		

Of the 119 Opens held so far, twenty Scots have won, eighteen Americans, sixteen English, three Australians, two South Africans and one each from France, Ireland, New Zealand, Argentina and Spain. The Scots have won thirty-nine times but only twice since Braid in 1910 (Duncan in 1920 and Lyle in 1985), the USA thirty-one times, England twenty-eight times, Australia and South Africa seven times each, Spain three times and each of the others once. Since the triumvirate's day ended, the only Englishmen to win more than once have been Sir Henry Cotton with three victories and Nick Faldo, twice champion. The Americans have won thirty out of the last sixty-three Opens played.

It will be seen that certain nationalities tend to dominate for a decade or so; the Scots until 1893, then the English until 1914, the USA in the 1920s and until 1933 when the English had a short resuscitation. The Commonwealth were to the fore from 1949 to 1965 (Locke, Thomson, Nagle and Charles) with the Americans coming back

again to win in 13 out of 18 years between 1966 and 1983. Equally dominating in their periods were Hagen and Jones in the twenties, Cotton in the thirties, Locke and Thomson the fifties, and thereafter Palmer, Nicklaus, Player, Trevino, Watson and Ballesteros.

Open Courses

Only fourteen courses have accommodated the Open. Prestwick, discarded after 1925 as unsuitable for large crowds and St Andrews share the lead, each having staged the championship on 24 occasions. The second group comprises Muirfield with thirteen, Royal St George's, Sandwich eleven and Hoylake with ten. Hoylake's last Open was in 1967; that it is not used now is due not to any lack of quality of the course but to lack of space. Deal appeared in 1909 and 1920, and was due again in 1949 but the sea broke across the course, and Sandwich came in for the last time until 1981. Troon and Lytham St Annes each held an Open between the wars, Carnoustie two and Princes, Sandwich, when Sarazen won in 1932, one; this course, which was used as a tank training ground during the Second World War, has not been asked again. In 1951, Portrush, the only Irish course to stage an Open, also provided the only English winner between Cotton and Jacklin in Max Faulkner. Birkdale and Turnberry are firmly established in the rota which appears to have settled at four Scottish courses, St Andrews, Muirfield, Troon and Turnberry, and three in England, Lytham St Annes, Birkdale and Royal St George's, Sandwich.

Traditionally the Open is only played on Links courses. While there may yet be new venues by the sea capable of being stretched and groomed to be worthy of holding an Open, the many other considerations to be weighed, such as an adequate road system to carry vast crowds and nearly as many acres as the course covers to accommodate the tented village and services, it is not easy to see where the Championship Committee will turn.

Qualifying

How does one qualify to play in an Open? Since qualifying was first introduced in 1914, there have been numerous changes. Regional qualifying was tried for a year in 1926. At one of the courses used, Sunningdale, Bobby Jones (and even he had to qualify!) played what many consider the classic round of golf: a 66, all 4s and 3s, never over par, 8 birdies, 33 putts and 33 other shots.

Until 1963 all competitors, even the holder, had to play two qualifying rounds on the Open course on the Monday and Tuesday of the Open week. The qualifiers then had one round on Wednesday, one on Thursday and the leading group of between 40 and 60 players finished with two rounds on Friday. In 1963 certain exemptions from qualifying were introduced. The two rounds on the Friday were dropped in 1966 in favour of one round each on Friday and Saturday; not until 1980 was the first round played on Thursday and the last on Sunday. As the entry continued to increase, in 1970 nearby courses were used for qualifying and in 1977 regional qualifying was reintroduced in the previous week with final qualifying on nearby courses later.

There have been surprisingly few ties involving a play-off, only twelve in 119 Championships. The first should have been in 1876 involving David Strath and Bob Martin. However, Strath took umbrage over a complaint against him and refused to play again, Martin being declared the winner. Until 1963 ties were decided over 36 holes; the last two, between Nicklaus and Sanders at St Andrews in 1971 and Watson and Newton at Carnoustie in 1975, were played over 18. Later it was decided that in the event of a tie, the winner would be found immediately by a play-off over specified holes, followed by 'sudden death' if necessary. This happened in 1989 when Calcavecchia beat Norman and Grady over 4 holes after finishing level on 275.

Prize Money

In 1863 the total prize money was £10, its distribution among the fourteen entrants, six of whom were amateurs, is unknown. A year later it had risen by over 50% to £16, with the winner taking £6. By 1990 the total prize fund had risen to £827,700 of which Nick Faldo received £85,000. All 72 qualifiers for the last day received £2700 or more. Additionally winners of the qualifying rounds won smaller amounts. Until about 1955, the winner's and leaders' rewards were very modest; even in 1939 the cheque for the first man was £100 out of a total of £500. With some justification the prestige of winning the Open then was adjudged to be of much more value than any monetary award. The growth since the 1950s has been astonishing and is evidence that, while it is still a tremendous asset for any man to have won the Open, the authorities have recognised that it will not maintain its leading place without substantial reward.

The rapid advance of the Open to the major spectacle it has become is due to a combination of factors. Not least of these is the TV presentation of the BBC, acknowledged as the world's best in golf, the interest and enthusiasm of thousands of spectators keen to watch on the spot rather than on the box, and the Royal &

Ancient's promotion of this world showpiece of golf that it has become. Behind it all has been the foresight of successive Championship Committees and, in the late 1960s and 1970s, the masterly spreading of the gospel by Keith Mackenzie, Secretary of the R&A in 1966-82, that is so ably continued by his successor, Michael Bonallack.

Laurence Viney

The Amateur Championship

Early History

Golf has always been a competitive game and club medals have been keenly contested since the nineteenth century. Many of the leading amateurs were members of several clubs and, aided by an excellent railway system, they competed against each other at such venues as St Andrews, Prestwick, Hoylake and Musselburgh. An embryonic *open amateur competition* was held in the late 1850s (the first being won by Robert Chambers, the publisher, in 1858) but there seems to have been little enthusiasm for such an event and it died around the time of the first Open Championship (1860). The best amateurs began to enter the Open from 1861. By the 1870s, there was increased interest in organising a tournament for amateurs only but nothing happened, probably because no one club took a strong enough lead. A proposal in 1877 to the membership of the R&A that it sponsor a sort of Amateur Championship (involving club members and others nominated by members) was defeated.

It fell to the Hoylake golfers to set in motion the championship we now know as *The Amateur*. In 1884 the Secretary of Royal Liverpool, Thomas Potter, proposed that an event – open to all amateurs – should be organised. This original intention was not carried out until 1886 and so the winner of 1885 (AF Macfie) triumphed over a strong but limited field drawn from certain clubs. The clubs which were responsible for the running of the championship until the R&A took over in 1920 – and who made contributions for the purchase of the trophy – were:

Royal & Ancient
Royal Burgess Golfing Society of Edinburgh
Royal Liverpool
Royal St George's
Royal Albert, Montrose
Royal North Devon

Royal Aberdeen
Royal Blackheath
Royal Wimbledon
Royal Dublin
Alnmouth
North Berwick, New Club
Panmure, Dundee
Prestwick
Bruntsfield Links Golfing Society, Edinburgh
Dalhousie
Gullane
Formby
Honourable Company of Edinburgh Golfers
Innerleven
King James VI, Perth
Kilspindie
Luffness
Tantallon
Troon
West Lancashire

The first championship was not without its teething troubles. The format which was adopted allowed both golfers to proceed to the next round if their match was halved, so the first championship had three semi-finalists – and Macfie got a bye into the final. From 1886, the usual format was adopted.

More serious than the problem of an idiosyncratic draw, however, was the question of amateur status, raised for the first time in 1886.

The committee had to decide if it should accept the entries of John Ball III and Douglas Rolland. As a 15-year-old, Ball had finished fourth in the 1878 Open at Prestwick and on the advice of Jack Morris he accepted the prize money of 10s (50p). Rolland, a stonemason, had accepted second prize in the 1884 Open. Rolland's entry to the Amateur was refused while Ball's was accepted. Ball went on to win the championship a record eight times and the Open Championship of 1890.

The Format

After such a difficult start, the format of 18-hole matches with a 36-hole final remained until 1956. This arrangement made for many closely fought matches, as shown in 1930, the year of RT Jones' Grand Slam triumph. Jones' only victory in the event came in the right year and it is worth pointing out that, in making his way to the final, he won in the fourth round at the 19th (by laying a stymie) against Cyril Tolley, the holder, and his victories in the sixth round and in the semi-final were by the narrowest of margins. In addition, the fact that the draw was not seeded sometimes meant early meetings between top golfers; for example, in 1926 the visiting American Walker Cup Team members, von Elm and Ouimet, met

in the second round and von Elm went on to meet Jesse Sweetser in the third. As a result of such events, there was some pressure for the introduction of seeding the draw but it was not until 1958 that the practice was officially adopted. In the fifties and sixties there were other changes in format in an attempt to satisfy large numbers of golfers who wished to play and to ensure a worthy winner.

The popularity of the championship has posed difficulties for the R&A. The mathematically ideal number of entrants to be fitted into a convenient format is 256. In 1950, 324 entered the championship causing golf to be played on the Old Course for 14 hours a day. In order to restrict the numbers turning up to the championship proper, an experiment in regional qualifying was held in 1958 (again a St Andrews year) and 488 players with handicaps of 5 and under played 36 holes of stroke play on 14 courses. This system was quickly replaced and in 1961 the handicap limit was lowered (to 3) and a balloting-out of higher handicaps was introduced so that 256 were left to play for the trophy. This method was followed until 1983 with the introduction of 36 holes of stroke play to find 64 players for match play, from which to find the eventual winner.

There was also pressure for the introduction of 36-hole matches. As early as 1922 the R&A's championship committee canvassed the opinion of the 252 men who played that year. Nineteen of these voted in favour of 36-hole matches, seven for district qualification, fifty-two voted for a stroke play qualification followed by 18-hole matches and the others who replied wanted no change to the system. In 1956 and 1957 the last 3 rounds were played over 36 holes, in 1958 and 1959 the semi-final and final were over 36 holes and then the old format returned.

There is constant pressure on the organisers to find a format to satisfy the needs of large numbers of home and foreign players, to take into account differences in national handicapping systems, to preserve the atmosphere of the championship, to maintain match play as a central feature of top-level amateur golf and even to take into account the vagaries of the weather. The task is almost impossible.

The Winners

Any man who wins the Amateur is a considerable golfer but attention should be paid to certain outstanding champions. John Ball of Royal Liverpool won the title eight times between 1888 and 1912.

It is interesting to note that he never successfully defended his title Michael Bonallack triumphed five times between 1961 and 1970, including an incredible hat-trick of final victories in which he successively beat Joe Carr and Bill Hyndman twice.

Several golfers have successfully defended their title: Horace Hutchinson, Harold Hilton, Lawson Little, Peter McEvoy and Philip Parkin, while others have won twice or more – Johnny Laidlay, Freddie Tait, Bob Maxwell, Cyril Tolley, Edward Holderness, Frank Stranahan, Joe Carr and Trevor Homer.

The oldest man to win was the Hon Michael Scott, at the age of 54 in 1933. The youngest winners – John Beharrell and Bobby Cole – were both 18 years and 1 month old. Cole's victory over Ronnie Shade was achieved over 18 holes – play being affected by poor visibility. The first overseas winner was Walter Travis who won in 1904 – one consequence of his victory was the banning of the use of centre-shafted putters. The first continental winner was the Frenchman, Philippe Ploujoux, who won in 1981. A visiting Walker Cup team always makes for an exciting championship and from fifteen visits to Great Britain the title has crossed the Atlantic twelve times. Indeed, on six occasions the final was an all-American affair.

No doubt there have been hundreds of thrilling matches played in the championship but few can have been as pulsating as the 1899 final at Prestwick where Johnny Ball beat Freddie Tait at the 37th hole. The victory must have been a sweet one for Ball, since Tait, the hero of Scotland, had won the previous year over Ball's home links of Hoylake. Tait was killed the following year in the Boer War. *The great battle* as Jones described his 4th round tie against Tolley in 1930 rivals the Ball-Tait final for tense excitement and for sheer brilliance of scoring Michael Bonallack's 1st round in the final of 1968 must take pride of place.

The Amateur Championship was 100 years old in 1985 and in essence it has changed remarkably little. How will the Championship react to changes such as the increasing popularity of the game at home and abroad, the lure of the professional ranks with its dependence on stroke play and the increasing commercialism of all sport? There is every reason to believe that it will continue to stand for all that is great in golf.

David Christie

Famous Players of the Past

In making the difficult choice of the names to be included, effort has been made to acknowledge the outstanding players and personalities of each successive era from the early pioneers to the stars of recent times.

Anderson, Jamie

Born 1842, died 1912. Winner of three consecutive Open Championships (1877-78-79). Born at St Andrews, he was the son of *Old Daw*, a St Andrews caddie and character. Jamie began golf when 10 years old, and rapidly developed into a fine player, noted for straight hitting and good putting. Anderson's method was to play steadily and on one occasion at St Andrews he remarked that he had played 90 consecutive holes without a bad shot or one stroke made otherwise than he had intended. He was for a period professional to Ardeer Club, but returned to St Andrews to follow his vocation of playing professional.

Anderson, Willie

Born in Scotland, 1878, died 1910. One of the Scottish emigrants to America, his flat swing won him the US Open in 1901, 1903, 1904 and 1905. He shares the record of four Open titles with Jones, Hogan and Nicklaus, and remains the only man to win three in a row.

Armour, Thomas D

Born Edinburgh, 1896. Died 1968. Open Champion, 1931. US Open Champion, 1927. USPGA 1930. He had a distinguished amateur career – including the French Open Amateur and tied first place in the Canadian Open. He had the unique distinction of playing in 1921 for Britain against the US as an amateur and in 1925 as a professional for the US against Britain in the unofficial international matches that preceded the inception of the Walker Cup and Ryder Cup events. When he came to the end of his tournament career he quickly gained an outstanding reputation as a coach, and books he wrote on the technique of the game were best-sellers.

Auchterlonie, William

Born St Andrews in 1872, died 1963. Won the Open title at Prestwick at the age of 21 with a set of seven clubs which he had made himself and shortly afterwards founded the famous club-making firm in St Andrews. He never played with more than his seven clubs and was a great believer that a golfer had to be master of the half, three-quarter and full shots with each club. As professional to the Royal & Ancient Golf Club from 1935 to his death he saw one of his ambitions fulfilled – the Centenary Open at St Andrews in 1960.

Ball, John

One of the greatest amateur golfers of all time. Born at Hoylake, 24th December, 1862, his father owned the Royal Hotel, Hoylake, prior to the formation of the golf links and when there was a small racecourse on the land later formed into the Royal Liverpool Links. The links became John Ball's playground. In 1878, when fifteen years old, he competed in the Open Championship, finished fourth, eight strokes behind the winner and ahead of many famous Scottish professionals of that time. Between 1888 and 1912 he won the Amateur Championship eight times. In 1890 he was the first amateur to win the Open Championship. He played for England against Scotland continuously from 1902 to 1911, captaining the side each year. He was Amateur Champion in 1899 when war with South Africa broke out and Ball served in that campaign with the Cheshire Yeomanry and did not compete in the Championships of 1900-01-02. In the First World War he served in the Home Forces. He played in his last Amateur Championship in 1921, the year of the first American invasion, and he reached the fifth round although in his fifty-eighth year. Modest and retiring, he rarely spoke about his golf. On the morning of his last round in the Championship he remarked to a friend in the clubhouse, *If only a storm of wind and rain would sweep across the links from the Welsh hills I feel I could beat all of them once again.* But it was a week of torrid heat and he failed. He retired to his farm in North Wales, where he died in December 1940.

Barton, Miss Pamela

Born London, 4th March, 1917. Died 13th November, 1943. At the age of twenty-two when the Second World War broke out, Miss Pamela Barton had already achieved great fame in the golfing world. She won the Ladies' Championship, 1936-39, runner-up, 1934-35, the American Ladies' Championship, 1936 and the French Ladies' Championship, 1934. In 1936, at the age of nineteen, she held both the British and American Ladies' Championships, the first person to do so since 1909. Miss Barton played for England in the home internationals in 1935-36-37-38-39; for Great Britain *v* United States in 1934-36; *v* France, 1934-36-37-38-39. She was a member of the Ladies' Golf Union teams which toured Canada and America, 1934, and Australia and New Zealand in 1935. Of a charming and cheerful disposition, Miss Barton, who became a Flight-Officer in the WAAF, was killed in a plane crash at an RAF airfield in Kent.

Braid, James

Born Elie, Fife, 6th February, 1870. Died London, 27th November, 1950. One of the greatest figures in golf of all times, James Braid, with Harry Vardon and JH Taylor, made up the Triumvirate which dominated British professional golf for twenty years before the First World War. He was the first person to win the Open Championship five times. This record was later equalled by Taylor and beaten by Vardon. Braid's achievements were remarkable for the short time in which they were accomplished. In ten years he won five times and was second on three occasions. His victories were in 1901, 1905, 1906, 1908, 1910. He won the Match Play Tournament four times, 1903-5-7-11, a record which was unequalled till 1950, and the French Open Championship in 1910. He played for Scotland *v* England in 1903-4-5-6-7-9-10-12 and for Great Britain against America, 1921. A joiner by trade, Braid played as an amateur in Fife and Edinburgh and in 1893 went to London and worked as a club-maker. Taylor and Vardon were well established in the golfing world before Braid turned professional in 1896 and he quickly came into prominence by finishing level with Taylor, who by that time had been Champion twice, in a challenge match. In a historic international foursomes, Braid partnered by Alex Herd lost to Vardon and Taylor in a match for £400 over four courses. A tall powerful player who lashed the ball with *divine* fury, he was famous for his imperturbability; no matter how the game was progressing he always appeared outwardly calm and it was this serenity of temperament which assisted him to his Championship victories on two occasions. A man of few words, it was once said that *Nobody could be as wise as James Braid looked.* One of the founder members of the Professional Golfers' Association, Braid did much to elevate the status of the professional golfer. Braid made a major contribution to golf architecture; Gleneagles, Rosemount, Carnoustie and Dalmahoy all bear his stamp. He was admired and respected by all who knew him, as much for his modest and kindly nature as for his prowess as a golfer. He was professional at Romford for eight years and at Walton Heath for forty-five, and was for twenty-five years an honorary member of the latter club, becoming one of its directors. He was made an honorary member of the Royal & Ancient Golf Club in the last years of his life and had the distinction of being the only honorary member of the Parliamentary Golfing Society.

Campbell, Miss Dorothy Iona

Born Edinburgh, 1883. Died in America, 1946. Won British Ladies' Championship, 1909-11; Scottish Ladies' Championship, 1905-6-8; American Ladies' Championship, 1909-10; Canadian Ladies' Championship 1910-11-12. One of only two women golfers to win the British, American and Canadian Championships, the other being Marlene Stewart (Mrs M Stewart Streit). Played for Scotland in international matches and for British Ladies *v* American Ladies.

Campbell, Willie

A native of Musselburgh, Willie Campbell never shirked a match anywhere or with anybody, and it was only on rare occasions that he did not win. He was a tall, strapping fellow, and was regarded as one of the finest match players of the time, fearless and courageous. In 1887 Campbell was professional at Prestwick, and in the Open Championship of that year he seemed destined to win but took eight strokes with three holes left. He joined the outflow of Scots professionals to the USA in 1891 where he died at the age of 33.

Compston, Archie Edward Wones

Born Penn, Wolverhampton, 14th January, 1893, died September, 1962. One of the outstanding personalities of British golf in the years between the two World Wars who fought hard to resist the developing dominance of the American invasion. He played in three Ryder Cup matches – in 1927, 1929 and 1931. In a 72 hole Challenge match he beat Hagen by 18 and 17 in 1928 at Moor Park and in the Open which followed he finished third to Hagen. He tied for second place in the Open of 1925.

Cotton, Sir Henry

Henry Cotton, born in Cheshire in 1907, bestrode the British professional scene as player, teacher, writer, course architect and encourager of youth from 1930 until his death in December 1987, a few days before his well-deserved knighthood was announced. The only Briton to win the Open more than once between 1914 and 1989, his three victories at Sandwich in 1934, Carnoustie in 1937 and Muirfield in 1948 were pinnacles in a dedicated, sometimes controversial, but highly successful career. All three victories contained at least one memorable round. His 65 at Sandwich, after which a golf ball was named, his last round 71 at Carnoustie in a downpour and his record 66 at Muirfield, with King George VI among the spectators, showed a style of play and life admired by all. No man did more to raise the status of the professional golfer. His insistence of Honorary Membership of clubs to which he was attached – Waterloo Brussels, Ashridge, Royal Mid-Surrey and Temple near Maidenhead – began a practice now followed by many clubs with their professionals. As Ryder Cup player and Captain, founder-member of the Golf Foundation, and his Rookie of the Year award, he led by example. His reward, which many would say came too late, was the first knighthood given for service to golf. His many playing successes included winning 11 Continental Opens, five finals in the News of the World Match-play Tournament, which at the time was second only in prestige to the Open. He won this twice, was four times selected for the Ryder Cup team, being Captain in 1937 and non-playing Captain in 1953. Captain of the PGA in 1934 and 1954, he had many other lesser tournament wins. During the war, in which he served in the RAF, he played exhibition matches in aid of the Red Cross and encouraged his fellow professionals to do likewise. After he retired from Championship play, he devoted his time to writing articles for the golf press, several books, support for the Golf Foundation and the development of his beloved Penina in Portugal where he spent much of his last years. He was elected to Honorary Membership of the Royal & Ancient Club in 1968 and was aware of his coming knighthood when he died a few days before it was announced.

Darwin, Bernard

One of the most respected and widely known personalities in the game died soon after his 85th birthday in 1961. As a graceful and authoritative writer on golf and golfers he had no equal. He knew intimately every player and every course of note throughout the world, and his phenomenal memory, fluent pen and gentle humour established him as the top historian of the game over many years. In 1937 he was awarded the CBE for his services to literature, which included journalism, books of children's stories and other sports besides golf. He was captain of the Royal & Ancient Club in 1934-35, and played internationally for England from 1902 until 1924 and in the first Walker Cup match (1922). He had travelled to the US to report the match for The Times and had been called in to play and captain the side when Robert Harris fell ill. During his playing career he won many amateur titles and trophies. He was a grandson of Charles Darwin.

The Dolemans

Four brothers, natives of Musselburgh, who were associated with golf for seventy years. John, born 1826, died at Musselburgh 1918; AH, born 1836, died at Blackpool 1914; William born 1838, died at Glasgow 1918, and Frank born Musselburgh 1848, died Edinburgh, 1929. William was the best player. He was first amateur in the Open Championship in 1865-68, 1870 and 1872. He played in nearly every Amateur Championship up to 1911, and at Hoylake in 1910, when 73 years of age, he won his tie in the first round. AH was one of the pioneers of golf in England, and founder of golf at Lytham and St Annes. John, the eldest, introduced golf to Nottingham. In 1908 he took part in an octogenarian foursome, which was continued annually until 1914. Frank was a club-maker and for many years he carried on a golf club-making business at the ancient Wright's Houses, Bruntsfield Links, Edinburgh.

Duncan, George

Died on 15th January, 1964, aged 80. He was the last Scottish-born winner of the Open title domiciled in Britain. He won the title in 1920 and his victory was achieved after two opening rounds of 80 which left him 13 strokes behind the leader. Two years later, at Sandwich, he finished second to Hagen after one of the most exciting finishes up to that time. Hagen had finished and was already being hailed as the winner when Duncan, a very late starter, reached the 18th hole needing a 4 to tie. He failed but his round was notable as the only one under 70 in that Open and the first to break 70 in the Open since 1904. Prior to the first war, Duncan was a prominent challenger to the established Triumvirate and would probably have achieved greater fame but for the war years during which he would have been at his prime. One of the fastest players of all time, he wasted no time especially on the greens and his book Golf at a Gallop was appropriately titled.

The Dunns

The twin brothers Dunn, born at Musselburgh in 1821, were prominent in golf between 1840 and 1860. In 1849, old Willie Dunn and Jamie Dunn played their great match against Allan Robertson and old Tom Morris. Willie Dunn became custodian in the Blackheath Links until 1864, and he then returned to Leith, and later to North Berwick, where he died at the age of 59. Willie Dunn was celebrated for the peculiar grace of his style and, as the longest driver of his day, he was a doughty match fighter, and one of his famous games was with Allan Robertson in 1843, when he played the St Andrews champion 20 rounds, and lost by 2 rounds and 1 to play. Another famous match was in 1852, when, partnered by Sir Robert Hay, he played Allan Robertson and Old Tom. Jamie Dunn, his twin brother, was also a fine player. Willie's son went to America, and won the first Championship of America in 1894. He was among the first to experiment with the idea of steel shafts. About 1900 he inserted thin steel rods in split cane and lancewood shafts. He invented a coneshaped paper tee, the forerunner of the wooden tee, and was a pioneer of indoor golf schools. He died in London in 1952.

Ferguson, Bob

Born Musselburgh, 1848. Died 1915. Started to caddie on Musselburgh when aged 8. In 1866, when 18, he won the first prize in the Leith Tournament, in which all the great professionals of the day took part. The late Sir Charles Tennant put up the money for young Ferguson, who, in 1868 and 1869, beat Tom Morris six times. In 1875, at Hoylake, with young Tom Morris representing Scotland in a foursome, he beat Bob Kirk, Blackheath, and John Allan, Westward Ho! representing England. He won the Open Championship in 1880, 1881, and 1882. In 1883 he tied with Willie Fernie, losing the 36-hole play-off by one stroke. After this Championship he became ill with typhoid, and was never able to reproduce his great form. He became the custodian of the Musselburgh links, taught the young and was widely respected in the community.

Fernie, Willie

Born St Andrews 1851; died Troon, June 1924. In 1880 he went to Dumfries as greenkeeper. In 1882 he was second to Bob Ferguson in the Open Championship and after a tie with the same player he won the Open Championship in 1883 at Musselburgh after a 36-hole play-off. He became professional to Felixstowe and Ardeer and in 1887 to Troon, and was there as professional until February, 1924. He was a very stylish player and in great demand as a teacher. He played in many important stake matches, the two biggest being against Andrew Kirkaldy over Troon, Prestwick and St Andrews which he won by 4 and 3, and against Willie Park over Musselburgh and Troon which he lost by 13 and 12. He played for Scotland against England in 1904.

Hagen, Walter C

Born Rochester, New York, 21st December, 1892. Died October, 1969. The first of the great golfers with star quality. People flocked to see him as much because he was a *character* as for his outstanding skill and many achievements. He did not want to be a millionaire, but merely to live like one, and this he did in dramatic style as when he used a hired Rolls-Royce as a changing room at the Open because professionals were not admitted to the clubhouse, and when he gave the whole of his first prize in the Open to his caddie. He also pioneered stylish dressing on the course. As a player he had great mastery of the recovery shot, nerves of steel beneath his debonair exterior and a fine putting touch. His best achievement was probably his four consecutive wins in the USPGA championship when the event was decided by matchplay over 36 holes. He won the US Open in 1914 and 1919 and the Open in 1922-24-28-29 and represented the US against Britain on seven occasions. His world tours with Kirkwood, his extrovert approach and the entertainment he provided on and off the course were the forerunners of the spectacular development of golf as a spectator sport. In spite of his being a contemporary of the immortal Bobby Jones, his personality was such that he was never overshadowed.

Herd, Alexander (Sandy)

Born at St Andrews in 1868, died London, 18th February, 1944. His life in the forefront of the game was more prolonged than his contemporaries of the Victorian era, and when he took part in his last Open at St Andrews in 1939 he was 71 and his appearances in the Championship covered a span of 54 years. A brilliant shot player, success often eluded him as he was prone to leave his putts short and to indecision. On his first appearance in the Open, at the age of 17, he possessed only four clubs and although he was frequently in contention it was not until 1902 that he won the Championship. He was the first player to win the Open using a rubber-cored ball. In 1920 at Deal and again the following year at St Andrews he was joint leader in the Open after three rounds. In 1926, aged 58, he won the PGA match-play tournament at Royal Mid-Surrey in a 36-hole final, having played five rounds in the previous three days to reach it. Those three achievements when he was in his fifties are con-

vincing proof of the longevity of his game. His life in golf brought him into competition with all the great Victorians – Taylor, Vardon, Kirkaldy, Braid and Park – and continued through the Jones and Hagen era up to the days of Locke, Cotton, Rees and Sarazen and others who, over 100 years after Herd's birth, were still playing Open Championship golf.

Hilton, Harold Horsfall

Born at West Kirby, a few miles from Hoylake, 12th January, 1869. Died 5th March, 1942. He was one of the most scientific of golfers. He learned his game at Royal Liverpool, where he won success in Boys' Competitions. In 1892, the year the Open Championship was extended to 72 holes, he won, and again in 1897. He won the Amateur Championship and the Irish Open Championship four times each, the St George's Cup twice, the American Amateur Championship once and became the first player, and the only Britisher, to hold both the US and British Amateur titles at the same time. He was small, 5 feet 7 inches, but immensely powerful in build. Hilton made a major contribution to golf literature as the first editor of Golf Monthly.

Hunter, Charles

Born Prestwick, 1836; died Prestwick, 24th January, 1921. A caddie and club-maker under old Tom Morris at Prestwick, he was for three years professional at the Blackheath Club, London, and succeeded old Tom as the Prestwick Club professional in 1864. He played in the first Open Championship at Prestwick in 1860, and he was a conspicuous figure at every championship and tournament held at Prestwick, acting as starter and in charge of the house flag up till the time of his death. He did not take much part in professional competitions, preferring to attend to his club-making and his members. In fact, during one championship round, while playing a niblick shot, he received word that the Lord Ailsa wished him to come at once and pick him out a set of clubs. He put his niblick back in his bag, pocketed his ball and returned to his workshop. In 1919 he was presented with his portrait in oils by the Prestwick Club, and a replica hangs in the Club. At the Open Championship of 1914 at Prestwick, he was the recipient of a presentation from his brother professionals. As a man of fine integrity, his friendship was valued by all golfers of his time.

Hutchinson, Horatio Gordon

Born London, 16th May, 1859, died in London, 28th July, 1932; an eminent golfer from the early eighties until 1907. He was a stylish and attractive player. Won the Amateur Championship in 1886

and 1887, runner-up 1885 (the first year of the Championship), and he was in the final in 1903. He was a semi-finalist in 1896, 1901, and 1904. He represented England v Scotland 1902-3-4-6-7, and was chosen in 1905 but illness prevented him taking his place. His career in the front rank of the game extended over twenty years. He was a voluminous and pleasant writer on golf and outdoor life. He was the first Englishman to captain the Royal & Ancient. In other years he was also Captain of Royal Liverpool, Royal St George's and President of Royal North Devon.

Jones, Robert Tyre

Born Atlanta, Georgia, USA, 17th March 1902. Died 18th December, 1971 after many years of a crippling spinal disease. By the time he retired from competitive golf in 1930 at the age of 28, Jones had established himself as one of the greatest golfers of all time, if not the greatest. He represented America in the Walker Cup from its inauguration in 1922 until 1930 and played in the match against Great Britain in 1921. His victories included the US Open in 1923-26-29-30 (tied in 1925 and 1928 but lost the play-off; second in 1922 and 1924); US Amateur 1924-25-27-28-30 (runner-up in 1919 and 1926); Open Championship 1926-27-30; Amateur Championship 1930. In 1930, Jones reached a pinnacle which will probably never be equalled when he achieved the Grand Slam – winning in one year the Open and Amateur Championships of America and Britain. He then retired from championship golf. His stylish swing was the subject of admiration wherever he went – full, flowing, smooth, graceful and rhythmical. Yet he was of such a nervous disposition that he was frequently physically sick and unable to eat during a championship. During his championship winning years, Jones was also a keen scholar and gained first-class honours degrees in law, English literature and mechanical engineering at three different universities. He finally settled on a legal career with his own practice in Atlanta. It was there that he and his friend Clifford Roberts conceived and developed the idea of the great Augusta National course and the Masters tournament, now a fitting memorial to the Master Golfer himself. In recognition of his great skill and courage, and the esteem in which he was held in Britain and St Andrews, he was made an honorary member of the Royal & Ancient in 1956 and two years later, when in St Andrews as captain of the US team in the inaugural competition for the Eisenhower Trophy, he was given the Freedom of the Burgh of St Andrews. As a final tribute, a memorial service was held for him in St Andrews. The 10th hole of the Old Course, St Andrews (previously nameless) is now called after him.

Kirkaldy, Andrew

Born Denhead, near St Andrews, 18th March, 1860. Died St Andrews, 16th April, 1934. A rugged type of the old school of Scottish professionals, he was the last survivor of that race. After army service in Egypt and India he was appointed professional at Winchester. He had no liking for the steady sedate life of an English professional and after six weeks returned to his native St Andrews, where he lived the rest of his days acting as a playing professional until he was appointed professional to the Royal and Ancient Golf Club. He was a man of powerful physique. He was a beautiful golfer to watch, particularly his iron shots. In the Open Championship, 1889, he tied with Willie Park at Musselburgh, but lost on the replay. He played in many money matches and the most notable was in 1895. JH Taylor had won the Open Championship in 1894, the first English professional to do so, and prior to the Open Championship, at St Andrews in 1895, the young English champion challenged the world for £50 a-side. Kirkaldy accepted and won by a hole. Candid, outspoken, sometimes uncouth, Kirkaldy in his old age was respected by princes and peers.

Laidlay, John Ernest

Born in East Lothian in 1860, Johnny Laidlay played high-quality golf for fifty years – a testimony to his technique and temperament. In all, he won more than 130 medals. At a time when golf was booming and the opposition tough, he won the Amateur Championship twice (1889, 1891) was runner-up three times and beaten semi-finalist three times. He was second in the 1893 Open Championship when his characteristically good putting failed. He played for Scotland every year from 1902 until 1911, when he was fifty-one. The longevity of his very individual swing was perhaps due to his early golfing experiences at Musselburgh where he saw Young Tom Morris, knew Willie Park well and played a lot with Bob Ferguson (including a famous round by moonlight). His contribution to the game was the overlapping grip – known erroneously as the Vardon grip. Laidlay played cricket for Scotland (vs Yorkshire – taking 6 wickets for 18 runs); he was a pioneer of wildlife photography and carved beautiful furniture. He died at Sunningdale in 1940.

Leitch, Miss Charlotte Cecilia Pitcairn (Cecil)

Born Silloth, Cumbria, 13th April, 1891. Died London, 16th September, 1977. Although Cecil Leitch had reached the semi-final of the British Ladies' Championship in 1908 at the age of 17 and had won the French Ladies' Championship in 1912, it was in 1914 that she really established herself as Britain's dominant woman golfer when she won the English Ladies', the French Ladies' and the British Ladies'. She retained each of these titles when they were next held after the First World War (the English in 1919 and the British and French in 1920) and who can say how many times she might have won them in the intervening years. In all she won the French Ladies' in 1912-14-20-21-24, the English Ladies' in 1914-19, the British Ladies' in 1914-20-21-26 and the Canadian Ladies' in 1921. Her total of four victories in the British Ladies' has never been bettered and has been equalled only by her great rival Joyce Wethered, against whom in the 1920s she had many memorable matches. Miss Leitch was an outspoken person who occasionally battled with the golfing authorities. Her strong attacking play mirrored her personality. Aged 19, in 1910 she accepted the challenge from Harold Hilton, at his peak, to take on any woman golfer over 72 holes giving half a stroke (a stroke at every second hole). Miss Leitch won this famous challenge match by 2 and 1 and later also beat John Ball, eight times Amateur Champion. Right to the end of her life, Cecil Leitch took an active interest in golf, attending major events whenever possible.

Little, W Lawson, Jun

Born Newport, RI, 23rd June, 1910, died February, 1968. As an amateur he established two records in that he won both the Amateur and American Amateur Championships in 1934 and again in 1935. In the final of the 1934 Amateur he won by the margin of 14 and 13 and for the 23 holes played he was ten under 4's. He turned professional in 1936 and won the Canadian Open in the same year and in 1940, won the US Open after a play-off.

Locke, Arthur D'Arcy

Bobby Locke, the son of Northern Irish emigrants, was born near Johannesburg on 20th November 1917 and died on 9th March 1987. He turned professional in 1938 after a very successful amateur career, in which he won the South African Boys' Championship, the South African Amateur (twice) and Open Championship (twice) as well as finishing leading amateur in the Open Championships of 1936 and 1937. As a result of his visits to Britain, he developed a characteristic hook to increase his length and although never a long hitter, his deadly short game made him a formidable competitor. In his first year as a professional he won the Irish, Transvaal, South African and New Zealand Open Championships as well as the South African Pro-

fessional title. During the war, Locke flew Liberator bombers for nearly 2000 hours. He left the South African Air Force weighing four stones heavier and immediately resumed his winning way. Second to Snead at St Andrews in the 1946 Open, he was encouraged to visit America where he was greatly successful. He beat Snead 12–2 in a series of matches and won five tournaments in 1947, two in 1948, three in 1949 and one in 1950. Locke had bad relations with the USPGA who disliked his success and they banned him from their tournaments. Locke concentrated his efforts on Europe. He won the Open Championship four times – 1949-50-52-59 – as well as the Open Championships of Canada (1947), France (1952-53), Germany (1954), Switzerland (1954), Egypt (1954) and South Africa (six times as a professional). He also won a number of British titles including the Dunlop Masters, Spalding, the Lotus, Daks and Bowmaker Tournaments. The 1957 Open Championship was the first to be shown on television and the first in which the leaders went out last. Locke won by 3 strokes and his score of 279 was the first time 280 had been beaten at St Andrews. Locke had to mark his ball on the 72nd hole and in front of the cameras replaced it on the wrong spot. The R & A decided to let his score stand as he had derived no advantage from his technical error and disqualification would have been inequitable and against the spirit of the game. Bobby Locke will be remembered as a beautifully dressed golfer – plus fours, white shirt and tie – with a superb temperament, especially after a disastrous hole, great self discipline, the highest standards of behaviour and a wonderful short game. He was virtually in retirement when he had a serious car crash. On recovery he continued to play golf but his competitive career was at an end. He was made an honorary member of the R & A in 1976.

Longhurst, Henry

Died 22nd July, 1978, aged 69. After leaving Cambridge University, he acquired a job as a golf writer in which he could indulge his love of the game and be paid for it. He never ceased to be amazed at his own good fortune. His regular weekly article in the *Sunday Times* became compulsory reading for the golfing cognoscenti. From writing he became involved in radio and, later, television, through which he became world famous as a commentator. Television was the perfect medium for his talents. His humour, easy manner, gifted observation and perception, mellow voice, calm delivery and economy of word were all perfectly suited to a slow-moving sport, and from his vast knowledge and understanding of the game, he was always able to fill in any gaps in the action with an apt story or two. Longhurst also wrote several amusing books about different periods of his life, including a brief spell as an MP. He was awarded the CBE for his services to golf and was one of only a handful of people to be made an honorary member of the Royal & Ancient Golf Club. His own golf was good enough to have won the German Open Amateur in 1936 and to be runner-up in the French Open Amateur in 1937.

Massy, Arnaud

Born Biarritz in 1877, died 1958. Was the first overseas player to win the Open in 1907 from Taylor, Vardon and Braid; tied with Vardon in 1911 and lost play-off, conceding on the 35th hole.

Micklem, Gerald

Gerald Micklem, born in 1911, devoted so much of his life to the benefit of golf, both as player and administrator, that he will always be remembered for his dedication to the cause of amateurs and professionals alike. He was one of the last true Corinthians, an almost forgotten appellation, who gave his time unsparingly to the game's development, whether locally at his favourite Sunningdale, at the Royal & Ancient or on the international scene. After a pre-war Oxford Blue, he was English Champion in 1947 and 1953, four times in the Walker Cup side between 1947 and 1955 and non-playing Captain in 1957 and 1959, and 12 years a Home International from 1947. He was second in the Brabazon and also won the St George's Challenge Cup, the Berkshire Trophy, the President's Putter and several Royal & Ancient Members' medals. When he ceased to play in tournaments, his administrative responsibilities were legion. Captain of many English and British teams in European and International events, he took a leading part in the development of the Open, being Chairman of the Championship Committee of the Royal & Ancient during a key period. It was in this appointment that he made his greatest contribution to the future of the game. It was his vision and enterprise which led to the spectacle that the Open is today, as the most prestigious and best organised Championship anywhere in the world. He was Captain of the Royal & Ancient Club in 1968. To the end of his life he lent his support to most golf ventures and many were the amateurs and professionals whom he helped and who were made welcome at his home, close to Sunningdale, and who remember his generosity and advice given, based on his wide knowledge of the game.

Mitchell, Abe

Born East Grinstead, 1887, died 1947. *The finest player who never won an Open Championship* was the tribute paid by JH Taylor. He finished in the first 6 five times in the Open and was 3 times winner of the Match Play Championship. Along with Duncan and later Compston, he was one of the few British hopes against the American invasion of the twenties.

The Morrises

Old Tom Morris and his son, young Tom Morris, played a prominent part in golf in the period from 1850 to 1875. The father was born at St Andrews on 16th June, 1821. At the age of eighteen, he was apprenticed to Allan Robertson in the ball-making trade. When Morris was thirty years of age, Colonel Fairlie of Coodham took him to Prestwick, and he remained there until 1865, when he returned to St Andrews and became greenkeeper to the Royal & Ancient Golf Club, a position he held until 1904. Young Tom was born at St Andrews in 1851, and exhibited early remarkable powers as a golfer. At the age of sixteen he won the Open Professional Tournament at Montrose against the best players in the country, and he won the Championship Belt outright by scoring three successive victories in 1868-9-70. The Championship lapsed for a year, but when it was resumed in 1872, young Tom scored his fourth successive victory. There is no doubt that young Tom was the finest golfer of his time, but the tragic death of his wife, while he was engaged playing with his father in a great golf match at North Berwick against the brothers Willie and Mungo Park, had a most depressing effect on him, and he only survived his wife by a few months. Near the finish of this match, a telegram reached North Berwick intimating that, following her confinement, young Tom's wife was dangerously ill. The telegram was held over by Provost Brodie and not handed to young Tom until the end of the match. The yacht of John Lewis, an Edinburgh golfer, was put at the service of the Morrises but before the party embarked, a second telegram brought the sad news to young Tom that his wife had died. It was a mournful party that made the voyage across the Forth to St Andrews. The brilliant young golfer never recovered from the shock, and he died on Christmas Day of the same year, 1875, at the age of twenty-four. There was a second son, JOF Morris, who played in professional tournaments, but, although a fine golfer, he never approached the brilliant execution of his elder brother. Old Tom competed in every Open Golf Championship up to and including 1896, which, curiously, was the year Harry Vardon scored his first victory in the Open Championship. Old Tom died at St Andrews in

1908. He was respected throughout the golfing world for his honest, sturdy qualities. His portrait hangs in the Royal & Ancient Clubhouse, and the home green at St Andrews is named in his memory. A monument, with a sculpted figure of Young Tom, in golfing pose, was erected by public subscription in St Andrews Cathedral Churchyard and a smaller memorial stone was placed on the grave when Old Tom died.

Ouimet, Francis D

Born Brookline, Mass, 1893, died 1967. Described as the player who started the golf boom in the US when as a young amateur he tied with Vardon and Ray for the 1913 US Open and then won the play-off. In an illustrious career he won the US Amateur twice and was a member of every Walker Cup team from 1922 to 1934 and was non-playing Captain from then until 1949. The first non-British national, to be elected Captain of the Royal & Ancient Golf Club in 1951. He was prominent in golf legislation and administration in America and a committee member of the USGA for many years.

The Parks

Brothers Willie and Mungo Park of Musselburgh are famous in the annals of golf for the numerous money matches they played. Willie had the distinction of winning the very first Open Championship in 1860 and repeated his victory in 1863, 1866 and 1875. For twenty years Willie had a standing challenge in *Bell's Life*, London, to play any man in the world for £100 a side. Willie took part in numerous matches against Tom Morris for very large stakes and in the last of these at Musselburgh in 1882, the match came to an abrupt end when Park was 2 up with 6 to play. The referee stopped play because spectators were interfering with the balls. Morris and the referee retired to Foreman's public house. Park sent a message saying if Morris did not come out and finish the match he would play the remaining holes alone and claim the stakes. This he did. Mungo followed in his brother's footsteps by winning the Open Championship in 1874. He was for many years greenkeeper and professional at Alnmouth. Willie's son, Willie Jun, kept up the golfing tradition of the family by winning the Open in 1887 and 1889. He designed many golf courses in Europe and America, sometimes in conjunction with property development as at Sunningdale, and was the pioneer of the modern ideas of golf course construction. Like his forebears he took part in many private challenge matches, the one against Harry Vardon at North Berwick in 1899 being watched by the greatest crowd ever for that time and for many years afterwards. Willie Jun died in 1925 aged 61. The

third generation of this golfing family sustained a prominent golf association through Miss Doris Park (Mrs Aylmer Porter), daughter of Willie Jun, who had a distinguished record in ladies' international and championship golf.

Philp, Hugh

The master craftsman among the half-dozen club-makers located in St Andrews in the early days of the nineteenth century. He was especially skilled in making a wooden putter with a long head of pear shaped design. He is believed to have made not many more than one hundred putters. The wooden putter was for centuries a favoured club at St Andrews for long approach putting. The creations of Hugh Philp are highly prized by golf club collectors. After his death in 1856 his business was carried on by Robert Forgan.

Ray, Edward

Born Jersey in 1877, died 1943. His early days coincided with the famous Triumvirate and it was not until 1912 that he won the Open and was runner-up the following year to Taylor. He was again runner-up in 1925 at the age of 48. In 1913 he tied for the US Open with Ouimet and Vardon, but lost the play-off. After the war he returned to America and won the US Open title in 1920 and was the last British player to hold the title until Tony Jacklin, in 1970. He and Vardon were the only British players to win both the US Open and the Open until they were joined by Jacklin. Noted for his long driving and powers of recovery, he was invariably to be seen playing with a pipe clenched between his teeth.

Rees, David James

One of Britain's outstanding golfers from the 1930s to the 1960s. He played in nine Ryder Cup matches between 1937 and 1961, and was also non-playing captain in 1967. In 1957, he captained the only British PGA team to win the Ryder Cup since 1933. He was three times a runner-up in the Open Championship and once third, and won the PGA Match-Play Championship four times, and the Dunlop Masters twice, in addition to numerous other tournament successes in Britain, on the Continent of Europe, and in Australasia. At the age of 60, in 1973, he finished third in the Martini Tournament. He was made an honorary member of the Royal & Ancient Golf Club in 1976. Born in March, 1913, he died in November, 1983.

Robertson, Allan

Born St Andrews, 1815, died 1858. According to tradition, he was never beaten in an individual stake match on level terms. A short, thick-set man, he had a beautiful well-timed swing, and several golfers who could recall Robertson, and who saw Harry Vardon at his best, were of the opinion that there was considerable similarity in the elegance and grace of the two players. Tom Morris, senior, worked in Allan Robertson's shop, where the principal trade was making feather balls. A disagreement occurred between Robertson and Morris on the advent of the gutta ball, because Old Tom decided to play with the invention, and Allan considered the gutta might damage his trade in featheries. Allan, through agents, endeavoured to buy up all gutta balls in order to protect his industry of feather balls. Allan Robertson and Tom Morris never seem to have come together in any single match for large stakes, but it is recorded that they never lost a foursome in which they were partners.

Sayers, Bernard

Born Leith, 1857, died at North Berwick, 9th March, 1924. Of very small stature, one of the smallest professionals, and light of build, he nevertheless took a leading position in the game for over forty years with his outstanding skill and rigid physical training. He engaged in numerous stake matches and played for Scotland against England in every match form 1903 to 1913, except 1911. He played in every Open Championship from 1880 to 1923. Of a bright and sunny disposition, he contributed much to the merriment of championship and professional gatherings. He taught princes and nobles to play the game, was presented to King Edward, and received a presentation from King George, when Duke of York.

Smith, Mrs Frances
(née Bunty Stephens)

Died July 1978, aged 53. Dominated post war women's golf by winning the British Ladies' Championship in 1949 and 1954 (runner-up 1951-52), the English Ladies' in 1948-54-55 (runner-up 1959) and the French Ladies' in 1949. She represented Great Britain in the Curtis Cup on six consecutive occasions form 1950 to 1960. A pronounced pause at the top of her swing made her style most distinctive. She was awarded the OBE for her services to golf and was president of the English Ladies' Golf Association at the time of her death.

Smith, Horton

Died October, 1963, aged 55. Came to notice first from Joplin, Missouri, when 20 years old, and brilliantly embarked on the professional circuit in the winter of 1929 when he won all but one of the open tournaments in which he played. He was promoted to that year's Ryder Cup team and also played in 1933 and 1935. He won the first US Masters Tournament in 1934 and again in 1936 as well as more than thirty other major events. On his 21st birthday he won the French Open. He was President of the American PGA, 1952-54 and received two national distinctions; the Ben Hogan Award for overcoming illness or injury, and the Bobby Jones Award for distinguished sportsmanship in golf. The day after the Ryder Cup match which he attended in Atlanta in 1963 he collapsed and died in a Detroit hospital.

Smith, Macdonald

Born at Carnoustie in 1890, died at Los Angeles in 1949. Was one of the great golfers who never won the Open Championship, in which he consistently finished in a high place, coming second in 1930 and 1932, third in 1923 and 1924, fourth in 1925 and 1934 and fifth in 1931. He went to America before he was twenty. In the Open Championship at Prestwick in 1925 he entered the last round with a lead of five strokes over the field, but a wildly enthusiastic Scottish crowd of 20,000 engulfed and overwhelmed him. The sequel to these unruly scenes was the introduction of gate money the following year and Prestwick was dropped from the rota for the Open.

Tait, Frederick Guthrie

Freddie Tait was born at 17 Drummond Place, Edinburgh (his father PG Tait was a Professor in Edinburgh University), on 11th January, 1870. He was killed in the South African War at Koodoosberg Drift, 7th February, 1900. He joined the Royal & Ancient in 1890 and on 5th August that year he beat all previous amateur records for St Andrews by holing the course in 77, and in 1894 he reduced the record to 72. He was first amateur in the Open Championship in 1894 (Sandwich), 1896 (Muirfield), 1899 (Sandwich). He was third in 1896 and 1897. He won the Amateur Championship in 1896 at Sandwich, beating in successive rounds GC Broadwood, Charles Hutchings, JE Laidlay, John Ball, Horace Hutchinson, and HH Hilton, the strongest amateurs of the day. He repeated his victory in 1898 at Hoylake, and in 1899 he fought and lost at the 37th the historic final with John Ball at Prestwick. There is a Freddie Tait Cup given annually to the best amateur in the South African Open Championship. This cup was purchased from the surplus of the fund collected during the visit of the British amateur golfers to South Africa in 1928.

Taylor, John Henry

Last survivor of the famous Triumvirate – Taylor, Braid and Vardon – died at his Devonshire home in February, 1963, within a month of his 92nd birthday. He was born at Northam, North Devon, 19th March, 1871, and had been professional at Burnham, Winchester and Royal Mid-Surrey. JH won the Open Championship five times – in 1894-95-1900-09-13 – and also tied with Harry Vardon in 1896, but lost the replay. He was runner-up also in 1904-05-06-14. His brilliant career included the French and German Open Championships and he was second in the US Open in 1900. Among the many honours he received were honorary membership of the Royal & Ancient Golf Club in 1949. He was regarded as the pioneer of British professionalism and helped to start the Professional Golfers' Association. He did much to raise the whole status of the professional and, in the words of Bernard Darwin, *turned a feckless company into a self-respecting and respected body of men.* On his retirement in 1957 the Royal North Devon Golf Club paid him their greatest compliment by electing him President.

Tolley, Cyril James Hastings

Born in 1896, Tolley was a dominant figure in amateur golf in the inter-war period. He won the first of two Amateur Championships in 1920 while still a student at Oxford and continued to win championships and represent England and Britain until 1938. Among other titles he won the Welsh Open (1921 and 1923) and remains the only amateur to have won the French Open (1924 and 1929). A powerful hitter with a delicate touch, Tolley was a crowd pleaser. He is remembered as much for a match he lost as much as for some of his victories. Having won the Amateur Championship in 1929, Tolley was a favourite to win at St Andrews in 1930. The draw was unseeded and he met Bobby Jones in the fourth round. A huge crowd turned out to watch an extremely exciting match which Jones won on the 19th with a stymie. The rest is history. Tolley was elected Captain of the R & A in 1948. He died in 1978.

Travis, Walter J

Born in Australia in 1862, died in New York 1925. Travis was the first overseas golfer to win the British Amateur, at Sandwich in 1904. He won the title using a centre-shafted putter, which was subsequently banned for many years. He won the US Amateur Championship in 1900, having taken up

the game four years previously at the age of 35. He repeated his victory in 1901 and 1903 and was a semi-finalist five times between 1898 and 1914, winning also the stroke competition six times between 1900 and 1908. The *Old Man* as he was known is reckoned to have been one of the finest judges of distance who ever played golf.

Vardon, Harry

Born Grouville, Jersey, died at South Herts on 20th March, 1937. Created a record by winning the Open Championship six times, his wins being in 1896, 1898, 1899, 1903, 1911 and 1914. He also won the American Open in 1900 and tied in 1913, subsequently losing the play-off. He had a serious illness in 1903 and it was said that he never quite regained his former dominance, particularly on the putting green. That he was the foremost golfer of his time cannot be disputed and he innovated the modern upright swing and popularised the over-lapping grip invented by JE Laidlay. Had it not been for ill-health and the intervention of the First World War, his outstanding records both in the UK and America would almost certainly have been added to in later years. But in any event his profound influence on the game lives on. More than 100 years after his birth his achievements are still the standard of comparison with the latter day giants of the game.

Wethered, Roger H

Born 3rd January, 1899, in Malden, Surrey and died in 1983, aged 84. He was one of the outstanding amateurs of the period between the two World Wars, winning the Amateur Championship in 1923, and being runner-up in 1928 and 1930. He won the President's Putter of the Oxford and Cambridge GS five times (once a tie) between 1926 and 1936, played against the United States six times between 1921 and 1934, and for England against Scotland every year from 1922 to 1930. He was captain of the Royal & Ancient in 1946. But he will probably be best remembered for the fact that he tied with Jock Hutchison, a Scot who had settled in the United States, for first place in the 1921 Open Championship at St Andrews, having incurred a penalty stroke in the course of the event by inadvertently stepping backwards and treading on his ball, while Hutchison, in the first round, had had a hole in one. Wethered was reluctant to stay on for the 36-hole play-off the following day because of a cricket engagement in England, but was persuaded to do so, only to be beaten by nine strokes, 150 to 159. No British amateur has come so close to winning the Open Championship since.

Wood, Craig Ralph

Born Lake Placid, New York, 18th November, 1901. Died 1968. Visited Great Britain for first time in 1933, and tied for Open Championship with Denny Shute, but lost on replay. Won American Open Championship, 1941; US Masters' Tournament, 1941; Canadian Open Championship, 1942; runner-up American PGA Championship, 1934. In 1936 second in USPGA Championship. A member of the American Ryder Cup team, 1931-33-35, and US Australian team, 1937. In 1939 tied for US Open, but lost on replay.

Zaharias, Mrs George (Mildred Babe Didrikson)

Born at Port Arthur, Texas, USA, in June 1915, and died of cancer at Galveston in September 1956. In the 1932 Olympic Games she established three world records for women: 80 metres hurdles, javelin, and high jump. On giving up athletics she took up golf and won the Texas Women's Open in 1940-45-46; Western Open, 1940-44-45-50; US National Women's Amateur, 1946. In 1947 won the Ladies' Championship, being the first American to do so. In August 1947 she turned professional and went on to win the US National Women's Open, 1948-50. In winning the Tampa Open, 1951, she set up a then women's world record aggregate of 288 for 72 holes. She was voted Woman Athlete of the year 1932-45-46-47-50, and in 1949 was voted Greatest Female Athlete of the Half-Century. First woman to hold the post of head professional to a golf club. The *Babe* was a courageous and fighting character who left her mark in the world of sport.

The British Golf Museum

Peter Lewis MA, MPhil, MBIM, Museum Director

The British Golf Museum, located opposite the Royal & Ancient Club House, is truly in the centre of the 'home of golf' – St Andrews. It opened its doors to the public on 25 June 1990 and then was officially opened by Viscount Whitelaw three months later. As its name implies, the museum tells the story of golf in Britain and British influence on golf abroad from the Middle Ages to the present day.

The museum is set out chronologically, taking the visitor from the earliest surviving written reference to golf, in 1457, right up to the 1990s. Each gallery has a well-defined theme. The tour begins with the origins of the game in Scotland under the Stuart monarchs, through the eighteenth century to the nineteenth century. The beginnings of the Open Championship, from 1860 to 1891, are covered in depth, as are the early years of the Amateur Championship, which began in 1885. The story then moves on to golf in the period 1890 to 1914, with an emphasis on equipment development and the Open Championship. There is a gallery devoted to the administration of golf and another on the growth of the game between the two world wars. The largest gallery in the museum is the one dealing with golf since 1946. There is also a section charting the development of ladies' golf, a temporary exhibition gallery, a 48-seat audiovisual theatre and a shop.

Dramatic tableaux depict two eighteenth century gentlemen making bets before playing a round of golf; Allan Robertson making feather balls in his kitchen, c1840; the changes in ladies' fashions from 1890 to 1990 and Willie and Laurie Auchterlonie designing clubs in their workshop in about 1946.

The whole museum is brought to life by the use of touch screens. At the touch of a fingertip, visitors can activate choices of programs, ranging from biographies of famous players to accounts of epic golf matches; from the role of caddies to the role of the Royal & Ancient Golf Club; from nineteenth century fashions to fashionable modern golfers. For the truly dedicated visitor there is on offer a plethora of statistics of major championships, and two quizzes – on the Rules of Golf and the History of Golf. In all there

Peter Lewis, Director of the British Golf Museum.

© APS Group

are 11 work stations spread throughout the galleries containing 138 program choices. All the hardware and software in the museum were kindly supplied by Philips Electronics, using the most advanced optical disc technology in the world – Compact Disk Interactive (CD–I).

The exhibits themselves constitute the finest public display of golfing memorabilia in Britain. Major changes in equipment can be seen in their historical context and their impact on the game visibly measured. The clubs range from long-nosed spoons with hickory shafts hand-made by master clubmakers such as Hugh Philp, John Jackson and the McEwans to computer-designed metal woods with graphite shafts. Feather balls, gutta-percha balls, early wound core rubber balls and modern two-piece balls all have their places in the displays.

The fruits of victory are, of course, much in evidence: the 131 medals won by John Laidlay, James Robb's Amateur Championship medals, JH Taylor's five Open medals, James Braid's five Open medals, one of Walter Hagen's Open medals, Robert Wethered's medal collection and a superb range of medals and trophies from the ladies' game. The driving putter used by Tom Morris when he won the 1867 Open is here, as are Bobby Jones' driver from the 1920s and clubs used by Arnold Palmer in the 1960 Open. Old and Young Tom Morris, John Ball, Harry Var-

don, JH Taylor, James Braid, Henry Cotton, Walter Hagen and Joyce Wethered are just some of the other great personalities and champions of the game represented in the museum by displays of items that belonged to them.

The lighter side of golf is on display too. Visitors can see, among other wonders, a stuffed bird, killed by a ball at the R&A Spring Meeting in 1890; cigarette cards and flicker books of the 1930s; a nineteenth-century club membership ballot box; Bateman cartoons on ceramic pieces; the earliest known golfing bet, dated 1504 and the first known explanation of handicapping in 1687.

All of this is contained in an exhibition area of about 6500 square feet. The galleries were designed by Leslie Gooday and Associates and the touch screen programs were designed by APS Advertising and Marketing. All the text and captions for the displays as well as the scripts for the touch screens were supplied by myself.

The museum, a purpose-built building of about 11,000 square feet received planning permission in March 1989 and construction began that May. Sandy Sinclair, then Captain of the R&A, cut the first divot. Thirteen months later, he was the first customer through the doors of the completed museum.

The British Golf Museum is an independent enterprise, owned by the Royal & Ancient Golf Club of St Andrews Trust. Most of the funding came from the Royal & Ancient Golf Club along with a grant from the Scottish Tourist Board and a major contribution from Philips Interactive Media Systems via a sponsorship arrangement.

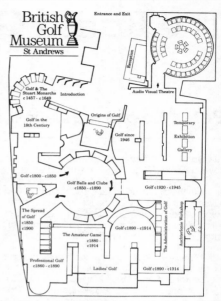

© Artis Associates

The museum, laid out over 6500 square feet, includes an audiovisual theatre and combines in its displays vivid historical tableaux and the latest computer technology.

A tour of the museum begins with an introduction to the game's origins, computerised touch-screens complemented by remarkable collections of historic equipment, such as these early clubs.

© APS Group

Part VII
Interesting Facts and Record Scoring

Interesting Facts and Unusual Incidents

Royal Golf Clubs

● The right to the designation *Royal* is bestowed by the favour of the Sovereign or a member of the Royal House. In most cases the title is granted along with the bestowal of royal patronage on the club. The Perth Golfing Society was the first to receive the designation *Royal*. That was accorded in June 1833. King William IV bestowed the honour on the Royal & Ancient Club in 1834. The most recent Club to be so designated is the Royal Troon in 1978.

Royal and Presidential Golfers

● In the long history of the Royal and Ancient game no reigning British monarch has played in an open competition. The Duke of Windsor, when Prince of Wales in 1922, competed in the Royal & Ancient Autumn Medal at St Andrews. He also took part in competitions at Mid-Surrey, Sunningdale, Royal St George's and in the Parliamentary Handicap. He also occasionally competed in American events, sometimes partnered by a professional, and on a private visit to London in 1952 he competed in the Autumn competition of Royal St George's at Sandwich scoring 97. As Prince of Wales he had played on courses all over the world and, after his abdication, as Duke of Windsor he continued to enjoy the game for many years.

● King George VI (when Duke of York) in 1930 and the Duke of Kent in 1937 also competed in the Autumn Meeting of the Royal & Ancient, these occasions being after they had formally played themselves into the Captaincy of the Club and each returned his card in the medal round.

● King Leopold of Belgium played in the Belgian Amateur Championship at Le Zoute, the only reigning monarch ever to have played in a national championship. The Belgian King played in many competitions subsequent to his abdication. In 1949 he reached the quarter-finals of the French Amateur Championship at St Cloud, playing as Count de Rethy.

● King Baudouin of Belgium in 1958 played in the triangular match Belgium-France-Holland and won his match against a Dutch player. He also took part in the Gleneagles Hotel tournament (playing as Mr B de Rethy), partnered by Dai Rees in 1959.

● United States President George Bush accepted an invitation in 1990 to become an Honorary Member of the Royal & Ancient Golf Club of St Andrews. The honour recognised his long connection and that of his family with golf and the R&A. Both President Bush's father, Prescott Bush Sr, and his grandfather, George Herbert Walker – who donated the Walker Cup – were presidents of the United States Golf Association. Other Honorary Members of the R&A are the Duke of Edinburgh, the Duke of Kent, Kel Nagle, Jack Nicklaus, Arnold Palmer, Gene Sarazen, Peter Thomson and Roberto De Vicenzo.

First Lady Golfer

● Mary Queen of Scots, who was beheaded on 8th February, 1587, was probably the first lady golfer so mentioned by name. As evidence of her indifference to the fate of Darnley, her husband who was murdered at Kirk o' Field, Edinburgh, she was charged at her trial with having played at golf in the fields beside Seton a few days after his death.

Record Championship Victories

● In the Amateur Championship at Muirfield, 1920, Captain Carter, an Irish golfer, defeated an American entrant by 10 and 8. This is the only known instance where a player has won every hole in an Amateur Championship tie.

● In the final of the Canadian Ladies Championship at Rivermead, Ottawa, 1921, Cecil Leitch defeated Mollie McBride by 17 and 15. Miss Leitch only lost 1 hole in the match, the ninth. She was 14 up at the end of the first round, and only 3 holes were necessary in the second round, Miss Leitch winning them all. She won 18 holes out of 21 played, lost 1, and halved 2.

● In the final of the French Ladies' Open Championship at Le Touquet in 1927, Mlle de la Chaume (St Cloud) defeated Mrs Alex Johnston (Moor Park) by 15 and 14, the largest victory in a European golf championship.

● At Prestwick in 1934, W Lawson Little, Presidio, San Francisco, defeated James Wallace, Troon Portland, by 14 and 13 in the final of the Amateur Championship, the record victory in the Amateur Championship. Wallace failed to win a single hole.

● The largest victory in the Walker Cup in 18-hole matches was in 1979 when American Scott Hoch beat Jim Buckley by 9 and 7. Buckley had a back injury.

Players who have won Two or More Major Championships since 1916

● (The first Masters Tournament was played in 1934.)

1922 Gene Sarazen – USPGA, US Open
1924 Walter Hagen – USPGA, Open
1926 Bobby Jones – US Open, Open
1930 Bobby Jones – US Open, Open (Bobby Jones also won the US Amateur and British Amateur in this year.)
1932 Gene Sarazen – US Open, Open
1941 Craig Wood – Masters, US Open
1948 Ben Hogan – USPGA, US Open
1949 Sam Snead – USPGA, Masters
1951 Ben Hogan – Masters, US Open
1953 Ben Hogan – Masters, US Open, Open
1956 Jack Burke – USPGA, Masters
1960 Arnold Palmer – Masters, US Open
1962 Arnold Palmer – Masters, Open
1963 Jack Nicklaus – USPGA, Masters
1966 Jack Nicklaus – Masters, Open
1971 Lee Trevino – US Open, Open
1972 Jack Nicklaus – Masters, Open
1974 Gary Player – Masters, Open
1975 Jack Nicklaus – USPGA, Masters
1977 Tom Watson – Masters, Open
1980 Jack Nicklaus – USPGA, US Open
1982 Tom Watson – US Open, Open
1990 Nick Faldo – Masters, Open

Outstanding Records in Championships, International Matches and on the Professional Circuit

● The record number of victories in the Open Championship is six, held by Harry Vardon who won in 1896-98-99-1903-11-14.

● Five-time winners of the Championship are JH Taylor in 1894-95-1900-09-13; James Braid in 1901-05-06-08-10; Peter Thomson in 1954-55-56-58-65 and Tom Watson in 1975-77-80-82-83. Thomson's 1965 win was achieved when the Championship had become a truly international event. In 1957 he finished second behind Bobby Locke. By winning again in 1958 Thomson was prevented only by Bobby Locke from winning five consecutive Open Championships.

● Four successive victories in the Open by Young Tom Morris is a record so far never equalled. He won in 1868-69-70-72. (The Championship was not played in 1871.) Other four-time winners are Bobby Locke in 1949-50-52-57, Walter Hagen in 1922-24-28-29, Willie Park 1860-63-66-75, and Old Tom Morris 1861-62-64-67.

● Since the Championship began in 1860, players who have won three times in succession are Jamie Anderson, Bob Ferguson, and Peter Thomson.

● Robert Tyre Jones won the Open three times in 1926-27-30; the Amateur in 1930; the American Open in 1923-26-29-30; and the American Amateur in 1924-25-27-28-30. In winning the four major golf titles of the world in one year (1930) he achieved a feat unlikely ever to be equalled. Jones retired from competitive golf after winning the 1930 American Open, the last of these Championships, at the age of 28.

● Jack Nicklaus has had the most wins (six) in the US Masters Tournament, followed by Arnold Palmer with four.

● In modern times there are four championships generally regarded as standing above all others – the Open, US Open, US Masters, and USPGA. Four players have held all these titles, Gene Sarazen, Ben Hogan, Gary Player, and Jack Nicklaus, who in 1978 became the first player to have held each of them at least three times. His record in these events is – Open 1966-70-78; US Open 1962-67-72-80; US Masters 1963-65-66-72-75-86; USPGA 1963-71-73-75-80. His total of major championships is now 18.

The nearest approach to achieving the Grand Slam of the Open, US Open, US Masters and USPGA in one year was by Ben Hogan in 1953 when he won the first three and could not compete in the USPGA as it then overlapped with the Open Championship.

● In 1975 Jack Nicklaus came very near to winning the Grand Slam, winning the Masters and the USPGA and finishing only two shots and one shot behind the winning scores in the US Open and the Open Championship respectively.

● The record number of victories in the US Open is four, held by W Anderson, Bobby Jones, Ben Hogan and Jack Nicklaus.

● Bobby Jones (amateur), Gene Sarazen, Ben Hogan, Lee Trevino and Tom Watson are the only players to have won the Open and US Open Championships in the same year. Tony Jacklin won the Open in 1969 and the US Open in 1970 and for a few weeks was the holder of both.

● John Ball holds the record number of victories in the Amateur Championship, which he won eight times. Next comes Michael Bonallack (who was internationally known as The Duke) with five wins.

● In winning the Amateur Championship in 1970 Michael Bonallack became the first player to win in three consecutive years.

● The English Amateur record number of victories is held by Michael Bonallack, who won the title five times.

● Cecil Leitch and Joyce Wethered each won the British Ladies' title four times.

● The Scottish Amateur record is held by Ronnie Shade, who won five titles in successive years – 1963-64-65-66-67. His long reign as Champion ended when he was beaten in the fourth round of the 1968 Championship after winning 44 consecutive matches.

● Joyce Wethered established an unbeaten record by winning the English Ladies' in five successive years from 1920 to 1924 inclusive.

● In winning the Amateur Championships of Britain and America in 1934 and 1935 Lawson Little won 31 consecutive matches. Other dual winners of these championships in the same year are RT Jones (1930) and Bob Dickson (1967).

● Gary Player won the South African Open for the 13th time in 1981. He has also won the Australian Open seven times.

● Peter Thomson's victory in the 1971 New Zealand Open Championship was his ninth in that championship.

● In a four week spell in 1971, Lee Trevino won in succession the US Open, the Canadian Open and the Open Championships.

● The finalists in the 1970 Amateur Championship, Michael Bonallack and Bill Hyndman, were the same as in 1969. This was the first time the same two players reached the final in successive years.

● Seve Ballesteros holds the record for most wins in one year on the European Tour, six in 1986; this followed his record equalling number in 1985. The best British players have been Bernard Hunt in 1963, Nick Faldo in 1983, and Ian Woosnam in 1987, each with five victories.

● On the US professional circuit the greatest number of consecutive victories is 11, achieved by Byron Nelson in 1945. Nelson also holds the record for most victories in one calendar year, again in 1945 when he won a total of 18 tournaments.

● Jack Nicklaus and the late Walter Hagen have had five wins each in the USPGA Championship. All Hagen's wins were in successive years and at match play; all Nicklaus's at stroke play.

● In 1953 Flori van Donck of Belgium had seven major victories in Europe, including the Open Championships of Switzerland, Italy, Holland, Germany and Belgium.

● In 1947 Norman von Nida (Australia) had seven tournament victories in England.

● Mrs Anne Sander won four major amateur titles each under a different name. She won the US Ladies' in 1958 as Miss Quast, in 1961 as Mrs Decker, in 1963 as Mrs Welts and the British Ladies' in 1980 as Mrs Sander.

● The highest number of appearances in the Ryder Cup matches is held by Christy O'Connor who made his tenth appearance in 1973.

● The greatest number of appearances in the Walker Cup matches is held by Irishman Joe Carr who made his tenth appearance in 1967.

● In the Curtis Cup Mary McKenna made her ninth consecutive appearance in 1986.

● Players who have represented their country in both Walker and Ryder Cup matches are Fred Haas, Ken Venturi, Gene Littler, Jack Nicklaus, Tommy Aaron, Mason Rudolph, Bob Murphy, Lanny Wadkins, Tom Kite, Jerry Pate, Craig Stadler, Jay Haas, Bill Rodgers, Hal Sutton and Curtis Strange (US), and Norman Drew, Peter Townsend, Clive Clark, Peter Oosterhuis, Howard Clark, Mark James, Michael King, Paul Way, Ronan Rafferty and Sandy Lyle (Great Britain and Ireland).

Remarkable Recoveries in Match Play

● There have been two remarkable recoveries in the Walker Cup Matches. In 1930 at Sandwich, JA Stout, Great Britain, round in 68, was 4 up at the end of the first round against Donald Moe. Stout started in the second round, 3, 3, 3, and was 7 up. He was still 7 up with 13 to play. Moe, who went round in 67, won back the 7 holes to draw

level at the 17th green. At the 18th or 36th of the match, Moe, after a long drive placed his iron shot within three feet of the hole and won the match by 1 hole.

● In 1936 at Pine Valley, George Voigt and Harry Girvan for America were 7 up with 11 to play against Alec Hill and Cecil Ewing. The British pair drew level at the 17th hole, or the 35th of the match, and the last hole was halved.

● In the 1965 Piccadilly Match-Play Championship Gary Player beat Tony Lema after being 7 down with 17 to play.

● Bobby Cruickshank, the old Edinburgh player, had an extraordinary recovery in a 36-hole match in a USPGA Championship for he defeated Al Watrous after being 11 down with 12 to play.

● In a match at the Army GC, Aldershot, on 5th July, 1974, for the Gradoville Bowl, MC Smart was eight down with eight to play against Mike Cook. Smart succeeded in winning all the remaining holes and the 19th for victory.

Oldest Champions

Open Championship

Belt: 46 years. Tom Morris in 1867.
Cup: 44 years 93 days. Roberto De Vicenzo in 1967.
    44 years 42 days. Harry Vardon in 1914.
    42 years 97 days. JH Taylor in 1913.
Amateur Championship: Hon Michael Scott, 54 years, Hoylake 1933.
British Ladies Amateur: Mrs Jessie Valentine, 43 years, Hunstanton 1958.
Scottish Amateur: JM Cannon, 53 years, Troon 1969.
English Amateur: Terry Shingler, 41 years 11 months, Walton Heath 1977. Gerald Micklem, 41 years 8 months, Royal Birkdale 1947.
US Open: Hale Irwin, 45 years, Medinah, Illinois, 1990.
US Amateur: Jack Westland, 47 years, Seattle 1952. Westland was defeated in the 1931 final, 21 years previously, by Francis Ouimet at Beverley, Chicago, Illinois.
US Masters: Jack Nicklaus, 46 years, in 1986.
USPGA: Julius Boros, 48 years, in 1968. Lee Trevino, 43 years, in 1984.
USPGA Tour: Sam Snead, 52 years, Greensborough Open in 1965. Julius Boros lost play-off in Westchester Classic 1975. Sam Snead, 61 years, equal second in Glen Campbell Open 1974.

Youngest Champions

Open Championship

Belt: 17 years 5 months. Tom Morris, Jr in 1868.

Cup: 21 years 25 days. Willie Auchterlonie in 1893.
21 years 5 months. Tom Morris, Jr in 1872.
22 years 103 days. Severiano Ballesteros in 1979.
Amateur Championship: JC Beharrell, 18 years 1 month, Troon 1956. R Cole (S Africa) 18 years 1 month, Carnoustie 1966.
British Ladies Amateur: May Hezlett, 17 years, Newcastle Co Down 1899. Michelle Walker, 18 years, Alwoodley 1971.
English Amateur: Nick Faldo, 18 years, Lytham St Annes 1975. Paul Downes, 18 years, Birkdale 1978.
English Amateur Stroke Play: Ronan Rafferty, 16 years, Hunstanton 1980.
British Ladies Open Stroke Play: Helen Dobson, 18 years, Southerness, 1989.

Disqualifications

Disqualifications are now numerous, usually for some irregularity over signing a scorecard or for late arrival at the first tee. We therefore show here only incidents in major events involving famous players or players who were in a winning position or, alternatively, incidents which were in themselves unusual.

● JJ McDermott, the American Open Champion 1911-12, arrived for the Open Championship at Prestwick in 1914 to discover that he had made a mistake of a week in the date the championship began. The American could not play as the qualifying rounds were completed on the day he arrived.

● In the Amateur Championship at Sandwich in 1937, Brigadier-General Critchley, arriving from New York at Southampton on the *Queen Mary*, which had been delayed by fog, flew by specially chartered aeroplane to Sandwich. He circled over the clubhouse, so that the officials knew he was nearly there, but he arrived six minutes late, and his name had been struck out. At the same championship a player, entered from Burma, who had travelled across the Pacific and the American Continent, and also was on the *Queen Mary*, travelled from Southampton by motor car and arrived four hours after his starting time to find after journeying more than halfway round the world he was *struck out.*

● An unprecedented disqualification was that of A Murray in the New Zealand Open Championship, 1937. Murray, who was New Zealand Champion in 1935, was playing with JP Hornabrook, New Zealand Amateur Champion, and at the 8th hole in the last round, while waiting for his partner to putt, Murray dropped a ball on the edge of the green and made a practice putt along the edge. Murray returned the lowest score in the championship, but he was disqualified for taking the practice putt.

● At the Open Championship at St Andrews in 1946, John Panton, Glenbervie, in the evening practised putting on a green on the New Course, which was one of the qualifying courses. He himself reported his inadvertence to the Royal & Ancient and he was disqualified.

● At the Open Championship, Sandwich, 1949, C Rotar, an American, qualified by four strokes to compete in the championship but he was disqualified because he had used a putter which did not conform to the accepted form and make of a golf club, the socket being bent over the centre of the club head. This is the only case where a player has been disqualified in the Open Championship for using an illegal club.

● In the 1957 American Women's Open Championship, Mrs Jackie Pung had the lowest score, 298 over four rounds, but lost the championship. The card she signed for the final round read *five* at the 4th hole instead of the correct *six*. Her total of 72 was correct but the error, under rigid rules, resulted in her disqualification. Betty Jameson, who partnered Mrs Pung and also returned a wrong score, was also disqualified.

Longest Match

● WR Chamberlain, a retired farmer, and George New, a postmaster at Chilton Foliat, on 1st August, 1922, met at Littlecote, the 9-hole course of Sir Ernest Wills, and they agreed to play every Thursday afternoon over the course. This they did until New's sudden death on 13th January, 1938. An accurate record of the matches was kept giving details of each round including wind direction and playing conditions. In the elaborate system nearly two million facts were recorded. They played 814 rounds, and aggregated 86,397 strokes, of which Chamberlain took 44,008 and New 42,371. New, therefore, was 1,637 strokes up. The last round of all was halved, a suitable end to such an unusual contest.

Longest Ties

● The longest known ties in 18-hole match play rounds in major events were in an early round of the News of the World Match Play Championship at Turnberry in 1960, when WS Collins beat WJ Branch at the 31st hole and in the third round of the same tournament at Walton Heath in 1961 when Harold Henning beat Peter Alliss also at the 31st hole.

● In the 1970 Scottish Amateur Championship at Balgownie, Aberdeen, E Hammond beat J McIvor at the 29th hole in their second round tie.

● CA Palmer beat Lionel Munn at the 28th hole at Sandwich in 1908. This is the record tie of the British Amateur Championship. Munn has also been engaged in two other extended ties in the Amateur Championship. At Muirfield, in 1932, in

the semi-final, he was defeated by John de Forest, the ultimate winner, at the 26th hole, and at St Andrews, in 1936, in the second round he was defeated by JL Mitchell, again at the 26th hole.

The following examples of long ties are in a different category for they occurred in competitions, either stroke play or match play, where the conditions stipulated that in the event of a tie, a further stated number of holes had to be played – in some cases 36 holes, but mostly 18. With this method a vast number of extra holes was sometimes necessary to settle ties.

● The longest known was between two American women in a tournament at Peterson (New Jersey) when 88 extra holes were required before Mrs Edwin Labaugh emerged as winner.

● In a match on the Queensland course, Australia, in October, 1933, HB Bonney and Col HCH Robertson versus BJ Canniffe and Dr Wallis Hoare required to play a further four 18-hole matches after being level at the end of the original 18 holes. In the fourth replay Hoare and Caniffe won by 3 and 2 which meant that 70 extra holes had been necessary to decide the tie.

● After finishing all square in the final of the Dudley GC's foursomes competition in 1950, FW Mannell and AG Walker played a further three 18-hole replays against T Poole and E Jones, each time finishing all square. A further 9 holes were then arranged when Mannell and Walker won by 3 and 2 making a total of 61 extra holes to decide the tie.

● RA Whitcombe and Mark Seymour tied for first prize in the Penfold £750 Tournament at St Annes-on-Sea, in 1934. They had to play off over 36 holes and tied again. They were then required to play another 9 holes when Whitcombe won with 34 against 36. The tournament was over 72 holes. The first tie added 36 holes and the extra 9 holes made an aggregate of 117 holes to decide the winner. This is a record in first-class British golf but in no way compares with other long ties as it involved only two replays – one of 36 holes and one of 9.

● In the American Open Championship at Toledo, Ohio, in 1931, G Von Elm and Billy Burke tied for the title. Each required aggregates of 292. On the first replay both finished in 149 for 36 holes but on the second replay Burke won with a score of 148 against 149. This is a record tie in a national open championship.

● Paul Downes was beaten by Robin Davenport at the 9th extra hole in the 4th round of the 1981 English Amateur Championship. A record marathon match for the championship.

● Severiano Ballesteros was beaten by Johnny Miller at the 9th extra hole of a sudden-death play-off at the 1982 million dollar Sun City

Challenge, a record for any 72 hole professional event.

● José Maria Olazabal beat Ronan Rafferty at the 9th extra hole to win the 1989 Dutch Open on the Kennemer Golf and Country Club course.

Long Drives

It is impossible to state with any certainty what is the longest ever drive. Many long drives have never been measured and many others have most likely never been brought to our attention. Then there are several outside factors which can produce freakishly long drives, such as a strong following wind, downhill terrain or bonehard ground. Where all three of these favourable conditions prevail outstandingly long drives can be achieved. Another consideration is that a long drive made during a tournament is a different proposition from one made for length alone, either on the practice ground, a long driving competition or in a game of no consequence. All this should be borne in mind when considering the long drives shown here.

● Tommie Campbell of Portmarnock hit a drive of 392 yards at Dun Laoghaire GC in July 1964.

● Playing in Australia, American George Bayer is reported to have driven to within chipping distance of a 589 yards hole. *It was certainly a drive of over 500 yards,* said Bayer acknowledging the strong following wind, sharp downslope where his ball landed and the bonehard ground.

● In September, 1934, over the East Devon course, THV Haydon, Wimbledon, drove to the edge of the 9th green which was a hole of 465 yards, giving a drive of not less than 450 yards. The hole was downhill and presumably other favourable conditions were also present. Haydon is also reported to have nearly driven the 15th hole (420 yards) at Royal Wimbledon in October, 1929. The ball finished just short of the green on a hole which was slightly uphill all the way and when the following wind was described as only a breeze.

● EC Bliss drove 445 yards at Herne Bay in August, 1913. The drive was measured by a Government Surveyor who also measured the drop in height from tee to resting place of the ball at 57 feet.

● George Johnson in 1972, with the assistance of a following wind, drove a ball 413 yards at the 8th hole at Delamere Forest.

Long Carries

● At Sitwell Park, Rotherham, in 1935, W Smithson, the home professional, drove a ball which carried a dyke at 380 yards from the 2nd tee.

● George Bell, of Penrith GC, New South Wales,

Australia, using a number 2 wood drove across the Nepean River, a certified carry of 309 yards in a driving contest in 1964.

● After the 1986 Irish Professional Championship at Waterville, Co. Kerry, four long-hitting professionals tried for the longest-carry record over water, across a lake in the Waterville Hotel grounds. Liam Higgins, the local professional, carried 310 yards and Paul Leonard 311, beating the previous record by 2 yards.

● In the 1972 Algarve Open at Penina, Henry Cotton vouched for a carry of 305 yards over a ditch at the 18th hole by long-hitting Spanish professional Francisco Abreu. There was virtually no wind assistance.

● At the Home International matches at Portmarnock in 1949 a driving competition was held in which all the players in the English, Scottish, Welsh and Irish teams competed. The actual carry was measured. The longest was 280 yards by Jimmy Bruen.

● When Walter Hagen was in Britain for the Open Championship in 1928, he drove a ball from the roof of the Savoy Hotel to the other side of the Thames.

● On 6th April, 1976, Tony Jacklin hit a number of balls into Vancouver harbour, Canada, from the 495-foot high roof of a new building complex. The longest carry was measured at 389 yards.

Long Hitting

There have been numerous long hits, not on golf courses, where an outside agency has assisted the length of the shot. Such an example was a 'drive' by Liam Higgins in 1986, on the Airport runway at Baldonal, near Dublin, of 632 yards.

Longest Albatrosses

● The longest-known albatrosses (three under par) recorded at par 5 holes are:

● 609 yards-15th hole at Mahaka Inn West Course, Hawaii, by John Eakin of California on 12th November, 1972.

● 602 yards-16th hole at Whiting Field Golf Course, Milton, Florida, by 27-year-old Bill Graham with a drive and a 3-wood, aided by a 25 mph tail wind.

● The longest-known albatrosses in Open Championships are:

580 yards-14th hole at Crans-sur-Sierre, by American Billy Casper in the 1971 Swiss Open.

558 yards-5th hole at Muirfield by American Johnny Miller in the 1972 Open Championship.

Eagles (Multiple and Consecutive)

● Wilf Jones scored three consecutive eagles at the first three holes at Moor Hall GC when playing in a competition there on August Bank

Holiday Monday 1968. He scored 3, 1, 2 at holes measuring 529 yards, 176 yards and 302 yards.

● In a round of the 1980 Jubilee Cup, a mixed foursomes match play event of Colchester GC, Mrs Nora Booth and her son Brendan scored three consecutive gross eagles of 1, 3, 2 at the 8th, 9th and 10th holes.

● Three players in a four-ball match at Kington GC, Herefordshire, on 22nd July, 1948, all had eagle 2s at the 18th hole (272 yards). They were RN Bird, R Morgan and V Timson.

● Four Americans from Wisconsin on holiday at Gleneagles in 1977 scored three eagles and a birdie at the 300-yard par-4 14th hole on the King's course. The birdie was by Dr Kim Lulloff and the eagles by Dr Gordon Meiklejohn, Richard Johnson and Jack Kubitz.

● In an open competition at Glen Innes GC, Australia on 13th November, 1977, three players in a four-ball scored eagle 3s at the 9th hole (442 metres). They were Terry Marshall, Roy McHarg and Jack Rohleder.

Speed of Golf Ball and Club Head and Effect of Wind and Temperature

● In *The Search for the Perfect Swing*, a scientific study of the golf swing, a first class golfer is said to have the club head travelling at 100 mph at impact. This will cause the ball to leave the club at 135 mph. An outstandingly long hitter might manage to have the club head travelling at 130 mph which would produce a ball send-off speed of 175 mph. The resultant shot would carry 280 yards.

● According to Thomas Hardman, Wilson's director of research and development, wind will reduce or increase the flight of a golf ball by approximately 1½ yards for every mile per hour of wind. Every two degrees of temperature will make a yard difference in a ball's flight.

Highest Golf Courses

● The highest golf course in the world is thought to be the Tuctu GC in Peru which is 14,335 feet above sea-level. High courses are also found in Bolivia with the La Paz GC being about 13,500 feet. In the Himalayas, near the border with Tibet, a 9-hole course at 12,800 feet has been laid out by keen golfers in the Indian Army.

● The highest known course in Europe is at Sestriere in the Italian Alps, 6,500 feet above sea-level.

● The highest courses in Great Britain are Leadhills in Scotland at 1,500 feet, Tredegar in Wales rising to 1,300 feet and Church Stretton in England at 1,250 feet.

Lowest Courses

● The lowest known course in the world was at Kallia, south of Jericho. No longer in existence, this 9-hole course, running along the shore of the Dead Sea, lay 1,250 feet below normal sea-level.

Most Northerly Course

● The most northerly course is the Akureyri Golf Club in Iceland which is situated 65°40' North of the equator. Not far south is the Luleö course in Sweden, at 65°35' North.

Longest Courses

● The longest course in the world is Dub's Dread GC, Piper, Kansas, USA measuring 8,101 yards (par 78).

● The longest course for the Open Championship was 7,252 yards at Carnoustie in 1968.

Longest Holes

● The longest hole in the world, as far as is known, is the 6th hole measuring 782 metres (860 yards) at Koolan Island GC, Western Australia. The par of the hole is 7. There are several holes over 700 yards throughout the world. At Teyateyaneng, South Africa, one hole measures 619 yards.

● The longest hole for the Open Championship was 577 yards (6th hole) at Troon in 1973.

Longest Tournaments

● The longest tournament held was over 144 holes in the World Open at Pinehurst, N Carolina, USA, first held in 1973. Play was over two weeks with a cut imposed at the halfway mark.

● An annual tournament is played in Germany on the longest day of the year, comprising 100 holes' medal play. The best return, in 1968, was 417 strokes.

Largest Entries

The Open – 1707, St Andrews, 1990.
The Amateur – 488, St Andrews, 1958.
British Youths' – 244, Woodhall Spa, 1979.

The Boys' – 247, Formby, 1980.
Ladies' British Open Amateur – 157, St Andrews, 1975.
British Ladies Stroke Play – 120, Formby, 1985.
British Girls'–94, Hesketh, 1985.
English Amateur – 370, Moortown, 1980, also Woodhall Spa, 1984.
English Open Amateur Stroke Play – 313, Royal Cinque Ports, Deal 1984.
Irish Amateur – 302, Portmarnock, 1974.
Scottish Amateur – 244, Gullane, 1983.
Scottish Open Amateur Stroke Play – 249, Dunbar, North Berwick, 1985.
Scottish Boys' – 354, North Berwick, 1973.
Welsh Amateur – 108, Prestatyn, 1980.
Welsh Boys' – 112, Glamorganshire, 1975.
● US Open – The US Open of 1990 received a record 6198 entries.
● The largest entry for a PGA European Tour event was 398 for the 1978 Colgate PGA Championship. Since 1985, when the all-exempt ruling was introduced, all PGA tournaments have had 144 competitors, slightly more or less.
● In 1952, Bobby Locke, the Open Champion, played a round at Wentworth, against any golfer in Britain. Cards costing 2s. 6d. each (12½p), were taken out by 24,000 golfers. The challenge was to beat the local par by more than Locke beat the par at Wentworth; 1,641 competitors, including women, succeeded in *beating* the Champion and each received a certificate signed by him. As a result of this challenge the British Golf Foundation benefited to the extent of £3,026, the proceeds from the sale of cards. A similar tournament was held in the United States and Canada when 87,094 golfers participated; 14,667 players bettered Ben Hogan's score under handicap. The fund benefited by $80,024.

Largest Prize Money

● The largest prize money for an event in Britain was $1,018,000 in the Dunhill Cup at St Andrews in 1990.
● In 1990 the total prize money at the Open at St Andrews was £825,000, with a first prize of £85,000.
● The Machrie Tournament of 1901 was the first tournament with a first prize of £100. It was won by JH Taylor, then Open Champion, who beat James Braid in the final.
● The world's richest tournament was the $2,515,000 Nabisco Championships held in 1990 at Houston, Texas.
● (For prize money in the Open Championship see under Conditions and History of Open Championship.)

Holing-in-One

Holing-in-One – Odds Against

● At the Wanderers Club, Johannesburg in January, 1951, forty-nine amateurs and professionals each played three balls at a hole 146 yards long. Of the 147 balls hit, the nearest was by Koos de Beer, professional at Reading Country Club, which finished 10½ inches from the hole. Harry Bradshaw, the Irish professional who was touring with the British team in South Africa, touched the pin with his second shot, but the ball rolled on and stopped 3 feet 2 inches from the cup.
● A competition on similar lines was held in 1951 in New York when 1,409 players who had done a hole-in-one held a competition over several days at short holes on three New York golf courses. Each player was allowed a total of five shots, giving an aggregate of 7,045 shots. No player holed-in-one, and the nearest ball finished 3½ inches from the hole.
● A further illustration of the element of luck in holing-in-one is derived from an effort by Harry Gonder, an American professional, who in 1940 stood for 16 hours 25 minutes and hit 1,817 balls trying to do a 160 yard hole-in-one. He had two official witnesses and caddies to tee and retrieve the balls and count the strokes. His 1,756th shot struck the hole but stopped an inch from the hole. This was his nearest effort.
● From this and other similar information an estimate of the odds against holing-in-one at any particular hole within the range of one shot was made at somewhere between 1,500 and 2,000 to 1 by a proficient player. Subsequently, however, statistical analysis in America has come up with the following odds: a male professional or top amateur 3,708 to 1; a female professional or top amateur 4,648 to 1; an average golfer 42,952 to 1.

Hole-in-One First Recorded

● Earliest recorded hole-in-one was in 1868 at the Open Championship when Tom Morris (Young Tom) did the 8th hole 145 yards Prestwick in one stroke. This was the first of four Open Championships won successively by Young Tom.
● The first hole-in-one recorded with the 1.66 in ball was in 1972 by John G Salvesen, a member of the R & A Championship Committee. At the time this size of ball was only experimental. Salvesen used a 7-iron for his historical feat at the 11th hole on the Old Course, St Andrews.

Holing-in-One in Important Events

Since the day of the first known hole-in-one by Tom Morris jun, at the 8th hole (145 yards) at Prestwick in the 1868 Open Championship,

holes-in-one, even in championships, have become too numerous for each to be recorded. Only where other unusual or interesting circumstances prevailed are the instances shown here.

● 1878–Jamie Anderson, competing in the Open Championship at Prestwick, holed the 17th hole in one. Anderson was playing the next to last hole, and though it seemed then that he was winning easily, it turned out afterwards that if he had not taken this hole in one stroke he would very likely have lost. Anderson was just about to make his tee shot when Andy Stuart (winner of the first Irish Open Championship in 1892), who was acting as marker to Anderson, remarked he was standing outside the teeing ground, and that if he played the stroke from there he would be disqualified. Anderson picked up his ball and teed it in a proper place. Then he holed-in-one. He won the Championship by one stroke.

● 1885–AF Macfie in the fourth round of the initial competition at Hoylake for the Amateur Championship, holed the 14th or *Rushes* hole in one. Since then this particular hole at Hoylake has strangely enough been the scene of several holes-in-one in major championships – in 1898 by S Winkley Smith, West Middlesex, in the Amateur Championship; in 1902 by Daniel Brown, Musselburgh, in the Open Championship; and in 1925 by GNP Humphries, Stourbridge, in the English Amateur Championship.

● 1906–R Johnston, North Berwick, competing in the Open Championship, did the 14th hole at Muirfield in one. Johnston played with only one club throughout – an adjustable head club.

● 1925–JH Taylor, in his second round in the Open Championship at Prestwick, did the 2nd hole in one stroke. In contrast, Murdoch (Troon Municipal), who played with Taylor, took 14 at the 1st hole.

● 1933–In the final round of the Irish Open Championship over 36 holes at Newcastle, Co Down, on 23rd September, 1933, Eric Fiddian, Stourbridge, who was boy champion in 1927 and English champion in 1932, was opposed to Jack McLean. In the first round Fiddian did the 7th hole, 128 yards, in one stroke, and in the second round he did the 14th hole, 205 yards, also in one stroke. These remarkable strokes did not carry Fiddian to victory for he was defeated by 3 and 2.

● 1959–The first hole-in-one in the US Women's Open Championship was recorded. It was by Patty Berg on the 7th hole (170 yards) at Churchill Valley CC, Pittsburgh.

● 1962–On 6th April, playing in the second round of the Schweppes Close Championship at Little Aston, H Middleton of Shandon Park, Belfast, holed his tee shot at the 159 yards 5th hole, winning a prize of £1,000. Ten minutes later, playing two matches ahead of Middleton, RA Jowle, son of the professional, Frank Jowle, holed his tee shot at the 179 yards 9th hole. As an amateur he was rewarded by the sponsors with a £30 voucher.

● 1963–By holing out in one stroke at the 18th hole (156 yards) at Moor Park on the first day of the Esso Golden round-robin tournament, HR Henning, South Africa, won the £10,000 prize offered for this feat.

● 1967–Tony Jacklin in winning the Masters tournament at St George's, Sandwich, did the 16th hole in one. His ace has an exceptional place in the records for it was seen by millions on TV, the ball in view in its flight till it went into the hole in his final round of 64.

● 1971–John Hudson, 25-year-old professional at Hendon, achieved a near miracle when he holed two consecutive holes-in-one in the Martini Tournament at Norwich. They were at the 11th and 12th holes (195 yards and 311 yards respectively) in the second round.

● 1971–In the Open Championship at Birkdale, Lionel Platts holed-in-one at the 212-yard 4th hole in the second round. This was the first instance of an Open Championship hole-in-one being recorded by television. It was incidentally Platts' seventh ace of his career.

● 1972–Two holes-in-one were recorded at the 180-yard 5th hole at Pebble Beach in the US Open. They were achieved by Jerry McGee in the third round and Bobby Mitchell in the final round.

● 1973–Peter Butler achieved what is thought to be the first hole-in-one in the Ryder Cup when he holed out at the 16th hole at Muirfield in the 1973 match.

● 1973–In the 1973 Open Championship at Troon, two holes-in-one were recorded, both at the 8th hole, known as the Postage Stamp, in the first round. They were achieved by Gene Sarazen and amateur David Russell, who were by coincidence respectively the oldest and youngest competitors.

● Mrs Argea Tissies, whose husband Hermann took 15 at Royal Troon's Postage Stamp 8th hole in the 1950 Open, scored a hole-in-one at the 2nd hole at Punta Ala in the second round of the Italian Ladies Senior Open of 1978. Exactly 5 years later on the same date, at the same time of day, in the same round of the same tournament at the same hole, she did it again with the same club.

● In less than two hours play in the second round of the 1989 US Open at Oak Hill Country Club, Rochester, New York, four competitors – Doug Weaver, Mark Wiebe, Jerry Pate and Nick Price – each holed the 167 yards 6th hole in one. The odds against four professionals achieving such a record in a field of 156 are reckoned at 332,000 to 1.

Holing-in-One – Longest Holes

● Bob Mitera, when a 21-year-old American student, standing 5 feet 6 inches and weighing under 12 stones, claimed the world record for the longest hole-in-one. Playing over the appropriately named Miracle Hill course at Omaha, on 7th October, 1965, Bob holed his drive at the 10th hole, 447 yards long. The ground sloped sharply downhill.

● Two longer holes-in-one have been achieved, but because they were at dog-leg holes they were not generally accepted as being the longest holes-in-one. They were 480 yards (5th hole, Hope CC, Arkansas) by L Bruce on 15th November, 1962 and 477 yards (14th hole, Martin County CC, Stuart, Florida) by Billy Newman on 13th August, 1972. The estimated length by cutting the corner was around 360 yards.

● In March, 1961, Lou Kretlow holed his tee shot at the 427 yards 16th hole at Lake Hefner course, Oklahoma City, USA.

● The longest known hole-in-one in Great Britain was the 393-yard 7th hole at West Lancashire GC, where in 1972 the assistant professional Peter Parkinson holed his tee shot.

● Other long holes-in-one recorded in Great Britain have been 380 yards (5th hole at Tankersley Park) by David Hulley in 1961; 380 yards (12th hole at White Webbs) by Danny Dunne on 30th July, 1976; 370 yards (17th hole at Chilwell Manor, distance from the forward tee) by Ray Newton in 1977; 365 yards (10th hole at Harewood Downs) by K Saunders in 1965; 365 yards (7th hole at Catterick Garrison GC) by Leslie Bruckner on 18th July, 1980.

● The longest-recorded hole-in-one by a woman was that accomplished in September, 1949 by Marie Robie – the 393-yard hole at Furnace Brook course, Wollaston, Mass, USA.

● In April 1988, Mary Anderson, a bio-chemistry student at Trinity College, Dublin, holed-in-one at the 290-yard 6th hole at the Island GC, Co Dublin, the longest known hole-in-one by a woman in Great Britain.

Holing-in-One – Greatest Number by One Person

47–Amateur Norman Manley of Long Beach, California.

42–US professional Art Wall between 1936 and April 1979.

35–Mancil Davis, professional at the Trophy Club, Forth Worth, Texas. Davis achieved his last in 1979 at the age of 25.

31–British professional CT le Chevalier who died in 1973.

20–British amateur, Jim Hay of Kirkintilloch GC.

10–Mrs Olga Penman, formerly of Harewood Downs GC.

At One Hole

10–Joe Vitullo at 16th hole of Hubbard GC, Ohio.

5–Left-hander, the late Fred Francis at 7th (now 16th) hole of Cardigan GC.

Holing-in-One – Greatest Frequency

● The greatest number of holes-in-one in a calendar year is 11, by JO Boydstone of California in 1962.

● John Putt of Frilford Heath GC had six holes-in-one in 1970, followed by three in 1971.

● Douglas Porteous, of Ruchill GC, Glasgow, achieved seven holes-in-one in the space of eight months. Four of them were scored in a five-day period from 26th to 30th September, 1974, in three consecutive rounds of golf. The first two were achieved at Ruchill GC in one round, third there two days later, and the fourth at Clydebank and District GC after another two days. The following May, Porteous had three holes-in-one, the first at Linn Park GC incredibly followed by two more in the one round at Clober GC.

● Mrs Kathleen Hetherington of West Essex has holed-in-one five times, four being at the 15th hole at West Essex. Four of her five aces were within seven months in 1966.

● Mrs Dorothy Hill of Dumfries and Galloway GC holed-in-one three times in 11 days in 1977.

● James C Reid of Brodick, aged 59 and 8 handicap in 1987, has achieved 14 holes-in-one, all but one on Isle of Arran courses. His success, in spite of severe physical handicaps of a stiff left knee, a damaged right ankle, two discs removed from his back and a hip replacement is remarkable. He plays regularly, walks the course, but uses a walking stick for balance.

Holing Successive Holes-in-One

● Successive holes-in-one are rare; successive par 4 holes-in-one may be classed as near miracles. NL Manley performed the most incredible feat in September, 1964, at Del Valle Country Club, Saugus, California, USA. The par 4 7th (330 yards) and 8th (290 yards) are both slightly downhill, dog-leg holes. Manley had *aces* at both, en route to a course record of 61 (par 71).

● The first recorded example in Britain of a player holing-in-one stroke at each of two successive holes was achieved on 6th February, 1964, at the Walmer and Kingsdown course, Kent. The young assistant professional at that club, Roger Game (aged 17) holed out with a No. 4 wood at the 244-yard 7th hole, and repeated the feat at the 256-yard 8th hole, using a No. 5 iron.

● The first occasion of holing-in-one at consecutive holes in a major professional event occurred

when John Hudson, 25-year-old professional at Hendon, holed-in-one at the 11th and 12th holes at Norwich during the second round of the 1971 Martini tournament. Hudson used a 4-iron at the 195-yard 11th and a driver at the 311-yard downhill 12th hole.

● Assistant professional Tom Doty (23 years), playing in a friendly match on a course near Chicago in October, 1971 had a remarkable four hole score which included two consecutive holes-in-one, sandwiched either side by an albatross and an eagle: 4th hole (500 yards)-2; 5th hole (360 yards dog-leg)-1; 6th hole (175 yards)-1; 7th hole (375 yards)-2. Thus he was 10 under par for four consecutive holes.

Holing-in-One Twice (or more) in Same Round by Same Person

What might be thought to be a very rare feat indeed – that of holing-in-one twice in the same round – has in fact happened on many occasions as the following instances show. It is, nevertheless, compared to the number of golfers in the world, still something of an outstanding achievement. The first known occasion was in 1907 when J Ireland playing in a three-ball match at Worlington holed the 5th and 18th holes in one stroke and two years later in 1909 HC Josecelyne holed the 3rd (175 yards) and the 14th (115 yards) at Acton on 24th November.

● The Rev Harold Snider, aged 75, scored his first hole-in-one on 9th June, 1976 at the 8th hole of the Ironwood course, near Phoenix. By the end of his round he had scored three holes-in-one,

the other two being at the 13th (110 yards) and 14th (135 yards). Ironwood is a par-3 course, giving more opportunity of scoring holes-in-one, but, nevertheless, three holes-in-one in one round on any type of course is an outstanding achievement.

● The first mention of two holes-in-one in a round by a woman is of special note in that it was followed later by a similar feat by another lady at the same club. On 19th May, 1942, Mrs W Driver, of Balgowlah Golf Club, New South Wales, holed out in one at the 3rd and 8th holes in the same round, while on 29th July, 1948, Mrs F Burke at the same club holed out in one at the 2nd and 8th holes.

● The youngest-known person to have had two holes-in-one in one round was a 14-year-old American, Peter Townsend.

● The youngest British player was Ian Robertson in June, 1972, at Torphin Hill GC, Edinburgh, when 15 years old. The holes were the 252-yard 9th and 210-yard 14th.

● The youngest woman to have performed the feat was a 17-year-old, Marjorie Merchant, playing at the Lomas Athletic GC, Argentina, at the 4th (170 yards) and 8th (130 yards) holes.

Holes-in-One on the Same Day

● In July 1987, at the Skerries Club, Co Dublin, Rank Xerox sponsored two tournaments, a men's 18-hole four-ball with 134 pairs competing and a 9-hole mixed foursomes with 33. During the day each of the four par-3 holes on the course were holed-in-one, the 2nd by Noel Bollard, 5th by Bart Reynolds, 12th by Jackie Carr and 15th by Gerry Ellis.

Two Holes-in-One at Same Hole in Same Game

First in World
● George Stewart and Fred Spellmeyer at the 18th hole, Forest Hills, New Jersey, USA in October 1919.

First in Great Britain
● Miss G Clutterbuck and Mrs HM Robinson at the 15th hole (120 yards), St Augustine GC, Ramsgate, on 8th May, 1925.

First in Denmark
● In a Club match in August 1987 at Himmerland, Steffan Jacobsen of Aalborg and Peter Forsberg of Himmerland halved the 15th hole in one shot, the first known occasion in Denmark.

First in Australia
● Dr & Mrs B Rankine, playing in a mixed 'Canadian foursome' event at the Osmond Club near Adelaide, South Australia in April 1987,

holed-in-one in consecutive shots at the 2nd hole (162 metres), he from the men's tee with a 3-iron and his wife from the Ladies' tee with a 1½ wood.

Holing-in-One — Miscellaneous Incidents

● The late Harry Vardon, who scored the greatest number of victories in the Open Championship, only once did a hole-in-one. That was in 1903 at Mundesley, Norfolk, where Vardon was convalescing from a long illness.

● Walter Hagen, one of the greatest and most colourful golfers of all time, in his long career also did only one hole-in-one – at the 6th hole at Worcester, Mass, in 1925. It was the first shot played with a new ball, he used a No 1 iron and it was the first of July.

● In April 1984 Joseph McCaffrey and his son, Gordon, each holed-in-one in the Spring Medal at the 164 yard 12th hole at Vale of Leven Club, Dunbartonshire.

● Identical twins, John and Desmond Rosser scored holes-in-one in consecutive rounds at Auckland GC, New Zealand. Playing in a medal competition on Saturday 15th March, 1975 with his twin and two other members, John, the elder twin, holed-in-one at the 10th hole with his wedge. In their next game, the following Wednesday, the twins were again playing in a four-ball with two other members when Desmond holed-in-one at the 13th hole using his driver.

● In 1977, 14-year-old Gillian Field after a series of lessons holed-in-one at the 10th hole at Moor Place GC in her first round of golf.

● Robert Patterson, aged 15, holed his tee shot at Hazlemere G&CC's 383-yard 1st hole using a 3-wood, on 18th April, 1990.

● Having taken some golf lessons in Britain, Mrs Joan Birtley of Flamstead, Herts., accompanied her husband on a business trip to America in 1977. At Doral CC, Miami, Mrs Birtley hired some clubs and played her first-ever round of golf. At the 4th hole (116 yards) she holed-in-one.

● By holing-in-one at the 2nd hole in a match against D Graham in the 1979 Suntory World Match Play at Wentworth, Japanese professional Isao Aoki won himself a Bovis home at Gleneagles worth, inclusive of furnishings, £55,000.

● When he holed-in-one at the 105-yard 14th hole at Tahoe Paradise course, USA, in the Harrah Invitational Tournament in 1965, Dick Kolbus, from Oakland, California, won a Rolls-Royce car.

● JoAnn Washam twice holed-in-one in the 1979 Kemper Open, a USLPGA Tournament.

● On the morning after being elected captain for 1973 of the Norwich GC, JS Murray hit his first shot as captain straight into the hole at the 169 yards first hole.

● Using the same club and ball, 11-handicap left-hander Christopher Smyth holed-in-one at the 2nd hole (170 yards) in two consecutive medal competitions at Headfort GC, Co Meath, in January, 1976.

● In a knock-out competition at Ely, Cambridgeshire, on 13th October, 1962, Mr Challis drove to within four feet of the 1st hole (170 yards). His opponent, Mr Delwage, pitched his second shot; his ball struck that of Mr Challis, knocking it into the hole and giving him the hole-in-one.

● In an RAF outing in 1973 at Peterborough Milton GC two holes-in-one were made with the same ball but not by the same person. The first was in the morning singles by Des Tuson at the 142-yard 11th hole. Then in the afternoon, playing in a greensome competition, his partner, Keith Schofield, holed-in-one at the 174-yard 2nd hole. The ball was then carefully put away.

● Joe Kirkwood holed-in-one on 11 occasions including one when doing a Newsreel Movie at the 5th (168 yards), Sea Island, Georgia, and another when he was performing trick shots off the face of a watch at the 1st (268 yards), Cedar Rapids, Iowa.

● At Royal Hong Kong Golf Club, Susan Tonroe, aged 16, and her brother, aged 11, each did the 7th hole in one in junior competitions in the same week.

● Playing over Rickmansworth course at Easter, 1960, Mrs AE (Paddy) Martin achieved a remarkable sequence of *aces*. On Good Friday she sank her tee shot at the third hole (125 yards). The next day, using the same ball and the same No. 8 iron, at the same hole, she scored another *one*. And on the Monday (same ball, same club, same hole) she again holed out from the tee.

● Playing in the Eastern Inter-County Foursomes in May 1974, RJ Taylor holed-in-one at the 188-yards 16th hole at Hunstanton on three consecutive days. Leading Bookmakers reckoned the odds against such a feat at 5 million to one.

● Joan Jankins, aged 12, achieved a hole-in-one at the 240-yard 3rd hole at Abersoch, Gwynedd, in October 1984.

● In January 1985 Otto Bucher of Switzerland, aged 99, holed-in-one at the 130-yard 12th hole at the La Manga Championship South course in Spain.

● At Barton-on-Sea in February 1989 Mrs Dorothy Huntley-Flindt, aged 91, holed in one at the par 3 13th. The following day Mr John Chape, a fellow member in his 80s, holed the par 3 5th in one.

● In 1988 senior citizen Mrs Joan Hall twice holed in one in 19 days at the 12th at Immingham and the 5th at Market Rasen. Three months later she achieved a third ace at Immingham's 17th.

Challenge Matches

One of the first recorded professional challenge matches was in 1843 when Allan Robertson beat Willie Dunn in a 20-round match at St Andrews over 360 holes by 2 rounds and 1 to play. Thereafter until about 1905 many matches are recorded, some for up to £200 a side – a considerable sum for the time. The Morrises, the Dunns and the Parks were the main protagonists until Vardon, Braid and Taylor took over in the 1890s. Often matches were on a home-and-away basis over 72 holes or more, with many spectators; Vardon and Willie Park Jr attracted over 10,000 at North Berwick in 1899.

Between the wars Walter Hagen, Archie Compston, Henry Cotton and Bobby Locke all played several such matches. Compston surprisingly beat Hagen by 18 up and 17 to play at Moor Park in 1928; yet typically Hagen went on to win the Open the following week at Sandwich. Cotton played classic golf at Walton Heath in 1937 when he beat Densmore Shute for £500 a side at Walton Heath by 6 and 5 over 72 holes.

After 1945 the appeal of Challenge matches waned, mainly due to the increasing number of professional tournaments available.

Curious and Large Wagers
(See also bets recorded under Cross-Country Matches, and in Challenge Matches)

● In the Royal and Ancient Club minutes an entry on 3rd November, 1870 was made in the following terms: *Sir David Moncreiffe, Bart, of Moncrieffe, backs his life against the life of John Whyte-Melville, Esq, of Strathkinnes, for a new silver club as a present to the St Andrews Golf Club, the price of the club to be paid by the survivor and the arms of the parties to be engraved on the club, and the present bet inscribed on it. No balls to be attached to it. In testimony of which this bet is subscribed by the parties thereto.* Thirteen years later, Mr Whyte-Melville, in a feeling and appropriate speech, expressed his deep regret at the lamented death of Sir Robert Moncrieffe, one of the most distinguished and zealous supporters of the club. Whyte-Melville, while lamenting the cause that led to it, had pleasure in fulfilling the duty imposed upon him by the bet, and accordingly delivered to the captain the silver putter. Whyte-Melville in 1883 was elected captain of the club a second time; he died in his eighty-sixth year in July, 1883, before he could take office and the captaincy remained vacant for a year. His portrait hangs in the Royal & Ancient clubhouse and is one of the finest and most distinguished pictures in the smoking room.

● In 1914 Francis Ouimet, who in the previous autumn had won the American Open Championship after a triangular tie with Harry Vardon and Ted Ray, came to Great Britain with Jerome D Travers, the holder of the American amateur title, to compete in the British Amateur Championship at Sandwich. An American syndicate took a bet of £30,000 to £10,000 that one or other of the two United States champions would be the winner. It only took two rounds to decide the bet against the Americans. Ouimet was beaten by a then quite unknown player, HS Tubbs, while Travers was defeated by Charles Palmer, who was fifty-six years of age at the time.

● 1907 John Ball for a wager undertook to go round Hoylake during a dense fog in under 90, in not more than two and a quarter hours and without losing a ball. Ball played with a black ball, went round in 81, and also beat the time.

● The late Ben Sayers, for a wager, played the eighteen holes of the Burgess Society course scoring a four at every hole. Sayers was about to start against an American, when his opponent asked him what he could do the course in. *Fours* replied Sayers, meaning 72, or an average of 4s for the round. A bet was made and the American then added, *Remember a three or a five is not a four.* There were eight bogey 5s and two 3s on the Burgess course at the time Old Ben achieved his feat.

● Cross-country and freak matches, embraced on another page, have been fruitful of many wagers, and matches have been played between distinguished golfers using only a putting cleek against players carrying all their clubs. At Hoylake a match was fixed between a scratch golfer and a handicap 6 player. They played level, the handicap player having the right to say *Boo* three times on the round. He said *Boo* at the 13th hole and won the match easily with two *Boos* in hand, the scratch player, of course, being affected by always anticipating the *Boo*.

● In June, 1950, Bryan Field, vice-president of the Delaware Park racecourse, USA, who had not played golf for several years, accepted a wager that, without practice, he would not go round Pine Valley, rated one of the hardest courses in the world, in less than 300 shots. With borrowed clubs, he set off at 8am planning to finish in time for lunch. He started 7, 9, 4, 11, and when he got a 10 at the 5th, one of the most testing on the course, after putting three tee shots into the lake, it was obvious that he was well on the way to winning the bet. With an 11 at the 8th, another difficult hole he reached the turn in 73. Coming home in 75, Mr Field holed the course in 148 and won his wager with 152 strokes in hand. He took two hours, fifty minutes to complete the round.

Feats of Endurance

Although golf is not a game where endurance, in the ordinary sense in which the term is employed in sport, is required, there are several

instances of feats on the links which demanded great physical exertion.

● In 1971 during a 24-hour period from 6 pm on 27th November until 5.15 pm on 28th November, Ian Colston completed 401 holes over the 6,061 yards Bendigo course, Victoria, Australia. Colston was a top marathon athlete but was not a golfer. However prior to his golfing marathon he took some lessons and became adept with a 6-iron, the only club he used throughout the 401 holes. The only assistance Colston had was a team of harriers to carry his 6-iron and look for his ball, and a band of motor cyclists who provided light during the night. This is, as far as is known, the greatest number of holes played in 24 hours on foot on a full-size course.

● In 1934 Col Bill Farnham played 376 holes in 24 hours 10 minutes at the Guildford Lake Course, Guildford, Connecticut, using only a mashie and a putter.

● To raise funds for extending the Skipton GC course from 12 to 18 holes, the club professional, 24-year-old Graham Webster, played 277 holes in the hours of daylight on Monday 20th June, 1977. Playing with nothing longer than a 5-iron he averaged 81 per 18-hole round. Included in his marathon was a hole-in-one.

● Michael Moore, a 7 handicap 26-year-old member of Okehampton GC, completed on foot 15 rounds 6 holes (276 holes) there on Sunday, 25th June, 1972, in the hours of daylight. He started at 4.15 am and stopped at 9.15 pm. The distance covered was estimated at 56 miles. Nine brief stoppages for salty soup were made. His time for 6 rounds was 6 hours 2 minutes; for 12 rounds, 12 hours 58 minutes.

● On 21st June, 1976, 5-handicapper Sandy Small played 15 rounds (270 holes) over his home course Cosby GC, length 6,128 yards, to raise money for the Society of Physically Handicapped Children. Using only a 5-iron, 9-iron and putter, Small started at 4.10 am and completed his 270th hole at 10.39 pm with the aid of car headlights. His fastest round was his first (40 minutes) and slowest his last (82 minutes). His best round of 76 was achieved in the second round.

● In 1957, Bert L Scoggins, a US serviceman, played 260 holes in one day on the American golf course at Berlin. He started out at 2.30 am and played continuously for 18 hours, walking 56 miles in the course of his marathon feat. His lowest single round score was 84.

● Bill Falkingham, Jr, of Amstel GC, Victoria, Australia, played 257 holes between 12.30 am and 6.15 pm on 14th December, 1968. The first three holes were played in darkness. He was accompanied by his brother and a friend who held a torch to assist direction. Ten balls were lost but the first ball lasted eight rounds. His best round was 90 over a course measuring 6,673 yards, par 73, over which a gale force wind blew

all day, in a temperature of 90 degrees. During the morning he trod on a snake but did not stop to kill it. He was sustained by only sandwiches and soft drinks and although completely exhausted when he finished he had completely recovered next morning and went out for another round.

● During the weekend of 20th-21st June, 1970, Peter Chambers of Yorkshire completed over 14 rounds of golf over the Scarborough South Cliff course. In a non-stop marathon lasting just under 24 hours, Chambers played 257 holes in 1,168 strokes, an average of 84.4 strokes per round.

● Stan Gard, a member of North Brighton Golf Club, New South Wales, in 1938 completed fourteen rounds and four holes on his home course. Gard started his marathon performance at 12.55 am, and finished with the aid of car lights at 9.30 pm. He played consistent golf, his best being 78 in the tenth round, and his worst 92 in the second round.

● Bruce Sutherland, on the Craiglockhart Links, Edinburgh, started at 8.15 pm on 21st June, 1927, and played almost continuously until 7.30 pm on 22nd June, 1927. During the night four caddies with acetylene lamps lit the way, and lost balls were reduced to a minimum. He completed fourteen rounds. Mr Sutherland, who was a physical culture teacher, never recovered from the physical strain and died a few years later.

● Sidney Gleave, motor cycle racer, and Ernest Smith, golf professional, Davyhulme Club, Manchester, on 12th June, 1939, played five rounds of golf in five different countries – Scotland, Ireland, Isle of Man, England and Wales. Smith had to play the five rounds under 80 in one day to win the £100 wager. They travelled by plane, and the following was their programme with time taken and Smith's score:

Start–Prestwick St Nicholas (Scotland), 3.40 am. Score 70. Time taken, 1 hour 35 minutes. 2nd

Course–Bangor (Ireland), 7.15 am. Score 76. Time taken, 1 hour 30 minutes. 3rd Course – Castletown (Isle of Man), 10.15 am. Score 76. Time taken, 1 hour 40 minutes. 4th Course – Blackpool, Stanley Park (England), 1.30 pm. Score 72. Time taken, 1 hour 55 minutes. 5th Course – Hawarden (Wales), 6 pm. Score 68 (record). Time taken, 2 hours 15 minutes.

● On Wednesday, 3rd July, 1974, ES Wilson, Whitehead, Co Antrim and Dr GW Donaldson, Newry, Co Down, played a nine-hole match in each of seven countries in the one day. The first 9 holes was at La Moye (Channel Islands) followed by Hawarden (Wales), Chester (England), Turnberry (Scotland), Castletown (Isle of Man), Dundalk (Eire) and Warrenpoint (N Ireland). They started their first round at 4.25 am and their last round at 9.25 pm. Wilson piloted his own plane throughout.

● Rick Garcia and Don Tanner from Gallup, New Mexico, played 18 holes, selected from seven States, in one day in 1976 to raise money for muscular dystrophy. The States concerned were Texas, New Mexico, Colorado, Utah, Arizona, California and Nevada. A distance of over 2,000 miles was covered by private plane.

● In June 1986 to raise money for the upkeep of his medieval church, the Rector of Mark with Allerton, Somerset, the Rev Michael Pavey, played a sponsored 18 holes on 18 different courses in the Bath & Wells Diocese. With his partner, the well-known broadcaster on music, Antony Hopkins, they played the 1st at Minehead at 5.55 am and finished playing the 18th at Burnham and Berrow at 6.05 pm. They covered 240 miles in the 'round' including the distances to reach the correct tee for the 'next' hole on each course. Par for the 'round' was 70. Together the pair raised £10,500 for the church.

● To raise funds for the Marlborough Club's centenary year (1988), Laurence Ross, the Club professional, in June 1987, played 8 rounds in 12 hours. Against a par of 72, he completed the 576 holes in 3 under par, playing from back tees and walking all the way.

Fastest Rounds

● Dick Kimbrough, 41, completed a round on foot on 8th August, 1972, at North Platte CC, Nebraska (6,068 yards) in 30 minutes 10 seconds. He carried only a 3-iron. Earlier the same year Kimbrough played 364 holes in 24 hours.

● At Mowbray Course, Cape Town, November 1931, Len Richardson, who had represented South Africa in the Olympic Games, played a round which measured 6,248 yards in 31 minutes 22 seconds.

● The women's all-time record for a round played on a course of at least 5,250 yards is held by Dianne Taylor, 37, Jacksonville, Florida. She played the 5,692 yards University GC at Jacksonville in 55 minutes 54 seconds on 7th April, 1980.

● Faster rounds have been recorded, but they have not been done on foot. The fastest of these was achieved by 3 handicap Ken Wildey at Calcot Park GC on 20th July, 1980. Wildey, riding in a motorised cart, completed the 6,010 yards course in 24 minutes 3 seconds.

The sole purpose in each of the above instances was speed. The following are examples of fast rounds in a match or competition.

● On 14th June, 1922, Jock Hutchison and Joe Kirkwood (Australia) played round the Old Course at St Andrews in 1 hour 20 minutes. Hutchison, out in 37, led by three holes at the ninth and won by 4 and 3.

● In April, 1934, after attending a wedding in Bournemouth, Hants, Captain Gerald Moxom hurried to his club, West Hill in Surrey, to play in the captain's prize competition. With daylight fading and still dressed in his morning suit, he went round in 65 minutes and won the competition with a net 71 into the bargain.

● Fastest rounds can also take another form – the time taken for a ball to be propelled round 18 holes. The fastest known round of this type is

8 minutes 53.8 seconds on 25th August, 1979 by 42 members at Ridgemount CC Rochester, New York, a course measuring 6,161 yards. The Rules of Golf were observed but a ball was available on the following tee to be driven off the instant the ball had been holed at the preceding hole.

Slow Play

Standards have changed dramatically over the years as to what constitutes slow play as the following statement, which first appeared in the 1949 Golfer's Handbook, shows: *Slow motion golf has marred many championships, and notorious tortoises have been known to take three-and-a-half hours in a championship tie.*

Nowadays a round taking three-and-a half hours is commonplace, but for the sake of history we record here examples of what was considered very slow play up to 1950.

● When Henry Cotton and RA Whitcombe played Bobby Locke and Sid Brews at Walton Heath, 1938, for a stake of £500 a side, the match made headlines with the slowness of play. Locke, who was engaging in his first important professional match in Great Britain, was ultra-careful, and the marshalling of the crowd — there were 5,000 spectators present during the second round – caused many delays, sometimes as much as 10 minutes being required for the players to leave one green and play off the next tee. The first round took three hours 40 minutes and the second round four hours 15 minutes. Cotton and Whitcombe won by 2 and 1. Locke, although on the defeated side, played phenomenal golf. He went round in 63. Walton Heath tees were far extended and it was a cruel test.

● In the Scottish Amateur Championship, 1922, at St Andrews, a competitor was deplorably slow and in one tie his opponent, in the hope of shaming the sloth into quickening his play brought to the links a camp bed, which was carried round by others who had been playing in the championship. The camp bed was placed at the side of each green, and while the tortoise crawled about studying the line of the putt, his opponent reclined on the bed and nonchalantly observed the antics of his rival. The attempt to secure a speed-up in the play was unsuccessful and the tortoise was even more deliberate in his play.

● The Amateur Championship, St Andrews, 1950, was remarkable for slowness of play and the inordinate time taken by some players to play their shots. The main cause of the slowness was the time taken to study putts. In some cases five minutes were spent over a stroke on the greens, although the record entry of 324 and the huge double greens of the Championship Course were also contributory to the sluggish pace. Many matches took four hours to complete and five couples waited at some tees. A record for the championship was made on the third day when play in the third and fourth rounds occupied 14 hours. The first ball was struck at 8 am and the last match finished on the 17th green in the lamplit dusk shortly before 10 pm. In the final between FR Stranahan and RD Chapman the first nine holes of the morning round took an hour and 50 minutes to play. A field telephone message was sent to the referee, Colonel CO Hezlet, Portrush, to warn the players that the second round would start at the scheduled time. This increased the pace slightly and the round was finished in three hours 40 minutes, the slowest round in the final of the championship at that time.

Curious Scoring

● Three threes, four fours, five fives and six sixes is one of only two progressive combinations that can work out for 18 holes. A player in a South African competition had this sequence and noticed the curiosity in scoring. The other combination is five fives, six sixes and seven sevens.

● RH Corbett, playing in the semi-final of the Tangye Cup at Mullim in 1916, did a score of 27. The remarkable part of Corbett's score was that it was made up of nine successive 3s, bogey being 5, 3, 4, 4, 5, 3, 4, 4, 3.

● At Little Chalfont in June 1985 Adrian Donkersley played six successive holes in 6, 5, 4, 3, 2, 1 from the 9th to the 14th holes against a par of 4, 4, 3, 4, 3, 3.

● On 2nd September, 1920, playing over Torphin, near Edinburgh, William Ingle did the first five holes in 1, 2, 3, 4, 5.

● In the summer of 1970, Keith McMillan, on holiday at Cullen, had a remarkable series of 1, 2, 3, 4, 5 at the 11th to 15th holes.

● Playing at Addington Palace, July, 1934, Ronald Jones, a member of Hendon Club, holed five consecutive holes in 5, 4, 3, 2, 1.

● Harry Dunderdale of Lincoln GC scored 5, 4, 3, 2, 1 in five consecutive holes during the first round of his club championship in 1978. The hole-in-one was the 7th, measuring 294 yards.

● At Westerhope near Newcastle in January 1986 Alan Crosby, the Club professional, played the first four holes in 4, 3, 2, 1 against the par of 4, 4, 3, 4.

● At the Open Amateur Tournament of the Royal Ashdown Forest in 1936 Bobby Locke in his morning round had a score of 72, accomplishing every hole in 4.

● Severiano Ballesteros in winning the 1978 Swiss Open scored four rounds of 68.

● Henry Cotton told of one of the most extraordinary scoring feats ever. With some other professionals he was at Sestrieres in the thirties for the Italian Open Championship and Joe Ezar, a colourful character in those days on both sides of the Atlantic, accepted a wager from a club official – 1,000 lira for a 66 to break the course record; 2,000 for a 65; and 4,000 for a 64. *I'll do 64*, said Ezar, and proceeded to jot down the hole-by-hole score figures he would do next day for that total. With the exception of the ninth and tenth holes where his predicted score was 3, 4 and the actual score was 4, 3, he accomplished this amazing feat exactly as nominated.

● Nick Faldo scored par figures at all 18 holes in the final round of the 1987 Open Championship at Muirfield to win the title.

High Scores

● In the qualifying competition at Formby for the 1976 Open Championship, Maurice Flitcroft, a 46-year-old crane driver from Barrow-in-Furness, took 121 strokes for the first round and then withdrew saying, *I have no chance of qualifying.* Flitcroft entered as a professional but had never before played 18 holes. He had taken the game up 18 months previously but, as he was not a member of a club, had been limited to practising on a local beach. His round was made up thus: 7, 5, 6, 6, 6, 6, 12, 6, 7-61; 11, 5, 6, 8, 4, 9, 5, 7, 5-60, total 121. After his round Flitcroft said, *I've made a lot of progress in the last few months and I'm sorry I did not do better. I was trying too hard at the beginning but began to put things together at the end of the round.* R & A officials who were not amused by the bogus professional's efforts, refunded the £30 entry money to Flitcroft's two fellow-competitors.

● Playing in the qualifying rounds of the 1965 Open Championship at Southport, an American self-styled professional entrant from Milwaukee, Walter Danecki, achieved the inglorious feat of scoring a total of 221 strokes for 36 holes, 81 over par. His first round over the Hillside course was 108, followed by a second round of 113. Walter, who afterwards admitted he felt a *little discouraged and sad*, declared that he entered because he was *after the money*.

● The highest individual scoring ever known in the rounds connected with the Open Championship occurred at Muirfield, 1935, when a Scottish professional started 7, 10, 5, 10, and took 65 to reach the 9th hole. Another 10 came at the 11th and the player decided to retire at the 12th hole. There he was in a bunker, and after playing four shots he had not regained the fairway.

● In 1883 in the Open Championship at Musselburgh, Willie Fernie, the winner, had a 10, the only time double figures appeared on the card of the Open Champion of the year. Fernie won after a tie with Bob Ferguson, and his score for the last hole in the tie was 2. He holed from just off the green to win by one stroke.

● In the first Open Championship at Prestwick in 1860 a competitor took 21, the highest score for one hole ever recorded in this event. The record is preserved in the archives of the Prestwick Golf Club, where the championship was founded.

● In the first round of the 1980 US Masters, Tom Weiskopf hit his ball into the water hazard in front of the par-3 12th hole five times and scored 13 for the hole.

● In the French Open at St Cloud, in 1968, Brian Barnes took 15 for the short 8th hole in the second round. After missing putts at which he hurriedly snatched while the ball was moving he penalised himself further by standing astride the line of a putt. The amazing result was that he actually took 12 strokes from about three feet from the hole.

● US professional Dave Hill 6-putted the fifth green at Oakmont in the 1962 US Open Championship.

● Many high scores have been made at the Road Hole at St Andrews. Davie Ayton, on one occasion, was coming in a certain winner of the Open Championship when he got on the road and took 11. In 1921, at the Open Championship, one professional took 13. In 1923, competing for the Autumn Medal of the Royal & Ancient, JB Anderson required a five and a four to win the second award, but he took 13 at the Road Hole. Anderson was close to the green in two, was twice in the bunkers in the face of the green, and once on the road. In 1935, RH Oppenheimer tied for the Royal Medal (the first award) in the Autumn Meeting of the Royal & Ancient. On the play-off he was one stroke behind Captain Aitken when they stood on the 17th tee. Oppenheimer drove three balls out of bounds and eventually took 11 to the Road Hole.

● British professional Mark James scored 111 in the second round of the 1978 Italian Open. He played the closing holes with only his right hand due to an injury to his left hand.

● In the 1927 Shawnee Open, Tommy Armour took 23 strokes to the 17th hole. Armour had won the American Open Championship a week earlier. In an effort to play the hole in a particular

way, Armour hooked ball after ball out of bounds and finished with a 21 on the card. There was some doubt about the accuracy of this figure and on reaching the clubhouse Armour stated that it should be 23. This is the highest score by a professional in a tournament.

Freak Matches

● In 1912, the late Harry Dearth, an eminent vocalist, attired in a complete suit of heavy armour, played a match at Bushey Hall. He was beaten 2 and 1.

● In 1914, at the start of the First World War, JN Farrar, a native of Hoylake, was stationed at Royston, Herts. A bet was made of 10-1 that he would not go round Royston under 100 strokes, equipped in full infantry marching order, water bottle, full field kit and haversack. Farrar went round in 94. At the camp were several golfers, including professionals, who tried the same feat but failed.

● Captain Pennington, who was killed in an air crash in 1933, took part in a match *from the air* against AJ Young, the professional at Sonning. Captain Pennington, with 80 golf balls in the locker of his machine, had to find the Sonning greens by dropping the balls as he circled over the course. The balls were covered in white cloth to ensure that they did not bounce once they struck the ground. The airman completed the course in 40 minutes, taking 29 *strokes*, while Young occupied two hours for his round of 68.

● In April 1924, at Littlehampton, Harry Rowntree, an amateur golfer, played the better ball of Edward Ray and George Duncan, receiving an allowance of 150 yards to use as he required during the round. Rowntree won by 6 and 5 and had used only 50 yards 2 feet of his handicap. At

one hole Duncan had a two – Rowntree, who was 25 yards from the hole, took this distance from his handicap and won the hole in one. Ray (died 1945) afterwards declared that, conceded a handicap of one yard per round, he could win every championship in the world. And he might, when reckoning is taken of the number of times a putt just stops an inch or two or how much difference to a shot three inches will make for the lie of the ball, either in a bunker or on the fairway. Many single matches on the same system have been played. An 18 handicap player opposed to a scratch player should make a close match with an allowance of 50 yards.

● The first known instance of a golf match by telephone occurred in 1957, when the Cotswold Hills Golf Club, Cheltenham, England, won a golf tournament against the Cheltenham Golf Club, Melbourne, Australia, by six strokes. A large crowd assembled at the English club to wait for the 12,000 miles telephone call from Australia. The match had been played at the suggestion of a former member of the Cotswold Hills Club, Harry Davies, and was open to every member of the two clubs. The result of the match was decided on the aggregate of the eight best scores on each side and the English club won by 564 strokes to 570.

Golf Matches Against Other Sports

● HH Hilton and Percy Ashworth, many times racket champion, contested a driving match, the former driving a golf ball with a driver, and the latter a golf ball with a racket. Best distances: Against breeze – Golfer 182 yards; Racket player 125 yards. Down wind – Golfer 230 yards; Racket player 140 yards. Afterwards Ashworth hit a golf ball with the racket and got a greater distance than with the racket ball, but was still a long way behind the ball driven by Hilton.

● In 1913, at Wellington, Shropshire, a match between a golfer and a fisherman casting a 2½ oz weight was played. The golfer, Rupert May, took 87; the fisherman JJD Mackinlay, required 102. The fisherman's difficulty was in his short casts. His longest cast, 105 yards, was within 12 yards of the world record at the time, held by a French angler, Decautelle. When within a rod's length of a hole he ran the weight to the rod end and dropped into the hole. Five times he broke his line, and was allowed another shot without penalty.

● In December, 1913, FMA Webster, of the London Athletic Club, and Dora Roberts, with javelins, played a match with the late Harry Vardon and Mrs Gordon Robertson, who used the regulation clubs and golf balls. The golfers conceded two-thirds in the matter of distance, and they won by 5 up and 4 to play in a contest of 18 holes. The javelin throwers had a mark of two feet square in which to *hole out* while the golfers

had to get their ball into the ordinary golf hole. Mr Webster's best throw was one of 160 feet.

● Several matches have taken place between a golfer on the one side and an archer on the other. The wielder of the bow and arrow has nearly always proved the victor. In 1953 at Kirkhill Golf Course, Lanarkshire, five archers beat six golfers by two games to one. There were two special rules for the match; when an archer's arrow landed six feet from the hole or the golfer's ball three feet from the hole, they were counted as holed. When the arrows landed in bunkers or in the rough, archers lifted their arrow and added a stroke. The sixth archer in this match called off and one archer shot two arrows from each of the 18 tees.

● In 1954, at the Southbroom Club, South Africa, a match over 9 holes was played between an archer and a fisherman against two golfers. The participants were all champions of their own sphere and consisted of Vernon Adams (archer), Dennis Burd (fisherman), Jeanette Wahl (champion of Southbroom and Port Shepstone), and Ron Burd (professional at Southbroom). The conditions were that the archer had holed out when his arrows struck a small leather bag placed on the green beside the hole and in the event of his placing his approach shot within a bow's length of the pin he was deemed to have 1-putted. The fisherman, to achieve a 1-putt, had to land his sinker within a rod's length of the pin. The two golfers were ahead for brief spells, but it was the opposition who led at the deciding 9th hole where *Robin Hood* played a perfect approach for a birdie.

● An *Across England* combined match was begun on 11th October, 1965, by four golfers and two archers from Crowborough Beacon Golf Club, Sussex, accompanied by *Penny*, a white Alsatian dog, whose duty it was to find lost balls. They teed *off* from Carlisle Castle via Hadrian's Wall, the Pennine Way, finally holing out in the 18th hole at Newcastle United Golf Club in 612 teed shots. Casualties included 110 lost golf balls and 19 lost or broken arrows. The match took five-and-a-half days, and the distance travelled was about 60 miles. The golfers were Miss P Ward, K Meaney, K Ashdown and CA Macey; the archers were WH Hulme and T Scott. The first arrow was fired from the battlements of Carlisle Castle, a distance of nearly 300 yards, by Cumberland Champion R Willis, who also fired the second arrow right across the River Eden. R Clough, president of Newcastle United GC, holed the last two putts. The match was in aid of *Guide Dogs for the Blind* and *Friends of Crowborough Hospital.*

Cross-country Matches

● Taking 1 year, 114 days, Floyd Rood golfed his way from coast to coast across the United States. He took 114,737 shots including 3,511 penalty shots for the 3,397 mile *course.*

● Two Californian teenagers, Bob Aube (17) and Phil Marrone (18) went on a golfing safari in 1974 from San Francisco to Los Angeles, a trip of over 500 miles lasting 16 days. The first six days they played alongside motorways. Over 1,000 balls were used.

● In 1830, the Gold Medal winner of the Royal & Ancient backed himself for 10 sovereigns to drive from the 1st hole at St Andrews to the toll bar at Cupar, distance nine miles, in 200 teed shots. He won easily.

● In 1848, two Edinburgh golfers played a match from Bruntsfield Links to the top of Arthur's Seat – an eminence overlooking the Scottish capital, 822 feet above sea level.

● On a winter's day in 1898, Freddie Tait backed himself to play a gutta ball in 40 teed shots from Royal St George's Clubhouse, Sandwich, to the Cinque Ports Club, Deal. He was to hole out by hitting any part of the Deal Clubhouse. The distance as the crow flies was three miles. The redoubtable Tait holed out with his 32nd shot, so effectively that the ball went through a window.

● On 3rd December, 1920, P Rupert Phillips and W Raymond Thomas teed up on the first tee of the Radyr Golf Club and played to the last hole at Southerndown. The distance as the crow flies was 15½ miles, but circumventing swamps, woods, and plough, they covered, approximately, 20 miles. The wager was that they would not do the *hole* in 1,000 strokes, but they holed out at their 608th stroke two days later. They carried large ordnance maps.

● In 1900 three members of the Hackensack (NJ) Club played a game of four-and-a-half hours over an extemporised course six miles long, which stretched from Hackensack to Paterson. Despite rain, cornfields, and wide streams, the three golfers – JW Hauleebeek, Dr ER Pfaare, and Eugene Crassons – completed the round, the first and the last named taking 305 strokes each, and Dr Pfaare 327 strokes. The players used only two clubs, the mashie and the cleek.

● On 12th March, 1921, A Stanley Turner, Macclesfield, played from his house to the Cat and Fiddle Inn, five miles distance, in 64 strokes. The route was broken and hilly with a rise of nearly 1,000 feet. Turner was allowed to tee up within two club lengths after each shot and the wagering was 6-4 against his doing the distance in 170 strokes.

● In 1919, a golfer drove a ball from Piccadilly Circus and, proceeding via the Strand, Fleet Street and Ludgate Hill, *holed out* at the Royal Exchange, London. The player drove off at 8 am on a Sunday, a time when the usually thronged thoroughfares were deserted.

● On 23rd April, 1939, Richard Sutton, a London stockbroker, played from Tower Bridge, London,

to White's Club, St James's Street, in 142 strokes. The bet was he would not do *the course* in under 200 shots. Sutton used a putter, crossed the Thames at Southwark Bridge, and hit the ball short distances to keep out of trouble.

● Golfers produced the most original event in Ireland's three-week national festival of An Tostal, 1953 – a cross-country competition with an advertised £1,000,000 for the man who could hole out in one. The 150 golfers drove off from the first tee at Kildare Club to hole out eventually on the 18th green, five miles away, on the nearby Curragh course, a distance of 8,800 yards. The unusual hazards to be negotiated included the main Dublin-Cork railway line and highway, the Curragh Racecourse, hoofprints left by Irish thoroughbred racehorses out exercising on the plains from nearby stables, army tank tracks and about 150 telephone lines. The Golden Ball Trophy, which is played for annually – a standard size golf ball in gold, mounted on a black marble pillar beside the silver figure of a golfer on a green marble base, designed by Captain Maurice Cogan, Army GHQ, Dublin — was for the best gross. And it went to one of the longest hitters in international golf – Amateur Champion, Irish internationalist and British Walker Cup player Joe Carr, with the remarkable score of 52.

● Four Aberdeen University students (as a 1961 Charities Week stunt) set out to golf their way up Ben Nevis (4,406 feet). After losing 63 balls and expending 659 strokes, the quartet, about halfway up, conceded victory to Britain's highest mountain.

Long-lived Golfers

● The oldest golfer who ever lived we believe was Arthur Thompson of British Columbia, Canada. He equalled his age when 103 at Uplands GC, a course of over 6,000 yards. He died two years later aged 105.

● Nathaniel Vickers celebrated his 103rd birthday on Sunday, 9th October, 1949, and died the following day. He was the oldest member of the United States Senior Golf Association and until 1942 he competed regularly in their events and won many trophies in the various age divisions. When 100 years old, he apologised for being able to play only 9 holes a day. Vickers predicted he would live until 103 and he died a few hours after he had celebrated his birthday.

● American George Miller, who died in 1979 aged 102, played regularly when 100 years old.

● In his 93rd year, the Rev Harcourt Just had a daily round of six to 10 holes at St Andrews. In 1950, the Town Council gave him the *Courtesy of the Course*, which excused the venerable minister paying the yearly charge.

● George Swanwick, a member of Wallasey, celebrated his 90th birthday with a luncheon at the club on 1st April, 1971. He played golf several times a week, carrying his own clubs and had holed-in-one at the ages of 75 and 85. His ambition was to complete the sequence aged 95 . . . but he died in 1973 aged 92.

● The 10th Earl of Wemyss played a round on his 92nd birthday, in 1910, at Craigielaw. When 87 the Earl was partnered by Harry Vardon in a match at Kilspindie, the golf course on his East Lothian estate at Gosford. The venerable earl, after playing his ball, mounted a pony and rode to the next shot. He died on 30th June, 1914, in his 96th year.

● FL Callender, aged 78, in September 1932, played nine consecutive rounds in the Jubilee Vase, St Andrews. He was defeated in the ninth, the final round, by 4 and 2. Callender's handicap was 12. This is the best known achievement of a septuagenarian in golf.

● Mr Bernard Matthews, aged 82, of Banstead Downs Club, handicap 6, holed the course in 72 gross in August 1988. A week later he holed it in 70, twelve shots below his age. He came back in 31, finishing 4, 3, 3, 2, 3, against a par of 5, 4, 3, 3, 4. Mr Matthews's eclectic score at his Club is 37, or one over 2's.

Playing in the Dark

On numerous occasions it has been necessary to hold lamps, lighted candles, or torches at holes in order that players might finish a competition. Large entries, slow play, early darkness and an eclipse of the sun have all been causes of playing in darkness.

● Since 1972, the Whitburn Golf Club at South Shields, Tyne and Wear, has held an annual Summer Solstice Competition. All competitors, who draw lots for starting tees, must begin before 4.24 and 13 seconds am, the time the sun rises over the first hole on the longest day of the year.

● At the Open Championship in Musselburgh in November 1889 many players finished when the light had so far gone that the adjacent street lamps were lit. The cards were checked by candlelight. Several players who had no chance of the championship were paid small sums to withdraw in order to permit others who had a chance to finish in daylight. This was the last championship at Musselburgh.

● At the Southern Section of the PGA tournament on 25th September, 1907, at Burnham Beeches, several players concluded the round by the aid of torch lights placed near the holes.

● In the Irish Open Championship at Portmarnock in September, 1907, a tie in the third round between WC Pickeman and A Jeffcott was postponed owing to darkness, at the 22nd hole. Pickeman on the following morning won at the 24th.

● The qualifying round of the American Amateur Championship in 1910 could not be

finished in one day, and several competitors had to stop their round on account of darkness, and complete it early in the morning of the following day.

● On 10th January, 1926, in the final of the President's Putter, at Rye, EF Storey and RH Wethered were all square at the 24th hole. It was then 5 pm and so dark that, although a fair crowd was present, the balls could not be followed, and the tie was abandoned and the Putter held jointly for the year. The winner of the Putter each year affixes the ball he played; for 1926 there are two balls, respectively engraved with the names of the finalists.

● In the 1932 Walker Cup contest at Brooklyn, a total eclipse of the sun occurred.

● At Perth, on 14th September, 1932, a competition was in progress under good clear evening light, and a full bright moon. The moon rose at 7.10 and an hour later came under eclipse to the earth's surface. The light then became so bad that on the last three greens competitors holed out by the aid of the light from matches.

● At Carnoustie, 1932, in the competition for the *Craw's Nest* the large entry necessitated competitors being sent off in 3-ball matches. The late players had to be assisted by electric torches flashed on the greens.

● In February, 1950, Max Faulkner and his partner, R Dolman, in a Guildford Alliance event finished their round in complete darkness. A photographer's flash bulbs were used at the last hole to direct Faulkner's approach. Several others of more than 100 competitors also finished in the darkness. At the last hole they had only the light from the clubhouse to aim at and one played his approach so boldly that he put his ball through the hall doorway and almost into the dressing room.

● On the second day of the 1969 Ryder Cup contest, the last 4-ball match ended in near total darkness on the 18th green at Birkdale. With the help of the clubhouse lights the two American players, Lee Trevino and Miller Barber, and Tony Jacklin for Britain each faced putts of around five feet to win their match. All missed and their game was halved.

● The occasions mentioned above all occurred in competitions where it was not intended to play in the dark. There are, however, numerous instances where players set out to play in the dark either for bets or for novelty.

● On 29th November, 1878, RW Brown backed himself to go round the Hoylake links in 150 strokes, starting at 11 pm. The conditions of the match were that Mr Brown was only to be penalised *loss of distance* for a lost ball, and that no one was to help him to find it. He went round in 147 strokes, and won his bet by the narrow margin of three strokes.

● In 1876 David Strath backed himself to go round St Andrews under 100, in moonlight. He took 95, and did not lose a ball.

● In September 1928, at St Andrews, the first and last holes were illuminated by lanterns, and at 11 pm four members of the Royal and Ancient set out to play a foursome over the 2 holes. Electric lights, lanterns, and rockets were used to brighten the fairway, and the headlights of motor cars parked on Links Place formed a helpful battery. The 1st hole was won in four, and each side got a five at the 18th. About 1,000 spectators followed the freak match, which was played to celebrate the appointment of Angus Hambro to the captaincy of the club.

● In 1931, Rufus Stewart, professional, Kooyonga Club, South Australia, and former Australian Open Champion, played 18 holes of exhibition golf at night without losing a single ball over the Kooyonga course, and completed the round in 77.

● At Ashley Wood Golf Club, Blandford, Dorset, a night-time golf tournament is arranged annually with up to 180 golfers taking part over four nights. Over £6000 has been raised in four years for the Muscular Dystrophy Charity.

● At Pannal, 3rd July, 1937, RH Locke, playing in bright moonlight, holed his tee shot at the 15th hole, distance 220 yards, the only known case of holing-in-one under such conditions.

● In August, 1970, a group of Canadians held a stroke competition at the Summit Golf and Country Club, Ontario, in total darkness. Organised by Peter Kennedy, seven competitors took part, starting at midnight. Special rules drawn up included only a 1-stroke penalty for a lost ball, but if 12 balls were lost the competitor had to retire. The best score was 84 by Lief Pettersen.

Fatal and Other Accidents on the Links

The history of golf is, unfortunately, marred by a great number of fatal accidents on or near the course. In the vast majority of such cases they have been caused either by careless swinging of the club or by an uncontrolled shot when the ball

has struck a spectator or bystander. In addition to the fatal accidents there is an even larger number on record which have resulted in serious injury or blindness. We do not propose to list these accidents except where they have some unusual feature. We would remind all golfers of the tragic consequences which have so often been caused by momentary carelessness. The fatal accidents which follow have an unusual cause and other accidents given may have their humorous aspect.

● In July, 1971, 43-year-old Rudolph Roy was killed at a Montreal course when, in playing out of woods, the shaft of his club snapped, rebounded off a tree and the jagged edge plunged into his body.

● Harold Wallace, aged 75, playing at Lundin Links with two friends in 1950, was crossing the railway line which separates the fifth green and sixth tee, when a light engine knocked him down and he was killed instantly.

● In the summer of 1963, Harold Kalles, of Toronto, Canada, died six days after his throat had been cut by a golf club shaft, which broke against a tree as he was trying to play out of a bunker.

● At Jacksonville, Florida, on 18th March, 1952, two women golfers were instantly killed when hit simultaneously by the whirling propellor of a navy fighter plane. They were playing together when the plane with a dead engine coming in out of control, hit them from behind.

● In September, 1956, Myrl G Hanmore, aged 50, died from an accident at the Riviera Country Club, Los Angeles, apparently caused when he lost control of a golf car on a steep incline and was crushed between the vehicle he was driving and one he was towing from the first tee to a storage barn.

● At Knott End Golf Club, on 20th June, 1953, Charles Langley, playing in a competition for the Captain's Prize, hit his tee shot from the 10th and struck the cone-shaped wood marker at the ladies' tee, which was approximately nine feet from where Mr Langley had teed his ball. The ball rebounded at lightning speed striking and destroying Mr Langley's left eye.

Lightning on the Links

There have been a considerable number of fatal and serious accidents through players and caddies having been struck by lightning on the course. The Royal & Ancient and the USGA have, since 1952, provided for discontinuance of play during lightning storms under the Rules of Golf (Rule 37, 6) and the United States Golf Association have given the following guide for personal safety during thunderstorms:

(a) Do not go out of doors or remain out during thunderstorms unless it is necessary. Stay inside of a building where it is dry, preferably away from fireplaces, stoves, and other metal objects.

(b) If there is any choice of shelter, choose in the following order:
  1. Large metal or metal-frame buildings.
  2. Dwellings or other buildings which are protected against lightning.
  3. Large unprotected buildings.
  4. Small unprotected buildings.

(c) If remaining out of doors is unavoidable, keep away from:
  1. Small sheds and shelters if in an exposed location.
  2. Isolated trees.
  3. Wire fences.
  4. Hilltops and wide open spaces.

(d) Seek shelter in:
  1. A cave.
  2. A depression in the ground.
  3. A deep valley or canyon.
  4. The foot of a steep or overhanging cliff.
  5. Dense woods.
  6. A grove of trees.

Note – Raising golf clubs or umbrellas above the head is dangerous.

● A serious incident with lightning involving well-known golfers was at the 1975 Western Open in Chicago when Lee Trevino, Jerry Heard and Bobby Nichols were all struck and had to be taken to hospital. At the same time Tony Jacklin had a club thrown 15 feet out of his hands.

● Two well-known competitors were struck by lightning in European events in 1977. They were Mark James of Britain in the Swiss Open and Severiano Ballesteros of Spain in the Scandinavian Open. Fortunately neither appeared to be badly injured.

Spectators Interfering with Balls

● Deliberate interference by spectators with balls in play during important money matches was not unknown in the old days when there was intense rivalry between the schools of Musselburgh, St Andrews, and North Berwick, and disputes arose in stake matches caused by the action of spectators in kicking the ball into either a favourable or an unfavourable position.

● Tom Morris, in his last match with Willie Park at Musselburgh, refused to go on because of interference by the spectators, and in the match on the same course about 40 years later, in 1895, between Willie Park junior and JH Taylor, the barracking of the crowd and interference with play was so bad that when the Park-Vardon match came to be arranged in 1899, Vardon refused to accept Musselburgh as a venue.

● Even in modern times spectators have been known to interfere deliberately with players' balls, though it is usually by children. In the 1972

Penfold Tournament at Queen's Park, Bournemouth, Christy O'Connor jun had his ball stolen by a young boy, but not being told of this at the time had to take the penalty for a lost ball. O'Connor finished in a tie for first place, but lost the play-off.

● In 1912 in the last round of the final of the Amateur Championship at Westward Ho! between Abe Mitchell and John Ball, the drive of the former to the short 14th hit an open umbrella held by a lady protecting herself from the heavy rain, and instead of landing on the green the ball was diverted into a bunker. Mitchell, who was leading at the time by 2 holes, lost the hole and Ball won the Championship at the 38th hole.

● In the match between the professionals of Great Britain and America at Southport in 1937 a dense crowd collected round the 15th green waiting for the Sarazen-Alliss match. The American's ball landed in the lap of a woman, who picked it up and threw it so close to the hole that Sarazen got a two against Alliss' three.

● In a memorable tie between Bobby Jones and Cyril Tolley in the 1930 Amateur Championship at St Andrews, Jones' approach to the 17th green struck spectators massed at the left end of the green and led to controversy as to whether it would otherwise have gone on to the famous road. Jones himself had deliberately played for that part of the green and had requested stewards to get the crowd back. Had the ball gone on to the road, the historic Jones Quadrilateral of the year – the Open and Amateur Championships of Britain and the United States – might not have gone into the records.

● In the 1983 Suntory World Match-play Championship at Wentworth Nick Faldo hit his second shot over the green at the 16th hole into a group of spectators. To everyone's astonishment and discomfiture the ball reappeared on the green about 30 ft from the hole, propelled there by a thoroughly misguided and anonymous spectator. The referee ruled that Faldo play the ball where it lay on the green. Faldo's opponent, Graham Marsh, understandably upset by the incident, took three putts against Faldo's two, thus losing a hole he might well otherwise have won. Faldo won the match 2 and 1, but lost in the final to Marsh's fellow Australian Greg Norman by 3 and 2.

Golf Balls Killing Animals and Fish, and Incidents with Animals

● An astounding fatality to an animal through being hit by a golf ball occurred at St Margaret's-at-Cliffe Golf Club, Kent on 13th June, 1934, when WJ Robinson, the professional, killed a cow with his tee shot to the 18th hole. The cow was standing in the fairway about 100 yards from the tee, and the ball struck her on the back of the head. She fell like a log, but staggered to her feet and

walked about 50 yards before dropping again. When the players reached her she was dead.

● JW Perret, of Ystrad Mynach, playing with Chas R Halliday, of Ralston, in the qualifying rounds of the Society of One Armed Golfers' Championship over the Darley course, Troon, on 27th August, 1935, killed two gulls at successive holes with his second shots. The *deadly* shots were at the 1st and 2nd holes.

● On the first day of grouse shooting of the 1975 season (12th August), 11-year-old schoolboy, Willie Fraser, of Kingussie, beat all the guns when he killed a grouse with his tee shot on the local course.

● On 10th June, 1904, while playing in the Edinburgh High Constables' Competition at Kilspindie, Captain Ferguson sent a long ball into the rough at the Target hole, and on searching for it found that it had struck and killed a young hare.

● Playing in a mixed open tournament at the Waimairi Beach Golf Club in Christchurch, New Zealand, in the summer of 1961, Mrs RT Challis found her ball in fairly long spongy grass where a placing rule applied. She picked up, placed the ball and played her stroke. A young hare leaped into the air and fell dead at her feet. She had placed the ball on the leveret without seeing it and without disturbing it.

● In 1906 in the Border Championship at Hawick, a gull and a weasel were killed by balls during the afternoon's play.

● A golfer at Newark, in May, 1907, drove his ball into the river. The ball struck a trout 2lb in weight and killed it.

● On 24th April, 1975, at Scunthorpe GC, Jim Tollan's drive at the 14th hole, called *The Mallard*, struck and killed a female mallard duck in flight. The duck was stuffed and is displayed in the Scunthorpe Clubhouse.

● A Samuel, Melbourne Club, at Sandringham,

was driving with an iron club from the 17th tee, when a kitten, which had been playing in the long grass, sprang suddenly at the ball. Kitten and club arrived at the objective simultaneously, with the result that the kitten took an unexpected flight through the air, landing some 20 yards away.

● As Susan Rowlands was lining up a vital putt in the closing stages of the final of the 1978 Welsh Girls' Championship at Abergele, a tiny mouse scampered up her trouser leg. After holing the putt, the mouse ran down again. Susan, who won the final admitted that she fortunately had not known it was there.

Interference by Birds and Animals

● Crows, ravens, hawks and seagulls frequently carry off golf balls, sometimes dropping the ball actually on the green, and it is a common incident for a cow to swallow a golf ball. A plague of crows on the Liverpool course at Hoylake are addicted to golf balls – they stole 26 in one day – selecting only new balls. It was suggested that members should carry shotguns as a 15th club!

● A match was approaching a hole in a rather low-lying course, when one of the players made a crisp chip from about 30 yards from the hole. The ball trickled slowly across the green and eventually disappeared into the hole. After a momentary pause, the ball was suddenly ejected on to the green, and out jumped a large frog.

● In Massachusetts a goose, having been hit rather hard by a golf ball which then came to rest by the side of a water hazard, took revenge by waddling over to the ball and kicking it into the water.

● A large black crow named Jasper which frequented the Lithgow GC in New South Wales, Australia, stole 30 golf balls in the club's 1972 Easter Tournament.

● As Mrs Molly Whitaker was playing from a bunker at Beachwood course, Natal, South Africa, a large monkey leaped from a bush and clutched her round the neck. A caddie drove it off by clipping it with an iron club.

● In the summer of 1963, SC King had a good drive to the 10th hole at the Guernsey Club. His partner, RW Clark, was in the rough, and King helped him to search. Returning to his ball, he found a cow eating it. Next day, at the same hole, the positions were reversed, and King was in the rough. Clark placed his woollen hat over his ball, remarking, *I'll make sure the cow doesn't eat mine.* On his return he found the cow thoroughly enjoying his hat; nothing was left but the pom-pom.

Armless, One-armed, Legless and Ambidextrous Players

● In September, 1933, at Burgess Golfing Society of Edinburgh, the first championship for one-armed golfers was held. There were 43 entries and 37 of the competitors had lost an arm in the 1914-18 war. Play was over two rounds and the championship was won by WE Thomson, East-wood, Glasgow, with a score of 169 (82 and 87) for two rounds. The Burgess course was 6,300 yards long. Thomson drove the last green, 260 yards. The championship and an international match are played annually.

● In the Boys' Amateur Championship 1923, at Dunbar and 1949 at St Andrews, there were competitors each with one arm. The competitor in 1949, RP Reid, Cupar, Fife, who lost his arm working a machine in a butcher's shop, got through to the third round.

● There have been cases of persons with no arms playing golf. One, Thomas McAuliffe, who held the club between his right shoulder and cheek, once went round Buffalo CC, USA, in 108.

● Group Captain Bader, who lost both legs in a flying accident prior to the World War 1939-45, took part in golf competitions and reached a single-figure handicap in spite of his disability.

● In 1909, Scott of Silloth, and John Haskins of Hoylake, both one-armed golfers, played a home and away match for £20 a side. Scott finished five up at Silloth. He was seven up and 14 to play at Hoylake but Haskins played so well that Scott eventually only won by 3 and 1. This was the first match between one-armed golfers. Haskins in 1919 was challenged by Mr Mycock, of Buxton, another one-armed player. The match was 36 holes, home and away. The first half was played over the Buxton and High Peak Links, and the latter half over the Liverpool Links, and resulted in a win for Haskins by 11 and 10. Later in the same year Haskins received another challenge to play against Alexander Smart of Aberdeen. The match was 18 holes over the Balgownie Course, and ended in favour of Haskins.

● In a match, November, 1926, between the Geduld and Sub Nigel Clubs – two golf clubs connected with the South African gold mines of the same names – each club had two players minus an arm. The natural consequence was that the quartet were matched. The players were – AWP Charteris and E Mitchell, Sub Nigel; and EP Coles and J Kirby, Geduld. This is the first record of four one-armed players in a foursome.

● At Joliet Country Club, USA, a one-armed golfer named DR Anderson drove a ball 300 yards.

● Left-handedness, but playing golf right-handed, is prevalent and for a man to throw with his left hand and play golf right-handed is considered an advantage, for Bobby Jones, Jesse Sweetser, Walter Hagen, Jim Barnes, Joe Kirkwood and more recently Johnny Miller were eminent golfers who were left-handed and ambidextrous.

● In a practice round for the Open Championship in July, 1927, at St Andrews, Len Nettlefold and Joe Kirkwood changed sets of clubs at the 9th hole. Nettlefold was a left-handed golfer and Kirkwood right-handed. They played the last nine, Kirkwood with the left-handed clubs and Nettlefold with the right-handed clubs.

● The late Harry Vardon, when he was at Ganton, got tired of giving impossible odds to his members and beating them, so he collected a set of left-handed clubs, and rating himself at scratch, conceded the handicap odds to them. He won with the same monotonous regularity.

● Ernest Jones, who was professional at the Chislehurst Club, was badly wounded in the war in France in 1916 and his right leg had to be amputated below the knee. He persevered with the game, and before the end of the year he went round the Clacton course balanced on his one leg in 72. Jones later settled in the United States

where he built fame and fortune as a golf teacher.

● Major Alexander McDonald Fraser of Edinburgh had the distinction of holding two handicaps simultaneously in the same club – one when he played left-handed and the other for his right-handed play. In medal competitions he had to state before teeing up which method he would use.

● Former England test cricketer Brian Close once held a handicap of 2 playing right-handed, but after retiring from cricket in 1977 decided to apply himself as a left-handed player. His left-handed handicap at the time of his retirement was 7. Close had the distinction of once beating Ted Dexter, another distinguished test cricketer and noted golfer twice in the one day, playing right-handed in the morning and left-handed in the afternoon.

Blind and Blindfolded Golf

● Major Towse, VC, whose eyes were shot out during the South African War, 1899, was probably the first blind man to play golf. His only stipulations when playing the game were that he should be allowed to touch the ball with his hands to ascertain its position, and that his caddie could ring a small bell to indicate the position of the hole. Major Towse, who played with considerable skill, was also an expert oarsman and bridge player. He died in 1945, aged 81.

● The United States Blind Golfers' Association in 1946 promoted an Invitational Golf Tournament for the blind at Country Club, Inglewood, California. This competition is held annually and in 1953 there were 24 competitors and 11 players completed the two rounds of 36 holes. The winner was Charley Boswell who lost his eyesight leading a tank unit in Germany in 1944.

● In July, 1954, at Lambton Golf and Country Club, Toronto, the first international championship for the blind was held. It resulted in a win for Joe Lazaro, of Waltham, Mass, with a score of 220 for the two rounds. He drove the 215-yard 16th hole and just missed an ace, his ball stopping 18 inches from the hole. Charley Boswell, who won the United States Blind Golfers' Association Tournament in 1953, was second. The same Charles Boswell, of Birmingham, Alabama holed the 141-yard 14th hole at the Vestavia CC in one in October, 1970.

● Another blind person to have holed-in-one was American Ben Thomas while on holiday in South Carolina in 1978.

● Rick Sorenson undertook a bet in which, playing 18 holes blindfolded at Meadowbrook Course, Minneapolis, on 25th May, 1973, he was to pay $10 for every hole over par and receive $100 for every hole in par or better. He went round in 86 losing $70 on the deal.

● Alfred Toogood played in a match at Sunningdale in 1912 blindfolded. His opponent was Tin-

dal Atkinson, and Toogood was beaten 8 and 7. I Millar, Newcastle-upon-Tyne, played a match, blindfolded, against AT Broughton, Birkdale, at Newcastle, County Down, in 1908. Putting matches while blindfolded have been frequently played.

● Wing-Commander *Laddie* Lucas, DSO, DFC, MP, played over Sandy Lodge golf course in Hertfordshire on 7th August, 1954, completely blindfolded and had a score of 87.

Trick Shots

● Joe Kirkwood, Australia, specialised in public exhibitions of trick and fancy shots. He played all kinds of strokes after nominating them, and among his ordinary strokes nothing was more impressive than those hit for low flight. He played a full drive from the face of a wristlet watch, and the toe of a spectator's shoe, full strokes at a suspended ball, and played for slice and pull at will, and exhibited his ambidexterity by playing left-handed strokes with right-handed clubs. Holing six balls, stymieing, a full shot at a ball catching it as it descended, and hitting 12 full shots in rapid succession, with his face turned away from the ball, were shots among his repertoire. In playing the last named Kirkwood placed the balls in a row, about six inches apart, and moved quickly along the line. Kirkwood, who was born in Aus-

tralia lived for many years in America. He died in November, 1970 aged 73.

● Joe Ezar, an American professional, who specialised in trick shots, included in his show a number of clowning acts with balls.

● On 2nd April, 1894, a 3-ball match was played over Musselburgh course between Messrs Grant, Bowden, and Waggot, the clubmaker, the latter teeing on the face of a watch at each tee. He finished the round in 41 the watch being undamaged in any way.

● At Westbrook, USA, in 1901, ET Knapp drove a ball off the top of a hen's egg. The egg was slightly dented on one end to afford a hold for the ball.

● At Esher, 23rd November, 1931, George Ashdown, the club professional, in a match played his tee shot for each of the 18 holes from a rubber tee strapped to the forehead of Miss Ena Shaw.

● EA Forrest, a South African professional in a music hall turn of trick golf shots, played blindfolded shots, one being from the ball teed on the chin of his recumbent partner.

● The late Paul Hahn, an American trick specialist could hit four balls with two clubs Holding a club in each hand he hit two balls, hooking one and slicing the other with the same swing. Hahn had a repertoire of 30 trick shots. In 1955 he flew round the world, exhibiting in 14 countries and on all five continents.

Balls Colliding and Touching

● Competing in the 1980 Corfu International Championship, Sharon Peachey drove from one tee and her ball collided in mid-air with one from a competitor playing another hole. Her ball ended in a pond.

● Playing in the Cornish team championship in 1973 at West Cornwall GC Tom Scott-Brown, of West Cornwall GC, and Paddy Bradley, of Tehidy GC, saw their drives from the fourth and eighth tees collide in mid-air.

● Playing in a 4-ball match at Guernsey Club in June, 1966, all four players were near the 13th green from the tee. Two of them – DG Hare and S Machin – chipped up simultaneously; the balls collided in mid-air; Machin's ball hit the green, then the flagstick, and dropped into the hole for a birdie 2.

● In May, 1926, during the meeting of the Army Golfing Society at St Andrews, Colonel Howard and Lieutenant-Colonel Buchanan Dunlop, while playing in the foursomes against J Rodger and J Mackie, hit full iron shots for the seconds to the 16th green. Each thought he had to play his ball first, and hidden by a bunker the players struck their balls simultaneously. The balls, going towards the hole about 20 yards from the pin and five feet in the air, met with great force and dropped either side of the hole five yards apart.

● In 1972, before a luncheon celebrating the centenary of the Ladies' Section of Royal Wimbledon GC, a 12-hole competition was held during which two competitors, Mrs L Champion and Mrs A McKendrick, driving from the eighth and ninth tees respectively, saw their balls collide in mid-air.

● In 1928, at Wentworth Falls, Australia, Dr Alcorn and EA Avery, of the Leura Club, were playing with the professional, E Barnes. The tee shots of Avery and Barnes at the 9th hole finished on opposite sides of the fairway. Unknown to each other, both players hit their seconds (chip shots) at the same time. Dr Alcorn, standing at the pin, suddenly saw two balls approaching the hole from different angles. They met in the air and then dropped into the hole.

● At Rugby, 1931, playing in a 4-ball match, H Fraser pulled his drive from the 10th tee in the direction of the ninth tee. Simultaneously a club member, driving from the ninth tee, pulled his drive. The tees were about 350 yards apart. The two balls collided in mid-air.

● Two golf balls, being played in opposite directions, collided in flight over Longniddry Golf Course on 27th June, 1953. Immediately after Stewart Elder, of Longniddry, had driven from the third tee, another ball, which had been pulled off line from the second fairway, which runs alongside the third, struck his ball about 20 feet above the ground. SJ Fleming, of Tranent, who was playing with Elder, heard a loud crack and thought Elder's ball had exploded. The balls were found undamaged about 70 yards apart.

Three and Two Balls Dislodged by One Shot

● In 1934 on the short 3rd hole (now the 13th) of Olton Course, Warwickshire, JR Horden, a scratch golfer of the club, sent his tee shot into long wet grass a few feet over the back of the green. When he played an *explosion* shot three balls dropped on to the putting green, his own and two others.

● AM Chevalier, playing at Hale, Cheshire, March, 1935, drove his ball into a grass bunker, and when he reached it there was only part of it showing. He played the shot with a niblick and to his amazement not one but three balls shot into the air. They all dropped back into the bunker and came to rest within a foot of each other. Then came another surprise. One of the *finds* was of the same manufacture and bore the same number as the ball he was playing with.

● Playing to the 9th hole, at Osborne House Club, Isle of Wight, George A Sherman lost his ball which had sunk out of sight on the sodden fairway. A few weeks later, playing from the same tee, his ball again was plugged, only the top showing. Under a local rule he lifted his ball to place it, and exactly under it lay the ball he had lost previously.

Balls in Strange Places

● Playing at the John O' Gaunt Club, Sutton, near Biggleswade (Bedfordshire), a member drove a ball which did not touch the ground until it reached London – over 40 miles away. The ball landed in a vegetable lorry which was passing the golf course and fell out of a package of cabbages when they were unloaded at Covent Garden, London.

● In the English Open Amateur Stroke Play at Moortown in 1974, Nigel Denham, a Yorkshire County player, in the first round saw his overhit second shot to the 18th green bounce up some steps into the clubhouse. His ball went through an open door, ricochetted off a wall and came to rest in the men's bar, 20 feet from the windows. As the clubhouse was not out of bounds Denham decided to play the shot back to the green and opened a window 4 feet by 2 feet through which he pitched his ball to 12 feet from the flag. (Several weeks later the R & A declared that Denham should have been penalised two shots for opening the window. The clubhouse was an immovable obstruction and no part of it should have been moved.)

● In the Open Championship at Sandwich, 1949, Harry Bradshaw, Kilcroney, Dublin, at the

5th hole in his second round, drove into the rough and found his ball inside a beer bottle with the neck and shoulder broken off and four sharp points sticking up. Bradshaw, if he had treated the ball as in an unplayable lie might have been involved in a disqualification, so he decided to play it where it lay. With his blaster he smashed the bottle and sent the ball about 30 yards. The hole, a par 4, cost him 6.

● Kevin Sharman of Woodbridge GC hit a low, very straight drive at the club's 8th hole in 1979. After some minutes' searching, his ball was found embedded in a plastic sphere on top of the direction post.

● On the Dublin Course, 16th July, 1936, in the Irish Open Championship, AD Locke, the South African, played his tee shot at the 100-yard 12th hole, but the ball could not be found on arrival at the green. The marker removed the pin and it was discovered that the ball had been entangled in the flag. It dropped near the edge of the hole and Locke holed the short putt for a *birdie* two.

● While playing a round on the Geelong Golf Club Course, Australia, Easter, 1923, Captain Charteris topped his tee shot to the short 2nd hole, which lies over a creek with deep and steep clay banks. His ball came to rest on the near slope of the creek bank. He elected to play the ball as it lay, and took his niblick. After the shot, the ball was nowhere to be seen. It was afterwards found embedded in a mass of gluey clay stuck fast to the face of the niblick. It could not be shaken off. Charteris did what was afterwards approved by the R&A, cleaned the ball and dropped it behind without penalty.

● In October, 1929, at Blackmoor Golf Club, Bordon, Hants, a player driving from the first tee holed out his ball in the chimney of a house some 120 yards distant and some 40 yards out of bounds on the right. The owner and his wife were sitting in front of the fire when they heard a rattle in the chimney and were astonished to see a golf ball drop into the fire.

● A similar incident occurred in an inter-club match between Musselburgh and Lothianburn at Prestongrange in 1938 when a member of the former team hooked his ball at the 2nd hole and gave it up for lost. To his amazement a woman emerged from one of the houses adjacent to this part of the course and handed back the ball which she said had come down the chimney and landed on a pot which was on the fire.

● In July, 1955, J Lowrie, starter at the Eden Course, St Andrews, witnessed a freak shot. A visitor drove from the first tee just as a north-bound train was passing. He sliced the shot and the ball disappeared through an open window of a passenger compartment. Almost immediately the ball emerged again, having been thrown back on to the fairway by a man in the compartment, who waved a greeting which presumably

indicated that no one was hurt.

● Many balls have been hit into the pockets of spectators, stewards, other competitors and even the players' own pockets. They have also been found in trouser turn-ups and in the folds of sweaters and waterproofs.

● At Coombe Wood Golf Club a player hit a ball towards the 16th green where it landed in the vertical exhaust of a tractor which was mowing the fairway. The greenkeeper was somewhat surprised to find a temporary loss of power in the tractor. When sufficient compression had built up in the exhaust system, the ball was forced out with tremendous velocity, hit the roof of a house nearby, bounced off and landed some three feet from the pin on the green.

● There have been many occasions when mis-directed shots have finished in strange places after an unusual line of flight and bounce. At Ashford, Middlesex, John Miller, aged 69, hit his tee shot out of bounds at the 12th hole (237 yards). It struck a parked car, passed through a copse, hit more cars, jumped a canopy, flew through the clubhouse kitchen window, finishing in a cooking stock-pot, without once touching the ground. Mr Miller had previously done the hole-in-one on four occasions.

Balls Hit to and from Great Heights

● In 1798 two Edinburgh golfers undertook to drive a ball over the spire of St Giles' Cathedral, Edinburgh, for a wager. Mr Sceales, of Leith, and Mr Smellie, a printer, were each allowed six shots and succeeded in sending the balls well over the weather-cock, a height of more than 160 feet from the ground.

● Some years later Donald McLean, an Edinburgh lawyer, won a substantial bet by driving a ball over the Melville Monument in St Andrew Square, Edinburgh – height, 154 feet.

● Tom Morris in 1860, at the famous bridge of Ballochmyle, stood in the quarry beneath and, from a stick elevated horizontally, attempted to send golf balls over the bridge. He could raise them only to the pathway, 400 feet high, which was in itself a great feat with the gutta ball.

● Captain Ernest Carter, on 28th September, 1922, drove a ball from the roadway at the 1st tee on Harlech Links against the wall of Harlech Castle. The embattlements are 200 feet over the level of the roadway, and the point where the ball struck the embattlements was 180 yards from the point where the ball was teed. Captain Carter, who was laid odds of £100 to £1, used a baffy.

● In 1896 Freddie Tait, then a subaltern in the Black Watch, drove a ball from the Rookery, the highest building on Edinburgh Castle, in a match against a brother officer to hole out in the fountain in Princes Street Gardens 350 feet below and about 300 yards distant.

● Prior to the 1977 Lancôme Tournament in Paris, Arnold Palmer hit three balls from the second stage of the Eiffel Tower, over 300 feet above ground. The longest was measured at 403 yards. One ball was hooked and hit a bus but no serious damage was done as all traffic had been stopped for safety reasons.

● Long drives have been made from mountain peaks, across the gorge at Victoria Falls, from the Pyramids, high buildings in New York, and from many other similar places. As an illustration of such freakish *drives* a member of the New York Rangers' Hockey Team from the top of Mount Edith Cavell, 11,033 feet high, drove a ball which struck the Ghost Glacier 5,000 feet below and bounced off the rocky ledge another 1,000 feet – a total drop of 2,000 yards. Later, in June, 1968, from Pikes Peak, Colorado (14,110 feet), Arthur Lynskey hit a ball which travelled 200 yards horizontally but 2 miles vertically.

Remarkable Shots

● Remarkable shots are to be numbered as the grains of sand; around every 19th hole, legends are recalled of astounding shots. One shot is commemorated by a memorial tablet at the 17th hole at the Lytham and St Annes Club. It was made by Bobby Jones in the final round of the Open Championship in 1926. He was partnered by Al Watrous, another American player. They had been running neck and neck and at the end of the third round, Watrous was just leading Jones with 215 against 217. At the 16th Jones drew level then on the 17th he drove into a sandy lie in broken ground. Watrous reached the green with his second. Jones took a mashie-iron (the equivalent to a No. 4 iron today) and hit a magnificent shot to the green to get his 4. This remarkable recovery unnerved Watrous, who 3-putted, and Jones, getting another 4 at the last hole against 5, won his first Open Championship with 291 against Watrous' 293. The tablet is near the spot where Jones played his second shot.

● Arnold Palmer (USA), playing in the second round of the Australian Wills Masters tournament at Melbourne, in October, 1964, hooked his second shot at the 9th hole high into the fork of a gum tree. Climbing 20 feet up the tree, Palmer, with the head of his No. 1 iron reversed, played a *hammer* stroke and knocked the ball some 30 yards forward, followed by a brilliant chip to the green and a putt.

● In the foursome during the Ryder Cup at Moortown in 1929, Joe Turnesa hooked the American side's second shot at the last hole behind the marquee adjoining the clubhouse, Johnny Farrel then pitched the ball over the marquee on to the green only feet away from the pin and Turnesa holed out for a 4.

● In 1922, Peter Robertson, Braid Hills, Edinburgh, holed the Road Hole, St Andrews (17th, Old Course) in two shots, a drive and a brassie.

● Lew Worsham, in the *World's Championship* at Tam O'Shanter, 9th August, 1953, at the last hole from a distance of 135 yards, holed a wedge shot for a two at the 410-yard hole. This incredible shot made him the winner by one stroke and gave him the greatest jackpot in golf at that time, $25,000. The difference between the first and third prizes was equivalent to £5,000.

Miscellaneous Incidents and Strange Golfing Facts

● Gary Player of South Africa was honoured by his country by having his portrait on new postage stamps which were issued on 12th December, 1976. It was the first time a specific golfer had ever been depicted on any country's postage stamps. In 1981 the US Postal Service introduced stamps featuring Bobby Jones and Babe Zaharias. They are the first golfers to be thus honoured by the United States.

● Prior to the 1976 Curtis Cup Match, members of the British Isles and United States teams were presented to the Queen at Buckingham Palace, the first occasion this has occurred.

● In February, 1971, the first ever golf shots on the moon's surface were played by Captain Alan Shepard, commander of the Apollo 14 spacecraft. Captain Shepard hit two balls with an iron head attached to a makeshift shaft. With a one-handed swing he claimed he hit the first ball 200 yards aided by the reduced force of gravity on the moon. Subsequent findings put this distance in doubt. The second was a shank. Acknowledging the occasion the R&A sent Captain Shepard the following telegram: *Warmest congratulations to all of you on your great achievement and safe return. Please refer to Rules of Golf section on etiquette, paragraph 6, quote – before leaving a bunker a player should carefully fill up all holes made by him therein, unquote.* Shepard presented the club to the USGA Museum in 1974.

● Charles (Chick) Evans competed in every US Amateur Championship held between 1907 and 1962 by which time he was 72 years old. This amounted to 50 consecutive occasions discounting the six years of the two World Wars when the championship was not held.

● In winning the 1977 US Open at Southern Hills CC, Tulsa, Oklahoma, Hubert Green had to contend with a death threat. Coming off the 14th green in the final round, he was advised by USGA officials that a phone call had been received saying that he would be killed. Green decided that play should continue and happily he went on to win, unharmed.

● It was discovered at the 1977 USPGA Championship that the clubs with which Tom Watson had won the Open Championship and the US

Masters earlier in the year were illegal, having grooves which exceeded the permitted specifications. The set he used in winning the 1975 Open Championship were then flown out to him and they too were found to be illegal. No retrospective action was taken.

● Mrs Fred Daly, wife of the former Open champion, saved the clubhouse of Balmoral GC, Belfast, from destruction when three men entered the professionals' shop on 5th August, 1976 and left a bag containing a bomb outside the shop beside the clubhouse when refused money. Mrs Daly carried the bag over to a hedge some distance away where the bomb exploded 15 minutes later. The only damage was broken windows. On the same day several hours afterwards, Dungannon GC in Co Tyrone suffered extensive damage to the clubhouse from terrorist bombs. Co Down GC, proposed venue of the 1979 home international matches suffered bomb damage in May that year and through fear for the safety of team members the 1979 matches were cancelled.

● The Army Golfing Society and St Andrews on 21st April, 1934, played a match 200-a-side, the largest golf match ever played. Play was by foursomes. The Army won 58, St Andrews 31 and 11 were halved.

● On the eve of the 1979 World Cup in Greece, Dale Hayes and Hugh Baiocchi, representing South Africa, were compelled to withdraw when the Greek government, on a demand from the anti-apartheid committee of the United Nations, refused permission for them to compete.

● In November, 1983, as John Gallacher (39), a 9-handicap player, was driving off at the 9th hole at Machrihanish in a winter league 4-ball tie, a Hercules transport plane from Germany coming in to land at the adjoining RAF airfield passed overhead, and was struck by Gallacher's ball. A mark that could have been caused by a golf ball was subsequently found on the aircraft's fuselage, but Gallacher's ball was never found.

● In 1986 Alistair Risk and three colleagues on the 17th green at Brora, Sutherland, watched a cow giving birth to twin calves between the markers on the 18th tee, causing them to play their next tee shots from in front of the tee. Their application for a ruling from the R & A brought a Rules Committee reply that while technically a rule had been broken, their action was considered within the spirit of the game and there should be no penalty. The Secretary added that the Rules Committee hoped that mother and twins were doing well.

● In view of the increasing number of people crossing the road (known as Granny Clark's Wynd) which runs across the first and 18th fairways of the Old Course, St Andrews, as a right of way, the St Andrews Links committee decided in 1969 to control the flow by erecting traffic lights, with appropriate green for go, yellow for caution

and red for stop. The lights are controlled from the starter's box on the first tee. Golfers on the first tee must wait until the lights turn to green before driving off and a notice has been erected at the Wynd warning pedestrians not to cross at yellow or stop.

● A traffic light for golfers was also installed in 1971 on one of Japan's most congested courses. After putting on the uphill 9th hole of the Fukuoka course in Southern Japan, players have to switch on a go-ahead signal for following golfers waiting to play their shots to the green.

● A 22-year-old professional at Brett Essex GC, Brentwood, David Moore, who was playing in the Mufulira Open in Zambia in 1976, was shot dead it is alleged by the man with whom he was staying for the duration of the tournament. It appeared his host then shot himself.

● The first round of the Amateur Championship in 1887 and again in 1953, both strangely enough at Hoylake, consisted of only one tie, all the other competitors receiving byes. The first round of the English Ladies' in 1924 and the Scottish Amateur in 1932 also consisted of only one tie.

● Patricia Shepherd has won the ladies' club championship at Turriff GC Aberdeenshire 30 consecutive times from 1959 to 1988.

● Mrs Jackie Mercer won the South African Ladies' Championship in 1979, 31 years after her first victory in the event as Miss Jacqueline Smith.

● During the Royal & Ancient medal meeting on 25th September, 1907, a member of the Royal & Ancient drove a ball which struck the sharp point of a hatpin in the hat of a lady who was crossing the course. The ball was so firmly impaled that it remained in position. The lady was not hurt.

● John Cook, professional at Brickendon Grange, and former English Amateur champion, narrowly escaped death during an attempted coup against King Hassan of Morocco in July 1971. Cook had been playing in a tournament arranged by King Hassan, a keen golfer, and was at the King's birthday party in Rabat when rebels

broke into the party demanding that the king give up his throne. Cook and many others present were taken hostage. Over 200 people were killed before King Hassan surrendered minutes before the group which included Cook was due for the firing squad.

● When playing from the 9th tee at Lossiemouth golf course in June, 1971, Martin Robertson struck a Royal Navy jet aircraft which was coming in to land at the nearby airfield. The plane was not damaged.

● At a court in Inglewood, California, in 1978, Jim Brown was convicted of beating and choking an opponent during a dispute over where a ball should have been placed on the green.

● During the Northern Ireland troubles a home-made hand grenade was found in a bunker at Dungannon GC, Co Tyrone, on Sunday, 12th September, 1976.

● At Rhymney and Tredegar, South Wales, on 10th September, 1934, the hard felt hat of a pedestrian who was crossing the fairway was hit by the drive of a golfer. The man fell, but his head was only slightly grazed. The ball had gone right through the hat and was found 20 yards farther on.

● To mark the centenary of the Jersey Golf Club in 1978, the Jersey Post Office issued a set of four special stamps featuring Jersey's most famous golfer, Harry Vardon. The background of the 13p stamp was a brief biography of Vardon's career reproduced from the Golfer's Handbook.

● Forty-one-year-old John Mosley went for a round of golf at Delaware Park GC, Buffalo, New York, in July, 1972. He stepped on to the first tee and was challenged over a green fee by an official guard. A scuffle developed, a shot was fired and Mosley, a bullet in his chest, died on the way to hospital. His wife was awarded $131,250 in an action against the City of Buffalo and the guard. The guard was sentenced to 7½ years for second-degree manslaughter.

● When three competitors in a pro-am event in 1968 in Pennsylvania were about to drive from the 16th tee, two bandits (one with pistol) suddenly emerged from the bushes, struck one of the players and robbed them of wrist watches and $300.

● A 5-hole miniature course has been built on top of a seven-storey garage at Pompano Beach, Florida.

● In the 1932 Walker Cup match at Brooklyn, Leonard Crawley succeeded in denting the cup. An errant iron shot to the 18th green hit the cup, which was on display outside the clubhouse.

● A mayor in an English Midland town at the opening ceremony of a new course had to putt on the 18th green. The unfortunate man missed the ball completely.

● There has rarely been a man who played better golf than the late Harry Vardon played in 1898 and 1899. All the same, at Wheaton, Illinois,

in the American Open Championship, in 1900, which he won, he made the humiliating mistake of regarding a six-inch putt with such indifference that, in trying to knock it gaily into the hole, he missed the ball entirely, and struck his club into the ground, thus counting a stroke.

● Three golf officials appeared in court in Johannesburg, South Africa, accused of violating a 75-year-old Sunday Observance Law by staging the final round of the South African PGA championship on Sunday, 28th February, 1971. The championship should have been completed on the Saturday but heavy rain prevented any play.

● At the 11th hole at Troon in the 1962 Open Championship, Max Faulkner carelessly tapped the ball against his foot, and the hole ultimately cost him 11 strokes.

● In the Open Championship of 1876, at St Andrews, Bob Martin and David Strath tied at 176. A protest was lodged against Strath alleging he played his approach to the 17th green and struck a spectator. The Royal & Ancient ordered the replay, but Strath refused to play off the tie until a decision had been given on the protest. No decision was given and Bob Martin was declared the Champion.

● At Rose Bay, New South Wales, on 11th July, 1931, DJ Bayly MacArthur, on stepping into a bunker, began to sink. MacArthur, who weighed 14 stone, shouted for help. He was rescued when up to the armpits. He had stepped on a patch of quicksand, aggravated by excess of moisture.

● The late Bobby Cruickshank was the victim of his own jubilation in the 1934 US Open at Merion. In the 4th round while in with a chance of winning he half-topped his second shot at the 11th hole. The ball was heading for a pond in front of the green but instead of ending up in the water it hit a rock and bounced on to the green. In his delight Cruickshank threw his club into the air only to receive a resounding blow on the head as it returned to earth.

● A dog with an infallible nose for finding lost golf balls was, in 1971, given honorary membership of the Waihi GC, Hamilton, New Zealand. The dog, called Chico, was trained to search for lost balls, to be sold back to the members, the money being put into the club funds.

● By 1980 Waddy, an 11-year-old beagle belonging to Bob Inglis, the secretary of Brokenhurst Manor GC, had found over 35,000 golf balls.

● On 6th July, 1938, N Bathie, playing on Downfield, Dundee, was about to hit an iron shot when the ball was suddenly whisked away. The player was spun completely round. He had been caught in the fringe of a whirlwind. The whirlwind lifted a wooden shelter 60 feet into the air and burst it into smithereens over the 11th green. A haystack was uprooted and a tree razed.

● In a match over Queen's Park, Bournemouth,

Archie Compston, finding that his ball had finished in the branches of a tree, played a shot with his club at the full stretch of his arms, above his head. The result was a wonderful shot which almost reached the green.

● Donald Grant, a competitor in the Dornoch Open Amateur Tournament in 1939, cycled from London and tied for second place in the first round of the competition with 74.

● Herbert M Hepworth, Headingley, Leeds, Lord Mayor of Leeds in 1906, scored one thousand holes in 2, a feat which took him 30 years to accomplish. It was celebrated by a dinner in 1931 at the Leeds club. The first 2 of all was scored on 12th June, 1901, at Cobble Hall Course, Leeds, and the 1,000th in 1931 at Alwoodley, Leeds. Hepworth died in November, 1942.

● Fiona MacDonald was the first female to play in the Oxford and Cambridge University match at Ganton in 1986.

● Mrs Sara Gibbon won the Farnham (Surrey) Club's Grandmother's competition 48 hours after her first grand-child was born.

● Mrs Joy Traill of Kloof CC, South Africa, holed from off the green six times in a round there on 20th October, 1977 at the age of 70.

● Nineteen-year-old Ron Stutesman holed chips at five consecutive holes in a round at Orchard Hills CC, Washougal, USA in January, 1978.

● On Saturday, 12th July, 1975, 16-year-old, 3-handicap Colin Smith, of Cowal GC broke his handicap on three different courses. Playing in the Glasgow Youths' Championship at Cawder he scored 73 over the Cawder Course (SSS 71) and 70 over the Keir Course (SSS 68). Then in the evening in the Poseidon Trophy at his home club he scored 70 (SSS 70).

● At Carnoustie in the first qualifying round for the 1952 Scottish Amateur Championship a competitor drove three balls in succession out of bounds at the 1st hole and thereupon withdrew.

Strange Local Rules

● The Duke of Windsor, who played on an extraordinary variety of the world's courses, once took advantage of a local rule at Jinja in Uganda to lift his ball from a hippo's footprint without penalty.

● Another local rule in Uganda read: *If a ball comes to rest in dangerous proximity to a crocodile, another ball may be dropped.*

● At the Glen Canyon course in Arizona a local rule provides that *If your ball lands within a club length of a rattlesnake you are allowed to move the ball.*

● The 6th hole at Koolan Island GC, Western Australia also serves as a local air strip and a local rule reads *Aircraft and vehicular traffic have right of way at all times.*

● A local rule at the RAF Waddington GC reads *When teeing off from the 2nd, right of way must be given to taxi-ing aircraft.*

Record Scoring

Records of the Open Championship

Most Victories

6—Harry Vardon, 1896-98-99-1903-11-14
5—James Braid, 1901-05-06-08-10; JH Taylor, 1984-95-1900-09-13; Peter Thomson, 1954-55-56-58-65; Tom Watson, 1975-77-80-82-83

Most Times Runner-up or Joint Runner-up

7—Jack Nicklaus, 1964-67-68-72-76-77-79
6—JH Taylor, 1896-1904-05-06-07-14

Oldest Winner

Old Tom Morris, 46 years 99 days, 1867
Roberto De Vicenzo, 44 years 93 days, 1967

Youngest Winner

Young Tom Morris, 17 years 5 months 8 days, 1868
Willie Auchterlonie, 21 years 24 days, 1893
Severiano Ballesteros, 22 years 3 months 12 days, 1979

Youngest and Oldest Competitor

John Ball, 14 years, 1878
Gene Sarazen, 71 years 4 months 13 days, 1973

Biggest Margin of Victory

13 strokes, Old Tom Morris, 1862
12 strokes, Young Tom Morris, 1870
8 strokes, JH Taylor, 1900 and 1913; James Braid, 1908
6 strokes, Bobby Jones, 1927; Walter Hagen, 1929; Arnold Palmer, 1962; Johnny Miller, 1976

Lowest Winning Aggregates

268 (68, 70, 65, 65), Tom Watson, Turnberry, 1977
270 (67, 65, 67, 71), Nick Faldo, St Andrews 1990
271 (68, 70, 64, 69), Tom Watson, Muirfield, 1980

Lowest Aggregate by Runner-Up

269 (68, 70, 65, 66), Jack Nicklaus, Turnberry, 1977

Lowest Aggregate by an Amateur

283 (74, 70, 71, 68), Guy Wolstenholme, St Andrews, 1960

Lowest Individual Round

63—Mark Hayes, second round, Turnberry, 1977; Isao Aoki, third round, Muirfield, 1980; Greg Norman, second round, Turnberry, 1986

Lowest Individual Round by an Amateur

66—Frank Stranahan, fourth round, Troon, 1950

Lowest First Round

64—Craig Stadler, Royal Birkdale, 1983; Christy O'Connor Jr, Royal St George's, 1985; Rodger Davis, Muirfield, 1987

Lowest Second Round

63—Mark Hayes, Turnberry, 1977; Greg Norman, Turnberry, 1986

Lowest Third Round

63—Isao Aoki, Muirfield, 1980; Paul Broadhurst, St Andrews 1990

Lowest Fourth Round

64—Graham Marsh, Royal Birkdale, 1983; Severiano Ballesteros, Turnberry, 1986; Greg Norman, Royal Troon, 1989

Lowest First 36 Holes

132, (67, 65), Henry Cotton, Sandwich, 1934;
Nick Faldo (67, 65) and Greg Norman (66, 66),
St Andrews, 1990

Lowest Second 36 Holes

130 (65, 65), Tom Watson, Turnberry, 1977

Lowest First 54 Holes

199 (67, 65, 67) Nick Faldo, St Andrews, 1990
202, (68, 70, 64), Tom Watson, Muirfield, 1980
203 (68, 70, 65), Jack Nicklaus and Tom Watson,
Turnberry, 1977

Lowest Final 54 Holes

200 (70, 65, 65), Tom Watson, Turnberry, 1977

Lowest 9 Holes

28—Denis Durnian, first 9, Royal Birkdale, 1983

Champions in Three Decades

Harry Vardon, 1986, 1903, 1911
JH Taylor, 1894, 1900, 1913
Gary Player, 1959, 1968, 1974

Biggest Span Between First and Last Victories

19 years, JH Taylor, 1894-1913
18 years, Harry Vardon, 1896-1914
15 years, Gary Player, 1959-74
14 years, Henry Cotton, 1934-48

Successive Victories

4—Young Tom Morris, 1868-72. No
championship in 1871
3—Jamie Anderson, 1877-79; Bob Ferguson,
1880-82, Peter Thomson, 1954-56
2—Old Tom Morris, 1861-62; JH Taylor, 1894-95;
Harry Vardon, 1898-99; James Braid, 1905-06;
Bobby Jones, 1926-27; Walter Hagen, 1928-29;
Bobby Locke, 1949-50; Arnold Palmer, 1961-62;
Lee Trevino, 1971-72; Tom Watson, 1982-83

Victories by Amateurs

3—Bobby Jones, 1926-27-30
2—Harold Hilton, 1892-97
1—John Ball, 1890
Roger Wethered lost a play-off in 1921

Highest Number of Top Five Finishes

16—JH Taylor and Jack Nicklaus
15—Harry Vardon and James Braid

Highest Number of Rounds Under 70

29—Jack Nicklaus
21—Tom Watson
19—Lee Trevino
19—Nick Faldo
15—Peter Thomson
14—Severiano Ballesteros
13—Gary Player
13—Ben Crenshaw
12—Bobby Locke, Arnold Palmer

Outright Leader after Every Round

Willie Auchterlonie, 1893; JH Taylor, 1894 and
1900; James Braid, 1908; Ted Ray, 1912; Bobby
Jones, 1927; Gene Sarazen, 1932; Henry Cotton,
1934; Tom Weiskopf, 1973

Record Leads (Since 1892)

After 18 holes:
4 strokes, James Braid, 1908; Bobby Jones,
1927; Henry Cotton, 1934; Christy O'Connor Jr,
1985
After 36 holes:
9 strokes, Henry Cotton, 1934
After 54 holes:
10 strokes, Henry Cotton, 1934
7 strokes, Tony Lema, 1964
6 strokes, James Braid, 1908
5 strokes, Arnold Palmer, 1962; Bill Rogers,
1981; Nick Faldo 1990

Champions with Each Round Lower than Previous One

Jack White, 1904, Sandwich, 80, 75, 72, 69
James Braid, 1906, Muirfield, 77, 76, 74, 73
Ben Hogan, 1953, Carnoustie, 73, 71, 70, 68
Gary Player, 1959, Muirfield, 75, 71, 70, 68

Champion with Four Rounds the Same

Densmore Shute, 1933, St Andrews, 73, 73, 73,
73 (excluding the play-off)

Biggest Variation Between Rounds of a Champion

14 strokes, Henry Cotton, 1934, second round
65, fourth round 79
11 strokes, Jack White, 1904, first round 80,
fourth round 69; Greg Norman, 1986, first round
74, second round 63, third round 74

Biggest Variation Between Two Rounds

17 strokes, Jack Nicklaus, 1981, first round 83,
second round 66; Ian Baker-Finch, 1986, first
round 86, second round 69

Best Comeback by Champions

After 18 holes:
Harry Vardon, 1896, 11 strokes behind the leader

After 36 holes:
George Duncan, 1920, 13 strokes behind the leader

After 54 holes:
Jim Barnes, 1925, 5 strokes behind the leader
Of non-champions, Greg Norman, 1989, seven strokes behind the leader and lost in a play-off

Champions with Four Rounds Under 70

None
Arnold Palmer, 1962, Tom Watson, 1977 and 1980, Severiano Ballesteros, 1984, Mark Calcavecchia, 1989, and Nick Faldo, 1990 had three rounds under 70

Best Finishing Round by a Champion

65—Tom Watson, Turnberry, 1977; Severiano Ballesteros, Royal Lytham, 1988
66—Johnny Miller, Royal Birkdale, 1976

Worst Finishing Round by a Champion since 1920

79—Henry Cotton, Sandwich, 1934
78—Reg Whitcombe, Sandwich, 1938
77—Walter Hagen, Hoylake, 1924

Worst Opening Round by a Champion since 1919

80—George Duncan, Deal, 1920 (he also had a second round of 80)
77—Walter Hagen, Hoylake, 1924

Best Opening Round by a Champion

66—Peter Thomson, Royal Lytham, 1958
67—Henry Cotton, Sandwich, 1934; Tom Watson, Royal Birkdale, 1983; Severiano Ballesteros, Royal Lytham, 1988; Nick Faldo, St Andrews, 1990

Biggest Recovery in 18 Holes by a Champion

George Duncan, Deal, 1920, was 13 strokes behind the leader, Abe Mitchell, after 36 holes and level after 54

Most Appearances on Final Day (Since 1892)

30, JH Taylor
27, Harry Vardon, James Braid, Jack Nicklaus

26, Peter Thomson
24, Gary Player
23, Dai Rees
22, Henry Cotton

Championship since 1946 with the Fewest Rounds Under 70

St Andrews, 1946; Hoylake, 1947; Portrush, 1951; Hoylake, 1956; Carnoustie, 1968. All had only two rounds under 70

Longest Course

Carnoustie, 1968, 7252 yd (6631m)

Courses most often used

Prestwick, 24 (but not since 1925); St Andrews, 24; Muirfield, 13; Sandwich, 11; Hoylake, 10; Royal Lytham, 8; Royal Troon, Musselburgh and Royal Birkdale, 6; Carnoustie, 5; Deal and Turnberry, 2; Royal Portrush and Prince's, 1

Prize Money

Year	Total	First Prize £
1860	nil	nil
1863	10	nil
1864	16	6
1876	20	20
1889	22	8
1891	28.50	10
1892	110	(Amateur winner)
1893	100	30
1910	125	50
1920	225	75
1927	275	100
1930	400	100
1931	500	100
1946	1,000	150
1949	1,700	300
1953	2,450	500
1954	3,500	750
1955	3,750	1,000
1958	4,850	1,000
1959	5,000	1,000
1960	7,000	1,250
1961	8,500	1,400
1963	8,500	1,500
1965	10,000	1,750
1966	15,000	2,100
1968	20,000	3,000
1969	30,000	4,250
1970	40,000	5,250
1971	45,000	5,500
1972	50,000	5,500
1975	75,000	7,500
1977	100,000	10,000
1978	125,000	12,500
1979	155,000	15,500

1980	200,000	25,000
1982	250,000	32,000
1983	300,000	40,000
1984	451,000	55,000
1985	530,000	65,000
1986	600,000	70,000
1987	650,000	75,000
1988	700,000	80,000
1989	750,000	80,000
1990	815,000	85,000

Attendance

Year	Attendance
1962	37,098
1963	24,585
1964	35,954
1965	32,927
1966	40,182
1967	29,880
1968	51,819
1969	46,001
1970	82,593
1971	70,076
1972	84,746
1973	78,810
1974	92,796
1975	85,258
1976	92,021
1977	87,615
1978	125,271
1979	134,501
1980	131,610
1981	111,987
1982	133,299
1983	142,892
1984	193,126
1985	141,619
1986	134,261
1987	139,189
1988	191,334
1989	160,639
1990	207,000

European PGA Tour

Lowest 72 Hole Aggregate

258 (14 under par) by David Llewellyn (Wales) in 1988 AGF Biarritz Open; 259 (25 under par) by Mark McNulty (Zimbabwe) in 1987 German Open at Frankfurt.

Lowest 9 Holes

27 (9 under par) by José María Canizares (Spain) in 1978 Swiss Open at Crans-sur-Sierre; 27 (7 under par) by Robert Lee (England) in

1985 Johnnie Walker Monte Carlo Open at Mont Agel; 27 (6 under par) by Robert Lee in 1987 Portuguese Open at Estoril.

Lowest 18 Holes

60 (11 under par) by Baldovino Dassu (Italy) in 1971 Swiss Open at Crans-sur-Sierre; 60 by David Llewellyn (Wales) in 1988 AGF Biarritz Open. 60 (9 under par) by Ian Woosnam (Wales) in 1990, Torras Monte Carlo Open at Mont Agel.

Lowest 36 Holes

125 (13 under par) by Sam Torrance (Scotland) in 1985 Johnnie Walker Monte Carlo Open at Mont Agel; 125 (13 under par) by Lu Liang Huan (Taiwan) in 1971 French Open at Biarritz; 125 (11 under par) by David Llewellyn in 1988 AGF Biarritz Open. 125 (13 under par) by Ian Woosnam in 1990 Torras Monte Carlo Open at Mont Agel.

Lowest 54 Holes

192 (24 under par) by Anders Forbrand (Sweden) in 1987 Ebel European Masters Swiss Open at Crans-sur-Sierre.

Largest Winning Margin

17 strokes by Bernhard Langer in the 1979 Cacharel Under-25s' Championship in Nîmes.

Highest Winning Score

306 by Peter Butler (England) in 1963 Schweppes PGA Close Championship at Royal Birkdale.

Miscellaneous British

The Professional Golfers' Association in Britain claimed a women's world record for the score of 62 by Janice Arnold during a WPGA tournament in September 1990. Miss Arnold, a New Zealand professional, won the 36-hole event by 12 shots with a 17 under par total of 131 on a course of 5815 yards at the Coventry Golf Club. The record first-round 62 with 31 out and back included seven birdies, one eagle 3 and holing of a five-iron shot for an albatross 2.

Andrew Brooks recorded a 72-hole aggregate of 259 in winning the Skol (Scotland) tournament at Williamwood in 1974.

Playing the ladies' course (4,020 yards) at Sunningdale on 26th September, 1961, Arthur Lees, the professional there, went round in 52, 10 under par. He went out in 26 (2, 3, 3, 4, 3, 3, 3, 3,

2) and came back in 26 (2, 3, 3, 3, 2, 3, 4, 3, 3).

AE Smith, the Woolacombe Bay professional, recorded a score of 55 in a game there with a club member on 1st January, 1936. The course measured 4,248 yards. Smith went out in 29 and came back in 26 finishing with a hole-in-one at the 18th hole.

Other low scores recorded in Britain are by CC Aylmer, an English International who went round Ranelagh in 56; George Duncan, Axenfels in 56; Harry Bannerman, Banchory in 56 in 1971; Ian Connelly, Welwyn Garden City in 56 in 1972; James Braid, Hedderwick near Dunbar in 57; H Hardman, Wirral in 58; Norman Quigley, Windermere in 58 in 1937; Robert Webster, Eaglescliffe in 58, in 1970.

Harry Weetman scored 58 in a round at Croham Hurst on 30th January, 1956. The course measured 6,171 yards.

D Sewell had a round of 60 in an Alliance Meeting at Ferndown, Bournemouth, a full-size course. He scored 30 for each half and had a total of 26 putts.

In September 1986, Jeffrey Burn, handicap 1 of Shrewsbury GC scored 60 in a club competition, made up of 8 birdies, an eagle and 9 pars. He was 30 out and 30 home and no 5 on his card.

Andrew Sherborne, a 20-year-old amateur, went round Cirencester in 60 strokes.

Dennis Gray completed a round at Broome Manor, Swindon (6,906 yards, SSS 73) in the summer of 1976 in 60 (28 out, 32 in).

Playing over Aberdour on 13th June, 1936, Hector Thomson, British Amateur champion, 1936, and Jack McLean, former Scottish Amateur champion, each did 61 in the second round of an exhibition. McLean in his first round had a 63, which gave him an aggregate 124 for 36 holes.

Steve Tredinnick in a friendly match against business tycoon Joe Hyman scored a 61 over West Sussex (6,211 yards) in 1970. It included a hole-in-one at the 12th (198 yards) and a 2 at the 17th (445 yards).

Another round of 61 on a full-size course was achieved by 18-year-old Michael Jones on his home course, Worthing GC (6,274 yards) in the first round of the President's Cup in May, 1974.

In the Second City Pro-Am tournament in 1970, at Handsworth, Simon Fogarty did the second 9 holes in 27 against the par of 36.

In the second round of a 36-hole open amateur competition at Sandyhills GC on 10th September, 1978, Barclay Howard completed the last 9 holes in 27.

RH Corbett, in 1916, in the semi-final of the Tangye Cup at Mullim did 9 holes in 27 as did Dr James Stothers of Ralston over the 2,056 yards 9-hole course at Carradale, Argyll, during the summer of 1971. In each case the total was made up of nine 3s.

US Open

Lowest 72 Hole Aggregate

272 by Jack Nicklaus at Baltusrol in 1980.

Lowest 18 Holes

63 by Johnny Miller at Oakmont in 1973 in the final round and by Jack Nicklaus and Tom Weiskopf at Baltusrol in 1980, both in the first round.

Lowest 9 Holes

30 by Jimmy McHale in 1947, Arnold Palmer in 1960, Ken Venturi in 1964, Bob Charles and Tom Shaw in 1971, and Raymond Floyd in 1980.

Lowest 36 Holes

134 by Jack Nicklaus at Baltusrol in 1980.

Lowest 54 Holes

204 by Jack Nicklaus and Isao Aoki at Baltusrol in 1980.

US Professional events

Lowest 72 Hole Aggregate

257 (60, 68, 64, 65) by Mike Souchak in the 1955 Texas Open.

Lowest 18 Holes

59 by Sam Snead in the third round of the Greenbrier Open (Sam Snead Festival) at White Sulphur Springs, West Virginia in 1959 and by Al Geiberger in the second round of the 1977 Danny Thomas Memphis Classic at Colonial CC when preferred lies were in operation.

Lowest 9 Holes

27 by Mike Souchak in the 1955 Texas Open and by Andy North in the 1975 BC Open.

Lowest First 36 Holes

126 by Tommy Bolt in 1954. (On the US mini-tour a 36-hole score of 123 was achieved by Bob Risch in the 1978 Mesa Centennial Open.)

Lowest Final 36 Holes

122 by Sam Snead in the Greenbrier Open (Sam Snead Festival) in 1959. On the USPGA Tour it is 125 by Ron Streck in the 1978 Texas Open.

Lowest 54 Holes

189 by Chandler Harper in the 1954 Texas Open (last three rounds).
192 by Bob Gilder in the 1982 Westchester Classic (first three rounds).

Largest Winning Margin

16 strokes by J Douglas Edgar in the 1919 Canadian Open Championship and by Bobby Locke in the 1948 Chicago Victory National Championship.

Miscellaneous USA

The lowest scores recorded for 18 holes in America are 55 by EF Staugaard in 1935 over the 6,419 yards Montebello Park, California, and 55 by Homero Blancas in 1962 over the 5,002 yards Premier course in Longview, Texas. Staugaard in his round had 2 eagles, 13 birdies and 3 pars.

Equally outstanding is a round of 58 (13 under par) achieved by a 13-year-old boy, Douglas Beecher, on 6th July, 1976 at Pitman CC, New Jersey. The course measured 6,180 yards from the back tees, and the middle tees, off which Douglas played, were estimated by the club professional to reduce the yardage by under 180 yards.

In 1941 at a course in Portsmouth, Virginia, measuring 6,100 yards, Chandler Harper scored 58.

Jack Nicklaus in an exhibition match at Breakers Club, Palm Beach, California, in 1973 scored 59 over the 6,200 yards course.

Ben Hogan, practising on a 7,006-yard course at Palm Beach, Florida, went round in 61 – 11 under par.

The lowest 9-hole score in America is 25, held jointly by Bill Burke over the second half of the 6,384 yards Normandie CC, St Louis in May, 1970 at the age of 29; by Daniel Cavin who had seven 3s and two 2s on the par 36 Bill Brewer Course, Texas in September, 1959; and by Douglas Beecher over the second half of Pitman CC, New Jersey on 6th July, 1976 at the amazingly young age of 13. The back 9 holes of the Pitman course measured 3,150 yards (par 35) from the back tees, but even though Douglas played off the middle tees, the yardage was still over 3,000 yards for the 9 holes. He scored 8 birdies and 1 eagle.

Horton Smith scored 119 for two consecutive rounds in winning the Catalina Open in California in December, 1928. The course, however, measured only 4,700 yards.

National Opens – excluding Europe and USA

Lowest 72 Hole Aggregate

255 by Peter Tupling in the Nigerian Open at Lagos, 1981.

Lowest 36 Hole Aggregate

124 (18 under par) by Sandy Lyle in the 1978 Nigerian Open at Ikoyi GC, Lagos. (Lyle was in his first year as a professional.)

Lowest 18 Holes

59 by Gary Player in the second round of the 1974 Brazilian Open at Gavea GC (6,185 yards), Rio de Janeiro.

Professional Events – excluding GB and USA

Lowest 72 Hole Aggregate

260 (66, 62, 69, 63) by Bob Charles in the Spalding Masters at Tauranga, New Zealand, in 1969.

Lowest 18 Hole Aggregate

60 by Australian Billy Dunk at Merewether, NSW in November, 1970.

Lowest 9 Hole Aggregate

27 by American Bill Brask at Tauranga in the New Zealand PGA in 1976.

Miscellaneous – excluding GB and USA

Tony Jacklin won the 1973 Los Lagartos Open with an aggregate of 261, 27 under par.

Henry Cotton in 1950 had a round of 56 at Monte Carlo (29 out, 27 in).

In a Pro-Am tournament prior to the 1973 Nigerian Open, British professional David Jagger went round in 59.

Max Banbury recorded a 9-hole score of 26 at Woodstock, Ontario, playing in a competition in 1952.

Women

The lowest score recorded on a full-size course by a woman is 62 by Mary (Mickey) Wright of Dallas, Texas. This was achieved on the Hogan Park course (6,286 yards) at Midland, Texas, in November, 1964. It was equalled by 16-year-old Rae Rothfelder on 9th July, 1978 at Diamond Oak G&CC, Fort Worth, Texas, a course measuring 6,124 yards.

The lowest 72-hole score on the US Ladies' PGA circuit is 271 by Hollis Stacy in the 1977 Rail Muscular Dystrophy.

The lowest 9-hole score on the US Ladies' PGA circuit is 29, first achieved by Marlene Bauer Hagge in 1971 and equalled by Carol Mann (1975), Pat Bradley (1978 and again in 1979), Alexandra Reinhardt (1978), and Silvia Bertolaccini (1979).

The lowest score for 36 holes on the USLPGA circuit is 131 achieved by Kathy Martin in the 1976 Birmingham Classic and by Silvia Bertolaccini in the 1977 Lady Keystone Open.

The lowest 9-hole score on the WPGA circuit is 30 by Susan Moon at Valbonne in 1979.

In the Women's World Team Championship in Mexico in 1966, Mrs Belle Robertson, playing for the British team, was the only player to break 70. She scored 69 in the third round.

At Westgate-on-Sea GC (measuring 5,002 yards), Wanda Morgan scored 60 in an open tournament in 1929.

Since scores cannot properly be taken in match play no stroke records can be made in match play events. Nevertheless we record here two outstanding examples of low scoring in the finals of national championships. Mrs Catherine Lacoste de Prado is credited with a score of 62 in the first round of the 36-hole final of the 1972 French Ladies' Open Championship at Morfontaine. She went out in 29 and came back in 33 on a course measuring 5,933 yards.

In the final of the English Ladies' Championship at Woodhall Spa in 1954, Frances Stephens (later Mrs Smith) did the first nine holes against Elizabeth Price (later Mrs Fisher) in 30. It included a hole-in-one at the 5th. The nine holes measured 3,280 yards.

Amateur National Championships

The following examples of low scoring cannot be regarded as genuine stroke play records since they took place in match play. Nevertheless they are recorded here as being worthy of note.

Michael Bonallack in beating D Kelley in the final of the English championship in 1968 at Ganton did the first 18 holes in 61 with only one putt under two feet conceded. He was out in 32 and home in 29. The par of the course was 71.

Charles McFarlane, playing in the fourth round of the Amateur Championship at Sandwich in 1914 against Charles Evans did the first nine holes in 31, winning by 6 and 5.

This score of 31 at Sandwich was equalled on several occasions in later years there. Then, in 1948, Richard Chapman of America went out in 29 in the fourth round eventually beating Hamilton McInally, Scottish Champion in 1937, 1939 and 1947, by 9 and 7.

In the fourth round of the Amateur Championship at Hoylake in 1953, Harvie Ward, the holder, did the first nine holes against Frank Stranahan in 32. The total yardage for the holes was 3,474 yards and included one hole of 527 yards and five holes over 400 yards. Ward won by one hole.

Francis Ouimet in the first round of the American Amateur Championship in 1932 against George Voigt did the first nine holes in 30. Ouimet won by 6 and 5.

Low scores by Amateurs in Open competitions

The 1970 South African Dunlop Masters Tournament was won by an amateur, John Fourie, with a score of 266, 14 under par. He led from start to finish with rounds of 65, 68, 65, 68, finally winning by six shots from Gary Player.

Jim Ferrier, Manly, won the New South Wales championship at Sydney in 1935 with 266. His rounds were: 67, 65, 70, 64, giving an aggregate 16 strokes better than that of the runner-up. At the time he did this amazing score Ferrier was 20 years old and an amateur.

Most holes below par

EF Staugaard in a round of 55 over the 6,419 yards Montbello Park, California, in 1935, had 2 eagles, 13 birdies and 3 pars.

American Jim Clouette scored 14 birdies in a round at Longhills GC, Arkansas, in 1974. The course measured 6,257 yards.

Jimmy Martin in his round of 63 in the Swallow-Penfold at Stoneham in 1961 had 1 eagle and 11 birdies.

In the Ricarton Rose Bowl at Hamilton, Scotland, in August, 1981, Wilma Aitken, a women's amateur internationalist, had 11 birdies in a round of 64, including 9 consecutive birdies from the 3rd to the 11th.

Mrs Donna Young scored 9 birdies and 1 eagle in one round in the 1975 Colgate European Women's Open.

Consecutive holes below par

Lionel Platts had 10 consecutive birdies from the 8th to 17th holes at Blairgowrie GC during a practice round for the 1973 Sumrie Better-Ball tournament.

Roberto De Vicenzo in the Argentine Centre of the Republic Championship in April, 1974 at the Cordoba GC, Villa Allende, broke par at each of the first 9 holes. (By starting his round at the 10th hole they were in fact the second 9 holes played by Vicenzo.) He had 1 eagle (at the 7th hole) and 8 birdies. The par for the 3,602 yards half was 37, completed by Vicenzo in 27.

Nine consecutive holes under par have been recorded by Claude Harmon in a friendly match over Winged Foot GC, Mamaroneck, NY, in 1931; by Les Hardie at Eastern GC, Melbourne, in April, 1934; by Jimmy Smith at McCabe GC, Nashville, Tenn, in 1969; by Jim DeForest on a 9-hole sand-green course at New Salem, North Dakota, in August, 1974; by 13-year-old Douglas Beecher, in 1976, at Pitman CC, New Jersey; and by Rick Sigda at Greenfield CC, Mass, in 1979.

TW Egan in winning the East of Ireland Championship in 1962 at Baltray had 8 consecutive birdies (2nd to 9th) in the third round.

On the USPGA circuit 8 consecutive holes below par have been achieved twice – by Bob Goalby in the 1961 St Petersburg Open, and by Fuzzy Zoeller in the 1976 Quad Cities Open.

Seven successive birdies have been recorded by Peter Thomson at Wentworth in the 1958 Dunlop; by Bernard Hunt at Wentworth in the 1958 Daks; by Angel Miguel at Wentworth (East) in the 1960 Daks; by Peter Butler at Fulford in the 1971 Benson and Hedges; by Peter Townsend at Wentworth in 1974 Viyella PGA; and by Brian Waites at the RAC in the 1980 Bob Hope Classic.

The United States Ladies' PGA record is 7 consecutive holes below par achieved by Carol Mann in the Borden Classic at Columbus, Ohio in 1975.

Miss Wilma Aitken recorded 9 successive birdies (from the 3rd to the 11th) in the 1981 Ricarton Rose Bowl.

Low scoring rarities

In the qualifying rounds of the 1956 Dunlop Tournament at Sunningdale, Arthur Lees, the resident professional, played 27 consecutive holes without taking more than a 4 at any hole. His first round was 65 and his second 69.

At Standerton GC, South Africa, in May, 1937, FF Bennett, playing for Standerton against Witwatersrand University, did the 2nd hole, 110 yards, in three 2s and a 1. Standerton is a 9-hole course, and in the match Bennett had to play four rounds.

In 1973 in the 36-hole Club Championship at Mufulira GC, Zambia, Amateur HG McQuillan, completed two rounds in 65 and 66 for a winning score of 131.

In 1957 a four-ball comprising HJ Marr, E Stevenson, C Bennett and WS May completed the 2nd hole (160 yards) in the grand total of 6 strokes. Marr and Stevenson both holed in 1 while Bennett and May both made 2.

The old Meadow Brook Club of Long Island, USA, had five par 3 holes and George Low in a round there in the 1950s scored 2 at each of them.

In a friendly match on a course near Chicago in 1971, assistant professional Tom Doty (23 years) had a remarkable low run over four consecutive holes: 4th (500 yards) 2; 5th (360 yards, dogleg) 1; 6th (175 yards) 1; 7th (375 yards) 2.

RW Bishop, playing in the Oxley Park, July medal competition in 1966, scored three consecutive 2s. They occurred at the 12th, 13th and 14th holes which measured 151, 500 and 136 yards respectively.

In the 1959 PGA Close Championship at Ashburnham, Bob Boobyer scored five 2s in one of the rounds.

American Art Wall scored three consecutive 2s in the first round of the US Masters in 1974. They were at the 4th, 5th and 6th holes, the par of which was 3, 4 and 3.

Nine consecutive 3s have been recorded by RH Corbett in 1916 in the semi-final of the Tangye Cup; by Dr James Stothers of Ralston GC over the 2,056 yards 9-hole course at Carradale, Argyll during the summer of 1971; by Irish internationalist Brian Kissock in the Homebright Open at Carnalea GC, Bangor in June, 1975; and by American club professional Ben Toski.

The most consecutive 3s in a British PGA event is seven by Eric Brown in the Dunlop at Gleneagles (Queen's Course) in 1960.

Hubert Green scored eight consecutive 3s in a round in the 1980 US Open.

The greatest number of 3s in one round in a British PGA event is 11 by Brian Barnes in the 1977 Skol Lager tournament at Gleneagles.

Fewest putts

The lowest known number of putts in one round is 14, achieved by Colin Collen-Smith in a round at Betchworth Park, Dorking in June, 1947. He single-putted 14 greens and chipped into the hole on four occasions. Professional Richard Stanwood in a round at Riverside GC, Pocatello, Idaho on 17th May, 1976 took 15 putts, chipping into the hole on five occasions. Several instances of 16 putts in one round have been recorded in friendly games.

For 9 holes, the fewest putts is 5 by Ron Stutes-

man for the first 9 holes at Orchard Hills G&CC, Washington, USA in 1978.

Walter Hagen in nine consecutive holes on one occasion took only seven putts. He holed long putts on seven greens and chips at the other two holes.

In competitive stroke rounds in Britain and Ireland, the lowest known number of putts in one round is 18, in a medal round at Portpatrick Dunskey GC, Wilmslow GC professional Fred Taggart is reported to have taken 20 putts in one round of the 1934 Open Championship. Padraigh Hogan (Elm Park), when competing in the Junior Scratch Cup at Carlow in 1976, took only 20 putts in a round of 67.

The fewest putts in a British PGA event is believed to be 22 by Bill Large in a qualifying round over Moor Park High Course for the 1972 Benson and Hedges Match Play.

Overseas, outside the United States of America, the fewest putts is 19 achieved by Robert Wynn (GB) in a round in the 1973 Nigerian Open and by Mary Bohen (US) in the final round of the 1977 South Australian Open at Adelaide.

The USPGA record for fewest putts in one round is 18, held by Sam Trahan in the 4th round of the 1979 Philadelphia Classic. For 9 holes the USPGA record is 8, by Jim Colbert in the 1967 Greater Jacksonville Open.

The fewest putts recorded for a 72-hole USPGA tournament is 94 by George Archer in the 1980 Heritage Classic.

The fewest putts recorded by a woman is 17, by Joan Joyce in the Lady Michelob tournament, Georgia in May, 1982.

Index